Qi Men Dun Jia Made Easy

(奇门遁甲)

Simplifying the Ancient Art

Calvin Yap

Copyright © 2019 by Calvin Yap

All rights reserved worldwide.
First Edition 2019

The authors can be reached at:

Email: Calvin Yap (calvin_yap@yahoo.com)

Website: http://www.fengshui-hacks.com/

Edited by: Denise Yap May Yee

Warning and Disclaimer

The information in this book is based on the author's knowledge and personal experience. It is presented for educational purposes to assist the reader in expanding his or her knowledge on Chinese Meta-physics. The techniques and practices are not to be used without any proper training. The author is not responsible in any manner whatsoever for any loses or damages caused or alleged to be caused directly or indirectly from using the information contained in this book.
The author provides onsite courses for those who are keen to learn. Please contact the author for arrangement.

Dedication and Acknowledgement

For my family:

To my wife Lucy & my 2 daughters: Denise & Sherry for their understanding and support.

Contents

Table

Figures

Author's Note

Traditionally, students spent years staying with their master to learn this art. Some of them spent 30-40 years being guided by the master in learning and sharpening one faction of Chinese Meta-Physics before becoming a master.

In the digital era, everything has to be fast, and that includes learning. Some students spent 3 days attending a class, and the next day, claim to be Fengshui Master. I don't advocate such practice as I strongly believe that to excel, you need constant guidance from someone, and with experience, help others and share the knowledge later.

I was a student of Chinese Meta-Physics for many years before I mastered the art and started teaching. I completely understand the difficulties in learning this art. As such, the purpose of writing this book is to simplify the art for easy learning. A word of caution is that Qi Men Dun Jia covers a lot of areas, and this book only presents the tip of the tip of the iceberg. I also made it easier to learn by stripping away all the advanced content. However, the advanced content is still important to mastering Qi Men Dun Jia, but it will be covered in depth in my class.

I hope that this book will help you started with Qi Men Dun Jia.

Calvin Yap
calvin_yap@yahoo.com
http://www.fengshui-hacks.com

Other books from Author:

1. Control Your Destiny by Mastering Qi Men Dun Jia (ISBN: 978-981-08-7136-9)
2. Qi Men Dun Jia (奇门遁甲) Chāi Bù (拆布) English Calendar 2011 – 2020 (ISBN: 978-981-08-7386-8)
3. Practical Application of Qi Men Dun Jia (ISBN: 978-981-08-9837-3)
4. Qi Men Dun Jia Compendium Series Volume 1 - English Chai Bu & Zhi Run Calendar 1930 – 2020 (ISBN: 978-981-07-0509-1)
5. Qi Men Dun Jia Compendium Series Volume 2 - 540 Yang Dun Chart (ISBN: 978-981-07-0510-7)
6. Qi Men Dun Jia Compendium Series Volume 3 - 540 Yin Dun Chart (ISBN: 978-981-07-0511-4)
7. FengShui at Your Fingertips (ISBN: 978-981-07-1670-7)
8. Destiny Analysis of Famous People using Qi Men Dun Jia (not available to public)
9. Controla Mejor Tu Destino Dominando Qi Men Dun Jia: Qi Men Dun Jia (Spanish Edition) (ISBN: 978-981-11-1618-6)
10. Le FengShui sur le bout des doigts (French Edition) (ISBN : 978-981-11-0436-7)
11. Better Control of Your Destiny by Mastering Qi Men Dun Jia (ISBN: 978-981-09-2079-1)
12. Fundamentals of Chinese Meta-Physics (ISBN: 978-981-11-3809-6)

Translation by Author:

1. Basic Qi Men Dun Jia - How to become a Fengshui Master by Master Ye (ISBN: 978-981-07-1745-2)
2. Destiny Analysis Using Qi Men Dun Jia by Master Ye (not available to public)
3. Date Selection Using Qi Men Dun Jia by Master Ye (not available to public)

Introduction to Qi Men Dun Jia

奇门遁甲 (Qí Mén Dùn Jiǎ) is an ancient form of Chinese Meta-Physics which is still used in modern times. As in the name Qi Men, which loosely translates to Mystical Door, it gives a sense of mystic or magic to people who do not know otherwise. Qi Men Dun Jia may be applied to business, crime-solving, marriage and matchmaking, medical divination, Feng Shui, military affairs, finding missing people, travel, personal fortune divination etc.

It was recorded in Chinese history that Qi Men Dun Jia, together with Da Liu Ren and Tai Yi Shen Shu are the epitome peak of the Three Arts or Three Styles (三式 sān shì) in Chinese Meta-physics. It was said that these Arts can only be practiced by the Emperor or their advisors. Commoners caught practicing these Three Arts run the risk of being executed!

According to legend, Qi Men Dun Jia was taught to 黃帝 (the Yellow Emperor, Huáng Dì- 2697 BC to 2597 BC) by a fairy, 九天玄女 (Jiǔ Tiān Xuán Nǚ). During that time, the Yellow Emperor was fighting against a rebel called 蚩尤 (Chī Yóu). Chī Yóu was familiar with the art of Yin & Yang and had developed the capability to summon the wind and rain. It was rumoured that his head was as strong as copper and his arms were like iron (铜头铁臂) and he was able to win any wars. During the ensuing battles with Chī Yóu, the Yellow Emperor exhausted all means to defeat him. 九天玄女 (Jiǔ Tiān Xuán Nǚ) took pity on the Yellow Emperor and taught the art of Qi Men Dun Jia to the Yellow Emperor. Harnessing the knowledge of Qi Men Dun Jia, the Yellow Emperor invented the 指南车 (South Pointing Chariot) to win the war against Chī Yóu.

Zhūgě Liàng [1]

诸葛亮 (Zhūgě Liàng), 181–234 was the Chancellor of Shu Han during the Three Kingdoms period of China. He is often recognized as the greatest and most accomplished strategist of his era. It was said that he used the technique in Qi Men Dun Jia to win battles.

Using straw boats to borrow arrows

Before the Battle of Red Cliffs, Zhūgě Liàng visited the Wu camp to assist 周瑜 (Zhōu Yú). 周瑜 (Zhōu Yú) saw Zhūgě Liàng as a threat to Eastern Wu and was also jealous of Zhūgě Liàng 's talent. He assigned Zhūgě Liàng the task of making 100,000 arrows in ten days or face execution for failure in duties under military law. Zhūgě Liàng promised that he will finish this seemingly impossible task in three days. He requested 20 large boats; each manned by a few soldiers and filled with straw human-like figures. Before dawn, with river fog cloaking his movements, Zhūgě Liàng deployed his ships. He ordered

---

[1] Adopted from wikipedia

his soldiers to beat war drums and shout orders so as to imitate the noise of an attack.

Upon hearing the drums, the Wei soldiers rushed out to meet the "attack". Zhūgě Liàng drank wine with Lu Su on one of the boats. The Wei soldiers were unable to see through the fog and fired volleys of arrows at the sound of the drums. The straw figures were soon penetrated by many arrows, which became stuck in the straw. Zhūgě Liàng returned to Wu in triumph. After removing the arrows from the straw figures' bodies, Zhūgě Liàng discovered there were over 100,000 arrows.

It was said that Zhūgě Liàng used Qi Men Dun Jia to get the correct timing and direction of river fog.

赤壁之戰 (Battle of Red Cliffs)

In the battle of the Red Cliffs (赤壁之戰), 诸葛亮 Zhuge Liang said: 万事俱备，只欠东风 (All matters are ready, except for east wind). In the battle of Red Cliffs, he wanted to burn up 曹操 (Cáo Cāo)'s fleet of chained ships and knew that it could only be done by launching arrows with fire with the help of east wind. He used Qi Men to predict the timing of the east wind so that they can launch the attack. So, this is the 天时 – Heaven aspect. Putting the battle of the Red Cliffs in the Heaven, Earth, Man context:

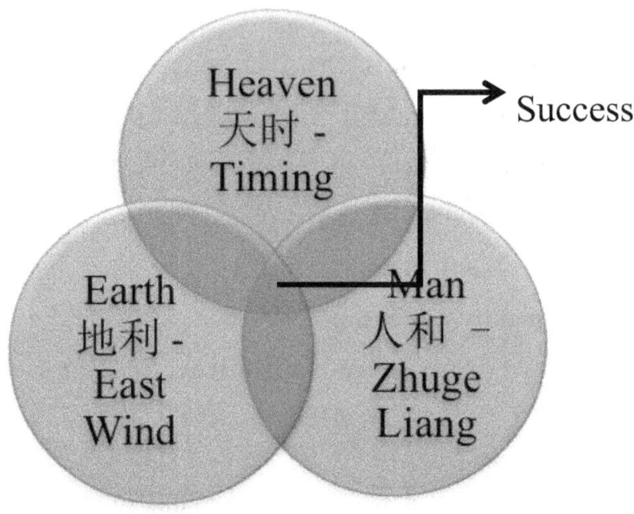

Figure 1 - Heaven, Earth & Man

Zhuge Liang and his army (Man 人和), with the help of East Wind (Earth 地利), initiated the battle at the exact timing (Heaven 天时). In this combination, he executed the battle at the right time with the right environment and the correct people. Hence, the success of the battle depended on the quality of these three components as well as the interaction between these three components.

Jiāng Zǐyá [2]

姜子牙 (Jiāng Zǐyá), was a Chinese historical and legendary figure who resided next to the Weishui River about 3,000 years ago. The region was the feudal estate of King Wen of Zhou. The last ruler of the Shang dynasty, King Zhou of Shang (16th - 11th century BC) was a tyrannical and debauched slave owner who spent his days carousing with his favourite concubine Daji and mercilessly executing or punishing upright officials and all others who objected to his ways. Jiāng Zǐyá had once served the Shang king and had come to hate him with all his heart. He was an expert in military affairs (i.e. Qi Men Dun Jia) and hoped that someday someone would call on him to help overthrow the king. He waited and waited till he was 80 years old, continuing placidly with his fishing in a tributary of the Weihe River (near today's Xi'an) using a barbless hook or even no hook at all, on the theory that the fish would come to him on their own volition when they were ready.

King Wen of the Zhou state, (central Shaanxi), found Jiāng fishing. King Wen, following the advice of his father and grandfather before him, was in search of talented people. In fact, he had been told by his grandfather, the Grand Duke of Zhou, that one day a sage would appear to help rule the Zhou state.

When King Wen saw Jiang, at first sight, he felt that this was an unusual old man and began to converse with him. He discovered that this white-haired fisherman was actually an astute political thinker and military strategist. This, he felt, must be the man his grandfather was waiting for. He took Jiang in his coach to the court and appointed him prime minister and gave him the title Jiang Taigongwang ("The Great

---

[2] Adopted from wikipedia

Duke's Hope", or "The expected of the Great Duke") in reference to a prophetic dream Danfu, grandfather of Wenwang, had had many years before. This was later shortened to Jiang Taigong.

Zhāng Liáng (Western Han)[3]

張良 (Zhāng Liáng) 262 BC – 189 BC, was a strategist and statesman of the early Han Dynasty period of Chinese history. He is also known as one of the "Three Heroes of the early Han Dynasty" (漢初三傑), along with Han Xin and Xiao He. Zhāng Liáng contributed greatly to the founding of the Han Dynasty.

To avenge the fall of his native state, Zhāng Liáng dedicated his efforts to hire assassins to kill Qin Shi Huang. Qin Shi Huang survived the assassination attempt, after which he issued an order for the arrest of Zhāng Liáng. As a wanted man by the government, Zhāng Liáng travelled to Xiapi and stayed there for some time, using fake identities to evade the authorities. One day, Zhāng Liáng took a stroll at the Yishui Bridge and met an old man there. The man walked towards Zhāng and chucked his shoe down the bridge on purpose, after which he yelled at Zhāng, "Hey boy, go down and fetch me my shoe!" Zhāng Liáng was astonished and unhappy but he obeyed silently. The old man then lifted his foot and ordered Zhāng Liáng to put on the shoe for him. Zhāng Liáng was furious but he controlled his temper and meekly obliged. The old man did not show any sign of gratitude and walked

---

[3] Adopted from wikipedia

away in laughter. The old man came back after walking a distance and praised Zhāng Liáng, "This child can be taught!" and he asked Zhāng Liáng to meet him at the bridge again at dawn five days later. Zhāng Liáng was confused but he agreed.

Five days later, Zhāng Liáng rushed to the bridge at the stroke of dawn but the old man was already waiting for him there. The old man chided him, "How can you be late for a meeting with an elderly man? Come back again five days later!" Zhāng Liáng tried his best to be punctual the second time but the old man still arrived earlier than him, and he was scorned by the old man once more and told to return again five days later. The third time, Zhāng Liáng went to the bridge at midnight and waited until the old man appeared. This time, the old man was impressed with Zhāng Liáng's fortitude that he presented Zhāng Liáng with a book, saying, "You can become the tutor of a ruler after reading this book. In ten years' time the world will become chaotic, and you can use your knowledge from this book to bring peace and prosperity to the empire. Meet me again thirteen years later. I'm the yellow rock at the foot of Mount Gucheng." The old man was 黃石公 (Huang Shigong; aka "Yellow Rock Old Man") of the legendary "Four Haos of Mount Shang" (商山四皓), a group of four reclusive wise men. The book was titled 太公兵法 (The Art of War by Taigong) and believed to be the Six Secret Teachings by Jiāng Zǐyá.

Liu Bowen

Liu Ji (1311 - 1375), style name Bowen, was a key military consultant of Zhu Yuanzhang, the founder of Ming dynasty. It was said that Liu Bowen used Qi Men Dun Jia skill to bring the Ming dynasty to the throne.

Liu Bowen sat for imperial examination and obtained the position of jinshi. He served the Yuan dynasty as an official for 25 years. One of rebels managed to bribe his way into the government favour and Liu Bowen being an honest and straight person, was not happy with the event. He was subsequently demoted and finally left to retire in his ancestral homeland. In 1360, Liu Bowen was introduced to Zhu Yuanzhang, a former leader of White Lotus rebellion and leader of anti-Yuan rebellion. Liu Bowen then served under Zhu Yuanzhang and became his commanding officer on land and water.

Mao Zedong

毛泽东 Máo Zédōng (December 26, 1893 – September 9, 1976) was a Chinese revolutionary, political theorist and communist leader. He led the People's Republic of China (PRC) from its establishment in 1949 until his death in 1976. It was rumoured that Mao actually used Qi Men Dun Jia to win his battle against Kuomintang. In some of the battles, Mao actually dictated the actual timing and direction for the troops to be deployed, which is a key signature of Qi Men Dun Jia.

What is 奇门遁甲 (Qí Mén Dùn Jiǎ)?

In the nutshell, a Qi Men Dun Jia practitioner needs to plot a Qi Men Dun Jia chart based on the Chinese Year, Month, Day and Hour. There are four families of 奇门遁甲 (Qí Mén Dùn Jiǎ). They are:

- Year Qi Men (年家奇门)

- Month Qi Men (月家奇门)

- Day Qi Men (日家奇门)

- Hour Qi Men (时家奇门)

The most popular is Hour Qi Men, which is the basis of this book. Year Qi Men is mainly used for country- level analysis or prediction for major events. Month Qi Men uses the month and Year as the basis to plot the chart. Likewise, Day Qi Men uses the Day as the basis to plot Qi Men chart.

For Hour Qi Men, there are 1080 Qi Men Dun Jia charts that are divided into 580 Yang Dun and 580 Yin Dun. Each Dun is divided into 9 categories (1 to 9) where each chart represents 60 JiaZi Hour. To summarise:

- In 1 Dun, there are 60 charts.

- There are 9 Yang Dun and 9 Yin Dun

- 9 X 60 = 580 Yang Dun, 9 X 60 = 580 Yin Dun, total 1080 charts.

Yang Dun and Yin Dun are the markers for Solar events where the Sun is at a certain position relative to the earth. For example, Yang Dun begins around 21st or 22nd Dec every year, where the Winter Solstice (冬至 - Dōng Zhì) starts. This is when the Sun is at a 270° angle relative to Earth in the Celestial Longitude. Yin Dun begins around 21st or 22nd June every year where Summer Solstice (夏至 - Xià Zhì) starts. This is when the Sun is at a 90° angle relative to Earth in the Celestial Longitude.

Please refer to the following books if you like to go deeper into how Qi Men Dun Jia system works and how to plot chart:

- Fundamentals of Chinese Meta-Physics
- Better Control of your Destiny by mastering Qi Men Dun Jia

To make things simpler for beginners, I have included the calendar and Qi Men Dun Jia charts at the end of this book so that you would not have to plot the chart manually. In addition, you can go to my website at http://www.fengshui-hacks.com/ to plot charts as well.

Before you can learn how to interpret Qi Men Dun Jia charts, you would need to know the structure of Qi Men Dun Jia charts. Qi Men Dun Jia charts use Post-Heaven Ba Gua as the basis. See the next section on Qi Men Dun Jia chart and structure for more information.

As there are different families of 奇门遁甲 (Qí Mén Dùn Jiǎ), there are various methods of plotting 奇门遁甲 (Qí Mén Dùn Jiǎ) charts. The most popular methods are Chāi Bù (拆布) and Zhí Rùn (直闰) method.

There are other methods not mentioned here, but that does not mean that they are not used. Another thing to note is that there might be slight variances in the manner of practice even within Chāi Bù or Zhí Rùn method between Masters.

Usage of Qi Men Dun Jia

Qi Men Dun Jia can be used for:

- Divination
- Application
- Destiny Analysis
- Change Name
- Fengshui Prescription
- Religious Matter
- Personal Wellbeing

Divination

For those who had learnt Qi Men Dun Jia before, this is the most basic fundamental of Qi Men Dun Jia. You can use Qi Men Dun Jia Divination to forecast:

- Relationship Matters: divorce, 3rd party affair, scandal and legal entanglement.
- Wealth and Investment: status of current wealth, join venture, investment into business.
- Interview and Academic: whether the interview or exam will be successful.
- Accuracy of information: whether the person is lying or had provided fake information.
- Perform Fengshui audit and destiny analysis using divination.
- Mundane things such as finding lost items and weather forecast. My student even used Qi Men Dun Jia to find the whereabouts of his wife in the shopping mall.

Application

This is where the real deal of Qi Men Dun Jia comes in. Application means choosing a good date or time and the proper action to make things happen. This is where the concept of Heaven, Earth & Man (天时, 地利, 人和) comes in.

So, what can Qi Men Dun Jia do for you? There are 2 parts to this:

1. Based on the date or time of the certain endeavour, find out what are the possible problems or issues.
2. Choose a good date or time for the important endeavour.

Please note that there are not many Qi Men masters are teaching this as this is regarded as a guarded secret that is not to be easily revealed.

Marriage

For some married couples, certain (bad) things start to happen after marriage. This could be due to the wrong date or time used for their marriage. With the date and time chosen for marriage, we can use Qi Men Dun Jia to find out what are the problems or issues that the couple has or will have. Some problems includes: inability to conceive, 3rd party coming into the picture, divorce, sickness or even death.

For those who are going to get married, we can use Qi Men Dun Jia to choose a good date or time for their marriage in order to ensure good results (e.g. kids or harmony)

House Renovation

Sometimes choosing a wrong date for house renovation can cause dire consequences. Based on the date or time used, we can use Qi Men Dun Jia to find out what are the dire consequences (e.g. injury at work, bankruptcy etc.)

On the other hand, using Qi Men Dun Jia to choose a good date or time for house renovation would allow us to ensure good returns (harmony, wealth etc.).

Burial or Yin (阴) Fengshui

Sometimes the same type of calamity (e.g. same type of sickness) might befall on some of the family members after the burial of their ancestor. This could be due to the wrong date or time used for the burial. From the date or time used for the burial, the cause of the calamity and the affected family members can be determined using Qi Men Dun Jia.

By using Qi Men Dun Jia, we can choose a good date or time for the re-burial in order to ensure good blessings for descendants.

Move-in to new house

Bad things could happen if the wrong date or time is used for the move-in ceremony. There could be potential health issue, injury, loss of job, loss of wealth etc. because of the wrong date or time used. Based on the date or time used, all these consequences can be derived using Qi Men Dun Jia.

To ensure prosperity, good health and wealth, a good Qi Men Dun Jia date or time can be used for the move-in ceremony.

Some masters brand the above techniques as "Qi Men Dun Jia Fengshui", but to me, this is just a simple divination based on the date or time used for move-in. A "real" Qi Men Dun Jia Fengshui uses a person's Qi Men Dun Jia Bazi to match to the person's house. This includes the direction of bed as well as the suitable colour scheme for the people staying in the house.

Opening Ceremony for Business

The key focus of business is to make money. If there are no customers patronizing, then it affects the profits. As such, choosing a good date or time for business opening is also as important. Choosing a wrong date or time for business opening has dire consequences on the business.

For example, choosing a time where the hour is in "Kong" will result in poor customers' patronage. We can use Qi Men Dun Jia to choose a prosperous date or time for business opening, by factoring in business facing or sitting[4], owner's bazi and good date to optimize Heaven, Earth & Man effect (天时, 地利, 人和).

---

[4] This is a more advanced technique in Qi Men Dun Jia usage with Fengshui.

Interview or Exam

Finding a good job and passing exams are important milestones for a person. Sometimes, going for interview or exam on the wrong date and time will lead to the failure in getting the job or failure in the exam. Therefore, choosing a good date or time is very important.

You can use Qi Men Dun Jia Divination to find the chances of passing, and based on that, use Qi Men Dun Jia Fengshui to mediate in order to improve your chances. Alternatively, you can choose a good date or time to go for an interview or exam. You can further supplement it by using Qi Men Dun Jia Fengshui technique to ensure optimum results.

Assembly of Bed

Qi Men Dun Jia has a built-in compass. Therefore, we can use it to "correct" certain condition. Assembly of bed is another method specially designed by my predecessors to do such correction. Basically, prior to the date selected, dissemble the bed and leave the mattress up on the wall for at least 24 hours. At the specific date and time, re-assemble the bed to the correct direction.

The date and time is chosen to achieve the specific results that the person desires. For example, for those who are always sick, they can chose a date or time that would help to improve their health.

Other forms of application

You can use Qi Men Dun Jia to:

- Choose a good date or time to seek wealth to ensure good returns.
- Choose a good date or time for horse betting, 4D betting, casino gambling, asking favour from boss, negotiation, court hearing, filing of lawsuit etc.
- Based on current date and time, find a good direction or location to hide, escape (avoid being arrested).

Destiny Analysis

Qi Men Dun Jia can be used for destiny analysis. Like Zi Ping bazi or Zi Wei Dou Shou, you can use your birth date and time to plot the Qi Men Dun Jia chart. You can see the same things (or more) as in Zi Ping bazi.

Your Qi Men Dun Jia Bazi chart is basically like your life compass. It tells you:

- How good is your wealth, both direct and indirect wealth?
- How good are your relationships? For example, your relationship with your spouse, kids, parents, siblings, boss. You even see who are the people that will potentially sabotage you (小人), who are your noblemen etc.
- Major events that are happening to your spouse, kids, parents or siblings based on your Qi Men Dun Jia bazi.
- You can use it to choose a house that suits your bazi and use Qi Men Dun Jia Fengshui to further enhance it.

- Your health status and where are your weak organs. When will your sickness manifest.
- Your career; type of career that best suits you, relationship with your boss and the environment. The location of your office that suits your bazi.
- Business acumen, if you are more suitable to have your own business or simply stay employed.
- The colour scheme that suits you based on your Qi Men Dun Jia Bazi.
- Sequences of events that are happening or going to happen in your entire life.
- Time of Death.

Change Name

The Chinese believed that the following impacts a person life:

一命, 二运, 三风水, 四积功德, 五读书, 六名, 七相, 八敬神, 九交贵人, 十养生.

Translated to:

1-Destiny, 2-Luck, 3-Fengshui, 4-Do good deeds, 5-Education, 6-Name, 7-Appearance, 8-respect God, 9-networking, 10-Life cultivation.

So, a good name is ranked 6th in the hierarchy of influence. As such, based on your Qi Men Dun Jia Destiny chart, you can use Qi Men Dun Jia to change your name into one that compliments your Destiny chart and therefore enhance your life.

Fengshui

I can use Qi Men Dun Jia divination to find out the Fengshui condition of your house without knowing where you stay and prescribe a Qi Men Dun Jia Fengshui remedy to you based on the divination made. I can derive the condition or situation of the people living in the house without knowing their birth date or time.

Using your Qi Men Dun Jia Destiny chart, I will be able to tell the flaw in your chart and prescribe a Qi Men Dun Jia Fengshui remedy for you. From this, we can see how Bazi does the diagnosis and Fengshui does the prescription.

Any flaws, issues and problems can be fixed using the assembly of bed method. For example, when a perfectly healthy couple was unable to have children despite having nothing wrong with their bazi (according to Qi Men Dun Jia Destiny Analysis), the problem could be due to the wrong date that was used for their wedding. Another example is that after moving into the new house, the husband lost his job, and this is attributed to the wrong move-in date used. So, by disassembling and reassembling the bed again on a good Qi Men date or time, we can change a person's luck. I have helped my clients who were on the verge of bankruptcy using this technique.

For those who are in dire state, we can also use the Qi Men Dun Jia Life Changing method to turn the luck around. This technique is used by certified practitioners to help client change their luck.

Religious Matter

Last but not least, Qi Men Dun Jia can be used for spiritual or religious matters. There is a Qi Men Dun Jia Talisman that can be used as a remedy. A good date and time is selected to "bless" the Talisman to ensure its effectiveness. Qi Men Dun Jia Date Selection can be used to choose a good date and time to perform religious matters.

In addition, you can also choose a good date and time and sector for spiritual matters. This can be further enhanced by being at a good Fengshui place.

Your Qi Men Dun Jia Destiny chart can be used to read information about your past life(s). This is more related to the karma effect. Things happening in this life are related to what you did in your past life.

Part I – Basic

Here are some basic that you need to know to learn 奇门遁甲 (Qí Mén Dùn Jiǎ).

Basics

Five Elements

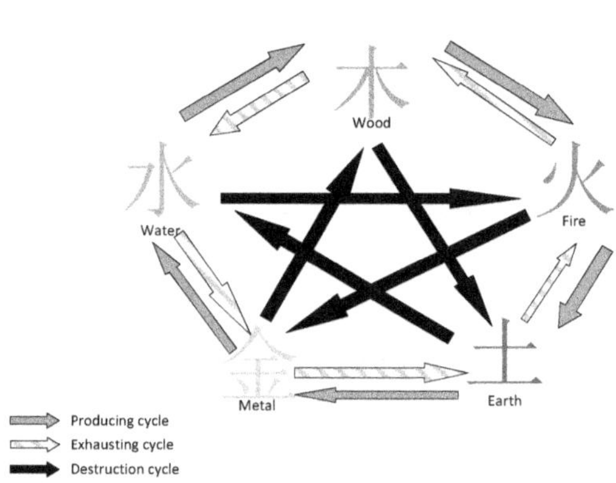

Figure 2 - Five Elements

The concept of the Five Elements (五行) is the most basic fundamental as well as the most important concept to understand the basic art of Chinese meta-physics. Ancient Chinese Sage derived that the universe is consists of five building blocks of elements; i.e. Earth, Metal, Water, Wood and Fire. Each element has its own attributes and characteristics. These five elements follow the law of nature as describe below:

- Wood produces Fire, exhausts Water and controls Earth.

- Fire produces Earth, exhausts Wood and controls Metal.

- Earth produces Metal, exhausts Fire and controls Water.

- Metal produces Water, exhausts Earth and controls Wood.

- Water produces Wood, exhausts Metal and controls Fire.

He Tu (River Map)

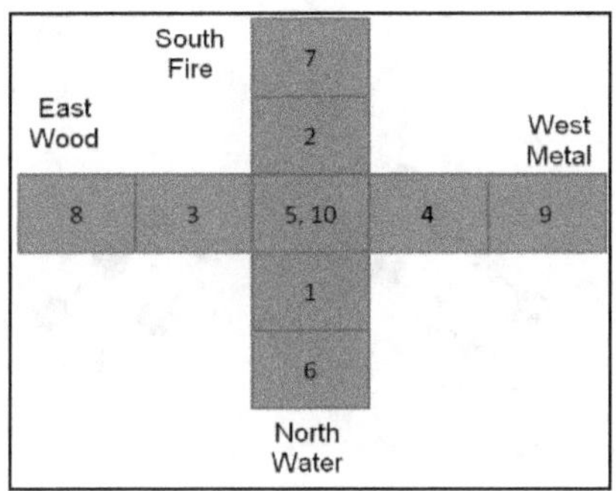

Figure 3 - He Tu (River Map)

It was said that the He Tu or River Map was derived from a mystical creature that emerged from the Yellow River – hence it is called River Map. On the back of this creature were black and white dots which formed a pattern.

The He Tu describes that 1 & 6 are North and Water element. It can be described that a combination of 1 & 6 become Water. The same apply for 2 & 7, which is Fire element and the resulting combination is also Fire. 3 & 8 or combination of both is Wood element. 4 & 9 or combination of both is Metal element. Finally, 5 & 10 combine to become Earth element.

Luo Shu (Magic Squares)

According to the legend, it was said that a giant tortoise emerged from the river. Inscribed on its back were circular dots in 3x3 grid pattern. It is also known as Magic Squares.

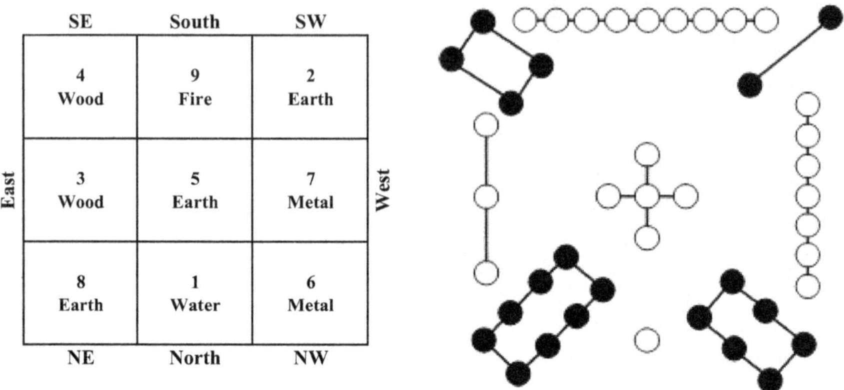

	SE	South	SW	
	4 Wood	9 Fire	2 Earth	
East	3 Wood	5 Earth	7 Metal	West
	8 Earth	1 Water	6 Metal	
	NE	North	NW	

Figure 4 - Luo Shu

Ba Gua (Trigram)

It was claimed that Fu Xi is the person who invented the Ba Gua. There are 2 types of Ba Gua; Pre-Heaven and Post-Heaven. The tips to memorize the Ba Gua as follow:

Ba Gua	Symbol	Memorizing (in Chinese)	Translation
乾 qián (Father)	—————— —————— ——————	乾 qián 三 sān 连 lián	Qián is 3 links
兑 duì (Youngest Daughter)	—— —— —————— ——————	兑 duì 上 shàng 缺 quē	Duì lack of top
離 lí (Middle Daughter)	—————— —— —— ——————	離 lí 中 zhōng 虛 xū	Lí middle void
震 zhèn (Eldest Son)	—— —— —— —— ——————	震 zhèn 仰 yǎng	Zhèn is upward-facing jar

		孟 yú	
巽 xùn (Eldest Daughter)	━━━━ ━━━━ ━━ ━━	巽 xùn 下 xià 断 duàn	Xùn is broken off at the bottom
坎 kǎn (Middle Son)	━━ ━━ ━━━━ ━━ ━━	坎 kǎn 中 zhōng 满 mǎn	Kǎn is full in the middle
艮 gèn (Youngest Son)	━━━━ ━━ ━━ ━━ ━━	艮 gèn 覆 fù 碗 wǎn	Gèn is upside down bowl
坤 kūn (Mother)	━━ ━━ ━━ ━━ ━━ ━━	坤 kūn 六 liù 断 duàn	Kūn is 6 broken-off line

Table 1 - Ba Gua (Trigram)

In Chinese Meta-physics, the Post-Heaven Ba Gua is mostly used. The Pre-Heaven Ba Gua is used to supplement any formula if needed.

The lines are derived from the Taiji where the Chinese believe that the universe is made of positive and negative energy balancing each other. When there is sunlight, there will be darkness; when there is strong, there is weak.

The Taiji shows that everything is in virtuous cycle with the blending of Yin and Yang influences. This is the inter-locking black and white as shown in the Taiji symbol. The stronger element is denoted as Yang. Therefore, sunlight is Yang where darkness is Yin. Movement is Yang and stationary is Yin. Therefore, in Feng Shui, mountain is considered as Yin, while water is considered as Yang. In a natural environment, water collects in mountain and forms river. Therefore, it can be said that mountain produce water.

In Taiji you will notice that in Yin there is Yang and in Yang there is Yin. Looking at the Taiji chart, you will find that within the black there is white and within the white there is black. This is the meaning. The Taiji is further derived into solid and broken line. The solid line denotes Yang or Male and the broken line denotes Yin or Female.

__________ This is a Yang line and it denotes Male. ＼ ＿ This is a Yin line and it denotes Female. Then the solid line and broken line are further arranged to form the Ba Gua. The Pre-Heaven Ba Gua layout on 3 X 3 grids as follow:

兌 duì Youngest Daughter Metal, 4 Lake	乾 qián Father Metal, 9 Heaven	巽 xùn Eldest Daughter Wood, 2 Wind
離 lí Middle Daughter Fire, 3 Fire	5	坎 kǎn Middle Son Water, 7 Water
震 zhèn Eldest Son Wood, 8 Thunder	坤 kūn Mother Earth, 1 Earth	艮 gèn Youngest Son Earth, 6 Mountain

Table 2 - Pre-Heaven Ba Gua

The Post-Heaven Ba Gua layout on 3 X 3 grids as follow:

巽 xùn Eldest Daughter Wood, 4 Wind	離 lí Middle Daughter Fire, 9 Fire	坤 kūn Mother Earth, 2 Earth
震 zhèn Eldest Son Wood, 3 Thunder	5	兌 duì Youngest Daughter Metal, 7 Lake
艮 gèn Youngest Son Earth, 8 Mountain	坎 kǎn Middle Son Water, 1 Water	乾 qián Father Metal, 6 Heaven

Table 3 - Post-Heaven Ba Gua

Qi Men Dun Jia uses both Pre & Post-Heaven Ba Gua as references. Charts are plotted using the Post-Heaven Ba Gua as a base.

Ten Heavenly Stems

The attributes of Ten Heavenly Stems as follow:

Heavenly Stems	Attribute
Jia (甲)	Yang Wood
Yi (乙)	Yin Wood
Bing (丙)	Yang Fire
Ding (丁)	Yin Fire
Wu/ Ji (戊 / 己)	Yang Earth / Yin Earth
Geng (庚)	Yang Metal
Xin (辛)	Yin Metal
Ren (壬)	Yang Water
Gui (癸)	Yin Water

Table 4- 10 Heavenly Stems

Twelve Earthly Branches

The attributes of twelve earthly branches as follow:

Earthly Branches	Element	Animal	Time
子 (Zi)	Yang Water	Rat	23:00 – 00:59
丑 (Chou)	Yin Earth	Ox	01:00 – 02:59
寅 (Yin)	Yang Wood	Tiger	03:00 – 04:59
卯 (Mao)	Yin Wood	Rabbit	05:00 – 06:59
辰 (Chen)	Yang Earth	Dragon	07:00 – 08:59
巳 (Si)	Yin Fire	Snake	09:00 – 10:59
午 (Wu)	Yang Fire	Horse	11:00 – 12:59
未 (Wei)	Yin Earth	Goat	13:00 – 14:59
申 (Shen)	Yang Metal	Monkey	15:00 – 16:59
酉 (You)	Yin Metal	Rooster	17:00 – 18:59
戌 (Xu)	Yang Earth	Dog	19:00 – 20:59
亥 (Hai)	Yin Water	Pig	21:00 – 22:59

Table 5 - 12 Earthly Branches

In the nutshell, a Qi Men Dun Jia chart looks like this:

<table>
<tr><td colspan="3">Yang (阳) Dun# 1 Hour: JiaZi ; 直符(ZhíFú): 天蓬(TiānPéng) 直使(ZhíShǐ): 休门(XiūMén) ; 旬首(XúnShǒu): JiaZiWu</td></tr>
<tr>
<td>六合 (Liù Hé)
天辅 (Tiān Fǔ)
杜门 (Dù Mén)
Xun 4   Xin
Xin</td>
<td>白虎 (Bái Hǔ)
天英 (Tiān Yīng)
景门 (Jǐng Mén)
Li 9   Yi
Yi</td>
<td>玄武 (Xuán Wǔ)
禽芮 (Qín Ruì)
死门 (Sǐ Mén)
Kun 2   Ji/Ren
Ji/Ren</td>
</tr>
<tr>
<td>太阴 (Tài Yīn)
天冲 (Tiān Chōng)
伤门 (Shāng Mén)
Zhen 3   Geng
Geng</td>
<td>Yang (阳) Dun# 1
Hour: JiaZi
Fu Yin
©Calvin Yap</td>
<td>九地 (Jiǔ Dì)
天柱 (Tiān Zhù)
惊门 (Jīng Mén)
Dui 7   Ding
Ding</td>
</tr>
<tr>
<td>螣蛇 (Téng Shé)
天任 (Tiān Rèn)
生门 (Shēng Mén)
Gen 8   Bing
Bing</td>
<td>值符 (Zhí Fú)
天蓬 (Tiān Péng)
休门 (Xiū Mén)
Kan 1   Wu
Wu</td>
<td>九天 (Jiǔ Tiān)
天心 (Tiān Xīn)
开门 (Kāi Mén)
Qian 6   Gui
Gui</td>
</tr>
</table>

Figure 5 - Example chart (Yang Dun#1 JiaZi)

Note: explanation of various plates will be based on this example chart (Yang Dun#1 JiaZi Hour)

A Qi Men Dun Jia chart consists of many layer of plates. There are:

- Post-Heaven Ba Gua or Earth Plate

- Human Plate

- Heaven Plate

- God Plate

- Earth Plate Heavenly Stems

- Heaven Plate Heavenly Stems

Breaking up the Qi Men Dun Jia chart, you can see the plates as follow:

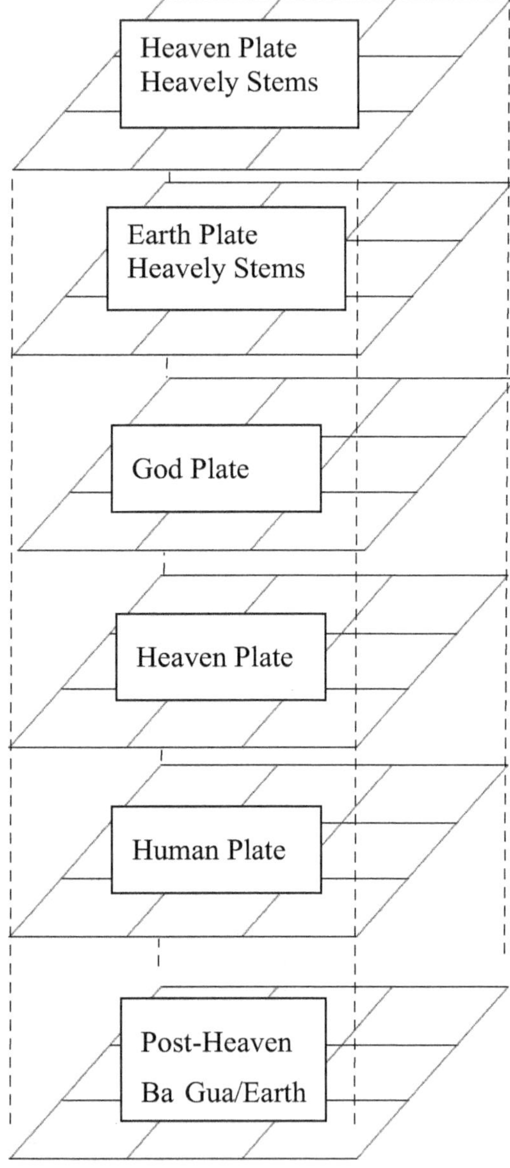

Figure 6 - breakdown of Qi Men Dun Jia Chart

Post-Heaven Ba Gua / Earth Plate

The Post Heaven Ba Gua and Earth Plate consists of 3 X 3 grid called palace (宫). The arrangement as follow:

	SE (东南)	South (正南)	SW (西南)	
	巳 (Si) 巽四宫 (Xun 4) Wood 辰 (Chen)	午 (Wu) 离九宫 (Li 9) Fire	未 (Wei) 坤二宫 (Kun 2) Earth (Shen) 申	
East (正东)	震三宫 (Zhen 3) Wood 卯 (Mao)		兑七宫 (Dui 7) Metal (You) 酉	West (正西)
	寅 (Yin) 艮八宫 (Gen 8) Earth 丑 (Chou)	坎一宫 (Kan 1) Water 子 (Zi)	(Xu) 戌 乾六宫 (Qian 6) Metal 亥 (Hai)	
	NE (东北)	North (正北)	NW (西北)	

Figure 7 - Post-Heaven Ba Gua / Earth Plate

This arrangement is fixed and will not change. The attributes of each Palace as follow:

Palace	Direction	Element	Earthly Branches	Relationship representative
Xun 4	South East	Wood	Chen & Si	Eldest Daughter
Li 9	South	Fire	Wu	Middle Daughter
Kun 2	South West	Earth	Wei & Shen	Mother or Lady Master
Zhen 3	East	Wood	Mao	Eldest Son
Dui 7	West	Metal	You	Youngest Daughter
Gen 8	North East	Earth	Yin & Chou	Youngest Son
Kan 1	North	Water	Zi	Middle Son
Qian 6	North West	Metal	Xu & Hai	Father or Male Master

Table 6 - Earth Plate attributes

The Post-Heaven Ba Gua / Earth Plate forms the basis for all the plate above. The Human, Heaven, God, Earth Heavenly Stem and Heaven Heavenly Stem Plates are arranged on top of the Post-Heaven Ba Gua / Earth Plate; i.e. the 3 X 3 grid.

Relationship between palaces

The following shows the five elements relationship between the palaces in order to find out if it is auspicious or inauspicious. This is used when evaluating relationship between 2 palaces. For example, the comparison is done on items (Heavenly Stems, 八神 (8 God - bā shén), 九星 (Jiǔ Xīng) or 八门 (Bā Mén)) in Kan 1 Palace (which is Water) against items in Kun 2 Palace (Earth).

Kan 1 Palace (North - Water)

Other Palace	Element	Relationship	Auspiciousness
Kun 2 (SW)	Earth	Earth controls Water. Kun 2 controls Kan 1.	Inauspicious
Zhen 3 (East)	Wood	Water gives birth to Wood. Kan 1supports Zhen 3.	Auspicious
Xun 4 (SE)	Wood	Water gives birth to Wood. Kan 1 supports Xun 4.	Auspicious
Qian 6 (NW)	Metal	Metal gives birth to Water. Qian 6 supports Kan 1.	Auspicious
Dui 7 (West)	Metal	Metal gives birth to Water. Dui 7 supports Kan 1.	Auspicious
Gen 8 (NE)	Earth	Earth controls Water. Gen 8 controls Kan 1.	Inauspicious
Li 9 (South)	Fire	Water controls Fire. Kan 1 controls Li 9.	Inauspicious

Kun 2 Palace (SW - Earth)

Other Palace	Element	Relationship	Auspiciousness
Kan 1 (North)	Water	Earth controls Water. Kun 2 controls Kan 1.	Inauspicious
Zhen 3 (East)	Wood	Wood controls Earth. Zhen 3 controls Kun 2.	Inauspicious
Xun 4 (SE)	Wood	Wood controls Earth. Xun 4 controls Kun 2.	Inauspicious
Qian 6 (NW)	Metal	Earth gives birth to	Auspicious

		Metal. Kun 2 supports Qian 6.	
Dui 7 (West)	Metal	Earth gives birth to Metal. Kun 2 supports Dui 7.	Auspicious
Gen 8 (NE)	Earth	Same element. Gen 8 supports Kun 2.	Auspicious
Li 9 (South)	Fire	Fire gives birth to Earth. Li 9 supports Kun 2.	Auspicious

Zhen 3 Palace (East - Wood)

Other Palace	Element	Relationship	Auspiciousness
Kan 1 (North)	Water	Water gives birth to Wood. Kan 1 supports Zhen 3.	Auspicious
Kun 2 (SW)	Earth	Wood controls Earth. Zhen 3 controls Kun 2.	Inauspicious
Xun 4 (SE)	Wood	Same element. Xun 4 supports Zhen 3.	Auspicious
Qian 6 (NW)	Metal	Metal controls Wood. Qian 6 controls Zhen 3.	Inauspicious
Dui 7 (West)	Metal	Metal controls Wood. Dui 7 controls Zhen 3.	Inauspicious
Gen 8 (NE)	Earth	Wood controls Earth. Zhen 3 controls Gen 8.	Inauspicious
Li 9 (South)	Fire	Wood gives birth to Fire. Zhen 3 supports Li 9.	Auspicious

Xun 4 Palace (SE - Wood)

Other Palace	Element	Relationship	Auspiciousness
Kan 1 (North)	Water	Water gives birth to Wood. Kan 1 supports Xun 4.	Auspicious
Kun 2 (SW)	Earth	Wood controls Earth. Xun 4 controls Kun 2.	Inauspicious
Zhen 3 (East)	Wood	Same element. Zhen 3 supports Xun 4.	Auspicious
Qian 6 (NW)	Metal	Metal controls Wood. Qian 6 controls Xun 4.	Inauspicious
Dui 7 (West)	Metal	Metal controls Wood. Dui 7 controls Xun 4.	Inauspicious
Gen 8 (NE)	Earth	Wood controls Earth. Xun 4 controls Gen 8.	Inauspicious
Li 9 (South)	Fire	Wood gives birth to Fire. Xun 4 supports Li 9.	Auspicious

Qian 6 Palace (NW - Metal)

Other Palace	Element	Relationship	Auspiciousness
Kan 1 (North)	Water	Metal gives birth to Water. Qian 6 supports Kan 1.	Auspicious
Kun 2 (SW)	Earth	Earth gives birth to Metal. Kun 2 support Qian 6.	Auspicious
Zhen 3 (East)	Wood	Metal controls Wood. Qian 6 controls Zhen 3.	Inauspicious
Xun 4 (SE)	Wood	Metal controls Wood. Qian 6 controls Xun 4.	Inauspicious
Dui 7 (West)	Metal	Same element. Dui 7 supports Qian 6.	Auspicious
Gen 8 (NE)	Earth	Earth gives birth to Metal. Gen 8 supports Qian 6.	Auspicious
Li 9 (South)	Fire	Fire controls Metal. Li 9 controls Qian 6.	Inauspicious

Dui 7 Palace (West - Metal)

Other Palace	Element	Relationship	Auspiciousness
Kan 1 (North)	Water	Metal gives birth to Water. Dui 7 supports Kan 1.	Auspicious
Kun 2 (SW)	Earth	Earth gives birth to Metal. Kun 2 supports Dui 7.	Auspicious
Zhen 3 (East)	Wood	Metal controls Wood. Dui 7 controls Zhen 3.	Inauspicious
Xun 4 (SE)	Wood	Metal controls Wood. Dui 7 controls Xun 4.	Inauspicious
Qian 6 (NW)	Metal	Same element. Dui 7 supports Qian 6.	Auspicious
Gen 8 (NE)	Earth	Earth gives birth to Metal. Gen 8 supports Dui 7.	Auspicious
Li 9 (South)	Fire	Fire controls Metal. Li 9 controls Dui 7.	Inauspicious

Gen 8 Palace (NE- Earth)

Other Palace	Element	Relationship	Auspiciousness
Kan 1 (North)	Water	Earth controls Water. Gen 8 controls Kan 1.	Inauspicious
Kun 2 (SW)	Earth	Same element. Kun 2 supports Gen 8.	Auspicious
Zhen 3 (East)	Wood	Wood controls Earth. Zhen 3 controls Gen 8.	Inauspicious
Xun 4 (SE)	Wood	Wood controls Earth. Xun 4 controls Gen 8.	Inauspicious
Qian 6 (NW)	Metal	Earth gives birth to Metal. Gen 8 supports Qian 6.	Auspicious
Dui 7 (West)	Metal	Earth gives birth to Metal. Gen 8 supports Dui 7.	Auspicious
Li 9 (South)	Fire	Fire gives birth to Earth.	Auspicious

		Li 9 Supports Gen 8.	

Li 9 Palace (South - Fire)

Other Palace	Element	Relationship	Auspiciousness
Kan 1 (North)	Water	Water controls Fire. Kan 1 controls Li 9.	Inauspicious
Kun 2 (SW)	Earth	Fire gives birth to Earth. Li 9 supports Kun 2.	Auspicious
Zhen 3 (East)	Wood	Wood gives birth to Fire. Zhen 3 supports Li 9.	Auspicious
Xun 4 (SE)	Wood	Wood gives birth to Fire. Xun 4 supports Li 9.	Auspicious
Qian 6 (NW)	Metal	Fire controls Metal. Li 9 controls Qian 6.	Inauspicious
Dui 7 (West)	Metal	Fire controls Metal. Li 9 controls Dui 7.	Inauspicious
Gen 8 (NE)	Earth	Fire gives birth to Earth. Gen 8 supports Li 9.	Auspicious

Human Plate

The Human Plate is also known as 8 door or Ba Men (八门), which consists of 8 elements spread out in the 3 X 3 grid or palaces. The 8 elements are: 开门 (Kāi Mén), 休门 (Xiū Mén), 生门 (Shēng Mén), 伤门 (Shāng Mén), 杜门 (Dù Mén), 景门 (Jǐng Mén), 死门 (Sǐ Mén), 惊门 (Jīng Mén).

Based on the sample chart (Yang Dun #1 JiaZi), the Human Plate looks like this:

<table>
<tr><td>SE (东南)</td><td>South (正南)</td><td>SW(西南)</td></tr>
<tr><td>杜门 (Dù Mén)</td><td>景门 (Jǐng Mén)</td><td>死门 (Sǐ Mén)</td></tr>
<tr><td>伤门 (Shāng Mén)</td><td></td><td>惊门 (Jīng Mén)</td></tr>
<tr><td>生门 (Shēng Mén)</td><td>休门 (Xiū Mén)</td><td>开门 (Kāi Mén)</td></tr>
<tr><td>NE (东北)</td><td>North (正北)</td><td>NW (西北)</td></tr>
</table>

East (正东) — left side; West (正西) — right side

Figure 8 - Sample Human Plate

This is also known as the original position of **Fu Yin** position of the Human Plate.

The position of each door relative to each other is fixed. For example, going in clock-wise pattern from North, we have 休门 (Xiū Mén) then follow by 生门 (Shēng Mén) at North East and then 伤门 (Shāng Mén) and so forth in the following pattern: 开门 (Kāi Mén) → 休门 (Xiū Mén) → 生门 (Shēng Mén) → 伤门 (Shāng Mén) → 杜门 (Dù Mén) → 景门 (Jǐng Mén) → 死门 (Sǐ Mén) → 惊门 (Jīng Mén).

So, if 休门 (Xiū Mén) is at East Palace, then the Human Plate will look like this:

	SE (东南)	South (正南)	SW (西南)	
	生门 (Shēng Mén)	伤门 (Shāng Mén)	杜门 (Dù Mén)	
East (正东)	休门 (Xiū Mén)		景门 (Jǐng Mén)	West (正西)
	开门 (Kāi Mén)	惊门 (Jīng Mén)	死门 (Sǐ Mén)	
	NE (东北)	North (正北)	NW (西北)	

The simplified attributes of each 8 door or Ba Men is as follow:

8 Door	English meaning	Representation
开门 (Kāi Mén)	Open Door	Leader, judge, job, career, shop front.
休门 (Xiū Mén)	Rest Door	Family, relax living.
生门 (Shēng Mén)	Growth Door	Business transaction, profit, wealth luck
伤门 (Shāng Mén)	Hurt Door	Transportation, indirect wealth, gambling, hurt.
杜门 (Dù Mén)	Stuck Door	Stuck, concealment, hiding, hard to get.
景门 (Jǐng Mén)	Scenery Door	Blood related calamity, gorgeous place, dispute, examination paper, documents, management.
死门 (Sǐ Mén)	Dead Door	Bad luck, dead man, tomb, land.
惊门 (Jīng Mén)	Shock Door	Dispute, scandal, law suit, lawyer, panic.

Table 7 - Human Plate Attribute

The level of auspiciousness of the 8 door as follow:

8 Door	Auspiciousness
开门 (Kāi Mén)	Good
休门 (Xiū Mén)	Good
生门 (Shēng Mén)	Good
伤门 (Shāng Mén)	Bad
杜门 (Dù Mén)	Middle
景门 (Jǐng Mén)	Middle
死门 (Sǐ Mén)	Very Bad
惊门 (Jīng Mén)	Bad

Table 8 - 8 door auspiciousness

From the example, the Human Plate together with Post-Heaven Bagua/Earth Plate will be as follow:

杜门 (Dù Mén) Xun 4	景门 (Jǐng Mén) Li 9	死门 (Sǐ Mén) Kun 2
伤门 (Shāng Mén) Zhen 3		惊门 (Jīng Mén) Dui 7
生门 (Shēng Mén) Gen 8	休门 (Xiū Mén) Kan 1	开门 (Kāi Mén) Qian 6

Heaven Plate

The Heaven Plate consists of 九星 (Jiǔ Xīng) or 9 Stars. They are 天心 (Tiān Xīn), 天蓬 (Tiān Péng), 天任 (Tiān Rèn), 天冲 (Tiān Chōng), 天辅 (Tiān Fǔ), 天英 (Tiān Yīng), 天禽 (Tiān Qín), 天芮 (Tiān Ruì), 天柱 (Tiān Zhù). Because there are 9 of them, one of them will be in the middle. Therefore, the middle element, which is 天禽 (Tiān Qín), will be moved to be together with 天芮 (Tiān Ruì). Most of the time, 天禽 (Tiān Qín) is not used in the interpretation.

The simplified attributes of 9 stars is as follow:

9 Stars	English meaning	Representation
天心 (Tiān Xīn)	Doctor	Doctor, round object, scheming person.
天蓬 (Tiān Péng)	Marshall	Hugh wealth loss, big robber, murderer, lechery, fat, leader.
天任 (Tiān Rèn)	Post	Auspiciousness, kind, honest, frank.
天冲 (Tiān Chōng)	Clash	Athlete, martial artist, clash, conflict, impulsive, do things speedily.
天辅 (Tiān Fǔ)	Assistance	Wisdom, civilized, academic, teacher, examination officer, interviewer.

天英 (Tiān Yīng)	Hero	Strong character, blood related issue.
天禽 (Tiān Qín)	Bird	Honest frank.
天芮 (Tiān Ruì)	Disease	Illness, issue, student, religious, Chinese Meta-physics.
天柱 (Tiān Zhù)	Pillar	Adverse calamity, ruin, dispute, gossip, scandal.

Table 9 - 9 Stars attributes

The level of auspiciousness of the 9 stars as follow:

9 Stars	Auspiciousness
天心 (Tiān Xīn)	Good
天蓬 (Tiān Péng)	Bad
天任 (Tiān Rèn)	Middle
天冲 (Tiān Chōng)	Middle
天辅 (Tiān Fǔ)	Good
天英 (Tiān Yīng)	Bad
天禽 (Tiān Qín)	Good
天芮 (Tiān Ruì)	Bad
天柱 (Tiān Zhù)	Bad

Table 10 - 9 Stars Auspiciousness

From the example, the Heaven Plate together with Post-Heaven Bagua/Earth Plate will be as follow:

天辅 (Tiān Fǔ) Xun 4	天英 (Tiān Yīng) Li 9	禽芮 (Qín Ruì) Kun 2
天冲 (Tiān Chōng) Zhen 3		天柱 (Tiān Zhù) Dui 7
天任 (Tiān Rèn) Gen 8	天蓬 (Tiān Péng) Kan 1	天心 (Tiān Xīn) Qian 6

Combining with Human Plate, the chart as follow:

天辅 (Tiān Fǔ) 杜门 (Dù Mén) Xun 4	天英 (Tiān Yīng) 景门 (Jǐng Mén) Li 9	禽芮 (Qín Ruì) 死门 (Sǐ Mén) Kun 2
天冲 (Tiān Chōng) 伤门 (Shāng Mén) Zhen 3		天柱 (Tiān Zhù) 惊门 (Jīng Mén) Dui 7
天任 (Tiān Rèn) 生门 (Shēng Mén) Gen 8	天蓬 (Tiān Péng) 休门 (Xiū Mén) Kan 1	天心 (Tiān Xīn) 开门 (Kāi Mén) Qian 6

God Plate

The God Plate is also known as 8 Gods or Bā Shén (八神). The 8 Gods consists of 值符 (Zhí Fú), 螣蛇 (Téng Shé), 太阴 (Tài Yīn), 六合 (Liù Hé), 白虎 (Bái Hǔ), 玄武 (Xuán Wǔ), 九地 (Jiǔ Dì), 九天 (Jiǔ Tiān).

Based on the sample chart (Yang Dun #1 JiaZi), the God Plate looks like this:

	SE (东南)	South (正南)	SW(西南)	
	六合 (Liù Hé)	白虎 (Bái Hǔ)	玄武 (Xuán Wǔ)	
East (正东)	太阴 (Tài Yīn)		九地 (Jiǔ Dì)	West (正西)
	螣蛇 (Téng Shé)	值符 (Zhí Fú)	九天 (Jiǔ Tiān)	
	NE (东北)	North (正北)	NW (西北)	

The simplified attributes of each 8 door or Ba Men is as follow:

8 God	English meaning	Representation
值符 (Zhí Fú)	Leader	Authority, leader, boss, valuable, precious.
螣蛇 (Téng Shé)	Winged Snake	Vexed, worried, fake, cunning, agile, nimble.
太阴 (Tài Yīn)	Moon	Dark, gloomy, gentle, quiet.
六合 (Liù Hé)	Six Combine	Marriage, cooperation, evidence.
白虎 (Bái Hǔ)	White Tiger	Fierce, ferocious, traffic accident, bad-temper, temperamental.
玄武 (Xuán Wǔ)	Dark Martiality	Financial loss, thief, fake, false, petty.
九地 (Jiǔ Dì)	Nine Earth	Short, slow, depressed, slow-moving, solid, firm.
九天 (Jiǔ Tiān)	Nine Heaven	Tall, sky, heaven, high object, extrovert, impulsive.

Table 11 - 8 Gods representation

The level of auspiciousness of the 8 Gods as follow:

8 God	Auspiciousness
值符 (Zhí Fú)	Good
螣蛇 (Téng Shé)	Bad
太阴 (Tài Yīn)	Medium
六合 (Liù Hé)	Good
白虎 (Bái Hǔ)	Bad
玄武 (Xuán Wǔ)	Bad
九地 (Jiǔ Dì)	Medium
九天 (Jiǔ Tiān)	Good

Table 12 - 8 God auspiciousness

From the example, the God Plate together with Post-Heaven Bagua/Earth Plate will be as follow:

六合 (Liù Hé) Xun 4	白虎 (Bái Hǔ) Li 9	玄武 (Xuán Wǔ) Kun 2
太阴 (Tài Yīn) Zhen 3		九地 (Jiǔ Dì) Dui 7
螣蛇 (Téng Shé) Gen 8	值符 (Zhí Fú) Kan 1	九天 (Jiǔ Tiān) Qian 6

Combining with Earth, Human and Heaven Plate, the chart as follow:

六合 (Liù Hé) 天辅 (Tiān Fǔ) 杜门 (Dù Mén) Xun 4	白虎 (Bái Hǔ) 天英 (Tiān Yīng) 景门 (Jǐng Mén) Li 9	玄武 (Xuán Wǔ) 禽芮 (Qín Ruì) 死门 (Sǐ Mén) Kun 2
太阴 (Tài Yīn) 天冲 (Tiān Chōng) 伤门 (Shāng Mén) Zhen 3		九地 (Jiǔ Dì) 天柱 (Tiān Zhù) 惊门 (Jīng Mén) Dui 7
螣蛇 (Téng Shé) 天任 (Tiān Rèn) 生门 (Shēng Mén) Gen 8	值符 (Zhí Fú) 天蓬 (Tiān Péng) 休门 (Xiū Mén) Kan 1	九天 (Jiǔ Tiān) 天心 (Tiān Xīn) 开门 (Kāi Mén) Qian 6

Earth Plate Heavenly Stems

The Earth Plate Heavenly Stems consists of 9 out of the 10 Heavenly Stems placed around the plate. Why 9 and not 10? This is because **Qi Men Dun Jia**, and the **Dun Jia** means "to hide the **Jia**". Therefore, **Jia** Heavenly Stem is hidden. **Jia** is like the king in chess where it is hidden and protected.

From the example, the Earth Plate Heavenly Stems looks like this:

Xun 4 Xin	Li 9 Yi	Kun 2 Ji/Ren
Zhen 3 Geng		Dui 7 Ding
Gen 8 Bing	Kan 1 Wu	Qian 6 Gui

The Earth Plate Heavenly Stems is derived based on the solar information.

Combining the Earth, Human and Heaven Plate, the chart is as follow:

<table>
<tr>
<td>六合 (Liù Hé)
天辅 (Tiān Fǔ)
杜门 (Dù Mén)
Xun 4
Xin</td>
<td>白虎 (Bái Hǔ)
天英 (Tiān Yīng)
景门 (Jǐng Mén)
Li 9
Yi</td>
<td>玄武 (Xuán Wǔ)
禽芮 (Qín Ruì)
死门 (Sǐ Mén)
Kun 2
Ji/Ren</td>
</tr>
<tr>
<td>太阴 (Tài Yīn)
天冲 (Tiān Chōng)
伤门 (Shāng Mén)
Zhen 3
Geng</td>
<td></td>
<td>九地 (Jiǔ Dì)
天柱 (Tiān Zhù)
惊门 (Jīng Mén)
Dui 7
Ding</td>
</tr>
<tr>
<td>螣蛇 (Téng Shé)
天任 (Tiān Rèn)
生门 (Shēng Mén)
Gen 8
Bing</td>
<td>值符 (Zhí Fú)
天蓬 (Tiān Péng)
休门 (Xiū Mén)
Kan 1
Wu</td>
<td>九天 (Jiǔ Tiān)
天心 (Tiān Xīn)
开门 (Kāi Mén)
Qian 6
Gui</td>
</tr>
</table>

Heaven Plate Heavenly Stems

Like the Earth Plate Heavenly Stems, the Heaven Plate Heavenly Stems is 9 Heavenly Stems placed around the plate. The Heaven Plate Heavenly Stems are derived from the Earth Plate Heavenly Stems.

From the example, the Heaven Plate Heavenly Stems looks like this:

Xun 4 Xin	Li 9 Yi	Kun 2 Ji/Ren
Zhen 3 Geng		Dui 7 Ding
Gen 8 Bing	Kan 1 Wu	Qian 6 Gui

Combining the Earth, Human, Heaven and Earth Plate Heavenly Stems, the chart is as follow:

六合 (Liù Hé) 天辅 (Tiān Fǔ) 杜门 (Dù Mén) 　　　Xun 4　　Xin 　　　　　　　Xin	白虎 (Bái Hǔ) 天英 (Tiān Yīng) 景门 (Jǐng Mén) 　　Li　9　　　Yi 　　　　　　　Yi	玄武 (Xuán Wǔ) 禽芮 (Qín Ruì) 死门 (Sǐ Mén) Kun　2　　Ji/Ren 　　　　　Ji/Ren
太阴 (Tài Yīn) 天冲 (Tiān Chōng) 伤门 (Shāng Mén) Zhen　3　　Geng 　　　　　　Geng		九地 (Jiǔ Dì) 天柱 (Tiān Zhù) 惊门 (Jīng Mén) 　Dui　7　　Ding 　　　　　　Ding
螣蛇 (Téng Shé) 天任 (Tiān Rèn) 生门 (Shēng Mén) Gen　8　　Bing 　　　　　Bing	值符 (Zhí Fú) 天蓬 (Tiān Péng) 休门 (Xiū Mén) Kan　1　　Wu 　　　　　Wu	九天 (Jiǔ Tiān) 天心 (Tiān Xīn) 开门 (Kāi Mén) Qian　6　　Gui 　　　　　Gui

Other elements

There are still other elements that you need to be aware of before you can start reading Qi Men Dun Jia.

Horse

The Horse star is marked with the character 马 in the chart. It is also known as Travelling Horse or Yì Mǎ (驿马). It has the meaning of movement, running away or changes.

Emptiness

The Emptiness star is marked with the character **O** in the chart. It is also known as Kōng (空).When there is Kong in the palace, it means all the Earth, Human, Heaven and God elements will be only 20% auspicious or inauspicious. When the time attributed to the palace arrives at the palace where there is a Kōng (空), the full 100% capability will be regained.

Fu Yin

A chart can be categorised as a normal chart, Fu Yin Chart or Fan Yin Chart. A Fu Yin chart is indicated by the word **Fu Yin** at the middle of palace.

<table>
<tr>
<td>六合 (Liù Hé)
天辅 (Tiān Fǔ)
杜门 (Dù Mén)

Xun 4   Xin
      Xin</td>
<td>白虎 (Bái Hǔ)
天英 (Tiān Yīng)
景门 (Jǐng Mén)

Li 9   Yi
      Yi</td>
<td>玄武 (Xuán Wǔ)
禽芮 (Qin Rui)
死门 (Sǐ Mén)

Kun 2   Ji/Ren
      Ji/Ren</td>
</tr>
<tr>
<td>太阴 (Tài Yīn)
天冲 (Tiān Chōng)
伤门 (Shāng Mén)

Zhen 3   Geng
      Geng</td>
<td>Yang (阳) Dun# 1
Hour: Jia Zi
Fu Yin
©Calvin Yap</td>
<td>九地 (Jiǔ Dì)
天柱 (Tiān Zhù)
惊门 (Jǐng Mén)

Dui 7   Ding
      Ding</td>
</tr>
<tr>
<td>螣蛇 (Téng Shé)
天任 (Tiān Rèn)
生门 (Shēng Mén)

Gen 8   Bing
      Bing</td>
<td>值符 (Zhí Fú)
天蓬 (Tiān Péng)
休门 (Xiū Mén)

Kan 1   Wu
      Wu</td>
<td>九天 (Jiǔ Tiān)
天心 (Tiān Xīn)
开门 (Kāi Mén)

Qian 6   Gui
      Gui</td>
</tr>
</table>

Figure 9 - Fu Yin

A Fu Yin (伏吟) chart means that it is stagnant, and there is no change or suffering.

Fan Yin

A Fan Yin (反吟) chart is indicated by the word **Fan Yin** at the middle palace.

Figure 10 - Fan Yin

A Fan Yin chart means fickle, uncertainty, changes, and a 50-50 chance.

Other than Fu Yin and Fan Yin chart, there are the normal charts.

Four Pillars with Qi Men Dun Jia chart

A Qi Men Dun Jia chart has to be read together with Four Pillars that is derived from the Year, Month, Day and Hour. The Four Pillars consists of Year Pillar, Month Pillar, Day Pillar and Hour Pillar. Hence it is called the Four Pillars.

Hour Pillar	Day Pillar	Month Pillar	Year Pillar
Hour Heavenly Stem	Day Heavenly Stem	Month Heavenly Stem	Year Heavenly Stem
Hour Earthly Branch	Day Earthly Branch	Month Earthly Branch	Year Earthly Branch

Each Pillar is made out from a combination of Heavenly Stem and Earthly Branch that is known as 60 Jia Zi. The top is called Heavenly Stem and the bottom is called Earthly Branch.

For more information on this, please refer to the book, ***Fundamental of Chinese Meta-Physics, Chinese Calendar System***.

For example, 28th Dec 2018 at Jia Zi hour is as follow:

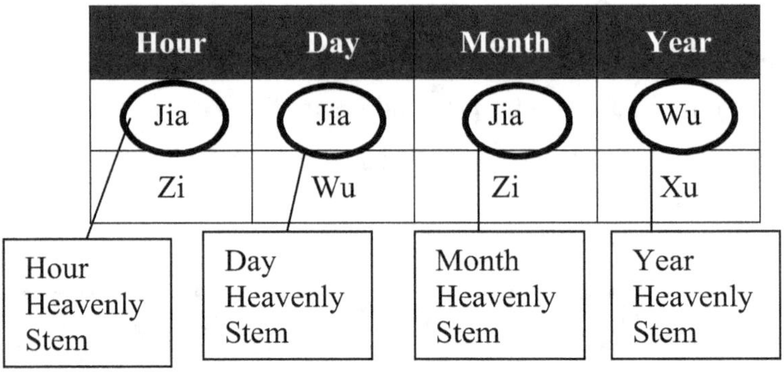

Hour	Day	Month	Year
Jia	Jia	Jia	Wu
Zi	Wu	Zi	Xu
Hour Heavenly Stem	Day Heavenly Stem	Month Heavenly Stem	Year Heavenly Stem

And the Qi Men Dun Jia Chart as follow:

六合 (Liù Hé) 天辅 (Tiān Fǔ) 杜门 (Dù Mén) 　　Xun 4　　Xin 　　　　　　Xin	白虎 (Bái Hǔ) 天英 (Tiān Yīng) 景门 (Jǐng Mén) 　　Li 9　　Yi 　　　　　Yi	玄武 (Xuán Wǔ) 禽芮 (Qín Ruì) 死门 (Sǐ Mén) Kun 2　　Ji/Ren 　　　　Ji/Ren
太阴 (Tài Yīn) 天冲 (Tiān Chōng) 伤门 (Shāng Mén) 　Zhen 3　　Geng 　　　　　Geng	Yang (阳) Dun# 1 Hour: **JiaZi** **Fu Yin** ©Calvin Yap	九地 (Jiǔ Dì) 天柱 (Tiān Zhù) 惊门 (Jīng Mén) 　Dui 7　　Ding 　　　　　Ding
螣蛇 (Téng Shé) 天任 (Tiān Rèn) 生门 (Shēng Mén) 　Gen 8　　Bing 　　　　　Bing	值符 (Zhí Fú) 天蓬 (Tiān Péng) 休门 (Xiū Mén) 　Kan 1　　Wu 　　　　　Wu	九天 (Jiǔ Tiān) 天心 (Tiān Xīn) 开门 (Kāi Mén) 　Qian 6　　Gui 　　　　　Gui

- Hour Heavenly Stem = the matter asked or the offspring or subordinate of the person asking.

- Day Heavenly Stem = the person asking.

- Month Heavenly Stem = the sibling, friend or colleague of the person asking.

- Year Heavenly Stem = the parents or ancestors of the person asking.

- Heaven Plate Heavenly Stem– to see the current situation. For example, if you are asking about what is going to happen, then look for Heaven Plate Heavenly Stem in the chart.

The hidden Jia

From the example above, the Hour Heavenly Stem is Jia but it is not found in the Qi Men Dun Jia chart. So, where is it hidden? As mentioned previously, Jia is like the King in chess, and it has to be protected and hidden from enemy. So, Jia is hidden as follow:

Jia	Hidden at
Jia Zi	**Wu**
Jia Xu	**Ji**
Jia Shen	**Geng**
Jia Wu	**Xin**
Jia Chen	**Ren**
Jia Yin	**Gui**

Table 13 - hidden Jia

For the example above: Hour Pillar is Jia Zi, so Jia is hidden at Wu. Wu Heavenly Stem will represent Hour Heavenly Stem. Day Pillar is Jia Wu, so Jia is hidden at Xin. Xin Heavenly Stem will represent Day Heavenly Stem. Likewise, Month Pillar is Jia Zi, so Jia is hidden at

Wu. Therefore, Wu Heavenly Stem will represent Month Heavenly Stem as well.

Distribution of Qi Men Dun Jia Chart

There are 1080 charts Qi Men Dun Jia chart that are divided into 580 Yang Dun and 580 Yin Dun. Each Dun is divided into 9 categories (1 to 9) where each chart represents 60 JiaZi Hour. To summarise:

- In 1 Dun, there are 60 charts.
- There are 9 Yang Dun and 9 Yin Dun
- 9 X 60 = 580 Yang Dun, 9 X 60 = 580 Yin Dun, total 1080 charts.

Yang Dun and Yin Dun are the marker for Solar events where the Sun is at a certain position relative to the earth. For example, Yang Dun begins around 21st or 22nd Dec every year, where the Winter Solstice (冬至 - Dōng Zhì) starts. This is when the Sun is at a 270° angle relative to Earth in the Celestial Longitude. Yin Dun begins around 21st or 22nd June every year where Summer Solstice (夏至 - Xià Zhì) starts. This is when the Sun is at a 90° angle relative to Earth in the Celestial Longitude.

Each Dun consists of 60 charts which are based on 60 JiaZi hour as follow:

JiaZi, YiChou, BingYin, DingMao, WuChen, JiSi, GengWu, XinWei, RenShen, GuiYou, JiaXu, YiHai, BingZi, DingChou, WuYin, JiMao, GengChen, XinSi, RenWu, GuiWei, JiaShen, YiYou, BingXu, DingHai, WuZi, JiChou, GengYin, XinMao, RenChen, GuiSi, JiaWu, YiWei, BingShen, DingYou, WuXu,

JiHai, GengZi, XinChou, RenYin, GuiMao, JiaChen, YiSi, BingWu, DingWei, WuShen, JiYou, GengXu, XinHai, RenZi, GuiChou, JiaYin, YiMao, BingChen, DingSi, WuWu, JiWei, GengShen, XinYou, RenXu, GuiHai

Mth	二十四节气 (24 sub season - èr shí sì jié qì)	Start Date	Dun
First month (Yin)	立春 (Beginning of Spring - lì chūn), 雨水 (Rain Water - yǔ shuǐ)	Feb 4, 5 Feb 18, 19	Yang
2nd Month (Mao)	惊蛰 (Insect Awakening - jīng zhé), 春分 (Spring Equinox - chūn fēn)	Mar 5, 6 Mar 20, 21	Yang
3rd Month (Chen)	清明 (Pure Brightness - qīng míng), 谷雨 (Grain Rain - gǔ yǔ)	Apr 4, 5 Apr 20, 21	Yang
4th Month (Si)	立夏 (Beginning of Summer - lì xià), 小满 (Small Grain - xiǎo mǎn)	May 5, 6 May 21, 22	Yang
5th Month (Wu)	芒种 (Summer Harvest - máng zhòng), 夏至 (Summer Solstice - xià zhì)	Jun 5, 6 Jun 21, 22	Yang Yin
6th Month (Wei)	小署 (Mild Summer - xiǎo shǔ), 大署 (Extreme Summer - dà shǔ)	July 7, 8 July 22, 23	Yin
7th Month (Shen)	立秋 (Beginning of Autumn - lì qiū), 外署 (Outer Heat - wài shǔ)	Aug 7, 8 Aug 23, 24	Yin
8th Month (You)	白露 (White Dew - bái lù), 秋分 (Autumn Equinox - qiū fēn)	Sep 7, 8 Sep 23, 24	Yin
9th Month (Xu)	寒露 (Cold Dew - hán lù), 霜降 (Frost - shuāng jiàng)	Oct 8, 9 Oct 23, 24	Yin
10th Month (Hai)	立冬 (Beginning of Winter - lì dōng), 小雪 (Mild Snow - xiǎo xuě)	Nov 7, 8 Nov 22, 23	Yin

11th Month (Zi)	大雪 (Extreme Snow - dà xuě), 冬至 (Winter Solstice - dōng zhì)	Dec 7, 8 Dec 21, 22	Yin Yang
12th Month (Chou)	小寒 (Mild Cold - xiǎo hán), 大寒 (Extreme Cold - dà hán)	Jan 5, 6 Jan 20, 21	Yang

Table 14 - Distribution of QMDJ Charts

Rules of Divination

In ancient times, our forefathers had laid down the following rules when asking for divination. The rules are stated as **three do not divine** (三不占).

The rules are:

1. No movement, don't divine (Wú gù bù zhàn 无故不占)
2. Nothing surprising, don't divine (Wú yì bù zhàn 无异不占)
3. Don't ask, don't divine (Wú wèn bù zhàn 无问不占)

No movement, don't divine (Wú Gù Bù Zhàn 无故不占)

Movement is indication of something is happening. For example, asking for temple lot – need to shake the lot holder for the lot to drop out. As such, if there is no indication (e.g. movement or something happening) don't do the divination.

Nothing surprising, don't divine (Wú Yì Bù Zhàn 无异不占)

"Surprise" affects human emotion, which affect human 6th sense. "Surprise" will cause changes in human mood. Since there is change, it means there is movement. So, you should only do divination when there is slight hint or triggering of the 6th sense.

Don't ask, don't divine (Wú Wèn Bù Zhàn 无问不占)

If people don't ask you, don't divine. It affects the Cause and Effect (Karma). Things happen for a reason. If you can help but if the person didn't ask for help, then it is the person's karma. However, if you insist on helping, you are essentially violating the laws of nature.

Ti Yong (体用)

Chinese Meta-Physics emphasises a lot on the concept of Ti 体 (Body) and Yong 用 (Use). Some websites translates this as "Essence" and "Function" (Ti 体 = Essence and Yong 用 = Function).

In the nutshell, Ti Yong (体用) talks about the reference point and its relationship with the surroundings. See the diagram below:

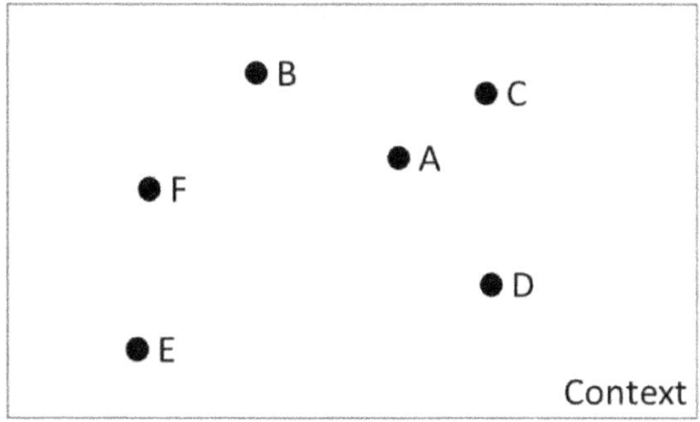

Figure 11 - Ti Yong

Within this context, there is A, B, C, D, E and F. If we use "A" as the **Point of Reference**, then we evaluate the attributes of B, C, D, E and F with reference to "A". Therefore:

- Point of Reference = (Ti 体)

- Attributes with reference to Point of Reference = Yong (用)

Using the above example, if the Context is distance and using "A" as Ti (体), then "C" is the nearest while "E" is the furthest, where both are the Yong (用). If we use "F" as Ti (体), then "D" is the furthest as Yong (用).

Part II –Qi Men Dun Jia Divination

In this section, you will be taught basic Qi Men Dun Jia divination and how to interpret simple questions. For more advanced techniques, you are advised to sign up for the class.

Steps in Qi Men Dun Jia Divination

Qi Men Dun Jia Divination can done easily by following these 5 steps:

Collect → Plot → Determine → Identify → Interpret

1. **Collect** all the questions that a person wants to ask before plotting the Qi Men Dun Jia chart. The questions have to be precise and not open-ended. (e.g. will I get rich is not an acceptable question)

2. **Plot** the Qi Men Dun Jia chart once you have finished collecting the questions. Use the current time with no time adjustment. The art of divination is to look for the indicator of current date and time. This is when the Heaven connects with the Earth and the Man is in between to receive the message.

   You can refer to the end of this book for calendar and chart or simply go to my website:

   http://www.fengshui-hacks.com/ and click on **plot chart**.

   Alternatively, you can also download my Android Application:

3. **Determine** the Ti (体) or point of reference based on the questions asked. For example, for relationships, we look for 六合 (Liù Hé). For profit or capital, use Wu.

   Here are some basic points of reference, but please note that this list is not exhaustive:

Reference Point, Ti (体)	Qi Men Dun Jia element
Career	开门 (Kāi Mén)
Business transaction, profit, wealth luck	生门 (Shēng Mén)
Examiner, interviewer	天辅 (Tiān Fǔ)
Illness	天芮 (Tiān Ruì) or 禽芮 (Qín Ruì)
Marriage	六合 (Liù Hé)
Person asking	Day Heavenly Stem

Table 15 - Reference Point

Apart from above, there is specific element for specific scenario:

Specific scenario: Career

Item	Qi Men Dun Jia element
Career	开门 (Kāi Mén)
Boss	值符 (Zhí Fú)
Person asking	Day Heavenly Stem

Table 16 - Specific Scenario: Career

Specific scenario: Relationship

Item	Qi Men Dun Jia element
3rd Party Male	Bing
3rd Party Female	Ding
Person asking	Day Heavenly Stem

Table 17 - Specific scenario: Relationship

For divination, we would sometimes need to evaluate the relationship between the person asking and his/her spouse. The table below lists the Day Heavenly Stem vs the spouse. For Jia Heavenly Stem, since it is hidden, we need to see the Jia Earthly Branch of the day. For example, if the day pillar is Jia Zi, then Wu is use.

Day Heavenly Stem	Qi Men Dun Jia element for Spouse
Jia Zi = Wu	Ji
Jia Xu = Ji	Wu
Jia Shen = Geng	Yi
Jia Chen = Ren	Ding
Jia Yin = Gui	Wu
Wu	Ji

Ji	Wu
Geng	Yi
Xin	Bing
Ren	Ding
Gui	Wu
Yi	Geng
Bing	Xin
Ding	Ren

Table 18 - Relationship: Spouse

Specific scenario: Business

Item	Qi Men Dun Jia element
Business	生门 (Shēng Mén)
Partnership	六合 (Liù Hé)
Profit	Wu
Customer	Hour Heavenly Stem
Person asking	Day Heavenly Stem

Table 19 - Specific Scenario: Business

Specific scenario: Illness

Item	Qi Men Dun Jia element

Illness	禽芮 (Qín Ruì)
Doctor	天心 (Tiān Xīn)
Operation	景门 (Jǐng Mén)
Growth	Xin (small growth) or Geng (big growth)
Person asking	Day Heavenly Stem

Table 20 - Specific scenario: illness

Palace	Sickness
Kan 1	• Kidney • Urinal track • Lower abdomen
Kun 2	• Stomach • Intestine • Spleen • Internal organ • Right arm
Zhen 3	• Liver • Gall bladder • Left rib • Muscle • Left breast • Waist
Xun 4	• Shoulder • Neck • Left arm
Qian 6	• Heart • Internal organs • Right foot

Dui 7	• Lung • Right rib • Throat • Mouth • Right breast • Skin
Gen 8	• Left foot
Li 9	• Heart • Arteries • Head

Table 21 - Palace vs Sickness

4. **<u>Identify</u>** where the Ti (体) or point of reference is in the chart.

   • Which Palace is the Ti (体) in?

   • What is the attribute or Yong (用) based on 八神 (8 God – bā shén), 九星 (Jiǔ Xīng), 八门 (Bā Mén)?

   • The interaction between 八神 (8 God – bā shén), 九星 (Jiǔ Xīng) and 八门 (Bā Mén) using the Ti Yong concept.

   • The interaction between palaces to see if the relationship is good or not.

5. **<u>Interpret</u>** based on the information gathered in step 4. You can use it to conclude your interpretation and provide advice to your client.

It is much easier to explain the 5 steps with example.

Example 1:

Collect

A lady came to consult asking about her current working situation where things are not going smoothly.

Plot

The date and time asking is 22nd Mar 2010 at Wei Hour. The Four Pillar of that date and time as follow:

Hour	Day	Month	Year
Ding	Ding	Ji	Geng
Wei	Mao	Mao	Yin

Based on the Qi Men Dun Jia Calendar, it is a Yang Dun #1, Ding Wei hour chart:

<table>
<tr><td colspan="3">Yang (阳) Dun# 1 Hour: DingWei ; 直符(ZhíFú): 天禽(TiānQín)
直使(ZhíShǐ): 死门(SǐMén) ; 旬首(XúnShǒu): JiaChenRen</td></tr>
<tr>
<td>玄武 (Xuán Wǔ)
天冲 (Tiān Chōng)
开门 (Kāi Mén)
Xun 4   Geng
Xin</td>
<td>九地 (Jiǔ Dì)
天辅 (Tiān Fǔ)
休门 (Xiū Mén)
Li 9   Xin
Yi</td>
<td>九天 (Jiǔ Tiān)
天英 (Tiān Yīng)
生门 (Shēng Mén)
Kun 2   Yi
Ji/Ren</td>
</tr>
<tr>
<td>白虎 (Bái Hǔ)
天任 (Tiān Rèn)
惊门 (Jīng Mén)
Zhen 3   Bing
Geng</td>
<td>Yang (阳) Dun# 1
Hour: **DingWei**

©Calvin Yap</td>
<td>值符 (Zhí Fú)
禽芮 (Qín Ruì)
伤门 (Shāng Mén)
Dui 7   Ji/Ren
Ding</td>
</tr>
<tr>
<td>六合 (Liù Hé)
天蓬 (Tiān Péng)
死门 (Sǐ Mén)
Gen 8   Wu
Bing</td>
<td>太阴 (Tài Yīn)
天心 (Tiān Xīn)
景门 (Jǐng Mén)
Kan 1   Gui
Wu</td>
<td>腾蛇 (Téng Shé)
天柱 (Tiān Zhù)
杜门 (Dù Mén)
Qian 6   Ding
Gui</td>
</tr>
</table>

Determine

Based on the question asked, determine the reference point or Ti (体).

The lady was asking about her career, so the reference point or Ti (体)

is 开门 **(Kāi Mén)** (see Table 15 - Reference Point

).

In addition, Day Heavenly Stem at Heaven Plate represents the person

asking.

Identify

Based on the Reference Point, identify where the reference point is in

the chart:

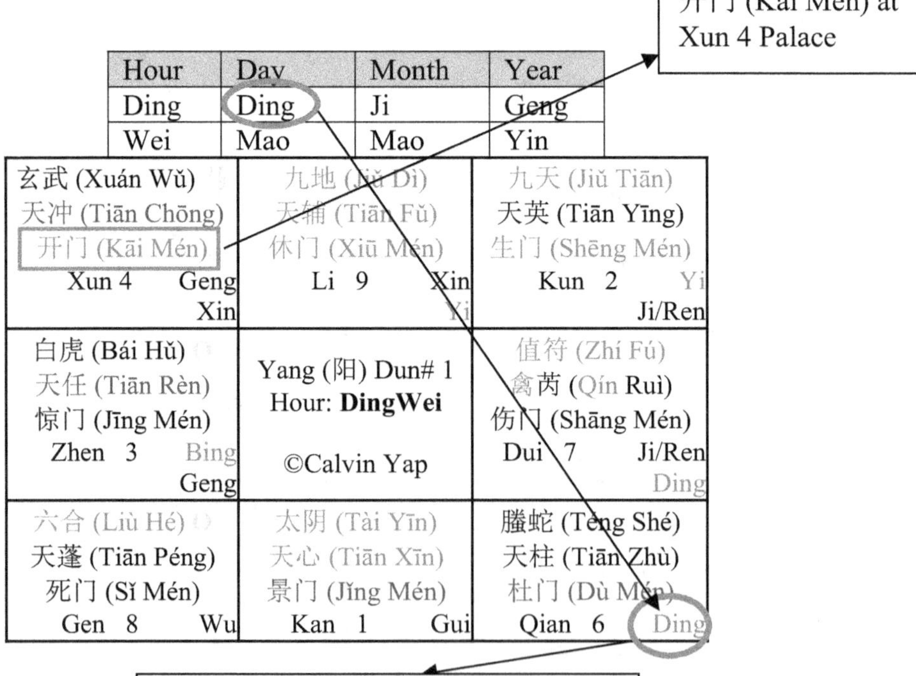

...Men Dun Jia Made Easy

Bing	Wu	Gui

Career is represented by 开门 **(Kāi Mén)** at Xun 4 Palace. Using 开门 **(Kāi Mén)** as Ti (体)，together with 天冲 (Tiān Chōng), 玄武 (Xuán Wǔ) and Horse as Yong (用).

Another reference point is the person, which is represented by Day Heavenly Stem. In this case, it is Ding and it is located at Qian 6 Palace with 杜门 (Dù Mén), 腾蛇 (Téng Shé), 天柱 (Tiān Zhù).

Interpret

Now, with all the information collected, you can then start your interpretation and conclusion. Since, the question is about career, so, the reference point is career or 开门 **(Kāi Mén).**

Career:

开门 **(Kāi Mén)** as Ti (体) is at Xun 4 Palace with 天冲 (Tiān Chōng), 玄武 (Xuán Wǔ) and Horse as Yong (用). Since it is on the same palace, this information provides the **condition** of the question asked, which in this case is Career.

- Career (开门 **(Kāi Mén)**) with 天冲 (Tiān Chōng), there is a lot of conflict in the workplace or job as 天冲 (Tiān Chōng)[5] represents conflict or clash.

- Career (开门 (Kāi Mén)) with 玄武 (Xuán Wǔ)[6], there is a lot of petty people in the workplace or job as 玄武 (Xuán Wǔ) represents petty.

- Career (开门 (Kāi Mén)) with Horse[7], the job requires a lot of running around. (Note: if Career with Horse and Kong, then the job could be made redundant, where the person might be retrenched).

The Person:

The person who came for consult is represented by the four pillars Day Heavenly Stem of the day the chart plotted. For example, on 22nd Mar 2010, the Day Heavenly Stem is **"Ding"**. For 23rd Mar 2010, the Day Heavenly Stem is **"Wu"** and 24th Mar 2010, the day Heavenly Stem is **"Ji"**. So for this case, the person came for consult on 22nd Mar 2010 and the Day Heavenly Stem is **"Ding"**, so **"Ding"** represents the person asking[8].

---

[5] See **Table 9 - 9 Stars attributes** for information

[6] See **Table 11 - 8 Gods representation** for information

[7] See **Other elements** for information

[8] Note: each Heavenly Stem has its own representation. Information is provided in the class

"Ding" is at Qian 6 Palace with 螣蛇 (Téng Shé), 天柱 (Tiān Zhù) and 杜门 (Dù Mén). Qian 6 Palace tells the condition/feeling of the person asking.

- The person with 螣蛇 (Téng Shé)[9], the person is currently vexed and worried.
- The person with 天柱 (Tiān Zhù)[10], the person is entangled in gossip or scandal.
- The person with 杜门 (Dù Mén)[11], the person is currently stuck or does not know what to do.

The person vs Career:

In here, we see the interaction between the person and her career. The person is represented by Ding at Qian 6 Palace. Career is represented by 开门 **(Kāi Mén)** at Xun 4 Palace. The relationship between palaces is Qian 6 vs Xun 4. See **Relationship between palaces** for information.

Qian 6 Palace (NW - Metal)

---

[9] See **Table 11 - 8 Gods representation** for information

[10] See **Table 9 - 9 Stars attributes** for information

[11] See **Table 6 - Earth Plate attributes** for information

Other Palace	Element	Relationship	Auspiciousness
Kan 1 (North)	Water	Metal gives birth to Water. Qian 6 supports Kan 1.	Auspicious
Kun 2 (SW)	Earth	Earth gives birth to Metal. Kun 2 support Qian 6.	Auspicious
Zhen 3 (East)	Wood	Metal controls Wood. Qian 6 controls Zhen 3.	Inauspicious
Xun 4 (SE)	Wood	Metal controls Wood. Qian 6 controls Xun 4.	Inauspicious
Dui 7 (West)	Metal	Same element. Dui 7 supports Qian 6.	Auspicious
Gen 8 (NE)	Earth	Earth gives birth to Metal. Gen 8 supports Qian 6.	Auspicious
Li 9 (South)	Fire	Fire controls Metal. Li 9 controls Qian 6.	Inauspicious

From the table above, you can see that Qian 6 vs Xun 4 is **Inauspicious**. Therefore, we can conclude that the relationship between the person and Career is **Inauspicious**. This will means that either the person is not happy with her job or the job is not suitable for the person.

Other factor(s):

We can also look at other factors, such as if her boss is supportive or not. The boss reference point is 值符 (Zhí Fú)[12]. 值符 (Zhí Fú) is at Dui 7 Palace.

Is the boss supportive of the person? Then we see Dui 7 vs Qian 6 (as the person, Ding is at Qian 6). From the **Relationship between palaces**

---

[12] See **Table 16 - Specific Scenario: Career**

we can see that Dui 7 vs Qian 6 is **auspicious**, so the boss is supportive of the person asking.

Is the boss supportive of the situation at work? Then we see Dui 7 vs Xun 4. From **Relationship between palaces**, we can see that Dui 7 vs Xun 4 is Inauspicious. So we can deduce that the boss is not helping with the situation at work.

Analysis:

From here there is a lot of information can be extracted. The lady asking is not happy with her job as there seems to be a lot of conflict and gossip going around in the office. Although the boss is supportive of her, he/she is not doing anything to mediate the situation at work.

Example 2:

Collect

A lady asking about her son's job situation.

Plot

The date and time she asked is 17th Mar 2010 at Xu Hour. The Four Pillar of that date and time as follow:

Hour	Day	Month	Year
Wu	Bing	Ji	Geng
Xu	Yin	Mao	Yin

Based on the Qi Men Dun Jia Calendar, it is a Yang Dun #1, Wu Xu hour chart:

<table>
<tr><td colspan="3">Yang (阳) Dun# 1 Hour: WuXu；直符(ZhíFú): 天辅(TiānFǔ)
直使(ZhíShǐ): 杜门(DùMén)；旬首(XúnShǒu): JiaWu/Xin</td></tr>
<tr>
<td>六合 (Liù Hé)
天柱 (Tiān Zhù)
死门 (Sǐ Mén)
Xun 4   Ding
      Xin</td>
<td>白虎 (Bái Hǔ)
天心 (Tiān Xīn)
惊门 (Jīng Mén)
Li 9   Gui
      Yi</td>
<td>玄武 (Xuán Wǔ)
天蓬 (Tiān Péng)
开门 (Kāi Mén)
Kun 2   Wu
      Ji/Ren</td>
</tr>
<tr>
<td>太阴 (Tài Yīn)
禽芮 (Qín Ruì)
景门 (Jǐng Mén)
Zhen 3   Ji/Ren
      Geng</td>
<td>Yang (阳) Dun# 1
Hour: WuXu

©Calvin Yap</td>
<td>九地 (Jiǔ Dì)
天任 (Tiān Rèn)
休门 (Xiū Mén)
Dui 7   Bing
      Ding</td>
</tr>
<tr>
<td>螣蛇 (Téng Shé)
天英 (Tiān Yīng)
杜门 (Dù Mén)
Gen 8   Yi
      Bing</td>
<td>值符 (Zhí Fú)
天辅 (Tiān Fǔ)
伤门 (Shāng Mén)
Kan 1   Xin
      Wu</td>
<td>九天 (Jiǔ Tiān)
天冲 (Tiān Chōng)
生门 (Shēng Mén)
Qian 6   Geng
      Gui</td>
</tr>
</table>

Determine

Based on the question asked, determine the reference point or Ti (体).

The question asked is about her son's career, so the reference point or Ti (体) is 开门 **(Kāi Mén)** (see Table 15 - Reference Point

).

In addition, Day Heavenly Stem at Heaven Plate represents the person asking.

Identify

Based on the Reference Point, identify where the reference point is in the chart:

Hour	Day	Month	Year
Wu	Bing	Ji	Geng
Xu	Yin	Mao	Yin

开门 (Kāi Mén) at Kun 2 Palace

Yang (阳) Dun# 1 Hour: **WuXu** ; 直符(ZhíFú): 天辅(TiānFǔ)
直使(ZhíShǐ): 杜门(DùMén) ; 旬首(XúnShǒu): JiaWu/Xin

六合 (Liù Hé) 天柱 (Tiān Zhù) 死门 (Sǐ Mén) Xun 4　　Ding 　　　　Xin	白虎 (Bái Hǔ) 天心 (Tiān Xīn) 惊门 (Jīng Mén) Li 9　　Gui 　　　　Yi	玄武 (Xuán Wǔ) 天蓬 (Tiān Péng) 开门 (Kāi Mén) Kun 2　　Wu 　　　　Ji/Ren
太阴 (Tài Yīn) 禽芮 (Qín Ruì) 景门 (Jǐng Mén) Zhen 3　　Ji/Ren 　　　　Geng	Yang (阳) Dun# 1 Hour: **WuXu** ©Calvin Yap	九地 (Jiǔ Dì) 天任 (Tiān Rèn) 休门 (Xiū Mén) Dui 7　　Bing 　　　　Ding
螣蛇 (Téng Shé) 天英 (Tiān Yīng) 杜门 (Dù Mén) Gen 8　　Yi 　　　　Bing	值符 (Zhí Fú) 天辅 (Tiān Fǔ) 伤门 (Shāng Mén) Kan 1　　Xin 　　　　Wu	九天 (Jiǔ Tiān) 天冲 (Tiān Chōng) 生门 (Shēng Mén) Qian 6　　Geng 　　　　Gui

Heaven Plate Day Heavenly Stem

Interpret

Now, with all the information collected, you can then start your interpretation and conclusion. Since, the question is about career, so, the reference point is career or 开门 (Kāi Mén).

Career:

开门 (Kāi Mén) as Ti (体) is at Kun 2 with 天蓬 (Tiān Péng), 玄武 (Xuán Wǔ) and Horse as Yong (用). Since it is on the same palace, this information provides the **condition** of the question asked, which in this case is Career.

- Career (开门 (Kāi Mén)) with 天蓬 (Tiān Péng), there is people coming to steal the job as 天蓬 (Tiān Péng)[13] represents big robber.

- Career (开门 (Kāi Mén)) with 玄武 (Xuán Wǔ)[14], there is a lot of petty people in the workplace or job as 玄武 (Xuán Wǔ) represents petty.

---

[13] See **Table 9 - 9 Stars attributes** for information

[14] See **Table 11 - 8 Gods representation** for information

- Career (开门 (Kāi Mén)) with Horse[15], the job requires a lot of running around. (Note: if Career with Horse and Kong, then the job could be made redundant).

The Person:

The person who came for consult is represented by the four pillars Day Heavenly Stem of the day the chart being ploted. So for this case, the person came for consult on 17th Mar 2010 and the Day Heavenly Stem is "**Bing**", so "**Bing**" represents the person asking.

"**Bing**" is at Dui 7 Palace with 九地 (Jiǔ Dì), 天任(Tiān Rèn) and 休门 (Xiū Mén). Dui 7 Palace tells the condition/feeling of the person asking.

- The person with 九地 (Jiǔ Dì)[16], the person is currently depressed.
- The person with 天任(Tiān Rèn) [17], the person is kind and compasionate.
- The person with 休门 (Xiū Mén)[18], the person is relaxed.

---

[15] See **Other elements** for information

[16] See **Table 11 - 8 Gods representation** for information

[17] See **Table 9 - 9 Stars attributes** for information

The person vs Career:

In here, we see the interaction between the person and her career. The person is represented by Bing at Dui 7 Palace. Career is represented by 开门 **(Kāi Mén)** at Kun 2 Palace. The relationship between palaces is Dui 7 and Kun 2. See **Relationship between palaces** for information.

Dui 7 Palace (West - Metal)

Other Palace	Element	Relationship	Auspiciousness
Kan 1 (North)	Water	Metal gives birth to Water. Dui 7 supports Kan 1	Auspicious
Kun 2 (SW)	Earth	Earth gives birth to Metal. Kun 2 supports Dui 7.	Auspicious
Zhen 3 (East)	Wood	Metal controls Wood. Dui 7 controls Zhen 3.	Inauspicious
Xun 4 (SE)	Wood	Metal controls Wood. Dui 7 controls Xun 4.	Inauspicious
Qian 6 (NW)	Metal	Same element. Dui 7 supports Qian 6.	Auspicious
Gen 8 (NE)	Earth	Earth gives birth to Metal. Gen 8 supports Dui 7.	Auspicious
Li 9 (South)	Fire	Fire controls Metal. Li 9 controls Dui 7.	Inauspicious

From the table above, you can see that Dui 7 vs Kun 2 is **Auspicious**. Therefore, we can conclude that the relationship between the person and Career is **Auspicious**. This will means that the job is supporting the

---

[18] See **Table 6 - Earth Plate attributes** for information

---

person. However, the Career palace itself is inauspicious (with天蓬 (Tiān Péng), 玄武 (Xuán Wǔ) and Horse). So, having inauspicious Career Palace supporting the person, it is not good.

Analysis:

From here there is a lot of information can be extracted. The lady's son seems to resent the fact that there are a lot of gossip at his office and there are people eying his job. Therefore, there will not be any career progression for him.

Outcome:

In the end, the lady's son quit his job and went overseas to study. Subsequently, he graduated, found a wife and settled down overseas.

Example 3:

Collect

A man asking about taking new job offer as the General Manager reporting directly to Chairman.

Plot

The date and time asking is 2nd Mar 2015 at Xu Hour. The Four Pillar of that date and time as follow:

Hour	Day	Month	Year
Geng	Ding	Wu	Yi
Xu	Chou	Yin	Wei

Based on the Qi Men Dun Jia Calendar, it is a Yang Dun #3, Geng Xu hour chart:

<table>
<tr><td colspan="3">Yang (阳) Dun# 3 Hour: GengXu ；直符(ZhíFú): 天柱(TiānZhù)
直使(ZhíShǐ): 惊门(JīngMén) ；旬首(XúnShǒu): JiaChenRen</td></tr>
<tr>
<td>九地 (Jiǔ Dì)
天英 (Tiān Yīng)
惊门 (Jīng Mén)
Xun 4   Ding
    Ji</td>
<td>九天 (Jiǔ Tiān)
禽芮 (Qín Ruì)
开门 (Kāi Mén)
Li 9   Yi/Geng
    Ding</td>
<td>值符 (Zhí Fú)
天柱 (Tiān Zhù)
休门 (Xiū Mén)
Kun 2   Ren
    Yi/Geng</td>
</tr>
<tr>
<td>玄武 (Xuán Wǔ)
天辅 (Tiān Fǔ)
死门 (Sǐ Mén)
Zhen 3   Ji
    Wu</td>
<td>Yang (阳) Dun# 3
Hour: GengXu

©Calvin Yap</td>
<td>螣蛇 (Téng Shé)
天心 (Tiān Xīn)
生门 (Shēng Mén)
Dui 7   Xin
    Ren</td>
</tr>
<tr>
<td>白虎 (Bái Hǔ)
天冲 (Tiān Chōng)
景门 (Jǐng Mén)
Gen 8   Wu
    Gui</td>
<td>六合 (Liù Hé)
天任 (Tiān Rèn)
杜门 (Dù Mén)
Kan 1   Gui
    Bing</td>
<td>太阴 (Tài Yīn)
天蓬 (Tiān Péng)
伤门 (Shāng Mén)
Qian 6   Bing
    Xin</td>
</tr>
</table>

Determine

Based on the question asked, determine the reference point or Ti (体).

The question asked is about her son's career, so the reference point or Ti (体) is 开门 **(Kāi Mén)** (see Table 15 - Reference Point

).

In addition, Day Heavenly Stem at Heaven Plate represents the person asking.

Identify

Based on the Reference Point, identify where the reference point is in the chart:

Hour	Day	Month	Year
Geng	Ding	Wu	Yi
Xu	Chou	Yin	Wei

开门 (Kāi Mén) at Li 9 Palace

Yang (阳) Dun# 3 Hour: **GengXu** ; 直符(ZhíFú): 天柱(TiānZhù)
直使(ZhíShǐ): 惊门(JīngMén) ; 旬首(XúnShǒu): JiaChenRen

九地 (Jiǔ Dì) 天英 (Tiān Yīng) 惊门 (Jīng Mén) Xun 4 Ding Ji	九天 (Jiǔ Tiān) 禽芮 (Qín Ruì) 开门 (Kāi Mén) Li 9 Yi/Geng Ding	值符 (Zhí Fú) 天柱 (Tiān Zhù) 休门 (Xiū Mén) Kun 2 Ren Yi/Geng
玄武 (Xuán Wǔ) 天辅 (Tiān Fǔ) 死门 (Sǐ Mén) Zhen 3 Ji Wu	Yang (阳) Dun# 3 Hour: **GengXu** ©Calvin Yap	腾蛇 (Téng Shé) 天心 (Tiān Xīn) 生门 (Shēng Mén) Dui 7 Xin Ren
白虎 (Bái Hǔ) 天冲 (Tiān Chōng) 景门 (Jǐng Mén) Gen 8 Wu Gui	六合 (Liù Hé) 天任 (Tiān Rèn) 杜门 (Dù Mén) Kan 1 Gui Bing	太阴 (Tài Yīn) 天蓬 (Tiān Péng) 伤门 (Shāng Mén) Qian 6 Bing Xin

Heaven Plate Day Heavenly Stem

Interpretation

Now, with all the information collected, you can then start your interpretation and conclusion. Since, the question is about career, so, the reference point is career or 开门 **(Kāi Mén).**

Career:

开门 **(Kāi Mén)** as Ti (体) is at Li 9 with 禽芮 (Qín Ruì) and 九天 (Jiǔ Tiān) as Yong (用). This information provides the **condition** of the question asked, which in this case is Career.

- Career (开门 **(Kāi Mén)**) with 禽芮 (Qín Ruì), this job is problematic as 天芮 (Tiān Ruì)[19] represents issues.
- Career (开门 (Kāi Mén)) with 九天 (Jiǔ Tiān)[20], means this job is a high position (i.e. General Manager) as 九天 (Jiǔ Tiān) represents high objective.

The Person:

---

[19] See **Table 9 - 9 Stars attributes** for information

[20] See **Table 11 - 8 Gods representation** for information

The person who came for consult is represented by the four pillars Day Heavenly Stem of the day the chart being ploted. So for this case, the person came for consult on is 2nd Mar 2015 and the Day Heavenly Stem is "**Ding**", so "**Ding**" represents the person asking.

"**Ding**" is at Xun 4 Palace with 九地 (Jiǔ Dì), 天英 (Tiān Yīng) and 惊门 (Jīng Mén). Xun 4 Palace tells the condition/feeling of the person asking.

- The person with 九地 (Jiǔ Dì)[21], the person is currently depressed.
- The person with 天英 (Tiān Yīng)[22], the person has a strong character.
- The person with 惊门 (Jīng Mén)[23], the person is in panic or shock.

The person vs Career:

In here, we see the interaction between the person and her career. The person is represented by Ding at Xun 4 Palace. Career is represented by

---

[21] See **Table 11 - 8 Gods representation** for information

[22] See **Table 9 - 9 Stars attributes** for information

[23] See **Table 6 - Earth Plate attributes** for information

开门 **(Kāi Mén)** at Li 9 Palace. The relationship between palaces is Xun 4 and Li 9. See **Relationship between palaces** for information.

You can see that Xun 4 vs Li 9 is **Auspicious**. Therefore, we can conclude that the relationship between the person and Career is **Auspicious**. This will means that the job is supporting the person.

Other factors:

We can also look at other factor like whether the boss is supportive or not. The boss reference point is 值符 (Zhí Fú)[24]. 值符 (Zhí Fú) is at Kun 2 Palace.

Is the boss supportive of the person? Then we see Xun 4 vs Kun 2 (as the person, Ding is at Xun 4). From the **Relationship between palaces** we can see that Xun 4 vs Kun 2 is **inauspicious**, so the boss is not supportive of the person asking, should the person take on the job.

Analysis:

From here, there is a lot of information that can be extracted. The job will be a very demanding job, and although the job and the person asking is supportive of the job, but during the course of doing his job, he will run into conflicts with his boss.

---

[24] See **Table 16 - Specific Scenario: Career**

Outcome:

The person asking decided to take on the job despite my advise against it. In the end, he got into argument with his boss and resigned after working there for less than 1 year.

Example 4:

Collect

A lady asking about taking new job offer (internal transfer).

Plot

The date and time asking is 16th June 2014 at Shen Hour. The Four Pillar of that date and time as follow:

Hour	Day	Month	Year
Geng	Wu	Geng	Jia
Shen	Wu	Wu	Wu

Based on the Qi Men Dun Jia Calendar, it is a Yang Dun #3, Geng Shen hour chart:

<table>
<tr><td colspan="3">Yang (阳) Dun# 3 Hour: GengShen；直符(ZhíFú): 天任(TiānRèn) 直使(ZhíShǐ): 生门(ShēngMén)；旬首(XúnShǒu): JiaYinGui</td></tr>
<tr>
<td>九地 (Jiǔ Dì)
天心 (Tiān Xīn)
开门 (Kāi Mén)
Xun 4   Xin
     Ji</td>
<td>九天 (Jiǔ Tiān)
天蓬 (Tiān Péng)
休门 (Xiū Mén)
Li 9   Bing
     Ding</td>
<td>值符 (Zhí Fú)
天任 (Tiān Rèn)
生门 (Shēng Mén)
Kun 2   Gui
     Yi/Geng</td>
</tr>
<tr>
<td>玄武 (Xuán Wǔ)
天柱 (Tiān Zhù)
惊门 (Jīng Mén)
Zhen 3   Ren
     Wu</td>
<td>Yang (阳) Dun# 3
Hour: GengShen
Fan Yin
©Calvin Yap</td>
<td>螣蛇 (Téng Shé)
天冲 (Tiān Chōng)
伤门 (Shāng Mén)
Dui 7   Wu
     Ren</td>
</tr>
<tr>
<td>白虎 (Bái Hǔ)
禽芮 (Qín Ruì)
死门 (Sǐ Mén)
Gen 8   Yi/Geng
     Gui</td>
<td>六合 (Liù Hé)
天英 (Tiān Yīng)
景门 (Jǐng Mén)
Kan 1   Ding
     Bing</td>
<td>太阴 (Tài Yīn)
天辅 (Tiān Fǔ)
杜门 (Dù Mén)
Qian 6   Ji
     Xin</td>
</tr>
</table>

Determine

Based on the question asked, determine the reference point or Ti (体).

The question asked is about her son's career, so the reference point or Ti (体) is 开门 **(Kāi Mén)** (see Table 15 - Reference Point

).

In addition, Day Heavenly Stem at Heaven Plate represents the person asking.

Identify

Based on the Reference Point, identify where the reference point is in the chart:

Hour	Day	Month	Year
Geng	Wu	Geng	Jia
Shen	Wu	Wu	Wu

开门(Kāi Mén) at Xun 4 Palace

Yang (阳) Dun# 3 Hour: **GengShen** ; 直符(ZhíFú): 天任(TiānRèn) 直使(ZhíShǐ): 生门(ShēngMén) ; 旬首(XúnShǒu): JiaYinGui

九地 (Jiǔ Dì) 天心 (Tiān Xīn) 开门 (Kāi Mén) Xun 4　　Xin 　　　　Ji	九天 (Jiǔ Tiān) 天蓬 (Tiān Péng) 休门 (Xiū Mén) Li 9　　　Bing 　　　　Ding	值符 (Zhí Fú) 天任 (Tiān Rèn) 生门 (Shēng Mén) Kun 2　　Gui 　　　Yi/Geng
玄武 (Xuán Wǔ) 天柱 (Tiān Zhù) 惊门 (Jīng Mén) Zhen 3　　Ren 　　　　Wu	Yang (阳) Dun# 3 Hour: **GengShen** **Fan Yin** ©Calvin Yap	螣蛇 (Téng Shé) 天冲 (Tiān Chōng) 伤门 (Shāng Mén) Dui 7　　Wu 　　　　Ren
白虎 (Bái Hǔ) 禽芮 (Qín Ruì) 死门 (Sǐ Mén) Gen 8　　Yi/Geng	六合 (Liù Hé) 天英 (Tiān Yīng) 景门 (Jǐng Mén) Kan 1　　Ding	太阴 (Tài Yīn) 天辅 (Tiān Fǔ) 杜门 (Dù Mén) Qian 6　　Ji

Heaven Plate Day Heavenly Stem

Gui	Bing	Xin	

Interpret

Now, with all the information collected, you can then start your interpretation and conclusion. Since, the question is about career, so, the reference point is career or 开门 **(Kāi Mén).**

Career:

开门 **(Kāi Mén)** as Ti (体) is at Xun 4 with 天心 (Tiān Xīn) and 九地 (Jiǔ Dì) as Yong (用). This information provides the **condition** of the question asked, which in this case is Career.

- Career (开门 **(Kāi Mén)**) with 天心 (Tiān Xīn), this job is auspicious.
- Career (开门 (Kāi Mén)) with 九地 (Jiǔ Dì)[25], means this job is a slow- moving or backend type of job.

The Person:

The person who came for consult is represented by the four pillars Day Heavenly Stem of the day the chart being ploted. So for this case, the

---

[25] See **Table 11 - 8 Gods representation** for information

---

person came for consult on is 16th June 2014 and the Day Heavenly Stem is "**Wu**", so "**Wu**" represents the person asking.

"**Wu**" is at Dui 7 Palace with 螣蛇 (Téng Shé), 天冲 (Tiān Chōng) and 伤门 (Shāng Mén). Dui 7 Palace tells the condition/feeling of the person asking.

- The person with 螣蛇 (Téng Shé)[26], the person is currently vexed and worried.
- The person with 天冲 (Tiān Chōng)[27], the person is impulsive.
- The person with 伤门 (Shāng Mén)[28], the person is hurt.

The person vs Career:

In here, we see the interaction between the person and her career. The person is represented by Wu at Dui 7 Palace. Career is represented by 开门 **(Kāi Mén)** at Xun 4 Palace. The relationship between palaces is Xun 4 and Dui 7. See **Relationship between palaces** for information.

---

[26] See **Table 11 - 8 Gods representation** for information

[27] See **Table 9 - 9 Stars attributes** for information

[28] See **Table 6 - Earth Plate attributes** for information

You can see that Xun 4 vs Dui 7 is **inauspicious**. Therefore, we can conclude that the relationship between the person and Career is **inauspicious**. This will mean that the job is not supporting the person.

Other factors:

We can also look at other factors like whether the boss is supportive or not. The boss reference point is 值符 (Zhí Fú)[29]. 值符 (Zhí Fú) is at Kun 2 Palace.

Is the boss supportive of the person? Then we see Dui 7 vs Kun 2 (as the person, Wu is at Dui 7). From the **Relationship between palaces** we can see that Dui 7 vs Kun 2 is **auspicious**, so the boss is supportive of the person asking, if the person takes on the job. That could explain why the boss offered her the opportunity to transfer.

However, this Qi Men Dun Jia chart is a **Fan Yin** chart. A Fan Yin chart means fickle, uncertainty and changes.

Analysis:

From here there is a lot of information that can be extracted. The job is not supportive of the person asking, so if she decided to take on the job,

---

[29] See **Table 16 - Specific Scenario: Career**

she will not be happy. In addition, this is also a Fan Yin chart, so the job scope might change later.

Outcome:

The person asking did not take on the job and it was offered to her colleague. However, due to change in the job scope, her colleague left the position.

Example 5:

Collect

A lady asked about her marriage situation.

Plot

The date and time asking is 9th Feb 2010 at Wu Hour. The Four Pillar of that date and time as follow:

Hour	Day	Month	Year
Ren	Geng	Wu	Geng
Wu	Yin	Yin	Yin

Based on the Qi Men Dun Jia Calendar, it is a Yang Dun #2, Ren Wu hour chart:

Yang (阳) Dun# 2 Hour: RenWu ； 直符(ZhíFú): 天冲(TiānChōng) 直使(ZhíShǐ): 伤门(ShāngMén) ； 旬首(XúnShǒu): JiaXuJi		
白虎 (Bái Hǔ) 天柱 (Tiān Zhù) 休门 (Xiū Mén) Xun 4　　Gui 　　Geng	玄武 (Xuán Wǔ) 天心 (Tiān Xīn) 生门 (Shēng Mén) Li　9　　Ren 　　Bing	九地 (Jiǔ Dì) 天蓬 (Tiān Péng) 伤门 (Shāng Mén) Kun　2　　Yi 　　Wu/Xin
六合 (Liù Hé) 禽芮 (Qín Ruì) 开门 (Kāi Mén) Zhen　3　　Wu/Xin 　　Ji	Yang (阳) Dun# 2 Hour: **RenWu** ©Calvin Yap	九天 (Jiǔ Tiān) 天任 (Tiān Rèn) 杜门 (Dù Mén) Dui　7　　Ding 　　Gui
太阴 (Tài Yīn) 天英 (Tiān Yīng) 惊门 (Jīng Mén) Gen　8　　Bing 　　Ding	螣蛇 (Téng Shé) 天辅 (Tiān Fǔ) 死门 (Sǐ Mén) Kan　1　　Geng 　　Yi	值符 (Zhí Fú) 天冲 (Tiān Chōng) 景门 (Jǐng Mén) Qian　6　　Ji 　　Ren

Determine

Based on the question asked, determine the reference point or Ti (体). The lady was asking about her relationship, so the reference point or Ti (体) is 六合 (Liù Hé) (see Table 15 - Reference Point

).

In addition, Day Heavenly Stem at Heaven Plate represents the person asking and the associate Heavenly Stem that represent the spouse.

Identify

Based on the Reference Point, identify where the reference point is in the chart:

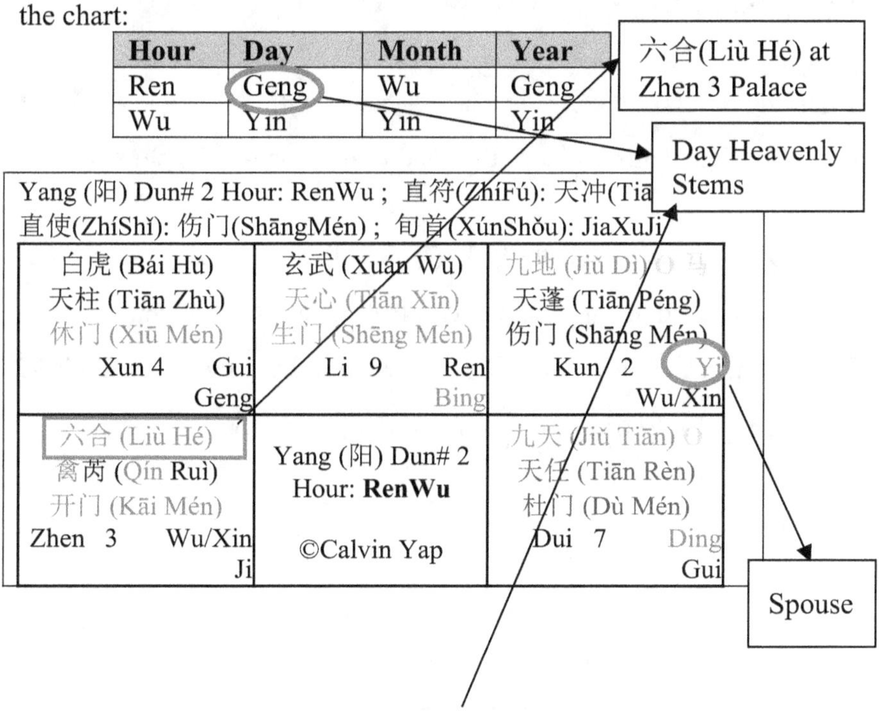

Hour	Day	Month	Year
Ren	Geng	Wu	Geng
Wu	Yin	Yin	Yin

六合(Liù Hé) at Zhen 3 Palace

Day Heavenly Stems

Yang (阳) Dun# 2 Hour: RenWu ; 直符(ZhíFú): 天冲(Tiā ; 直使(ZhíShǐ): 伤门(ShāngMén) ; 旬首(XúnShǒu): JiaXuJi

白虎 (Bái Hǔ) 天柱 (Tiān Zhù) 休门 (Xiū Mén) Xun 4　　Gui 　　　　Geng	玄武 (Xuán Wǔ) 天心 (Tiān Xīn) 生门 (Shēng Mén) Li 9　　Ren 　　　Bing	九地 (Jiǔ Dì) 天蓬 (Tiān Péng) 伤门 (Shāng Mén) Kun 2　　Yi 　　　Wu/Xin
六合 (Liù Hé) 禽芮 (Qín Ruì) 开门 (Kāi Mén) Zhen 3　　Wu/Xin 　　　　Ji	Yang (阳) Dun# 2 Hour: **RenWu** ©Calvin Yap	九天 (Jiǔ Tiān) 天任 (Tiān Rèn) 杜门 (Dù Mén) Dui 7　　Ding 　　　Gui

Spouse

太阴 (Tài Yīn) 天英 (Tiān Yīng) 惊门 (Jīng Mén) Gen 8 Bing Ding	螣蛇 (Téng Shé) 天辅 (Tiān Fǔ) 死门 (Sǐ Mén) Kan 1 Geng Yi	值符 (Zhí Fú) 天冲 (Tiān Chōng) 景门 (Jǐng Mén) Qian 6 Ji Ren

Interpretation

Now, with all the information collected, you can then start your interpretation and conclusion. Since, the question is about relationship, so, the reference point is 六合 **(Liù Hé)**. (see **Table 15 - Reference Point**

)

Relationship:

六合 **(Liù Hé)** as Ti (体) is at Zhen 3 Palace with 禽芮 (Qín Ruì) and 开门 (Kāi Mén). This provides the condition of the relationship.

- 六合 **(Liù Hé)** with 禽芮 (Qín Ruì) means there is problem with relationship as 禽芮 (Qín Ruì) represents problem.
- 六合 **(Liù Hé)** with 开门 (Kāi Mén) means the relationship is open for 3rd party as 开门 (Kāi Mén) means open.

The person:

The person who came for consult is represented by the four pillars Day Heavenly Stem of the day the chart being ploted. In this case, **"Geng"** represents the person asking. **"Geng"** is at Kan 1 Palace with 螣蛇

(Téng Shé), 天辅 (Tiān Fǔ) and 死门 (Sǐ Mén). Kan 1 Palace tells the condition/feeling of the person asking.

- The person with 螣蛇 (Téng Shé)[30], the person is currently vexed and worried.
- The person with 天辅 (Tiān Fǔ)[31] means the person has wisdom (maybe that is why she came for consult)
- The person with 死门 (Sǐ Mén)[32] means the person is currently in bad luck.

Person's Spouse:

The person's Spouse is represented by **"Yi"**[33]. **"Yi"** is at Kun 2 Palace with 九地 (Jiǔ Dì), 天蓬 (Tiān Péng), 伤门 (Shāng Mén), Horse and Kong. Kun2 Palace tells the condition/feeling of the person asking.

- Person's spouse with 九地 (Jiǔ Dì), the spouse is feeling low at the moment.
- Spouse with 天蓬 (Tiān Péng), the spouse is lechery.

---

[30] See **Table 11 - 8 Gods representation** for information

[31] See **Table 9 - 9 Stars attributes** for more information.

[32] See **Table 7 - Human Plate Attribute** for more information.

[33] See **Table 18 - Relationship: Spouse** for the mapping.

- Spouse with 伤门 (Shāng Mén), the spouse is feeling hurt.

- Spouse with Horse and Kong, the spouse is no longer with the person.

The person vs Relationship:

Next we evaluate the person vs the relationship. The person is at Kan 1 Palace and relationship is at Zhen 3 Palace. Between Kan 1 Palace and Zhen 3 Palace is an **auspicious** relationship. Therefore, we can conclude that the person cherishes the relationship.

The Spouse vs Relationship:

The spouse is at Kun 2 Palace and the relationship is at Zhen 3 Palace. Between Kun 2 palace and Zhen 3 Palace is an **inauspicious** relationship. Therefore, we can conclude that the spouse does not cherish the relationship.

The Person vs the Spouse

The person is at Kan 1 Palace and the Spouse is at Kun 2 Palace. Between Kan 1 and Kun 2 Palaces, it is an **inauspicious** relationship. Therefore, we can conclude that both the person and the spouse do not have feeling for each other.

Reading further:

The Spouse is at Kun 2 Palace. 3rd Party female is represented by Ding at Dui 7 Palace. Between Kun 2 and Dui 7 palaces, it is an auspicious relationship. We can conclude that the spouse is having an affair outside.

Conclusion:

Based on the interpretation above, we can conclude that the person's relationship is not good. Her husband has already left her, and he is having an affair outside.

In actual situation, she is in the process of divorcing her husband as her husband is having affair outside.

Example 6:

Collect

A married lady was asking about her marriage. She was worried that her husband might divorce her.

Plot

The date and time asking is 24th Feb 2010 at Wu Hour. The Four Pillar of that date and time as follow:

Hour	Day	Month	Year
Ren	Yi	Wu	Geng
Wu	Si	Yin	Yin

Based on the Qi Men Dun Jia Calendar, it is a Yang Dun #3, Ren Wu hour chart:

<table>
<tr><td colspan="3">Yang (阳) Dun# 3 Hour: RenWu ; 直符(ZhíFú): 天辅(TiānFǔ)
直使(ZhíShǐ): 杜门(DùMén) ; 旬首(XúnShǒu): JiaXuJi</td></tr>
<tr>
<td>玄武 (Xuán Wǔ)
天蓬 (Tiān Péng)
景门 (Jǐng Mén)
Xun 4   Bing
Ji</td>
<td>九地 (Jiǔ Dì)
天任 (Tiān Rèn)
死门 (Sǐ Mén)
Li 9   Gui
Ding</td>
<td>九天 (Jiǔ Tiān)
天冲 (Tiān Chōng)
惊门 (Jīng Mén)
Kun 2   Wu
Yi/Geng</td>
</tr>
<tr>
<td>白虎 (Bái Hǔ)
天心 (Tiān Xīn)
杜门 (Dù Mén)
Zhen 3   Xin
Wu</td>
<td>Yang (阳) Dun# 3
Hour: RenWu

©Calvin Yap</td>
<td>值符 (Zhí Fú)
天辅 (Tiān Fǔ)
开门 (Kāi Mén)
Dui 7   Ji
Ren</td>
</tr>
<tr>
<td>六合 (Liù Hé)
天柱 (Tiān Zhù)
伤门 (Shāng Mén)
Gen 8   Ren
Gui</td>
<td>太阴 (Tài Yīn)
禽芮 (Qín Ruì)
生门 (Shēng Mén)
Kan 1   Yi/Geng
Bing</td>
<td>腾蛇 (Téng Shé)
天英 (Tiān Yīng)
休门 (Xiū Mén)
Qian 6   Ding
Xin</td>
</tr>
</table>

Determine

Based on the question asked, determine the reference point or Ti (体). The lady was asking about her relationship, so the reference point or Ti (体) is 六合 **(Liù Hé).** (see **Table 15 - Reference Point**

).

In addition, Day Heavenly Stem at Heaven Plate represents the person asking and the associate Heavenly Stem that represent the spouse.

Identify

Based on the Reference Point, identify where the reference point in the chart:

Hour	Day	Month	Year
Ren	Yi	Wu	Geng
Wu	Si	Yin	Yin

六合(Liù Hé) at Gen 8 Palace

Day Heavenly Stems

Spouse

Yang (阳) Dun# 3 Hour: **RenWu** ; 直符(ZhíFú):
直使(ZhíShǐ): 杜门(DùMén) ; 旬首(XúnShǒu): J

玄武 (Xuán Wǔ)
天蓬 (Tiān Péng)
景门 (Jǐng Mén)
Xun 4   Bing
    Ji
	九地 (Jiǔ Dì)
	天任 (Tiān Rèn)
	死门 (Sǐ Mén)
	Li 9 Gui
	    Ding
		九天 (Jiǔ Tiān)
		天冲 (Tiān Chōng)
		惊门 (Jīng Mén)
		Kun 2 Wu
		    Yi/Geng

白虎 (Bái Hǔ)
天心 (Tiān Xīn)
杜门 (Dù Mén)
Zhen 3   Xin
    Wu
	Yang (阳) Dun# 3
	Hour: **RenWu**
	
	©Calvin Yap
		值符 (Zhí Fú)
		天辅 (Tiān Fǔ)
		开门 (Kāi Mén)
		Dui 7 Ji
		    Ren

六合 (Liù Hé) 天柱 (Tiān Zhù)	太阴 (Tài Yīn) 禽芮 (Qín Ruì)	螣蛇 (Téng Shé) 天英 (Tiān Yīng)

伤门 (Shāng Mén)	生门 (Shēng Mén)	休门 (Xiū Mén)	
Gen 8　　　Ren 　　　　　Gui	Kan 1　　　Yi/Geng 　　　　　Bing	Qian 6　　　Ding 　　　　　Xin	

Interpret

Now, with all the information collected, you can then start your interpretation and conclusion. Since, the question is about relationship, so, the reference point is 六合 **(Liù Hé).** (see **Table 15 - Reference Point**

)

Relationship:

六合 **(Liù Hé)** as Ti (体) is at Gen 8 Palace with 天柱 (Tiān Zhù) and 伤门 (Shāng Mén). This provides the condition of the relationship.

- 六合 (Liù Hé) with 天柱 (Tiān Zhù) means relationship is ruined as 天柱 (Tiān Zhù) means ruin, dispute, gossip, scandal.
- 六合 (Liù Hé) with 伤门 (Shāng Mén) means relationship is hurt as 伤门 (Shāng Mén) means hurt.

The person and Spouse

The person who came for consult is represented by the four pillars Day Heavenly Stem of the day the chart being ploted. In this case, **"Yi"** represents the person asking. **"Yi"** is at Kan 1 Palace with 太阴 (Tài Yīn), 禽芮 (Qín Ruì) and 生门 (Shēng Mén).

The person's spouse is represented by **"Geng"**, which is at the same palace as the person asking.

So, we can deduce that both of them still have feelings for each other.

The person and Spouse vs Relationship:

The person and Spouse are both at Kan 1 Palace and the relationship is at Gen 8 Palace. Between Kan 1 Palace and Gen 8 Palace (see **Relationship between palaces**):

Kan 1 Palace (North - Water)

Other Palace	Element	Relationship	Auspiciousness
Kun 2 (SW)	Earth	Earth controls Water. Kun 2 controls Kan 1.	Inauspicious
Zhen 3 (East)	Wood	Water gives birth to Wood. Kan 1supports Zhen 3.	Auspicious
Xun 4 (SE)	Wood	Water gives birth to Wood. Kan 1 supports Xun 4.	Auspicious
Qian 6 (NW)	Metal	Metal gives birth to Water. Qian 6 supports Kan 1.	Auspicious
Dui 7 (West)	Metal	Metal gives birth to Water. Dui 7 supports Kan 1.	Auspicious
Gen 8 (NE)	Earth	Earth controls Water. Gen 8 controls Kan 1.	Inauspicious
Li 9 (South)	Fire	Water controls Fire. Kan 1 controls Li 9.	Inauspicious

Kan 1 vs Gen 8 is inauspicious. Therefore, both of them vs Relationship are inauspicious. That will mean that both of them wants to end the relationship.

Reading further:

The Spouse is "**Geng**" at Kan 1 Palace. 3rd Party female is represented by "**Ding**" at Qian 6 Palace. Between Kan 1 and Qian 6, it is an auspicious relationship. We can conclude that the spouse is having an affair outside.

Conclusion:

Based on the information above, we can conclude that the husband is indeed having an affair outside and both of them wants to end the relationship. However, it seems like both of them still have feelings for each other. Therefore, it is advisable to suggest that she should sit down with her husband to discuss this:

- Husband to end the affair with 3rd party and get back together
- Carry on with the divorce.

Example 7:

Collect

A lady came for consult regarding relationship. She found out that her husband is having an affair outside, and wants to know whether they will end up divorcing.

Plot

The date and time asking is 28th May 2011 at Si Hour. The Four Pillar of that date and time as follow:

Hour	Day	Month	Year
Ding	Gui	Gui	Xin
Si	Wei	Si	Mao

Based on the Qi Men Dun Jia Calendar, it is a Yang Dun #5, Ding Si hour chart:

<table>
<tr><td colspan="3">Yang (阳) Dun# 5 Hour: DingSi；直符(ZhíFú): 天蓬(TiānPéng)
直使(ZhíShǐ): 休门(XiūMén)；旬首(XúnShǒu): JiaYinGui</td></tr>
<tr>
<td>九地 (Jiǔ Dì)
天柱 (Tiān Zhù)
休门 (Xiū Mén)
Xun 4   Geng
Yi</td>
<td>九天 (Jiǔ Tiān)
天心 (Tiān Xīn)
生门 (Shēng Mén)
Li 9   Ji
Ren</td>
<td>值符 (Zhí Fú)
天蓬 (Tiān Péng)
伤门 (Shāng Mén)
Kun 2   Gui
Ding/Wu</td>
</tr>
<tr>
<td>玄武 (Xuán Wǔ)
禽芮 (Qín Ruì)
开门 (Kāi Mén)
Zhen 3   Ding/Wu
Bing</td>
<td>Yang (阳) Dun# 5
Hour: DingSi

©Calvin Yap</td>
<td>螣蛇 (Téng Shé)
天任 (Tiān Rèn)
杜门 (Dù Mén)
Dui 7   Xin
Geng</td>
</tr>
<tr>
<td>白虎 (Bái Hǔ)
天英 (Tiān Yīng)
惊门 (Jīng Mén)
Gen 8   Ren
Xin</td>
<td>六合 (Liù Hé)
天辅 (Tiān Fǔ)
死门 (Sǐ Mén)
Kan 1   Yi
Gui</td>
<td>太阴 (Tài Yīn)
天冲 (Tiān Chōng)
景门 (Jǐng Mén)
Qian 6   Bing
Ji</td>
</tr>
</table>

Determine

Based on the question asked, determine the reference point or Ti (体). The lady was asking about her relationship, so the reference point or Ti (体) is 六合 **(Liù Hé)**. (see **Table 15 - Reference Point**

).

In addition, Day Heavenly Stem at Heaven Plate represents the person asking and the associate Heavenly Stem that represent the spouse.

Identify

Based on the Reference Point, identify where the reference point is in the chart:

Hour	Day	Month	Year
Ding	Gui	Gui	Xin
Si	Wei	Si	Mao

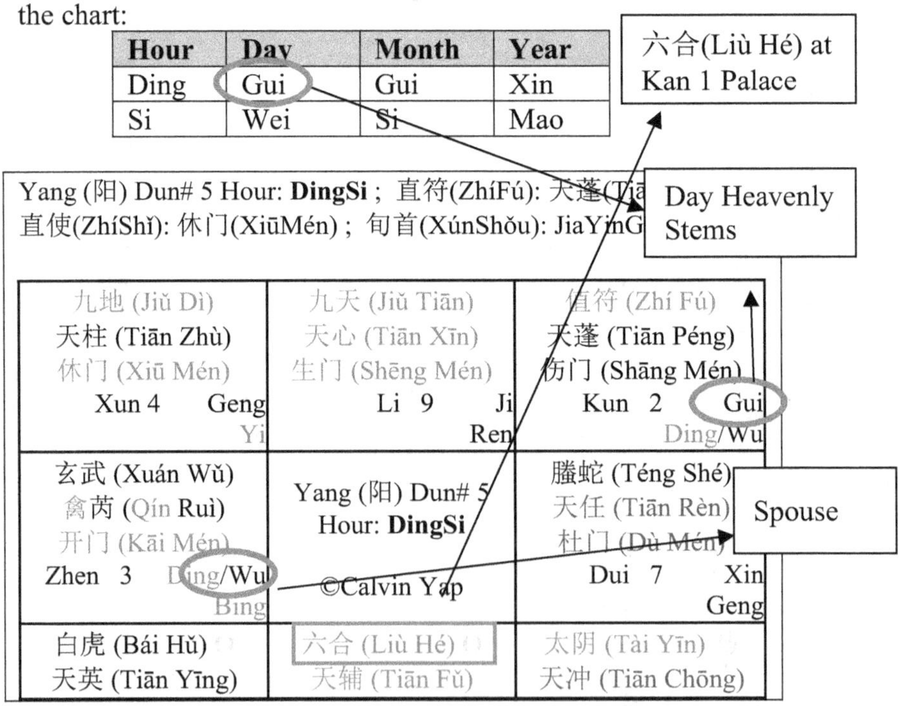

六合(Liù Hé) at Kan 1 Palace

Yang (阳) Dun# 5 Hour: **DingSi**；直符(ZhíFú): 天蓬(Tiā
直使(ZhíShǐ): 休门(XiūMén)；旬首(XúnShǒu): JiaYinG

Day Heavenly Stems

九地 (Jiǔ Dì) 天柱 (Tiān Zhù) 休门 (Xiū Mén) Xun 4　　Geng 　　　　Yi	九天 (Jiǔ Tiān) 天心 (Tiān Xīn) 生门 (Shēng Mén) Li 9　　Ji 　　　Ren	值符 (Zhí Fú) 天蓬 (Tiān Péng) 伤门 (Shāng Mén) Kun 2　　Gui 　　　Ding/Wu
玄武 (Xuán Wǔ) 禽芮 (Qín Ruì) 开门 (Kāi Mén) Zhen 3　　Ding/Wu 　　　Bing	Yang (阳) Dun# 5 Hour: **DingSi** ©Calvin Yap	螣蛇 (Téng Shé) 天任 (Tiān Rèn) 杜门 (Dù Mén) Dui 7　　Xin 　　　Geng
白虎 (Bái Hǔ) 天英 (Tiān Yīng)	六合 (Liù Hé) 天辅 (Tiān Fǔ)	太阴 (Tài Yīn) 天冲 (Tiān Chōng)

Spouse

惊门 (Jīng Mén) Gen 8　　Ren 　　　　Xin	死门 (Sǐ Mén) Kan 1　　Yi 　　　　Gui	景门 (Jǐng Mén) Qian 6　　Bing 　　　　Ji

Interpret

Now, with all the information collected, you can then start your interpretation and conclusion. Since, the question is about relationship, so, the reference point is 六合 **(Liù Hé).** (see **Table 15 - Reference Point**

)

Relationship:

六合 **(Liù Hé)** as Ti (体) is at Kan 1 Palace with 天辅 (Tiān Fǔ), 死门 (Sǐ Mén) and Kong.

- 六合 (Liù Hé) with 天辅 (Tiān Fǔ) is auspicious.

- 六合 (Liù Hé) with 死门 (Sǐ Mén) is very inauspicious. It means the relationship is death, where both of them have no feeling for each other.

- 六合 (Liù Hé) with Kong means relationship is not there anymore.

The person and Spouse

The person who came for consult is represented by the four pillars Day Heavenly Stem of the day the chart being ploted. In this case, **"Gui"** represents the person asking. **"Gui"** is at Kun 2 Palace.

The person's spouse is represented by "**Wu**" at Zhen 3 Palace. Between Kun 2 and Zhen 3, it is an inauspicious relationship. Therefore, we can deduce that both of them do not have feelings for each other.

The person vs Relationship:

The person asking is at Kun 2 Palace. Relationship is at Kan 1 Palace. Between Kun 2 and Kan 1 Palaces, it is an inauspicious relationship. Therefore, can deduce that the person asking wants to end the relationship.

Reading further:

The Spouse is "**Wu**" at Zhen 3 Palace. 3rd Party female is represented by "**Ding**", which is at Zhen 3 Palace as well. Therefore, we can deduce that the spouse is already together with the 3rd party.

Conclusion:

Since the spouse is having an affair and is already together with the 3rd party, and that the person asking is not in favour of the relationship, we can conclude that the divorce will be successful.

Example 8:

Collect

A lady is going to get married but is having doubts. She wants to know whether this marriage will work out.

Plot

The date and time asking is 20th May 2015 at Shen Hour. The Four Pillar of that date and time as follow:

Hour	Day	Month	Year
Bing	Bing	Xin	Yi
Shen	Shen	Si	Wei

Based on the Qi Men Dun Jia Calendar, it is a Yang Dun #4, Bing Shen hour chart:

<table>
<tr><td colspan="3">Yang (阳) Dun# 4 Hour: BingShen ; 直符(ZhíFú): 天柱(TiānZhù)
直使(ZhíShǐ): 惊门(JīngMén) ; 旬首(XúnShǒu): JiaWu/Xin</td></tr>
<tr>
<td>九地 (Jiǔ Dì)
天英 (Tiān Yīng)
死门 (Sǐ Mén)
Xun 4   Gui
      Wu</td>
<td>九天 (Jiǔ Tiān)
禽芮 (Qín Ruì)
惊门 (Jīng Mén)
Li 9   Bing/Ji
      Gui</td>
<td>值符 (Zhí Fú)
天柱 (Tiān Zhù)
开门 (Kāi Mén)
Kun 2   Xin
      Bing/Ji</td>
</tr>
<tr>
<td>玄武 (Xuán Wǔ)
天辅 (Tiān Fǔ)
景门 (Jǐng Mén)
Zhen 3   Wu
      Yi</td>
<td>Yang (阳) Dun# 4
Hour: BingShen

©Calvin Yap</td>
<td>螣蛇 (Téng Shé)
天心 (Tiān Xīn)
休门 (Xiū Mén)
Dui 7   Geng
      Xin</td>
</tr>
<tr>
<td>白虎 (Bái Hǔ)
天冲 (Tiān Chōng)
杜门 (Dù Mén)
Gen 8   Yi
      Ren</td>
<td>六合 (Liù Hé)
天任 (Tiān Rèn)
伤门 (Shāng Mén)
Kan 1   Ren
      Ding</td>
<td>太阴 (Tài Yīn)
天蓬 (Tiān Péng)
生门 (Shēng Mén)
Qian 6   Ding
      Geng</td>
</tr>
</table>

Determine

Based on the question asked, determine the reference point or Ti (体).
The lady was asking about her relationship, so the reference point or Ti
(体) is 六合 **(Liù Hé).** (see **Table 15 - Reference Point**

).

In addition, Day Heavenly Stem at Heaven Plate represents the person
asking and the associated Heavenly Stem that represents the spouse.

Identify

Based on the Reference Point, identify where the reference point is in
the chart:

Hour	Day	Month	Year
Bing	Bing	Xin	Yi
Shen	Shen	Si	Wei

六合(Liù Hé) at Kan 1 Palace

Day Heavenly Stems

Spouse

Yang (阳) Dun# 4 Hour: **BingShen** ; 直符(ZhíFú): 天柱(TiānZhù)
直使(ZhíShǐ): 惊门(JīngMén) ; 旬首(XúnShǒu): JiaWu/Xi

九地 (Jiǔ Dì) 天英 (Tiān Yīng) 死门 (Sǐ Mén) Xun 4 Gui Wu	九天 (Jiǔ Tiān) 禽芮 (Qín Ruì) 惊门 (Jīng Mén) Li 9 Bing/Ji Gui	值符 (Zhí Fú) 天柱 (Tiān Zhù) 开门 (Kāi Mén) Kun 2 Xin Bing/Ji
玄武 (Xuán Wǔ) 天辅 (Tiān Fǔ) 景门 (Jǐng Mén) Zhen 3 Wu Yi	Yang (阳) Dun# 4 Hour: **BingShen** ©Calvin Yap	腾蛇 (Téng Shé) 天心 (Tiān Xīn) 休门 (Xiū Mén) Dui 7 Geng Xin
白虎 (Bái Hǔ) 天冲 (Tiān Chōng) 杜门 (Dù Mén) Gen 8 Yi Ren	六合 (Liù Hé) 天任 (Tiān Rèn) 伤门 (Shāng Mén) Kan 1 Ren Ding	太阴 (Tài Yīn) 天蓬 (Tiān Péng) 生门 (Shēng Mén) Qian 6 Ding Geng

Interpret

Now, with all the information collected, you can then start your interpretation and conclusion. Since, the question is about relationship, so, the reference point is 六合 **(Liù Hé).** (see **Table 15 - Reference Point**

)

Relationship:

六合 **(Liù Hé)** as Ti (体）is at Kan 1 Palace with 天任 (Tiān Rèn) and 伤门 (Shāng Mén).

- 六合 (Liù Hé) with 天任 (Tiān Rèn) is auspicious.
- 六合 (Liù Hé) with 伤门 (Shāng Mén) is inauspicious. It means that the relationship is hurt.

The person and Spouse

The person who came for consult is represented by the four pillars Day Heavenly Stem of the day the chart being ploted. In this case, **"Bing"** represents the person asking. **"Bing"** is at Li 9 Palace.

The person's spouse is represented by **"Xin"** at Kun 2 Palace. Between Kun 2 and Li 9, it is an auspicious relationship. Therefore, we can deduce that both of them have feelings for each other.

The person vs Relationship:

The person asking is at Li 9 Palace. Relationship is at Kan 1 Palace. Between Li 9 and Kan 1 Palaces, it is an inauspicious relationship. Therefore, we can deduce that the person asking has doubts that the relationship will work.

The Spouse vs Relationship:

The Spouse is "**Xin**" at Kun 2 Palace. Between Kun 2 and Kan 1 Palaces, there is an inauspicious relationship. Therefore, the Spouse is also doubting that the relationship will work.

Conclusion:

Although both of them love each other, both of them doubt that the relationship will work. Thus, both of them would need to work harder for the relationship to work.

Example 9:

Collect

A friend has been asked to invest in business as partnership. He asked the author whether it is advisable to do so.

Plot

The date and time asking is 3rd Feb 2010 at Shen Hour. The Four Pillar of that date and time as follow:

Hour	Day	Month	Year
Ren	Jia	Ding	Ji
Shen	Shen	Chou	Chou

Based on the Qi Men Dun Jia Calendar, it is a Yang Dun #9, Ren Shen hour chart:

<table>
<tr><td colspan="3">Yang (阳) Dun# 9 Hour: RenShen ; 直符(ZhíFú): 天英(TiānYīng)
直使(ZhíShǐ): 景门(JǐngMén) ; 旬首(XúnShǒu): JiaZiWu</td></tr>
<tr>
<td>值符 (Zhí Fú)
天英 (Tiān Yīng)
惊门 (Jīng Mén)
Xun 4   Wu
     Ren</td>
<td>螣蛇 (Téng Shé)
禽芮 (Qín Ruì)
开门 (Kāi Mén)
Li 9   Geng/Gui
     Wu</td>
<td>太阴 (Tài Yīn)
天柱 (Tiān Zhù)
休门 (Xiū Mén)
Kun 2   Bing
     Geng/Gui</td>
</tr>
<tr>
<td>九天 (Jiǔ Tiān)
天辅 (Tiān Fǔ)
死门 (Sǐ Mén)
Zhen 3   Ren
     Xin</td>
<td>Yang (阳) Dun# 9
Hour: RenShen

©Calvin Yap</td>
<td>六合 (Liù Hé)
天心 (Tiān Xīn)
生门 (Shēng Mén)
Dui 7   Ding
     Bing</td>
</tr>
<tr>
<td>九地 (Jiǔ Dì)
天冲 (Tiān Chōng)
景门 (Jǐng Mén)
Gen 8   Xin
     Yi</td>
<td>玄武 (Xuán Wǔ)
天任 (Tiān Rèn)
杜门 (Dù Mén)
Kan 1   Yi
     Ji</td>
<td>白虎 (Bái Hǔ)
天蓬 (Tiān Péng)
伤门 (Shāng Mén)
Qian 6   Ji
     Ding</td>
</tr>
</table>

Determine

Based on the question asked, determine the reference point or Ti (体). The person is asking about business investment and partnership, so the reference point or Ti (体) is 生门 (Shēng Mén). In addition, there are other elements to consider (see **Table 19 - Specific Scenario: Business**):

- Partnership: 六合 (Liù Hé)
- Profit: Wu Heavenly Stem
- Customer: Hour Heavenly Stem
- Person asking: Day Heavenly Stem

Identify

Identify the reference point in the chart:

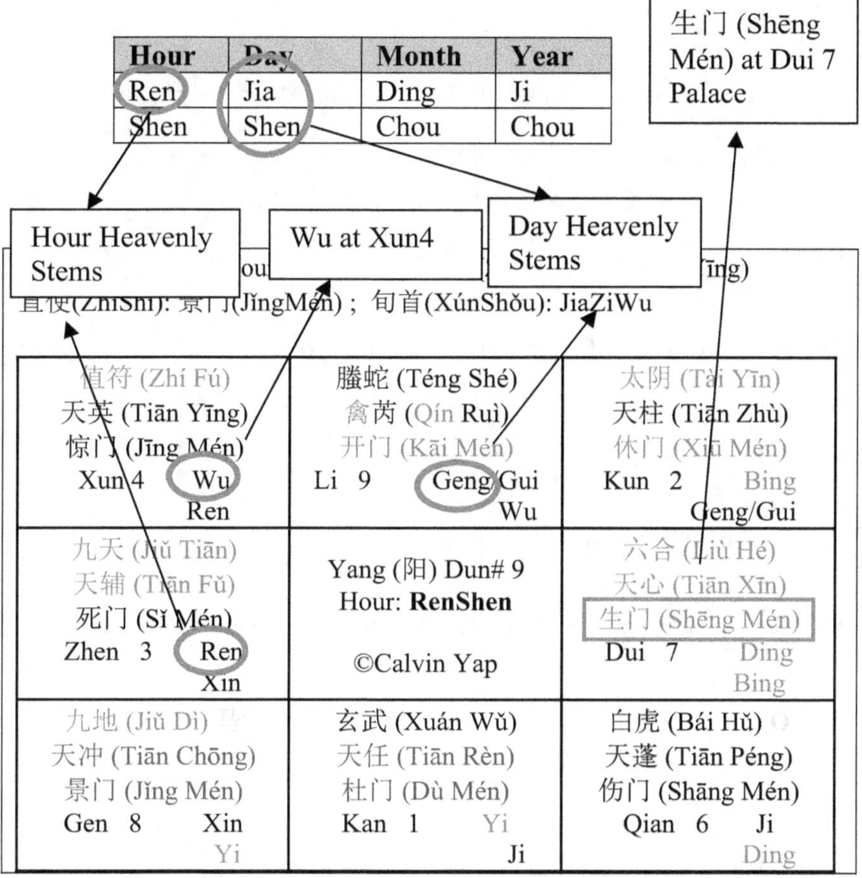

- 生门 (Shēng Mén) at Dui 7 Palace with 六合 (Liù Hé) and 天心 (Tiān Xīn)

- 六合 (Liù Hé) at Dui 7 Palace with 生门 (Shēng Mén) and 天心 (Tiān Xīn)

- Day Heavenly Stem, "**Geng**" at Li 9 Palace with 螣蛇 (Téng Shé), 禽芮 (Qín Ruì) and 开门 (Kāi Mén)

- **Wu** Heavenly Stem at Xun 4 Palace with 值符 (Zhí Fú), 天英 (Tiān Yīng) and 惊门 (Jīng Mén)

- Hour Heavenly Stem at Zhen 3 with 九天 (Jiǔ Tiān), 天辅 (Tiān Fǔ) and 死门 (Sǐ Mén).

Interpret

Now, with all the information collected, you can then start your interpretation and conclusion. Firstly, the question asked is about business and partnership.

Business and partnership:

Both Business and Partnership reference point is at Dui 7 Palace.

- 生门 (Shēng Mén) at Dui 7 Palace with 六合 (Liù Hé) and 天心 (Tiān Xīn) means business will be good with this partnership.

- 六合 (Liù Hé) at Dui 7 Palace with 生门 (Shēng Mén) and 天心 (Tiān Xīn) means partnership is good for the business.

The person:

The person who came for consult is represented by the four pillars Day Heavenly Stem of the day the chart being ploted. In this case, it is Jia

Shen[34], which is "**Geng**". "**Geng**" is at Li 9 Palace with 螣蛇 (Téng Shé), 禽芮 (Qín Ruì) and 开门 (Kāi Mén).

- The person with 螣蛇 (Téng Shé) means the person is vexed.
- The person with 禽芮 (Qín Ruì) means the person is troubled.
- The person with 开门 (Kāi Mén) means the person is open.

Business/Partnership vs Profit:

Business and Partnership is at Dui 7 Palace. Representing profit, Wu is at Xun 4 Palace. Between Dui 7 and Xun 4 Palace is in an inauspicious relationship. Therefore, we can deduce that the business is not doing well.

Business/Partnership vs the person:

Business and Partnership is at Dui 7 Palace. The person asking is "**Geng**" at Li 9 Palace. Between Dui 7 and Li 9 Palaces, it is in an inauspicious relationship. Therefore, the business and partnership is not favourable to the person asking.

Business vs customer:

Business is at Dui 7 Palace and representing customer is Hour Heavenly Stem "**Ren**" at Zhen 3 Palace. Between Dui 7 and Zhen 3, it is in an inauspicious relationship.

---

[34] See **Table 13 - hidden Jia**.

Conclusion:

Although the business will be good with this partnership, if the person asking joins the business and partnership, the business profit will not be good and customers will not come. Therefore, if he decides to invest in this business, he will lose all of his investment. In the end, the person did not carry out with the business plan.

Example 10:

Collect

A client asked about his financial situation.

Plot

The date and time asking is 8th June 2011 at Shen hour. The Four Pillar of that date and time as follow:

Hour	Day	Month	Year
Ren	Jia	Jia	Xin
Shen	Wu	Wu	Mao

Based on the Qi Men Dun Jia Calendar, it is a Yang Dun #6, Ren Shen hour chart:

<table>
<tr><td colspan="3">Yang (阳) Dun# 6 Hour: RenShen；直符(ZhíFú): 天心(TiānXīn) 直使(ZhíShǐ): 开门(KāiMén)；旬首(XúnShǒu): JiaZiWu</td></tr>
<tr>
<td>六合 (Liù Hé)
天冲 (Tiān Chōng)
死门 (Sǐ Mén)
Xun 4　　Ding
　　　　Bing</td>
<td>白虎 (Bái Hǔ)
天辅 (Tiān Fǔ)
惊门 (Jīng Mén)
Li 9　　Bing
　　　　Xin</td>
<td>玄武 (Xuán Wǔ)
天英 (Tiān Yīng)
开门 (Kāi Mén)
Kun 2　　Xin
　　　　Gui/Yi</td>
</tr>
<tr>
<td>太阴 (Tài Yīn)
天任 (Tiān Rèn)
景门 (Jǐng Mén)
Zhen 3　　Geng
　　　　Ding</td>
<td>Yang (阳) Dun# 6
Hour: RenShen

©Calvin Yap</td>
<td>九地 (Jiǔ Dì)
禽芮 (Qín Ruì)
休门 (Xiū Mén)
Dui 7　　Gui/Yi
　　　　Ji</td>
</tr>
<tr>
<td>螣蛇 (Téng Shé)
天蓬 (Tiān Péng)
杜门 (Dù Mén)
Gen 8　　Ren
　　　　Geng</td>
<td>值符 (Zhí Fú)
天心 (Tiān Xīn)
伤门 (Shāng Mén)
Kan 1　　Wu
　　　　Ren</td>
<td>九天 (Jiǔ Tiān)
天柱 (Tiān Zhù)
生门 (Shēng Mén)
Qian 6　　Ji
　　　　Wu</td>
</tr>
</table>

Determine

Based on the question asked, determine the reference point or Ti (体).
The person is asking about financial situation, so the reference point or
Ti (体) is 生门 (Shēng Mén).

Identify

Identify the reference point in the chart:

Hour	Day	Month	Year
Ren	Jia	Jia	Xin
Shen	Wu	Wu	Mao

生门 (Shēng Mén) at Dui 7 Palace

Yang (阳) Dun# 6 Hour: **RenShen** 直符(ZhíFú) 天心(TiānXīn)
直使(ZhíShǐ): 开门(KāiMén) ; 旬首 Wu

Day Heavenly Stems

六合 (Liù Hé) 天冲 (Tiān Chōng) 死门 (Sǐ Mén) Xun 4　　Ding 　　　　Bing	白虎 (Bái Hǔ) 天辅 (Tiān Fǔ) 惊门 (Jīng Mén) Li 9　　Bing 　　　　Xin	玄武 (Xuán Wǔ) 天英 (Tiān Yīng) 开门 (Kāi Mén) Kun 2　　Xin 　　　　Gui/Yi
太阴 (Tài Yīn) 天任 (Tiān Rèn) 景门 (Jǐng Mén) Zhen 3　　Geng 　　　　Ding	Yang (阳) Dun# 6 Hour: **RenShen** ©Calvin Yap	九地 (Jiǔ Dì) 禽芮 (Qín Ruì) 休门 (Xiū Mén) Dui 7　　Gui/Yi 　　　　Ji
螣蛇 (Téng Shé) 天蓬 (Tiān Péng) 杜门 (Dù Mén) Gen 8　　Ren 　　　　Geng	值符 (Zhí Fú) 天心 (Tiān Xīn) 伤门 (Shāng Mén) Kan 1　　Wu 　　　　Ren	九天 (Jiǔ Tiān) 天柱 (Tiān Zhù) 生门 (Shēng Mén) Qian 6　　Ji 　　　　Wu

- 生门 (Shēng Mén) at Qian 6 with 九天 (Jiǔ Tiān), 天柱 (Tiān Zhù) and Kong.

- Day Heavenly Stem is Jia, so we have to look at the whole pillar, which is Jia Wu. Jia Wu is "hidden" at **"Xin"**. So, **"Xin"** represent Day Heavenly Stem at Kun 2 Palace with 玄武 (Xuán Wǔ), 天英 (Tiān Yīng) and 开门 (Kāi Mén).

Interpret

Now, with all the information collected, you can then start your interpretation and conclusion. Firstly, the question asked is about financial situation.

Financial Situation:

Representing financial situation is 生门 (Shēng Mén) at Qian 6 with 九天 (Jiǔ Tiān), 天柱 (Tiān Zhù) and Kong.

- 生门 (Shēng Mén) with Kong means that it is only 20% capable. That means that financially, the person is not doing well.

- 生门 (Shēng Mén) with 天柱 (Tiān Zhù) means that financially, the person is in adverse calamity.

- 生门 (Shēng Mén) with 九天 (Jiǔ Tiān) means high and extreme. Combining all the readings, it means that financially, the person is in extreme adverse calamity.

The person:

The person who came for consult is represented by the four pillars Day Heavenly Stem of the day the chart being plotted. In this case, it is Jia Wu or "**Xin**". "**Xin**" is at Kun 2 Palace with 玄武 (Xuán Wǔ), 天英 (Tiān Yīng) and 开门 (Kāi Mén). "Xin" is with 玄武 (Xuán Wǔ), and 玄武 (Xuán Wǔ) means financial loss.

Conclusion:

The financial situation for the person asking is not very good and he is facing advance calamity. The person needs to examine and re-evaluate his investment choices.

Example 11:

Collect

A client goes overseas frequently for business. He wanted to know whether it is good for him financially.

Plot

The date and time when this customer asked was on 4th June 2011 at Wu Hour. The Four Pillar of that date and time as follow:

Hour	Day	Month	Year
Ren	Geng	Gui	Xin
Wu	Yin	Si	Mao

Based on the Qi Men Dun Jia Calendar, it is a Yang Dun #8, Ren Wu hour chart:

<table>
<tr><td colspan="3">Yang (阳) Dun# 8 Hour: RenWu；直符(ZhíFú): 天英(TiānYīng) 直使(ZhíShǐ): 景门(JǐngMén)；旬首(XúnShǒu): JiaXuJi</td></tr>
<tr>
<td>螣蛇 (Téng Shé)
禽芮 (Qín Ruì)
惊门 (Jīng Mén)
Xun 4   Xin/Ding
        Gui</td>
<td>太阴 (Tài Yīn)
天柱 (Tiān Zhù)
开门 (Kāi Mén)
Li 9   Yi
      Ji</td>
<td>六合 (Liù Hé)
天心 (Tiān Xīn)
休门 (Xiū Mén)
Kun 2   Bing
      Xin/Ding</td>
</tr>
<tr>
<td>值符 (Zhí Fú)
天英 (Tiān Yīng)
死门 (Sǐ Mén)
Zhen 3   Ji
      Ren</td>
<td>Yang (阳) Dun# 8
Hour: RenWu

©Calvin Yap</td>
<td>白虎 (Bái Hǔ)
天蓬 (Tiān Péng)
生门 (Shēng Mén)
Dui 7   Geng
      Yi</td>
</tr>
<tr>
<td>九天 (Jiǔ Tiān)
天辅 (Tiān Fǔ)
景门 (Jǐng Mén)
Gen 8   Gui</td>
<td>九地 (Jiǔ Dì)
天冲 (Tiān Chōng)
杜门 (Dù Mén)
Kan 1   Ren</td>
<td>玄武 (Xuán Wǔ)
天任 (Tiān Rèn)
伤门 (Shāng Mén)
Qian 6   Wu</td>
</tr>
</table>

	Wu	Geng	Bing

Determine

Based on the question asked, determine the reference point or Ti (体).

The person is asking about financial situation, so the reference point or Ti (体) is 生门 (Shēng Mén).

Identify

Identify the reference point in the chart:

Hour	Day	Month	Year
Ren	Geng	Gui	Xin
Wu	Yin	Si	Mao

生门 (Shēng Mén) at Dui 7 Palace

Day Heavenly Stems

Yang (阳) Dun# 8 Hour: **RenWu**；直符(ZhíFú): 天英(TiānYīng) 直使(ZhíShǐ): 景门(JǐngMén)；旬首(XúnShǒu): JiaXuJi

螣蛇 (Téng Shé) 禽芮 (Qín Ruì) 惊门 (Jīng Mén) Xun 4　　Xin/Ding　　　　Gui	太阴 (Tài Yīn) 天柱 (Tiān Zhù) 开门 (Kāi Mén) Li 9　　　Yi　　　　Ji	六合 (Liù Hé) 天心 (Tiān Xīn) 休门 (Xiū Mén) Kun 2　　Bing　　　Xin/Ding
值符 (Zhí Fú) 天英 (Tiān Yīng) 死门 (Sǐ Mén) Zhen 3　　Ji　　　　　Ren	Yang (阳) Dun# 8 Hour: **RenWu** ©Calvin Yap	白虎 (Bái Hǔ) 天蓬 (Tiān Péng) 生门 (Shēng Mén) Dui 7　　Geng　　　Yi
九天 (Jiǔ Tiān) 天辅 (Tiān Fǔ) 景门 (Jǐng Mén) Gen 8　　Gui　　　Wu	九地 (Jiǔ Dì) 天冲 (Tiān Chōng) 杜门 (Dù Mén) Kan 1　　Ren　　　Geng	玄武 (Xuán Wǔ) 天任 (Tiān Rèn) 伤门 (Shāng Mén) Qian 6　　Wu　　　Bing

- 生门 (Shēng Mén) at Dui 7 with 白虎 (Bái Hǔ), 天蓬 (Tiān Péng) and Kong.

- Day Heavenly Stem is "**Geng**", which is at the same palace as 生门 (Shēng Mén) which is at Dui 7.

Interpret

Now, with all the information collected, you can then start your interpretation and conclusion. Firstly, we would check whether all the travelling is good for his business.

Business:

Representing business is 生门 (Shēng Mén) at Dui 7 with 白虎 (Bái Hǔ), 天蓬 (Tiān Péng) and Kong.

- 生门 (Shēng Mén) with Kong means that it is only 20% capable. This will means that all the travelling will not yield good business results.

- 生门 (Shēng Mén) with 天蓬 (Tiān Péng) means that his business will lose money big time, and together with 白虎 (Bái Hǔ), it means that he will lose money ferociously.

The person:

The person is represented by Day Heavenly Stem "**Geng**" at Dui 7 Palace, which is the same palace of 生门 (Shēng Mén). Together with 白虎 (Bái Hǔ), 天蓬 (Tiān Péng) and Kong, it also means that his business is losing money.

Conclusion:

Therefore, we can tell him that all his frequent flying overseas is not favourable and will not benefit his business. We can then advise him to concentrate on his domestic business instead.

Example 12:

Collect

A lady is asking whether or not it is okay to open a fashion retail shop.

Plot

The date and time when this customer asked was on 14th June 2011 at Wei hour. The Four Pillar as follow:

Hour	Day	Month	Year
Gui	Geng	Jia	Xin
Wei	Zi	Wu	Mao

Based on the Qi Men Dun Jia Calendar, it is a Yang Dun #3, Gui Wei hour chart:

Yang (阳) Dun# 3 Hour: **GuiWei** ; 直符(ZhíFú): 天辅(TiānFǔ)
直使(ZhíShǐ): 杜门(DùMén) ; 旬首(XúnShǒu): JiaXuJi

太阴 (Tài Yīn) 禽芮 (Qín Ruì) 杜门 (Dù Mén) Xun 4　　Yi/Geng 　　　　　　Ji	六合 (Liù Hé) 天柱 (Tiān Zhù) 景门 (Jǐng Mén) Li 9　　　Ren 　　　　　Ding	白虎 (Bái Hǔ) 天心 (Tiān Xīn) 死门 (Sǐ Mén) Kun 2　　　Xin 　　　　　Yi/Geng
螣蛇 (Téng Shé) 天英 (Tiān Yīng) 伤门 (Shāng Mén) Zhen 3　　Ding 　　　　　Wu	Yang (阳) Dun# 3 Hour: **GuiWei** ©Calvin Yap	玄武 (Xuán Wǔ) 天蓬 (Tiān Péng) 惊门 (Jīng Mén) Dui 7　　　Bing 　　　　　Ren
值符 (Zhí Fú) 天辅 (Tiān Fǔ) 生门 (Shēng Mén) Gen 8　　　Ji 　　　　　Gui	九天 (Jiǔ Tiān) 天冲 (Tiān Chōng) 休门 (Xiū Mén) Kan 1　　　Wu 　　　　　Bing	九地 (Jiǔ Dì) 天任 (Tiān Rèn) 开门 (Kāi Mén) Qian 6　　Gui 　　　　　Xin

Determine

Based on the question asked, determine the reference point or Ti (体).
The lady is asking about investing in business, so the reference point or
Ti (体) is 生门 (Shēng Mén).

In addition, Day Heavenly Stem at Heaven Plate represents the person
asking.

Identify

Identify the reference point in the chart:

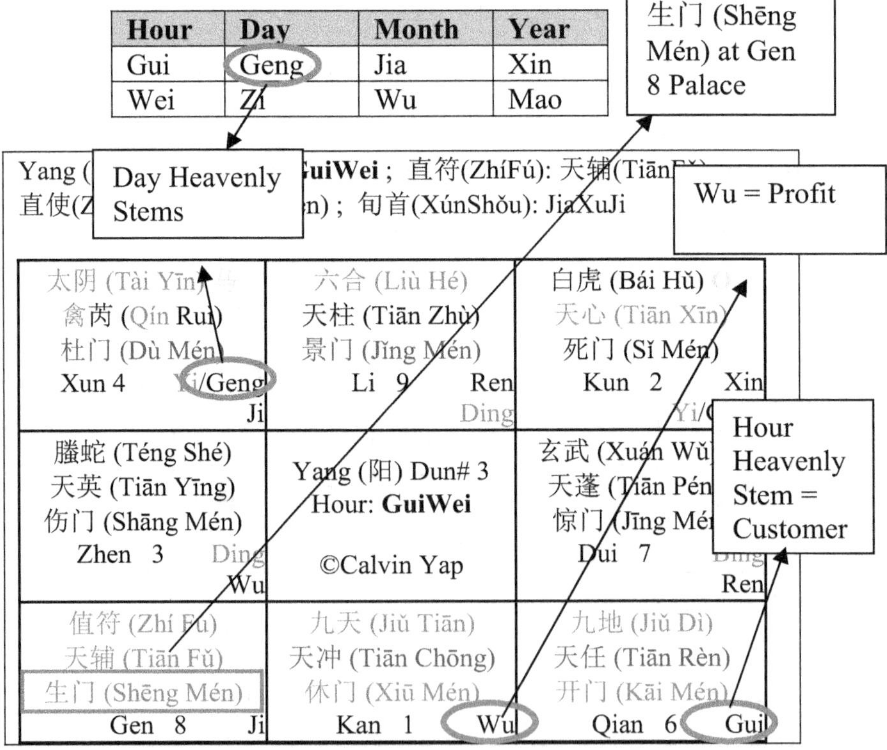

Interpret[35]

Now, with all the information collected, you can then start your interpretation and conclusion. Since, the question is about investing in business, so the reference point is 生门 (Shēng Mén).

生门 (Shēng Mén) at Gen 8 Palace with 值符 (Zhí Fú) and 天辅 (Tiān Fǔ), which is auspicious.

Profit is represented by **"Wu"** at Kan 1 Palace with 九天 (Jiǔ Tiān), 天冲 (Tiān Chōng) and 休门 (Xiū Mén), which is auspicious.

The person vs Profit:

The person is represented by Day Heavenly Stem, which is **"Geng"** at Xun 4 Palace. Profit is represented by **"Wu"** at Kan 1 Palace. Between Kan 1 and Xun 4 Palace, it is in an auspicious relationship. Therefore, the person will gain profits.

The business vs Customer:

The business is represented by 生门 (Shēng Mén) at Gen 8 Palace. Customer is represented by Hour Heavenly Stem, which is **"Gui"** at Qian 6 Palace. Between Gen 8 and Qian 6, it is an auspicious

---

[35] See **Table 19 - Specific Scenario: Business**

relationship. Therefore, there will be customers patronising the business.

Conclusion:

As such, investment into this business is good and the person will gain good profits as there will be a lot of customers patronizing the shop.

Example 13:

Collect

A lady asked about her health.

Plot

The date and time asking is 5th Feb 2010 at Wei Hour. The Four Pillar of that date and time as follow:

Hour	Day	Month	Year
Yi	Bing	Wu	Geng
Wei	Xu	Yin	Yin

Based on the Qi Men Dun Jia Calendar, it is a Yang Dun #5, Yi Wei hour chart:

<table>
<tr><td colspan="3">Yang (阳) Dun# 5 Hour: YiWei；直符(ZhíFú): 天任(TiānRèn)
直使(ZhíShǐ): 生门(ShēngMén)；旬首(XúnShǒu): JiaWu/Xin</td></tr>
<tr>
<td>值符 (Zhí Fú)
天任 (Tiān Rèn)
休门 (Xiū Mén)
Xun 4   Xin
Yi</td>
<td>螣蛇 (Téng Shé)
天冲 (Tiān Chōng)
生门 (Shēng Mén)
Li 9   Bing
Ren</td>
<td>太阴 (Tài Yīn)
天辅 (Tiān Fǔ)
伤门 (Shāng Mén)
Kun 2   Yi
Ding/Wu</td>
</tr>
<tr>
<td>九天 (Jiǔ Tiān)
天蓬 (Tiān Péng)
开门 (Kāi Mén)
Zhen 3   Gui
Bing</td>
<td>Yang (阳) Dun# 5
Hour: YiWei

©Calvin Yap</td>
<td>六合 (Liù Hé)
天英 (Tiān Yīng)
杜门 (Dù Mén)
Dui 7   Ren
Geng</td>
</tr>
<tr>
<td>九地 (Jiǔ Dì)
天心 (Tiān Xīn)
惊门 (Jīng Mén)
Gen 8   Ji</td>
<td>玄武 (Xuán Wǔ)
天柱 (Tiān Zhù)
死门 (Sǐ Mén)
Kan 1   Geng</td>
<td>白虎 (Bái Hǔ)
禽芮 (Qín Ruì)
景门 (Jǐng Mén)
Qian 6   Ding/Wu</td>
</tr>
</table>

Xin	Gui	Ji

Determine

Based on the question asked, determine the reference point or Ti (体). Since she is asking about her health, the reference point or Ti (体) for illness is 禽芮 (Qín Ruì)[36]. In addition, Day Heavenly Stem at Heaven Plate represents the person asking. 天心 (Tiān Xīn)[37] also represents doctor.

---

[36] See **Table 15 - Reference Point**

[37] See **Table 20 - Specific scenario: illness**

Identify

Based on the Reference Point, identify where the reference point is in
the chart:

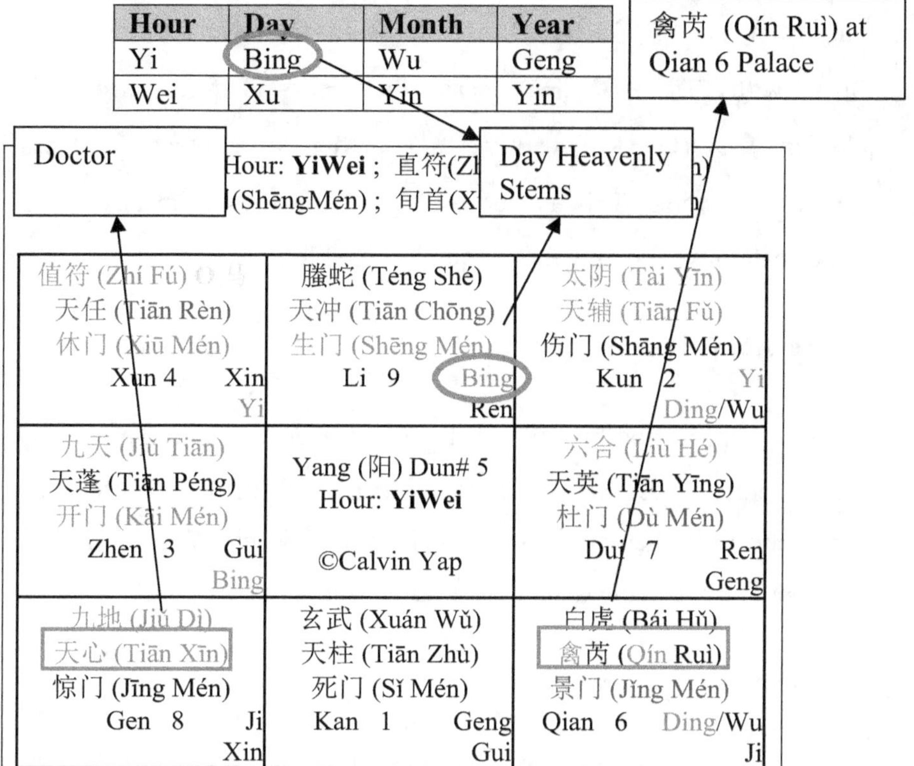

Interpretation

Illness:

Illness is represented by 禽芮 (Qín Ruì) at Qian 6 Palace with 景门 (Jǐng Mén) and 白虎 (Bái Hǔ). 白虎 (Bái Hǔ) means ferocious, so illness with 白虎 (Bái Hǔ) means the illness is quite serious. In addition, 禽芮 (Qín Ruì) with 景门 (Jǐng Mén) means that the illness requires operation. This is because 景门 (Jǐng Mén) means blood related calamity; and operation require to see blood.

The person vs Doctor:

Doctor is represented by 天心 (Tiān Xīn) at Gen 8 Palace. The person is represented by Day Heavenly Stem **"Bing"** at Li 9 Palace. Between Gen 8 and Li 9, they are in an auspicious relationship. We can deduce that doctor will be able to help the person asking.

Conclusion:

The person asking is worried about her health, but from the information gathered above, she should be ok.

Example 14:

Collect

A student called to cancel meeting as her mother is hospitalised due to pain at the chest. The doctor couldn't accertain what is the problem.

Plot

The date and time asking is 12th July 2013 at Chen Hour. The Four Pillar of that date and time as follow:

Hour	Day	Month	Year
Wu	Ji	Ji	Gui
Chen	Mao	Wei	Si

Based on the Qi Men Dun Jia Calendar, it is a Yin Dun #8, Wu Chen hour chart:

Yin (阴) Dun# 8 Hour: **WuChen** ；直符(ZhíFú): 天任(TiānRèn)
直使(ZhíShǐ): 生门(ShēngMén) ；旬首(XúnShǒu): JiaZiWu

九地 (Jiǔ Dì) 天辅 (Tiān Fǔ) 生门 (Shēng Mén) Xun 4　　Ren 　　　　Ren	玄武 (Xuán Wǔ) 天英 (Tiān Yīng) 伤门 (Shāng Mén) Li 9　　　Yi 　　　　Yi	白虎 (Bái Hǔ) 禽芮 (Qín Ruì) 杜门 (Dù Mén) Kun 2　　Ding/Xin 　　　　Ding/Xin
九天 (Jiǔ Tiān) 天冲 (Tiān Chōng) 休门 (Xiū Mén) Zhen 3　　Gui 　　　　Gui	Yin (阴) Dun# 8 Hour: **WuChen** **Fu Yin** ©Calvin Yap	六合 (Liù Hé) 天柱 (Tiān Zhù) 景门 (Jǐng Mén) Dui 7　　Ji 　　　　Ji
值符 (Zhí Fú) 天任 (Tiān Rèn) 开门 (Kāi Mén) Gen 8　　Wu 　　　　Wu	螣蛇 (Téng Shé) 天蓬 (Tiān Péng) 惊门 (Jīng Mén) Kan 1　　Bing 　　　　Bing	太阴 (Tài Yīn) 天心 (Tiān Xīn) 死门 (Sǐ Mén) Qian 6　　Geng 　　　　Geng

Determine

Based on the question asked, determine the reference point or Ti (体). Since she is asking about her health, the reference point or Ti (体) for illness is 禽芮 (Qín Ruì)[38]. In addition, Day Heavenly Stem at Heaven Plate represents the person asking. 天心 (Tiān Xīn)[39] also represents doctor.

In addition, based on the location of 禽芮 (Qín Ruì), we can determine the problematic organ as per **Table 21 - Palace vs Sickness.**

---

[38] See **Table 15 - Reference Point**

[39] See **Table 20 - Specific scenario: illness**

Identify

Based on the Reference Point, identify where the reference point in the chart:

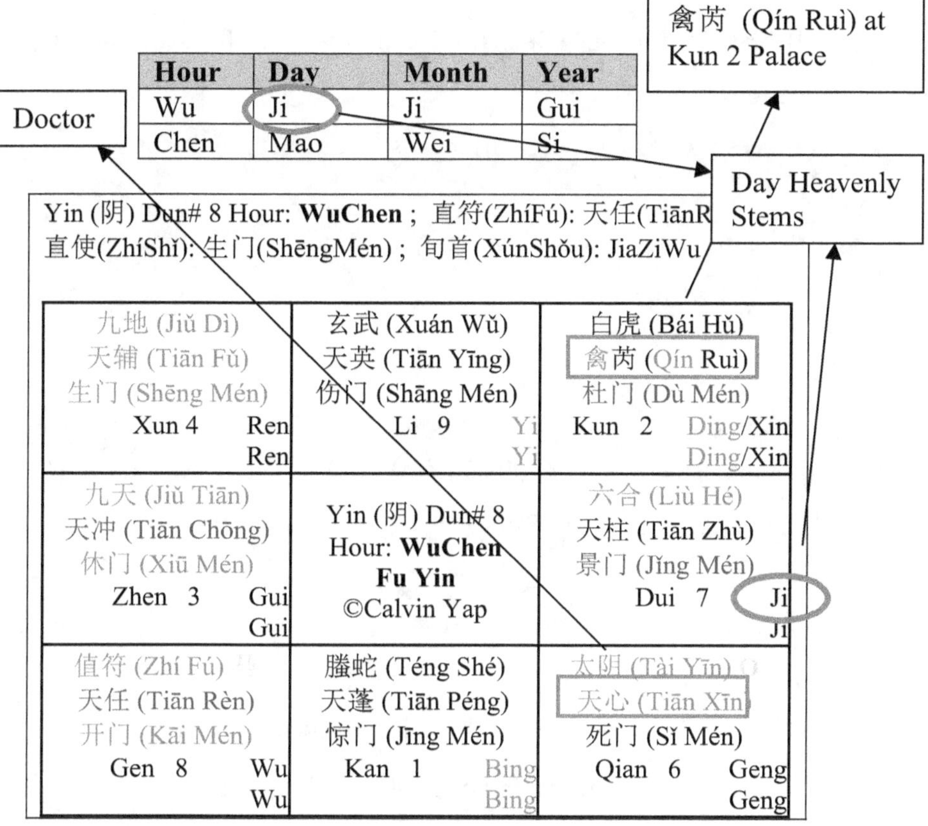

Interpretation

Illness:

Illness is represented by 禽芮 (Qín Ruì) at Kun 2 Palace with 白虎 (Bái Hǔ) and 杜门 (Dù Mén).

- As per **Table 21 - Palace vs Sickness**, Kun 2 Palace is referring to Stomach, Intestine or Spleen.
- There is "**Xin**" at Kun 2 Palace, so there might be small growth there.
- Illness with 白虎 (Bái Hǔ) means that the illness could be serious.
- Illness with 杜门 (Dù Mén) means that something is stuck.

Therefore, can deduce that there might be a growth stuck at the stomach, spleen or intestine area.

Doctor:

Doctor is represented by 天心 (Tiān Xīn) at Qian 6 Palace with 太阴 (Tài Yīn), 死门 (Sǐ Mén) and Kong.

- 天心 (Tiān Xīn) with 太阴 (Tài Yīn), means that doctor might not be in his/her top form.
- 天心 (Tiān Xīn) with 死门 (Sǐ Mén), means that doctor is in bad luck, so he/she might not be able to detect the problem.
- 天心 (Tiān Xīn) with Kong, Kong means that there is only 20% capability. So, the doctor might be absentminded.

Conclusion:

Based on the information provided above, it was advised that a scan to be done at the stomach, spleen or intestine area. Originally, the doctor refused to do it but after my student's insistence, the doctor decided to perform a scan, and discovered polyp or soft stone near the gall bladder.

Example 15:

Collect

A person asked whether he has heart issue.

Plot

The date and time asking is 19th Dec 2014 at Si Hour. The Four Pillar of that date and time as follow:

Hour	Day	Month	Year
Ji	Jia	Bing	Jia
Si	Zi	Zi	Wu

Based on the Qi Men Dun Jia Calendar, it is a Yin Dun #4, Ji Si hour chart:

<table>
<tr><td colspan="3">Yin (阴) Dun# 4 Hour: JiSi；直符(ZhíFú): 天辅(TiānFǔ)
直使(ZhíShǐ): 杜门(DùMén)；旬首(XúnShǒu): JiaZiWu</td></tr>
<tr>
<td>九天 (Jiǔ Tiān)
天英 (Tiān Yīng)
死门 (Sǐ Mén)
Xun 4   Ren
    Wu</td>
<td>九地 (Jiǔ Dì)
禽芮 (Qín Ruì)
惊门 (Jīng Mén)
Li 9   Geng/Yi
    Ren</td>
<td>玄武 (Xuán Wǔ)
天柱 (Tiān Zhù)
开门 (Kāi Mén)
Kun 2   Ding
    Geng/Yi</td>
</tr>
<tr>
<td>值符 (Zhí Fú)
天辅 (Tiān Fǔ)
景门 (Jǐng Mén)
Zhen 3   Wu
    Ji</td>
<td>Yin (阴) Dun# 4
Hour: JiSi

©Calvin Yap</td>
<td>白虎 (Bái Hǔ)
天心 (Tiān Xīn)
休门 (Xiū Mén)
Dui 7   Bing
    Ding</td>
</tr>
<tr>
<td>螣蛇 (Téng Shé)
天冲 (Tiān Chōng)
杜门 (Dù Mén)
Gen 8   Ji
    Gui</td>
<td>太阴 (Tài Yīn)
天任 (Tiān Rèn)
伤门 (Shāng Mén)
Kan 1   Gui
    Xin</td>
<td>六合 (Liù Hé)
天蓬 (Tiān Péng)
生门 (Shēng Mén)
Qian 6   Xin
    Bing</td>
</tr>
</table>

Determine

Based on the question asked, determine the reference point or Ti (体). Since she is asking about her health, the reference point or Ti (体) for illness is 禽芮 (Qín Ruì)[40]. In addition, Day Heavenly Stem at Heaven Plate represents the person asking. 天心 (Tiān Xīn)[41] also represents doctor.

In addition, based on the location of 禽芮 (Qín Ruì), we can determine the problematic organ as per **Table 21 - Palace vs Sickness.**

[40] See **Table 15 - Reference Point**

[41] See **Table 20 - Specific scenario: illness**

Identify

Based on the Reference Point, identify where the reference point in the chart:

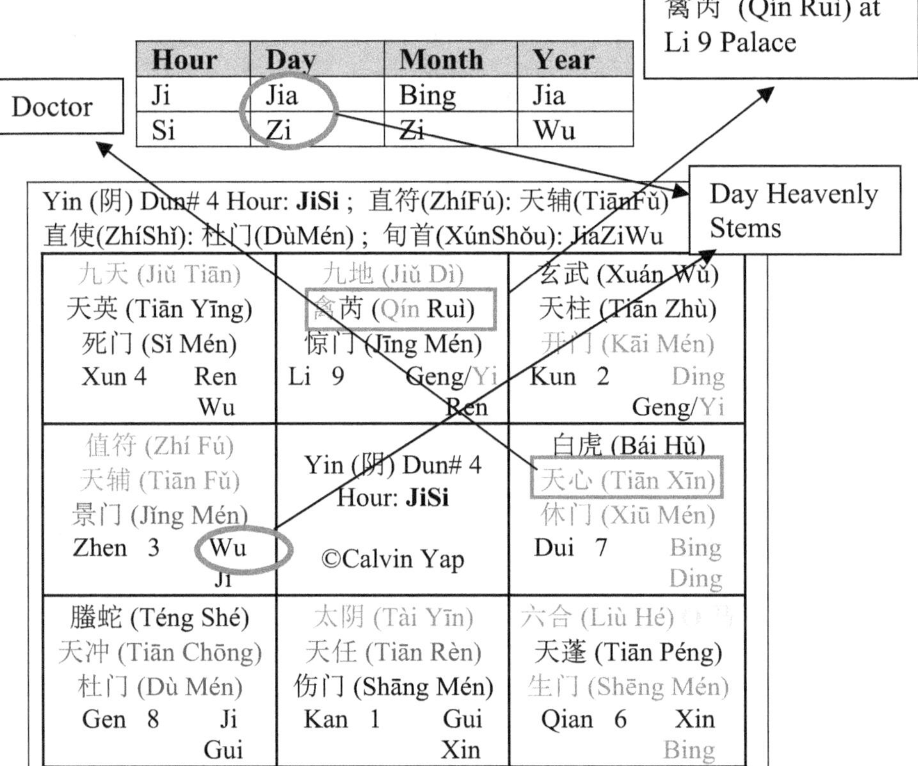

Interpretation

Illness:

Illness is represented by 禽芮 (Qín Ruì) at Li 9 Palace with 九地 (Jiǔ Dì) and 惊门 (Jīng Mén).

- As per **Table 21 - Palace vs Sickness**, Li 9 Palace is referring to heart, arteries and head.

- Illness with 九地 (Jiǔ Dì) means that the illness could be slow or difficult to detect.

- Illness with 惊门 (Jīng Mén) means complication.

Therefore, can deduce that the person might have heart problem.

Doctor:

Doctor is represented by 天心 (Tiān Xīn) at Dui 7 Palace with 白虎 (Bái Hǔ) and 休门 (Xiū Mén).

- 天心 (Tiān Xīn) with 白虎 (Bái Hǔ), means that the doctor might be aggressive in his/her diagnostic.

- 天心 (Tiān Xīn) with 休门 (Xiū Mén), means that the doctor might not check things in detail.

The Person:

The person is represented by Day Heavenly Stem, which is **"Jia"**. However, **"Jia"** is hidden in Qi Men Dun Jia. As per **Table 13 - hidden Jia**, **"Jia Zi"** is represented by **"Wu"** at Zhen 3 Palace with 景门 (Jǐng Mén), 天辅 (Tiān Fǔ) and 值符 (Zhí Fú).

- The person with 景门 (Jǐng Mén) means there will be blood related calamity. This will means that he would require surgery.

- The person with 天辅 (Tiān Fǔ) is auspicious.

- The person with 值符 (Zhí Fú) means there will be nobleman coming to help.

Outcome:

Subsequent cardiological examination confirmed that there is heart issue and surgery is required.

Part III – Qi Men Dun Jia Calendar

Qi Men Dun Jia Calendar and 1080 charts for you to plot chart.

Calendar

The calendar is organized using Qi Men Dun Jia Season starting from Yang Dun. Example as follow:

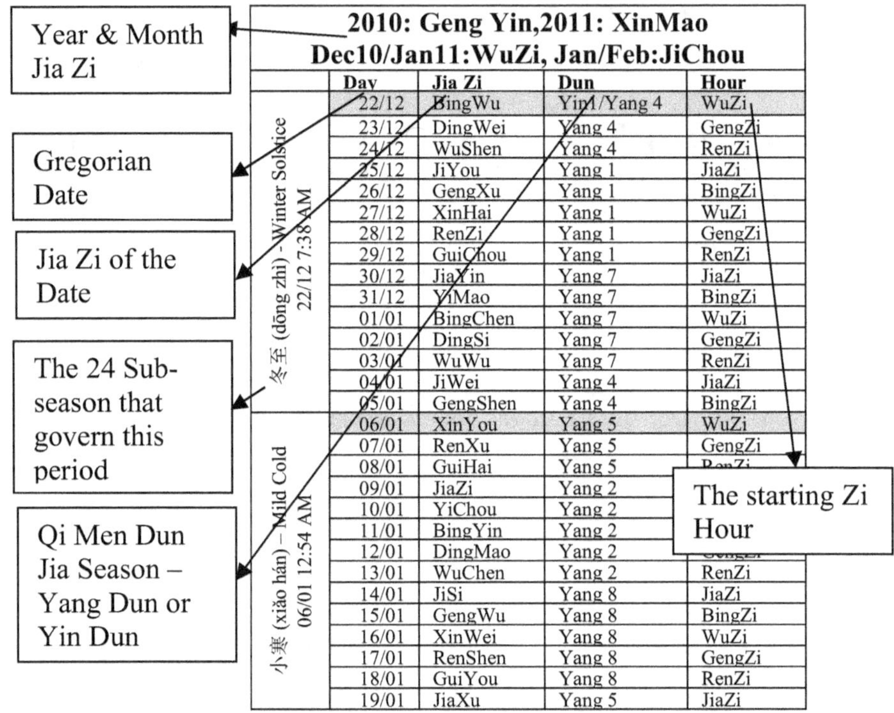

2010: Geng Yin, 2011: XinMao
Dec10/Jan11:WuZi, Jan/Feb:JiChou

Day	Jia Zi	Dun	Hour
22/12	BingWu	Yin1/Yang 4	WuZi
23/12	DingWei	Yang 4	GengZi
24/12	WuShen	Yang 4	RenZi
25/12	JiYou	Yang 1	JiaZi
26/12	GengXu	Yang 1	BingZi
27/12	XinHai	Yang 1	WuZi
28/12	RenZi	Yang 1	GengZi
29/12	GuiChou	Yang 1	RenZi
30/12	JiaYin	Yang 7	JiaZi
31/12	YiMao	Yang 7	BingZi
01/01	BingChen	Yang 7	WuZi
02/01	DingSi	Yang 7	GengZi
03/01	WuWu	Yang 7	RenZi
04/01	JiWei	Yang 4	JiaZi
05/01	GengShen	Yang 4	BingZi
06/01	XinYou	Yang 5	WuZi
07/01	RenXu	Yang 5	GengZi
08/01	GuiHai	Yang 5	RenZi
09/01	JiaZi	Yang 2	[illegible]
10/01	YiChou	Yang 2	[illegible]
11/01	BingYin	Yang 2	[illegible]
12/01	DingMao	Yang 2	GengZi
13/01	WuChen	Yang 2	RenZi
14/01	JiSi	Yang 8	JiaZi
15/01	GengWu	Yang 8	BingZi
16/01	XinWei	Yang 8	WuZi
17/01	RenShen	Yang 8	GengZi
18/01	GuiYou	Yang 8	RenZi
19/01	JiaXu	Yang 5	JiaZi

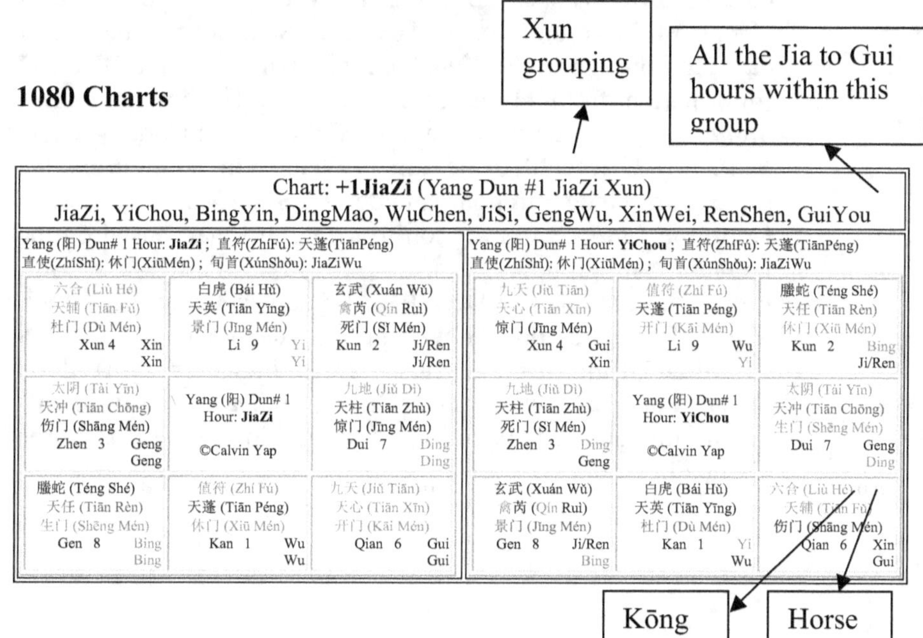

Inverse is where 立春 (Beginning of Spring - lì chūn) starts. This is when the JiaZi of Year and Month change to the next.

立春 (lì chūn) – Beginning of Spring
04/02 12:32 PM

	04/02	GengYin	Yang 6/2	BingZi
	05/02	XinMao	Yang 2	WuZi
	06/02	RenChen	Yang 2	GengZi
	07/02	GuiSi	Yang 2	RenZi
	08/02	JiaWu	Yang 8	JiaZi
	09/02	YiWei	Yang 8	BingZi
	10/02	BingShen	Yang 8	WuZi
	11/02	DingYou	Yang 8	GengZi
	12/02	WuXu	Yang 8	RenZi
	13/02	JiHai	Yang 5	JiaZi
	14/02	GengZi	Yang 5	BingZi
	15/02	XinChou	Yang 5	WuZi
	16/02	RenYin	Yang 5	GengZi
	17/02	GuiMao	Yang 5	RenZi
	18/02	JiaChen	Yang 2	JiaZi

1080 Charts

Xun grouping

All the Jia to Gui hours within this group

Chart: +1JiaZi (Yang Dun #1 JiaZi Xun)

JiaZi, YiChou, BingYin, DingMao, WuChen, JiSi, GengWu, XinWei, RenShen, GuiYou

Yang (阳) Dun# 1 Hour: **JiaZi** ; 直符(ZhíFú): 天蓬(TiānPéng)
直使(ZhíShǐ): 休门(XiūMén) ; 旬首(XúnShǒu): JiaZiWu

六合 (Liù Hé) 天辅 (Tiān Fǔ) 杜门 (Dù Mén) Xun 4 Xin Xin	白虎 (Bái Hǔ) 天英 (Tiān Yīng) 景门 (Jǐng Mén) Li 9 Yi Yi	玄武 (Xuán Wǔ) 禽芮 (Qín Ruì) 死门 (SǏ Mén) Kun 2 Ji/Ren Ji/Ren
太阴 (Tài Yīn) 天冲 (Tiān Chōng) 伤门 (Shāng Mén) Zhen 3 Geng Geng	Yang (阳) Dun# 1 Hour: **JiaZi** ©Calvin Yap	九地 (Jiǔ Dì) 天柱 (Tiān Zhù) 惊门 (Jǐng Mén) Dui 7 Ding Ding
螣蛇 (Téng Shé) 天任 (Tiān Rèn) 生门 (Shēng Mén) Gen 8 Bing Bing	值符 (Zhí Fú) 天蓬 (Tiān Péng) 休门 (Xiū Mén) Kan 1 Wu Wu	九天 (Jiǔ Tiān) 天心 (Tiān Xīn) 开门 (Kāi Mén) Qian 6 Gui Gui

Yang (阳) Dun# 1 Hour: **YiChou** ; 直符(ZhíFú): 天蓬(TiānPéng)
直使(ZhíShǐ): 休门(XiūMén) ; 旬首(XúnShǒu): JiaZiWu

九天 (Jiǔ Tiān) 天心 (Tiān Xīn) 惊门 (Jǐng Mén) Xun 4 Gui Xin	值符 (Zhí Fú) 天蓬 (Tiān Péng) 开门 (Kāi Mén) Li 9 Wu Yi	螣蛇 (Téng Shé) 天任 (Tiān Rèn) 休门 (Xiū Mén) Kun 2 Bing Ji/Ren
九地 (Jiǔ Dì) 天柱 (Tiān Zhù) 死门 (SǏ Mén) Zhen 3 Ding Geng	Yang (阳) Dun# 1 Hour: **YiChou** ©Calvin Yap	太阴 (Tài Yīn) 天冲 (Tiān Chōng) 生门 (Shēng Mén) Dui 7 Geng Ding
玄武 (Xuán Wǔ) 禽芮 (Qín Ruì) 景门 (Jǐng Mén) Gen 8 Ji/Ren Bing	白虎 (Bái Hǔ) 天英 (Tiān Yīng) 杜门 (Dù Mén) Kan 1 Yi Wu	六合 (Liù Hé) 天辅 (Tiān Fǔ) 伤门 (Shāng Mén) Qian 6 Xin Gui

Kōng

Horse

Steps in finding a Qi Men Dun Jia chart

1. Obtain the Gregorian date and time. Note that the start of a day is on 23:00 the day before. If you are looking for a chart between 23:00 – 24:00, use the next day Zi hour. See the ***Hour Reference*** for more information.

2. Go to the ***Hour Reference*** to obtain the Earthly Branches of the time.

3. Go to the ***Calendar*** section to locate the **day**, **JiaZi** and **Hour**. Using the information from **Hour** and ***Xun Shou*** chart, look for the particular time Heavenly Stems and Xun.

4. For example, 22/Dec/2010 3-5 am (Yin hour), 22/Dec/2010 is the date where Winter Solstice starts at 7:38am. Therefore, 3-5am is still in Yin Dun. (see ***24 Sub Season*** under ***Basic Information***). From the ***Calendar*** section, the **Dun** column is "**Yin 1**" and the **Hour** column is "**Wu Zi**". The JiaZi for this date is "**Bing Wu**". The month is "**Wu Zi**" and the Year is "**Geng Yin**". To look for the Heavenly Stem for that particular day Yin hour, go to the ***Xun Shou*** chart and look for "**Wu Zi**" (information from **Hour** column) and walk down the ***Xun Shou*** chart till you reach Yin hour. (Wu Zi -> Ji Chou -> Geng Yin). So, 22/Dec/2010 3-5 am is **Geng Yin** hour. From the same chart, **Geng Yin** hour is under **Jia Shen Xun**.

5. Go to the ***1080 Charts*** section to locate the chart based on the **Dun** and **Xun** group.

6. From the example, 22/Dec/2010 3-5 am is **Geng Yin** Hour, **Yin 1** Dun and **Jia Shen** Xun. So, the chart is under "**-1JiaShen**". (minus = Yin, plus = Yang, JiaShen = Xun). Look under **Yin Dun,** where the **Chart:** indicates "**-1JiaShen**". Within this group, look for Yin hour and in this case it will be **Geng Yin** Hour.

Another example:

- To look for 13/Jan/2011 12pm (Wu hour) chart:
  - 13/Jan/2011 is **Wu Chen** Day.
  - Since it has not pass 立春 (Beginning of Spring - lì chūn), it is in **Ji Chou** Month and **Geng Yin** Year.
  - The Dun is **Yang 2** Dun.
  - The calendar **Hour** is "**RenZi**". Look for "Ren Zi" in **Xun Shou** table under **Basic Information**, and start counting until you reach Wu Hour. (Ren Zi -> Gui Chou -> Jia Yin -> Yi Mao -> Bing Chen -> Ding Si -> Wu Wu) The Heavenly Stems is Wu, and the time is **Wu Wu**. **Wu Wu** is under **Jia Yin** Xun from the **Xun Shou** table. So, the bazi for **13/Jan/2011 12pm** is:

Hour	Day	Month	Year
Wu	Wu	Ji	Geng
Wu	Chen	Chou	Yin

  - The Qi Men Dun Jia chart is **Yang 2** Dun, **Jia Yin** Xun which is "**+2JiaYin**", **Wu Wu** hour.

Yang (阳) Dun# 2 Hour: **WuWu** ; 直符(ZhíFú): 天柱(TiānZhù)

直使(ZhíShǐ): 惊门(JǐngMén) ; 旬首(XúnShǒu): JiaYinGui

<table>
<tr><td>九地 (Jiǔ Dì)
天英 (Tiān Yīng)
景门 (Jǐng Mén)
Xun 4   Bing
Geng</td><td>九天 (Jiǔ Tiān)
禽芮 (Qín Ruì)
死门 (Sǐ Mén)
Li 9   Wu/Xin
Bing</td><td>值符 (Zhí Fú)
天柱 (Tiān Zhù)
惊门 (Jǐng Mén)
Kun 2   Gui
Wu/Xin</td></tr>
<tr><td>玄武 (Xuán Wǔ)
天辅 (Tiān Fǔ)
杜门 (Dù Mén)
Zhen 3   Geng
Ji</td><td>Yang (阳) Dun# 2
Hour: **WuWu**

©Calvin Yap</td><td>螣蛇 (Téng Shé)
天心 (Tiān Xīn)
开门 (Kāi Mén)
Dui 7   Ren
Gui</td></tr>
<tr><td>白虎 (Bái Hǔ)
天冲 (Tiān Chōng)
伤门 (Shāng Mén)
Gen 8   Ji
Ding</td><td>六合 (Liù Hé)
天任 (Tiān Rèn)
生门 (Shēng Mén)
Kan 1   Ding
Yi</td><td>太阴 (Tài Yīn)
天蓬 (Tiān Péng)
休门 (Xiū Mén)
Qian 6   Yi
Ren</td></tr>
</table>

Basic information

24 Sub Season

Month	二十四节气 (24 sub season - èr shí sì jié qì)	Start Date	Dun
First month (Yin)	立春 (Beginning of Spring - lì chūn), 雨水 (Rain Water - yǔ shuǐ)	Feb 4, 5 Feb 18, 19	Yang
2nd Month (Mao)	惊蛰 (Insect Awakening - jīng zhé), 春分 (Spring Equinox - chūn fēn)	Mar 5, 6 Mar 20, 21	Yang
3rd Month (Chen)	清明 (Pure Brightness - qīng míng), 谷雨 (Grain Rain - gǔ yǔ)	Apr 4, 5 Apr 20, 21	Yang
4th Month (Si)	立夏 (Beginning of Summer - lì xià), 小满 (Small Grain - xiǎo mǎn)	May 5, 6 May 21, 22	Yang
5th Month (Wu)	芒种 (Summer Harvest - máng zhòng), 夏至 (Summer Solstice - xià zhì)	Jun 5, 6 Jun 21, 22	Yang Yin
6th Month (Wei)	小署 (Mild Summer - xiǎo shǔ), 大署 (Extreme Summer - dà shǔ)	July 7, 8 July 22, 23	Yin
7th Month (Shen)	立秋 (Beginning of Autumn - lì qiū), 外署 (Outer Heat - wài shǔ)	Aug 7, 8 Aug 23, 24	Yin
8th Month (You)	白露 (White Dew - bái lù), 秋分 (Autumn Equinox - qiū fēn)	Sep 7, 8 Sep 23, 24	Yin
9th Month (Xu)	寒露 (Cold Dew - hán lù), 霜降 (Frost - shuāng jiàng)	Oct 8, 9 Oct 23, 24	Yin
10th Month (Hai)	立冬 (Beginning of Winter - lì dōng), 小雪 (Mild Snow - xiǎo xuě)	Nov 7, 8 Nov 22, 23	Yin
11th Month (Zi)	大雪 (Extreme Snow - dà xuě), 冬至 (Winter Solstice - dōng zhì)	Dec 7, 8 Dec 21, 22	Yin Yang
12th Month (Chou)	小 寒 (Mild Cold - xiǎo hán), 大寒 (Extreme Cold - dà hán)	Jan 5, 6 Jan 20, 21	Yang

Note: Yin Dun starts around Jun 21 or 22 till Dec 20 or 21. Yang Dun starts around Dec 21 or 22 till Jun 20 or 21.

Hour reference

Earthly Branches	Time
子(Zi)	23:00 – 00:59
丑(Chou)	01:00 – 02:59
寅(Yin)	03:00 – 04:59
卯(Mao)	05:00 – 06:59
辰(Chen)	07:00 – 08:59
巳(Si)	09:00 – 10:59
午(Wu)	11:00 – 12:59
未(Wei)	13:00 – 14:59
申(Shen)	15:00 – 16:59
酉(You)	17:00 – 18:59
戌(Xu)	19:00 – 20:59
亥(Hai)	21:00 – 22:59

Xun Shou

Xun	Jia Zi Xun	Jia Xu Xun	Jia Shen Xun	Jia Wu Xun	Jia Chen Xun	Jia Yin Xun
60 Jia Zi	甲(Jia) 子(Zi)	甲(Jia) 戌(Xu)	甲(Jia) 申(Shen)	甲(Jia) 午(Wu)	甲(Jia) 辰(Chen)	甲(Jia) 寅(Yin)
	乙(Yi) 丑(Chou)	乙(Yi) 亥(Hai)	乙(Yi) 酉(You)	乙(Yi) 未(Wei)	乙(Yi) 巳(Si)	乙(Yi) 卯(Mao)
	丙(Bing) 寅(Yin)	丙(Bing) 子(Zi)	丙(Bing) 戌(Xu)	丙(Bing) 申(Shen)	丙(Bing) 午(Wu)	丙(Bing) 辰(Chen)
	丁(Ding) 卯(Mao)	丁(Ding) 丑(Chou)	丁(Ding) 亥(Hai)	丁(Ding) 酉(You)	丁(Ding) 未(Wei)	丁(Ding) 巳(Si)
	戊(Wu) 辰(Chen)	戊(Wu) 寅(Yin)	戊(Wu) 子(Zi)	戊(Wu) 戌(Xu)	戊(Wu) 申(Shen)	戊(Wu) 午(Wu)
	己(Ji) 巳(Si)	己(Ji) 卯(Mao)	己(Ji) 丑(Chou)	己(Ji) 亥(Hai)	己(Ji) 酉(You)	己(Ji) 未(Wei)
	庚(Geng) 午(Wu)	庚(Geng) 辰(Chen)	庚(Geng) 寅(Yin)	庚(Geng) 子(Zi)	庚(Geng) 戌(Xu)	庚(Geng) 申(Shen)
	辛(Xin) 未(Wei)	辛(Xin) 巳(Si)	辛(Xin) 卯(Mao)	辛(Xin) 丑(Chou)	辛(Xin) 亥(Hai)	辛(Xin) 酉(You)
	壬(Ren)	壬(Ren)	壬(Ren)	壬(Ren)	壬(Ren)	壬(Ren)

	申(Shen)	午(Wu)	辰(Chen)	寅(Yin)	子(Zi)	戌(Xu)
	癸(Gui) 酉(You)	癸(Gui) 未(Wei)	癸(Gui) 巳(Si)	癸(Gui) 卯(Mao)	癸(Gui) 丑(Chou)	癸(Gui) 亥(Hai)
旬首 (Xún Shǒu)	戊(Wu)	己(Ji)	庚(Geng)	辛(Xin)	壬(Ren)	癸(Gui)

In Hour Qi Men method, the key is which Xun group a particular time is. Each Xun is grouped from Jia to Gui. For example, Jia Zi Xun is from Jia Zi hour to Gui You hour. In a day, there are 12 Hours and therefore, in a day there will be in 2 Xun groups.

2018:WuXu, 2019:JiHai

	2018:WuXu, 2019:JiHai Dec18/Jan19:JiaZi, Jan/Feb:YiChou					2019:JiHai Feb/Mar:BingYin, Mar/Apr:DingMao			
	Day	Jia Zi	Dun	Hour		Day	Jia Zi	Dun	Hour
冬至 (dōng zhì) -Winter Solstice 22/12 6:22 AM	22/12	WuZi	Yin 7/Yang 7	RenZi	雨水 (yǔ shuǐ) -Rain Water 19/02 7:03 AM	19/02	DingHai	Yang 5/6	GengZi
	23/12	JiChou	Yang 4	JiaZi		20/02	WuZi	Yang 6	RenZi
	24/12	GengYin	Yang 4	BingZi		21/02	JiChou	Yang 3	JiaZi
	25/12	XinMao	Yang 4	WuZi		22/02	GengYin	Yang 3	BingZi
	26/12	RenChen	Yang 4	GengZi		23/02	XinMao	Yang 3	WuZi
	27/12	GuiSi	Yang 4	RenZi		24/02	RenChen	Yang 3	GengZi
	28/12	JiaWu	Yang 1	JiaZi		25/02	GuiSi	Yang 3	RenZi
	29/12	YiWei	Yang 1	BingZi		26/02	JiaWu	Yang 9	JiaZi
	30/12	BingShen	Yang 1	WuZi		27/02	YiWei	Yang 9	BingZi
	31/12	DingYou	Yang 1	GengZi		28/02	BingShen	Yang 9	WuZi
	01/01	WuXu	Yang 1	RenZi		01/03	DingYou	Yang 9	GengZi
	02/01	JiHai	Yang 7	JiaZi		02/03	WuXu	Yang 9	RenZi
	03/01	GengZi	Yang 7	BingZi		03/03	JiHai	Yang 6	JiaZi
	04/01	XinChou	Yang 7	WuZi		04/03	GengZi	Yang 6	BingZi
小寒 (xiǎo hán) -Mild Cold 05/01 11:38 PM	05/01	RenYin	Yang 7/8	GengZi		05/03	XinChou	Yang 6	WuZi
	06/01	GuiMao	Yang 8	RenZi	惊蛰 (jīng zhé) -Insect Awakening 06/03 5:09 AM	06/03	RenYin	Yang 6/7	GengZi
	07/01	JiaChen	Yang 5	JiaZi		07/03	GuiMao	Yang 7	RenZi
	08/01	YiSi	Yang 5	BingZi		08/03	JiaChen	Yang 4	JiaZi
	09/01	BingWu	Yang 5	WuZi		09/03	YiSi	Yang 4	BingZi
	10/01	DingWei	Yang 5	GengZi		10/03	BingWu	Yang 4	WuZi
	11/01	WuShen	Yang 5	RenZi		11/03	DingWei	Yang 4	GengZi
	12/01	JiYou	Yang 2	JiaZi		12/03	WuShen	Yang 4	RenZi
	13/01	GengXu	Yang 2	BingZi		13/03	JiYou	Yang 1	JiaZi
	14/01	XinHai	Yang 2	WuZi		14/03	GengXu	Yang 1	BingZi
	15/01	RenZi	Yang 2	GengZi		15/03	XinHai	Yang 1	WuZi
	16/01	GuiChou	Yang 2	RenZi		16/03	RenZi	Yang 1	GengZi
	17/01	JiaYin	Yang 8	JiaZi		17/03	GuiChou	Yang 1	RenZi
	18/01	YiMao	Yang 8	BingZi		18/03	JiaYin	Yang 7	JiaZi
	19/01	BingChen	Yang 8	WuZi		19/03	YiMao	Yang 7	BingZi
大寒 (dà hán) -Extreme Cold 20/01 4:59 PM	20/01	DingSi	Yang 8/9	GengZi		20/03	BingChen	Yang 7	WuZi
	21/01	WuWu	Yang 9	RenZi	春分 (chūn fēn) -Spring Equinox 21/03 5:58 AM	21/03	DingSi	Yang 7/9	GengZi
	22/01	JiWei	Yang 6	JiaZi		22/03	WuWu	Yang 9	RenZi
	23/01	GengShen	Yang 6	BingZi		23/03	JiWei	Yang 6	JiaZi
	24/01	XinYou	Yang 6	WuZi		24/03	GengShe	Yang 6	BingZi
	25/01	RenXu	Yang 6	GengZi		25/03	XinYou	Yang 6	WuZi
	26/01	GuiHai	Yang 6	RenZi		26/03	RenXu	Yang 6	GengZi
	27/01	JiaZi	Yang 3	JiaZi		27/03	GuiHai	Yang 6	RenZi
	28/01	YiChou	Yang 3	BingZi		28/03	JiaZi	Yang 3	JiaZi
	29/01	BingYin	Yang 3	WuZi		29/03	YiChou	Yang 3	BingZi
	30/01	DingMao	Yang 3	GengZi		30/03	BingYin	Yang 3	WuZi
	31/01	WuChen	Yang 3	RenZi		31/03	DingMao	Yang 3	GengZi
	01/02	JiSi	Yang 9	JiaZi		01/04	WuChen	Yang 3	RenZi
	02/02	GengWu	Yang 9	BingZi		02/04	JiSi	Yang 9	JiaZi
	03/02	XinWei	Yang 9	WuZi		03/04	GengWu	Yang 9	BingZi
立春 (lì chūn) -Beginning of Spring 04/02 11:14 AM	04/02	RenShen	Yang 9/5	GengZi		04/04	XinWei	Yang 9	WuZi
	05/02	GuiYou	Yang 5	RenZi	清明 (qīng míng) -Pure Brightness 05/04 9:51 AM	05/04	RenShen	Yang 9/1	GengZi
	06/02	JiaXu	Yang 2	JiaZi		06/04	GuiYou	Yang 1	RenZi
	07/02	YiHai	Yang 2	BingZi		07/04	JiaXu	Yang 7	JiaZi
	08/02	BingZi	Yang 2	WuZi		08/04	YiHai	Yang 7	BingZi
	09/02	DingChou	Yang 2	GengZi		09/04	BingZi	Yang 7	WuZi
	10/02	WuYin	Yang 2	RenZi		10/04	DingCho	Yang 7	GengZi
	11/02	JiMao	Yang 8	JiaZi		11/04	WuYin	Yang 7	RenZi
	12/02	GengChen	Yang 8	BingZi		12/04	JiMao	Yang 4	JiaZi
	13/02	XinSi	Yang 8	WuZi		13/04	GengChe	Yang 4	BingZi
	14/02	RenWu	Yang 8	GengZi		14/04	XinSi	Yang 4	WuZi
	15/02	GuiWei	Yang 8	RenZi		15/04	RenWu	Yang 4	GengZi
	16/02	JiaShen	Yang 5	JiaZi		16/04	GuiWei	Yang 4	RenZi
	17/02	YiYou	Yang 5	BingZi		17/04	JiaShen	Yang 1	JiaZi
	18/02	BingXu	Yang 5	WuZi		18/04	YiYou	Yang 1	BingZi
						19/04	BingXu	Yang 1	WuZi

2019:JiHai — Apr/May:WuChen, May/Jun:JiSi

Solar Term	Day	Jia Zi	Dun	Hour
谷雨 (gǔ yǔ) -Grain Rain 20/04 4:55 PM	20/04	DingHai	Yang 1/2	GengZi
	21/04	WuZi	Yang 2	RenZi
	22/04	JiChou	Yang 8	JiaZi
	23/04	GengYin	Yang 8	BingZi
	24/04	XinMao	Yang 8	WuZi
	25/04	RenChen	Yang 8	GengZi
	26/04	GuiSi	Yang 8	RenZi
	27/04	JiaWu	Yang 5	JiaZi
	28/04	YiWei	Yang 5	BingZi
	29/04	BingShen	Yang 5	WuZi
	30/04	DingYou	Yang 5	GengZi
	01/05	WuXu	Yang 5	RenZi
	02/05	JiHai	Yang 2	JiaZi
	03/05	GengZi	Yang 2	BingZi
	04/05	XinChou	Yang 2	WuZi
	05/05	RenYin	Yang 2	GengZi
立夏 (lì xià) -Beginning of Summer 06/05 3:02 AM	06/05	GuiMao	Yang 2/1	RenZi
	07/05	JiaChen	Yang 7	JiaZi
	08/05	YiSi	Yang 7	BingZi
	09/05	BingWu	Yang 7	WuZi
	10/05	DingWei	Yang 7	GengZi
	11/05	WuShen	Yang 7	RenZi
	12/05	JiYou	Yang 4	JiaZi
	13/05	GengXu	Yang 4	BingZi
	14/05	XinHai	Yang 4	WuZi
	15/05	RenZi	Yang 4	GengZi
	16/05	GuiChou	Yang 4	RenZi
	17/05	JiaYin	Yang 1	JiaZi
	18/05	YiMao	Yang 1	BingZi
	19/05	BingChen	Yang 1	WuZi
	20/05	DingSi	Yang 1	GengZi
小满 (xiǎo mǎn) -Small Grain 21/05 3:59 PM	21/05	WuWu	Yang 1/2	RenZi
	22/05	JiWei	Yang 8	JiaZi
	23/05	GengShe	Yang 8	BingZi
	24/05	XinYou	Yang 8	WuZi
	25/05	RenXu	Yang 8	GengZi
	26/05	GuiHai	Yang 8	RenZi
	27/05	JiaZi	Yang 5	JiaZi
	28/05	YiChou	Yang 5	BingZi
	29/05	BingYin	Yang 5	WuZi
	30/05	DingMao	Yang 5	GengZi
	31/05	WuChen	Yang 5	RenZi
	01/06	JiSi	Yang 2	JiaZi
	02/06	GengWu	Yang 2	BingZi
	03/06	XinWei	Yang 2	WuZi
	04/06	RenShen	Yang 2	GengZi
	05/06	GuiYou	Yang 2	RenZi
芒种 (máng zhòng) -Summer Harvest 06/06 7:06 AM	06/06	JiaXu	Yang 8/9	JiaZi
	07/06	YiHai	Yang 9	BingZi
	08/06	BingZi	Yang 9	WuZi
	09/06	DingCho	Yang 9	GengZi
	10/06	WuYin	Yang 9	RenZi
	11/06	JiMao	Yang 6	JiaZi
	12/06	GengChe	Yang 6	BingZi
	13/06	XinSi	Yang 6	WuZi
	14/06	RenWu	Yang 6	GengZi
	15/06	GuiWei	Yang 6	RenZi
	16/06	JiaShen	Yang 3	JiaZi
	17/06	YiYou	Yang 3	BingZi
	18/06	BingXu	Yang 3	WuZi
	19/06	DingHai	Yang 3	GengZi
	20/06	WuZi	Yang 3	RenZi

2019:JiHai — Jun/July:GengWu, Jul/Aug:XinWei

Solar Term	Day	Jia Zi	Dun	Hour
夏至 (xià zhì) -Summer Solstice 21/06 11:54 PM	21/06	JiChou	Yang 9/Yin 6	JiaZi
	22/06	GengYin	Yin 6	BingZi
	23/06	XinMao	Yin 6	WuZi
	24/06	RenChen	Yin 6	GengZi
	25/06	GuiSi	Yin 6	RenZi
	26/06	JiaWu	Yin 9	JiaZi
	27/06	YiWei	Yin 9	BingZi
	28/06	BingShen	Yin 9	WuZi
	29/06	DingYou	Yin 9	GengZi
	30/06	WuXu	Yin 9	RenZi
	01/07	JiHai	Yin 3	JiaZi
	02/07	GengZi	Yin 3	BingZi
	03/07	XinChou	Yin 3	WuZi
	04/07	RenYin	Yin 3	GengZi
	05/07	GuiMao	Yin 3	RenZi
	06/07	JiaChen	Yin 6	JiaZi
小暑 (xiǎo shǔ) -Mild Summer 07/07 5:20 PM	07/07	YiSi	Yin 6/5	BingZi
	08/07	BingWu	Yin 5	WuZi
	09/07	DingWei	Yin 5	GengZi
	10/07	WuShen	Yin 5	RenZi
	11/07	JiYou	Yin 8	JiaZi
	12/07	GengXu	Yin 8	BingZi
	13/07	XinHai	Yin 8	WuZi
	14/07	RenZi	Yin 8	GengZi
	15/07	GuiChou	Yin 8	RenZi
	16/07	JiaYin	Yin 2	JiaZi
	17/07	YiMao	Yin 2	BingZi
	18/07	BingChen	Yin 2	WuZi
	19/07	DingSi	Yin 2	GengZi
	20/07	WuWu	Yin 2	RenZi
	21/07	JiWei	Yin 5	JiaZi
	22/07	GengShen	Yin 5	BingZi
大暑 (dà shǔ) -Extreme Summer 23/07 10:50 AM	23/07	XinYou	Yin 5/4	WuZi
	24/07	RenXu	Yin 4	GengZi
	25/07	GuiHai	Yin 4	RenZi
	26/07	JiaZi	Yin 7	JiaZi
	27/07	YiChou	Yin 7	BingZi
	28/07	BingYin	Yin 7	WuZi
	29/07	DingMao	Yin 7	GengZi
	30/07	WuChen	Yin 7	RenZi
	31/07	JiSi	Yin 1	JiaZi
	01/08	GengWu	Yin 1	BingZi
	02/08	XinWei	Yin 1	WuZi
	03/08	RenShen	Yin 1	GengZi
	04/08	GuiYou	Yin 1	RenZi
	05/08	JiaXu	Yin 4	JiaZi
	06/08	YiHai	Yin 4	BingZi
	07/08	BingZi	Yin 4	WuZi
立秋 (lì qiū) -Beginning of Autumn 08/08 3:12 AM	08/08	DingChou	Yin 4/8	GengZi
	09/08	WuYin	Yin 8	RenZi
	10/08	JiMao	Yin 2	JiaZi
	11/08	GengChen	Yin 2	BingZi
	12/08	XinSi	Yin 2	WuZi
	13/08	RenWu	Yin 2	GengZi
	14/08	GuiWei	Yin 2	RenZi
	15/08	JiaShen	Yin 5	JiaZi
	16/08	YiYou	Yin 5	BingZi
	17/08	BingXu	Yin 5	WuZi
	18/08	DingHai	Yin 5	GengZi
	19/08	WuZi	Yin 5	RenZi
	20/08	JiChou	Yin 8	JiaZi
	21/08	GengYin	Yin 8	BingZi
	22/08	XinMao	Yin 8	WuZi

2019:JiHai — Aug/Sep:RenShen, Sep/Oct:GuiYou

Solar Term	Day	Jia Zi	Dun	Hour
处暑 (chǔ shǔ) -Outer Heat 23/08 6:01 PM	23/08	RenChen	Yin 8/7	GengZi
	24/08	GuiSi	Yin 7	RenZi
	25/08	JiaWu	Yin 1	JiaZi
	26/08	YiWei	Yin 1	BingZi
	27/08	BingShen	Yin 1	WuZi
	28/08	DingYou	Yin 1	GengZi
	29/08	WuXu	Yin 1	RenZi
	30/08	JiHai	Yin 4	JiaZi
	31/08	GengZi	Yin 4	BingZi
	01/09	XinChou	Yin 4	WuZi
	02/09	RenYin	Yin 4	GengZi
	03/09	GuiMao	Yin 4	RenZi
	04/09	JiaChen	Yin 7	JiaZi
	05/09	YiSi	Yin 7	BingZi
	06/09	BingWu	Yin 7	WuZi
	07/09	DingWei	Yin 7	GengZi
白露 (bái lù) -White Dew 08/09 6:16 AM	08/09	WuShen	Yin 7/6	RenZi
	09/09	JiYou	Yin 9	JiaZi
	10/09	GengXu	Yin 9	BingZi
	11/09	XinHai	Yin 9	WuZi
	12/09	RenZi	Yin 9	GengZi
	13/09	GuiChou	Yin 9	RenZi
	14/09	JiaYin	Yin 3	JiaZi
	15/09	YiMao	Yin 3	BingZi
	16/09	BingChen	Yin 3	WuZi
	17/09	DingSi	Yin 3	GengZi
	18/09	WuWu	Yin 3	RenZi
	19/09	JiWei	Yin 6	JiaZi
	20/09	GengShen	Yin 6	BingZi
	21/09	XinYou	Yin 6	WuZi
	22/09	RenXu	Yin 6	GengZi
秋分 (qiū fēn) -Autumn Equinox 23/09 3:50 PM	23/09	GuiHai	Yin 6/4	RenZi
	24/09	JiaZi	Yin 7	JiaZi
	25/09	YiChou	Yin 7	BingZi
	26/09	BingYin	Yin 7	WuZi
	27/09	DingMao	Yin 7	GengZi
	28/09	WuChen	Yin 7	RenZi
	29/09	JiSi	Yin 1	JiaZi
	30/09	GengWu	Yin 1	BingZi
	01/10	XinWei	Yin 1	WuZi
	02/10	RenShen	Yin 1	GengZi
	03/10	GuiYou	Yin 1	RenZi
	04/10	JiaXu	Yin 4	JiaZi
	05/10	YiHai	Yin 4	BingZi
	06/10	BingZi	Yin 4	WuZi
	07/10	DingChou	Yin 4	GengZi
寒露 (hán lù) -Cold Dew 08/10 10:05 PM	08/10	WuYin	Yin 4/6	RenZi
	09/10	JiMao	Yin 6	JiaZi
	10/10	GengChen	Yin 6	BingZi
	11/10	XinSi	Yin 6	WuZi
	12/10	RenWu	Yin 6	GengZi
	13/10	GuiWei	Yin 6	RenZi
	14/10	JiaShen	Yin 9	JiaZi
	15/10	YiYou	Yin 9	BingZi
	16/10	BingXu	Yin 9	WuZi
	17/10	DingHai	Yin 9	GengZi
	18/10	WuZi	Yin 9	RenZi
	19/10	JiChou	Yin 3	JiaZi
	20/10	GengYin	Yin 3	BingZi
	21/10	XinMao	Yin 3	WuZi
	22/10	RenChen	Yin 3	GengZi
	23/10	GuiSi	Yin 3	RenZi

2019:JiHai — Oct/Nov:JiaXu, Nov/Dec:YiHai

Solar Term	Day	Jia Zi	Dun	Hour
霜降 (shuāng jiàng) -Frost 24/10 1:19 AM	24/10	JiaWu	Yin	JiaZi
	25/10	YiWei	Yin 5	BingZi
	26/10	BingShen	Yin 5	WuZi
	27/10	DingYou	Yin 5	GengZi
	28/10	WuXu	Yin 5	RenZi
	29/10	JiHai	Yin 8	JiaZi
	30/10	GengZi	Yin 8	BingZi
	31/10	XinChou	Yin 8	WuZi
	01/11	RenYin	Yin 8	GengZi
	02/11	GuiMao	Yin 8	RenZi
	03/11	JiaChen	Yin 2	JiaZi
	04/11	YiSi	Yin 2	BingZi
	05/11	BingWu	Yin 2	WuZi
	06/11	DingWei	Yin 2	GengZi
	07/11	WuShen	Yin 2	RenZi
立冬 (lì dōng) -Beginning of Winter 08/11 1:24 AM	08/11	JiYou	Yin	JiaZi
	09/11	GengXu	Yin 6	BingZi
	10/11	XinHai	Yin 6	WuZi
	11/11	RenZi	Yin 6	GengZi
	12/11	GuiChou	Yin 6	RenZi
	13/11	JiaYin	Yin 9	JiaZi
	14/11	YiMao	Yin 9	BingZi
	15/11	BingChen	Yin 9	WuZi
	16/11	DingSi	Yin 9	GengZi
	17/11	WuWu	Yin 9	RenZi
	18/11	JiWei	Yin 3	JiaZi
	19/11	GengShen	Yin 3	BingZi
	20/11	XinYou	Yin 3	WuZi
	21/11	RenXu	Yin 3	GengZi
小雪 (xiǎo xuě) -Mild Snow 22/11 10:58 PM	22/11	GuiHai	Yin	RenZi
	23/11	JiaZi	Yin 5	JiaZi
	24/11	YiChou	Yin 5	BingZi
	25/11	BingYin	Yin 5	WuZi
	26/11	DingMao	Yin 5	GengZi
	27/11	WuChen	Yin 5	RenZi
	28/11	JiSi	Yin 8	JiaZi
	29/11	GengWu	Yin 8	BingZi
	30/11	XinWei	Yin 8	WuZi
	01/12	RenShen	Yin 8	GengZi
	02/12	GuiYou	Yin 8	RenZi
	03/12	JiaXu	Yin 2	JiaZi
	04/12	YiHai	Yin 2	BingZi
	05/12	BingZi	Yin 2	WuZi
	06/12	DingChou	Yin 2	GengZi
大雪 (dà xuě) -Extreme Snow 07/12 6:18 PM	07/12	WuYin	Yin	RenZi
	08/12	JiMao	Yin 4	JiaZi
	09/12	GengChen	Yin 4	BingZi
	10/12	XinSi	Yin 4	WuZi
	11/12	RenWu	Yin 4	GengZi
	12/12	GuiWei	Yin 4	RenZi
	13/12	JiaShen	Yin 7	JiaZi
	14/12	YiYou	Yin 7	BingZi
	15/12	BingXu	Yin 7	WuZi
	16/12	DingHai	Yin 7	GengZi
	17/12	WuZi	Yin 7	RenZi
	18/12	JiChou	Yin 1	JiaZi
	19/12	GengYin	Yin 1	BingZi
	20/12	XinMao	Yin 1	WuZi
	21/12	RenChen	Yin 1	GengZi

2019:JiHai, 2020:GengZi

2019:JiHai, 2020:GengZi
Dec11/Jan12:BingZi, Jan/Feb:DingChou

Solar Term	Day	Jia Zi	Dun	Hour
冬至 (dōng zhì) -Winter Solstice 22/12 12:19 PM	22/12	GuiSi	Yin 1/Yang 4	RenZi
	23/12	JiaWu	Yang 1	JiaZi
	24/12	YiWei	Yang 1	BingZi
	25/12	BingShen	Yang 1	WuZi
	26/12	DingYou	Yang 1	GengZi
	27/12	WuXu	Yang 1	RenZi
	28/12	JiHai	Yang 7	JiaZi
	29/12	GengZi	Yang 7	BingZi
	30/12	XinChou	Yang 7	WuZi
	31/12	RenYin	Yang 7	GengZi
	01/01	GuiMao	Yang 7	RenZi
	02/01	JiaChen	Yang 4	JiaZi
	03/01	YiSi	Yang 4	BingZi
	04/01	BingWu	Yang 4	WuZi
	05/01	DingWei	Yang 4	GengZi
小寒 (xiǎo hán) -Mild Cold 06/01 5:29 AM	06/01	WuShen	Yang 4/5	RenZi
	07/01	JiYou	Yang 2	JiaZi
	08/01	GengXu	Yang 2	BingZi
	09/01	XinHai	Yang 2	WuZi
	10/01	RenZi	Yang 2	GengZi
	11/01	GuiChou	Yang 2	RenZi
	12/01	JiaYin	Yang 8	JiaZi
	13/01	YiMao	Yang 8	BingZi
	14/01	BingChen	Yang 8	WuZi
	15/01	DingSi	Yang 8	GengZi
	16/01	WuWu	Yang 8	RenZi
	17/01	JiWei	Yang 5	JiaZi
	18/01	GengShen	Yang 5	BingZi
	19/01	XinYou	Yang 5	WuZi
大寒 (dà hán) -Extreme Cold 20/01 10:54 PM	20/01	RenXu	Yang 5/6	GengZi
	21/01	GuiHai	Yang 6	RenZi
	22/01	JiaZi	Yang 3	JiaZi
	23/01	YiChou	Yang 3	BingZi
	24/01	BingYin	Yang 3	WuZi
	25/01	DingMao	Yang 3	GengZi
	26/01	WuChen	Yang 3	RenZi
	27/01	JiSi	Yang 9	JiaZi
	28/01	GengWu	Yang 9	BingZi
	29/01	XinWei	Yang 9	WuZi
	30/01	RenShen	Yang 9	GengZi
	31/01	GuiYou	Yang 9	RenZi
	01/02	JiaXu	Yang 6	JiaZi
	02/02	YiHai	Yang 6	BingZi
	03/02	BingZi	Yang 6	WuZi
立春 (lì chūn) -Beginning of Spring 04/02 5:03 PM	04/02	DingChou	Yang 6/2	GengZi
	05/02	WuYin	Yang 2	RenZi
	06/02	JiMao	Yang 8	JiaZi
	07/02	GengChen	Yang 8	BingZi
	08/02	XinSi	Yang 8	WuZi
	09/02	RenWu	Yang 8	GengZi
	10/02	GuiWei	Yang 8	RenZi
	11/02	JiaShen	Yang 5	JiaZi
	12/02	YiYou	Yang 5	BingZi
	13/02	BingXu	Yang 5	WuZi
	14/02	DingHai	Yang 5	GengZi
	15/02	WuZi	Yang 5	RenZi
	16/02	JiChou	Yang 2	JiaZi
	17/02	GengYin	Yang 2	BingZi
	18/02	XinMao	Yang 2	WuZi

2020:GengZi
Feb/Mar:WuYin, Mar/Apr:JiMao

Solar Term	Day	Jia Zi	Dun	Hour
雨水 (yǔ shuǐ) -Rain Water 19/02 12:56 PM	19/02	RenChen	Yang 2/3	GengZi
	20/02	GuiSi	Yang 3	RenZi
	21/02	JiaWu	Yang 9	JiaZi
	22/02	YiWei	Yang 9	BingZi
	23/02	BingShen	Yang 9	WuZi
	24/02	DingYou	Yang 9	GengZi
	25/02	WuXu	Yang 9	RenZi
	26/02	JiHai	Yang 6	JiaZi
	27/02	GengZi	Yang 6	BingZi
	28/02	XinChou	Yang 6	WuZi
	29/02	RenYin	Yang 6	GengZi
	01/03	GuiMao	Yang 6	RenZi
	02/03	JiaChen	Yang 3	JiaZi
	03/03	YiSi	Yang 3	BingZi
	04/03	BingWu	Yang 3	WuZi
惊蛰 (jīng zhé) -Insect Awakening 05/03 10:56 AM	05/03	DingWei	Yang 3/4	GengZi
	06/03	WuShen	Yang 4	RenZi
	07/03	JiYou	Yang 1	JiaZi
	08/03	GengXu	Yang 1	BingZi
	09/03	XinHai	Yang 1	WuZi
	10/03	RenZi	Yang 1	GengZi
	11/03	GuiChou	Yang 1	RenZi
	12/03	JiaYin	Yang 7	JiaZi
	13/03	YiMao	Yang 7	BingZi
	14/03	BingChen	Yang 7	WuZi
	15/03	DingSi	Yang 7	GengZi
	16/03	WuWu	Yang 7	RenZi
	17/03	JiWei	Yang 4	JiaZi
	18/03	GengShe	Yang 4	BingZi
	19/03	XinYou	Yang 4	WuZi
春分 (chūn fēn) -Spring Equinox 20/03 11:49 AM	20/03	RenXu	Yang 4/6	GengZi
	21/03	GuiHai	Yang 6	RenZi
	22/03	JiaZi	Yang 3	JiaZi
	23/03	YiChou	Yang 3	BingZi
	24/03	BingYin	Yang 3	WuZi
	25/03	DingMao	Yang 3	GengZi
	26/03	WuChen	Yang 3	RenZi
	27/03	JiSi	Yang 9	JiaZi
	28/03	GengWu	Yang 9	BingZi
	29/03	XinWei	Yang 9	WuZi
	30/03	RenShen	Yang 9	GengZi
	31/03	GuiYou	Yang 9	RenZi
	01/04	JiaXu	Yang 6	JiaZi
	02/04	YiHai	Yang 6	BingZi
	03/04	BingZi	Yang 6	WuZi
清明 (qīng míng) -Pure Brightness 04/04 3:38 PM	04/04	DingCho	Yang 6/7	GengZi
	05/04	WuYin	Yang 7	RenZi
	06/04	JiMao	Yang 4	JiaZi
	07/04	GengChe	Yang 4	BingZi
	08/04	XinSi	Yang 4	WuZi
	09/04	RenWu	Yang 4	GengZi
	10/04	GuiWei	Yang 4	RenZi
	11/04	JiaShen	Yang 1	JiaZi
	12/04	YiYou	Yang 1	BingZi
	13/04	BingXu	Yang 1	WuZi
	14/04	DingHai	Yang 1	GengZi
	15/04	WuZi	Yang 1	RenZi
	16/04	JiChou	Yang 7	JiaZi
	17/04	GengYin	Yang 7	BingZi
	18/04	XinMao	Yang 7	WuZi

2020:GengZi — Apr/May:GengChen, May/Jun:XinSi

Solar Term	Day	Jia Zi	Dun	Hour
谷雨 (gǔ yǔ) -Grain Rain 19/04 10:45 PM	19/04	RenChen	Yang 7/8	GengZ
	20/04	GuiSi	Yang 8	RenZi
	21/04	JiaWu	Yang 5	JiaZi
	22/04	YiWei	Yang 5	BingZi
	23/04	BingShen	Yang 5	WuZi
	24/04	DingYou	Yang 5	GengZ
	25/04	WuXu	Yang 5	RenZi
	26/04	JiHai	Yang 2	JiaZi
	27/04	GengZi	Yang 2	BingZi
	28/04	XinChou	Yang 2	WuZi
	29/04	RenYin	Yang 2	GengZ
	30/04	GuiMao	Yang 2	RenZi
	01/05	JiaChen	Yang 8	JiaZi
	02/05	YiSi	Yang 8	BingZi
	03/05	BingWu	Yang 8	WuZi
	04/05	DingWei	Yang 8	GengZ
立夏 (lì xià) -Beginning of Summer 05/05 8:51 AM	05/05	WuShen	Yang 8/7	RenZi
	06/05	JiYou	Yang 4	JiaZi
	07/05	GengXu	Yang 4	BingZi
	08/05	XinHai	Yang 4	WuZi
	09/05	RenZi	Yang 4	GengZ
	10/05	GuiChou	Yang 4	RenZi
	11/05	JiaYin	Yang 1	JiaZi
	12/05	YiMao	Yang 1	BingZi
	13/05	BingChen	Yang 1	WuZi
	14/05	DingSi	Yang 1	GengZ
	15/05	WuWu	Yang 1	RenZi
	16/05	JiWei	Yang 7	JiaZi
	17/05	GengShen	Yang 7	BingZi
	18/05	XinYou	Yang 7	WuZi
	19/05	RenXu	Yang 7	GengZ
小满 (xiǎo mǎn) -Small Grain 20/05 9:49 PM	20/05	GuiHai	Yang 7/8	RenZi
	21/05	JiaZi	Yang 5	JiaZi
	22/05	YiChou	Yang 5	BingZi
	23/05	BingYin	Yang 5	WuZi
	24/05	DingMao	Yang 5	GengZ
	25/05	WuChen	Yang 5	RenZi
	26/05	JiSi	Yang 2	JiaZi
	27/05	GengWu	Yang 2	BingZi
	28/05	XinWei	Yang 2	WuZi
	29/05	RenShen	Yang 2	GengZ
	30/05	GuiYou	Yang 2	RenZi
	31/05	JiaXu	Yang 8	JiaZi
	01/06	YiHai	Yang 8	BingZi
	02/06	BingZi	Yang 8	WuZi
	03/06	DingChou	Yang 8	GengZ
	04/06	WuYin	Yang 8	RenZi
芒种 (máng zhòng) -Summer Harvest 05/06 12:58 PM	05/06	JiMao	Yang 5/6	JiaZi
	06/06	GengChen	Yang 6	BingZi
	07/06	XinSi	Yang 6	WuZi
	08/06	RenWu	Yang 6	GengZ
	09/06	GuiWei	Yang 6	RenZi
	10/06	JiaShen	Yang 3	JiaZi
	11/06	YiYou	Yang 3	BingZi
	12/06	BingXu	Yang 3	WuZi
	13/06	DingHai	Yang 3	GengZ
	14/06	WuZi	Yang 3	RenZi
	15/06	JiChou	Yang 9	JiaZi
	16/06	GengYin	Yang 9	BingZi
	17/06	XinMao	Yang 9	WuZi
	18/06	RenChen	Yang 9	GengZ
	19/06	GuiSi	Yang 9	RenZi
	20/06	JiaWu	Yang 6	JiaZi

2020:GengZi — Jun/July:RenWu, Jul/Aug:GuiWei

Solar Term	Day	Jia Zi	Dun	Hour
夏至 (xià zhì) -Summer Solstice 21/06 5:43 AM	21/06	YiWei	Yang 6/Yin 9	BingZi
	22/06	BingShen	Yin 9	WuZi
	23/06	DingYou	Yin 9	GengZi
	24/06	WuXu	Yin 9	RenZi
	25/06	JiHai	Yin 3	JiaZi
	26/06	GengZi	Yin 3	BingZi
	27/06	XinChou	Yin 3	WuZi
	28/06	RenYin	Yin 3	GengZi
	29/06	GuiMao	Yin 3	RenZi
	30/06	JiaChen	Yin 6	JiaZi
	01/07	YiSi	Yin 6	BingZi
	02/07	BingWu	Yin 6	WuZi
	03/07	DingWei	Yin 6	GengZi
	04/07	WuShen	Yin 6	RenZi
	05/07	JiYou	Yin 9	JiaZi
小暑 (xiǎo shǔ) -Mild Summer 06/07 11:14 PM	06/07	GengXu	Yin 9/8	BingZi
	07/07	XinHai	Yin 8	WuZi
	08/07	RenZi	Yin 8	GengZi
	09/07	GuiChou	Yin 8	RenZi
	10/07	JiaYin	Yin 2	JiaZi
	11/07	YiMao	Yin 2	BingZi
	12/07	BingChen	Yin 2	WuZi
	13/07	DingSi	Yin 2	GengZi
	14/07	WuWu	Yin 2	RenZi
	15/07	JiWei	Yin 5	JiaZi
	16/07	GengShe	Yin 5	BingZi
	17/07	XinYou	Yin 5	WuZi
	18/07	RenXu	Yin 5	GengZi
	19/07	GuiHai	Yin 5	RenZi
	20/07	JiaZi	Yin 8	JiaZi
	21/07	YiChou	Yin 8	BingZi
大暑 (dà shǔ) -Extreme Summer 22/07 4:36 PM	22/07	BingYin	Yin 8/7	WuZi
	23/07	DingMao	Yin 7	GengZi
	24/07	WuChen	Yin 7	RenZi
	25/07	JiSi	Yin 1	JiaZi
	26/07	GengWu	Yin 1	BingZi
	27/07	XinWei	Yin 1	WuZi
	28/07	RenShen	Yin 1	GengZi
	29/07	GuiYou	Yin 1	RenZi
	30/07	JiaXu	Yin 4	JiaZi
	31/07	YiHai	Yin 4	BingZi
	01/08	BingZi	Yin 4	WuZi
	02/08	DingCho	Yin 4	GengZi
	03/08	WuYin	Yin 4	RenZi
	04/08	JiMao	Yin 7	JiaZi
	05/08	GengChe	Yin 7	BingZi
	06/08	XinSi	Yin 7	WuZi
立秋 (lì qiū) -Beginning of Autumn 07/08 9:06 AM	07/08	RenWu	Yin 7/2	GengZi
	08/08	GuiWei	Yin 2	RenZi
	09/08	JiaShen	Yin 5	JiaZi
	10/08	YiYou	Yin 5	BingZi
	11/08	BingXu	Yin 5	WuZi
	12/08	DingHai	Yin 5	GengZi
	13/08	WuZi	Yin 5	RenZi
	14/08	JiChou	Yin 8	JiaZi
	15/08	GengYin	Yin 8	BingZi
	16/08	XinMao	Yin 8	WuZi
	17/08	RenChen	Yin 8	GengZi
	18/08	GuiSi	Yin 8	RenZi
	19/08	JiaWu	Yin 2	JiaZi
	20/08	YiWei	Yin 2	BingZi
	21/08	BingShen	Yin 2	WuZi

	Day	Jia Zi	Dun	Hour		Day	Jia Zi	Dun	Hour
		2020:GengZi					**2020:GengZi**		
		Aug/Sep:JiaShen, Sep/Oct:YiYou					Oct/Nov:BingXu, Nov/Dec:DingHai		
处暑 (chǔ shǔ) -Outer Heat 22/08 11:44 PM	22/08	DingYou	Yin 2/1	GengZi	霜降 (shuāng jiàng) -Frost 23/10 6:59 AM	23/10	JiHai	Yin 9/8	JiaZi
	23/08	WuXu	Yin 1	RenZi		24/10	GengZi	Yin 8	BingZi
	24/08	JiHai	Yin 4	JiaZi		25/10	XinChou	Yin 8	WuZi
	25/08	GengZi	Yin 4	BingZi		26/10	RenYin	Yin 8	GengZi
	26/08	XinChou	Yin 4	WuZi		27/10	GuiMao	Yin 8	RenZi
	27/08	RenYin	Yin 4	GengZi		28/10	JiaChen	Yin 2	JiaZi
	28/08	GuiMao	Yin 4	RenZi		29/10	YiSi	Yin 2	BingZi
	29/08	JiaChen	Yin 7	JiaZi		30/10	BingWu	Yin 2	WuZi
	30/08	YiSi	Yin 7	BingZi		31/10	DingWei	Yin 2	GengZi
	31/08	BingWu	Yin 7	WuZi		01/11	WuShen	Yin 2	RenZi
	01/09	DingWei	Yin 7	GengZi		02/11	JiYou	Yin 5	JiaZi
	02/09	WuShen	Yin 7	RenZi		03/11	GengXu	Yin 5	BingZi
	03/09	JiYou	Yin 1	JiaZi		04/11	XinHai	Yin 5	WuZi
	04/09	GengXu	Yin 1	BingZi		05/11	RenZi	Yin 5	GengZi
	05/09	XinHai	Yin 1	WuZi		06/11	GuiChou	Yin 5	RenZi
	06/09	RenZi	Yin 1	GengZi	立冬 (lì dōng) -Beginning of Winter 07/11 7:13 AM	07/11	JiaYin	Yin 8/9	JiaZi
白露 (bái lù) -White Dew 07/09 12:07 PM	07/09	GuiChou	Yin 1/9	RenZi		08/11	YiMao	Yin 9	BingZi
	08/09	JiaYin	Yin 3	JiaZi		09/11	BingChen	Yin 9	WuZi
	09/09	YiMao	Yin 3	BingZi		10/11	DingSi	Yin 9	GengZi
	10/09	BingChen	Yin 3	WuZi		11/11	WuWu	Yin 9	RenZi
	11/09	DingSi	Yin 3	GengZi		12/11	JiWei	Yin 3	JiaZi
	12/09	WuWu	Yin 3	RenZi		13/11	GengShe	Yin 3	BingZi
	13/09	JiWei	Yin 6	JiaZi		14/11	XinYou	Yin 3	WuZi
	14/09	GengShen	Yin 6	BingZi		15/11	RenXu	Yin 3	GengZi
	15/09	XinYou	Yin 6	WuZi		16/11	GuiHai	Yin 3	RenZi
	16/09	RenXu	Yin 6	GengZi		17/11	JiaZi	Yin 6	JiaZi
	17/09	GuiHai	Yin 6	RenZi		18/11	YiChou	Yin 6	BingZi
	18/09	JiaZi	Yin 9	JiaZi		19/11	BingYin	Yin 6	WuZi
	19/09	YiChou	Yin 9	BingZi		20/11	DingMao	Yin 6	GengZi
	20/09	BingYin	Yin 9	WuZi		21/11	WuChen	Yin 6	RenZi
	21/09	DingMao	Yin 9	GengZi	小雪 (xiǎo xuě) -Mild Snow 22/11 4:39 AM	22/11	JiSi	Yin 9/8	JiaZi
秋分 (qiū fēn) -Autumn Equinox 22/09 9:30 PM	22/09	WuChen	Yin 9/7	RenZi		23/11	GengWu	Yin 8	BingZi
	23/09	JiSi	Yin 1	JiaZi		24/11	XinWei	Yin 8	WuZi
	24/09	GengWu	Yin 1	BingZi		25/11	RenShen	Yin 8	GengZi
	25/09	XinWei	Yin 1	WuZi		26/11	GuiYou	Yin 8	RenZi
	26/09	RenShen	Yin 1	GengZi		27/11	JiaXu	Yin 2	JiaZi
	27/09	GuiYou	Yin 1	RenZi		28/11	YiHai	Yin 2	BingZi
	28/09	JiaXu	Yin 4	JiaZi		29/11	BingZi	Yin 2	WuZi
	29/09	YiHai	Yin 4	BingZi		30/11	DingCho	Yin 2	GengZi
	30/09	BingZi	Yin 4	WuZi		01/12	WuYin	Yin 2	RenZi
	01/10	DingChou	Yin 4	GengZi		02/12	JiMao	Yin 5	JiaZi
	02/10	WuYin	Yin 4	RenZi		03/12	GengChe	Yin 5	BingZi
	03/10	JiMao	Yin 7	JiaZi		04/12	XinSi	Yin 5	WuZi
	04/10	GengChen	Yin 7	BingZi		05/12	RenWu	Yin 5	GengZi
	05/10	XinSi	Yin 7	WuZi		06/12	GuiWei	Yin 5	RenZi
	06/10	RenWu	Yin 7	GengZi	大雪 (dà xuě) -Extreme Snow 07/12 12:09 AM	07/12	JiaShen	Yin 8/7	JiaZi
	07/10	GuiWei	Yin 7	RenZi		08/12	YiYou	Yin 7	BingZi
寒露 (hán lù) -Cold Dew 08/10 3:55 AM	08/10	JiaShen	Yin 1/9	JiaZi		09/12	BingXu	Yin 7	WuZi
	09/10	YiYou	Yin 9	BingZi		10/12	DingHai	Yin 7	GengZi
	10/10	BingXu	Yin 9	WuZi		11/12	WuZi	Yin 7	RenZi
	11/10	DingHai	Yin 9	GengZi		12/12	JiChou	Yin 1	JiaZi
	12/10	WuZi	Yin 9	RenZi		13/12	GengYin	Yin 1	BingZi
	13/10	JiChou	Yin 3	JiaZi		14/12	XinMao	Yin 1	WuZi
	14/10	GengYin	Yin 3	BingZi		15/12	RenChen	Yin 1	GengZi
	15/10	XinMao	Yin 3	WuZi		16/12	GuiSi	Yin 1	RenZi
	16/10	RenChen	Yin 3	GengZi		17/12	JiaWu	Yin 4	JiaZi
	17/10	GuiSi	Yin 3	RenZi		18/12	YiWei	Yin 4	BingZi
	18/10	JiaWu	Yin 6	JiaZi		19/12	BingShen	Yin 4	WuZi
	19/10	YiWei	Yin 6	BingZi		20/12	DingYou	Yin 4	GengZi
	20/10	BingShen	Yin 6	WuZi					
	21/10	DingYou	Yin 6	GengZi					
	22/10	WuXu	Yin 6	RenZi					

2020: GengZi,2021: XinChou

2020: GengZi,2021: XinChou
Dec20/Jan21:Wu Zi, Jan/Feb:JiChou

Solar Term	Day	Jia Zi	Dun	Hour
冬至 (dōng zhì) - Winter Solstice 21/12 6:02 AM	21/12	WuXu	Yin 4/Yang 1	RenZi
	22/12	JiHai	Yang 7	JiaZi
	23/12	GengZi	Yang 7	BingZi
	24/12	XinChou	Yang 7	WuZi
	25/12	RenYin	Yang 7	GengZi
	26/12	GuiMao	Yang 7	RenZi
	27/12	JiaChen	Yang 4	JiaZi
	28/12	YiSi	Yang 4	BingZi
	29/12	BingWu	Yang 4	WuZi
	30/12	DingWei	Yang 4	GengZi
	31/12	WuShen	Yang 4	RenZi
	01/01	JiYou	Yang 1	JiaZi
	02/01	GengXu	Yang 1	BingZi
	03/01	XinHai	Yang 1	WuZi
	04/01	RenZi	Yang 1	GengZi
小寒 (xiǎo hán) - Mild Cold 05/01 11:23 AM	05/01	GuiChou	Yang 1/Yang 2	RenZi
	06/01	JiaYin	Yang 8	JiaZi
	07/01	YiMao	Yang 8	BingZi
	08/01	BingChen	Yang 8	WuZi
	09/01	DingSi	Yang 8	GengZi
	10/01	WuWu	Yang 8	RenZi
	11/01	JiWei	Yang 5	JiaZi
	12/01	GengShen	Yang 5	BingZi
	13/01	XinYou	Yang 5	WuZi
	14/01	RenXu	Yang 5	GengZi
	15/01	GuiHai	Yang 5	RenZi
	16/01	JiaZi	Yang 2	JiaZi
	17/01	YiChou	Yang 2	BingZi
	18/01	BingYin	Yang 2	WuZi
	19/01	DingMao	Yang 2	GengZi
大寒 (dà hán) - Extreme Cold 20/01 4:39 AM	20/01	WuChen	Yang 2/Yang 3	RenZi
	21/01	JiSi	Yang 9	JiaZi
	22/01	GengWu	Yang 9	BingZi
	23/01	XinWei	Yang 9	WuZi
	24/01	RenShen	Yang 9	GengZi
	25/01	GuiYou	Yang 9	RenZi
	26/01	JiaXu	Yang 6	JiaZi
	27/01	YiHai	Yang 6	BingZi
	28/01	BingZi	Yang 6	WuZi
	29/01	DingChou	Yang 6	GengZi
	30/01	WuYin	Yang 6	RenZi
	31/01	JiMao	Yang 3	JiaZi
	01/02	GengChen	Yang 3	BingZi
	02/02	XinSi	Yang 3	WuZi
立春 (lì chūn) - Beginning of Spring 03/02 10:58 PM	03/02	RenWu	Yang 3/Yang 8	GengZi
	04/02	GuiWei	Yang 8	RenZi
	05/02	JiaShen	Yang 5	JiaZi
	06/02	YiYou	Yang 5	BingZi
	07/02	BingXu	Yang 5	WuZi
	08/02	DingHai	Yang 5	GengZi
	09/02	WuZi	Yang 5	RenZi
	10/02	JiChou	Yang 2	JiaZi
	11/02	GengYin	Yang 2	BingZi
	12/02	XinMao	Yang 2	WuZi
	13/02	RenChen	Yang 2	GengZi
	14/02	GuiSi	Yang 2	RenZi
	15/02	JiaWu	Yang 8	JiaZi
	16/02	YiWei	Yang 8	BingZi
	17/02	BingShen	Yang 8	WuZi

2021: XinChou
Feb/Mar: GengYin, Mar/Apr:XinMao

Solar Term	Day	Jia Zi	Dun	Hour
雨水 (yǔ shuǐ) - Rain Water 18/02 6:43 PM	18/02	DingYou	Yang 8/Yang	GengZi
	19/02	WuXu	Yang 9	RenZi
	20/02	JiHai	Yang 6	JiaZi
	21/02	GengZi	Yang 6	BingZi
	22/02	XinChou	Yang 6	WuZi
	23/02	RenYin	Yang 6	GengZi
	24/02	GuiMao	Yang 6	RenZi
	25/02	JiaChen	Yang 3	JiaZi
	26/02	YiSi	Yang 3	BingZi
	27/02	BingWu	Yang 3	WuZi
	28/02	DingWei	Yang 3	GengZi
	01/03	WuShen	Yang 3	RenZi
	02/03	JiYou	Yang 9	JiaZi
	03/03	GengXu	Yang 9	BingZi
	04/03	XinHai	Yang 9	WuZi
惊蛰 (jīng zhé) - Insect Awakening 05/03 4:53 PM	05/03	RenZi	Yang 9/Yang	GengZi
	06/03	GuiChou	Yang 1	RenZi
	07/03	JiaYin	Yang 7	JiaZi
	08/03	YiMao	Yang 7	BingZi
	09/03	BingChen	Yang 7	WuZi
	10/03	DingSi	Yang 7	GengZi
	11/03	WuWu	Yang 7	RenZi
	12/03	JiWei	Yang 4	JiaZi
	13/03	GengShen	Yang 4	BingZi
	14/03	XinYou	Yang 4	WuZi
	15/03	RenXu	Yang 4	GengZi
	16/03	GuiHai	Yang 4	RenZi
	17/03	JiaZi	Yang 1	JiaZi
	18/03	YiChou	Yang 1	BingZi
	19/03	BingYin	Yang 1	WuZi
春分 (chūn fēn) - Spring Equinox 20/03 5:37 PM	20/03	DingMao	Yang 1/Yang	GengZi
	21/03	WuChen	Yang 3	RenZi
	22/03	JiSi	Yang 9	JiaZi
	23/03	GengWu	Yang 9	BingZi
	24/03	XinWei	Yang 9	WuZi
	25/03	RenShen	Yang 9	GengZi
	26/03	GuiYou	Yang 9	RenZi
	27/03	JiaXu	Yang 6	JiaZi
	28/03	YiHai	Yang 6	BingZi
	29/03	BingZi	Yang 6	WuZi
	30/03	DingChou	Yang 6	GengZi
	31/03	WuYin	Yang 6	RenZi
	01/04	JiMao	Yang 3	JiaZi
	02/04	GengChen	Yang 3	BingZi
	03/04	XinSi	Yang 3	WuZi
清明 (qīng míng) - Pure Brightness 04/04 9:34 PM	04/04	RenWu	Yang 3/Yang	GengZi
	05/04	GuiWei	Yang 4	RenZi
	06/04	JiaShen	Yang 1	JiaZi
	07/04	YiYou	Yang 1	BingZi
	08/04	BingXu	Yang 1	WuZi
	09/04	DingHai	Yang 1	GengZi
	10/04	WuZi	Yang 1	RenZi
	11/04	JiChou	Yang 7	JiaZi
	12/04	GengYin	Yang 7	BingZi
	13/04	XinMao	Yang 7	WuZi
	14/04	RenChen	Yang 7	GengZi
	15/04	GuiSi	Yang 7	RenZi
	16/04	JiaWu	Yang 4	JiaZi
	17/04	YiWei	Yang 4	BingZi
	18/04	BingShen	Yang 4	WuZi
	19/04	DingYou	Yang 4	GengZi

2021: XinChou — Apr/May:RenChen, May/Jun:GuiSi

Solar Term	Day	Jia Zi	Dun	Hour
谷雨 (gǔ yǔ) - Grain Rain — 20/04 4:33 AM	20/04	WuXu	Yang 4/Yang 5	RenZi
	21/04	JiHai	Yang 2	JiaZi
	22/04	GengZi	Yang 2	BingZi
	23/04	XinChou	Yang 2	WuZi
	24/04	RenYin	Yang 2	GengZi
	25/04	GuiMao	Yang 2	RenZi
	26/04	JiaChen	Yang 8	JiaZi
	27/04	YiSi	Yang 8	BingZi
	28/04	BingWu	Yang 8	WuZi
	29/04	DingWei	Yang 8	GengZi
	30/04	WuShen	Yang 8	RenZi
	01/05	JiYou	Yang 5	JiaZi
	02/05	GengXu	Yang 5	BingZi
	03/05	XinHai	Yang 5	WuZi
	04/05	RenZi	Yang 5	GengZi
立夏 (lì xià) - Beginning of Summer — 05/05 2:47 PM	05/05	GuiChou	Yang 5/Yang 4	RenZi
	06/05	JiaYin	Yang 1	JiaZi
	07/05	YiMao	Yang 1	BingZi
	08/05	BingChen	Yang 1	WuZi
	09/05	DingSi	Yang 1	GengZi
	10/05	WuWu	Yang 1	RenZi
	11/05	JiWei	Yang 7	JiaZi
	12/05	GengShen	Yang 7	BingZi
	13/05	XinYou	Yang 7	WuZi
	14/05	RenXu	Yang 7	GengZi
	15/05	GuiHai	Yang 7	RenZi
	16/05	JiaZi	Yang 4	JiaZi
	17/05	YiChou	Yang 4	BingZi
	18/05	BingYin	Yang 4	WuZi
	19/05	DingMao	Yang 4	GengZi
	20/05	WuChen	Yang 4	RenZi
小满 (xiǎo mǎn) - Small Grain — 21/05 3:36 AM	21/05	JiSi	Yang 1/Yang 2	JiaZi
	22/05	GengWu	Yang 2	BingZi
	23/05	XinWei	Yang 2	WuZi
	24/05	RenShen	Yang 2	GengZi
	25/05	GuiYou	Yang 2	RenZi
	26/05	JiaXu	Yang 8	JiaZi
	27/05	YiHai	Yang 8	BingZi
	28/05	BingZi	Yang 8	WuZi
	29/05	DingChou	Yang 8	GengZi
	30/05	WuYin	Yang 8	RenZi
	31/05	JiMao	Yang 5	JiaZi
	01/06	GengChe	Yang 5	BingZi
	02/06	XinSi	Yang 5	WuZi
	03/06	RenWu	Yang 5	GengZi
	04/06	GuiWei	Yang 5	RenZi
芒种 (máng zhòng) - Summer Harvest — 05/06 6:51 PM	05/06	JiaShen	Yang 2/Yang 3	JiaZi
	06/06	YiYou	Yang 3	BingZi
	07/06	BingXu	Yang 3	WuZi
	08/06	DingHai	Yang 3	GengZi
	09/06	WuZi	Yang 3	RenZi
	10/06	JiChou	Yang 9	JiaZi
	11/06	GengYin	Yang 9	BingZi
	12/06	XinMao	Yang 9	WuZi
	13/06	RenChen	Yang 9	GengZi
	14/06	GuiSi	Yang 9	RenZi
	15/06	JiaWu	Yang 6	JiaZi
	16/06	YiWei	Yang 6	BingZi
	17/06	BingShen	Yang 6	WuZi
	18/06	DingYou	Yang 6	GengZi
	19/06	WuXu	Yang 6	RenZi
	20/06	JiHai	Yang 3	JiaZi

2021: XinChou — Jun/July:JiaWu, Jul/Aug:YiWei

Solar Term	Day	Jia Zi	Dun	Hour
夏至 (xià zhì) - Summer Solstice — 21/06 11:31 AM	21/06	GengZi	Yang 3/Yin 3	BingZi
	22/06	XinChou	Yin 3	WuZi
	23/06	RenYin	Yin 3	GengZi
	24/06	GuiMao	Yin 3	RenZi
	25/06	JiaChen	Yin 6	JiaZi
	26/06	YiSi	Yin 6	BingZi
	27/06	BingWu	Yin 6	WuZi
	28/06	DingWei	Yin 6	GengZi
	29/06	WuShen	Yin 6	RenZi
	30/06	JiYou	Yin 9	JiaZi
	01/07	GengXu	Yin 9	BingZi
	02/07	XinHai	Yin 9	WuZi
	03/07	RenZi	Yin 9	GengZi
	04/07	GuiChou	Yin 9	RenZi
	05/07	JiaYin	Yin 3	JiaZi
	06/07	YiMao	Yin 3	BingZi
小暑 (xiǎo shǔ) - Mild Summer — 07/07 5:05 AM	07/07	BingChen	Yin 3/Yin 2	WuZi
	08/07	DingSi	Yin 2	GengZi
	09/07	WuWu	Yin 2	RenZi
	10/07	JiWei	Yin 5	JiaZi
	11/07	GengShen	Yin 5	BingZi
	12/07	XinYou	Yin 5	WuZi
	13/07	RenXu	Yin 5	GengZi
	14/07	GuiHai	Yin 5	RenZi
	15/07	JiaZi	Yin 8	JiaZi
	16/07	YiChou	Yin 8	BingZi
	17/07	BingYin	Yin 8	WuZi
	18/07	DingMao	Yin 8	GengZi
	19/07	WuChen	Yin 8	RenZi
	20/07	JiSi	Yin 2	JiaZi
	21/07	GengWu	Yin 2	BingZi
大暑 (dà shǔ) - Extreme Summer — 22/07 10:26 PM	22/07	XinWei	Yin 2/Yin 1	WuZi
	23/07	RenShen	Yin 1	GengZi
	24/07	GuiYou	Yin 1	RenZi
	25/07	JiaXu	Yin 4	JiaZi
	26/07	YiHai	Yin 4	BingZi
	27/07	BingZi	Yin 4	WuZi
	28/07	DingChou	Yin 4	GengZi
	29/07	WuYin	Yin 4	RenZi
	30/07	JiMao	Yin 7	JiaZi
	31/07	GengChe	Yin 7	BingZi
	01/08	XinSi	Yin 7	WuZi
	02/08	RenWu	Yin 7	GengZi
	03/08	GuiWei	Yin 7	RenZi
	04/08	JiaShen	Yin 1	JiaZi
	05/08	YiYou	Yin 1	BingZi
立秋 (lì qiū) - Beginning of Autumn — 07/08 2:53 PM	06/08	BingXu	Yin 1	WuZi
	07/08	DingHai	Yin 1/Yin 5	GengZi
	08/08	WuZi	Yin 5	RenZi
	09/08	JiChou	Yin 8	JiaZi
	10/08	GengYin	Yin 8	BingZi
	11/08	XinMao	Yin 8	WuZi
	12/08	RenChen	Yin 8	GengZi
	13/08	GuiSi	Yin 8	RenZi
	14/08	JiaWu	Yin 2	JiaZi
	15/08	YiWei	Yin 2	BingZi
	16/08	BingShen	Yin 2	WuZi
	17/08	DingYou	Yin 2	GengZi
	18/08	WuXu	Yin 2	RenZi
	19/08	JiHai	Yin 5	JiaZi
	20/08	GengZi	Yin 5	BingZi
	21/08	XinChou	Yin 5	WuZi
	22/08	RenYin	Yin 5	GengZi

2021: XinChou — Aug/Sep:BingShen, Sep/Oct:DingYou

Solar Term	Day	Jia Zi	Chai Bu	Hour
外署 (wài shǔ) - Outer Heat 23/08 5:34 AM	23/08	GuiMao	Yin 5/Yin 4	RenZi
	24/08	JiaChen	Yin 7	JiaZi
	25/08	YiSi	Yin 7	BingZi
	26/08	BingWu	Yin 7	WuZi
	27/08	DingWei	Yin 7	GengZi
	28/08	WuShen	Yin 7	RenZi
	29/08	JiYou	Yin 1	JiaZi
	30/08	GengXu	Yin 1	BingZi
	31/08	XinHai	Yin 1	WuZi
	01/09	RenZi	Yin 1	GengZi
	02/09	GuiChou	Yin 1	RenZi
	03/09	JiaYin	Yin 4	JiaZi
	04/09	YiMao	Yin 4	BingZi
	05/09	BingChen	Yin 4	WuZi
	06/09	DingSi	Yin 4	GengZi
白露 (bái lù) - White Dew 07/09 5:52 PM	07/09	WuWu	Yin 4/Yin 3	RenZi
	08/09	JiWei	Yin 6	JiaZi
	09/09	GengShen	Yin 6	BingZi
	10/09	XinYou	Yin 6	WuZi
	11/09	RenXu	Yin 6	GengZi
	12/09	GuiHai	Yin 6	RenZi
	13/09	JiaZi	Yin 9	JiaZi
	14/09	YiChou	Yin 9	BingZi
	15/09	BingYin	Yin 9	WuZi
	16/09	DingMao	Yin 9	GengZi
	17/09	WuChen	Yin 9	RenZi
	18/09	JiSi	Yin 3	JiaZi
	19/09	GengWu	Yin 3	BingZi
	20/09	XinWei	Yin 3	WuZi
	21/09	RenShen	Yin 3	GengZi
	22/09	GuiYou	Yin 3	RenZi
秋分 (qiū fēn) - Autumn Equinox 23/09 3:20 AM	23/09	JiaXu	Yin 6/Yin 4	JiaZi
	24/09	YiHai	Yin 4	BingZi
	25/09	BingZi	Yin 4	WuZi
	26/09	DingChou	Yin 4	GengZi
	27/09	WuYin	Yin 4	RenZi
	28/09	JiMao	Yin 7	JiaZi
	29/09	GengChen	Yin 7	BingZi
	30/09	XinSi	Yin 7	WuZi
	01/10	RenWu	Yin 7	GengZi
	02/10	GuiWei	Yin 7	RenZi
	03/10	JiaShen	Yin 1	JiaZi
	04/10	YiYou	Yin 1	BingZi
	05/10	BingXu	Yin 1	WuZi
	06/10	DingHai	Yin 1	GengZi
	07/10	WuZi	Yin 1	RenZi
寒露 (hán lù) - Cold Dew 08/10 9:38 AM	08/10	JiChou	Yin 4/Yin 3	JiaZi
	09/10	GengYin	Yin 3	BingZi
	10/10	XinMao	Yin 3	WuZi
	11/10	RenChen	Yin 3	GengZi
	12/10	GuiSi	Yin 3	RenZi
	13/10	JiaWu	Yin 6	JiaZi
	14/10	YiWei	Yin 6	BingZi
	15/10	BingShen	Yin 6	WuZi
	16/10	DingYou	Yin 6	GengZi
	17/10	WuXu	Yin 6	RenZi
	18/10	JiHai	Yin 9	JiaZi
	19/10	GengZi	Yin 9	BingZi
	20/10	XinChou	Yin 9	WuZi
	21/10	RenYin	Yin 9	GengZi
	22/10	GuiMao	Yin 9	RenZi

2021: XinChou — Oct/Nov:WuXu, Nov/Dec:JiHai

Solar Term	Day	Jia Zi	Chai Bu	Hour
霜降 (shuāng jiàng) - Frost 23/10 12:50 PM	23/10	JiaChen	Yin 3/Yin 2	JiaZi
	24/10	YiSi	Yin 2	BingZi
	25/10	BingWu	Yin 2	WuZi
	26/10	DingWei	Yin 2	GengZi
	27/10	WuShen	Yin 2	RenZi
	28/10	JiYou	Yin 5	JiaZi
	29/10	GengXu	Yin 5	BingZi
	30/10	XinHai	Yin 5	WuZi
	31/10	RenZi	Yin 5	GengZi
	01/11	GuiChou	Yin 5	RenZi
	02/11	JiaYin	Yin 8	JiaZi
	03/11	YiMao	Yin 8	BingZi
	04/11	BingChen	Yin 8	WuZi
	05/11	DingSi	Yin 8	GengZi
	06/11	WuWu	Yin 8	RenZi
立冬 (lì dōng) - Beginning of Winter 07/11 12:58 PM	07/11	JiWei	Yin 2/Yin 3	JiaZi
	08/11	GengShen	Yin 3	BingZi
	09/11	XinYou	Yin 3	WuZi
	10/11	RenXu	Yin 3	GengZi
	11/11	GuiHai	Yin 3	RenZi
	12/11	JiaZi	Yin 6	JiaZi
	13/11	YiChou	Yin 6	BingZi
	14/11	BingYin	Yin 6	WuZi
	15/11	DingMao	Yin 6	GengZi
	16/11	WuChen	Yin 6	RenZi
	17/11	JiSi	Yin 9	JiaZi
	18/11	GengWu	Yin 9	BingZi
	19/11	XinWei	Yin 9	WuZi
	20/11	RenShen	Yin 9	GengZi
	21/11	GuiYou	Yin 9	RenZi
小雪 (xiǎo xuě) - Mild Snow 22/11 10:33 AM	22/11	JiaXu	Yin 3/Yin 2	JiaZi
	23/11	YiHai	Yin 2	BingZi
	24/11	BingZi	Yin 2	WuZi
	25/11	DingChou	Yin 2	GengZi
	26/11	WuYin	Yin 2	RenZi
	27/11	JiMao	Yin 5	JiaZi
	28/11	GengChen	Yin 5	BingZi
	29/11	XinSi	Yin 5	WuZi
	30/11	RenWu	Yin 5	GengZi
	01/12	GuiWei	Yin 5	RenZi
	02/12	JiaShen	Yin 8	JiaZi
	03/12	YiYou	Yin 8	BingZi
	04/12	BingXu	Yin 8	WuZi
	05/12	DingHai	Yin 8	GengZi
	06/12	WuZi	Yin 8	RenZi
大雪 (dà xuě) - Extreme Snow 07/12 5:56 AM	07/12	JiChou	Yin 2/Yin 1	JiaZi
	08/12	GengYin	Yin 1	BingZi
	09/12	XinMao	Yin 1	WuZi
	10/12	RenChen	Yin 1	GengZi
	11/12	GuiSi	Yin 1	RenZi
	12/12	JiaWu	Yin 4	JiaZi
	13/12	YiWei	Yin 4	BingZi
	14/12	BingShen	Yin 4	WuZi
	15/12	DingYou	Yin 4	GengZi
	16/12	WuXu	Yin 4	RenZi
	17/12	JiHai	Yin 7	JiaZi
	18/12	GengZi	Yin 7	BingZi
	19/12	XinChou	Yin 7	WuZi
	20/12	RenYin	Yin 7	GengZi

2021: XinChou,2022: RenYin

2021: XinChou,2022: RenYin Dec21/Jan22:GengZi, Jan/Feb:XinChou	Day	Jia Zi	Dun	Hour	2022: RenYin Feb/Mar:RenYin, Mar/Apr:GuiMao	Day	Jia Zi	Dun	Hour
冬至 (dōng zhì) - Winter Solstice 21/12 11:59 PM	21/12	GuiMao	Yin 7/Yang 7	RenZi	雨水 (yǔ shuǐ) - Rain Water 19/02 12:42 AM	19/02	GuiMao	Yang 5/Yang 6	RenZi
	22/12	JiaChen	Yang 4	JiaZi		20/02	JiaChen	Yang 3	JiaZi
	23/12	YiSi	Yang 4	BingZi		21/02	YiSi	Yang 3	BingZi
	24/12	BingWu	Yang 4	WuZi		22/02	BingWu	Yang 3	WuZi
	25/12	DingWei	Yang 4	GengZi		23/02	DingWei	Yang 3	GengZi
	26/12	WuShen	Yang 4	RenZi		24/02	WuShen	Yang 3	RenZi
	27/12	JiYou	Yang 1	JiaZi		25/02	JiYou	Yang 9	JiaZi
	28/12	GengXu	Yang 1	BingZi		26/02	GengXu	Yang 9	BingZi
	29/12	XinHai	Yang 1	WuZi		27/02	XinHai	Yang 9	WuZi
	30/12	RenZi	Yang 1	GengZi		28/02	RenZi	Yang 9	GengZi
	31/12	GuiChou	Yang 1	RenZi		01/03	GuiChou	Yang 9	RenZi
	01/01	JiaYin	Yang 7	JiaZi		02/03	JiaYin	Yang 6	JiaZi
	02/01	YiMao	Yang 7	BingZi		03/03	YiMao	Yang 6	BingZi
	03/01	BingChen	Yang 7	WuZi		04/03	BingChen	Yang 6	WuZi
	04/01	DingSi	Yang 7	GengZi		05/03	DingSi	Yang 6/Yang 7	GengZi
小寒 (xiǎo hán) - Mild Cold 05/01 5:13 PM	05/01	WuWu	Yang 7/Yang 8	RenZi	驚蟄 (jīng zhé) - Insect Awakening 05/03 10:43 PM	06/03	WuWu	Yang 7	RenZi
	06/01	JiWei	Yang 5	JiaZi		07/03	JiWei	Yang 4	JiaZi
	07/01	GengShen	Yang 5	BingZi		08/03	GengShen	Yang 4	BingZi
	08/01	XinYou	Yang 5	WuZi		09/03	XinYou	Yang 4	WuZi
	09/01	RenXu	Yang 5	GengZi		10/03	RenXu	Yang 4	GengZi
	10/01	GuiHai	Yang 5	RenZi		11/03	GuiHai	Yang 4	RenZi
	11/01	JiaZi	Yang 2	JiaZi		12/03	JiaZi	Yang 1	JiaZi
	12/01	YiChou	Yang 2	BingZi		13/03	YiChou	Yang 1	BingZi
	13/01	BingYin	Yang 2	WuZi		14/03	BingYin	Yang 1	WuZi
	14/01	DingMao	Yang 2	GengZi		15/03	DingMao	Yang 1	GengZi
	15/01	WuChen	Yang 2	RenZi		16/03	WuChen	Yang 1	RenZi
	16/01	JiSi	Yang 8	JiaZi		17/03	JiSi	Yang 7	JiaZi
	17/01	GengWu	Yang 8	BingZi		18/03	GengWu	Yang 7	BingZi
	18/01	XinWei	Yang 8	WuZi		19/03	XinWei	Yang 7	WuZi
	19/01	RenShen	Yang 8	GengZi		20/03	RenShen	Yang 7/Yang 9	GengZi
大寒 (dà hán) - Extreme Cold 20/01 10:38 AM	20/01	GuiYou	Yang 8/Yang 9	RenZi	春分 (chūn fēn) - Spring Equinox 20/03 11:33 PM	21/03	GuiYou	Yang 9	RenZi
	21/01	JiaXu	Yang 6	JiaZi		22/03	JiaXu	Yang 6	JiaZi
	22/01	YiHai	Yang 6	BingZi		23/03	YiHai	Yang 6	BingZi
	23/01	BingZi	Yang 6	WuZi		24/03	BingZi	Yang 6	WuZi
	24/01	DingChou	Yang 6	GengZi		25/03	DingChou	Yang 6	GengZi
	25/01	WuYin	Yang 6	RenZi		26/03	WuYin	Yang 6	RenZi
	26/01	JiMao	Yang 3	JiaZi		27/03	JiMao	Yang 3	JiaZi
	27/01	GengChen	Yang 3	BingZi		28/03	GengChen	Yang 3	BingZi
	28/01	XinSi	Yang 3	WuZi		29/03	XinSi	Yang 3	WuZi
	29/01	RenWu	Yang 3	GengZi		30/03	RenWu	Yang 3	GengZi
	30/01	GuiWei	Yang 3	RenZi		31/03	GuiWei	Yang 3	RenZi
	31/01	JiaShen	Yang 9	JiaZi		01/04	JiaShen	Yang 9	JiaZi
	01/02	YiYou	Yang 9	BingZi		02/04	YiYou	Yang 9	BingZi
	02/02	BingXu	Yang 9	WuZi		03/04	BingXu	Yang 9	WuZi
	03/02	DingHai	Yang 9	GengZi		04/04	DingHai	Yang 9	GengZi
立春 (lì chūn) - Beginning of Spring 04/02 4:50 AM	04/02	WuZi	Yang 9/Yang 5	RenZi	清明 (qīng míng) - Pure Brightness 05/04 3:20 AM	05/04	WuZi	Yang 9/Yang 1	RenZi
	05/02	JiChou	Yang 2	JiaZi		06/04	JiChou	Yang 7	JiaZi
	06/02	GengYin	Yang 2	BingZi		07/04	GengYin	Yang 7	BingZi
	07/02	XinMao	Yang 2	WuZi		08/04	XinMao	Yang 7	WuZi
	08/02	RenChen	Yang 2	GengZi		09/04	RenChen	Yang 7	GengZi
	09/02	GuiSi	Yang 2	RenZi		10/04	GuiSi	Yang 7	RenZi
	10/02	JiaWu	Yang 8	JiaZi		11/04	JiaWu	Yang 4	JiaZi
	11/02	YiWei	Yang 8	BingZi		12/04	YiWei	Yang 4	BingZi
	12/02	BingShen	Yang 8	WuZi		13/04	BingShen	Yang 4	WuZi
	13/02	DingYou	Yang 8	GengZi		14/04	DingYou	Yang 4	GengZi
	14/02	WuXu	Yang 8	RenZi		15/04	WuXu	Yang 4	RenZi
	15/02	JiHai	Yang 5	JiaZi		16/04	JiHai	Yang 1	JiaZi
	16/02	GengZi	Yang 5	BingZi		17/04	GengZi	Yang 1	BingZi
	17/02	XinChou	Yang 5	WuZi		18/04	XinChou	Yang 1	WuZi
	18/02	RenYin	Yang 5	GengZi		19/04	RenYin	Yang 1	GengZi

	Day	Jia Zi	Dun	Hour		Day	Jia Zi	Dun	Hour
		2022: RenYin — Apr/May:JiaChen, May/Jun:YiSi					2022: RenYin — Jun/July:BingWu, Jul/Aug:DingWei		
谷雨 (gǔ yǔ) - Grain Rain 20/04 10:24 AM	20/04	GuiMao	Yang 1/Yang 2	RenZi	夏至 (xià zhì) - Summer Solstice 21/06 5:13 PM	21/06	YiSi	Yang 9/Yin 6	BingZi
	21/04	JiaChen	Yang 8	JiaZi		22/06	BingWu	Yin 6	WuZi
	22/04	YiSi	Yang 8	BingZi		23/06	DingWei	Yin 6	GengZi
	23/04	BingWu	Yang 8	WuZi		24/06	WuShen	Yin 6	RenZi
	24/04	DingWei	Yang 8	GengZi		25/06	JiYou	Yin 9	JiaZi
	25/04	WuShen	Yang 8	RenZi		26/06	GengXu	Yin 9	BingZi
	26/04	JiYou	Yang 5	JiaZi		27/06	XinHai	Yin 9	WuZi
	27/04	GengXu	Yang 5	BingZi		28/06	RenZi	Yin 9	GengZi
	28/04	XinHai	Yang 5	WuZi		29/06	GuiChou	Yin 9	RenZi
	29/04	RenZi	Yang 5	GengZi		30/06	JiaYin	Yin 3	JiaZi
	30/04	GuiChou	Yang 5	RenZi		01/07	YiMao	Yin 3	BingZi
	01/05	JiaYin	Yang 2	JiaZi		02/07	BingChen	Yin 3	WuZi
	02/05	YiMao	Yang 2	BingZi		03/07	DingSi	Yin 3	GengZi
	03/05	BingChen	Yang 2	WuZi		04/07	WuWu	Yin 3	RenZi
	04/05	DingSi	Yang 2	GengZi		05/07	JiWei	Yin 6	JiaZi
立夏 (lì xià) - Beginning of Summer 05/05 8:25 PM	05/05	WuWu	Yang 2/Yang 1	RenZi		06/07	GengShen	Yin 6	BingZi
	06/05	JiWei	Yang 7	JiaZi	小暑 (xiǎo shǔ) - Mild Summer 07/07 10:37 AM	07/07	XinYou	Yin 6/Yin 5	WuZi
	07/05	GengShen	Yang 7	BingZi		08/07	RenXu	Yin 5	GengZi
	08/05	XinYou	Yang 7	WuZi		09/07	GuiHai	Yin 5	RenZi
	09/05	RenXu	Yang 7	GengZi		10/07	JiaZi	Yin 8	JiaZi
	10/05	GuiHai	Yang 7	RenZi		11/07	YiChou	Yin 8	BingZi
	11/05	JiaZi	Yang 4	JiaZi		12/07	BingYin	Yin 8	WuZi
	12/05	YiChou	Yang 4	BingZi		13/07	DingMao	Yin 8	GengZi
	13/05	BingYin	Yang 4	WuZi		14/07	WuChen	Yin 8	RenZi
	14/05	DingMao	Yang 4	GengZi		15/07	JiSi	Yin 2	JiaZi
	15/05	WuChen	Yang 4	RenZi		16/07	GengWu	Yin 2	BingZi
	16/05	JiSi	Yang 1	JiaZi		17/07	XinWei	Yin 2	WuZi
	17/05	GengWu	Yang 1	BingZi		18/07	RenShen	Yin 2	GengZi
	18/05	XinWei	Yang 1	WuZi		19/07	GuiYou	Yin 2	RenZi
	19/05	RenShen	Yang 1	GengZi		20/07	JiaXu	Yin 5	JiaZi
	20/05	GuiYou	Yang 1	RenZi		21/07	YiHai	Yin 5	BingZi
小满 (xiǎo mǎn) - Small Grain 21/05 9:22 AM	21/05	JiaXu	Yang 7/Yang 8	JiaZi		22/07	BingZi	Yin 5	WuZi
	22/05	YiHai	Yang 8	BingZi	大暑 (dà shǔ) - Extreme Summer 23/07 4:06 AM	23/07	DingChou	Yin 5/Yin 4	GengZi
	23/05	BingZi	Yang 8	WuZi		24/07	WuYin	Yin 4	RenZi
	24/05	DingChou	Yang 8	GengZi		25/07	JiMao	Yin 7	JiaZi
	25/05	WuYin	Yang 8	RenZi		26/07	GengChe	Yin 7	BingZi
	26/05	JiMao	Yang 5	JiaZi		27/07	XinSi	Yin 7	WuZi
	27/05	GengChe	Yang 5	BingZi		28/07	RenWu	Yin 7	GengZi
	28/05	XinSi	Yang 5	WuZi		29/07	GuiWei	Yin 7	RenZi
	29/05	RenWu	Yang 5	GengZi		30/07	JiaShen	Yin 1	JiaZi
	30/05	GuiWei	Yang 5	RenZi		31/07	YiYou	Yin 1	BingZi
	31/05	JiaShen	Yang 2	JiaZi		01/08	BingXu	Yin 1	WuZi
	01/06	YiYou	Yang 2	BingZi		02/08	DingHai	Yin 1	GengZi
	02/06	BingXu	Yang 2	WuZi		03/08	WuZi	Yin 1	RenZi
	03/06	DingHai	Yang 2	GengZi		04/08	JiChou	Yin 4	JiaZi
	04/06	WuZi	Yang 2	RenZi		05/08	GengYin	Yin 4	BingZi
	05/06	JiChou	Yang 8	JiaZi		06/08	XinMao	Yin 4	WuZi
芒种 (máng zhòng) - Summer Harvest 06/06 12:25 AM	06/06	GengYin	Yang 8/Yang 9	BingZi	立秋 (lì qiū) - Beginning of Autumn 07/08 8:28 PM	07/08	RenChen	Yin 4/Yin 8	GengZi
	07/06	XinMao	Yang 9	WuZi		08/08	GuiSi	Yin 8	RenZi
	08/06	RenChen	Yang 9	GengZi		09/08	JiaWu	Yin 2	JiaZi
	09/06	GuiSi	Yang 9	RenZi		10/08	YiWei	Yin 2	BingZi
	10/06	JiaWu	Yang 6	JiaZi		11/08	BingShen	Yin 2	WuZi
	11/06	YiWei	Yang 6	BingZi		12/08	DingYou	Yin 2	GengZi
	12/06	BingShen	Yang 6	WuZi		13/08	WuXu	Yin 2	RenZi
	13/06	DingYou	Yang 6	GengZi		14/08	JiHai	Yin 5	JiaZi
	14/06	WuXu	Yang 6	RenZi		15/08	GengZi	Yin 5	BingZi
	15/06	JiHai	Yang 3	JiaZi		16/08	XinChou	Yin 5	WuZi
	16/06	GengZi	Yang 3	BingZi		17/08	RenYin	Yin 5	GengZi
	17/06	XinChou	Yang 3	WuZi		18/08	GuiMao	Yin 5	RenZi
	18/06	RenYin	Yang 3	GengZi		19/08	JiaChen	Yin 8	JiaZi
	19/06	GuiMao	Yang 3	RenZi		20/08	YiSi	Yin 8	BingZi
	20/06	JiaChen	Yang 9	JiaZi		21/08	BingWu	Yin 8	WuZi
						22/08	DingWei	Yin 8	GengZi

2022: RenYin — Aug/Sep:WuShen, Sep/Oct:JiYou

外暑 (wài shǔ) - Outer Heat — 23/08 11:15 AM

Day	Jia Zi	Dun	Hour
23/08	WuShen	Yin 8/Yin 7	RenZi
24/08	JiYou	Yin 1	JiaZi
25/08	GengXu	Yin 1	BingZi
26/08	XinHai	Yin 1	WuZi
27/08	RenZi	Yin 1	GengZi
28/08	GuiChou	Yin 1	RenZi
29/08	JiaYin	Yin 4	JiaZi
30/08	YiMao	Yin 4	BingZi
31/08	BingChen	Yin 4	WuZi
01/09	DingSi	Yin 4	GengZi
02/09	WuWu	Yin 4	RenZi
03/09	JiWei	Yin 7	JiaZi
04/09	GengShen	Yin 7	BingZi
05/09	XinYou	Yin 7	WuZi
06/09	RenXu	Yin 7	GengZi

白露 (bái lù) - White Dew — 07/09 11:32 PM

Day	Jia Zi	Dun	Hour
07/09	GuiHai	Yin 7/Yin 6	RenZi
08/09	JiaZi	Yin 9	JiaZi
09/09	YiChou	Yin 9	BingZi
10/09	BingYin	Yin 9	WuZi
11/09	DingMao	Yin 9	GengZi
12/09	WuChen	Yin 9	RenZi
13/09	JiSi	Yin 3	JiaZi
14/09	GengWu	Yin 3	BingZi
15/09	XinWei	Yin 3	WuZi
16/09	RenShen	Yin 3	GengZi
17/09	GuiYou	Yin 3	RenZi
18/09	JiaXu	Yin 6	JiaZi
19/09	YiHai	Yin 6	BingZi
20/09	BingZi	Yin 6	WuZi
21/09	DingChou	Yin 6	GengZi
22/09	WuYin	Yin 6	RenZi

秋分 (qiū fēn) - Autumn Equinox — 23/09 9:03 AM

Day	Jia Zi	Dun	Hour
23/09	JiMao	Yin 9/Yin 7	JiaZi
24/09	GengChen	Yin 7	BingZi
25/09	XinSi	Yin 7	WuZi
26/09	RenWu	Yin 7	GengZi
27/09	GuiWei	Yin 7	RenZi
28/09	JiaShen	Yin 1	JiaZi
29/09	YiYou	Yin 1	BingZi
30/09	BingXu	Yin 1	WuZi
01/10	DingHai	Yin 1	GengZi
02/10	WuZi	Yin 1	RenZi
03/10	JiChou	Yin 4	JiaZi
04/10	GengYin	Yin 4	BingZi
05/10	XinMao	Yin 4	WuZi
06/10	RenChen	Yin 4	GengZi
07/10	GuiSi	Yin 4	RenZi

寒露 (hán lù) - Cold Dew — 08/10 3:22 PM

Day	Jia Zi	Dun	Hour
08/10	JiaWu	Yin 7/Yin 6	JiaZi
09/10	YiWei	Yin 6	BingZi
10/10	BingShen	Yin 6	WuZi
11/10	DingYou	Yin 6	GengZi
12/10	WuXu	Yin 6	RenZi
13/10	JiHai	Yin 9	JiaZi
14/10	GengZi	Yin 9	BingZi
15/10	XinChou	Yin 9	WuZi
16/10	RenYin	Yin 9	GengZi
17/10	GuiMao	Yin 9	RenZi
18/10	JiaChen	Yin 3	JiaZi
19/10	YiSi	Yin 3	BingZi
20/10	BingWu	Yin 3	WuZi
21/10	DingWei	Yin 3	GengZi
22/10	WuShen	Yin 3	RenZi

2022: RenYin — Oct/Nov:GengXu, Nov/Dec:XinHai

霜降 (shuāng jiàng) - Frost — 23/10 6:35 PM

Day	Jia Zi	Dun	Hour
23/10	JiYou	Yin 6/Yin 5	JiaZi
24/10	GengXu	Yin 5	BingZi
25/10	XinHai	Yin 5	WuZi
26/10	RenZi	Yin 5	GengZi
27/10	GuiChou	Yin 5	RenZi
28/10	JiaYin	Yin 8	JiaZi
29/10	YiMao	Yin 8	BingZi
30/10	BingChen	Yin 8	WuZi
31/10	DingSi	Yin 8	GengZi
01/11	WuWu	Yin 8	RenZi
02/11	JiWei	Yin 2	JiaZi
03/11	GengShen	Yin 2	BingZi
04/11	XinYou	Yin 2	WuZi
05/11	RenXu	Yin 2	GengZi
06/11	GuiHai	Yin 2	RenZi

立冬 (lì dōng) - Beginning of Winter — 07/11 6:45 PM

Day	Jia Zi	Dun	Hour
07/11	JiaZi	Yin 5/Yin 6	JiaZi
08/11	YiChou	Yin 6	BingZi
09/11	BingYin	Yin 6	WuZi
10/11	DingMao	Yin 6	GengZi
11/11	WuChen	Yin 6	RenZi
12/11	JiSi	Yin 9	JiaZi
13/11	GengWu	Yin 9	BingZi
14/11	XinWei	Yin 9	WuZi
15/11	RenShen	Yin 9	GengZi
16/11	GuiYou	Yin 9	RenZi
17/11	JiaXu	Yin 3	JiaZi
18/11	YiHai	Yin 3	BingZi
19/11	BingZi	Yin 3	WuZi
20/11	DingChou	Yin 3	GengZi
21/11	WuYin	Yin 3	RenZi

小雪 (xiǎo xuě) - Mild Snow — 22/11 4:20 PM

Day	Jia Zi	Dun	Hour
22/11	JiMao	Yin 6/Yin 5	JiaZi
23/11	GengChen	Yin 5	BingZi
24/11	XinSi	Yin 5	WuZi
25/11	RenWu	Yin 5	GengZi
26/11	GuiWei	Yin 5	RenZi
27/11	JiaShen	Yin 8	JiaZi
28/11	YiYou	Yin 8	BingZi
29/11	BingXu	Yin 8	WuZi
30/11	DingHai	Yin 8	GengZi
01/12	WuZi	Yin 8	RenZi
02/12	JiChou	Yin 2	JiaZi
03/12	GengYin	Yin 2	BingZi
04/12	XinMao	Yin 2	WuZi
05/12	RenChen	Yin 2	GengZi
06/12	GuiSi	Yin 2	RenZi

大雪 (dà xuě) - Extreme Snow — 07/12 11:46 AM

Day	Jia Zi	Dun	Hour
07/12	JiaWu	Yin 5/Yin 4	JiaZi
08/12	YiWei	Yin 4	BingZi
09/12	BingShen	Yin 4	WuZi
10/12	DingYou	Yin 4	GengZi
11/12	WuXu	Yin 4	RenZi
12/12	JiHai	Yin 7	JiaZi
13/12	GengZi	Yin 7	BingZi
14/12	XinChou	Yin 7	WuZi
15/12	RenYin	Yin 7	GengZi
16/12	GuiMao	Yin 7	RenZi
17/12	JiaChen	Yin 1	JiaZi
18/12	YiSi	Yin 1	BingZi
19/12	BingWu	Yin 1	WuZi
20/12	DingWei	Yin 1	GengZi
21/12	WuShen	Yin 1	RenZi

2022: RenYin,2023: GuiMao

	Day	Jia Zi	Dun	Hour		Day	Jia Zi	Dun	Hour
2022: RenYin,2023: GuiMao Dec22/Jan23:RenZi, Jan/Feb:GuiChou					**2023: GuiMao** Feb/Mar:JiaYin, Mar/Apr:YiMao				
冬至 (dōng zhì) - Winter Solstice 22/12 5:48 AM	22/12	JiYou	Yin 4/Yang 1	JiaZi	雨水 (yǔ shuǐ) - Rain Water 19/02 6:34 AM	19/02	WuShen	Yang 2/Yang 3	RenZi
	23/12	GengXu	Yang 1	BingZi		20/02	JiYou	Yang 9	JiaZi
	24/12	XinHai	Yang 1	WuZi		21/02	GengXu	Yang 9	BingZi
	25/12	RenZi	Yang 1	GengZi		22/02	XinHai	Yang 9	WuZi
	26/12	GuiChou	Yang 1	RenZi		23/02	RenZi	Yang 9	GengZi
	27/12	JiaYin	Yang 7	JiaZi		24/02	GuiChou	Yang 9	RenZi
	28/12	YiMao	Yang 7	BingZi		25/02	JiaYin	Yang 6	JiaZi
	29/12	BingChen	Yang 7	WuZi		26/02	YiMao	Yang 6	BingZi
	30/12	DingSi	Yang 7	GengZi		27/02	BingChen	Yang 6	WuZi
	31/12	WuWu	Yang 7	RenZi		28/02	DingSi	Yang 6	GengZi
	01/01	JiWei	Yang 4	JiaZi		01/03	WuWu	Yang 6	RenZi
	02/01	GengShen	Yang 4	BingZi		02/03	JiWei	Yang 3	JiaZi
	03/01	XinYou	Yang 4	WuZi		03/03	GengShen	Yang 3	BingZi
	04/01	RenXu	Yang 4	GengZi		04/03	XinYou	Yang 3	WuZi
小寒 (xiǎo hán) - Mild Cold 05/01 11:04 PM	05/01	GuiHai	Yang 4/Yang 5	RenZi		05/03	RenXu	Yang 3	GengZi
	06/01	JiaZi	Yang 2	JiaZi	惊蛰 (jīng zhé) - Insect Awakening 06/03 4:36 AM	06/03	GuiHai	Yang 3/Yang 4	RenZi
	07/01	YiChou	Yang 2	BingZi		07/03	JiaZi	Yang 1	JiaZi
	08/01	BingYin	Yang 2	WuZi		08/03	YiChou	Yang 1	BingZi
	09/01	DingMao	Yang 2	GengZi		09/03	BingYin	Yang 1	WuZi
	10/01	WuChen	Yang 2	RenZi		10/03	DingMao	Yang 1	GengZi
	11/01	JiSi	Yang 8	JiaZi		11/03	WuChen	Yang 1	RenZi
	12/01	GengWu	Yang 8	BingZi		12/03	JiSi	Yang 7	JiaZi
	13/01	XinWei	Yang 8	WuZi		13/03	GengWu	Yang 7	BingZi
	14/01	RenShen	Yang 8	GengZi		14/03	XinWei	Yang 7	WuZi
	15/01	GuiYou	Yang 8	RenZi		15/03	RenShen	Yang 7	GengZi
	16/01	JiaXu	Yang 5	JiaZi		16/03	GuiYou	Yang 7	RenZi
	17/01	YiHai	Yang 5	BingZi		17/03	JiaXu	Yang 4	JiaZi
	18/01	BingZi	Yang 5	WuZi		18/03	YiHai	Yang 4	BingZi
	19/01	DingChou	Yang 5	GengZi		19/03	BingZi	Yang 4	WuZi
大寒 (dà hán) - Extreme Cold 20/01 4:29 PM	20/01	WuYin	Yang 5/Yang 6	RenZi		20/03	DingChou	Yang 4	GengZi
	21/01	JiMao	Yang 3	JiaZi	春分 (chūn fēn) - Spring Equinox 21/03 5:24 AM	21/03	WuYin	Yang 4/Yang 6	RenZi
	22/01	GengChen	Yang 3	BingZi		22/03	JiMao	Yang 3	JiaZi
	23/01	XinSi	Yang 3	WuZi		23/03	GengChen	Yang 3	BingZi
	24/01	RenWu	Yang 3	GengZi		24/03	XinSi	Yang 3	WuZi
	25/01	GuiWei	Yang 3	RenZi		25/03	RenWu	Yang 3	GengZi
	26/01	JiaShen	Yang 9	JiaZi		26/03	GuiWei	Yang 3	RenZi
	27/01	YiYou	Yang 9	BingZi		27/03	JiaShen	Yang 9	JiaZi
	28/01	BingXu	Yang 9	WuZi		28/03	YiYou	Yang 9	BingZi
	29/01	DingHai	Yang 9	GengZi		29/03	BingXu	Yang 9	WuZi
	30/01	WuZi	Yang 9	RenZi		30/03	DingHai	Yang 9	GengZi
	31/01	JiChou	Yang 6	JiaZi		31/03	WuZi	Yang 9	RenZi
	01/02	GengYin	Yang 6	BingZi		01/04	JiChou	Yang 6	JiaZi
	02/02	XinMao	Yang 6	WuZi		02/04	GengYin	Yang 6	BingZi
	03/02	RenChen	Yang 6	GengZi		03/04	XinMao	Yang 6	WuZi
立春 (lì chūn) - Beginning of Spring 04/02 10:42 AM	04/02	GuiSi	Yang 6/Yang 2	RenZi		04/04	RenChen	Yang 6	GengZi
	05/02	JiaWu	Yang 8	JiaZi	清明 (qīng míng) - Pure Brightness 05/04 9:12 AM	05/04	GuiSi	Yang 6/Yang 7	RenZi
	06/02	YiWei	Yang 8	BingZi		06/04	JiaWu	Yang 4	JiaZi
	07/02	BingShen	Yang 8	WuZi		07/04	YiWei	Yang 4	BingZi
	08/02	DingYou	Yang 8	GengZi		08/04	BingShen	Yang 4	WuZi
	09/02	WuXu	Yang 8	RenZi		09/04	DingYou	Yang 4	GengZi
	10/02	JiHai	Yang 5	JiaZi		10/04	WuXu	Yang 4	RenZi
	11/02	GengZi	Yang 5	BingZi		11/04	JiHai	Yang 1	JiaZi
	12/02	XinChou	Yang 5	WuZi		12/04	GengZi	Yang 1	BingZi
	13/02	RenYin	Yang 5	GengZi		13/04	XinChou	Yang 1	WuZi
	14/02	GuiMao	Yang 5	RenZi		14/04	RenYin	Yang 1	GengZi
	15/02	JiaChen	Yang 2	JiaZi		15/04	GuiMao	Yang 1	RenZi
	16/02	YiSi	Yang 2	BingZi		16/04	JiaChen	Yang 7	JiaZi
	17/02	BingWu	Yang 2	WuZi		17/04	YiSi	Yang 7	BingZi
	18/02	DingWei	Yang 2	GengZi		18/04	BingWu	Yang 7	WuZi
						19/04	DingWei	Yang 7	GengZi

2023: GuiMao — Apr/May:BingChen, May/Jun:DingSi

Solar Term	Day	Jia Zi	Dun	Hour
谷雨 (gǔ yǔ) - Grain Rain — 20/04 4:13 PM	20/04	WuShen	Yang 7/Yang 8	RenZi
	21/04	JiYou	Yang 5	JiaZi
	22/04	GengXu	Yang 5	BingZi
	23/04	XinHai	Yang 5	WuZi
	24/04	RenZi	Yang 5	GengZi
	25/04	GuiChou	Yang 5	RenZi
	26/04	JiaYin	Yang 2	JiaZi
	27/04	YiMao	Yang 2	BingZi
	28/04	BingChen	Yang 2	WuZi
	29/04	DingSi	Yang 2	GengZi
	30/04	WuWu	Yang 2	RenZi
	01/05	JiWei	Yang 8	JiaZi
	02/05	GengShen	Yang 8	BingZi
	03/05	XinYou	Yang 8	WuZi
	04/05	RenXu	Yang 8	GengZi
	05/05	GuiHai	Yang 8	RenZi
立夏 (lì xià) - Beginning of Summer — 06/05 2:18 AM	06/05	JiaZi	Yang 5/Yang 4	JiaZi
	07/05	YiChou	Yang 4	BingZi
	08/05	BingYin	Yang 4	WuZi
	09/05	DingMao	Yang 4	GengZi
	10/05	WuChen	Yang 4	RenZi
	11/05	JiSi	Yang 1	JiaZi
	12/05	GengWu	Yang 1	BingZi
	13/05	XinWei	Yang 1	WuZi
	14/05	RenShen	Yang 1	GengZi
	15/05	GuiYou	Yang 1	RenZi
	16/05	JiaXu	Yang 7	JiaZi
	17/05	YiHai	Yang 7	BingZi
	18/05	BingZi	Yang 7	WuZi
	19/05	DingChou	Yang 7	GengZi
	20/05	WuYin	Yang 7	RenZi
小満 (xiǎo mǎn) - Small Grain — 21/05 3:08 PM	21/05	JiMao	Yang 4/Yang 5	JiaZi
	22/05	GengChen	Yang 5	BingZi
	23/05	XinSi	Yang 5	WuZi
	24/05	RenWu	Yang 5	GengZi
	25/05	GuiWei	Yang 5	RenZi
	26/05	JiaShen	Yang 2	JiaZi
	27/05	YiYou	Yang 2	BingZi
	28/05	BingXu	Yang 2	WuZi
	29/05	DingHai	Yang 2	GengZi
	30/05	WuZi	Yang 2	RenZi
	31/05	JiChou	Yang 8	JiaZi
	01/06	GengYin	Yang 8	BingZi
	02/06	XinMao	Yang 8	WuZi
	03/06	RenChen	Yang 8	GengZi
	04/06	GuiSi	Yang 8	RenZi
	05/06	JiaWu	Yang 5	JiaZi
芒種 (máng zhòng) - Summer Harvest — 06/06 6:18 AM	06/06	YiWei	Yang 5/Yang 6	BingZi
	07/06	BingShen	Yang 6	WuZi
	08/06	DingYou	Yang 6	GengZi
	09/06	WuXu	Yang 6	RenZi
	10/06	JiHai	Yang 3	JiaZi
	11/06	GengZi	Yang 3	BingZi
	12/06	XinChou	Yang 3	WuZi
	13/06	RenYin	Yang 3	GengZi
	14/06	GuiMao	Yang 3	RenZi
	15/06	JiaChen	Yang 9	JiaZi
	16/06	YiSi	Yang 9	BingZi
	17/06	BingWu	Yang 9	WuZi
	18/06	DingWei	Yang 9	GengZi
	19/06	WuShen	Yang 9	RenZi
	20/06	JiYou	Yang 6	JiaZi

2023: GuiMao — Jun/July:WuWu, Jul/Aug:JiWei

Solar Term	Day	Jia Zi	Dun	Hour
夏至 (xià zhì) - Summer Solstice — 21/06 10:57 PM	21/06	GengXu	Yang 6/Yin 9	BingZi
	22/06	XinHai	Yin 9	WuZi
	23/06	RenZi	Yin 9	GengZi
	24/06	GuiChou	Yin 9	RenZi
	25/06	JiaYin	Yin 3	JiaZi
	26/06	YiMao	Yin 3	BingZi
	27/06	BingChen	Yin 3	WuZi
	28/06	DingSi	Yin 3	GengZi
	29/06	WuWu	Yin 3	RenZi
	30/06	JiWei	Yin 6	JiaZi
	01/07	GengShen	Yin 6	BingZi
	02/07	XinYou	Yin 6	WuZi
	03/07	RenXu	Yin 6	GengZi
	04/07	GuiHai	Yin 6	RenZi
	05/07	JiaZi	Yin 9	JiaZi
	06/07	YiChou	Yin 9	BingZi
小暑 (xiǎo shǔ) - Mild Summer — 07/07 4:30 PM	07/07	BingYin	Yin 9/Yin 8	WuZi
	08/07	DingMao	Yin 8	GengZi
	09/07	WuChen	Yin 8	RenZi
	10/07	JiSi	Yin 2	JiaZi
	11/07	GengWu	Yin 2	BingZi
	12/07	XinWei	Yin 2	WuZi
	13/07	RenShen	Yin 2	GengZi
	14/07	GuiYou	Yin 2	RenZi
	15/07	JiaXu	Yin 5	JiaZi
	16/07	YiHai	Yin 5	BingZi
	17/07	BingZi	Yin 5	WuZi
	18/07	DingChou	Yin 5	GengZi
	19/07	WuYin	Yin 5	RenZi
	20/07	JiMao	Yin 8	JiaZi
	21/07	GengChen	Yin 8	BingZi
	22/07	XinSi	Yin 8	WuZi
大暑 (dà shǔ) - Extreme Summer — 23/07 9:50 AM	23/07	RenWu	Yin 8/Yin 7	GengZi
	24/07	GuiWei	Yin 7	RenZi
	25/07	JiaShen	Yin 1	JiaZi
	26/07	YiYou	Yin 1	BingZi
	27/07	BingXu	Yin 1	WuZi
	28/07	DingHai	Yin 1	GengZi
	29/07	WuZi	Yin 1	RenZi
	30/07	JiChou	Yin 4	JiaZi
	31/07	GengYin	Yin 4	BingZi
	01/08	XinMao	Yin 4	WuZi
	02/08	RenChen	Yin 4	GengZi
	03/08	GuiSi	Yin 4	RenZi
	04/08	JiaWu	Yin 7	JiaZi
	05/08	YiWei	Yin 7	BingZi
	06/08	BingShen	Yin 7	WuZi
	07/08	DingYou	Yin 7	GengZi
立秋 (lì qiū) - Beginning of Autumn — 08/08 2:22 AM	08/08	WuXu	Yin 7/Yin 2	RenZi
	09/08	JiHai	Yin 5	JiaZi
	10/08	GengZi	Yin 5	BingZi
	11/08	XinChou	Yin 5	WuZi
	12/08	RenYin	Yin 5	GengZi
	13/08	GuiMao	Yin 5	RenZi
	14/08	JiaChen	Yin 8	JiaZi
	15/08	YiSi	Yin 8	BingZi
	16/08	BingWu	Yin 8	WuZi
	17/08	DingWei	Yin 8	GengZi
	18/08	WuShen	Yin 8	RenZi
	19/08	JiYou	Yin 2	JiaZi
	20/08	GengXu	Yin 2	BingZi
	21/08	XinHai	Yin 2	WuZi
	22/08	RenZi	Yin 2	GengZi

2023: GuiMao — Aug/Sep:GengShen, Sep/Oct:XinYou

Solar Term	Day	Jia Zi	Dun	Hour
外署 (wài shǔ) - Outer Heat 23/08 5:01 PM	23/08	GuiChou	Yin 2/Yin 1	RenZi
	24/08	JiaYin	Yin 4	JiaZi
	25/08	YiMao	Yin 4	BingZi
	26/08	BingChen	Yin 4	WuZi
	27/08	DingSi	Yin 4	GengZi
	28/08	WuWu	Yin 4	RenZi
	29/08	JiWei	Yin 7	JiaZi
	30/08	GengShen	Yin 7	BingZi
	31/08	XinYou	Yin 7	WuZi
	01/09	RenXu	Yin 7	GengZi
	02/09	GuiHai	Yin 7	RenZi
	03/09	JiaZi	Yin 1	JiaZi
	04/09	YiChou	Yin 1	BingZi
	05/09	BingYin	Yin 1	WuZi
	06/09	DingMao	Yin 1	GengZi
	07/09	WuChen	Yin 1	RenZi
白露 (bái lù) - White Dew 08/09 5:26 AM	08/09	JiSi	Yin 4/Yin 3	JiaZi
	09/09	GengWu	Yin 3	BingZi
	10/09	XinWei	Yin 3	WuZi
	11/09	RenShen	Yin 3	GengZi
	12/09	GuiYou	Yin 3	RenZi
	13/09	JiaXu	Yin 6	JiaZi
	14/09	YiHai	Yin 6	BingZi
	15/09	BingZi	Yin 6	WuZi
	16/09	DingChou	Yin 6	GengZi
	17/09	WuYin	Yin 6	RenZi
	18/09	JiMao	Yin 9	JiaZi
	19/09	GengChen	Yin 9	BingZi
	20/09	XinSi	Yin 9	WuZi
	21/09	RenWu	Yin 9	GengZi
	22/09	GuiWei	Yin 9	RenZi
秋分 (qiū fēn) - Autumn Equinox 23/09 2:49 PM	23/09	JiaShen	Yin 3/Yin 1	JiaZi
	24/09	YiYou	Yin 1	BingZi
	25/09	BingXu	Yin 1	WuZi
	26/09	DingHai	Yin 1	GengZi
	27/09	WuZi	Yin 1	RenZi
	28/09	JiChou	Yin 4	JiaZi
	29/09	GengYin	Yin 4	BingZi
	30/09	XinMao	Yin 4	WuZi
	01/10	RenChen	Yin 4	GengZi
	02/10	GuiSi	Yin 4	RenZi
	03/10	JiaWu	Yin 7	JiaZi
	04/10	YiWei	Yin 7	BingZi
	05/10	BingShen	Yin 7	WuZi
	06/10	DingYou	Yin 7	GengZi
	07/10	WuXu	Yin 7	RenZi
寒露 (hán lù) - Cold Dew 08/10 9:15 PM	08/10	JiHai	Yin 1/Yin 9	JiaZi
	09/10	GengZi	Yin 9	BingZi
	10/10	XinChou	Yin 9	WuZi
	11/10	RenYin	Yin 9	GengZi
	12/10	GuiMao	Yin 9	RenZi
	13/10	JiaChen	Yin 3	JiaZi
	14/10	YiSi	Yin 3	BingZi
	15/10	BingWu	Yin 3	WuZi
	16/10	DingWei	Yin 3	GengZi
	17/10	WuShen	Yin 3	RenZi
	18/10	JiYou	Yin 6	JiaZi
	19/10	GengXu	Yin 6	BingZi
	20/10	XinHai	Yin 6	WuZi
	21/10	RenZi	Yin 6	GengZi
	22/10	GuiChou	Yin 6	RenZi
	23/10	JiaYin	Yin 9	JiaZi

2023: GuiMao — Oct/Nov:RenXu, Nov/Dec:GuiHai

Solar Term	Day	Jia Zi	Dun	Hour
霜降 (shuāng jiàng) - Frost 24/10 12:20 AM	24/10	YiMao	Yin 9/Yin 8	BingZi
	25/10	BingChen	Yin 8	WuZi
	26/10	DingSi	Yin 8	GengZi
	27/10	WuWu	Yin 8	RenZi
	28/10	JiWei	Yin 2	JiaZi
	29/10	GengShen	Yin 2	BingZi
	30/10	XinYou	Yin 2	WuZi
	31/10	RenXu	Yin 2	GengZi
	01/11	GuiHai	Yin 2	RenZi
	02/11	JiaZi	Yin 5	JiaZi
	03/11	YiChou	Yin 5	BingZi
	04/11	BingYin	Yin 5	WuZi
	05/11	DingMao	Yin 5	GengZi
	06/11	WuChen	Yin 5	RenZi
	07/11	JiSi	Yin 8	JiaZi
立冬 (lì dōng) - Beginning of Winter 08/11 12:35 AM	08/11	GengWu	Yin 8/Yin 9	BingZi
	09/11	XinWei	Yin 9	WuZi
	10/11	RenShen	Yin 9	GengZi
	11/11	GuiYou	Yin 9	RenZi
	12/11	JiaXu	Yin 3	JiaZi
	13/11	YiHai	Yin 3	BingZi
	14/11	BingZi	Yin 3	WuZi
	15/11	DingChou	Yin 3	GengZi
	16/11	WuYin	Yin 3	RenZi
	17/11	JiMao	Yin 6	JiaZi
	18/11	GengChen	Yin 6	BingZi
	19/11	XinSi	Yin 6	WuZi
	20/11	RenWu	Yin 6	GengZi
	21/11	GuiWei	Yin 6	RenZi
小雪 (xiǎo xuě) - Mild Snow 22/11 10:02 PM	22/11	JiaShen	Yin 9/Yin 8	JiaZi
	23/11	YiYou	Yin 8	BingZi
	24/11	BingXu	Yin 8	WuZi
	25/11	DingHai	Yin 8	GengZi
	26/11	WuZi	Yin 8	RenZi
	27/11	JiChou	Yin 2	JiaZi
	28/11	GengYin	Yin 2	BingZi
	29/11	XinMao	Yin 2	WuZi
	30/11	RenChen	Yin 2	GengZi
	01/12	GuiSi	Yin 2	RenZi
	02/12	JiaWu	Yin 5	JiaZi
	03/12	YiWei	Yin 5	BingZi
	04/12	BingShen	Yin 5	WuZi
	05/12	DingYou	Yin 5	GengZi
	06/12	WuXu	Yin 5	RenZi
大雪 (dà xuě) - Extreme Snow 07/12 5:32 PM	07/12	JiHai	Yin 8/Yin 7	JiaZi
	08/12	GengZi	Yin 7	BingZi
	09/12	XinChou	Yin 7	WuZi
	10/12	RenYin	Yin 7	GengZi
	11/12	GuiMao	Yin 7	RenZi
	12/12	JiaChen	Yin 1	JiaZi
	13/12	YiSi	Yin 1	BingZi
	14/12	BingWu	Yin 1	WuZi
	15/12	DingWei	Yin 1	GengZi
	16/12	WuShen	Yin 1	RenZi
	17/12	JiYou	Yin 4	JiaZi
	18/12	GengXu	Yin 4	BingZi
	19/12	XinHai	Yin 4	WuZi
	20/12	RenZi	Yin 4	GengZi
	21/12	GuiChou	Yin 4	RenZi

2023: GuiMao,2024: JiaChen

2023: GuiMao,2024: JiaChen — Dec23/Jan24:JiaZi, Jan/Feb:YiChou

Solar terms (left block):
- 冬至 (dōng zhì) - Winter Solstice 22/12 11:27 AM
- 小寒 (xiǎo hán) - Mild Cold 06/01 4:49 AM
- 大寒 (dà hán) - Extreme Cold 20/01 10:07 PM
- 立春 (lì chūn) - Beginning of Spring 04/02 4:26 PM

Day	Jia Zi	Dun	Hour
22/12	JiaYin	Yin 7/Yang 7	JiaZi
23/12	YiMao	Yang 7	BingZi
24/12	BingChen	Yang 7	WuZi
25/12	DingSi	Yang 7	GengZi
26/12	WuWu	Yang 7	RenZi
27/12	JiWei	Yang 4	JiaZi
28/12	GengShen	Yang 4	BingZi
29/12	XinYou	Yang 4	WuZi
30/12	RenXu	Yang 4	GengZi
31/12	GuiHai	Yang 4	RenZi
01/01	JiaZi	Yang 1	JiaZi
02/01	YiChou	Yang 1	BingZi
03/01	BingYin	Yang 1	WuZi
04/01	DingMao	Yang 1	GengZi
05/01	WuChen	Yang 1	RenZi
06/01	JiSi	Yang 7/Yang 8	JiaZi
07/01	GengWu	Yang 8	BingZi
08/01	XinWei	Yang 8	WuZi
09/01	RenShen	Yang 8	GengZi
10/01	GuiYou	Yang 8	RenZi
11/01	JiaXu	Yang 5	JiaZi
12/01	YiHai	Yang 5	BingZi
13/01	BingZi	Yang 5	WuZi
14/01	DingChou	Yang 5	GengZi
15/01	WuYin	Yang 5	RenZi
16/01	JiMao	Yang 2	JiaZi
17/01	GengChen	Yang 2	BingZi
18/01	XinSi	Yang 2	WuZi
19/01	RenWu	Yang 2	GengZi
20/01	GuiWei	Yang 2/Yang 3	RenZi
21/01	JiaShen	Yang 9	JiaZi
22/01	YiYou	Yang 9	BingZi
23/01	BingXu	Yang 9	WuZi
24/01	DingHai	Yang 9	GengZi
25/01	WuZi	Yang 9	RenZi
26/01	JiChou	Yang 6	JiaZi
27/01	GengYin	Yang 6	BingZi
28/01	XinMao	Yang 6	WuZi
29/01	RenChen	Yang 6	GengZi
30/01	GuiSi	Yang 6	RenZi
31/01	JiaWu	Yang 3	JiaZi
01/02	YiWei	Yang 3	BingZi
02/02	BingShen	Yang 3	WuZi
03/02	DingYou	Yang 3	GengZi
04/02	WuXu	Yang 3/Yang 8	RenZi
05/02	JiHai	Yang 5	JiaZi
06/02	GengZi	Yang 5	BingZi
07/02	XinChou	Yang 5	WuZi
08/02	RenYin	Yang 5	GengZi
09/02	GuiMao	Yang 5	RenZi
10/02	JiaChen	Yang 2	JiaZi
11/02	YiSi	Yang 2	BingZi
12/02	BingWu	Yang 2	WuZi
13/02	DingWei	Yang 2	GengZi
14/02	WuShen	Yang 2	RenZi
15/02	JiYou	Yang 8	JiaZi
16/02	GengXu	Yang 8	BingZi
17/02	XinHai	Yang 8	WuZi
18/02	RenZi	Yang 8	GengZi

2024: JiaChen — Feb/Mar:BingYin, Mar/Apr:DingMao

Solar terms (right block):
- 雨水 (yǔ shuǐ) - Rain Water 19/02 12:12 PM
- 惊蛰 (jīng zhé) - Insect Awakening 05/03 10:22 AM
- 春分 (chūn fēn) - Spring Equinox 20/03 11:06 AM
- 清明 (qīng míng) - Pure Brightness 04/04 3:02 PM

Day	Jia Zi	Dun	Hour
19/02	GuiChou	Yang 8/Yang 9	RenZi
20/02	JiaYin	Yang 6	JiaZi
21/02	YiMao	Yang 6	BingZi
22/02	BingChen	Yang 6	WuZi
23/02	DingSi	Yang 6	GengZi
24/02	WuWu	Yang 6	RenZi
25/02	JiWei	Yang 3	JiaZi
26/02	GengShen	Yang 3	BingZi
27/02	XinYou	Yang 3	WuZi
28/02	RenXu	Yang 3	GengZi
29/02	GuiHai	Yang 3	RenZi
01/03	JiaZi	Yang 9	JiaZi
02/03	YiChou	Yang 9	BingZi
03/03	BingYin	Yang 9	WuZi
04/03	DingMao	Yang 9	GengZi
05/03	WuChen	Yang 9/Yang 1	RenZi
06/03	JiSi	Yang 7	JiaZi
07/03	GengWu	Yang 7	BingZi
08/03	XinWei	Yang 7	WuZi
09/03	RenShen	Yang 7	GengZi
10/03	GuiYou	Yang 7	RenZi
11/03	JiaXu	Yang 4	JiaZi
12/03	YiHai	Yang 4	BingZi
13/03	BingZi	Yang 4	WuZi
14/03	DingChou	Yang 4	GengZi
15/03	WuYin	Yang 4	RenZi
16/03	JiMao	Yang 1	JiaZi
17/03	GengChen	Yang 1	BingZi
18/03	XinSi	Yang 1	WuZi
19/03	RenWu	Yang 1	GengZi
20/03	GuiWei	Yang 1/Yang 3	RenZi
21/03	JiaShen	Yang 9	JiaZi
22/03	YiYou	Yang 9	BingZi
23/03	BingXu	Yang 9	WuZi
24/03	DingHai	Yang 9	GengZi
25/03	WuZi	Yang 9	RenZi
26/03	JiChou	Yang 6	JiaZi
27/03	GengYin	Yang 6	BingZi
28/03	XinMao	Yang 6	WuZi
29/03	RenChen	Yang 6	GengZi
30/03	GuiSi	Yang 6	RenZi
31/03	JiaWu	Yang 3	JiaZi
01/04	YiWei	Yang 3	BingZi
02/04	BingShen	Yang 3	WuZi
03/04	DingYou	Yang 3	GengZi
04/04	WuXu	Yang 3/Yang 4	RenZi
05/04	JiHai	Yang 1	JiaZi
06/04	GengZi	Yang 1	BingZi
07/04	XinChou	Yang 1	WuZi
08/04	RenYin	Yang 1	GengZi
09/04	GuiMao	Yang 1	RenZi
10/04	JiaChen	Yang 7	JiaZi
11/04	YiSi	Yang 7	BingZi
12/04	BingWu	Yang 7	WuZi
13/04	DingWei	Yang 7	GengZi
14/04	WuShen	Yang 7	RenZi
15/04	JiYou	Yang 4	JiaZi
16/04	GengXu	Yang 4	BingZi
17/04	XinHai	Yang 4	WuZi
18/04	RenZi	Yang 4	GengZi

Solar Term	Day	Jia Zi	Dun	Hour
2024: JiaChen — Apr/May: WuChen, May/Jun: JiSi				
谷雨 (gǔ yǔ) - Grain Rain 19/04 9:59 PM	19/04	GuiChou	Yang 4/Yang 5	RenZi
	20/04	JiaYin	Yang 2	JiaZi
	21/04	YiMao	Yang 2	BingZi
	22/04	BingChen	Yang 2	WuZi
	23/04	DingSi	Yang 2	GengZi
	24/04	WuWu	Yang 2	RenZi
	25/04	JiWei	Yang 8	JiaZi
	26/04	GengShen	Yang 8	BingZi
	27/04	XinYou	Yang 8	WuZi
	28/04	RenXu	Yang 8	GengZi
	29/04	GuiHai	Yang 8	RenZi
	30/04	JiaZi	Yang 5	JiaZi
	01/05	YiChou	Yang 5	BingZi
	02/05	BingYin	Yang 5	WuZi
	03/05	DingMao	Yang 5	GengZi
	04/05	WuChen	Yang 5	RenZi
立夏 (lì xià) - Beginning of Summer 05/05 8:09 AM	05/05	JiSi	Yang 2/Yang 1	JiaZi
	06/05	GengWu	Yang 1	BingZi
	07/05	XinWei	Yang 1	WuZi
	08/05	RenShen	Yang 1	GengZi
	09/05	GuiYou	Yang 1	RenZi
	10/05	JiaXu	Yang 7	JiaZi
	11/05	YiHai	Yang 7	BingZi
	12/05	BingZi	Yang 7	WuZi
	13/05	DingChou	Yang 7	GengZi
	14/05	WuYin	Yang 7	RenZi
	15/05	JiMao	Yang 4	JiaZi
	16/05	GengChen	Yang 4	BingZi
	17/05	XinSi	Yang 4	WuZi
	18/05	RenWu	Yang 4	GengZi
	19/05	GuiWei	Yang 4	RenZi
小满 (xiǎo mǎn) - Small Grain 20/05 8:59 PM	20/05	JiaShen	Yang 1/Yang 2	JiaZi
	21/05	YiYou	Yang 2	BingZi
	22/05	BingXu	Yang 2	WuZi
	23/05	DingHai	Yang 2	GengZi
	24/05	WuZi	Yang 2	RenZi
	25/05	JiChou	Yang 8	JiaZi
	26/05	GengYin	Yang 8	BingZi
	27/05	XinMao	Yang 8	WuZi
	28/05	RenChen	Yang 8	GengZi
	29/05	GuiSi	Yang 8	RenZi
	30/05	JiaWu	Yang 5	JiaZi
	31/05	YiWei	Yang 5	BingZi
	01/06	BingShen	Yang 5	WuZi
	02/06	DingYou	Yang 5	GengZi
	03/06	WuXu	Yang 5	RenZi
	04/06	JiHai	Yang 2	JiaZi
芒种 (máng zhòng) - Summer Harvest 05/06 12:09 PM	05/06	GengZi	Yang 2/Yang 3	BingZi
	06/06	XinChou	Yang 3	WuZi
	07/06	RenYin	Yang 3	GengZi
	08/06	GuiMao	Yang 3	RenZi
	09/06	JiaChen	Yang 9	JiaZi
	10/06	YiSi	Yang 9	BingZi
	11/06	BingWu	Yang 9	WuZi
	12/06	DingWei	Yang 9	GengZi
	13/06	WuShen	Yang 9	RenZi
	14/06	JiYou	Yang 6	JiaZi
	15/06	GengXu	Yang 6	BingZi
	16/06	XinHai	Yang 6	WuZi
	17/06	RenZi	Yang 6	GengZi
	18/06	GuiChou	Yang 6	RenZi
	19/06	JiaYin	Yang 3	JiaZi
	20/06	YiMao	Yang 3	BingZi

Solar Term	Day	Jia Zi	Dun	Hour
2024: JiaChen — Jun/July: GengWu, Jul/Aug: XinWei				
夏至 (xià zhì) - Summer Solstice 21/06 4:50 AM	21/06	BingChen	Yang 3/Yin 3	WuZi
	22/06	DingSi	Yin 3	GengZi
	23/06	WuWu	Yin 3	RenZi
	24/06	JiWei	Yin 6	JiaZi
	25/06	GengShen	Yin 6	BingZi
	26/06	XinYou	Yin 6	WuZi
	27/06	RenXu	Yin 6	GengZi
	28/06	GuiHai	Yin 6	RenZi
	29/06	JiaZi	Yin 9	JiaZi
	30/06	YiChou	Yin 9	BingZi
	01/07	BingYin	Yin 9	WuZi
	02/07	DingMao	Yin 9	GengZi
	03/07	WuChen	Yin 9	RenZi
	04/07	JiSi	Yin 3	JiaZi
	05/07	GengWu	Yin 3	BingZi
小暑 (xiǎo shǔ) - Mild Summer 06/07 10:19 PM	06/07	XinWei	Yin 3/Yin 2	WuZi
	07/07	RenShen	Yin 2	GengZi
	08/07	GuiYou	Yin 2	RenZi
	09/07	JiaXu	Yin 5	JiaZi
	10/07	YiHai	Yin 5	BingZi
	11/07	BingZi	Yin 5	WuZi
	12/07	DingChou	Yin 5	GengZi
	13/07	WuYin	Yin 5	RenZi
	14/07	JiMao	Yin 8	JiaZi
	15/07	GengChen	Yin 8	BingZi
	16/07	XinSi	Yin 8	WuZi
	17/07	RenWu	Yin 8	GengZi
	18/07	GuiWei	Yin 8	RenZi
	19/07	JiaShen	Yin 2	JiaZi
	20/07	YiYou	Yin 2	BingZi
	21/07	BingXu	Yin 2	WuZi
大暑 (dà shǔ) - Extreme Summer 22/07 3:44 PM	22/07	DingHai	Yin 2/Yin 1	GengZi
	23/07	WuZi	Yin 1	RenZi
	24/07	JiChou	Yin 4	JiaZi
	25/07	GengYin	Yin 4	BingZi
	26/07	XinMao	Yin 4	WuZi
	27/07	RenChen	Yin 4	GengZi
	28/07	GuiSi	Yin 4	RenZi
	29/07	JiaWu	Yin 7	JiaZi
	30/07	YiWei	Yin 7	BingZi
	31/07	BingShen	Yin 7	WuZi
	01/08	DingYou	Yin 7	GengZi
	02/08	WuXu	Yin 7	RenZi
	03/08	JiHai	Yin 1	JiaZi
	04/08	GengZi	Yin 1	BingZi
	05/08	XinChou	Yin 1	WuZi
	06/08	RenYin	Yin 1	GengZi
立秋 (lì qiū) - Beginning of Autumn 07/08 8:09 AM	07/08	GuiMao	Yin 1/Yin 5	RenZi
	08/08	JiaChen	Yin 8	JiaZi
	09/08	YiSi	Yin 8	BingZi
	10/08	BingWu	Yin 8	WuZi
	11/08	DingWei	Yin 8	GengZi
	12/08	WuShen	Yin 8	RenZi
	13/08	JiYou	Yin 2	JiaZi
	14/08	GengXu	Yin 2	BingZi
	15/08	XinHai	Yin 2	WuZi
	16/08	RenZi	Yin 2	GengZi
	17/08	GuiChou	Yin 2	RenZi
	18/08	JiaYin	Yin 5	JiaZi
	19/08	YiMao	Yin 5	BingZi
	20/08	BingChen	Yin 5	WuZi
	21/08	DingSi	Yin 5	GengZi

2024: JiaChen — Aug/Sep:RenShen, Sep/Oct:GuiYou

Solar Term	Day	Jia Zi	Dun	Hour
外暑 (wài shǔ) - Outer Heat 22/08 10:54 PM	22/08	WuWu	Yin 5/Yin 4	RenZi
	23/08	JiWei	Yin 7	JiaZi
	24/08	GengShen	Yin 7	BingZi
	25/08	XinYou	Yin 7	WuZi
	26/08	RenXu	Yin 7	GengZi
	27/08	GuiHai	Yin 7	RenZi
	28/08	JiaZi	Yin 1	JiaZi
	29/08	YiChou	Yin 1	BingZi
	30/08	BingYin	Yin 1	WuZi
	31/08	DingMao	Yin 1	GengZi
	01/09	WuChen	Yin 1	RenZi
	02/09	JiSi	Yin 4	JiaZi
	03/09	GengWu	Yin 4	BingZi
	04/09	XinWei	Yin 4	WuZi
	05/09	RenShen	Yin 4	GengZi
	06/09	GuiYou	Yin 4	RenZi
白露 (bái lù) - White Dew 07/09 11:11 AM	07/09	JiaXu	Yin 7/Yin 6	JiaZi
	08/09	YiHai	Yin 6	BingZi
	09/09	BingZi	Yin 6	WuZi
	10/09	DingChou	Yin 6	GengZi
	11/09	WuYin	Yin 6	RenZi
	12/09	JiMao	Yin 9	JiaZi
	13/09	GengChen	Yin 9	BingZi
	14/09	XinSi	Yin 9	WuZi
	15/09	RenWu	Yin 9	GengZi
	16/09	GuiWei	Yin 9	RenZi
	17/09	JiaShen	Yin 3	JiaZi
	18/09	YiYou	Yin 3	BingZi
	19/09	BingXu	Yin 3	WuZi
	20/09	DingHai	Yin 3	GengZi
	21/09	WuZi	Yin 3	RenZi
秋分 (qiū fēn) - Autumn Equinox 22/09 8:43 PM	22/09	JiChou	Yin 6/Yin 4	JiaZi
	23/09	GengYin	Yin 4	BingZi
	24/09	XinMao	Yin 4	WuZi
	25/09	RenChen	Yin 4	GengZi
	26/09	GuiSi	Yin 4	RenZi
	27/09	JiaWu	Yin 7	JiaZi
	28/09	YiWei	Yin 7	BingZi
	29/09	BingShen	Yin 7	WuZi
	30/09	DingYou	Yin 7	GengZi
	01/10	WuXu	Yin 7	RenZi
	02/10	JiHai	Yin 1	JiaZi
	03/10	GengZi	Yin 1	BingZi
	04/10	XinChou	Yin 1	WuZi
	05/10	RenYin	Yin 1	GengZi
	06/10	GuiMao	Yin 1	RenZi
	07/10	JiaChen	Yin 4	JiaZi
寒露 (hán lù) - Cold Dew 08/10 2:59 AM	08/10	YiSi	Yin 4/Yin 3	BingZi
	09/10	BingWu	Yin 3	WuZi
	10/10	DingWei	Yin 3	GengZi
	11/10	WuShen	Yin 3	RenZi
	12/10	JiYou	Yin 6	JiaZi
	13/10	GengXu	Yin 6	BingZi
	14/10	XinHai	Yin 6	WuZi
	15/10	RenZi	Yin 6	GengZi
	16/10	GuiChou	Yin 6	RenZi
	17/10	JiaYin	Yin 9	JiaZi
	18/10	YiMao	Yin 9	BingZi
	19/10	BingChen	Yin 9	WuZi
	20/10	DingSi	Yin 9	GengZi
	21/10	WuWu	Yin 9	RenZi
	22/10	JiWei	Yin 3	JiaZi

2024: JiaChen — Oct/Nov:JiaXu, Nov/Dec:YiHai

Solar Term	Day	Jia Zi	Dun	Hour
霜降 (shuāng jiàng) - Frost 23/10 6:14 AM	23/10	GengShen	Yin 3/Yin 2	BingZi
	24/10	XinYou	Yin 2	WuZi
	25/10	RenXu	Yin 2	GengZi
	26/10	GuiHai	Yin 2	RenZi
	27/10	JiaZi	Yin 5	JiaZi
	28/10	YiChou	Yin 5	BingZi
	29/10	BingYin	Yin 5	WuZi
	30/10	DingMao	Yin 5	GengZi
	31/10	WuChen	Yin 5	RenZi
	01/11	JiSi	Yin 8	JiaZi
	02/11	GengWu	Yin 8	BingZi
	03/11	XinWei	Yin 8	WuZi
	04/11	RenShen	Yin 8	GengZi
	05/11	GuiYou	Yin 8	RenZi
	06/11	JiaXu	Yin 2	JiaZi
立冬 (lì dōng) - Beginning of Winter 07/11 6:19 AM	07/11	YiHai	Yin 2/Yin 3	BingZi
	08/11	BingZi	Yin 3	WuZi
	09/11	DingChou	Yin 3	GengZi
	10/11	WuYin	Yin 3	RenZi
	11/11	JiMao	Yin 6	JiaZi
	12/11	GengChen	Yin 6	BingZi
	13/11	XinSi	Yin 6	WuZi
	14/11	RenWu	Yin 6	GengZi
	15/11	GuiWei	Yin 6	RenZi
	16/11	JiaShen	Yin 9	JiaZi
	17/11	YiYou	Yin 9	BingZi
	18/11	BingXu	Yin 9	WuZi
	19/11	DingHai	Yin 9	GengZi
	20/11	WuZi	Yin 9	RenZi
	21/11	JiChou	Yin 3	JiaZi
小雪 (xiǎo xuě) - Mild Snow 22/11 3:56 AM	22/11	GengYin	Yin 3/Yin 2	BingZi
	23/11	XinMao	Yin 2	WuZi
	24/11	RenChen	Yin 2	GengZi
	25/11	GuiSi	Yin 2	RenZi
	26/11	JiaWu	Yin 5	JiaZi
	27/11	YiWei	Yin 5	BingZi
	28/11	BingShen	Yin 5	WuZi
	29/11	DingYou	Yin 5	GengZi
	30/11	WuXu	Yin 5	RenZi
	01/12	JiHai	Yin 8	JiaZi
	02/12	GengZi	Yin 8	BingZi
	03/12	XinChou	Yin 8	WuZi
	04/12	RenYin	Yin 8	GengZi
	05/12	GuiMao	Yin 8	RenZi
大雪 (dà xuě) - Extreme Snow 06/12 11:16 PM	06/12	JiaChen	Yin 2/Yin 1	JiaZi
	07/12	YiSi	Yin 1	BingZi
	08/12	BingWu	Yin 1	WuZi
	09/12	DingWei	Yin 1	GengZi
	10/12	WuShen	Yin 1	RenZi
	11/12	JiYou	Yin 4	JiaZi
	12/12	GengXu	Yin 4	BingZi
	13/12	XinHai	Yin 4	WuZi
	14/12	RenZi	Yin 4	GengZi
	15/12	GuiChou	Yin 4	RenZi
	16/12	JiaYin	Yin 7	JiaZi
	17/12	YiMao	Yin 7	BingZi
	18/12	BingChen	Yin 7	WuZi
	19/12	DingSi	Yin 7	GengZi
	20/12	WuWu	Yin 7	RenZi

2024: JiaChen,2025: YiSi

2024: JiaChen,2025: YiSi — Dec24/Jan25:BingZi, Jan/Feb:DingChou

Solar Term	Day	Jia Zi	Dun	Hour
冬至 (dōng zhì) - Winter Solstice 21/12 5:20 PM	21/12	JiWei	Yin 1/Yang 4	JiaZi
	22/12	GengShen	Yang 4	BingZi
	23/12	XinYou	Yang 4	WuZi
	24/12	RenXu	Yang 4	GengZi
	25/12	GuiHai	Yang 4	RenZi
	26/12	JiaZi	Yang 1	JiaZi
	27/12	YiChou	Yang 1	BingZi
	28/12	BingYin	Yang 1	WuZi
	29/12	DingMao	Yang 1	GengZi
	30/12	WuChen	Yang 1	RenZi
	31/12	JiSi	Yang 7	JiaZi
	01/01	GengWu	Yang 7	BingZi
	02/01	XinWei	Yang 7	WuZi
	03/01	RenShen	Yang 7	GengZi
	04/01	GuiYou	Yang 7	RenZi
小寒 (xiǎo hán) - Mild Cold 05/01 10:32 AM	05/01	JiaXu	Yang 4/Yang 5	JiaZi
	06/01	YiHai	Yang 5	BingZi
	07/01	BingZi	Yang 5	WuZi
	08/01	DingChou	Yang 5	GengZi
	09/01	WuYin	Yang 5	RenZi
	10/01	JiMao	Yang 2	JiaZi
	11/01	GengChen	Yang 2	BingZi
	12/01	XinSi	Yang 2	WuZi
	13/01	RenWu	Yang 2	GengZi
	14/01	GuiWei	Yang 2	RenZi
	15/01	JiaShen	Yang 8	JiaZi
	16/01	YiYou	Yang 8	BingZi
	17/01	BingXu	Yang 8	WuZi
	18/01	DingHai	Yang 8	GengZi
	19/01	WuZi	Yang 8	RenZi
大寒 (dà hán) - Extreme Cold 20/01 3:59 AM	20/01	JiChou	Yang 5/Yang 6	JiaZi
	21/01	GengYin	Yang 6	BingZi
	22/01	XinMao	Yang 6	WuZi
	23/01	RenChen	Yang 6	GengZi
	24/01	GuiSi	Yang 6	RenZi
	25/01	JiaWu	Yang 3	JiaZi
	26/01	YiWei	Yang 3	BingZi
	27/01	BingShen	Yang 3	WuZi
	28/01	DingYou	Yang 3	GengZi
	29/01	WuXu	Yang 3	RenZi
	30/01	JiHai	Yang 9	JiaZi
	31/01	GengZi	Yang 9	BingZi
	01/02	XinChou	Yang 9	WuZi
	02/02	RenYin	Yang 9	GengZi
立春 (lì chūn) - Beginning of Spring 03/02 10:10 PM	03/02	GuiMao	Yang 9/Yang 5	RenZi
	04/02	JiaChen	Yang 2	JiaZi
	05/02	YiSi	Yang 2	BingZi
	06/02	BingWu	Yang 2	WuZi
	07/02	DingWei	Yang 2	GengZi
	08/02	WuShen	Yang 2	RenZi
	09/02	JiYou	Yang 8	JiaZi
	10/02	GengXu	Yang 8	BingZi
	11/02	XinHai	Yang 8	WuZi
	12/02	RenZi	Yang 8	GengZi
	13/02	GuiChou	Yang 8	RenZi
	14/02	JiaYin	Yang 5	JiaZi
	15/02	YiMao	Yang 5	BingZi
	16/02	BingChen	Yang 5	WuZi
	17/02	DingSi	Yang 5	GengZi

2025: YiSi — Feb/Mar:WuYin, Mar/Apr:JiMao

Solar Term	Day	Jia Zi	Dun	Hour
雨水 (yǔ shuǐ) - Rain Water 18/02 6:06 PM	18/02	WuWu	Yang 5/Yang 6	RenZi
	19/02	JiWei	Yang 3	JiaZi
	20/02	GengShen	Yang 3	BingZi
	21/02	XinYou	Yang 3	WuZi
	22/02	RenXu	Yang 3	GengZi
	23/02	GuiHai	Yang 3	RenZi
	24/02	JiaZi	Yang 9	JiaZi
	25/02	YiChou	Yang 9	BingZi
	26/02	BingYin	Yang 9	WuZi
	27/02	DingMao	Yang 9	GengZi
	28/02	WuChen	Yang 9	RenZi
	01/03	JiSi	Yang 6	JiaZi
	02/03	GengWu	Yang 6	BingZi
	03/03	XinWei	Yang 6	WuZi
	04/03	RenShen	Yang 6	GengZi
惊蛰 (jīng zhé) - Insect Awakening 05/03 4:07 PM	05/03	GuiYou	Yang 6/Yang 7	RenZi
	06/03	JiaXu	Yang 4	JiaZi
	07/03	YiHai	Yang 4	BingZi
	08/03	BingZi	Yang 4	WuZi
	09/03	DingChou	Yang 4	GengZi
	10/03	WuYin	Yang 4	RenZi
	11/03	JiMao	Yang 1	JiaZi
	12/03	GengChen	Yang 1	BingZi
	13/03	XinSi	Yang 1	WuZi
	14/03	RenWu	Yang 1	GengZi
	15/03	GuiWei	Yang 1	RenZi
	16/03	JiaShen	Yang 7	JiaZi
	17/03	YiYou	Yang 7	BingZi
	18/03	BingXu	Yang 7	WuZi
	19/03	DingHai	Yang 7	GengZi
春分 (chūn fēn) - Spring Equinox 20/03 5:01 PM	20/03	WuZi	Yang 7/Yang 9	RenZi
	21/03	JiChou	Yang 6	JiaZi
	22/03	GengYin	Yang 6	BingZi
	23/03	XinMao	Yang 6	WuZi
	24/03	RenChen	Yang 6	GengZi
	25/03	GuiSi	Yang 6	RenZi
	26/03	JiaWu	Yang 3	JiaZi
	27/03	YiWei	Yang 3	BingZi
	28/03	BingShen	Yang 3	WuZi
	29/03	DingYou	Yang 3	GengZi
	30/03	WuXu	Yang 3	RenZi
	31/03	JiHai	Yang 9	JiaZi
	01/04	GengZi	Yang 9	BingZi
	02/04	XinChou	Yang 9	WuZi
	03/04	RenYin	Yang 9	GengZi
清明 (qīng míng) - Pure Brightness 04/04 8:48 PM	04/04	GuiMao	Yang 9/Yang 1	RenZi
	05/04	JiaChen	Yang 7	JiaZi
	06/04	YiSi	Yang 7	BingZi
	07/04	BingWu	Yang 7	WuZi
	08/04	DingWei	Yang 7	GengZi
	09/04	WuShen	Yang 7	RenZi
	10/04	JiYou	Yang 4	JiaZi
	11/04	GengXu	Yang 4	BingZi
	12/04	XinHai	Yang 4	WuZi
	13/04	RenZi	Yang 4	GengZi
	14/04	GuiChou	Yang 4	RenZi
	15/04	JiaYin	Yang 1	JiaZi
	16/04	YiMao	Yang 1	BingZi
	17/04	BingChen	Yang 1	WuZi
	18/04	DingSi	Yang 1	GengZi
	19/04	WuWu	Yang 1	RenZi

2025: YiSi — Apr/May:GengChen, May/Jun:XinSi

Solar Term	Day	Jia Zi	Dun	Hour
谷雨 (gǔ yǔ) - Grain Rain 20/04 3:55 AM	20/04	JiWei	Yang 7/Yang 8	JiaZi
	21/04	GengShen	Yang 8	BingZi
	22/04	XinYou	Yang 8	WuZi
	23/04	RenXu	Yang 8	GengZi
	24/04	GuiHai	Yang 8	RenZi
	25/04	JiaZi	Yang 5	JiaZi
	26/04	YiChou	Yang 5	BingZi
	27/04	BingYin	Yang 5	WuZi
	28/04	DingMao	Yang 5	GengZi
	29/04	WuChen	Yang 5	RenZi
	30/04	JiSi	Yang 2	JiaZi
	01/05	GengWu	Yang 2	BingZi
	02/05	XinWei	Yang 2	WuZi
	03/05	RenShen	Yang 2	GengZi
	04/05	GuiYou	Yang 2	RenZi
立夏 (lì xià) - Beginning of Summer 05/05 1:56 PM	05/05	JiaXu	Yang 8/Yang 7	JiaZi
	06/05	YiHai	Yang 7	BingZi
	07/05	BingZi	Yang 7	WuZi
	08/05	DingChou	Yang 7	GengZi
	09/05	WuYin	Yang 7	RenZi
	10/05	JiMao	Yang 4	JiaZi
	11/05	GengChen	Yang 4	BingZi
	12/05	XinSi	Yang 4	WuZi
	13/05	RenWu	Yang 4	GengZi
	14/05	GuiWei	Yang 4	RenZi
	15/05	JiaShen	Yang 1	JiaZi
	16/05	YiYou	Yang 1	BingZi
	17/05	BingXu	Yang 1	WuZi
	18/05	DingHai	Yang 1	GengZi
	19/05	WuZi	Yang 1	RenZi
	20/05	JiChou	Yang 7	JiaZi
小满 (xiǎo mǎn) - Small Grain 21/05 2:54 AM	21/05	GengYin	Yang 7/Yang 8	BingZi
	22/05	XinMao	Yang 8	WuZi
	23/05	RenChen	Yang 8	GengZi
	24/05	GuiSi	Yang 8	RenZi
	25/05	JiaWu	Yang 5	JiaZi
	26/05	YiWei	Yang 5	BingZi
	27/05	BingShen	Yang 5	WuZi
	28/05	DingYou	Yang 5	GengZi
	29/05	WuXu	Yang 5	RenZi
	30/05	JiHai	Yang 2	JiaZi
	31/05	GengZi	Yang 2	BingZi
	01/06	XinChou	Yang 2	WuZi
	02/06	RenYin	Yang 2	GengZi
	03/06	GuiMao	Yang 2	RenZi
	04/06	JiaChen	Yang 8	JiaZi
芒种 (máng zhòng) - Summer Harvest 05/06 5:56 PM	05/06	YiSi	Yang 8/Yang 9	BingZi
	06/06	BingWu	Yang 9	WuZi
	07/06	DingWei	Yang 9	GengZi
	08/06	WuShen	Yang 9	RenZi
	09/06	JiYou	Yang 6	JiaZi
	10/06	GengXu	Yang 6	BingZi
	11/06	XinHai	Yang 6	WuZi
	12/06	RenZi	Yang 6	GengZi
	13/06	GuiChou	Yang 6	RenZi
	14/06	JiaYin	Yang 3	JiaZi
	15/06	YiMao	Yang 3	BingZi
	16/06	BingChen	Yang 3	WuZi
	17/06	DingSi	Yang 3	GengZi
	18/06	WuWu	Yang 3	RenZi
	19/06	JiWei	Yang 9	JiaZi
	20/06	GengShen	Yang 9	BingZi

2025: YiSi — Jun/July:RenWu, Jul/Aug:GuiWei

Solar Term	Day	Jia Zi	Dun	Hour
夏至 (xià zhi) - Summer Solstice 21/06 10:42 AM	21/06	XinYou	Yang 9/Yin 6	WuZi
	22/06	RenXu	Yin 6	GengZi
	23/06	GuiHai	Yin 6	RenZi
	24/06	JiaZi	Yin 9	JiaZi
	25/06	YiChou	Yin 9	BingZi
	26/06	BingYin	Yin 9	WuZi
	27/06	DingMao	Yin 9	GengZi
	28/06	WuChen	Yin 9	RenZi
	29/06	JiSi	Yin 3	JiaZi
	30/06	GengWu	Yin 3	BingZi
	01/07	XinWei	Yin 3	WuZi
	02/07	RenShen	Yin 3	GengZi
	03/07	GuiYou	Yin 3	RenZi
	04/07	JiaXu	Yin 6	JiaZi
	05/07	YiHai	Yin 6	BingZi
	06/07	BingZi	Yin 6	WuZi
小暑 (xiǎo shǔ) - Mild Summer 07/07 4:04 AM	07/07	DingChou	Yin 6/Yin 5	GengZi
	08/07	WuYin	Yin 5	RenZi
	09/07	JiMao	Yin 8	JiaZi
	10/07	GengChen	Yin 8	BingZi
	11/07	XinSi	Yin 8	WuZi
	12/07	RenWu	Yin 8	GengZi
	13/07	GuiWei	Yin 8	RenZi
	14/07	JiaShen	Yin 2	JiaZi
	15/07	YiYou	Yin 2	BingZi
	16/07	BingXu	Yin 2	WuZi
	17/07	DingHai	Yin 2	GengZi
	18/07	WuZi	Yin 2	RenZi
	19/07	JiChou	Yin 5	JiaZi
	20/07	GengYin	Yin 5	BingZi
	21/07	XinMao	Yin 5	WuZi
大暑 (dà shǔ) - Extreme Summer 22/07 9:29 PM	22/07	RenChen	Yin 5/Yin 4	GengZi
	23/07	GuiSi	Yin 4	RenZi
	24/07	JiaWu	Yin 7	JiaZi
	25/07	YiWei	Yin 7	BingZi
	26/07	BingShen	Yin 7	WuZi
	27/07	DingYou	Yin 7	GengZi
	28/07	WuXu	Yin 7	RenZi
	29/07	JiHai	Yin 1	JiaZi
	30/07	GengZi	Yin 1	BingZi
	31/07	XinChou	Yin 1	WuZi
	01/08	RenYin	Yin 1	GengZi
	02/08	GuiMao	Yin 1	RenZi
	03/08	JiaChen	Yin 4	JiaZi
	04/08	YiSi	Yin 4	BingZi
	05/08	BingWu	Yin 4	WuZi
	06/08	DingWei	Yin 4	GengZi
立秋 (lì qiū) - Beginning of Autumn 07/08 1:51 PM	07/08	WuShen	Yin 4/Yin 8	RenZi
	08/08	JiYou	Yin 2	JiaZi
	09/08	GengXu	Yin 2	BingZi
	10/08	XinHai	Yin 2	WuZi
	11/08	RenZi	Yin 2	GengZi
	12/08	GuiChou	Yin 2	RenZi
	13/08	JiaYin	Yin 5	JiaZi
	14/08	YiMao	Yin 5	BingZi
	15/08	BingChen	Yin 5	WuZi
	16/08	DingSi	Yin 5	GengZi
	17/08	WuWu	Yin 5	RenZi
	18/08	JiWei	Yin 8	JiaZi
	19/08	GengShen	Yin 8	BingZi
	20/08	XinYou	Yin 8	WuZi
	21/08	RenXu	Yin 8	GengZi
	22/08	GuiHai	Yin 8	RenZi

	2025: YiSi Aug/Sep:JiaShen, Sep/Oct:YiYou				2025: YiSi Oct/Nov:BingXu, Nov/Dec:DingHai			
	Day	Jia Zi	Dun	Hour		Day	Jia Zi	Dun	Hour
外暑 (wài shǔ) - Outer Heat 23/08 4:33 AM	23/08	JiaZi	Yin 2/Yin 1	JiaZi	霜降 (shuāng jiàng) - Frost 23/10 11:50 AM	23/10	YiChou	Yin 6/Yin 5	BingZi
	24/08	YiChou	Yin 1	BingZi		24/10	BingYin	Yin 5	WuZi
	25/08	BingYin	Yin 1	WuZi		25/10	DingMao	Yin 5	GengZ
	26/08	DingMao	Yin 1	GengZ		26/10	WuChen	Yin 5	RenZi
	27/08	WuChen	Yin 1	RenZi		27/10	JiSi	Yin 8	JiaZi
	28/08	JiSi	Yin 4	JiaZi		28/10	GengWu	Yin 8	BingZi
	29/08	GengWu	Yin 4	BingZi		29/10	XinWei	Yin 8	WuZi
	30/08	XinWei	Yin 4	WuZi		30/10	RenShen	Yin 8	GengZ
	31/08	RenShen	Yin 4	GengZ		31/10	GuiYou	Yin 8	RenZi
	01/09	GuiYou	Yin 4	RenZi		01/11	JiaXu	Yin 2	JiaZi
	02/09	JiaXu	Yin 7	JiaZi		02/11	YiHai	Yin 2	BingZi
	03/09	YiHai	Yin 7	BingZi		03/11	BingZi	Yin 2	WuZi
	04/09	BingZi	Yin 7	WuZi		04/11	DingChou	Yin 2	GengZ
	05/09	DingChou	Yin 7	GengZ		05/11	WuYin	Yin 2	RenZi
	06/09	WuYin	Yin 7	RenZi		06/11	JiMao	Yin 5	JiaZi
白露 (bái lù) - White Dew 07/09 4:51 PM	07/09	JiMao	Yin 1/Yin 9	JiaZi	立冬 (lì dōng) - Beginning of Winter 07/11 12:03 PM	07/11	GengChen	Yin 5/Yin 6	BingZi
	08/09	GengChen	Yin 9	BingZi		08/11	XinSi	Yin 6	WuZi
	09/09	XinSi	Yin 9	WuZi		09/11	RenWu	Yin 6	GengZ
	10/09	RenWu	Yin 9	GengZ		10/11	GuiWei	Yin 6	RenZi
	11/09	GuiWei	Yin 9	RenZi		11/11	JiaShen	Yin 9	JiaZi
	12/09	JiaShen	Yin 3	JiaZi		12/11	YiYou	Yin 9	BingZi
	13/09	YiYou	Yin 3	BingZi		13/11	BingXu	Yin 9	WuZi
	14/09	BingXu	Yin 3	WuZi		14/11	DingHai	Yin 9	GengZ
	15/09	DingHai	Yin 3	GengZ		15/11	WuZi	Yin 9	RenZi
	16/09	WuZi	Yin 3	RenZi		16/11	JiChou	Yin 3	JiaZi
	17/09	JiChou	Yin 6	JiaZi		17/11	GengYin	Yin 3	BingZi
	18/09	GengYin	Yin 6	BingZi		18/11	XinMao	Yin 3	WuZi
	19/09	XinMao	Yin 6	WuZi		19/11	RenChen	Yin 3	GengZ
	20/09	RenChen	Yin 6	GengZ		20/11	GuiSi	Yin 3	RenZi
	21/09	GuiSi	Yin 6	RenZi		21/11	JiaWu	Yin 6	JiaZi
	22/09	JiaWu	Yin 9	JiaZi		22/11	YiWei	Yin 6/Yin 5	BingZi
秋分 (qiū fēn) - Autumn Equinox 23/09 2:19 AM	23/09	YiWei	Yin 9/Yin 7	BingZi	小雪 (xiǎo xuě) - Mild Snow 22/11 9:35 AM	23/11	BingShen	Yin 5	WuZi
	24/09	BingShen	Yin 7	WuZi		24/11	DingYou	Yin 5	GengZ
	25/09	DingYou	Yin 7	GengZ		25/11	WuXu	Yin 5	RenZi
	26/09	WuXu	Yin 7	RenZi		26/11	JiHai	Yin 8	JiaZi
	27/09	JiHai	Yin 1	JiaZi		27/11	GengZi	Yin 8	BingZi
	28/09	GengZi	Yin 1	BingZi		28/11	XinChou	Yin 8	WuZi
	29/09	XinChou	Yin 1	WuZi		29/11	RenYin	Yin 8	GengZ
	30/09	RenYin	Yin 1	GengZ		30/11	GuiMao	Yin 8	RenZi
	01/10	GuiMao	Yin 1	RenZi		01/12	JiaChen	Yin 2	JiaZi
	02/10	JiaChen	Yin 4	JiaZi		02/12	YiSi	Yin 2	BingZi
	03/10	YiSi	Yin 4	BingZi		03/12	BingWu	Yin 2	WuZi
	04/10	BingWu	Yin 4	WuZi		04/12	DingWei	Yin 2	GengZ
	05/10	DingWei	Yin 4	GengZ		05/12	WuShen	Yin 2	RenZi
	06/10	WuShen	Yin 4	RenZi		06/12	JiYou	Yin 5	JiaZi
寒露 (hán lù) - Cold Dew 08/10 8:40 AM	07/10	JiYou	Yin 7	JiaZi	大雪 (dà xuě) - Extreme Snow 07/12 5:04 AM	07/12	GengXu	Yin 5/Yin 4	BingZi
	08/10	GengXu	Yin 7/Yin 6	BingZi		08/12	XinHai	Yin 4	WuZi
	09/10	XinHai	Yin 6	WuZi		09/12	RenZi	Yin 4	GengZ
	10/10	RenZi	Yin 6	GengZ		10/12	GuiChou	Yin 4	RenZi
	11/10	GuiChou	Yin 6	RenZi		11/12	JiaYin	Yin 7	JiaZi
	12/10	JiaYin	Yin 9	JiaZi		12/12	YiMao	Yin 7	BingZi
	13/10	YiMao	Yin 9	BingZi		13/12	BingChen	Yin 7	WuZi
	14/10	BingChen	Yin 9	WuZi		14/12	DingSi	Yin 7	GengZ
	15/10	DingSi	Yin 9	GengZ		15/12	WuWu	Yin 7	RenZi
	16/10	WuWu	Yin 9	RenZi		16/12	JiWei	Yin 1	JiaZi
	17/10	JiWei	Yin 3	JiaZi		17/12	GengShen	Yin 1	BingZi
	18/10	GengShen	Yin 3	BingZi		18/12	XinYou	Yin 1	WuZi
	19/10	XinYou	Yin 3	WuZi		19/12	RenXu	Yin 1	GengZ
	20/10	RenXu	Yin 3	GengZ		20/12	GuiHai	Yin 1	RenZi
	21/10	GuiHai	Yin 3	RenZi					
	22/10	JiaZi	Yin 6	JiaZi					

2025: YiSi, 2026: BingWu

		2025: YiSi, 2026: BingWu Dec25/Jan26: WuZi, Jan/Feb: JiChou				2026: BingWu Feb/Mar: GengYin, Mar/Apr: XinMao		
	Day	Jia Zi	Dun	Hour	Day	Jia Zi	Dun	Hour
冬至 (dōng zhì) - Winter Solstice 21/12 11:02 PM	21/12	JiaZi	Yin 4/Yang 1	JiaZi	18/02	GuiHai	Yang 2/Yang 3	RenZi
	22/12	YiChou	Yang 1	BingZi	19/02	JiaZi	Yang 9	JiaZi
	23/12	BingYin	Yang 1	WuZi	20/02	YiChou	Yang 9	BingZi
	24/12	DingMao	Yang 1	GengZi	21/02	BingYin	Yang 9	WuZi
	25/12	WuChen	Yang 1	RenZi	22/02	DingMao	Yang 9	GengZi
	26/12	JiSi	Yang 7	JiaZi	23/02	WuChen	Yang 9	RenZi
	27/12	GengWu	Yang 7	BingZi	24/02	JiSi	Yang 6	JiaZi
	28/12	XinWei	Yang 7	WuZi	25/02	GengWu	Yang 6	BingZi
	29/12	RenShen	Yang 7	GengZi	26/02	XinWei	Yang 6	WuZi
	30/12	GuiYou	Yang 7	RenZi	27/02	RenShen	Yang 6	GengZi
	31/12	JiaXu	Yang 4	JiaZi	28/02	GuiYou	Yang 6	RenZi
	01/01	YiHai	Yang 4	BingZi	01/03	JiaXu	Yang 3	JiaZi
	02/01	BingZi	Yang 4	WuZi	02/03	YiHai	Yang 3	BingZi
	03/01	DingChou	Yang 4	GengZi	03/03	BingZi	Yang 3	WuZi
	04/01	WuYin	Yang 4	RenZi	04/03	DingChou	Yang 3	GengZi
小寒 (xiǎo hán) - Mild Cold 05/01 4:22 PM	05/01	JiMao	Yang 1/Yang 2	JiaZi	05/03	WuYin	Yang 3/Yang 4	RenZi
	06/01	GengChen	Yang 2	BingZi	06/03	JiMao	Yang 1	JiaZi
	07/01	XinSi	Yang 2	WuZi	07/03	GengChen	Yang 1	BingZi
	08/01	RenWu	Yang 2	GengZi	08/03	XinSi	Yang 1	WuZi
	09/01	GuiWei	Yang 2	RenZi	09/03	RenWu	Yang 1	GengZi
	10/01	JiaShen	Yang 8	JiaZi	10/03	GuiWei	Yang 1	RenZi
	11/01	YiYou	Yang 8	BingZi	11/03	JiaShen	Yang 7	JiaZi
	12/01	BingXu	Yang 8	WuZi	12/03	YiYou	Yang 7	BingZi
	13/01	DingHai	Yang 8	GengZi	13/03	BingXu	Yang 7	WuZi
	14/01	WuZi	Yang 8	RenZi	14/03	DingHai	Yang 7	GengZi
	15/01	JiChou	Yang 5	JiaZi	15/03	WuZi	Yang 7	RenZi
	16/01	GengYin	Yang 5	BingZi	16/03	JiChou	Yang 4	JiaZi
	17/01	XinMao	Yang 5	WuZi	17/03	GengYin	Yang 4	BingZi
	18/01	RenChen	Yang 5	GengZi	18/03	XinMao	Yang 4	WuZi
	19/01	GuiSi	Yang 5	RenZi	19/03	RenChen	Yang 4	GengZi
大寒 (dà hán) - Extreme Cold 20/01 9:44 AM	20/01	JiaWu	Yang 2/Yang 3	JiaZi	20/03	GuiSi	Yang 4/Yang 6	RenZi
	21/01	YiWei	Yang 3	BingZi	21/03	JiaWu	Yang 3	JiaZi
	22/01	BingShen	Yang 3	WuZi	22/03	YiWei	Yang 3	BingZi
	23/01	DingYou	Yang 3	GengZi	23/03	BingShen	Yang 3	WuZi
	24/01	WuXu	Yang 3	RenZi	24/03	DingYou	Yang 3	GengZi
	25/01	JiHai	Yang 9	JiaZi	25/03	WuXu	Yang 3	RenZi
	26/01	GengZi	Yang 9	BingZi	26/03	JiHai	Yang 9	JiaZi
	27/01	XinChou	Yang 9	WuZi	27/03	GengZi	Yang 9	BingZi
	28/01	RenYin	Yang 9	GengZi	28/03	XinChou	Yang 9	WuZi
	29/01	GuiMao	Yang 9	RenZi	29/03	RenYin	Yang 9	GengZi
	30/01	JiaChen	Yang 6	JiaZi	30/03	GuiMao	Yang 9	RenZi
	31/01	YiSi	Yang 6	BingZi	31/03	JiaChen	Yang 6	JiaZi
	01/02	BingWu	Yang 6	WuZi	01/04	YiSi	Yang 6	BingZi
	02/02	DingWei	Yang 6	GengZi	02/04	BingWu	Yang 6	WuZi
	03/02	WuShen	Yang 6	RenZi	03/04	DingWei	Yang 6	GengZi
立春 (lì chūn) - Beginning of Spring 04/02 4:01 AM	04/02	JiYou	Yang 3/Yang 8	JiaZi	04/04	WuShen	Yang 6	RenZi
	05/02	GengXu	Yang 8	BingZi	05/04	JiYou	Yang 3/Yang 4	JiaZi
	06/02	XinHai	Yang 8	WuZi	06/04	GengXu	Yang 4	BingZi
	07/02	RenZi	Yang 8	GengZi	07/04	XinHai	Yang 4	WuZi
	08/02	GuiChou	Yang 8	RenZi	08/04	RenZi	Yang 4	GengZi
	09/02	JiaYin	Yang 5	JiaZi	09/04	GuiChou	Yang 4	RenZi
	10/02	YiMao	Yang 5	BingZi	10/04	JiaYin	Yang 1	JiaZi
	11/02	BingChen	Yang 5	WuZi	11/04	YiMao	Yang 1	BingZi
	12/02	DingSi	Yang 5	GengZi	12/04	BingChen	Yang 1	WuZi
	13/02	WuWu	Yang 5	RenZi	13/04	DingSi	Yang 1	GengZi
	14/02	JiWei	Yang 2	JiaZi	14/04	WuWu	Yang 1	RenZi
	15/02	GengShen	Yang 2	BingZi	15/04	JiWei	Yang 7	JiaZi
	16/02	XinYou	Yang 2	WuZi	16/04	GengShen	Yang 7	BingZi
	17/02	RenXu	Yang 2	GengZi	17/04	XinYou	Yang 7	WuZi
					18/04	RenXu	Yang 7	GengZi
					19/04	GuiHai	Yang 7	RenZi

The vertical solar-term labels in the right-hand column group read:
- 雨水 (yǔ shuǐ) - Rain Water, 18/02 11:51 PM
- 惊蛰 (jīng zhé) - Insect Awakening, 05/03 9:58 PM
- 春分 (chūn fēn) - Spring Equinox, 20/03 10:45 PM
- 清明 (qīng míng) - Pure Brightness, 05/04 2:39 AM

2026: BingWu — Apr/May:RenChen, May/Jun:GuiSi

Solar Term	Day	Jia Zi	Dun	Hour
谷雨 (gǔ yǔ) - Grain Rain 20/04 9:38 AM	20/04	JiaZi	Yang 4/Yang 5	JiaZi
	21/04	YiChou	Yang 5	BingZi
	22/04	BingYin	Yang 5	WuZi
	23/04	DingMao	Yang 5	GengZi
	24/04	WuChen	Yang 5	RenZi
	25/04	JiSi	Yang 2	JiaZi
	26/04	GengWu	Yang 2	BingZi
	27/04	XinWei	Yang 2	WuZi
	28/04	RenShen	Yang 2	GengZi
	29/04	GuiYou	Yang 2	RenZi
	30/04	JiaXu	Yang 8	JiaZi
	01/05	YiHai	Yang 8	BingZi
	02/05	BingZi	Yang 8	WuZi
	03/05	DingChou	Yang 8	GengZi
	04/05	WuYin	Yang 8	RenZi
立夏 (lì xià) - Beginning of Summer 05/05 7:48 PM	05/05	JiMao	Yang 5/Yang 4	JiaZi
	06/05	GengChe	Yang 4	BingZi
	07/05	XinSi	Yang 4	WuZi
	08/05	RenWu	Yang 4	GengZi
	09/05	GuiWei	Yang 4	RenZi
	10/05	JiaShen	Yang 1	JiaZi
	11/05	YiYou	Yang 1	BingZi
	12/05	BingXu	Yang 1	WuZi
	13/05	DingHai	Yang 1	GengZi
	14/05	WuZi	Yang 1	RenZi
	15/05	JiChou	Yang 7	JiaZi
	16/05	GengYin	Yang 7	BingZi
	17/05	XinMao	Yang 7	WuZi
	18/05	RenChen	Yang 7	GengZi
	19/05	GuiSi	Yang 7	RenZi
	20/05	JiaWu	Yang 4	JiaZi
小滿 (xiǎo mǎn) - Small Grain 21/05 8:36 AM	21/05	YiWei	Yang 4/Yang 5	BingZi
	22/05	BingShen	Yang 5	WuZi
	23/05	DingYou	Yang 5	GengZi
	24/05	WuXu	Yang 5	RenZi
	25/05	JiHai	Yang 2	JiaZi
	26/05	GengZi	Yang 2	BingZi
	27/05	XinChou	Yang 2	WuZi
	28/05	RenYin	Yang 2	GengZi
	29/05	GuiMao	Yang 2	RenZi
	30/05	JiaChen	Yang 8	JiaZi
	31/05	YiSi	Yang 8	BingZi
	01/06	BingWu	Yang 8	WuZi
	02/06	DingWei	Yang 8	GengZi
	03/06	WuShen	Yang 8	RenZi
	04/06	JiYou	Yang 5	JiaZi
芒種 (máng zhòng) - Summer Harvest 05/06 11:48 PM	05/06	GengXu	Yang 5/Yang 6	BingZi
	06/06	XinHai	Yang 6	WuZi
	07/06	RenZi	Yang 6	GengZi
	08/06	GuiChou	Yang 6	RenZi
	09/06	JiaYin	Yang 3	JiaZi
	10/06	YiMao	Yang 3	BingZi
	11/06	BingChen	Yang 3	WuZi
	12/06	DingSi	Yang 3	GengZi
	13/06	WuWu	Yang 3	RenZi
	14/06	JiWei	Yang 9	JiaZi
	15/06	GengShen	Yang 9	BingZi
	16/06	XinYou	Yang 9	WuZi
	17/06	RenXu	Yang 9	GengZi
	18/06	GuiHai	Yang 9	RenZi
	19/06	JiaZi	Yang 6	JiaZi
	20/06	YiChou	Yang 6	BingZi

2026: BingWu — Jun/July:JiaWu, Jul/Aug:YiWei

Solar Term	Day	Jia Zi	Dun	Hour
夏至 (xià zhì) - Summer Solstice 21/06 4:24 PM	21/06	BingYin	Yang 6/Yin 9	WuZi
	22/06	DingMao	Yin 9	GengZi
	23/06	WuChen	Yin 9	RenZi
	24/06	JiSi	Yin 3	JiaZi
	25/06	GengWu	Yin 3	BingZi
	26/06	XinWei	Yin 3	WuZi
	27/06	RenShen	Yin 3	GengZi
	28/06	GuiYou	Yin 3	RenZi
	29/06	JiaXu	Yin 6	JiaZi
	30/06	YiHai	Yin 6	BingZi
	01/07	BingZi	Yin 6	WuZi
	02/07	DingChou	Yin 6	GengZi
	03/07	WuYin	Yin 6	RenZi
	04/07	JiMao	Yin 9	JiaZi
	05/07	GengChe	Yin 9	BingZi
	06/07	XinSi	Yin 9	WuZi
小暑 (xiǎo shǔ) - Mild Summer 07/07 9:56 AM	07/07	RenWu	Yin 9/Yin 8	GengZi
	08/07	GuiWei	Yin 8	RenZi
	09/07	JiaShen	Yin 2	JiaZi
	10/07	YiYou	Yin 2	BingZi
	11/07	BingXu	Yin 2	WuZi
	12/07	DingHai	Yin 2	GengZi
	13/07	WuZi	Yin 2	RenZi
	14/07	JiChou	Yin 5	JiaZi
	15/07	GengYin	Yin 5	BingZi
	16/07	XinMao	Yin 5	WuZi
	17/07	RenChen	Yin 5	GengZi
	18/07	GuiSi	Yin 5	RenZi
	19/07	JiaWu	Yin 8	JiaZi
	20/07	YiWei	Yin 8	BingZi
	21/07	BingShen	Yin 8	WuZi
	22/07	DingYou	Yin 8	GengZi
大暑 (dà shǔ) - Extreme Summer 23/07 3:12 AM	23/07	WuXu	Yin 8/Yin 7	RenZi
	24/07	JiHai	Yin 1	JiaZi
	25/07	GengZi	Yin 1	BingZi
	26/07	XinChou	Yin 1	WuZi
	27/07	RenYin	Yin 1	GengZi
	28/07	GuiMao	Yin 1	RenZi
	29/07	JiaChen	Yin 4	JiaZi
	30/07	YiSi	Yin 4	BingZi
	31/07	BingWu	Yin 4	WuZi
	01/08	DingWei	Yin 4	GengZi
	02/08	WuShen	Yin 4	RenZi
	03/08	JiYou	Yin 7	JiaZi
	04/08	GengXu	Yin 7	BingZi
	05/08	XinHai	Yin 7	WuZi
	06/08	RenZi	Yin 7	GengZi
立秋 (lì qiū) - Beginning of Autumn 07/08 7:42 PM	07/08	GuiChou	Yin 7/Yin 2	RenZi
	08/08	JiaYin	Yin 5	JiaZi
	09/08	YiMao	Yin 5	BingZi
	10/08	BingChen	Yin 5	WuZi
	11/08	DingSi	Yin 5	GengZi
	12/08	WuWu	Yin 5	RenZi
	13/08	JiWei	Yin 8	JiaZi
	14/08	GengShen	Yin 8	BingZi
	15/08	XinYou	Yin 8	WuZi
	16/08	RenXu	Yin 8	GengZi
	17/08	GuiHai	Yin 8	RenZi
	18/08	JiaZi	Yin 2	JiaZi
	19/08	YiChou	Yin 2	BingZi
	20/08	BingYin	Yin 2	WuZi
	21/08	DingMao	Yin 2	GengZi
	22/08	WuChen	Yin 2	RenZi

		2026: BingWu Aug/Sep:BingShen, Sep/Oct:DingYou					2026: BingWu Oct/Nov:WuXu, Nov/Dec:JiHai		
	Day	Jia Zi	Dun	Hour		Day	Jia Zi	Dun	Hour
外暑 (wài shǔ) - Outer Heat 23/08 10:18 AM	23/0	JiSi	Yin 5/Yin 4	JiaZi	霜降 (shuāng jiàng) - Frost 23/10 5:37 PM	23/10	GengWu	Yin 9/Yin 8	BingZi
	24/0	GengWu	Yin 4	BingZi		24/10	XinWei	Yin 8	WuZi
	25/0	XinWei	Yin 4	WuZi		25/10	RenShen	Yin 8	GengZi
	26/0	RenShen	Yin 4	GengZi		26/10	GuiYou	Yin 8	RenZi
	27/0	GuiYou	Yin 4	RenZi		27/10	JiaXu	Yin 2	JiaZi
	28/0	JiaXu	Yin 7	JiaZi		28/10	YiHai	Yin 2	BingZi
	29/0	YiHai	Yin 7	BingZi		29/10	BingZi	Yin 2	WuZi
	30/0	BingZi	Yin 7	WuZi		30/10	DingChou	Yin 2	GengZi
	31/0	DingChou	Yin 7	GengZi		31/10	WuYin	Yin 2	RenZi
	01/0	WuYin	Yin 7	RenZi		01/11	JiMao	Yin 5	JiaZi
	02/0	JiMao	Yin 1	JiaZi		02/11	GengChen	Yin 5	BingZi
	03/0	GengChen	Yin 1	BingZi		03/11	XinSi	Yin 5	WuZi
	04/0	XinSi	Yin 1	WuZi		04/11	RenWu	Yin 5	GengZi
	05/0	RenWu	Yin 1	GengZi		05/11	GuiWei	Yin 5	RenZi
	06/0	GuiWei	Yin 1	RenZi		06/11	JiaShen	Yin 8	JiaZi
白露 (bái lù) - White Dew 07/09 10:40 PM	07/0	JiaShen	Yin 4/Yin 3	JiaZi	立冬 (lì dōng) - Beginning of Winter 07/11 5:51 PM	07/11	YiYou	Yin 8/Yin 9	BingZi
	08/0	YiYou	Yin 3	BingZi		08/11	BingXu	Yin 9	WuZi
	09/0	BingXu	Yin 3	WuZi		09/11	DingHai	Yin 9	GengZi
	10/0	DingHai	Yin 3	GengZi		10/11	WuZi	Yin 9	RenZi
	11/0	WuZi	Yin 3	RenZi		11/11	JiChou	Yin 3	JiaZi
	12/0	JiChou	Yin 6	JiaZi		12/11	GengYin	Yin 3	BingZi
	13/0	GengYin	Yin 6	BingZi		13/11	XinMao	Yin 3	WuZi
	14/0	XinMao	Yin 6	WuZi		14/11	RenChen	Yin 3	GengZi
	15/0	RenChen	Yin 6	GengZi		15/11	GuiSi	Yin 3	RenZi
	16/0	GuiSi	Yin 6	RenZi		16/11	JiaWu	Yin 6	JiaZi
	17/0	JiaWu	Yin 9	JiaZi		17/11	YiWei	Yin 6	BingZi
	18/0	YiWei	Yin 9	BingZi		18/11	BingShen	Yin 6	WuZi
	19/0	BingShen	Yin 9	WuZi		19/11	DingYou	Yin 6	GengZi
	20/0	DingYou	Yin 9	GengZi		20/11	WuXu	Yin 6	RenZi
	21/0	WuXu	Yin 9	RenZi		21/11	JiHai	Yin 9	JiaZi
	22/0	JiHai	Yin 3	JiaZi		22/11	GengZi	Yin 9/Yin 8	BingZi
秋分 (qiū fēn) - Autumn Equinox 23/09 8:04 AM	23/0	GengZi	Yin 3/Yin 1	BingZi	小雪 (xiǎo xuě) - Mild Snow 22/11 3:23 PM	23/11	XinChou	Yin 8	WuZi
	24/0	XinChou	Yin 1	WuZi		24/11	RenYin	Yin 8	GengZi
	25/0	RenYin	Yin 1	GengZi		25/11	GuiMao	Yin 8	RenZi
	26/0	GuiMao	Yin 1	RenZi		26/11	JiaChen	Yin 2	JiaZi
	27/0	JiaChen	Yin 4	JiaZi		27/11	YiSi	Yin 2	BingZi
	28/0	YiSi	Yin 4	BingZi		28/11	BingWu	Yin 2	WuZi
	29/0	BingWu	Yin 4	WuZi		29/11	DingWei	Yin 2	GengZi
	30/0	DingWei	Yin 4	GengZi		30/11	WuShen	Yin 2	RenZi
	01/1	WuShen	Yin 4	RenZi		01/12	JiYou	Yin 5	JiaZi
	02/1	JiYou	Yin 7	JiaZi		02/12	GengXu	Yin 5	BingZi
	03/1	GengXu	Yin 7	BingZi		03/12	XinHai	Yin 5	WuZi
	04/1	XinHai	Yin 7	WuZi		04/12	RenZi	Yin 5	GengZi
	05/1	RenZi	Yin 7	GengZi		05/12	GuiChou	Yin 5	RenZi
	06/1	GuiChou	Yin 7	RenZi		06/12	JiaYin	Yin 8	JiaZi
	07/1	JiaYin	Yin 1	JiaZi		07/12	YiMao	Yin 8/Yin 7	BingZi
寒露 (hán lù) - Cold Dew 08/10 2:28 PM	08/1	YiMao	Yin 1/Yin 9	BingZi	大雪 (dà xuě) - Extreme Snow 07/12 10:52 AM	08/12	BingChen	Yin 7	WuZi
	09/1	BingChen	Yin 9	WuZi		09/12	DingSi	Yin 7	GengZi
	10/1	DingSi	Yin 9	GengZi		10/12	WuWu	Yin 7	RenZi
	11/1	WuWu	Yin 9	RenZi		11/12	JiWei	Yin 1	JiaZi
	12/1	JiWei	Yin 3	JiaZi		12/12	GengShen	Yin 1	BingZi
	13/1	GengShen	Yin 3	BingZi		13/12	XinYou	Yin 1	WuZi
	14/1	XinYou	Yin 3	WuZi		14/12	RenXu	Yin 1	GengZi
	15/1	RenXu	Yin 3	GengZi		15/12	GuiHai	Yin 1	RenZi
	16/1	GuiHai	Yin 3	RenZi		16/12	JiaZi	Yin 4	JiaZi
	17/1	JiaZi	Yin 6	JiaZi		17/12	YiChou	Yin 4	BingZi
	18/1	YiChou	Yin 6	BingZi		18/12	BingYin	Yin 4	WuZi
	19/1	BingYin	Yin 6	WuZi		19/12	DingMao	Yin 4	GengZi
	20/1	DingMao	Yin 6	GengZi		20/12	WuChen	Yin 4	RenZi
	21/1	WuChen	Yin 6	RenZi		21/12	JiSi	Yin 7	JiaZi
	22/1	JiSi	Yin 9	JiaZi					

2026: BingWu, 2027: DingWei

	2026: BingWu, 2027: DingWei Dec26/Jan27:GengZi, Jan/Feb:XinChou					2027: DingWei Feb/Mar:RenYin, Mar/Apr:GuiMao			
Term	Day	Jia Zi	Dun	Hour	Term	Day	Jia Zi	Dun	Hour
冬至 (dōng zhì) - Winter Solstice 22/12 4:49 AM	22/12	GengWu	Yin 7/Yang 7	BingZi	雨水 (yǔ shuǐ) - Rain Water 19/02 5:33 AM	19/02	JiSi	Yang 5/Yang 6	JiaZi
	23/12	XinWei	Yang 7	WuZi		20/02	GengWu	Yang 6	BingZi
	24/12	RenShen	Yang 7	GengZi		21/02	XinWei	Yang 6	WuZi
	25/12	GuiYou	Yang 7	RenZi		22/02	RenShen	Yang 6	GengZi
	26/12	JiaXu	Yang 4	JiaZi		23/02	GuiYou	Yang 6	RenZi
	27/12	YiHai	Yang 4	BingZi		24/02	JiaXu	Yang 3	JiaZi
	28/12	BingZi	Yang 4	WuZi		25/02	YiHai	Yang 3	BingZi
	29/12	DingChou	Yang 4	GengZi		26/02	BingZi	Yang 3	WuZi
	30/12	WuYin	Yang 4	RenZi		27/02	DingChou	Yang 3	GengZi
	31/12	JiMao	Yang 1	JiaZi		28/02	WuYin	Yang 3	RenZi
	01/01	GengChen	Yang 1	BingZi		01/03	JiMao	Yang 9	JiaZi
	02/01	XinSi	Yang 1	WuZi		02/03	GengChen	Yang 9	BingZi
	03/01	RenWu	Yang 1	GengZi		03/03	XinSi	Yang 9	WuZi
	04/01	GuiWei	Yang 1	RenZi		04/03	RenWu	Yang 9	GengZi
小寒 (xiǎo hán) - Mild Cold 05/01 10:09 PM	05/01	JiaShen	Yang 7/Yang 8	JiaZi		05/03	GuiWei	Yang 9	RenZi
	06/01	YiYou	Yang 8	BingZi	惊蛰 (jīng zhé) - Insect Awakening 06/03 3:39 AM	06/03	JiaShen	Yang 6/Yang 7	JiaZi
	07/01	BingXu	Yang 8	WuZi		07/03	YiYou	Yang 7	BingZi
	08/01	DingHai	Yang 8	GengZi		08/03	BingXu	Yang 7	WuZi
	09/01	WuZi	Yang 8	RenZi		09/03	DingHai	Yang 7	GengZi
	10/01	JiChou	Yang 5	JiaZi		10/03	WuZi	Yang 7	RenZi
	11/01	GengYin	Yang 5	BingZi		11/03	JiChou	Yang 4	JiaZi
	12/01	XinMao	Yang 5	WuZi		12/03	GengYin	Yang 4	BingZi
	13/01	RenChen	Yang 5	GengZi		13/03	XinMao	Yang 4	WuZi
	14/01	GuiSi	Yang 5	RenZi		14/03	RenChen	Yang 4	GengZi
	15/01	JiaWu	Yang 2	JiaZi		15/03	GuiSi	Yang 4	RenZi
	16/01	YiWei	Yang 2	BingZi		16/03	JiaWu	Yang 1	JiaZi
	17/01	BingShen	Yang 2	WuZi		17/03	YiWei	Yang 1	BingZi
	18/01	DingYou	Yang 2	GengZi		18/03	BingShen	Yang 1	WuZi
	19/01	WuXu	Yang 2	RenZi		19/03	DingYou	Yang 1	GengZi
大寒 (dà hán) - Extreme Cold 20/01 3:29 PM	20/01	JiHai	Yang 8/Yang 9	JiaZi		20/03	WuXu	Yang 1	RenZi
	21/01	GengZi	Yang 9	BingZi	春分 (chūn fēn) - Spring Equinox 21/03 4:24 AM	21/03	JiHai	Yang 7/Yang 9	JiaZi
	22/01	XinChou	Yang 9	WuZi		22/03	GengZi	Yang 9	BingZi
	23/01	RenYin	Yang 9	GengZi		23/03	XinChou	Yang 9	WuZi
	24/01	GuiMao	Yang 9	RenZi		24/03	RenYin	Yang 9	GengZi
	25/01	JiaChen	Yang 6	JiaZi		25/03	GuiMao	Yang 9	RenZi
	26/01	YiSi	Yang 6	BingZi		26/03	JiaChen	Yang 6	JiaZi
	27/01	BingWu	Yang 6	WuZi		27/03	YiSi	Yang 6	BingZi
	28/01	DingWei	Yang 6	GengZi		28/03	BingWu	Yang 6	WuZi
	29/01	WuShen	Yang 6	RenZi		29/03	DingWei	Yang 6	GengZi
	30/01	JiYou	Yang 3	JiaZi		30/03	WuShen	Yang 6	RenZi
	31/01	GengXu	Yang 3	BingZi		31/03	JiYou	Yang 3	JiaZi
	01/02	XinHai	Yang 3	WuZi		01/04	GengXu	Yang 3	BingZi
	02/02	RenZi	Yang 3	GengZi		02/04	XinHai	Yang 3	WuZi
	03/02	GuiChou	Yang 3	RenZi		03/04	RenZi	Yang 3	GengZi
立春 (lì chūn) - Beginning of Spring 04/02 9:45 AM	04/02	JiaYin	Yang 9/Yang 5	JiaZi		04/04	GuiChou	Yang 3	RenZi
	05/02	YiMao	Yang 5	BingZi	清明 (qīng míng) - Pure Brightness 05/04 8:17 AM	05/04	JiaYin	Yang 9/Yang 1	JiaZi
	06/02	BingChen	Yang 5	WuZi		06/04	YiMao	Yang 1	BingZi
	07/02	DingSi	Yang 5	GengZi		07/04	BingChen	Yang 1	WuZi
	08/02	WuWu	Yang 5	RenZi		08/04	DingSi	Yang 1	GengZi
	09/02	JiWei	Yang 2	JiaZi		09/04	WuWu	Yang 1	RenZi
	10/02	GengShen	Yang 2	BingZi		10/04	JiWei	Yang 7	JiaZi
	11/02	XinYou	Yang 2	WuZi		11/04	GengShen	Yang 7	BingZi
	12/02	RenXu	Yang 2	GengZi		12/04	XinYou	Yang 7	WuZi
	13/02	GuiHai	Yang 2	RenZi		13/04	RenXu	Yang 7	GengZi
	14/02	JiaZi	Yang 8	JiaZi		14/04	GuiHai	Yang 7	RenZi
	15/02	YiChou	Yang 8	BingZi		15/04	JiaZi	Yang 4	JiaZi
	16/02	BingYin	Yang 8	WuZi		16/04	YiChou	Yang 4	BingZi
	17/02	DingMao	Yang 8	GengZi		17/04	BingYin	Yang 4	WuZi
	18/02	WuChen	Yang 8	RenZi		18/04	DingMao	Yang 4	GengZi
						19/04	WuChen	Yang 4	RenZi

027: DingWei — Apr/May:JiaChen, May/Jun:YiSi

谷雨 (gǔ yǔ) - Grain Rain — 20/04 3:17 PM

Day	Jia Zi	Dun	Hour
20/04	JiSi	Yang 1/Yang 2	JiaZi
21/04	GengWu	Yang 2	BingZi
22/04	XinWei	Yang 2	WuZi
23/04	RenShen	Yang 2	GengZi
24/04	GuiYou	Yang 2	RenZi
25/04	JiaXu	Yang 8	JiaZi
26/04	YiHai	Yang 8	BingZi
27/04	BingZi	Yang 8	WuZi
28/04	DingChou	Yang 8	GengZi
29/04	WuYin	Yang 8	RenZi
30/04	JiMao	Yang 5	JiaZi
01/05	GengChe	Yang 5	BingZi
02/05	XinSi	Yang 5	WuZi
03/05	RenWu	Yang 5	GengZi
04/05	GuiWei	Yang 5	RenZi
05/05	JiaShen	Yang 2	JiaZi

立夏 (lì xià) - Beginning of Summer — 06/05 1:24 AM

Day	Jia Zi	Dun	Hour
06/05	YiYou	Yang 2/Yang 1	BingZi
07/05	BingXu	Yang 1	WuZi
08/05	DingHai	Yang 1	GengZi
09/05	WuZi	Yang 1	RenZi
10/05	JiChou	Yang 7	JiaZi
11/05	GengYin	Yang 7	BingZi
12/05	XinMao	Yang 7	WuZi
13/05	RenChen	Yang 7	GengZi
14/05	GuiSi	Yang 7	RenZi
15/05	JiaWu	Yang 4	JiaZi
16/05	YiWei	Yang 4	BingZi
17/05	BingShen	Yang 4	WuZi
18/05	DingYou	Yang 4	GengZi
19/05	WuXu	Yang 4	RenZi
20/05	JiHai	Yang 1	JiaZi

小滿 (xiǎo mǎn) - Small Grain — 21/05 2:17 PM

Day	Jia Zi	Dun	Hour
21/05	GengZi	Yang 1/Yang 2	BingZi
22/05	XinChou	Yang 2	WuZi
23/05	RenYin	Yang 2	GengZi
24/05	GuiMao	Yang 2	RenZi
25/05	JiaChen	Yang 8	JiaZi
26/05	YiSi	Yang 8	BingZi
27/05	BingWu	Yang 8	WuZi
28/05	DingWei	Yang 8	GengZi
29/05	WuShen	Yang 8	RenZi
30/05	JiYou	Yang 5	JiaZi
31/05	GengXu	Yang 5	BingZi
01/06	XinHai	Yang 5	WuZi
02/06	RenZi	Yang 5	GengZi
03/06	GuiChou	Yang 5	RenZi
04/06	JiaYin	Yang 2	JiaZi
05/06	YiMao	Yang 2	BingZi

芒種 (máng zhǒng) - Summer Harvest — 06/06 5:25 AM

Day	Jia Zi	Dun	Hour
06/06	BingChen	Yang 2/Yang 3	WuZi
07/06	DingSi	Yang 3	GengZi
08/06	WuWu	Yang 3	RenZi
09/06	JiWei	Yang 9	JiaZi
10/06	GengShen	Yang 9	BingZi
11/06	XinYou	Yang 9	WuZi
12/06	RenXu	Yang 9	GengZi
13/06	GuiHai	Yang 9	RenZi
14/06	JiaZi	Yang 6	JiaZi
15/06	YiChou	Yang 6	BingZi
16/06	BingYin	Yang 6	WuZi
17/06	DingMao	Yang 6	GengZi
18/06	WuChen	Yang 6	RenZi
19/06	JiSi	Yang 3	JiaZi
20/06	GengWu	Yang 3	BingZi

2027: DingWei — Jun/July:BingWu, Jul/Aug:DingWei

夏至 (xià zhì) - Summer Solstice — 21/06 10:10 PM

Day	Jia Zi	Dun	Hour
21/06	XinWei	Yang 3/Yin 3	WuZi
22/06	RenShen	Yin 3	GengZi
23/06	GuiYou	Yin 3	RenZi
24/06	JiaXu	Yin 6	JiaZi
25/06	YiHai	Yin 6	BingZi
26/06	BingZi	Yin 6	WuZi
27/06	DingChou	Yin 6	GengZi
28/06	WuYin	Yin 6	RenZi
29/06	JiMao	Yin 9	JiaZi
30/06	GengChe	Yin 9	BingZi
01/07	XinSi	Yin 9	WuZi
02/07	RenWu	Yin 9	GengZi
03/07	GuiWei	Yin 9	RenZi
04/07	JiaShen	Yin 3	JiaZi
05/07	YiYou	Yin 3	BingZi
06/07	BingXu	Yin 3	WuZi

小暑 (xiǎo shǔ) - Mild Summer — 07/07 3:36 PM

Day	Jia Zi	Dun	Hour
07/07	DingHai	Yin 3/Yin 2	GengZi
08/07	WuZi	Yin 2	RenZi
09/07	JiChou	Yin 5	JiaZi
10/07	GengYin	Yin 5	BingZi
11/07	XinMao	Yin 5	WuZi
12/07	RenChen	Yin 5	GengZi
13/07	GuiSi	Yin 5	RenZi
14/07	JiaWu	Yin 8	JiaZi
15/07	YiWei	Yin 8	BingZi
16/07	BingShen	Yin 8	WuZi
17/07	DingYou	Yin 8	GengZi
18/07	WuXu	Yin 8	RenZi
19/07	JiHai	Yin 2	JiaZi
20/07	GengZi	Yin 2	BingZi
21/07	XinChou	Yin 2	WuZi
22/07	RenYin	Yin 2	GengZi

大暑 (dà shǔ) - Extreme Summer — 23/07 9:04 AM

Day	Jia Zi	Dun	Hour
23/07	GuiMao	Yin 2/Yin 1	RenZi
24/07	JiaChen	Yin 4	JiaZi
25/07	YiSi	Yin 4	BingZi
26/07	BingWu	Yin 4	WuZi
27/07	DingWei	Yin 4	GengZi
28/07	WuShen	Yin 4	RenZi
29/07	JiYou	Yin 7	JiaZi
30/07	GengXu	Yin 7	BingZi
31/07	XinHai	Yin 7	WuZi
01/08	RenZi	Yin 7	GengZi
02/08	GuiChou	Yin 7	RenZi
03/08	JiaYin	Yin 1	JiaZi
04/08	YiMao	Yin 1	BingZi
05/08	BingChen	Yin 1	WuZi
06/08	DingSi	Yin 1	GengZi

立秋 (lì qiū) - Beginning of Autumn — 08/08 1:26 AM

Day	Jia Zi	Dun	Hour
07/08	WuWu	Yin 1	RenZi
08/08	JiWei	Yin 4/Yin 8	JiaZi
09/08	GengShen	Yin 8	BingZi
10/08	XinYou	Yin 8	WuZi
11/08	RenXu	Yin 8	GengZi
12/08	GuiHai	Yin 8	RenZi
13/08	JiaZi	Yin 2	JiaZi
14/08	YiChou	Yin 2	BingZi
15/08	BingYin	Yin 2	WuZi
16/08	DingMao	Yin 2	GengZi
17/08	WuChen	Yin 2	RenZi
18/08	JiSi	Yin 5	JiaZi
19/08	GengWu	Yin 5	BingZi
20/08	XinWei	Yin 5	WuZi
21/08	RenShen	Yin 5	GengZi
22/08	GuiYou	Yin 5	RenZi

2027: DingWei — Aug/Sep:WuShen, Sep/Oct:JiYou

Solar Term	Day	Jia Zi	Dun	Hour
外暑 (wài shǔ) - Outer Heat 23/08 4:13 PM	23/0	JiaXu	Yin 8/Yin 7	JiaZi
	24/0	YiHai	Yin 7	BingZi
	25/0	BingZi	Yin 7	WuZi
	26/0	DingChou	Yin 7	GengZi
	27/0	WuYin	Yin 7	RenZi
	28/0	JiMao	Yin 1	JiaZi
	29/0	GengChen	Yin 1	BingZi
	30/0	XinSi	Yin 1	WuZi
	31/0	RenWu	Yin 1	GengZi
	01/0	GuiWei	Yin 1	RenZi
	02/0	JiaShen	Yin 4	JiaZi
	03/0	YiYou	Yin 4	BingZi
	04/0	BingXu	Yin 4	WuZi
	05/0	DingHai	Yin 4	GengZi
	06/0	WuZi	Yin 4	RenZi
	07/0	JiChou	Yin 7	JiaZi
白露 (bái lù) - White Dew 08/09 4:28 AM	08/0	GengYin	Yin 7/Yin 6	BingZi
	09/0	XinMao	Yin 6	WuZi
	10/0	RenChen	Yin 6	GengZi
	11/0	GuiSi	Yin 6	RenZi
	12/0	JiaWu	Yin 9	JiaZi
	13/0	YiWei	Yin 9	BingZi
	14/0	BingShen	Yin 9	WuZi
	15/0	DingYou	Yin 9	GengZi
	16/0	WuXu	Yin 9	RenZi
	17/0	JiHai	Yin 3	JiaZi
	18/0	GengZi	Yin 3	BingZi
	19/0	XinChou	Yin 3	WuZi
	20/0	RenYin	Yin 3	GengZi
	21/0	GuiMao	Yin 3	RenZi
	22/0	JiaChen	Yin 6	JiaZi
秋分 (qiū fēn) - Autumn Equinox 23/09 2:01 PM	23/0	YiSi	Yin 6/Yin 4	BingZi
	24/0	BingWu	Yin 4	WuZi
	25/0	DingWei	Yin 4	GengZi
	26/0	WuShen	Yin 4	RenZi
	27/0	JiYou	Yin 7	JiaZi
	28/0	GengXu	Yin 7	BingZi
	29/0	XinHai	Yin 7	WuZi
	30/0	RenZi	Yin 7	GengZi
	01/1	GuiChou	Yin 7	RenZi
	02/1	JiaYin	Yin 1	JiaZi
	03/1	YiMao	Yin 1	BingZi
	04/1	BingChen	Yin 1	WuZi
	05/1	DingSi	Yin 1	GengZi
	06/1	WuWu	Yin 1	RenZi
	07/1	JiWei	Yin 4	JiaZi
寒露 (hán lù) - Cold Dew 08/10 8:16 PM	08/1	GengShen	Yin 4/Yin 3	BingZi
	09/1	XinYou	Yin 3	WuZi
	10/1	RenXu	Yin 3	GengZi
	11/1	GuiHai	Yin 3	RenZi
	12/1	JiaZi	Yin 6	JiaZi
	13/1	YiChou	Yin 6	BingZi
	14/1	BingYin	Yin 6	WuZi
	15/1	DingMao	Yin 6	GengZi
	16/1	WuChen	Yin 6	RenZi
	17/1	JiSi	Yin 9	JiaZi
	18/1	GengWu	Yin 9	BingZi
	19/1	XinWei	Yin 9	WuZi
	20/1	RenShen	Yin 9	GengZi
	21/1	GuiYou	Yin 9	RenZi
	22/1	JiaXu	Yin 3	JiaZi

2027: DingWei — Oct/Nov:GengXu, Nov/Dec:XinHai

Solar Term	Day	Jia Zi	Dun	Hour
霜降 (shuāng jiàng) - Frost 23/10 11:32 PM	23/10	YiHai	Yin 3/Yin 2	BingZi
	24/10	BingZi	Yin 2	WuZi
	25/10	DingChou	Yin 2	GengZi
	26/10	WuYin	Yin 2	RenZi
	27/10	JiMao	Yin 5	JiaZi
	28/10	GengChen	Yin 5	BingZi
	29/10	XinSi	Yin 5	WuZi
	30/10	RenWu	Yin 5	GengZi
	31/10	GuiWei	Yin 5	RenZi
	01/11	JiaShen	Yin 8	JiaZi
	02/11	YiYou	Yin 8	BingZi
	03/11	BingXu	Yin 8	WuZi
	04/11	DingHai	Yin 8	GengZi
	05/11	WuZi	Yin 8	RenZi
	06/11	JiChou	Yin 2	JiaZi
立冬 (lì dōng) - Beginning of Winter 07/11 11:38 PM	07/11	GengYin	Yin 2/Yin 3	BingZi
	08/11	XinMao	Yin 3	WuZi
	09/11	RenChen	Yin 3	GengZi
	10/11	GuiSi	Yin 3	RenZi
	11/11	JiaWu	Yin 6	JiaZi
	12/11	YiWei	Yin 6	BingZi
	13/11	BingShen	Yin 6	WuZi
	14/11	DingYou	Yin 6	GengZi
	15/11	WuXu	Yin 6	RenZi
	16/11	JiHai	Yin 9	JiaZi
	17/11	GengZi	Yin 9	BingZi
	18/11	XinChou	Yin 9	WuZi
	19/11	RenYin	Yin 9	GengZi
	20/11	GuiMao	Yin 9	RenZi
	21/11	JiaChen	Yin 3	JiaZi
小雪 (xiǎo xuě) - Mild Snow 22/11 9:15 PM	22/11	YiSi	Yin 3/Yin 2	BingZi
	23/11	BingWu	Yin 2	WuZi
	24/11	DingWei	Yin 2	GengZi
	25/11	WuShen	Yin 2	RenZi
	26/11	JiYou	Yin 5	JiaZi
	27/11	GengXu	Yin 5	BingZi
	28/11	XinHai	Yin 5	WuZi
	29/11	RenZi	Yin 5	GengZi
	30/11	GuiChou	Yin 5	RenZi
	01/12	JiaYin	Yin 8	JiaZi
	02/12	YiMao	Yin 8	BingZi
	03/12	BingChen	Yin 8	WuZi
	04/12	DingSi	Yin 8	GengZi
	05/12	WuWu	Yin 8	RenZi
	06/12	JiWei	Yin 2	JiaZi
大雪 (dà xuě) - Extreme Snow 07/12 4:37 PM	07/12	GengShen	Yin 2/Yin 1	BingZi
	08/12	XinYou	Yin 1	WuZi
	09/12	RenXu	Yin 1	GengZi
	10/12	GuiHai	Yin 1	RenZi
	11/12	JiaZi	Yin 4	JiaZi
	12/12	YiChou	Yin 4	BingZi
	13/12	BingYin	Yin 4	WuZi
	14/12	DingMao	Yin 4	GengZi
	15/12	WuChen	Yin 4	RenZi
	16/12	JiSi	Yin 7	JiaZi
	17/12	GengWu	Yin 7	BingZi
	18/12	XinWei	Yin 7	WuZi
	19/12	RenShen	Yin 7	GengZi
	20/12	GuiYou	Yin 7	RenZi
	21/12	JiaXu	Yin 1	JiaZi

2027: DingWei, 2028: WuShen

2027: DingWei, 2028: WuShen — Dec27/Jan28:RenZi, Jan/Feb:GuiChou

Solar Term	Day	Jia Zi	Dun	Hour
冬至 (dōng zhì) - Winter Solstice 22/12 10:41 AM	22/12	YiHai	Yin 1/Yang 4	BingZi
	23/12	BingZi	Yang 4	WuZi
	24/12	DingChou	Yang 4	GengZi
	25/12	WuYin	Yang 4	RenZi
	26/12	JiMao	Yang 1	JiaZi
	27/12	GengChen	Yang 1	BingZi
	28/12	XinSi	Yang 1	WuZi
	29/12	RenWu	Yang 1	GengZi
	30/12	GuiWei	Yang 1	RenZi
	31/12	JiaShen	Yang 7	JiaZi
	01/01	YiYou	Yang 7	BingZi
	02/01	BingXu	Yang 7	WuZi
	03/01	DingHai	Yang 7	GengZi
	04/01	WuZi	Yang 7	RenZi
	05/01	JiChou	Yang 4	JiaZi
小寒 (xiǎo hán) - Mild Cold 06/01 3:54 AM	06/01	GengYin	Yang 4/Yang 5	BingZi
	07/01	XinMao	Yang 5	WuZi
	08/01	RenChen	Yang 5	GengZi
	09/01	GuiSi	Yang 5	RenZi
	10/01	JiaWu	Yang 2	JiaZi
	11/01	YiWei	Yang 2	BingZi
	12/01	BingShen	Yang 2	WuZi
	13/01	DingYou	Yang 2	GengZi
	14/01	WuXu	Yang 2	RenZi
	15/01	JiHai	Yang 8	JiaZi
	16/01	GengZi	Yang 8	BingZi
	17/01	XinChou	Yang 8	WuZi
	18/01	RenYin	Yang 8	GengZi
	19/01	GuiMao	Yang 8	RenZi
大寒 (dà hán) - Extreme Cold 20/01 9:21 PM	20/01	JiaChen	Yang 5/Yang 6	JiaZi
	21/01	YiSi	Yang 6	BingZi
	22/01	BingWu	Yang 6	WuZi
	23/01	DingWei	Yang 6	GengZi
	24/01	WuShen	Yang 6	RenZi
	25/01	JiYou	Yang 3	JiaZi
	26/01	GengXu	Yang 3	BingZi
	27/01	XinHai	Yang 3	WuZi
	28/01	RenZi	Yang 3	GengZi
	29/01	GuiChou	Yang 3	RenZi
	30/01	JiaYin	Yang 9	JiaZi
	31/01	YiMao	Yang 9	BingZi
	01/02	BingChen	Yang 9	WuZi
	02/02	DingSi	Yang 9	GengZi
	03/02	WuWu	Yang 9	RenZi
立春 (lì chūn) - Beginning of Spring 04/02 3:30 PM	04/02	JiWei	Yang 6/Yang 2	JiaZi
	05/02	GengShen	Yang 2	BingZi
	06/02	XinYou	Yang 2	WuZi
	07/02	RenXu	Yang 2	GengZi
	08/02	GuiHai	Yang 2	RenZi
	09/02	JiaZi	Yang 8	JiaZi
	10/02	YiChou	Yang 8	BingZi
	11/02	BingYin	Yang 8	WuZi
	12/02	DingMao	Yang 8	GengZi
	13/02	WuChen	Yang 8	RenZi
	14/02	JiSi	Yang 5	JiaZi
	15/02	GengWu	Yang 5	BingZi
	16/02	XinWei	Yang 5	WuZi
	17/02	RenShen	Yang 5	GengZi
	18/02	GuiYou	Yang 5	RenZi

2028: WuShen — Feb/Mar:JiaYin, Mar/Apr:YiMao

Solar Term	Day	Jia Zi	Dun	Hour
雨水 (yǔ shuǐ) - Rain Water 19/02 11:25 AM	19/02	JiaXu	Yang 2/Yang 3	JiaZi
	20/02	YiHai	Yang 3	BingZi
	21/02	BingZi	Yang 3	WuZi
	22/02	DingChou	Yang 3	GengZi
	23/02	WuYin	Yang 3	RenZi
	24/02	JiMao	Yang 9	JiaZi
	25/02	GengChen	Yang 9	BingZi
	26/02	XinSi	Yang 9	WuZi
	27/02	RenWu	Yang 9	GengZi
	28/02	GuiWei	Yang 9	RenZi
	29/02	JiaShen	Yang 6	JiaZi
	01/03	YiYou	Yang 6	BingZi
	02/03	BingXu	Yang 6	WuZi
	03/03	DingHai	Yang 6	GengZi
	04/03	WuZi	Yang 6	RenZi
惊蛰 (jīng zhé) - Insect Awakening 05/03 9:24 AM	05/03	JiChou	Yang 3/Yang 4	JiaZi
	06/03	GengYin	Yang 4	BingZi
	07/03	XinMao	Yang 4	WuZi
	08/03	RenChen	Yang 4	GengZi
	09/03	GuiSi	Yang 4	RenZi
	10/03	JiaWu	Yang 1	JiaZi
	11/03	YiWei	Yang 1	BingZi
	12/03	BingShen	Yang 1	WuZi
	13/03	DingYou	Yang 1	GengZi
	14/03	WuXu	Yang 1	RenZi
	15/03	JiHai	Yang 7	JiaZi
	16/03	GengZi	Yang 7	BingZi
	17/03	XinChou	Yang 7	WuZi
	18/03	RenYin	Yang 7	GengZi
	19/03	GuiMao	Yang 7	RenZi
春分 (chūn fēn) - Spring Equinox 20/03 10:16 AM	20/03	JiaChen	Yang 4/Yang 6	JiaZi
	21/03	YiSi	Yang 6	BingZi
	22/03	BingWu	Yang 6	WuZi
	23/03	DingWei	Yang 6	GengZi
	24/03	WuShen	Yang 6	RenZi
	25/03	JiYou	Yang 3	JiaZi
	26/03	GengXu	Yang 3	BingZi
	27/03	XinHai	Yang 3	WuZi
	28/03	RenZi	Yang 3	GengZi
	29/03	GuiChou	Yang 3	RenZi
	30/03	JiaYin	Yang 9	JiaZi
	31/03	YiMao	Yang 9	BingZi
	01/04	BingChen	Yang 9	WuZi
	02/04	DingSi	Yang 9	GengZi
	03/04	WuWu	Yang 9	RenZi
清明 (qīng míng) - Pure Brightness 04/04 2:02 PM	04/04	JiWei	Yang 6/Yang 7	JiaZi
	05/04	GengShen	Yang 7	BingZi
	06/04	XinYou	Yang 7	WuZi
	07/04	RenXu	Yang 7	GengZi
	08/04	GuiHai	Yang 7	RenZi
	09/04	JiaZi	Yang 4	JiaZi
	10/04	YiChou	Yang 4	BingZi
	11/04	BingYin	Yang 4	WuZi
	12/04	DingMao	Yang 4	GengZi
	13/04	WuChen	Yang 4	RenZi
	14/04	JiSi	Yang 1	JiaZi
	15/04	GengWu	Yang 1	BingZi
	16/04	XinWei	Yang 1	WuZi
	17/04	RenShen	Yang 1	GengZi
	18/04	GuiYou	Yang 1	RenZi

2028: WuShen — Apr/May:BingChen, May/Jun:DingSi

Solar Term	Day	Jia Zi	Dun	Hour
谷雨 (gǔ yǔ) - Grain Rain 19/04 9:09 PM	19/04	JiaXu	Yang 7/Yang 8	JiaZi
	20/04	YiHai	Yang 8	BingZi
	21/04	BingZi	Yang 8	WuZi
	22/04	DingChou	Yang 8	GengZi
	23/04	WuYin	Yang 8	RenZi
	24/04	JiMao	Yang 5	JiaZi
	25/04	GengChen	Yang 5	BingZi
	26/04	XinSi	Yang 5	WuZi
	27/04	RenWu	Yang 5	GengZi
	28/04	GuiWei	Yang 5	RenZi
	29/04	JiaShen	Yang 2	JiaZi
	30/04	YiYou	Yang 2	BingZi
	01/05	BingXu	Yang 2	WuZi
	02/05	DingHai	Yang 2	GengZi
	03/05	WuZi	Yang 2	RenZi
立夏 (lì xià) - Beginning of Summer 05/05 7:11 AM	04/05	JiChou	Yang 8	JiaZi
	05/05	GengYin	Yang 8/Yang 7	BingZi
	06/05	XinMao	Yang 7	WuZi
	07/05	RenChen	Yang 7	GengZi
	08/05	GuiSi	Yang 7	RenZi
	09/05	JiaWu	Yang 4	JiaZi
	10/05	YiWei	Yang 4	BingZi
	11/05	BingShen	Yang 4	WuZi
	12/05	DingYou	Yang 4	GengZi
	13/05	WuXu	Yang 4	RenZi
	14/05	JiHai	Yang 1	JiaZi
	15/05	GengZi	Yang 1	BingZi
	16/05	XinChou	Yang 1	WuZi
	17/05	RenYin	Yang 1	GengZi
	18/05	GuiMao	Yang 1	RenZi
	19/05	JiaChen	Yang 7	JiaZi
小满 (xiǎo mǎn) - Small Grain 20/05 8:09 PM	20/05	YiSi	Yang 7/Yang 8	BingZi
	21/05	BingWu	Yang 8	WuZi
	22/05	DingWei	Yang 8	GengZi
	23/05	WuShen	Yang 8	RenZi
	24/05	JiYou	Yang 5	JiaZi
	25/05	GengXu	Yang 5	BingZi
	26/05	XinHai	Yang 5	WuZi
	27/05	RenZi	Yang 5	GengZi
	28/05	GuiChou	Yang 5	RenZi
	29/05	JiaYin	Yang 2	JiaZi
	30/05	YiMao	Yang 2	BingZi
	31/05	BingChen	Yang 2	WuZi
	01/06	DingSi	Yang 2	GengZi
	02/06	WuWu	Yang 2	RenZi
	03/06	JiWei	Yang 8	JiaZi
	04/06	GengShen	Yang 8	BingZi
芒种 (máng zhòng) - Summer Harvest 05/06 11:15 AM	05/06	XinYou	Yang 8/Yang 9	WuZi
	06/06	RenXu	Yang 9	GengZi
	07/06	GuiHai	Yang 9	RenZi
	08/06	JiaZi	Yang 6	JiaZi
	09/06	YiChou	Yang 6	BingZi
	10/06	BingYin	Yang 6	WuZi
	11/06	DingMao	Yang 6	GengZi
	12/06	WuChen	Yang 6	RenZi
	13/06	JiSi	Yang 3	JiaZi
	14/06	GengWu	Yang 3	BingZi
	15/06	XinWei	Yang 3	WuZi
	16/06	RenShen	Yang 3	GengZi
	17/06	GuiYou	Yang 3	RenZi
	18/06	JiaXu	Yang 9	JiaZi
	19/06	YiHai	Yang 9	BingZi
	20/06	BingZi	Yang 9	WuZi

2028: WuShen — Jun/July:WuWu, Jul/Aug:JiWei

Solar Term	Day	Jia Zi	Dun	Hour
夏至 (xià zhì) - Summer Solstice 21/06 4:01 AM	21/06	DingChou	Yang 9/Yin 6	GengZi
	22/06	WuYin	Yin 6	RenZi
	23/06	JiMao	Yin 9	JiaZi
	24/06	GengChen	Yin 9	BingZi
	25/06	XinSi	Yin 9	WuZi
	26/06	RenWu	Yin 9	GengZi
	27/06	GuiWei	Yin 9	RenZi
	28/06	JiaShen	Yin 3	JiaZi
	29/06	YiYou	Yin 3	BingZi
	30/06	BingXu	Yin 3	WuZi
	01/07	DingHai	Yin 3	GengZi
	02/07	WuZi	Yin 3	RenZi
	03/07	JiChou	Yin 6	JiaZi
	04/07	GengYin	Yin 6	BingZi
	05/07	XinMao	Yin 6	WuZi
小暑 (xiǎo shǔ) - Mild Summer 06/07 9:29 PM	06/07	RenChen	Yin 6/Yin 5	GengZi
	07/07	GuiSi	Yin 5	RenZi
	08/07	JiaWu	Yin 8	JiaZi
	09/07	YiWei	Yin 8	BingZi
	10/07	BingShen	Yin 8	WuZi
	11/07	DingYou	Yin 8	GengZi
	12/07	WuXu	Yin 8	RenZi
	13/07	JiHai	Yin 2	JiaZi
	14/07	GengZi	Yin 2	BingZi
	15/07	XinChou	Yin 2	WuZi
	16/07	RenYin	Yin 2	GengZi
	17/07	GuiMao	Yin 2	RenZi
	18/07	JiaChen	Yin 5	JiaZi
	19/07	YiSi	Yin 5	BingZi
	20/07	BingWu	Yin 5	WuZi
	21/07	DingWei	Yin 5	GengZi
大暑 (dà shǔ) - Extreme Summer 22/07 2:53 PM	22/07	WuShen	Yin 5/Yin 4	RenZi
	23/07	JiYou	Yin 7	JiaZi
	24/07	GengXu	Yin 7	BingZi
	25/07	XinHai	Yin 7	WuZi
	26/07	RenZi	Yin 7	GengZi
	27/07	GuiChou	Yin 7	RenZi
	28/07	JiaYin	Yin 1	JiaZi
	29/07	YiMao	Yin 1	BingZi
	30/07	BingChen	Yin 1	WuZi
	31/07	DingSi	Yin 1	GengZi
	01/08	WuWu	Yin 1	RenZi
	02/08	JiWei	Yin 4	JiaZi
	03/08	GengShen	Yin 4	BingZi
	04/08	XinYou	Yin 4	WuZi
	05/08	RenXu	Yin 4	GengZi
	06/08	GuiHai	Yin 4	RenZi
立秋 (lì qiū) - Beginning of Autumn 07/08 7:20 AM	07/08	JiaZi	Yin 7/Yin 2	JiaZi
	08/08	YiChou	Yin 2	BingZi
	09/08	BingYin	Yin 2	WuZi
	10/08	DingMao	Yin 2	GengZi
	11/08	WuChen	Yin 2	RenZi
	12/08	JiSi	Yin 5	JiaZi
	13/08	GengWu	Yin 5	BingZi
	14/08	XinWei	Yin 5	WuZi
	15/08	RenShen	Yin 5	GengZi
	16/08	GuiYou	Yin 5	RenZi
	17/08	JiaXu	Yin 8	JiaZi
	18/08	YiHai	Yin 8	BingZi
	19/08	BingZi	Yin 8	WuZi
	20/08	DingChou	Yin 8	GengZi
	21/08	WuYin	Yin 8	RenZi

2028: WuShen — Aug/Sep:GengShen, Sep/Oct:XinYou

Solar Term	Day	Jia Zi	Dun	Hour
外暑 (wài shǔ) - Outer Heat 22/08 10:00 PM	22/08	JiMao	Yin 2/Yin 1	JiaZi
	23/08	GengChen	Yin 1	BingZi
	24/08	XinSi	Yin 1	WuZi
	25/08	RenWu	Yin 1	GengZi
	26/08	GuiWei	Yin 1	RenZi
	27/08	JiaShen	Yin 4	JiaZi
	28/08	YiYou	Yin 4	BingZi
	29/08	BingXu	Yin 4	WuZi
	30/08	DingHai	Yin 4	GengZi
	31/08	WuZi	Yin 4	RenZi
	01/09	JiChou	Yin 7	JiaZi
	02/09	GengYin	Yin 7	BingZi
	03/09	XinMao	Yin 7	WuZi
	04/09	RenChen	Yin 7	GengZi
	05/09	GuiSi	Yin 7	RenZi
	06/09	JiaWu	Yin 1	JiaZi
白露 (bái lù) - White Dew 07/09 10:21 AM	07/09	YiWei	Yin 1/Yin 9	BingZi
	08/09	BingShen	Yin 9	WuZi
	09/09	DingYou	Yin 9	GengZi
	10/09	WuXu	Yin 9	RenZi
	11/09	JiHai	Yin 3	JiaZi
	12/09	GengZi	Yin 3	BingZi
	13/09	XinChou	Yin 3	WuZi
	14/09	RenYin	Yin 3	GengZi
	15/09	GuiMao	Yin 3	RenZi
	16/09	JiaChen	Yin 6	JiaZi
	17/09	YiSi	Yin 6	BingZi
	18/09	BingWu	Yin 6	WuZi
	19/09	DingWei	Yin 6	GengZi
	20/09	WuShen	Yin 6	RenZi
	21/09	JiYou	Yin 9	JiaZi
秋分 (qiū fēn) - Autumn Equinox 22/09 7:44 PM	22/09	GengXu	Yin 9/Yin 7	BingZi
	23/09	XinHai	Yin 7	WuZi
	24/09	RenZi	Yin 7	GengZi
	25/09	GuiChou	Yin 7	RenZi
	26/09	JiaYin	Yin 1	JiaZi
	27/09	YiMao	Yin 1	BingZi
	28/09	BingChen	Yin 1	WuZi
	29/09	DingSi	Yin 1	GengZi
	30/09	WuWu	Yin 1	RenZi
	01/10	JiWei	Yin 4	JiaZi
	02/10	GengShen	Yin 4	BingZi
	03/10	XinYou	Yin 4	WuZi
	04/10	RenXu	Yin 4	GengZi
	05/10	GuiHai	Yin 4	RenZi
	06/10	JiaZi	Yin 7	JiaZi
	07/10	YiChou	Yin 7	BingZi
寒露 (hán lù) - Cold Dew 08/10 2:08 AM	08/10	BingYin	Yin 7/Yin 6	WuZi
	09/10	DingMao	Yin 6	GengZi
	10/10	WuChen	Yin 6	RenZi
	11/10	JiSi	Yin 9	JiaZi
	12/10	GengWu	Yin 9	BingZi
	13/10	XinWei	Yin 9	WuZi
	14/10	RenShen	Yin 9	GengZi
	15/10	GuiYou	Yin 9	RenZi
	16/10	JiaXu	Yin 3	JiaZi
	17/10	YiHai	Yin 3	BingZi
	18/10	BingZi	Yin 3	WuZi
	19/10	DingChou	Yin 3	GengZi
	20/10	WuYin	Yin 3	RenZi
	21/10	JiMao	Yin 6	JiaZi
	22/10	GengChen	Yin 6	BingZi

2028: WuShen — Oct/Nov:RenXu, Nov/Dec:GuiHai

Solar Term	Day	Jia Zi	Dun	Hour
霜降 (shuāng jiàng) - Frost 23/10 5:13 AM	23/10	XinSi	Yin 6/Yin 5	WuZi
	24/10	RenWu	Yin 5	GengZi
	25/10	GuiWei	Yin 5	RenZi
	26/10	JiaShen	Yin 8	JiaZi
	27/10	YiYou	Yin 8	BingZi
	28/10	BingXu	Yin 8	WuZi
	29/10	DingHai	Yin 8	GengZi
	30/10	WuZi	Yin 8	RenZi
	31/10	JiChou	Yin 2	JiaZi
	01/11	GengYin	Yin 2	BingZi
	02/11	XinMao	Yin 2	WuZi
	03/11	RenChen	Yin 2	GengZi
	04/11	GuiSi	Yin 2	RenZi
	05/11	JiaWu	Yin 5	JiaZi
	06/11	YiWei	Yin 5	BingZi
立冬 (lì dōng) - Beginning of Winter 07/11 5:26 AM	07/11	BingShen	Yin 5/Yin 6	WuZi
	08/11	DingYou	Yin 6	GengZi
	09/11	WuXu	Yin 6	RenZi
	10/11	JiHai	Yin 9	JiaZi
	11/11	GengZi	Yin 9	BingZi
	12/11	XinChou	Yin 9	WuZi
	13/11	RenYin	Yin 9	GengZi
	14/11	GuiMao	Yin 9	RenZi
	15/11	JiaChen	Yin 3	JiaZi
	16/11	YiSi	Yin 3	BingZi
	17/11	BingWu	Yin 3	WuZi
	18/11	DingWei	Yin 3	GengZi
	19/11	WuShen	Yin 3	RenZi
	20/11	JiYou	Yin 6	JiaZi
	21/11	GengXu	Yin 6	BingZi
小雪 (xiǎo xuě) - Mild Snow 22/11 2:54 AM	22/11	XinHai	Yin 6/Yin 5	WuZi
	23/11	RenZi	Yin 5	GengZi
	24/11	GuiChou	Yin 5	RenZi
	25/11	JiaYin	Yin 8	JiaZi
	26/11	YiMao	Yin 8	BingZi
	27/11	BingChen	Yin 8	WuZi
	28/11	DingSi	Yin 8	GengZi
	29/11	WuWu	Yin 8	RenZi
	30/11	JiWei	Yin 2	JiaZi
	01/12	GengShen	Yin 2	BingZi
	02/12	XinYou	Yin 2	WuZi
	03/12	RenXu	Yin 2	GengZi
	04/12	GuiHai	Yin 2	RenZi
	05/12	JiaZi	Yin 5	JiaZi
大雪 (dà xuě) - Extreme Snow 06/12 10:24 PM	06/12	YiChou	Yin 5/Yin 4	BingZi
	07/12	BingYin	Yin 4	WuZi
	08/12	DingMao	Yin 4	GengZi
	09/12	WuChen	Yin 4	RenZi
	10/12	JiSi	Yin 7	JiaZi
	11/12	GengWu	Yin 7	BingZi
	12/12	XinWei	Yin 7	WuZi
	13/12	RenShen	Yin 7	GengZi
	14/12	GuiYou	Yin 7	RenZi
	15/12	JiaXu	Yin 1	JiaZi
	16/12	YiHai	Yin 1	BingZi
	17/12	BingZi	Yin 1	WuZi
	18/12	DingChou	Yin 1	GengZi
	19/12	WuYin	Yin 1	RenZi
	20/12	JiMao	Yin 4	JiaZi

2028: WuShen, 2029:JiYou

2028: WuShen, 2029:JiYou
Dec28/Jan29:JiaZi, Jan/Feb:YiChou

Solar Term	Day	Jia Zi	Dun	Hour
冬至 (dōng zhì) - Winter Solstice 21/12 4:19 PM	21/12	GengChen	Yin 4/Yang 1	BingZi
	22/12	XinSi	Yang 1	WuZi
	23/12	RenWu	Yang 1	GengZi
	24/12	GuiWei	Yang 1	RenZi
	25/12	JiaShen	Yang 7	JiaZi
	26/12	YiYou	Yang 7	BingZi
	27/12	BingXu	Yang 7	WuZi
	28/12	DingHai	Yang 7	GengZi
	29/12	WuZi	Yang 7	RenZi
	30/12	JiChou	Yang 4	JiaZi
	31/12	GengYin	Yang 4	BingZi
	01/01	XinMao	Yang 4	WuZi
	02/01	RenChen	Yang 4	GengZi
	03/01	GuiSi	Yang 4	RenZi
	04/01	JiaWu	Yang 1	JiaZi
小寒 (xiǎo hán) - Mild Cold 05/01 9:41 AM	05/01	YiWei	Yang 1/Yang 2	BingZi
	06/01	BingShen	Yang 2	WuZi
	07/01	DingYou	Yang 2	GengZi
	08/01	WuXu	Yang 2	RenZi
	09/01	JiHai	Yang 8	JiaZi
	10/01	GengZi	Yang 8	BingZi
	11/01	XinChou	Yang 8	WuZi
	12/01	RenYin	Yang 8	GengZi
	13/01	GuiMao	Yang 8	RenZi
	14/01	JiaChen	Yang 5	JiaZi
	15/01	YiSi	Yang 5	BingZi
	16/01	BingWu	Yang 5	WuZi
	17/01	DingWei	Yang 5	GengZi
	18/01	WuShen	Yang 5	RenZi
	19/01	JiYou	Yang 2	JiaZi
大寒 (dà hán) - Extreme Cold 20/01 3:00 AM	20/01	GengXu	Yang 2/Yang 3	BingZi
	21/01	XinHai	Yang 3	WuZi
	22/01	RenZi	Yang 3	GengZi
	23/01	GuiChou	Yang 3	RenZi
	24/01	JiaYin	Yang 9	JiaZi
	25/01	YiMao	Yang 9	BingZi
	26/01	BingChen	Yang 9	WuZi
	27/01	DingSi	Yang 9	GengZi
	28/01	WuWu	Yang 9	RenZi
	29/01	JiWei	Yang 6	JiaZi
	30/01	GengShen	Yang 6	BingZi
	31/01	XinYou	Yang 6	WuZi
	01/02	RenXu	Yang 6	GengZi
	02/02	GuiHai	Yang 6	RenZi
立春 (lì chūn) - Beginning of Spring 03/02 9:20 PM	03/02	JiaZi	Yang 3/Yang 8	JiaZi
	04/02	YiChou	Yang 8	BingZi
	05/02	BingYin	Yang 8	WuZi
	06/02	DingMao	Yang 8	GengZi
	07/02	WuChen	Yang 8	RenZi
	08/02	JiSi	Yang 5	JiaZi
	09/02	GengWu	Yang 5	BingZi
	10/02	XinWei	Yang 5	WuZi
	11/02	RenShen	Yang 5	GengZi
	12/02	GuiYou	Yang 5	RenZi
	13/02	JiaXu	Yang 2	JiaZi
	14/02	YiHai	Yang 2	BingZi
	15/02	BingZi	Yang 2	WuZi
	16/02	DingChou	Yang 2	GengZi
	17/02	WuYin	Yang 2	RenZi

2021: XinChou
Feb/Mar:BingYin, Mar/Apr:DingMao

Solar Term	Day	Jia Zi	Dun	Hour
雨水 (yǔ shuǐ) - Rain Water 18/02 5:07 PM	18/02	JiMao	Yang 8/Yang 9	JiaZi
	19/02	GengChen	Yang 9	BingZi
	20/02	XinSi	Yang 9	WuZi
	21/02	RenWu	Yang 9	GengZi
	22/02	GuiWei	Yang 9	RenZi
	23/02	JiaShen	Yang 6	JiaZi
	24/02	YiYou	Yang 6	BingZi
	25/02	BingXu	Yang 6	WuZi
	26/02	DingHai	Yang 6	GengZi
	27/02	WuZi	Yang 6	RenZi
	28/02	JiChou	Yang 3	JiaZi
	01/03	GengYin	Yang 3	BingZi
	02/03	XinMao	Yang 3	WuZi
	03/03	RenChen	Yang 3	GengZi
	04/03	GuiSi	Yang 3	RenZi
驚蟄 (jīng zhé) - Insect Awakening 05/03 3:17 PM	05/03	JiaWu	Yang 9/Yang 1	JiaZi
	06/03	YiWei	Yang 1	BingZi
	07/03	BingShen	Yang 1	WuZi
	08/03	DingYou	Yang 1	GengZi
	09/03	WuXu	Yang 1	RenZi
	10/03	JiHai	Yang 7	JiaZi
	11/03	GengZi	Yang 7	BingZi
	12/03	XinChou	Yang 7	WuZi
	13/03	RenYin	Yang 7	GengZi
	14/03	GuiMao	Yang 7	RenZi
	15/03	JiaChen	Yang 4	JiaZi
	16/03	YiSi	Yang 4	BingZi
	17/03	BingWu	Yang 4	WuZi
	18/03	DingWei	Yang 4	GengZi
	19/03	WuShen	Yang 4	RenZi
春分 (chūn fēn) - Spring Equinox 20/03 4:01 PM	20/03	JiYou	Yang 1/Yang 3	JiaZi
	21/03	GengXu	Yang 3	BingZi
	22/03	XinHai	Yang 3	WuZi
	23/03	RenZi	Yang 3	GengZi
	24/03	GuiChou	Yang 3	RenZi
	25/03	JiaYin	Yang 9	JiaZi
	26/03	YiMao	Yang 9	BingZi
	27/03	BingChen	Yang 9	WuZi
	28/03	DingSi	Yang 9	GengZi
	29/03	WuWu	Yang 9	RenZi
	30/03	JiWei	Yang 6	JiaZi
	31/03	GengShen	Yang 6	BingZi
	01/04	XinYou	Yang 6	WuZi
	02/04	RenXu	Yang 6	GengZi
	03/04	GuiHai	Yang 6	RenZi
清明 (qīng míng) - Pure Brightness 04/04 7:58 PM	04/04	JiaZi	Yang 3/Yang 4	JiaZi
	05/04	YiChou	Yang 4	BingZi
	06/04	BingYin	Yang 4	WuZi
	07/04	DingMao	Yang 4	GengZi
	08/04	WuChen	Yang 4	RenZi
	09/04	JiSi	Yang 1	JiaZi
	10/04	GengWu	Yang 1	BingZi
	11/04	XinWei	Yang 1	WuZi
	12/04	RenShen	Yang 1	GengZi
	13/04	GuiYou	Yang 1	RenZi
	14/04	JiaXu	Yang 7	JiaZi
	15/04	YiHai	Yang 7	BingZi
	16/04	BingZi	Yang 7	WuZi
	17/04	DingChou	Yang 7	GengZi
	18/04	WuYin	Yang 7	RenZi
	19/04	JiMao	Yang 4	JiaZi

2021: XinChou — Apr/May:WuChen, May/Jun:JiSi

Solar Term	Day	Jia Zi	Dun	Hour
谷雨 (gǔ yǔ) - Grain Rain 20/04 2:55 AM	20/04	GengChen	Yang 4/Yang 5	BingZi
	21/04	XinSi	Yang 5	WuZi
	22/04	RenWu	Yang 5	GengZi
	23/04	GuiWei	Yang 5	RenZi
	24/04	JiaShen	Yang 2	JiaZi
	25/04	YiYou	Yang 2	BingZi
	26/04	BingXu	Yang 2	WuZi
	27/04	DingHai	Yang 2	GengZi
	28/04	WuZi	Yang 2	RenZi
	29/04	JiChou	Yang 8	JiaZi
	30/04	GengYin	Yang 8	BingZi
	01/05	XinMao	Yang 8	WuZi
	02/05	RenChen	Yang 8	GengZi
	03/05	GuiSi	Yang 8	RenZi
	04/05	JiaWu	Yang 5	JiaZi
立夏 (lì xià) - Beginning of Summer 05/05 1:07 PM	05/05	YiWei	Yang 5/Yang 4	BingZi
	06/05	BingShen	Yang 4	WuZi
	07/05	DingYou	Yang 4	GengZi
	08/05	WuXu	Yang 4	RenZi
	09/05	JiHai	Yang 1	JiaZi
	10/05	GengZi	Yang 1	BingZi
	11/05	XinChou	Yang 1	WuZi
	12/05	RenYin	Yang 1	GengZi
	13/05	GuiMao	Yang 1	RenZi
	14/05	JiaChen	Yang 7	JiaZi
	15/05	YiSi	Yang 7	BingZi
	16/05	BingWu	Yang 7	WuZi
	17/05	DingWei	Yang 7	GengZi
	18/05	WuShen	Yang 7	RenZi
	19/05	JiYou	Yang 4	JiaZi
	20/05	GengXu	Yang 4	BingZi
小满 (xiǎo mǎn) - Small Grain 21/05 1:55 AM	21/05	XinHai	Yang 4/Yang 5	WuZi
	22/05	RenZi	Yang 5	GengZi
	23/05	GuiChou	Yang 5	RenZi
	24/05	JiaYin	Yang 2	JiaZi
	25/05	YiMao	Yang 2	BingZi
	26/05	BingChen	Yang 2	WuZi
	27/05	DingSi	Yang 2	GengZi
	28/05	WuWu	Yang 2	RenZi
	29/05	JiWei	Yang 8	JiaZi
	30/05	GengShen	Yang 8	BingZi
	31/05	XinYou	Yang 8	WuZi
	01/06	RenXu	Yang 8	GengZi
	02/06	GuiHai	Yang 8	RenZi
	03/06	JiaZi	Yang 5	JiaZi
	04/06	YiChou	Yang 5	BingZi
芒种 (máng zhòng) - Summer Harvest 05/06 5:09 PM	05/06	BingYin	Yang 5/Yang 6	WuZi
	06/06	DingMao	Yang 6	GengZi
	07/06	WuChen	Yang 6	RenZi
	08/06	JiSi	Yang 3	JiaZi
	09/06	GengWu	Yang 3	BingZi
	10/06	XinWei	Yang 3	WuZi
	11/06	RenShen	Yang 3	GengZi
	12/06	GuiYou	Yang 3	RenZi
	13/06	JiaXu	Yang 9	JiaZi
	14/06	YiHai	Yang 9	BingZi
	15/06	BingZi	Yang 9	WuZi
	16/06	DingChou	Yang 9	GengZi
	17/06	WuYin	Yang 9	RenZi
	18/06	JiMao	Yang 6	JiaZi
	19/06	GengChen	Yang 6	BingZi
	20/06	XinSi	Yang 6	WuZi

2021: XinChou — Jun/July:GengWu, Jul/Aug:XinWei

Solar Term	Day	Jia Zi	Dun	Hour
夏至 (xià zhì) - Summer Solstice 21/06 9:47 AM	21/06	RenWu	Yang 6/Yin 9	GengZi
	22/06	GuiWei	Yin 9	RenZi
	23/06	JiaShen	Yin 3	JiaZi
	24/06	YiYou	Yin 3	BingZi
	25/06	BingXu	Yin 3	WuZi
	26/06	DingHai	Yin 3	GengZi
	27/06	WuZi	Yin 3	RenZi
	28/06	JiChou	Yin 6	JiaZi
	29/06	GengYin	Yin 6	BingZi
	30/06	XinMao	Yin 6	WuZi
	01/07	RenChen	Yin 6	GengZi
	02/07	GuiSi	Yin 6	RenZi
	03/07	JiaWu	Yin 9	JiaZi
	04/07	YiWei	Yin 9	BingZi
	05/07	BingShen	Yin 9	WuZi
	06/07	DingYou	Yin 9	GengZi
小暑 (xiǎo shǔ) - Mild Summer 07/07 3:22 AM	07/07	WuXu	Yin 9/Yin 8	RenZi
	08/07	JiHai	Yin 2	JiaZi
	09/07	GengZi	Yin 2	BingZi
	10/07	XinChou	Yin 2	WuZi
	11/07	RenYin	Yin 2	GengZi
	12/07	GuiMao	Yin 2	RenZi
	13/07	JiaChen	Yin 5	JiaZi
	14/07	YiSi	Yin 5	BingZi
	15/07	BingWu	Yin 5	WuZi
	16/07	DingWei	Yin 5	GengZi
	17/07	WuShen	Yin 5	RenZi
	18/07	JiYou	Yin 8	JiaZi
	19/07	GengXu	Yin 8	BingZi
	20/07	XinHai	Yin 8	WuZi
	21/07	RenZi	Yin 8	GengZi
大暑 (dà shǔ) - Extreme Summer 22/07 8:41 PM	22/07	GuiChou	Yin 8/Yin 7	RenZi
	23/07	JiaYin	Yin 1	JiaZi
	24/07	YiMao	Yin 1	BingZi
	25/07	BingChen	Yin 1	WuZi
	26/07	DingSi	Yin 1	GengZi
	27/07	WuWu	Yin 1	RenZi
	28/07	JiWei	Yin 4	JiaZi
	29/07	GengShen	Yin 4	BingZi
	30/07	XinYou	Yin 4	WuZi
	31/07	RenXu	Yin 4	GengZi
	01/08	GuiHai	Yin 4	RenZi
	02/08	JiaZi	Yin 7	JiaZi
	03/08	YiChou	Yin 7	BingZi
	04/08	BingYin	Yin 7	WuZi
	05/08	DingMao	Yin 7	GengZi
	06/08	WuChen	Yin 7	RenZi
立秋 (lì qiū) - Beginning of Autumn 07/08 1:11 PM	07/08	JiSi	Yin 1/Yin 5	JiaZi
	08/08	GengWu	Yin 5	BingZi
	09/08	XinWei	Yin 5	WuZi
	10/08	RenShen	Yin 5	GengZi
	11/08	GuiYou	Yin 5	RenZi
	12/08	JiaXu	Yin 8	JiaZi
	13/08	YiHai	Yin 8	BingZi
	14/08	BingZi	Yin 8	WuZi
	15/08	DingChou	Yin 8	GengZi
	16/08	WuYin	Yin 8	RenZi
	17/08	JiMao	Yin 2	JiaZi
	18/08	GengChen	Yin 2	BingZi
	19/08	XinSi	Yin 2	WuZi
	20/08	RenWu	Yin 2	GengZi
	21/08	GuiWei	Yin 2	RenZi
	22/08	JiaShen	Yin 5	JiaZi

2021: XinChou — Aug/Sep:RenShen, Sep/Oct:GuiYou

Solar Term	Day	Jia Zi	Dun	Hour
外署 (wài shǔ) - Outer Heat 23/08 3:51 AM	23/08	YiYou	Yin 5/Yin 4	BingZi
	24/08	BingXu	Yin 4	WuZi
	25/08	DingHai	Yin 4	GengZi
	26/08	WuZi	Yin 4	RenZi
	27/08	JiChou	Yin 7	JiaZi
	28/08	GengYin	Yin 7	BingZi
	29/08	XinMao	Yin 7	WuZi
	30/08	RenChen	Yin 7	GengZi
	31/08	GuiSi	Yin 7	RenZi
	01/09	JiaWu	Yin 1	JiaZi
	02/09	YiWei	Yin 1	BingZi
	03/09	BingShen	Yin 1	WuZi
	04/09	DingYou	Yin 1	GengZi
	05/09	WuXu	Yin 1	RenZi
	06/09	JiHai	Yin 4	JiaZi
白露 (bái lù) - White Dew 07/09 4:11 PM	07/09	GengZi	Yin 4/Yin 3	BingZi
	08/09	XinChou	Yin 3	WuZi
	09/09	RenYin	Yin 3	GengZi
	10/09	GuiMao	Yin 3	RenZi
	11/09	JiaChen	Yin 6	JiaZi
	12/09	YiSi	Yin 6	BingZi
	13/09	BingWu	Yin 6	WuZi
	14/09	DingWei	Yin 6	GengZi
	15/09	WuShen	Yin 6	RenZi
	16/09	JiYou	Yin 9	JiaZi
	17/09	GengXu	Yin 9	BingZi
	18/09	XinHai	Yin 9	WuZi
	19/09	RenZi	Yin 9	GengZi
	20/09	GuiChou	Yin 9	RenZi
	21/09	JiaYin	Yin 3	JiaZi
	22/09	YiMao	Yin 3	BingZi
秋分 (qiū fēn) - Autumn Equinox 23/09 1:38 AM	23/09	BingChen	Yin 3/Yin 1	WuZi
	24/09	DingSi	Yin 1	GengZi
	25/09	WuWu	Yin 1	RenZi
	26/09	JiWei	Yin 4	JiaZi
	27/09	GengShen	Yin 4	BingZi
	28/09	XinYou	Yin 4	WuZi
	29/09	RenXu	Yin 4	GengZi
	30/09	GuiHai	Yin 4	RenZi
	01/10	JiaZi	Yin 7	JiaZi
	02/10	YiChou	Yin 7	BingZi
	03/10	BingYin	Yin 7	WuZi
	04/10	DingMao	Yin 7	GengZi
	05/10	WuChen	Yin 7	RenZi
	06/10	JiSi	Yin 1	JiaZi
	07/10	GengWu	Yin 1	BingZi
寒露 (hán lù) - Cold Dew 08/10 7:57 AM	08/10	XinWei	Yin 1/Yin 9	WuZi
	09/10	RenShen	Yin 9	GengZi
	10/10	GuiYou	Yin 9	RenZi
	11/10	JiaXu	Yin 3	JiaZi
	12/10	YiHai	Yin 3	BingZi
	13/10	BingZi	Yin 3	WuZi
	14/10	DingChou	Yin 3	GengZi
	15/10	WuYin	Yin 3	RenZi
	16/10	JiMao	Yin 6	JiaZi
	17/10	GengChen	Yin 6	BingZi
	18/10	XinSi	Yin 6	WuZi
	19/10	RenWu	Yin 6	GengZi
	20/10	GuiWei	Yin 6	RenZi
	21/10	JiaShen	Yin 9	JiaZi
	22/10	YiYou	Yin 9	BingZi

2021: XinChou — Oct/Nov:JiaXu, Nov/Dec:YiHai

Solar Term	Day	Jia Zi	Dun	Hour
霜降 (shuāng jiàng) - Frost 23/10 11:07 AM	23/10	BingXu	Yin 9/Yin 8	WuZi
	24/10	DingHai	Yin 8	GengZi
	25/10	WuZi	Yin 8	RenZi
	26/10	JiChou	Yin 2	JiaZi
	27/10	GengYin	Yin 2	BingZi
	28/10	XinMao	Yin 2	WuZi
	29/10	RenChen	Yin 2	GengZi
	30/10	GuiSi	Yin 2	RenZi
	31/10	JiaWu	Yin 5	JiaZi
	01/11	YiWei	Yin 5	BingZi
	02/11	BingShen	Yin 5	WuZi
	03/11	DingYou	Yin 5	GengZi
	04/11	WuXu	Yin 5	RenZi
	05/11	JiHai	Yin 8	JiaZi
	06/11	GengZi	Yin 8	BingZi
立冬 (lì dōng) - Beginning of Winter 07/11 11:16 AM	07/11	XinChou	Yin 8/Yin 9	WuZi
	08/11	RenYin	Yin 9	GengZi
	09/11	GuiMao	Yin 9	RenZi
	10/11	JiaChen	Yin 3	JiaZi
	11/11	YiSi	Yin 3	BingZi
	12/11	BingWu	Yin 3	WuZi
	13/11	DingWei	Yin 3	GengZi
	14/11	WuShen	Yin 3	RenZi
	15/11	JiYou	Yin 6	JiaZi
	16/11	GengXu	Yin 6	BingZi
	17/11	XinHai	Yin 6	WuZi
	18/11	RenZi	Yin 6	GengZi
	19/11	GuiChou	Yin 6	RenZi
	20/11	JiaYin	Yin 9	JiaZi
	21/11	YiMao	Yin 9	BingZi
小雪 (xiǎo xuě) - Mild Snow 22/11 8:49 AM	22/11	BingChen	Yin 9/Yin 8	WuZi
	23/11	DingSi	Yin 8	GengZi
	24/11	WuWu	Yin 8	RenZi
	25/11	JiWei	Yin 2	JiaZi
	26/11	GengShen	Yin 2	BingZi
	27/11	XinYou	Yin 2	WuZi
	28/11	RenXu	Yin 2	GengZi
	29/11	GuiHai	Yin 2	RenZi
	30/11	JiaZi	Yin 5	JiaZi
	01/12	YiChou	Yin 5	BingZi
	02/12	BingYin	Yin 5	WuZi
	03/12	DingMao	Yin 5	GengZi
	04/12	WuChen	Yin 5	RenZi
	05/12	JiSi	Yin 8	JiaZi
	06/12	GengWu	Yin 8	BingZi
大雪 (dà xuě) - Extreme Snow 07/12 4:13 AM	07/12	XinWei	Yin 8/Yin 7	WuZi
	08/12	RenShen	Yin 7	GengZi
	09/12	GuiYou	Yin 7	RenZi
	10/12	JiaXu	Yin 1	JiaZi
	11/12	YiHai	Yin 1	BingZi
	12/12	BingZi	Yin 1	WuZi
	13/12	DingChou	Yin 1	GengZi
	14/12	WuYin	Yin 1	RenZi
	15/12	JiMao	Yin 4	JiaZi
	16/12	GengChen	Yin 4	BingZi
	17/12	XinSi	Yin 4	WuZi
	18/12	RenWu	Yin 4	GengZi
	19/12	GuiWei	Yin 4	RenZi
	20/12	JiaShen	Yin 7	JiaZi

2029:JiYou, 2030:GengXu

	Day	Jia Zi	Dun	Hour		Day	Jia Zi	Dun	Hour
2029:JiYou, 2030:GengXu Dec29/Jan30:BingZi, Jan/Feb:DingChou					**2030:GengXu** Feb/Mar:WuYin, Mar/Apr:JiMao				
冬至 (dōng zhì) - Winter Solstice 21/12 10:13 PM	21/12	YiYou	Yin 7/Yang 7	BingZi	雨水 (yǔ shuǐ) - Rain Water 18/02 10:59 PM	18/02	JiaShen	Yang 5/Yang 6	JiaZi
	22/12	BingXu	Yang 7	WuZi		19/02	YiYou	Yang 6	BingZi
	23/12	DingHai	Yang 7	GengZi		20/02	BingXu	Yang 6	WuZi
	24/12	WuZi	Yang 7	RenZi		21/02	DingHai	Yang 6	GengZi
	25/12	JiChou	Yang 4	JiaZi		22/02	WuZi	Yang 6	RenZi
	26/12	GengYin	Yang 4	BingZi		23/02	JiChou	Yang 3	JiaZi
	27/12	XinMao	Yang 4	WuZi		24/02	GengYin	Yang 3	BingZi
	28/12	RenChen	Yang 4	GengZi		25/02	XinMao	Yang 3	WuZi
	29/12	GuiSi	Yang 4	RenZi		26/02	RenChen	Yang 3	GengZi
	30/12	JiaWu	Yang 1	JiaZi		27/02	GuiSi	Yang 3	RenZi
	31/12	YiWei	Yang 1	BingZi		28/02	JiaWu	Yang 9	JiaZi
	01/01	BingShen	Yang 1	WuZi		01/03	YiWei	Yang 9	BingZi
	02/01	DingYou	Yang 1	GengZi		02/03	BingShen	Yang 9	WuZi
	03/01	WuXu	Yang 1	RenZi		03/03	DingYou	Yang 9	GengZi
	04/01	JiHai	Yang 7	JiaZi		04/03	WuXu	Yang 9	RenZi
小寒 (xiǎo hán) - Mild Cold 05/01 3:30 PM	05/01	GengZi	Yang 7/Yang 8	BingZi	惊蛰 (jīng zhé) - Insect Awakening 05/03 9:02 PM	05/03	JiHai	Yang 6/Yang 7	JiaZi
	06/01	XinChou	Yang 8	WuZi		06/03	GengZi	Yang 7	BingZi
	07/01	RenYin	Yang 8	GengZi		07/03	XinChou	Yang 7	WuZi
	08/01	GuiMao	Yang 8	RenZi		08/03	RenYin	Yang 7	GengZi
	09/01	JiaChen	Yang 5	JiaZi		09/03	GuiMao	Yang 7	RenZi
	10/01	YiSi	Yang 5	BingZi		10/03	JiaChen	Yang 4	JiaZi
	11/01	BingWu	Yang 5	WuZi		11/03	YiSi	Yang 4	BingZi
	12/01	DingWei	Yang 5	GengZi		12/03	BingWu	Yang 4	WuZi
	13/01	WuShen	Yang 5	RenZi		13/03	DingWei	Yang 4	GengZi
	14/01	JiYou	Yang 2	JiaZi		14/03	WuShen	Yang 4	RenZi
	15/01	GengXu	Yang 2	BingZi		15/03	JiYou	Yang 1	JiaZi
	16/01	XinHai	Yang 2	WuZi		16/03	GengXu	Yang 1	BingZi
	17/01	RenZi	Yang 2	GengZi		17/03	XinHai	Yang 1	WuZi
	18/01	GuiChou	Yang 2	RenZi		18/03	RenZi	Yang 1	GengZi
	19/01	JiaYin	Yang 8	JiaZi		19/03	GuiChou	Yang 1	RenZi
大寒 (dà hán) - Extreme Cold 20/01 8:53 AM	20/01	YiMao	Yang 8/Yang 9	BingZi	春分 (chūn fēn) - Spring Equinox 20/03 9:51 PM	20/03	JiaYin	Yang 7/Yang 9	JiaZi
	21/01	BingChen	Yang 9	WuZi		21/03	YiMao	Yang 9	BingZi
	22/01	DingSi	Yang 9	GengZi		22/03	BingChen	Yang 9	WuZi
	23/01	WuWu	Yang 9	RenZi		23/03	DingSi	Yang 9	GengZi
	24/01	JiWei	Yang 6	JiaZi		24/03	WuWu	Yang 9	RenZi
	25/01	GengShen	Yang 6	BingZi		25/03	JiWei	Yang 6	JiaZi
	26/01	XinYou	Yang 6	WuZi		26/03	GengShen	Yang 6	BingZi
	27/01	RenXu	Yang 6	GengZi		27/03	XinYou	Yang 6	WuZi
	28/01	GuiHai	Yang 6	RenZi		28/03	RenXu	Yang 6	GengZi
	29/01	JiaZi	Yang 3	JiaZi		29/03	GuiHai	Yang 6	RenZi
	30/01	YiChou	Yang 3	BingZi		30/03	JiaZi	Yang 3	JiaZi
	31/01	BingYin	Yang 3	WuZi		31/03	YiChou	Yang 3	BingZi
	01/02	DingMao	Yang 3	GengZi		01/04	BingYin	Yang 3	WuZi
	02/02	WuChen	Yang 3	RenZi		02/04	DingMao	Yang 3	GengZi
	03/02	JiSi	Yang 9	JiaZi		03/04	WuChen	Yang 3	RenZi
立春 (lì chūn) - Beginning of Spring 04/02 3:08 AM	04/02	GengWu	Yang 9/Yang 5	BingZi	清明 (qīng míng) - Pure Brightness 05/04 1:40 AM	04/04	JiSi	Yang 9	JiaZi
	05/02	XinWei	Yang 5	WuZi		05/04	GengWu	Yang 9/Yang 1	BingZi
	06/02	RenShen	Yang 5	GengZi		06/04	XinWei	Yang 1	WuZi
	07/02	GuiYou	Yang 5	RenZi		07/04	RenShen	Yang 1	GengZi
	08/02	JiaXu	Yang 2	JiaZi		08/04	GuiYou	Yang 1	RenZi
	09/02	YiHai	Yang 2	BingZi		09/04	JiaXu	Yang 7	JiaZi
	10/02	BingZi	Yang 2	WuZi		10/04	YiHai	Yang 7	BingZi
	11/02	DingChou	Yang 2	GengZi		11/04	BingZi	Yang 7	WuZi
	12/02	WuYin	Yang 2	RenZi		12/04	DingChou	Yang 7	GengZi
	13/02	JiMao	Yang 8	JiaZi		13/04	WuYin	Yang 7	RenZi
	14/02	GengChen	Yang 8	BingZi		14/04	JiMao	Yang 4	JiaZi
	15/02	XinSi	Yang 8	WuZi		15/04	GengChen	Yang 4	BingZi
	16/02	RenWu	Yang 8	GengZi		16/04	XinSi	Yang 4	WuZi
	17/02	GuiWei	Yang 8	RenZi		17/04	RenWu	Yang 4	GengZi
						18/04	GuiWei	Yang 4	RenZi
						19/04	JiaShen	Yang 1	JiaZi

2030:GengXu — Apr/May:GengChen, May/Jun:XinSi

Solar Term	Day	Jia Zi	Dun	Hour
谷雨 (gǔ yǔ) - Grain Rain 20/04 8:43 AM	20/04	YiYou	Yang 1/Yang 2	BingZi
	21/04	BingXu	Yang 2	WuZi
	22/04	DingHai	Yang 2	GengZi
	23/04	WuZi	Yang 2	RenZi
	24/04	JiChou	Yang 8	JiaZi
	25/04	GengYin	Yang 8	BingZi
	26/04	XinMao	Yang 8	WuZi
	27/04	RenChen	Yang 8	GengZi
	28/04	GuiSi	Yang 8	RenZi
	29/04	JiaWu	Yang 5	JiaZi
	30/04	YiWei	Yang 5	BingZi
	01/05	BingShen	Yang 5	WuZi
	02/05	DingYou	Yang 5	GengZi
	03/05	WuXu	Yang 5	RenZi
	04/05	JiHai	Yang 2	JiaZi
立夏 (lì xià) - Beginning of Summer 05/05 6:45 PM	05/05	GengZi	Yang 2/Yang 1	BingZi
	06/05	XinChou	Yang 1	WuZi
	07/05	RenYin	Yang 1	GengZi
	08/05	GuiMao	Yang 1	RenZi
	09/05	JiaChen	Yang 7	JiaZi
	10/05	YiSi	Yang 7	BingZi
	11/05	BingWu	Yang 7	WuZi
	12/05	DingWei	Yang 7	GengZi
	13/05	WuShen	Yang 7	RenZi
	14/05	JiYou	Yang 4	JiaZi
	15/05	GengXu	Yang 4	BingZi
	16/05	XinHai	Yang 4	WuZi
	17/05	RenZi	Yang 4	GengZi
	18/05	GuiChou	Yang 4	RenZi
	19/05	JiaYin	Yang 1	JiaZi
	20/05	YiMao	Yang 1	BingZi
小满 (xiǎo mǎn) - Small Grain 21/05 7:40 AM	21/05	BingChen	Yang 1/Yang 2	WuZi
	22/05	DingSi	Yang 2	GengZi
	23/05	WuWu	Yang 2	RenZi
	24/05	JiWei	Yang 8	JiaZi
	25/05	GengShen	Yang 8	BingZi
	26/05	XinYou	Yang 8	WuZi
	27/05	RenXu	Yang 8	GengZi
	28/05	GuiHai	Yang 8	RenZi
	29/05	JiaZi	Yang 5	JiaZi
	30/05	YiChou	Yang 5	BingZi
	31/05	BingYin	Yang 5	WuZi
	01/06	DingMao	Yang 5	GengZi
	02/06	WuChen	Yang 5	RenZi
	03/06	JiSi	Yang 2	JiaZi
	04/06	GengWu	Yang 2	BingZi
芒种 (máng zhòng) - Summer Harvest 05/06 10:44 PM	05/06	XinWei	Yang 2/Yang 3	WuZi
	06/06	RenShen	Yang 3	GengZi
	07/06	GuiYou	Yang 3	RenZi
	08/06	JiaXu	Yang 9	JiaZi
	09/06	YiHai	Yang 9	BingZi
	10/06	BingZi	Yang 9	WuZi
	11/06	DingChou	Yang 9	GengZi
	12/06	WuYin	Yang 9	RenZi
	13/06	JiMao	Yang 6	JiaZi
	14/06	GengChen	Yang 6	BingZi
	15/06	XinSi	Yang 6	WuZi
	16/06	RenWu	Yang 6	GengZi
	17/06	GuiWei	Yang 6	RenZi
	18/06	JiaShen	Yang 3	JiaZi
	19/06	YiYou	Yang 3	BingZi
	20/06	BingXu	Yang 3	WuZi

2030:GengXu — Jun/July:RenWu, Jul/Aug:GuiWei

Solar Term	Day	Jia Zi	Dun	Hour
夏至 (xià zhì) - Summer Solstice 21/06 3:30 PM	21/06	DingHai	Yang 3/Yin 3	GengZi
	22/06	WuZi	Yin 3	RenZi
	23/06	JiChou	Yin 6	JiaZi
	24/06	GengYin	Yin 6	BingZi
	25/06	XinMao	Yin 6	WuZi
	26/06	RenChen	Yin 6	GengZi
	27/06	GuiSi	Yin 6	RenZi
	28/06	JiaWu	Yin 9	JiaZi
	29/06	YiWei	Yin 9	BingZi
	30/06	BingShen	Yin 9	WuZi
	01/07	DingYou	Yin 9	GengZi
	02/07	WuXu	Yin 9	RenZi
	03/07	JiHai	Yin 3	JiaZi
	04/07	GengZi	Yin 3	BingZi
	05/07	XinChou	Yin 3	WuZi
	06/07	RenYin	Yin 3	GengZi
小暑 (xiǎo shǔ) - Mild Summer 07/07 8:55 AM	07/07	GuiMao	Yin 3/Yin 2	RenZi
	08/07	JiaChen	Yin 5	JiaZi
	09/07	YiSi	Yin 5	BingZi
	10/07	BingWu	Yin 5	WuZi
	11/07	DingWei	Yin 5	GengZi
	12/07	WuShen	Yin 5	RenZi
	13/07	JiYou	Yin 8	JiaZi
	14/07	GengXu	Yin 8	BingZi
	15/07	XinHai	Yin 8	WuZi
	16/07	RenZi	Yin 8	GengZi
	17/07	GuiChou	Yin 8	RenZi
	18/07	JiaYin	Yin 2	JiaZi
	19/07	YiMao	Yin 2	BingZi
	20/07	BingChen	Yin 2	WuZi
	21/07	DingSi	Yin 2	GengZi
	22/07	WuWu	Yin 2	RenZi
大暑 (dà shǔ) - Extreme Summer 23/07 2:24 AM	23/07	JiWei	Yin 5/Yin 4	JiaZi
	24/07	GengShen	Yin 4	BingZi
	25/07	XinYou	Yin 4	WuZi
	26/07	RenXu	Yin 4	GengZi
	27/07	GuiHai	Yin 4	RenZi
	28/07	JiaZi	Yin 7	JiaZi
	29/07	YiChou	Yin 7	BingZi
	30/07	BingYin	Yin 7	WuZi
	31/07	DingMao	Yin 7	GengZi
	01/08	WuChen	Yin 7	RenZi
	02/08	JiSi	Yin 1	JiaZi
	03/08	GengWu	Yin 1	BingZi
	04/08	XinWei	Yin 1	WuZi
	05/08	RenShen	Yin 1	GengZi
	06/08	GuiYou	Yin 1	RenZi
立秋 (lì qiū) - Beginning of Autumn 07/08 6:46 PM	07/08	JiaXu	Yin 4/Yin 8	JiaZi
	08/08	YiHai	Yin 8	BingZi
	09/08	BingZi	Yin 8	WuZi
	10/08	DingChou	Yin 8	GengZi
	11/08	WuYin	Yin 8	RenZi
	12/08	JiMao	Yin 2	JiaZi
	13/08	GengChen	Yin 2	BingZi
	14/08	XinSi	Yin 2	WuZi
	15/08	RenWu	Yin 2	GengZi
	16/08	GuiWei	Yin 2	RenZi
	17/08	JiaShen	Yin 5	JiaZi
	18/08	YiYou	Yin 5	BingZi
	19/08	BingXu	Yin 5	WuZi
	20/08	DingHai	Yin 5	GengZi
	21/08	WuZi	Yin 5	RenZi
	22/08	JiChou	Yin 8	JiaZi

2030:GengXu — Aug/Sep:JiaShen, Sep/Oct:YiYou

Term	Day	Jia Zi	Dun	Hour
外暑 (wài shǔ) - Outer Heat 23/08 9:36 AM	23/0	GengYin	Yin 8/Yin 7	BingZi
	24/0	XinMao	Yin 7	WuZi
	25/0	RenChen	Yin 7	GengZi
	26/0	GuiSi	Yin 7	RenZi
	27/0	JiaWu	Yin 1	JiaZi
	28/0	YiWei	Yin 1	BingZi
	29/0	BingShen	Yin 1	WuZi
	30/0	DingYou	Yin 1	GengZi
	31/0	WuXu	Yin 1	RenZi
	01/0	JiHai	Yin 4	JiaZi
	02/0	GengZi	Yin 4	BingZi
	03/0	XinChou	Yin 4	WuZi
	04/0	RenYin	Yin 4	GengZi
	05/0	GuiMao	Yin 4	RenZi
	06/0	JiaChen	Yin 7	JiaZi
白露 (bái lù) - White Dew 07/09 9:52 PM	07/0	YiSi	Yin 7/Yin 6	BingZi
	08/0	BingWu	Yin 6	WuZi
	09/0	DingWei	Yin 6	GengZi
	10/0	WuShen	Yin 6	RenZi
	11/0	JiYou	Yin 9	JiaZi
	12/0	GengXu	Yin 9	BingZi
	13/0	XinHai	Yin 9	WuZi
	14/0	RenZi	Yin 9	GengZi
	15/0	GuiChou	Yin 9	RenZi
	16/0	JiaYin	Yin 3	JiaZi
	17/0	YiMao	Yin 3	BingZi
	18/0	BingChen	Yin 3	WuZi
	19/0	DingSi	Yin 3	GengZi
	20/0	WuWu	Yin 3	RenZi
	21/0	JiWei	Yin 6	JiaZi
	22/0	GengShen	Yin 6	BingZi
秋分 (qiū fēn) - Autumn Equinox 23/09 7:26 AM	23/0	XinYou	Yin 6/Yin 4	WuZi
	24/0	RenXu	Yin 4	GengZi
	25/0	GuiHai	Yin 4	RenZi
	26/0	JiaZi	Yin 7	JiaZi
	27/0	YiChou	Yin 7	BingZi
	28/0	BingYin	Yin 7	WuZi
	29/0	DingMao	Yin 7	GengZi
	30/0	WuChen	Yin 7	RenZi
	01/1	JiSi	Yin 1	JiaZi
	02/1	GengWu	Yin 1	BingZi
	03/1	XinWei	Yin 1	WuZi
	04/1	RenShen	Yin 1	GengZi
	05/1	GuiYou	Yin 1	RenZi
	06/1	JiaXu	Yin 4	JiaZi
	07/1	YiHai	Yin 4	BingZi
寒露 (hán lù) - Cold Dew 08/10 1:44 PM	08/1	BingZi	Yin 4/Yin 3	WuZi
	09/1	DingChou	Yin 3	GengZi
	10/1	WuYin	Yin 3	RenZi
	11/1	JiMao	Yin 6	JiaZi
	12/1	GengChen	Yin 6	BingZi
	13/1	XinSi	Yin 6	WuZi
	14/1	RenWu	Yin 6	GengZi
	15/1	GuiWei	Yin 6	RenZi
	16/1	JiaShen	Yin 9	JiaZi
	17/1	YiYou	Yin 9	BingZi
	18/1	BingXu	Yin 9	WuZi
	19/1	DingHai	Yin 9	GengZi
	20/1	WuZi	Yin 9	RenZi
	21/1	JiChou	Yin 3	JiaZi
	22/1	GengYin	Yin 3	BingZi

2030:GengXu — Oct/Nov:BingXu, Nov/Dec:DingHai

Term	Day	Jia Zi	Dun	Hour
霜降 (shuāng jiàng) - Frost 23/10 5:00 PM	23/10	XinMao	Yin 3/Yin 2	WuZi
	24/10	RenChen	Yin 2	GengZi
	25/10	GuiSi	Yin 2	RenZi
	26/10	JiaWu	Yin 5	JiaZi
	27/10	YiWei	Yin 5	BingZi
	28/10	BingShen	Yin 5	WuZi
	29/10	DingYou	Yin 5	GengZi
	30/10	WuXu	Yin 5	RenZi
	31/10	JiHai	Yin 8	JiaZi
	01/11	GengZi	Yin 8	BingZi
	02/11	XinChou	Yin 8	WuZi
	03/11	RenYin	Yin 8	GengZi
	04/11	GuiMao	Yin 8	RenZi
	05/11	JiaChen	Yin 2	JiaZi
	06/11	YiSi	Yin 2	BingZi
立冬 (lì dōng) - Beginning of Winter 07/11 5:08 PM	07/11	BingWu	Yin 2/Yin 3	WuZi
	08/11	DingWei	Yin 3	GengZi
	09/11	WuShen	Yin 3	RenZi
	10/11	JiYou	Yin 6	JiaZi
	11/11	GengXu	Yin 6	BingZi
	12/11	XinHai	Yin 6	WuZi
	13/11	RenZi	Yin 6	GengZi
	14/11	GuiChou	Yin 6	RenZi
	15/11	JiaYin	Yin 9	JiaZi
	16/11	YiMao	Yin 9	BingZi
	17/11	BingChen	Yin 9	WuZi
	18/11	DingSi	Yin 9	GengZi
	19/11	WuWu	Yin 9	RenZi
	20/11	JiWei	Yin 3	JiaZi
	21/11	GengShen	Yin 3	BingZi
小雪 (xiǎo xuě) - Mild Snow 22/11 2:44 PM	22/11	XinYou	Yin 3/Yin 2	WuZi
	23/11	RenXu	Yin 2	GengZi
	24/11	GuiHai	Yin 2	RenZi
	25/11	JiaZi	Yin 5	JiaZi
	26/11	YiChou	Yin 5	BingZi
	27/11	BingYin	Yin 5	WuZi
	28/11	DingMao	Yin 5	GengZi
	29/11	WuChen	Yin 5	RenZi
	30/11	JiSi	Yin 8	JiaZi
	01/12	GengWu	Yin 8	BingZi
	02/12	XinWei	Yin 8	WuZi
	03/12	RenShen	Yin 8	GengZi
	04/12	GuiYou	Yin 8	RenZi
	05/12	JiaXu	Yin 2	JiaZi
	06/12	YiHai	Yin 2	BingZi
大雪 (dà xuě) - Extreme Snow 07/12 10:07 AM	07/12	BingZi	Yin 2/Yin 1	WuZi
	08/12	DingChou	Yin 1	GengZi
	09/12	WuYin	Yin 1	RenZi
	10/12	JiMao	Yin 4	JiaZi
	11/12	GengChen	Yin 4	BingZi
	12/12	XinSi	Yin 4	WuZi
	13/12	RenWu	Yin 4	GengZi
	14/12	GuiWei	Yin 4	RenZi
	15/12	JiaShen	Yin 7	JiaZi
	16/12	YiYou	Yin 7	BingZi
	17/12	BingXu	Yin 7	WuZi
	18/12	DingHai	Yin 7	GengZi
	19/12	WuZi	Yin 7	RenZi
	20/12	JiChou	Yin 1	JiaZi
	21/12	GengYin	Yin 1	BingZi

1080 Charts

Yang Dun#1

<table>
<tr><td colspan="6" align="center">Chart: +1JiaZi (Yang Dun #1 JiaZi Xun)
JiaZi, YiChou, BingYin, DingMao, WuChen, JiSi, GengWu, XinWei, RenShen, GuiYou</td></tr>
<tr>
<td colspan="3">Yang (阳) Dun# 1 Hour: JiaZi；直符(ZhíFú): 天蓬(TiānPéng)
直使(ZhíShǐ): 休门(XiūMén)；旬首(XúnShǒu): JiaZiWu</td>
<td colspan="3">Yang (阳) Dun# 1 Hour: YiChou；直符(ZhíFú): 天蓬(TiānPéng)
直使(ZhíShǐ): 休门(XiūMén)；旬首(XúnShǒu): JiaZiWu</td>
</tr>
<tr>
<td>六合 (Liù Hé)
天辅 (Tiān Fǔ)
杜门 (Dù Mén)
Xun 4　　Xin
　　　　Xin</td>
<td>白虎 (Bái Hǔ)
天英 (Tiān Yīng)
景门 (Jǐng Mén)
Li 9　　Yi
　　　　Yi</td>
<td>玄武 (Xuán Wǔ)
禽芮 (Qín Ruì)
死门 (Sǐ Mén)
Kun 2　　Ji/Ren
　　　　Ji/Ren</td>
<td>九天 (Jiǔ Tiān)
天心 (Tiān Xīn)
惊门 (Jīng Mén)
Xun 4　　Gui
　　　　Xin</td>
<td>侦符 (Zhí Fú)
天蓬 (Tiān Péng)
开门 (Kāi Mén)
Li 9　　Wu
　　　　Yi</td>
<td>腾蛇 (Téng Shé)
天任 (Tiān Rèn)
休门 (Xiū Mén)
Kun 2　　Bing
　　　　Ji/Ren</td>
</tr>
<tr>
<td>太阴 (Tài Yīn)
天冲 (Tiān Chōng)
伤门 (Shāng Mén)
Zhen 3　　Geng
　　　　Geng</td>
<td>Yang (阳) Dun# 1
Hour: JiaZi
Fu Yin
©Calvin Yap</td>
<td>九地 (Jiǔ Dì)
天柱 (Tiān Zhù)
惊门 (Jīng Mén)
Dui 7　　Ding
　　　　Ding</td>
<td>九地 (Jiǔ Dì)
天柱 (Tiān Zhù)
死门 (Sǐ Mén)
Zhen 3　　Ding
　　　　Geng</td>
<td>Yang (阳) Dun# 1
Hour: YiChou
Fan Yin
©Calvin Yap</td>
<td>太阴 (Tài Yīn)
天冲 (Tiān Chōng)
生门 (Shēng Mén)
Dui 7　　Geng
　　　　Ding</td>
</tr>
<tr>
<td>腾蛇 (Téng Shé)
天任 (Tiān Rèn)
生门 (Shēng Mén)
Gen 8　　Bing
　　　　Bing</td>
<td>侦符 (Zhí Fú)
天蓬 (Tiān Péng)
休门 (Xiū Mén)
Kan 1　　Wu
　　　　Wu</td>
<td>九天 (Jiǔ Tiān)
天心 (Tiān Xīn)
开门 (Kāi Mén)
Qian 6　　Gui
　　　　Gui</td>
<td>玄武 (Xuán Wǔ)
禽芮 (Qín Ruì)
景门 (Jǐng Mén)
Gen 8　　Ji/Ren
　　　　Bing</td>
<td>白虎 (Bái Hǔ)
天英 (Tiān Yīng)
杜门 (Dù Mén)
Kan 1　　Yi
　　　　Wu</td>
<td>六合 (Liù Hé)
天辅 (Tiān Fǔ)
伤门 (Shāng Mén)
Qian 6　　Xin
　　　　Gui</td>
</tr>
<tr>
<td colspan="3">Yang (阳) Dun# 1 Hour: BingYin；直符(ZhíFú): 天蓬(TiānPéng)
直使(ZhíShǐ): 休门(XiūMén)；旬首(XúnShǒu): JiaZiWu</td>
<td colspan="3">Yang (阳) Dun# 1 Hour: DingMao；直符(ZhíFú): 天蓬(TiānPéng)
直使(ZhíShǐ): 休门(XiūMén)；旬首(XúnShǒu): JiaZiWu</td>
</tr>
<tr>
<td>太阴 (Tài Yīn)
天冲 (Tiān Chōng)
生门 (Shēng Mén)
Xun 4　　Geng
　　　　Xin</td>
<td>六合 (Liù Hé)
天辅 (Tiān Fǔ)
伤门 (Shāng Mén)
Li 9　　Xin
　　　　Yi</td>
<td>白虎 (Bái Hǔ)
天英 (Tiān Yīng)
杜门 (Dù Mén)
Kun 2　　Yi
　　　　Ji/Ren</td>
<td>玄武 (Xuán Wǔ)
禽芮 (Qín Ruì)
休门 (Xiū Mén)
Xun 4　　Ji/Ren
　　　　Xin</td>
<td>九地 (Jiǔ Dì)
天柱 (Tiān Zhù)
生门 (Shēng Mén)
Li 9　　Ding
　　　　Yi</td>
<td>九天 (Jiǔ Tiān)
天心 (Tiān Xīn)
伤门 (Shāng Mén)
Kun 2　　Gui
　　　　Ji/Ren</td>
</tr>
<tr>
<td>腾蛇 (Téng Shé)
天任 (Tiān Rèn)
休门 (Xiū Mén)
Zhen 3　　Bing
　　　　Geng</td>
<td>Yang (阳) Dun# 1
Hour: BingYin

©Calvin Yap</td>
<td>玄武 (Xuán Wǔ)
禽芮 (Qín Ruì)
景门 (Jǐng Mén)
Dui 7　　Ji/Ren
　　　　Ding</td>
<td>白虎 (Bái Hǔ)
天英 (Tiān Yīng)
开门 (Kāi Mén)
Zhen 3　　Yi
　　　　Geng</td>
<td>Yang (阳) Dun# 1
Hour: DingMao

©Calvin Yap</td>
<td>侦符 (Zhí Fú)
天蓬 (Tiān Péng)
杜门 (Dù Mén)
Dui 7　　Wu
　　　　Ding</td>
</tr>
<tr>
<td>侦符 (Zhí Fú)
天蓬 (Tiān Péng)
开门 (Kāi Mén)
Gen 8　　Wu
　　　　Bing</td>
<td>九天 (Jiǔ Tiān)
天心 (Tiān Xīn)
惊门 (Jīng Mén)
Kan 1　　Gui
　　　　Wu</td>
<td>九地 (Jiǔ Dì)
天柱 (Tiān Zhù)
死门 (Sǐ Mén)
Qian 6　　Ding
　　　　Gui</td>
<td>六合 (Liù Hé)
天辅 (Tiān Fǔ)
惊门 (Jīng Mén)
Gen 8　　Xin
　　　　Bing</td>
<td>太阴 (Tài Yīn)
天冲 (Tiān Chōng)
死门 (Sǐ Mén)
Kan 1　　Geng
　　　　Wu</td>
<td>腾蛇 (Téng Shé)
天任 (Tiān Rèn)
景门 (Jǐng Mén)
Qian 6　　Bing
　　　　Gui</td>
</tr>
<tr>
<td colspan="3">Yang (阳) Dun# 1 Hour: WuChen；直符(ZhíFú): 天蓬(TiānPéng)
直使(ZhíShǐ): 休门(XiūMén)；旬首(XúnShǒu): JiaZiWu</td>
<td colspan="3">Yang (阳) Dun# 1 Hour: JiSi；直符(ZhíFú): 天蓬(TiānPéng)
直使(ZhíShǐ): 休门(XiūMén)；旬首(XúnShǒu): JiaZiWu</td>
</tr>
<tr>
<td>六合 (Liù Hé)
天辅 (Tiān Fǔ)
惊门 (Jīng Mén)
Xun 4　　Xin
　　　　Xin</td>
<td>白虎 (Bái Hǔ)
天英 (Tiān Yīng)
开门 (Kāi Mén)
Li 9　　Yi
　　　　Yi</td>
<td>玄武 (Xuán Wǔ)
禽芮 (Qín Ruì)
休门 (Xiū Mén)
Kun 2　　Ji/Ren
　　　　Ji/Ren</td>
<td>九地 (Jiǔ Dì)
天柱 (Tiān Zhù)
景门 (Jǐng Mén)
Xun 4　　Ding
　　　　Xin</td>
<td>九天 (Jiǔ Tiān)
天心 (Tiān Xīn)
死门 (Sǐ Mén)
Li 9　　Gui
　　　　Yi</td>
<td>侦符 (Zhí Fú)
天蓬 (Tiān Péng)
惊门 (Jīng Mén)
Kun 2　　Wu
　　　　Ji/Ren</td>
</tr>
<tr>
<td>太阴 (Tài Yīn)
天冲 (Tiān Chōng)
死门 (Sǐ Mén)
Zhen 3　　Geng
　　　　Geng</td>
<td>Yang (阳) Dun# 1
Hour: WuChen
Fu Yin
©Calvin Yap</td>
<td>九地 (Jiǔ Dì)
天柱 (Tiān Zhù)
生门 (Shēng Mén)
Dui 7　　Ding
　　　　Ding</td>
<td>玄武 (Xuán Wǔ)
禽芮 (Qín Ruì)
杜门 (Dù Mén)
Zhen 3　　Ji/Ren
　　　　Geng</td>
<td>Yang (阳) Dun# 1
Hour: JiSi

©Calvin Yap</td>
<td>腾蛇 (Téng Shé)
天任 (Tiān Rèn)
开门 (Kāi Mén)
Dui 7　　Bing
　　　　Ding</td>
</tr>
<tr>
<td>腾蛇 (Téng Shé)
天任 (Tiān Rèn)
景门 (Jǐng Mén)
Gen 8　　Bing
　　　　Bing</td>
<td>侦符 (Zhí Fú)
天蓬 (Tiān Péng)
杜门 (Dù Mén)
Kan 1　　Wu
　　　　Wu</td>
<td>九天 (Jiǔ Tiān)
天心 (Tiān Xīn)
伤门 (Shāng Mén)
Qian 6　　Gui
　　　　Gui</td>
<td>白虎 (Bái Hǔ)
天英 (Tiān Yīng)
伤门 (Shāng Mén)
Gen 8　　Yi
　　　　Bing</td>
<td>六合 (Liù Hé)
天辅 (Tiān Fǔ)
生门 (Shēng Mén)
Kan 1　　Xin
　　　　Wu</td>
<td>太阴 (Tài Yīn)
天冲 (Tiān Chōng)
休门 (Xiū Mén)
Qian 6　　Geng
　　　　Gui</td>
</tr>
</table>

Yang (阳) Dun# 1 Hour: GengWu；直符(ZhíFú): 天蓬(TiānPéng)
直使(ZhíShǐ): 休门(XiūMén)；旬首(XúnShǒu): JiaZiWu

螣蛇 (Téng Shé) 天任 (Tiān Rèn) 死门 (Sǐ Mén) Xun 4 — Bing Xin	太阴 (Tài Yīn) 天冲 (Tiān Chōng) 惊门 (Jīng Mén) Li 9 — Geng Yi	六合 (Liù Hé) 天辅 (Tiān Fǔ) 开门 (Kāi Mén) Kun 2 — Xin Ji/Ren
值符 (Zhí Fú) 天蓬 (Tiān Péng) 景门 (Jǐng Mén) Zhen 3 — Wu Geng	Yang (阳) Dun# 1 Hour: **GengWu** ©Calvin Yap	白虎 (Bái Hǔ) 天英 (Tiān Yīng) 休门 (Xiū Mén) Dui 7 — Yi Ding
九天 (Jiǔ Tiān) 天心 (Tiān Xīn) 杜门 (Dù Mén) Gen 8 — Gui Bing	九地 (Jiǔ Dì) 天柱 (Tiān Zhù) 伤门 (Shāng Mén) Kan 1 — Ding Wu	玄武 (Xuán Wǔ) 禽芮 (Qín Ruì) 生门 (Shēng Mén) Qian 6 — Ji/Ren Gui

Yang (阳) Dun# 1 Hour: XinWei；直符(ZhíFú): 天蓬(TiānPéng)
直使(ZhíShǐ): 休门(XiūMén)；旬首(XúnShǒu): JiaZiWu

值符 (Zhí Fú) 天蓬 (Tiān Péng) 伤门 (Shāng Mén) Xun 4 — Wu Xin	螣蛇 (Téng Shé) 天任 (Tiān Rèn) 杜门 (Dù Mén) Li 9 — Bing Yi	太阴 (Tài Yīn) 天冲 (Tiān Chōng) 景门 (Jǐng Mén) Kun 2 Ji/Ren
九天 (Jiǔ Tiān) 天心 (Tiān Xīn) 生门 (Shēng Mén) Zhen 3 — Gui Geng	Yang (阳) Dun# 1 Hour: **XinWei** ©Calvin Yap	六合 (Liù Hé) 天辅 (Tiān Fǔ) 死门 (Sǐ Mén) Dui 7 Xin
九地 (Jiǔ Dì) 天柱 (Tiān Zhù) 休门 (Xiū Mén) Gen 8 — Ding	玄武 (Xuán Wǔ) 禽芮 (Qín Ruì) 开门 (Kāi Mén) Kan 1 — Ji/Ren Wu	白虎 (Bái Hǔ) 天英 (Tiān Yīng) 惊门 (Jīng Mén) Qian 6 — Yi Gui

Yang (阳) Dun# 1 Hour: RenShen；直符(ZhíFú): 天蓬(TiānPéng)
直使(ZhíShǐ): 休门(XiūMén)；旬首(XúnShǒu): JiaZiWu

九地 (Jiǔ Dì) 天柱 (Tiān Zhù) 开门 (Kāi Mén) Xun 4 — Ding Xin	九天 (Jiǔ Tiān) 天心 (Tiān Xīn) 休门 (Xiū Mén) Li 9 — Gui Yi	值符 (Zhí Fú) 天蓬 (Tiān Péng) 生门 (Shēng Mén) Kun 2 — Wu Ji/Ren
玄武 (Xuán Wǔ) 禽芮 (Qín Ruì) 惊门 (Jīng Mén) Zhen 3 — Ji/Ren Geng	Yang (阳) Dun# 1 Hour: **RenShen** ©Calvin Yap	螣蛇 (Téng Shé) 天任 (Tiān Rèn) 伤门 (Shāng Mén) Dui 7 — Bing Ding
白虎 (Bái Hǔ) 天英 (Tiān Yīng) 死门 (Sǐ Mén) Gen 8 — Yi Bing	六合 (Liù Hé) 天辅 (Tiān Fǔ) 景门 (Jǐng Mén) Kan 1 — Xin Wu	太阴 (Tài Yīn) 天冲 (Tiān Chōng) 杜门 (Dù Mén) Qian 6 — Geng Gui

Yang (阳) Dun# 1 Hour: GuiYou；直符(ZhíFú): 天蓬(TiānPéng)
直使(ZhíShǐ): 休门(XiūMén)；旬首(XúnShǒu): JiaZiWu

白虎 (Bái Hǔ) 天英 (Tiān Yīng) 杜门 (Dù Mén) Xun 4 — Yi Xin	玄武 (Xuán Wǔ) 禽芮 (Qín Ruì) 景门 (Jǐng Mén) Li 9 — Ji/Ren Yi	九地 (Jiǔ Dì) 天柱 (Tiān Zhù) 死门 (Sǐ Mén) Kun 2 — Ding Ji/Ren
六合 (Liù Hé) 天辅 (Tiān Fǔ) 伤门 (Shāng Mén) Zhen 3 — Xin Geng	Yang (阳) Dun# 1 Hour: **GuiYou** ©Calvin Yap	九天 (Jiǔ Tiān) 天心 (Tiān Xīn) 惊门 (Jīng Mén) Dui 7 — Gui Ding
太阴 (Tài Yīn) 天冲 (Tiān Chōng) 生门 (Shēng Mén) Gen 8 — Geng Bing	螣蛇 (Téng Shé) 天任 (Tiān Rèn) 休门 (Xiū Mén) Kan 1 — Bing Wu	值符 (Zhí Fú) 天蓬 (Tiān Péng) 开门 (Kāi Mén) Qian 6 — Wu Gui

---

Chart: +1JiaXu (Yang Dun #1 JiaXu Xun)
JiaXu, YiHai, BingZi, DingChou, WuYin, JiMao, GengChen, XinSi, RenWu, GuiWei

Yang (阳) Dun# 1 Hour: JiaXu；直符(ZhíFú): 天芮(TiānRuì)
直使(ZhíShǐ): 死门(SǐMén)；旬首(XúnShǒu): JiaXuJi

九地 (Jiǔ Dì) 天辅 (Tiān Fǔ) 杜门 (Dù Mén) Xun 4 — Xin Xin	九天 (Jiǔ Tiān) 天英 (Tiān Yīng) 景门 (Jǐng Mén) Li 9 Yi	值符 (Zhí Fú) 禽芮 (Qín Ruì) 死门 (Sǐ Mén) Kun 2 Ji/Ren
玄武 (Xuán Wǔ) 天冲 (Tiān Chōng) 伤门 (Shāng Mén) Zhen 3 — Geng Geng	Yang (阳) Dun# 1 Hour: **JiaXu** **Fu Yin** ©Calvin Yap	螣蛇 (Téng Shé) 天柱 (Tiān Zhù) 惊门 (Jīng Mén) Dui 7 — Ding Ding
白虎 (Bái Hǔ) 天任 (Tiān Rèn) 生门 (Shēng Mén) Gen 8 — Bing Bing	六合 (Liù Hé) 天蓬 (Tiān Péng) 休门 (Xiū Mén) Kan 1 Wu	太阴 (Tài Yīn) 天心 (Tiān Xīn) 开门 (Kāi Mén) Qian 6 Gui

Yang (阳) Dun# 1 Hour: YiHai；直符(ZhíFú): 天芮(TiānRuì)
直使(ZhíShǐ): 死门(SǐMén)；旬首(XúnShǒu): JiaXuJi

九天 (Jiǔ Tiān) 天英 (Tiān Yīng) 惊门 (Jīng Mén) Xun 4 — Yi Xin	值符 (Zhí Fú) 禽芮 (Qín Ruì) 开门 (Kāi Mén) Li 9 — Ji/Ren	螣蛇 (Téng Shé) 天柱 (Tiān Zhù) 休门 (Xiū Mén) Kun 2 — Ding Ji/Ren
九地 (Jiǔ Dì) 天辅 (Tiān Fǔ) 死门 (Sǐ Mén) Zhen 3 — Xin Geng	Yang (阳) Dun# 1 Hour: **YiHai** ©Calvin Yap	太阴 (Tài Yīn) 天心 (Tiān Xīn) 生门 (Shēng Mén) Dui 7 — Gui Ding
玄武 (Xuán Wǔ) 天冲 (Tiān Chōng) 景门 (Jǐng Mén) Gen 8 — Geng Bing	白虎 (Bái Hǔ) 天任 (Tiān Rèn) 杜门 (Dù Mén) Kan 1 — Bing Wu	六合 (Liù Hé) 天蓬 (Tiān Péng) 伤门 (Shāng Mén) Qian 6 — Wu Gui

Yang (阳) Dun# 1 Hour: BingZi；直符(ZhíFú): 天芮(TiānRuì)
直使(ZhíShǐ): 死门(SǐMén)；旬首(XúnShǒu): JiaXuJi

太阴 (Tài Yīn) 天心 (Tiān Xīn) 死门 (Sǐ Mén) Xun 4　Gui Xin	六合 (Liù Hé) 天蓬 (Tiān Péng) 惊门 (Jīng Mén) Li 9　Wu Yi	白虎 (Bái Hǔ) 天任 (Tiān Rèn) 开门 (Kāi Mén) Kun 2　Bing Ji/Ren
螣蛇 (Téng Shé) 天柱 (Tiān Zhù) 景门 (Jǐng Mén) Zhen 3　Ding Geng	Yang (阳) Dun# 1 Hour: **BingZi** **Fan Yin** ©Calvin Yap	玄武 (Xuán Wǔ) 天冲 (Tiān Chōng) 休门 (Xiū Mén) Dui 7　Geng Ding
值符 (Zhí Fú) 禽芮 (Qín Ruì) 杜门 (Dù Mén) Gen 8　Ji/Ren Bing	九天 (Jiǔ Tiān) 天英 (Tiān Yīng) 伤门 (Shāng Mén) Kan 1　Yi Wu	九地 (Jiǔ Dì) 天辅 (Tiān Fǔ) 生门 (Shēng Mén) Qian 6　Xin Gui

Yang (阳) Dun# 1 Hour: DingChou；直符(ZhíFú): 天芮(TiānRuì)
直使(ZhíShǐ): 死门(SǐMén)；旬首(XúnShǒu): JiaXuJi

玄武 (Xuán Wǔ) 天冲 (Tiān Chōng) 杜门 (Dù Mén) Xun 4　Geng Xin	九地 (Jiǔ Dì) 天辅 (Tiān Fǔ) 景门 (Jǐng Mén) Li 9　Xin Yi	九天 (Jiǔ Tiān) 天英 (Tiān Yīng) 死门 (Sǐ Mén) Kun 2 Ji/Ren
白虎 (Bái Hǔ) 天任 (Tiān Rèn) 伤门 (Shāng Mén) Zhen 3 Geng	Yang (阳) Dun# 1 Hour: **DingChou** ©Calvin Yap	值符 (Zhí Fú) 禽芮 (Qín Ruì) 惊门 (Jīng Mén) Dui 7　Ji/Ren Ding
六合 (Liù Hé) 天蓬 (Tiān Péng) 生门 (Shēng Mén) Gen 8　Wu	太阴 (Tài Yīn) 天心 (Tiān Xīn) 休门 (Xiū Mén) Kan 1　Gui Wu	螣蛇 (Téng Shé) 天柱 (Tiān Zhù) 开门 (Kāi Mén) Qian 6　Ding Gui

Yang (阳) Dun# 1 Hour: WuYin；直符(ZhíFú): 天芮(TiānRuì)
直使(ZhíShǐ): 死门(SǐMén)；旬首(XúnShǒu): JiaXuJi

六合 (Liù Hé) 天蓬 (Tiān Péng) 生门 (Shēng Mén) Xun 4　Wu Xin	白虎 (Bái Hǔ) 天任 (Tiān Rèn) 伤门 (Shāng Mén) Li 9　Bing Yi	玄武 (Xuán Wǔ) 天冲 (Tiān Chōng) 杜门 (Dù Mén) Kun 2　Geng Ji/Ren
太阴 (Tài Yīn) 天心 (Tiān Xīn) 休门 (Xiū Mén) Zhen 3　Gui Geng	Yang (阳) Dun# 1 Hour: **WuYin** ©Calvin Yap	九地 (Jiǔ Dì) 天辅 (Tiān Fǔ) 景门 (Jǐng Mén) Dui 7　Xin Ding
螣蛇 (Téng Shé) 天柱 (Tiān Zhù) 开门 (Kāi Mén) Gen 8　Ding Bing	值符 (Zhí Fú) 禽芮 (Qín Ruì) 惊门 (Jīng Mén) Kan 1　Ji/Ren Wu	九天 (Jiǔ Tiān) 天英 (Tiān Yīng) 死门 (Sǐ Mén) Qian 6　Yi Gui

Yang (阳) Dun# 1 Hour: JiMao；直符(ZhíFú): 天芮(TiānRuì)
直使(ZhíShǐ): 死门(SǐMén)；旬首(XúnShǒu): JiaXuJi

九地 (Jiǔ Dì) 天辅 (Tiān Fǔ) 伤门 (Shāng Mén) Xun 4 Xin	九天 (Jiǔ Tiān) 天英 (Tiān Yīng) 杜门 (Dù Mén) Li 9 Yi	值符 (Zhí Fú) 禽芮 (Qín Ruì) 景门 (Jǐng Mén) Kun 2　Ji/Ren Ji/Ren
玄武 (Xuán Wǔ) 天冲 (Tiān Chōng) 生门 (Shēng Mén) Zhen 3　Geng Geng	Yang (阳) Dun# 1 Hour: **JiMao** **Fu Yin** ©Calvin Yap	螣蛇 (Téng Shé) 天柱 (Tiān Zhù) 死门 (Sǐ Mén) Dui 7 Ding
白虎 (Bái Hǔ) 天任 (Tiān Rèn) 休门 (Xiū Mén) Gen 8　Bing Bing	六合 (Liù Hé) 天蓬 (Tiān Péng) 开门 (Kāi Mén) Kan 1　Wu Wu	太阴 (Tài Yīn) 天心 (Tiān Xīn) 惊门 (Jīng Mén) Qian 6　Gui Gui

Yang (阳) Dun# 1 Hour: GengChen；直符(ZhíFú): 天芮(TiānRuì)
直使(ZhíShǐ): 死门(SǐMén)；旬首(XúnShǒu): JiaXuJi

螣蛇 (Téng Shé) 天柱 (Tiān Zhù) 开门 (Kāi Mén) Xun 4　Ding Xin	太阴 (Tài Yīn) 天心 (Tiān Xīn) 休门 (Xiū Mén) Li 9　Gui Yi	六合 (Liù Hé) 天蓬 (Tiān Péng) 生门 (Shēng Mén) Kun 2　Wu Ji/Ren
值符 (Zhí Fú) 禽芮 (Qín Ruì) 惊门 (Jīng Mén) Zhen 3　Ji/Ren Geng	Yang (阳) Dun# 1 Hour: **GengChen** ©Calvin Yap	白虎 (Bái Hǔ) 天任 (Tiān Rèn) 伤门 (Shāng Mén) Dui 7　Bing Ding
九天 (Jiǔ Tiān) 天英 (Tiān Yīng) 死门 (Sǐ Mén) Gen 8　Yi Bing	九地 (Jiǔ Dì) 天辅 (Tiān Fǔ) 景门 (Jǐng Mén) Kan 1　Xin Wu	玄武 (Xuán Wǔ) 天冲 (Tiān Chōng) 杜门 (Dù Mén) Qian 6　Geng Gui

Yang (阳) Dun# 1 Hour: XinSi；直符(ZhíFú): 天芮(TiānRuì)
直使(ZhíShǐ): 死门(SǐMén)；旬首(XúnShǒu): JiaXuJi

值符 (Zhí Fú) 禽芮 (Qín Ruì) 景门 (Jǐng Mén) Xun 4　Ji/Ren Xin	螣蛇 (Téng Shé) 天柱 (Tiān Zhù) 死门 (Sǐ Mén) Li 9　Ding	太阴 (Tài Yīn) 天心 (Tiān Xīn) 惊门 (Jīng Mén) Kun 2　Gui Ji/Ren
九天 (Jiǔ Tiān) 天英 (Tiān Yīng) 杜门 (Dù Mén) Zhen 3　Yi Geng	Yang (阳) Dun# 1 Hour: **XinSi** ©Calvin Yap	六合 (Liù Hé) 天蓬 (Tiān Péng) 开门 (Kāi Mén) Dui 7　Wu Ding
九地 (Jiǔ Dì) 天辅 (Tiān Fǔ) 伤门 (Shāng Mén) Gen 8　Xin Bing	玄武 (Xuán Wǔ) 天冲 (Tiān Chōng) 生门 (Shēng Mén) Kan 1　Geng Wu	白虎 (Bái Hǔ) 天任 (Tiān Rèn) 休门 (Xiū Mén) Qian 6　Bing Gui

Yang (阳) Dun# 1 Hour: RenWu；直符(ZhíFú): 天芮(TiānRuì)
直使(ZhíShǐ): 死门(SǐMén)；旬首(XúnShǒu): JiaXuJi

九地 (Jiǔ Dì)	九天 (Jiǔ Tiān)	值符 (Zhí Fú)

Yang (阳) Dun# 1 Hour: GuiWei；直符(ZhíFú): 天芮(TiānRuì)
直使(ZhíShǐ): 死门(SǐMén)；旬首(XúnShǒu): JiaXuJi

白虎 (Bái Hǔ)	玄武 (Xuán Wǔ)	九地 (Jiǔ Dì)

Hour: RenWu — Fu Yin — ©Calvin Yap (Yang (阳) Dun# 1)

天辅 (Tiān Fǔ) 休门 (Xiū Mén) Xun 4 — Xin — Xin	天英 (Tiān Yīng) 生门 (Shēng Mén) Li 9 — Yi — Yi	禽芮 (Qín Ruì) 伤门 (Shāng Mén) Kun 2 — Ji/Ren — Ji/Ren
玄武 (Xuán Wǔ) 天冲 (Tiān Chōng) 开门 (Kāi Mén) Zhen 3 — Geng — Geng	Yang (阳) Dun# 1 Hour: **RenWu** **Fu Yin** ©Calvin Yap	螣蛇 (Téng Shé) 天柱 (Tiān Zhù) 杜门 (Dù Mén) Dui 7 — Ding — Ding
白虎 (Bái Hǔ) 天任 (Tiān Rèn) 惊门 (Jīng Mén) Gen 8 — Bing — Bing	六合 (Liù Hé) 天蓬 (Tiān Péng) 死门 (Sǐ Mén) Kan 1 — Wu — Wu	太阴 (Tài Yīn) 天心 (Tiān Xīn) 景门 (Jǐng Mén) Qian 6 — Gui — Gui

Hour: GuiWei — ©Calvin Yap (Yang (阳) Dun# 1)

天任 (Tiān Rèn) 杜门 (Dù Mén) Xun 4 — Bing — Xin	天冲 (Tiān Chōng) 景门 (Jǐng Mén) Li 9 — Geng — Yi	天辅 (Tiān Fǔ) 死门 (Sǐ Mén) Kun 2 — Xin — Ji/Ren
六合 (Liù Hé) 天蓬 (Tiān Péng) 伤门 (Shāng Mén) Zhen 3 — Wu — Geng	Yang (阳) Dun# 1 Hour: **GuiWei** ©Calvin Yap	九天 (Jiǔ Tiān) 天英 (Tiān Yīng) 惊门 (Jīng Mén) Dui 7 — Yi — Ding
太阴 (Tài Yīn) 天心 (Tiān Xīn) 生门 (Shēng Mén) Gen 8 — Gui — Bing	螣蛇 (Téng Shé) 天柱 (Tiān Zhù) 休门 (Xiū Mén) Kan 1 — Ding — Wu	值符 (Zhí Fú) 禽芮 (Qín Ruì) 开门 (Kāi Mén) Qian 6 — Ji/Ren — Gui

---

Chart: +1JiaShen (Yang Dun #1 JiaShen Xun)
JiaShen, YiYou, BingXu, DingHai, WuZi, JiChou, GengYin, XinMao, RenChen, GuiSi

Yang (阳) Dun# 1 Hour: JiaShen ; 直符(ZhíFú): 天冲(TiānChōng)
直使(ZhíShǐ): 伤门(ShāngMén) ; 旬首(XúnShǒu): JiaShenGeng

螣蛇 (Téng Shé) 天辅 (Tiān Fǔ) 杜门 (Dù Mén) Xun 4 — Xin — Xin	太阴 (Tài Yīn) 天英 (Tiān Yīng) 景门 (Jǐng Mén) Li 9 — Yi — Yi	六合 (Liù Hé) 禽芮 (Qín Ruì) 死门 (Sǐ Mén) Kun 2 — Ji/Ren — Ji/Ren
值符 (Zhí Fú) 天冲 (Tiān Chōng) 伤门 (Shāng Mén) Zhen 3 — Geng — Geng	Yang (阳) Dun# 1 Hour: **JiaShen** **Fu Yin** ©Calvin Yap	白虎 (Bái Hǔ) 天柱 (Tiān Zhù) 惊门 (Jīng Mén) Dui 7 — Ding — Ding
九天 (Jiǔ Tiān) 天任 (Tiān Rèn) 生门 (Shēng Mén) Gen 8 — Bing — Bing	九地 (Jiǔ Dì) 天蓬 (Tiān Péng) 休门 (Xiū Mén) Kan 1 — Wu — Wu	玄武 (Xuán Wǔ) 天心 (Tiān Xīn) 开门 (Kāi Mén) Qian 6 — Gui — Gui

Yang (阳) Dun# 1 Hour: YiYou ; 直符(ZhíFú): 天冲(TiānChōng)
直使(ZhíShǐ): 伤门(ShāngMén) ; 旬首(XúnShǒu): JiaShenGeng

九天 (Jiǔ Tiān) 天任 (Tiān Rèn) 伤门 (Shāng Mén) Xun 4 — Bing — Xin	值符 (Zhí Fú) 天冲 (Tiān Chōng) 杜门 (Dù Mén) Li 9 — Geng — Yi	螣蛇 (Téng Shé) 天辅 (Tiān Fǔ) 景门 (Jǐng Mén) Kun 2 — Xin — Ji/Ren
九地 (Jiǔ Dì) 天蓬 (Tiān Péng) 生门 (Shēng Mén) Zhen 3 — Wu — Geng	Yang (阳) Dun# 1 Hour: **YiYou** ©Calvin Yap	太阴 (Tài Yīn) 天英 (Tiān Yīng) 死门 (Sǐ Mén) Dui 7 — Yi — Ding
玄武 (Xuán Wǔ) 天心 (Tiān Xīn) 休门 (Xiū Mén) Gen 8 — Gui — Bing	白虎 (Bái Hǔ) 天柱 (Tiān Zhù) 开门 (Kāi Mén) Kan 1 — Ding — Wu	六合 (Liù Hé) 禽芮 (Qín Ruì) 惊门 (Jīng Mén) Qian 6 — Ji/Ren — Gui

Yang (阳) Dun# 1 Hour: BingXu ; 直符(ZhíFú): 天冲(TiānChōng)
直使(ZhíShǐ): 伤门(ShāngMén) ; 旬首(XúnShǒu): JiaShenGeng

太阴 (Tài Yīn) 天英 (Tiān Yīng) 休门 (Xiū Mén) Xun 4 — Yi — Xin	六合 (Liù Hé) 禽芮 (Qín Ruì) 生门 (Shēng Mén) Li 9 — Ji/Ren — Yi	白虎 (Bái Hǔ) 天柱 (Tiān Zhù) 伤门 (Shāng Mén) Kun 2 — Ding — Ji/Ren
螣蛇 (Téng Shé) 天辅 (Tiān Fǔ) 开门 (Kāi Mén) Zhen 3 — Xin — Geng	Yang (阳) Dun# 1 Hour: **BingXu** ©Calvin Yap	玄武 (Xuán Wǔ) 天心 (Tiān Xīn) 杜门 (Dù Mén) Dui 7 — Gui — Ding
值符 (Zhí Fú) 天冲 (Tiān Chōng) 惊门 (Jīng Mén) Gen 8 — Geng — Geng	九天 (Jiǔ Tiān) 天任 (Tiān Rèn) 死门 (Sǐ Mén) Kan 1 — Bing — Wu	九地 (Jiǔ Dì) 天蓬 (Tiān Péng) 景门 (Jǐng Mén) Qian 6 — Wu — Gui

Yang (阳) Dun# 1 Hour: DingHai ; 直符(ZhíFú): 天冲(TiānChōng)
直使(ZhíShǐ): 伤门(ShāngMén) ; 旬首(XúnShǒu): JiaShenGeng

玄武 (Xuán Wǔ) 天心 (Tiān Xīn) 惊门 (Jīng Mén) Xun 4 — Gui — Xin	九地 (Jiǔ Dì) 天蓬 (Tiān Péng) 开门 (Kāi Mén) Li 9 — Wu — Yi	九天 (Jiǔ Tiān) 天任 (Tiān Rèn) 休门 (Xiū Mén) Kun 2 — Bing — Ji/Ren
白虎 (Bái Hǔ) 天柱 (Tiān Zhù) 死门 (Sǐ Mén) Zhen 3 — Ding — Geng	Yang (阳) Dun# 1 Hour: **DingHai** **Fan Yin** ©Calvin Yap	值符 (Zhí Fú) 天冲 (Tiān Chōng) 生门 (Shēng Mén) Dui 7 — Geng — Ding
六合 (Liù Hé) 禽芮 (Qín Ruì) 景门 (Jǐng Mén) Gen 8 — Ji/Ren — Bing	太阴 (Tài Yīn) 天英 (Tiān Yīng) 杜门 (Dù Mén) Kan 1 — Yi — Wu	螣蛇 (Téng Shé) 天辅 (Tiān Fǔ) 伤门 (Shāng Mén) Qian 6 — Xin — Gui

Yang (阳) Dun# 1 Hour: WuZi ; 直符(ZhíFú): 天冲(TiānChōng)
直使(ZhíShǐ): 伤门(ShāngMén) ; 旬首(XúnShǒu): JiaShenGeng

六合 (Liù Hé) 禽芮 (Qín Ruì) 开门 (Kāi Mén) Xun 4　Ji/Ren	白虎 (Bái Hǔ) 天柱 (Tiān Zhù) 休门 (Xiū Mén) Li 9　Ding	玄武 (Xuán Wǔ) 天心 (Tiān Xīn) 生门 (Shēng Mén) Kun 2　Gui
Xin	Yi	Ji/Ren
太阴 (Tài Yīn) 天英 (Tiān Yīng) 惊门 (Jīng Mén) Zhen 3　Yi	**Yang (阳) Dun# 1** Hour: **WuZi** ©Calvin Yap	九地 (Jiǔ Dì) 天蓬 (Tiān Péng) 伤门 (Shāng Mén) Dui 7　Wu
Geng		Ding
螣蛇 (Téng Shé) 天辅 (Tiān Fǔ) 死门 (Sǐ Mén) Gen 8　Xin	值符 (Zhí Fú) 天冲 (Tiān Chōng) 景门 (Jīng Mén) Kan 1　Geng	九天 (Jiǔ Tiān) 天任 (Tiān Rèn) 杜门 (Dù Mén) Qian 6　Bing
Bing	Wu	Gui

Yang (阳) Dun# 1 Hour: JiChou ; 直符(ZhíFú): 天冲(TiānChōng)
直使(ZhíShǐ): 伤门(ShāngMén) ; 旬首(XúnShǒu): JiaShenGeng

九地 (Jiǔ Dì) 天蓬 (Tiān Péng) 景门 (Jīng Mén) Xun 4　Wu	九天 (Jiǔ Tiān) 天任 (Tiān Rèn) 死门 (Sǐ Mén) Li 9　Bing	值符 (Zhí Fú) 天冲 (Tiān Chōng) 惊门 (Jīng Mén) Kun 2　Geng
Xin	Yi	Ji/Ren
玄武 (Xuán Wǔ) 天心 (Tiān Xīn) 杜门 (Dù Mén) Zhen 3　Gui	**Yang (阳) Dun# 1** Hour: **JiChou** ©Calvin Yap	螣蛇 (Téng Shé) 天辅 (Tiān Fǔ) 开门 (Kāi Mén) Dui 7　Xin
Geng		Ding
白虎 (Bái Hǔ) 天柱 (Tiān Zhù) 伤门 (Shāng Mén) Gen 8　Ding	六合 (Liù Hé) 禽芮 (Qín Ruì) 生门 (Shēng Mén) Kan 1　Ji/Ren	太阴 (Tài Yīn) 天英 (Tiān Yīng) 休门 (Xiū Mén) Qian 6　Yi
Bing	Wu	Gui

Yang (阳) Dun# 1 Hour: GengYin ; 直符(ZhíFú): 天冲(TiānChōng)
直使(ZhíShǐ): 伤门(ShāngMén) ; 旬首(XúnShǒu): JiaShenGeng

螣蛇 (Téng Shé) 天辅 (Tiān Fǔ) 生门 (Shēng Mén) Xun 4　Xin	太阴 (Tài Yīn) 天英 (Tiān Yīng) 伤门 (Shāng Mén) Li 9　Yi	六合 (Liù Hé) 禽芮 (Qín Ruì) 杜门 (Dù Mén) Kun 2　Ji/Ren
Xin	Yi	Ji/Ren
值符 (Zhí Fú) 天冲 (Tiān Chōng) 休门 (Xiū Mén) Zhen 3　Geng	**Yang (阳) Dun# 1** Hour: **GengYin** **Fu Yin** ©Calvin Yap	白虎 (Bái Hǔ) 天柱 (Tiān Zhù) 景门 (Jīng Mén) Dui 7　Ding
Geng		Ding
九天 (Jiǔ Tiān) 天任 (Tiān Rèn) 开门 (Kāi Mén) Gen 8　Bing	九地 (Jiǔ Dì) 天蓬 (Tiān Péng) 惊门 (Jīng Mén) Kan 1　Wu	玄武 (Xuán Wǔ) 天心 (Tiān Xīn) 死门 (Sǐ Mén) Qian 6　Gui
Bing	Wu	Gui

Yang (阳) Dun# 1 Hour: XinMao ; 直符(ZhíFú): 天冲(TiānChōng)
直使(ZhíShǐ): 伤门(ShāngMén) ; 旬首(XúnShǒu): JiaShenGeng

值符 (Zhí Fú) 天冲 (Tiān Chōng) 死门 (Sǐ Mén) Xun 4　Geng	螣蛇 (Téng Shé) 天辅 (Tiān Fǔ) 惊门 (Jīng Mén) Li 9　Xin	太阴 (Tài Yīn) 天英 (Tiān Yīng) 开门 (Kāi Mén) Kun 2　Yi
Xin	Yi	Ji/Ren
九天 (Jiǔ Tiān) 天任 (Tiān Rèn) 景门 (Jīng Mén) Zhen 3　Bing	**Yang (阳) Dun# 1** Hour: **XinMao** ©Calvin Yap	六合 (Liù Hé) 禽芮 (Qín Ruì) 休门 (Xiū Mén) Dui 7　Ji/Ren
Geng		Ding
九地 (Jiǔ Dì) 天蓬 (Tiān Péng) 杜门 (Dù Mén) Gen 8　Wu	玄武 (Xuán Wǔ) 天心 (Tiān Xīn) 伤门 (Shāng Mén) Kan 1　Gui	白虎 (Bái Hǔ) 天柱 (Tiān Zhù) 生门 (Shēng Mén) Qian 6　Ding
Bing	Wu	Gui

Yang (阳) Dun# 1 Hour: RenChen ; 直符(ZhíFú): 天冲(TiānChōng)
直使(ZhíShǐ): 伤门(ShāngMén) ; 旬首(XúnShǒu): JiaShenGeng

九地 (Jiǔ Dì) 天蓬 (Tiān Péng) 休门 (Xiū Mén) Xun 4　Wu	九天 (Jiǔ Tiān) 天任 (Tiān Rèn) 生门 (Shēng Mén) Li 9　Bing	值符 (Zhí Fú) 天冲 (Tiān Chōng) 伤门 (Shāng Mén) Kun 2　Geng
Xin	Yi	Ji/Ren
玄武 (Xuán Wǔ) 天心 (Tiān Xīn) 开门 (Kāi Mén) Zhen 3　Gui	**Yang (阳) Dun# 1** Hour: **RenChen** ©Calvin Yap	螣蛇 (Téng Shé) 天辅 (Tiān Fǔ) 杜门 (Dù Mén) Dui 7　Xin
Geng		Ding
白虎 (Bái Hǔ) 天柱 (Tiān Zhù) 惊门 (Jīng Mén) Gen 8　Ding	六合 (Liù Hé) 禽芮 (Qín Ruì) 死门 (Sǐ Mén) Kan 1　Ji/Ren	太阴 (Tài Yīn) 天英 (Tiān Yīng) 景门 (Jīng Mén) Qian 6　Yi
Bing	Wu	Gui

Yang (阳) Dun# 1 Hour: GuiSi ; 直符(ZhíFú): 天冲(TiānChōng)
直使(ZhíShǐ): 伤门(ShāngMén) ; 旬首(XúnShǒu): JiaShenGeng

白虎 (Bái Hǔ) 天柱 (Tiān Zhù) 杜门 (Dù Mén) Xun 4　Ding	玄武 (Xuán Wǔ) 天心 (Tiān Xīn) 景门 (Jīng Mén) Li 9　Gui	九地 (Jiǔ Dì) 天蓬 (Tiān Péng) 死门 (Sǐ Mén) Kun 2　Wu
Xin	Yi	Ji/Ren
六合 (Liù Hé) 禽芮 (Qín Ruì) 伤门 (Shāng Mén) Zhen 3　Ji/Ren	**Yang (阳) Dun# 1** Hour: **GuiSi** ©Calvin Yap	九天 (Jiǔ Tiān) 天任 (Tiān Rèn) 惊门 (Jīng Mén) Dui 7　Bing
Geng		Ding
太阴 (Tài Yīn) 天英 (Tiān Yīng) 生门 (Shēng Mén) Gen 8　Yi	螣蛇 (Téng Shé) 天辅 (Tiān Fǔ) 休门 (Xiū Mén) Kan 1　Xin	值符 (Zhí Fú) 天冲 (Tiān Chōng) 开门 (Kāi Mén) Qian 6　Geng
Bing	Wu	Gui

Chart: +1JiaWu (Yang Dun #1 JiaWu Xun)
JiaWu, YiWei, BingShen, DingYou, WuXu, JiHai, GengZi, XinChou, RenYin, GuiMao

Yang (阳) Dun# 1 Hour: JiaWu ; 直符(ZhíFú): 天辅(TiānFǔ)
直使(ZhíShǐ): 杜门(DùMén) ; 旬首(XúnShǒu): JiaWu/Xin

值符 (Zhí Fú) 天辅 (Tiān Fǔ) 杜门 (Dù Mén) Xun 4 Xin Xin	螣蛇 (Téng Shé) 天英 (Tiān Yīng) 景门 (Jǐng Mén) Li 9 Yi Yi	太阴 (Tài Yīn) 禽芮 (Qín Ruì) 死门 (Sǐ Mén) Kun 2 Ji/Ren Ji/Ren
九天 (Jiǔ Tiān) 天冲 (Tiān Chōng) 伤门 (Shāng Mén) Zhen 3 Geng Geng	Yang (阳) Dun# 1 Hour: **JiaWu** **Fu Yin** ©Calvin Yap	六合 (Liù Hé) 天柱 (Tiān Zhù) 惊门 (Jīng Mén) Dui 7 Ding Ding
九地 (Jiǔ Dì) 天任 (Tiān Rèn) 生门 (Shēng Mén) Gen 8 Bing Bing	玄武 (Xuán Wǔ) 天蓬 (Tiān Péng) 休门 (Xiū Mén) Kan 1 Wu Wu	白虎 (Bái Hǔ) 天心 (Tiān Xīn) 开门 (Kāi Mén) Qian 6 Gui Gui

Yang (阳) Dun# 1 Hour: YiWei ; 直符(ZhíFú): 天辅(TiānFǔ)
直使(ZhíShǐ): 杜门(DùMén) ; 旬首(XúnShǒu): JiaWu/Xin

九天 (Jiǔ Tiān) 天冲 (Tiān Chōng) 生门 (Shēng Mén) Xun 4 Geng Xin	值符 (Zhí Fú) 天辅 (Tiān Fǔ) 伤门 (Shāng Mén) Li 9 Xin	螣蛇 (Téng Shé) 天英 (Tiān Yīng) 杜门 (Dù Mén) Kun 2 Yi Ji/Ren
九地 (Jiǔ Dì) 天任 (Tiān Rèn) 休门 (Xiū Mén) Zhen 3 Bing Geng	Yang (阳) Dun# 1 Hour: **YiWei** ©Calvin Yap	太阴 (Tài Yīn) 禽芮 (Qín Ruì) 景门 (Jǐng Mén) Dui 7 Ji/Ren Ding
玄武 (Xuán Wǔ) 天蓬 (Tiān Péng) 开门 (Kāi Mén) Gen 8 Wu Bing	白虎 (Bái Hǔ) 天心 (Tiān Xīn) 惊门 (Jīng Mén) Kan 1 Gui Wu	六合 (Liù Hé) 天柱 (Tiān Zhù) 死门 (Sǐ Mén) Qian 6 Ding Gui

Yang (阳) Dun# 1 Hour: BingShen ; 直符(ZhíFú): 天辅(TiānFǔ)
直使(ZhíShǐ): 杜门(DùMén) ; 旬首(XúnShǒu): JiaWu/Xin

太阴 (Tài Yīn) 禽芮 (Qín Ruì) 开门 (Kāi Mén) Xun 4 Ji/Ren Xin	六合 (Liù Hé) 天柱 (Tiān Zhù) 休门 (Xiū Mén) Li 9 Ding Yi	白虎 (Bái Hǔ) 天心 (Tiān Xīn) 生门 (Shēng Mén) Kun 2 Gui Ji/Ren
螣蛇 (Téng Shé) 天英 (Tiān Yīng) 惊门 (Jīng Mén) Zhen 3 Yi Geng	Yang (阳) Dun# 1 Hour: **BingShen** ©Calvin Yap	玄武 (Xuán Wǔ) 天蓬 (Tiān Péng) 伤门 (Shāng Mén) Dui 7 Wu Ding
值符 (Zhí Fú) 天辅 (Tiān Fǔ) 死门 (Sǐ Mén) Gen 8 Xin Bing	九天 (Jiǔ Tiān) 天冲 (Tiān Chōng) 景门 (Jǐng Mén) Kan 1 Geng Wu	九地 (Jiǔ Dì) 天任 (Tiān Rèn) 杜门 (Dù Mén) Qian 6 Bing Gui

Yang (阳) Dun# 1 Hour: DingYou ; 直符(ZhíFú): 天辅(TiānFǔ)
直使(ZhíShǐ): 杜门(DùMén) ; 旬首(XúnShǒu): JiaWu/Xin

玄武 (Xuán Wǔ) 天蓬 (Tiān Péng) 休门 (Xiū Mén) Xun 4 Wu Xin	九地 (Jiǔ Dì) 天任 (Tiān Rèn) 生门 (Shēng Mén) Li 9 Bing Yi	九天 (Jiǔ Tiān) 天冲 (Tiān Chōng) 伤门 (Shāng Mén) Kun 2 Geng Ji/Ren
白虎 (Bái Hǔ) 天心 (Tiān Xīn) 开门 (Kāi Mén) Zhen 3 Gui Geng	Yang (阳) Dun# 1 Hour: **DingYou** ©Calvin Yap	值符 (Zhí Fú) 天辅 (Tiān Fǔ) 杜门 (Dù Mén) Dui 7 Xin Ding
六合 (Liù Hé) 天柱 (Tiān Zhù) 惊门 (Jīng Mén) Gen 8 Ding Bing	太阴 (Tài Yīn) 禽芮 (Qín Ruì) 死门 (Sǐ Mén) Kan 1 Ji/Ren Wu	螣蛇 (Téng Shé) 天英 (Tiān Yīng) 景门 (Jǐng Mén) Qian 6 Yi Gui

Yang (阳) Dun# 1 Hour: WuXu ; 直符(ZhíFú): 天辅(TiānFǔ)
直使(ZhíShǐ): 杜门(DùMén) ; 旬首(XúnShǒu): JiaWu/Xin

六合 (Liù Hé) 天柱 (Tiān Zhù) 死门 (Sǐ Mén) Xun 4 Ding Xin	白虎 (Bái Hǔ) 天心 (Tiān Xīn) 惊门 (Jīng Mén) Li 9 Gui Yi	玄武 (Xuán Wǔ) 天蓬 (Tiān Péng) 开门 (Kāi Mén) Kun 2 Wu Ji/Ren
太阴 (Tài Yīn) 禽芮 (Qín Ruì) 景门 (Jǐng Mén) Zhen 3 Ji/Ren Geng	Yang (阳) Dun# 1 Hour: **WuXu** ©Calvin Yap	九地 (Jiǔ Dì) 天任 (Tiān Rèn) 休门 (Xiū Mén) Dui 7 Bing Ding
螣蛇 (Téng Shé) 天英 (Tiān Yīng) 杜门 (Dù Mén) Gen 8 Yi Bing	值符 (Zhí Fú) 天辅 (Tiān Fǔ) 伤门 (Shāng Mén) Kan 1 Xin Wu	九天 (Jiǔ Tiān) 天冲 (Tiān Chōng) 生门 (Shēng Mén) Qian 6 Geng Gui

Yang (阳) Dun# 1 Hour: JiHai ; 直符(ZhíFú): 天辅(TiānFǔ)
直使(ZhíShǐ): 杜门(DùMén) ; 旬首(XúnShǒu): JiaWu/Xin

九地 (Jiǔ Dì) 天任 (Tiān Rèn) 伤门 (Shāng Mén) Xun 4 Bing Xin	九天 (Jiǔ Tiān) 天冲 (Tiān Chōng) 杜门 (Dù Mén) Li 9 Geng Yi	值符 (Zhí Fú) 天辅 (Tiān Fǔ) 景门 (Jǐng Mén) Kun 2 Xin Ji/Ren
玄武 (Xuán Wǔ) 天蓬 (Tiān Péng) 生门 (Shēng Mén) Zhen 3 Wu Geng	Yang (阳) Dun# 1 Hour: **JiHai** ©Calvin Yap	螣蛇 (Téng Shé) 天英 (Tiān Yīng) 死门 (Sǐ Mén) Dui 7 Yi Ding
白虎 (Bái Hǔ) 天心 (Tiān Xīn) 休门 (Xiū Mén) Gen 8 Gui Bing	六合 (Liù Hé) 天柱 (Tiān Zhù) 开门 (Kāi Mén) Kan 1 Ding Wu	太阴 (Tài Yīn) 禽芮 (Qín Ruì) 惊门 (Jīng Mén) Qian 6 Ji/Ren Gui

---

Yang (阳) Dun# 1 Hour: GengZi ; 直符(ZhíFú): 天辅(TiānFǔ)
直使(ZhíShǐ): 杜门(DùMén) ; 旬首(XúnShǒu): JiaWu/Xin

螣蛇 (Téng Shé) 天英 (Tiān Yīng) 惊门 (Jīng Mén) Xun 4 Yi / Xin	太阴 (Tài Yīn) 禽芮 (Qín Ruì) 开门 (Kāi Mén) Li 9 Ji/Ren / Yi	六合 (Liù Hé) 天柱 (Tiān Zhù) 休门 (Xiū Mén) Kun 2 Ding / Ji/Ren
值符 (Zhí Fú) 天辅 (Tiān Fǔ) 死门 (Sǐ Mén) Zhen 3 Xin / Geng	Yang (阳) Dun# 1 Hour: **GengZi** ©Calvin Yap	白虎 (Bái Hǔ) 天心 (Tiān Xīn) 生门 (Shēng Mén) Dui 7 Gui / Ding
九天 (Jiǔ Tiān) 天冲 (Tiān Chōng) 景门 (Jǐng Mén) Gen 8 Geng / Bing	九地 (Jiǔ Dì) 天任 (Tiān Rèn) 杜门 (Dù Mén) Kan 1 Bing / Wu	玄武 (Xuán Wǔ) 天蓬 (Tiān Péng) 伤门 (Shāng Mén) Qian 6 Wu / Gui

Yang (阳) Dun# 1 Hour: XinChou ; 直符(ZhíFú): 天辅(TiānFǔ)
直使(ZhíShǐ): 杜门(DùMén) ; 旬首(XúnShǒu): JiaWu/Xin

值符 (Zhí Fú) 天辅 (Tiān Fǔ) 生门 (Shēng Mén) Xun 4 Xin / Xin	螣蛇 (Téng Shé) 天英 (Tiān Yīng) 伤门 (Shāng Mén) Li 9 Yi / Yi	太阴 (Tài Yīn) 禽芮 (Qín Ruì) 杜门 (Dù Mén) Kun 2 Ji/Ren / Ji/Ren
九天 (Jiǔ Tiān) 天冲 (Tiān Chōng) 休门 (Xiū Mén) Zhen 3 Geng / Geng	Yang (阳) Dun# 1 Hour: **XinChou** **Fu Yin** ©Calvin Yap	六合 (Liù Hé) 天柱 (Tiān Zhù) 景门 (Jǐng Mén) Dui 7 Ding / Ding
九地 (Jiǔ Dì) 天任 (Tiān Rèn) 开门 (Kāi Mén) Gen 8 Bing / Bing	玄武 (Xuán Wǔ) 天蓬 (Tiān Péng) 惊门 (Jīng Mén) Kan 1 Wu / Wu	白虎 (Bái Hǔ) 天心 (Tiān Xīn) 死门 (Sǐ Mén) Qian 6 Gui / Gui

Yang (阳) Dun# 1 Hour: RenYin ; 直符(ZhíFú): 天辅(TiānFǔ)
直使(ZhíShǐ): 杜门(DùMén) ; 旬首(XúnShǒu): JiaWu/Xin

九地 (Jiǔ Dì) 天任 (Tiān Rèn) 景门 (Jǐng Mén) Xun 4 Bing / Xin	九天 (Jiǔ Tiān) 天冲 (Tiān Chōng) 死门 (Sǐ Mén) Li 9 Geng / Yi	值符 (Zhí Fú) 天辅 (Tiān Fǔ) 惊门 (Jīng Mén) Kun 2 Xin / Ji/Ren
玄武 (Xuán Wǔ) 天蓬 (Tiān Péng) 杜门 (Dù Mén) Zhen 3 Wu / Geng	Yang (阳) Dun# 1 Hour: **RenYin** ©Calvin Yap	螣蛇 (Téng Shé) 天英 (Tiān Yīng) 开门 (Kāi Mén) Dui 7 Yi / Ding
白虎 (Bái Hǔ) 天心 (Tiān Xīn) 伤门 (Shāng Mén) Gen 8 Gui / Bing	六合 (Liù Hé) 天柱 (Tiān Zhù) 生门 (Shēng Mén) Kan 1 Ding / Wu	太阴 (Tài Yīn) 禽芮 (Qín Ruì) 休门 (Xiū Mén) Qian 6 Ji/Ren / Gui

Yang (阳) Dun# 1 Hour: GuiMao ; 直符(ZhíFú): 天辅(TiānFǔ)
直使(ZhíShǐ): 杜门(DùMén) ; 旬首(XúnShǒu): JiaWu/Xin

白虎 (Bái Hǔ) 天心 (Tiān Xīn) 杜门 (Dù Mén) Xun 4 Gui / Xin	玄武 (Xuán Wǔ) 天蓬 (Tiān Péng) 景门 (Jǐng Mén) Li 9 Wu / Yi	九地 (Jiǔ Dì) 天任 (Tiān Rèn) 死门 (Sǐ Mén) Kun 2 Bing / Ji/Ren
六合 (Liù Hé) 天柱 (Tiān Zhù) 伤门 (Shāng Mén) Zhen 3 Ding / Geng	Yang (阳) Dun# 1 Hour: **GuiMao** **Fan Yin** ©Calvin Yap	九天 (Jiǔ Tiān) 天冲 (Tiān Chōng) 惊门 (Jīng Mén) Dui 7 Geng / Ding
太阴 (Tài Yīn) 禽芮 (Qín Ruì) 生门 (Shēng Mén) Gen 8 Ji/Ren / Bing	螣蛇 (Téng Shé) 天英 (Tiān Yīng) 休门 (Xiū Mén) Kan 1 Yi / Wu	值符 (Zhí Fú) 天辅 (Tiān Fǔ) 开门 (Kāi Mén) Qian 6 Xin / Gui

Chart: +1JiaChen (Yang Dun #1 JiaChen Xun)
JiaChen, YiSi, BingWu, DingWei, WuShen, JiYou, GengXu, XinHai, RenZi, GuiChou

Yang (阳) Dun# 1 Hour: JiaChen ; 直符(ZhíFú): 天禽(TiānQín)
直使(ZhíShǐ): 死门(SǐMén) ; 旬首(XúnShǒu): JiaChenRen

九地 (Jiǔ Dì) 天辅 (Tiān Fǔ) 杜门 (Dù Mén) Xun 4 Xin / Xin	九天 (Jiǔ Tiān) 天英 (Tiān Yīng) 景门 (Jǐng Mén) Li 9 Yi / Yi	值符 (Zhí Fú) 禽芮 (Qín Ruì) 死门 (Sǐ Mén) Kun 2 Ji/Ren / Ji/Ren
玄武 (Xuán Wǔ) 天冲 (Tiān Chōng) 伤门 (Shāng Mén) Zhen 3 Geng / Geng	Yang (阳) Dun# 1 Hour: **JiaChen** **Fu Yin** ©Calvin Yap	螣蛇 (Téng Shé) 天柱 (Tiān Zhù) 惊门 (Jīng Mén) Dui 7 Ding / Ding
白虎 (Bái Hǔ) 天任 (Tiān Rèn) 生门 (Shēng Mén) Gen 8 Bing / Bing	六合 (Liù Hé) 天蓬 (Tiān Péng) 休门 (Xiū Mén) Kan 1 Wu / Wu	太阴 (Tài Yīn) 天心 (Tiān Xīn) 开门 (Kāi Mén) Qian 6 Gui / Gui

Yang (阳) Dun# 1 Hour: YiSi ; 直符(ZhíFú): 天禽(TiānQín)
直使(ZhíShǐ): 死门(SǐMén) ; 旬首(XúnShǒu): JiaChenRen

九天 (Jiǔ Tiān) 天英 (Tiān Yīng) 生门 (Shēng Mén) Xun 4 Yi / Xin	值符 (Zhí Fú) 禽芮 (Qín Ruì) 伤门 (Shāng Mén) Li 9 Ji/Ren / Yi	螣蛇 (Téng Shé) 天柱 (Tiān Zhù) 杜门 (Dù Mén) Kun 2 Ding / Ji/Ren
九地 (Jiǔ Dì) 天辅 (Tiān Fǔ) 休门 (Xiū Mén) Zhen 3 Xin / Geng	Yang (阳) Dun# 1 Hour: **YiSi** ©Calvin Yap	太阴 (Tài Yīn) 天心 (Tiān Xīn) 景门 (Jǐng Mén) Dui 7 Gui / Ding
玄武 (Xuán Wǔ) 天冲 (Tiān Chōng) 开门 (Kāi Mén) Gen 8 Geng / Bing	白虎 (Bái Hǔ) 天任 (Tiān Rèn) 惊门 (Jīng Mén) Kan 1 Bing / Wu	六合 (Liù Hé) 天蓬 (Tiān Péng) 死门 (Sǐ Mén) Qian 6 Wu / Gui

---

Yang (阳) Dun# 1 Hour: BingWu ; 直符(ZhíFú): 天禽(TiānQín)
直使(ZhíShǐ): 死门(SǏMén) ; 旬首(XúnShǒu): JiaChenRen

太阴 (Tài Yīn) 天心 (Tiān Xīn) 伤门 (Shāng Mén) Xun 4　Gui Xin	六合 (Liù Hé) 天蓬 (Tiān Péng) 杜门 (Dù Mén) Li 9　Wu Yi	白虎 (Bái Hǔ) 天任 (Tiān Rèn) 景门 (Jǐng Mén) Kun 2　Bing Ji/Ren
螣蛇 (Téng Shé) 天柱 (Tiān Zhù) 生门 (Shēng Mén) Zhen 3　Ding Geng	Yang (阳) Dun# 1 Hour: **BingWu** **Fan Yin** ©Calvin Yap	玄武 (Xuán Wǔ) 天冲 (Tiān Chōng) 死门 (SǏ Mén) Dui 7　Geng Ding
值符 (Zhí Fú) 禽芮 (Qín Ruì) 休门 (Xiū Mén) Gen 8　Ji/Ren Bing	九天 (Jiǔ Tiān) 天英 (Tiān Yīng) 开门 (Kāi Mén) Kan 1　Yi Wu	九地 (Jiǔ Dì) 天辅 (Tiān Fǔ) 惊门 (Jǐng Mén) Qian 6　Xin Gui

Yang (阳) Dun# 1 Hour: DingWei ; 直符(ZhíFú): 天禽(TiānQín)
直使(ZhíShǐ): 死门(SǏMén) ; 旬首(XúnShǒu): JiaChenRen

玄武 (Xuán Wǔ) 天冲 (Tiān Chōng) 开门 (Kāi Mén) Xun 4　Geng Xin	九地 (Jiǔ Dì) 天辅 (Tiān Fǔ) 休门 (Xiū Mén) Li 9　Xin Yi	九天 (Jiǔ Tiān) 天英 (Tiān Yīng) 生门 (Shēng Mén) Kun 2　Yi Ji/Ren
白虎 (Bái Hǔ) 天任 (Tiān Rèn) 惊门 (Jǐng Mén) Zhen 3　Bing Geng	Yang (阳) Dun# 1 Hour: **DingWei** ©Calvin Yap	值符 (Zhí Fú) 禽芮 (Qín Ruì) 伤门 (Shāng Mén) Dui 7　Ji/Ren Ding
六合 (Liù Hé) 天蓬 (Tiān Péng) 死门 (SǏ Mén) Gen 8　Wu Bing	太阴 (Tài Yīn) 天心 (Tiān Xīn) 景门 (Jǐng Mén) Kan 1　Gui Wu	螣蛇 (Téng Shé) 天柱 (Tiān Zhù) 杜门 (Dù Mén) Qian 6　Ding Gui

Yang (阳) Dun# 1 Hour: WuShen ; 直符(ZhíFú): 天禽(TiānQín)
直使(ZhíShǐ): 死门(SǏMén) ; 旬首(XúnShǒu): JiaChenRen

六合 (Liù Hé) 天蓬 (Tiān Péng) 景门 (Jǐng Mén) Xun 4　Wu Xin	白虎 (Bái Hǔ) 天任 (Tiān Rèn) 死门 (SǏ Mén) Li 9　Bing Yi	玄武 (Xuán Wǔ) 天冲 (Tiān Chōng) 惊门 (Jǐng Mén) Kun 2　Geng Ji/Ren
太阴 (Tài Yīn) 天心 (Tiān Xīn) 杜门 (Dù Mén) Zhen 3　Gui Geng	Yang (阳) Dun# 1 Hour: **WuShen** ©Calvin Yap	九地 (Jiǔ Dì) 天辅 (Tiān Fǔ) 开门 (Kāi Mén) Dui 7　Xin Ding
螣蛇 (Téng Shé) 天柱 (Tiān Zhù) 伤门 (Shāng Mén) Gen 8　Ding Bing	值符 (Zhí Fú) 禽芮 (Qín Ruì) 生门 (Shēng Mén) Kan 1　Ji/Ren Wu	九天 (Jiǔ Tiān) 天英 (Tiān Yīng) 休门 (Xiū Mén) Qian 6　Yi Gui

Yang (阳) Dun# 1 Hour: JiYou ; 直符(ZhíFú): 天禽(TiānQín)
直使(ZhíShǐ): 死门(SǏMén) ; 旬首(XúnShǒu): JiaChenRen

九地 (Jiǔ Dì) 天辅 (Tiān Fǔ) 休门 (Xiū Mén) Xun 4　Xin Xin	九天 (Jiǔ Tiān) 天英 (Tiān Yīng) 生门 (Shēng Mén) Li 9　Yi Yi	值符 (Zhí Fú) 禽芮 (Qín Ruì) 伤门 (Shāng Mén) Kun 2　Ji/Ren Ji/Ren
玄武 (Xuán Wǔ) 天冲 (Tiān Chōng) 开门 (Kāi Mén) Zhen 3　Geng Geng	Yang (阳) Dun# 1 Hour: **JiYou** **Fu Yin** ©Calvin Yap	螣蛇 (Téng Shé) 天柱 (Tiān Zhù) 杜门 (Dù Mén) Dui 7　Ding
白虎 (Bái Hǔ) 天任 (Tiān Rèn) 惊门 (Jǐng Mén) Gen 8　Bing Bing	六合 (Liù Hé) 天蓬 (Tiān Péng) 死门 (SǏ Mén) Kan 1　Wu Wu	太阴 (Tài Yīn) 天心 (Tiān Xīn) 景门 (Jǐng Mén) Qian 6　Gui Gui

Yang (阳) Dun# 1 Hour: GengXu ; 直符(ZhíFú): 天禽(TiānQín)
直使(ZhíShǐ): 死门(SǏMén) ; 旬首(XúnShǒu): JiaChenRen

螣蛇 (Téng Shé) 天柱 (Tiān Zhù) 杜门 (Dù Mén) Xun 4　Ding Xin	太阴 (Tài Yīn) 天心 (Tiān Xīn) 景门 (Jǐng Mén) Li 9　Gui Yi	六合 (Liù Hé) 天蓬 (Tiān Péng) 死门 (SǏ Mén) Kun 2　Wu Ji/Ren
值符 (Zhí Fú) 禽芮 (Qín Ruì) 伤门 (Shāng Mén) Zhen 3　Ji/Ren Geng	Yang (阳) Dun# 1 Hour: **GengXu** ©Calvin Yap	白虎 (Bái Hǔ) 天任 (Tiān Rèn) 惊门 (Jǐng Mén) Dui 7　Bing Ding
九天 (Jiǔ Tiān) 天英 (Tiān Yīng) 生门 (Shēng Mén) Gen 8　Yi Bing	九地 (Jiǔ Dì) 天辅 (Tiān Fǔ) 休门 (Xiū Mén) Kan 1　Xin Wu	玄武 (Xuán Wǔ) 天冲 (Tiān Chōng) 开门 (Kāi Mén) Qian 6　Geng Gui

Yang (阳) Dun# 1 Hour: XinHai ; 直符(ZhíFú): 天禽(TiānQín)
直使(ZhíShǐ): 死门(SǏMén) ; 旬首(XúnShǒu): JiaChenRen

值符 (Zhí Fú) 禽芮 (Qín Ruì) 惊门 (Jǐng Mén) Xun 4　Ji/Ren Xin	螣蛇 (Téng Shé) 天柱 (Tiān Zhù) 开门 (Kāi Mén) Li 9　Ding Yi	太阴 (Tài Yīn) 天心 (Tiān Xīn) 休门 (Xiū Mén) Kun 2　Gui Ji/Ren
九天 (Jiǔ Tiān) 天英 (Tiān Yīng) 死门 (SǏ Mén) Zhen 3　Yi Geng	Yang (阳) Dun# 1 Hour: **XinHai** ©Calvin Yap	六合 (Liù Hé) 天蓬 (Tiān Péng) 生门 (Shēng Mén) Dui 7　Wu Ding
九地 (Jiǔ Dì) 天辅 (Tiān Fǔ) 景门 (Jǐng Mén) Gen 8　Xin Bing	玄武 (Xuán Wǔ) 天冲 (Tiān Chōng) 杜门 (Dù Mén) Kan 1　Geng Wu	白虎 (Bái Hǔ) 天任 (Tiān Rèn) 伤门 (Shāng Mén) Qian 6　Bing Gui

Yang (阳) Dun# 1 Hour: RenZi ; 直符(ZhíFú): 天禽(TiānQín)
直使(ZhíShǐ): 死门(SǐMén) ; 旬首(XúnShǒu): JiaChenRen

九地 (Jiǔ Dì) 天辅 (Tiān Fǔ) 死门 (SǐMén) Xun 4　Xin Xin	九天 (Jiǔ Tiān) 天英 (Tiān Yīng) 惊门 (Jīng Mén) Li 9　Yi Yi	值符 (Zhí Fú) 禽芮 (Qín Ruì) 开门 (Kāi Mén) Kun 2　Ji/Ren Ji/Ren
玄武 (Xuán Wǔ) 天冲 (Tiān Chōng) 景门 (Jǐng Mén) Zhen 3　Geng Geng	Yang (阳) Dun# 1 Hour: **RenZi** **Fu Yin** ©Calvin Yap	腾蛇 (Téng Shé) 天柱 (Tiān Zhù) 休门 (Xiū Mén) Dui 7　Ding Ding
白虎 (Bái Hǔ) 天任 (Tiān Rèn) 杜门 (Dù Mén) Gen 8　Bing Bing	六合 (Liù Hé) 天蓬 (Tiān Péng) 伤门 (Shāng Mén) Kan 1　Wu Wu	太阴 (Tài Yīn) 天心 (Tiān Xīn) 生门 (Shēng Mén) Qian 6　Gui Gui

Yang (阳) Dun# 1 Hour: GuiChou ; 直符(ZhíFú): 天禽(TiānQín)
直使(ZhíShǐ): 死门(SǐMén) ; 旬首(XúnShǒu): JiaChenRen

白虎 (Bái Hǔ) 天任 (Tiān Rèn) 杜门 (Dù Mén) Xun 4　Bing Xin	玄武 (Xuán Wǔ) 天冲 (Tiān Chōng) 景门 (Jǐng Mén) Li 9　Geng Yi	九地 (Jiǔ Dì) 天辅 (Tiān Fǔ) 死门 (SǐMén) Kun 2　Xin Ji/Ren
六合 (Liù Hé) 天蓬 (Tiān Péng) 伤门 (Shāng Mén) Zhen 3　Wu Geng	Yang (阳) Dun# 1 Hour: **GuiChou** ©Calvin Yap	九天 (Jiǔ Tiān) 天英 (Tiān Yīng) 惊门 (Jīng Mén) Dui 7　Yi Ding
太阴 (Tài Yīn) 天心 (Tiān Xīn) 生门 (Shēng Mén) Gen 8　Gui Bing	腾蛇 (Téng Shé) 天柱 (Tiān Zhù) 休门 (Xiū Mén) Kan 1　Ding Wu	值符 (Zhí Fú) 禽芮 (Qín Ruì) 开门 (Kāi Mén) Qian 6　Ji/Ren Gui

Chart: +1JiaYin (Yang Dun #1 JiaYin Xun)
JiaYin, YiMao, BingChen, DingSi, WuWu, JiWei, GengShen, XinYou, RenXu, GuiHai

Yang (阳) Dun# 1 Hour: JiaYin ; 直符(ZhíFú): 天心(TiānXīn)
直使(ZhíShǐ): 开门(KāiMén) ; 旬首(XúnShǒu): JiaYinGui

白虎 (Bái Hǔ) 天辅 (Tiān Fǔ) 杜门 (Dù Mén) Xun 4　Xin Xin	玄武 (Xuán Wǔ) 天英 (Tiān Yīng) 景门 (Jǐng Mén) Li 9　Yi Yi	九地 (Jiǔ Dì) 禽芮 (Qín Ruì) 死门 (SǐMén) Kun 2　Ji/Ren Ji/Ren
六合 (Liù Hé) 天冲 (Tiān Chōng) 伤门 (Shāng Mén) Zhen 3　Geng Geng	Yang (阳) Dun# 1 Hour: **JiaYin** **Fu Yin** ©Calvin Yap	九天 (Jiǔ Tiān) 天柱 (Tiān Zhù) 惊门 (Jīng Mén) Dui 7　Ding Ding
太阴 (Tài Yīn) 天任 (Tiān Rèn) 生门 (Shēng Mén) Gen 8　Bing Bing	腾蛇 (Téng Shé) 天蓬 (Tiān Péng) 休门 (Xiū Mén) Kan 1　Wu Wu	值符 (Zhí Fú) 天心 (Tiān Xīn) 开门 (Kāi Mén) Qian 6　Gui Gui

Yang (阳) Dun# 1 Hour: YiMao ; 直符(ZhíFú): 天心(TiānXīn)
直使(ZhíShǐ): 开门(KāiMén) ; 旬首(XúnShǒu): JiaYinGui

九天 (Jiǔ Tiān) 天柱 (Tiān Zhù) 景门 (Jǐng Mén) Xun 4　Ding Xin	值符 (Zhí Fú) 天心 (Tiān Xīn) 死门 (SǐMén) Li 9　Gui Yi	腾蛇 (Téng Shé) 天蓬 (Tiān Péng) 惊门 (Jīng Mén) Kun 2　Wu Ji/Ren
九地 (Jiǔ Dì) 禽芮 (Qín Ruì) 杜门 (Dù Mén) Zhen 3　Ji/Ren Geng	Yang (阳) Dun# 1 Hour: **YiMao** ©Calvin Yap	太阴 (Tài Yīn) 天任 (Tiān Rèn) 开门 (Kāi Mén) Dui 7　Bing Ding
玄武 (Xuán Wǔ) 天英 (Tiān Yīng) 伤门 (Shāng Mén) Gen 8　Yi Bing	白虎 (Bái Hǔ) 天辅 (Tiān Fǔ) 生门 (Shēng Mén) Kan 1　Xin Wu	六合 (Liù Hé) 天冲 (Tiān Chōng) 休门 (Xiū Mén) Qian 6　Geng Gui

Yang (阳) Dun# 1 Hour: BingChen ; 直符(ZhíFú): 天心(TiānXīn)
直使(ZhíShǐ): 开门(KāiMén) ; 旬首(XúnShǒu): JiaYinGui

太阴 (Tài Yīn) 天任 (Tiān Rèn) 生门 (Shēng Mén) Xun 4　Bing Xin	六合 (Liù Hé) 天冲 (Tiān Chōng) 伤门 (Shāng Mén) Li 9　Geng Yi	白虎 (Bái Hǔ) 天辅 (Tiān Fǔ) 杜门 (Dù Mén) Kun 2　Xin Ji/Ren
腾蛇 (Téng Shé) 天蓬 (Tiān Péng) 休门 (Xiū Mén) Zhen 3　Wu Geng	Yang (阳) Dun# 1 Hour: **BingChen** ©Calvin Yap	玄武 (Xuán Wǔ) 天英 (Tiān Yīng) 景门 (Jǐng Mén) Dui 7　Yi Ding
值符 (Zhí Fú) 天心 (Tiān Xīn) 开门 (Kāi Mén) Gen 8　Gui Bing	九天 (Jiǔ Tiān) 天柱 (Tiān Zhù) 惊门 (Jīng Mén) Kan 1　Ding Wu	九地 (Jiǔ Dì) 禽芮 (Qín Ruì) 死门 (SǐMén) Qian 6　Ji/Ren Gui

Yang (阳) Dun# 1 Hour: DingSi ; 直符(ZhíFú): 天心(TiānXīn)
直使(ZhíShǐ): 开门(KāiMén) ; 旬首(XúnShǒu): JiaYinGui

玄武 (Xuán Wǔ) 天英 (Tiān Yīng) 惊门 (Jīng Mén) Xun 4　Yi Xin	九地 (Jiǔ Dì) 禽芮 (Qín Ruì) 开门 (Kāi Mén) Li 9　Ji/Ren Yi	九天 (Jiǔ Tiān) 天柱 (Tiān Zhù) 休门 (Xiū Mén) Kun 2　Ding Ji/Ren
白虎 (Bái Hǔ) 天辅 (Tiān Fǔ) 死门 (SǐMén) Zhen 3　Xin Geng	Yang (阳) Dun# 1 Hour: **DingSi** ©Calvin Yap	值符 (Zhí Fú) 天心 (Tiān Xīn) 生门 (Shēng Mén) Dui 7　Gui Ding
六合 (Liù Hé) 天冲 (Tiān Chōng) 景门 (Jǐng Mén) Gen 8　Geng Bing	太阴 (Tài Yīn) 天任 (Tiān Rèn) 杜门 (Dù Mén) Kan 1　Bing Wu	腾蛇 (Téng Shé) 天蓬 (Tiān Péng) 伤门 (Shāng Mén) Qian 6　Wu Gui

Yang (阳) Dun# 1 Hour: WuWu ; 直符(ZhíFú): 天心(TiānXīn)
直使(ZhíShǐ): 开门(KāiMén) ; 旬首(XúnShǒu): JiaYinGui

六合 (Liù Hé) 天冲 (Tiān Chōng) 伤门 (Shāng Mén) Xun 4　Geng　Xin	白虎 (Bái Hǔ) 天辅 (Tiān Fǔ) 杜门 (Dù Mén) Li 9　Xin　Yi	玄武 (Xuán Wǔ) 天英 (Tiān Yīng) 景门 (Jǐng Mén) Kun 2　Yi　Ji/Ren
太阴 (Tài Yīn) 天任 (Tiān Rèn) 生门 (Shēng Mén) Zhen 3　Bing　Geng	Yang (阳) Dun# 1 Hour: **WuWu** ©Calvin Yap	九地 (Jiǔ Dì) 禽芮 (Qín Ruì) 死门 (Sǐ Mén) Dui 7　Ji/Ren　Ding
螣蛇 (Téng Shé) 天蓬 (Tiān Péng) 休门 (Xiū Mén) Gen 8　Wu　Bing	值符 (Zhí Fú) 天心 (Tiān Xīn) 开门 (Kāi Mén) Kan 1　Gui　Wu	九天 (Jiǔ Tiān) 天柱 (Tiān Zhù) 惊门 (Jīng Mén) Qian 6　Ding　Gui

Yang (阳) Dun# 1 Hour: JiWei ; 直符(ZhíFú): 天心(TiānXīn)
直使(ZhíShǐ): 开门(KāiMén) ; 旬首(XúnShǒu): JiaYinGui

九地 (Jiǔ Dì) 禽芮 (Qín Ruì) 死门 (Sǐ Mén) Xun 4　Ji/Ren　Xin	九天 (Jiǔ Tiān) 天柱 (Tiān Zhù) 惊门 (Jīng Mén) Li 9　Ding　Yi	值符 (Zhí Fú) 天心 (Tiān Xīn) 开门 (Kāi Mén) Kun 2　Gui　Ji/Ren
玄武 (Xuán Wǔ) 天英 (Tiān Yīng) 景门 (Jǐng Mén) Zhen 3　Yi　Geng	Yang (阳) Dun# 1 Hour: **JiWei** ©Calvin Yap	螣蛇 (Téng Shé) 天蓬 (Tiān Péng) 休门 (Xiū Mén) Dui 7　Wu　Ding
白虎 (Bái Hǔ) 天辅 (Tiān Fǔ) 杜门 (Dù Mén) Gen 8　Xin　Bing	六合 (Liù Hé) 天冲 (Tiān Chōng) 伤门 (Shāng Mén) Kan 1　Geng　Wu	太阴 (Tài Yīn) 天任 (Tiān Rèn) 生门 (Shēng Mén) Qian 6　Bing　Gui

Yang (阳) Dun# 1 Hour: GengShen ; 直符(ZhíFú): 天心(TiānXīn)
直使(ZhíShǐ): 开门(KāiMén) ; 旬首(XúnShǒu): JiaYinGui

螣蛇 (Téng Shé) 天蓬 (Tiān Péng) 休门 (Xiū Mén) Xun 4　Wu　Xin	太阴 (Tài Yīn) 天任 (Tiān Rèn) 生门 (Shēng Mén) Li 9　Bing　Yi	六合 (Liù Hé) 天冲 (Tiān Chōng) 伤门 (Shāng Mén) Kun 2　Geng　Ji/Ren
值符 (Zhi Fú) 天心 (Tiān Xīn) 开门 (Kāi Mén) Zhen 3　Gui　Geng	Yang (阳) Dun# 1 Hour: **GengShen** ©Calvin Yap	白虎 (Bái Hǔ) 天辅 (Tiān Fǔ) 杜门 (Dù Mén) Dui 7　Xin　Ding
九天 (Jiǔ Tiān) 天柱 (Tiān Zhù) 惊门 (Jīng Mén) Gen 8　Ding　Bing	九地 (Jiǔ Dì) 禽芮 (Qín Ruì) 死门 (Sǐ Mén) Kan 1　Ji/Ren　Wu	玄武 (Xuán Wǔ) 天英 (Tiān Yīng) 景门 (Jǐng Mén) Qian 6　Yi　Gui

Yang (阳) Dun# 1 Hour: XinYou ; 直符(ZhíFú): 天心(TiānXīn)
直使(ZhíShǐ): 开门(KāiMén) ; 旬首(XúnShǒu): JiaYinGui

值符 (Zhí Fú) 天心 (Tiān Xīn) 开门 (Kāi Mén) Xun 4　Gui　Xin	螣蛇 (Téng Shé) 天蓬 (Tiān Péng) 休门 (Xiū Mén) Li 9　Wu　Yi	太阴 (Tài Yīn) 天任 (Tiān Rèn) 生门 (Shēng Mén) Kun 2　Bing　Ji/Ren
九天 (Jiǔ Tiān) 天柱 (Tiān Zhù) 惊门 (Jīng Mén) Zhen 3　Ding　Geng	Yang (阳) Dun# 1 Hour: **XinYou** **Fan Yin** ©Calvin Yap	六合 (Liù Hé) 天冲 (Tiān Chōng) 伤门 (Shāng Mén) Dui 7　Geng　Ding
九地 (Jiǔ Dì) 禽芮 (Qín Ruì) 死门 (Sǐ Mén) Gen 8　Ji/Ren　Bing	玄武 (Xuán Wǔ) 天英 (Tiān Yīng) 景门 (Jǐng Mén) Kan 1　Yi　Wu	白虎 (Bái Hǔ) 天辅 (Tiān Fǔ) 杜门 (Dù Mén) Qian 6　Xin　Gui

Yang (阳) Dun# 1 Hour: RenXu ; 直符(ZhíFú): 天心(TiānXīn)
直使(ZhíShǐ): 开门(KāiMén) ; 旬首(XúnShǒu): JiaYinGui

九地 (Jiǔ Dì) 禽芮 (Qín Ruì) 死门 (Sǐ Mén) Xun 4　Ji/Ren　Xin	九天 (Jiǔ Tiān) 天柱 (Tiān Zhù) 惊门 (Jīng Mén) Li 9　Ding　Yi	值符 (Zhí Fú) 天心 (Tiān Xīn) 开门 (Kāi Mén) Kun 2　Gui　Ji/Ren
玄武 (Xuán Wǔ) 天英 (Tiān Yīng) 景门 (Jǐng Mén) Zhen 3　Yi　Geng	Yang (阳) Dun# 1 Hour: **RenXu** ©Calvin Yap	螣蛇 (Téng Shé) 天蓬 (Tiān Péng) 休门 (Xiū Mén) Dui 7　Wu　Ding
白虎 (Bái Hǔ) 天辅 (Tiān Fǔ) 杜门 (Dù Mén) Gen 8　Xin　Bing	六合 (Liù Hé) 天冲 (Tiān Chōng) 伤门 (Shāng Mén) Kan 1　Geng　Wu	太阴 (Tài Yīn) 天任 (Tiān Rèn) 生门 (Shēng Mén) Qian 6　Bing　Gui

Yang (阳) Dun# 1 Hour: GuiHai ; 直符(ZhíFú): 天心(TiānXīn)
直使(ZhíShǐ): 开门(KāiMén) ; 旬首(XúnShǒu): JiaYinGui

白虎 (Bái Hǔ) 天辅 (Tiān Fǔ) 杜门 (Dù Mén) Xun 4　Xin　Xin	玄武 (Xuán Wǔ) 天英 (Tiān Yīng) 景门 (Jǐng Mén) Li 9　Yi　Yi	九地 (Jiǔ Dì) 禽芮 (Qín Ruì) 死门 (Sǐ Mén) Kun 2　Ji/Ren　Ji/Ren
六合 (Liù Hé) 天冲 (Tiān Chōng) 伤门 (Shāng Mén) Zhen 3　Geng　Geng	Yang (阳) Dun# 1 Hour: **GuiHai** **Fu Yin** ©Calvin Yap	九天 (Jiǔ Tiān) 天柱 (Tiān Zhù) 惊门 (Jīng Mén) Dui 7　Ding　Ding
太阴 (Tài Yīn) 天任 (Tiān Rèn) 生门 (Shēng Mén) Gen 8　Bing　Bing	螣蛇 (Téng Shé) 天蓬 (Tiān Péng) 休门 (Xiū Mén) Kan 1　Wu　Wu	值符 (Zhí Fú) 天心 (Tiān Xīn) 开门 (Kāi Mén) Qian 6　Gui　Gui

Yang Dun#2

Chart: +2JiaZi (Yang Dun #2 JiaZi Xun)
JiaZi, YiChou, BingYin, DingMao, WuChen, JiSi, GengWu, XinWei, RenShen, GuiYou

Yang (阳) Dun# 2 Hour: JiaZi ；直符(ZhíFú):天芮(TiānRuì) 直使(ZhíShǐ): 死门(SǐMén) ；旬首(XúnShǒu): JiaZiWu

九地 (Jiǔ Dì) 天辅 (Tiān Fǔ) 杜门 (Dù Mén) Xun 4　Geng　Geng	九天 (Jiǔ Tiān) 天英 (Tiān Yīng) 景门 (Jǐng Mén) Li 9　Bing　Bing	值符 (Zhí Fú) 禽芮 (Qín Ruì) 死门 (Sǐ Mén) Kun 2　Wu/Xin　Wu/Xin
玄武 (Xuán Wǔ) 天冲 (Tiān Chōng) 伤门 (Shāng Mén) Zhen 3　Ji　Ji	Yang (阳) Dun# 2 Hour: JiaZi Fu Yin ©Calvin Yap	螣蛇 (Téng Shé) 天柱 (Tiān Zhù) 惊门 (Jīng Mén) Dui 7　Gui　Gui
白虎 (Bái Hǔ) 天任 (Tiān Rèn) 生门 (Shēng Mén) Gen 8　Ding　Ding	六合 (Liù Hé) 天蓬 (Tiān Péng) 休门 (Xiū Mén) Kan 1　Yi　Yi	太阴 (Tài Yīn) 天心 (Tiān Xīn) 开门 (Kāi Mén) Qian 6　Ren　Ren

Yang (阳) Dun# 2 Hour: YiChou ；直符(ZhíFú): 天芮(TiānRuì) 直使(ZhíShǐ): 死门(SǐMén) ；旬首(XúnShǒu): JiaZiWu

六合 (Liù Hé) 天蓬 (Tiān Péng) 惊门 (Jīng Mén) Xun 4　Yi　Geng	白虎 (Bái Hǔ) 天任 (Tiān Rèn) 开门 (Kāi Mén) Li 9　Ding　Bing	玄武 (Xuán Wǔ) 天冲 (Tiān Chōng) 休门 (Xiū Mén) Kun 2　Ji　Wu/Xin
太阴 (Tài Yīn) 天心 (Tiān Xīn) 死门 (Sǐ Mén) Zhen 3　Ren　Ji	Yang (阳) Dun# 2 Hour: YiChou ©Calvin Yap	九地 (Jiǔ Dì) 天辅 (Tiān Fǔ) 生门 (Shēng Mén) Dui 7　Geng　Gui
螣蛇 (Téng Shé) 天柱 (Tiān Zhù) 景门 (Jǐng Mén) Gen 8　Gui　Ding	值符 (Zhí Fú) 禽芮 (Qín Ruì) 杜门 (Dù Mén) Kan 1　Wu/Xin　Yi	九天 (Jiǔ Tiān) 天英 (Tiān Yīng) 伤门 (Shāng Mén) Qian 6　Bing　Ren

Yang (阳) Dun# 2 Hour: BingYin ；直符(ZhíFú):天芮(TiānRuì) 直使(ZhíShǐ): 死门(SǐMén) ；旬首(XúnShǒu): JiaZiWu

九天 (Jiǔ Tiān) 天英 (Tiān Yīng) 死门 (Sǐ Mén) Xun 4　Bing　Geng	值符 (Zhí Fú) 禽芮 (Qín Ruì) 惊门 (Jīng Mén) Li 9　Wu/Xin　Bing	螣蛇 (Téng Shé) 天柱 (Tiān Zhù) 开门 (Kāi Mén) Kun 2　Gui　Wu/Xin
九地 (Jiǔ Dì) 天辅 (Tiān Fǔ) 景门 (Jǐng Mén) Zhen 3　Geng　Ji	Yang (阳) Dun# 2 Hour: BingYin ©Calvin Yap	太阴 (Tài Yīn) 天心 (Tiān Xīn) 休门 (Xiū Mén) Dui 7　Ren　Gui
玄武 (Xuán Wǔ) 天冲 (Tiān Chōng) 杜门 (Dù Mén) Gen 8　Ji　Ding	白虎 (Bái Hǔ) 天任 (Tiān Rèn) 伤门 (Shāng Mén) Kan 1　Ding　Yi	六合 (Liù Hé) 天蓬 (Tiān Péng) 生门 (Shēng Mén) Qian 6　Yi　Ren

Yang (阳) Dun# 2 Hour: DingMao ；直符(ZhíFú): 天芮(TiānRuì) 直使(ZhíShǐ): 死门(SǐMén) ；旬首(XúnShǒu): JiaZiWu

太阴 (Tài Yīn) 天心 (Tiān Xīn) 杜门 (Dù Mén) Xun 4　Ren　Geng	六合 (Liù Hé) 天蓬 (Tiān Péng) 景门 (Jǐng Mén) Li 9　Yi　Bing	白虎 (Bái Hǔ) 天任 (Tiān Rèn) 死门 (Sǐ Mén) Kun 2　Ding　Wu/Xin
螣蛇 (Téng Shé) 天柱 (Tiān Zhù) 伤门 (Shāng Mén) Zhen 3　Gui　Ji	Yang (阳) Dun# 2 Hour: DingMao Fan Yin ©Calvin Yap	玄武 (Xuán Wǔ) 天冲 (Tiān Chōng) 惊门 (Jīng Mén) Dui 7　Ji　Gui
值符 (Zhí Fú) 禽芮 (Qín Ruì) 生门 (Shēng Mén) Gen 8　Wu/Xin　Ding	九天 (Jiǔ Tiān) 天英 (Tiān Yīng) 休门 (Xiū Mén) Kan 1　Bing　Yi	九地 (Jiǔ Dì) 天辅 (Tiān Fǔ) 开门 (Kāi Mén) Qian 6　Geng　Ren

Yang (阳) Dun# 2 Hour: WuChen ；直符(ZhíFú): 天芮(TiānRuì) 直使(ZhíShǐ): 死门(SǐMén) ；旬首(XúnShǒu): JiaZiWu

九地 (Jiǔ Dì) 天辅 (Tiān Fǔ) 生门 (Shēng Mén) Xun 4　Geng　Geng	九天 (Jiǔ Tiān) 天英 (Tiān Yīng) 伤门 (Shāng Mén) Li 9　Bing　Bing	值符 (Zhí Fú) 禽芮 (Qín Ruì) 杜门 (Dù Mén) Kun 2　Wu/Xin　Wu/Xin
玄武 (Xuán Wǔ) 天冲 (Tiān Chōng) 休门 (Xiū Mén) Zhen 3　Ji　Ji	Yang (阳) Dun# 2 Hour: WuChen Fu Yin ©Calvin Yap	螣蛇 (Téng Shé) 天柱 (Tiān Zhù) 景门 (Jǐng Mén) Dui 7　Gui　Gui
白虎 (Bái Hǔ) 天任 (Tiān Rèn) 开门 (Kāi Mén) Gen 8　Ding　Ding	六合 (Liù Hé) 天蓬 (Tiān Péng) 惊门 (Jīng Mén) Kan 1　Yi　Yi	太阴 (Tài Yīn) 天心 (Tiān Xīn) 死门 (Sǐ Mén) Qian 6　Ren　Ren

Yang (阳) Dun# 2 Hour: JiSi ；直符(ZhíFú): 天芮(TiānRuì) 直使(ZhíShǐ): 死门(SǐMén) ；旬首(XúnShǒu): JiaZiWu

螣蛇 (Téng Shé) 天柱 (Tiān Zhù) 伤门 (Shāng Mén) Xun 4　Gui　Geng	太阴 (Tài Yīn) 天心 (Tiān Xīn) 杜门 (Dù Mén) Li 9　Ren　Bing	六合 (Liù Hé) 天蓬 (Tiān Péng) 景门 (Jǐng Mén) Kun 2　Yi　Wu/Xin
值符 (Zhí Fú) 禽芮 (Qín Ruì) 生门 (Shēng Mén) Zhen 3　Wu/Xin　Ji	Yang (阳) Dun# 2 Hour: JiSi ©Calvin Yap	白虎 (Bái Hǔ) 天任 (Tiān Rèn) 死门 (Sǐ Mén) Dui 7　Ding　Gui
九天 (Jiǔ Tiān) 天英 (Tiān Yīng) 休门 (Xiū Mén) Gen 8　Bing　Ding	九地 (Jiǔ Dì) 天辅 (Tiān Fǔ) 开门 (Kāi Mén) Kan 1　Geng　Yi	玄武 (Xuán Wǔ) 天冲 (Tiān Chōng) 惊门 (Jīng Mén) Qian 6　Ji　Ren

Yang (阳) Dun# 2 Hour: **GengWu** ; 直符(ZhíFú): 天芮(TiānRuì)
直使(ZhíShǐ): 死门(SǐMén) ; 旬首(XúnShǒu): JiaZiWu

值符 (Zhí Fú) 禽芮 (Qín Ruì) 开门 (Kāi Mén) Xun 4 Wu/Xin Geng	螣蛇 (Téng Shé) 天柱 (Tiān Zhù) 休门 (Xiū Mén) Li 9 Gui Bing	太阴 (Tài Yīn) 天心 (Tiān Xīn) 生门 (Shēng Mén) Kun 2 Ren Wu/Xin
九天 (Jiǔ Tiān) 天英 (Tiān Yīng) 惊门 (Jīng Mén) Zhen 3 Bing Ji	Yang (阳) Dun# 2 Hour: **GengWu** ©Calvin Yap	六合 (Liù Hé) 天蓬 (Tiān Péng) 伤门 (Shāng Mén) Dui 7 Yi Gui
九地 (Jiǔ Dì) 天辅 (Tiān Fǔ) 死门 (Sǐ Mén) Gen 8 Geng Ding	玄武 (Xuán Wǔ) 天冲 (Tiān Chōng) 景门 (Jǐng Mén) Kan 1 Ji Yi	白虎 (Bái Hǔ) 天任 (Tiān Rèn) 杜门 (Dù Mén) Qian 6 Ding Ren

Yang (阳) Dun# 2 Hour: **XinWei** ; 直符(ZhíFú): 天芮(TiānRuì)
直使(ZhíShǐ): 死门(SǐMén) ; 旬首(XúnShǒu): JiaZiWu

九地 (Jiǔ Dì) 天辅 (Tiān Fǔ) 景门 (Jǐng Mén) Xun 4 Geng Geng	九天 (Jiǔ Tiān) 天英 (Tiān Yīng) 死门 (Sǐ Mén) Li 9 Bing	值符 (Zhí Fú) 禽芮 (Qín Ruì) 惊门 (Jīng Mén) Kun 2 Wu/Xin Wu/Xin
玄武 (Xuán Wǔ) 天冲 (Tiān Chōng) 杜门 (Dù Mén) Zhen 3 Ji Ji	Yang (阳) Dun# 2 Hour: **XinWei** **Fu Yin** ©Calvin Yap	螣蛇 (Téng Shé) 天柱 (Tiān Zhù) 开门 (Kāi Mén) Dui 7 Gui Gui
白虎 (Bái Hǔ) 天任 (Tiān Rèn) 伤门 (Shāng Mén) Gen 8 Ding Ding	六合 (Liù Hé) 天蓬 (Tiān Péng) 生门 (Shēng Mén) Kan 1 Yi Yi	太阴 (Tài Yīn) 天心 (Tiān Xīn) 休门 (Xiū Mén) Qian 6 Ren Ren

Yang (阳) Dun# 2 Hour: **RenShen** ; 直符(ZhíFú): 天芮(TiānRuì)
直使(ZhíShǐ): 死门(SǐMén) ; 旬首(XúnShǒu): JiaZiWu

白虎 (Bái Hǔ) 天任 (Tiān Rèn) 休门 (Xiū Mén) Xun 4 Ding Geng	玄武 (Xuán Wǔ) 天冲 (Tiān Chōng) 生门 (Shēng Mén) Li 9 Ji Bing	九地 (Jiǔ Dì) 天辅 (Tiān Fǔ) 伤门 (Shāng Mén) Kun 2 Geng Wu/Xin
六合 (Liù Hé) 天蓬 (Tiān Péng) 开门 (Kāi Mén) Zhen 3 Yi Ji	Yang (阳) Dun# 2 Hour: **RenShen** ©Calvin Yap	九天 (Jiǔ Tiān) 天英 (Tiān Yīng) 杜门 (Dù Mén) Dui 7 Bing Gui
太阴 (Tài Yīn) 天心 (Tiān Xīn) 惊门 (Jīng Mén) Gen 8 Ren Ding	螣蛇 (Téng Shé) 天柱 (Tiān Zhù) 死门 (Sǐ Mén) Kan 1 Gui Yi	值符 (Zhí Fú) 禽芮 (Qín Ruì) 景门 (Jǐng Mén) Qian 6 Wu/Xin Ren

Yang (阳) Dun# 2 Hour: **GuiYou** ; 直符(ZhíFú): 天芮(TiānRuì)
直使(ZhíShǐ): 死门(SǐMén) ; 旬首(XúnShǒu): JiaZiWu

玄武 (Xuán Wǔ) 天冲 (Tiān Chōng) 杜门 (Dù Mén) Xun 4 Ji Geng	九地 (Jiǔ Dì) 天辅 (Tiān Fǔ) 景门 (Jǐng Mén) Li 9 Geng Bing	九天 (Jiǔ Tiān) 天英 (Tiān Yīng) 死门 (Sǐ Mén) Kun 2 Bing Wu/Xin
白虎 (Bái Hǔ) 天任 (Tiān Rèn) 伤门 (Shāng Mén) Zhen 3 Ding Ji	Yang (阳) Dun# 2 Hour: **GuiYou** ©Calvin Yap	值符 (Zhí Fú) 禽芮 (Qín Ruì) 惊门 (Jīng Mén) Dui 7 Wu/Xin Gui
六合 (Liù Hé) 天蓬 (Tiān Péng) 生门 (Shēng Mén) Gen 8 Yi Ding	太阴 (Tài Yīn) 天心 (Tiān Xīn) 休门 (Xiū Mén) Kan 1 Ren Yi	螣蛇 (Téng Shé) 天柱 (Tiān Zhù) 开门 (Kāi Mén) Qian 6 Gui Ren

---

Chart: +2JiaXu (Yang Dun #2 JiaXu Xun)
JiaXu, YiHai, BingZi, DingChou, WuYin, JiMao, GengChen, XinSi, RenWu, GuiWei

Yang (阳) Dun# 2 Hour: **JiaXu** ; 直符(ZhíFú): 天冲(TiānChōng)
直使(ZhíShǐ): 伤门(ShāngMén) ; 旬首(XúnShǒu): JiaXuJi

螣蛇 (Téng Shé) 天辅 (Tiān Fǔ) 杜门 (Dù Mén) Xun 4 Geng Geng	太阴 (Tài Yīn) 天英 (Tiān Yīng) 景门 (Jǐng Mén) Li 9 Bing Bing	六合 (Liù Hé) 禽芮 (Qín Ruì) 死门 (Sǐ Mén) Kun 2 Wu/Xin Wu/Xin
值符 (Zhí Fú) 天冲 (Tiān Chōng) 伤门 (Shāng Mén) Zhen 3 Ji Ji	Yang (阳) Dun# 2 Hour: **JiaXu** **Fu Yin** ©Calvin Yap	白虎 (Bái Hǔ) 天柱 (Tiān Zhù) 惊门 (Jīng Mén) Dui 7 Gui Gui
九天 (Jiǔ Tiān) 天任 (Tiān Rèn) 生门 (Shēng Mén) Gen 8 Ding Ding	九地 (Jiǔ Dì) 天蓬 (Tiān Péng) 休门 (Xiū Mén) Kan 1 Yi Yi	玄武 (Xuán Wǔ) 天心 (Tiān Xīn) 开门 (Kāi Mén) Qian 6 Ren Ren

Yang (阳) Dun# 2 Hour: **YiHai** ; 直符(ZhíFú): 天冲(TiānChōng)
直使(ZhíShǐ): 伤门(ShāngMén) ; 旬首(XúnShǒu): JiaXuJi

六合 (Liù Hé) 禽芮 (Qín Ruì) 伤门 (Shāng Mén) Xun 4 Wu/Xin Geng	白虎 (Bái Hǔ) 天柱 (Tiān Zhù) 杜门 (Dù Mén) Li 9 Gui Bing	玄武 (Xuán Wǔ) 天心 (Tiān Xīn) 景门 (Jǐng Mén) Kun 2 Ren Wu/Xin
太阴 (Tài Yīn) 天英 (Tiān Yīng) 生门 (Shēng Mén) Zhen 3 Bing Ji	Yang (阳) Dun# 2 Hour: **YiHai** ©Calvin Yap	九地 (Jiǔ Dì) 天蓬 (Tiān Péng) 死门 (Sǐ Mén) Dui 7 Yi Gui
螣蛇 (Téng Shé) 天辅 (Tiān Fǔ) 休门 (Xiū Mén) Gen 8 Geng Ding	值符 (Zhí Fú) 天冲 (Tiān Chōng) 开门 (Kāi Mén) Kan 1 Ji Yi	九天 (Jiǔ Tiān) 天任 (Tiān Rèn) 惊门 (Jīng Mén) Qian 6 Ding Ren

Yang (阳) Dun# 2 Hour: **BingZi** ; 直符(ZhíFú): 天冲(TiānChōng)
直使(ZhíShǐ): 伤门(ShāngMén) ; 旬首(XúnShǒu): JiaXuJi

九天 (Jiǔ Tiān) 天任 (Tiān Rèn) 休门 (Xiū Mén) Xun 4　Ding Geng	值符 (Zhi Fú) 天冲 (Tiān Chōng) 生门 (Shēng Mén) Li 9　Ji Bing	螣蛇 (Téng Shé) 天辅 (Tiān Fǔ) 伤门 (Shāng Mén) Kun 2　Geng Wu/Xin
九地 (Jiǔ Dì) 天蓬 (Tiān Péng) 开门 (Kāi Mén) Zhen 3　Yi Ji	Yang (阳) Dun# 2 Hour: **BingZi** ©Calvin Yap	太阴 (Tài Yīn) 天英 (Tiān Yīng) 杜门 (Dù Mén) Dui 7　Bing Gui
玄武 (Xuán Wǔ) 天心 (Tiān Xīn) 惊门 (Jīng Mén) Gen 8　Ren Ding	白虎 (Bái Hǔ) 天柱 (Tiān Zhù) 死门 (Sǐ Mén) Kan 1　Gui Yi	六合 (Liù Hé) 禽芮 (Qín Ruì) 景门 (Jǐng Mén) Qian 6　Wu/Xin Ren

Yang (阳) Dun# 2 Hour:**DingChou** ; 直符(ZhíFú): 冲(TiānChōng)
直使(ZhíShǐ): 伤门(ShāngMén) ; 旬首(XúnShǒu): JiaXuJi

太阴 (Tài Yīn) 天英 (Tiān Yīng) 惊门 (Jīng Mén) Xun 4　Bing Geng	六合 (Liù Hé) 禽芮 (Qín Ruì) 开门 (Kāi Mén) Li 9　Wu/Xin Bing	白虎 (Bái Hǔ) 天柱 (Tiān Zhù) 休门 (Xiū Mén) Kun 2　Gui Wu/Xin
螣蛇 (Téng Shé) 天辅 (Tiān Fǔ) 死门 (Sǐ Mén) Zhen 3　Geng Ji	Yang (阳) Dun# 2 Hour: **DingChou** ©Calvin Yap	玄武 (Xuán Wǔ) 天心 (Tiān Xīn) 生门 (Shēng Mén) Dui 7　Ren Gui
值符 (Zhí Fú) 天冲 (Tiān Chōng) 景门 (Jǐng Mén) Gen 8　Ji Ding	九天 (Jiǔ Tiān) 天任 (Tiān Rèn) 杜门 (Dù Mén) Kan 1　Ding Yi	九地 (Jiǔ Dì) 天蓬 (Tiān Péng) 伤门 (Shāng Mén) Qian 6　Yi Ren

Yang (阳) Dun# 2 Hour: **WuYin** ; 直符(ZhíFú): 天冲(TiānChōng)
直使(ZhíShǐ): 伤门(ShāngMén) ; 旬首(XúnShǒu): JiaXuJi

九地 (Jiǔ Dì) 天蓬 (Tiān Péng) 开门 (Kāi Mén) Xun 4　Yi Geng	九天 (Jiǔ Tiān) 天任 (Tiān Rèn) 休门 (Xiū Mén) Li 9　Ding Bing	值符 (Zhí Fú) 天冲 (Tiān Chōng) 生门 (Shēng Mén) Kun 2　Ji Wu/Xin
玄武 (Xuán Wǔ) 天心 (Tiān Xīn) 惊门 (Jīng Mén) Zhen 3　Ren Ji	Yang (阳) Dun# 2 Hour: **WuYin** ©Calvin Yap	螣蛇 (Téng Shé) 天辅 (Tiān Fǔ) 伤门 (Shāng Mén) Dui 7　Geng Gui
白虎 (Bái Hǔ) 天柱 (Tiān Zhù) 死门 (Sǐ Mén) Gen 8　Gui Ding	六合 (Liù Hé) 禽芮 (Qín Ruì) 景门 (Jǐng Mén) Kan 1　Wu/Xin Yi	太阴 (Tài Yīn) 天英 (Tiān Yīng) 杜门 (Dù Mén) Qian 6　Bing Ren

Yang (阳) Dun# 2 Hour: **JiMao** ; 直符(ZhíFú): 天冲(TiānChōng)
直使(ZhíShǐ): 伤门(ShāngMén) ; 旬首(XúnShǒu): JiaXuJi

螣蛇 (Téng Shé) 天辅 (Tiān Fǔ) 景门 (Jǐng Mén) Xun 4　Geng Geng	太阴 (Tài Yīn) 天英 (Tiān Yīng) 死门 (Sǐ Mén) Li 9　Bing Bing	六合 (Liù Hé) 禽芮 (Qín Ruì) 惊门 (Jīng Mén) Kun 2　Wu/Xin Wu/Xin
值符 (Zhí Fú) 天冲 (Tiān Chōng) 杜门 (Dù Mén) Zhen 3　Ji Ji	Yang (阳) Dun# 2 Hour: **JiMao** **Fu Yin** ©Calvin Yap	白虎 (Bái Hǔ) 天柱 (Tiān Zhù) 开门 (Kāi Mén) Dui 7　Gui Gui
九天 (Jiǔ Tiān) 天任 (Tiān Rèn) 伤门 (Shāng Mén) Gen 8　Ding Ding	九地 (Jiǔ Dì) 天蓬 (Tiān Péng) 生门 (Shēng Mén) Kan 1　Yi Yi	玄武 (Xuán Wǔ) 天心 (Tiān Xīn) 休门 (Xiū Mén) Qian 6　Ren Ren

Yang (阳) Dun# 2 Hour: **GengChen**; 直符(ZhíFú): 冲(TiānChōng)
直使(ZhíShǐ): 伤门(ShāngMén) ; 旬首(XúnShǒu): JiaXuJi

值符 (Zhí Fú) 天冲 (Tiān Chōng) 生门 (Shēng Mén) Xun 4　Ji Geng	螣蛇 (Téng Shé) 天辅 (Tiān Fǔ) 伤门 (Shāng Mén) Li 9　Geng Bing	太阴 (Tài Yīn) 天英 (Tiān Yīng) 杜门 (Dù Mén) Kun 2　Bing Wu/Xin
九天 (Jiǔ Tiān) 天任 (Tiān Rèn) 休门 (Xiū Mén) Zhen 3　Ding Ji	Yang (阳) Dun# 2 Hour: **GengChen** ©Calvin Yap	六合 (Liù Hé) 禽芮 (Qín Ruì) 景门 (Jǐng Mén) Dui 7　Wu/Xin Gui
九地 (Jiǔ Dì) 天蓬 (Tiān Péng) 开门 (Kāi Mén) Gen 8　Yi Ding	玄武 (Xuán Wǔ) 天心 (Tiān Xīn) 惊门 (Jīng Mén) Kan 1　Ren Yi	白虎 (Bái Hǔ) 天柱 (Tiān Zhù) 死门 (Sǐ Mén) Qian 6　Gui Ren

Yang (阳) Dun# 2 Hour: **XinSi** ; 直符(ZhíFú): 天冲(TiānChōng)
直使(ZhíShǐ): 伤门(ShāngMén) ; 旬首(XúnShǒu): JiaXuJi

九地 (Jiǔ Dì) 天蓬 (Tiān Péng) 死门 (Sǐ Mén) Xun 4　Yi Geng	九天 (Jiǔ Tiān) 天任 (Tiān Rèn) 惊门 (Jīng Mén) Li 9　Ding Bing	值符 (Zhí Fú) 天冲 (Tiān Chōng) 开门 (Kāi Mén) Kun 2　Ji Wu/Xin
玄武 (Xuán Wǔ) 天心 (Tiān Xīn) 景门 (Jǐng Mén) Zhen 3　Ren Ji	Yang (阳) Dun# 2 Hour: **XinSi** ©Calvin Yap	螣蛇 (Téng Shé) 天辅 (Tiān Fǔ) 休门 (Xiū Mén) Dui 7　Geng Gui
白虎 (Bái Hǔ) 天柱 (Tiān Zhù) 杜门 (Dù Mén) Gen 8　Gui Ding	六合 (Liù Hé) 禽芮 (Qín Ruì) 伤门 (Shāng Mén) Kan 1　Wu/Xin Yi	太阴 (Tài Yīn) 天英 (Tiān Yīng) 生门 (Shēng Mén) Qian 6　Bing Ren

Yang (阳) Dun# 2 Hour: RenWu ; 直符(ZhíFú): 天冲(TiānChōng)
直使(ZhíShǐ): 伤门(ShāngMén) ; 旬首(XúnShǒu): JiaXuJi

白虎 (Bái Hǔ) 天柱 (Tiān Zhù) 休门 (Xiū Mén) Xun 4 Gui Geng	玄武 (Xuán Wǔ) 天心 (Tiān Xīn) 生门 (Shēng Mén) Li 9 Ren Bing	九地 (Jiǔ Dì) 天蓬 (Tiān Péng) 伤门 (Shāng Mén) Kun 2 Yi Wu/Xin
六合 (Liù Hé) 禽芮 (Qín Ruì) 开门 (Kāi Mén) Zhen 3 Wu/Xin Ji	Yang (阳) Dun# 2 Hour: **RenWu** ©Calvin Yap	九天 (Jiǔ Tiān) 天任 (Tiān Rèn) 杜门 (Dù Mén) Dui 7 Ding Gui
太阴 (Tài Yīn) 天英 (Tiān Yīng) 惊门 (Jīng Mén) Gen 8 Bing Ding	螣蛇 (Téng Shé) 天辅 (Tiān Fǔ) 死门 (Sǐ Mén) Kan 1 Geng Yi	值符 (Zhí Fú) 天冲 (Tiān Chōng) 景门 (Jǐng Mén) Qian 6 Ji Ren

Yang (阳) Dun# 2 Hour: GuiWei ; 直符(ZhíFú): 天冲(TiānChōng)
直使(ZhíShǐ): 伤门(ShāngMén) ; 旬首(XúnShǒu): JiaXuJi

玄武 (Xuán Wǔ) 天心 (Tiān Xīn) 杜门 (Dù Mén) Xun 4 Ren Geng	九地 (Jiǔ Dì) 天蓬 (Tiān Péng) 景门 (Jǐng Mén) Li 9 Yi Bing	九天 (Jiǔ Tiān) 天任 (Tiān Rèn) 死门 (Sǐ Mén) Kun 2 Ding Wu/Xin
白虎 (Bái Hǔ) 天柱 (Tiān Zhù) 伤门 (Shāng Mén) Zhen 3 Gui Ji	Yang (阳) Dun# 2 Hour: **GuiWei** **Fan Yin** ©Calvin Yap	值符 (Zhí Fú) 天冲 (Tiān Chōng) 惊门 (Jīng Mén) Dui 7 Ji Gui
六合 (Liù Hé) 禽芮 (Qín Ruì) 生门 (Shēng Mén) Gen 8 Wu/Xin Ding	太阴 (Tài Yīn) 天英 (Tiān Yīng) 休门 (Xiū Mén) Kan 1 Bing Yi	螣蛇 (Téng Shé) 天辅 (Tiān Fǔ) 开门 (Kāi Mén) Qian 6 Geng Ren

Chart: +2JiaShen (Yang Dun #2 JiaShen Xun)
JiaShen, YiYou, BingXu, DingHai, WuZi, JiChou, GengYin, XinMao, RenChen, GuiSi

Yang (阳) Dun# 2 Hour: JiaShen ; 直符(ZhíFú): 天辅(TiānFǔ)
直使(ZhíShǐ): 杜门(DùMén) ; 旬首(XúnShǒu): JiaShenGeng

值符 (Zhí Fú) 天辅 (Tiān Fǔ) 杜门 (Dù Mén) Xun 4 Geng Geng	螣蛇 (Téng Shé) 天英 (Tiān Yīng) 景门 (Jǐng Mén) Li 9 Bing Bing	太阴 (Tài Yīn) 禽芮 (Qín Ruì) 死门 (Sǐ Mén) Kun 2 Wu/Xin Wu/Xin
九天 (Jiǔ Tiān) 天冲 (Tiān Chōng) 伤门 (Shāng Mén) Zhen 3 Ji Ji	Yang (阳) Dun# 2 Hour: **JiaShen** **Fu Yin** ©Calvin Yap	六合 (Liù Hé) 天柱 (Tiān Zhù) 惊门 (Jīng Mén) Dui 7 Gui Gui
九地 (Jiǔ Dì) 天任 (Tiān Rèn) 生门 (Shēng Mén) Gen 8 Ding Ding	玄武 (Xuán Wǔ) 天蓬 (Tiān Péng) 休门 (Xiū Mén) Kan 1 Yi Yi	白虎 (Bái Hǔ) 天心 (Tiān Xīn) 开门 (Kāi Mén) Qian 6 Ren Ren

Yang (阳) Dun# 2 Hour: YiYou ; 直符(ZhíFú): 天辅(TiānFǔ)
直使(ZhíShǐ): 杜门(DùMén) ; 旬首(XúnShǒu): JiaShenGeng

六合 (Liù Hé) 天柱 (Tiān Zhù) 生门 (Shēng Mén) Xun 4 Gui Geng	白虎 (Bái Hǔ) 天心 (Tiān Xīn) 伤门 (Shāng Mén) Li 9 Ren Bing	玄武 (Xuán Wǔ) 天蓬 (Tiān Péng) 杜门 (Dù Mén) Kun 2 Yi Wu/Xin
太阴 (Tài Yīn) 禽芮 (Qín Ruì) 休门 (Xiū Mén) Zhen 3 Wu/Xin Ji	Yang (阳) Dun# 2 Hour: **YiYou** ©Calvin Yap	九地 (Jiǔ Dì) 天任 (Tiān Rèn) 景门 (Jǐng Mén) Dui 7 Ding Gui
螣蛇 (Téng Shé) 天英 (Tiān Yīng) 开门 (Kāi Mén) Gen 8 Bing Ding	值符 (Zhí Fú) 天辅 (Tiān Fǔ) 惊门 (Jīng Mén) Kan 1 Geng Yi	九天 (Jiǔ Tiān) 天冲 (Tiān Chōng) 死门 (Sǐ Mén) Qian 6 Ji Ren

Yang (阳) Dun# 2 Hour: BingXu ; 直符(ZhíFú): 天辅(TiānFǔ)
直使(ZhíShǐ): 杜门(DùMén) ; 旬首(XúnShǒu): JiaShenGeng

九天 (Jiǔ Tiān) 天冲 (Tiān Chōng) 开门 (Kāi Mén) Xun 4 Ji Geng	值符 (Zhí Fú) 天辅 (Tiān Fǔ) 休门 (Xiū Mén) Li 9 Geng Bing	螣蛇 (Téng Shé) 天英 (Tiān Yīng) 生门 (Shēng Mén) Kun 2 Bing Wu/Xin
九地 (Jiǔ Dì) 天任 (Tiān Rèn) 惊门 (Jīng Mén) Zhen 3 Ding Ji	Yang (阳) Dun# 2 Hour: **BingXu** ©Calvin Yap	太阴 (Tài Yīn) 禽芮 (Qín Ruì) 伤门 (Shāng Mén) Dui 7 Wu/Xin Gui
玄武 (Xuán Wǔ) 天蓬 (Tiān Péng) 死门 (Sǐ Mén) Gen 8 Yi Ding	白虎 (Bái Hǔ) 天心 (Tiān Xīn) 景门 (Jǐng Mén) Kan 1 Ren Yi	六合 (Liù Hé) 天柱 (Tiān Zhù) 杜门 (Dù Mén) Qian 6 Gui Ren

Yang (阳) Dun# 2 Hour: DingHai ; 直符(ZhíFú): 天辅(TiānFǔ)
直使(ZhíShǐ): 杜门(DùMén) ; 旬首(XúnShǒu): JiaShenGeng

太阴 (Tài Yīn) 禽芮 (Qín Ruì) 休门 (Xiū Mén) Xun 4 Wu/Xin Geng	六合 (Liù Hé) 天柱 (Tiān Zhù) 生门 (Shēng Mén) Li 9 Gui Bing	白虎 (Bái Hǔ) 天心 (Tiān Xīn) 伤门 (Shāng Mén) Kun 2 Ren Wu/Xin
螣蛇 (Téng Shé) 天英 (Tiān Yīng) 开门 (Kāi Mén) Zhen 3 Bing Ji	Yang (阳) Dun# 2 Hour: **DingHai** ©Calvin Yap	玄武 (Xuán Wǔ) 天蓬 (Tiān Péng) 杜门 (Dù Mén) Dui 7 Yi Gui
值符 (Zhí Fú) 天辅 (Tiān Fǔ) 惊门 (Jīng Mén) Gen 8 Geng Ding	九天 (Jiǔ Tiān) 天冲 (Tiān Chōng) 死门 (Sǐ Mén) Kan 1 Ji Yi	九地 (Jiǔ Dì) 天任 (Tiān Rèn) 景门 (Jǐng Mén) Qian 6 Ding Ren

Yang (阳) Dun# 2 Hour: **WuZi** ; 直符(ZhíFú): 天辅(TiānFǔ)
直使(ZhíShǐ): 杜门(DùMén) ; 旬首(XúnShǒu): JiaShenGeng

九地 (Jiǔ Dì) 天任 (Tiān Rèn) 死门 (Sǐ Mén) Xun 4　Ding Geng	九天 (Jiǔ Tiān) 天冲 (Tiān Chōng) 惊门 (Jīng Mén) Li 9　Ji Bing	值符 (Zhí Fú) 天辅 (Tiān Fǔ) 开门 (Kāi Mén) Kun 2　Geng Wu/Xin
玄武 (Xuán Wǔ) 天蓬 (Tiān Péng) 景门 (Jīng Mén) Zhen 3　Yi Ji	Yang (阳) Dun# 2 Hour: **WuZi** ©Calvin Yap	螣蛇 (Téng Shé) 天英 (Tiān Yīng) 休门 (Xiū Mén) Dui 7　Bing Gui
白虎 (Bái Hǔ) 天心 (Tiān Xīn) 杜门 (Dù Mén) Gen 8　Ren Ding	六合 (Liù Hé) 天柱 (Tiān Zhù) 伤门 (Shāng Mén) Kan 1　Gui Yi	太阴 (Tài Yīn) 禽芮 (Qín Ruì) 生门 (Shēng Mén) Qian 6　Wu/Xin Ren

Yang (阳) Dun# 2 Hour: **JiChou** ; 直符(ZhíFú): 天辅(TiānFǔ)
直使(ZhíShǐ): 杜门(DùMén) ; 旬首(XúnShǒu): JiaShenGeng

螣蛇 (Téng Shé) 天英 (Tiān Yīng) 伤门 (Shāng Mén) Xun 4　Bing Geng	太阴 (Tài Yīn) 禽芮 (Qín Ruì) 杜门 (Dù Mén) Li 9　Wu/Xin Bing	六合 (Liù Hé) 天柱 (Tiān Zhù) 景门 (Jīng Mén) Kun 2　Gui Wu/Xin
值符 (Zhí Fú) 天辅 (Tiān Fǔ) 生门 (Shēng Mén) Zhen 3　Geng Ji	Yang (阳) Dun# 2 Hour: **JiChou** ©Calvin Yap	白虎 (Bái Hǔ) 天心 (Tiān Xīn) 死门 (Sǐ Mén) Dui 7　Ren Gui
九天 (Jiǔ Tiān) 天冲 (Tiān Chōng) 休门 (Xiū Mén) Gen 8　Ji Ding	九地 (Jiǔ Dì) 天任 (Tiān Rèn) 开门 (Kāi Mén) Kan 1　Ding Yi	玄武 (Xuán Wǔ) 天蓬 (Tiān Péng) 惊门 (Jīng Mén) Qian 6　Yi Ren

Yang (阳) Dun# 2 Hour: **GengYin** ; 直符(ZhíFú): 天辅(TiānFǔ)
直使(ZhíShǐ): 杜门(DùMén) ; 旬首(XúnShǒu): JiaShenGeng

值符 (Zhí Fú) 天辅 (Tiān Fǔ) 惊门 (Jīng Mén) Xun 4　Geng Geng	螣蛇 (Téng Shé) 天英 (Tiān Yīng) 开门 (Kāi Mén) Li 9　Bing Bing	太阴 (Tài Yīn) 禽芮 (Qín Ruì) 休门 (Xiū Mén) Kun 2　Wu/Xin Wu/Xin
九天 (Jiǔ Tiān) 天冲 (Tiān Chōng) 死门 (Sǐ Mén) Zhen 3　Ji Ji	Yang (阳) Dun# 2 Hour: **GengYin** **Fu Yin** ©Calvin Yap	六合 (Liù Hé) 天柱 (Tiān Zhù) 生门 (Shēng Mén) Dui 7　Gui Gui
九地 (Jiǔ Dì) 天任 (Tiān Rèn) 景门 (Jīng Mén) Gen 8　Ding Ding	玄武 (Xuán Wǔ) 天蓬 (Tiān Péng) 杜门 (Dù Mén) Kan 1　Yi Yi	白虎 (Bái Hǔ) 天心 (Tiān Xīn) 伤门 (Shāng Mén) Qian 6　Ren Ren

Yang (阳) Dun# 2 Hour: **XinMao** ; 直符(ZhíFú): 天辅(TiānFǔ)
直使(ZhíShǐ): 杜门(DùMén) ; 旬首(XúnShǒu): JiaShenGeng

九地 (Jiǔ Dì) 天任 (Tiān Rèn) 生门 (Shēng Mén) Xun 4　Ding Geng	九天 (Jiǔ Tiān) 天冲 (Tiān Chōng) 伤门 (Shāng Mén) Li 9　Ji Bing	值符 (Zhí Fú) 天辅 (Tiān Fǔ) 杜门 (Dù Mén) Kun 2　Geng Wu/Xin
玄武 (Xuán Wǔ) 天蓬 (Tiān Péng) 休门 (Xiū Mén) Zhen 3　Yi Ji	Yang (阳) Dun# 2 Hour: **XinMao** ©Calvin Yap	螣蛇 (Téng Shé) 天英 (Tiān Yīng) 景门 (Jīng Mén) Dui 7　Bing Gui
白虎 (Bái Hǔ) 天心 (Tiān Xīn) 开门 (Kāi Mén) Gen 8　Ren Ding	六合 (Liù Hé) 天柱 (Tiān Zhù) 惊门 (Jīng Mén) Kan 1　Gui Yi	太阴 (Tài Yīn) 禽芮 (Qín Ruì) 死门 (Sǐ Mén) Qian 6　Wu/Xin Ren

Yang (阳) Dun# 2 Hour: **RenChen** ; 直符(ZhíFú): 天辅(TiānFǔ)
直使(ZhíShǐ): 杜门(DùMén) ; 旬首(XúnShǒu): JiaShenGeng

白虎 (Bái Hǔ) 天心 (Tiān Xīn) 景门 (Jīng Mén) Xun 4　Ren Geng	玄武 (Xuán Wǔ) 天蓬 (Tiān Péng) 死门 (Sǐ Mén) Li 9　Yi Bing	九地 (Jiǔ Dì) 天任 (Tiān Rèn) 惊门 (Jīng Mén) Kun 2　Ding Wu/Xin
六合 (Liù Hé) 天柱 (Tiān Zhù) 杜门 (Dù Mén) Zhen 3　Gui Ji	Yang (阳) Dun# 2 Hour: **RenChen** **Fan Yin** ©Calvin Yap	九天 (Jiǔ Tiān) 天冲 (Tiān Chōng) 开门 (Kāi Mén) Dui 7　Ji Gui
太阴 (Tài Yīn) 禽芮 (Qín Ruì) 伤门 (Shāng Mén) Gen 8　Wu/Xin Ding	螣蛇 (Téng Shé) 天英 (Tiān Yīng) 生门 (Shēng Mén) Kan 1　Bing Yi	值符 (Zhí Fú) 天辅 (Tiān Fǔ) 休门 (Xiū Mén) Qian 6　Geng Ren

Yang (阳) Dun# 2 Hour: **GuiSi** ; 直符(ZhíFú): 天辅(TiānFǔ)
直使(ZhíShǐ): 杜门(DùMén) ; 旬首(XúnShǒu): JiaShenGeng

玄武 (Xuán Wǔ) 天蓬 (Tiān Péng) 杜门 (Dù Mén) Xun 4　Yi Geng	九地 (Jiǔ Dì) 天任 (Tiān Rèn) 景门 (Jīng Mén) Li 9　Ding Bing	九天 (Jiǔ Tiān) 天冲 (Tiān Chōng) 死门 (Sǐ Mén) Kun 2　Ji Wu/Xin
白虎 (Bái Hǔ) 天心 (Tiān Xīn) 伤门 (Shāng Mén) Zhen 3　Ren Ji	Yang (阳) Dun# 2 Hour: **GuiSi** ©Calvin Yap	值符 (Zhí Fú) 天辅 (Tiān Fǔ) 惊门 (Jīng Mén) Dui 7　Geng Gui
六合 (Liù Hé) 天柱 (Tiān Zhù) 生门 (Shēng Mén) Gen 8　Gui Ding	太阴 (Tài Yīn) 禽芮 (Qín Ruì) 休门 (Xiū Mén) Kan 1　Wu/Xin Yi	螣蛇 (Téng Shé) 天英 (Tiān Yīng) 开门 (Kāi Mén) Qian 6　Bing Ren

Chart: **+2JiaWu** (Yang Dun #2 JiaWu Xun)
JiaWu, YiWei, BingShen, DingYou, WuXu, JiHai, GengZi, XinChou, RenYin, GuiMao

Yang (阳) Dun# 2 Hour: **JiaWu** ; 直符(ZhíFú): 天禽(TiānQín)
直使(ZhíShǐ): 死门(SǐMén) ; 旬首(XúnShǒu): JiaWu/Xin

九地 (Jiǔ Dì) 天辅 (Tiān Fǔ) 杜门 (Dù Mén) Xun 4 Geng Geng	九天 (Jiǔ Tiān) 天英 (Tiān Yīng) 景门 (Jǐng Mén) Li 9 Bing Bing	值符 (Zhí Fú) 禽芮 (Qín Ruì) 死门 (Sǐ Mén) Kun 2 Wu/Xin Wu/Xin
玄武 (Xuán Wǔ) 天冲 (Tiān Chōng) 伤门 (Shāng Mén) Zhen 3 Ji Ji	Yang (阳) Dun# 2 Hour: **JiaWu** **Fu Yin** ©Calvin Yap	螣蛇 (Téng Shé) 天柱 (Tiān Zhù) 惊门 (Jīng Mén) Dui 7 Gui Gui
白虎 (Bái Hǔ) 天任 (Tiān Rèn) 生门 (Shēng Mén) Gen 8 Ding Ding	六合 (Liù Hé) 天蓬 (Tiān Péng) 休门 (Xiū Mén) Kan 1 Yi Yi	太阴 (Tài Yīn) 天心 (Tiān Xīn) 开门 (Kāi Mén) Qian 6 Ren Ren

Yang (阳) Dun# 2 Hour: **YiWei** ; 直符(ZhíFú): 天禽(TiānQín)
直使(ZhíShǐ): 死门(SǐMén) ; 旬首(XúnShǒu): JiaWu/Xin

六合 (Liù Hé) 天蓬 (Tiān Péng) 生门 (Shēng Mén) Xun 4 Yi Geng	白虎 (Bái Hǔ) 天任 (Tiān Rèn) 伤门 (Shāng Mén) Li 9 Ding Bing	玄武 (Xuán Wǔ) 天冲 (Tiān Chōng) 杜门 (Dù Mén) Kun 2 Ji Wu/Xin
太阴 (Tài Yīn) 天心 (Tiān Xīn) 休门 (Xiū Mén) Zhen 3 Ren	Yang (阳) Dun# 2 Hour: **YiWei** ©Calvin Yap	九地 (Jiǔ Dì) 天辅 (Tiān Fǔ) 景门 (Jǐng Mén) Dui 7 Geng Gui
螣蛇 (Téng Shé) 天柱 (Tiān Zhù) 开门 (Kāi Mén) Gen 8 Gui Ding	值符 (Zhí Fú) 禽芮 (Qín Ruì) 惊门 (Jīng Mén) Kan 1 Wu/Xin Yi	九天 (Jiǔ Tiān) 天英 (Tiān Yīng) 死门 (Sǐ Mén) Qian 6 Bing Ren

Yang (阳) Dun# 2 Hour: **BingShen** ; 直符(ZhíFú): 天禽(TiānQín)
直使(ZhíShǐ): 死门(SǐMén) ; 旬首(XúnShǒu): JiaWu/Xin

九天 (Jiǔ Tiān) 天英 (Tiān Yīng) 伤门 (Shāng Mén) Xun 4 Bing Geng	值符 (Zhí Fú) 禽芮 (Qín Ruì) 杜门 (Dù Mén) Li 9 Wu/Xin Bing	螣蛇 (Téng Shé) 天柱 (Tiān Zhù) 景门 (Jǐng Mén) Kun 2 Gui Wu/Xin
九地 (Jiǔ Dì) 天辅 (Tiān Fǔ) 生门 (Shēng Mén) Zhen 3 Geng Ji	Yang (阳) Dun# 2 Hour: **BingShen** ©Calvin Yap	太阴 (Tài Yīn) 天心 (Tiān Xīn) 死门 (Sǐ Mén) Dui 7 Ren Gui
玄武 (Xuán Wǔ) 天冲 (Tiān Chōng) 休门 (Xiū Mén) Gen 8 Ji Ding	白虎 (Bái Hǔ) 天任 (Tiān Rèn) 开门 (Kāi Mén) Kan 1 Ding Yi	六合 (Liù Hé) 天蓬 (Tiān Péng) 惊门 (Jīng Mén) Qian 6 Yi Ren

Yang (阳) Dun# 2 Hour: **DingYou** ; 直符(ZhíFú): 天禽(TiānQín)
直使(ZhíShǐ): 死门(SǐMén) ; 旬首(XúnShǒu): JiaWu/Xin

太阴 (Tài Yīn) 天心 (Tiān Xīn) 开门 (Kāi Mén) Xun 4 Ren Geng	六合 (Liù Hé) 天蓬 (Tiān Péng) 休门 (Xiū Mén) Li 9 Yi Bing	白虎 (Bái Hǔ) 天任 (Tiān Rèn) 生门 (Shēng Mén) Kun 2 Ding Wu/Xin
螣蛇 (Téng Shé) 天柱 (Tiān Zhù) 惊门 (Jīng Mén) Zhen 3 Gui	Yang (阳) Dun# 2 Hour: **DingYou** **Fan Yin** ©Calvin Yap	玄武 (Xuán Wǔ) 天冲 (Tiān Chōng) 伤门 (Shāng Mén) Dui 7 Ji Gui
值符 (Zhí Fú) 禽芮 (Qín Ruì) 死门 (Sǐ Mén) Gen 8 Wu/Xin Ding	九天 (Jiǔ Tiān) 天英 (Tiān Yīng) 景门 (Jǐng Mén) Kan 1 Bing	九地 (Jiǔ Dì) 天辅 (Tiān Fǔ) 杜门 (Dù Mén) Qian 6 Geng Ren

Yang (阳) Dun# 2 Hour: **WuXu** ; 直符(ZhíFú): 天禽(TiānQín)
直使(ZhíShǐ): 死门(SǐMén) ; 旬首(XúnShǒu): JiaWu/Xin

九地 (Jiǔ Dì) 天辅 (Tiān Fǔ) 景门 (Jǐng Mén) Xun 4 Geng Geng	九天 (Jiǔ Tiān) 天英 (Tiān Yīng) 死门 (Sǐ Mén) Li 9 Bing Bing	值符 (Zhí Fú) 禽芮 (Qín Ruì) 惊门 (Jīng Mén) Kun 2 Wu/Xin Wu/Xin
玄武 (Xuán Wǔ) 天冲 (Tiān Chōng) 杜门 (Dù Mén) Zhen 3 Ji Ji	Yang (阳) Dun# 2 Hour: **WuXu** **Fu Yin** ©Calvin Yap	螣蛇 (Téng Shé) 天柱 (Tiān Zhù) 开门 (Kāi Mén) Dui 7 Gui Gui
白虎 (Bái Hǔ) 天任 (Tiān Rèn) 伤门 (Shāng Mén) Gen 8 Ding Ding	六合 (Liù Hé) 天蓬 (Tiān Péng) 生门 (Shēng Mén) Kan 1 Yi Yi	太阴 (Tài Yīn) 天心 (Tiān Xīn) 休门 (Xiū Mén) Qian 6 Ren Ren

Yang (阳) Dun# 2 Hour: **JiHai** ; 直符(ZhíFú): 天禽(TiānQín)
直使(ZhíShǐ): 死门(SǐMén) ; 旬首(XúnShǒu): JiaWu/Xin

螣蛇 (Téng Shé) 天柱 (Tiān Zhù) 休门 (Xiū Mén) Xun 4 Gui Geng	太阴 (Tài Yīn) 天心 (Tiān Xīn) 生门 (Shēng Mén) Li 9 Ren Bing	六合 (Liù Hé) 天蓬 (Tiān Péng) 伤门 (Shāng Mén) Kun 2 Yi Wu/Xin
值符 (Zhí Fú) 禽芮 (Qín Ruì) 开门 (Kāi Mén) Zhen 3 Wu/Xin Ji	Yang (阳) Dun# 2 Hour: **JiHai** ©Calvin Yap	白虎 (Bái Hǔ) 天任 (Tiān Rèn) 杜门 (Dù Mén) Dui 7 Ding Gui
九天 (Jiǔ Tiān) 天英 (Tiān Yīng) 惊门 (Jīng Mén) Gen 8 Bing Ding	九地 (Jiǔ Dì) 天辅 (Tiān Fǔ) 死门 (Sǐ Mén) Kan 1 Geng Yi	玄武 (Xuán Wǔ) 天冲 (Tiān Chōng) 景门 (Jǐng Mén) Qian 6 Ji Ren

Yang (阳) Dun# 2 Hour: **GengZi** ; 直符(ZhíFú): 天禽(TiānQín)
直使(ZhíShǐ): 死门(SǐMén) ; 旬首(XúnShǒu): JiaWu/Xin

值符 (Zhí Fú) 禽芮 (Qín Ruì) 杜门 (Dù Mén) Xun 4　Wu/Xin Geng	螣蛇 (Téng Shé) 天柱 (Tiān Zhù) 景门 (Jǐng Mén) Li 9　Gui Bing	太阴 (Tài Yīn) 天心 (Tiān Xīn) 死门 (Sǐ Mén) Kun 2　Ren Wu/Xin
九天 (Jiǔ Tiān) 天英 (Tiān Yīng) 伤门 (Shāng Mén) Zhen 3　Bing Ji	Yang (阳) Dun# 2 Hour: **GengZi** ©Calvin Yap	六合 (Liù Hé) 天蓬 (Tiān Péng) 惊门 (Jīng Mén) Dui 7　Yi Gui
九地 (Jiǔ Dì) 天辅 (Tiān Fǔ) 生门 (Shēng Mén) Gen 8　Geng Ding	玄武 (Xuán Wǔ) 天冲 (Tiān Chōng) 休门 (Xiū Mén) Kan 1　Ji Yi	白虎 (Bái Hǔ) 天任 (Tiān Rèn) 开门 (Kāi Mén) Qian 6　Ding Ren

Yang (阳) Dun# 2 Hour: **XinChou** ; 直符(ZhíFú): 天禽(TiānQín)
直使(ZhíShǐ): 死门(SǐMén) ; 旬首(XúnShǒu): JiaWu/Xin

九地 (Jiǔ Dì) 天辅 (Tiān Fǔ) 惊门 (Jīng Mén) Xun 4　Geng Geng	九天 (Jiǔ Tiān) 天英 (Tiān Yīng) 开门 (Kāi Mén) Li 9　Bing	值符 (Zhí Fú) 禽芮 (Qín Ruì) 休门 (Xiū Mén) Kun 2　Wu/Xin Wu/Xin
玄武 (Xuán Wǔ) 天冲 (Tiān Chōng) 死门 (Sǐ Mén) Zhen 3　Ji Ji	Yang (阳) Dun# 2 Hour: **XinChou** **Fu Yin** ©Calvin Yap	螣蛇 (Téng Shé) 天柱 (Tiān Zhù) 生门 (Shēng Mén) Dui 7　Gui Gui
白虎 (Bái Hǔ) 天任 (Tiān Rèn) 景门 (Jǐng Mén) Gen 8　Ding Ding	六合 (Liù Hé) 天蓬 (Tiān Péng) 杜门 (Dù Mén) Kan 1　Yi Yi	太阴 (Tài Yīn) 天心 (Tiān Xīn) 伤门 (Shāng Mén) Qian 6　Ren Ren

Yang (阳) Dun# 2 Hour: **RenYin** ; 直符(ZhíFú): 天禽(TiānQín)
直使(ZhíShǐ): 死门(SǐMén) ; 旬首(XúnShǒu): JiaWu/Xin

白虎 (Bái Hǔ) 天任 (Tiān Rèn) 死门 (Sǐ Mén) Xun 4　Ding Geng	玄武 (Xuán Wǔ) 天冲 (Tiān Chōng) 惊门 (Jīng Mén) Li 9　Ji Bing	九地 (Jiǔ Dì) 天辅 (Tiān Fǔ) 开门 (Kāi Mén) Kun 2　Geng Wu/Xin
六合 (Liù Hé) 天蓬 (Tiān Péng) 景门 (Jǐng Mén) Zhen 3　Yi Ji	Yang (阳) Dun# 2 Hour: **RenYin** ©Calvin Yap	九天 (Jiǔ Tiān) 天英 (Tiān Yīng) 休门 (Xiū Mén) Dui 7　Bing Gui
太阴 (Tài Yīn) 天心 (Tiān Xīn) 杜门 (Dù Mén) Gen 8　Ren Ding	螣蛇 (Téng Shé) 天柱 (Tiān Zhù) 伤门 (Shāng Mén) Kan 1　Gui Yi	值符 (Zhí Fú) 禽芮 (Qín Ruì) 生门 (Shēng Mén) Qian 6　Wu/Xin Ren

Yang (阳) Dun# 2 Hour: **GuiMao** ; 直符(ZhíFú): 天禽(TiānQín)
直使(ZhíShǐ): 死门(SǐMén) ; 旬首(XúnShǒu): JiaWu/Xin

玄武 (Xuán Wǔ) 天冲 (Tiān Chōng) 杜门 (Dù Mén) Xun 4　Ji Geng	九地 (Jiǔ Dì) 天辅 (Tiān Fǔ) 景门 (Jǐng Mén) Li 9　Geng Bing	九天 (Jiǔ Tiān) 天英 (Tiān Yīng) 死门 (Sǐ Mén) Kun 2　Bing Wu/Xin
白虎 (Bái Hǔ) 天任 (Tiān Rèn) 伤门 (Shāng Mén) Zhen 3　Ding Ji	Yang (阳) Dun# 2 Hour: **GuiMao** ©Calvin Yap	值符 (Zhí Fú) 禽芮 (Qín Ruì) 惊门 (Jīng Mén) Dui 7　Wu/Xin Gui
六合 (Liù Hé) 天蓬 (Tiān Péng) 生门 (Shēng Mén) Gen 8　Yi Ding	太阴 (Tài Yīn) 天心 (Tiān Xīn) 休门 (Xiū Mén) Kan 1　Ren Yi	螣蛇 (Téng Shé) 天柱 (Tiān Zhù) 开门 (Kāi Mén) Qian 6　Gui Ren

---

Chart: +2JiaChen (Yang Dun #2 JiaChen Xun)
JiaChen, YiSi, BingWu, DingWei, WuShen, JiYou, GengXu, XinHai, RenZi, GuiChou

Yang (阳) Dun# 2 Hour: **JiaChen** ; 直符(ZhíFú): 天心(TiānXīn)
直使(ZhíShǐ): 开门(KāiMén) ; 旬首(XúnShǒu): JiaChenRen

白虎 (Bái Hǔ) 天辅 (Tiān Fǔ) 杜门 (Dù Mén) Xun 4　Geng Geng	玄武 (Xuán Wǔ) 天英 (Tiān Yīng) 景门 (Jǐng Mén) Li 9　Bing Bing	九地 (Jiǔ Dì) 禽芮 (Qín Ruì) 死门 (Sǐ Mén) Kun 2　Wu/Xin Wu/Xin
六合 (Liù Hé) 天冲 (Tiān Chōng) 伤门 (Shāng Mén) Zhen 3　Ji Ji	Yang (阳) Dun# 2 Hour: **JiaChen** **Fu Yin** ©Calvin Yap	九天 (Jiǔ Tiān) 天柱 (Tiān Zhù) 惊门 (Jīng Mén) Dui 7　Gui Gui
太阴 (Tài Yīn) 天任 (Tiān Rèn) 生门 (Shēng Mén) Gen 8　Ding Ding	螣蛇 (Téng Shé) 天蓬 (Tiān Péng) 休门 (Xiū Mén) Kan 1　Yi Yi	值符 (Zhí Fú) 天心 (Tiān Xīn) 开门 (Kāi Mén) Qian 6　Ren Ren

Yang (阳) Dun# 2 Hour: **YiSi** ; 直符(ZhíFú): 天心(TiānXīn)
直使(ZhíShǐ): 开门(KāiMén) ; 旬首(XúnShǒu): JiaChenRen

六合 (Liù Hé) 天冲 (Tiān Chōng) 景门 (Jǐng Mén) Xun 4　Ji Geng	白虎 (Bái Hǔ) 天辅 (Tiān Fǔ) 死门 (Sǐ Mén) Li 9　Geng Bing	玄武 (Xuán Wǔ) 天英 (Tiān Yīng) 惊门 (Jīng Mén) Kun 2　Bing Wu/Xin
太阴 (Tài Yīn) 天任 (Tiān Rèn) 杜门 (Dù Mén) Zhen 3　Ding Ji	Yang (阳) Dun# 2 Hour: **YiSi** ©Calvin Yap	九地 (Jiǔ Dì) 禽芮 (Qín Ruì) 开门 (Kāi Mén) Dui 7　Wu/Xin Gui
螣蛇 (Téng Shé) 天蓬 (Tiān Péng) 伤门 (Shāng Mén) Gen 8　Yi Ding	值符 (Zhí Fú) 天心 (Tiān Xīn) 生门 (Shēng Mén) Kan 1　Ren Yi	九天 (Jiǔ Tiān) 天柱 (Tiān Zhù) 休门 (Xiū Mén) Qian 6　Gui Ren

Chart 1 (top-left)

Yang (阳) Dun# 2 Hour: **BingWu**；直符(ZhíFú): 天心(TiānXīn)
直使(ZhíShǐ): 开门(KāiMén)；旬首(XúnShǒu): JiaChenRen

九天 (Jiǔ Tiān)	值符 (Zhí Fú)	螣蛇 (Téng Shé)
天柱 (Tiān Zhù)	天心 (Tiān Xīn)	天蓬 (Tiān Péng)
生门 (Shēng Mén)	伤门 (Shāng Mén)	杜门 (Dù Mén)
Xun 4　Gui　Geng	Li 9　Ren　Bing	Kun 2　Yi　Wu/Xin
九地 (Jiǔ Dì)		太阴 (Tài Yīn)
禽芮 (Qín Ruì)	Yang (阳) Dun# 2	天任 (Tiān Rèn)
休门 (Xiū Mén)	Hour: **BingWu**	景门 (Jǐng Mén)
Zhen 3　Wu/Xin　Ji	©Calvin Yap	Dui 7　Ding　Gui
玄武 (Xuán Wǔ)	白虎 (Bái Hǔ)	六合 (Liù Hé)
天英 (Tiān Yīng)	天辅 (Tiān Fǔ)	天冲 (Tiān Chōng)
开门 (Kāi Mén)	惊门 (Jīng Mén)	死门 (Sǐ Mén)
Gen 8　Bing　Ding	Kan 1　Geng　Yi	Qian 6　Ji　Ren

Chart 2 (top-right)

Yang (阳) Dun# 2 Hour: **DingWei**；直符(ZhíFú): 天心(TiānXīn)
直使(ZhíShǐ): 开门(KāiMén)；旬首(XúnShǒu): JiaChenRen

太阴 (Tài Yīn)	六合 (Liù Hé)	白虎 (Bái Hǔ)
天任 (Tiān Rèn)	天冲 (Tiān Chōng)	天辅 (Tiān Fǔ)
惊门 (Jīng Mén)	开门 (Kāi Mén)	休门 (Xiū Mén)
Xun 4　Ding　Geng	Li 9　Ji　Bing	Kun 2　Geng　Wu/Xin
螣蛇 (Téng Shé)		玄武 (Xuán Wǔ)
天蓬 (Tiān Péng)	Yang (阳) Dun# 2	天英 (Tiān Yīng)
死门 (Sǐ Mén)	Hour: **DingWei**	生门 (Shēng Mén)
Zhen 3　Yi　Ji	©Calvin Yap	Dui 7　Bing　Gui
值符 (Zhí Fú)	九天 (Jiǔ Tiān)	九地 (Jiǔ Dì)
天心 (Tiān Xīn)	天柱 (Tiān Zhù)	禽芮 (Qín Ruì)
景门 (Jǐng Mén)	杜门 (Dù Mén)	伤门 (Shāng Mén)
Gen 8　Ren　Ding	Kan 1　Gui　Yi	Qian 6　Wu/Xin　Ren

Chart 3 (middle-left)

Yang (阳) Dun# 2 Hour: **WuShen**；直符(ZhíFú): 天心(TiānXīn)
直使(ZhíShǐ): 开门(KāiMén)；旬首(XúnShǒu): JiaChenRen

九地 (Jiǔ Dì)	九天 (Jiǔ Tiān)	值符 (Zhí Fú)
禽芮 (Qín Ruì)	天柱 (Tiān Zhù)	天心 (Tiān Xīn)
伤门 (Shāng Mén)	杜门 (Dù Mén)	景门 (Jǐng Mén)
Xun 4　Wu/Xin　Geng	Li 9　Gui　Bing	Kun 2　Ren　Wu/Xin
玄武 (Xuán Wǔ)		螣蛇 (Téng Shé)
天英 (Tiān Yīng)	Yang (阳) Dun# 2	天蓬 (Tiān Péng)
生门 (Shēng Mén)	Hour: **WuShen**	死门 (Sǐ Mén)
Zhen 3　Bing　Ji	©Calvin Yap	Dui 7　Yi　Gui
白虎 (Bái Hǔ)	六合 (Liù Hé)	太阴 (Tài Yīn)
天辅 (Tiān Fǔ)	天冲 (Tiān Chōng)	天任 (Tiān Rèn)
休门 (Xiū Mén)	开门 (Kāi Mén)	惊门 (Jīng Mén)
Gen 8　Geng　Ding	Kan 1　Ji　Yi	Qian 6　Ding　Ren

Chart 4 (middle-right)

Yang (阳) Dun# 2 Hour: **JiYou**；直符(ZhíFú): 天心(TiānXīn)
直使(ZhíShǐ): 开门(KāiMén)；旬首(XúnShǒu): JiaChenRen

螣蛇 (Téng Shé)	太阴 (Tài Yīn)	六合 (Liù Hé)
天蓬 (Tiān Péng)	天任 (Tiān Rèn)	天冲 (Tiān Chōng)
死门 (Sǐ Mén)	惊门 (Jīng Mén)	开门 (Kāi Mén)
Xun 4　Yi　Geng	Li 9　Ding　Bing	Kun 2　Ji　Wu/Xin
值符 (Zhí Fú)		白虎 (Bái Hǔ)
天心 (Tiān Xīn)	Yang (阳) Dun# 2	天辅 (Tiān Fǔ)
景门 (Jǐng Mén)	Hour: **JiYou**	休门 (Xiū Mén)
Zhen 3　Ren　Ji	©Calvin Yap	Dui 7　Geng　Gui
九天 (Jiǔ Tiān)	九地 (Jiǔ Dì)	玄武 (Xuán Wǔ)
天柱 (Tiān Zhù)	禽芮 (Qín Ruì)	天英 (Tiān Yīng)
杜门 (Dù Mén)	伤门 (Shāng Mén)	生门 (Shēng Mén)
Gen 8　Gui　Ding	Kan 1　Wu/Xin　Yi	Qian 6　Bing　Ren

Chart 5 (bottom-left)

Yang (阳) Dun# 2 Hour: **GengXu**；直符(ZhíFú): 天心(TiānXīn)
直使(ZhíShǐ): 开门(KāiMén)；旬首(XúnShǒu): JiaChenRen

值符 (Zhí Fú)	螣蛇 (Téng Shé)	太阴 (Tài Yīn)
天心 (Tiān Xīn)	天蓬 (Tiān Péng)	天任 (Tiān Rèn)
休门 (Xiū Mén)	生门 (Shēng Mén)	伤门 (Shāng Mén)
Xun 4　Ren　Geng	Li 9　Yi　Bing	Kun 2　Ding　Wu/Xin
九天 (Jiǔ Tiān)		六合 (Liù Hé)
天柱 (Tiān Zhù)	Yang (阳) Dun# 2	天冲 (Tiān Chōng)
开门 (Kāi Mén)	Hour: **GengXu** **Fan Yin**	杜门 (Dù Mén)
Zhen 3　Gui　Ji	©Calvin Yap	Dui 7　Ji　Gui
九地 (Jiǔ Dì)	玄武 (Xuán Wǔ)	白虎 (Bái Hǔ)
禽芮 (Qín Ruì)	天英 (Tiān Yīng)	天辅 (Tiān Fǔ)
惊门 (Jīng Mén)	死门 (Sǐ Mén)	景门 (Jǐng Mén)
Gen 8　Wu/Xin　Ding	Kan 1　Bing　Yi	Qian 6　Geng　Ren

Chart 6 (bottom-right)

Yang (阳) Dun# 2 Hour: **XinHai**；直符(ZhíFú): 天心(TiānXīn)
直使(ZhíShǐ): 开门(KāiMén)；旬首(XúnShǒu): JiaChenRen

九地 (Jiǔ Dì)	九天 (Jiǔ Tiān)	值符 (Zhí Fú)
禽芮 (Qín Ruì)	天柱 (Tiān Zhù)	天心 (Tiān Xīn)
开门 (Kāi Mén)	休门 (Xiū Mén)	生门 (Shēng Mén)
Xun 4　Wu/Xin　Geng	Li 9　Gui　Bing	Kun 2　Ren　Wu/Xin
玄武 (Xuán Wǔ)		螣蛇 (Téng Shé)
天英 (Tiān Yīng)	Yang (阳) Dun# 2	天蓬 (Tiān Péng)
惊门 (Jīng Mén)	Hour: **XinHai**	伤门 (Shāng Mén)
Zhen 3　Bing　Ji	©Calvin Yap	Dui 7　Yi　Gui
白虎 (Bái Hǔ)	六合 (Liù Hé)	太阴 (Tài Yīn)
天辅 (Tiān Fǔ)	天冲 (Tiān Chōng)	天任 (Tiān Rèn)
死门 (Sǐ Mén)	景门 (Jǐng Mén)	杜门 (Dù Mén)
Gen 8　Geng　Ding	Kan 1　Ji　Yi	Qian 6　Ding　Ren

Yang (阳) Dun# 2 Hour: RenZi ; 直符(ZhíFú): 天心(TiānXīn)
直使(ZhíShǐ): 开门(KāiMén) ; 旬首(XúnShǒu): JiaChenRen

白虎 (Bái Hǔ) 天辅 (Tiān Fǔ) 死门 (Sǐ Mén) Xun 4　Geng Geng	玄武 (Xuán Wǔ) 天英 (Tiān Yīng) 惊门 (Jīng Mén) Li 9　Bing Bing	九地 (Jiǔ Dì) 禽芮 (Qín Ruì) 开门 (Kāi Mén) Kun 2　Wu/Xin Wu/Xin
六合 (Liù Hé) 天冲 (Tiān Chōng) 景门 (Jǐng Mén) Zhen 3　Ji Ji	Yang (阳) Dun# 2 Hour: **RenZi** **Fu Yin** ©Calvin Yap	九天 (Jiǔ Tiān) 天柱 (Tiān Zhù) 休门 (Xiū Mén) Dui 7　Gui Gui
太阴 (Tài Yīn) 天任 (Tiān Rèn) 杜门 (Dù Mén) Gen 8　Ding Ding	螣蛇 (Téng Shé) 天蓬 (Tiān Péng) 伤门 (Shāng Mén) Kan 1　Yi Yi	值符 (Zhí Fú) 天心 (Tiān Xīn) 生门 (Shēng Mén) Qian 6　Ren Ren

Yang (阳) Dun# 2 Hour: GuiChou ; 直符(ZhíFú): 天心(TiānXīn)
直使(ZhíShǐ): 开门(KāiMén) ; 旬首(XúnShǒu): JiaChenRen

玄武 (Xuán Wǔ) 天英 (Tiān Yīng) 杜门 (Dù Mén) Xun 4　Bing Geng	九地 (Jiǔ Dì) 禽芮 (Qín Ruì) 景门 (Jǐng Mén) Li 9　Wu/Xin	九天 (Jiǔ Tiān) 天柱 (Tiān Zhù) 死门 (Sǐ Mén) Kun 2　Gui Wu/Xin
白虎 (Bái Hǔ) 天辅 (Tiān Fǔ) 伤门 (Shāng Mén) Zhen 3　Geng Ji	Yang (阳) Dun# 2 Hour: **GuiChou** ©Calvin Yap	值符 (Zhí Fú) 天心 (Tiān Xīn) 惊门 (Jīng Mén) Dui 7　Ren Gui
六合 (Liù Hé) 天冲 (Tiān Chōng) 生门 (Shēng Mén) Gen 8　Ji Ding	太阴 (Tài Yīn) 天任 (Tiān Rèn) 休门 (Xiū Mén) Kan 1　Ding Yi	螣蛇 (Téng Shé) 天蓬 (Tiān Péng) 开门 (Kāi Mén) Qian 6　Yi Ren

Chart: +2JiaYin (Yang Dun #2 JiaYin Xun)
JiaYin, YiMao, BingChen, DingSi, WuWu, JiWei, GengShen, XinYou, RenXu, GuiHai

Yang (阳) Dun# 2 Hour: JiaYin ; 直符(ZhíFú): 天柱(TiānZhù)
直使(ZhíShǐ): 惊门(JīngMén) ; 旬首(XúnShǒu): JiaYinGui

玄武 (Xuán Wǔ) 天辅 (Tiān Fǔ) 杜门 (Dù Mén) Xun 4　Geng Geng	九地 (Jiǔ Dì) 天英 (Tiān Yīng) 景门 (Jǐng Mén) Li 9　Bing Bing	九天 (Jiǔ Tiān) 禽芮 (Qín Ruì) 死门 (Sǐ Mén) Kun 2　Wu/Xin Wu/Xin
白虎 (Bái Hǔ) 天冲 (Tiān Chōng) 伤门 (Shāng Mén) Zhen 3　Ji Ji	Yang (阳) Dun# 2 Hour: **JiaYin** **Fu Yin** ©Calvin Yap	值符 (Zhí Fú) 天柱 (Tiān Zhù) 惊门 (Jīng Mén) Dui 7　Gui Gui
六合 (Liù Hé) 天任 (Tiān Rèn) 生门 (Shēng Mén) Gen 8　Ding Ding	太阴 (Tài Yīn) 天蓬 (Tiān Péng) 休门 (Xiū Mén) Kan 1　Yi Yi	螣蛇 (Téng Shé) 天心 (Tiān Xīn) 开门 (Kāi Mén) Qian 6　Ren Ren

Yang (阳) Dun# 2 Hour: YiMao ; 直符(ZhíFú): 天柱(TiānZhù)
直使(ZhíShǐ): 惊门(JīngMén) ; 旬首(XúnShǒu): JiaYinGui

六合 (Liù Hé) 天任 (Tiān Rèn) 休门 (Xiū Mén) Xun 4　Ding Geng	白虎 (Bái Hǔ) 天冲 (Tiān Chōng) 生门 (Shēng Mén) Li 9　Ji Bing	玄武 (Xuán Wǔ) 天辅 (Tiān Fǔ) 伤门 (Shāng Mén) Kun 2　Geng Wu/Xin
太阴 (Tài Yīn) 天蓬 (Tiān Péng) 开门 (Kāi Mén) Zhen 3　Yi Ji	Yang (阳) Dun# 2 Hour: **YiMao** ©Calvin Yap	九地 (Jiǔ Dì) 天英 (Tiān Yīng) 杜门 (Dù Mén) Dui 7　Bing Gui
螣蛇 (Téng Shé) 天心 (Tiān Xīn) 惊门 (Jīng Mén) Gen 8　Ren Ding	值符 (Zhí Fú) 天柱 (Tiān Zhù) 死门 (Sǐ Mén) Kan 1　Gui Yi	九天 (Jiǔ Tiān) 禽芮 (Qín Ruì) 景门 (Jǐng Mén) Qian 6　Wu/Xin Ren

Yang (阳) Dun# 2 Hour: BingChen ; 直符(ZhíFú): 天柱(TiānZhù)
直使(ZhíShǐ): 惊门(JīngMén) ; 旬首(XúnShǒu): JiaYinGui

九天 (Jiǔ Tiān) 禽芮 (Qín Ruì) 死门 (Sǐ Mén) Xun 4　Wu/Xin Geng	值符 (Zhí Fú) 天柱 (Tiān Zhù) 惊门 (Jīng Mén) Li 9　Gui Bing	螣蛇 (Téng Shé) 天心 (Tiān Xīn) 开门 (Kāi Mén) Kun 2　Ren Wu/Xin
九地 (Jiǔ Dì) 天英 (Tiān Yīng) 景门 (Jǐng Mén) Zhen 3　Bing Ji	Yang (阳) Dun# 2 Hour: **BingChen** ©Calvin Yap	太阴 (Tài Yīn) 天蓬 (Tiān Péng) 休门 (Xiū Mén) Dui 7　Yi Gui
玄武 (Xuán Wǔ) 天辅 (Tiān Fǔ) 杜门 (Dù Mén) Gen 8　Geng Ding	白虎 (Bái Hǔ) 天冲 (Tiān Chōng) 伤门 (Shāng Mén) Kan 1　Ji Yi	六合 (Liù Hé) 天任 (Tiān Rèn) 生门 (Shēng Mén) Qian 6　Ding Ren

Yang (阳) Dun# 2 Hour: DingSi ; 直符(ZhíFú): 天柱(TiānZhù)
直使(ZhíShǐ): 惊门(JīngMén) ; 旬首(XúnShǒu): JiaYinGui

太阴 (Tài Yīn) 天蓬 (Tiān Péng) 生门 (Shēng Mén) Xun 4　Yi Geng	六合 (Liù Hé) 天任 (Tiān Rèn) 伤门 (Shāng Mén) Li 9　Ding Bing	白虎 (Bái Hǔ) 天冲 (Tiān Chōng) 杜门 (Dù Mén) Kun 2　Ji Wu/Xin
螣蛇 (Téng Shé) 天心 (Tiān Xīn) 休门 (Xiū Mén) Zhen 3　Ren Ji	Yang (阳) Dun# 2 Hour: **DingSi** ©Calvin Yap	玄武 (Xuán Wǔ) 天辅 (Tiān Fǔ) 景门 (Jǐng Mén) Dui 7　Geng Gui
值符 (Zhí Fú) 天柱 (Tiān Zhù) 开门 (Kāi Mén) Gen 8　Gui Ding	九天 (Jiǔ Tiān) 禽芮 (Qín Ruì) 惊门 (Jīng Mén) Kan 1　Wu/Xin Yi	九地 (Jiǔ Dì) 天英 (Tiān Yīng) 死门 (Sǐ Mén) Qian 6　Bing Ren

Yang (阳) Dun# 2 Hour: WuWu

Yang (阳) Dun# 2 Hour: **WuWu**；直符(ZhíFú): 天柱(TiānZhù)
直使(ZhíShǐ): 惊门(JīngMén)；旬首(XúnShǒu): JiaYinGui

九地 (Jiǔ Dì) 天英 (Tiān Yīng) 景门 (Jǐng Mén) Xun 4　Bing　Geng	九天 (Jiǔ Tiān) 禽芮 (Qín Ruì) 死门 (Sǐ Mén) Li 9　Bing	值符 (Zhí Fú) 天柱 (Tiān Zhù) 惊门 (Jīng Mén) Kun 2　Gui　Wu/Xin
玄武 (Xuán Wǔ) 天辅 (Tiān Fǔ) 杜门 (Dù Mén) Zhen 3　Geng　Ji	Yang (阳) Dun# 2 Hour: **WuWu** ©Calvin Yap	螣蛇 (Téng Shé) 天心 (Tiān Xīn) 开门 (Kāi Mén) Dui 7　Ren　Gui
白虎 (Bái Hǔ) 天冲 (Tiān Chōng) 伤门 (Shāng Mén) Gen 8　Ji　Ding	六合 (Liù Hé) 天任 (Tiān Rèn) 生门 (Shēng Mén) Kan 1　Ding　Yi	太阴 (Tài Yīn) 天蓬 (Tiān Péng) 休门 (Xiū Mén) Qian 6　Yi　Ren

Yang (阳) Dun# 2 Hour: JiWei

Yang (阳) Dun# 2 Hour: **JiWei**；直符(ZhíFú): 天柱(TiānZhù)
直使(ZhíShǐ): 惊门(JīngMén)；旬首(XúnShǒu): JiaYinGui

螣蛇 (Téng Shé) 天心 (Tiān Xīn) 开门 (Kāi Mén) Xun 4　Ren　Geng	太阴 (Tài Yīn) 天蓬 (Tiān Péng) 休门 (Xiū Mén) Li 9　Yi　Bing	六合 (Liù Hé) 天任 (Tiān Rèn) 生门 (Shēng Mén) Kun 2　Ding　Wu/Xin
值符 (Zhí Fú) 天柱 (Tiān Zhù) 惊门 (Jīng Mén) Zhen 3　Gui　Ji	Yang (阳) Dun# 2 Hour: **JiWei** **Fan Yin** ©Calvin Yap	白虎 (Bái Hǔ) 天冲 (Tiān Chōng) 伤门 (Shāng Mén) Dui 7　Ji　Gui
九天 (Jiǔ Tiān) 禽芮 (Qín Ruì) 死门 (Sǐ Mén) Gen 8　Wu/Xin　Ding	九地 (Jiǔ Dì) 天英 (Tiān Yīng) 景门 (Jǐng Mén) Kan 1　Bing　Yi	玄武 (Xuán Wǔ) 天辅 (Tiān Fǔ) 杜门 (Dù Mén) Qian 6　Geng　Ren

Yang (阳) Dun# 2 Hour: GengShen

Yang (阳) Dun# 2 Hour: **GengShen**；直符(ZhíFú): 天柱(TiānZhù)
直使(ZhíShǐ): 惊门(JīngMén)；旬首(XúnShǒu): JiaYinGui

值符 (Zhí Fú) 天柱 (Tiān Zhù) 惊门 (Jīng Mén) Xun 4　Gui　Geng	螣蛇 (Téng Shé) 天心 (Tiān Xīn) 开门 (Kāi Mén) Li 9　Ren　Bing	太阴 (Tài Yīn) 天蓬 (Tiān Péng) 休门 (Xiū Mén) Kun 2　Yi　Wu/Xin
九天 (Jiǔ Tiān) 禽芮 (Qín Ruì) 死门 (Sǐ Mén) Zhen 3　Wu/Xin　Ji	Yang (阳) Dun# 2 Hour: **GengShen** ©Calvin Yap	六合 (Liù Hé) 天任 (Tiān Rèn) 生门 (Shēng Mén) Dui 7　Ding　Gui
九地 (Jiǔ Dì) 天英 (Tiān Yīng) 景门 (Jǐng Mén) Gen 8　Bing　Ding	玄武 (Xuán Wǔ) 天辅 (Tiān Fǔ) 杜门 (Dù Mén) Kan 1　Geng　Yi	白虎 (Bái Hǔ) 天冲 (Tiān Chōng) 伤门 (Shāng Mén) Qian 6　Ji　Ren

Yang (阳) Dun# 2 Hour: XinYou

Yang (阳) Dun# 2 Hour: **XinYou**；直符(ZhíFú): 天柱(TiānZhù)
直使(ZhíShǐ): 惊门(JīngMén)；旬首(XúnShǒu): JiaYinGui

九地 (Jiǔ Dì) 天英 (Tiān Yīng) 景门 (Jǐng Mén) Xun 4　Bing　Geng	九天 (Jiǔ Tiān) 禽芮 (Qín Ruì) 死门 (Sǐ Mén) Li 9　Wu/Xin　Bing	值符 (Zhí Fú) 天柱 (Tiān Zhù) 惊门 (Jīng Mén) Kun 2　Gui　Wu/Xin
玄武 (Xuán Wǔ) 天辅 (Tiān Fǔ) 杜门 (Dù Mén) Zhen 3　Geng　Ji	Yang (阳) Dun# 2 Hour: **XinYou** ©Calvin Yap	螣蛇 (Téng Shé) 天心 (Tiān Xīn) 开门 (Kāi Mén) Dui 7　Ren　Gui
白虎 (Bái Hǔ) 天冲 (Tiān Chōng) 伤门 (Shāng Mén) Gen 8　Ji　Ding	六合 (Liù Hé) 天任 (Tiān Rèn) 生门 (Shēng Mén) Kan 1　Ding　Yi	太阴 (Tài Yīn) 天蓬 (Tiān Péng) 休门 (Xiū Mén) Qian 6　Yi　Ren

Yang (阳) Dun# 2 Hour: RenXu

Yang (阳) Dun# 2 Hour: **RenXu**；直符(ZhíFú): 天柱(TiānZhù)
直使(ZhíShǐ): 惊门(JīngMén)；旬首(XúnShǒu): JiaYinGui

白虎 (Bái Hǔ) 天冲 (Tiān Chōng) 伤门 (Shāng Mén) Xun 4　Ji　Geng	玄武 (Xuán Wǔ) 天辅 (Tiān Fǔ) 杜门 (Dù Mén) Li 9　Geng　Bing	九地 (Jiǔ Dì) 天英 (Tiān Yīng) 景门 (Jǐng Mén) Kun 2　Bing　Wu/Xin
六合 (Liù Hé) 天任 (Tiān Rèn) 生门 (Shēng Mén) Zhen 3　Ding　Ji	Yang (阳) Dun# 2 Hour: **RenXu** ©Calvin Yap	九天 (Jiǔ Tiān) 禽芮 (Qín Ruì) 死门 (Sǐ Mén) Dui 7　Wu/Xin　Gui
太阴 (Tài Yīn) 天蓬 (Tiān Péng) 休门 (Xiū Mén) Gen 8　Yi　Ding	螣蛇 (Téng Shé) 天心 (Tiān Xīn) 开门 (Kāi Mén) Kan 1　Ren　Yi	值符 (Zhí Fú) 天柱 (Tiān Zhù) 惊门 (Jīng Mén) Qian 6　Gui　Ren

Yang (阳) Dun# 2 Hour: GuiHai

Yang (阳) Dun# 2 Hour: **GuiHai**；直符(ZhíFú): 天柱(TiānZhù)
直使(ZhíShǐ): 惊门(JīngMén)；旬首(XúnShǒu): JiaYinGui

玄武 (Xuán Wǔ) 天辅 (Tiān Fǔ) 杜门 (Dù Mén) Xun 4　Geng　Geng	九地 (Jiǔ Dì) 天英 (Tiān Yīng) 景门 (Jǐng Mén) Li 9　Bing　Bing	九天 (Jiǔ Tiān) 禽芮 (Qín Ruì) 死门 (Sǐ Mén) Kun 2　Wu/Xin　Wu/Xin
白虎 (Bái Hǔ) 天冲 (Tiān Chōng) 伤门 (Shāng Mén) Zhen 3　Ji　Ji	Yang (阳) Dun# 2 Hour: **GuiHai** **Fu Yin** ©Calvin Yap	值符 (Zhí Fú) 天柱 (Tiān Zhù) 惊门 (Jīng Mén) Dui 7　Gui　Gui
六合 (Liù Hé) 天任 (Tiān Rèn) 生门 (Shēng Mén) Gen 8　Ding　Ding	太阴 (Tài Yīn) 天蓬 (Tiān Péng) 休门 (Xiū Mén) Kan 1　Yi　Yi	螣蛇 (Téng Shé) 天心 (Tiān Xīn) 开门 (Kāi Mén) Qian 6　Ren　Ren

Yang Dun#3

Chart: +3JiaZi (Yang Dun #3 JiaZi Xun)
JiaZi, YiChou, BingYin, DingMao, WuChen, JiSi, GengWu, XinWei, RenShen, GuiYou

Yang (阳) Dun# 3 Hour: **JiaZi**；直符(ZhíFú): 天冲(TiānChōng)
直使(ZhíShǐ): 伤门(ShāngMén)；旬首(XúnShǒu): JiaZiWu

螣蛇 (Téng Shé) 天辅 (Tiān Fǔ) 杜门 (Dù Mén) Xun 4 — Ji Ji	太阴 (Tài Yīn) 天英 (Tiān Yīng) 景门 (Jǐng Mén) Li 9 — Ding Ding	六合 (Liù Hé) 禽芮 (Qín Ruì) 死门 (Sǐ Mén) Kun 2 — Yi/Geng Yi/Geng
值符 (Zhí Fú) 天冲 (Tiān Chōng) 伤门 (Shāng Mén) Zhen 3 — Wu Wu	Yang (阳) Dun# 3 Hour: **JiaZi** **Fu Yin** ©Calvin Yap	白虎 (Bái Hǔ) 天柱 (Tiān Zhù) 惊门 (Jīng Mén) Dui 7 — Ren Ren
九天 (Jiǔ Tiān) 天任 (Tiān Rèn) 生门 (Shēng Mén) Gen 8 — Gui Gui	九地 (Jiǔ Dì) 天蓬 (Tiān Péng) 休门 (Xiū Mén) Kan 1 — Bing	玄武 (Xuán Wǔ) 天心 (Tiān Xīn) 开门 (Kāi Mén) Qian 6 — Xin Xin

Yang (阳) Dun# 3 Hour: **YiChou**；直符(ZhíFú): 天冲(TiānChōng)
直使(ZhíShǐ): 伤门(ShāngMén)；旬首(XúnShǒu): JiaZiWu

九地 (Jiǔ Dì) 天蓬 (Tiān Péng) 伤门 (Shāng Mén) Xun 4 — Bing Ji	九天 (Jiǔ Tiān) 天任 (Tiān Rèn) 杜门 (Dù Mén) Li 9 — Gui Ding	值符 (Zhí Fú) 天冲 (Tiān Chōng) 景门 (Jǐng Mén) Kun 2 — Wu Yi/Geng
玄武 (Xuán Wǔ) 天心 (Tiān Xīn) 生门 (Shēng Mén) Zhen 3 — Xin Wu	Yang (阳) Dun# 3 Hour: **YiChou** ©Calvin Yap	螣蛇 (Téng Shé) 天辅 (Tiān Fǔ) 死门 (Sǐ Mén) Dui 7 — Ji Ren
白虎 (Bái Hǔ) 天柱 (Tiān Zhù) 休门 (Xiū Mén) Gen 8 — Ren Gui	六合 (Liù Hé) 禽芮 (Qín Ruì) 开门 (Kāi Mén) Kan 1 — Yi/Geng Bing	太阴 (Tài Yīn) 天英 (Tiān Yīng) 惊门 (Jīng Mén) Qian 6 — Ding Xin

Yang (阳) Dun# 3 Hour: **BingYin**；直符(ZhíFú): 天冲(TiānChōng)
直使(ZhíShǐ): 伤门(ShāngMén)；旬首(XúnShǒu): JiaZiWu

六合 (Liù Hé) 禽芮 (Qín Ruì) 休门 (Xiū Mén) Xun 4 — Yi/Geng Ji	白虎 (Bái Hǔ) 天柱 (Tiān Zhù) 生门 (Shēng Mén) Li 9 — Ren Ding	玄武 (Xuán Wǔ) 天心 (Tiān Xīn) 伤门 (Shāng Mén) Kun 2 — Xin Yi/Geng
太阴 (Tài Yīn) 天英 (Tiān Yīng) 开门 (Kāi Mén) Zhen 3 — Ding Wu	Yang (阳) Dun# 3 Hour: **BingYin** ©Calvin Yap	九地 (Jiǔ Dì) 天蓬 (Tiān Péng) 杜门 (Dù Mén) Dui 7 — Bing Ren
螣蛇 (Téng Shé) 天辅 (Tiān Fǔ) 惊门 (Jīng Mén) Gen 8 — Ji Gui	值符 (Zhí Fú) 天冲 (Tiān Chōng) 死门 (Sǐ Mén) Kan 1 — Wu Bing	九天 (Jiǔ Tiān) 天任 (Tiān Rèn) 景门 (Jǐng Mén) Qian 6 — Gui Xin

Yang (阳) Dun# 3 Hour: **DingMao**；直符(ZhíFú): 天冲(TiānChōng)
直使(ZhíShǐ): 伤门(ShāngMén)；旬首(XúnShǒu): JiaZiWu

九天 (Jiǔ Tiān) 天任 (Tiān Rèn) 惊门 (Jīng Mén) Xun 4 — Gui Ji	值符 (Zhí Fú) 天冲 (Tiān Chōng) 开门 (Kāi Mén) Li 9 — Wu Ding	螣蛇 (Téng Shé) 天辅 (Tiān Fǔ) 休门 (Xiū Mén) Kun 2 — Ji Yi/Geng
九地 (Jiǔ Dì) 天蓬 (Tiān Péng) 死门 (Sǐ Mén) Zhen 3 — Bing Wu	Yang (阳) Dun# 3 Hour: **DingMao** ©Calvin Yap	太阴 (Tài Yīn) 天英 (Tiān Yīng) 生门 (Shēng Mén) Dui 7 — Ding Ren
玄武 (Xuán Wǔ) 天心 (Tiān Xīn) 景门 (Jǐng Mén) Gen 8 — Xin Gui	白虎 (Bái Hǔ) 天柱 (Tiān Zhù) 杜门 (Dù Mén) Kan 1 — Ren Bing	六合 (Liù Hé) 禽芮 (Qín Ruì) 伤门 (Shāng Mén) Qian 6 — Yi/Geng Xin

Yang (阳) Dun# 3 Hour: **WuChen**；直符(ZhíFú): 天冲(TiānChōng)
直使(ZhíShǐ): 伤门(ShāngMén)；旬首(XúnShǒu): JiaZiWu

螣蛇 (Téng Shé) 天辅 (Tiān Fǔ) 开门 (Kāi Mén) Xun 4 — Ji Ji	太阴 (Tài Yīn) 天英 (Tiān Yīng) 休门 (Xiū Mén) Li 9 — Ding Ding	六合 (Liù Hé) 禽芮 (Qín Ruì) 生门 (Shēng Mén) Kun 2 — Yi/Geng Yi/Geng
值符 (Zhí Fú) 天冲 (Tiān Chōng) 惊门 (Jīng Mén) Zhen 3 — Wu Wu	Yang (阳) Dun# 3 Hour: **WuChen** **Fu Yin** ©Calvin Yap	白虎 (Bái Hǔ) 天柱 (Tiān Zhù) 伤门 (Shāng Mén) Dui 7 — Ren Ren
九天 (Jiǔ Tiān) 天任 (Tiān Rèn) 死门 (Sǐ Mén) Gen 8 — Gui Gui	九地 (Jiǔ Dì) 天蓬 (Tiān Péng) 景门 (Jǐng Mén) Kan 1 — Bing Bing	玄武 (Xuán Wǔ) 天心 (Tiān Xīn) 杜门 (Dù Mén) Qian 6 — Xin Xin

Yang (阳) Dun# 3 Hour: **JiSi**；直符(ZhíFú): 天冲(TiānChōng)
直使(ZhíShǐ): 伤门(ShāngMén)；旬首(XúnShǒu): JiaZiWu

值符 (Zhí Fú) 天冲 (Tiān Chōng) 景门 (Jǐng Mén) Xun 4 — Wu Ji	螣蛇 (Téng Shé) 天辅 (Tiān Fǔ) 死门 (Sǐ Mén) Li 9 — Ji Ding	太阴 (Tài Yīn) 天英 (Tiān Yīng) 惊门 (Jīng Mén) Kun 2 — Ding Yi/Geng
九天 (Jiǔ Tiān) 天任 (Tiān Rèn) 杜门 (Dù Mén) Zhen 3 — Gui Wu	Yang (阳) Dun# 3 Hour: **JiSi** ©Calvin Yap	六合 (Liù Hé) 禽芮 (Qín Ruì) 开门 (Kāi Mén) Dui 7 — Yi/Geng Ren
九地 (Jiǔ Dì) 天蓬 (Tiān Péng) 伤门 (Shāng Mén) Gen 8 — Bing Gui	玄武 (Xuán Wǔ) 天心 (Tiān Xīn) 生门 (Shēng Mén) Kan 1 — Xin Bing	白虎 (Bái Hǔ) 天柱 (Tiān Zhù) 休门 (Xiū Mén) Qian 6 — Ren Xin

Yang (阳) Dun# 3 Hour: GengWu；直符(ZhíFú): 天冲(TiānChōng)
直使(ZhíShǐ): 伤门(ShāngMén)；旬首(XúnShǒu): JiaZiWu

九地 (Jiŭ Dì) 天蓬 (Tiān Péng) 生门 (Shēng Mén) Xun 4　　Bing Ji	九天 (Jiŭ Tiān) 天任 (Tiān Rèn) 伤门 (Shāng Mén) Li 9　　Gui Ding	值符 (Zhí Fú) 天冲 (Tiān Chōng) 杜门 (Dù Mén) Kun 2　　Wu Yi/Geng
玄武 (Xuán Wŭ) 天心 (Tiān Xīn) 休门 (Xiū Mén) Zhen 3　　Xin Wu	Yang (阳) Dun# 3 Hour: **GengWu** ©Calvin Yap	螣蛇 (Téng Shé) 天辅 (Tiān Fŭ) 景门 (Jĭng Mén) Dui 7　　Ji Ren
白虎 (Bái Hŭ) 天柱 (Tiān Zhù) 开门 (Kāi Mén) Gen 8　　Ren Gui	六合 (Liù Hé) 禽芮 (Qín Ruì) 惊门 (Jīng Mén) Kan 1　　Yi/Geng Bing	太阴 (Tài Yīn) 天英 (Tiān Yīng) 死门 (Sĭ Mén) Qian 6　　Ding Xin

Yang (阳) Dun# 3 Hour: XinWei；直符(ZhíFú): 天冲(TiānChōng)
直使(ZhíShǐ): 伤门(ShāngMén)；旬首(XúnShǒu): JiaZiWu

白虎 (Bái Hŭ) 天柱 (Tiān Zhù) 死门 (Sĭ Mén) Xun 4　　Ren Ji	玄武 (Xuán Wŭ) 天心 (Tiān Xīn) 惊门 (Jīng Mén) Li 9　　Xin Ding	九地 (Jiŭ Dì) 天蓬 (Tiān Péng) 开门 (Kāi Mén) Kun 2　　Bing Yi/Geng
六合 (Liù Hé) 禽芮 (Qín Ruì) 景门 (Jĭng Mén) Zhen 3　　Yi/Geng Wu	Yang (阳) Dun# 3 Hour: **XinWei** ©Calvin Yap	九天 (Jiŭ Tiān) 天任 (Tiān Rèn) 休门 (Xiū Mén) Dui 7　　Gui Ren
太阴 (Tài Yīn) 天英 (Tiān Yīng) 杜门 (Dù Mén) Gen 8　　Ding Gui	螣蛇 (Téng Shé) 天辅 (Tiān Fŭ) 伤门 (Shāng Mén) Kan 1　　Ji Bing	值符 (Zhí Fú) 天冲 (Tiān Chōng) 生门 (Shēng Mén) Qian 6　　Wu Xin

Yang (阳) Dun# 3 Hour: RenShen；直符(ZhíFú): 天冲(TiānChōng)
直使(ZhíShǐ): 伤门(ShāngMén)；旬首(XúnShǒu): JiaZiWu

玄武 (Xuán Wŭ) 天心 (Tiān Xīn) 休门 (Xiū Mén) Xun 4　　Xin Ji	九地 (Jiŭ Dì) 天蓬 (Tiān Péng) 生门 (Shēng Mén) Li 9　　Bing Ding	九天 (Jiŭ Tiān) 天任 (Tiān Rèn) 伤门 (Shāng Mén) Kun 2　　Gui Yi/Geng
白虎 (Bái Hŭ) 天柱 (Tiān Zhù) 开门 (Kāi Mén) Zhen 3　　Ren Wu	Yang (阳) Dun# 3 Hour: **RenShen** **Fan Yin** ©Calvin Yap	值符 (Zhí Fú) 天冲 (Tiān Chōng) 杜门 (Dù Mén) Dui 7　　Wu Ren
六合 (Liù Hé) 禽芮 (Qín Ruì) 惊门 (Jīng Mén) Gen 8　　Yi/Geng Gui	太阴 (Tài Yīn) 天英 (Tiān Yīng) 死门 (Sĭ Mén) Kan 1　　Ding Bing	螣蛇 (Téng Shé) 天辅 (Tiān Fŭ) 景门 (Jĭng Mén) Qian 6　　Ji Xin

Yang (阳) Dun# 3 Hour: GuiYou；直符(ZhíFú): 天冲(TiānChōng)
直使(ZhíShǐ): 伤门(ShāngMén)；旬首(XúnShǒu): JiaZiWu

太阴 (Tài Yīn) 天英 (Tiān Yīng) 杜门 (Dù Mén) Xun 4　　Ding Ji	六合 (Liù Hé) 禽芮 (Qín Ruì) 景门 (Jĭng Mén) Li 9　　Yi/Geng Ding	白虎 (Bái Hŭ) 天柱 (Tiān Zhù) 死门 (Sĭ Mén) Kun 2　　Ren Yi/Geng
螣蛇 (Téng Shé) 天辅 (Tiān Fŭ) 伤门 (Shāng Mén) Zhen 3　　Ji Wu	Yang (阳) Dun# 3 Hour: **GuiYou** ©Calvin Yap	玄武 (Xuán Wŭ) 天心 (Tiān Xīn) 惊门 (Jīng Mén) Dui 7　　Xin Ren
值符 (Zhí Fú) 天冲 (Tiān Chōng) 生门 (Shēng Mén) Gen 8　　Wu Gui	九天 (Jiŭ Tiān) 天任 (Tiān Rèn) 休门 (Xiū Mén) Kan 1　　Gui Bing	九地 (Jiŭ Dì) 天蓬 (Tiān Péng) 开门 (Kāi Mén) Qian 6　　Bing Xin

---

Chart: +3JiaXu (Yang Dun #3 JiaXu Xun)
JiaXu, YiHai, BingZi, DingChou, WuYin, JiMao, GengChen, XinSi, RenWu, GuiWei

Yang (阳) Dun# 3 Hour: JiaXu；直符(ZhíFú): 天辅(TiānFŭ)
直使(ZhíShǐ): 杜门(DùMén)；旬首(XúnShǒu): JiaXuJi

值符 (Zhí Fú) 天辅 (Tiān Fŭ) 杜门 (Dù Mén) Xun 4　　Ji Ji	螣蛇 (Téng Shé) 天英 (Tiān Yīng) 景门 (Jĭng Mén) Li 9　　Ding Ding	太阴 (Tài Yīn) 禽芮 (Qín Ruì) 死门 (Sĭ Mén) Kun 2　　Yi/Geng Yi/Geng
九天 (Jiŭ Tiān) 天冲 (Tiān Chōng) 伤门 (Shāng Mén) Zhen 3　　Wu Wu	Yang (阳) Dun# 3 Hour: **JiaXu** **Fu Yin** ©Calvin Yap	六合 (Liù Hé) 天柱 (Tiān Zhù) 惊门 (Jīng Mén) Dui 7　　Ren Ren
九地 (Jiŭ Dì) 天任 (Tiān Rèn) 生门 (Shēng Mén) Gen 8　　Gui Gui	玄武 (Xuán Wŭ) 天蓬 (Tiān Péng) 休门 (Xiū Mén) Kan 1　　Bing Bing	白虎 (Bái Hŭ) 天心 (Tiān Xīn) 开门 (Kāi Mén) Qian 6　　Xin Xin

Yang (阳) Dun# 3 Hour: YiHai；直符(ZhíFú): 天辅(TiānFŭ)
直使(ZhíShǐ): 杜门(DùMén)；旬首(XúnShǒu): JiaXuJi

九地 (Jiŭ Dì) 天任 (Tiān Rèn) 生门 (Shēng Mén) Xun 4　　Gui Ji	九天 (Jiŭ Tiān) 天冲 (Tiān Chōng) 伤门 (Shāng Mén) Li 9　　Wu Wu	值符 (Zhí Fú) 天辅 (Tiān Fŭ) 杜门 (Dù Mén) Kun 2　　Ji Yi/Geng
玄武 (Xuán Wŭ) 天蓬 (Tiān Péng) 休门 (Xiū Mén) Zhen 3　　Bing Wu	Yang (阳) Dun# 3 Hour: **YiHai** ©Calvin Yap	螣蛇 (Téng Shé) 天英 (Tiān Yīng) 景门 (Jĭng Mén) Dui 7　　Ding Ren
白虎 (Bái Hŭ) 天心 (Tiān Xīn) 开门 (Kāi Mén) Gen 8　　Xin Gui	六合 (Liù Hé) 天柱 (Tiān Zhù) 惊门 (Jīng Mén) Kan 1　　Ren Bing	太阴 (Tài Yīn) 禽芮 (Qín Ruì) 死门 (Sĭ Mén) Qian 6　　Yi/Geng Xin

Yang (阳) Dun# 3 Hour: BingZi ; 直符(ZhíFú): 天辅(TiānFǔ)
直使(ZhíShǐ): 杜门(DùMén) ; 旬首(XúnShǒu): JiaXuJi

六合 (Liù Hé) 天柱 (Tiān Zhù) 开门 (Kāi Mén) Xun 4　Ren　Ji	白虎 (Bái Hǔ) 天心 (Tiān Xīn) 休门 (Xiū Mén) Li 9　Xin　Ding	玄武 (Xuán Wǔ) 天蓬 (Tiān Péng) 生门 (Shēng Mén) Kun 2　Bing　Yi/Geng
太阴 (Tài Yīn) 禽芮 (Qín Ruì) 惊门 (Jīng Mén) Zhen 3　Yi/Geng　Wu	Yang (阳) Dun# 3 Hour: **BingZi** ©Calvin Yap	九地 (Jiǔ Dì) 天任 (Tiān Rèn) 伤门 (Shāng Mén) Dui 7　Gui　Ren
腾蛇 (Téng Shé) 天英 (Tiān Yīng) 死门 (Sǐ Mén) Gen 8　Ding　Gui	值符 (Zhí Fú) 天辅 (Tiān Fǔ) 景门 (Jǐng Mén) Kan 1　Ji　Bing	九天 (Jiǔ Tiān) 天冲 (Tiān Chōng) 杜门 (Dù Mén) Qian 6　Wu　Xin

Yang (阳) Dun# 3 Hour: DingChou ; 直符(ZhíFú): 天辅(TiānFǔ)
直使(ZhíShǐ): 杜门(DùMén) ; 旬首(XúnShǒu): JiaXuJi

九天 (Jiǔ Tiān) 天冲 (Tiān Chōng) 休门 (Xiū Mén) Xun 4　Wu　Ji	值符 (Zhí Fú) 天辅 (Tiān Fǔ) 生门 (Shēng Mén) Li 9　Ji　Ding	腾蛇 (Téng Shé) 天英 (Tiān Yīng) 伤门 (Shāng Mén) Kun 2　Ding　Yi/Geng
九地 (Jiǔ Dì) 天任 (Tiān Rèn) 开门 (Kāi Mén) Zhen 3　Gui　Wu	Yang (阳) Dun# 3 Hour: **DingChou** ©Calvin Yap	太阴 (Tài Yīn) 禽芮 (Qín Ruì) 杜门 (Dù Mén) Dui 7　Yi/Geng　Ren
玄武 (Xuán Wǔ) 天蓬 (Tiān Péng) 惊门 (Jīng Mén) Gen 8　Bing　Gui	白虎 (Bái Hǔ) 天心 (Tiān Xīn) 死门 (Sǐ Mén) Kan 1　Xin　Bing	六合 (Liù Hé) 天柱 (Tiān Zhù) 景门 (Jǐng Mén) Qian 6　Ren　Xin

Yang (阳) Dun# 3 Hour: WuYin ; 直符(ZhíFú): 天辅(TiānFǔ)
直使(ZhíShǐ): 杜门(DùMén) ; 旬首(XúnShǒu): JiaXuJi

腾蛇 (Téng Shé) 天英 (Tiān Yīng) 死门 (Sǐ Mén) Xun 4　Ding　Ji	太阴 (Tài Yīn) 禽芮 (Qín Ruì) 惊门 (Jīng Mén) Li 9　Yi/Geng　Ding	六合 (Liù Hé) 天柱 (Tiān Zhù) 开门 (Kāi Mén) Kun 2　Ren　Yi/Geng
值符 (Zhí Fú) 天辅 (Tiān Fǔ) 景门 (Jǐng Mén) Zhen 3　Ji　Wu	Yang (阳) Dun# 3 Hour: **WuYin** ©Calvin Yap	白虎 (Bái Hǔ) 天心 (Tiān Xīn) 休门 (Xiū Mén) Dui 7　Xin　Ren
九天 (Jiǔ Tiān) 天冲 (Tiān Chōng) 杜门 (Dù Mén) Gen 8　Wu　Gui	九地 (Jiǔ Dì) 天任 (Tiān Rèn) 伤门 (Shāng Mén) Kan 1　Gui　Bing	玄武 (Xuán Wǔ) 天蓬 (Tiān Péng) 生门 (Shēng Mén) Qian 6　Bing　Xin

Yang (阳) Dun# 3 Hour: JiMao ; 直符(ZhíFú): 天辅(TiānFǔ)
直使(ZhíShǐ): 杜门(DùMén) ; 旬首(XúnShǒu): JiaXuJi

值符 (Zhí Fú) 天辅 (Tiān Fǔ) 伤门 (Shāng Mén) Xun 4　Ji　Ji	腾蛇 (Téng Shé) 天英 (Tiān Yīng) 杜门 (Dù Mén) Li 9　Ding　Ding	太阴 (Tài Yīn) 禽芮 (Qín Ruì) 景门 (Jǐng Mén) Kun 2　Yi/Geng　Yi/Geng
九天 (Jiǔ Tiān) 天冲 (Tiān Chōng) 生门 (Shēng Mén) Zhen 3　Wu　Wu	Yang (阳) Dun# 3 Hour: **JiMao** **Fu Yin** ©Calvin Yap	六合 (Liù Hé) 天柱 (Tiān Zhù) 死门 (Sǐ Mén) Dui 7　Ren　Ren
九地 (Jiǔ Dì) 天任 (Tiān Rèn) 休门 (Xiū Mén) Gen 8　Gui　Gui	玄武 (Xuán Wǔ) 天蓬 (Tiān Péng) 开门 (Kāi Mén) Kan 1　Bing　Bing	白虎 (Bái Hǔ) 天心 (Tiān Xīn) 惊门 (Jīng Mén) Qian 6　Xin　Xin

Yang (阳) Dun# 3 Hour: GengChen ; 直符(ZhíFú): 天辅(TiānFǔ)
直使(ZhíShǐ): 杜门(DùMén) ; 旬首(XúnShǒu): JiaXuJi

九地 (Jiǔ Dì) 天任 (Tiān Rèn) 惊门 (Jīng Mén) Xun 4　Gui　Ji	九天 (Jiǔ Tiān) 天冲 (Tiān Chōng) 开门 (Kāi Mén) Li 9　Wu　Ding	值符 (Zhí Fú) 天辅 (Tiān Fǔ) 休门 (Xiū Mén) Kun 2　Ji　Yi/Geng
玄武 (Xuán Wǔ) 天蓬 (Tiān Péng) 死门 (Sǐ Mén) Zhen 3　Bing　Wu	Yang (阳) Dun# 3 Hour: **GengChen** ©Calvin Yap	腾蛇 (Téng Shé) 天英 (Tiān Yīng) 生门 (Shēng Mén) Dui 7　Ding　Ren
白虎 (Bái Hǔ) 天心 (Tiān Xīn) 景门 (Jǐng Mén) Gen 8　Xin　Gui	六合 (Liù Hé) 天柱 (Tiān Zhù) 杜门 (Dù Mén) Kan 1　Ren　Bing	太阴 (Tài Yīn) 禽芮 (Qín Ruì) 伤门 (Shāng Mén) Qian 6　Yi/Geng　Xin

Yang (阳) Dun# 3 Hour: XinSi ; 直符(ZhíFú): 天辅(TiānFǔ)
直使(ZhíShǐ): 杜门(DùMén) ; 旬首(XúnShǒu): JiaXuJi

白虎 (Bái Hǔ) 天心 (Tiān Xīn) 生门 (Shēng Mén) Xun 4　Xin　Ji	玄武 (Xuán Wǔ) 天蓬 (Tiān Péng) 伤门 (Shāng Mén) Li 9　Bing　Ding	九地 (Jiǔ Dì) 天任 (Tiān Rèn) 杜门 (Dù Mén) Kun 2　Gui　Yi/Geng
六合 (Liù Hé) 天柱 (Tiān Zhù) 休门 (Xiū Mén) Zhen 3　Ren　Wu	Yang (阳) Dun# 3 Hour: **XinSi** **Fan Yin** ©Calvin Yap	九天 (Jiǔ Tiān) 天冲 (Tiān Chōng) 景门 (Jǐng Mén) Dui 7　Wu　Ren
太阴 (Tài Yīn) 禽芮 (Qín Ruì) 开门 (Kāi Mén) Gen 8　Yi/Geng　Gui	腾蛇 (Téng Shé) 天英 (Tiān Yīng) 惊门 (Jīng Mén) Kan 1　Ding　Bing	值符 (Zhí Fú) 天辅 (Tiān Fǔ) 死门 (Sǐ Mén) Qian 6　Ji　Xin

Yang (阳) Dun# 3 Hour: **RenWu**；直符(ZhíFú): 天辅(TiānFǔ)
直使(ZhíShǐ): 杜门(DùMén)；旬首(XúnShǒu): JiaXuJi

玄武 (Xuán Wǔ) 天蓬 (Tiān Péng) 景门 (Jǐng Mén) Xun 4　Bing Ji	九地 (Jiǔ Dì) 天任 (Tiān Rèn) 死门 (Sǐ Mén) Li 9　Gui Ding	九天 (Jiǔ Tiān) 天冲 (Tiān Chōng) 惊门 (Jīng Mén) Kun 2　Wu Yi/Geng
白虎 (Bái Hǔ) 天心 (Tiān Xīn) 杜门 (Dù Mén) Zhen 3　Xin Wu	Yang (阳) Dun# 3 Hour: **RenWu** ©Calvin Yap	值符 (Zhí Fú) 天辅 (Tiān Fǔ) 开门 (Kāi Mén) Dui 7　Ji Ren
六合 (Liù Hé) 天柱 (Tiān Zhù) 伤门 (Shāng Mén) Gen 8　Ren Gui	太阴 (Tài Yīn) 禽芮 (Qín Ruì) 生门 (Shēng Mén) Kan 1　Yi/Geng Bing	螣蛇 (Téng Shé) 天英 (Tiān Yīng) 休门 (Xiū Mén) Qian 6　Ding Xin

Yang (阳) Dun# 3 Hour: **GuiWei**；直符(ZhíFú): 天辅(TiānFǔ)
直使(ZhíShǐ): 杜门(DùMén)；旬首(XúnShǒu): JiaXuJi

太阴 (Tài Yīn) 禽芮 (Qín Ruì) 杜门 (Dù Mén) Xun 4　Yi/Geng Ji	六合 (Liù Hé) 天柱 (Tiān Zhù) 景门 (Jǐng Mén) Li 9 Ren	白虎 (Bái Hǔ) 天心 (Tiān Xīn) 死门 (Sǐ Mén) Kun 2　Xin Yi/Geng
螣蛇 (Téng Shé) 天英 (Tiān Yīng) 伤门 (Shāng Mén) Zhen 3　Ding Wu	Yang (阳) Dun# 3 Hour: **GuiWei** ©Calvin Yap	玄武 (Xuán Wǔ) 天蓬 (Tiān Péng) 惊门 (Jīng Mén) Dui 7　Bing Ren
值符 (Zhí Fú) 天辅 (Tiān Fǔ) 生门 (Shēng Mén) Gen 8　Ji Gui	九天 (Jiǔ Tiān) 天冲 (Tiān Chōng) 休门 (Xiū Mén) Kan 1　Wu	九地 (Jiǔ Dì) 天任 (Tiān Rèn) 开门 (Kāi Mén) Qian 6　Gui Xin

Chart: +3JiaShen (Yang Dun #3 JiaShen Xun)
JiaShen, YiYou, BingXu, DingHai, WuZi, JiChou, GengYin, XinMao, RenChen, GuiSi

Yang (阳) Dun# 3 Hour: **JiaShen**；直符(ZhíFú): 天禽(TiānQín)
直使(ZhíShǐ): 死门(SǐMén)；旬首(XúnShǒu): JiaShenGeng

九地 (Jiǔ Dì) 天辅 (Tiān Fǔ) 杜门 (Dù Mén) Xun 4　Ji Ji	九天 (Jiǔ Tiān) 天英 (Tiān Yīng) 景门 (Jǐng Mén) Li 9　Ding Ding	值符 (Zhí Fú) 禽芮 (Qín Ruì) 死门 (Sǐ Mén) Kun 2　Yi/Geng Yi/Geng
玄武 (Xuán Wǔ) 天冲 (Tiān Chōng) 伤门 (Shāng Mén) Zhen 3　Wu Wu	Yang (阳) Dun# 3 Hour: **JiaShen** **Fu Yin** ©Calvin Yap	螣蛇 (Téng Shé) 天柱 (Tiān Zhù) 惊门 (Jīng Mén) Dui 7　Ren Ren
白虎 (Bái Hǔ) 天任 (Tiān Rèn) 生门 (Shēng Mén) Gen 8　Gui Gui	六合 (Liù Hé) 天蓬 (Tiān Péng) 休门 (Xiū Mén) Kan 1　Bing Bing	太阴 (Tài Yīn) 天心 (Tiān Xīn) 开门 (Kāi Mén) Qian 6　Xin Xin

Yang (阳) Dun# 3 Hour: **YiYou**；直符(ZhíFú): 天禽(TiānQín)
直使(ZhíShǐ): 死门(SǐMén)；旬首(XúnShǒu): JiaShenGeng

九地 (Jiǔ Dì) 天辅 (Tiān Fǔ) 生门 (Shēng Mén) Xun 4　Ji Ji	九天 (Jiǔ Tiān) 天英 (Tiān Yīng) 伤门 (Shāng Mén) Li 9　Ding Ding	值符 (Zhí Fú) 禽芮 (Qín Ruì) 杜门 (Dù Mén) Kun 2　Yi/Geng Yi/Geng
玄武 (Xuán Wǔ) 天冲 (TiānChōng) 休门 (Xiū Mén) Zhen 3　Wu Wu	Yang (阳) Dun# 3 Hour: **YiYou** **Fu Yin** ©Calvin Yap	螣蛇 (Téng Shé) 天柱 (Tiān Zhù) 景门 (Jǐng Mén) Dui 7　Ren Ren
白虎 (Bái Hǔ) 天任 (Tiān Rèn) 开门 (Kāi Mén) Gen 8　Gui Gui	六合 (Liù Hé) 天蓬 (Tiān Péng) 惊门 (Jīng Mén) Kan 1　Bing Bing	太阴 (Tài Yīn) 天心 (Tiān Xīn) 死门 (Sǐ Mén) Qian 6　Xin Xin

Yang (阳) Dun# 3 Hour: **BingXu**；直符(ZhíFú): 天禽(TiānQín)
直使(ZhíShǐ): 死门(SǐMén)；旬首(XúnShǒu): JiaShenGeng

六合 (Liù Hé) 天蓬 (Tiān Péng) 伤门 (Shāng Mén) Xun 4　Bing Ji	白虎 (Bái Hǔ) 天任 (Tiān Rèn) 杜门 (Dù Mén) Li 9　Gui Ding	玄武 (Xuán Wǔ) 天冲 (Tiān Chōng) 景门 (Jǐng Mén) Kun 2　Wu Yi/Geng
太阴 (Tài Yīn) 天心 (Tiān Xīn) 生门 (Shēng Mén) Zhen 3　Xin Wu	Yang (阳) Dun# 3 Hour: **BingXu** ©Calvin Yap	九地 (Jiǔ Dì) 天辅 (Tiān Fǔ) 死门 (Sǐ Mén) Dui 7　Ji Ren
螣蛇 (Téng Shé) 天柱 (Tiān Zhù) 休门 (Xiū Mén) Gen 8　Ren Gui	值符 (Zhí Fú) 禽芮 (Qín Ruì) 开门 (Kāi Mén) Kan 1　Yi/Geng Bing	九天 (Jiǔ Tiān) 天英 (Tiān Yīng) 惊门 (Jīng Mén) Qian 6　Ding Xin

Yang (阳) Dun# 3 Hour: **DingHai**；直符(ZhíFú): 天禽(TiānQín)
直使(ZhíShǐ): 死门(SǐMén)；旬首(XúnShǒu): JiaShenGeng

九天 (Jiǔ Tiān) 天英 (Tiān Yīng) 开门 (Kāi Mén) Xun 4　Ding Ji	值符 (Zhí Fú) 禽芮 (Qín Ruì) 休门 (Xiū Mén) Li 9　Yi/Geng Ding	螣蛇 (Téng Shé) 天柱 (Tiān Zhù) 生门 (Shēng Mén) Kun 2　Ren Yi/Geng
九地 (Jiǔ Dì) 天辅 (Tiān Fǔ) 惊门 (Jīng Mén) Zhen 3　Ji Wu	Yang (阳) Dun# 3 Hour: **DingHai** ©Calvin Yap	太阴 (Tài Yīn) 天心 (Tiān Xīn) 伤门 (Shāng Mén) Dui 7　Xin Ren
玄武 (Xuán Wǔ) 天冲 (Tiān Chōng) 死门 (Sǐ Mén) Gen 8　Wu Gui	白虎 (Bái Hǔ) 天任 (Tiān Rèn) 景门 (Jǐng Mén) Kan 1　Gui Bing	六合 (Liù Hé) 天蓬 (Tiān Péng) 杜门 (Dù Mén) Qian 6　Bing Xin

Yang (阳) Dun# 3 Hour: **WuZi**；直符(ZhíFú): 天禽(TiānQín)
直使(ZhíShǐ): 死门(SǐMén)；旬首(XúnShǒu): JiaShenGeng

螣蛇 (Téng Shé) 天柱 (Tiān Zhù) 景门 (Jǐng Mén) Xun 4　Ren Ji	太阴 (Tài Yīn) 天心 (Tiān Xīn) 死门 (Sǐ Mén) Li 9　Xin	六合 (Liù Hé) 天蓬 (Tiān Péng) 惊门 (Jīng Mén) Kun 2　Bing Ding
值符 (Zhi Fú) 禽芮 (Qín Ruì) 杜门 (Dù Mén) Zhen3 Yi/Geng Wu	Yang (阳) Dun# 3 Hour: **WuZi** ©Calvin Yap	白虎 (Bái Hǔ) 天任 (Tiān Rèn) 开门 (Kāi Mén) Dui 7　Gui Ren
九天 (Jiǔ Tiān) 天英 (Tiān Yīng) 伤门 (Shāng Mén) Gen 8　Ding Gui	九地 (Jiǔ Dì) 天辅 (Tiān Fǔ) 生门 (Shēng Mén) Kan 1　Ji Bing	玄武 (Xuán Wǔ) 天冲 (Tiān Chōng) 休门 (Xiū Mén) Qian 6　Wu Xin

Yang (阳) Dun# 3 Hour: **JiChou**；直符(ZhíFú): 天禽(TiānQín)
直使(ZhíShǐ): 死门(SǐMén)；旬首(XúnShǒu): JiaShenGeng

值符 (Zhi Fú) 禽芮 (Qín Ruì) 休门 (Xiū Mén) Xun 4　Yi/Geng Ji	螣蛇 (Téng Shé) 天柱 (Tiān Zhù) 生门 (Shēng Mén) Li 9　Ren Ding	太阴 (Tài Yīn) 天心 (Tiān Xīn) 伤门 (Shāng Mén) Kun 2　Xin Yi/Geng
九天 (Jiǔ Tiān) 天英 (Tiān Yīng) 开门 (Kāi Mén) Zhen 3　Ding Wu	Yang (阳) Dun# 3 Hour: **JiChou** ©Calvin Yap	六合 (Liù Hé) 天蓬 (Tiān Péng) 杜门 (Dù Mén) Dui 7　Bing Ren
九地 (Jiǔ Dì) 天辅 (Tiān Fǔ) 惊门 (Jīng Mén) Gen 8　Ji Gui	玄武 (Xuán Wǔ) 天冲 (Tiān Chōng) 死门 (Sǐ Mén) Kan 1　Wu Bing	白虎 (Bái Hǔ) 天任 (Tiān Rèn) 景门 (Jǐng Mén) Qian 6　Gui Xin

Yang (阳) Dun# 3 Hour: **GengYin**；直符(ZhíFú): 天禽(TiānQín)
直使(ZhíShǐ): 死门(SǐMén)；旬首(XúnShǒu): JiaShenGeng

九地 (Jiǔ Dì) 天辅 (Tiān Fǔ) 杜门 (Dù Mén) Xun 4　Ji Ji	九天 (Jiǔ Tiān) 天英 (Tiān Yīng) 景门 (Jǐng Mén) Li 9　Ding Ding	值符 (Zhi Fú) 禽芮 (Qín Ruì) 死门 (Sǐ Mén) Kun 2　Yi/Geng Yi/Geng
玄武 (Xuán Wǔ) 天冲 (Tiān Chōng) 伤门 (Shāng Mén) Zhen 3　Wu Wu	Yang (阳) Dun# 3 Hour: **GengYin** **Fu Yin** ©Calvin Yap	螣蛇 (Téng Shé) 天柱 (Tiān Zhù) 惊门 (Jīng Mén) Dui 7　Ren Ren
白虎 (Bái Hǔ) 天任 (Tiān Rèn) 生门 (Shēng Mén) Gen 8　Gui Gui	六合 (Liù Hé) 天蓬 (Tiān Péng) 休门 (Xiū Mén) Kan 1　Bing Bing	太阴 (Tài Yīn) 天心 (Tiān Xīn) 开门 (Kāi Mén) Qian 6　Xin Xin

Yang (阳) Dun# 3 Hour: **XinMao**；直符(ZhíFú): 天禽(TiānQín)
直使(ZhíShǐ): 死门(SǐMén)；旬首(XúnShǒu): JiaShenGeng

白虎 (Bái Hǔ) 天任 (Tiān Rèn) 惊门 (Jīng Mén) Xun 4　Gui Ji	玄武 (Xuán Wǔ) 天冲 (Tiān Chōng) 开门 (Kāi Mén) Li 9　Wu Ding	九地 (Jiǔ Dì) 天辅 (Tiān Fǔ) 休门 (Xiū Mén) Kun 2　Ji Yi/Geng
六合 (Liù Hé) 天蓬 (Tiān Péng) 死门 (Sǐ Mén) Zhen 3　Bing Wu	Yang (阳) Dun# 3 Hour: **XinMao** ©Calvin Yap	九天 (Jiǔ Tiān) 天英 (Tiān Yīng) 生门 (Shēng Mén) Dui 7　Ding Ren
太阴 (Tài Yīn) 天心 (Tiān Xīn) 景门 (Jǐng Mén) Gen 8　Xin Gui	螣蛇 (Téng Shé) 天柱 (Tiān Zhù) 杜门 (Dù Mén) Kan 1　Ren Bing	值符 (Zhi Fú) 禽芮 (Qín Ruì) 伤门 (Shāng Mén) Qian6 Yi/Geng Xin

Yang (阳) Dun# 3 Hour: **RenChen**；直符(ZhíFú): 天禽(TiānQín)
直使(ZhíShǐ): 死门(SǐMén)；旬首(XúnShǒu): JiaShenGeng

玄武 (Xuán Wǔ) 天冲 (Tiān Chōng) 死门 (Sǐ Mén) Xun 4　Wu Ji	九地 (Jiǔ Dì) 天辅 (Tiān Fǔ) 惊门 (Jīng Mén) Li 9　Ji Ding	九天 (Jiǔ Tiān) 天英 (Tiān Yīng) 开门 (Kāi Mén) Kun 2　Ding Yi/Geng
白虎 (Bái Hǔ) 天任 (Tiān Rèn) 景门 (Jǐng Mén) Zhen 3　Gui Wu	Yang (阳) Dun# 3 Hour: **RenChen** ©Calvin Yap	值符 (Zhi Fú) 禽芮 (Qín Ruì) 休门 (Xiū Mén) Dui 7　Yi/Geng Ren
六合 (Liù Hé) 天蓬 (Tiān Péng) 杜门 (Dù Mén) Gen 8　Bing Gui	太阴 (Tài Yīn) 天心 (Tiān Xīn) 伤门 (Shāng Mén) Kan 1　Xin Bing	螣蛇 (Téng Shé) 天柱 (Tiān Zhù) 生门 (Shēng Mén) Qian 6　Ren Xin

Yang (阳) Dun# 3 Hour: **GuiSi**；直符(ZhíFú): 天禽(TiānQín)
直使(ZhíShǐ): 死门(SǐMén)；旬首(XúnShǒu): JiaShenGeng

太阴 (Tài Yīn) 天心 (Tiān Xīn) 杜门 (Dù Mén) Xun 4　Xin Ji	六合 (Liù Hé) 天蓬 (Tiān Péng) 景门 (Jǐng Mén) Li 9　Bing Ding	白虎 (Bái Hǔ) 天任 (Tiān Rèn) 死门 (Sǐ Mén) Kun 2　Gui Yi/Geng
螣蛇 (Téng Shé) 天柱 (Tiān Zhù) 伤门 (Shāng Mén) Zhen 3　Ren Wu	Yang (阳) Dun# 3 Hour: **GuiSi** **Fan Yin** ©Calvin Yap	玄武 (Xuán Wǔ) 天冲 (TiānChōng) 惊门 (Jīng Mén) Dui 7　Wu Ren
值符 (Zhi Fú) 禽芮 (Qín Ruì) 生门 (Shēng Mén) Gen 8　Yi/Geng Gui	九天 (Jiǔ Tiān) 天英 (Tiān Yīng) 休门 (Xiū Mén) Kan 1　Ding Bing	九地 (Jiǔ Dì) 天辅 (Tiān Fǔ) 开门 (Kāi Mén) Qian 6　Ji Xin

*Chart: **+3JiaWu** (Yang Dun #3 JiaWu Xun)*
JiaWu, YiWei, BingShen, DingYou, WuXu, JiHai, GengZi, XinChou, RenYin, GuiMao

---

Yang (阳) Dun# 3 Hour: **JiaWu** ; 直符(ZhíFú): 天心(TiānXīn)
直使(ZhíShǐ): 开门(KāiMén) ; 旬首(XúnShǒu): JiaWu/Xin

白虎 (Bái Hǔ) 天辅 (Tiān Fǔ) 杜门 (Dù Mén) Xun 4　　Ji Ji	玄武 (Xuán Wǔ) 天英 (Tiān Yīng) 景门 (Jǐng Mén) Li 9　　Ding Ding	九地 (Jiǔ Dì) 禽芮 (Qín Ruì) 死门 (Sǐ Mén) Kun 2　　Yi/Geng Yi/Geng
六合 (Liù Hé) 天冲 (Tiān Chōng) 伤门 (Shāng Mén) Zhen 3　　Wu Wu	Yang (阳) Dun# 3 Hour: **JiaWu** **Fu Yin** ©Calvin Yap	九天 (Jiǔ Tiān) 天柱 (Tiān Zhù) 惊门 (Jīng Mén) Dui 7　　Ren Ren
太阴 (Tài Yīn) 天任 (Tiān Rèn) 生门 (Shēng Mén) Gen 8　　Gui Gui	腾蛇 (Téng Shé) 天蓬 (Tiān Péng) 休门 (Xiū Mén) Kan 1　　Bing Bing	值符 (Zhí Fú) 天心 (Tiān Xīn) 开门 (Kāi Mén) Qian 6　　Xin Xin

Yang (阳) Dun# 3 Hour: **YiWei** ; 直符(ZhíFú): 天心(TiānXīn)
直使(ZhíShǐ): 开门(KāiMén) ; 旬首(XúnShǒu): JiaWu/Xin

九地 (Jiǔ Dì) 禽芮 (Qín Ruì) 景门 (Jǐng Mén) Xun 4　　Yi/Geng Ji	九天 (Jiǔ Tiān) 天柱 (Tiān Zhù) 死门 (Sǐ Mén) Li 9　　Ren	值符 (Zhí Fú) 天心 (Tiān Xīn) 惊门 (Jīng Mén) Kun 2　　Xin Yi/Geng
玄武 (Xuán Wǔ) 天英 (Tiān Yīng) 杜门 (Dù Mén) Zhen 3　　Ding Wu	Yang (阳) Dun# 3 Hour: **YiWei** ©Calvin Yap	腾蛇 (Téng Shé) 天蓬 (Tiān Péng) 开门 (Kāi Mén) Dui 7　　Bing Ren
白虎 (Bái Hǔ) 天辅 (Tiān Fǔ) 伤门 (Shāng Mén) Gen 8　　Ji Gui	六合 (Liù Hé) 天冲 (Tiān Chōng) 生门 (Shēng Mén) Kan 1　　Wu	太阴 (Tài Yīn) 天任 (Tiān Rèn) 休门 (Xiū Mén) Qian 6　　Gui Xin

Yang (阳) Dun# 3 Hour: **BingShen** ; 直符(ZhíFú): 天心(TiānXīn)
直使(ZhíShǐ): 开门(KāiMén) ; 旬首(XúnShǒu): JiaWu/Xin

六合 (Liù Hé) 天冲 (Tiān Chōng) 生门 (Shēng Mén) Xun 4　　Wu Ji	白虎 (Bái Hǔ) 天辅 (Tiān Fǔ) 伤门 (Shāng Mén) Li 9　　Ji Ding	玄武 (Xuán Wǔ) 天英 (Tiān Yīng) 杜门 (Dù Mén) Kun 2　　Ding Yi/Geng
太阴 (Tài Yīn) 天任 (Tiān Rèn) 休门 (Xiū Mén) Zhen 3　　Gui Wu	Yang (阳) Dun# 3 Hour: **BingShen** ©Calvin Yap	九地 (Jiǔ Dì) 禽芮 (Qín Ruì) 景门 (Jǐng Mén) Dui 7　　Yi/Geng Ren
腾蛇 (Téng Shé) 天蓬 (Tiān Péng) 开门 (Kāi Mén) Gen 8　　Bing Gui	值符 (Zhí Fú) 天心 (Tiān Xīn) 惊门 (Jīng Mén) Kan 1　　Xin Bing	九天 (Jiǔ Tiān) 天柱 (Tiān Zhù) 死门 (Sǐ Mén) Qian 6　　Ren Xin

Yang (阳) Dun# 3 Hour: **DingYou** ; 直符(ZhíFú): 天心(TiānXīn)
直使(ZhíShǐ): 开门(KāiMén) ; 旬首(XúnShǒu): JiaWu/Xin

九天 (Jiǔ Tiān) 天柱 (Tiān Zhù) 惊门 (Jīng Mén) Xun 4　　Ren Ji	值符 (Zhí Fú) 天心 (Tiān Xīn) 开门 (Kāi Mén) Li 9　　Xin Ding	腾蛇 (Téng Shé) 天蓬 (Tiān Péng) 休门 (Xiū Mén) Kun 2　　Bing Yi/Geng
九地 (Jiǔ Dì) 禽芮 (Qín Ruì) 死门 (Sǐ Mén) Zhen 3　　Yi/Geng Wu	Yang (阳) Dun# 3 Hour: **DingYou** ©Calvin Yap	太阴 (Tài Yīn) 天任 (Tiān Rèn) 生门 (Shēng Mén) Dui 7　　Gui Ren
玄武 (Xuán Wǔ) 天英 (Tiān Yīng) 景门 (Jǐng Mén) Gen 8　　Ding Gui	白虎 (Bái Hǔ) 天辅 (Tiān Fǔ) 杜门 (Dù Mén) Kan 1　　Ji Bing	六合 (Liù Hé) 天冲 (Tiān Chōng) 伤门 (Shāng Mén) Qian 6　　Wu Xin

Yang (阳) Dun# 3 Hour: **WuXu** ; 直符(ZhíFú): 天心(TiānXīn)
直使(ZhíShǐ): 开门(KāiMén) ; 旬首(XúnShǒu): JiaWu/Xin

腾蛇 (Téng Shé) 天蓬 (Tiān Péng) 伤门 (Shāng Mén) Xun 4　　Bing Ji	太阴 (Tài Yīn) 天任 (Tiān Rèn) 杜门 (Dù Mén) Li 9　　Gui Ding	六合 (Liù Hé) 天冲 (Tiān Chōng) 景门 (Jǐng Mén) Kun 2　　Wu Yi/Geng
值符 (Zhí Fú) 天心 (Tiān Xīn) 生门 (Shēng Mén) Zhen 3　　Xin Wu	Yang (阳) Dun# 3 Hour: **WuXu** ©Calvin Yap	白虎 (Bái Hǔ) 天辅 (Tiān Fǔ) 死门 (Sǐ Mén) Dui 7　　Ji Ren
九天 (Jiǔ Tiān) 天柱 (Tiān Zhù) 休门 (Xiū Mén) Gen 8　　Ren Gui	九地 (Jiǔ Dì) 禽芮 (Qín Ruì) 开门 (Kāi Mén) Kan 1　　Yi/Geng Bing	玄武 (Xuán Wǔ) 天英 (Tiān Yīng) 惊门 (Jīng Mén) Qian 6　　Ding Xin

Yang (阳) Dun# 3 Hour: **JiHai** ; 直符(ZhíFú): 天心(TiānXīn)
直使(ZhíShǐ): 开门(KāiMén) ; 旬首(XúnShǒu): JiaWu/Xin

值符 (Zhí Fú) 天心 (Tiān Xīn) 死门 (Sǐ Mén) Xun 4　　Xin Ji	腾蛇 (Téng Shé) 天蓬 (Tiān Péng) 惊门 (Jīng Mén) Li 9　　Bing Ding	太阴 (Tài Yīn) 天任 (Tiān Rèn) 开门 (Kāi Mén) Kun 2　　Gui Yi/Geng
九天 (Jiǔ Tiān) 天柱 (Tiān Zhù) 景门 (Jǐng Mén) Zhen 3　　Ren Wu	Yang (阳) Dun# 3 Hour: **JiHai** **Fan Yin** ©Calvin Yap	六合 (Liù Hé) 天冲 (Tiān Chōng) 休门 (Xiū Mén) Dui 7　　Wu Ren
九地 (Jiǔ Dì) 禽芮 (Qín Ruì) 杜门 (Dù Mén) Gen 8　　Yi/Geng Gui	玄武 (Xuán Wǔ) 天英 (Tiān Yīng) 伤门 (Shāng Mén) Kan 1　　Ding Bing	白虎 (Bái Hǔ) 天辅 (Tiān Fǔ) 生门 (Shēng Mén) Qian 6　　Ji Xin

Yang (阳) Dun# 3 Hour: GengZi ；直符(ZhíFú): 天心(TiānXīn)
直使(ZhíShǐ): 开门(KāiMén)；旬首(XúnShǒu): JiaWu/Xin

九地 (Jiǔ Dì) 禽芮 (Qín Ruì) 休门 (Xiū Mén) Xun 4 　Yi/Geng Ji	九天 (Jiǔ Tiān) 天柱 (Tiān Zhù) 生门 (Shēng Mén) Li 9 　Ren	值符 (Zhí Fú) 天心 (Tiān Xīn) 伤门 (Shāng Mén) Kun 2 　Xin Yi/Geng
玄武 (Xuán Wǔ) 天英 (Tiān Yīng) 开门 (Kāi Mén) Zhen 3 　Ding Wu	Yang (阳) Dun# 3 Hour: **GengZi** ©Calvin Yap	螣蛇 (Téng Shé) 天蓬 (Tiān Péng) 杜门 (Dù Mén) Dui 7 　Bing Ren
白虎 (Bái Hǔ) 天辅 (Tiān Fǔ) 惊门 (Jīng Mén) Gen 8 　Ji Gui	六合 (Liù Hé) 天冲 (Tiān Chōng) 死门 (Sǐ Mén) Kan 1 　Wu Bing	太阴 (Tài Yīn) 天任 (Tiān Rèn) 景门 (Jǐng Mén) Qian 6 　Gui Xin

Yang (阳) Dun# 3 Hour: XinChou ；直符(ZhíFú): 天心(TiānXīn)
直使(ZhíShǐ): 开门(KāiMén)；旬首(XúnShǒu): JiaWu/Xin

白虎 (Bái Hǔ) 天辅 (Tiān Fǔ) 开门 (Kāi Mén) Xun 4 　Ji	玄武 (Xuán Wǔ) 天英 (Tiān Yīng) 休门 (Xiū Mén) Li 9 　Ding	九地 (Jiǔ Dì) 禽芮 (Qín Ruì) 生门 (Shēng Mén) Kun 2 　Yi/Geng Yi/Geng
六合 (Liù Hé) 天冲 (Tiān Chōng) 惊门 (Jīng Mén) Zhen 3 　Wu Wu	Yang (阳) Dun# 3 Hour: **XinChou** **Fu Yin** ©Calvin Yap	九天 (Jiǔ Tiān) 天柱 (Tiān Zhù) 伤门 (Shāng Mén) Dui 7 　Ren Ren
太阴 (Tài Yīn) 天任 (Tiān Rèn) 死门 (Sǐ Mén) Gen 8 　Gui Gui	螣蛇 (Téng Shé) 天蓬 (Tiān Péng) 景门 (Jǐng Mén) Kan 1 　Bing Bing	值符 (Zhí Fú) 天心 (Tiān Xīn) 杜门 (Dù Mén) Qian 6 　Xin Xin

Yang (阳) Dun# 3 Hour: RenYin ；直符(ZhíFú): 天心(TiānXīn)
直使(ZhíShǐ): 开门(KāiMén)；旬首(XúnShǒu): JiaWu/Xin

玄武 (Xuán Wǔ) 天英 (Tiān Yīng) 死门 (Sǐ Mén) Xun 4 　Ding Ji	九地 (Jiǔ Dì) 禽芮 (Qín Ruì) 惊门 (Jīng Mén) Li 9 　Yi/Geng Ding	九天 (Jiǔ Tiān) 天柱 (Tiān Zhù) 开门 (Kāi Mén) Kun 2 　Ren Yi/Geng
白虎 (Bái Hǔ) 天辅 (Tiān Fǔ) 景门 (Jǐng Mén) Zhen 3 　Ji Wu	Yang (阳) Dun# 3 Hour: **RenYin** ©Calvin Yap	值符 (Zhí Fú) 天心 (Tiān Xīn) 休门 (Xiū Mén) Dui 7 　Xin Ren
六合 (Liù Hé) 天冲 (Tiān Chōng) 杜门 (Dù Mén) Gen 8 　Wu Gui	太阴 (Tài Yīn) 天任 (Tiān Rèn) 伤门 (Shāng Mén) Kan 1 　Gui Bing	螣蛇 (Téng Shé) 天蓬 (Tiān Péng) 生门 (Shēng Mén) Qian 6 　Bing Xin

Yang (阳) Dun# 3 Hour: GuiMao ；直符(ZhíFú): 天心(TiānXīn)
直使(ZhíShǐ): 开门(KāiMén)；旬首(XúnShǒu): JiaWu/Xin

太阴 (Tài Yīn) 天任 (Tiān Rèn) 杜门 (Dù Mén) Xun 4 　Gui Ji	六合 (Liù Hé) 天冲 (Tiān Chōng) 景门 (Jǐng Mén) Li 9 　Wu Ding	白虎 (Bái Hǔ) 天辅 (Tiān Fǔ) 死门 (Sǐ Mén) Kun 2 　Ji Yi/Geng
螣蛇 (Téng Shé) 天蓬 (Tiān Péng) 伤门 (Shāng Mén) Zhen 3 　Bing Wu	Yang (阳) Dun# 3 Hour: **GuiMao** ©Calvin Yap	玄武 (Xuán Wǔ) 天英 (Tiān Yīng) 惊门 (Jīng Mén) Dui 7 　Ding Ren
值符 (Zhí Fú) 天心 (Tiān Xīn) 生门 (Shēng Mén) Gen 8 　Xin Gui	九天 (Jiǔ Tiān) 天柱 (Tiān Zhù) 休门 (Xiū Mén) Kan 1 　Ren Bing	九地 (Jiǔ Dì) 禽芮 (Qín Ruì) 开门 (Kāi Mén) Qian 6 　Yi/Geng Xin

Chart: +3JiaChen (Yang Dun #3 JiaChen Xun)
JiaChen, YiSi, BingWu, DingWei, WuShen, JiYou, GengXu, XinHai, RenZi, GuiChou

Yang (阳) Dun# 3 Hour: JiaChen ；直符(ZhíFú): 天柱(TiānZhù)
直使(ZhíShǐ): 惊门(JīngMén)；旬首(XúnShǒu): JiaChenRen

玄武 (Xuán Wǔ) 天辅 (Tiān Fǔ) 杜门 (Dù Mén) Xun 4 　Ji Ji	九地 (Jiǔ Dì) 天英 (Tiān Yīng) 景门 (Jǐng Mén) Li 9 　Ding Ding	九天 (Jiǔ Tiān) 禽芮 (Qín Ruì) 死门 (Sǐ Mén) Kun 2 　Yi/Geng Yi/Geng
白虎 (Bái Hǔ) 天冲 (Tiān Chōng) 伤门 (Shāng Mén) Zhen 3 　Wu Wu	Yang (阳) Dun# 3 Hour: **JiaChen** **Fu Yin** ©Calvin Yap	值符 (Zhí Fú) 天柱 (Tiān Zhù) 惊门 (Jīng Mén) Dui 7 　Ren Ren
六合 (Liù Hé) 天任 (Tiān Rèn) 生门 (Shēng Mén) Gen 8 　Gui Gui	太阴 (Tài Yīn) 天蓬 (Tiān Péng) 休门 (Xiū Mén) Kan 1 　Bing Bing	螣蛇 (Téng Shé) 天心 (Tiān Xīn) 开门 (Kāi Mén) Qian 6 　Xin Xin

Yang (阳) Dun# 3 Hour: YiSi ；直符(ZhíFú): 天柱(TiānZhù)
直使(ZhíShǐ): 惊门(JīngMén)；旬首(XúnShǒu): JiaChenRen

九地 (Jiǔ Dì) 天英 (Tiān Yīng) 休门 (Xiū Mén) Xun 4 　Ding Ji	九天 (Jiǔ Tiān) 禽芮 (Qín Ruì) 生门 (Shēng Mén) Li 9 　Yi/Geng Ding	值符 (Zhí Fú) 天柱 (Tiān Zhù) 伤门 (Shāng Mén) Kun 2 　Ren Yi/Geng
玄武 (Xuán Wǔ) 天辅 (Tiān Fǔ) 开门 (Kāi Mén) Zhen 3 　Ji Wu	Yang (阳) Dun# 3 Hour: **YiSi** ©Calvin Yap	螣蛇 (Téng Shé) 天心 (Tiān Xīn) 杜门 (Dù Mén) Dui 7 　Xin Ren
白虎 (Bái Hǔ) 天冲 (Tiān Chōng) 惊门 (Jīng Mén) Gen 8 　Wu Gui	六合 (Liù Hé) 天任 (Tiān Rèn) 死门 (Sǐ Mén) Kan 1 　Gui Bing	太阴 (Tài Yīn) 天蓬 (Tiān Péng) 景门 (Jǐng Mén) Qian 6 　Bing Xin

Chart 1

Yang (阳) Dun# 3 Hour: **BingWu**；直符(ZhíFú): 天柱(TiānZhù)
直使(ZhíShǐ): 惊门(JīngMén)；旬首(XúnShǒu): JiaChenRen

六合 (Liù Hé) 天任 (Tiān Rèn) 死门 (Sǐ Mén) Xun 4　　Gui 　　　Ji	白虎 (Bái Hǔ) 天冲 (Tiān Chōng) 惊门 (Jīng Mén) Li 9　　Wu	玄武 (Xuán Wǔ) 天辅 (Tiān Fǔ) 开门 (Kāi Mén) Kun 2　　Ji 　　Yi/Geng
太阴 (Tài Yīn) 天蓬 (Tiān Péng) 景门 (Jǐng Mén) Zhen 3　　Bing Wu	Yang (阳) Dun# 3 Hour: **BingWu** ©Calvin Yap	九地 (Jiǔ Dì) 天英 (Tiān Yīng) 休门 (Xiū Mén) Dui 7　　Ding 　　Ren
螣蛇 (Téng Shé) 天心 (Tiān Xīn) 杜门 (Dù Mén) Gen 8　　Xin Gui	值符 (Zhí Fú) 天柱 (Tiān Zhù) 伤门 (Shāng Mén) Kan 1　　Ren Bing	九天 (Jiǔ Tiān) 禽芮 (Qín Ruì) 生门 (Shēng Mén) Qian 6　　Yi/Geng Xin

Chart 2

Yang (阳) Dun# 3 Hour: **DingWei**；直符(ZhíFú): 天柱(TiānZhù)
直使(ZhíShǐ): 惊门(JīngMén)；旬首(XúnShǒu): JiaChenRen

九天 (Jiǔ Tiān) 禽芮 (Qín Ruì) 生门 (Shēng Mén) Xun 4　　Yi/Geng 　　Ji	值符 (Zhí Fú) 天柱 (Tiān Zhù) 伤门 (Shāng Mén) Li 9　　Ren Ding	螣蛇 (Téng Shé) 天心 (Tiān Xīn) 杜门 (Dù Mén) Kun 2　　Xin 　　Yi/Geng
九地 (Jiǔ Dì) 天英 (Tiān Yīng) 休门 (Xiū Mén) Zhen 3　　Ding Wu	Yang (阳) Dun# 3 Hour: **DingWei** ©Calvin Yap	太阴 (Tài Yīn) 天蓬 (Tiān Péng) 景门 (Jǐng Mén) Dui 7　　Bing 　　Ren
玄武 (Xuán Wǔ) 天辅 (Tiān Fǔ) 开门 (Kāi Mén) Gen 8　　Ji Gui	白虎 (Bái Hǔ) 天冲 (Tiān Chōng) 惊门 (Jīng Mén) Kan 1　　Wu Bing	六合 (Liù Hé) 天任 (Tiān Rèn) 死门 (Sǐ Mén) Qian 6　　Gui Xin

Chart 3

Yang (阳) Dun# 3 Hour: **WuShen**；直符(ZhíFú): 天柱(TiānZhù)
直使(ZhíShǐ): 惊门(JīngMén)；旬首(XúnShǒu): JiaChenRen

螣蛇 (Téng Shé) 天心 (Tiān Xīn) 景门 (Jǐng Mén) Xun 4　　Xin 　　Ji	太阴 (Tài Yīn) 天蓬 (Tiān Péng) 死门 (Sǐ Mén) Li 9　　Bing Ding	六合 (Liù Hé) 天任 (Tiān Rèn) 惊门 (Jīng Mén) Kun 2　　Gui 　　Yi/Geng
值符 (Zhí Fú) 天柱 (Tiān Zhù) 杜门 (Dù Mén) Zhen 3　　Ren Wu	Yang (阳) Dun# 3 Hour: **WuShen** **Fan Yin** ©Calvin Yap	白虎 (Bái Hǔ) 天冲 (Tiān Chōng) 开门 (Kāi Mén) Dui 7　　Wu 　　Ren
九天 (Jiǔ Tiān) 禽芮 (Qín Ruì) 伤门 (Shāng Mén) Gen 8　　Yi/Geng Gui	九地 (Jiǔ Dì) 天英 (Tiān Yīng) 生门 (Shēng Mén) Kan 1　　Ding Bing	玄武 (Xuán Wǔ) 天辅 (Tiān Fǔ) 休门 (Xiū Mén) Qian 6　　Ji Xin

Chart 4

Yang (阳) Dun# 3 Hour: **JiYou**；直符(ZhíFú): 天柱(TiānZhù)
直使(ZhíShǐ): 惊门(JīngMén)；旬首(XúnShǒu): JiaChenRen

值符 (Zhí Fú) 天柱 (Tiān Zhù) 开门 (Kāi Mén) Xun 4　　Ren 　　Ji	螣蛇 (Téng Shé) 天心 (Tiān Xīn) 休门 (Xiū Mén) Li 9　　Xin Ding	太阴 (Tài Yīn) 天蓬 (Tiān Péng) 生门 (Shēng Mén) Kun 2　　Bing 　　Yi/Geng
九天 (Jiǔ Tiān) 禽芮 (Qín Ruì) 惊门 (Jīng Mén) Zhen 3　　Yi/Geng Wu	Yang (阳) Dun# 3 Hour: **JiYou** ©Calvin Yap	六合 (Liù Hé) 天任 (Tiān Rèn) 伤门 (Shāng Mén) Dui 7　　Gui 　　Ren
九地 (Jiǔ Dì) 天英 (Tiān Yīng) 死门 (Sǐ Mén) Gen 8　　Ding Gui	玄武 (Xuán Wǔ) 天辅 (Tiān Fǔ) 景门 (Jǐng Mén) Kan 1　　Ji Bing	白虎 (Bái Hǔ) 天冲 (Tiān Chōng) 杜门 (Dù Mén) Qian 6　　Wu Xin

Chart 5

Yang (阳) Dun# 3 Hour: **GengXu**；直符(ZhíFú): 天柱(TiānZhù)
直使(ZhíShǐ): 惊门(JīngMén)；旬首(XúnShǒu): JiaChenRen

九地 (Jiǔ Dì) 天英 (Tiān Yīng) 惊门 (Jīng Mén) Xun 4　　Ding 　　Ji	九天 (Jiǔ Tiān) 禽芮 (Qín Ruì) 开门 (Kāi Mén) Li 9　　Yi/Geng Ding	值符 (Zhí Fú) 天柱 (Tiān Zhù) 休门 (Xiū Mén) Kun 2　　Ren 　　Yi/Geng
玄武 (Xuán Wǔ) 天辅 (Tiān Fǔ) 死门 (Sǐ Mén) Zhen 3　　Ji Wu	Yang (阳) Dun# 3 Hour: **GengXu** ©Calvin Yap	螣蛇 (Téng Shé) 天心 (Tiān Xīn) 生门 (Shēng Mén) Dui 7　　Xin 　　Ren
白虎 (Bái Hǔ) 天冲 (Tiān Chōng) 景门 (Jǐng Mén) Gen 8　　Wu Gui	六合 (Liù Hé) 天任 (Tiān Rèn) 杜门 (Dù Mén) Kan 1　　Gui Bing	太阴 (Tài Yīn) 天蓬 (Tiān Péng) 伤门 (Shāng Mén) Qian 6　　Bing Xin

Chart 6

Yang (阳) Dun# 3 Hour: **XinHai**；直符(ZhíFú): 天柱(TiānZhù)
直使(ZhíShǐ): 惊门(JīngMén)；旬首(XúnShǒu): JiaChenRen

白虎 (Bái Hǔ) 天冲 (Tiān Chōng) 景门 (Jǐng Mén) Xun 4　　Wu 　　Ji	玄武 (Xuán Wǔ) 天辅 (Tiān Fǔ) 死门 (Sǐ Mén) Li 9　　Ji Ding	九地 (Jiǔ Dì) 天英 (Tiān Yīng) 惊门 (Jīng Mén) Kun 2　　Ding 　　Yi/Geng
六合 (Liù Hé) 天任 (Tiān Rèn) 杜门 (Dù Mén) Zhen 3　　Gui Wu	Yang (阳) Dun# 3 Hour: **XinHai** ©Calvin Yap	九天 (Jiǔ Tiān) 禽芮 (Qín Ruì) 开门 (Kāi Mén) Dui 7　　Yi/Geng 　　Ren
太阴 (Tài Yīn) 天蓬 (Tiān Péng) 伤门 (Shāng Mén) Gen 8　　Bing Gui	螣蛇 (Téng Shé) 天心 (Tiān Xīn) 生门 (Shēng Mén) Kan 1　　Xin Bing	值符 (Zhí Fú) 天柱 (Tiān Zhù) 休门 (Xiū Mén) Qian 6　　Ren Xin

Yang (阳) Dun# 3 Hour: RenZi ; 直符(ZhíFú): 天柱(TiānZhù)
直使(ZhíShǐ): 惊门(JǐngMén) ; 旬首(XúnShǒu): JiaChenRen

玄武 (Xuán Wǔ) 天辅 (Tiān Fǔ) 伤门 (Shāng Mén) Xun 4　Ji Ji	九地 (Jiǔ Dì) 天英 (Tiān Yīng) 杜门 (Dù Mén) Li 9　Ding Ding	九天 (Jiǔ Tiān) 禽芮 (Qín Ruì) 景门 (Jǐng Mén) Kun 2　Yi/Geng Yi/Geng
白虎 (Bái Hǔ) 天冲 (Tiān Chōng) 生门 (Shēng Mén) Zhen 3　Wu Wu	Yang (阳) Dun# 3 Hour: **RenZi** **Fu Yin** ©Calvin Yap	值符 (Zhí Fú) 天柱 (Tiān Zhù) 死门 (Sǐ Mén) Dui 7　Ren Ren
六合 (Liù Hé) 天任 (Tiān Rèn) 休门 (Xiū Mén) Gen 8　Gui Gui	太阴 (Tài Yīn) 天蓬 (Tiān Péng) 开门 (Kāi Mén) Kan 1　Bing Bing	螣蛇 (Téng Shé) 天心 (Tiān Xīn) 惊门 (Jǐng Mén) Qian 6　Xin Xin

Yang (阳) Dun# 3 Hour: GuiChou ; 直符(ZhíFú): 天柱(TiānZhù)
直使(ZhíShǐ): 惊门(JǐngMén) ; 旬首(XúnShǒu): JiaChenRen

太阴 (Tài Yīn) 天蓬 (Tiān Péng) 杜门 (Dù Mén) Xun 4　Bing Ji	六合 (Liù Hé) 天任 (Tiān Rèn) 景门 (Jǐng Mén) Li 9　Gui Ding	白虎 (Bái Hǔ) 天冲 (Tiān Chōng) 死门 (Sǐ Mén) Kun 2　Wu Yi/Geng
螣蛇 (Téng Shé) 天心 (Tiān Xīn) 伤门 (Shāng Mén) Zhen 3　Xin Wu	Yang (阳) Dun# 3 Hour: **GuiChou** ©Calvin Yap	玄武 (Xuán Wǔ) 天辅 (Tiān Fǔ) 惊门 (Jǐng Mén) Dui 7　Ji Ren
值符 (Zhí Fú) 天柱 (Tiān Zhù) 生门 (Shēng Mén) Gen 8　Ren Gui	九天 (Jiǔ Tiān) 禽芮 (Qín Ruì) 休门 (Xiū Mén) Kan 1　Yi/Geng Bing	九地 (Jiǔ Dì) 天英 (Tiān Yīng) 开门 (Kāi Mén) Qian 6　Ding Xin

---

*Chart: **+3JiaYin** (Yang Dun #3 JiaYin Xun)*
JiaYin, YiMao, BingChen, DingSi, WuWu, JiWei, GengShen, XinYou, RenXu, GuiHai

Yang (阳) Dun# 3 Hour: JiaYin ; 直符(ZhíFú): 天任(TiānRèn)
直使(ZhíShǐ): 生门(ShēngMén) ; 旬首(XúnShǒu): JiaYinGui

太阴 (Tài Yīn) 天辅 (Tiān Fǔ) 杜门 (Dù Mén) Xun 4　Ji Ji	六合 (Liù Hé) 天英 (Tiān Yīng) 景门 (Jǐng Mén) Li 9　Ding Ding	白虎 (Bái Hǔ) 禽芮 (Qín Ruì) 死门 (Sǐ Mén) Kun 2　Yi/Geng Yi/Geng
螣蛇 (Téng Shé) 天冲 (Tiān Chōng) 伤门 (Shāng Mén) Zhen 3　Wu Wu	Yang (阳) Dun# 3 Hour: **JiaYin** **Fu Yin** ©Calvin Yap	玄武 (Xuán Wǔ) 天柱 (Tiān Zhù) 惊门 (Jǐng Mén) Dui 7　Ren Ren
值符 (Zhí Fú) 天任 (Tiān Rèn) 生门 (Shēng Mén) Gen 8　Gui Gui	九天 (Jiǔ Tiān) 天蓬 (Tiān Péng) 休门 (Xiū Mén) Kan 1　Bing Bing	九地 (Jiǔ Dì) 天心 (Tiān Xīn) 开门 (Kāi Mén) Qian 6　Xin Xin

Yang (阳) Dun# 3 Hour: YiMao ; 直符(ZhíFú): 天任(TiānRèn)
直使(ZhíShǐ): 生门(ShēngMén) ; 旬首(XúnShǒu): JiaYinGui

九地 (Jiǔ Dì) 天心 (Tiān Xīn) 休门 (Xiū Mén) Xun 4　Xin Ji	九天 (Jiǔ Tiān) 天蓬 (Tiān Péng) 生门 (Shēng Mén) Li 9　Bing Ding	值符 (Zhí Fú) 天任 (Tiān Rèn) 伤门 (Shāng Mén) Kun 2　Gui Yi/Geng
玄武 (Xuán Wǔ) 天柱 (Tiān Zhù) 开门 (Kāi Mén) Zhen 3　Ren Wu	Yang (阳) Dun# 3 Hour: **YiMao** **Fan Yin** ©Calvin Yap	螣蛇 (Téng Shé) 天冲 (Tiān Chōng) 杜门 (Dù Mén) Dui 7　Wu Ren
白虎 (Bái Hǔ) 禽芮 (Qín Ruì) 惊门 (Jǐng Mén) Gen 8　Yi/Geng Gui	六合 (Liù Hé) 天英 (Tiān Yīng) 死门 (Sǐ Mén) Kan 1　Ding Bing	太阴 (Tài Yīn) 天辅 (Tiān Fǔ) 景门 (Jǐng Mén) Qian 6　Ji Xin

Yang (阳) Dun# 3 Hour: BingChen ; 直符(ZhíFú): 天任(TiānRèn)
直使(ZhíShǐ): 生门(ShēngMén) ; 旬首(XúnShǒu): JiaYinGui

六合 (Liù Hé) 天英 (Tiān Yīng) 景门 (Jǐng Mén) Xun 4　Ding Ji	白虎 (Bái Hǔ) 禽芮 (Qín Ruì) 死门 (Sǐ Mén) Li 9　Yi/Geng Ding	玄武 (Xuán Wǔ) 天柱 (Tiān Zhù) 惊门 (Jǐng Mén) Kun 2　Ren Yi/Geng
太阴 (Tài Yīn) 天辅 (Tiān Fǔ) 杜门 (Dù Mén) Zhen 3　Ji Wu	Yang (阳) Dun# 3 Hour: **BingChen** ©Calvin Yap	九地 (Jiǔ Dì) 天心 (Tiān Xīn) 开门 (Kāi Mén) Dui 7　Xin Ren
螣蛇 (Téng Shé) 天冲 (Tiān Chōng) 伤门 (Shāng Mén) Gen 8　Wu Gui	值符 (Zhí Fú) 天任 (Tiān Rèn) 生门 (Shēng Mén) Kan 1　Gui Bing	九天 (Jiǔ Tiān) 天蓬 (Tiān Péng) 休门 (Xiū Mén) Qian 6　Bing Xin

Yang (阳) Dun# 3 Hour: DingSi ; 直符(ZhíFú): 天任(TiānRèn)
直使(ZhíShǐ): 生门(ShēngMén) ; 旬首(XúnShǒu): JiaYinGui

九天 (Jiǔ Tiān) 天蓬 (Tiān Péng) 开门 (Kāi Mén) Xun 4　Bing Ji	值符 (Zhí Fú) 天任 (Tiān Rèn) 休门 (Xiū Mén) Li 9　Gui Ding	螣蛇 (Téng Shé) 天冲 (Tiān Chōng) 生门 (Shēng Mén) Kun 2　Wu Yi/Geng
九地 (Jiǔ Dì) 天心 (Tiān Xīn) 惊门 (Jǐng Mén) Zhen 3　Xin Wu	Yang (阳) Dun# 3 Hour: **DingSi** ©Calvin Yap	太阴 (Tài Yīn) 天辅 (Tiān Fǔ) 伤门 (Shāng Mén) Dui 7　Ji Ren
玄武 (Xuán Wǔ) 天柱 (Tiān Zhù) 死门 (Sǐ Mén) Gen 8　Ren Gui	白虎 (Bái Hǔ) 禽芮 (Qín Ruì) 景门 (Jǐng Mén) Kan 1　Yi/Geng Bing	六合 (Liù Hé) 天英 (Tiān Yīng) 杜门 (Dù Mén) Qian 6　Ding Xin

Yang (阳) Dun# 3 Hour: **WuWu**；直符(ZhíFú): 天任(TiānRèn)
直使(ZhíShǐ): 生门(ShēngMén)；旬首(XúnShǒu): JiaYinGui

螣蛇 (Téng Shé) 天冲 (Tiān Chōng) 伤门 (Shāng Mén) Xun 4　Wu　Ji	太阴 (Tài Yīn) 天辅 (Tiān Fǔ) 杜门 (Dù Mén) Li 9　Ji	六合 (Liù Hé) 天英 (Tiān Yīng) 景门 (Jīng Mén) Kun 2　Ding　Yi/Geng
值符 (Zhí Fú) 天任 (Tiān Rèn) 生门 (Shēng Mén) Zhen 3　Gui　Wu	Yang (阳) Dun# 3 Hour: **WuWu** ©Calvin Yap	白虎 (Bái Hǔ) 禽芮 (Qín Ruì) 死门 (Sǐ Mén) Dui 7　Yi/Geng　Ren
九天 (Jiǔ Tiān) 天蓬 (Tiān Péng) 休门 (Xiū Mén) Gen 8　Bing　Gui	九地 (Jiǔ Dì) 天心 (Tiān Xīn) 开门 (Kāi Mén) Kan 1　Xin　Bing	玄武 (Xuán Wǔ) 天柱 (Tiān Zhù) 惊门 (Jīng Mén) Qian 6　Ren　Xin

Yang (阳) Dun# 3 Hour: **JiWei**；直符(ZhíFú): 天任(TiānRèn)
直使(ZhíShǐ): 生门(ShēngMén)；旬首(XúnShǒu): JiaYinGui

值符 (Zhí Fú) 天任 (Tiān Rèn) 生门 (Shēng Mén) Xun 4　Gui　Ji	螣蛇 (Téng Shé) 天冲 (Tiān Chōng) 伤门 (Shāng Mén) Li 9　Wu　Ding	太阴 (Tài Yīn) 天辅 (Tiān Fǔ) 杜门 (Dù Mén) Kun 2　Ji　Yi/Geng
九天 (Jiǔ Tiān) 天蓬 (Tiān Péng) 休门 (Xiū Mén) Zhen 3　Bing　Wu	Yang (阳) Dun# 3 Hour: **JiWei** ©Calvin Yap	六合 (Liù Hé) 天英 (Tiān Yīng) 景门 (Jīng Mén) Dui 7　Ding　Ren
九地 (Jiǔ Di) 天心 (Tiān Xīn) 开门 (Kāi Mén) Gen 8　Xin　Gui	玄武 (Xuán Wǔ) 天柱 (Tiān Zhù) 惊门 (Jīng Mén) Kan 1　Ren　Bing	白虎 (Bái Hǔ) 禽芮 (Qín Ruì) 死门 (Sǐ Mén) Qian 6　Yi/Geng　Xin

Yang (阳) Dun# 3 Hour: **GengShen**；直符(ZhíFú): 天任(TiānRèn)
直使(ZhíShǐ): 生门(ShēngMén)；旬首(XúnShǒu): JiaYinGui

九地 (Jiǔ Dì) 天心 (Tiān Xīn) 开门 (Kāi Mén) Xun 4　Xin　Ji	九天 (Jiǔ Tiān) 天蓬 (Tiān Péng) 休门 (Xiū Mén) Li 9　Bing　Ding	值符 (Zhí Fú) 天任 (Tiān Rèn) 生门 (Shēng Mén) Kun 2　Gui　Yi/Geng
玄武 (Xuán Wǔ) 天柱 (Tiān Zhù) 惊门 (Jīng Mén) Zhen 3　Ren　Wu	Yang (阳) Dun# 3 Hour: **GengShen** **Fan Yin** ©Calvin Yap	螣蛇 (Téng Shé) 天冲 (Tiān Chōng) 伤门 (Shāng Mén) Dui 7　Wu　Ren
白虎 (Bái Hǔ) 禽芮 (Qín Ruì) 死门 (Sǐ Mén) Gen 8　Yi/Geng　Gui	六合 (Liù Hé) 天英 (Tiān Yīng) 景门 (Jīng Mén) Kan 1　Ding　Bing	太阴 (Tài Yīn) 天辅 (Tiān Fǔ) 杜门 (Dù Mén) Qian 6　Ji　Xin

Yang (阳) Dun# 3 Hour: **XinYou**；直符(ZhíFú): 天任(TiānRèn)
直使(ZhíShǐ): 生门(ShēngMén)；旬首(XúnShǒu): JiaYinGui

白虎 (Bái Hǔ) 禽芮 (Qín Ruì) 死门 (Sǐ Mén) Xun 4　Yi/Geng　Ji	玄武 (Xuán Wǔ) 天柱 (Tiān Zhù) 惊门 (Jīng Mén) Li 9　Ren　Ding	九地 (Jiǔ Dì) 天心 (Tiān Xīn) 开门 (Kāi Mén) Kun 2　Xin　Yi/Geng
六合 (Liù Hé) 天英 (Tiān Yīng) 景门 (Jīng Mén) Zhen 3　Ding　Wu	Yang (阳) Dun# 3 Hour: **XinYou** ©Calvin Yap	九天 (Jiǔ Tiān) 天蓬 (Tiān Péng) 休门 (Xiū Mén) Dui 7　Bing　Ren
太阴 (Tài Yīn) 天辅 (Tiān Fǔ) 杜门 (Dù Mén) Gen 8　Ji　Gui	螣蛇 (Téng Shé) 天冲 (Tiān Chōng) 伤门 (Shāng Mén) Kan 1　Wu　Bing	值符 (Zhí Fú) 天任 (Tiān Rèn) 生门 (Shēng Mén) Qian 6　Gui　Xin

Yang (阳) Dun# 3 Hour: **RenXu**；直符(ZhíFú): 天任(TiānRèn)
直使(ZhíShǐ): 生门(ShēngMén)；旬首(XúnShǒu): JiaYinGui

玄武 (Xuán Wǔ) 天柱 (Tiān Zhù) 惊门 (Jīng Mén) Xun 4　Ren　Ji	九地 (Jiǔ Di) 天心 (Tiān Xīn) 开门 (Kāi Mén) Li 9　Xin　Ding	九天 (Jiǔ Tiān) 天蓬 (Tiān Péng) 休门 (Xiū Mén) Kun 2　Bing　Yi/Geng
白虎 (Bái Hǔ) 禽芮 (Qín Ruì) 死门 (Sǐ Mén) Zhen 3　Yi/Geng　Wu	Yang (阳) Dun# 3 Hour: **RenXu** ©Calvin Yap	值符 (Zhí Fú) 天任 (Tiān Rèn) 生门 (Shēng Mén) Dui 7　Gui　Ren
六合 (Liù Hé) 天英 (Tiān Yīng) 景门 (Jīng Mén) Gen 8　Ding　Gui	太阴 (Tài Yīn) 天辅 (Tiān Fǔ) 杜门 (Dù Mén) Kan 1　Ji　Bing	螣蛇 (Téng Shé) 天冲 (Tiān Chōng) 伤门 (Shāng Mén) Qian 6　Wu　Xin

Yang (阳) Dun# 3 Hour: **GuiHai**；直符(ZhíFú): 天任(TiānRèn)
直使(ZhíShǐ): 生门(ShēngMén)；旬首(XúnShǒu): JiaYinGui

太阴 (Tài Yīn) 天辅 (Tiān Fǔ) 杜门 (Dù Mén) Xun 4　Ji　Ji	六合 (Liù Hé) 天英 (Tiān Yīng) 景门 (Jīng Mén) Li 9　Ding　Ding	白虎 (Bái Hǔ) 禽芮 (Qín Ruì) 死门 (Sǐ Mén) Kun 2　Yi/Geng　Yi/Geng
螣蛇 (Téng Shé) 天冲 (Tiān Chōng) 伤门 (Shāng Mén) Zhen 3　Wu　Wu	Yang (阳) Dun# 3 Hour: **GuiHai** **Fu Yin** ©Calvin Yap	玄武 (Xuán Wǔ) 天柱 (Tiān Zhù) 惊门 (Jīng Mén) Dui 7　Ren　Ren
值符 (Zhí Fú) 天任 (Tiān Rèn) 生门 (Shēng Mén) Gen 8　Gui　Gui	九天 (Jiǔ Tiān) 天蓬 (Tiān Péng) 休门 (Xiū Mén) Kan 1　Bing　Bing	九地 (Jiǔ Dì) 天心 (Tiān Xīn) 开门 (Kāi Mén) Qian 6　Xin　Xin

Yang Dun#4

Chart: +4JiaZi (Yang Dun #4 JiaZi Xun)
JiaZi, YiChou, BingYin, DingMao, WuChen, JiSi, GengWu, XinWei, RenShen, GuiYou

Yang (阳) Dun# 4 Hour: **JiaZi** ; 直符(ZhíFú): 天辅(TiānFǔ)
直使(ZhíShǐ): 杜门(DùMén) ; 旬首(XúnShǒu): JiaZiWu

值符(Zhi Fú) 天辅(Tiān Fú) 杜门(Dù Mén) Xun 4　Wu 　Wu	螣蛇(Téng Shé) 天英(Tiān Yīng) 景门(Jǐng Mén) Li 9　Gui 　Gui	太阴(Tài Yīn) 禽芮(Qín Ruì) 死门(Sǐ Mén) Kun 2　Bing/Ji 　Bing/Ji
九天(Jiǔ Tiān) 天冲(Tiān Chōng) 伤门(Shāng Mén) Zhen 3　Yi 　Yi	Yang (阳) Dun# 4 Hour: **JiaZi** **Fu Yin** ©Calvin Yap	六合(Liù Hé) 天柱(Tiān Zhù) 惊门(Jīng Mén) Dui 7　Xin 　Xin
九地(Jiǔ Dì) 天任(Tiān Rèn) 生门(Shēng Mén) Gen 8　Ren 　Ren	玄武(Xuán Wǔ) 天蓬(Tiān Péng) 休门(Xiū Mén) Kan 1　Ding 　Ding	白虎(Bái Hǔ) 天心(Tiān Xīn) 开门(Kāi Mén) Qian 6　Geng 　Geng

Yang (阳) Dun# 4 Hour: **YiChou** ; 直符(ZhíFú): 天辅(TiānFǔ)
直使(ZhíShǐ): 杜门(DùMén) ; 旬首(XúnShǒu): JiaZiWu

螣蛇(Téng Shé) 天英(Tiān Yīng) 生门(Shēng Mén) Xun 4　Gui 　Wu	太阴(Tài Yīn) 禽芮(Qín Ruì) 伤门(Shāng Mén) Li 9　Bing/Ji 　Gui	六合(Liù Hé) 天柱(Tiān Zhù) 杜门(Dù Mén) Kun 2　Xin 　Bing/Ji
值符(Zhi Fú) 天辅(Tiān Fú) 休门(Xiū Mén) Zhen 3　Wu 　Yi	Yang (阳) Dun# 4 Hour: **YiChou** ©Calvin Yap	白虎(Bái Hǔ) 天心(Tiān Xīn) 景门(Jǐng Mén) Dui 7　Geng 　Xin
九天(Jiǔ Tiān) 天冲(Tiān Chōng) 开门(Kāi Mén) Gen 8　Yi 　Ren	九地(Jiǔ Dì) 天任(Tiān Rèn) 惊门(Jīng Mén) Kan 1　Ren 　Ding	玄武(Xuán Wǔ) 天蓬(Tiān Péng) 死门(Sǐ Mén) Qian 6　Ding 　Geng

Yang (阳) Dun# 4 Hour: **BingYin** ; 直符(ZhíFú): 天辅(TiānFǔ)
直使(ZhíShǐ): 杜门(DùMén) ; 旬首(XúnShǒu): JiaZiWu

九地(Jiǔ Dì) 天任(Tiān Rèn) 开门(Kāi Mén) Xun 4　Ren 　Wu	九天(Jiǔ Tiān) 天冲(Tiān Chōng) 休门(Xiū Mén) Li 9　Yi 　Gui	值符(Zhi Fú) 天辅(Tiān Fú) 生门(Shēng Mén) Kun 2　Wu 　Bing/Ji
玄武(Xuán Wǔ) 天蓬(Tiān Péng) 惊门(Jīng Mén) Zhen 3　Ding 　Yi	Yang (阳) Dun# 4 Hour: **BingYin** ©Calvin Yap	螣蛇(Téng Shé) 天英(Tiān Yīng) 伤门(Shāng Mén) Dui 7　Gui 　Xin
白虎(Bái Hǔ) 天心(Tiān Xīn) 死门(Sǐ Mén) Gen 8　Geng 　Ren	六合(Liù Hé) 天柱(Tiān Zhù) 景门(Jǐng Mén) Kan 1　Xin 　Ding	太阴(Tài Yīn) 禽芮(Qín Ruì) 杜门(Dù Mén) Qian 6　Bing/Ji 　Geng

Yang (阳) Dun# 4 Hour: **DingMao** ; 直符(ZhíFú): 天辅(TiānFǔ)
直使(ZhíShǐ): 杜门(DùMén) ; 旬首(XúnShǒu): JiaZiWu

六合(Liù Hé) 天柱(Tiān Zhù) 休门(Xiū Mén) Xun 4　Xin 　Wu	白虎(Bái Hǔ) 天心(Tiān Xīn) 生门(Shēng Mén) Li 9　Geng 　Gui	玄武(Xuán Wǔ) 天蓬(Tiān Péng) 伤门(Shāng Mén) Kun 2　Ding 　Bing/Ji
太阴(Tài Yīn) 禽芮(Qín Ruì) 开门(Kāi Mén) Zhen 3　Bing/Ji 　Yi	Yang (阳) Dun# 4 Hour: **DingMao** ©Calvin Yap	九地(Jiǔ Dì) 天任(Tiān Rèn) 杜门(Dù Mén) Dui 7　Ren 　Xin
螣蛇(Téng Shé) 天英(Tiān Yīng) 惊门(Jīng Mén) Gen 8　Gui 　Ren	值符(Zhi Fú) 天辅(Tiān Fú) 死门(Sǐ Mén) Kan 1　Wu 　Ding	九天(Jiǔ Tiān) 天冲(Tiān Chōng) 景门(Jǐng Mén) Qian 6　Yi 　Geng

Yang (阳) Dun# 4 Hour: **WuChen** ; 直符(ZhíFú): 天辅(TiānFǔ)
直使(ZhíShǐ): 杜门(DùMén) ; 旬首(XúnShǒu): JiaZiWu

值符(Zhi Fú) 天辅(Tiān Fú) 死门(Sǐ Mén) Xun 4　Wu 　Wu	螣蛇(Téng Shé) 天英(Tiān Yīng) 惊门(Jīng Mén) Li 9　Gui 　Gui	太阴(Tài Yīn) 禽芮(Qín Ruì) 开门(Kāi Mén) Kun 2　Bing/Ji 　Bing/Ji
九天(Jiǔ Tiān) 天冲(Tiān Chōng) 景门(Jǐng Mén) Zhen 3　Yi 　Yi	Yang (阳) Dun# 4 Hour: **WuChen** **Fu Yin** ©Calvin Yap	六合(Liù Hé) 天柱(Tiān Zhù) 休门(Xiū Mén) Dui 7　Xin 　Xin
九地(Jiǔ Dì) 天任(Tiān Rèn) 杜门(Dù Mén) Gen 8　Ren 　Ren	玄武(Xuán Wǔ) 天蓬(Tiān Péng) 伤门(Shāng Mén) Kan 1　Ding 　Ding	白虎(Bái Hǔ) 天心(Tiān Xīn) 生门(Shēng Mén) Qian 6　Geng 　Geng

Yang (阳) Dun# 4 Hour: **JiSi** ; 直符(ZhíFú): 天辅(TiānFǔ)
直使(ZhíShǐ): 杜门(DùMén) ; 旬首(XúnShǒu): JiaZiWu

九地(Jiǔ Dì) 天任(Tiān Rèn) 伤门(Shāng Mén) Xun 4　Ren 　Wu	九天(Jiǔ Tiān) 天冲(Tiān Chōng) 杜门(Dù Mén) Li 9　Yi 　Gui	值符(Zhi Fú) 天辅(Tiān Fú) 景门(Jǐng Mén) Kun 2　Wu 　Bing/Ji
玄武(Xuán Wǔ) 天蓬(Tiān Péng) 生门(Shēng Mén) Zhen 3　Ding 　Yi	Yang (阳) Dun# 4 Hour: **JiSi** ©Calvin Yap	螣蛇(Téng Shé) 天英(Tiān Yīng) 死门(Sǐ Mén) Dui 7　Gui 　Xin
白虎(Bái Hǔ) 天心(Tiān Xīn) 休门(Xiū Mén) Gen 8　Geng 　Ren	六合(Liù Hé) 天柱(Tiān Zhù) 开门(Kāi Mén) Kan 1　Xin 　Ding	太阴(Tài Yīn) 禽芮(Qín Ruì) 惊门(Jīng Mén) Qian 6　Bing/Ji 　Geng

Yang (阳) Dun# 4 Hour: GengWu；直符(ZhíFú): 天辅(TiānFǔ)
直使(ZhíShǐ): 杜门(DùMén)；旬首(XúnShǒu): JiaZiWu

白虎 (Bái Hǔ) 天心 (Tiān Xīn) 惊门 (Jīng Mén) Xun 4　Geng Wu	玄武 (Xuán Wǔ) 天蓬 (Tiān Péng) 开门 (Kāi Mén) Li 9　Ding Gui	九地 (Jiǔ Dì) 天任 (Tiān Rèn) 休门 (Xiū Mén) Kun 2　Ren Bing/Ji
六合 (Liù Hé) 天柱 (Tiān Zhù) 死门 (Sǐ Mén) Zhen 3　Xin Yi	Yang (阳) Dun# 4 Hour: **GengWu** **Fan Yin** ©Calvin Yap	九天 (Jiǔ Tiān) 天冲 (Tiān Chōng) 生门 (Shēng Mén) Dui 7　Yi Xin
太阴 (Tài Yīn) 禽芮 (Qín Ruì) 景门 (Jǐng Mén) Gen 8　Bing/Ji Ren	螣蛇 (Téng Shé) 天英 (Tiān Yīng) 杜门 (Dù Mén) Kan 1　Gui Ding	值符 (Zhí Fú) 天辅 (Tiān Fǔ) 伤门 (Shāng Mén) Qian 6　Wu Geng

Yang (阳) Dun# 4 Hour: XinWei；直符(ZhíFú): 天辅(TiānFǔ)
直使(ZhíShǐ): 杜门(DùMén)；旬首(XúnShǒu): JiaZiWu

玄武 (Xuán Wǔ) 天蓬 (Tiān Péng) 生门 (Shēng Mén) Xun 4　Ding Wu	九地 (Jiǔ Dì) 天任 (Tiān Rèn) 伤门 (Shāng Mén) Li 9　Ren Gui	九天 (Jiǔ Tiān) 天冲 (Tiān Chōng) 杜门 (Dù Mén) Kun 2　Yi Bing/Ji
白虎 (Bái Hǔ) 天心 (Tiān Xīn) 休门 (Xiū Mén) Zhen 3　Geng Yi	Yang (阳) Dun# 4 Hour: **XinWei** ©Calvin Yap	值符 (Zhí Fú) 天辅 (Tiān Fǔ) 景门 (Jǐng Mén) Dui 7　Wu Xin
六合 (Liù Hé) 天柱 (Tiān Zhù) 开门 (Kāi Mén) Gen 8　Xin Ren	太阴 (Tài Yīn) 禽芮 (Qín Ruì) 惊门 (Jīng Mén) Kan 1　Bing/Ji Ding	螣蛇 (Téng Shé) 天英 (Tiān Yīng) 死门 (Sǐ Mén) Qian 6　Gui Geng

Yang (阳) Dun# 4 Hour: RenShen；直符(ZhíFú): 天辅(TiānFǔ)
直使(ZhíShǐ): 杜门(DùMén)；旬首(XúnShǒu): JiaZiWu

太阴 (Tài Yīn) 禽芮 (Qín Ruì) 景门 (Jǐng Mén) Xun 4　Bing/Ji Wu	六合 (Liù Hé) 天柱 (Tiān Zhù) 死门 (Sǐ Mén) Li 9　Xin Gui	白虎 (Bái Hǔ) 天心 (Tiān Xīn) 惊门 (Jīng Mén) Kun 2　Geng Bing/Ji
螣蛇 (Téng Shé) 天英 (Tiān Yīng) 杜门 (Dù Mén) Zhen 3　Gui Yi	Yang (阳) Dun# 4 Hour: **RenShen** ©Calvin Yap	玄武 (Xuán Wǔ) 天蓬 (Tiān Péng) 开门 (Kāi Mén) Dui 7　Ding Xin
值符 (Zhí Fú) 天辅 (Tiān Fǔ) 伤门 (Shāng Mén) Gen 8　Wu Ren	九天 (Jiǔ Tiān) 天冲 (Tiān Chōng) 生门 (Shēng Mén) Kan 1　Yi Ding	九地 (Jiǔ Dì) 天任 (Tiān Rèn) 休门 (Xiū Mén) Qian 6　Ren Geng

Yang (阳) Dun# 4 Hour: GuiYou；直符(ZhíFú): 天辅(TiānFǔ)
直使(ZhíShǐ): 杜门(DùMén)；旬首(XúnShǒu): JiaZiWu

九天 (Jiǔ Tiān) 天冲 (Tiān Chōng) 杜门 (Dù Mén) Xun 4　Yi Wu	值符 (Zhí Fú) 天辅 (Tiān Fǔ) 景门 (Jǐng Mén) Li 9　Wu Gui	螣蛇 (Téng Shé) 天英 (Tiān Yīng) 死门 (Sǐ Mén) Kun 2　Gui Bing/Ji
九地 (Jiǔ Dì) 天任 (Tiān Rèn) 伤门 (Shāng Mén) Zhen 3　Ren Yi	Yang (阳) Dun# 4 Hour: **GuiYou** ©Calvin Yap	太阴 (Tài Yīn) 禽芮 (Qín Ruì) 惊门 (Jīng Mén) Dui 7　Bing/Ji Xin
玄武 (Xuán Wǔ) 天蓬 (Tiān Péng) 生门 (Shēng Mén) Gen 8　Ding Ren	白虎 (Bái Hǔ) 天心 (Tiān Xīn) 休门 (Xiū Mén) Kan 1　Geng Ding	六合 (Liù Hé) 天柱 (Tiān Zhù) 开门 (Kāi Mén) Qian 6　Xin Geng

Chart: +4JiaXu (Yang Dun #4 JiaXu Xun)
JiaXu, YiHai, BingZi, DingChou, WuYin, JiMao, GengChen, XinSi, RenWu, GuiWei

Yang (阳) Dun# 4 Hour: JiaXu；直符(ZhíFú): 天禽(TiānQín)
直使(ZhíShǐ): 死门(SǐMén)；旬首(XúnShǒu): JiaXuJi

九地 (Jiǔ Dì) 天辅 (Tiān Fǔ) 杜门 (Dù Mén) Xun 4　Wu Wu	九天 (Jiǔ Tiān) 天英 (Tiān Yīng) 景门 (Jǐng Mén) Li 9　Gui Gui	值符 (Zhí Fú) 禽芮 (Qín Ruì) 死门 (Sǐ Mén) Kun 2　Bing/Ji Bing/Ji
玄武 (Xuán Wǔ) 天冲 (Tiān Chōng) 伤门 (Shāng Mén) Zhen 3　Yi Yi	Yang (阳) Dun# 4 Hour: **JiaXu** **Fu Yin** ©Calvin Yap	螣蛇 (Téng Shé) 天柱 (Tiān Zhù) 惊门 (Jīng Mén) Dui 7　Xin Xin
白虎 (Bái Hǔ) 天任 (Tiān Rèn) 生门 (Shēng Mén) Gen 8　Ren Ren	六合 (Liù Hé) 天蓬 (Tiān Péng) 休门 (Xiū Mén) Kan 1　Ding Ding	太阴 (Tài Yīn) 天心 (Tiān Xīn) 开门 (Kāi Mén) Qian 6　Geng Geng

Yang (阳) Dun# 4 Hour: YiHai；直符(ZhíFú): 天禽(TiānQín)
直使(ZhíShǐ): 死门(SǐMén)；旬首(XúnShǒu): JiaXuJi

螣蛇 (Téng Shé) 天柱 (Tiān Zhù) 生门 (Shēng Mén) Xun 4　Xin Wu	太阴 (Tài Yīn) 天心 (Tiān Xīn) 伤门 (Shāng Mén) Li 9　Geng Gui	六合 (Liù Hé) 天蓬 (Tiān Péng) 杜门 (Dù Mén) Kun 2　Ding Bing/Ji
值符 (Zhí Fú) 禽芮 (Qín Ruì) 休门 (Xiū Mén) Zhen 3　Bing/Ji Yi	Yang (阳) Dun# 4 Hour: **YiHai** ©Calvin Yap	白虎 (Bái Hǔ) 天任 (Tiān Rèn) 景门 (Jǐng Mén) Dui 7　Ren Xin
九天 (Jiǔ Tiān) 天英 (Tiān Yīng) 开门 (Kāi Mén) Gen 8　Gui Ren	九地 (Jiǔ Dì) 天辅 (Tiān Fǔ) 惊门 (Jīng Mén) Kan 1　Wu Ding	玄武 (Xuán Wǔ) 天冲 (Tiān Chōng) 死门 (Sǐ Mén) Qian 6　Yi Geng

Yang (阳) Dun# 4 Hour: **BingZi**；直符(ZhíFú): 天禽(TiānQín)
直使(ZhíShǐ): 死门(SǐMén)；旬首(XúnShǒu): JiaXuJi

九地 (Jiǔ Dì) 天辅 (Tiān Fǔ) 伤门 (Shāng Mén) Xun 4　Wu Wu	九天 (Jiǔ Tiān) 天英 (Tiān Yīng) 杜门 (Dù Mén) Li 9　Gui Gui	值符 (Zhí Fú) 禽芮 (Qín Ruì) 景门 (Jīng Mén) Kun 2　Bing/Ji Bing/Ji
玄武 (Xuán Wǔ) 天冲 (Tiān Chōng) 生门 (Shēng Mén) Zhen 3　Yi Yi	Yang (阳) Dun# 4 Hour: **BingZi** **Fu Yin** ©Calvin Yap	螣蛇 (Téng Shé) 天柱 (Tiān Zhù) 死门 (Sǐ Mén) Dui 7　Xin Xin
白虎 (Bái Hǔ) 天任 (Tiān Rèn) 休门 (Xiū Mén) Gen 8　Ren Ren	六合 (Liù Hé) 天蓬 (Tiān Péng) 开门 (Kāi Mén) Kan 1　Ding Ding	太阴 (Tài Yīn) 天心 (Tiān Xīn) 惊门 (Jīng Mén) Qian 6　Geng Geng

Yang (阳) Dun# 4 Hour: **DingChou**；直符(ZhíFú): 天禽(TiānQín)
直使(ZhíShǐ): 死门(SǐMén)；旬首(XúnShǒu): JiaXuJi

六合 (Liù Hé) 天蓬 (Tiān Péng) 开门 (Kāi Mén) Xun 4　Ding Wu	白虎 (Bái Hǔ) 天任 (Tiān Rèn) 休门 (Xiū Mén) Li 9　Ren Gui	玄武 (Xuán Wǔ) 天冲 (Tiān Chōng) 生门 (Shēng Mén) Kun 2　Yi Bing/Ji
太阴 (Tài Yīn) 天心 (Tiān Xīn) 惊门 (Jīng Mén) Zhen 3　Geng Yi	Yang (阳) Dun# 4 Hour: **DingChou** ©Calvin Yap	九地 (Jiǔ Dì) 天辅 (Tiān Fǔ) 伤门 (Shāng Mén) Dui 7　Wu Xin
螣蛇 (Téng Shé) 天柱 (Tiān Zhù) 死门 (Sǐ Mén) Gen 8　Xin Ren	值符 (Zhí Fú) 禽芮 (Qín Ruì) 景门 (Jīng Mén) Kan 1　Bing/Ji Ding	九天 (Jiǔ Tiān) 天英 (Tiān Yīng) 杜门 (Dù Mén) Qian 6　Gui Geng

Yang (阳) Dun# 4 Hour: **WuYin**；直符(ZhíFú): 天禽(TiānQín)
直使(ZhíShǐ): 死门(SǐMén)；旬首(XúnShǒu): JiaXuJi

值符 (Zhí Fú) 禽芮 (Qín Ruì) 景门 (Jīng Mén) Xun 4　Bing/Ji Wu	螣蛇 (Téng Shé) 天柱 (Tiān Zhù) 死门 (Sǐ Mén) Li 9　Xin Gui	太阴 (Tài Yīn) 天心 (Tiān Xīn) 惊门 (Jīng Mén) Kun 2　Geng Bing/Ji
九天 (Jiǔ Tiān) 天英 (Tiān Yīng) 杜门 (Dù Mén) Zhen 3　Gui Yi	Yang (阳) Dun# 4 Hour: **WuYin** ©Calvin Yap	六合 (Liù Hé) 天蓬 (Tiān Péng) 开门 (Kāi Mén) Dui 7　Ding Xin
九地 (Jiǔ Dì) 天辅 (Tiān Fǔ) 伤门 (Shāng Mén) Gen 8　Wu Ren	玄武 (Xuán Wǔ) 天冲 (Tiān Chōng) 生门 (Shēng Mén) Kan 1　Yi Ding	白虎 (Bái Hǔ) 天任 (Tiān Rèn) 休门 (Xiū Mén) Qian 6　Ren Geng

Yang (阳) Dun# 4 Hour: **JiMao**；直符(ZhíFú): 天禽(TiānQín)
直使(ZhíShǐ): 死门(SǐMén)；旬首(XúnShǒu): JiaXuJi

九地 (Jiǔ Dì) 天辅 (Tiān Fǔ) 休门 (Xiū Mén) Xun 4　Wu Wu	九天 (Jiǔ Tiān) 天英 (Tiān Yīng) 生门 (Shēng Mén) Li 9　Gui Gui	值符 (Zhí Fú) 禽芮 (Qín Ruì) 伤门 (Shāng Mén) Kun 2　Bing/Ji Bing/Ji
玄武 (Xuán Wǔ) 天冲 (Tiān Chōng) 开门 (Kāi Mén) Zhen 3　Yi Yi	Yang (阳) Dun# 4 Hour: **JiMao** **Fu Yin** ©Calvin Yap	螣蛇 (Téng Shé) 天柱 (Tiān Zhù) 杜门 (Dù Mén) Dui 7　Xin Xin
白虎 (Bái Hǔ) 天任 (Tiān Rèn) 惊门 (Jīng Mén) Gen 8　Ren Ren	六合 (Liù Hé) 天蓬 (Tiān Péng) 死门 (Sǐ Mén) Kan 1　Ding Ding	太阴 (Tài Yīn) 天心 (Tiān Xīn) 景门 (Jīng Mén) Qian 6　Geng Geng

Yang (阳) Dun# 4 Hour: **GengChen**；直符(ZhíFú): 天禽(TiānQín)
直使(ZhíShǐ): 死门(SǐMén)；旬首(XúnShǒu): JiaXuJi

白虎 (Bái Hǔ) 天任 (Tiān Rèn) 杜门 (Dù Mén) Xun 4　Ren Wu	玄武 (Xuán Wǔ) 天冲 (Tiān Chōng) 景门 (Jīng Mén) Li 9　Yi Gui	九地 (Jiǔ Dì) 天辅 (Tiān Fǔ) 死门 (Sǐ Mén) Kun 2　Wu Bing/Ji
六合 (Liù Hé) 天蓬 (Tiān Péng) 伤门 (Shāng Mén) Zhen 3　Ding Yi	Yang (阳) Dun# 4 Hour: **GengChen** ©Calvin Yap	九天 (Jiǔ Tiān) 天英 (Tiān Yīng) 惊门 (Jīng Mén) Dui 7　Gui Xin
太阴 (Tài Yīn) 天心 (Tiān Xīn) 生门 (Shēng Mén) Gen 8　Geng Ren	螣蛇 (Téng Shé) 天柱 (Tiān Zhù) 休门 (Xiū Mén) Kan 1　Xin Ding	值符 (Zhí Fú) 禽芮 (Qín Ruì) 开门 (Kāi Mén) Qian 6　Bing/Ji Geng

Yang (阳) Dun# 4 Hour: **XinSi**；直符(ZhíFú): 天禽(TiānQín)
直使(ZhíShǐ): 死门(SǐMén)；旬首(XúnShǒu): JiaXuJi

玄武 (Xuán Wǔ) 天冲 (Tiān Chōng) 惊门 (Jīng Mén) Xun 4　Yi Wu	九地 (Jiǔ Dì) 天辅 (Tiān Fǔ) 开门 (Kāi Mén) Li 9　Wu Gui	九天 (Jiǔ Tiān) 天英 (Tiān Yīng) 休门 (Xiū Mén) Kun 2　Gui Bing/Ji
白虎 (Bái Hǔ) 天任 (Tiān Rèn) 死门 (Sǐ Mén) Zhen 3　Ren Yi	Yang (阳) Dun# 4 Hour: **XinSi** ©Calvin Yap	值符 (Zhí Fú) 禽芮 (Qín Ruì) 生门 (Shēng Mén) Dui 7　Bing/Ji Xin
六合 (Liù Hé) 天蓬 (Tiān Péng) 景门 (Jīng Mén) Gen 8　Ding Ren	太阴 (Tài Yīn) 天心 (Tiān Xīn) 杜门 (Dù Mén) Kan 1　Geng Ding	螣蛇 (Téng Shé) 天柱 (Tiān Zhù) 伤门 (Shāng Mén) Qian 6　Xin Geng

Yang (阳) Dun# 4 Hour: **RenWu** ; 直符(ZhíFú): 天禽(TiānQín)
直使(ZhíShǐ): 死门(SǐMén) ; 旬首(XúnShǒu): JiaXuJi

太阴 (Tài Yīn) 天心 (Tiān Xīn) 死门 (Sǐ Mén) Xun 4 Wu	六合 (Liù Hé) 天蓬 (Tiān Péng) 惊门 (Jīng Mén) Li 9 Ding Gui	白虎 (Bái Hǔ) 天任 (Tiān Rèn) 开门 (Kāi Mén) Kun 2 Ren Bing/Ji
螣蛇 (Téng Shé) 天柱 (Tiān Zhù) 景门 (Jǐng Mén) Zhen 3 Xin Yi	Yang (阳) Dun# 4 Hour: **RenWu** **Fan Yin** ©Calvin Yap	玄武 (Xuán Wǔ) 天冲 (Tiān Chōng) 休门 (Xiū Mén) Dui 7 Yi Xin
值符 (Zhí Fú) 禽芮 (Qín Ruì) 杜门 (Dù Mén) Gen 8 Bing/Ji Ren	九天 (Jiǔ Tiān) 天英 (Tiān Yīng) 伤门 (Shāng Mén) Kan 1 Gui Ding	九地 (Jiǔ Dì) 天辅 (Tiān Fǔ) 生门 (Shēng Mén) Qian 6 Wu Geng

Yang (阳) Dun# 4 Hour: **GuiWei** ; 直符(ZhíFú): 天禽(TiānQín)
直使(ZhíShǐ): 死门(SǐMén) ; 旬首(XúnShǒu): JiaXuJi

九天 (Jiǔ Tiān) 天英 (Tiān Yīng) 杜门 (Dù Mén) Xun 4 Gui Wu	值符 (Zhí Fú) 禽芮 (Qín Ruì) 景门 (Jǐng Mén) Li 9 Bing/Ji Gui	螣蛇 (Téng Shé) 天柱 (Tiān Zhù) 死门 (Sǐ Mén) Kun 2 Xin Bing/Ji
九地 (Jiǔ Dì) 天辅 (Tiān Fǔ) 伤门 (Shāng Mén) Zhen 3 Wu Yi	Yang (阳) Dun# 4 Hour: **GuiWei** ©Calvin Yap	太阴 (Tài Yīn) 天心 (Tiān Xīn) 惊门 (Jīng Mén) Dui 7 Geng Xin
玄武 (Xuán Wǔ) 天冲 (Tiān Chōng) 生门 (Shēng Mén) Gen 8 Yi Ren	白虎 (Bái Hǔ) 天任 (Tiān Rèn) 休门 (Xiū Mén) Kan 1 Ren Ding	六合 (Liù Hé) 天蓬 (Tiān Péng) 开门 (Kāi Mén) Qian 6 Ding Geng

Chart: +4JiaShen (Yang Dun #4 JiaShen Xun)
JiaShen, YiYou, BingXu, DingHai, WuZi, JiChou, GengYin, XinMao, RenChen, GuiSi

Yang (阳) Dun# 4 Hour: **JiaShen** ; 直符(ZhíFú): 天心(TiānXīn)
直使(ZhíShǐ): 开门(KāiMén) ; 旬首(XúnShǒu): JiaShenGeng

白虎 (Bái Hǔ) 天辅 (Tiān Fǔ) 杜门 (Dù Mén) Xun 4 Wu Wu	玄武 (Xuán Wǔ) 天英 (Tiān Yīng) 景门 (Jǐng Mén) Li 9 Gui Gui	九地 (Jiǔ Dì) 禽芮 (Qín Ruì) 死门 (Sǐ Mén) Kun 2 Bing/Ji Bing/Ji
六合 (Liù Hé) 天冲 (Tiān Chōng) 伤门 (Shāng Mén) Zhen 3 Yi Yi	Yang (阳) Dun# 4 Hour: **JiaShen** **Fu Yin** ©Calvin Yap	九天 (Jiǔ Tiān) 天柱 (Tiān Zhù) 惊门 (Jīng Mén) Dui 7 Xin Xin
太阴 (Tài Yīn) 天任 (Tiān Rèn) 生门 (Shēng Mén) Gen 8 Ren Ren	螣蛇 (Téng Shé) 天蓬 (Tiān Péng) 休门 (Xiū Mén) Kan 1 Ding Ding	值符 (Zhí Fú) 天心 (Tiān Xīn) 开门 (Kāi Mén) Qian 6 Geng Geng

Yang (阳) Dun# 4 Hour: **YiYou** ; 直符(ZhíFú): 天心(TiānXīn)
直使(ZhíShǐ): 开门(KāiMén) ; 旬首(XúnShǒu): JiaShenGeng

螣蛇 (Téng Shé) 天蓬 (Tiān Péng) 景门 (Jǐng Mén) Xun 4 Ding Wu	太阴 (Tài Yīn) 天任 (Tiān Rèn) 死门 (Sǐ Mén) Li 9 Ren Gui	六合 (Liù Hé) 天冲 (Tiān Chōng) 惊门 (Jīng Mén) Kun 2 Yi Bing/Ji
值符 (Zhí Fú) 天心 (Tiān Xīn) 杜门 (Dù Mén) Zhen 3 Geng Yi	Yang (阳) Dun# 4 Hour: **YiYou** ©Calvin Yap	白虎 (Bái Hǔ) 天辅 (Tiān Fǔ) 开门 (Kāi Mén) Dui 7 Wu Xin
九天 (Jiǔ Tiān) 天柱 (Tiān Zhù) 伤门 (Shāng Mén) Gen 8 Xin Ren	九地 (Jiǔ Dì) 禽芮 (Qín Ruì) 生门 (Shēng Mén) Kan 1 Bing/Ji Ding	玄武 (Xuán Wǔ) 天英 (Tiān Yīng) 休门 (Xiū Mén) Qian 6 Gui Geng

Yang (阳) Dun# 4 Hour: **BingXu** ; 直符(ZhíFú): 天心(TiānXīn)
直使(ZhíShǐ): 开门(KāiMén) ; 旬首(XúnShǒu): JiaShenGeng

九地 (Jiǔ Dì) 禽芮 (Qín Ruì) 生门 (Shēng Mén) Xun 4 Bing/Ji Wu	九天 (Jiǔ Tiān) 天柱 (Tiān Zhù) 伤门 (Shāng Mén) Li 9 Xin Gui	值符 (Zhí Fú) 天心 (Tiān Xīn) 杜门 (Dù Mén) Kun 2 Geng Bing/Ji
玄武 (Xuán Wǔ) 天英 (Tiān Yīng) 休门 (Xiū Mén) Zhen 3 Gui Yi	Yang (阳) Dun# 4 Hour: **BingXu** ©Calvin Yap	螣蛇 (Téng Shé) 天蓬 (Tiān Péng) 景门 (Jǐng Mén) Dui 7 Ding Xin
白虎 (Bái Hǔ) 天辅 (Tiān Fǔ) 开门 (Kāi Mén) Gen 8 Wu Ren	六合 (Liù Hé) 天冲 (Tiān Chōng) 惊门 (Jīng Mén) Kan 1 Yi Ding	太阴 (Tài Yīn) 天任 (Tiān Rèn) 死门 (Sǐ Mén) Qian 6 Ren Geng

Yang (阳) Dun# 4 Hour: **DingHai** ; 直符(ZhíFú): 天心(TiānXīn)
直使(ZhíShǐ): 开门(KāiMén) ; 旬首(XúnShǒu): JiaShenGeng

六合 (Liù Hé) 天冲 (Tiān Chōng) 惊门 (Jīng Mén) Xun 4 Yi Wu	白虎 (Bái Hǔ) 天辅 (Tiān Fǔ) 开门 (Kāi Mén) Li 9 Wu Gui	玄武 (Xuán Wǔ) 天英 (Tiān Yīng) 休门 (Xiū Mén) Kun 2 Gui Bing/Ji
太阴 (Tài Yīn) 天任 (Tiān Rèn) 死门 (Sǐ Mén) Zhen 3 Ren Yi	Yang (阳) Dun# 4 Hour: **DingHai** ©Calvin Yap	九地 (Jiǔ Dì) 禽芮 (Qín Ruì) 生门 (Shēng Mén) Dui 7 Bing/Ji Xin
螣蛇 (Téng Shé) 天蓬 (Tiān Péng) 景门 (Jǐng Mén) Gen 8 Ding Ren	值符 (Zhí Fú) 天心 (Tiān Xīn) 杜门 (Dù Mén) Kan 1 Geng Ding	九天 (Jiǔ Tiān) 天柱 (Tiān Zhù) 伤门 (Shāng Mén) Qian 6 Xin Geng

Yang (阳) Dun# 4 Hour: WuZi；直符(ZhíFú): 天心(TiānXīn)
直使(ZhíShǐ): 开门(KāiMén)；旬首(XúnShǒu): JiaShenGeng

值符 (Zhí Fú) 天心 (Tiān Xīn) 伤门 (Shāng Mén) Xun 4　　Geng 　　　　　Wu	腾蛇 (Téng Shé) 天蓬 (Tiān Péng) 杜门 (Dù Mén) Li 9　　Ding 　　　Gui	太阴 (Tài Yīn) 天任 (Tiān Rèn) 景门 (Jǐng Mén) Kun 2　　Ren 　　　Bing/Ji
九天 (Jiǔ Tiān) 天柱 (Tiān Zhù) 生门 (Shēng Mén) Zhen 3　　Xin 　　　　　Yi	Yang (阳) Dun# 4 Hour: **WuZi** **Fan Yin** ©Calvin Yap	六合 (Liù Hé) 天冲 (Tiān Chōng) 死门 (Sǐ Mén) Dui 7　　Yi 　　　Xin
九地 (Jiǔ Dì) 禽芮 (Qín Ruì) 休门 (Xiū Mén) Gen 8　Bing/Ji 　　　Ren	玄武 (Xuán Wǔ) 天英 (Tiān Yīng) 开门 (Kāi Mén) Kan 1　　Gui 　　　Ding	白虎 (Bái Hǔ) 天辅 (Tiān Fǔ) 惊门 (Jīng Mén) Qian 6　　Wu 　　　Geng

Yang (阳) Dun# 4 Hour: JiChou；直符(ZhíFú): 天心(TiānXīn)
直使(ZhíShǐ): 开门(KāiMén)；旬首(XúnShǒu): JiaShenGeng

九地 (Jiǔ Dì) 禽芮 (Qín Ruì) 死门 (Sǐ Mén) Xun 4　Bing/Ji 　　　Wu	九天 (Jiǔ Tiān) 天柱 (Tiān Zhù) 惊门 (Jīng Mén) Li 9　　Xin 　　　Gui	值符 (Zhí Fú) 天心 (Tiān Xīn) 开门 (Kāi Mén) Kun 2　　Geng 　　　Bing/Ji
玄武 (Xuán Wǔ) 天英 (Tiān Yīng) 景门 (Jǐng Mén) Zhen 3　　Gui 　　　　　Yi	Yang (阳) Dun# 4 Hour: **JiChou** ©Calvin Yap	腾蛇 (Téng Shé) 天蓬 (Tiān Péng) 休门 (Xiū Mén) Dui 7　　Ding 　　　Xin
白虎 (Bái Hǔ) 天辅 (Tiān Fǔ) 杜门 (Dù Mén) Gen 8　　Wu 　　　Ren	六合 (Liù Hé) 天冲 (Tiān Chōng) 伤门 (Shāng Mén) Kan 1　　Yi 　　　Ding	太阴 (Tài Yīn) 天任 (Tiān Rèn) 生门 (Shēng Mén) Qian 6　　Ren 　　　Geng

Yang (阳) Dun# 4 Hour: GengYin；直符(ZhíFú): 天心(TiānXīn)
直使(ZhíShǐ): 开门(KāiMén)；旬首(XúnShǒu): JiaShenGeng

白虎 (Bái Hǔ) 天辅 (Tiān Fǔ) 休门 (Xiū Mén) Xun 4　　Wu 　　　　　Wu	玄武 (Xuán Wǔ) 天英 (Tiān Yīng) 生门 (Shēng Mén) Li 9　　Gui 　　　Gui	九地 (Jiǔ Dì) 禽芮 (Qín Ruì) 伤门 (Shāng Mén) Kun 2　Bing/Ji 　　　Bing/Ji
六合 (Liù Hé) 天冲 (Tiān Chōng) 开门 (Kāi Mén) Zhen 3　　Yi	Yang (阳) Dun# 4 Hour: **GengYin** **Fu Yin** ©Calvin Yap	九天 (Jiǔ Tiān) 天柱 (Tiān Zhù) 杜门 (Dù Mén) Dui 7　　Xin 　　　Xin
太阴 (Tài Yīn) 天任 (Tiān Rèn) 惊门 (Jīng Mén) Gen 8　　Ren 　　　Ren	腾蛇 (Téng Shé) 天蓬 (Tiān Péng) 死门 (Sǐ Mén) Kan 1　　Ding 　　　Ding	值符 (Zhí Fú) 天心 (Tiān Xīn) 景门 (Jǐng Mén) Qian 6　　Geng 　　　Geng

Yang (阳) Dun# 4 Hour: XinMao；直符(ZhíFú): 天心(TiānXīn)
直使(ZhíShǐ): 开门(KāiMén)；旬首(XúnShǒu): JiaShenGeng

玄武 (Xuán Wǔ) 天英 (Tiān Yīng) 开门 (Kāi Mén) Xun 4　　Gui 　　　　　Wu	九地 (Jiǔ Dì) 禽芮 (Qín Ruì) 休门 (Xiū Mén) Li 9　Bing/Ji 　　　Gui	九天 (Jiǔ Tiān) 天柱 (Tiān Zhù) 生门 (Shēng Mén) Kun 2　　Xin 　　　Bing/Ji
白虎 (Bái Hǔ) 天辅 (Tiān Fǔ) 惊门 (Jīng Mén) Zhen 3　　Wu 　　　　　Yi	Yang (阳) Dun# 4 Hour: **XinMao** ©Calvin Yap	值符 (Zhí Fú) 天心 (Tiān Xīn) 伤门 (Shāng Mén) Dui 7　　Geng 　　　Xin
六合 (Liù Hé) 天冲 (Tiān Chōng) 死门 (Sǐ Mén) Gen 8　　Yi 　　　Ren	太阴 (Tài Yīn) 天任 (Tiān Rèn) 景门 (Jǐng Mén) Kan 1　　Ren 　　　Ding	腾蛇 (Téng Shé) 天蓬 (Tiān Péng) 杜门 (Dù Mén) Qian 6　　Ding 　　　Geng

Yang (阳) Dun# 4 Hour: RenChen；直符(ZhíFú): 天心(TiānXīn)
直使(ZhíShǐ): 开门(KāiMén)；旬首(XúnShǒu): JiaShenGeng

太阴 (Tài Yīn) 天任 (Tiān Rèn) 死门 (Sǐ Mén) Xun 4　　Ren 　　　　　Wu	六合 (Liù Hé) 天冲 (Tiān Chōng) 惊门 (Jīng Mén) Li 9　　Yi 　　　Gui	白虎 (Bái Hǔ) 天辅 (Tiān Fǔ) 开门 (Kāi Mén) Kun 2　　Wu 　　　Bing/Ji
腾蛇 (Téng Shé) 天蓬 (Tiān Péng) 景门 (Jǐng Mén) Zhen 3　　Ding 　　　　　Yi	Yang (阳) Dun# 4 Hour: **RenChen** ©Calvin Yap	玄武 (Xuán Wǔ) 天英 (Tiān Yīng) 休门 (Xiū Mén) Dui 7　　Gui 　　　Xin
值符 (Zhí Fú) 天心 (Tiān Xīn) 杜门 (Dù Mén) Gen 8　　Geng 　　　Ren	九天 (Jiǔ Tiān) 天柱 (Tiān Zhù) 伤门 (Shāng Mén) Kan 1　　Xin 　　　Ding	九地 (Jiǔ Dì) 禽芮 (Qín Ruì) 生门 (Shēng Mén) Qian 6　Bing/Ji 　　　Geng

Yang (阳) Dun# 4 Hour: GuiSi；直符(ZhíFú): 天心(TiānXīn)
直使(ZhíShǐ): 开门(KāiMén)；旬首(XúnShǒu): JiaShenGeng

九天 (Jiǔ Tiān) 天柱 (Tiān Zhù) 杜门 (Dù Mén) Xun 4　　Xin 　　　　　Wu	值符 (Zhí Fú) 天心 (Tiān Xīn) 景门 (Jǐng Mén) Li 9　　Geng 　　　Gui	腾蛇 (Téng Shé) 天蓬 (Tiān Péng) 死门 (Sǐ Mén) Kun 2　　Ding 　　　Bing/Ji
九地 (Jiǔ Dì) 禽芮 (Qín Ruì) 伤门 (Shāng Mén) Zhen 3　Bing/Ji 　　　　　Yi	Yang (阳) Dun# 4 Hour: **GuiSi** ©Calvin Yap	太阴 (Tài Yīn) 天任 (Tiān Rèn) 惊门 (Jīng Mén) Dui 7　　Ren 　　　Xin
玄武 (Xuán Wǔ) 天英 (Tiān Yīng) 生门 (Shēng Mén) Gen 8　　Gui 　　　Ren	白虎 (Bái Hǔ) 天辅 (Tiān Fǔ) 休门 (Xiū Mén) Kan 1　　Wu 　　　Ding	六合 (Liù Hé) 天冲 (Tiān Chōng) 开门 (Kāi Mén) Qian 6　　Yi 　　　Geng

Chart: +4JiaWu (Yang Dun #4 JiaWu Xun)
JiaWu, YiWei, BingShen, DingYou, WuXu, JiHai, GengZi, XinChou, RenYin, GuiMao

Yang (阳) Dun# 4 Hour: **JiaWu**；直符(ZhíFú): 天柱(TiānZhù)
直使(ZhíShǐ): 惊门(JǐngMén)；旬首(XúnShǒu): JiaWu/Xin

玄武 (Xuán Wǔ) 天辅 (Tiān Fǔ) 杜门 (Dù Mén) Xun 4　　Wu 　　　　Wu	九地 (Jiǔ Dì) 天英 (Tiān Yīng) 景门 (Jǐng Mén) Li 9　　Gui 　　　Gui	九天 (Jiǔ Tiān) 禽芮 (Qín Ruì) 死门 (Sǐ Mén) Kun 2　　Bing/Ji 　　　　Bing/Ji
白虎 (Bái Hǔ) 天冲 (Tiān Chōng) 伤门 (Shāng Mén) Zhen 3　　Yi 　　　　Yi	Yang (阳) Dun# 4 Hour: **JiaWu** **Fu Yin** ©Calvin Yap	值符 (Zhí Fú) 天柱 (Tiān Zhù) 惊门 (Jǐng Mén) Dui 7　　Xin 　　　　Xin
六合 (Liù Hé) 天任 (Tiān Rèn) 生门 (Shēng Mén) Gen 8　　Ren 　　　　Ren	太阴 (Tài Yīn) 天蓬 (Tiān Péng) 休门 (Xiū Mén) Kan 1　　Ding 　　　　Ding	螣蛇 (Téng Shé) 天心 (Tiān Xīn) 开门 (Kāi Mén) Qian 6　　Geng 　　　　Geng

Yang (阳) Dun# 4 Hour: **YiWei**；直符(ZhíFú): 天柱(TiānZhù)
直使(ZhíShǐ): 惊门(JǐngMén)；旬首(XúnShǒu): JiaWu/Xin

螣蛇 (Téng Shé) 天心 (Tiān Xīn) 休门 (Xiū Mén) Xun 4　　Wu	太阴 (Tài Yīn) 天蓬 (Tiān Péng) 生门 (Shēng Mén) Li 9　　Gui	六合 (Liù Hé) 天任 (Tiān Rèn) 伤门 (Shāng Mén) Kun 2　　Ren 　　　　Bing/Ji
值符 (Zhí Fú) 天柱 (Tiān Zhù) 开门 (Kāi Mén) Zhen 3　　Xin 　　　　Yi	Yang (阳) Dun# 4 Hour: **YiWei** **Fan Yin** ©Calvin Yap	白虎 (Bái Hǔ) 天冲 (Tiān Chōng) 杜门 (Dù Mén) Dui 7　　Yi 　　　　Xin
九天 (Jiǔ Tiān) 禽芮 (Qín Ruì) 惊门 (Jǐng Mén) Gen 8　　Bing/Ji 　　　　Ren	九地 (Jiǔ Dì) 天英 (Tiān Yīng) 死门 (Sǐ Mén) Kan 1　　Gui 　　　　Ding	玄武 (Xuán Wǔ) 天辅 (Tiān Fǔ) 景门 (Jǐng Mén) Qian 6　　Wu 　　　　Geng

Yang (阳) Dun# 4 Hour: **BingShen**；直符(ZhíFú): 天柱(TiānZhù)
直使(ZhíShǐ): 惊门(JǐngMén)；旬首(XúnShǒu): JiaWu/Xin

九地 (Jiǔ Dì) 天英 (Tiān Yīng) 死门 (Sǐ Mén) Xun 4　　Gui 　　　　Wu	九天 (Jiǔ Tiān) 禽芮 (Qín Ruì) 惊门 (Jǐng Mén) Li 9　　Bing/Ji 　　　Gui	值符 (Zhí Fú) 天柱 (Tiān Zhù) 开门 (Kāi Mén) Kun 2　　Xin 　　　　Bing/Ji
玄武 (Xuán Wǔ) 天辅 (Tiān Fǔ) 景门 (Jǐng Mén) Zhen 3　　Wu 　　　　Yi	Yang (阳) Dun# 4 Hour: **BingShen** ©Calvin Yap	螣蛇 (Téng Shé) 天心 (Tiān Xīn) 休门 (Xiū Mén) Dui 7　　Geng 　　　　Xin
白虎 (Bái Hǔ) 天冲 (Tiān Chōng) 杜门 (Dù Mén) Gen 8　　Yi 　　　　Ren	六合 (Liù Hé) 天任 (Tiān Rèn) 伤门 (Shāng Mén) Kan 1　　Ren 　　　　Ding	太阴 (Tài Yīn) 天蓬 (Tiān Péng) 生门 (Shēng Mén) Qian 6　　Ding 　　　　Geng

Yang (阳) Dun# 4 Hour: **DingYou**；直符(ZhíFú): 天柱(TiānZhù)
直使(ZhíShǐ): 惊门(JǐngMén)；旬首(XúnShǒu): JiaWu/Xin

六合 (Liù Hé) 天任 (Tiān Rèn) 生门 (Shēng Mén) Xun 4　　Ren 　　　　Wu	白虎 (Bái Hǔ) 天冲 (Tiān Chōng) 伤门 (Shāng Mén) Li 9　　Yi 　　　Gui	玄武 (Xuán Wǔ) 天辅 (Tiān Fǔ) 杜门 (Dù Mén) Kun 2　　Wu 　　　　Bing/Ji
太阴 (Tài Yīn) 天蓬 (Tiān Péng) 休门 (Xiū Mén) Zhen 3　　Ding 　　　　Yi	Yang (阳) Dun# 4 Hour: **DingYou** ©Calvin Yap	九地 (Jiǔ Dì) 天英 (Tiān Yīng) 景门 (Jǐng Mén) Dui 7　　Gui 　　　　Xin
螣蛇 (Téng Shé) 天心 (Tiān Xīn) 开门 (Kāi Mén) Gen 8　　Geng 　　　　Ren	值符 (Zhí Fú) 天柱 (Tiān Zhù) 惊门 (Jǐng Mén) Kan 1　　Xin 　　　　Ding	九天 (Jiǔ Tiān) 禽芮 (Qín Ruì) 死门 (Sǐ Mén) Qian 6　　Bing/Ji 　　　　Geng

Yang (阳) Dun# 4 Hour: **WuXu**；直符(ZhíFú): 天柱(TiānZhù)
直使(ZhíShǐ): 惊门(JǐngMén)；旬首(XúnShǒu): JiaWu/Xin

值符 (Zhí Fú) 天柱 (Tiān Zhù) 景门 (Jǐng Mén) Xun 4　　Xin 　　　　Wu	螣蛇 (Téng Shé) 天心 (Tiān Xīn) 死门 (Sǐ Mén) Li 9　　Geng 　　　Gui	太阴 (Tài Yīn) 天蓬 (Tiān Péng) 惊门 (Jǐng Mén) Kun 2　　Ding 　　　　Bing/Ji
九天 (Jiǔ Tiān) 禽芮 (Qín Ruì) 杜门 (Dù Mén) Zhen 3　　Bing/Ji	Yang (阳) Dun# 4 Hour: **WuXu** ©Calvin Yap	六合 (Liù Hé) 天任 (Tiān Rèn) 开门 (Kāi Mén) Dui 7　　Ren 　　　　Xin
九地 (Jiǔ Dì) 天英 (Tiān Yīng) 伤门 (Shāng Mén) Gen 8　　Gui 　　　　Ren	玄武 (Xuán Wǔ) 天辅 (Tiān Fǔ) 生门 (Shēng Mén) Kan 1　　Wu 　　　　Ding	白虎 (Bái Hǔ) 天冲 (Tiān Chōng) 休门 (Xiū Mén) Qian 6　　Yi 　　　　Geng

Yang (阳) Dun# 4 Hour: **JiHai**；直符(ZhíFú): 天柱(TiānZhù)
直使(ZhíShǐ): 惊门(JǐngMén)；旬首(XúnShǒu): JiaWu/Xin

九地 (Jiǔ Dì) 天英 (Tiān Yīng) 开门 (Kāi Mén) Xun 4　　Gui 　　　　Wu	九天 (Jiǔ Tiān) 禽芮 (Qín Ruì) 休门 (Xiū Mén) Li 9　　Bing/Ji 　　　Gui	值符 (Zhí Fú) 天柱 (Tiān Zhù) 生门 (Shēng Mén) Kun 2　　Xin 　　　　Bing/Ji
玄武 (Xuán Wǔ) 天辅 (Tiān Fǔ) 惊门 (Jǐng Mén) Zhen 3　　Wu	Yang (阳) Dun# 4 Hour: **JiHai** ©Calvin Yap	螣蛇 (Téng Shé) 天心 (Tiān Xīn) 伤门 (Shāng Mén) Dui 7　　Geng 　　　　Xin
白虎 (Bái Hǔ) 天冲 (Tiān Chōng) 死门 (Sǐ Mén) Gen 8　　Yi 　　　　Ren	六合 (Liù Hé) 天任 (Tiān Rèn) 景门 (Jǐng Mén) Kan 1　　Ren 　　　　Ding	太阴 (Tài Yīn) 天蓬 (Tiān Péng) 杜门 (Dù Mén) Qian 6　　Ding 　　　　Geng

Yang (阳) Dun# 4 Hour: **GengZi** ; 直符(ZhíFú): 天柱(TiānZhù)
直使(ZhíShǐ): 惊门(JīngMén) ; 旬首(XúnShǒu): JiaWu/Xin

白虎 (Bái Hǔ) 天冲 (Tiān Chōng) 惊门 (Jīng Mén) Xun 4 · Yi Wu	玄武 (Xuán Wǔ) 天辅 (Tiān Fǔ) 开门 (Kāi Mén) Li 9 · Wu Gui	九地 (Jiǔ Dì) 天英 (Tiān Yīng) 休门 (Xiū Mén) Kun 2 · Gui Bing/Ji
六合 (Liù Hé) 天任 (Tiān Rèn) 死门 (Sǐ Mén) Zhen 3 · Ren Yi	Yang (阳) Dun# 4 Hour: GengZi ©Calvin Yap	九天 (Jiǔ Tiān) 禽芮 (Qín Ruì) 生门 (Shēng Mén) Dui 7 · Bing/Ji Xin
太阴 (Tài Yīn) 天蓬 (Tiān Péng) 景门 (Jǐng Mén) Gen 8 · Ding Ren	螣蛇 (Téng Shé) 天心 (Tiān Xīn) 杜门 (Dù Mén) Kan 1 · Geng Ding	值符 (Zhí Fú) 天柱 (Tiān Zhù) 伤门 (Shāng Mén) Qian 6 · Xin Geng

Yang (阳) Dun# 4 Hour: **XinChou** ; 直符(ZhíFú): 天柱(TiānZhù)
直使(ZhíShǐ): 惊门(JīngMén) ; 旬首(XúnShǒu): JiaWu/Xin

玄武 (Xuán Wǔ) 天辅 (Tiān Fǔ) 景门 (Jǐng Mén) Xun 4 · Wu Wu	九地 (Jiǔ Dì) 天英 (Tiān Yīng) 死门 (Sǐ Mén) Li 9 · Gui Gui	九天 (Jiǔ Tiān) 禽芮 (Qín Ruì) 惊门 (Jīng Mén) Kun 2 · Bing/Ji Bing/Ji
白虎 (Bái Hǔ) 天冲 (Tiān Chōng) 杜门 (Dù Mén) Zhen 3 · Yi	Yang (阳) Dun# 4 Hour: XinChou Fu Yin ©Calvin Yap	值符 (Zhí Fú) 天柱 (Tiān Zhù) 开门 (Kāi Mén) Dui 7 · Xin Xin
六合 (Liù Hé) 天任 (Tiān Rèn) 伤门 (Shāng Mén) Gen 8 · Ren Ren	太阴 (Tài Yīn) 天蓬 (Tiān Péng) 生门 (Shēng Mén) Kan 1 · Ding Ding	螣蛇 (Téng Shé) 天心 (Tiān Xīn) 休门 (Xiū Mén) Qian 6 · Geng Geng

Yang (阳) Dun# 4 Hour: **RenYin** ; 直符(ZhíFú): 天柱(TiānZhù)
直使(ZhíShǐ): 惊门(JīngMén) ; 旬首(XúnShǒu): JiaWu/Xin

太阴 (Tài Yīn) 天蓬 (Tiān Péng) 伤门 (Shāng Mén) Xun 4 · Ding Wu	六合 (Liù Hé) 天任 (Tiān Rèn) 杜门 (Dù Mén) Li 9 · Ren Gui	白虎 (Bái Hǔ) 天冲 (Tiān Chōng) 景门 (Jǐng Mén) Kun 2 · Yi Bing/Ji
螣蛇 (Téng Shé) 天心 (Tiān Xīn) 生门 (Shēng Mén) Zhen 3 · Geng Yi	Yang (阳) Dun# 4 Hour: RenYin ©Calvin Yap	玄武 (Xuán Wǔ) 天辅 (Tiān Fǔ) 死门 (Sǐ Mén) Dui 7 · Wu Xin
值符 (Zhí Fú) 天柱 (Tiān Zhù) 休门 (Xiū Mén) Gen 8 · Xin Ren	九天 (Jiǔ Tiān) 禽芮 (Qín Ruì) 开门 (Kāi Mén) Kan 1 · Bing/Ji Ding	九地 (Jiǔ Dì) 天英 (Tiān Yīng) 惊门 (Jīng Mén) Qian 6 · Gui Geng

Yang (阳) Dun# 4 Hour: **GuiMao** ; 直符(ZhíFú): 天柱(TiānZhù)
直使(ZhíShǐ): 惊门(JīngMén) ; 旬首(XúnShǒu): JiaWu/Xin

九天 (Jiǔ Tiān) 禽芮 (Qín Ruì) 杜门 (Dù Mén) Xun 4 · Bing/Ji Wu	值符 (Zhí Fú) 天柱 (Tiān Zhù) 景门 (Jǐng Mén) Li 9 · Xin Gui	螣蛇 (Téng Shé) 天心 (Tiān Xīn) 死门 (Sǐ Mén) Kun 2 · Geng Bing/Ji
九地 (Jiǔ Dì) 天英 (Tiān Yīng) 伤门 (Shāng Mén) Zhen 3 · Gui Yi	Yang (阳) Dun# 4 Hour: GuiMao ©Calvin Yap	太阴 (Tài Yīn) 天蓬 (Tiān Péng) 惊门 (Jīng Mén) Dui 7 · Ding Xin
玄武 (Xuán Wǔ) 天辅 (Tiān Fǔ) 生门 (Shēng Mén) Gen 8 · Wu Ren	白虎 (Bái Hǔ) 天冲 (Tiān Chōng) 休门 (Xiū Mén) Kan 1 · Yi Ding	六合 (Liù Hé) 天任 (Tiān Rèn) 开门 (Kāi Mén) Qian 6 · Ren Geng

Chart: +4JiaChen (Yang Dun #4 JiaChen Xun)
JiaChen, YiSi, BingWu, DingWei, WuShen, JiYou, GengXu, XinHai, RenZi, GuiChou

Yang (阳) Dun# 4 Hour: **JiaChen** ; 直符(ZhíFú): 天任(TiānRèn)
直使(ZhíShǐ): 生门(ShēngMén) ; 旬首(XúnShǒu): JiaChenRen

太阴 (Tài Yīn) 天辅 (Tiān Fǔ) 杜门 (Dù Mén) Xun 4 · Wu Wu	六合 (Liù Hé) 天英 (Tiān Yīng) 景门 (Jǐng Mén) Li 9 · Gui Gui	白虎 (Bái Hǔ) 禽芮 (Qín Ruì) 死门 (Sǐ Mén) Kun 2 · Bing/Ji Bing/Ji
螣蛇 (Téng Shé) 天冲 (Tiān Chōng) 伤门 (Shāng Mén) Zhen 3 · Yi Yi	Yang (阳) Dun# 4 Hour: JiaChen Fu Yin ©Calvin Yap	玄武 (Xuán Wǔ) 天柱 (Tiān Zhù) 惊门 (Jīng Mén) Dui 7 · Xin Xin
值符 (Zhí Fú) 天任 (Tiān Rèn) 生门 (Shēng Mén) Gen 8 · Ren Ren	九天 (Jiǔ Tiān) 天蓬 (Tiān Péng) 休门 (Xiū Mén) Kan 1 · Ding Ding	九地 (Jiǔ Dì) 天心 (Tiān Xīn) 开门 (Kāi Mén) Qian 6 · Geng Geng

Yang (阳) Dun# 4 Hour: **YiSi** ; 直符(ZhíFú): 天任(TiānRèn)
直使(ZhíShǐ): 生门(ShēngMén) ; 旬首(XúnShǒu): JiaChenRen

螣蛇 (Téng Shé) 天冲 (Tiān Chōng) 休门 (Xiū Mén) Xun 4 · Yi Wu	太阴 (Tài Yīn) 天辅 (Tiān Fǔ) 生门 (Shēng Mén) Li 9 · Wu Gui	六合 (Liù Hé) 天英 (Tiān Yīng) 伤门 (Shāng Mén) Kun 2 · Gui Bing/Ji
值符 (Zhí Fú) 天任 (Tiān Rèn) 开门 (Kāi Mén) Zhen 3 · Ren Yi	Yang (阳) Dun# 4 Hour: YiSi ©Calvin Yap	白虎 (Bái Hǔ) 禽芮 (Qín Ruì) 杜门 (Dù Mén) Dui 7 · Bing/Ji Xin
九天 (Jiǔ Tiān) 天蓬 (Tiān Péng) 惊门 (Jīng Mén) Gen 8 · Ding Ren	九地 (Jiǔ Dì) 天心 (Tiān Xīn) 死门 (Sǐ Mén) Kan 1 · Geng Ding	玄武 (Xuán Wǔ) 天柱 (Tiān Zhù) 景门 (Jǐng Mén) Qian 6 · Xin Geng

Yang (阳) Dun# 4 Hour: **BingWu** ; 直符(ZhíFú): 天任(TiānRèn) ; 直使(ZhíShǐ): 生门(ShēngMén) ; 旬首(XúnShǒu): JiaChenRen

九地 (Jiǔ Dì) 天心 (Tiān Xīn) 景门 (Jǐng Mén) Xun 4　Geng　Wu	九天 (Jiǔ Tiān) 天蓬 (Tiān Péng) 死门 (Sǐ Mén) Li 9　Ding　Gui	值符 (Zhí Fú) 天任 (Tiān Rèn) 惊门 (Jīng Mén) Kun 2　Ren　Bing/Ji
玄武 (Xuán Wǔ) 天柱 (Tiān Zhù) 杜门 (Dù Mén) Zhen 3　Xin　Yi	Yang (阳) Dun# 4 Hour: **BingWu** **Fan Yin** ©Calvin Yap	螣蛇 (Téng Shé) 天冲 (Tiān Chōng) 开门 (Kāi Mén) Dui 7　Yi　Xin
白虎 (Bái Hǔ) 禽芮 (Qín Ruì) 伤门 (Shāng Mén) Gen 8　Bing/Ji　Ren	六合 (Liù Hé) 天英 (Tiān Yīng) 生门 (Shēng Mén) Kan 1　Gui　Ding	太阴 (Tài Yīn) 天辅 (Tiān Fǔ) 休门 (Xiū Mén) Qian 6　Wu　Geng

Yang (阳) Dun# 4 Hour: **DingWei** ; 直符(ZhíFú): 天任(TiānRèn) ; 直使(ZhíShǐ): 生门(ShēngMén) ; 旬首(XúnShǒu): JiaChenRen

六合 (Liù Hé) 天英 (Tiān Yīng) 开门 (Kāi Mén) Xun 4　Gui　Wu	白虎 (Bái Hǔ) 禽芮 (Qín Ruì) 休门 (Xiū Mén) Li 9　Bing/Ji　Gui	玄武 (Xuán Wǔ) 天柱 (Tiān Zhù) 生门 (Shēng Mén) Kun 2　Xin　Bing/Ji
太阴 (Tài Yīn) 天辅 (Tiān Fǔ) 惊门 (Jīng Mén) Zhen 3　Wu　Yi	Yang (阳) Dun# 4 Hour: **DingWei** ©Calvin Yap	九地 (Jiǔ Dì) 天心 (Tiān Xīn) 伤门 (Shāng Mén) Dui 7　Geng　Xin
螣蛇 (Téng Shé) 天冲 (Tiān Chōng) 死门 (Sǐ Mén) Gen 8　Yi　Ren	值符 (Zhí Fú) 天任 (Tiān Rèn) 景门 (Jǐng Mén) Kan 1　Ren　Ding	九天 (Jiǔ Tiān) 天蓬 (Tiān Péng) 杜门 (Dù Mén) Qian 6　Ding　Geng

Yang (阳) Dun# 4 Hour: **WuShen** ; 直符(ZhíFú): 天任(TiānRèn) ; 直使(ZhíShǐ): 生门(ShēngMén) ; 旬首(XúnShǒu): JiaChenRen

值符 (Zhí Fú) 天任 (Tiān Rèn) 伤门 (Shāng Mén) Xun 4　Ren　Wu	螣蛇 (Téng Shé) 天冲 (Tiān Chōng) 杜门 (Dù Mén) Li 9　Yi　Gui	太阴 (Tài Yīn) 天辅 (Tiān Fǔ) 景门 (Jǐng Mén) Kun 2　Wu　Bing/Ji
九天 (Jiǔ Tiān) 天蓬 (Tiān Péng) 生门 (Shēng Mén) Zhen 3　Ding　Yi	Yang (阳) Dun# 4 Hour: **WuShen** ©Calvin Yap	六合 (Liù Hé) 天英 (Tiān Yīng) 死门 (Sǐ Mén) Dui 7　Gui　Xin
九地 (Jiǔ Dì) 天心 (Tiān Xīn) 休门 (Xiū Mén) Gen 8　Geng　Ren	玄武 (Xuán Wǔ) 天柱 (Tiān Zhù) 开门 (Kāi Mén) Kan 1　Xin　Ding	白虎 (Bái Hǔ) 禽芮 (Qín Ruì) 惊门 (Jīng Mén) Qian 6　Bing/Ji　Geng

Yang (阳) Dun# 4 Hour: **JiYou** ; 直符(ZhíFú): 天任(TiānRèn) ; 直使(ZhíShǐ): 生门(ShēngMén) ; 旬首(XúnShǒu): JiaChenRen

九地 (Jiǔ Dì) 天心 (Tiān Xīn) 生门 (Shēng Mén) Xun 4　Geng　Wu	九天 (Jiǔ Tiān) 天蓬 (Tiān Péng) 伤门 (Shāng Mén) Li 9　Ding　Gui	值符 (Zhí Fú) 天任 (Tiān Rèn) 杜门 (Dù Mén) Kun 2　Ren　Bing/Ji
玄武 (Xuán Wǔ) 天柱 (Tiān Zhù) 休门 (Xiū Mén) Zhen 3　Xin　Yi	Yang (阳) Dun# 4 Hour: **JiYou** **Fan Yin** ©Calvin Yap	螣蛇 (Téng Shé) 天冲 (Tiān Chōng) 景门 (Jǐng Mén) Dui 7　Yi　Xin
白虎 (Bái Hǔ) 禽芮 (Qín Ruì) 开门 (Kāi Mén) Gen 8　Bing/Ji　Ren	六合 (Liù Hé) 天英 (Tiān Yīng) 惊门 (Jīng Mén) Kan 1　Gui　Ding	太阴 (Tài Yīn) 天辅 (Tiān Fǔ) 死门 (Sǐ Mén) Qian 6　Wu　Geng

Yang (阳) Dun# 4 Hour: **GengXu** ; 直符(ZhíFú): 天任(TiānRèn) ; 直使(ZhíShǐ): 生门(ShēngMén) ; 旬首(XúnShǒu): JiaChenRen

白虎 (Bái Hǔ) 禽芮 (Qín Ruì) 开门 (Kāi Mén) Xun 4　Bing/Ji　Wu	玄武 (Xuán Wǔ) 天柱 (Tiān Zhù) 休门 (Xiū Mén) Li 9　Xin　Gui	九地 (Jiǔ Dì) 天心 (Tiān Xīn) 生门 (Shēng Mén) Kun 2　Geng　Bing/Ji
六合 (Liù Hé) 天英 (Tiān Yīng) 惊门 (Jīng Mén) Zhen 3　Gui　Yi	Yang (阳) Dun# 4 Hour: **GengXu** ©Calvin Yap	九天 (Jiǔ Tiān) 天蓬 (Tiān Péng) 伤门 (Shāng Mén) Dui 7　Ding　Xin
太阴 (Tài Yīn) 天辅 (Tiān Fǔ) 死门 (Sǐ Mén) Gen 8　Wu　Ren	螣蛇 (Téng Shé) 天冲 (Tiān Chōng) 景门 (Jǐng Mén) Kan 1　Yi　Ding	值符 (Zhí Fú) 天任 (Tiān Rèn) 杜门 (Dù Mén) Qian 6　Ren　Geng

Yang (阳) Dun# 4 Hour: **XinHai** ; 直符(ZhíFú): 天任(TiānRèn) ; 直使(ZhíShǐ): 生门(ShēngMén) ; 旬首(XúnShǒu): JiaChenRen

玄武 (Xuán Wǔ) 天柱 (Tiān Zhù) 死门 (Sǐ Mén) Xun 4　Xin　Wu	九地 (Jiǔ Dì) 天心 (Tiān Xīn) 惊门 (Jīng Mén) Li 9　Geng　Gui	九天 (Jiǔ Tiān) 天蓬 (Tiān Péng) 开门 (Kāi Mén) Kun 2　Ding　Bing/Ji
白虎 (Bái Hǔ) 禽芮 (Qín Ruì) 景门 (Jǐng Mén) Zhen 3　Bing/Ji　Yi	Yang (阳) Dun# 4 Hour: **XinHai** ©Calvin Yap	值符 (Zhí Fú) 天任 (Tiān Rèn) 休门 (Xiū Mén) Dui 7　Ren　Xin
六合 (Liù Hé) 天英 (Tiān Yīng) 杜门 (Dù Mén) Gen 8　Gui　Ren	太阴 (Tài Yīn) 天辅 (Tiān Fǔ) 伤门 (Shāng Mén) Kan 1　Wu　Ding	螣蛇 (Téng Shé) 天冲 (Tiān Chōng) 生门 (Shēng Mén) Qian 6　Yi　Geng

Yang (阳) Dun# 4 Hour: **RenZi** ; 直符(ZhíFú): 天任(TiānRèn)
直使(ZhíShǐ): 生门(ShēngMén) ; 旬首(XúnShǒu): JiaChenRen

太阴 (Tài Yīn) 天辅 (Tiān Fǔ) 惊门 (Jīng Mén) Xun 4　Wu Wu	六合 (Liù Hé) 天英 (Tiān Yīng) 开门 (Kāi Mén) Li 9　Gui Gui	白虎 (Bái Hǔ) 禽芮 (Qín Ruì) 休门 (Xiū Mén) Kun 2　Bing/Ji Bing/Ji
螣蛇 (Téng Shé) 天冲 (Tiān Chōng) 死门 (Sǐ Mén) Zhen 3　Yi Yi	Yang (阳) Dun# 4 Hour: **RenZi** **Fu Yin** ©Calvin Yap	玄武 (Xuán Wǔ) 天柱 (Tiān Zhù) 生门 (Shēng Mén) Dui 7　Xin Xin
值符 (Zhí Fú) 天任 (Tiān Rèn) 景门 (Jǐng Mén) Gen 8　Ren Ren	九天 (Jiǔ Tiān) 天蓬 (Tiān Péng) 杜门 (Dù Mén) Kan 1　Ding Ding	九地 (Jiǔ Dì) 天心 (Tiān Xīn) 伤门 (Shāng Mén) Qian 6　Geng Geng

Yang (阳) Dun# 4 Hour: **GuiChou** ; 直符(ZhíFú): 天任(TiānRèn)
直使(ZhíShǐ): 生门(ShēngMén) ; 旬首(XúnShǒu): JiaChenRen

九天 (Jiǔ Tiān) 天蓬 (Tiān Péng) 杜门 (Dù Mén) Xun 4　Ding Wu	值符 (Zhí Fú) 天任 (Tiān Rèn) 景门 (Jǐng Mén) Li 9　Ren Gui	螣蛇 (Téng Shé) 天冲 (Tiān Chōng) 死门 (Sǐ Mén) Kun 2　Yi Bing/Ji
九地 (Jiǔ Dì) 天心 (Tiān Xīn) 伤门 (Shāng Mén) Zhen 3　Geng Yi	Yang (阳) Dun# 4 Hour: **GuiChou** ©Calvin Yap	太阴 (Tài Yīn) 天辅 (Tiān Fǔ) 惊门 (Jīng Mén) Dui 7　Wu Xin
玄武 (Xuán Wǔ) 天柱 (Tiān Zhù) 生门 (Shēng Mén) Gen 8　Xin Ren	白虎 (Bái Hǔ) 禽芮 (Qín Ruì) 休门 (Xiū Mén) Kan 1　Bing/Ji Ding	六合 (Liù Hé) 天英 (Tiān Yīng) 开门 (Kāi Mén) Qian 6　Gui Geng

Chart: **+4JiaYin** (Yang Dun #4 JiaYin Xun)
JiaYin, YiMao, BingChen, DingSi, WuWu, JiWei, GengShen, XinYou, RenXu, Gui

Yang (阳) Dun# 4 Hour: **JiaYin** ; 直符(ZhíFú): 天英(TiānYīng)
直使(ZhíShǐ): 景门(JǐngMén) ; 旬首(XúnShǒu): JiaYinGui

九天 (Jiǔ Tiān) 天辅 (Tiān Fǔ) 杜门 (Dù Mén) Xun 4　Wu Wu	值符 (Zhí Fú) 天英 (Tiān Yīng) 景门 (Jǐng Mén) Li 9　Gui Gui	螣蛇 (Téng Shé) 禽芮 (Qín Ruì) 死门 (Sǐ Mén) Kun 2　Bing/Ji Bing/Ji
九地 (Jiǔ Dì) 天冲 (Tiān Chōng) 伤门 (Shāng Mén) Zhen 3　Yi Yi	Yang (阳) Dun# 4 Hour: **JiaYin** **Fu Yin** ©Calvin Yap	太阴 (Tài Yīn) 天柱 (Tiān Zhù) 惊门 (Jīng Mén) Dui 7　Xin Xin
玄武 (Xuán Wǔ) 天任 (Tiān Rèn) 生门 (Shēng Mén) Gen 8　Ren Ren	白虎 (Bái Hǔ) 天蓬 (Tiān Péng) 休门 (Xiū Mén) Kan 1　Ding Ding	六合 (Liù Hé) 天心 (Tiān Xīn) 开门 (Kāi Mén) Qian 6　Geng Geng

Yang (阳) Dun# 4 Hour: **YiMao** ; 直符(ZhíFú): 天英(TiānYīng)
直使(ZhíShǐ): 景门(JǐngMén) ; 旬首(XúnShǒu): JiaYinGui

螣蛇 (Téng Shé) 禽芮 (Qín Ruì) 开门 (Kāi Mén) Xun 4　Bing/Ji Wu	太阴 (Tài Yīn) 天柱 (Tiān Zhù) 休门 (Xiū Mén) Li 9　Xin Gui	六合 (Liù Hé) 天心 (Tiān Xīn) 生门 (Shēng Mén) Kun 2　Geng Bing/Ji
值符 (Zhí Fú) 天英 (Tiān Yīng) 惊门 (Jīng Mén) Zhen 3　Gui Yi	Yang (阳) Dun# 4 Hour: **YiMao** ©Calvin Yap	白虎 (Bái Hǔ) 天蓬 (Tiān Péng) 伤门 (Shāng Mén) Dui 7　Ding Xin
九天 (Jiǔ Tiān) 天辅 (Tiān Fǔ) 死门 (Sǐ Mén) Gen 8　Wu Ren	九地 (Jiǔ Dì) 天冲 (Tiān Chōng) 景门 (Jǐng Mén) Kan 1　Yi Ding	玄武 (Xuán Wǔ) 天任 (Tiān Rèn) 杜门 (Dù Mén) Qian 6　Ren Geng

Yang (阳) Dun# 4 Hour: **BingChen** ; 直符(ZhíFú): 天英(TiānYīng)
直使(ZhíShǐ): 景门(JǐngMén) ; 旬首(XúnShǒu): JiaYinGui

九地 (Jiǔ Dì) 天冲 (Tiān Chōng) 伤门 (Shāng Mén) Xun 4　Yi Wu	九天 (Jiǔ Tiān) 天辅 (Tiān Fǔ) 杜门 (Dù Mén) Li 9　Wu Gui	值符 (Zhí Fú) 天英 (Tiān Yīng) 景门 (Jǐng Mén) Kun 2　Gui Bing/Ji
玄武 (Xuán Wǔ) 天任 (Tiān Rèn) 生门 (Shēng Mén) Zhen 3　Ren Yi	Yang (阳) Dun# 4 Hour: **BingChen** ©Calvin Yap	螣蛇 (Téng Shé) 禽芮 (Qín Ruì) 死门 (Sǐ Mén) Dui 7　Bing/Ji Xin
白虎 (Bái Hǔ) 天蓬 (Tiān Péng) 休门 (Xiū Mén) Gen 8　Ding Ren	六合 (Liù Hé) 天心 (Tiān Xīn) 开门 (Kāi Mén) Kan 1　Geng Ding	太阴 (Tài Yīn) 天柱 (Tiān Zhù) 惊门 (Jīng Mén) Qian 6　Xin Geng

Yang (阳) Dun# 4 Hour: **DingSi** ; 直符(ZhíFú): 天英(TiānYīng)
直使(ZhíShǐ): 景门(JǐngMén) ; 旬首(XúnShǒu): JiaYinGui

六合 (Liù Hé) 天心 (Tiān Xīn) 死门 (Sǐ Mén) Xun 4　Geng Wu	白虎 (Bái Hǔ) 天蓬 (Tiān Péng) 惊门 (Jīng Mén) Li 9　Ding Gui	玄武 (Xuán Wǔ) 天任 (Tiān Rèn) 开门 (Kāi Mén) Kun 2　Ren Bing/Ji
太阴 (Tài Yīn) 天柱 (Tiān Zhù) 景门 (Jǐng Mén) Zhen 3　Xin Yi	Yang (阳) Dun# 4 Hour: **DingSi** **Fan Yin** ©Calvin Yap	九地 (Jiǔ Dì) 天冲 (Tiān Chōng) 休门 (Xiū Mén) Dui 7　Yi Xin
螣蛇 (Téng Shé) 禽芮 (Qín Ruì) 杜门 (Dù Mén) Gen 8　Bing/Ji Ren	值符 (Zhí Fú) 天英 (Tiān Yīng) 伤门 (Shāng Mén) Kan 1　Gui Ding	九天 (Jiǔ Tiān) 天辅 (Tiān Fǔ) 生门 (Shēng Mén) Qian 6　Wu Geng

Yang (阳) Dun# 4 Hour: **WuWu** ; 直符(ZhíFú): 天英(TiānYīng)
直使(ZhíShǐ): 景门(JǐngMén) ; 旬首(XúnShǒu): JiaYinGui

值符 (Zhí Fú) 天英 (Tiān Yīng) 景门 (Jǐng Mén) Xun 4 — Gui / Wu	螣蛇 (Téng Shé) 禽芮 (Qín Ruì) 死门 (Sǐ Mén) Li 9 — Bing/Ji / Gui	太阴 (Tài Yīn) 天柱 (Tiān Zhù) 惊门 (Jīng Mén) Kun 2 — Xin / Bing/Ji
九天 (Jiǔ Tiān) 天辅 (Tiān Fǔ) 杜门 (Dù Mén) Zhen 3 — Wu / Yi	Yang (阳) Dun# 4 Hour: **WuWu** ©Calvin Yap	六合 (Liù Hé) 天心 (Tiān Xīn) 开门 (Kāi Mén) Dui 7 — Geng / Xin
九地 (Jiǔ Dì) 天冲 (Tiān Chōng) 伤门 (Shāng Mén) Gen 8 — Yi / Ren	玄武 (Xuán Wǔ) 天任 (Tiān Rèn) 生门 (Shēng Mén) Kan 1 — Ren / Ding	白虎 (Bái Hǔ) 天蓬 (Tiān Péng) 休门 (Xiū Mén) Qian 6 — Ding / Geng

Yang (阳) Dun# 4 Hour: **JiWei** ; 直符(ZhíFú): 天英(TiānYīng)
直使(ZhíShǐ): 景门(JǐngMén) ; 旬首(XúnShǒu): JiaYinGui

九地 (Jiǔ Dì) 天冲 (Tiān Chōng) 伤门 (Shāng Mén) Xun 4 — Yi / Wu	九天 (Jiǔ Tiān) 天辅 (Tiān Fǔ) 杜门 (Dù Mén) Li 9 — Wu / Gui	值符 (Zhí Fú) 天英 (Tiān Yīng) 景门 (Jǐng Mén) Kun 2 — Gui / Bing/Ji
玄武 (Xuán Wǔ) 天任 (Tiān Rèn) 生门 (Shēng Mén) Zhen 3 — Ren / Yi	Yang (阳) Dun# 4 Hour: **JiWei** ©Calvin Yap	螣蛇 (Téng Shé) 禽芮 (Qín Ruì) 死门 (Sǐ Mén) Dui 7 — Bing/Ji / Xin
白虎 (Bái Hǔ) 天蓬 (Tiān Péng) 休门 (Xiū Mén) Gen 8 — Ding / Ren	六合 (Liù Hé) 天心 (Tiān Xīn) 开门 (Kāi Mén) Kan 1 — Geng / Ding	太阴 (Tài Yīn) 天柱 (Tiān Zhù) 惊门 (Jīng Mén) Qian 6 — Xin / Geng

Yang (阳) Dun# 4 Hour: **GengShen** ; 直符(ZhíFú): 天英(TiānYīng)
直使(ZhíShǐ): 景门(JǐngMén) ; 旬首(XúnShǒu): JiaYinGui

白虎 (Bái Hǔ) 天蓬 (Tiān Péng) 休门 (Xiū Mén) Xun 4 — Ding / Wu	玄武 (Xuán Wǔ) 天任 (Tiān Rèn) 生门 (Shēng Mén) Li 9 — Ren / Gui	九地 (Jiǔ Dì) 天冲 (Tiān Chōng) 伤门 (Shāng Mén) Kun 2 — Yi / Bing/Ji
六合 (Liù Hé) 天心 (Tiān Xīn) 开门 (Kāi Mén) Zhen 3 — Geng / Yi	Yang (阳) Dun# 4 Hour: **GengShen** ©Calvin Yap	九天 (Jiǔ Tiān) 天辅 (Tiān Fǔ) 杜门 (Dù Mén) Dui 7 — Wu / Xin
太阴 (Tài Yīn) 天柱 (Tiān Zhù) 惊门 (Jīng Mén) Gen 8 — Xin / Ren	螣蛇 (Téng Shé) 禽芮 (Qín Ruì) 死门 (Sǐ Mén) Kan 1 — Bing/Ji / Ding	值符 (Zhí Fú) 天英 (Tiān Yīng) 景门 (Jǐng Mén) Qian 6 — Gui / Geng

Yang (阳) Dun# 4 Hour: **XinYou** ; 直符(ZhíFú): 天英(TiānYīng)
直使(ZhíShǐ): 景门(JǐngMén) ; 旬首(XúnShǒu): JiaYinGui

玄武 (Xuán Wǔ) 天任 (Tiān Rèn) 生门 (Shēng Mén) Xun 4 — Ren / Wu	九地 (Jiǔ Dì) 天冲 (Tiān Chōng) 伤门 (Shāng Mén) Li 9 — Yi / Gui	九天 (Jiǔ Tiān) 天辅 (Tiān Fǔ) 杜门 (Dù Mén) Kun 2 — Wu / Bing/Ji
白虎 (Bái Hǔ) 天蓬 (Tiān Péng) 休门 (Xiū Mén) Zhen 3 — Ding / Yi	Yang (阳) Dun# 4 Hour: **XinYou** ©Calvin Yap	值符 (Zhí Fú) 天英 (Tiān Yīng) 景门 (Jǐng Mén) Dui 7 — Gui / Xin
六合 (Liù Hé) 天心 (Tiān Xīn) 开门 (Kāi Mén) Gen 8 — Geng / Ren	太阴 (Tài Yīn) 天柱 (Tiān Zhù) 惊门 (Jīng Mén) Kan 1 — Xin / Ding	螣蛇 (Téng Shé) 禽芮 (Qín Ruì) 死门 (Sǐ Mén) Qian 6 — Bing/Ji / Geng

Yang (阳) Dun# 4 Hour: **RenXu** ; 直符(ZhíFú): 天英(TiānYīng)
直使(ZhíShǐ): 景门(JǐngMén) ; 旬首(XúnShǒu): JiaYinGui

太阴 (Tài Yīn) 天柱 (Tiān Zhù) 惊门 (Jīng Mén) Xun 4 — Xin / Wu	六合 (Liù Hé) 天心 (Tiān Xīn) 开门 (Kāi Mén) Li 9 — Geng / Gui	白虎 (Bái Hǔ) 天蓬 (Tiān Péng) 休门 (Xiū Mén) Kun 2 — Ding / Bing/Ji
螣蛇 (Téng Shé) 禽芮 (Qín Ruì) 死门 (Sǐ Mén) Zhen 3 — Bing/Ji / Yi	Yang (阳) Dun# 4 Hour: **RenXu** ©Calvin Yap	玄武 (Xuán Wǔ) 天任 (Tiān Rèn) 生门 (Shēng Mén) Dui 7 — Ren / Xin
值符 (Zhí Fú) 天英 (Tiān Yīng) 景门 (Jǐng Mén) Gen 8 — Gui / Ren	九天 (Jiǔ Tiān) 天辅 (Tiān Fǔ) 杜门 (Dù Mén) Kan 1 — Wu / Ding	九地 (Jiǔ Dì) 天冲 (Tiān Chōng) 伤门 (Shāng Mén) Qian 6 — Yi / Geng

Yang (阳) Dun# 4 Hour: **GuiHai** ; 直符(ZhíFú): 天英(TiānYīng)
直使(ZhíShǐ): 景门(JǐngMén) ; 旬首(XúnShǒu): JiaYinGui

九天 (Jiǔ Tiān) 天辅 (Tiān Fǔ) 杜门 (Dù Mén) Xun 4 — Wu / Wu	值符 (Zhí Fú) 天英 (Tiān Yīng) 景门 (Jǐng Mén) Li 9 — Gui / Gui	螣蛇 (Téng Shé) 禽芮 (Qín Ruì) 死门 (Sǐ Mén) Kun 2 — Bing/Ji / Bing/Ji
九地 (Jiǔ Dì) 天冲 (Tiān Chōng) 伤门 (Shāng Mén) Zhen 3 — Yi / Yi	Yang (阳) Dun# 4 Hour: **GuiHai** **Fu Yin** ©Calvin Yap	太阴 (Tài Yīn) 天柱 (Tiān Zhù) 惊门 (Jīng Mén) Dui 7 — Xin / Xin
玄武 (Xuán Wǔ) 天任 (Tiān Rèn) 生门 (Shēng Mén) Gen 8 — Ren / Ren	白虎 (Bái Hǔ) 天蓬 (Tiān Péng) 休门 (Xiū Mén) Kan 1 — Ding / Ding	六合 (Liù Hé) 天心 (Tiān Xīn) 开门 (Kāi Mén) Qian 6 — Geng / Geng

Yang Dun#5

<table>
<tr><td colspan="6" align="center">Chart: +5JiaZi (Yang Dun #5 JiaZi Xun)
JiaZi, YiChou, BingYin, DingMao, WuChen, JiSi, GengWu, XinWei, RenShen, GuiYou</td></tr>
</table>

Yang (阳) Dun# 5 Hour: JiaZi ; 直符(ZhíFú): 天禽(TiānQín)
直使(ZhíShǐ): 死门(SǐMén) **;** 旬首(XúnShǒu): JiaZiWu

九地 (Jiǔ Dì) 天辅 (Tiān Fǔ) 杜门 (Dù Mén) Xun 4 — Yi / Yi	九天 (Jiǔ Tiān) 天英 (Tiān Yīng) 景门 (Jǐng Mén) Li 9 — Ren / Ren	值符 (Zhí Fú) 禽芮 (Qín Ruì) 死门 (Sǐ Mén) Kun 2 — Ding/Wu / Ding/Wu
玄武 (Xuán Wǔ) 天冲 (Tiān Chōng) 伤门 (Shāng Mén) Zhen 3 — Bing / Bing	Yang (阳) Dun# 5 Hour: **JiaZi** **Fu Yin** ©Calvin Yap	螣蛇 (Téng Shé) 天柱 (Tiān Zhù) 惊门 (Jīng Mén) Dui 7 — Geng / Geng
白虎 (Bái Hǔ) 天任 (Tiān Rèn) 生门 (Shēng Mén) Gen 8 — Xin / Xin	六合 (Liù Hé) 天蓬 (Tiān Péng) 休门 (Xiū Mén) Kan 1 — Gui / Gui	太阴 (Tài Yīn) 天心 (Tiān Xīn) 开门 (Kāi Mén) Qian 6 — Ji / Ji

Yang (阳) Dun# 5 Hour: YiChou ; 直符(ZhíFú): 天禽(TiānQín)
直使(ZhíShǐ): 死门(SǐMén) **;** 旬首(XúnShǒu): JiaZiWu

值符 (Zhí Fú) 禽芮 (Qín Ruì) 生门 (Shēng Mén) Xun 4 — Ding/Wu / Yi	螣蛇 (Téng Shé) 天柱 (Tiān Zhù) 伤门 (Shāng Mén) Li 9 — Geng / Ren	太阴 (Tài Yīn) 天心 (Tiān Xīn) 杜门 (Dù Mén) Kun 2 — Ji / Ding/Wu
九天 (Jiǔ Tiān) 天英 (Tiān Yīng) 休门 (Xiū Mén) Zhen 3 — Ren / Bing	Yang (阳) Dun# 5 Hour: **YiChou** ©Calvin Yap	六合 (Liù Hé) 天蓬 (Tiān Péng) 景门 (Jǐng Mén) Dui 7 — Gui / Geng
九地 (Jiǔ Dì) 天辅 (Tiān Fǔ) 开门 (Kāi Mén) Gen 8 — Yi / Gui	玄武 (Xuán Wǔ) 天冲 (Tiān Chōng) 惊门 (Jīng Mén) Kan 1 — Bing	白虎 (Bái Hǔ) 天任 (Tiān Rèn) 死门 (Sǐ Mén) Qian 6 — Xin / Ji

Yang (阳) Dun# 5 Hour: BingYin ; 直符(ZhíFú): 天禽(TiānQín)
直使(ZhíShǐ): 死门(SǐMén) **;** 旬首(XúnShǒu): JiaZiWu

螣蛇 (Téng Shé) 天柱 (Tiān Zhù) 伤门 (Shāng Mén) Xun 4 — Geng / Yi	太阴 (Tài Yīn) 天心 (Tiān Xīn) 杜门 (Dù Mén) Li 9 — Ji / Ren	六合 (Liù Hé) 天蓬 (Tiān Péng) 景门 (Jǐng Mén) Kun 2 — Gui / Ding/Wu
值符 (Zhí Fú) 禽芮 (Qín Ruì) 生门 (Shēng Mén) Zhen 3 — Ding/Wu / Bing	Yang (阳) Dun# 5 Hour: **BingYin** ©Calvin Yap	白虎 (Bái Hǔ) 天任 (Tiān Rèn) 死门 (Sǐ Mén) Dui 7 — Xin / Geng
九天 (Jiǔ Tiān) 天英 (Tiān Yīng) 休门 (Xiū Mén) Gen 8 — Ren / Xin	九地 (Jiǔ Dì) 天辅 (Tiān Fǔ) 开门 (Kāi Mén) Kan 1 — Yi / Gui	玄武 (Xuán Wǔ) 天冲 (Tiān Chōng) 惊门 (Jīng Mén) Qian 6 — Bing / Ji

Yang (阳) Dun# 5 Hour: DingMao ; 直符(ZhíFú): 天禽(TiānQín)
直使(ZhíShǐ): 死门(SǐMén) **;** 旬首(XúnShǒu): JiaZiWu

九地 (Jiǔ Dì) 天辅 (Tiān Fǔ) 开门 (Kāi Mén) Xun 4 — Yi / Yi	九天 (Jiǔ Tiān) 天英 (Tiān Yīng) 休门 (Xiū Mén) Li 9 — Ren / Ren	值符 (Zhí Fú) 禽芮 (Qín Ruì) 生门 (Shēng Mén) Kun 2 — Ding/Wu / Ding/Wu
玄武 (Xuán Wǔ) 天冲 (Tiān Chōng) 惊门 (Jīng Mén) Zhen 3 — Bing	Yang (阳) Dun# 5 Hour: **DingMao** **Fu Yin** ©Calvin Yap	螣蛇 (Téng Shé) 天柱 (Tiān Zhù) 伤门 (Shāng Mén) Dui 7 — Geng / Geng
白虎 (Bái Hǔ) 天任 (Tiān Rèn) 死门 (Sǐ Mén) Gen 8 — Xin / Xin	六合 (Liù Hé) 天蓬 (Tiān Péng) 景门 (Jǐng Mén) Kan 1 — Gui / Gui	太阴 (Tài Yīn) 天心 (Tiān Xīn) 杜门 (Dù Mén) Qian 6 — Ji / Ji

Yang (阳) Dun# 5 Hour: WuChen ; 直符(ZhíFú): 天禽(TiānQín)
直使(ZhíShǐ): 死门(SǐMén) **;** 旬首(XúnShǒu): JiaZiWu

九地 (Jiǔ Dì) 天辅 (Tiān Fǔ) 景门 (Jǐng Mén) Xun 4 — Yi / Yi	九天 (Jiǔ Tiān) 天英 (Tiān Yīng) 死门 (Sǐ Mén) Li 9 — Ren / Ren	值符 (Zhí Fú) 禽芮 (Qín Ruì) 惊门 (Jīng Mén) Kun 2 — Ding/Wu / Ding/Wu
玄武 (Xuán Wǔ) 天冲 (Tiān Chōng) 杜门 (Dù Mén) Zhen 3 — Bing / Bing	Yang (阳) Dun# 5 Hour: **WuChen** **Fu Yin** ©Calvin Yap	螣蛇 (Téng Shé) 天柱 (Tiān Zhù) 开门 (Kāi Mén) Dui 7 — Geng / Geng
白虎 (Bái Hǔ) 天任 (Tiān Rèn) 伤门 (Shāng Mén) Gen 8 — Xin / Xin	六合 (Liù Hé) 天蓬 (Tiān Péng) 生门 (Shēng Mén) Kan 1 — Gui / Gui	太阴 (Tài Yīn) 天心 (Tiān Xīn) 休门 (Xiū Mén) Qian 6 — Ji / Ji

Yang (阳) Dun# 5 Hour: JiSi ; 直符(ZhíFú): 天禽(TiānQín)
直使(ZhíShǐ): 死门(SǐMén) **;** 旬首(XúnShǒu): JiaZiWu

白虎 (Bái Hǔ) 天任 (Tiān Rèn) 休门 (Xiū Mén) Xun 4 — Xin / Yi	玄武 (Xuán Wǔ) 天冲 (Tiān Chōng) 生门 (Shēng Mén) Li 9 — Bing / Ren	九地 (Jiǔ Dì) 天辅 (Tiān Fǔ) 伤门 (Shāng Mén) Kun 2 — Yi / Ding/Wu
六合 (Liù Hé) 天蓬 (Tiān Péng) 开门 (Kāi Mén) Zhen 3 — Gui / Bing	Yang (阳) Dun# 5 Hour: **JiSi** ©Calvin Yap	九天 (Jiǔ Tiān) 天英 (Tiān Yīng) 杜门 (Dù Mén) Dui 7 — Ren / Geng
太阴 (Tài Yīn) 天心 (Tiān Xīn) 惊门 (Jīng Mén) Gen 8 — Ji / Xin	螣蛇 (Téng Shé) 天柱 (Tiān Zhù) 死门 (Sǐ Mén) Kan 1 — Geng / Gui	值符 (Zhí Fú) 禽芮 (Qín Ruì) 景门 (Jǐng Mén) Qian 6 — Ding/Wu / Ji

Yang (阳) Dun# 5 Hour: GengWu ；直符(ZhíFú): 天禽(TiānQín)
直使(ZhíShǐ): 死门(SǐMén)；旬首(XúnShǒu): JiaZiWu

玄武 (Xuán Wǔ) 天冲 (Tiān Chōng) 杜门 (Dù Mén) Xun 4　Bing Yi	九地 (Jiǔ Dì) 天辅 (Tiān Fǔ) 景门 (Jǐng Mén) Li 9　Yi Ren	九天 (Jiǔ Tiān) 天英 (Tiān Yīng) 死门 (Sǐ Mén) Kun 2　Ren Ding/Wu
白虎 (Bái Hǔ) 天任 (Tiān Rèn) 伤门 (Shāng Mén) Zhen 3　Xin Bing	Yang (阳) Dun# 5 Hour: **GengWu** ©Calvin Yap	禽芮 (Qín Ruì) 惊门 (Jīng Mén) Dui 7　Ding/Wu Geng
六合 (Liù Hé) 天蓬 (Tiān Péng) 生门 (Shēng Mén) Gen 8　Gui Xin	太阴 (Tài Yīn) 天心 (Tiān Xīn) 休门 (Xiū Mén) Kan 1　Ji Gui	腾蛇 (Téng Shé) 天柱 (Tiān Zhù) 开门 (Kāi Mén) Qian 6　Geng Ji

Yang (阳) Dun# 5 Hour: XinWei ；直符(ZhíFú): 天禽(TiānQín)
直使(ZhíShǐ): 死门(SǐMén)；旬首(XúnShǒu): JiaZiWu

太阴 (Tài Yīn) 天心 (Tiān Xīn) 惊门 (Jīng Mén) Xun 4　Ji Yi	六合 (Liù Hé) 天蓬 (Tiān Péng) 开门 (Kāi Mén) Li 9　Gui Ren	白虎 (Bái Hǔ) 天任 (Tiān Rèn) 休门 (Xiū Mén) Kun 2　Xin Ding/Wu
腾蛇 (Téng Shé) 天柱 (Tiān Zhù) 死门 (Sǐ Mén) Zhen 3　Geng Bing	Yang (阳) Dun# 5 Hour: **XinWei** **Fan Yin** ©Calvin Yap	玄武 (Xuán Wǔ) 天冲 (Tiān Chōng) 生门 (Shēng Mén) Dui 7　Bing Geng
值符 (Zhí Fú) 禽芮 (Qín Ruì) 景门 (Jǐng Mén) Gen 8　Ding/Wu Xin	九天 (Jiǔ Tiān) 天英 (Tiān Yīng) 杜门 (Dù Mén) Kan 1　Ren Gui	九地 (Jiǔ Dì) 天辅 (Tiān Fǔ) 伤门 (Shāng Mén) Qian 6　Yi Ji

Yang (阳) Dun# 5 Hour: RenShen ；直符(ZhíFú): 天禽(TiānQín)
直使(ZhíShǐ): 死门(SǐMén)；旬首(XúnShǒu): JiaZiWu

九天 (Jiǔ Tiān) 天英 (Tiān Yīng) 死门 (Sǐ Mén) Xun 4　Ren Yi	值符 (Zhí Fú) 禽芮 (Qín Ruì) 惊门 (Jīng Mén) Li 9　Ding/Wu Ren	腾蛇 (Téng Shé) 天柱 (Tiān Zhù) 开门 (Kāi Mén) Kun 2　Geng Ding/Wu
九地 (Jiǔ Dì) 天辅 (Tiān Fǔ) 景门 (Jǐng Mén) Zhen 3　Yi Bing	Yang (阳) Dun# 5 Hour: **RenShen** ©Calvin Yap	太阴 (Tài Yīn) 天心 (Tiān Xīn) 休门 (Xiū Mén) Dui 7　Ji Geng
玄武 (Xuán Wǔ) 天冲 (Tiān Chōng) 杜门 (Dù Mén) Gen 8　Bing Xin	白虎 (Bái Hǔ) 天任 (Tiān Rèn) 伤门 (Shāng Mén) Kan 1　Xin Gui	六合 (Liù Hé) 天蓬 (Tiān Péng) 生门 (Shēng Mén) Qian 6　Gui Ji

Yang (阳) Dun# 5 Hour: GuiYou ；直符(ZhíFú): 天禽(TiānQín)
直使(ZhíShǐ): 死门(SǐMén)；旬首(XúnShǒu): JiaZiWu

六合 (Liù Hé) 天蓬 (Tiān Péng) 杜门 (Dù Mén) Xun 4　Gui Yi	白虎 (Bái Hǔ) 天任 (Tiān Rèn) 景门 (Jǐng Mén) Li 9　Xin Ren	玄武 (Xuán Wǔ) 天冲 (Tiān Chōng) 死门 (Sǐ Mén) Kun 2　Bing Ding/Wu
太阴 (Tài Yīn) 天心 (Tiān Xīn) 伤门 (Shāng Mén) Zhen 3　Ji Bing	Yang (阳) Dun# 5 Hour: **GuiYou** ©Calvin Yap	九地 (Jiǔ Dì) 天辅 (Tiān Fǔ) 惊门 (Jīng Mén) Dui 7　Yi Geng
腾蛇 (Téng Shé) 天柱 (Tiān Zhù) 生门 (Shēng Mén) Gen 8　Geng Xin	值符 (Zhí Fú) 禽芮 (Qín Ruì) 休门 (Xiū Mén) Kan 1　Ding/Wu Gui	九天 (Jiǔ Tiān) 天英 (Tiān Yīng) 开门 (Kāi Mén) Qian 6　Ren Ji

Chart: +5JiaXu (Yang Dun #5 JiaXu Xun)
JiaXu, YiHai, BingZi, DingChou, WuYin, JiMao, GengChen, XinSi, RenWu, GuiWei

Yang (阳) Dun# 5 Hour: JiaXu ；直符(ZhíFú): 天心(TiānXīn)
直使(ZhíShǐ): 开门(KāiMén)；旬首(XúnShǒu): JiaXuJi

白虎 (Bái Hǔ) 天辅 (Tiān Fǔ) 杜门 (Dù Mén) Xun 4　Yi Yi	玄武 (Xuán Wǔ) 天英 (Tiān Yīng) 景门 (Jǐng Mén) Li 9　Ren Ren	九地 (Jiǔ Dì) 禽芮 (Qín Ruì) 死门 (Sǐ Mén) Kun 2　Ding/Wu Ding/Wu
六合 (Liù Hé) 天冲 (Tiān Chōng) 伤门 (Shāng Mén) Zhen 3　Bing Bing	Yang (阳) Dun# 5 Hour: **JiaXu** **Fu Yin** ©Calvin Yap	九天 (Jiǔ Tiān) 天柱 (Tiān Zhù) 惊门 (Jīng Mén) Dui 7　Geng Geng
太阴 (Tài Yīn) 天任 (Tiān Rèn) 生门 (Shēng Mén) Gen 8　Xin Xin	腾蛇 (Téng Shé) 天蓬 (Tiān Péng) 休门 (Xiū Mén) Kan 1　Gui Gui	值符 (Zhí Fú) 天心 (Tiān Xīn) 开门 (Kāi Mén) Qian 6　Ji Ji

Yang (阳) Dun# 5 Hour: YiHai ；直符(ZhíFú): 天心(TiānXīn)
直使(ZhíShǐ): 开门(KāiMén)；旬首(XúnShǒu): JiaXuJi

值符 (Zhí Fú) 天心 (Tiān Xīn) 景门 (Jǐng Mén) Xun 4　Ji Yi	腾蛇 (Téng Shé) 天蓬 (Tiān Péng) 死门 (Sǐ Mén) Li 9　Gui Ren	太阴 (Tài Yīn) 天任 (Tiān Rèn) 惊门 (Jīng Mén) Kun 2　Xin Ding/Wu
九天 (Jiǔ Tiān) 天柱 (Tiān Zhù) 杜门 (Dù Mén) Zhen 3　Geng Bing	Yang (阳) Dun# 5 Hour: **YiHai** **Fan Yin** ©Calvin Yap	六合 (Liù Hé) 天冲 (Tiān Chōng) 开门 (Kāi Mén) Dui 7　Bing Geng
九地 (Jiǔ Dì) 禽芮 (Qín Ruì) 伤门 (Shāng Mén) Gen 8　Ding/Wu Xin	玄武 (Xuán Wǔ) 天英 (Tiān Yīng) 生门 (Shēng Mén) Kan 1　Ren Gui	白虎 (Bái Hǔ) 天辅 (Tiān Fǔ) 休门 (Xiū Mén) Qian 6　Yi Ji

Yang (阳) Dun# 5 Hour: BingZi ；直符(ZhíFú): 天心(TiānXīn)
直使(ZhíShǐ): 开门(KāiMén) ；旬首(XúnShǒu): JiaXuJi

螣蛇 (Téng Shé) 天蓬 (Tiān Péng) 生门 (Shēng Mén) Xun 4　Gui Yi	太阴 (Tài Yīn) 天任 (Tiān Rèn) 伤门 (Shāng Mén) Li 9　Xin Ren	六合 (Liù Hé) 天冲 (Tiān Chōng) 杜门 (Dù Mén) Kun 2　Bing Ding/Wu
值符 (Zhí Fú) 天心 (Tiān Xīn) 休门 (Xiū Mén) Zhen 3　Ji Bing	Yang (阳) Dun# 5 Hour: **BingZi** ©Calvin Yap	白虎 (Bái Hǔ) 天辅 (Tiān Fǔ) 景门 (Jǐng Mén) Dui 7　Yi Geng
九天 (Jiǔ Tiān) 天柱 (Tiān Zhù) 开门 (Kāi Mén) Gen 8　Geng Xin	九地 (Jiǔ Dì) 禽芮 (Qín Ruì) 惊门 (Jīng Mén) Kan 1　Ding/Wu Gui	玄武 (Xuán Wǔ) 天英 (Tiān Yīng) 死门 (Sǐ Mén) Qian 6　Ren Ji

Yang (阳) Dun# 5 Hour: DingChou ；直符(ZhíFú): 天心(TiānXīn)
直使(ZhíShǐ): 开门(KāiMén) ；旬首(XúnShǒu): JiaXuJi

九地 (Jiǔ Dì) 禽芮 (Qín Ruì) 惊门 (Jīng Mén) Xun 4　Ding/Wu Yi	九天 (Jiǔ Tiān) 天柱 (Tiān Zhù) 开门 (Kāi Mén) Li 9　Geng Ren	值符 (Zhí Fú) 天心 (Tiān Xīn) 休门 (Xiū Mén) Kun 2　Ji Ding/Wu
玄武 (Xuán Wǔ) 天英 (Tiān Yīng) 死门 (Sǐ Mén) Zhen 3　Ren Bing	Yang (阳) Dun# 5 Hour: **DingChou** ©Calvin Yap	螣蛇 (Téng Shé) 天蓬 (Tiān Péng) 生门 (Shēng Mén) Dui 7　Gui Geng
白虎 (Bái Hǔ) 天辅 (Tiān Fǔ) 景门 (Jǐng Mén) Gen 8　Yi Xin	六合 (Liù Hé) 天冲 (Tiān Chōng) 杜门 (Dù Mén) Kan 1　Bing Gui	太阴 (Tài Yīn) 天任 (Tiān Rèn) 伤门 (Shāng Mén) Qian 6　Xin Ji

Yang (阳) Dun# 5 Hour: WuYin ；直符(ZhíFú): 天心(TiānXīn)
直使(ZhíShǐ): 开门(KāiMén) ；旬首(XúnShǒu): JiaXuJi

九地 (Jiǔ Dì) 禽芮 (Qín Ruì) 伤门 (Shāng Mén) Xun 4　Ding/Wu Yi	九天 (Jiǔ Tiān) 天柱 (Tiān Zhù) 杜门 (Dù Mén) Li 9　Geng Ren	值符 (Zhí Fú) 天心 (Tiān Xīn) 景门 (Jǐng Mén) Kun 2　Ji Ding/Wu
玄武 (Xuán Wǔ) 天英 (Tiān Yīng) 生门 (Shēng Mén) Zhen 3　Ren Bing	Yang (阳) Dun# 5 Hour: **WuYin** ©Calvin Yap	螣蛇 (Téng Shé) 天蓬 (Tiān Péng) 死门 (Sǐ Mén) Dui 7　Gui Geng
白虎 (Bái Hǔ) 天辅 (Tiān Fǔ) 休门 (Xiū Mén) Gen 8　Yi Xin	六合 (Liù Hé) 天冲 (Tiān Chōng) 开门 (Kāi Mén) Kan 1　Bing Gui	太阴 (Tài Yīn) 天任 (Tiān Rèn) 惊门 (Jīng Mén) Qian 6　Xin Ji

Yang (阳) Dun# 5 Hour: JiMao ；直符(ZhíFú): 天心(TiānXīn)
直使(ZhíShǐ): 开门(KāiMén) ；旬首(XúnShǒu): JiaXuJi

白虎 (Bái Hǔ) 天辅 (Tiān Fǔ) 死门 (Sǐ Mén) Xun 4　Yi Yi	玄武 (Xuán Wǔ) 天英 (Tiān Yīng) 惊门 (Jīng Mén) Li 9　Ren Ren	九地 (Jiǔ Dì) 禽芮 (Qín Ruì) 开门 (Kāi Mén) Kun 2　Ding/Wu Ding/Wu
六合 (Liù Hé) 天冲 (Tiān Chōng) 景门 (Jǐng Mén) Zhen 3　Bing Bing	Yang (阳) Dun# 5 Hour: **JiMao** **Fu Yin** ©Calvin Yap	九天 (Jiǔ Tiān) 天柱 (Tiān Zhù) 休门 (Xiū Mén) Dui 7　Geng Geng
太阴 (Tài Yīn) 天任 (Tiān Rèn) 杜门 (Dù Mén) Gen 8　Xin Xin	螣蛇 (Téng Shé) 天蓬 (Tiān Péng) 伤门 (Shāng Mén) Kan 1　Gui Gui	值符 (Zhí Fú) 天心 (Tiān Xīn) 生门 (Shēng Mén) Qian 6　Ji Ji

Yang (阳) Dun# 5 Hour: GengChen ；直符(ZhíFú): 天心(TiānXīn)
直使(ZhíShǐ): 开门(KāiMén) ；旬首(XúnShǒu): JiaXuJi

玄武 (Xuán Wǔ) 天英 (Tiān Yīng) 休门 (Xiū Mén) Xun 4　Ren Yi	九地 (Jiǔ Dì) 禽芮 (Qín Ruì) 生门 (Shēng Mén) Li 9　Ding/Wu Ren	九天 (Jiǔ Tiān) 天柱 (Tiān Zhù) 伤门 (Shāng Mén) Kun 2　Geng Ding/Wu
白虎 (Bái Hǔ) 天辅 (Tiān Fǔ) 开门 (Kāi Mén) Zhen 3　Yi Bing	Yang (阳) Dun# 5 Hour: **GengChen** ©Calvin Yap	值符 (Zhí Fú) 天心 (Tiān Xīn) 杜门 (Dù Mén) Dui 7　Ji Geng
六合 (Liù Hé) 天冲 (Tiān Chōng) 惊门 (Jīng Mén) Gen 8　Bing Xin	太阴 (Tài Yīn) 天任 (Tiān Rèn) 死门 (Sǐ Mén) Kan 1　Xin Gui	螣蛇 (Téng Shé) 天蓬 (Tiān Péng) 景门 (Jǐng Mén) Qian 6　Gui Ji

Yang (阳) Dun# 5 Hour: XinSi ；直符(ZhíFú): 天心(TiānXīn)
直使(ZhíShǐ): 开门(KāiMén) ；旬首(XúnShǒu): JiaXuJi

太阴 (Tài Yīn) 天任 (Tiān Rèn) 开门 (Kāi Mén) Xun 4　Xin Yi	六合 (Liù Hé) 天冲 (Tiān Chōng) 休门 (Xiū Mén) Li 9　Bing Ren	白虎 (Bái Hǔ) 天辅 (Tiān Fǔ) 生门 (Shēng Mén) Kun 2　Yi Ding/Wu
螣蛇 (Téng Shé) 天蓬 (Tiān Péng) 惊门 (Jīng Mén) Zhen 3　Gui Bing	Yang (阳) Dun# 5 Hour: **XinSi** ©Calvin Yap	玄武 (Xuán Wǔ) 天英 (Tiān Yīng) 伤门 (Shāng Mén) Dui 7　Ren Geng
值符 (Zhí Fú) 天心 (Tiān Xīn) 死门 (Sǐ Mén) Gen 8　Ji Xin	九天 (Jiǔ Tiān) 天柱 (Tiān Zhù) 景门 (Jǐng Mén) Kan 1　Geng Gui	九地 (Jiǔ Dì) 禽芮 (Qín Ruì) 杜门 (Dù Mén) Qian 6　Ding/Wu Ji

Yang (阳) Dun# 5 Hour: RenWu ; 直符(ZhíFú): 天心(TiānXīn)
直使(ZhíShǐ): 开门(KāiMén) ; 旬首(XúnShǒu): JiaXuJi

九天 (Jiǔ Tiān) 天柱 (Tiān Zhù) 死门 (Sǐ Mén) Xun 4　Geng Yi	值符 (Zhí Fú) 天心 (Tiān Xīn) 惊门 (Jīng Mén) Li 9　Ji Ren	腾蛇 (Téng Shé) 天蓬 (Tiān Péng) 开门 (Kāi Mén) Kun 2　Gui Ding/Wu
九地 (Jiǔ Dì) 禽芮 (Qín Ruì) 景门 (Jǐng Mén) Zhen 3　Ding/Wu Bing	Yang (阳) Dun# 5 Hour: **RenWu** ©Calvin Yap	太阴 (Tài Yīn) 天任 (Tiān Rèn) 休门 (Xiū Mén) Dui 7　Xin
玄武 (Xuán Wǔ) 天英 (Tiān Yīng) 杜门 (Dù Mén) Gen 8　Ren Xin	白虎 (Bái Hǔ) 天辅 (Tiān Fǔ) 伤门 (Shāng Mén) Kan 1　Yi Gui	六合 (Liù Hé) 天冲 (Tiān Chōng) 生门 (Shēng Mén) Qian 6　Bing Ji

Yang (阳) Dun# 5 Hour: GuiWei ; 直符(ZhíFú): 天心(TiānXīn)
直使(ZhíShǐ): 开门(KāiMén) ; 旬首(XúnShǒu): JiaXuJi

六合 (Liù Hé) 天冲 (Tiān Chōng) 杜门 (Dù Mén) Xun 4　Bing Yi	白虎 (Bái Hǔ) 天辅 (Tiān Fǔ) 景门 (Jǐng Mén) Li 9　Yi Ren	玄武 (Xuán Wǔ) 天英 (Tiān Yīng) 死门 (Sǐ Mén) Kun 2　Ren Ding/Wu
太阴 (Tài Yīn) 天任 (Tiān Rèn) 伤门 (Shāng Mén) Zhen 3　Xin Bing	Yang (阳) Dun# 5 Hour: **GuiWei** ©Calvin Yap	九地 (Jiǔ Dì) 禽芮 (Qín Ruì) 惊门 (Jīng Mén) Dui 7　Ding/Wu Geng
腾蛇 (Téng Shé) 天蓬 (Tiān Péng) 生门 (Shēng Mén) Gen 8　Gui Xin	值符 (Zhí Fú) 天心 (Tiān Xīn) 休门 (Xiū Mén) Kan 1　Ji Gui	九天 (Jiǔ Tiān) 天柱 (Tiān Zhù) 开门 (Kāi Mén) Qian 6　Geng Ji

Chart: +5JiaShen (Yang Dun #5 JiaShen Xun)
JiaShen, YiYou, BingXu, DingHai, WuZi, JiChou, GengYin, XinMao, RenChen, GuiSi

Yang (阳) Dun# 5 Hour: JiaShen ; 直符(ZhíFú): 天柱(TiānZhù)
直使(ZhíShǐ): 惊门(JīngMén) ; 旬首(XúnShǒu): JiaShenGeng

玄武 (Xuán Wǔ) 天辅 (Tiān Fǔ) 杜门 (Dù Mén) Xun 4　Yi Yi	九地 (Jiǔ Dì) 天英 (Tiān Yīng) 景门 (Jǐng Mén) Li 9　Ren Ren	九天 (Jiǔ Tiān) 禽芮 (Qín Ruì) 死门 (Sǐ Mén) Kun 2　Ding/Wu Ding/Wu
白虎 (Bái Hǔ) 天冲 (Tiān Chōng) 伤门 (Shāng Mén) Zhen 3　Bing Bing	Yang (阳) Dun# 5 Hour: **JiaShen** **Fu Yin** ©Calvin Yap	值符 (Zhí Fú) 天柱 (Tiān Zhù) 惊门 (Jīng Mén) Dui 7　Geng Geng
六合 (Liù Hé) 天任 (Tiān Rèn) 生门 (Shēng Mén) Gen 8　Xin Xin	太阴 (Tài Yīn) 天蓬 (Tiān Péng) 休门 (Xiū Mén) Kan 1　Gui Gui	腾蛇 (Téng Shé) 天心 (Tiān Xīn) 开门 (Kāi Mén) Qian 6　Ji Ji

Yang (阳) Dun# 5 Hour: YiYou ; 直符(ZhíFú): 天柱(TiānZhù)
直使(ZhíShǐ): 惊门(JīngMén) ; 旬首(XúnShǒu): JiaShenGeng

值符 (Zhí Fú) 天柱 (Tiān Zhù) 休门 (Xiū Mén) Xun 4　Geng Yi	腾蛇 (Téng Shé) 天心 (Tiān Xīn) 生门 (Shēng Mén) Li 9　Ji Ren	太阴 (Tài Yīn) 天蓬 (Tiān Péng) 伤门 (Shāng Mén) Kun 2　Gui Ding/Wu
九天 (Jiǔ Tiān) 禽芮 (Qín Ruì) 开门 (Kāi Mén) Zhen 3　Ding/Wu Bing	Yang (阳) Dun# 5 Hour: **YiYou** ©Calvin Yap	六合 (Liù Hé) 天任 (Tiān Rèn) 杜门 (Dù Mén) Dui 7　Xin Geng
九地 (Jiǔ Dì) 天英 (Tiān Yīng) 惊门 (Jīng Mén) Gen 8　Ren Xin	玄武 (Xuán Wǔ) 天辅 (Tiān Fǔ) 死门 (Sǐ Mén) Kan 1　Yi Gui	白虎 (Bái Hǔ) 天冲 (Tiān Chōng) 景门 (Jǐng Mén) Qian 6　Bing Ji

Yang (阳) Dun# 5 Hour: BingXu ; 直符(ZhíFú): 天柱(TiānZhù)
直使(ZhíShǐ): 惊门(JīngMén) ; 旬首(XúnShǒu): JiaShenGeng

腾蛇 (Téng Shé) 天心 (Tiān Xīn) 死门 (Sǐ Mén) Xun 4　Ji Yi	太阴 (Tài Yīn) 天蓬 (Tiān Péng) 惊门 (Jīng Mén) Li 9　Gui Ren	六合 (Liù Hé) 天任 (Tiān Rèn) 开门 (Kāi Mén) Kun 2　Xin Ding/Wu
值符 (Zhí Fú) 天柱 (Tiān Zhù) 景门 (Jǐng Mén) Zhen 3　Geng Bing	Yang (阳) Dun# 5 Hour: **BingXu** **Fan Yin** ©Calvin Yap	白虎 (Bái Hǔ) 天冲 (Tiān Chōng) 休门 (Xiū Mén) Dui 7　Bing Geng
九天 (Jiǔ Tiān) 禽芮 (Qín Ruì) 杜门 (Dù Mén) Gen 8　Ding/Wu Xin	九地 (Jiǔ Dì) 天英 (Tiān Yīng) 伤门 (Shāng Mén) Kan 1　Ren Gui	玄武 (Xuán Wǔ) 天辅 (Tiān Fǔ) 生门 (Shēng Mén) Qian 6　Yi Ji

Yang (阳) Dun# 5 Hour: DingHai ; 直符(ZhíFú): 天柱(TiānZhù)
直使(ZhíShǐ): 惊门(JīngMén) ; 旬首(XúnShǒu): JiaShenGeng

九地 (Jiǔ Dì) 天英 (Tiān Yīng) 生门 (Shēng Mén) Xun 4　Ren Yi	九天 (Jiǔ Tiān) 禽芮 (Qín Ruì) 伤门 (Shāng Mén) Li 9　Ding/Wu Ren	值符 (Zhí Fú) 天柱 (Tiān Zhù) 杜门 (Dù Mén) Kun 2　Geng Ding/Wu
玄武 (Xuán Wǔ) 天辅 (Tiān Fǔ) 休门 (Xiū Mén) Zhen 3　Yi Bing	Yang (阳) Dun# 5 Hour: **DingHai** ©Calvin Yap	腾蛇 (Téng Shé) 天心 (Tiān Xīn) 景门 (Jǐng Mén) Dui 7　Ji Geng
白虎 (Bái Hǔ) 天冲 (Tiān Chōng) 开门 (Kāi Mén) Gen 8　Bing Xin	六合 (Liù Hé) 天任 (Tiān Rèn) 惊门 (Jīng Mén) Kan 1　Xin Gui	太阴 (Tài Yīn) 天蓬 (Tiān Péng) 死门 (Sǐ Mén) Qian 6　Gui Ji

Yang (阳) Dun# 5 Hour: WuZi ; 直符(ZhíFú): 天柱(TiānZhù)
直使(ZhíShǐ): 惊门(JīngMén) ; 旬首(XúnShǒu): JiaShenGeng

九地 (Jiǔ Dì) 天英 (Tiān Yīng) 景门 (Jǐng Mén) Xun 4　Ren Yi	九天 (Jiǔ Tiān) 禽芮 (Qín Ruì) 死门 (Sǐ Mén) Li 9　Ding/Wu Ren	值符 (Zhí Fú) 天柱 (Tiān Zhù) 惊门 (Jīng Mén) Kun 2　Geng Ding/Wu
玄武 (Xuán Wǔ) 天辅 (Tiān Fǔ) 杜门 (Dù Mén) Zhen 3　Yi Bing	Yang (阳) Dun# 5 Hour: **WuZi** ©Calvin Yap	螣蛇 (Téng Shé) 天心 (Tiān Xīn) 开门 (Kāi Mén) Dui 7　Ji Geng
白虎 (Bái Hǔ) 天冲 (Tiān Chōng) 伤门 (Shāng Mén) Gen 8　Bing Xin	六合 (Liù Hé) 天任 (Tiān Rèn) 生门 (Shēng Mén) Kan 1　Xin Gui	太阴 (Tài Yīn) 天蓬 (Tiān Péng) 休门 (Xiū Mén) Qian 6　Gui Ji

Yang (阳) Dun# 5 Hour: JiChou ; 直符(ZhíFú): 天柱(TiānZhù)
直使(ZhíShǐ): 惊门(JīngMén) ; 旬首(XúnShǒu): JiaShenGeng

白虎 (Bái Hǔ) 天冲 (Tiān Chōng) 开门 (Kāi Mén) Xun 4　Bing Yi	玄武 (Xuán Wǔ) 天辅 (Tiān Fǔ) 休门 (Xiū Mén) Li 9　Yi Ren	九地 (Jiǔ Dì) 天英 (Tiān Yīng) 生门 (Shēng Mén) Kun 2　Ren Ding/Wu
六合 (Liù Hé) 天任 (Tiān Rèn) 惊门 (Jīng Mén) Zhen 3　Xin Bing	Yang (阳) Dun# 5 Hour: **JiChou** ©Calvin Yap	九天 (Jiǔ Tiān) 禽芮 (Qín Ruì) 伤门 (Shāng Mén) Dui 7　Ding/Wu Geng
太阴 (Tài Yīn) 天蓬 (Tiān Péng) 死门 (Sǐ Mén) Gen 8　Gui Xin	螣蛇 (Téng Shé) 天心 (Tiān Xīn) 景门 (Jǐng Mén) Kan 1　Ji Gui	值符 (Zhí Fú) 天柱 (Tiān Zhù) 杜门 (Dù Mén) Qian 6　Geng Ji

Yang (阳) Dun# 5 Hour: GengYin ; 直符(ZhíFú): 天柱(TiānZhù)
直使(ZhíShǐ): 惊门(JīngMén) ; 旬首(XúnShǒu): JiaShenGeng

玄武 (Xuán Wǔ) 天辅 (Tiān Fǔ) 惊门 (Jīng Mén) Xun 4　Yi Yi	九地 (Jiǔ Dì) 天英 (Tiān Yīng) 开门 (Kāi Mén) Li 9　Ren Ren	九天 (Jiǔ Tiān) 禽芮 (Qín Ruì) 休门 (Xiū Mén) Kun 2　Ding/Wu Ding/Wu
白虎 (Bái Hǔ) 天冲 (Tiān Chōng) 死门 (Sǐ Mén) Zhen 3　Bing Bing	Yang (阳) Dun# 5 Hour: **GengYin** **Fu Yin** ©Calvin Yap	值符 (Zhí Fú) 天柱 (Tiān Zhù) 生门 (Shēng Mén) Dui 7　Geng Geng
六合 (Liù Hé) 天任 (Tiān Rèn) 景门 (Jǐng Mén) Gen 8　Xin Xin	太阴 (Tài Yīn) 天蓬 (Tiān Péng) 杜门 (Dù Mén) Kan 1　Gui Gui	螣蛇 (Téng Shé) 天心 (Tiān Xīn) 伤门 (Shāng Mén) Qian 6　Ji Ji

Yang (阳) Dun# 5 Hour: XinMao ; 直符(ZhíFú): 天柱(TiānZhù)
直使(ZhíShǐ): 惊门(JīngMén) ; 旬首(XúnShǒu): JiaShenGeng

太阴 (Tài Yīn) 天蓬 (Tiān Péng) 景门 (Jǐng Mén) Xun 4　Gui Yi	六合 (Liù Hé) 天任 (Tiān Rèn) 死门 (Sǐ Mén) Li 9　Xin Ren	白虎 (Bái Hǔ) 天冲 (Tiān Chōng) 惊门 (Jīng Mén) Kun 2　Bing Ding/Wu
螣蛇 (Téng Shé) 天心 (Tiān Xīn) 杜门 (Dù Mén) Zhen 3　Ji Bing	Yang (阳) Dun# 5 Hour: **XinMao** ©Calvin Yap	玄武 (Xuán Wǔ) 天辅 (Tiān Fǔ) 开门 (Kāi Mén) Dui 7　Yi Geng
值符 (Zhí Fú) 天柱 (Tiān Zhù) 伤门 (Shāng Mén) Gen 8　Geng Xin	九天 (Jiǔ Tiān) 禽芮 (Qín Ruì) 生门 (Shēng Mén) Kan 1　Ding/Wu Gui	九地 (Jiǔ Dì) 天英 (Tiān Yīng) 休门 (Xiū Mén) Qian 6　Ren Ji

Yang (阳) Dun# 5 Hour: RenChen ; 直符(ZhíFú): 天柱(TiānZhù)
直使(ZhíShǐ): 惊门(JīngMén) ; 旬首(XúnShǒu): JiaShenGeng

九天 (Jiǔ Tiān) 禽芮 (Qín Ruì) 伤门 (Shāng Mén) Xun 4　Ding/Wu Yi	值符 (Zhí Fú) 天柱 (Tiān Zhù) 杜门 (Dù Mén) Li 9　Geng Ren	螣蛇 (Téng Shé) 天心 (Tiān Xīn) 景门 (Jǐng Mén) Kun 2　Ji Ding/Wu
九地 (Jiǔ Dì) 天英 (Tiān Yīng) 生门 (Shēng Mén) Zhen 3　Ren Bing	Yang (阳) Dun# 5 Hour: **RenChen** ©Calvin Yap	太阴 (Tài Yīn) 天蓬 (Tiān Péng) 死门 (Sǐ Mén) Dui 7　Gui Geng
玄武 (Xuán Wǔ) 天辅 (Tiān Fǔ) 休门 (Xiū Mén) Gen 8　Yi Xin	白虎 (Bái Hǔ) 天冲 (Tiān Chōng) 开门 (Kāi Mén) Kan 1　Bing Gui	六合 (Liù Hé) 天任 (Tiān Rèn) 惊门 (Jīng Mén) Qian 6　Xin Ji

Yang (阳) Dun# 5 Hour: GuiSi ; 直符(ZhíFú): 天柱(TiānZhù)
直使(ZhíShǐ): 惊门(JīngMén) ; 旬首(XúnShǒu): JiaShenGeng

六合 (Liù Hé) 天任 (Tiān Rèn) 杜门 (Dù Mén) Xun 4　Xin Yi	白虎 (Bái Hǔ) 天冲 (Tiān Chōng) 景门 (Jǐng Mén) Li 9　Bing Ren	玄武 (Xuán Wǔ) 天辅 (Tiān Fǔ) 死门 (Sǐ Mén) Kun 2　Yi Ding/Wu
太阴 (Tài Yīn) 天蓬 (Tiān Péng) 伤门 (Shāng Mén) Zhen 3　Gui Bing	Yang (阳) Dun# 5 Hour: **GuiSi** ©Calvin Yap	九地 (Jiǔ Dì) 天英 (Tiān Yīng) 惊门 (Jīng Mén) Dui 7　Ren Geng
螣蛇 (Téng Shé) 天心 (Tiān Xīn) 生门 (Shēng Mén) Gen 8　Ji Xin	值符 (Zhí Fú) 天柱 (Tiān Zhù) 休门 (Xiū Mén) Kan 1　Geng Gui	九天 (Jiǔ Tiān) 禽芮 (Qín Ruì) 开门 (Kāi Mén) Qian 6　Ding/Wu Ji

Chart: +5JiaWu (Yang Dun #5 JiaWu Xun)
JiaWu, YiWei, BingShen, DingYou, WuXu, JiHai, GengZi, XinChou, RenYin, GuiMao

Yang (阳) Dun# 5 Hour: JiaWu ; 直符(ZhíFú): 天任(TiānRèn)
直使(ZhíShǐ): 生门(ShēngMén) ; 句首(XúnShǒu): JiaWu/Xin

太阴 (Tài Yīn) 天辅 (Tiān Fǔ) 杜门 (Dù Mén) Xun 4 — Yi — Yi	六合 (Liù Hé) 天英 (Tiān Yīng) 景门 (Jǐng Mén) Li 9 — Ren — Ren	白虎 (Bái Hǔ) 禽芮 (Qín Ruì) 死门 (Sǐ Mén) Kun 2 — Ding/Wu — Ding/Wu
螣蛇 (Téng Shé) 天冲 (Tiān Chōng) 伤门 (Shāng Mén) Zhen 3 — Bing — Bing	Yang (阳) Dun# 5 Hour: **JiaWu** **Fu Yin** ©Calvin Yap	玄武 (Xuán Wǔ) 天柱 (Tiān Zhù) 惊门 (Jīng Mén) Dui 7 — Geng — Geng
值符 (Zhí Fú) 天任 (Tiān Rèn) 生门 (Shēng Mén) Gen 8 — Xin — Xin	九天 (Jiǔ Tiān) 天蓬 (Tiān Péng) 休门 (Xiū Mén) Kan 1 — Gui — Gui	九地 (Jiǔ Dì) 天心 (Tiān Xīn) 开门 (Kāi Mén) Qian 6 — Ji — Ji

Yang (阳) Dun# 5 Hour: YiWei ; 直符(ZhíFú): 天任(TiānRèn)
直使(ZhíShǐ): 生门(ShēngMén) ; 句首(XúnShǒu): JiaWu/Xin

值符 (Zhí Fú) 天任 (Tiān Rèn) 休门 (Xiū Mén) Xun 4 — Xin — Yi	螣蛇 (Téng Shé) 天冲 (Tiān Chōng) 生门 (Shēng Mén) Li 9 — Bing — Ren	太阴 (Tài Yīn) 天辅 (Tiān Fǔ) 伤门 (Shāng Mén) Kun 2 — Yi — Ding/Wu
九天 (Jiǔ Tiān) 天蓬 (Tiān Péng) 开门 (Kāi Mén) Zhen 3 — Gui — Bing	Yang (阳) Dun# 5 Hour: **YiWei** ©Calvin Yap	六合 (Liù Hé) 天英 (Tiān Yīng) 杜门 (Dù Mén) Dui 7 — Ren — Geng
九地 (Jiǔ Dì) 天心 (Tiān Xīn) 惊门 (Jīng Mén) Gen 8 — Xin — Xin	玄武 (Xuán Wǔ) 天柱 (Tiān Zhù) 死门 (Sǐ Mén) Kan 1 — Geng — Gui	白虎 (Bái Hǔ) 禽芮 (Qín Ruì) 景门 (Jǐng Mén) Qian 6 — Ding/Wu — Ji

Yang (阳) Dun# 5 Hour: BingShen ; 直符(ZhíFú): 天任(TiānRèn)
直使(ZhíShǐ): 生门(ShēngMén) ; 句首(XúnShǒu): JiaWu/Xin

螣蛇 (Téng Shé) 天冲 (Tiān Chōng) 景门 (Jǐng Mén) Xun 4 — Bing — Yi	太阴 (Tài Yīn) 天辅 (Tiān Fǔ) 死门 (Sǐ Mén) Li 9 — Yi — Ren	六合 (Liù Hé) 天英 (Tiān Yīng) 惊门 (Jīng Mén) Kun 2 — Ren — Ding/Wu
值符 (Zhí Fú) 天任 (Tiān Rèn) 杜门 (Dù Mén) Zhen 3 — Xin — Bing	Yang (阳) Dun# 5 Hour: **BingShen** ©Calvin Yap	白虎 (Bái Hǔ) 禽芮 (Qín Ruì) 开门 (Kāi Mén) Dui 7 — Ding/Wu — Geng
九天 (Jiǔ Tiān) 天蓬 (Tiān Péng) 伤门 (Shāng Mén) Gen 8 — Gui — Xin	九地 (Jiǔ Dì) 天心 (Tiān Xīn) 生门 (Shēng Mén) Kan 1 — Ji — Gui	玄武 (Xuán Wǔ) 天柱 (Tiān Zhù) 休门 (Xiū Mén) Qian 6 — Geng — Ji

Yang (阳) Dun# 5 Hour: DingYou ; 直符(ZhíFú): 天任(TiānRèn)
直使(ZhíShǐ): 生门(ShēngMén) ; 句首(XúnShǒu): JiaWu/Xin

九地 (Jiǔ Dì) 天心 (Tiān Xīn) 开门 (Kāi Mén) Xun 4 — Ji — Yi	九天 (Jiǔ Tiān) 天蓬 (Tiān Péng) 休门 (Xiū Mén) Li 9 — Gui — Ren	值符 (Zhí Fú) 天任 (Tiān Rèn) 生门 (Shēng Mén) Kun 2 — Xin — Ding/Wu
玄武 (Xuán Wǔ) 天柱 (Tiān Zhù) 惊门 (Jīng Mén) Zhen 3 — Geng — Bing	Yang (阳) Dun# 5 Hour: **DingYou** **Fan Yin** ©Calvin Yap	螣蛇 (Téng Shé) 天冲 (Tiān Chōng) 伤门 (Shāng Mén) Dui 7 — Bing — Geng
白虎 (Bái Hǔ) 禽芮 (Qín Ruì) 死门 (Sǐ Mén) Gen 8 — Ding/Wu — Xin	六合 (Liù Hé) 天英 (Tiān Yīng) 景门 (Jǐng Mén) Kan 1 — Ren — Gui	太阴 (Tài Yīn) 天辅 (Tiān Fǔ) 杜门 (Dù Mén) Qian 6 — Yi — Ji

Yang (阳) Dun# 5 Hour: WuXu ; 直符(ZhíFú): 天任(TiānRèn)
直使(ZhíShǐ): 生门(ShēngMén) ; 句首(XúnShǒu): JiaWu/Xin

九地 (Jiǔ Dì) 天心 (Tiān Xīn) 伤门 (Shāng Mén) Xun 4 — Ji — Yi	九天 (Jiǔ Tiān) 天蓬 (Tiān Péng) 杜门 (Dù Mén) Li 9 — Gui — Ren	值符 (Zhí Fú) 天任 (Tiān Rèn) 景门 (Jǐng Mén) Kun 2 — Xin — Ding/Wu
玄武 (Xuán Wǔ) 天柱 (Tiān Zhù) 生门 (Shēng Mén) Zhen 3 — Geng — Bing	Yang (阳) Dun# 5 Hour: **WuXu** **Fan Yin** ©Calvin Yap	螣蛇 (Téng Shé) 天冲 (Tiān Chōng) 死门 (Sǐ Mén) Dui 7 — Bing — Geng
白虎 (Bái Hǔ) 禽芮 (Qín Ruì) 休门 (Xiū Mén) Gen 8 — Ding/Wu — Xin	六合 (Liù Hé) 天英 (Tiān Yīng) 开门 (Kāi Mén) Kan 1 — Ren — Gui	太阴 (Tài Yīn) 天辅 (Tiān Fǔ) 惊门 (Jīng Mén) Qian 6 — Yi — Ji

Yang (阳) Dun# 5 Hour: JiHai ; 直符(ZhíFú): 天任(TiānRèn)
直使(ZhíShǐ): 生门(ShēngMén) ; 句首(XúnShǒu): JiaWu/Xin

白虎 (Bái Hǔ) 禽芮 (Qín Ruì) 生门 (Shēng Mén) Xun 4 — Ding/Wu — Yi	玄武 (Xuán Wǔ) 天柱 (Tiān Zhù) 伤门 (Shāng Mén) Li 9 — Geng — Ren	九地 (Jiǔ Dì) 天心 (Tiān Xīn) 杜门 (Dù Mén) Kun 2 — Ji — Ding/Wu
六合 (Liù Hé) 天英 (Tiān Yīng) 休门 (Xiū Mén) Zhen 3 — Ren — Bing	Yang (阳) Dun# 5 Hour: **JiHai** ©Calvin Yap	九天 (Jiǔ Tiān) 天蓬 (Tiān Péng) 景门 (Jǐng Mén) Dui 7 — Gui — Geng
太阴 (Tài Yīn) 天辅 (Tiān Fǔ) 开门 (Kāi Mén) Gen 8 — Yi — Xin	螣蛇 (Téng Shé) 天冲 (Tiān Chōng) 惊门 (Jīng Mén) Kan 1 — Bing — Gui	值符 (Zhí Fú) 天任 (Tiān Rèn) 死门 (Sǐ Mén) Qian 6 — Xin — Ji

Yang (阳) Dun# 5 Hour: **GengZi** ; 直符(ZhíFú): 天任(TiānRèn)
直使(ZhíShǐ): 生门(ShēngMén) ; 旬首(XúnShǒu): JiaWu/Xin

玄武 (Xuán Wǔ) 天柱 (Tiān Zhù) 开门 (Kāi Mén) Xun 4　Geng Yi	九地 (Jiǔ Dì) 天心 (Tiān Xīn) 休门 (Xiū Mén) Li 9　Ji Ren	九天 (Jiǔ Tiān) 天蓬 (Tiān Péng) 生门 (Shēng Mén) Kun 2　Gui Ding/Wu
白虎 (Bái Hǔ) 禽芮 (Qín Ruì) 惊门 (Jīng Mén) Zhen 3　Ding/Wu Bing	Yang (阳) Dun# 5 Hour: **GengZi** ©Calvin Yap	值符 (Zhí Fú) 天任 (Tiān Rèn) 伤门 (Shāng Mén) Dui 7　Xin Geng
六合 (Liù Hé) 天英 (Tiān Yīng) 死门 (Sǐ Mén) Gen 8　Ren Xin	太阴 (Tài Yīn) 天辅 (Tiān Fú) 景门 (Jǐng Mén) Kan 1　Yi Gui	腾蛇 (Téng Shé) 天冲 (Tiān Chōng) 杜门 (Dù Mén) Qian 6　Bing Ji

Yang (阳) Dun# 5 Hour: **XinChou** ; 直符(ZhíFú): 天任(TiānRèn)
直使(ZhíShǐ): 生门(ShēngMén) ; 旬首(XúnShǒu): JiaWu/Xin

太阴 (Tài Yīn) 天辅 (Tiān Fú) 死门 (Sǐ Mén) Xun 4　Yi Yi	六合 (Liù Hé) 天英 (Tiān Yīng) 惊门 (Jīng Mén) Li 9　Ren Ren	白虎 (Bái Hǔ) 禽芮 (Qín Ruì) 开门 (Kāi Mén) Kun 2　Ding/Wu Ding/Wu
腾蛇 (Téng Shé) 天冲 (Tiān Chōng) 景门 (Jǐng Mén) Zhen 3　Bing Bing	Yang (阳) Dun# 5 Hour: **XinChou** **Fu Yin** ©Calvin Yap	玄武 (Xuán Wǔ) 天柱 (Tiān Zhù) 休门 (Xiū Mén) Dui 7　Geng Geng
值符 (Zhí Fú) 天任 (Tiān Rèn) 杜门 (Dù Mén) Gen 8　Xin Xin	九天 (Jiǔ Tiān) 天蓬 (Tiān Péng) 伤门 (Shāng Mén) Kan 1　Gui Gui	九地 (Jiǔ Dì) 天心 (Tiān Xīn) 生门 (Shēng Mén) Qian 6　Ji Ji

Yang (阳) Dun# 5 Hour: **RenYin** ; 直符(ZhíFú): 天任(TiānRèn)
直使(ZhíShǐ): 生门(ShēngMén) ; 旬首(XúnShǒu): JiaWu/Xin

九天 (Jiǔ Tiān) 天蓬 (Tiān Péng) 惊门 (Jīng Mén) Xun 4　Gui Yi	值符 (Zhí Fú) 天任 (Tiān Rèn) 开门 (Kāi Mén) Li 9　Xin Ren	腾蛇 (Téng Shé) 天冲 (Tiān Chōng) 休门 (Xiū Mén) Kun 2　Bing Ding/Wu
九地 (Jiǔ Dì) 天心 (Tiān Xīn) 死门 (Sǐ Mén) Zhen 3　Ji Bing	Yang (阳) Dun# 5 Hour: **RenYin** ©Calvin Yap	太阴 (Tài Yīn) 天辅 (Tiān Fú) 生门 (Shēng Mén) Dui 7　Yi Geng
玄武 (Xuán Wǔ) 天柱 (Tiān Zhù) 景门 (Jǐng Mén) Gen 8　Geng Xin	白虎 (Bái Hǔ) 禽芮 (Qín Ruì) 杜门 (Dù Mén) Kan 1　Ding/Wu Gui	六合 (Liù Hé) 天英 (Tiān Yīng) 伤门 (Shāng Mén) Qian 6　Ren Ji

Yang (阳) Dun# 5 Hour: **GuiMao** ; 直符(ZhíFú): 天任(TiānRèn)
直使(ZhíShǐ): 生门(ShēngMén) ; 旬首(XúnShǒu): JiaWu/Xin

六合 (Liù Hé) 天英 (Tiān Yīng) 杜门 (Dù Mén) Xun 4　Ren Yi	白虎 (Bái Hǔ) 禽芮 (Qín Ruì) 景门 (Jǐng Mén) Li 9　Ding/Wu Ren	玄武 (Xuán Wǔ) 天柱 (Tiān Zhù) 死门 (Sǐ Mén) Kun 2　Geng Ding/Wu
太阴 (Tài Yīn) 天辅 (Tiān Fú) 伤门 (Shāng Mén) Zhen 3　Yi Bing	Yang (阳) Dun# 5 Hour: **GuiMao** ©Calvin Yap	九地 (Jiǔ Dì) 天心 (Tiān Xīn) 惊门 (Jīng Mén) Dui 7　Ji Geng
腾蛇 (Téng Shé) 天冲 (Tiān Chōng) 生门 (Shēng Mén) Gen 8　Bing Xin	值符 (Zhí Fú) 天任 (Tiān Rèn) 休门 (Xiū Mén) Kan 1　Xin Gui	九天 (Jiǔ Tiān) 天蓬 (Tiān Péng) 开门 (Kāi Mén) Qian 6　Gui Ji

Chart: +5JiaChen (Yang Dun #5 JiaChen Xun)
JiaChen, YiSi, BingWu, DingWei, WuShen, JiYou, GengXu, XinHai, RenZi, GuiChou

Yang (阳) Dun# 5 Hour: **JiaChen** ; 直符(ZhíFú): 天英(TiānYīng)
直使(ZhíShǐ): 景门(JǐngMén) ; 旬首(XúnShǒu): JiaChenRen

九天 (Jiǔ Tiān) 天辅 (Tiān Fú) 杜门 (Dù Mén) Xun 4　Yi Yi	值符 (Zhí Fú) 天英 (Tiān Yīng) 景门 (Jǐng Mén) Li 9　Ren Ren	腾蛇 (Téng Shé) 禽芮 (Qín Ruì) 死门 (Sǐ Mén) Kun 2　Ding/Wu Ding/Wu
九地 (Jiǔ Dì) 天冲 (Tiān Chōng) 伤门 (Shāng Mén) Zhen 3　Bing Bing	Yang (阳) Dun# 5 Hour: **JiaChen** **Fu Yin** ©Calvin Yap	太阴 (Tài Yīn) 天柱 (Tiān Zhù) 惊门 (Jīng Mén) Dui 7　Geng Geng
玄武 (Xuán Wǔ) 天任 (Tiān Rèn) 生门 (Shēng Mén) Gen 8　Xin Xin	白虎 (Bái Hǔ) 天蓬 (Tiān Péng) 休门 (Xiū Mén) Kan 1　Gui Gui	六合 (Liù Hé) 天心 (Tiān Xīn) 开门 (Kāi Mén) Qian 6　Ji Ji

Yang (阳) Dun# 5 Hour: **YiSi** ; 直符(ZhíFú): 天英(TiānYīng)
直使(ZhíShǐ): 景门(JǐngMén) ; 旬首(XúnShǒu): JiaChenRen

值符 (Zhí Fú) 天英 (Tiān Yīng) 开门 (Kāi Mén) Xun 4　Ren Yi	腾蛇 (Téng Shé) 禽芮 (Qín Ruì) 休门 (Xiū Mén) Li 9　Ding/Wu Ren	太阴 (Tài Yīn) 天柱 (Tiān Zhù) 生门 (Shēng Mén) Kun 2　Geng Ding/Wu
九天 (Jiǔ Tiān) 天辅 (Tiān Fú) 惊门 (Jīng Mén) Zhen 3　Yi Bing	Yang (阳) Dun# 5 Hour: **YiSi** ©Calvin Yap	六合 (Liù Hé) 天心 (Tiān Xīn) 伤门 (Shāng Mén) Dui 7　Ji Geng
九地 (Jiǔ Dì) 天冲 (Tiān Chōng) 死门 (Sǐ Mén) Gen 8　Bing Xin	玄武 (Xuán Wǔ) 天任 (Tiān Rèn) 景门 (Jǐng Mén) Kan 1　Xin Gui	白虎 (Bái Hǔ) 天蓬 (Tiān Péng) 杜门 (Dù Mén) Qian 6　Gui Ji

Yang (阳) Dun# 5 Hour: **BingWu**；直符(ZhíFú): 天英(TiānYīng)
直使(ZhíShǐ): 景门(JǐngMén)；旬首(XúnShǒu): JiaChenRen

螣蛇 (Téng Shé) 禽芮 (Qín Ruì) 伤门 (Shāng Mén) Xun 4　Ding/Wu Yi	太阴 (Tài Yīn) 天柱 (Tiān Zhù) 杜门 (Dù Mén) Li 9　Geng Ren	六合 (Liù Hé) 天心 (Tiān Xīn) 景门 (Jǐng Mén) Kun 2　Ji Ding/Wu
值符 (Zhí Fú) 天英 (Tiān Yīng) 生门 (Shēng Mén) Zhen 3　Ren Bing	Yang (阳) Dun# 5 Hour: **BingWu** ©Calvin Yap	白虎 (Bái Hǔ) 天蓬 (Tiān Péng) 死门 (Sǐ Mén) Dui 7　Gui Geng
九天 (Jiǔ Tiān) 天辅 (Tiān Fǔ) 休门 (Xiū Mén) Gen 8　Yi Xin	九地 (Jiǔ Dì) 天冲 (Tiān Chōng) 开门 (Kāi Mén) Kan 1　Bing Gui	玄武 (Xuán Wǔ) 天任 (Tiān Rèn) 惊门 (Jīng Mén) Qian 6　Xin Ji

Yang (阳) Dun# 5 Hour: **DingWei**；直符(ZhíFú): 天英(TiānYīng)
直使(ZhíShǐ): 景门(JǐngMén)；旬首(XúnShǒu): JiaChenRen

九地 (Jiǔ Dì) 天冲 (Tiān Chōng) 死门 (Sǐ Mén) Xun 4　Bing Yi	九天 (Jiǔ Tiān) 天辅 (Tiān Fǔ) 惊门 (Jīng Mén) Li 9　Yi Ren	值符 (Zhí Fú) 天英 (Tiān Yīng) 开门 (Kāi Mén) Kun 2　Ren Ding/Wu
玄武 (Xuán Wǔ) 天任 (Tiān Rèn) 景门 (Jǐng Mén) Zhen 3　Xin Bing	Yang (阳) Dun# 5 Hour: **DingWei** ©Calvin Yap	螣蛇 (Téng Shé) 禽芮 (Qín Ruì) 休门 (Xiū Mén) Dui 7　Ding/Wu Geng
白虎 (Bái Hǔ) 天蓬 (Tiān Péng) 杜门 (Dù Mén) Gen 8　Gui Xin	六合 (Liù Hé) 天心 (Tiān Xīn) 伤门 (Shāng Mén) Kan 1　Ji Gui	太阴 (Tài Yīn) 天柱 (Tiān Zhù) 生门 (Shēng Mén) Qian 6　Geng Ji

Yang (阳) Dun# 5 Hour: **WuShen**；直符(ZhíFú): 天英(TiānYīng)
直使(ZhíShǐ): 景门(JǐngMén)；旬首(XúnShǒu): JiaChenRen

九地 (Jiǔ Dì) 天冲 (Tiān Chōng) 景门 (Jǐng Mén) Xun 4　Bing Yi	九天 (Jiǔ Tiān) 天辅 (Tiān Fǔ) 死门 (Sǐ Mén) Li 9　Yi Ren	值符 (Zhí Fú) 天英 (Tiān Yīng) 惊门 (Jīng Mén) Kun 2　Ren Ding/Wu
玄武 (Xuán Wǔ) 天任 (Tiān Rèn) 杜门 (Dù Mén) Zhen 3　Xin Bing	Yang (阳) Dun# 5 Hour: **WuShen** ©Calvin Yap	螣蛇 (Téng Shé) 禽芮 (Qín Ruì) 开门 (Kāi Mén) Dui 7　Ding/Wu Geng
白虎 (Bái Hǔ) 天蓬 (Tiān Péng) 伤门 (Shāng Mén) Gen 8　Gui Xin	六合 (Liù Hé) 天心 (Tiān Xīn) 生门 (Shēng Mén) Kan 1　Ji Gui	太阴 (Tài Yīn) 天柱 (Tiān Zhù) 休门 (Xiū Mén) Qian 6　Geng Ji

Yang (阳) Dun# 5 Hour: **JiYou**；直符(ZhíFú): 天英(TiānYīng)
直使(ZhíShǐ): 景门(JǐngMén)；旬首(XúnShǒu): JiaChenRen

白虎 (Bái Hǔ) 天蓬 (Tiān Péng) 伤门 (Shāng Mén) Xun 4　Gui Yi	玄武 (Xuán Wǔ) 天任 (Tiān Rèn) 杜门 (Dù Mén) Li 9　Xin Ren	九地 (Jiǔ Dì) 天冲 (Tiān Chōng) 景门 (Jǐng Mén) Kun 2　Bing Ding/Wu
六合 (Liù Hé) 天心 (Tiān Xīn) 生门 (Shēng Mén) Zhen 3　Ji Bing	Yang (阳) Dun# 5 Hour: **JiYou** ©Calvin Yap	九天 (Jiǔ Tiān) 天辅 (Tiān Fǔ) 死门 (Sǐ Mén) Dui 7　Yi Geng
太阴 (Tài Yīn) 天柱 (Tiān Zhù) 休门 (Xiū Mén) Gen 8　Geng Xin	螣蛇 (Téng Shé) 禽芮 (Qín Ruì) 开门 (Kāi Mén) Kan 1　Ding/Wu Gui	值符 (Zhí Fú) 天英 (Tiān Yīng) 惊门 (Jīng Mén) Qian 6　Ren Ji

Yang (阳) Dun# 5 Hour: **GengXu**；直符(ZhíFú): 天英(TiānYīng)
直使(ZhíShǐ): 景门(JǐngMén)；旬首(XúnShǒu): JiaChenRen

玄武 (Xuán Wǔ) 天任 (Tiān Rèn) 休门 (Xiū Mén) Xun 4　Xin Yi	九地 (Jiǔ Dì) 天冲 (Tiān Chōng) 生门 (Shēng Mén) Li 9　Bing Ren	九天 (Jiǔ Tiān) 天辅 (Tiān Fǔ) 伤门 (Shāng Mén) Kun 2　Yi Ding/Wu
白虎 (Bái Hǔ) 天蓬 (Tiān Péng) 开门 (Kāi Mén) Zhen 3　Gui Bing	Yang (阳) Dun# 5 Hour: **GengXu** ©Calvin Yap	值符 (Zhí Fú) 天英 (Tiān Yīng) 杜门 (Dù Mén) Dui 7　Ren Geng
六合 (Liù Hé) 天心 (Tiān Xīn) 惊门 (Jīng Mén) Gen 8　Ji Xin	太阴 (Tài Yīn) 天柱 (Tiān Zhù) 死门 (Sǐ Mén) Kan 1　Geng Gui	螣蛇 (Téng Shé) 禽芮 (Qín Ruì) 景门 (Jǐng Mén) Qian 6　Ding/Wu Ji

Yang (阳) Dun# 5 Hour: **XinHai**；直符(ZhíFú): 天英(TiānYīng)
直使(ZhíShǐ): 景门(JǐngMén)；旬首(XúnShǒu): JiaChenRen

太阴 (Tài Yīn) 天柱 (Tiān Zhù) 生门 (Shēng Mén) Xun 4　Geng Yi	六合 (Liù Hé) 天心 (Tiān Xīn) 伤门 (Shāng Mén) Li 9　Ji Ren	白虎 (Bái Hǔ) 天蓬 (Tiān Péng) 杜门 (Dù Mén) Kun 2　Gui Ding/Wu
螣蛇 (Téng Shé) 禽芮 (Qín Ruì) 休门 (Xiū Mén) Zhen 3　Ding/Wu Bing	Yang (阳) Dun# 5 Hour: **XinHai** ©Calvin Yap	玄武 (Xuán Wǔ) 天任 (Tiān Rèn) 景门 (Jǐng Mén) Dui 7　Xin Geng
值符 (Zhí Fú) 天英 (Tiān Yīng) 开门 (Kāi Mén) Gen 8　Ren Xin	九天 (Jiǔ Tiān) 天辅 (Tiān Fǔ) 惊门 (Jīng Mén) Kan 1　Yi Gui	九地 (Jiǔ Dì) 天冲 (Tiān Chōng) 死门 (Sǐ Mén) Qian 6　Bing Ji

Yang (阳) Dun# 5 Hour: **RenZi** ; 直符(ZhíFú): 天英(TiānYīng)
直使(ZhíShǐ): 景门(JǐngMén) ; 旬首(XúnShǒu): JiaChenRen

九天 (Jiǔ Tiān) 天辅 (Tiān Fǔ) 惊门 (Jīng Mén) Xun 4　Yi　Yi	值符 (Zhí Fú) 天英 (Tiān Yīng) 开门 (Kāi Mén) Li 9　Ren　Ren	螣蛇 (Téng Shé) 禽芮 (Qín Ruì) 休门 (Xiū Mén) Kun 2　Ding/Wu　Ding/Wu
九地 (Jiǔ Dì) 天冲 (Tiān Chōng) 死门 (Sǐ Mén) Zhen 3　Bing　Bing	Yang (阳) Dun# 5 Hour: **RenZi** **Fu Yin** ©Calvin Yap	太阴 (Tài Yīn) 天柱 (Tiān Zhù) 生门 (Shēng Mén) Dui 7　Geng　Geng
玄武 (XuánWǔ) 天任 (Tiān Rèn) 景门 (Jīng Mén) Gen 8　Xin　Xin	白虎 (Bái Hǔ) 天蓬 (Tiān Péng) 杜门 (Dù Mén) Kan 1　Gui　Gui	六合 (Liù Hé) 天心 (Tiān Xīn) 伤门 (Shāng Mén) Qian 6　Ji　Ji

Yang (阳) Dun# 5 Hour: **GuiChou** ; 直符(ZhíFú): 天英(TiānYīng)
直使(ZhíShǐ): 景门(JǐngMén) ; 旬首(XúnShǒu): JiaChenRen

六合 (Liù Hé) 天心 (Tiān Xīn) 杜门 (Dù Mén) Xun 4　Ji　Yi	白虎 (Bái Hǔ) 天蓬 (Tiān Péng) 景门 (Jīng Mén) Li 9　Gui　Ren	玄武 (Xuán Wǔ) 天任 (Tiān Rèn) 死门 (Sǐ Mén) Kun 2　Xin　Ding/Wu
太阴 (Tài Yīn) 天柱 (Tiān Zhù) 伤门 (Shāng Mén) Zhen 3　Geng　Bing	Yang (阳) Dun# 5 Hour: **GuiChou** **Fan Yin** ©Calvin Yap	九地 (Jiǔ Dì) 天冲 (Tiān Chōng) 惊门 (Jīng Mén) Dui 7　Bing　Geng
螣蛇 (Téng Shé) 禽芮 (Qín Ruì) 生门 (Shēng Mén) Gen 8　Ding/Wu　Xin	值符 (Zhí Fú) 天英 (Tiān Yīng) 休门 (Xiū Mén) Kan 1　Ren　Gui	九天 (Jiǔ Tiān) 天辅 (Tiān Fǔ) 开门 (Kāi Mén) Qian 6　Yi　Ji

Chart: +5JiaYin (Yang Dun #5 JiaYin Xun)
JiaYin, YiMao, BingChen, DingSi, WuWu, JiWei, GengShen, XinYou, RenXu, GuiHai

Yang (阳) Dun# 5 Hour: **JiaYin** ; 直符(ZhíFú): 天蓬(TiānPéng)
直使(ZhíShǐ): 休门(XiūMén) ; 旬首(XúnShǒu): JiaYinGui

六合 (Liù Hé) 天辅 (Tiān Fǔ) 杜门 (Dù Mén) Xun 4　Yi　Yi	白虎 (Bái Hǔ) 天英 (Tiān Yīng) 景门 (Jīng Mén) Li 9　Ren　Ren	玄武 (Xuán Wǔ) 禽芮 (Qín Ruì) 死门 (Sǐ Mén) Kun 2　Ding/Wu　Ding/Wu
太阴 (Tài Yīn) 天冲 (Tiān Chōng) 伤门 (Shāng Mén) Zhen 3　Bing　Bing	Yang (阳) Dun# 5 Hour: **JiaYin** **Fu Yin** ©Calvin Yap	九地 (Jiǔ Dì) 天柱 (Tiān Zhù) 惊门 (Jīng Mén) Dui 7　Geng　Geng
螣蛇 (Téng Shé) 天任 (Tiān Rèn) 生门 (Shēng Mén) Gen 8　Xin　Xin	值符 (Zhí Fú) 天蓬 (Tiān Péng) 休门 (Xiū Mén) Kan 1　Gui　Gui	九天 (Jiǔ Tiān) 天心 (Tiān Xīn) 开门 (Kāi Mén) Qian 6　Ji　Ji

Yang (阳) Dun# 5 Hour: **YiMao** ; 直符(ZhíFú): 天蓬(TiānPéng)
直使(ZhíShǐ): 休门(XiūMén) ; 旬首(XúnShǒu): JiaYinGui

值符 (Zhí Fú) 天蓬 (Tiān Péng) 惊门 (Jīng Mén) Xun 4　Gui　Yi	螣蛇 (Téng Shé) 天任 (Tiān Rèn) 开门 (Kāi Mén) Li 9　Xin　Ren	太阴 (Tài Yīn) 天冲 (Tiān Chōng) 休门 (Xiū Mén) Kun 2　Bing　Ding/Wu
九天 (Jiǔ Tiān) 天心 (Tiān Xīn) 死门 (Sǐ Mén) Zhen 3　Ji　Bing	Yang (阳) Dun# 5 Hour: **YiMao** ©Calvin Yap	六合 (Liù Hé) 天辅 (Tiān Fǔ) 生门 (Shēng Mén) Dui 7　Yi　Geng
九地 (Jiǔ Dì) 天柱 (Tiān Zhù) 景门 (Jīng Mén) Gen 8　Geng　Xin	玄武 (Xuán Wǔ) 禽芮 (Qín Ruì) 杜门 (Dù Mén) Kan 1　Ding/Wu　Gui	白虎 (Bái Hǔ) 天英 (Tiān Yīng) 伤门 (Shāng Mén) Qian 6　Ren　Ji

Yang (阳) Dun# 5 Hour: **BingChen** ; 直符(ZhíFú): 天蓬(TiānPéng)
直使(ZhíShǐ): 休门(XiūMén) ; 旬首(XúnShǒu): JiaYinGui

螣蛇 (Téng Shé) 天任 (Tiān Rèn) 生门 (Shēng Mén) Xun 4　Xin　Yi	太阴 (Tài Yīn) 天冲 (Tiān Chōng) 伤门 (Shāng Mén) Li 9　Bing　Ren	六合 (Liù Hé) 天辅 (Tiān Fǔ) 杜门 (Dù Mén) Kun 2　Yi　Ding/Wu
值符 (Zhí Fú) 天蓬 (Tiān Péng) 休门 (Xiū Mén) Zhen 3　Gui　Bing	Yang (阳) Dun# 5 Hour: **BingChen** ©Calvin Yap	白虎 (Bái Hǔ) 天英 (Tiān Yīng) 景门 (Jīng Mén) Dui 7　Ren　Geng
九天 (Jiǔ Tiān) 天心 (Tiān Xīn) 开门 (Kāi Mén) Gen 8　Ji　Xin	九地 (Jiǔ Dì) 天柱 (Tiān Zhù) 惊门 (Jīng Mén) Kan 1　Geng　Gui	玄武 (Xuán Wǔ) 禽芮 (Qín Ruì) 死门 (Sǐ Mén) Qian 6　Ding/Wu　Ji

Yang (阳) Dun# 5 Hour: **DingSi** ; 直符(ZhíFú): 天蓬(TiānPéng)
直使(ZhíShǐ): 休门(XiūMén) ; 旬首(XúnShǒu): JiaYinGui

九地 (Jiǔ Dì) 天柱 (Tiān Zhù) 休门 (Xiū Mén) Xun 4　Geng　Yi	九天 (Jiǔ Tiān) 天心 (Tiān Xīn) 生门 (Shēng Mén) Li 9　Ji　Ren	值符 (Zhí Fú) 天蓬 (Tiān Péng) 伤门 (Shāng Mén) Kun 2　Gui　Ding/Wu
玄武 (Xuán Wǔ) 禽芮 (Qín Ruì) 开门 (Kāi Mén) Zhen 3　Ding/Wu　Bing	Yang (阳) Dun# 5 Hour: **DingSi** ©Calvin Yap	螣蛇 (Téng Shé) 天任 (Tiān Rèn) 杜门 (Dù Mén) Dui 7　Xin　Geng
白虎 (Bái Hǔ) 天英 (Tiān Yīng) 惊门 (Jīng Mén) Gen 8　Ren　Xin	六合 (Liù Hé) 天辅 (Tiān Fǔ) 死门 (Sǐ Mén) Kan 1　Yi　Gui	太阴 (Tài Yīn) 天冲 (Tiān Chōng) 景门 (Jīng Mén) Qian 6　Bing　Ji

Yang (阳) Dun# 5 Hour: **WuWu** ; 直符(ZhíFú): 天蓬(TiānPéng)
直使(ZhíShǐ): 休门(XiūMén) ; 旬首(XúnShǒu): JiaYinGui

九地 (Jiǔ Dì) 天柱 (Tiān Zhù) 惊门 (Jīng Mén) Xun 4　Geng Yi	九天 (Jiǔ Tiān) 天心 (Tiān Xīn) 开门 (Kāi Mén) Li 9　Ji Ren	值符 (Zhí Fú) 天蓬 (Tiān Péng) 休门 (Xiū Mén) Kun 2　Gui Ding/Wu
玄武 (Xuán Wǔ) 禽芮 (Qín Ruì) 死门 (Sǐ Mén) Zhen 3　Ding/Wu Bing	Yang (阳) Dun# 5 Hour: **WuWu** ©Calvin Yap	螣蛇 (Téng Shé) 天任 (Tiān Rèn) 生门 (Shēng Mén) Dui 7　Xin Geng
白虎 (Bái Hǔ) 天英 (Tiān Yīng) 景门 (Jīng Mén) Gen 8　Ren Xin	六合 (Liù Hé) 天辅 (Tiān Fǔ) 杜门 (Dù Mén) Kan 1　Yi Gui	太阴 (Tài Yīn) 天冲 (Tiān Chōng) 伤门 (Shāng Mén) Qian 6　Bing Ji

Yang (阳) Dun# 5 Hour: **JiWei** ; 直符(ZhíFú): 天蓬(TiānPéng)
直使(ZhíShǐ): 休门(XiūMén) ; 旬首(XúnShǒu): JiaYinGui

白虎 (Bái Hǔ) 天英 (Tiān Yīng) 景门 (Jīng Mén) Xun 4　Ren Yi	玄武 (Xuán Wǔ) 禽芮 (Qín Ruì) 死门 (Sǐ Mén) Li 9　Ding/Wu Ren	九地 (Jiǔ Dì) 天柱 (Tiān Zhù) 惊门 (Jīng Mén) Kun 2　Geng Ding/Wu
六合 (Liù Hé) 天辅 (Tiān Fǔ) 杜门 (Dù Mén) Zhen 3　Yi Bing	Yang (阳) Dun# 5 Hour: **JiWei** ©Calvin Yap	九天 (Jiǔ Tiān) 天心 (Tiān Xīn) 开门 (Kāi Mén) Dui 7　Ji Geng
太阴 (Tài Yīn) 天冲 (Tiān Chōng) 伤门 (Shāng Mén) Gen 8　Bing Xin	螣蛇 (Téng Shé) 天任 (Tiān Rèn) 生门 (Shēng Mén) Kan 1　Xin Gui	值符 (Zhí Fú) 天蓬 (Tiān Péng) 休门 (Xiū Mén) Qian 6　Gui Ji

Yang (阳) Dun# 5 Hour:**GengShen** ;直符(ZhíFú): 天蓬(TiānPéng)
直使(ZhíShǐ): 休门(XiūMén) ; 旬首(XúnShǒu): JiaYinGui

玄武 (Xuán Wǔ) 禽芮 (Qín Ruì) 死门 (Sǐ Mén) Xun 4　Ding/Wu Yi	九地 (Jiǔ Dì) 天柱 (Tiān Zhù) 惊门 (Jīng Mén) Li 9　Geng Ren	九天 (Jiǔ Tiān) 天心 (Tiān Xīn) 开门 (Kāi Mén) Kun 2　Ji Ding/Wu
白虎 (Bái Hǔ) 天英 (Tiān Yīng) 景门 (Jīng Mén) Zhen 3　Ren Bing	Yang (阳) Dun# 5 Hour: **GengShen** ©Calvin Yap	值符 (Zhí Fú) 天蓬 (Tiān Péng) 休门 (Xiū Mén) Dui 7　Gui Geng
六合 (Liù Hé) 天辅 (Tiān Fǔ) 杜门 (Dù Mén) Gen 8　Yi Xin	太阴 (Tài Yīn) 天冲 (Tiān Chōng) 伤门 (Shāng Mén) Kan 1　Bing Gui	螣蛇 (Téng Shé) 天任 (Tiān Rèn) 生门 (Shēng Mén) Qian 6　Xin Ji

Yang (阳) Dun# 5 Hour: **XinYou** ; 直符(ZhíFú): 天蓬(TiānPéng)
直使(ZhíShǐ): 休门(XiūMén) ; 旬首(XúnShǒu): JiaYinGui

太阴 (Tài Yīn) 天冲 (Tiān Chōng) 伤门 (Shāng Mén) Xun 4　Bing Yi	六合 (Liù Hé) 天辅 (Tiān Fǔ) 杜门 (Dù Mén) Li 9　Yi Ren	白虎 (Bái Hǔ) 天英 (Tiān Yīng) 景门 (Jīng Mén) Kun 2　Ren Ding/Wu
螣蛇 (Téng Shé) 天任 (Tiān Rèn) 生门 (Shēng Mén) Zhen 3　Xin Bing	Yang (阳) Dun# 5 Hour: **XinYou** ©Calvin Yap	玄武 (Xuán Wǔ) 禽芮 (Qín Ruì) 死门 (Sǐ Mén) Dui 7　Ding/Wu Geng
值符 (Zhí Fú) 天蓬 (Tiān Péng) 休门 (Xiū Mén) Gen 8　Gui Xin	九天 (Jiǔ Tiān) 天心 (Tiān Xīn) 开门 (Kāi Mén) Kan 1　Ji Gui	九地 (Jiǔ Dì) 天柱 (Tiān Zhù) 惊门 (Jīng Mén) Qian 6　Geng Ji

Yang (阳) Dun# 5 Hour: **RenXu** ; 直符(ZhíFú): 天蓬(TiānPéng)
直使(ZhíShǐ): 休门(XiūMén) ; 旬首(XúnShǒu): JiaYinGui

九天 (Jiǔ Tiān) 天心 (Tiān Xīn) 开门 (Kāi Mén) Xun 4　Ji Yi	值符 (Zhí Fú) 天蓬 (Tiān Péng) 休门 (Xiū Mén) Li 9　Gui Ren	螣蛇 (Téng Shé) 天任 (Tiān Rèn) 生门 (Shēng Mén) Kun 2　Xin Ding/Wu
九地 (Jiǔ Dì) 天柱 (Tiān Zhù) 惊门 (Jīng Mén) Zhen 3　Geng Bing	Yang (阳) Dun# 5 Hour: **RenXu** **Fan Yin** ©Calvin Yap	太阴 (Tài Yīn) 天冲 (Tiān Chōng) 伤门 (Shāng Mén) Dui 7　Bing Geng
玄武 (Xuán Wǔ) 禽芮 (Qín Ruì) 死门 (Sǐ Mén) Gen 8　Ding/Wu Xin	白虎 (Bái Hǔ) 天英 (Tiān Yīng) 景门 (Jīng Mén) Kan 1　Ren Gui	六合 (Liù Hé) 天辅 (Tiān Fǔ) 杜门 (Dù Mén) Qian 6　Yi Ji

Yang (阳) Dun# 5 Hour: **GuiHai** ; 直符(ZhíFú): 天蓬(TiānPéng)
直使(ZhíShǐ): 休门(XiūMén) ; 旬首(XúnShǒu): JiaYinGui

六合 (Liù Hé) 天辅 (Tiān Fǔ) 杜门 (Dù Mén) Xun 4　Yi Yi	白虎 (Bái Hǔ) 天英 (Tiān Yīng) 景门 (Jīng Mén) Li 9　Ren Ren	玄武 (Xuán Wǔ) 禽芮 (Qín Ruì) 死门 (Sǐ Mén) Kun 2　Ding/Wu Ding/Wu
太阴 (Tài Yīn) 天冲 (Tiān Chōng) 伤门 (Shāng Mén) Zhen 3　Bing Bing	Yang (阳) Dun# 5 Hour: **GuiHai** **Fu Yin** ©Calvin Yap	九地 (Jiǔ Dì) 天柱 (Tiān Zhù) 惊门 (Jīng Mén) Dui 7　Geng Geng
螣蛇 (Téng Shé) 天任 (Tiān Rèn) 生门 (Shēng Mén) Gen 8　Xin Xin	值符 (Zhí Fú) 天蓬 (Tiān Péng) 休门 (Xiū Mén) Kan 1　Gui Gui	九天 (Jiǔ Tiān) 天心 (Tiān Xīn) 开门 (Kāi Mén) Qian 6　Ji Ji

Yang Dun#6

Chart: +6JiaZi (Yang Dun #6 JiaZi Xun)
JiaZi, YiChou, BingYin, DingMao, WuChen, JiSi, GengWu, XinWei, RenShen, GuiYou

Yang (阳) Dun# 6 Hour: JiaZi ; 直符(ZhíFú): 天心(TiānXīn)
直使(ZhíShǐ): 开门(KāiMén) ; 旬首(XúnShǒu): JiaZiWu

白虎 (Bái Hǔ) 天辅 (Tiān Fǔ) 杜门 (Dù Mén) Xun 4 Bing Bing	玄武 (Xuán Wǔ) 天英 (Tiān Yīng) 景门 (Jǐng Mén) Li 9 Xin	九地 (Jiǔ Dì) 禽芮 (Qín Ruì) 死门 (Sǐ Mén) Kun 2 Gui/Yi Gui/Yi
六合 (Liù Hé) 天冲 (Tiān Chōng) 伤门 (Shāng Mén) Zhen 3 Ding Ding	Yang (阳) Dun# 6 Hour: **JiaZi** **Fu Yin** ©Calvin Yap	九天 (Jiǔ Tiān) 天柱 (Tiān Zhù) 惊门 (Jǐng Mén) Dui 7 Ji Ji
太阴 (Tài Yīn) 天任 (Tiān Rèn) 生门 (Shēng Mén) Gen 8 Geng Geng	腾蛇 (Téng Shé) 天蓬 (Tiān Péng) 休门 (Xiū Mén) Kan 1 Ren Ren	值符 (Zhí Fú) 天心 (Tiān Xīn) 开门 (Kāi Mén) Qian 6 Wu Wu

Yang (阳) Dun# 6 Hour: YiChou ; 直符(ZhíFú): 天心(TiānXīn)
直使(ZhíShǐ): 开门(KāiMén) ; 旬首(XúnShǒu): JiaZiWu

九地 (Jiǔ Dì) 禽芮 (Qín Ruì) 景门 (Jǐng Mén) Xun 4 Gui/Yi Bing	九天 (Jiǔ Tiān) 天柱 (Tiān Zhù) 死门 (Sǐ Mén) Li 9 Xin	值符 (Zhí Fú) 天心 (Tiān Xīn) 惊门 (Jǐng Mén) Kun 2 Wu Gui/Yi
玄武 (Xuán Wǔ) 天英 (Tiān Yīng) 杜门 (Dù Mén) Zhen 3 Xin Ding	Yang (阳) Dun# 6 Hour: **YiChou** ©Calvin Yap	腾蛇 (Téng Shé) 天蓬 (Tiān Péng) 开门 (Kāi Mén) Dui 7 Ren Ji
白虎 (Bái Hǔ) 天辅 (Tiān Fǔ) 伤门 (Shāng Mén) Gen 8 Bing Geng	六合 (Liù Hé) 天冲 (Tiān Chōng) 生门 (Shēng Mén) Kan 1 Ding Ren	太阴 (Tài Yīn) 天任 (Tiān Rèn) 休门 (Xiū Mén) Qian 6 Geng Wu

Yang (阳) Dun# 6 Hour: BingYin ; 直符(ZhíFú): 天心(TiānXīn)
直使(ZhíShǐ): 开门(KāiMén) ; 旬首(XúnShǒu): JiaZiWu

值符 (Zhi Fú) 天心 (Tiān Xīn) 生门 (Shēng Mén) Xun 4 Wu Bing	腾蛇 (Téng Shé) 天蓬 (Tiān Péng) 伤门 (Shāng Mén) Li 9 Ren Xin	太阴 (Tài Yīn) 天任 (Tiān Rèn) 杜门 (Dù Mén) Kun 2 Geng Gui/Yi
九天 (Jiǔ Tiān) 天柱 (Tiān Zhù) 休门 (Xiū Mén) Zhen 3 Ji Ding	Yang (阳) Dun# 6 Hour: **BingYin** **Fan Yin** ©Calvin Yap	六合 (Liù Hé) 天冲 (Tiān Chōng) 景门 (Jǐng Mén) Dui 7 Ding Ji
九地 (Jiǔ Dì) 禽芮 (Qín Ruì) 开门 (Kāi Mén) Gen 8 Gui/Yi Geng	玄武 (Xuán Wǔ) 天英 (Tiān Yīng) 惊门 (Jǐng Mén) Kan 1 Xin Ren	白虎 (Bái Hǔ) 天辅 (Tiān Fǔ) 死门 (Sǐ Mén) Qian 6 Bing Wu

Yang (阳) Dun# 6 Hour: DingMao ; 直符(ZhíFú): 天心(TiānXīn)
直使(ZhíShǐ): 开门(KāiMén) ; 旬首(XúnShǒu): JiaZiWu

腾蛇 (Téng Shé) 天蓬 (Tiān Péng) 惊门 (Jīng Mén) Xun 4 Ren Bing	太阴 (Tài Yīn) 天任 (Tiān Rèn) 开门 (Kāi Mén) Li 9 Geng Xin	六合 (Liù Hé) 天冲 (Tiān Chōng) 休门 (Xiū Mén) Kun 2 Ding Gui/Yi
值符 (Zhí Fú) 天心 (Tiān Xīn) 死门 (Sǐ Mén) Zhen 3 Wu Ding	Yang (阳) Dun# 6 Hour: **DingMao** ©Calvin Yap	白虎 (Bái Hǔ) 天辅 (Tiān Fǔ) 生门 (Shēng Mén) Dui 7 Bing Ji
九天 (Jiǔ Tiān) 天柱 (Tiān Zhù) 景门 (Jǐng Mén) Gen 8 Ji Geng	九地 (Jiǔ Dì) 禽芮 (Qín Ruì) 杜门 (Dù Mén) Kan 1 Gui/Yi Ren	玄武 (Xuán Wǔ) 天英 (Tiān Yīng) 伤门 (Shāng Mén) Qian 6 Xin Wu

Yang (阳) Dun# 6 Hour: WuChen ; 直符(ZhíFú): 天心(TiānXīn)
直使(ZhíShǐ): 开门(KāiMén) ; 旬首(XúnShǒu): JiaZiWu

白虎 (Bái Hǔ) 天辅 (Tiān Fǔ) 伤门 (Shāng Mén) Xun 4 Bing Bing	玄武 (Xuán Wǔ) 天英 (Tiān Yīng) 杜门 (Dù Mén) Li 9 Xin	九地 (Jiǔ Dì) 禽芮 (Qín Ruì) 景门 (Jǐng Mén) Kun 2 Gui/Yi Gui/Yi
六合 (Liù Hé) 天冲 (Tiān Chōng) 生门 (Shēng Mén) Zhen 3 Ding Ding	Yang (阳) Dun# 6 Hour: **WuChen** **Fu Yin** ©Calvin Yap	九天 (Jiǔ Tiān) 天柱 (Tiān Zhù) 死门 (Sǐ Mén) Dui 7 Ji Ji
太阴 (Tài Yīn) 天任 (Tiān Rèn) 休门 (Xiū Mén) Gen 8 Geng Geng	腾蛇 (Téng Shé) 天蓬 (Tiān Péng) 开门 (Kāi Mén) Kan 1 Ren Ren	值符 (Zhí Fú) 天心 (Tiān Xīn) 惊门 (Jǐng Mén) Qian 6 Wu Wu

Yang (阳) Dun# 6 Hour: JiSi ; 直符(ZhíFú): 天心(TiānXīn)
直使(ZhíShǐ): 开门(KāiMén) ; 旬首(XúnShǒu): JiaZiWu

玄武 (Xuán Wǔ) 天英 (Tiān Yīng) 死门 (Sǐ Mén) Xun 4 Xin Bing	九地 (Jiǔ Dì) 禽芮 (Qín Ruì) 惊门 (Jīng Mén) Li 9 Gui/Yi Xin	九天 (Jiǔ Tiān) 天柱 (Tiān Zhù) 开门 (Kāi Mén) Kun 2 Ji Gui/Yi
白虎 (Bái Hǔ) 天辅 (Tiān Fǔ) 景门 (Jǐng Mén) Zhen 3 Bing Ding	Yang (阳) Dun# 6 Hour: **JiSi** ©Calvin Yap	值符 (Zhí Fú) 天心 (Tiān Xīn) 休门 (Xiū Mén) Dui 7 Wu Ji
六合 (Liù Hé) 天冲 (Tiān Chōng) 杜门 (Dù Mén) Gen 8 Ding Geng	太阴 (Tài Yīn) 天任 (Tiān Rèn) 伤门 (Shāng Mén) Kan 1 Geng Ren	腾蛇 (Téng Shé) 天蓬 (Tiān Péng) 生门 (Shēng Mén) Qian 6 Ren Wu

Yang (阳) Dun# 6 Hour: GengWu；直符(ZhíFú): 天心(TiānXīn)
直使(ZhíShǐ): 开门(KāiMén)；旬首(XúnShǒu): JiaZiWu

太阴 (Tài Yīn) 天任 (Tiān Rèn) 休门 (Xiū Mén) Xun 4 Bing Bing	六合 (Liù Hé) 天冲 (Tiān Chōng) 生门 (Shēng Mén) Li 9 Ding Xin	白虎 (Bái Hǔ) 天辅 (Tiān Fǔ) 伤门 (Shāng Mén) Kun 2 Bing Gui/Yi
螣蛇 (Téng Shé) 天蓬 (Tiān Péng) 开门 (Kāi Mén) Zhen 3 Ren Ding	Yang (阳) Dun# 6 Hour: **GengWu** ©Calvin Yap	玄武 (Xuán Wǔ) 天英 (Tiān Yīng) 杜门 (Dù Mén) Dui 7 Xin Ji
值符 (Zhí Fú) 天心 (Tiān Xīn) 惊门 (Jīng Mén) Gen 8 Wu Geng	九天 (Jiǔ Tiān) 天柱 (Tiān Zhù) 死门 (Sǐ Mén) Kan 1 Ji Ren	九地 (Jiǔ Dì) 禽芮 (Qín Ruì) 景门 (Jǐng Mén) Qian 6 Gui/Yi Wu

Yang (阳) Dun# 6 Hour: XinWei；直符(ZhíFú): 天心(TiānXīn)
直使(ZhíShǐ): 开门(KāiMén)；旬首(XúnShǒu): JiaZiWu

九天 (Jiǔ Tiān) 天柱 (Tiān Zhù) 开门 (Kāi Mén) Xun 4 Ji Bing	值符 (Zhí Fú) 天心 (Tiān Xīn) 休门 (Xiū Mén) Li 9 Wu Xin	螣蛇 (Téng Shé) 天蓬 (Tiān Péng) 生门 (Shēng Mén) Kun 2 Ren Gui/Yi
九地 (Jiǔ Dì) 禽芮 (Qín Ruì) 惊门 (Jīng Mén) Zhen 3 Gui/Yi Ding	Yang (阳) Dun# 6 Hour: **XinWei** ©Calvin Yap	太阴 (Tài Yīn) 天任 (Tiān Rèn) 伤门 (Shāng Mén) Dui 7 Geng Ji
玄武 (Xuán Wǔ) 天英 (Tiān Yīng) 死门 (Sǐ Mén) Gen 8 Xin Geng	白虎 (Bái Hǔ) 天辅 (Tiān Fǔ) 景门 (Jǐng Mén) Kan 1 Bing Ren	六合 (Liù Hé) 天冲 (Tiān Chōng) 杜门 (Dù Mén) Qian 6 Ding Wu

Yang (阳) Dun# 6 Hour: RenShen；直符(ZhíFú): 天心(TiānXīn)
直使(ZhíShǐ): 开门(KāiMén)；旬首(XúnShǒu): JiaZiWu

六合 (Liù Hé) 天冲 (Tiān Chōng) 死门 (Sǐ Mén) Xun 4 Ding Bing	白虎 (Bái Hǔ) 天辅 (Tiān Fǔ) 惊门 (Jīng Mén) Li 9 Bing Xin	玄武 (Xuán Wǔ) 天英 (Tiān Yīng) 开门 (Kāi Mén) Kun 2 Xin Gui/Yi
太阴 (Tài Yīn) 天任 (Tiān Rèn) 景门 (Jǐng Mén) Zhen 3 Geng Ding	Yang (阳) Dun# 6 Hour: **RenShen** ©Calvin Yap	九地 (Jiǔ Dì) 禽芮 (Qín Ruì) 休门 (Xiū Mén) Dui 7 Gui/Yi Ji
螣蛇 (Téng Shé) 天蓬 (Tiān Péng) 杜门 (Dù Mén) Gen 8 Ren Geng	值符 (Zhí Fú) 天心 (Tiān Xīn) 伤门 (Shāng Mén) Kan 1 Wu Ren	九天 (Jiǔ Tiān) 天柱 (Tiān Zhù) 生门 (Shēng Mén) Qian 6 Ji Wu

Yang (阳) Dun# 6 Hour: GuiYou；直符(ZhíFú): 天心(TiānXīn)
直使(ZhíShǐ): 开门(KāiMén)；旬首(XúnShǒu): JiaZiWu

九地 (Jiǔ Dì) 禽芮 (Qín Ruì) 杜门 (Dù Mén) Xun 4 Gui/Yi Bing	九天 (Jiǔ Tiān) 天柱 (Tiān Zhù) 景门 (Jǐng Mén) Li 9 Ji Xin	值符 (Zhí Fú) 天心 (Tiān Xīn) 死门 (Sǐ Mén) Kun 2 Wu Gui/Yi
玄武 (Xuán Wǔ) 天英 (Tiān Yīng) 伤门 (Shāng Mén) Zhen 3 Xin Ding	Yang (阳) Dun# 6 Hour: **GuiYou** ©Calvin Yap	螣蛇 (Téng Shé) 天蓬 (Tiān Péng) 惊门 (Jīng Mén) Dui 7 Ren Ji
白虎 (Bái Hǔ) 天辅 (Tiān Fǔ) 生门 (Shēng Mén) Gen 8 Bing Geng	六合 (Liù Hé) 天冲 (Tiān Chōng) 休门 (Xiū Mén) Kan 1 Ding Ren	太阴 (Tài Yīn) 天任 (Tiān Rèn) 开门 (Kāi Mén) Qian 6 Geng Wu

Chart: +6JiaXu (Yang Dun #6 JiaXu Xun)
JiaXu, YiHai, BingZi, DingChou, WuYin, JiMao, GengChen, XinSi, RenWu, GuiWei

Yang (阳) Dun# 6 Hour: JiaXu；直符(ZhíFú): 天柱(TiānZhù)
直使(ZhíShǐ): 惊门(JīngMén)；旬首(XúnShǒu): JiaXuJi

玄武 (Xuán Wǔ) 天辅 (Tiān Fǔ) 杜门 (Dù Mén) Xun 4 Bing Bing	九地 (Jiǔ Dì) 天英 (Tiān Yīng) 景门 (Jǐng Mén) Li 9 Xin Xin	九天 (Jiǔ Tiān) 禽芮 (Qín Ruì) 死门 (Sǐ Mén) Kun 2 Gui/Yi Gui/Yi
白虎 (Bái Hǔ) 天冲 (Tiān Chōng) 伤门 (Shāng Mén) Zhen 3 Ding Ding	Yang (阳) Dun# 6 Hour: **JiaXu** **Fu Yin** ©Calvin Yap	值符 (Zhí Fú) 天柱 (Tiān Zhù) 惊门 (Jīng Mén) Dui 7 Ji Ji
六合 (Liù Hé) 天任 (Tiān Rèn) 生门 (Shēng Mén) Gen 8 Geng Geng	太阴 (Tài Yīn) 天蓬 (Tiān Péng) 休门 (Xiū Mén) Kan 1 Ren Ren	螣蛇 (Téng Shé) 天心 (Tiān Xīn) 开门 (Kāi Mén) Qian 6 Wu Wu

Yang (阳) Dun# 6 Hour: YiHai；直符(ZhíFú): 天柱(TiānZhù)
直使(ZhíShǐ): 惊门(JīngMén)；旬首(XúnShǒu): JiaXuJi

九地 (Jiǔ Dì) 天英 (Tiān Yīng) 休门 (Xiū Mén) Xun 4 Xin Bing	九天 (Jiǔ Tiān) 禽芮 (Qín Ruì) 生门 (Shēng Mén) Li 9 Gui/Yi Xin	值符 (Zhí Fú) 天柱 (Tiān Zhù) 伤门 (Shāng Mén) Kun 2 Ji Gui/Yi
玄武 (Xuán Wǔ) 天辅 (Tiān Fǔ) 开门 (Kāi Mén) Zhen 3 Bing Ding	Yang (阳) Dun# 6 Hour: **YiHai** ©Calvin Yap	螣蛇 (Téng Shé) 天心 (Tiān Xīn) 杜门 (Dù Mén) Dui 7 Wu Ji
白虎 (Bái Hǔ) 天冲 (Tiān Chōng) 惊门 (Jīng Mén) Gen 8 Ding Geng	六合 (Liù Hé) 天任 (Tiān Rèn) 死门 (Sǐ Mén) Kan 1 Geng Ren	太阴 (Tài Yīn) 天蓬 (Tiān Péng) 景门 (Jǐng Mén) Qian 6 Ren Wu

Yang (阳) Dun# 6 Hour: BingZi ; 直符(ZhíFú): 天柱(TiānZhù)
直使(ZhíShǐ): 惊门(JīngMén) ; 旬首(XúnShǒu): JiaXuJi

值符 (Zhí Fú) 天柱 (Tiān Zhù) 死门 (Sǐ Mén) Xun 4 Ji	螣蛇 (Téng Shé) 天心 (Tiān Xīn) 惊门 (Jīng Mén) Li 9 Wu Xin	太阴 (Tài Yīn) 天蓬 (Tiān Péng) 开门 (Kāi Mén) Kun 2 Ren Gui/Yi
九天 (Jiǔ Tiān) 禽芮 (Qín Ruì) 景门 (Jǐng Mén) Zhen 3 Gui/Yi Ding	Yang (阳) Dun# 6 Hour: **BingZi** ©Calvin Yap	六合 (Liù Hé) 天任 (Tiān Rèn) 休门 (Xiū Mén) Dui 7 Geng Ji
九地 (Jiǔ Dì) 天英 (Tiān Yīng) 杜门 (Dù Mén) Gen 8 Xin Geng	玄武 (Xuán Wǔ) 天辅 (Tiān Fǔ) 伤门 (Shāng Mén) Kan 1 Bing Ren	白虎 (Bái Hǔ) 天冲 (Tiān Chōng) 生门 (Shēng Mén) Qian 6 Ding Wu

Yang (阳) Dun# 6 Hour: DingChou ; 直符(ZhíFú): 天柱(TiānZhù)
直使(ZhíShǐ): 惊门(JīngMén) ; 旬首(XúnShǒu): JiaXuJi

螣蛇 (Téng Shé) 天心 (Tiān Xīn) 生门 (Shēng Mén) Xun 4 Wu Bing	太阴 (Tài Yīn) 天蓬 (Tiān Péng) 伤门 (Shāng Mén) Li 9 Ren Xin	六合 (Liù Hé) 天任 (Tiān Rèn) 杜门 (Dù Mén) Kun 2 Geng Gui/Yi
值符 (Zhí Fú) 天柱 (Tiān Zhù) 休门 (Xiū Mén) Zhen 3 Ji Ding	Yang (阳) Dun# 6 Hour: **DingChou** **Fan Yin** ©Calvin Yap	白虎 (Bái Hǔ) 天冲 (Tiān Chōng) 景门 (Jǐng Mén) Dui 7 Ding Ji
九天 (Jiǔ Tiān) 禽芮 (Qín Ruì) 开门 (Kāi Mén) Gen 8 Gui/Yi Geng	九地 (Jiǔ Dì) 天英 (Tiān Yīng) 惊门 (Jīng Mén) Kan 1 Xin Ren	玄武 (Xuán Wǔ) 天辅 (Tiān Fǔ) 死门 (Sǐ Mén) Qian 6 Bing Wu

Yang (阳) Dun# 6 Hour: WuYin ; 直符(ZhíFú): 天柱(TiānZhù)
直使(ZhíShǐ): 惊门(JīngMén) ; 旬首(XúnShǒu): JiaXuJi

白虎 (Bái Hǔ) 天冲 (Tiān Chōng) 景门 (Jǐng Mén) Xun 4 Ding Bing	玄武 (Xuán Wǔ) 天辅 (Tiān Fǔ) 死门 (Sǐ Mén) Li 9 Bing Xin	九地 (Jiǔ Dì) 天英 (Tiān Yīng) 惊门 (Jīng Mén) Kun 2 Xin Gui/Yi
六合 (Liù Hé) 天任 (Tiān Rèn) 杜门 (Dù Mén) Zhen 3 Geng Ding	Yang (阳) Dun# 6 Hour: **WuYin** ©Calvin Yap	九天 (Jiǔ Tiān) 禽芮 (Qín Ruì) 开门 (Kāi Mén) Dui 7 Gui/Yi Ji
太阴 (Tài Yīn) 天蓬 (Tiān Péng) 伤门 (Shāng Mén) Gen 8 Ren Geng	螣蛇 (Téng Shé) 天心 (Tiān Xīn) 生门 (Shēng Mén) Kan 1 Wu Ren	值符 (Zhí Fú) 天柱 (Tiān Zhù) 休门 (Xiū Mén) Qian 6 Ji Wu

Yang (阳) Dun# 6 Hour: JiMao ; 直符(ZhíFú): 天柱(TiānZhù)
直使(ZhíShǐ): 惊门(JīngMén) ; 旬首(XúnShǒu): JiaXuJi

玄武 (Xuán Wǔ) 天辅 (Tiān Fǔ) 开门 (Kāi Mén) Xun 4 Bing Bing	九地 (Jiǔ Dì) 天英 (Tiān Yīng) 休门 (Xiū Mén) Li 9 Xin Xin	九天 (Jiǔ Tiān) 禽芮 (Qín Ruì) 生门 (Shēng Mén) Kun 2 Gui/Yi Gui/Yi
白虎 (Bái Hǔ) 天冲 (Tiān Chōng) 惊门 (Jīng Mén) Zhen 3 Ding Ding	Yang (阳) Dun# 6 Hour: **JiMao** **Fu Yin** ©Calvin Yap	值符 (Zhí Fú) 天柱 (Tiān Zhù) 伤门 (Shāng Mén) Dui 7 Ji Ji
六合 (Liù Hé) 天任 (Tiān Rèn) 死门 (Sǐ Mén) Gen 8 Geng Geng	太阴 (Tài Yīn) 天蓬 (Tiān Péng) 景门 (Jǐng Mén) Kan 1 Ren Ren	螣蛇 (Téng Shé) 天心 (Tiān Xīn) 杜门 (Dù Mén) Qian 6 Wu Wu

Yang (阳) Dun# 6 Hour: GengChen ; 直符(ZhíFú): 天柱(TiānZhù)
直使(ZhíShǐ): 惊门(JīngMén) ; 旬首(XúnShǒu): JiaXuJi

太阴 (Tài Yīn) 天蓬 (Tiān Péng) 惊门 (Jīng Mén) Xun 4 Ren Bing	六合 (Liù Hé) 天任 (Tiān Rèn) 开门 (Kāi Mén) Li 9 Geng Xin	白虎 (Bái Hǔ) 天冲 (Tiān Chōng) 休门 (Xiū Mén) Kun 2 Ding Gui/Yi
螣蛇 (Téng Shé) 天心 (Tiān Xīn) 死门 (Sǐ Mén) Zhen 3 Wu Ding	Yang (阳) Dun# 6 Hour: **GengChen** ©Calvin Yap	玄武 (Xuán Wǔ) 天辅 (Tiān Fǔ) 生门 (Shēng Mén) Dui 7 Bing Ji
值符 (Zhí Fú) 天柱 (Tiān Zhù) 景门 (Jǐng Mén) Gen 8 Ji Geng	九天 (Jiǔ Tiān) 禽芮 (Qín Ruì) 杜门 (Dù Mén) Kan 1 Gui/Yi Ren	九地 (Jiǔ Dì) 天英 (Tiān Yīng) 伤门 (Shāng Mén) Qian 6 Xin Wu

Yang (阳) Dun# 6 Hour: XinSi ; 直符(ZhíFú): 天柱(TiānZhù)
直使(ZhíShǐ): 惊门(JīngMén) ; 旬首(XúnShǒu): JiaXuJi

九天 (Jiǔ Tiān) 禽芮 (Qín Ruì) 景门 (Jǐng Mén) Xun 4 Gui/Yi Bing	值符 (Zhí Fú) 天柱 (Tiān Zhù) 死门 (Sǐ Mén) Li 9 Ji Xin	螣蛇 (Téng Shé) 天心 (Tiān Xīn) 惊门 (Jīng Mén) Kun 2 Wu Gui/Yi
九地 (Jiǔ Dì) 天英 (Tiān Yīng) 杜门 (Dù Mén) Zhen 3 Xin Ding	Yang (阳) Dun# 6 Hour: **XinSi** ©Calvin Yap	太阴 (Tài Yīn) 天蓬 (Tiān Péng) 开门 (Kāi Mén) Dui 7 Ren Ji
玄武 (Xuán Wǔ) 天辅 (Tiān Fǔ) 伤门 (Shāng Mén) Gen 8 Bing Geng	白虎 (Bái Hǔ) 天冲 (Tiān Chōng) 生门 (Shēng Mén) Kan 1 Ding Ren	六合 (Liù Hé) 天任 (Tiān Rèn) 休门 (Xiū Mén) Qian 6 Geng Wu

Yang (阳) Dun# 6 Hour: RenWu；直符(ZhíFú): 天柱(TiānZhù)
直使(ZhíShǐ): 惊门(JīngMén)；旬首(XúnShǒu): JiaXuJi

六合 (Liù Hé) 天任 (Tiān Rèn) 伤门 (Shāng Mén) Xun 4　Geng Bing	白虎 (Bái Hǔ) 天冲 (Tiān Chōng) 杜门 (Dù Mén) Li 9　Ding Xin	玄武(Xuán Wǔ) 天辅 (Tiān Fǔ) 景门 (Jǐng Mén) Kun 2　Bing Gui/Yi
太阴 (Tài Yīn) 天蓬 (Tiān Péng) 生门 (Shēng Mén) Zhen 3　Ren Ding	Yang (阳) Dun# 6 Hour: **RenWu** ©Calvin Yap	九地 (Jiǔ Dì) 天英 (Tiān Yīng) 死门 (Sǐ Mén) Dui 7　Xin Ji
螣蛇 (Téng Shé) 天心 (Tiān Xīn) 休门 (Xiū Mén) Gen 8　Wu Geng	值符 (Zhí Fú) 天柱 (Tiān Zhù) 开门 (Kāi Mén) Kan 1　Ji Ren	九天 (Jiǔ Tiān) 禽芮 (Qín Ruì) 惊门 (Jīng Mén) Qian 6　Gui/Yi Wu

Yang (阳) Dun# 6 Hour: GuiWei；直符(ZhíFú): 天柱(TiānZhù)
直使(ZhíShǐ): 惊门(JīngMén)；旬首(XúnShǒu): JiaXuJi

九地 (Jiǔ Dì) 天英 (Tiān Yīng) 杜门 (Dù Mén) Xun 4　Xin	九天 (Jiǔ Tiān) 禽芮 (Qín Ruì) 景门 (Jǐng Mén) Li 9　Gui/Yi Xin	值符 (Zhí Fú) 天柱 (Tiān Zhù) 死门 (Sǐ Mén) Kun 2　Ji Gui/Yi
玄武 (Xuán Wǔ) 天辅 (Tiān Fǔ) 伤门 (Shāng Mén) Zhen 3　Bing Ding	Yang (阳) Dun# 6 Hour: **GuiWei** ©Calvin Yap	螣蛇 (Téng Shé) 天心 (Tiān Xīn) 惊门 (Jīng Mén) Dui 7　Wu Ji
白虎 (Bái Hǔ) 天冲 (Tiān Chōng) 生门 (Shēng Mén) Gen 8　Ding Geng	六合 (Liù Hé) 天任 (Tiān Rèn) 休门 (Xiū Mén) Kan 1　Geng Ren	太阴 (Tài Yīn) 天蓬 (Tiān Péng) 开门 (Kāi Mén) Qian 6　Ren Wu

Chart: +6JiaShen (Yang Dun #6 JiaShen Xun)
JiaShen, YiYou, BingXu, DingHai, WuZi, JiChou, GengYin, XinMao, RenChen, GuiSi

Yang (阳) Dun# 6 Hour: JiaShen；直符(ZhíFú): 天任(TiānRèn)
直使(ZhíShǐ): 生门(ShēngMén)；旬首(XúnShǒu): JiaShenGeng

太阴 (Tài Yīn) 天辅 (Tiān Fǔ) 杜门 (Dù Mén) Xun 4　Bing Bing	六合 (Liù Hé) 天英 (Tiān Yīng) 景门 (Jǐng Mén) Li 9　Xin Xin	白虎 (Bái Hǔ) 禽芮 (Qín Ruì) 死门 (Sǐ Mén) Kun 2　Gui/Yi Gui/Yi
螣蛇 (Téng Shé) 天冲 (Tiān Chōng) 伤门 (Shāng Mén) Zhen 3　Ding Ding	Yang (阳) Dun# 6 Hour: **JiaShen** **Fu Yin** ©Calvin Yap	玄武 (Xuán Wǔ) 天柱 (Tiān Zhù) 惊门 (Jīng Mén) Dui 7　Ji Ji
值符 (Zhí Fú) 天任 (Tiān Rèn) 生门 (Shēng Mén) Gen 8　Geng Geng	九天 (Jiǔ Tiān) 天蓬 (Tiān Péng) 休门 (Xiū Mén) Kan 1　Ren Ren	九地 (Jiǔ Dì) 天心 (Tiān Xīn) 开门 (Kāi Mén) Qian 6　Wu Wu

Yang (阳) Dun# 6 Hour: YiYou；直符(ZhíFú): 天任(TiānRèn)
直使(ZhíShǐ): 生门(ShēngMén)；旬首(XúnShǒu): JiaShenGeng

九地 (Jiǔ Dì) 天心 (Tiān Xīn) 休门 (Xiū Mén) Xun 4　Wu Bing	九天 (Jiǔ Tiān) 天蓬 (Tiān Péng) 生门 (Shēng Mén) Li 9　Ren Xin	值符 (Zhí Fú) 天任 (Tiān Rèn) 伤门 (Shāng Mén) Kun 2　Geng Gui/Yi
玄武 (Xuán Wǔ) 天柱 (Tiān Zhù) 开门 (Kāi Mén) Zhen 3　Ji Ding	Yang (阳) Dun# 6 Hour: **YiYou** **Fan Yin** ©Calvin Yap	螣蛇 (Téng Shé) 天冲 (Tiān Chōng) 杜门 (Dù Mén) Dui 7　Ding Ji
白虎 (Bái Hǔ) 禽芮 (Qín Ruì) 惊门 (Jīng Mén) Gen 8　Gui/Yi Geng	六合 (Liù Hé) 天英 (Tiān Yīng) 死门 (Sǐ Mén) Kan 1　Xin Ren	太阴 (Tài Yīn) 天辅 (Tiān Fǔ) 景门 (Jǐng Mén) Qian 6　Bing Wu

Yang (阳) Dun# 6 Hour: BingXu；直符(ZhíFú): 天任(TiānRèn)
直使(ZhíShǐ): 生门(ShēngMén)；旬首(XúnShǒu): JiaShenGeng

值符 (Zhí Fú) 天任 (Tiān Rèn) 景门 (Jǐng Mén) Xun 4　Geng Bing	螣蛇 (Téng Shé) 天冲 (Tiān Chōng) 死门 (Sǐ Mén) Li 9　Ding Xin	太阴 (Tài Yīn) 天辅 (Tiān Fǔ) 惊门 (Jīng Mén) Kun 2　Bing Gui/Yi
九天 (Jiǔ Tiān) 天蓬 (Tiān Péng) 杜门 (Dù Mén) Zhen 3　Ren Ding	Yang (阳) Dun# 6 Hour: **BingXu** ©Calvin Yap	六合 (Liù Hé) 天英 (Tiān Yīng) 开门 (Kāi Mén) Dui 7　Xin Ji
九地 (Jiǔ Dì) 天心 (Tiān Xīn) 伤门 (Shāng Mén) Gen 8　Wu Geng	玄武 (Xuán Wǔ) 天柱 (Tiān Zhù) 生门 (Shēng Mén) Kan 1　Ji Ren	白虎 (Bái Hǔ) 禽芮 (Qín Ruì) 休门 (Xiū Mén) Qian 6　Gui/Yi Wu

Yang (阳) Dun# 6 Hour: DingHai；直符(ZhíFú): 天任(TiānRèn)
直使(ZhíShǐ): 生门(ShēngMén)；旬首(XúnShǒu): JiaShenGeng

螣蛇 (Téng Shé) 天冲 (Tiān Chōng) 开门 (Kāi Mén) Xun 4　Ding Bing	太阴 (Tài Yīn) 天辅 (Tiān Fǔ) 休门 (Xiū Mén) Li 9　Bing Xin	六合 (Liù Hé) 天英 (Tiān Yīng) 生门 (Shēng Mén) Kun 2　Xin Gui/Yi
值符 (Zhí Fú) 天任 (Tiān Rèn) 惊门 (Jīng Mén) Zhen 3　Geng Ding	Yang (阳) Dun# 6 Hour: **DingHai** ©Calvin Yap	白虎 (Bái Hǔ) 禽芮 (Qín Ruì) 伤门 (Shāng Mén) Dui 7　Gui/Yi Ji
九天 (Jiǔ Tiān) 天蓬 (Tiān Péng) 死门 (Sǐ Mén) Gen 8　Ren Geng	九地 (Jiǔ Dì) 天心 (Tiān Xīn) 景门 (Jǐng Mén) Kan 1　Wu Ren	玄武 (Xuán Wǔ) 天柱 (Tiān Zhù) 杜门 (Dù Mén) Qian 6　Ji Wu

Yang (阳) Dun# 6 Hour: WuZi ；直符(ZhíFú): 天任(TiānRèn)
直使(ZhíShǐ): 生门(ShēngMén) ；句首(XúnShǒu): JiaShenGeng

白虎 (Bái Hǔ) 禽芮 (Qín Ruì) 伤门 (Shāng Mén) Xun 4　Gui/Yi 　　　Bing	玄武 (Xuán Wǔ) 天柱 (Tiān Zhù) 杜门 (Dù Mén) Li 9　Ji 　　Xin	九地 (Jiǔ Dì) 天心 (Tiān Xīn) 景门 (Jǐng Mén) Kun 2　Wu 　　　Gui/Yi
六合 (Liù Hé) 天英 (Tiān Yīng) 生门 (Shēng Mén) Zhen 3　Xin 　　　Ding	Yang (阳) Dun# 6 Hour: WuZi ©Calvin Yap	九天 (Jiǔ Tiān) 天蓬 (Tiān Péng) 死门 (Sǐ Mén) Dui 7　Ren 　　　Ji
太阴 (Tài Yīn) 天辅 (Tiān Fǔ) 休门 (Xiū Mén) Gen 8　Bing 　　　Geng	螣蛇 (Téng Shé) 天冲 (Tiān Chōng) 开门 (Kāi Mén) Kan 1　Ding 　　　Ren	值符 (Zhí Fú) 天任 (Tiān Rèn) 惊门 (Jīng Mén) Qian 6　Geng 　　　Wu

Yang (阳) Dun# 6 Hour: JiChou ；直符(ZhíFú): 天任(TiānRèn)
直使(ZhíShǐ): 生门(ShēngMén) ；句首(XúnShǒu): JiaShenGeng

玄武 (Xuán Wǔ) 天柱 (Tiān Zhù) 生门 (Shēng Mén) Xun 4　Ji 　　　Bing	九地 (Jiǔ Dì) 天心 (Tiān Xīn) 伤门 (Shāng Mén) Li 9　Wu 　　Xin	九天 (Jiǔ Tiān) 天蓬 (Tiān Péng) 杜门 (Dù Mén) Kun 2　Ren 　　　Gui/Yi
白虎 (Bái Hǔ) 禽芮 (Qín Ruì) 休门 (Xiū Mén) Zhen 3　Gui/Yi 　　　Ding	Yang (阳) Dun# 6 Hour: JiChou ©Calvin Yap	值符 (Zhí Fú) 天任 (Tiān Rèn) 景门 (Jǐng Mén) Dui 7　Geng 　　　Ji
六合 (Liù Hé) 天英 (Tiān Yīng) 惊门 (Jīng Mén) Gen 8　Xin 　　　Geng	太阴 (Tài Yīn) 天辅 (Tiān Fǔ) 开门 (Kāi Mén) Kan 1　Bing 　　　Ren	螣蛇 (Téng Shé) 天冲 (Tiān Chōng) 死门 (Sǐ Mén) Qian 6　Ding 　　　Wu

Yang (阳) Dun# 6 Hour: GengYin ；直符(ZhíFú): 天任(TiānRèn)
直使(ZhíShǐ): 生门(ShēngMén) ；句首(XúnShǒu): JiaShenGeng

太阴 (Tài Yīn) 天辅 (Tiān Fǔ) 开门 (Kāi Mén) Xun 4　Bing 　　　Bing	六合 (Liù Hé) 天英 (Tiān Yīng) 休门 (Xiū Mén) Li 9　Xin 　　Xin	白虎 (Bái Hǔ) 禽芮 (Qín Ruì) 生门 (Shēng Mén) Kun 2　Gui/Yi 　　　Gui/Yi
螣蛇 (Téng Shé) 天冲 (Tiān Chōng) 惊门 (Jīng Mén) Zhen 3　Ding 　　　Ding	Yang (阳) Dun# 6 Hour: GengYin Fu Yin ©Calvin Yap	玄武 (Xuán Wǔ) 天柱 (Tiān Zhù) 伤门 (Shāng Mén) Dui 7　Ji 　　　Ji
值符 (Zhí Fú) 天任 (Tiān Rèn) 死门 (Sǐ Mén) Gen 8　Geng 　　　Geng	九天 (Jiǔ Tiān) 天蓬 (Tiān Péng) 景门 (Jǐng Mén) Kan 1　Ren 　　　Ren	九地 (Jiǔ Dì) 天心 (Tiān Xīn) 杜门 (Dù Mén) Qian 6　Wu 　　　Wu

Yang (阳) Dun# 6 Hour: XinMao ；直符(ZhíFú): 天任(TiānRèn)
直使(ZhíShǐ): 生门(ShēngMén) ；句首(XúnShǒu): JiaShenGeng

九天 (Jiǔ Tiān) 天蓬 (Tiān Péng) 死门 (Sǐ Mén) Xun 4　Ren 　　　Bing	值符 (Zhí Fú) 天任 (Tiān Rèn) 惊门 (Jīng Mén) Li 9　Geng 　　Xin	螣蛇 (Téng Shé) 天冲 (Tiān Chōng) 开门 (Kāi Mén) Kun 2　Ding 　　　Gui/Yi
九地 (Jiǔ Dì) 天心 (Tiān Xīn) 景门 (Jǐng Mén) Zhen 3　Wu 　　　Ding	Yang (阳) Dun# 6 Hour: XinMao ©Calvin Yap	太阴 (Tài Yīn) 天辅 (Tiān Fǔ) 休门 (Xiū Mén) Dui 7　Bing 　　　Ji
玄武 (Xuán Wǔ) 天柱 (Tiān Zhù) 杜门 (Dù Mén) Gen 8　Ji 　　　Geng	白虎 (Bái Hǔ) 禽芮 (Qín Ruì) 伤门 (Shāng Mén) Kan 1　Gui/Yi 　　　Ren	六合 (Liù Hé) 天英 (Tiān Yīng) 生门 (Shēng Mén) Qian 6　Xin 　　　Wu

Yang (阳) Dun# 6 Hour: RenChen ；直符(ZhíFú): 天任(TiānRèn)
直使(ZhíShǐ): 生门(ShēngMén) ；句首(XúnShǒu): JiaShenGeng

六合 (Liù Hé) 天英 (Tiān Yīng) 惊门 (Jīng Mén) Xun 4　Xin 　　　Bing	白虎 (Bái Hǔ) 禽芮 (Qín Ruì) 开门 (Kāi Mén) Li 9　Gui/Yi 　　Xin	玄武 (Xuán Wǔ) 天柱 (Tiān Zhù) 休门 (Xiū Mén) Kun 2　Ji 　　　Gui/Yi
太阴 (Tài Yīn) 天辅 (Tiān Fǔ) 死门 (Sǐ Mén) Zhen 3　Bing 　　　Ding	Yang (阳) Dun# 6 Hour: RenChen ©Calvin Yap	九地 (Jiǔ Dì) 天心 (Tiān Xīn) 生门 (Shēng Mén) Dui 7　Wu 　　　Ji
螣蛇 (Téng Shé) 天冲 (Tiān Chōng) 景门 (Jǐng Mén) Gen 8　Ding 　　　Geng	值符 (Zhí Fú) 天任 (Tiān Rèn) 杜门 (Dù Mén) Kan 1　Geng 　　　Ren	九天 (Jiǔ Tiān) 天蓬 (Tiān Péng) 伤门 (Shāng Mén) Qian 6　Ren 　　　Wu

Yang (阳) Dun# 6 Hour: GuiSi ；直符(ZhíFú): 天任(TiānRèn)
直使(ZhíShǐ): 生门(ShēngMén) ；句首(XúnShǒu): JiaShenGeng

九地 (Jiǔ Dì) 天心 (Tiān Xīn) 杜门 (Dù Mén) Xun 4　Wu 　　　Bing	九天 (Jiǔ Tiān) 天蓬 (Tiān Péng) 景门 (Jǐng Mén) Li 9　Ren 　　Xin	值符 (Zhí Fú) 天任 (Tiān Rèn) 死门 (Sǐ Mén) Kun 2　Geng 　　　Gui/Yi
玄武 (Xuán Wǔ) 天柱 (Tiān Zhù) 伤门 (Shāng Mén) Zhen 3　Ji 　　　Ding	Yang (阳) Dun# 6 Hour: GuiSi Fan Yin ©Calvin Yap	螣蛇 (Téng Shé) 天冲 (Tiān Chōng) 惊门 (Jīng Mén) Dui 7　Ding 　　　Ji
白虎 (Bái Hǔ) 禽芮 (Qín Ruì) 生门 (Shēng Mén) Gen 8　Gui/Yi 　　　Geng	六合 (Liù Hé) 天英 (Tiān Yīng) 休门 (Xiū Mén) Kan 1　Xin 　　　Ren	太阴 (Tài Yīn) 天辅 (Tiān Fǔ) 开门 (Kāi Mén) Qian 6　Bing 　　　Wu

Chart: +6JiaWu (Yang Dun #6 JiaWu Xun)
JiaWu, YiWei, BingShen, DingYou, WuXu, JiHai, GengZi, XinChou, RenYin, GuiMao

Yang (阳) Dun# 6 Hour: **JiaWu** ; 直符(ZhíFú): 天英(TiānYīng)
直使(ZhíShǐ): 景门(JǐngMén) ; 旬首(XúnShǒu): JiaWu/Xin

九天 (Jiǔ Tiān) 天辅 (Tiān Fǔ) 杜门 (Dù Mén) Xun 4 Bing Bing	值符 (Zhí Fú) 天英 (Tiān Yīng) 景门 (Jǐng Mén) Li 9 Xin Xin	螣蛇 (Téng Shé) 禽芮 (Qín Ruì) 死门 (Sǐ Mén) Kun 2 Gui/Yi Gui/Yi
九地 (Jiǔ Dì) 天冲 (Tiān Chōng) 伤门 (Shāng Mén) Zhen 3 Ding Ding	Yang (阳) Dun# 6 Hour: **JiaWu** **Fu Yin** ©Calvin Yap	太阴 (Tài Yīn) 天柱 (Tiān Zhù) 惊门 (Jīng Mén) Dui 7 Ji Ji
玄武 (Xuán Wǔ) 天任 (Tiān Rèn) 生门 (Shēng Mén) Gen 8 Geng Geng	白虎 (Bái Hǔ) 天蓬 (Tiān Péng) 休门 (Xiū Mén) Kan 1 Ren Ren	六合 (Liù Hé) 天心 (Tiān Xīn) 开门 (Kāi Mén) Qian 6 Wu Wu

Yang (阳) Dun# 6 Hour: **YiWei** ; 直符(ZhíFú): 天英(TiānYīng)
直使(ZhíShǐ): 景门(JǐngMén) ; 旬首(XúnShǒu): JiaWu/Xin

九地 (Jiǔ Dì) 天冲 (Tiān Chōng) 开门 (Kāi Mén) Xun 4 Ding Bing	九天 (Jiǔ Tiān) 天辅 (Tiān Fǔ) 休门 (Xiū Mén) Li 9 Bing Xin	值符 (Zhí Fú) 天英 (Tiān Yīng) 生门 (Shēng Mén) Kun 2 Xin Gui/Yi
玄武 (Xuán Wǔ) 天任 (Tiān Rèn) 惊门 (Jīng Mén) Zhen 3 Geng Ding	Yang (阳) Dun# 6 Hour: **YiWei** ©Calvin Yap	螣蛇 (Téng Shé) 禽芮 (Qín Ruì) 伤门 (Shāng Mén) Dui 7 Gui/Yi Ji
白虎 (Bái Hǔ) 天蓬 (Tiān Péng) 死门 (Sǐ Mén) Gen 8 Ren Geng	六合 (Liù Hé) 天心 (Tiān Xīn) 景门 (Jǐng Mén) Kan 1 Wu Ren	太阴 (Tài Yīn) 天柱 (Tiān Zhù) 杜门 (Dù Mén) Qian 6 Ji Wu

Yang (阳) Dun# 6 Hour: **BingShen** ; 直符(ZhíFú): 天英(TiānYīng)
直使(ZhíShǐ): 景门(JǐngMén) ; 旬首(XúnShǒu): JiaWu/Xin

值符 (Zhí Fú) 天英 (Tiān Yīng) 伤门 (Shāng Mén) Xun 4 Xin Bing	螣蛇 (Téng Shé) 禽芮 (Qín Ruì) 杜门 (Dù Mén) Li 9 Gui/Yi Xin	太阴 (Tài Yīn) 天柱 (Tiān Zhù) 景门 (Jǐng Mén) Kun 2 Ji Gui/Yi
九天 (Jiǔ Tiān) 天辅 (Tiān Fǔ) 生门 (Shēng Mén) Zhen 3 Bing Ding	Yang (阳) Dun# 6 Hour: **BingShen** ©Calvin Yap	六合 (Liù Hé) 天心 (Tiān Xīn) 死门 (Sǐ Mén) Dui 7 Wu Ji
九地 (Jiǔ Dì) 天冲 (Tiān Chōng) 休门 (Xiū Mén) Gen 8 Ding Geng	玄武 (Xuán Wǔ) 天任 (Tiān Rèn) 开门 (Kāi Mén) Kan 1 Geng Ren	白虎 (Bái Hǔ) 天蓬 (Tiān Péng) 惊门 (Jīng Mén) Qian 6 Ren Wu

Yang (阳) Dun# 6 Hour: **DingYou** ; 直符(ZhíFú): 天英(TiānYīng)
直使(ZhíShǐ): 景门(JǐngMén) ; 旬首(XúnShǒu): JiaWu/Xin

螣蛇 (Téng Shé) 禽芮 (Qín Ruì) 死门 (Sǐ Mén) Xun 4 Gui/Yi Bing	太阴 (Tài Yīn) 天柱 (Tiān Zhù) 惊门 (Jīng Mén) Li 9 Ji Xin	六合 (Liù Hé) 天心 (Tiān Xīn) 开门 (Kāi Mén) Kun 2 Wu Gui/Yi
值符 (Zhí Fú) 天英 (Tiān Yīng) 景门 (Jǐng Mén) Zhen 3 Xin Ding	Yang (阳) Dun# 6 Hour: **DingYou** ©Calvin Yap	白虎 (Bái Hǔ) 天蓬 (Tiān Péng) 休门 (Xiū Mén) Dui 7 Ren Ji
九天 (Jiǔ Tiān) 天辅 (Tiān Fǔ) 杜门 (Dù Mén) Gen 8 Bing Geng	九地 (Jiǔ Dì) 天冲 (Tiān Chōng) 伤门 (Shāng Mén) Kan 1 Ding Ren	玄武 (Xuán Wǔ) 天任 (Tiān Rèn) 生门 (Shēng Mén) Qian 6 Geng Wu

Yang (阳) Dun# 6 Hour: **WuXu** ; 直符(ZhíFú): 天英(TiānYīng)
直使(ZhíShǐ): 景门(JǐngMén) ; 旬首(XúnShǒu): JiaWu/Xin

白虎 (Bái Hǔ) 天蓬 (Tiān Péng) 景门 (Jǐng Mén) Xun 4 Ren Bing	玄武 (Xuán Wǔ) 天任 (Tiān Rèn) 死门 (Sǐ Mén) Li 9 Geng Xin	九地 (Jiǔ Dì) 天冲 (Tiān Chōng) 惊门 (Jīng Mén) Kun 2 Ding Gui/Yi
六合 (Liù Hé) 天心 (Tiān Xīn) 杜门 (Dù Mén) Zhen 3 Wu Ding	Yang (阳) Dun# 6 Hour: **WuXu** ©Calvin Yap	九天 (Jiǔ Tiān) 天辅 (Tiān Fǔ) 开门 (Kāi Mén) Dui 7 Bing Ji
太阴 (Tài Yīn) 天柱 (Tiān Zhù) 伤门 (Shāng Mén) Gen 8 Ji Geng	螣蛇 (Téng Shé) 禽芮 (Qín Ruì) 生门 (Shēng Mén) Kan 1 Gui/Yi Ren	值符 (Zhí Fú) 天英 (Tiān Yīng) 休门 (Xiū Mén) Qian 6 Xin Wu

Yang (阳) Dun# 6 Hour: **JiHai** ; 直符(ZhíFú): 天英(TiānYīng)
直使(ZhíShǐ): 景门(JǐngMén) ; 旬首(XúnShǒu): JiaWu/Xin

玄武 (Xuán Wǔ) 天任 (Tiān Rèn) 伤门 (Shāng Mén) Xun 4 Geng Bing	九地 (Jiǔ Dì) 天冲 (Tiān Chōng) 杜门 (Dù Mén) Li 9 Ding Xin	九天 (Jiǔ Tiān) 天辅 (Tiān Fǔ) 景门 (Jǐng Mén) Kun 2 Bing Gui/Yi
白虎 (Bái Hǔ) 天蓬 (Tiān Péng) 生门 (Shēng Mén) Zhen 3 Ren Ding	Yang (阳) Dun# 6 Hour: **JiHai** ©Calvin Yap	值符 (Zhí Fú) 天英 (Tiān Yīng) 死门 (Sǐ Mén) Dui 7 Xin Ji
六合 (Liù Hé) 天心 (Tiān Xīn) 休门 (Xiū Mén) Gen 8 Wu Geng	太阴 (Tài Yīn) 天柱 (Tiān Zhù) 开门 (Kāi Mén) Kan 1 Ji Ren	螣蛇 (Téng Shé) 禽芮 (Qín Ruì) 惊门 (Jīng Mén) Qian 6 Gui/Yi Wu

Yang (阳) Dun# 6 Hour: **GengZi** ; 直符(ZhíFú): 天英(TiānYīng)
直使(ZhíShǐ): 景门(JǐngMén) ; 旬首(XúnShǒu): JiaWu/Xin

太阴 (Tài Yīn) 天柱 (Tiān Zhù) 休门 (Xiū Mén) Xun 4　Ji Bing	六合 (Liù Hé) 天心 (Tiān Xīn) 生门 (Shēng Mén) Li 9　Wu	白虎 (Bái Hǔ) 天蓬 (Tiān Péng) 伤门 (Shāng Mén) Kun 2　Ren Xin　Gui/Yi
螣蛇 (Téng Shé) 禽芮 (Qín Ruì) 开门 (Kāi Mén) Zhen 3　Gui/Yi Ding	Yang (阳) Dun# 6 Hour: **GengZi** ©Calvin Yap	玄武 (Xuán Wǔ) 天任 (Tiān Rèn) 杜门 (Dù Mén) Dui 7　Geng Ji
值符 (Zhí Fú) 天英 (Tiān Yīng) 惊门 (Jīng Mén) Gen 8　Xin Geng	九天 (Jiǔ Tiān) 天辅 (Tiān Fǔ) 死门 (Sǐ Mén) Kan 1　Bing Ren	九地 (Jiǔ Dì) 天冲 (Tiān Chōng) 景门 (Jǐng Mén) Qian 6　Ding Wu

Yang (阳) Dun# 6 Hour: **XinChou** ; 直符(ZhíFú): 天英(TiānYīng)
直使(ZhíShǐ): 景门(JǐngMén) ; 旬首(XúnShǒu): JiaWu/Xin

九天 (Jiǔ Tiān) 天辅 (Tiān Fǔ) 生门 (Shēng Mén) Xun 4　Bing Bing	值符 (Zhí Fú) 天英 (Tiān Yīng) 伤门 (Shāng Mén) Li 9　Xin	螣蛇 (Téng Shé) 禽芮 (Qín Ruì) 杜门 (Dù Mén) Kun 2　Gui/Yi Gui/Yi
九地 (Jiǔ Dì) 天冲 (Tiān Chōng) 休门 (Xiū Mén) Zhen 3　Ding Ding	Yang (阳) Dun# 6 Hour: **XinChou** **Fu Yin** ©Calvin Yap	太阴 (Tài Yīn) 天柱 (Tiān Zhù) 景门 (Jǐng Mén) Dui 7　Ji Ji
玄武 (Xuán Wǔ) 天任 (Tiān Rèn) 开门 (Kāi Mén) Gen 8　Geng Geng	白虎 (Bái Hǔ) 天蓬 (Tiān Péng) 惊门 (Jīng Mén) Kan 1　Ren Ren	六合 (Liù Hé) 天心 (Tiān Xīn) 死门 (Sǐ Mén) Qian 6　Wu Wu

Yang (阳) Dun# 6 Hour: **RenYin** ; 直符(ZhíFú): 天英(TiānYīng)
直使(ZhíShǐ): 景门(JǐngMén) ; 旬首(XúnShǒu): JiaWu/Xin

六合 (Liù Hé) 天心 (Tiān Xīn) 惊门 (Jīng Mén) Xun 4　Wu Bing	白虎 (Bái Hǔ) 天蓬 (Tiān Péng) 开门 (Kāi Mén) Li 9　Ren Xin	玄武 (Xuán Wǔ) 天任 (Tiān Rèn) 休门 (Xiū Mén) Kun 2　Geng Gui/Yi
太阴 (Tài Yīn) 天柱 (Tiān Zhù) 死门 (Sǐ Mén) Zhen 3　Ji Ding	Yang (阳) Dun# 6 Hour: **RenYin** **Fan Yin** ©Calvin Yap	九地 (Jiǔ Dì) 天冲 (Tiān Chōng) 生门 (Shēng Mén) Dui 7　Ding Ji
螣蛇 (Téng Shé) 禽芮 (Qín Ruì) 景门 (Jǐng Mén) Gen 8　Gui/Yi Geng	值符 (Zhí Fú) 天英 (Tiān Yīng) 杜门 (Dù Mén) Kan 1　Xin Ren	九天 (Jiǔ Tiān) 天辅 (Tiān Fǔ) 伤门 (Shāng Mén) Qian 6　Bing Wu

Yang (阳) Dun# 6 Hour: **GuiMao** ; 直符(ZhíFú): 天英(TiānYīng)
直使(ZhíShǐ): 景门(JǐngMén) ; 旬首(XúnShǒu): JiaWu/Xin

九地 (Jiǔ Dì) 天冲 (Tiān Chōng) 杜门 (Dù Mén) Xun 4　Ding Bing	九天 (Jiǔ Tiān) 天辅 (Tiān Fǔ) 景门 (Jǐng Mén) Li 9　Bing Xin	值符 (Zhí Fú) 天英 (Tiān Yīng) 死门 (Sǐ Mén) Kun 2　Xin Gui/Yi
玄武 (Xuán Wǔ) 天任 (Tiān Rèn) 伤门 (Shāng Mén) Zhen 3　Geng Ding	Yang (阳) Dun# 6 Hour: **GuiMao** ©Calvin Yap	螣蛇 (Téng Shé) 禽芮 (Qín Ruì) 惊门 (Jīng Mén) Dui 7　Gui/Yi Ji
白虎 (Bái Hǔ) 天蓬 (Tiān Péng) 生门 (Shēng Mén) Gen 8　Ren Geng	六合 (Liù Hé) 天心 (Tiān Xīn) 休门 (Xiū Mén) Kan 1　Wu Ren	太阴 (Tài Yīn) 天柱 (Tiān Zhù) 开门 (Kāi Mén) Qian 6　Ji Wu

Chart: **+6JiaChen** (Yang Dun #6 JiaChen Xun)
JiaChen, YiSi, BingWu, DingWei, WuShen, JiYou, GengXu, XinHai, RenZi, GuiChou

Yang (阳) Dun# 6 Hour: **JiaChen** ; 直符(ZhíFú): 天蓬(TiānPéng)
直使(ZhíShǐ): 休门(XiūMén) ; 旬首(XúnShǒu): JiaChenRen

六合 (Liù Hé) 天辅 (Tiān Fǔ) 杜门 (Dù Mén) Xun 4　Bing Bing	白虎 (Bái Hǔ) 天英 (Tiān Yīng) 景门 (Jǐng Mén) Li 9　Xin Xin	玄武 (Xuán Wǔ) 禽芮 (Qín Ruì) 死门 (Sǐ Mén) Kun 2　Gui/Yi Gui/Yi
太阴 (Tài Yīn) 天冲 (Tiān Chōng) 伤门 (Shāng Mén) Zhen 3　Ding Ding	Yang (阳) Dun# 6 Hour: **JiaChen** **Fu Yin** ©Calvin Yap	九地 (Jiǔ Dì) 天柱 (Tiān Zhù) 惊门 (Jīng Mén) Dui 7　Ji Ji
螣蛇 (Téng Shé) 天任 (Tiān Rèn) 生门 (Shēng Mén) Gen 8　Geng Geng	值符 (Zhí Fú) 天蓬 (Tiān Péng) 休门 (Xiū Mén) Kan 1　Ren Ren	九天 (Jiǔ Tiān) 天心 (Tiān Xīn) 开门 (Kāi Mén) Qian 6　Wu Wu

Yang (阳) Dun# 6 Hour: **YiSi** ; 直符(ZhíFú): 天蓬(TiānPéng)
直使(ZhíShǐ): 休门(XiūMén) ; 旬首(XúnShǒu): JiaChenRen

九地 (Jiǔ Dì) 天柱 (Tiān Zhù) 惊门 (Jīng Mén) Xun 4　Ji Bing	九天 (Jiǔ Tiān) 天心 (Tiān Xīn) 开门 (Kāi Mén) Li 9　Wu Xin	值符 (Zhí Fú) 天蓬 (Tiān Péng) 休门 (Xiū Mén) Kun 2　Ren Gui/Yi
玄武 (Xuán Wǔ) 禽芮 (Qín Ruì) 死门 (Sǐ Mén) Zhen 3　Gui/Yi Ding	Yang (阳) Dun# 6 Hour: **YiSi** ©Calvin Yap	螣蛇 (Téng Shé) 天任 (Tiān Rèn) 生门 (Shēng Mén) Dui 7　Geng Ji
白虎 (Bái Hǔ) 天英 (Tiān Yīng) 景门 (Jǐng Mén) Gen 8　Xin Geng	六合 (Liù Hé) 天辅 (Tiān Fǔ) 杜门 (Dù Mén) Kan 1　Bing Ren	太阴 (Tài Yīn) 天冲 (Tiān Chōng) 伤门 (Shāng Mén) Qian 6　Ding Wu

Yang (阳) Dun# 6 Hour: **BingWu**；直符(ZhíFú): 天蓬(TiānPéng)；直使(ZhíShǐ): 休门(XiūMén)；旬首(XúnShǒu): JiaChenRen

值符 (Zhí Fú) 天蓬 (Tiān Péng) 生门 (Shēng Mén) Xun 4　Bing	螣蛇 (Téng Shé) 天任 (Tiān Rèn) 伤门 (Shāng Mén) Li 9　Geng　Xin	太阴 (Tài Yīn) 天冲 (Tiān Chōng) 杜门 (Dù Mén) Kun 2　Ding　Gui/Yi
九天 (Jiǔ Tiān) 天心 (Tiān Xīn) 休门 (Xiū Mén) Zhen 3　Wu　Ding	Yang (阳) Dun# 6 Hour: **BingWu** ©Calvin Yap	六合 (Liù Hé) 天辅 (Tiān Fǔ) 景门 (Jǐng Mén) Dui 7　Bing　Ji
九地 (Jiǔ Dì) 天柱 (Tiān Zhù) 开门 (Kāi Mén) Gen 8　Ji　Geng	玄武 (Xuán Wǔ) 禽芮 (Qín Ruì) 惊门 (Jīng Mén) Kan 1　Gui/Yi　Ren	白虎 (Bái Hǔ) 天英 (Tiān Yīng) 死门 (Sǐ Mén) Qian 6　Xin　Wu

Yang (阳) Dun# 6 Hour: **DingWei**；直符(ZhíFú): 天蓬(TiānPéng)；直使(ZhíShǐ): 休门(XiūMén)；旬首(XúnShǒu): JiaChenRen

螣蛇 (Téng Shé) 天任 (Tiān Rèn) 休门 (Xiū Mén) Xun 4　Geng　Bing	太阴 (Tài Yīn) 天冲 (Tiān Chōng) 生门 (Shēng Mén) Li 9　Ding　Xin	六合 (Liù Hé) 天辅 (Tiān Fǔ) 伤门 (Shāng Mén) Kun 2　Bing　Gui/Yi
值符 (Zhí Fú) 天蓬 (Tiān Péng) 开门 (Kāi Mén) Zhen 3　Ren　Ding	Yang (阳) Dun# 6 Hour: **DingWei** ©Calvin Yap	白虎 (Bái Hǔ) 天英 (Tiān Yīng) 杜门 (Dù Mén) Dui 7　Xin　Ji
九天 (Jiǔ Tiān) 天心 (Tiān Xīn) 惊门 (Jīng Mén) Gen 8　Wu　Geng	九地 (Jiǔ Dì) 天柱 (Tiān Zhù) 死门 (Sǐ Mén) Kan 1　Ji　Ren	玄武 (Xuán Wǔ) 禽芮 (Qín Ruì) 景门 (Jǐng Mén) Qian 6　Gui/Yi　Wu

Yang (阳) Dun# 6 Hour: **WuShen**；直符(ZhíFú): 天蓬(TiānPéng)；直使(ZhíShǐ): 休门(XiūMén)；旬首(XúnShǒu): JiaChenRen

白虎 (Bái Hǔ) 天英 (Tiān Yīng) 惊门 (Jīng Mén) Xun 4　Xin　Bing	玄武 (Xuán Wǔ) 禽芮 (Qín Ruì) 开门 (Kāi Mén) Li 9　Gui/Yi　Xin	九地 (Jiǔ Dì) 天柱 (Tiān Zhù) 休门 (Xiū Mén) Kun 2　Ji　Gui/Yi
六合 (Liù Hé) 天辅 (Tiān Fǔ) 死门 (Sǐ Mén) Zhen 3　Bing　Ding	Yang (阳) Dun# 6 Hour: **WuShen** ©Calvin Yap	九天 (Jiǔ Tiān) 天心 (Tiān Xīn) 生门 (Shēng Mén) Dui 7　Wu　Ji
太阴 (Tài Yīn) 天冲 (Tiān Chōng) 景门 (Jǐng Mén) Gen 8　Ding　Geng	螣蛇 (Téng Shé) 天任 (Tiān Rèn) 杜门 (Dù Mén) Kan 1　Geng　Ren	值符 (Zhí Fú) 天蓬 (Tiān Péng) 伤门 (Shāng Mén) Qian 6　Ren　Wu

Yang (阳) Dun# 6 Hour: **JiYou**；直符(ZhíFú): 天蓬(TiānPéng)；直使(ZhíShǐ): 休门(XiūMén)；旬首(XúnShǒu): JiaChenRen

玄武 (Xuán Wǔ) 禽芮 (Qín Ruì) 景门 (Jǐng Mén) Xun 4　Gui/Yi　Bing	九地 (Jiǔ Dì) 天柱 (Tiān Zhù) 死门 (Sǐ Mén) Li 9　Ji　Xin	九天 (Jiǔ Tiān) 天心 (Tiān Xīn) 惊门 (Jīng Mén) Kun 2　Wu　Gui/Yi
白虎 (Bái Hǔ) 天英 (Tiān Yīng) 杜门 (Dù Mén) Zhen 3　Xin　Ding	Yang (阳) Dun# 6 Hour: **JiYou** ©Calvin Yap	值符 (Zhí Fú) 天蓬 (Tiān Péng) 开门 (Kāi Mén) Dui 7　Ren　Ji
六合 (Liù Hé) 天辅 (Tiān Fǔ) 伤门 (Shāng Mén) Gen 8　Bing　Geng	太阴 (Tài Yīn) 天冲 (Tiān Chōng) 生门 (Shēng Mén) Kan 1　Ding　Ren	螣蛇 (Téng Shé) 天任 (Tiān Rèn) 休门 (Xiū Mén) Qian 6　Geng　Wu

Yang (阳) Dun# 6 Hour: **GengXu**；直符(ZhíFú): 天蓬(TiānPéng)；直使(ZhíShǐ): 休门(XiūMén)；旬首(XúnShǒu): JiaChenRen

太阴 (Tài Yīn) 天冲 (Tiān Chōng) 死门 (Sǐ Mén) Xun 4　Ding　Bing	六合 (Liù Hé) 天辅 (Tiān Fǔ) 惊门 (Jīng Mén) Li 9　Bing　Xin	白虎 (Bái Hǔ) 天英 (Tiān Yīng) 开门 (Kāi Mén) Kun 2　Xin　Gui/Yi
螣蛇 (Téng Shé) 天任 (Tiān Rèn) 景门 (Jǐng Mén) Zhen 3　Geng　Ding	Yang (阳) Dun# 6 Hour: **GengXu** ©Calvin Yap	玄武 (Xuán Wǔ) 禽芮 (Qín Ruì) 休门 (Xiū Mén) Dui 7　Gui/Yi　Ji
值符 (Zhí Fú) 天蓬 (Tiān Péng) 杜门 (Dù Mén) Gen 8　Ren　Geng	九天 (Jiǔ Tiān) 天心 (Tiān Xīn) 伤门 (Shāng Mén) Kan 1　Wu　Ren	九地 (Jiǔ Dì) 天柱 (Tiān Zhù) 生门 (Shēng Mén) Qian 6　Ji　Wu

Yang (阳) Dun# 6 Hour: **XinHai**；直符(ZhíFú): 天蓬(TiānPéng)；直使(ZhíShǐ): 休门(XiūMén)；旬首(XúnShǒu): JiaChenRen

九天 (Jiǔ Tiān) 天心 (Tiān Xīn) 伤门 (Shāng Mén) Xun 4　Wu　Bing	值符 (Zhí Fú) 天蓬 (Tiān Péng) 杜门 (Dù Mén) Li 9　Ren　Xin	螣蛇 (Téng Shé) 天任 (Tiān Rèn) 景门 (Jǐng Mén) Kun 2　Geng　Gui/Yi
九地 (Jiǔ Dì) 天柱 (Tiān Zhù) 生门 (Shēng Mén) Zhen 3　Ji　Ding	Yang (阳) Dun# 6 Hour: **XinHai** **Fan Yin** ©Calvin Yap	太阴 (Tài Yīn) 天冲 (Tiān Chōng) 死门 (Sǐ Mén) Dui 7　Ding　Ji
玄武 (Xuán Wǔ) 禽芮 (Qín Ruì) 休门 (Xiū Mén) Gen 8　Gui/Yi　Geng	白虎 (Bái Hǔ) 天英 (Tiān Yīng) 开门 (Kāi Mén) Kan 1　Xin　Ren	六合 (Liù Hé) 天辅 (Tiān Fǔ) 惊门 (Jīng Mén) Qian 6　Bing　Wu

Yang (阳) Dun# 6 Hour: RenZi；直符(ZhíFú): 天蓬(TiānPéng)
直使(ZhíShǐ): 休门(XiūMén)；旬首(XúnShǒu): JiaChenRen

六合 (Liù Hé) 天辅 (Tiān Fǔ) 开门 (Kāi Mén) Xun 4 Bing / Bing	白虎 (Bái Hǔ) 天英 (Tiān Yīng) 休门 (Xiū Mén) Li 9 Xin / Xin	玄武 (Xuán Wǔ) 禽芮 (Qín Ruì) 生门 (Shēng Mén) Kun 2 Gui/Yi / Gui/Yi
太阴 (Tài Yīn) 天冲 (Tiān Chōng) 惊门 (Jīng Mén) Zhen 3 Ding / Ding	Yang (阳) Dun# 6 Hour: **RenZi** **Fu Yin** ©Calvin Yap	九地 (Jiǔ Dì) 天柱 (Tiān Zhù) 伤门 (Shāng Mén) Dui 7 Ji / Ji
螣蛇 (Téng Shé) 天任 (Tiān Rèn) 死门 (Sǐ Mén) Gen 8 Geng / Geng	值符 (Zhí Fú) 天蓬 (Tiān Péng) 景门 (Jǐng Mén) Kan 1 Ren / Ren	九天 (Jiǔ Tiān) 天心 (Tiān Xīn) 杜门 (Dù Mén) Qian 6 Wu / Wu

Yang (阳) Dun# 6 Hour: GuiChou；直符(ZhíFú): 天蓬(TiānPéng)
直使(ZhíShǐ): 休门(XiūMén)；旬首(XúnShǒu): JiaChenRen

九地 (Jiǔ Dì) 天柱 (Tiān Zhù) 杜门 (Dù Mén) Xun 4 Ji	九天 (Jiǔ Tiān) 天心 (Tiān Xīn) 景门 (Jǐng Mén) Li 9 Wu / Xin	值符 (Zhí Fú) 天蓬 (Tiān Péng) 死门 (Sǐ Mén) Kun 2 Ren / Gui/Yi
玄武 (Xuán Wǔ) 禽芮 (Qín Ruì) 伤门 (Shāng Mén) Zhen 3 Gui/Yi	Yang (阳) Dun# 6 Hour: **GuiChou** ©Calvin Yap	螣蛇 (Téng Shé) 天任 (Tiān Rèn) 惊门 (Jīng Mén) Dui 7 Geng / Ji
白虎 (Bái Hǔ) 天英 (Tiān Yīng) 生门 (Shēng Mén) Gen 8 Xin / Geng	六合 (Liù Hé) 天辅 (Tiān Fǔ) 休门 (Xiū Mén) Kan 1 Bing / Ren	太阴 (Tài Yīn) 天冲 (Tiān Chōng) 开门 (Kāi Mén) Qian 6 Ding / Wu

Chart: +6JiaYin (Yang Dun #6 JiaYin Xun)
JiaYin, YiMao, BingChen, DingSi, WuWu, JiWei, GengShen, XinYou, RenXu, GuiHai

Yang (阳) Dun# 6 Hour: JiaYin；直符(ZhíFú): 天芮(TiānRuì)
直使(ZhíShǐ): 死门(SǐMén)；旬首(XúnShǒu): JiaYinGui

九地 (Jiǔ Dì) 天辅 (Tiān Fǔ) 杜门 (Dù Mén) Xun 4 Bing / Bing	九天 (Jiǔ Tiān) 天英 (Tiān Yīng) 景门 (Jǐng Mén) Li 9 Xin	值符 (Zhí Fú) 禽芮 (Qín Ruì) 死门 (Sǐ Mén) Kun 2 Gui/Yi / Gui/Yi
玄武 (Xuán Wǔ) 天冲 (Tiān Chōng) 伤门 (Shāng Mén) Zhen 3 Ding / Ding	Yang (阳) Dun# 6 Hour: **JiaYin** **Fu Yin** ©Calvin Yap	螣蛇 (Téng Shé) 天柱 (Tiān Zhù) 惊门 (Jīng Mén) Dui 7 Ji / Ji
白虎 (Bái Hǔ) 天任 (Tiān Rèn) 生门 (Shēng Mén) Gen 8 Geng / Geng	六合 (Liù Hé) 天蓬 (Tiān Péng) 休门 (Xiū Mén) Kan 1 Ren / Ren	太阴 (Tài Yīn) 天心 (Tiān Xīn) 开门 (Kāi Mén) Qian 6 Wu / Wu

Yang (阳) Dun# 6 Hour: YiMao；直符(ZhíFú): 天芮(TiānRuì)
直使(ZhíShǐ): 死门(SǐMén)；旬首(XúnShǒu): JiaYinGui

九地 (Jiǔ Dì) 天辅 (Tiān Fǔ) 惊门 (Jīng Mén) Xun 4 Bing / Bing	九天 (Jiǔ Tiān) 天英 (Tiān Yīng) 开门 (Kāi Mén) Li 9 Xin	值符 (Zhí Fú) 禽芮 (Qín Ruì) 休门 (Xiū Mén) Kun 2 Gui/Yi / Gui/Yi
玄武 (Xuán Wǔ) 天冲 (Tiān Chōng) 死门 (Sǐ Mén) Zhen 3 Ding / Ding	Yang (阳) Dun# 6 Hour: **YiMao** **Fu Yin** ©Calvin Yap	螣蛇 (Téng Shé) 天柱 (Tiān Zhù) 生门 (Shēng Mén) Dui 7 Ji / Ji
白虎 (Bái Hǔ) 天任 (Tiān Rèn) 景门 (Jǐng Mén) Gen 8 Geng / Geng	六合 (Liù Hé) 天蓬 (Tiān Péng) 杜门 (Dù Mén) Kan 1 Ren / Ren	太阴 (Tài Yīn) 天心 (Tiān Xīn) 伤门 (Shāng Mén) Qian 6 Wu / Wu

Yang (阳) Dun# 6 Hour: BingChen；直符(ZhíFú): 天芮(TiānRuì)
直使(ZhíShǐ): 死门(SǐMén)；旬首(XúnShǒu): JiaYinGui

值符 (Zhi Fú) 禽芮 (Qín Ruì) 死门 (Sǐ Mén) Xun 4 Gui/Yi / Bing	螣蛇 (Téng Shé) 天柱 (Tiān Zhù) 惊门 (Jīng Mén) Li 9 Ji / Xin	太阴 (Tài Yīn) 天心 (Tiān Xīn) 开门 (Kāi Mén) Kun 2 Wu / Gui/Yi
九天 (Jiǔ Tiān) 天英 (Tiān Yīng) 景门 (Jǐng Mén) Zhen 3 Xin / Ding	Yang (阳) Dun# 6 Hour: **BingChen** ©Calvin Yap	六合 (Liù Hé) 天蓬 (Tiān Péng) 休门 (Xiū Mén) Dui 7 Ren / Ji
九地 (Jiǔ Dì) 天辅 (Tiān Fǔ) 杜门 (Dù Mén) Gen 8 Bing / Geng	玄武 (Xuán Wǔ) 天冲 (Tiān Chōng) 伤门 (Shāng Mén) Kan 1 Ding / Ren	白虎 (Bái Hǔ) 天任 (Tiān Rèn) 生门 (Shēng Mén) Qian 6 Geng / Wu

Yang (阳) Dun# 6 Hour: DingSi；直符(ZhíFú): 天芮(TiānRuì)
直使(ZhíShǐ): 死门(SǐMén)；旬首(XúnShǒu): JiaYinGui

螣蛇 (Téng Shé) 天柱 (Tiān Zhù) 杜门 (Dù Mén) Xun 4 Ji	太阴 (Tài Yīn) 天心 (Tiān Xīn) 景门 (Jǐng Mén) Li 9 Wu / Xin	六合 (Liù Hé) 天蓬 (Tiān Péng) 死门 (Sǐ Mén) Kun 2 Ren / Gui/Yi
值符 (Zhí Fú) 禽芮 (Qín Ruì) 伤门 (Shāng Mén) Zhen 3 Gui/Yi	Yang (阳) Dun# 6 Hour: **DingSi** ©Calvin Yap	白虎 (Bái Hǔ) 天任 (Tiān Rèn) 惊门 (Jīng Mén) Dui 7 Geng / Ji
九天 (Jiǔ Tiān) 天英 (Tiān Yīng) 生门 (Shēng Mén) Gen 8 Xin / Geng	九地 (Jiǔ Dì) 天辅 (Tiān Fǔ) 休门 (Xiū Mén) Kan 1 Bing / Ren	玄武 (Xuán Wǔ) 天冲 (Tiān Chōng) 开门 (Kāi Mén) Qian 6 Ding / Wu

Yang (阳) Dun# 6 Hour: **WuWu** ; 直符(ZhíFú): 天芮(TiānRuì)
直使(ZhíShǐ): 死门(SǐMén) ; 旬首(XúnShǒu): JiaYinGui

白虎 (Bái Hǔ) 天任 (Tiān Rèn) 生门 (Shēng Mén) Xun 4 Geng Bing	玄武 (Xuán Wǔ) 天冲 (Tiān Chōng) 伤门 (Shāng Mén) Li 9 Ding Xin	九地 (Jiǔ Dì) 天辅 (Tiān Fǔ) 杜门 (Dù Mén) Kun 2 Bing Gui/Yi
六合 (Liù Hé) 天蓬 (Tiān Péng) 休门 (Xiū Mén) Zhen 3 Ren Ding	Yang (阳) Dun# 6 Hour: **WuWu** ©Calvin Yap	九天 (Jiǔ Tiān) 天英 (Tiān Yīng) 景门 (Jǐng Mén) Dui 7 Xin Ji
太阴 (Tài Yīn) 天心 (Tiān Xīn) 开门 (Kāi Mén) Gen 8 Wu Geng	螣蛇 (Téng Shé) 天柱 (Tiān Zhù) 惊门 (Jīng Mén) Kan 1 Ji Ren	值符 (Zhí Fú) 禽芮 (Qín Ruì) 死门 (Sǐ Mén) Qian 6 Gui/Yi Wu

Yang (阳) Dun# 6 Hour: **JiWei** ; 直符(ZhíFú): 天芮(TiānRuì)
直使(ZhíShǐ): 死门(SǐMén) ; 旬首(XúnShǒu): JiaYinGui

玄武 (Xuán Wǔ) 天冲 (Tiān Chōng) 伤门 (Shāng Mén) Xun 4 Ding Bing	九地 (Jiǔ Dì) 天辅 (Tiān Fǔ) 杜门 (Dù Mén) Li 9 Bing Xin	九天 (Jiǔ Tiān) 天英 (Tiān Yīng) 景门 (Jǐng Mén) Kun 2 Xin Gui/Yi
白虎 (Bái Hǔ) 天任 (Tiān Rèn) 生门 (Shēng Mén) Zhen 3 Geng Ding	Yang (阳) Dun# 6 Hour: **JiWei** ©Calvin Yap	值符 (Zhí Fú) 禽芮 (Qín Ruì) 死门 (Sǐ Mén) Dui 7 Gui/Yi Ji
六合 (Liù Hé) 天蓬 (Tiān Péng) 休门 (Xiū Mén) Gen 8 Ren Geng	太阴 (Tài Yīn) 天心 (Tiān Xīn) 开门 (Kāi Mén) Kan 1 Wu Ren	螣蛇 (Téng Shé) 天柱 (Tiān Zhù) 惊门 (Jīng Mén) Qian 6 Ji Wu

Yang (阳) Dun# 6 Hour: **GengShen** ; 直符(ZhíFú): 天芮(TiānRuì)
直使(ZhíShǐ): 死门(SǐMén) ; 旬首(XúnShǒu): JiaYinGui

太阴 (Tài Yīn) 天心 (Tiān Xīn) 开门 (Kāi Mén) Xun 4 Wu Bing	六合 (Liù Hé) 天蓬 (Tiān Péng) 休门 (Xiū Mén) Li 9 Ren Xin	白虎 (Bái Hǔ) 天任 (Tiān Rèn) 生门 (Shēng Mén) Kun 2 Geng Gui/Yi
螣蛇 (Téng Shé) 天柱 (Tiān Zhù) 惊门 (Jīng Mén) Zhen 3 Ji Ding	Yang (阳) Dun# 6 Hour: **GengShen** **Fan Yin** ©Calvin Yap	玄武 (Xuán Wǔ) 天冲 (Tiān Chōng) 伤门 (Shāng Mén) Dui 7 Ding Ji
值符 (Zhí Fú) 禽芮 (Qín Ruì) 死门 (Sǐ Mén) Gen 8 Gui/Yi Geng	九天 (Jiǔ Tiān) 天英 (Tiān Yīng) 景门 (Jǐng Mén) Kan 1 Xin Ren	九地 (Jiǔ Dì) 天辅 (Tiān Fǔ) 杜门 (Dù Mén) Qian 6 Bing Wu

Yang (阳) Dun# 6 Hour: **XinYou** ; 直符(ZhíFú): 天芮(TiānRuì)
直使(ZhíShǐ): 死门(SǐMén) ; 旬首(XúnShǒu): JiaYinGui

九天 (Jiǔ Tiān) 天英 (Tiān Yīng) 景门 (Jǐng Mén) Xun 4 Xin Bing	值符 (Zhí Fú) 禽芮 (Qín Ruì) 死门 (Sǐ Mén) Li 9 Gui/Yi Xin	螣蛇 (Téng Shé) 天柱 (Tiān Zhù) 惊门 (Jīng Mén) Kun 2 Ji Gui/Yi
九地 (Jiǔ Dì) 天辅 (Tiān Fǔ) 杜门 (Dù Mén) Zhen 3 Bing Ding	Yang (阳) Dun# 6 Hour: **XinYou** ©Calvin Yap	太阴 (Tài Yīn) 天心 (Tiān Xīn) 开门 (Kāi Mén) Dui 7 Wu Ji
玄武 (Xuán Wǔ) 天冲 (Tiān Chōng) 伤门 (Shāng Mén) Gen 8 Ding Geng	白虎 (Bái Hǔ) 天任 (Tiān Rèn) 生门 (Shēng Mén) Kan 1 Geng Ren	六合 (Liù Hé) 天蓬 (Tiān Péng) 休门 (Xiū Mén) Qian 6 Ren Wu

Yang (阳) Dun# 6 Hour: **RenXu** ; 直符(ZhíFú): 天芮(TiānRuì)
直使(ZhíShǐ): 死门(SǐMén) ; 旬首(XúnShǒu): JiaYinGui

六合 (Liù Hé) 天蓬 (Tiān Péng) 休门 (Xiū Mén) Xun 4 Ren Bing	白虎 (Bái Hǔ) 天任 (Tiān Rèn) 生门 (Shēng Mén) Li 9 Geng Xin	玄武 (Xuán Wǔ) 天冲 (Tiān Chōng) 伤门 (Shāng Mén) Kun 2 Ding Gui/Yi
太阴 (Tài Yīn) 天心 (Tiān Xīn) 开门 (Kāi Mén) Zhen 3 Wu Ding	Yang (阳) Dun# 6 Hour: **RenXu** ©Calvin Yap	九地 (Jiǔ Dì) 天辅 (Tiān Fǔ) 杜门 (Dù Mén) Dui 7 Bing Ji
螣蛇 (Téng Shé) 天柱 (Tiān Zhù) 惊门 (Jīng Mén) Gen 8 Ji Geng	值符 (Zhí Fú) 禽芮 (Qín Ruì) 死门 (Sǐ Mén) Kan 1 Gui/Yi Ren	九天 (Jiǔ Tiān) 天英 (Tiān Yīng) 景门 (Jǐng Mén) Qian 6 Xin Wu

Yang (阳) Dun# 6 Hour: **GuiHai** ; 直符(ZhíFú): 天芮(TiānRuì)
直使(ZhíShǐ): 死门(SǐMén) ; 旬首(XúnShǒu): JiaYinGui

九地 (Jiǔ Dì) 天辅 (Tiān Fǔ) 杜门 (Dù Mén) Xun 4 Bing Bing	九天 (Jiǔ Tiān) 天英 (Tiān Yīng) 景门 (Jǐng Mén) Li 9 Xin Xin	值符 (Zhí Fú) 禽芮 (Qín Ruì) 死门 (Sǐ Mén) Kun 2 Gui/Yi Gui/Yi
玄武 (Xuán Wǔ) 天冲 (Tiān Chōng) 伤门 (Shāng Mén) Zhen 3 Ding Ding	Yang (阳) Dun# 6 Hour: **GuiHai** **Fu Yin** ©Calvin Yap	螣蛇 (Téng Shé) 天柱 (Tiān Zhù) 惊门 (Jīng Mén) Dui 7 Ji Ji
白虎 (Bái Hǔ) 天任 (Tiān Rèn) 生门 (Shēng Mén) Gen 8 Geng Geng	六合 (Liù Hé) 天蓬 (Tiān Péng) 休门 (Xiū Mén) Kan 1 Ren Ren	太阴 (Tài Yīn) 天心 (Tiān Xīn) 开门 (Kāi Mén) Qian 6 Wu Wu

Yang Dun#7

<table>
<tr><td colspan="3" align="center">Chart: +7JiaZi (Yang Dun #7 JiaZi Xun)
JiaZi, YiChou, BingYin, DingMao, WuChen, JiSi, GengWu, XinWei, RenShen, GuiYou</td></tr>
</table>

Yang (阳) Dun# 7 Hour: **JiaZi** ; 直符(ZhíFú): 天柱(TiānZhù)
直使(ZhíShǐ): 惊门(JīngMén) ; 旬首(XúnShǒu): JiaZiWu

玄武 (Xuán Wǔ) 天辅 (Tiān Fǔ) 杜门 (Dù Mén) Xun 4　Ding 　　Ding	九地 (Jiǔ Dì) 天英 (Tiān Yīng) 景门 (Jǐng Mén) Li 9　Geng 　　Geng	九天 (Jiǔ Tiān) 禽芮 (Qín Ruì) 死门 (Sǐ Mén) Kun 2　Ren/Bing 　　Ren/Bing
白虎 (Bái Hǔ) 天冲 (Tiān Chōng) 伤门 (Shāng Mén) Zhen 3　Gui 　　Gui	Yang (阳) Dun# 7 Hour: **JiaZi** **Fu Yin** ©Calvin Yap	值符 (Zhí Fú) 天柱 (Tiān Zhù) 惊门 (Jīng Mén) Dui 7　Wu 　　Wu
六合 (Liù Hé) 天任 (Tiān Rèn) 生门 (Shēng Mén) Gen 8　Ji	太阴 (Tài Yīn) 天蓬 (Tiān Péng) 休门 (Xiū Mén) Kan 1　Xin	螣蛇 (Téng Shé) 天心 (Tiān Xīn) 开门 (Kāi Mén) Qian 6　Yi 　　Yi

Yang (阳) Dun# 7 Hour: **YiChou** ; 直符(ZhíFú): 天柱(TiānZhù)
直使(ZhíShǐ): 惊门(JīngMén) ; 旬首(XúnShǒu): JiaZiWu

白虎 (Bái Hǔ) 天冲 (Tiān Chōng) 休门 (Xiū Mén) Xun 4　Gui	玄武 (Xuán Wǔ) 天辅 (Tiān Fǔ) 生门 (Shēng Mén) Li 9　Ding 　　Geng	九地 (Jiǔ Dì) 天英 (Tiān Yīng) 伤门 (Shāng Mén) Kun 2　Geng 　　Ren/Bing
六合 (Liù Hé) 天任 (Tiān Rèn) 开门 (Kāi Mén) Zhen 3　Ji 　　Gui	Yang (阳) Dun# 7 Hour: **YiChou** ©Calvin Yap	九天 (Jiǔ Tiān) 禽芮 (Qín Ruì) 杜门 (Dù Mén) Dui 7　Ren/Bing 　　Wu
太阴 (Tài Yīn) 天蓬 (Tiān Péng) 惊门 (Jīng Mén) Gen 8　Xin 　　Ji	螣蛇 (Téng Shé) 天心 (Tiān Xīn) 死门 (Sǐ Mén) Kan 1　Xin	值符 (Zhí Fú) 天柱 (Tiān Zhù) 景门 (Jǐng Mén) Qian 6　Wu 　　Yi

Yang (阳) Dun# 7 Hour: **BingYin** ; 直符(ZhíFú): 天柱(TiānZhù)
直使(ZhíShǐ): 惊门(JīngMén) ; 旬首(XúnShǒu): JiaZiWu

九地 (Jiǔ Dì) 天英 (Tiān Yīng) 死门 (Sǐ Mén) Xun 4　Geng 　　Ding	九天 (Jiǔ Tiān) 禽芮 (Qín Ruì) 惊门 (Jīng Mén) Li 9　Ren/Bing 　　Geng	值符 (Zhí Fú) 天柱 (Tiān Zhù) 开门 (Kāi Mén) Kun 2　Wu 　　Ren/Bing
玄武 (Xuán Wǔ) 天辅 (Tiān Fǔ) 景门 (Jǐng Mén) Zhen 3　Ding 　　Gui	Yang (阳) Dun# 7 Hour: **BingYin** ©Calvin Yap	螣蛇 (Téng Shé) 天心 (Tiān Xīn) 休门 (Xiū Mén) Dui 7　Yi 　　Wu
白虎 (Bái Hǔ) 天冲 (Tiān Chōng) 杜门 (Dù Mén) Gen 8　Gui 　　Ji	六合 (Liù Hé) 天任 (Tiān Rèn) 伤门 (Shāng Mén) Kan 1　Ji	太阴 (Tài Yīn) 天蓬 (Tiān Péng) 生门 (Shēng Mén) Qian 6　Xin 　　Yi

Yang (阳) Dun# 7 Hour: **DingMao** ; 直符(ZhíFú): 天柱(TiānZhù)
直使(ZhíShǐ): 惊门(JīngMén) ; 旬首(XúnShǒu): JiaZiWu

值符 (Zhí Fú) 天柱 (Tiān Zhù) 生门 (Shēng Mén) Xun 4　Wu 　　Ding	螣蛇 (Téng Shé) 天心 (Tiān Xīn) 伤门 (Shāng Mén) Li 9　Yi 　　Geng	太阴 (Tài Yīn) 天蓬 (Tiān Péng) 杜门 (Dù Mén) Kun 2　Xin 　　Ren/Bing
九天 (Jiǔ Tiān) 禽芮 (Qín Ruì) 休门 (Xiū Mén) Zhen 3　Ren/Bing 　　Gui	Yang (阳) Dun# 7 Hour: **DingMao** ©Calvin Yap	六合 (Liù Hé) 天任 (Tiān Rèn) 景门 (Jǐng Mén) Dui 7　Ji 　　Wu
九地 (Jiǔ Dì) 天英 (Tiān Yīng) 开门 (Kāi Mén) Gen 8　Geng 　　Ji	玄武 (Xuán Wǔ) 天辅 (Tiān Fǔ) 惊门 (Jīng Mén) Kan 1　Ding 　　Xin	白虎 (Bái Hǔ) 天冲 (Tiān Chōng) 死门 (Sǐ Mén) Qian 6　Gui 　　Yi

Yang (阳) Dun# 7 Hour: **WuChen** ; 直符(ZhíFú): 天柱(TiānZhù)
直使(ZhíShǐ): 惊门(JīngMén) ; 旬首(XúnShǒu): JiaZiWu

玄武 (Xuán Wǔ) 天辅 (Tiān Fǔ) 景门 (Jǐng Mén) Xun 4　Ding 　　Ding	九地 (Jiǔ Dì) 天英 (Tiān Yīng) 死门 (Sǐ Mén) Li 9　Geng 　　Geng	九天 (Jiǔ Tiān) 禽芮 (Qín Ruì) 惊门 (Jīng Mén) Kun 2　Ren/Bing 　　Ren/Bing
白虎 (Bái Hǔ) 天冲 (Tiān Chōng) 杜门 (Dù Mén) Zhen 3　Gui 　　Gui	Yang (阳) Dun# 7 Hour: **WuChen** **Fu Yin** ©Calvin Yap	值符 (Zhí Fú) 天柱 (Tiān Zhù) 开门 (Kāi Mén) Dui 7　Wu 　　Wu
六合 (Liù Hé) 天任 (Tiān Rèn) 伤门 (Shāng Mén) Gen 8　Ji	太阴 (Tài Yīn) 天蓬 (Tiān Péng) 生门 (Shēng Mén) Kan 1　Xin	螣蛇 (Téng Shé) 天心 (Tiān Xīn) 休门 (Xiū Mén) Qian 6　Yi 　　Yi

Yang (阳) Dun# 7 Hour: **JiSi** ; 直符(ZhíFú): 天柱(TiānZhù)
直使(ZhíShǐ): 惊门(JīngMén) ; 旬首(XúnShǒu): JiaZiWu

太阴 (Tài Yīn) 天蓬 (Tiān Péng) 开门 (Kāi Mén) Xun 4　Xin 　　Ding	六合 (Liù Hé) 天任 (Tiān Rèn) 休门 (Xiū Mén) Li 9　Ji 　　Geng	白虎 (Bái Hǔ) 天冲 (Tiān Chōng) 生门 (Shēng Mén) Kun 2　Gui 　　Ren/Bing
螣蛇 (Téng Shé) 天心 (Tiān Xīn) 惊门 (Jīng Mén) Zhen 3　Yi 　　Gui	Yang (阳) Dun# 7 Hour: **JiSi** ©Calvin Yap	玄武 (Xuán Wǔ) 天辅 (Tiān Fǔ) 伤门 (Shāng Mén) Dui 7　Ding 　　Wu
值符 (Zhí Fú) 天柱 (Tiān Zhù) 死门 (Sǐ Mén) Gen 8　Wu 　　Ji	九天 (Jiǔ Tiān) 禽芮 (Qín Ruì) 景门 (Jǐng Mén) Kan 1　Ren/Bing 　　Xin	九地 (Jiǔ Dì) 天英 (Tiān Yīng) 杜门 (Dù Mén) Qian 6　Geng 　　Yi

Yang (阳) Dun# 7 Hour: **GengWu** ; 直符(ZhíFú): 天柱(TiānZhù)
直使(ZhíShǐ): 惊门(JīngMén) ; 旬首(XúnShǒu): JiaZiWu

九天 (Jiǔ Tiān) 禽芮 (Qín Ruì) 惊门 (Jīng Mén) Xun 4　　Ren/Bing Ding	值符 (Zhí Fú) 天柱 (Tiān Zhù) 开门 (Kāi Mén) Li 9　　Wu Geng	螣蛇 (Téng Shé) 天心 (Tiān Xīn) 休门 (Xiū Mén) Kun 2　　Yi Ren/Bing
九地 (Jiǔ Dì) 天英 (Tiān Yīng) 死门 (Sǐ Mén) Zhen 3　Geng Gui	Yang (阳) Dun# 7 Hour: **GengWu** ©Calvin Yap	太阴 (Tài Yīn) 天蓬 (Tiān Péng) 生门 (Shēng Mén) Dui 7　　Xin Wu
玄武 (Xuán Wǔ) 天辅 (Tiān Fǔ) 景门 (Jǐng Mén) Gen 8　Ding Ji	白虎 (Bái Hǔ) 天冲 (Tiān Chōng) 杜门 (Dù Mén) Kan 1　Gui Xin	六合 (Liù Hé) 天任 (Tiān Rèn) 伤门 (Shāng Mén) Qian 6　Ji Yi

Yang (阳) Dun# 7 Hour: **XinWei** ; 直符(ZhíFú): 天柱(TiānZhù)
直使(ZhíShǐ): 惊门(JīngMén) ; 旬首(XúnShǒu): JiaZiWu

六合 (Liù Hé) 天任 (Tiān Rèn) 景门 (Jǐng Mén) Xun 4　Ji Ding	白虎 (Bái Hǔ) 天冲 (Tiān Chōng) 死门 (Sǐ Mén) Li 9　　Gui Geng	玄武 (Xuán Wǔ) 天辅 (Tiān Fǔ) 惊门 (Jīng Mén) Kun 2　　Ding Ren/Bing
太阴 (Tài Yīn) 天蓬 (Tiān Péng) 杜门 (Dù Mén) Zhen 3　Xin Gui	Yang (阳) Dun# 7 Hour: **XinWei** ©Calvin Yap	九地 (Jiǔ Dì) 天英 (Tiān Yīng) 开门 (Kāi Mén) Dui 7　　Geng Wu
螣蛇 (Téng Shé) 天心 (Tiān Xīn) 伤门 (Shāng Mén) Gen 8　　Yi Ji	值符 (Zhí Fú) 天柱 (Tiān Zhù) 生门 (Shēng Mén) Kan 1　　Wu Xin	九天 (Jiǔ Tiān) 禽芮 (Qín Ruì) 休门 (Xiū Mén) Qian 6　Ren/Bing Yi

Yang (阳) Dun# 7 Hour: **RenShen** ; 直符(ZhíFú): 天柱(TiānZhù)
直使(ZhíShǐ): 惊门(JīngMén) ; 旬首(XúnShǒu): JiaZiWu

九地 (Jiǔ Dì) 天英 (Tiān Yīng) 伤门 (Shāng Mén) Xun 4　Geng Ding	九天 (Jiǔ Tiān) 禽芮 (Qín Ruì) 杜门 (Dù Mén) Li 9　　Ren/Bing Geng	值符 (Zhí Fú) 天柱 (Tiān Zhù) 景门 (Jǐng Mén) Kun 2　　Wu Ren/Bing
玄武 (Xuán Wǔ) 天辅 (Tiān Fǔ) 生门 (Shēng Mén) Zhen 3　Ding Gui	Yang (阳) Dun# 7 Hour: **RenShen** ©Calvin Yap	螣蛇 (Téng Shé) 天心 (Tiān Xīn) 死门 (Sǐ Mén) Dui 7　　Yi Wu
白虎 (Bái Hǔ) 天冲 (Tiān Chōng) 休门 (Xiū Mén) Gen 8　Gui Ji	六合 (Liù Hé) 天任 (Tiān Rèn) 开门 (Kāi Mén) Kan 1　Ji Xin	太阴 (Tài Yīn) 天蓬 (Tiān Péng) 惊门 (Jīng Mén) Qian 6　Xin Yi

Yang (阳) Dun# 7 Hour: **GuiYou** ; 直符(ZhíFú): 天柱(TiānZhù)
直使(ZhíShǐ): 惊门(JīngMén) ; 旬首(XúnShǒu): JiaZiWu

螣蛇 (Téng Shé) 天心 (Tiān Xīn) 杜门 (Dù Mén) Xun 4　Yi Ding	太阴 (Tài Yīn) 天蓬 (Tiān Péng) 景门 (Jǐng Mén) Li 9　　Xin Geng	六合 (Liù Hé) 天任 (Tiān Rèn) 死门 (Sǐ Mén) Kun 2　　Ji Ren/Bing
值符 (Zhí Fú) 天柱 (Tiān Zhù) 伤门 (Shāng Mén) Zhen 3　Wu Gui	Yang (阳) Dun# 7 Hour: **GuiYou** **Fan Yin** ©Calvin Yap	白虎 (Bái Hǔ) 天冲 (Tiān Chōng) 惊门 (Jīng Mén) Dui 7　　Gui Wu
九天 (Jiǔ Tiān) 禽芮 (Qín Ruì) 生门 (Shēng Mén) Gen 8　Ren/Bing Ji	九地 (Jiǔ Dì) 天英 (Tiān Yīng) 休门 (Xiū Mén) Kan 1　Geng Xin	玄武 (Xuán Wǔ) 天辅 (Tiān Fǔ) 开门 (Kāi Mén) Qian 6　Ding Yi

Chart: **+7JiaXu** (Yang Dun #7 JiaXu Xun)
JiaXu, YiHai, BingZi, DingChou, WuYin, JiMao, GengChen, XinSi, RenWu, GuiWei

Yang (阳) Dun# 7 Hour: **JiaXu** ; 直符(ZhíFú): 天任(TiānRèn)
直使(ZhíShǐ): 生门(ShēngMén) ; 旬首(XúnShǒu): JiaXuJi

太阴 (Tài Yīn) 天辅 (Tiān Fǔ) 杜门 (Dù Mén) Xun 4　Ding Ding	六合 (Liù Hé) 天英 (Tiān Yīng) 景门 (Jǐng Mén) Li 9　　Geng Geng	白虎 (Bái Hǔ) 禽芮 (Qín Ruì) 死门 (Sǐ Mén) Kun 2　　Ren/Bing Ren/Bing
螣蛇 (Téng Shé) 天冲 (Tiān Chōng) 伤门 (Shāng Mén) Zhen 3　Gui Gui	Yang (阳) Dun# 7 Hour: **JiaXu** **Fu Yin** ©Calvin Yap	玄武 (Xuán Wǔ) 天柱 (Tiān Zhù) 惊门 (Jīng Mén) Dui 7　　Wu Wu
值符 (Zhí Fú) 天任 (Tiān Rèn) 生门 (Shēng Mén) Gen 8　Ji Ji	九天 (Jiǔ Tiān) 天蓬 (Tiān Péng) 休门 (Xiū Mén) Kan 1　Xin Xin	九地 (Jiǔ Dì) 天心 (Tiān Xīn) 开门 (Kāi Mén) Qian 6　Yi Yi

Yang (阳) Dun# 7 Hour: **YiHai** ; 直符(ZhíFú): 天任(TiānRèn)
直使(ZhíShǐ): 生门(ShēngMén) ; 旬首(XúnShǒu): JiaXuJi

白虎 (Bái Hǔ) 禽芮 (Qín Ruì) 休门 (Xiū Mén) Xun 4　Ren/Bing Ding	玄武 (Xuán Wǔ) 天柱 (Tiān Zhù) 生门 (Shēng Mén) Li 9　　Wu Geng	九地 (Jiǔ Dì) 天心 (Tiān Xīn) 伤门 (Shāng Mén) Kun 2　　Yi Ren/Bing
六合 (Liù Hé) 天英 (Tiān Yīng) 开门 (Kāi Mén) Zhen 3　Geng Gui	Yang (阳) Dun# 7 Hour: **YiHai** ©Calvin Yap	九天 (Jiǔ Tiān) 天蓬 (Tiān Péng) 杜门 (Dù Mén) Dui 7　　Xin Wu
太阴 (Tài Yīn) 天辅 (Tiān Fǔ) 惊门 (Jīng Mén) Gen 8　Ding Ji	螣蛇 (Téng Shé) 天冲 (Tiān Chōng) 死门 (Sǐ Mén) Kan 1　Gui Xin	值符 (Zhí Fú) 天任 (Tiān Rèn) 景门 (Jǐng Mén) Qian 6　Ji Yi

Yang (阳) Dun# 7 Hour: BingZi ; 直符(ZhíFú): 天任(TiānRèn) ; 直使(ZhíShǐ): 生门(ShēngMén) ; 旬首(XúnShǒu): JiaXuJi

九地 (Jiǔ Dì) 天心 (Tiān Xīn) 景门 (Jǐng Mén) Xun 4 — Yi / Ding	九天 (Jiǔ Tiān) 天蓬 (Tiān Péng) 死门 (Sǐ Mén) Li 9 — Geng	值符 (Zhí Fú) 天任 (Tiān Rèn) 惊门 (Jīng Mén) Kun 2 — Ji / Ren/Bing
玄武 (Xuán Wǔ) 天柱 (Tiān Zhù) 杜门 (Dù Mén) Zhen 3 — Wu / Gui	Yang (阳) Dun# 7 Hour: BingZi **Fan Yin** ©Calvin Yap	螣蛇 (Téng Shé) 天冲 (Tiān Chōng) 开门 (Kāi Mén) Dui 7 — Gui / Wu
白虎 (Bái Hǔ) 禽芮 (Qín Ruì) 伤门 (Shāng Mén) Gen 8 — Ren/Bing / Ji	六合 (Liù Hé) 天英 (Tiān Yīng) 生门 (Shēng Mén) Kan 1 — Geng / Xin	太阴 (Tài Yīn) 天辅 (Tiān Fǔ) 休门 (Xiū Mén) Qian 6 — Ding / Yi

Yang (阳) Dun# 7 Hour: DingChou ; 直符(ZhíFú): 天任(TiānRèn) ; 直使(ZhíShǐ): 生门(ShēngMén) ; 旬首(XúnShǒu): JiaXuJi

值符 (Zhí Fú) 天任 (Tiān Rèn) 开门 (Kāi Mén) Xun 4 — Ji / Ding	螣蛇 (Téng Shé) 天冲 (Tiān Chōng) 休门 (Xiū Mén) Li 9 — Gui / Geng	太阴 (Tài Yīn) 天辅 (Tiān Fǔ) 生门 (Shēng Mén) Kun 2 — Ding / Ren/Bing
九天 (Jiǔ Tiān) 天蓬 (Tiān Péng) 惊门 (Jīng Mén) Zhen 3 — Xin / Gui	Yang (阳) Dun# 7 Hour: DingChou ©Calvin Yap	六合 (Liù Hé) 天英 (Tiān Yīng) 伤门 (Shāng Mén) Dui 7 — Geng / Wu
九地 (Jiǔ Dì) 天心 (Tiān Xīn) 死门 (Sǐ Mén) Gen 8 — Yi / Ji	玄武 (Xuán Wǔ) 天柱 (Tiān Zhù) 景门 (Jǐng Mén) Kan 1 — Wu / Xin	白虎 (Bái Hǔ) 禽芮 (Qín Ruì) 杜门 (Dù Mén) Qian 6 — Ren/Bing / Yi

Yang (阳) Dun# 7 Hour: WuYin ; 直符(ZhíFú): 天任(TiānRèn) ; 直使(ZhíShǐ): 生门(ShēngMén) ; 旬首(XúnShǒu): JiaXuJi

玄武 (Xuán Wǔ) 天柱 (Tiān Zhù) 伤门 (Shāng Mén) Xun 4 — Wu / Ding	九地 (Jiǔ Dì) 天心 (Tiān Xīn) 杜门 (Dù Mén) Li 9 — Yi / Geng	九天 (Jiǔ Tiān) 天蓬 (Tiān Péng) 景门 (Jǐng Mén) Kun 2 — Xin / Ren/Bing
白虎 (Bái Hǔ) 禽芮 (Qín Ruì) 生门 (Shēng Mén) Zhen 3 — Ren/Bing / Gui	Yang (阳) Dun# 7 Hour: WuYin ©Calvin Yap	值符 (Zhí Fú) 天任 (Tiān Rèn) 死门 (Sǐ Mén) Dui 7 — Ji / Wu
六合 (Liù Hé) 天英 (Tiān Yīng) 休门 (Xiū Mén) Gen 8 — Geng / Ji	太阴 (Tài Yīn) 天辅 (Tiān Fǔ) 开门 (Kāi Mén) Kan 1 — Ding / Xin	螣蛇 (Téng Shé) 天冲 (Tiān Chōng) 惊门 (Jīng Mén) Qian 6 — Gui / Yi

Yang (阳) Dun# 7 Hour: JiMao ; 直符(ZhíFú): 天任(TiānRèn) ; 直使(ZhíShǐ): 生门(ShēngMén) ; 旬首(XúnShǒu): JiaXuJi

太阴 (Tài Yīn) 天辅 (Tiān Fǔ) 生门 (Shēng Mén) Xun 4 — Ding / Ding	六合 (Liù Hé) 天英 (Tiān Yīng) 伤门 (Shāng Mén) Li 9 — Geng / Geng	白虎 (Bái Hǔ) 禽芮 (Qín Ruì) 杜门 (Dù Mén) Kun 2 — Ren/Bing / Ren/Bing
螣蛇 (Téng Shé) 天冲 (Tiān Chōng) 休门 (Xiū Mén) Zhen 3 — Gui / Gui	Yang (阳) Dun# 7 Hour: JiMao **Fu Yin** ©Calvin Yap	玄武 (Xuán Wǔ) 天柱 (Tiān Zhù) 景门 (Jǐng Mén) Dui 7 — Wu / Wu
值符 (Zhí Fú) 天任 (Tiān Rèn) 开门 (Kāi Mén) Gen 8 — Ji / Ji	九天 (Jiǔ Tiān) 天蓬 (Tiān Péng) 惊门 (Jīng Mén) Kan 1 — Xin / Xin	九地 (Jiǔ Dì) 天心 (Tiān Xīn) 死门 (Sǐ Mén) Qian 6 — Yi / Yi

Yang (阳) Dun# 7 Hour: GengChen ; 直符(ZhíFú): 天任(TiānRèn) ; 直使(ZhíShǐ): 生门(ShēngMén) ; 旬首(XúnShǒu): JiaXuJi

九天 (Jiǔ Tiān) 天蓬 (Tiān Péng) 开门 (Kāi Mén) Xun 4 — Xin / Ding	值符 (Zhí Fú) 天任 (Tiān Rèn) 休门 (Xiū Mén) Li 9 — Ji / Geng	螣蛇 (Téng Shé) 天冲 (Tiān Chōng) 生门 (Shēng Mén) Kun 2 — Gui / Ren/Bing
九地 (Jiǔ Dì) 天心 (Tiān Xīn) 惊门 (Jīng Mén) Zhen 3 — Yi / Gui	Yang (阳) Dun# 7 Hour: GengChen ©Calvin Yap	太阴 (Tài Yīn) 天辅 (Tiān Fǔ) 伤门 (Shāng Mén) Dui 7 — Ding / Wu
玄武 (Xuán Wǔ) 天柱 (Tiān Zhù) 死门 (Sǐ Mén) Gen 8 — Wu / Ji	白虎 (Bái Hǔ) 禽芮 (Qín Ruì) 景门 (Jǐng Mén) Kan 1 — Ren/Bing / Xin	六合 (Liù Hé) 天英 (Tiān Yīng) 杜门 (Dù Mén) Qian 6 — Geng / Yi

Yang (阳) Dun# 7 Hour: XinSi ; 直符(ZhíFú): 天任(TiānRèn) ; 直使(ZhíShǐ): 生门(ShēngMén) ; 旬首(XúnShǒu): JiaXuJi

六合 (Liù Hé) 天英 (Tiān Yīng) 死门 (Sǐ Mén) Xun 4 — Geng / Ding	白虎 (Bái Hǔ) 禽芮 (Qín Ruì) 惊门 (Jīng Mén) Li 9 — Ren/Bing / Geng	玄武 (Xuán Wǔ) 天柱 (Tiān Zhù) 开门 (Kāi Mén) Kun 2 — Wu / Ren/Bing
太阴 (Tài Yīn) 天辅 (Tiān Fǔ) 景门 (Jǐng Mén) Zhen 3 — Ding / Gui	Yang (阳) Dun# 7 Hour: XinSi ©Calvin Yap	九地 (Jiǔ Dì) 天心 (Tiān Xīn) 休门 (Xiū Mén) Dui 7 — Yi / Wu
螣蛇 (Téng Shé) 天冲 (Tiān Chōng) 杜门 (Dù Mén) Gen 8 — Gui / Ji	值符 (Zhí Fú) 天任 (Tiān Rèn) 伤门 (Shāng Mén) Kan 1 — Ji / Xin	九天 (Jiǔ Tiān) 天蓬 (Tiān Péng) 生门 (Shēng Mén) Qian 6 — Xin

Yang (阳) Dun# 7 Hour: **RenWu** ; 直符(ZhíFú): 天任(TiānRèn)
直使(ZhíShǐ): 生门(ShēngMén) ; 旬首(XúnShǒu): JiaXuJi

九地 (Jiǔ Dì) 天心 (Tiān Xīn) 惊门 (Jīng Mén) Xun 4　Yi Ding	九天 (Jiǔ Tiān) 天蓬 (Tiān Péng) 开门 (Kāi Mén) Li 9　Xin Geng	值符 (Zhí Fú) 天任 (Tiān Rèn) 休门 (Xiū Mén) Kun 2　Ji Ren/Bing
玄武 (Xuán Wǔ) 天柱 (Tiān Zhù) 死门 (Sǐ Mén) Zhen 3　Wu Gui	Yang (阳) Dun# 7 Hour: **RenWu** **Fan Yin** ©Calvin Yap	螣蛇 (Téng Shé) 天冲 (Tiān Chōng) 生门 (Shēng Mén) Dui 7　Gui Wu
白虎 (Bái Hǔ) 禽芮 (Qín Ruì) 景门 (Jǐng Mén) Gen 8　Ren/Bing Ji	六合 (Liù Hé) 天英 (Tiān Yīng) 杜门 (Dù Mén) Kan 1　Geng Xin	太阴 (Tài Yīn) 天辅 (Tiān Fǔ) 伤门 (Shāng Mén) Qian 6　Ding Yi

Yang (阳) Dun# 7 Hour: **GuiWei** ; 直符(ZhíFú): 天任(TiānRèn)
直使(ZhíShǐ): 生门(ShēngMén) ; 旬首(XúnShǒu): JiaXuJi

螣蛇 (Téng Shé) 天冲 (Tiān Chōng) 杜门 (Dù Mén) Xun 4　Gui Ding	太阴 (Tài Yīn) 天辅 (Tiān Fǔ) 景门 (Jǐng Mén) Li 9　Ding Geng	六合 (Liù Hé) 天英 (Tiān Yīng) 死门 (Sǐ Mén) Kun 2　Geng Ren/Bing
值符 (Zhí Fú) 天任 (Tiān Rèn) 伤门 (Shāng Mén) Zhen 3　Ji Gui	Yang (阳) Dun# 7 Hour: **GuiWei** ©Calvin Yap	白虎 (Bái Hǔ) 禽芮 (Qín Ruì) 惊门 (Jīng Mén) Dui 7　Ren/Bing Wu
九天 (Jiǔ Tiān) 天蓬 (Tiān Péng) 生门 (Shēng Mén) Gen 8　Xin Ji	九地 (Jiǔ Dì) 天心 (Tiān Xīn) 休门 (Xiū Mén) Kan 1　Yi Xin	玄武 (Xuán Wǔ) 天柱 (Tiān Zhù) 开门 (Kāi Mén) Qian 6　Wu Yi

Chart: +7JiaShen (Yang Dun #7 JiaShen Xun)
JiaShen, YiYou, BingXu, DingHai, WuZi, JiChou, GengYin, XinMao, RenChen, GuiSi

Yang (阳) Dun# 7 Hour: **JiaShen** ; 直符(ZhíFú): 天英(TiānYīng)
直使(ZhíShǐ): 景门(JǐngMén) ; 旬首(XúnShǒu): JiaShenGeng

九天 (Jiǔ Tiān) 天辅 (Tiān Fǔ) 杜门 (Dù Mén) Xun 4　Ding Ding	值符 (Zhí Fú) 天英 (Tiān Yīng) 景门 (Jǐng Mén) Li 9　Geng Geng	螣蛇 (Téng Shé) 禽芮 (Qín Ruì) 死门 (Sǐ Mén) Kun 2　Ren/Bing Ren/Bing
九地 (Jiǔ Dì) 天冲 (Tiān Chōng) 伤门 (Shāng Mén) Zhen 3　Gui Gui	Yang (阳) Dun# 7 Hour: **JiaShen** **Fu Yin** ©Calvin Yap	太阴 (Tài Yīn) 天柱 (Tiān Zhù) 惊门 (Jīng Mén) Dui 7　Wu Wu
玄武 (Xuán Wǔ) 天任 (Tiān Rèn) 生门 (Shēng Mén) Gen 8　Ji Ji	白虎 (Bái Hǔ) 天蓬 (Tiān Péng) 休门 (Xiū Mén) Kan 1　Xin Xin	六合 (Liù Hé) 天心 (Tiān Xīn) 开门 (Kāi Mén) Qian 6　Yi Yi

Yang (阳) Dun# 7 Hour: **YiYou** ; 直符(ZhíFú): 天英(TiānYīng)
直使(ZhíShǐ): 景门(JǐngMén) ; 旬首(XúnShǒu): JiaShenGeng

白虎 (Bái Hǔ) 天蓬 (Tiān Péng) 开门 (Kāi Mén) Xun 4　Xin	玄武 (Xuán Wǔ) 天任 (Tiān Rèn) 休门 (Xiū Mén) Li 9　Ji Geng	九地 (Jiǔ Dì) 天冲 (Tiān Chōng) 生门 (Shēng Mén) Kun 2　Gui Ren/Bing
六合 (Liù Hé) 天心 (Tiān Xīn) 惊门 (Jīng Mén) Zhen 3　Yi Gui	Yang (阳) Dun# 7 Hour: **YiYou** ©Calvin Yap	九天 (Jiǔ Tiān) 天辅 (Tiān Fǔ) 伤门 (Shāng Mén) Dui 7　Ding Wu
太阴 (Tài Yīn) 天柱 (Tiān Zhù) 死门 (Sǐ Mén) Gen 8　Wu Ji	螣蛇 (Téng Shé) 禽芮 (Qín Ruì) 景门 (Jǐng Mén) Kan 1　Ren/Bing Xin	值符 (Zhí Fú) 天英 (Tiān Yīng) 杜门 (Dù Mén) Qian 6　Geng Yi

Yang (阳) Dun# 7 Hour: **BingXu** ; 直符(ZhíFú): 天英(TiānYīng)
直使(ZhíShǐ): 景门(JǐngMén) ; 旬首(XúnShǒu): JiaShenGeng

九地 (Jiǔ Dì) 天冲 (Tiān Chōng) 伤门 (Shāng Mén) Xun 4　Gui Ding	九天 (Jiǔ Tiān) 天辅 (Tiān Fǔ) 杜门 (Dù Mén) Li 9　Ding Geng	值符 (Zhí Fú) 天英 (Tiān Yīng) 景门 (Jǐng Mén) Kun 2　Geng Ren/Bing
玄武 (Xuán Wǔ) 天任 (Tiān Rèn) 生门 (Shēng Mén) Zhen 3　Ji Gui	Yang (阳) Dun# 7 Hour: **BingXu** ©Calvin Yap	螣蛇 (Téng Shé) 禽芮 (Qín Ruì) 死门 (Sǐ Mén) Dui 7　Ren/Bing Wu
白虎 (Bái Hǔ) 天蓬 (Tiān Péng) 休门 (Xiū Mén) Gen 8　Xin Ji	六合 (Liù Hé) 天心 (Tiān Xīn) 开门 (Kāi Mén) Kan 1　Yi Xin	太阴 (Tài Yīn) 天柱 (Tiān Zhù) 惊门 (Jīng Mén) Qian 6　Wu Yi

Yang (阳) Dun# 7 Hour: **DingHai** ; 直符(ZhíFú): 天英(TiānYīng)
直使(ZhíShǐ): 景门(JǐngMén) ; 旬首(XúnShǒu): JiaShenGeng

值符 (Zhí Fú) 天英 (Tiān Yīng) 死门 (Sǐ Mén) Xun 4　Geng Ding	螣蛇 (Téng Shé) 禽芮 (Qín Ruì) 惊门 (Jīng Mén) Li 9　Ren/Bing Geng	太阴 (Tài Yīn) 天柱 (Tiān Zhù) 开门 (Kāi Mén) Kun 2　Wu Ren/Bing
九天 (Jiǔ Tiān) 天辅 (Tiān Fǔ) 景门 (Jǐng Mén) Zhen 3　Ding Gui	Yang (阳) Dun# 7 Hour: **DingHai** ©Calvin Yap	六合 (Liù Hé) 天心 (Tiān Xīn) 休门 (Xiū Mén) Dui 7　Yi Wu
九地 (Jiǔ Dì) 天冲 (Tiān Chōng) 杜门 (Dù Mén) Gen 8　Gui Ji	玄武 (Xuán Wǔ) 天任 (Tiān Rèn) 伤门 (Shāng Mén) Kan 1　Ji Xin	白虎 (Bái Hǔ) 天蓬 (Tiān Péng) 生门 (Shēng Mén) Qian 6　Xin Yi

Yang (阳) Dun# 7 Hour: **WuZi**；直符(ZhíFú): 天英(TiānYīng)
直使(ZhíShǐ): 景门(JǐngMén)；旬首(XúnShǒu): JiaShenGeng

玄武 (Xuán Wǔ) 天任 (Tiān Rèn) 景门 (Jǐng Mén) Xun 4　Ji Ding	九地 (Jiǔ Dì) 天冲 (Tiān Chōng) 死门 (Sǐ Mén) Li 9　Gui Geng	九天 (Jiǔ Tiān) 天辅 (Tiān Fǔ) 惊门 (Jīng Mén) Kun 2　Ding Ren/Bing
白虎 (Bái Hǔ) 天蓬 (Tiān Péng) 杜门 (Dù Mén) Zhen 3　Xin Gui	Yang (阳) Dun# 7 Hour: **WuZi** ©Calvin Yap	值符 (Zhí Fú) 天英 (Tiān Yīng) 开门 (Kāi Mén) Dui 7　Geng Wu
六合 (Liù Hé) 天心 (Tiān Xīn) 伤门 (Shāng Mén) Gen 8　Yi Ji	太阴 (Tài Yīn) 天柱 (Tiān Zhù) 生门 (Shēng Mén) Kan 1　Wu Xin	螣蛇 (Téng Shé) 禽芮 (Qín Ruì) 休门 (Xiū Mén) Qian 6　Ren/Bing Yi

Yang (阳) Dun# 7 Hour: **JiChou**；直符(ZhíFú): 天英(TiānYīng)
直使(ZhíShǐ): 景门(JǐngMén)；旬首(XúnShǒu): JiaShenGeng

太阴 (Tài Yīn) 天柱 (Tiān Zhù) 伤门 (Shāng Mén) Xun 4　Wu Ding	六合 (Liù Hé) 天心 (Tiān Xīn) 杜门 (Dù Mén) Li 9　Yi Geng	白虎 (Bái Hǔ) 天蓬 (Tiān Péng) 景门 (Jǐng Mén) Kun 2　Xin Ren/Bing
螣蛇 (Téng Shé) 禽芮 (Qín Ruì) 生门 (Shēng Mén) Zhen 3　Ren/Bing Gui	Yang (阳) Dun# 7 Hour: **JiChou** ©Calvin Yap	玄武 (Xuán Wǔ) 天任 (Tiān Rèn) 死门 (Sǐ Mén) Dui 7　Ji Wu
值符 (Zhí Fú) 天英 (Tiān Yīng) 休门 (Xiū Mén) Gen 8　Geng Ji	九天 (Jiǔ Tiān) 天辅 (Tiān Fǔ) 开门 (Kāi Mén) Kan 1　Ding Xin	九地 (Jiǔ Dì) 天冲 (Tiān Chōng) 惊门 (Jīng Mén) Qian 6　Gui Yi

Yang (阳) Dun# 7 Hour: **GengYin**；直符(ZhíFú): 天英(TiānYīng)
直使(ZhíShǐ): 景门(JǐngMén)；旬首(XúnShǒu): JiaShenGeng

九天 (Jiǔ Tiān) 天辅 (Tiān Fǔ) 休门 (Xiū Mén) Xun 4　Ding Ding	值符 (Zhí Fú) 天英 (Tiān Yīng) 生门 (Shēng Mén) Li 9　Geng Geng	螣蛇 (Téng Shé) 禽芮 (Qín Ruì) 伤门 (Shāng Mén) Kun 2　Ren/Bing Ren/Bing
九地 (Jiǔ Dì) 天冲 (Tiān Chōng) 开门 (Kāi Mén) Zhen 3　Gui Gui	Yang (阳) Dun# 7 Hour: **GengYin** Fu Yin ©Calvin Yap	太阴 (Tài Yīn) 天柱 (Tiān Zhù) 杜门 (Dù Mén) Dui 7　Wu Wu
玄武 (Xuán Wǔ) 天任 (Tiān Rèn) 惊门 (Jīng Mén) Gen 8　Ji Ji	白虎 (Bái Hǔ) 天蓬 (Tiān Péng) 死门 (Sǐ Mén) Kan 1　Xin Xin	六合 (Liù Hé) 天心 (Tiān Xīn) 景门 (Jǐng Mén) Qian 6　Yi Yi

Yang (阳) Dun# 7 Hour: **XinMao**；直符(ZhíFú): 天英(TiānYīng)
直使(ZhíShǐ): 景门(JǐngMén)；旬首(XúnShǒu): JiaShenGeng

六合 (Liù Hé) 天心 (Tiān Xīn) 生门 (Shēng Mén) Xun 4　Yi Ding	白虎 (Bái Hǔ) 天蓬 (Tiān Péng) 伤门 (Shāng Mén) Li 9　Xin Geng	玄武 (Xuán Wǔ) 天任 (Tiān Rèn) 杜门 (Dù Mén) Kun 2　Ji Ren/Bing
太阴 (Tài Yīn) 天柱 (Tiān Zhù) 休门 (Xiū Mén) Zhen 3　Wu Gui	Yang (阳) Dun# 7 Hour: **XinMao** Fan Yin ©Calvin Yap	九地 (Jiǔ Dì) 天冲 (Tiān Chōng) 景门 (Jǐng Mén) Dui 7　Gui Wu
螣蛇 (Téng Shé) 禽芮 (Qín Ruì) 开门 (Kāi Mén) Gen 8　Ren/Bing Ji	值符 (Zhí Fú) 天英 (Tiān Yīng) 惊门 (Jīng Mén) Kan 1　Geng Xin	九天 (Jiǔ Tiān) 天辅 (Tiān Fǔ) 死门 (Sǐ Mén) Qian 6　Ding Yi

Yang (阳) Dun# 7 Hour: **RenChen**；直符(ZhíFú): 天英(TiānYīng)
直使(ZhíShǐ): 景门(JǐngMén)；旬首(XúnShǒu): JiaShenGeng

九地 (Jiǔ Dì) 天冲 (Tiān Chōng) 惊门 (Jīng Mén) Xun 4　Gui Ding	九天 (Jiǔ Tiān) 天辅 (Tiān Fǔ) 开门 (Kāi Mén) Li 9　Ding Geng	值符 (Zhí Fú) 天英 (Tiān Yīng) 休门 (Xiū Mén) Kun 2　Geng Ren/Bing
玄武 (Xuán Wǔ) 天任 (Tiān Rèn) 死门 (Sǐ Mén) Zhen 3　Ji Gui	Yang (阳) Dun# 7 Hour: **RenChen** ©Calvin Yap	螣蛇 (Téng Shé) 禽芮 (Qín Ruì) 生门 (Shēng Mén) Dui 7　Ren/Bing Wu
白虎 (Bái Hǔ) 天蓬 (Tiān Péng) 景门 (Jǐng Mén) Gen 8　Xin Ji	六合 (Liù Hé) 天心 (Tiān Xīn) 杜门 (Dù Mén) Kan 1　Yi Xin	太阴 (Tài Yīn) 天柱 (Tiān Zhù) 伤门 (Shāng Mén) Qian 6　Wu Yi

Yang (阳) Dun# 7 Hour: **GuiSi**；直符(ZhíFú): 天英(TiānYīng)
直使(ZhíShǐ): 景门(JǐngMén)；旬首(XúnShǒu): JiaShenGeng

螣蛇 (Téng Shé) 禽芮 (Qín Ruì) 杜门 (Dù Mén) Xun 4　Ren/Bing Ding	太阴 (Tài Yīn) 天柱 (Tiān Zhù) 景门 (Jǐng Mén) Li 9　Wu Geng	六合 (Liù Hé) 天心 (Tiān Xīn) 死门 (Sǐ Mén) Kun 2　Yi Ren/Bing
值符 (Zhí Fú) 天英 (Tiān Yīng) 伤门 (Shāng Mén) Zhen 3　Geng Gui	Yang (阳) Dun# 7 Hour: **GuiSi** ©Calvin Yap	白虎 (Bái Hǔ) 天蓬 (Tiān Péng) 惊门 (Jīng Mén) Dui 7　Xin Wu
九天 (Jiǔ Tiān) 天辅 (Tiān Fǔ) 生门 (Shēng Mén) Gen 8　Ding Ji	九地 (Jiǔ Dì) 天冲 (Tiān Chōng) 休门 (Xiū Mén) Kan 1　Gui Xin	玄武 (Xuán Wǔ) 天任 (Tiān Rèn) 开门 (Kāi Mén) Qian 6　Ji Yi

Chart: +7JiaWu (Yang Dun #7 JiaWu Xun)
JiaWu, YiWei, BingShen, DingYou, WuXu, JiHai, GengZi, XinChou, RenYin, GuiMao

Yang (阳) Dun# 7 Hour: **JiaWu** ；直符(ZhíFú): 天蓬(TiānPéng)
直使(ZhíShǐ): 休门(XiūMén) ；旬首(XúnShǒu): JiaWu/Xin

六合 (Liù Hé) 天辅 (Tiān Fǔ) 杜门 (Dù Mén) Xun 4 — Ding / Ding	白虎 (Bái Hǔ) 天英 (Tiān Yīng) 景门 (Jǐng Mén) Li 9 — Geng / Geng	玄武 (Xuán Wǔ) 禽芮 (Qín Ruì) 死门 (Sǐ Mén) Kun 2 — Ren/Bing / Ren/Bing
太阴 (Tài Yīn) 天冲 (Tiān Chōng) 伤门 (Shāng Mén) Zhen 3 — Gui / Gui	Yang (阳) Dun# 7 Hour: **JiaWu** **Fu Yin** ©Calvin Yap	九地 (Jiǔ Dì) 天柱 (Tiān Zhù) 惊门 (Jīng Mén) Dui 7 — Wu / Wu
螣蛇 (Téng Shé) 天任 (Tiān Rèn) 生门 (Shēng Mén) Gen 8 — Ji / Ji	值符 (Zhí Fú) 天蓬 (Tiān Péng) 休门 (Xiū Mén) Kan 1 — Xin / Xin	九天 (Jiǔ Tiān) 天心 (Tiān Xīn) 开门 (Kāi Mén) Qian 6 — Yi / Yi

Yang (阳) Dun# 7 Hour: **YiWei** ；直符(ZhíFú): 天蓬(TiānPéng)
直使(ZhíShǐ): 休门(XiūMén) ；旬首(XúnShǒu): JiaWu/Xin

白虎 (Bái Hǔ) 天英 (Tiān Yīng) 惊门 (Jīng Mén) Xun 4 — Geng / Ding	玄武 (Xuán Wǔ) 禽芮 (Qín Ruì) 开门 (Kāi Mén) Li 9 — Ren/Bing / Geng	九地 (Jiǔ Dì) 天柱 (Tiān Zhù) 休门 (Xiū Mén) Kun 2 — Wu / Ren/Bing
六合 (Liù Hé) 天辅 (Tiān Fǔ) 死门 (Sǐ Mén) Zhen 3 — Ding / Gui	Yang (阳) Dun# 7 Hour: **YiWei** ©Calvin Yap	九天 (Jiǔ Tiān) 天心 (Tiān Xīn) 生门 (Shēng Mén) Dui 7 — Yi / Wu
太阴 (Tài Yīn) 天冲 (Tiān Chōng) 景门 (Jǐng Mén) Gen 8 — Gui	螣蛇 (Téng Shé) 天任 (Tiān Rèn) 杜门 (Dù Mén) Kan 1 — Ji / Xin	值符 (Zhí Fú) 天蓬 (Tiān Péng) 伤门 (Shāng Mén) Qian 6 — Xin / Yi

Yang (阳) Dun# 7 Hour: **BingShen** ；直符(ZhíFú): 天蓬(TiānPéng)
直使(ZhíShǐ): 休门(XiūMén) ；旬首(XúnShǒu): JiaWu/Xin

九地 (Jiǔ Dì) 天柱 (Tiān Zhù) 生门 (Shēng Mén) Xun 4 — Wu / Ding	九天 (Jiǔ Tiān) 天心 (Tiān Xīn) 伤门 (Shāng Mén) Li 9 — Yi / Geng	值符 (Zhí Fú) 天蓬 (Tiān Péng) 杜门 (Dù Mén) Kun 2 — Xin / Ren/Bing
玄武 (Xuán Wǔ) 禽芮 (Qín Ruì) 休门 (Xiū Mén) Zhen 3 — Ren/Bing / Gui	Yang (阳) Dun# 7 Hour: **BingShen** ©Calvin Yap	螣蛇 (Téng Shé) 天任 (Tiān Rèn) 景门 (Jǐng Mén) Dui 7 — Ji / Wu
白虎 (Bái Hǔ) 天英 (Tiān Yīng) 开门 (Kāi Mén) Gen 8 — Geng / Ji	六合 (Liù Hé) 天辅 (Tiān Fǔ) 惊门 (Jīng Mén) Kan 1 — Ding / Xin	太阴 (Tài Yīn) 天冲 (Tiān Chōng) 死门 (Sǐ Mén) Qian 6 — Gui / Yi

Yang (阳) Dun# 7 Hour: **DingYou** ；直符(ZhíFú): 天蓬(TiānPéng)
直使(ZhíShǐ): 休门(XiūMén) ；旬首(XúnShǒu): JiaWu/Xin

值符 (Zhí Fú) 天蓬 (Tiān Péng) 休门 (Xiū Mén) Xun 4 — Xin / Ding	螣蛇 (Téng Shé) 天任 (Tiān Rèn) 生门 (Shēng Mén) Li 9 — Ji / Geng	太阴 (Tài Yīn) 天冲 (Tiān Chōng) 伤门 (Shāng Mén) Kun 2 — Gui / Ren/Bing
九天 (Jiǔ Tiān) 天心 (Tiān Xīn) 开门 (Kāi Mén) Zhen 3 — Yi / Gui	Yang (阳) Dun# 7 Hour: **DingYou** ©Calvin Yap	六合 (Liù Hé) 天辅 (Tiān Fǔ) 杜门 (Dù Mén) Dui 7 — Ding / Wu
九地 (Jiǔ Dì) 天柱 (Tiān Zhù) 惊门 (Jīng Mén) Gen 8 — Wu / Ji	玄武 (Xuán Wǔ) 禽芮 (Qín Ruì) 死门 (Sǐ Mén) Kan 1 — Ren/Bing / Xin	白虎 (Bái Hǔ) 天英 (Tiān Yīng) 景门 (Jǐng Mén) Qian 6 — Geng / Yi

Yang (阳) Dun# 7 Hour: **WuXu** ；直符(ZhíFú): 天蓬(TiānPéng)
直使(ZhíShǐ): 休门(XiūMén) ；旬首(XúnShǒu): JiaWu/Xin

玄武 (Xuán Wǔ) 禽芮 (Qín Ruì) 惊门 (Jīng Mén) Xun 4 — Ren/Bing / Ding	九地 (Jiǔ Dì) 天柱 (Tiān Zhù) 开门 (Kāi Mén) Li 9 — Wu / Geng	九天 (Jiǔ Tiān) 天心 (Tiān Xīn) 休门 (Xiū Mén) Kun 2 — Yi / Ren/Bing
白虎 (Bái Hǔ) 天英 (Tiān Yīng) 死门 (Sǐ Mén) Zhen 3 — Geng / Gui	Yang (阳) Dun# 7 Hour: **WuXu** ©Calvin Yap	值符 (Zhí Fú) 天蓬 (Tiān Péng) 生门 (Shēng Mén) Dui 7 — Xin / Wu
六合 (Liù Hé) 天辅 (Tiān Fǔ) 景门 (Jǐng Mén) Gen 8 — Ding / Ji	太阴 (Tài Yīn) 天冲 (Tiān Chōng) 杜门 (Dù Mén) Kan 1 — Gui / Xin	螣蛇 (Téng Shé) 天任 (Tiān Rèn) 伤门 (Shāng Mén) Qian 6 — Ji / Xin

Yang (阳) Dun# 7 Hour: **JiHai** ；直符(ZhíFú): 天蓬(TiānPéng)
直使(ZhíShǐ): 休门(XiūMén) ；旬首(XúnShǒu): JiaWu/Xin

太阴 (Tài Yīn) 天冲 (Tiān Chōng) 景门 (Jǐng Mén) Xun 4 — Gui / Ding	六合 (Liù Hé) 天辅 (Tiān Fǔ) 死门 (Sǐ Mén) Li 9 — Ding / Geng	白虎 (Bái Hǔ) 天英 (Tiān Yīng) 惊门 (Jīng Mén) Kun 2 — Geng / Ren/Bing
螣蛇 (Téng Shé) 天任 (Tiān Rèn) 杜门 (Dù Mén) Zhen 3 — Ji / Gui	Yang (阳) Dun# 7 Hour: **JiHai** ©Calvin Yap	玄武 (Xuán Wǔ) 禽芮 (Qín Ruì) 开门 (Kāi Mén) Dui 7 — Ren/Bing / Wu
值符 (Zhí Fú) 天蓬 (Tiān Péng) 伤门 (Shāng Mén) Gen 8 — Xin / Ji	九天 (Jiǔ Tiān) 天心 (Tiān Xīn) 生门 (Shēng Mén) Kan 1 — Yi / Xin	九地 (Jiǔ Dì) 天柱 (Tiān Zhù) 休门 (Xiū Mén) Qian 6 — Wu / Yi

Yang (阳) Dun# 7 Hour: GengZi ; 直符(ZhíFú): 天蓬(TiānPéng)
直使(ZhíShǐ): 休门(XiūMén) ; 旬首(XúnShǒu): JiaWu/Xin

九天 (Jiǔ Tiān) 天心 (Tiān Xīn) 死门 (Sǐ Mén) Xun 4　Yi 　　Ding	值符 (Zhí Fú) 天蓬 (Tiān Péng) 惊门 (Jīng Mén) Li 9　Xin 　　Geng	螣蛇 (Téng Shé) 天任 (Tiān Rèn) 开门 (Kāi Mén) Kun 2　Ji 　　Ren/Bing
九地 (Jiǔ Dì) 天柱 (Tiān Zhù) 景门 (Jǐng Mén) Zhen 3　Wu 　　Gui	Yang (阳) Dun# 7 Hour: **GengZi** **Fan Yin** ©Calvin Yap	太阴 (Tài Yīn) 天冲 (Tiān Chōng) 休门 (Xiū Mén) Dui 7　Gui 　　Wu
玄武 (Xuán Wǔ) 禽芮 (Qín Ruì) 杜门 (Dù Mén) Gen 8　Ren/Bing 　　Ji	白虎 (Bái Hǔ) 天英 (Tiān Yīng) 伤门 (Shāng Mén) Kan 1　Geng 　　Xin	六合 (Liù Hé) 天辅 (Tiān Fǔ) 生门 (Shēng Mén) Qian 6　Ding 　　Yi

Yang (阳) Dun# 7 Hour: XinChou ; 直符(ZhíFú): 天蓬(TiānPéng)
直使(ZhíShǐ): 休门(XiūMén) ; 旬首(XúnShǒu): JiaWu/Xin

六合 (Liù Hé) 天辅 (Tiān Fǔ) 伤门 (Shāng Mén) Xun 4　Ding 　　Ding	白虎 (Bái Hǔ) 天英 (Tiān Yīng) 杜门 (Dù Mén) Li 9　Geng 　　Geng	玄武 (Xuán Wǔ) 禽芮 (Qín Ruì) 景门 (Jǐng Mén) Kun 2　Ren/Bing 　　Ren/Bing
太阴 (Tài Yīn) 天冲 (Tiān Chōng) 生门 (Shēng Mén) Zhen 3　Gui 　　Gui	Yang (阳) Dun# 7 Hour: **XinChou** **Fu Yin** ©Calvin Yap	九地 (Jiǔ Dì) 天柱 (Tiān Zhù) 死门 (Sǐ Mén) Dui 7　Wu 　　Wu
螣蛇 (Téng Shé) 天任 (Tiān Rèn) 休门 (Xiū Mén) Gen 8　Ji 　　Ji	值符 (Zhí Fú) 天蓬 (Tiān Péng) 开门 (Kāi Mén) Kan 1　Xin 　　Xin	九天 (Jiǔ Tiān) 天心 (Tiān Xīn) 惊门 (Jīng Mén) Qian 6　Yi 　　Yi

Yang (阳) Dun# 7 Hour: RenYin ; 直符(ZhíFú): 天蓬(TiānPéng)
直使(ZhíShǐ): 休门(XiūMén) ; 旬首(XúnShǒu): JiaWu/Xin

九地 (Jiǔ Dì) 天柱 (Tiān Zhù) 开门 (Kāi Mén) Xun 4　Wu 　　Ding	九天 (Jiǔ Tiān) 天心 (Tiān Xīn) 休门 (Xiū Mén) Li 9　Yi 　　Geng	值符 (Zhí Fú) 天蓬 (Tiān Péng) 生门 (Shēng Mén) Kun 2　Xin 　　Ren/Bing
玄武 (Xuán Wǔ) 禽芮 (Qín Ruì) 惊门 (Jīng Mén) Zhen 3　Ren/Bing 　　Gui	Yang (阳) Dun# 7 Hour: **RenYin** ©Calvin Yap	螣蛇 (Téng Shé) 天任 (Tiān Rèn) 伤门 (Shāng Mén) Dui 7　Ji 　　Wu
白虎 (Bái Hǔ) 天英 (Tiān Yīng) 死门 (Sǐ Mén) Gen 8　Geng 　　Ji	六合 (Liù Hé) 天辅 (Tiān Fǔ) 景门 (Jǐng Mén) Kan 1　Ding 　　Xin	太阴 (Tài Yīn) 天冲 (Tiān Chōng) 杜门 (Dù Mén) Qian 6　Gui 　　Yi

Yang (阳) Dun# 7 Hour: GuiMao ; 直符(ZhíFú): 天蓬(TiānPéng)
直使(ZhíShǐ): 休门(XiūMén) ; 旬首(XúnShǒu): JiaWu/Xin

螣蛇 (Téng Shé) 天任 (Tiān Rèn) 杜门 (Dù Mén) Xun 4　Ji 　　Ding	太阴 (Tài Yīn) 天冲 (Tiān Chōng) 景门 (Jǐng Mén) Li 9　Gui 　　Geng	六合 (Liù Hé) 天辅 (Tiān Fǔ) 死门 (Sǐ Mén) Kun 2　Ding 　　Ren/Bing
值符 (Zhí Fú) 天蓬 (Tiān Péng) 伤门 (Shāng Mén) Zhen 3　Xin 　　Gui	Yang (阳) Dun# 7 Hour: **GuiMao** ©Calvin Yap	白虎 (Bái Hǔ) 天英 (Tiān Yīng) 惊门 (Jīng Mén) Dui 7　Geng 　　Wu
九天 (Jiǔ Tiān) 天心 (Tiān Xīn) 生门 (Shēng Mén) Gen 8　Yi 　　Ji	九地 (Jiǔ Dì) 天柱 (Tiān Zhù) 休门 (Xiū Mén) Kan 1　Wu 　　Xin	玄武 (Xuán Wǔ) 禽芮 (Qín Ruì) 开门 (Kāi Mén) Qian 6　Ren/Bing 　　Yi

Chart: +7JiaChen (Yang Dun #7 JiaChen Xun)
JiaChen, YiSi, BingWu, DingWei, WuShen, JiYou, GengXu, XinHai, RenZi, GuiChou

Yang (阳) Dun# 7 Hour: JiaChen ; 直符(ZhíFú): 天芮(TiānRuì)
直使(ZhíShǐ): 死门(SǐMén) ; 旬首(XúnShǒu): JiaChenRen

九地 (Jiǔ Dì) 天辅 (Tiān Fǔ) 杜门 (Dù Mén) Xun 4　Ding 　　Ding	九天 (Jiǔ Tiān) 天英 (Tiān Yīng) 景门 (Jǐng Mén) Li 9　Geng 　　Geng	值符 (Zhí Fú) 禽芮 (Qín Ruì) 死门 (Sǐ Mén) Kun 2　Ren/Bing 　　Ren/Bing
玄武 (Xuán Wǔ) 天冲 (Tiān Chōng) 伤门 (Shāng Mén) Zhen 3　Gui 　　Gui	Yang (阳) Dun# 7 Hour: **JiaChen** **Fu Yin** ©Calvin Yap	螣蛇 (Téng Shé) 天柱 (Tiān Zhù) 惊门 (Jīng Mén) Dui 7　Wu 　　Wu
白虎 (Bái Hǔ) 天任 (Tiān Rèn) 生门 (Shēng Mén) Gen 8　Ji 　　Ji	六合 (Liù Hé) 天蓬 (Tiān Péng) 休门 (Xiū Mén) Kan 1　Xin 　　Xin	太阴 (Tài Yīn) 天心 (Tiān Xīn) 开门 (Kāi Mén) Qian 6　Yi 　　Yi

Yang (阳) Dun# 7 Hour: YiSi ; 直符(ZhíFú): 天芮(TiānRuì)
直使(ZhíShǐ): 死门(SǐMén) ; 旬首(XúnShǒu): JiaChenRen

白虎 (Bái Hǔ) 天任 (Tiān Rèn) 惊门 (Jīng Mén) Xun 4　Ji 　　Ding	玄武 (Xuán Wǔ) 天冲 (Tiān Chōng) 开门 (Kāi Mén) Li 9　Gui 　　Geng	九地 (Jiǔ Dì) 天辅 (Tiān Fǔ) 休门 (Xiū Mén) Kun 2　Ding 　　Ren/Bing
六合 (Liù Hé) 天蓬 (Tiān Péng) 死门 (Sǐ Mén) Zhen 3　Xin 　　Gui	Yang (阳) Dun# 7 Hour: **YiSi** ©Calvin Yap	九天 (Jiǔ Tiān) 天英 (Tiān Yīng) 生门 (Shēng Mén) Dui 7　Geng 　　Wu
太阴 (Tài Yīn) 天心 (Tiān Xīn) 景门 (Jǐng Mén) Gen 8　Yi 　　Ji	螣蛇 (Téng Shé) 天柱 (Tiān Zhù) 杜门 (Dù Mén) Kan 1　Wu 　　Xin	值符 (Zhí Fú) 禽芮 (Qín Ruì) 伤门 (Shāng Mén) Qian 6　Ren/Bing 　　Yi

Yang (阳) Dun# 7 Hour: BingWu ; 直符(ZhíFú): 天芮(TiānRuì)
直使(ZhíShǐ): 死门(SǐMén) ; 旬首(XúnShǒu): JiaChenRen

Yang (阳) Dun# 7 Hour: DingWei ; 直符(ZhíFú): 天芮(TiānRuì)
直使(ZhíShǐ): 死门(SǐMén) ; 旬首(XúnShǒu): JiaChenRen

Yang (阳) Dun# 7 Hour: BingWu Fu Yin

Xun 4	Li 9	Kun 2
九地 (Jiǔ Dì) 天辅 (Tiān Fǔ) 死门 (Sǐ Mén) Xun 4 — Ding / Ding	九天 (Jiǔ Tiān) 天英 (Tiān Yīng) 惊门 (Jīng Mén) Li 9 — Geng / Geng	值符 (Zhí Fú) 禽芮 (Qín Ruì) 开门 (Kāi Mén) Kun 2 — Ren/Bing / Ren/Bing
玄武 (Xuán Wǔ) 天冲 (Tiān Chōng) 景门 (Jǐng Mén) Zhen 3 — Gui / Gui	Yang (阳) Dun# 7 Hour: **BingWu** **Fu Yin** ©Calvin Yap	螣蛇 (Téng Shé) 天柱 (Tiān Zhù) 休门 (Xiū Mén) Dui 7 — Wu / Wu
白虎 (Bái Hǔ) 天任 (Tiān Rèn) 杜门 (Dù Mén) Gen 8 — Ji / Ji	六合 (Liù Hé) 天蓬 (Tiān Péng) 伤门 (Shāng Mén) Kan 1 — Xin / Xin	太阴 (Tài Yīn) 天心 (Tiān Xīn) 生门 (Shēng Mén) Qian 6 — Yi / Yi

Yang (阳) Dun# 7 Hour: DingWei

Xun 4	Li 9	Kun 2
值符 (Zhí Fú) 禽芮 (Qín Ruì) 杜门 (Dù Mén) Xun 4 — Ren/Bing / Ding	螣蛇 (Téng Shé) 天柱 (Tiān Zhù) 景门 (Jǐng Mén) Li 9 — Wu / Geng	太阴 (Tài Yīn) 天心 (Tiān Xīn) 死门 (Sǐ Mén) Kun 2 — Yi / Ren/Bing
九天 (Jiǔ Tiān) 天英 (Tiān Yīng) 伤门 (Shāng Mén) Zhen 3 — Geng / Gui	Yang (阳) Dun# 7 Hour: **DingWei** ©Calvin Yap	六合 (Liù Hé) 天蓬 (Tiān Péng) 惊门 (Jīng Mén) Dui 7 — Xin / Wu
九地 (Jiǔ Dì) 天辅 (Tiān Fǔ) 生门 (Shēng Mén) Gen 8 — Ding / Ji	玄武 (Xuán Wǔ) 天冲 (Tiān Chōng) 休门 (Xiū Mén) Kan 1 — Gui / Xin	白虎 (Bái Hǔ) 天任 (Tiān Rèn) 开门 (Kāi Mén) Qian 6 — Ji / Yi

Yang (阳) Dun# 7 Hour: **WuShen** ; 直符(ZhíFú): 天芮(TiānRuì)
直使(ZhíShǐ): 死门(SǐMén) ; 旬首(XúnShǒu): JiaChenRen

Xun 4	Li 9	Kun 2
玄武 (Xuán Wǔ) 天冲 (Tiān Chōng) 生门 (Shēng Mén) Xun 4 — Gui / Ding	九地 (Jiǔ Dì) 天辅 (Tiān Fǔ) 伤门 (Shāng Mén) Li 9 — Ding / Geng	九天 (Jiǔ Tiān) 天英 (Tiān Yīng) 杜门 (Dù Mén) Kun 2 — Geng / Ren/Bing
白虎 (Bái Hǔ) 天任 (Tiān Rèn) 休门 (Xiū Mén) Zhen 3 — Ji / Gui	Yang (阳) Dun# 7 Hour: **WuShen** ©Calvin Yap	值符 (Zhí Fú) 禽芮 (Qín Ruì) 景门 (Jǐng Mén) Dui 7 — Ren/Bing / Wu
六合 (Liù Hé) 天蓬 (Tiān Péng) 开门 (Kāi Mén) Gen 8 — Xin / Ji	太阴 (Tài Yīn) 天心 (Tiān Xīn) 惊门 (Jīng Mén) Kan 1 — Yi / Xin	螣蛇 (Téng Shé) 天柱 (Tiān Zhù) 死门 (Sǐ Mén) Qian 6 — Wu / Yi

Yang (阳) Dun# 7 Hour: **JiYou** ; 直符(ZhíFú): 天芮(TiānRuì)
直使(ZhíShǐ): 死门(SǐMén) ; 旬首(XúnShǒu): JiaChenRen

Xun 4	Li 9	Kun 2
太阴 (Tài Yīn) 天心 (Tiān Xīn) 伤门 (Shāng Mén) Xun 4 — Yi / Ding	六合 (Liù Hé) 天蓬 (Tiān Péng) 杜门 (Dù Mén) Li 9 — Xin / Geng	白虎 (Bái Hǔ) 天任 (Tiān Rèn) 景门 (Jǐng Mén) Kun 2 — Ji / Ren/Bing
螣蛇 (Téng Shé) 天柱 (Tiān Zhù) 生门 (Shēng Mén) Zhen 3 — Wu / Gui	Yang (阳) Dun# 7 Hour: **JiYou** **Fan Yin** ©Calvin Yap	玄武 (Xuán Wǔ) 天冲 (Tiān Chōng) 死门 (Sǐ Mén) Dui 7 — Gui / Wu
值符 (Zhí Fú) 禽芮 (Qín Ruì) 休门 (Xiū Mén) Gen 8 — Ren/Bing / Ji	九天 (Jiǔ Tiān) 天英 (Tiān Yīng) 开门 (Kāi Mén) Kan 1 — Geng / Xin	九地 (Jiǔ Dì) 天辅 (Tiān Fǔ) 惊门 (Jīng Mén) Qian 6 — Ding / Yi

Yang (阳) Dun# 7 Hour: **GengXu** ; 直符(ZhíFú): 天芮(TiānRuì)
直使(ZhíShǐ): 死门(SǐMén) ; 旬首(XúnShǒu): JiaChenRen

Xun 4	Li 9	Kun 2
九天 (Jiǔ Tiān) 天英 (Tiān Yīng) 开门 (Kāi Mén) Xun 4 — Geng / Ding	值符 (Zhí Fú) 禽芮 (Qín Ruì) 休门 (Xiū Mén) Li 9 — Ren/Bing / Geng	螣蛇 (Téng Shé) 天柱 (Tiān Zhù) 生门 (Shēng Mén) Kun 2 — Wu / Ren/Bing
九地 (Jiǔ Dì) 天辅 (Tiān Fǔ) 惊门 (Jīng Mén) Zhen 3 — Ding / Gui	Yang (阳) Dun# 7 Hour: **GengXu** ©Calvin Yap	太阴 (Tài Yīn) 天心 (Tiān Xīn) 伤门 (Shāng Mén) Dui 7 — Yi / Wu
玄武 (Xuán Wǔ) 天冲 (Tiān Chōng) 死门 (Sǐ Mén) Gen 8 — Gui / Ji	白虎 (Bái Hǔ) 天任 (Tiān Rèn) 景门 (Jǐng Mén) Kan 1 — Ji / Xin	六合 (Liù Hé) 天蓬 (Tiān Péng) 杜门 (Dù Mén) Qian 6 — Xin / Yi

Yang (阳) Dun# 7 Hour: **XinHai** ; 直符(ZhíFú): 天芮(TiānRuì)
直使(ZhíShǐ): 死门(SǐMén) ; 旬首(XúnShǒu): JiaChenRen

Xun 4	Li 9	Kun 2
六合 (Liù Hé) 天蓬 (Tiān Péng) 景门 (Jǐng Mén) Xun 4 — Xin / Ding	白虎 (Bái Hǔ) 天任 (Tiān Rèn) 死门 (Sǐ Mén) Li 9 — Ji / Geng	玄武 (Xuán Wǔ) 天冲 (Tiān Chōng) 惊门 (Jīng Mén) Kun 2 — Gui / Ren/Bing
太阴 (Tài Yīn) 天心 (Tiān Xīn) 杜门 (Dù Mén) Zhen 3 — Yi / Gui	Yang (阳) Dun# 7 Hour: **XinHai** ©Calvin Yap	九地 (Jiǔ Dì) 天辅 (Tiān Fǔ) 开门 (Kāi Mén) Dui 7 — Ding / Wu
螣蛇 (Téng Shé) 天柱 (Tiān Zhù) 伤门 (Shāng Mén) Gen 8 — Wu / Ji	值符 (Zhí Fú) 禽芮 (Qín Ruì) 生门 (Shēng Mén) Kan 1 — Ren/Bing / Xin	九天 (Jiǔ Tiān) 天英 (Tiān Yīng) 休门 (Xiū Mén) Qian 6 — Geng / Yi

Yang (阳) Dun# 7 Hour: **RenZi** ; 直符(ZhíFú): 天芮(TiānRuì)
直使(ZhíShǐ): 死门(SǐMén) ; 旬首(XúnShǒu): JiaChenRen

九地 (Jiǔ Dì) 天辅 (Tiān Fǔ) 休门 (Xiū Mén) Xun 4 — Ding Ding	九天 (Jiǔ Tiān) 天英 (Tiān Yīng) 生门 (Shēng Mén) Li 9 — Geng Geng	值符 (Zhí Fú) 禽芮 (Qín Ruì) 伤门 (Shāng Mén) Kun 2 — Ren/Bing Ren/Bing
玄武 (Xuán Wǔ) 天冲 (Tiān Chōng) 开门 (Kāi Mén) Zhen 3 — Gui Gui	Yang (阳) Dun# 7 Hour: **RenZi** **Fu Yin** ©Calvin Yap	螣蛇 (Téng Shé) 天柱 (Tiān Zhù) 杜门 (Dù Mén) Dui 7 — Wu Wu
白虎 (Bái Hǔ) 天任 (Tiān Rèn) 惊门 (Jīng Mén) Gen 8 — Ji Ji	六合 (Liù Hé) 天蓬 (Tiān Péng) 死门 (Sǐ Mén) Kan 1 — Xin Xin	太阴 (Tài Yīn) 天心 (Tiān Xīn) 景门 (Jǐng Mén) Qian 6 — Yi Yi

Yang (阳) Dun# 7 Hour: **GuiChou** ; 直符(ZhíFú): 天芮(TiānRuì)
直使(ZhíShǐ): 死门(SǐMén) ; 旬首(XúnShǒu): JiaChenRen

螣蛇 (Téng Shé) 天柱 (Tiān Zhù) 杜门 (Dù Mén) Xun 4 — Wu Ding	太阴 (Tài Yīn) 天心 (Tiān Xīn) 景门 (Jǐng Mén) Li 9 — Yi Geng	六合 (Liù Hé) 天蓬 (Tiān Péng) 死门 (Sǐ Mén) Kun 2 — Xin Ren/Bing
值符 (Zhí Fú) 禽芮 (Qín Ruì) 伤门 (Shāng Mén) Zhen 3 — Ren/Bing Gui	Yang (阳) Dun# 7 Hour: **GuiChou** ©Calvin Yap	白虎 (Bái Hǔ) 天任 (Tiān Rèn) 惊门 (Jīng Mén) Dui 7 — Ji Wu
九天 (Jiǔ Tiān) 天英 (Tiān Yīng) 生门 (Shēng Mén) Gen 8 — Geng Ji	九地 (Jiǔ Dì) 天辅 (Tiān Fǔ) 休门 (Xiū Mén) Kan 1 — Ding Xin	玄武 (Xuán Wǔ) 天冲 (Tiān Chōng) 开门 (Kāi Mén) Qian 6 — Gui Yi

Chart: **+7JiaYin** (Yang Dun #7 JiaYin Xun)
JiaYin, YiMao, BingChen, DingSi, WuWu, JiWei, GengShen, XinYou, RenXu, GuiHai

Yang (阳) Dun# 7 Hour: **JiaYin** ; 直符(ZhíFú): 天冲(TiānChōng)
直使(ZhíShǐ): 伤门(ShāngMén) ; 旬首(XúnShǒu): JiaYinGui

螣蛇 (Téng Shé) 天辅 (Tiān Fǔ) 杜门 (Dù Mén) Xun 4 — Ding Ding	太阴 (Tài Yīn) 天英 (Tiān Yīng) 景门 (Jǐng Mén) Li 9 — Geng Geng	六合 (Liù Hé) 禽芮 (Qín Ruì) 死门 (Sǐ Mén) Kun 2 — Ren/Bing Ren/Bing
值符 (Zhí Fú) 天冲 (Tiān Chōng) 伤门 (Shāng Mén) Zhen 3 — Gui Gui	Yang (阳) Dun# 7 Hour: **JiaYin** **Fu Yin** ©Calvin Yap	白虎 (Bái Hǔ) 天柱 (Tiān Zhù) 惊门 (Jīng Mén) Dui 7 — Wu Wu
九天 (Jiǔ Tiān) 天任 (Tiān Rèn) 生门 (Shēng Mén) Gen 8 — Ji Ji	九地 (Jiǔ Dì) 天蓬 (Tiān Péng) 休门 (Xiū Mén) Kan 1 — Xin Xin	玄武 (Xuán Wǔ) 天心 (Tiān Xīn) 开门 (Kāi Mén) Qian 6 — Yi Yi

Yang (阳) Dun# 7 Hour: **YiMao** ; 直符(ZhíFú): 天冲(TiānChōng)
直使(ZhíShǐ): 伤门(ShāngMén) ; 旬首(XúnShǒu): JiaYinGui

白虎 (Bái Hǔ) 天柱 (Tiān Zhù) 伤门 (Shāng Mén) Xun 4 — Wu Ding	玄武 (Xuán Wǔ) 天心 (Tiān Xīn) 杜门 (Dù Mén) Li 9 — Yi Geng	九地 (Jiǔ Dì) 天蓬 (Tiān Péng) 景门 (Jǐng Mén) Kun 2 — Xin Ren/Bing
六合 (Liù Hé) 禽芮 (Qín Ruì) 生门 (Shēng Mén) Zhen 3 — Ren/Bing Gui	Yang (阳) Dun# 7 Hour: **YiMao** ©Calvin Yap	九天 (Jiǔ Tiān) 天任 (Tiān Rèn) 死门 (Sǐ Mén) Dui 7 — Ji Wu
太阴 (Tài Yīn) 天英 (Tiān Yīng) 休门 (Xiū Mén) Gen 8 — Geng Ji	螣蛇 (Téng Shé) 天辅 (Tiān Fǔ) 开门 (Kāi Mén) Kan 1 — Ding Xin	值符 (Zhí Fú) 天冲 (Tiān Chōng) 惊门 (Jīng Mén) Qian 6 — Gui Yi

Yang (阳) Dun# 7 Hour: **BingChen** ; 直符(ZhíFú): 天冲(TiānChōng)
直使(ZhíShǐ): 伤门(ShāngMén) ; 旬首(XúnShǒu): JiaYinGui

九地 (Jiǔ Dì) 天蓬 (Tiān Péng) 休门 (Xiū Mén) Xun 4 — Xin Ding	九天 (Jiǔ Tiān) 天任 (Tiān Rèn) 生门 (Shēng Mén) Li 9 — Ji Geng	值符 (Zhí Fú) 天冲 (Tiān Chōng) 伤门 (Shāng Mén) Kun 2 — Gui Ren/Bing
玄武 (Xuán Wǔ) 天心 (Tiān Xīn) 开门 (Kāi Mén) Zhen 3 — Yi Gui	Yang (阳) Dun# 7 Hour: **BingChen** ©Calvin Yap	螣蛇 (Téng Shé) 天辅 (Tiān Fǔ) 杜门 (Dù Mén) Dui 7 — Ding Wu
白虎 (Bái Hǔ) 天柱 (Tiān Zhù) 惊门 (Jīng Mén) Gen 8 — Wu Ji	六合 (Liù Hé) 禽芮 (Qín Ruì) 死门 (Sǐ Mén) Kan 1 — Ren/Bing Xin	太阴 (Tài Yīn) 天英 (Tiān Yīng) 景门 (Jǐng Mén) Qian 6 — Geng Yi

Yang (阳) Dun# 7 Hour: **DingSi** ; 直符(ZhíFú): 天冲(TiānChōng)
直使(ZhíShǐ): 伤门(ShāngMén) ; 旬首(XúnShǒu): JiaYinGui

值符 (Zhí Fú) 天冲 (Tiān Chōng) 惊门 (Jīng Mén) Xun 4 — Gui Ding	螣蛇 (Téng Shé) 天辅 (Tiān Fǔ) 开门 (Kāi Mén) Li 9 — Ding Geng	太阴 (Tài Yīn) 天英 (Tiān Yīng) 休门 (Xiū Mén) Kun 2 — Geng Ren/Bing
九天 (Jiǔ Tiān) 天任 (Tiān Rèn) 死门 (Sǐ Mén) Zhen 3 — Ji Gui	Yang (阳) Dun# 7 Hour: **DingSi** ©Calvin Yap	六合 (Liù Hé) 禽芮 (Qín Ruì) 生门 (Shēng Mén) Dui 7 — Ren/Bing Wu
九地 (Jiǔ Dì) 天蓬 (Tiān Péng) 景门 (Jǐng Mén) Gen 8 — Xin Ji	玄武 (Xuán Wǔ) 天心 (Tiān Xīn) 杜门 (Dù Mén) Kan 1 — Yi Xin	白虎 (Bái Hǔ) 天柱 (Tiān Zhù) 伤门 (Shāng Mén) Qian 6 — Wu Yi

Chart 1

Yang (阳) Dun# 7 Hour: **WuWu** ; 直符(ZhíFú): 天冲(TiānChōng)
直使(ZhíShǐ): 伤门(ShāngMén) ; 旬首(XúnShǒu): JiaYinGui

玄武 (Xuán Wǔ) 天心 (Tiān Xīn) 开门 (Kāi Mén) Xun 4　Yi Ding	九地 (Jiǔ Dì) 天蓬 (Tiān Péng) 休门 (Xiū Mén) Li 9　Xin Geng	九天 (Jiǔ Tiān) 天任 (Tiān Rèn) 生门 (Shēng Mén) Kun 2　Ji Ren/Bing
白虎 (Bái Hǔ) 天柱 (Tiān Zhù) 惊门 (Jīng Mén) Zhen 3　Wu Gui	Yang (阳) Dun# 7 Hour: **WuWu** **Fan Yin** ©Calvin Yap	值符 (Zhí Fú) 天冲 (Tiān Chōng) 伤门 (Shāng Mén) Dui 7　Gui Wu
六合 (Liù Hé) 禽芮 (Qín Ruì) 死门 (Sǐ Mén) Gen 8　Ren/Bing Ji	太阴 (Tài Yīn) 天英 (Tiān Yīng) 景门 (Jǐng Mén) Kan 1　Geng Xin	螣蛇 (Téng Shé) 天辅 (Tiān Fǔ) 杜门 (Dù Mén) Qian 6　Ding Yi

Chart 2

Yang (阳) Dun# 7 Hour: **JiWei** ; 直符(ZhíFú): 天冲(TiānChōng)
直使(ZhíShǐ): 伤门(ShāngMén) ; 旬首(XúnShǒu): JiaYinGui

太阴 (Tài Yīn) 天英 (Tiān Yīng) 景门 (Jǐng Mén) Xun 4　Geng Ding	六合 (Liù Hé) 禽芮 (Qín Ruì) 死门 (Sǐ Mén) Li 9　Ren/Bing Geng	白虎 (Bái Hǔ) 天柱 (Tiān Zhù) 惊门 (Jīng Mén) Kun 2　Wu Ren/Bing
螣蛇 (Téng Shé) 天辅 (Tiān Fǔ) 杜门 (Dù Mén) Zhen 3　Ding Gui	Yang (阳) Dun# 7 Hour: **JiWei** ©Calvin Yap	玄武 (Xuán Wǔ) 天心 (Tiān Xīn) 开门 (Kāi Mén) Dui 7　Yi Wu
值符 (Zhí Fú) 天冲 (Tiān Chōng) 伤门 (Shāng Mén) Gen 8　Gui Ji	九天 (Jiǔ Tiān) 天任 (Tiān Rèn) 生门 (Shēng Mén) Kan 1　Ji Xin	九地 (Jiǔ Dì) 天蓬 (Tiān Péng) 休门 (Xiū Mén) Qian 6　Xin Yi

Chart 3

Yang (阳) Dun# 7 Hour: **GengShen** ; 直符(ZhíFú): 天冲(TiānChōng)
直使(ZhíShǐ): 伤门(ShāngMén) ; 旬首(XúnShǒu): JiaYinGui

九天 (Jiǔ Tiān) 天任 (Tiān Rèn) 生门 (Shēng Mén) Xun 4　Ji Ding	值符 (Zhí Fú) 天冲 (Tiān Chōng) 伤门 (Shāng Mén) Li 9　Gui Geng	螣蛇 (Téng Shé) 天辅 (Tiān Fǔ) 杜门 (Dù Mén) Kun 2　Ding Ren/Bing
九地 (Jiǔ Dì) 天蓬 (Tiān Péng) 休门 (Xiū Mén) Zhen 3　Xin Gui	Yang (阳) Dun# 7 Hour: **GengShen** ©Calvin Yap	太阴 (Tài Yīn) 天英 (Tiān Yīng) 景门 (Jǐng Mén) Dui 7　Geng Wu
玄武 (Xuán Wǔ) 天心 (Tiān Xīn) 开门 (Kāi Mén) Gen 8　Yi Ji	白虎 (Bái Hǔ) 天柱 (Tiān Zhù) 惊门 (Jīng Mén) Kan 1　Wu Xin	六合 (Liù Hé) 禽芮 (Qín Ruì) 死门 (Sǐ Mén) Qian 6　Ren/Bing Yi

Chart 4

Yang (阳) Dun# 7 Hour: **XinYou** ; 直符(ZhíFú): 天冲(TiānChōng)
直使(ZhíShǐ): 伤门(ShāngMén) ; 旬首(XúnShǒu): JiaYinGui

六合 (Liù Hé) 禽芮 (Qín Ruì) 死门 (Sǐ Mén) Xun 4　Ren/Bing Ding	白虎 (Bái Hǔ) 天柱 (Tiān Zhù) 惊门 (Jīng Mén) Li 9　Wu Geng	玄武 (Xuán Wǔ) 天心 (Tiān Xīn) 开门 (Kāi Mén) Kun 2　Yi Ren/Bing
太阴 (Tài Yīn) 天英 (Tiān Yīng) 景门 (Jǐng Mén) Zhen 3　Geng Gui	Yang (阳) Dun# 7 Hour: **XinYou** ©Calvin Yap	九地 (Jiǔ Dì) 天蓬 (Tiān Péng) 休门 (Xiū Mén) Dui 7　Xin Wu
螣蛇 (Téng Shé) 天辅 (Tiān Fǔ) 杜门 (Dù Mén) Gen 8　Ding Ji	值符 (Zhí Fú) 天冲 (Tiān Chōng) 伤门 (Shāng Mén) Kan 1　Gui Xin	九天 (Jiǔ Tiān) 天任 (Tiān Rèn) 生门 (Shēng Mén) Qian 6　Ji Yi

Chart 5

Yang (阳) Dun# 7 Hour: **RenXu** ; 直符(ZhíFú): 天冲(TiānChōng)
直使(ZhíShǐ): 伤门(ShāngMén) ; 旬首(XúnShǒu): JiaYinGui

九地 (Jiǔ Dì) 天蓬 (Tiān Péng) 休门 (Xiū Mén) Xun 4　Xin Ding	九天 (Jiǔ Tiān) 天任 (Tiān Rèn) 生门 (Shēng Mén) Li 9　Ji Geng	值符 (Zhí Fú) 天冲 (Tiān Chōng) 伤门 (Shāng Mén) Kun 2　Gui Ren/Bing
玄武 (Xuán Wǔ) 天心 (Tiān Xīn) 开门 (Kāi Mén) Zhen 3　Yi Gui	Yang (阳) Dun# 7 Hour: **RenXu** ©Calvin Yap	螣蛇 (Téng Shé) 天辅 (Tiān Fǔ) 杜门 (Dù Mén) Dui 7　Ding Wu
白虎 (Bái Hǔ) 天柱 (Tiān Zhù) 惊门 (Jīng Mén) Gen 8　Wu Ji	六合 (Liù Hé) 禽芮 (Qín Ruì) 死门 (Sǐ Mén) Kan 1　Ren/Bing Xin	太阴 (Tài Yīn) 天英 (Tiān Yīng) 景门 (Jǐng Mén) Qian 6　Geng Yi

Chart 6

Yang (阳) Dun# 7 Hour: **GuiHai** ; 直符(ZhíFú): 天冲(TiānChōng)
直使(ZhíShǐ): 伤门(ShāngMén) ; 旬首(XúnShǒu): JiaYinGui

螣蛇 (Téng Shé) 天辅 (Tiān Fǔ) 杜门 (Dù Mén) Xun 4　Ding Ding	太阴 (Tài Yīn) 天英 (Tiān Yīng) 景门 (Jǐng Mén) Li 9　Geng Geng	六合 (Liù Hé) 禽芮 (Qín Ruì) 死门 (Sǐ Mén) Kun 2　Ren/Bing Ren/Bing
值符 (Zhí Fú) 天冲 (Tiān Chōng) 伤门 (Shāng Mén) Zhen 3　Gui Gui	Yang (阳) Dun# 7 Hour: **GuiHai** **Fu Yin** ©Calvin Yap	白虎 (Bái Hǔ) 天柱 (Tiān Zhù) 惊门 (Jīng Mén) Dui 7　Wu Wu
九天 (Jiǔ Tiān) 天任 (Tiān Rèn) 生门 (Shēng Mén) Gen 8　Ji Ji	九地 (Jiǔ Dì) 天蓬 (Tiān Péng) 休门 (Xiū Mén) Kan 1　Xin Xin	玄武 (Xuán Wǔ) 天心 (Tiān Xīn) 开门 (Kāi Mén) Qian 6　Yi Yi

Yang Dun#8

Chart: **+8JiaZi** (Yang Dun #8 JiaZi Xun)
JiaZi, YiChou, BingYin, DingMao, WuChen, JiSi, GengWu, XinWei, RenShen, GuiYou

Yang (阳) Dun# 8 Hour: JiaZi ; 直符(ZhíFú): 天任(TiānRèn)
直使(ZhíShǐ): 生门(ShēngMén) ; 旬首(XúnShǒu): JiaZiWu

太阴 (Tài Yīn) 天辅 (Tiān Fǔ) 杜门 (Dù Mén) Xun 4　　Gui 　　　　Gui	六合 (Liù Hé) 天英 (Tiān Yīng) 景门 (Jǐng Mén) Li 9　　Ji 　　　Ji	白虎 (Bái Hǔ) 禽芮 (Qín Ruì) 死门 (Sǐ Mén) Kun 2　　Xin/Ding 　　　　Xin/Ding
螣蛇 (Téng Shé) 天冲 (Tiān Chōng) 伤门 (Shāng Mén) Zhen 3　　Ren 　　　　Ren	Yang (阳) Dun# 8 Hour: **JiaZi** **Fu Yin** ©Calvin Yap	玄武 (Xuán Wǔ) 天柱 (Tiān Zhù) 惊门 (Jǐng Mén) Dui 7　　Yi 　　　　Yi
值符 (Zhí Fú) 天任 (Tiān Rèn) 生门 (Shēng Mén) Gen 8　　Wu 　　　　Wu	九天 (Jiǔ Tiān) 天蓬 (Tiān Péng) 休门 (Xiū Mén) Kan 1　　Geng 　　　　Geng	九地 (Jiǔ Dì) 天心 (Tiān Xīn) 开门 (Kāi Mén) Qian 6　　Bing 　　　　Bing

Yang (阳) Dun# 8 Hour: YiChou ; 直符(ZhíFú): 天任(TiānRèn)
直使(ZhíShǐ): 生门(ShēngMén) ; 旬首(XúnShǒu): JiaZiWu

玄武 (Xuán Wǔ) 天柱 (Tiān Zhù) 休门 (Xiū Mén) Xun 4　　Gui	九地 (Jiǔ Dì) 天心 (Tiān Xīn) 生门 (Shēng Mén) Li 9　　Bing 　　　Ji	九天 (Jiǔ Tiān) 天蓬 (Tiān Péng) 伤门 (Shāng Mén) Kun 2　　Geng 　　　　Xin/Ding
白虎 (Bái Hǔ) 禽芮 (Qín Ruì) 开门 (Kāi Mén) Zhen 3　　Xin/Ding 　　　　Ren	Yang (阳) Dun# 8 Hour: **YiChou** ©Calvin Yap	值符 (Zhí Fú) 天任 (Tiān Rèn) 杜门 (Dù Mén) Dui 7　　Wu 　　　　Yi
六合 (Liù Hé) 天英 (Tiān Yīng) 惊门 (Jǐng Mén) Gen 8　　Ji 　　　Wu	太阴 (Tài Yīn) 天辅 (Tiān Fǔ) 死门 (Sǐ Mén) Kan 1　　Gui 　　　　Geng	螣蛇 (Téng Shé) 天冲 (Tiān Chōng) 景门 (Jǐng Mén) Qian 6　　Ren 　　　　Bing

Yang (阳) Dun# 8 Hour: BingYin ; 直符(ZhíFú): 天任(TiānRèn)
直使(ZhíShǐ): 生门(ShēngMén) ; 旬首(XúnShǒu): JiaZiWu

白虎 (Bái Hǔ) 禽芮 (Qín Ruì) 景门 (Jǐng Mén) Xun 4　　Xin/Ding 　　　　Gui	玄武 (Xuán Wǔ) 天柱 (Tiān Zhù) 死门 (Sǐ Mén) Li 9　　Yi 　　　Ji	九地 (Jiǔ Dì) 天心 (Tiān Xīn) 惊门 (Jǐng Mén) Kun 2　　Bing 　　　　Xin/Ding
六合 (Liù Hé) 天英 (Tiān Yīng) 杜门 (Dù Mén) Zhen 3　　Ji 　　　　Ren	Yang (阳) Dun# 8 Hour: **BingYin** ©Calvin Yap	九天 (Jiǔ Tiān) 天蓬 (Tiān Péng) 开门 (Kāi Mén) Dui 7　　Geng 　　　　Yi
太阴 (Tài Yīn) 天辅 (Tiān Fǔ) 伤门 (Shāng Mén) Gen 8　　Gui 　　　　Wu	螣蛇 (Téng Shé) 天冲 (Tiān Chōng) 生门 (Shēng Mén) Kan 1　　Ren 　　　　Geng	值符 (Zhí Fú) 天任 (Tiān Rèn) 休门 (Xiū Mén) Qian 6　　Wu 　　　　Bing

Yang (阳) Dun# 8 Hour: DingMao ; 直符(ZhíFú): 天任(TiānRèn)
直使(ZhíShǐ): 生门(ShēngMén) ; 旬首(XúnShǒu): JiaZiWu

九地 (Jiǔ Dì) 天心 (Tiān Xīn) 开门 (Kāi Mén) Xun 4　　Bing 　　　　Gui	九天 (Jiǔ Tiān) 天蓬 (Tiān Péng) 休门 (Xiū Mén) Li 9　　Geng 　　　Ji	值符 (Zhí Fú) 天任 (Tiān Rèn) 生门 (Shēng Mén) Kun 2　　Wu 　　　　Xin/Ding
玄武 (Xuán Wǔ) 天柱 (Tiān Zhù) 惊门 (Jǐng Mén) Zhen 3　　Yi 　　　　Ren	Yang (阳) Dun# 8 Hour: **DingMao** **Fan Yin** ©Calvin Yap	螣蛇 (Téng Shé) 天冲 (Tiān Chōng) 伤门 (Shāng Mén) Dui 7　　Ren 　　　　Yi
白虎 (Bái Hǔ) 禽芮 (Qín Ruì) 死门 (Sǐ Mén) Gen 8　　Xin/Ding 　　　　Wu	六合 (Liù Hé) 天英 (Tiān Yīng) 景门 (Jǐng Mén) Kan 1　　Ji 　　　　Geng	太阴 (Tài Yīn) 天辅 (Tiān Fǔ) 杜门 (Dù Mén) Qian 6　　Gui 　　　　Bing

Yang (阳) Dun# 8 Hour: WuChen ; 直符(ZhíFú): 天任(TiānRèn)
直使(ZhíShǐ): 生门(ShēngMén) ; 旬首(XúnShǒu): JiaZiWu

太阴 (Tài Yīn) 天辅 (Tiān Fǔ) 伤门 (Shāng Mén) Xun 4　　Gui 　　　　Gui	六合 (Liù Hé) 天英 (Tiān Yīng) 杜门 (Dù Mén) Li 9　　Ji 　　　Ji	白虎 (Bái Hǔ) 禽芮 (Qín Ruì) 景门 (Jǐng Mén) Kun 2　　Xin/Ding 　　　　Xin/Ding
螣蛇 (Téng Shé) 天冲 (Tiān Chōng) 生门 (Shēng Mén) Zhen 3　　Ren 　　　　Ren	Yang (阳) Dun# 8 Hour: **WuChen** **Fu Yin** ©Calvin Yap	玄武 (Xuán Wǔ) 天柱 (Tiān Zhù) 死门 (Sǐ Mén) Dui 7　　Yi 　　　　Yi
值符 (Zhí Fú) 天任 (Tiān Rèn) 休门 (Xiū Mén) Gen 8　　Wu 　　　　Wu	九天 (Jiǔ Tiān) 天蓬 (Tiān Péng) 开门 (Kāi Mén) Kan 1　　Geng 　　　　Geng	九地 (Jiǔ Dì) 天心 (Tiān Xīn) 惊门 (Jǐng Mén) Qian 6　　Bing 　　　　Bing

Yang (阳) Dun# 8 Hour: JiSi ; 直符(ZhíFú): 天任(TiānRèn)
直使(ZhíShǐ): 生门(ShēngMén) ; 旬首(XúnShǒu): JiaZiWu

九天 (Jiǔ Tiān) 天蓬 (Tiān Péng) 生门 (Shēng Mén) Xun 4　　Geng 　　　　Gui	值符 (Zhí Fú) 天任 (Tiān Rèn) 伤门 (Shāng Mén) Li 9　　Wu 　　　Ji	螣蛇 (Téng Shé) 天冲 (Tiān Chōng) 杜门 (Dù Mén) Kun 2　　Ren 　　　　Xin/Ding
九地 (Jiǔ Dì) 天心 (Tiān Xīn) 休门 (Xiū Mén) Zhen 3　　Bing 　　　　Ren	Yang (阳) Dun# 8 Hour: **JiSi** ©Calvin Yap	太阴 (Tài Yīn) 天辅 (Tiān Fǔ) 景门 (Jǐng Mén) Dui 7　　Gui 　　　　Yi
玄武 (Xuán Wǔ) 天柱 (Tiān Zhù) 开门 (Kāi Mén) Gen 8　　Yi 　　　　Wu	白虎 (Bái Hǔ) 禽芮 (Qín Ruì) 惊门 (Jǐng Mén) Kan 1　　Xin/Ding 　　　　Geng	六合 (Liù Hé) 天英 (Tiān Yīng) 死门 (Sǐ Mén) Qian 6　　Ji 　　　　Bing

Yang (阳) Dun# 8 Hour: **GengWu** ; 直符(ZhíFú): 天任(TiānRèn)
直使(ZhíShǐ): 生门(ShēngMén) ; 旬首(XúnShǒu): JiaZiWu

六合 (Liù Hé) 天英 (Tiān Yīng) 开门 (Kāi Mén) Xun 4　Ji Gui	白虎 (Bái Hǔ) 禽芮 (Qín Ruì) 休门 (Xiū Mén) Li 9　Xin/Ding Ji	玄武 (Xuán Wǔ) 天柱 (Tiān Zhù) 生门 (Shēng Mén) Kun 2　Yi Xin/Ding
太阴 (Tài Yīn) 天辅 (Tiān Fǔ) 惊门 (Jīng Mén) Zhen 3　Gui Ren	Yang (阳) Dun# 8 Hour: **GengWu** ©Calvin Yap	九地 (Jiǔ Dì) 天心 (Tiān Xīn) 伤门 (Shāng Mén) Dui 7　Bing Yi
螣蛇 (Téng Shé) 天冲 (Tiān Chōng) 死门 (Sǐ Mén) Gen 8　Ren Wu	值符 (Zhí Fú) 天任 (Tiān Rèn) 景门 (Jǐng Mén) Kan 1　Wu Geng	九天 (Jiǔ Tiān) 天蓬 (Tiān Péng) 杜门 (Dù Mén) Qian 6　Geng Bing

Yang (阳) Dun# 8 Hour: **XinWei** ; 直符(ZhíFú): 天任(TiānRèn)
直使(ZhíShǐ): 生门(ShēngMén) ; 旬首(XúnShǒu): JiaZiWu

九地 (Jiǔ Dì) 天心 (Tiān Xīn) 死门 (Sǐ Mén) Xun 4　Bing Gui	九天 (Jiǔ Tiān) 天蓬 (Tiān Péng) 惊门 (Jīng Mén) Li 9　Geng Ji	值符 (Zhí Fú) 天任 (Tiān Rèn) 开门 (Kāi Mén) Kun 2　Wu Xin/Ding
玄武 (Xuán Wǔ) 天柱 (Tiān Zhù) 景门 (Jǐng Mén) Zhen 3　Yi Ren	Yang (阳) Dun# 8 Hour: **XinWei** **Fan Yin** ©Calvin Yap	螣蛇 (Téng Shé) 天冲 (Tiān Chōng) 休门 (Xiū Mén) Dui 7　Ren Yi
白虎 (Bái Hǔ) 禽芮 (Qín Ruì) 杜门 (Dù Mén) Gen 8　Xin/Ding Wu	六合 (Liù Hé) 天英 (Tiān Yīng) 伤门 (Shāng Mén) Kan 1　Ji Geng	太阴 (Tài Yīn) 天辅 (Tiān Fǔ) 生门 (Shēng Mén) Qian 6　Gui Bing

Yang (阳) Dun# 8 Hour: **RenShen** ; 直符(ZhíFú): 天任(TiānRèn)
直使(ZhíShǐ): 生门(ShēngMén) ; 旬首(XúnShǒu): JiaZiWu

螣蛇 (Téng Shé) 天冲 (Tiān Chōng) 惊门 (Jīng Mén) Xun 4　Ren Gui	太阴 (Tài Yīn) 天辅 (Tiān Fǔ) 开门 (Kāi Mén) Li 9　Gui Ji	六合 (Liù Hé) 天英 (Tiān Yīng) 休门 (Xiū Mén) Kun 2　Ji Xin/Ding
值符 (Zhí Fú) 天任 (Tiān Rèn) 死门 (Sǐ Mén) Zhen 3　Wu Ren	Yang (阳) Dun# 8 Hour: **RenShen** ©Calvin Yap	白虎 (Bái Hǔ) 禽芮 (Qín Ruì) 生门 (Shēng Mén) Dui 7　Xin/Ding Yi
九天 (Jiǔ Tiān) 天蓬 (Tiān Péng) 景门 (Jǐng Mén) Gen 8　Geng Wu	九地 (Jiǔ Dì) 天心 (Tiān Xīn) 杜门 (Dù Mén) Kan 1　Geng	玄武 (Xuán Wǔ) 天柱 (Tiān Zhù) 伤门 (Shāng Mén) Qian 6　Yi Bing

Yang (阳) Dun# 8 Hour: **GuiYou** ; 直符(ZhíFú): 天任(TiānRèn)
直使(ZhíShǐ): 生门(ShēngMén) ; 旬首(XúnShǒu): JiaZiWu

值符 (Zhí Fú) 天任 (Tiān Rèn) 杜门 (Dù Mén) Xun 4　Wu Gui	螣蛇 (Téng Shé) 天冲 (Tiān Chōng) 景门 (Jǐng Mén) Li 9　Ren Ji	太阴 (Tài Yīn) 天辅 (Tiān Fǔ) 死门 (Sǐ Mén) Kun 2　Gui Xin/Ding
九天 (Jiǔ Tiān) 天蓬 (Tiān Péng) 伤门 (Shāng Mén) Zhen 3　Geng Ren	Yang (阳) Dun# 8 Hour: **GuiYou** ©Calvin Yap	六合 (Liù Hé) 天英 (Tiān Yīng) 惊门 (Jīng Mén) Dui 7　Ji Yi
九地 (Jiǔ Dì) 天心 (Tiān Xīn) 生门 (Shēng Mén) Gen 8　Bing Wu	玄武 (Xuán Wǔ) 天柱 (Tiān Zhù) 休门 (Xiū Mén) Kan 1　Yi Geng	白虎 (Bái Hǔ) 禽芮 (Qín Ruì) 开门 (Kāi Mén) Qian 6　Xin/Ding Bing

Chart: +8JiaXu (Yang Dun #8 JiaXu Xun)

JiaXu, YiHai, BingZi, DingChou, WuYin, JiMao, GengChen, XinSi, RenWu, GuiWei

Yang (阳) Dun# 8 Hour: **JiaXu** ; 直符(ZhíFú): 天英(TiānYīng)
直使(ZhíShǐ): 景门(JǐngMén) ; 旬首(XúnShǒu): JiaXuJi

九天 (Jiǔ Tiān) 天辅 (Tiān Fǔ) 杜门 (Dù Mén) Xun 4　Gui Gui	值符 (Zhí Fú) 天英 (Tiān Yīng) 景门 (Jǐng Mén) Li 9　Ji Ji	螣蛇 (Téng Shé) 禽芮 (Qín Ruì) 死门 (Sǐ Mén) Kun 2　Xin/Ding Xin/Ding
九地 (Jiǔ Dì) 天冲 (Tiān Chōng) 伤门 (Shāng Mén) Zhen 3　Ren Ren	Yang (阳) Dun# 8 Hour: **JiaXu** **Fu Yin** ©Calvin Yap	太阴 (Tài Yīn) 天柱 (Tiān Zhù) 惊门 (Jīng Mén) Dui 7　Yi Yi
玄武 (Xuán Wǔ) 天任 (Tiān Rèn) 生门 (Shēng Mén) Gen 8　Wu Wu	白虎 (Bái Hǔ) 天蓬 (Tiān Péng) 休门 (Xiū Mén) Kan 1　Geng Geng	六合 (Liù Hé) 天心 (Tiān Xīn) 开门 (Kāi Mén) Qian 6　Bing Bing

Yang (阳) Dun# 8 Hour: **YiHai** ; 直符(ZhíFú): 天英(TiānYīng)
直使(ZhíShǐ): 景门(JǐngMén) ; 旬首(XúnShǒu): JiaXuJi

玄武 (Xuán Wǔ) 天任 (Tiān Rèn) 开门 (Kāi Mén) Xun 4　Wu Gui	九地 (Jiǔ Dì) 天冲 (Tiān Chōng) 休门 (Xiū Mén) Li 9　Ren Ji	九天 (Jiǔ Tiān) 天辅 (Tiān Fǔ) 生门 (Shēng Mén) Kun 2　Gui Xin/Ding
白虎 (Bái Hǔ) 天蓬 (Tiān Péng) 惊门 (Jīng Mén) Zhen 3　Geng Ren	Yang (阳) Dun# 8 Hour: **YiHai** ©Calvin Yap	值符 (Zhí Fú) 天英 (Tiān Yīng) 伤门 (Shāng Mén) Dui 7　Ji Yi
六合 (Liù Hé) 天心 (Tiān Xīn) 死门 (Sǐ Mén) Gen 8　Bing Wu	太阴 (Tài Yīn) 天柱 (Tiān Zhù) 景门 (Jǐng Mén) Kan 1　Yi Geng	螣蛇 (Téng Shé) 禽芮 (Qín Ruì) 杜门 (Dù Mén) Qian 6　Xin/Ding Bing

Yang (阳) Dun# 8 Hour: BingZi；直符(ZhíFú): 天英(TiānYīng)
直使(ZhíShǐ): 景门(JǐngMén)；旬首(XúnShǒu): JiaXuJi

白虎 (Bái Hǔ) 天蓬 (Tiān Péng) 伤门 (Shāng Mén) Xun 4　Geng Gui	玄武 (Xuán Wǔ) 天任 (Tiān Rèn) 杜门 (Dù Mén) Li 9　Wu Ji	九地 (Jiǔ Dì) 天冲 (Tiān Chōng) 景门 (Jǐng Mén) Kun 2　Ren Xin/Ding
六合 (Liù Hé) 天心 (Tiān Xīn) 生门 (Shēng Mén) Zhen 3　Bing Ren	Yang (阳) Dun# 8 Hour: **BingZi** ©Calvin Yap	九天 (Jiǔ Tiān) 天辅 (Tiān Fǔ) 死门 (Sǐ Mén) Dui 7　Gui
太阴 (Tài Yīn) 天柱 (Tiān Zhù) 休门 (Xiū Mén) Gen 8　Yi Wu	螣蛇 (Téng Shé) 禽芮 (Qín Ruì) 开门 (Kāi Mén) Kan 1　Xin/Ding Geng	值符 (Zhí Fú) 天英 (Tiān Yīng) 惊门 (Jǐng Mén) Qian 6　Ji Bing

Yang (阳) Dun# 8 Hour: DingChou；直符(ZhíFú): 天英(TiānYīng)
直使(ZhíShǐ): 景门(JǐngMén)；旬首(XúnShǒu): JiaXuJi

九地 (Jiǔ Dì) 天冲 (Tiān Chōng) 死门 (Sǐ Mén) Xun 4　Ren Gui	九天 (Jiǔ Tiān) 天辅 (Tiān Fǔ) 惊门 (Jǐng Mén) Li 9　Gui Ji	值符 (Zhí Fú) 天英 (Tiān Yīng) 开门 (Kāi Mén) Kun 2　Ji Xin/Ding
玄武 (Xuán Wǔ) 天任 (Tiān Rèn) 景门 (Jǐng Mén) Zhen 3　Wu Ren	Yang (阳) Dun# 8 Hour: **DingChou** ©Calvin Yap	螣蛇 (Téng Shé) 禽芮 (Qín Ruì) 休门 (Xiū Mén) Dui 7　Xin/Ding Yi
白虎 (Bái Hǔ) 天蓬 (Tiān Péng) 杜门 (Dù Mén) Gen 8　Geng Wu	六合 (Liù Hé) 天心 (Tiān Xīn) 伤门 (Shāng Mén) Kan 1　Bing Geng	太阴 (Tài Yīn) 天柱 (Tiān Zhù) 生门 (Shēng Mén) Qian 6　Yi Bing

Yang (阳) Dun# 8 Hour: WuYin；直符(ZhíFú): 天英(TiānYīng)
直使(ZhíShǐ): 景门(JǐngMén)；旬首(XúnShǒu): JiaXuJi

太阴 (Tài Yīn) 天柱 (Tiān Zhù) 景门 (Jǐng Mén) Xun 4　Yi Gui	六合 (Liù Hé) 天心 (Tiān Xīn) 死门 (Sǐ Mén) Li 9　Bing Ji	白虎 (Bái Hǔ) 天蓬 (Tiān Péng) 惊门 (Jǐng Mén) Kun 2　Geng Xin/Ding
螣蛇 (Téng Shé) 禽芮 (Qín Ruì) 杜门 (Dù Mén) Zhen 3　Xin/Ding Ren	Yang (阳) Dun# 8 Hour: **WuYin** ©Calvin Yap	玄武 (Xuán Wǔ) 天任 (Tiān Rèn) 开门 (Kāi Mén) Dui 7　Wu Yi
值符 (Zhí Fú) 天英 (Tiān Yīng) 伤门 (Shāng Mén) Gen 8　Ji Wu	九天 (Jiǔ Tiān) 天辅 (Tiān Fǔ) 生门 (Shēng Mén) Kan 1　Gui Geng	九地 (Jiǔ Dì) 天冲 (Tiān Chōng) 休门 (Xiū Mén) Qian 6　Ren Bing

Yang (阳) Dun# 8 Hour: JiMao；直符(ZhíFú): 天英(TiānYīng)
直使(ZhíShǐ): 景门(JǐngMén)；旬首(XúnShǒu): JiaXuJi

九天 (Jiǔ Tiān) 天辅 (Tiān Fǔ) 伤门 (Shāng Mén) Xun 4　Gui Gui	值符 (Zhí Fú) 天英 (Tiān Yīng) 杜门 (Dù Mén) Li 9　Ji Ji	螣蛇 (Téng Shé) 禽芮 (Qín Ruì) 景门 (Jǐng Mén) Kun 2　Xin/Ding Xin/Ding
九地 (Jiǔ Dì) 天冲 (Tiān Chōng) 生门 (Shēng Mén) Zhen 3　Ren Ren	Yang (阳) Dun# 8 Hour: **JiMao** **Fu Yin** ©Calvin Yap	太阴 (Tài Yīn) 天柱 (Tiān Zhù) 死门 (Sǐ Mén) Dui 7　Yi Yi
玄武 (Xuán Wǔ) 天任 (Tiān Rèn) 休门 (Xiū Mén) Gen 8　Wu Wu	白虎 (Bái Hǔ) 天蓬 (Tiān Péng) 开门 (Kāi Mén) Kan 1　Geng Geng	六合 (Liù Hé) 天心 (Tiān Xīn) 惊门 (Jǐng Mén) Qian 6　Bing Bing

Yang (阳) Dun# 8 Hour: GengChen；直符(ZhíFú): 天英(TiānYīng)
直使(ZhíShǐ): 景门(JǐngMén)；旬首(XúnShǒu): JiaXuJi

六合 (Liù Hé) 天心 (Tiān Xīn) 休门 (Xiū Mén) Xun 4　Bing Gui	白虎 (Bái Hǔ) 天蓬 (Tiān Péng) 生门 (Shēng Mén) Li 9　Geng Ji	玄武 (Xuán Wǔ) 天任 (Tiān Rèn) 伤门 (Shāng Mén) Kun 2　Wu Xin/Ding
太阴 (Tài Yīn) 天柱 (Tiān Zhù) 开门 (Kāi Mén) Zhen 3　Yi Ren	Yang (阳) Dun# 8 Hour: **GengChen** **Fan Yin** ©Calvin Yap	九地 (Jiǔ Dì) 天冲 (Tiān Chōng) 杜门 (Dù Mén) Dui 7　Ren Yi
螣蛇 (Téng Shé) 禽芮 (Qín Ruì) 惊门 (Jǐng Mén) Gen 8　Xin/Ding Wu	值符 (Zhí Fú) 天英 (Tiān Yīng) 死门 (Sǐ Mén) Kan 1　Ji Geng	九天 (Jiǔ Tiān) 天辅 (Tiān Fǔ) 景门 (Jǐng Mén) Qian 6　Gui Bing

Yang (阳) Dun# 8 Hour: XinSi；直符(ZhíFú): 天英(TiānYīng)
直使(ZhíShǐ): 景门(JǐngMén)；旬首(XúnShǒu): JiaXuJi

九地 (Jiǔ Dì) 天冲 (Tiān Chōng) 生门 (Shēng Mén) Xun 4　Ren Gui	九天 (Jiǔ Tiān) 天辅 (Tiān Fǔ) 伤门 (Shāng Mén) Li 9　Gui Ji	值符 (Zhí Fú) 天英 (Tiān Yīng) 杜门 (Dù Mén) Kun 2　Ji Xin/Ding
玄武 (Xuán Wǔ) 天任 (Tiān Rèn) 休门 (Xiū Mén) Zhen 3　Wu Ren	Yang (阳) Dun# 8 Hour: **XinSi** ©Calvin Yap	螣蛇 (Téng Shé) 禽芮 (Qín Ruì) 景门 (Jǐng Mén) Dui 7　Xin/Ding Yi
白虎 (Bái Hǔ) 天蓬 (Tiān Péng) 开门 (Kāi Mén) Gen 8　Geng Wu	六合 (Liù Hé) 天心 (Tiān Xīn) 惊门 (Jǐng Mén) Kan 1　Bing Geng	太阴 (Tài Yīn) 天柱 (Tiān Zhù) 死门 (Sǐ Mén) Qian 6　Yi Bing

Yang (阳) Dun# 8 Hour: RenWu ; 直符(ZhíFú): 天英(TiānYīng)
直使(ZhíShǐ): 景门(JǐngMén) ; 旬首(XúnShǒu): JiaXuJi

螣蛇 (Téng Shé) 禽芮 (Qín Ruì) 惊门 (Jīng Mén) Xun 4 — Xin/Ding — Gui	太阴 (Tài Yīn) 天柱 (Tiān Zhù) 开门 (Kāi Mén) Li 9 — Yi — Ji	六合 (Liù Hé) 天心 (Tiān Xīn) 休门 (Xiū Mén) Kun 2 — Bing — Xin/Ding
值符 (Zhí Fú) 天英 (Tiān Yīng) 死门 (Sǐ Mén) Zhen 3 — Ji — Ren	Yang (阳) Dun# 8 Hour: **RenWu** ©Calvin Yap	白虎 (Bái Hǔ) 天蓬 (Tiān Péng) 生门 (Shēng Mén) Dui 7 — Geng — Yi
九天 (Jiǔ Tiān) 天辅 (Tiān Fǔ) 景门 (Jǐng Mén) Gen 8 — Gui — Wu	九地 (Jiǔ Dì) 天冲 (Tiān Chōng) 杜门 (Dù Mén) Kan 1 — Ren — Geng	玄武 (Xuán Wǔ) 天任 (Tiān Rèn) 伤门 (Shāng Mén) Qian 6 — Wu — Bing

Yang (阳) Dun# 8 Hour: GuiWei ; 直符(ZhíFú): 天英(TiānYīng)
直使(ZhíShǐ): 景门(JǐngMén) ; 旬首(XúnShǒu): JiaXuJi

值符 (Zhí Fú) 天英 (Tiān Yīng) 杜门 (Dù Mén) Xun 4 — Ji — Gui	螣蛇 (Téng Shé) 禽芮 (Qín Ruì) 景门 (Jǐng Mén) Li 9 — Xin/Ding — Ji	太阴 (Tài Yīn) 天柱 (Tiān Zhù) 死门 (Sǐ Mén) Kun 2 — Yi — Xin/Ding
九天 (Jiǔ Tiān) 天辅 (Tiān Fǔ) 伤门 (Shāng Mén) Zhen 3 — Gui — Ren	Yang (阳) Dun# 8 Hour: **GuiWei** ©Calvin Yap	六合 (Liù Hé) 天心 (Tiān Xīn) 惊门 (Jīng Mén) Dui 7 — Bing — Yi
九地 (Jiǔ Dì) 天冲 (Tiān Chōng) 生门 (Shēng Mén) Gen 8 — Ren — Wu	玄武 (Xuán Wǔ) 天任 (Tiān Rèn) 休门 (Xiū Mén) Kan 1 — Wu — Geng	白虎 (Bái Hǔ) 天蓬 (Tiān Péng) 开门 (Kāi Mén) Qian 6 — Geng — Bing

Chart: +8JiaShen (Yang Dun #8 JiaShen Xun)
JiaShen, YiYou, BingXu, DingHai, WuZi, JiChou, GengYin, XinMao, RenChen, GuiSi

Yang (阳) Dun# 8 Hour: JiaShen ; 直符(ZhíFú): 天蓬(TiānPéng)
直使(ZhíShǐ): 休门(XiūMén) ; 旬首(XúnShǒu): JiaShenGeng

六合 (Liù Hé) 天辅 (Tiān Fǔ) 杜门 (Dù Mén) Xun 4 — Gui — Gui	白虎 (Bái Hǔ) 天英 (Tiān Yīng) 景门 (Jǐng Mén) Li 9 — Ji — Ji	玄武 (Xuán Wǔ) 禽芮 (Qín Ruì) 死门 (Sǐ Mén) Kun 2 — Xin/Ding — Xin/Ding
太阴 (Tài Yīn) 天冲 (Tiān Chōng) 伤门 (Shāng Mén) Zhen 3 — Ren — Ren	Yang (阳) Dun# 8 Hour: **JiaShen** **Fu Yin** ©Calvin Yap	九地 (Jiǔ Dì) 天柱 (Tiān Zhù) 惊门 (Jīng Mén) Dui 7 — Yi — Yi
螣蛇 (Téng Shé) 天任 (Tiān Rèn) 生门 (Shēng Mén) Gen 8 — Wu — Wu	值符 (Zhí Fú) 天蓬 (Tiān Péng) 休门 (Xiū Mén) Kan 1 — Geng — Geng	九天 (Jiǔ Tiān) 天心 (Tiān Xīn) 开门 (Kāi Mén) Qian 6 — Bing — Bing

Yang (阳) Dun# 8 Hour: YiYou ; 直符(ZhíFú): 天蓬(TiānPéng)
直使(ZhíShǐ): 休门(XiūMén) ; 旬首(XúnShǒu): JiaShenGeng

玄武 (Xuán Wǔ) 禽芮 (Qín Ruì) 惊门 (Jīng Mén) Xun 4 — Xin/Ding — Gui	九地 (Jiǔ Dì) 天柱 (Tiān Zhù) 开门 (Kāi Mén) Li 9 — Yi — Ji	九天 (Jiǔ Tiān) 天心 (Tiān Xīn) 休门 (Xiū Mén) Kun 2 — Bing — Xin/Ding
白虎 (Bái Hǔ) 天英 (Tiān Yīng) 死门 (Sǐ Mén) Zhen 3 — Ji — Ren	Yang (阳) Dun# 8 Hour: **YiYou** ©Calvin Yap	值符 (Zhí Fú) 天蓬 (Tiān Péng) 生门 (Shēng Mén) Dui 7 — Geng — Yi
六合 (Liù Hé) 天辅 (Tiān Fǔ) 景门 (Jǐng Mén) Gen 8 — Gui — Wu	太阴 (Tài Yīn) 天冲 (Tiān Chōng) 杜门 (Dù Mén) Kan 1 — Ren — Geng	螣蛇 (Téng Shé) 天任 (Tiān Rèn) 伤门 (Shāng Mén) Qian 6 — Wu — Bing

Yang (阳) Dun# 8 Hour: BingXu ; 直符(ZhíFú): 天蓬(TiānPéng)
直使(ZhíShǐ): 休门(XiūMén) ; 旬首(XúnShǒu): JiaShenGeng

白虎 (Bái Hǔ) 天英 (Tiān Yīng) 生门 (Shēng Mén) Xun 4 — Ji — Gui	玄武 (Xuán Wǔ) 禽芮 (Qín Ruì) 伤门 (Shāng Mén) Li 9 — Xin/Ding — Ji	九地 (Jiǔ Dì) 天柱 (Tiān Zhù) 杜门 (Dù Mén) Kun 2 — Yi — Xin/Ding
六合 (Liù Hé) 天辅 (Tiān Fǔ) 休门 (Xiū Mén) Zhen 3 — Gui — Ren	Yang (阳) Dun# 8 Hour: **BingXu** ©Calvin Yap	九天 (Jiǔ Tiān) 天心 (Tiān Xīn) 景门 (Jǐng Mén) Dui 7 — Bing — Yi
太阴 (Tài Yīn) 天冲 (Tiān Chōng) 开门 (Kāi Mén) Gen 8 — Ren — Wu	螣蛇 (Téng Shé) 天任 (Tiān Rèn) 惊门 (Jīng Mén) Kan 1 — Wu — Geng	值符 (Zhí Fú) 天蓬 (Tiān Péng) 死门 (Sǐ Mén) Qian 6 — Geng — Bing

Yang (阳) Dun# 8 Hour: DingHai ; 直符(ZhíFú): 天蓬(TiānPéng)
直使(ZhíShǐ): 休门(XiūMén) ; 旬首(XúnShǒu): JiaShenGeng

九地 (Jiǔ Dì) 天柱 (Tiān Zhù) 休门 (Xiū Mén) Xun 4 — Yi — Gui	九天 (Jiǔ Tiān) 天心 (Tiān Xīn) 生门 (Shēng Mén) Li 9 — Bing — Ji	值符 (Zhí Fú) 天蓬 (Tiān Péng) 伤门 (Shāng Mén) Kun 2 — Geng — Xin/Ding
玄武 (Xuán Wǔ) 禽芮 (Qín Ruì) 开门 (Kāi Mén) Zhen 3 — Xin/Ding — Ren	Yang (阳) Dun# 8 Hour: **DingHai** ©Calvin Yap	螣蛇 (Téng Shé) 天任 (Tiān Rèn) 杜门 (Dù Mén) Dui 7 — Wu — Yi
白虎 (Bái Hǔ) 天英 (Tiān Yīng) 惊门 (Jīng Mén) Gen 8 — Ji — Wu	六合 (Liù Hé) 天辅 (Tiān Fǔ) 死门 (Sǐ Mén) Kan 1 — Gui — Geng	太阴 (Tài Yīn) 天冲 (Tiān Chōng) 景门 (Jǐng Mén) Qian 6 — Ren — Bing

Yang (阳) Dun# 8 Hour: **WuZi**；直符(ZhíFú): 天蓬(TiānPéng) 直使(ZhíShǐ): 休门(XiūMén)；旬首(XúnShǒu): JiaShenGeng

太阴 (Tài Yīn) 天冲 (Tiān Chōng) 惊门 (Jīng Mén) Xun 4　Ren Gui	六合 (Liù Hé) 天辅 (Tiān Fǔ) 开门 (Kāi Mén) Li 9　Gui Ji	白虎 (Bái Hǔ) 天英 (Tiān Yīng) 休门 (Xiū Mén) Kun 2　Ji Xin/Ding
螣蛇 (Téng Shé) 天任 (Tiān Rèn) 死门 (Sǐ Mén) Zhen 3　Wu Ren	Yang (阳) Dun# 8 Hour: **WuZi** ©Calvin Yap	玄武 (Xuán Wǔ) 禽芮 (Qín Ruì) 生门 (Shēng Mén) Dui 7　Xin/Ding Yi
值符 (Zhí Fú) 天蓬 (Tiān Péng) 景门 (Jǐng Mén) Gen 8　Geng Wu	九天 (Jiǔ Tiān) 天心 (Tiān Xīn) 杜门 (Dù Mén) Kan 1　Bing Geng	九地 (Jiǔ Dì) 天柱 (Tiān Zhù) 伤门 (Shāng Mén) Qian 6　Yi Bing

Yang (阳) Dun# 8 Hour: **JiChou**；直符(ZhíFú): 天蓬(TiānPéng) 直使(ZhíShǐ): 休门(XiūMén)；旬首(XúnShǒu): JiaShenGeng

九天 (Jiǔ Tiān) 天心 (Tiān Xīn) 景门 (Jǐng Mén) Xun 4　Bing Gui	值符 (Zhí Fú) 天蓬 (Tiān Péng) 死门 (Sǐ Mén) Li 9　Geng Ji	螣蛇 (Téng Shé) 天任 (Tiān Rèn) 惊门 (Jīng Mén) Kun 2　Wu Xin/Ding
九地 (Jiǔ Dì) 天柱 (Tiān Zhù) 杜门 (Dù Mén) Zhen 3　Yi Ren	Yang (阳) Dun# 8 Hour: **JiChou** **Fan Yin** ©Calvin Yap	太阴 (Tài Yīn) 天冲 (Tiān Chōng) 开门 (Kāi Mén) Dui 7　Ren Yi
玄武 (Xuán Wǔ) 禽芮 (Qín Ruì) 伤门 (Shāng Mén) Gen 8　Xin/Ding Wu	白虎 (Bái Hǔ) 天英 (Tiān Yīng) 生门 (Shēng Mén) Kan 1　Ji Geng	六合 (Liù Hé) 天辅 (Tiān Fǔ) 休门 (Xiū Mén) Qian 6　Gui Bing

Yang (阳) Dun# 8 Hour: **GengYin**；直符(ZhíFú): 天蓬(TiānPéng) 直使(ZhíShǐ): 休门(XiūMén)；旬首(XúnShǒu): JiaShenGeng

六合 (Liù Hé) 天辅 (Tiān Fǔ) 死门 (Sǐ Mén) Xun 4　Gui Gui	白虎 (Bái Hǔ) 天英 (Tiān Yīng) 惊门 (Jīng Mén) Li 9　Ji Ji	玄武 (Xuán Wǔ) 禽芮 (Qín Ruì) 开门 (Kāi Mén) Kun 2　Xin/Ding Xin/Ding
太阴 (Tài Yīn) 天冲 (Tiān Chōng) 景门 (Jǐng Mén) Zhen 3　Ren Ren	Yang (阳) Dun# 8 Hour: **GengYin** **Fu Yin** ©Calvin Yap	九地 (Jiǔ Dì) 天柱 (Tiān Zhù) 休门 (Xiū Mén) Dui 7　Yi Yi
螣蛇 (Téng Shé) 天任 (Tiān Rèn) 杜门 (Dù Mén) Gen 8　Wu Wu	值符 (Zhí Fú) 天蓬 (Tiān Péng) 伤门 (Shāng Mén) Kan 1　Geng Geng	九天 (Jiǔ Tiān) 天心 (Tiān Xīn) 生门 (Shēng Mén) Qian 6　Bing Bing

Yang (阳) Dun# 8 Hour: **XinMao**；直符(ZhíFú): 天蓬(TiānPéng) 直使(ZhíShǐ): 休门(XiūMén)；旬首(XúnShǒu): JiaShenGeng

九地 (Jiǔ Dì) 天柱 (Tiān Zhù) 伤门 (Shāng Mén) Xun 4　Yi Gui	九天 (Jiǔ Tiān) 天心 (Tiān Xīn) 杜门 (Dù Mén) Li 9　Bing Ji	值符 (Zhí Fú) 天蓬 (Tiān Péng) 景门 (Jǐng Mén) Kun 2　Geng Xin/Ding
玄武 (Xuán Wǔ) 禽芮 (Qín Ruì) 生门 (Shēng Mén) Zhen 3　Xin/Ding Ren	Yang (阳) Dun# 8 Hour: **XinMao** ©Calvin Yap	螣蛇 (Téng Shé) 天任 (Tiān Rèn) 死门 (Sǐ Mén) Dui 7　Wu Yi
白虎 (Bái Hǔ) 天英 (Tiān Yīng) 休门 (Xiū Mén) Gen 8　Ji Wu	六合 (Liù Hé) 天辅 (Tiān Fǔ) 开门 (Kāi Mén) Kan 1　Gui Geng	太阴 (Tài Yīn) 天冲 (Tiān Chōng) 惊门 (Jīng Mén) Qian 6　Ren Bing

Yang (阳) Dun# 8 Hour: **RenChen**；直符(ZhíFú): 天蓬(TiānPéng) 直使(ZhíShǐ): 休门(XiūMén)；旬首(XúnShǒu): JiaShenGeng

螣蛇 (Téng Shé) 天任 (Tiān Rèn) 开门 (Kāi Mén) Xun 4　Wu Gui	太阴 (Tài Yīn) 天冲 (Tiān Chōng) 休门 (Xiū Mén) Li 9　Ren Ji	六合 (Liù Hé) 天辅 (Tiān Fǔ) 生门 (Shēng Mén) Kun 2　Gui Xin/Ding
值符 (Zhí Fú) 天蓬 (Tiān Péng) 惊门 (Jīng Mén) Zhen 3　Geng Ren	Yang (阳) Dun# 8 Hour: **RenChen** ©Calvin Yap	白虎 (Bái Hǔ) 天英 (Tiān Yīng) 伤门 (Shāng Mén) Dui 7　Ji Yi
九天 (Jiǔ Tiān) 天心 (Tiān Xīn) 死门 (Sǐ Mén) Gen 8　Bing Wu	九地 (Jiǔ Dì) 天柱 (Tiān Zhù) 景门 (Jǐng Mén) Kan 1　Yi Geng	玄武 (Xuán Wǔ) 禽芮 (Qín Ruì) 杜门 (Dù Mén) Qian 6　Xin/Ding Bing

Yang (阳) Dun# 8 Hour: **GuiSi**；直符(ZhíFú): 天蓬(TiānPéng) 直使(ZhíShǐ): 休门(XiūMén)；旬首(XúnShǒu): JiaShenGeng

值符 (Zhí Fú) 天蓬 (Tiān Péng) 杜门 (Dù Mén) Xun 4　Geng Gui	螣蛇 (Téng Shé) 天任 (Tiān Rèn) 景门 (Jǐng Mén) Li 9　Wu Ji	太阴 (Tài Yīn) 天冲 (Tiān Chōng) 死门 (Sǐ Mén) Kun 2　Ren Xin/Ding
九天 (Jiǔ Tiān) 天心 (Tiān Xīn) 伤门 (Shāng Mén) Zhen 3　Bing Ren	Yang (阳) Dun# 8 Hour: **GuiSi** ©Calvin Yap	六合 (Liù Hé) 天辅 (Tiān Fǔ) 惊门 (Jīng Mén) Dui 7　Gui Yi
九地 (Jiǔ Dì) 天柱 (Tiān Zhù) 生门 (Shēng Mén) Gen 8　Yi Wu	玄武 (Xuán Wǔ) 禽芮 (Qín Ruì) 休门 (Xiū Mén) Kan 1　Xin/Ding Geng	白虎 (Bái Hǔ) 天英 (Tiān Yīng) 开门 (Kāi Mén) Qian 6　Ji Bing

Chart: +8JiaWu (Yang Dun #8 JiaWu Xun)
JiaWu, YiWei, BingShen, DingYou, WuXu, JiHai, GengZi, XinChou, RenYin, GuiMao

Yang (阳) Dun# 8 Hour: **JiaWu** ; 直符(ZhíFú): 天芮(TiānRuì)
直使(ZhíShǐ): 死门(SǏMén) ; 旬首(XúnShǒu): JiaWu/Xin

九地 (Jiǔ Dì) 天辅 (Tiān Fǔ) 杜门 (Dù Mén) Xun 4 　 Gui Gui	九天 (Jiǔ Tiān) 天英 (Tiān Yīng) 景门 (Jǐng Mén) Li 9 　 Ji Ji	值符 (Zhí Fú) 禽芮 (Qín Ruì) 死门 (SǏ Mén) Kun 2 　 Xin/Ding Xin/Ding
玄武 (Xuán Wǔ) 天冲 (Tiān Chōng) 伤门 (Shāng Mén) Zhen 3 　 Ren Ren	Yang (阳) Dun# 8 Hour: **JiaWu** **Fu Yin** ©Calvin Yap	螣蛇 (Téng Shé) 天柱 (Tiān Zhù) 惊门 (Jīng Mén) Dui 7 　 Yi Yi
白虎 (Bái Hǔ) 天任 (Tiān Rèn) 生门 (Shēng Mén) Gen 8 　 Wu Wu	六合 (Liù Hé) 天蓬 (Tiān Péng) 休门 (Xiū Mén) Kan 1 　 Geng Geng	太阴 (Tài Yīn) 天心 (Tiān Xīn) 开门 (Kāi Mén) Qian 6 　 Bing Bing

Yang (阳) Dun# 8 Hour: **YiWei** ; 直符(ZhíFú): 天芮(TiānRuì)
直使(ZhíShǐ): 死门(SǏMén) ; 旬首(XúnShǒu): JiaWu/Xin

玄武 (Xuán Wǔ) 天冲 (Tiān Chōng) 惊门 (Jīng Mén) Xun 4 　 Ren Gui	九地 (Jiǔ Dì) 天辅 (Tiān Fǔ) 开门 (Kāi Mén) Li 9 　 Gui Ji	九天 (Jiǔ Tiān) 天英 (Tiān Yīng) 休门 (Xiū Mén) Kun 2 　 Ji Xin/Ding
白虎 (Bái Hǔ) 天任 (Tiān Rèn) 死门 (SǏ Mén) Zhen 3 　 Wu Ren	Yang (阳) Dun# 8 Hour: **YiWei** ©Calvin Yap	值符 (Zhí Fú) 禽芮 (Qín Ruì) 生门 (Shēng Mén) Dui 7 　 Xin/Ding Yi
六合 (Liù Hé) 天蓬 (Tiān Péng) 景门 (Jǐng Mén) Gen 8 　 Geng Wu	太阴 (Tài Yīn) 天心 (Tiān Xīn) 杜门 (Dù Mén) Kan 1 　 Bing Geng	螣蛇 (Téng Shé) 天柱 (Tiān Zhù) 伤门 (Shāng Mén) Qian 6 　 Yi Bing

Yang (阳) Dun# 8 Hour: **BingShen** ; 直符(ZhíFú): 天芮(TiānRuì)
直使(ZhíShǐ): 死门(SǏMén) ; 旬首(XúnShǒu): JiaWu/Xin

白虎 (Bái Hǔ) 天任 (Tiān Rèn) 死门 (SǏ Mén) Xun 4 　 Wu Gui	玄武 (Xuán Wǔ) 天冲 (Tiān Chōng) 惊门 (Jīng Mén) Li 9 　 Ren Ji	九地 (Jiǔ Dì) 天辅 (Tiān Fǔ) 开门 (Kāi Mén) Kun 2 　 Gui Xin/Ding
六合 (Liù Hé) 天蓬 (Tiān Péng) 景门 (Jǐng Mén) Zhen 3 　 Geng Ren	Yang (阳) Dun# 8 Hour: **BingShen** ©Calvin Yap	九天 (Jiǔ Tiān) 天英 (Tiān Yīng) 休门 (Xiū Mén) Dui 7 　 Ji Yi
太阴 (Tài Yīn) 天心 (Tiān Xīn) 杜门 (Dù Mén) Gen 8 　 Bing Wu	螣蛇 (Téng Shé) 天柱 (Tiān Zhù) 伤门 (Shāng Mén) Kan 1 　 Yi Geng	值符 (Zhí Fú) 禽芮 (Qín Ruì) 生门 (Shēng Mén) Qian 6 　 Xin/Ding Bing

Yang (阳) Dun# 8 Hour: **DingYou** ; 直符(ZhíFú): 天芮(TiānRuì)
直使(ZhíShǐ): 死门(SǏMén) ; 旬首(XúnShǒu): JiaWu/Xin

九地 (Jiǔ Dì) 天辅 (Tiān Fǔ) 杜门 (Dù Mén) Xun 4 　 Gui Gui	九天 (Jiǔ Tiān) 天英 (Tiān Yīng) 景门 (Jǐng Mén) Li 9 　 Ji Ji	值符 (Zhí Fú) 禽芮 (Qín Ruì) 死门 (SǏ Mén) Kun 2 　 Xin/Ding Xin/Ding
玄武 (Xuán Wǔ) 天冲 (Tiān Chōng) 伤门 (Shāng Mén) Zhen 3 　 Ren Ren	Yang (阳) Dun# 8 Hour: **DingYou** **Fu Yin** ©Calvin Yap	螣蛇 (Téng Shé) 天柱 (Tiān Zhù) 惊门 (Jīng Mén) Dui 7 　 Yi Yi
白虎 (Bái Hǔ) 天任 (Tiān Rèn) 生门 (Shēng Mén) Gen 8 　 Wu Wu	六合 (Liù Hé) 天蓬 (Tiān Péng) 休门 (Xiū Mén) Kan 1 　 Geng Geng	太阴 (Tài Yīn) 天心 (Tiān Xīn) 开门 (Kāi Mén) Qian 6 　 Bing Bing

Yang (阳) Dun# 8 Hour: **WuXu** ; 直符(ZhíFú): 天芮(TiānRuì)
直使(ZhíShǐ): 死门(SǏMén) ; 旬首(XúnShǒu): JiaWu/Xin

太阴 (Tài Yīn) 天心 (Tiān Xīn) 生门 (Shēng Mén) Xun 4 　 Bing Gui	六合 (Liù Hé) 天蓬 (Tiān Péng) 伤门 (Shāng Mén) Li 9 　 Geng Ji	白虎 (Bái Hǔ) 天任 (Tiān Rèn) 杜门 (Dù Mén) Kun 2 　 Wu Xin/Ding
螣蛇 (Téng Shé) 天柱 (Tiān Zhù) 休门 (Xiū Mén) Zhen 3 　 Yi Ren	Yang (阳) Dun# 8 Hour: **WuXu** **Fan Yin** ©Calvin Yap	玄武 (Xuán Wǔ) 天冲 (Tiān Chōng) 景门 (Jǐng Mén) Dui 7 　 Ren Yi
值符 (Zhí Fú) 禽芮 (Qín Ruì) 开门 (Kāi Mén) Gen 8 　 Xin/Ding Wu	九天 (Jiǔ Tiān) 天英 (Tiān Yīng) 惊门 (Jīng Mén) Kan 1 　 Ji Geng	九地 (Jiǔ Dì) 天辅 (Tiān Fǔ) 死门 (SǏ Mén) Qian 6 　 Gui Bing

Yang (阳) Dun# 8 Hour: **JiHai** ; 直符(ZhíFú): 天芮(TiānRuì)
直使(ZhíShǐ): 死门(SǏMén) ; 旬首(XúnShǒu): JiaWu/Xin

九天 (Jiǔ Tiān) 天英 (Tiān Yīng) 伤门 (Shāng Mén) Xun 4 　 Ji Gui	值符 (Zhí Fú) 禽芮 (Qín Ruì) 杜门 (Dù Mén) Li 9 　 Xin/Ding Ji	螣蛇 (Téng Shé) 天柱 (Tiān Zhù) 景门 (Jǐng Mén) Kun 2 　 Yi Xin/Ding
九地 (Jiǔ Dì) 天辅 (Tiān Fǔ) 生门 (Shēng Mén) Zhen 3 　 Gui Ren	Yang (阳) Dun# 8 Hour: **JiHai** ©Calvin Yap	太阴 (Tài Yīn) 天心 (Tiān Xīn) 死门 (SǏ Mén) Dui 7 　 Bing Yi
玄武 (Xuán Wǔ) 天冲 (Tiān Chōng) 休门 (Xiū Mén) Gen 8 　 Ren Wu	白虎 (Bái Hǔ) 天任 (Tiān Rèn) 开门 (Kāi Mén) Kan 1 　 Wu Geng	六合 (Liù Hé) 天蓬 (Tiān Péng) 惊门 (Jīng Mén) Qian 6 　 Geng Bing

Yang (阳) Dun# 8 Hour: **GengZi**；直符(ZhíFú): 天芮(TiānRuì)
直使(ZhíShǐ): 死门(SǐMén)；旬首(XúnShǒu): JiaWu/Xin

六合 (Liù Hé) 天蓬 (Tiān Péng) 开门 (Kāi Mén) Xun 4　Geng Gui	白虎 (Bái Hǔ) 天任 (Tiān Rèn) 休门 (Xiū Mén) Li 9　Wu Ji	玄武 (Xuán Wǔ) 天冲 (Tiān Chōng) 生门 (Shēng Mén) Kun 2　Ren Xin/Ding
太阴 (Tài Yīn) 天心 (Tiān Xīn) 惊门 (Jīng Mén) Zhen 3　Bing Ren	Yang (阳) Dun# 8 Hour: **GengZi** ©Calvin Yap	九地 (Jiǔ Dì) 天辅 (Tiān Fǔ) 伤门 (Shāng Mén) Dui 7　Gui Yi
螣蛇 (Téng Shé) 天柱 (Tiān Zhù) 死门 (Sǐ Mén) Gen 8　Yi Wu	值符 (Zhí Fú) 禽芮 (Qín Ruì) 景门 (Jǐng Mén) Kan 1　Xin/Ding Geng	九天 (Jiǔ Tiān) 天英 (Tiān Yīng) 杜门 (Dù Mén) Qian 6　Ji Bing

Yang (阳) Dun# 8 Hour: **XinChou**；直符(ZhíFú): 天芮(TiānRuì)
直使(ZhíShǐ): 死门(SǐMén)；旬首(XúnShǒu): JiaWu/Xin

九地 (Jiǔ Dì) 天辅 (Tiān Fǔ) 景门 (Jǐng Mén) Xun 4　Gui Gui	九天 (Jiǔ Tiān) 天英 (Tiān Yīng) 死门 (Sǐ Mén) Li 9　Ji Ji	值符 (Zhí Fú) 禽芮 (Qín Ruì) 惊门 (Jīng Mén) Kun 2　Xin/Ding Xin/Ding
玄武 (Xuán Wǔ) 天冲 (Tiān Chōng) 杜门 (Dù Mén) Zhen 3　Ren Ren	Yang (阳) Dun# 8 Hour: **XinChou** **Fu Yin** ©Calvin Yap	螣蛇 (Téng Shé) 天柱 (Tiān Zhù) 开门 (Kāi Mén) Dui 7　Yi Yi
白虎 (Bái Hǔ) 天任 (Tiān Rèn) 伤门 (Shāng Mén) Gen 8　Wu Wu	六合 (Liù Hé) 天蓬 (Tiān Péng) 生门 (Shēng Mén) Kan 1　Geng Geng	太阴 (Tài Yīn) 天心 (Tiān Xīn) 休门 (Xiū Mén) Qian 6　Bing Bing

Yang (阳) Dun# 8 Hour: **RenYin**；直符(ZhíFú): 天芮(TiānRuì)
直使(ZhíShǐ): 死门(SǐMén)；旬首(XúnShǒu): JiaWu/Xin

螣蛇 (Téng Shé) 天柱 (Tiān Zhù) 休门 (Xiū Mén) Xun 4　Yi Gui	太阴 (Tài Yīn) 天心 (Tiān Xīn) 生门 (Shēng Mén) Li 9　Bing Ji	六合 (Liù Hé) 天蓬 (Tiān Péng) 伤门 (Shāng Mén) Kun 2　Geng Xin/Ding
值符 (Zhí Fú) 禽芮 (Qín Ruì) 开门 (Kāi Mén) Zhen 3　Xin/Ding Ren	Yang (阳) Dun# 8 Hour: **RenYin** ©Calvin Yap	白虎 (Bái Hǔ) 天任 (Tiān Rèn) 杜门 (Dù Mén) Dui 7　Wu Yi
九天 (Jiǔ Tiān) 天英 (Tiān Yīng) 惊门 (Jīng Mén) Gen 8　Ji Wu	九地 (Jiǔ Dì) 天辅 (Tiān Fǔ) 死门 (Sǐ Mén) Kan 1　Gui Geng	玄武 (Xuán Wǔ) 天冲 (Tiān Chōng) 景门 (Jǐng Mén) Qian 6　Ren Bing

Yang (阳) Dun# 8 Hour: **GuiMao**；直符(ZhíFú): 天芮(TiānRuì)
直使(ZhíShǐ): 死门(SǐMén)；旬首(XúnShǒu): JiaWu/Xin

值符 (Zhí Fú) 禽芮 (Qín Ruì) 杜门 (Dù Mén) Xun 4　Xin/Ding Gui	螣蛇 (Téng Shé) 天柱 (Tiān Zhù) 景门 (Jǐng Mén) Li 9　Yi Ji	太阴 (Tài Yīn) 天心 (Tiān Xīn) 死门 (Sǐ Mén) Kun 2　Bing Xin/Ding
九天 (Jiǔ Tiān) 天英 (Tiān Yīng) 伤门 (Shāng Mén) Zhen 3　Ji Ren	Yang (阳) Dun# 8 Hour: **GuiMao** ©Calvin Yap	六合 (Liù Hé) 天蓬 (Tiān Péng) 惊门 (Jīng Mén) Dui 7　Geng Yi
九地 (Jiǔ Dì) 天辅 (Tiān Fǔ) 生门 (Shēng Mén) Gen 8　Gui Wu	玄武 (Xuán Wǔ) 天冲 (Tiān Chōng) 休门 (Xiū Mén) Kan 1　Ren Geng	白虎 (Bái Hǔ) 天任 (Tiān Rèn) 开门 (Kāi Mén) Qian 6　Wu Bing

Chart: **+8JiaChen** (Yang Dun #8 JiaChen Xun)
JiaChen, YiSi, BingWu, DingWei, WuShen, JiYou, GengXu, XinHai, RenZi, GuiChou

Yang (阳) Dun# 8 Hour: **JiaChen**；直符(ZhíFú): 天冲(TiānChōng)
直使(ZhíShǐ): 伤门(ShāngMén)；旬首(XúnShǒu): JiaChenRen

螣蛇 (Téng Shé) 天辅 (Tiān Fǔ) 杜门 (Dù Mén) Xun 4　Gui Gui	太阴 (Tài Yīn) 天英 (Tiān Yīng) 景门 (Jǐng Mén) Li 9　Ji Ji	六合 (Liù Hé) 禽芮 (Qín Ruì) 死门 (Sǐ Mén) Kun 2　Xin/Ding Xin/Ding
值符 (Zhí Fú) 天冲 (Tiān Chōng) 伤门 (Shāng Mén) Zhen 3　Ren Ren	Yang (阳) Dun# 8 Hour: **JiaChen** **Fu Yin** ©Calvin Yap	白虎 (Bái Hǔ) 天柱 (Tiān Zhù) 惊门 (Jīng Mén) Dui 7　Yi Yi
九天 (Jiǔ Tiān) 天任 (Tiān Rèn) 生门 (Shēng Mén) Gen 8　Wu Wu	九地 (Jiǔ Dì) 天蓬 (Tiān Péng) 休门 (Xiū Mén) Kan 1　Geng Geng	玄武 (Xuán Wǔ) 天心 (Tiān Xīn) 开门 (Kāi Mén) Qian 6　Bing Bing

Yang (阳) Dun# 8 Hour: **YiSi**；直符(ZhíFú): 天冲(TiānChōng)
直使(ZhíShǐ): 伤门(ShāngMén)；旬首(XúnShǒu): JiaChenRen

玄武 (Xuán Wǔ) 天心 (Tiān Xīn) 伤门 (Shāng Mén) Xun 4　Bing Gui	九地 (Jiǔ Dì) 天蓬 (Tiān Péng) 杜门 (Dù Mén) Li 9　Geng Ji	九天 (Jiǔ Tiān) 天任 (Tiān Rèn) 景门 (Jǐng Mén) Kun 2　Wu Xin/Ding
白虎 (Bái Hǔ) 天柱 (Tiān Zhù) 生门 (Shēng Mén) Zhen 3　Yi Ren	Yang (阳) Dun# 8 Hour: **YiSi** **Fan Yin** ©Calvin Yap	值符 (Zhí Fú) 天冲 (Tiān Chōng) 死门 (Sǐ Mén) Dui 7　Ren Yi
六合 (Liù Hé) 禽芮 (Qín Ruì) 休门 (Xiū Mén) Gen 8　Xin/Ding Wu	太阴 (Tài Yīn) 天英 (Tiān Yīng) 开门 (Kāi Mén) Kan 1　Ji Geng	螣蛇 (Téng Shé) 天辅 (Tiān Fǔ) 惊门 (Jīng Mén) Qian 6　Gui Bing

Yang (阳) Dun# 8 Hour: **BingWu**；直符(ZhíFú): 天冲(TiānChōng)
直使(ZhíShǐ): 伤门(ShāngMén)；旬首(XúnShǒu): JiaChenRen

白虎 (Bái Hǔ) 天柱 (Tiān Zhù) 休门 (Xiū Mén) Xun 4　　Yi Gui	玄武 (Xuán Wǔ) 天心 (Tiān Xīn) 生门 (Shēng Mén) Li 9　　Bing Ji	九地 (Jiǔ Dì) 天蓬 (Tiān Péng) 伤门 (Shāng Mén) Kun 2　　Geng Xin/Ding
六合 (Liù Hé) 禽芮 (Qín Ruì) 开门 (Kāi Mén) Zhen 3　Xin/Ding Ren	Yang (阳) Dun# 8 Hour: **BingWu** ©Calvin Yap	九天 (Jiǔ Tiān) 天任 (Tiān Rèn) 杜门 (Dù Mén) Dui 7　　Wu Yi
太阴 (Tài Yīn) 天英 (Tiān Yīng) 惊门 (Jīng Mén) Gen 8　　Ji Wu	腾蛇 (Téng Shé) 天辅 (Tiān Fǔ) 死门 (Sǐ Mén) Kan 1　　Gui Geng	值符 (Zhí Fú) 天冲 (Tiān Chōng) 景门 (Jǐng Mén) Qian 6　　Ren Bing

Yang (阳) Dun# 8 Hour: **DingWei**；直符(ZhíFú): 天冲(TiānChōng)
直使(ZhíShǐ): 伤门(ShāngMén)；旬首(XúnShǒu): JiaChenRen

九地 (Jiǔ Dì) 天蓬 (Tiān Péng) 惊门 (Jīng Mén) Xun 4　　Geng Gui	九天 (Jiǔ Tiān) 天任 (Tiān Rèn) 开门 (Kāi Mén) Li 9　　Wu Ji	值符 (Zhí Fú) 天冲 (Tiān Chōng) 休门 (Xiū Mén) Kun 2　　Ren Xin/Ding
玄武 (Xuán Wǔ) 天心 (Tiān Xīn) 死门 (Sǐ Mén) Zhen 3　　Bing Ren	Yang (阳) Dun# 8 Hour: **DingWei** ©Calvin Yap	腾蛇 (Téng Shé) 天辅 (Tiān Fǔ) 生门 (Shēng Mén) Dui 7　　Gui Yi
白虎 (Bái Hǔ) 天柱 (Tiān Zhù) 景门 (Jǐng Mén) Gen 8　　Yi Wu	六合 (Liù Hé) 禽芮 (Qín Ruì) 杜门 (Dù Mén) Kan 1　Xin/Ding Geng	太阴 (Tài Yīn) 天英 (Tiān Yīng) 伤门 (Shāng Mén) Qian 6　　Ji Bing

Yang (阳) Dun# 8 Hour: **WuShen**；直符(ZhíFú): 天冲(TiānChōng)
直使(ZhíShǐ): 伤门(ShāngMén)；旬首(XúnShǒu): JiaChenRen

太阴 (Tài Yīn) 天英 (Tiān Yīng) 开门 (Kāi Mén) Xun 4　　Ji Gui	六合 (Liù Hé) 禽芮 (Qín Ruì) 休门 (Xiū Mén) Li 9　Xin/Ding Ji	白虎 (Bái Hǔ) 天柱 (Tiān Zhù) 生门 (Shēng Mén) Kun 2　　Yi Xin/Ding
腾蛇 (Téng Shé) 天辅 (Tiān Fǔ) 惊门 (Jīng Mén) Zhen 3　　Gui Ren	Yang (阳) Dun# 8 Hour: **WuShen** ©Calvin Yap	玄武 (Xuán Wǔ) 天心 (Tiān Xīn) 伤门 (Shāng Mén) Dui 7　　Bing Yi
值符 (Zhí Fú) 天冲 (Tiān Chōng) 死门 (Sǐ Mén) Gen 8　　Ren Wu	九天 (Jiǔ Tiān) 天任 (Tiān Rèn) 景门 (Jǐng Mén) Kan 1　　Wu Geng	九地 (Jiǔ Dì) 天蓬 (Tiān Péng) 杜门 (Dù Mén) Qian 6　　Geng Bing

Yang (阳) Dun# 8 Hour: **JiYou**；直符(ZhíFú): 天冲(TiānChōng)
直使(ZhíShǐ): 伤门(ShāngMén)；旬首(XúnShǒu): JiaChenRen

九天 (Jiǔ Tiān) 天任 (Tiān Rèn) 景门 (Jǐng Mén) Xun 4　　Wu Gui	值符 (Zhí Fú) 天冲 (Tiān Chōng) 死门 (Sǐ Mén) Li 9　　Ren Ji	腾蛇 (Téng Shé) 天辅 (Tiān Fǔ) 惊门 (Jīng Mén) Kun 2　　Gui Xin/Ding
九地 (Jiǔ Dì) 天蓬 (Tiān Péng) 杜门 (Dù Mén) Zhen 3　　Geng Ren	Yang (阳) Dun# 8 Hour: **JiYou** ©Calvin Yap	太阴 (Tài Yīn) 天英 (Tiān Yīng) 开门 (Kāi Mén) Dui 7　　Ji Yi
玄武 (Xuán Wǔ) 天心 (Tiān Xīn) 伤门 (Shāng Mén) Gen 8　　Bing Wu	白虎 (Bái Hǔ) 天柱 (Tiān Zhù) 生门 (Shēng Mén) Kan 1　　Yi Geng	六合 (Liù Hé) 禽芮 (Qín Ruì) 休门 (Xiū Mén) Qian 6　Xin/Ding Bing

Yang (阳) Dun# 8 Hour: **GengXu**；直符(ZhíFú): 天冲(TiānChōng)
直使(ZhíShǐ): 伤门(ShāngMén)；旬首(XúnShǒu): JiaChenRen

六合 (Liù Hé) 禽芮 (Qín Ruì) 生门 (Shēng Mén) Xun 4　Xin/Ding Gui	白虎 (Bái Hǔ) 天柱 (Tiān Zhù) 伤门 (Shāng Mén) Li 9　　Yi Ji	玄武 (Xuán Wǔ) 天心 (Tiān Xīn) 杜门 (Dù Mén) Kun 2　　Bing Xin/Ding
太阴 (Tài Yīn) 天英 (Tiān Yīng) 休门 (Xiū Mén) Zhen 3　　Ji Ren	Yang (阳) Dun# 8 Hour: **GengXu** ©Calvin Yap	九地 (Jiǔ Dì) 天蓬 (Tiān Péng) 景门 (Jǐng Mén) Dui 7　　Geng Yi
腾蛇 (Téng Shé) 天辅 (Tiān Fǔ) 开门 (Kāi Mén) Gen 8　　Gui Wu	值符 (Zhí Fú) 天冲 (Tiān Chōng) 惊门 (Jīng Mén) Kan 1　　Ren Geng	九天 (Jiǔ Tiān) 天任 (Tiān Rèn) 死门 (Sǐ Mén) Qian 6　　Wu Bing

Yang (阳) Dun# 8 Hour: **XinHai**；直符(ZhíFú): 天冲(TiānChōng)
直使(ZhíShǐ): 伤门(ShāngMén)；旬首(XúnShǒu): JiaChenRen

九地 (Jiǔ Dì) 天蓬 (Tiān Péng) 死门 (Sǐ Mén) Xun 4　　Geng Gui	九天 (Jiǔ Tiān) 天任 (Tiān Rèn) 惊门 (Jīng Mén) Li 9　　Wu Ji	值符 (Zhí Fú) 天冲 (Tiān Chōng) 开门 (Kāi Mén) Kun 2　　Ren Xin/Ding
玄武 (Xuán Wǔ) 天心 (Tiān Xīn) 景门 (Jǐng Mén) Zhen 3　　Bing Ren	Yang (阳) Dun# 8 Hour: **XinHai** ©Calvin Yap	腾蛇 (Téng Shé) 天辅 (Tiān Fǔ) 休门 (Xiū Mén) Dui 7　　Gui Yi
白虎 (Bái Hǔ) 天柱 (Tiān Zhù) 杜门 (Dù Mén) Gen 8　　Yi Wu	六合 (Liù Hé) 禽芮 (Qín Ruì) 伤门 (Shāng Mén) Kan 1　Xin/Ding Geng	太阴 (Tài Yīn) 天英 (Tiān Yīng) 生门 (Shēng Mén) Qian 6　　Ji Bing

Yang (阳) Dun# 8 Hour: **RenZi** ; 直符(ZhíFú): 天冲(TiānChōng)
直使(ZhíShǐ): 伤门(ShāngMén) ; 旬首(XúnShǒu): JiaChenRen

螣蛇 (Téng Shé) 天辅 (Tiān Fǔ) 休门 (Xiū Mén) Xun 4　　Gui Gui	太阴 (Tài Yīn) 天英 (Tiān Yīng) 生门 (Shēng Mén) Li 9　　Ji Ji	六合 (Liù Hé) 禽芮 (Qín Ruì) 伤门 (Shāng Mén) Kun 2　　Xin/Ding Xin/Ding
值符 (Zhí Fú) 天冲 (Tiān Chōng) 开门 (Kāi Mén) Zhen 3　　Ren Ren	Yang (阳) Dun# 8 Hour: **RenZi** **Fu Yin** ©Calvin Yap	白虎 (Bái Hǔ) 天柱 (Tiān Zhù) 杜门 (Dù Mén) Dui 7　　Yi Yi
九天 (Jiǔ Tiān) 天任 (Tiān Rèn) 惊门 (Jīng Mén) Gen 8　　Wu Wu	九地 (Jiǔ Dì) 天蓬 (Tiān Péng) 死门 (Sǐ Mén) Kan 1　　Geng Geng	玄武 (Xuán Wǔ) 天心 (Tiān Xīn) 景门 (Jǐng Mén) Qian 6　　Bing Bing

Yang (阳) Dun# 8 Hour: **GuiChou**; 直符(ZhíFú): 天冲(TiānChōng)
直使(ZhíShǐ): 伤门(ShāngMén) ; 旬首(XúnShǒu): JiaChenRen

值符 (Zhí Fú) 天冲 (Tiān Chōng) 杜门 (Dù Mén) Xun 4　　Ren Gui	螣蛇 (Téng Shé) 天辅 (Tiān Fǔ) 景门 (Jǐng Mén) Li 9　　Gui Ji	太阴 (Tài Yīn) 天英 (Tiān Yīng) 死门 (Sǐ Mén) Kun 2　　Ji Xin/Ding
九天 (Jiǔ Tiān) 天任 (Tiān Rèn) 伤门 (Shāng Mén) Zhen 3　　Wu Ren	Yang (阳) Dun# 8 Hour: **GuiChou** ©Calvin Yap	六合 (Liù Hé) 禽芮 (Qín Ruì) 惊门 (Jīng Mén) Dui 7　　Xin/Ding Yi
九地 (Jiǔ Dì) 天蓬 (Tiān Péng) 生门 (Shēng Mén) Gen 8　　Geng Wu	玄武 (Xuán Wǔ) 天心 (Tiān Xīn) 休门 (Xiū Mén) Kan 1　　Bing Geng	白虎 (Bái Hǔ) 天柱 (Tiān Zhù) 开门 (Kāi Mén) Qian 6　　Yi Bing

---

Chart: +8JiaYin (Yang Dun #8 JiaYin Xun)
JiaYin, YiMao, BingChen, DingSi, WuWu, JiWei, GengShen, XinYou, RenXu, GuiHai

---

Yang (阳) Dun# 8 Hour: **JiaYin** ; 直符(ZhíFú): 天辅(TiānFǔ)
直使(ZhíShǐ): 杜门(DùMén) ; 旬首(XúnShǒu): JiaYinGui

值符 (Zhí Fú) 天辅 (Tiān Fǔ) 杜门 (Dù Mén) Xun 4　　Gui Gui	螣蛇 (Téng Shé) 天英 (Tiān Yīng) 景门 (Jǐng Mén) Li 9　　Ji Ji	太阴 (Tài Yīn) 禽芮 (Qín Ruì) 死门 (Sǐ Mén) Kun 2　　Xin/Ding Xin/Ding
九天 (Jiǔ Tiān) 天冲 (Tiān Chōng) 伤门 (Shāng Mén) Zhen 3　　Ren Ren	Yang (阳) Dun# 8 Hour: **JiaYin** **Fu Yin** ©Calvin Yap	六合 (Liù Hé) 天柱 (Tiān Zhù) 惊门 (Jīng Mén) Dui 7　　Yi Yi
九地 (Jiǔ Dì) 天任 (Tiān Rèn) 生门 (Shēng Mén) Gen 8　　Wu Wu	玄武 (Xuán Wǔ) 天蓬 (Tiān Péng) 休门 (Xiū Mén) Kan 1　　Geng Geng	白虎 (Bái Hǔ) 天心 (Tiān Xīn) 开门 (Kāi Mén) Qian 6　　Bing Bing

Yang (阳) Dun# 8 Hour: **YiMao** ; 直符(ZhíFú): 天辅(TiānFǔ)
直使(ZhíShǐ): 杜门(DùMén) ; 旬首(XúnShǒu): JiaYinGui

玄武 (Xuán Wǔ) 天蓬 (Tiān Péng) 生门 (Shēng Mén) Xun 4　　Geng Gui	九地 (Jiǔ Dì) 天任 (Tiān Rèn) 伤门 (Shāng Mén) Li 9　　Wu Ji	九天 (Jiǔ Tiān) 天冲 (Tiān Chōng) 杜门 (Dù Mén) Kun 2　　Ren Xin/Ding
白虎 (Bái Hǔ) 天心 (Tiān Xīn) 休门 (Xiū Mén) Zhen 3　　Bing Ren	Yang (阳) Dun# 8 Hour: **YiMao** ©Calvin Yap	值符 (Zhí Fú) 天辅 (Tiān Fǔ) 景门 (Jǐng Mén) Dui 7　　Gui Yi
六合 (Liù Hé) 天柱 (Tiān Zhù) 开门 (Kāi Mén) Gen 8　　Yi Wu	太阴 (Tài Yīn) 禽芮 (Qín Ruì) 惊门 (Jīng Mén) Kan 1　　Xin/Ding Geng	螣蛇 (Téng Shé) 天英 (Tiān Yīng) 死门 (Sǐ Mén) Qian 6　　Ji Bing

Yang (阳) Dun# 8 Hour: **BingChen** ; 直符(ZhíFú): 天辅(TiānFǔ)
直使(ZhíShǐ): 杜门(DùMén) ; 旬首(XúnShǒu): JiaYinGui

白虎 (Bái Hǔ) 天心 (Tiān Xīn) 开门 (Kāi Mén) Xun 4　　Bing Gui	玄武 (Xuán Wǔ) 天蓬 (Tiān Péng) 休门 (Xiū Mén) Li 9　　Geng Ji	九地 (Jiǔ Dì) 天任 (Tiān Rèn) 生门 (Shēng Mén) Kun 2　　Wu Xin/Ding
六合 (Liù Hé) 天柱 (Tiān Zhù) 惊门 (Jīng Mén) Zhen 3　　Yi Ren	Yang (阳) Dun# 8 Hour: **BingChen** **Fan Yin** ©Calvin Yap	九天 (Jiǔ Tiān) 天冲 (Tiān Chōng) 伤门 (Shāng Mén) Dui 7　　Ren Yi
太阴 (Tài Yīn) 禽芮 (Qín Ruì) 死门 (Sǐ Mén) Gen 8　　Xin/Ding Wu	螣蛇 (Téng Shé) 天英 (Tiān Yīng) 景门 (Jǐng Mén) Kan 1　　Ji Geng	值符 (Zhí Fú) 天辅 (Tiān Fǔ) 杜门 (Dù Mén) Qian 6　　Gui Bing

Yang (阳) Dun# 8 Hour: **DingSi** ; 直符(ZhíFú): 天辅(TiānFǔ)
直使(ZhíShǐ): 杜门(DùMén) ; 旬首(XúnShǒu): JiaYinGui

九地 (Jiǔ Dì) 天任 (Tiān Rèn) 休门 (Xiū Mén) Xun 4　　Wu Gui	九天 (Jiǔ Tiān) 天冲 (Tiān Chōng) 生门 (Shēng Mén) Li 9　　Ren Ji	值符 (Zhí Fú) 天辅 (Tiān Fǔ) 伤门 (Shāng Mén) Kun 2　　Gui Xin/Ding
玄武 (Xuán Wǔ) 天蓬 (Tiān Péng) 开门 (Kāi Mén) Zhen 3　　Geng Ren	Yang (阳) Dun# 8 Hour: **DingSi** ©Calvin Yap	螣蛇 (Téng Shé) 天英 (Tiān Yīng) 杜门 (Dù Mén) Dui 7　　Ji Yi
白虎 (Bái Hǔ) 天心 (Tiān Xīn) 惊门 (Jīng Mén) Gen 8　　Bing Wu	六合 (Liù Hé) 天柱 (Tiān Zhù) 死门 (Sǐ Mén) Kan 1　　Yi Geng	太阴 (Tài Yīn) 禽芮 (Qín Ruì) 景门 (Jǐng Mén) Qian 6　　Xin/Ding Bing

Yang (阳) Dun# 8 Hour: WuWu；直符(ZhíFú): 天辅(TiānFǔ)
直使(ZhíShǐ): 杜门(DùMén)；旬首(XúnShǒu): JiaYinGui

太阴 (Tài Yīn) 禽芮 (Qín Ruì) 死门 (Sǐ Mén) Xun 4　Xin/Ding 　　　Gui	六合 (Liù Hé) 天柱 (Tiān Zhù) 惊门 (Jīng Mén) Li 9　Yi 　　Ji	白虎 (Bái Hǔ) 天心 (Tiān Xīn) 开门 (Kāi Mén) Kun 2　Bing 　　Xin/Ding
螣蛇 (Téng Shé) 天英 (Tiān Yīng) 景门 (Jǐng Mén) Zhen 3　Ji 　　Ren	Yang (阳) Dun# 8 Hour: **WuWu** ©Calvin Yap	玄武 (Xuán Wǔ) 天蓬 (Tiān Péng) 休门 (Xiū Mén) Dui 7　Geng 　　Yi
值符 (Zhí Fú) 天辅 (Tiān Fǔ) 杜门 (Dù Mén) Gen 8　Gui 　　Wu	九天 (Jiǔ Tiān) 天冲 (Tiān Chōng) 伤门 (Shāng Mén) Kan 1　Ren 　　Geng	九地 (Jiǔ Dì) 天任 (Tiān Rèn) 生门 (Shēng Mén) Qian 6　Wu 　　Bing

Yang (阳) Dun# 8 Hour: JiWei；直符(ZhíFú): 天辅(TiānFǔ)
直使(ZhíShǐ): 杜门(DùMén)；旬首(XúnShǒu): JiaYinGui

九天 (Jiǔ Tiān) 天冲 (Tiān Chōng) 伤门 (Shāng Mén) Xun 4　Ren 　　Gui	值符 (Zhí Fú) 天辅 (Tiān Fǔ) 杜门 (Dù Mén) Li 9　Gui 　　Ji	螣蛇 (Téng Shé) 天英 (Tiān Yīng) 景门 (Jǐng Mén) Kun 2　Ji 　　Xin/Ding
九地 (Jiǔ Dì) 天任 (Tiān Rèn) 生门 (Shēng Mén) Zhen 3　Wu 　　Ren	Yang (阳) Dun# 8 Hour: **JiWei** ©Calvin Yap	太阴 (Tài Yīn) 禽芮 (Qín Ruì) 死门 (Sǐ Mén) Dui 7　Xin/Ding 　　Yi
玄武 (Xuán Wǔ) 天蓬 (Tiān Péng) 休门 (Xiū Mén) Gen 8　Geng 　　Wu	白虎 (Bái Hǔ) 天心 (Tiān Xīn) 开门 (Kāi Mén) Kan 1　Bing 　　Geng	六合 (Liù Hé) 天柱 (Tiān Zhù) 惊门 (Jīng Mén) Qian 6　Yi 　　Bing

Yang (阳) Dun# 8 Hour: GengShen；直符(ZhíFú): 天辅(TiānFǔ)
直使(ZhíShǐ): 杜门(DùMén)；旬首(XúnShǒu): JiaYinGui

六合 (Liù Hé) 天柱 (Tiān Zhù) 惊门 (Jīng Mén) Xun 4　Yi 　　Gui	白虎 (Bái Hǔ) 天心 (Tiān Xīn) 开门 (Kāi Mén) Li 9　Bing 　　Ji	玄武 (Xuán Wǔ) 天蓬 (Tiān Péng) 休门 (Xiū Mén) Kun 2　Geng 　　Xin/Ding
太阴 (Tài Yīn) 禽芮 (Qín Ruì) 死门 (Sǐ Mén) Zhen 3　Xin/Ding 　　Ren	Yang (阳) Dun# 8 Hour: **GengShen** ©Calvin Yap	九地 (Jiǔ Dì) 天任 (Tiān Rèn) 生门 (Shēng Mén) Dui 7　Wu 　　Yi
螣蛇 (Téng Shé) 天英 (Tiān Yīng) 景门 (Jǐng Mén) Gen 8　Ji 　　Wu	值符 (Zhí Fú) 天辅 (Tiān Fǔ) 杜门 (Dù Mén) Kan 1　Gui 　　Geng	九天 (Jiǔ Tiān) 天冲 (Tiān Chōng) 伤门 (Shāng Mén) Qian 6　Ren 　　Bing

Yang (阳) Dun# 8 Hour: XinYou；直符(ZhíFú): 天辅(TiānFǔ)
直使(ZhíShǐ): 杜门(DùMén)；旬首(XúnShǒu): JiaYinGui

九地 (Jiǔ Dì) 天任 (Tiān Rèn) 生门 (Shēng Mén) Xun 4　Wu 　　Gui	九天 (Jiǔ Tiān) 天冲 (Tiān Chōng) 伤门 (Shāng Mén) Li 9　Ren 　　Ji	值符 (Zhí Fú) 天辅 (Tiān Fǔ) 杜门 (Dù Mén) Kun 2　Gui 　　Xin/Ding
玄武 (Xuán Wǔ) 天蓬 (Tiān Péng) 休门 (Xiū Mén) Zhen 3　Geng 　　Ren	Yang (阳) Dun# 8 Hour: **XinYou** ©Calvin Yap	螣蛇 (Téng Shé) 天英 (Tiān Yīng) 景门 (Jǐng Mén) Dui 7　Ji 　　Yi
白虎 (Bái Hǔ) 天心 (Tiān Xīn) 开门 (Kāi Mén) Gen 8　Bing 　　Wu	六合 (Liù Hé) 天柱 (Tiān Zhù) 惊门 (Jīng Mén) Kan 1　Yi 　　Geng	太阴 (Tài Yīn) 禽芮 (Qín Ruì) 死门 (Sǐ Mén) Qian 6　Xin/Ding 　　Bing

Yang (阳) Dun# 8 Hour: RenXu；直符(ZhíFú): 天辅(TiānFǔ)
直使(ZhíShǐ): 杜门(DùMén)；旬首(XúnShǒu): JiaYinGui

螣蛇 (Téng Shé) 天英 (Tiān Yīng) 景门 (Jǐng Mén) Xun 4　Ji 　　Gui	太阴 (Tài Yīn) 禽芮 (Qín Ruì) 死门 (Sǐ Mén) Li 9　Xin/Ding 　　Ji	六合 (Liù Hé) 天柱 (Tiān Zhù) 惊门 (Jīng Mén) Kun 2　Yi 　　Xin/Ding
值符 (Zhí Fú) 天辅 (Tiān Fǔ) 杜门 (Dù Mén) Zhen 3　Gui 　　Ren	Yang (阳) Dun# 8 Hour: **RenXu** ©Calvin Yap	白虎 (Bái Hǔ) 天心 (Tiān Xīn) 开门 (Kāi Mén) Dui 7　Bing 　　Yi
九天 (Jiǔ Tiān) 天冲 (Tiān Chōng) 伤门 (Shāng Mén) Gen 8　Ren 　　Wu	九地 (Jiǔ Dì) 天任 (Tiān Rèn) 生门 (Shēng Mén) Kan 1　Wu 　　Geng	玄武 (Xuán Wǔ) 天蓬 (Tiān Péng) 休门 (Xiū Mén) Qian 6　Geng 　　Bing

Yang (阳) Dun# 8 Hour: GuiHai；直符(ZhíFú): 天辅(TiānFǔ)
直使(ZhíShǐ): 杜门(DùMén)；旬首(XúnShǒu): JiaYinGui

值符 (Zhí Fú) 天辅 (Tiān Fǔ) 杜门 (Dù Mén) Xun 4　Gui 　　Gui	螣蛇 (Téng Shé) 天英 (Tiān Yīng) 景门 (Jǐng Mén) Li 9　Ji 　　Ji	太阴 (Tài Yīn) 禽芮 (Qín Ruì) 死门 (Sǐ Mén) Kun 2　Xin/Ding 　　Xin/Ding
九天 (Jiǔ Tiān) 天冲 (Tiān Chōng) 伤门 (Shāng Mén) Zhen 3　Ren 　　Ren	Yang (阳) Dun# 8 Hour: **GuiHai** **Fu Yin** ©Calvin Yap	六合 (Liù Hé) 天柱 (Tiān Zhù) 惊门 (Jīng Mén) Dui 7　Yi 　　Yi
九地 (Jiǔ Dì) 天任 (Tiān Rèn) 生门 (Shēng Mén) Gen 8　Wu 　　Wu	玄武 (Xuán Wǔ) 天蓬 (Tiān Péng) 休门 (Xiū Mén) Kan 1　Geng 　　Geng	白虎 (Bái Hǔ) 天心 (Tiān Xīn) 开门 (Kāi Mén) Qian 6　Bing 　　Bing

Yang Dun#9

Chart: +9JiaZi (Yang Dun #9 JiaZi Xun)
JiaZi, YiChou, BingYin, DingMao, WuChen, JiSi, GengWu, XinWei, RenShen, GuiYou

---

Yang (阳) Dun# 9 Hour: JiaZi；直符(ZhíFú): 天英(TiānYīng)
直使(ZhíShǐ): 景门(JǐngMén)；旬首(XúnShǒu): JiaZiWu

九天 (Jiǔ Tiān) 天辅 (Tiān Fǔ) 杜门 (Dù Mén) Xun 4 Ren	值符 (Zhí Fú) 天英 (Tiān Yīng) 景门 (Jǐng Mén) Li 9 Wu Wu	螣蛇 (Téng Shé) 禽芮 (Qín Ruì) 死门 (Sǐ Mén) Kun 2 Geng/Gui Geng/Gui
九地 (Jiǔ Dì) 天冲 (Tiān Chōng) 伤门 (Shāng Mén) Zhen 3 Xin Xin	Yang (阳) Dun# 9 Hour: **JiaZi** **Fu Yin** ©Calvin Yap	太阴 (Tài Yīn) 天柱 (Tiān Zhù) 惊门 (Jīng Mén) Dui 7 Bing Bing
玄武 (Xuán Wǔ) 天任 (Tiān Rèn) 生门 (Shēng Mén) Gen 8 Yi Yi	白虎 (Bái Hǔ) 天蓬 (Tiān Péng) 休门 (Xiū Mén) Kan 1 Ji Ji	六合 (Liù Hé) 天心 (Tiān Xīn) 开门 (Kāi Mén) Qian 6 Ding Ding

Yang (阳) Dun# 9 Hour: YiChou；直符(ZhíFú): 天英(TiānYīng)
直使(ZhíShǐ): 景门(JǐngMén)；旬首(XúnShǒu): JiaZiWu

太阴 (Tài Yīn) 天柱 (Tiān Zhù) 开门 (Kāi Mén) Xun 4 Bing Ren	六合 (Liù Hé) 天心 (Tiān Xīn) 休门 (Xiū Mén) Li 9 Ding Wu	白虎 (Bái Hǔ) 天蓬 (Tiān Péng) 生门 (Shēng Mén) Kun 2 Ji Geng/Gui
螣蛇 (Téng Shé) 禽芮 (Qín Ruì) 惊门 (Jīng Mén) Zhen 3 Geng/Gui Xin	Yang (阳) Dun# 9 Hour: **YiChou** ©Calvin Yap	玄武 (Xuán Wǔ) 天任 (Tiān Rèn) 伤门 (Shāng Mén) Dui 7 Yi Bing
值符 (Zhí Fú) 天英 (Tiān Yīng) 死门 (Sǐ Mén) Gen 8 Wu Yi	九天 (Jiǔ Tiān) 天辅 (Tiān Fǔ) 景门 (Jǐng Mén) Kan 1 Ren Ji	九地 (Jiǔ Dì) 天冲 (Tiān Chōng) 杜门 (Dù Mén) Qian 6 Xin Ding

Yang (阳) Dun# 9 Hour: BingYin；直符(ZhíFú): 天英(TiānYīng)
直使(ZhíShǐ): 景门(JǐngMén)；旬首(XúnShǒu): JiaZiWu

玄武 (Xuán Wǔ) 天任 (Tiān Rèn) 伤门 (Shāng Mén) Xun 4 Yi Ren	九地 (Jiǔ Dì) 天冲 (Tiān Chōng) 杜门 (Dù Mén) Li 9 Xin Wu	九天 (Jiǔ Tiān) 天辅 (Tiān Fǔ) 景门 (Jǐng Mén) Kun 2 Ren Geng/Gui
白虎 (Bái Hǔ) 天蓬 (Tiān Péng) 生门 (Shēng Mén) Zhen 3 Ji Xin	Yang (阳) Dun# 9 Hour: **BingYin** ©Calvin Yap	值符 (Zhí Fú) 天英 (Tiān Yīng) 死门 (Sǐ Mén) Dui 7 Wu Bing
六合 (Liù Hé) 天心 (Tiān Xīn) 休门 (Xiū Mén) Gen 8 Ding Yi	太阴 (Tài Yīn) 天柱 (Tiān Zhù) 开门 (Kāi Mén) Kan 1 Bing Ji	螣蛇 (Téng Shé) 禽芮 (Qín Ruì) 惊门 (Jīng Mén) Qian 6 Geng/Gui Ding

Yang (阳) Dun# 9 Hour: DingMao；直符(ZhíFú): 天英(TiānYīng)
直使(ZhíShǐ): 景门(JǐngMén)；旬首(XúnShǒu): JiaZiWu

白虎 (Bái Hǔ) 天蓬 (Tiān Péng) 死门 (Sǐ Mén) Xun 4 Ji Ren	玄武 (Xuán Wǔ) 天任 (Tiān Rèn) 惊门 (Jīng Mén) Li 9 Yi Wu	九地 (Jiǔ Dì) 天冲 (Tiān Chōng) 开门 (Kāi Mén) Kun 2 Xin Geng/Gui
六合 (Liù Hé) 天心 (Tiān Xīn) 景门 (Jǐng Mén) Zhen 3 Ding Xin	Yang (阳) Dun# 9 Hour: **DingMao** ©Calvin Yap	九天 (Jiǔ Tiān) 天辅 (Tiān Fǔ) 休门 (Xiū Mén) Dui 7 Ren Bing
太阴 (Tài Yīn) 天柱 (Tiān Zhù) 杜门 (Dù Mén) Gen 8 Bing Yi	螣蛇 (Téng Shé) 禽芮 (Qín Ruì) 伤门 (Shāng Mén) Kan 1 Geng/Gui Ji	值符 (Zhí Fú) 天英 (Tiān Yīng) 生门 (Shēng Mén) Qian 6 Wu Ding

Yang (阳) Dun# 9 Hour: WuChen；直符(ZhíFú): 天英(TiānYīng)
直使(ZhíShǐ): 景门(JǐngMén)；旬首(XúnShǒu): JiaZiWu

九天 (Jiǔ Tiān) 天辅 (Tiān Fǔ) 景门 (Jǐng Mén) Xun 4 Ren Ren	值符 (Zhí Fú) 天英 (Tiān Yīng) 死门 (Sǐ Mén) Li 9 Wu Wu	螣蛇 (Téng Shé) 禽芮 (Qín Ruì) 惊门 (Jīng Mén) Kun 2 Geng/Gui Geng/Gui
九地 (Jiǔ Dì) 天冲 (Tiān Chōng) 杜门 (Dù Mén) Zhen 3 Xin Xin	Yang (阳) Dun# 9 Hour: **WuChen** **Fu Yin** ©Calvin Yap	太阴 (Tài Yīn) 天柱 (Tiān Zhù) 开门 (Kāi Mén) Dui 7 Bing Bing
玄武 (Xuán Wǔ) 天任 (Tiān Rèn) 伤门 (Shāng Mén) Gen 8 Yi Yi	白虎 (Bái Hǔ) 天蓬 (Tiān Péng) 生门 (Shēng Mén) Kan 1 Ji Ji	六合 (Liù Hé) 天心 (Tiān Xīn) 休门 (Xiū Mén) Qian 6 Ding Ding

Yang (阳) Dun# 9 Hour: JiSi；直符(ZhíFú): 天英(TiānYīng)
直使(ZhíShǐ): 景门(JǐngMén)；旬首(XúnShǒu): JiaZiWu

六合 (Liù Hé) 天心 (Tiān Xīn) 伤门 (Shāng Mén) Xun 4 Ding Ren	白虎 (Bái Hǔ) 天蓬 (Tiān Péng) 杜门 (Dù Mén) Li 9 Ji Wu	玄武 (Xuán Wǔ) 天任 (Tiān Rèn) 景门 (Jǐng Mén) Kun 2 Yi Geng/Gui
太阴 (Tài Yīn) 天柱 (Tiān Zhù) 生门 (Shēng Mén) Zhen 3 Bing Xin	Yang (阳) Dun# 9 Hour: **JiSi** **Fan Yin** ©Calvin Yap	九地 (Jiǔ Dì) 天冲 (Tiān Chōng) 死门 (Sǐ Mén) Dui 7 Xin Bing
螣蛇 (Téng Shé) 禽芮 (Qín Ruì) 休门 (Xiū Mén) Gen 8 Geng/Gui Yi	值符 (Zhí Fú) 天英 (Tiān Yīng) 开门 (Kāi Mén) Kan 1 Wu Ji	九天 (Jiǔ Tiān) 天辅 (Tiān Fǔ) 惊门 (Jīng Mén) Qian 6 Ren Ding

Yang (阳) Dun# 9 Hour: GengWu ; 直符(ZhíFú): 天英(TiānYīng)
直使(ZhíShǐ): 景门(JǐngMén) ; 旬首(XúnShǒu): JiaZiWu

九地 (Jiǔ Dì) 天冲 (Tiān Chōng) 休门 (Xiū Mén) Xun 4　Xin Ren	九天 (Jiǔ Tiān) 天辅 (Tiān Fǔ) 生门 (Shēng Mén) Li 9　Ren Wu	值符 (Zhí Fú) 天英 (Tiān Yīng) 伤门 (Shāng Mén) Kun 2　Wu Geng/Gui
玄武 (Xuán Wǔ) 天任 (Tiān Rèn) 开门 (Kāi Mén) Zhen 3　Yi Xin	Yang (阳) Dun# 9 Hour: **GengWu** ©Calvin Yap	腾蛇 (Téng Shé) 禽芮 (Qin Ruì) 杜门 (Dù Mén) Dui 7　Geng/Gui Bing
白虎 (Bái Hǔ) 天蓬 (Tiān Péng) 惊门 (Jīng Mén) Gen 8　Ji Yi	六合 (Liù Hé) 天心 (Tiān Xīn) 死门 (Sǐ Mén) Kan 1　Ding Ji	太阴 (Tài Yīn) 天柱 (Tiān Zhù) 景门 (Jǐng Mén) Qian 6　Bing Ding

Yang (阳) Dun# 9 Hour: XinWei ; 直符(ZhíFú): 天英(TiānYīng)
直使(ZhíShǐ): 景门(JǐngMén) ; 旬首(XúnShǒu): JiaZiWu

腾蛇 (Téng Shé) 禽芮 (Qín Ruì) 生门 (Shēng Mén) Xun 4　Geng/Gui Ren	太阴 (Tài Yīn) 天柱 (Tiān Zhù) 伤门 (Shāng Mén) Li 9　Bing Wu	六合 (Liù Hé) 天心 (Tiān Xīn) 杜门 (Dù Mén) Kun 2　Ding Geng/Gui
值符 (Zhí Fú) 天英 (Tiān Yīng) 休门 (Xiū Mén) Zhen 3　Wu Xin	Yang (阳) Dun# 9 Hour: **XinWei** ©Calvin Yap	白虎 (Bái Hǔ) 天蓬 (Tiān Péng) 景门 (Jǐng Mén) Dui 7　Ji Bing
九天 (Jiǔ Tiān) 天辅 (Tiān Fǔ) 开门 (Kāi Mén) Gen 8　Ren Yi	九地 (Jiǔ Dì) 天冲 (Tiān Chōng) 惊门 (Jīng Mén) Kan 1　Xin Ji	玄武 (Xuán Wǔ) 天任 (Tiān Rèn) 死门 (Sǐ Mén) Qian 6　Yi Ding

Yang (阳) Dun# 9 Hour: RenShen ; 直符(ZhíFú): 天英(TiānYīng)
直使(ZhíShǐ): 景门(JǐngMén) ; 旬首(XúnShǒu): JiaZiWu

值符 (Zhí Fú) 天英 (Tiān Yīng) 惊门 (Jīng Mén) Xun 4　Wu Ren	腾蛇 (Téng Shé) 禽芮 (Qín Ruì) 开门 (Kāi Mén) Li 9　Geng/Gui Wu	太阴 (Tài Yīn) 天柱 (Tiān Zhù) 休门 (Xiū Mén) Kun 2　Bing Geng/Gui
九天 (Jiǔ Tiān) 天辅 (Tiān Fǔ) 死门 (Sǐ Mén) Zhen 3　Ren Xin	Yang (阳) Dun# 9 Hour: **RenShen** ©Calvin Yap	六合 (Liù Hé) 天心 (Tiān Xīn) 生门 (Shēng Mén) Dui 7　Ding Bing
九地 (Jiǔ Dì) 天冲 (Tiān Chōng) 景门 (Jǐng Mén) Gen 8　Xin Yi	玄武 (Xuán Wǔ) 天任 (Tiān Rèn) 杜门 (Dù Mén) Kan 1　Yi Ji	白虎 (Bái Hǔ) 天蓬 (Tiān Péng) 伤门 (Shāng Mén) Qian 6　Ji Ding

Yang (阳) Dun# 9 Hour: GuiYou ; 直符(ZhíFú): 天英(TiānYīng)
直使(ZhíShǐ): 景门(JǐngMén) ; 旬首(XúnShǒu): JiaZiWu

九地 (Jiǔ Dì) 天冲 (Tiān Chōng) 杜门 (Dù Mén) Xun 4　Xin Ren	九天 (Jiǔ Tiān) 天辅 (Tiān Fǔ) 景门 (Jǐng Mén) Li 9　Ren Wu	值符 (Zhí Fú) 天英 (Tiān Yīng) 死门 (Sǐ Mén) Kun 2　Wu Geng/Gui
玄武 (Xuán Wǔ) 天任 (Tiān Rèn) 伤门 (Shāng Mén) Zhen 3　Yi Xin	Yang (阳) Dun# 9 Hour: **GuiYou** ©Calvin Yap	腾蛇 (Téng Shé) 禽芮 (Qín Ruì) 惊门 (Jīng Mén) Dui 7　Geng/Gui Bing
白虎 (Bái Hǔ) 天蓬 (Tiān Péng) 生门 (Shēng Mén) Gen 8　Ji Yi	六合 (Liù Hé) 天心 (Tiān Xīn) 休门 (Xiū Mén) Kan 1　Ding Ji	太阴 (Tài Yīn) 天柱 (Tiān Zhù) 开门 (Kāi Mén) Qian 6　Bing Ding

Chart: +9JiaXu (Yang Dun #9 JiaXu Xun)
JiaXu, YiHai, BingZi, DingChou, WuYin, JiMao, GengChen, XinSi, RenWu, GuiWei

Yang (阳) Dun# 9 Hour: JiaXu ; 直符(ZhíFú): 天蓬(TiānPéng)
直使(ZhíShǐ): 休门(XiūMén) ; 旬首(XúnShǒu): JiaXuJi

六合 (Liù Hé) 天辅 (Tiān Fǔ) 杜门 (Dù Mén) Xun 4　Ren Ren	白虎 (Bái Hǔ) 天英 (Tiān Yīng) 景门 (Jǐng Mén) Li 9　Wu Wu	玄武 (Xuán Wǔ) 禽芮 (Qín Ruì) 死门 (Sǐ Mén) Kun 2　Geng/Gui Geng/Gui
太阴 (Tài Yīn) 天冲 (Tiān Chōng) 伤门 (Shāng Mén) Zhen 3　Xin Xin	Yang (阳) Dun# 9 Hour: **JiaXu** **Fu Yin** ©Calvin Yap	九地 (Jiǔ Dì) 天柱 (Tiān Zhù) 惊门 (Jīng Mén) Dui 7　Bing Bing
腾蛇 (Téng Shé) 天任 (Tiān Rèn) 生门 (Shēng Mén) Gen 8　Yi Yi	值符 (Zhí Fú) 天蓬 (Tiān Péng) 休门 (Xiū Mén) Kan 1　Ji Ji	九天 (Jiǔ Tiān) 天心 (Tiān Xīn) 开门 (Kāi Mén) Qian 6　Ding Ding

Yang (阳) Dun# 9 Hour: YiHai ; 直符(ZhíFú): 天蓬(TiānPéng)
直使(ZhíShǐ): 休门(XiūMén) ; 旬首(XúnShǒu): JiaXuJi

太阴 (Tài Yīn) 天冲 (Tiān Chōng) 惊门 (Jīng Mén) Xun 4　Xin Ren	六合 (Liù Hé) 天辅 (Tiān Fǔ) 开门 (Kāi Mén) Li 9　Ren Wu	白虎 (Bái Hǔ) 天英 (Tiān Yīng) 休门 (Xiū Mén) Kun 2　Wu Geng/Gui
腾蛇 (Téng Shé) 天任 (Tiān Rèn) 死门 (Sǐ Mén) Zhen 3　Yi Xin	Yang (阳) Dun# 9 Hour: **YiHai** ©Calvin Yap	玄武 (Xuán Wǔ) 禽芮 (Qín Ruì) 生门 (Shēng Mén) Dui 7　Geng/Gui Bing
值符 (Zhí Fú) 天蓬 (Tiān Péng) 景门 (Jǐng Mén) Gen 8　Ji Yi	九天 (Jiǔ Tiān) 天心 (Tiān Xīn) 杜门 (Dù Mén) Kan 1　Ding Ji	九地 (Jiǔ Dì) 天柱 (Tiān Zhù) 伤门 (Shāng Mén) Qian 6　Bing Ding

Yang (阳) Dun# 9 Hour: **BingZi**；直符(ZhíFú): 天蓬(TiānPéng)
直使(ZhíShǐ): 休门(XiūMén)；旬首(XúnShǒu): JiaXuJi

玄武 (Xuán Wǔ) 禽芮 (Qín Ruì) 生门 (Shēng Mén) Xun 4　　Geng/Gui Ren	九地 (Jiǔ Dì) 天柱 (Tiān Zhù) 伤门 (Shāng Mén) Li 9　　Bing Wu	九天 (Jiǔ Tiān) 天心 (Tiān Xīn) 杜门 (Dù Mén) Kun 2　　Ding Geng/Gui
白虎 (Bái Hǔ) 天英 (Tiān Yīng) 休门 (Xiū Mén) Zhen 3　Wu Xin	Yang (阳) Dun# 9 Hour: **BingZi** ©Calvin Yap	值符 (Zhí Fú) 天蓬 (Tiān Péng) 景门 (Jǐng Mén) Dui 7　　Ji Bing
六合 (Liù Hé) 天辅 (Tiān Fǔ) 开门 (Kāi Mén) Gen 8　　Ren Yi	太阴 (Tài Yīn) 天冲 (Tiān Chōng) 惊门 (Jīng Mén) Kan 1　　Xin Ji	腾蛇 (Téng Shé) 天任 (Tiān Rèn) 死门 (Sǐ Mén) Qian 6　　Yi Ding

Yang (阳) Dun# 9 Hour: **DingChou**；直符(ZhíFú): 天蓬(TiānPéng)
直使(ZhíShǐ): 休门(XiūMén)；旬首(XúnShǒu): JiaXuJi

白虎 (Bái Hǔ) 天英 (Tiān Yīng) 休门 (Xiū Mén) Xun 4　　Wu Ren	玄武 (Xuán Wǔ) 禽芮 (Qín Ruì) 生门 (Shēng Mén) Li 9　　Geng/Gui Wu	九地 (Jiǔ Dì) 天柱 (Tiān Zhù) 伤门 (Shāng Mén) Kun 2　　Bing Geng/Gui
六合 (Liù Hé) 天辅 (Tiān Fǔ) 开门 (Kāi Mén) Zhen 3　Ren Xin	Yang (阳) Dun# 9 Hour: **DingChou** ©Calvin Yap	九天 (Jiǔ Tiān) 天心 (Tiān Xīn) 杜门 (Dù Mén) Dui 7　　Ding Bing
太阴 (Tài Yīn) 天冲 (Tiān Chōng) 惊门 (Jīng Mén) Gen 8　　Xin Yi	腾蛇 (Téng Shé) 天任 (Tiān Rèn) 死门 (Sǐ Mén) Kan 1　　Yi Ji	值符 (Zhí Fú) 天蓬 (Tiān Péng) 景门 (Jǐng Mén) Qian 6　　Ji Ding

Yang (阳) Dun# 9 Hour: **WuYin**；直符(ZhíFú): 天蓬(TiānPéng)
直使(ZhíShǐ): 休门(XiūMén)；旬首(XúnShǒu): JiaXuJi

九天 (Jiǔ Tiān) 天心 (Tiān Xīn) 惊门 (Jīng Mén) Xun 4　　Ding Ren	值符 (Zhí Fú) 天蓬 (Tiān Péng) 开门 (Kāi Mén) Li 9　　Ji Wu	腾蛇 (Téng Shé) 天任 (Tiān Rèn) 休门 (Xiū Mén) Kun 2　　Yi Geng/Gui
九地 (Jiǔ Dì) 天柱 (Tiān Zhù) 死门 (Sǐ Mén) Zhen 3　Bing Xin	Yang (阳) Dun# 9 Hour: **WuYin** **Fan Yin** ©Calvin Yap	太阴 (Tài Yīn) 天冲 (Tiān Chōng) 生门 (Shēng Mén) Dui 7　Xin Bing
玄武 (Xuán Wǔ) 禽芮 (Qín Ruì) 景门 (Jǐng Mén) Gen 8　Geng/Gui Yi	白虎 (Bái Hǔ) 天英 (Tiān Yīng) 杜门 (Dù Mén) Kan 1　Wu Ji	六合 (Liù Hé) 天辅 (Tiān Fǔ) 伤门 (Shāng Mén) Qian 6　Ren Ding

Yang (阳) Dun# 9 Hour: **JiMao**；直符(ZhíFú): 天蓬(TiānPéng)
直使(ZhíShǐ): 休门(XiūMén)；旬首(XúnShǒu): JiaXuJi

六合 (Liù Hé) 天辅 (Tiān Fǔ) 景门 (Jǐng Mén) Xun 4　Ren Ren	白虎 (Bái Hǔ) 天英 (Tiān Yīng) 死门 (Sǐ Mén) Li 9　　Wu Wu	玄武 (Xuán Wǔ) 禽芮 (Qín Ruì) 惊门 (Jīng Mén) Kun 2　Geng/Gui Geng/Gui
太阴 (Tài Yīn) 天冲 (Tiān Chōng) 杜门 (Dù Mén) Zhen 3　Xin Xin	Yang (阳) Dun# 9 Hour: **JiMao** **Fu Yin** ©Calvin Yap	九地 (Jiǔ Dì) 天柱 (Tiān Zhù) 开门 (Kāi Mén) Dui 7　Bing Bing
腾蛇 (Téng Shé) 天任 (Tiān Rèn) 伤门 (Shāng Mén) Gen 8　Yi Ji	值符 (Zhí Fú) 天蓬 (Tiān Péng) 生门 (Shēng Mén) Kan 1　Ji Ji	九天 (Jiǔ Tiān) 天心 (Tiān Xīn) 休门 (Xiū Mén) Qian 6　Ding Ding

Yang (阳) Dun# 9 Hour: **GengChen**；直符(ZhíFú): 天蓬(TiānPéng)
直使(ZhíShǐ): 休门(XiūMén)；旬首(XúnShǒu): JiaXuJi

九地 (Jiǔ Dì) 天柱 (Tiān Zhù) 死门 (Sǐ Mén) Xun 4　Bing Ren	九天 (Jiǔ Tiān) 天心 (Tiān Xīn) 惊门 (Jīng Mén) Li 9　　Ding Wu	值符 (Zhí Fú) 天蓬 (Tiān Péng) 开门 (Kāi Mén) Kun 2　　Ji Geng/Gui
玄武 (Xuán Wǔ) 禽芮 (Qín Ruì) 景门 (Jǐng Mén) Zhen 3　Geng/Gui Xin	Yang (阳) Dun# 9 Hour: **GengChen** ©Calvin Yap	腾蛇 (Téng Shé) 天任 (Tiān Rèn) 休门 (Xiū Mén) Dui 7　　Yi Bing
白虎 (Bái Hǔ) 天英 (Tiān Yīng) 杜门 (Dù Mén) Gen 8　　Wu Yi	六合 (Liù Hé) 天辅 (Tiān Fǔ) 伤门 (Shāng Mén) Kan 1　　Ren Ji	太阴 (Tài Yīn) 天冲 (Tiān Chōng) 生门 (Shēng Mén) Qian 6　　Xin Ding

Yang (阳) Dun# 9 Hour: **XinSi**；直符(ZhíFú): 天蓬(TiānPéng)
直使(ZhíShǐ): 休门(XiūMén)；旬首(XúnShǒu): JiaXuJi

腾蛇 (Téng Shé) 天任 (Tiān Rèn) 伤门 (Shāng Mén) Xun 4　Yi Ren	太阴 (Tài Yīn) 天冲 (Tiān Chōng) 杜门 (Dù Mén) Li 9　　Xin Wu	六合 (Liù Hé) 天辅 (Tiān Fǔ) 景门 (Jǐng Mén) Kun 2　　Ren Geng/Gui
值符 (Zhí Fú) 天蓬 (Tiān Péng) 生门 (Shēng Mén) Zhen 3　Ji Xin	Yang (阳) Dun# 9 Hour: **XinSi** ©Calvin Yap	白虎 (Bái Hǔ) 天英 (Tiān Yīng) 死门 (Sǐ Mén) Dui 7　　Wu Bing
九天 (Jiǔ Tiān) 天心 (Tiān Xīn) 休门 (Xiū Mén) Gen 8　　Ding Yi	九地 (Jiǔ Dì) 天柱 (Tiān Zhù) 开门 (Kāi Mén) Kan 1　　Bing Ji	玄武 (Xuán Wǔ) 禽芮 (Qín Ruì) 惊门 (Jīng Mén) Qian 6　Geng/Gui Ding

Yang (阳) Dun# 9 Hour: **RenWu** ; 直符(ZhíFú): 天蓬(TiānPéng)
直使(ZhíShǐ): 休门(XiūMén) ; 旬首(XúnShǒu): JiaXuJi

值符 (Zhí Fú) 天蓬 (Tiān Péng) 开门 (Kāi Mén) Xun 4　Ji Ren	螣蛇 (Téng Shé) 天任 (Tiān Rèn) 休门 (Xiū Mén) Li 9　Yi Wu	太阴 (Tài Yīn) 天冲 (Tiān Chōng) 生门 (Shēng Mén) Kun 2　Xin Geng/Gui
九天 (Jiǔ Tiān) 天心 (Tiān Xīn) 惊门 (Jīng Mén) Zhen 3　Ding Xin	Yang (阳) Dun# 9 Hour: **RenWu** ©Calvin Yap	六合 (Liù Hé) 天辅 (Tiān Fǔ) 伤门 (Shāng Mén) Dui 7　Ren Bing
九地 (Jiǔ Dì) 天柱 (Tiān Zhù) 死门 (Sǐ Mén) Gen 8　Bing Yi	玄武 (Xuán Wǔ) 禽芮 (Qín Ruì) 景门 (Jīng Mén) Kan 1　Geng/Gui Ji	白虎 (Bái Hǔ) 天英 (Tiān Yīng) 杜门 (Dù Mén) Qian 6　Wu Ding

Yang (阳) Dun# 9 Hour: **GuiWei** ; 直符(ZhíFú): 天蓬(TiānPéng)
直使(ZhíShǐ): 休门(XiūMén) ; 旬首(XúnShǒu): JiaXuJi

九地 (Jiǔ Dì) 天柱 (Tiān Zhù) 杜门 (Dù Mén) Xun 4　Bing Ren	九天 (Jiǔ Tiān) 天心 (Tiān Xīn) 景门 (Jīng Mén) Li 9　Ding Wu	值符 (Zhí Fú) 天蓬 (Tiān Péng) 死门 (Sǐ Mén) Kun 2　Ji Geng/Gui
玄武 (Xuán Wǔ) 禽芮 (Qín Ruì) 伤门 (Shāng Mén) Zhen 3　Geng/Gui Xin	Yang (阳) Dun# 9 Hour: **GuiWei** ©Calvin Yap	螣蛇 (Téng Shé) 天任 (Tiān Rèn) 惊门 (Jīng Mén) Dui 7　Yi Bing
白虎 (Bái Hǔ) 天英 (Tiān Yīng) 生门 (Shēng Mén) Gen 8　Wu Yi	六合 (Liù Hé) 天辅 (Tiān Fǔ) 休门 (Xiū Mén) Kan 1　Ren Ji	太阴 (Tài Yīn) 天冲 (Tiān Chōng) 开门 (Kāi Mén) Qian 6　Xin Ding

Chart: **+9JiaShen** (Yang Dun #9 JiaShen Xun)
JiaShen, YiYou, BingXu, DingHai, WuZi, JiChou, GengYin, XinMao, RenChen, GuiSi

Yang (阳) Dun# 9 Hour: **JiaShen** ; 直符(ZhíFú): 天芮(TiānRuì)
直使(ZhíShǐ): 死门(SǐMén) ; 旬首(XúnShǒu): JiaShenGeng

九地 (Jiǔ Dì) 天辅 (Tiān Fǔ) 杜门 (Dù Mén) Xun 4　Ren Ren	九天 (Jiǔ Tiān) 天英 (Tiān Yīng) 景门 (Jīng Mén) Li 9　Wu Wu	值符 (Zhí Fú) 禽芮 (Qín Ruì) 死门 (Sǐ Mén) Kun 2　Geng/Gui Geng/Gui
玄武 (Xuán Wǔ) 天冲 (Tiān Chōng) 伤门 (Shāng Mén) Zhen 3　Xin Xin	Yang (阳) Dun# 9 Hour: **JiaShen** **Fu Yin** ©Calvin Yap	螣蛇 (Téng Shé) 天柱 (Tiān Zhù) 惊门 (Jīng Mén) Dui 7　Bing Bing
白虎 (Bái Hǔ) 天任 (Tiān Rèn) 生门 (Shēng Mén) Gen 8　Yi Yi	六合 (Liù Hé) 天蓬 (Tiān Péng) 休门 (Xiū Mén) Kan 1　Ji Ji	太阴 (Tài Yīn) 天心 (Tiān Xīn) 开门 (Kāi Mén) Qian 6　Ding Ding

Yang (阳) Dun# 9 Hour: **YiYou** ; 直符(ZhíFú): 天芮(TiānRuì)
直使(ZhíShǐ): 死门(SǐMén) ; 旬首(XúnShǒu): JiaShenGeng

太阴 (Tài Yīn) 天心 (Tiān Xīn) 惊门 (Jīng Mén) Xun 4　Ding Ren	六合 (Liù Hé) 天蓬 (Tiān Péng) 开门 (Kāi Mén) Li 9　Ji Wu	白虎 (Bái Hǔ) 天任 (Tiān Rèn) 休门 (Xiū Mén) Kun 2　Yi Geng/Gui
螣蛇 (Téng Shé) 天柱 (Tiān Zhù) 死门 (Sǐ Mén) Zhen 3　Bing Xin	Yang (阳) Dun# 9 Hour: **YiYou** **Fan Yin** ©Calvin Yap	玄武 (Xuán Wǔ) 天冲 (Tiān Chōng) 生门 (Shēng Mén) Dui 7　Xin Bing
值符 (Zhí Fú) 禽芮 (Qín Ruì) 景门 (Jīng Mén) Gen 8　Geng/Gui Yi	九天 (Jiǔ Tiān) 天英 (Tiān Yīng) 杜门 (Dù Mén) Kan 1　Wu Ji	九地 (Jiǔ Dì) 天辅 (Tiān Fǔ) 伤门 (Shāng Mén) Qian 6　Ren Ding

Yang (阳) Dun# 9 Hour: **BingXu** ; 直符(ZhíFú): 天芮(TiānRuì)
直使(ZhíShǐ): 死门(SǐMén) ; 旬首(XúnShǒu): JiaShenGeng

玄武 (Xuán Wǔ) 天冲 (Tiān Chōng) 死门 (Sǐ Mén) Xun 4　Xin Ren	九地 (Jiǔ Dì) 天辅 (Tiān Fǔ) 惊门 (Jīng Mén) Li 9　Ren Wu	九天 (Jiǔ Tiān) 天英 (Tiān Yīng) 开门 (Kāi Mén) Kun 2　Wu Geng/Gui
白虎 (Bái Hǔ) 天任 (Tiān Rèn) 景门 (Jīng Mén) Zhen 3　Yi Xin	Yang (阳) Dun# 9 Hour: **BingXu** ©Calvin Yap	值符 (Zhí Fú) 禽芮 (Qín Ruì) 休门 (Xiū Mén) Dui 7　Geng/Gui Bing
六合 (Liù Hé) 天蓬 (Tiān Péng) 杜门 (Dù Mén) Gen 8　Ji Yi	太阴 (Tài Yīn) 天心 (Tiān Xīn) 伤门 (Shāng Mén) Kan 1　Ding Ji	螣蛇 (Téng Shé) 天柱 (Tiān Zhù) 生门 (Shēng Mén) Qian 6　Bing Ding

Yang (阳) Dun# 9 Hour: **DingHai** ; 直符(ZhíFú): 天芮(TiānRuì)
直使(ZhíShǐ): 死门(SǐMén) ; 旬首(XúnShǒu): JiaShenGeng

白虎 (Bái Hǔ) 天任 (Tiān Rèn) 杜门 (Dù Mén) Xun 4　Yi Ren	玄武 (Xuán Wǔ) 天冲 (Tiān Chōng) 景门 (Jīng Mén) Li 9　Xin Wu	九地 (Jiǔ Dì) 天辅 (Tiān Fǔ) 死门 (Sǐ Mén) Kun 2　Ren Geng/Gui
六合 (Liù Hé) 天蓬 (Tiān Péng) 伤门 (Shāng Mén) Zhen 3　Ji Xin	Yang (阳) Dun# 9 Hour: **DingHai** ©Calvin Yap	九天 (Jiǔ Tiān) 天英 (Tiān Yīng) 惊门 (Jīng Mén) Dui 7　Wu Bing
太阴 (Tài Yīn) 天心 (Tiān Xīn) 生门 (Shēng Mén) Gen 8　Ding Yi	螣蛇 (Téng Shé) 天柱 (Tiān Zhù) 休门 (Xiū Mén) Kan 1　Bing Ji	值符 (Zhí Fú) 禽芮 (Qín Ruì) 开门 (Kāi Mén) Qian 6　Geng/Gui Ding

Yang (阳) Dun# 9 Hour: **WuZi**；直符(ZhíFú): 天芮(TiānRuì)
直使(ZhíShǐ): 死门(SǐMén)；旬首(XúnShǒu): JiaShenGeng

九天 (Jiǔ Tiān) 天英 (Tiān Yīng) 生门 (Shēng Mén) Xun 4　　Wu Ren	值符 (Zhí Fú) 禽芮 (Qín Ruì) 伤门 (Shāng Mén) Li 9　Geng/Gui Wu	螣蛇 (Téng Shé) 天柱 (Tiān Zhù) 杜门 (Dù Mén) Kun 2　　Bing Geng/Gui
九地 (Jiǔ Dì) 天辅 (Tiān Fǔ) 休门 (Xiū Mén) Zhen 3　Ren Xin	Yang (阳) Dun# 9 Hour: **WuZi** ©Calvin Yap	太阴 (Tài Yīn) 天心 (Tiān Xīn) 景门 (Jǐng Mén) Dui 7　Ding Bing
玄武 (Xuán Wǔ) 天冲 (Tiān Chōng) 开门 (Kāi Mén) Gen 8　Xin Yi	白虎 (Bái Hǔ) 天任 (Tiān Rèn) 惊门 (Jīng Mén) Kan 1　Yi Ji	六合 (Liù Hé) 天蓬 (Tiān Péng) 死门 (Sǐ Mén) Qian 6　Ji Ding

Yang (阳) Dun# 9 Hour: **JiChou**；直符(ZhíFú): 天芮(TiānRuì)
直使(ZhíShǐ): 死门(SǐMén)；旬首(XúnShǒu): JiaShenGeng

六合 (Liù Hé) 天蓬 (Tiān Péng) 伤门 (Shāng Mén) Xun 4　　Ji Ren	白虎 (Bái Hǔ) 天任 (Tiān Rèn) 杜门 (Dù Mén) Li 9　　Yi Wu	玄武 (Xuán Wǔ) 天冲 (Tiān Chōng) 景门 (Jǐng Mén) Kun 2　　Xin Geng/Gui
太阴 (Tài Yīn) 天心 (Tiān Xīn) 生门 (Shēng Mén) Zhen 3　Ding Xin	Yang (阳) Dun# 9 Hour: **JiChou** ©Calvin Yap	九地 (Jiǔ Dì) 天辅 (Tiān Fǔ) 死门 (Sǐ Mén) Dui 7　Ren Bing
螣蛇 (Téng Shé) 天柱 (Tiān Zhù) 休门 (Xiū Mén) Gen 8　Bing Yi	值符 (Zhí Fú) 禽芮 (Qín Ruì) 开门 (Kāi Mén) Kan 1　Geng/Gui Ji	九天 (Jiǔ Tiān) 天英 (Tiān Yīng) 惊门 (Jīng Mén) Qian 6　Wu Ding

Yang (阳) Dun# 9 Hour: **GengYin**；直符(ZhíFú): 天芮(TiānRuì)
直使(ZhíShǐ): 死门(SǐMén)；旬首(XúnShǒu): JiaShenGeng

九地 (Jiǔ Dì) 天辅 (Tiān Fǔ) 开门 (Kāi Mén) Xun 4　　Ren Ren	九天 (Jiǔ Tiān) 天英 (Tiān Yīng) 休门 (Xiū Mén) Li 9　　Wu Wu	值符 (Zhí Fú) 禽芮 (Qín Ruì) 生门 (Shēng Mén) Kun 2　Geng/Gui Geng/Gui
玄武 (Xuán Wǔ) 天冲 (Tiān Chōng) 惊门 (Jīng Mén) Zhen 3　Xin Xin	Yang (阳) Dun# 9 Hour: **GengYin** **Fu Yin** ©Calvin Yap	螣蛇 (Téng Shé) 天柱 (Tiān Zhù) 伤门 (Shāng Mén) Dui 7　Bing Bing
白虎 (Bái Hǔ) 天任 (Tiān Rèn) 死门 (Sǐ Mén) Gen 8　Yi Yi	六合 (Liù Hé) 天蓬 (Tiān Péng) 景门 (Jǐng Mén) Kan 1　Ji Ji	太阴 (Tài Yīn) 天心 (Tiān Xīn) 杜门 (Dù Mén) Qian 6　Ding Ding

Yang (阳) Dun# 9 Hour: **XinMao**；直符(ZhíFú): 天芮(TiānRuì)
直使(ZhíShǐ): 死门(SǐMén)；旬首(XúnShǒu): JiaShenGeng

螣蛇 (Téng Shé) 天柱 (Tiān Zhù) 景门 (Jǐng Mén) Xun 4　　Bing Ren	太阴 (Tài Yīn) 天心 (Tiān Xīn) 死门 (Sǐ Mén) Li 9　　Ding Wu	六合 (Liù Hé) 天蓬 (Tiān Péng) 惊门 (Jīng Mén) Kun 2　　Ji Geng/Gui
值符 (Zhí Fú) 禽芮 (Qín Ruì) 杜门 (Dù Mén) Zhen 3　Geng/Gui Xin	Yang (阳) Dun# 9 Hour: **XinMao** ©Calvin Yap	白虎 (Bái Hǔ) 天任 (Tiān Rèn) 开门 (Kāi Mén) Dui 7　Yi Bing
九天 (Jiǔ Tiān) 天英 (Tiān Yīng) 伤门 (Shāng Mén) Gen 8　Wu Yi	九地 (Jiǔ Dì) 天辅 (Tiān Fǔ) 生门 (Shēng Mén) Kan 1　Ren Ji	玄武 (Xuán Wǔ) 天冲 (Tiān Chōng) 休门 (Xiū Mén) Qian 6　Xin Ding

Yang (阳) Dun# 9 Hour: **RenChen**；直符(ZhíFú): 天芮(TiānRuì)
直使(ZhíShǐ): 死门(SǐMén)；旬首(XúnShǒu): JiaShenGeng

值符 (Zhí Fú) 禽芮 (Qín Ruì) 休门 (Xiū Mén) Xun 4　Geng/Gui Ren	螣蛇 (Téng Shé) 天柱 (Tiān Zhù) 生门 (Shēng Mén) Li 9　　Bing Wu	太阴 (Tài Yīn) 天心 (Tiān Xīn) 伤门 (Shāng Mén) Kun 2　　Ding Geng/Gui
九天 (Jiǔ Tiān) 天英 (Tiān Yīng) 开门 (Kāi Mén) Zhen 3　Wu Xin	Yang (阳) Dun# 9 Hour: **RenChen** ©Calvin Yap	六合 (Liù Hé) 天蓬 (Tiān Péng) 杜门 (Dù Mén) Dui 7　Ji Bing
九地 (Jiǔ Dì) 天辅 (Tiān Fǔ) 惊门 (Jīng Mén) Gen 8　Ren Yi	玄武 (Xuán Wǔ) 天冲 (Tiān Chōng) 死门 (Sǐ Mén) Kan 1　Xin Ji	白虎 (Bái Hǔ) 天任 (Tiān Rèn) 景门 (Jǐng Mén) Qian 6　Yi Bing

Yang (阳) Dun# 9 Hour: **GuiSi**；直符(ZhíFú): 天芮(TiānRuì)
直使(ZhíShǐ): 死门(SǐMén)；旬首(XúnShǒu): JiaShenGeng

九地 (Jiǔ Dì) 天辅 (Tiān Fǔ) 杜门 (Dù Mén) Xun 4　　Ren Ren	九天 (Jiǔ Tiān) 天英 (Tiān Yīng) 景门 (Jǐng Mén) Li 9　　Wu Wu	值符 (Zhí Fú) 禽芮 (Qín Ruì) 死门 (Sǐ Mén) Kun 2　Geng/Gui Geng/Gui
玄武 (Xuán Wǔ) 天冲 (Tiān Chōng) 伤门 (Shāng Mén) Zhen 3　Xin Xin	Yang (阳) Dun# 9 Hour: **GuiSi** **Fu Yin** ©Calvin Yap	螣蛇 (Téng Shé) 天柱 (Tiān Zhù) 惊门 (Jīng Mén) Dui 7　Bing Bing
白虎 (Bái Hǔ) 天任 (Tiān Rèn) 生门 (Shēng Mén) Gen 8　Yi Yi	六合 (Liù Hé) 天蓬 (Tiān Péng) 休门 (Xiū Mén) Kan 1　Ji Ji	太阴 (Tài Yīn) 天心 (Tiān Xīn) 开门 (Kāi Mén) Qian 6　Ding Ding

Chart: **+9JiaWu** (Yang Dun #9 JiaWu Xun)
JiaWu, YiWei, BingShen, DingYou, WuXu, JiHai, GengZi, XinChou, RenYin, GuiMao

Yang (阳) Dun# 9 Hour: **JiaWu**

直符(ZhíFú): 天冲(TiānChōng) ; 直使(ZhíShǐ): 伤门(ShāngMén) ; 旬首(XúnShǒu): JiaWu/Xin

螣蛇 (Téng Shé) 天辅 (Tiān Fǔ) 杜门 (Dù Mén) Xun 4 — Ren / Ren	太阴 (Tài Yīn) 天英 (Tiān Yīng) 景门 (Jǐng Mén) Li 9 — Wu / Wu	六合 (Liù Hé) 禽芮 (Qín Ruì) 死门 (Sǐ Mén) Kun 2 — Geng/Gui / Geng/Gui
值符 (Zhí Fú) 天冲 (Tiān Chōng) 伤门 (Shāng Mén) Zhen 3 — Xin / Xin	Yang (阳) Dun# 9 Hour: **JiaWu** **Fu Yin** ©Calvin Yap	白虎 (Bái Hǔ) 天柱 (Tiān Zhù) 惊门 (Jīng Mén) Dui 7 — Bing / Bing
九天 (Jiǔ Tiān) 天任 (Tiān Rèn) 生门 (Shēng Mén) Gen 8 — Yi / Yi	九地 (Jiǔ Dì) 天蓬 (Tiān Péng) 休门 (Xiū Mén) Kan 1 — Ji / Ji	玄武 (Xuán Wǔ) 天心 (Tiān Xīn) 开门 (Kāi Mén) Qian 6 — Ding / Ding

Yang (阳) Dun# 9 Hour: **YiWei**

直符(ZhíFú): 天冲(TiānChōng) ; 直使(ZhíShǐ): 伤门(ShāngMén) ; 旬首(XúnShǒu): JiaWu/Xin

太阴 (Tài Yīn) 天英 (Tiān Yīng) 伤门 (Shāng Mén) Xun 4 — Wu / Ren	六合 (Liù Hé) 禽芮 (Qín Ruì) 杜门 (Dù Mén) Li 9 — Geng/Gui / Wu	白虎 (Bái Hǔ) 天柱 (Tiān Zhù) 景门 (Jǐng Mén) Kun 2 — Bing / Geng/Gui
螣蛇 (Téng Shé) 天辅 (Tiān Fǔ) 生门 (Shēng Mén) Zhen 3 — Ren / Xin	Yang (阳) Dun# 9 Hour: **YiWei** ©Calvin Yap	玄武 (Xuán Wǔ) 天心 (Tiān Xīn) 死门 (Sǐ Mén) Dui 7 — Ding / Bing
值符 (Zhí Fú) 天冲 (Tiān Chōng) 休门 (Xiū Mén) Gen 8 — Xin / Yi	九天 (Jiǔ Tiān) 天任 (Tiān Rèn) 开门 (Kāi Mén) Kan 1 — Yi / Ji	九地 (Jiǔ Dì) 天蓬 (Tiān Péng) 惊门 (Jīng Mén) Qian 6 — Ji / Ding

Yang (阳) Dun# 9 Hour: **BingShen**

直符(ZhíFú): 天冲(TiānChōng) ; 直使(ZhíShǐ): 伤门(ShāngMén) ; 旬首(XúnShǒu): JiaWu/Xin

玄武 (Xuán Wǔ) 天心 (Tiān Xīn) 休门 (Xiū Mén) Xun 4 — Ding / Ren	九地 (Jiǔ Dì) 天蓬 (Tiān Péng) 生门 (Shēng Mén) Li 9 — Ji / Wu	九天 (Jiǔ Tiān) 天任 (Tiān Rèn) 伤门 (Shāng Mén) Kun 2 — Yi / Geng/Gui
白虎 (Bái Hǔ) 天柱 (Tiān Zhù) 开门 (Kāi Mén) Zhen 3 — Bing / Xin	Yang (阳) Dun# 9 Hour: **BingShen** **Fan Yin** ©Calvin Yap	值符 (Zhí Fú) 天冲 (Tiān Chōng) 杜门 (Dù Mén) Dui 7 — Xin / Bing
六合 (Liù Hé) 禽芮 (Qín Ruì) 惊门 (Jīng Mén) Gen 8 — Geng/Gui / Yi	太阴 (Tài Yīn) 天英 (Tiān Yīng) 死门 (Sǐ Mén) Kan 1 — Wu / Ji	螣蛇 (Téng Shé) 天辅 (Tiān Fǔ) 景门 (Jǐng Mén) Qian 6 — Ren / Ding

Yang (阳) Dun# 9 Hour: **DingYou**

直符(ZhíFú): 天冲(TiānChōng) ; 直使(ZhíShǐ): 伤门(ShāngMén) ; 旬首(XúnShǒu): JiaWu/Xin

白虎 (Bái Hǔ) 天柱 (Tiān Zhù) 惊门 (Jīng Mén) Xun 4 — Bing / Ren	玄武 (Xuán Wǔ) 天心 (Tiān Xīn) 开门 (Kāi Mén) Li 9 — Ding / Wu	九地 (Jiǔ Dì) 天蓬 (Tiān Péng) 休门 (Xiū Mén) Kun 2 — Ji / Geng/Gui
六合 (Liù Hé) 禽芮 (Qín Ruì) 死门 (Sǐ Mén) Zhen 3 — Geng/Gui / Xin	Yang (阳) Dun# 9 Hour: **DingYou** ©Calvin Yap	九天 (Jiǔ Tiān) 天任 (Tiān Rèn) 生门 (Shēng Mén) Dui 7 — Yi / Bing
太阴 (Tài Yīn) 天英 (Tiān Yīng) 景门 (Jǐng Mén) Gen 8 — Wu / Yi	螣蛇 (Téng Shé) 天辅 (Tiān Fǔ) 杜门 (Dù Mén) Kan 1 — Ren / Ji	值符 (Zhí Fú) 天冲 (Tiān Chōng) 伤门 (Shāng Mén) Qian 6 — Xin / Ding

Yang (阳) Dun# 9 Hour: **WuXu**

直符(ZhíFú): 天冲(TiānChōng) ; 直使(ZhíShǐ): 伤门(ShāngMén) ; 旬首(XúnShǒu): JiaWu/Xin

九天 (Jiǔ Tiān) 天任 (Tiān Rèn) 开门 (Kāi Mén) Xun 4 — Yi / Ren	值符 (Zhí Fú) 天冲 (Tiān Chōng) 休门 (Xiū Mén) Li 9 — Xin / Wu	螣蛇 (Téng Shé) 天辅 (Tiān Fǔ) 生门 (Shēng Mén) Kun 2 — Ren / Geng/Gui
九地 (Jiǔ Dì) 天蓬 (Tiān Péng) 惊门 (Jīng Mén) Zhen 3 — Ji / Xin	Yang (阳) Dun# 9 Hour: **WuXu** ©Calvin Yap	太阴 (Tài Yīn) 天英 (Tiān Yīng) 伤门 (Shāng Mén) Dui 7 — Wu / Bing
玄武 (Xuán Wǔ) 天心 (Tiān Xīn) 死门 (Sǐ Mén) Gen 8 — Ding / Yi	白虎 (Bái Hǔ) 天柱 (Tiān Zhù) 景门 (Jǐng Mén) Kan 1 — Bing / Ji	六合 (Liù Hé) 禽芮 (Qín Ruì) 杜门 (Dù Mén) Qian 6 — Geng/Gui / Ding

Yang (阳) Dun# 9 Hour: **JiHai**

直符(ZhíFú): 天冲(TiānChōng) ; 直使(ZhíShǐ): 伤门(ShāngMén) ; 旬首(XúnShǒu): JiaWu/Xin

六合 (Liù Hé) 禽芮 (Qín Ruì) 景门 (Jǐng Mén) Xun 4 — Geng/Gui / Ren	白虎 (Bái Hǔ) 天柱 (Tiān Zhù) 死门 (Sǐ Mén) Li 9 — Bing / Wu	玄武 (Xuán Wǔ) 天心 (Tiān Xīn) 惊门 (Jīng Mén) Kun 2 — Ding / Geng/Gui
太阴 (Tài Yīn) 天英 (Tiān Yīng) 杜门 (Dù Mén) Zhen 3 — Wu / Xin	Yang (阳) Dun# 9 Hour: **JiHai** ©Calvin Yap	九地 (Jiǔ Dì) 天蓬 (Tiān Péng) 开门 (Kāi Mén) Dui 7 — Ji / Bing
螣蛇 (Téng Shé) 天辅 (Tiān Fǔ) 伤门 (Shāng Mén) Gen 8 — Ren / Yi	值符 (Zhí Fú) 天冲 (Tiān Chōng) 生门 (Shēng Mén) Kan 1 — Xin / Ji	九天 (Jiǔ Tiān) 天任 (Tiān Rèn) 休门 (Xiū Mén) Qian 6 — Yi / Ding

Yang (阳) Dun# 9 Hour: GengZi

直符(ZhíFú): 天冲(TiānChōng) ; 直使(ZhíShǐ): 伤门(ShāngMén) ; 旬首(XúnShǒu): JiaWu/Xin

九地 (Jiǔ Dì) 天蓬 (Tiān Péng) 生门 (Shēng Mén) Xun 4　Ji Ren	九天 (Jiǔ Tiān) 天任 (Tiān Rèn) 伤门 (Shāng Mén) Li 9　Yi Wu	值符 (Zhí Fú) 天冲 (Tiān Chōng) 杜门 (Dù Mén) Kun 2　Xin Geng/Gui
玄武 (Xuán Wǔ) 天心 (Tiān Xīn) 休门 (Xiū Mén) Zhen 3　Ding Xin	Yang (阳) Dun# 9 Hour: **GengZi** ©Calvin Yap	螣蛇 (Téng Shé) 天辅 (Tiān Fǔ) 景门 (Jǐng Mén) Dui 7　Ren Bing
白虎 (Bái Hǔ) 天柱 (Tiān Zhù) 开门 (Kāi Mén) Gen 8　Bing Yi	六合 (Liù Hé) 禽芮 (Qín Ruì) 惊门 (Jīng Mén) Kan 1　Geng/Gui Ji	太阴 (Tài Yīn) 天英 (Tiān Yīng) 死门 (Sǐ Mén) Qian 6　Wu Ding

Yang (阳) Dun# 9 Hour: XinChou

直符(ZhíFú): 天冲(TiānChōng) ; 直使(ZhíShǐ): 伤门(ShāngMén) ; 旬首(XúnShǒu): JiaWu/Xin

螣蛇 (Téng Shé) 天辅 (Tiān Fǔ) 死门 (Sǐ Mén) Xun 4　Ren Ren	太阴 (Tài Yīn) 天英 (Tiān Yīng) 惊门 (Jīng Mén) Li 9　Wu Wu	六合 (Liù Hé) 禽芮 (Qín Ruì) 开门 (Kāi Mén) Kun 2　Geng/Gui Geng/Gui
值符 (Zhí Fú) 天冲 (Tiān Chōng) 景门 (Jǐng Mén) Zhen 3　Xin Xin	Yang (阳) Dun# 9 Hour: **XinChou** **Fu Yin** ©Calvin Yap	白虎 (Bái Hǔ) 天柱 (Tiān Zhù) 休门 (Xiū Mén) Dui 7　Bing Bing
九天 (Jiǔ Tiān) 天任 (Tiān Rèn) 杜门 (Dù Mén) Gen 8　Yi Yi	九地 (Jiǔ Dì) 天蓬 (Tiān Péng) 伤门 (Shāng Mén) Kan 1　Ji Ji	玄武 (Xuán Wǔ) 天心 (Tiān Xīn) 生门 (Shēng Mén) Qian 6　Ding Ding

Yang (阳) Dun# 9 Hour: RenYin

直符(ZhíFú): 天冲(TiānChōng) ; 直使(ZhíShǐ): 伤门(ShāngMén) ; 旬首(XúnShǒu): JiaWu/Xin

值符 (Zhí Fú) 天冲 (Tiān Chōng) 休门 (Xiū Mén) Xun 4　Xin Ren	螣蛇 (Téng Shé) 天辅 (Tiān Fǔ) 生门 (Shēng Mén) Li 9　Ren Wu	太阴 (Tài Yīn) 天英 (Tiān Yīng) 伤门 (Shāng Mén) Kun 2　Wu Geng/Gui
九天 (Jiǔ Tiān) 天任 (Tiān Rèn) 开门 (Kāi Mén) Zhen 3　Yi Xin	Yang (阳) Dun# 9 Hour: **RenYin** ©Calvin Yap	六合 (Liù Hé) 禽芮 (Qín Ruì) 杜门 (Dù Mén) Dui 7　Geng/Gui Bing
九地 (Jiǔ Dì) 天蓬 (Tiān Péng) 惊门 (Jīng Mén) Gen 8　Ji Yi	玄武 (Xuán Wǔ) 天心 (Tiān Xīn) 死门 (Sǐ Mén) Kan 1　Ding Ji	白虎 (Bái Hǔ) 天柱 (Tiān Zhù) 景门 (Jǐng Mén) Qian 6　Bing Ding

Yang (阳) Dun# 9 Hour: GuiMao

直符(ZhíFú): 天冲(TiānChōng) ; 直使(ZhíShǐ): 伤门(ShāngMén) ; 旬首(XúnShǒu): JiaWu/Xin

九地 (Jiǔ Dì) 天蓬 (Tiān Péng) 杜门 (Dù Mén) Xun 4　Ji Ren	九天 (Jiǔ Tiān) 天任 (Tiān Rèn) 景门 (Jǐng Mén) Li 9　Yi Wu	值符 (Zhí Fú) 天冲 (Tiān Chōng) 死门 (Sǐ Mén) Kun 2　Xin Geng/Gui
玄武 (Xuán Wǔ) 天心 (Tiān Xīn) 伤门 (Shāng Mén) Zhen 3　Ding Xin	Yang (阳) Dun# 9 Hour: **GuiMao** ©Calvin Yap	螣蛇 (Téng Shé) 天辅 (Tiān Fǔ) 惊门 (Jīng Mén) Dui 7　Ren Bing
白虎 (Bái Hǔ) 天柱 (Tiān Zhù) 生门 (Shēng Mén) Gen 8　Bing Yi	六合 (Liù Hé) 禽芮 (Qín Ruì) 休门 (Xiū Mén) Kan 1　Geng/Gui Ji	太阴 (Tài Yīn) 天英 (Tiān Yīng) 开门 (Kāi Mén) Qian 6　Wu Ding

---

Chart: **+9JiaChen** (Yang Dun #9 JiaChen Xun)

JiaChen, YiSi, BingWu, DingWei, WuShen, JiYou, GengXu, XinHai, RenZi, GuiChou

Yang (阳) Dun# 9 Hour: JiaChen

直符(ZhíFú): 天辅(TiānFǔ) ; 直使(ZhíShǐ): 杜门(DùMén) ; 旬首(XúnShǒu): JiaChenRen

值符 (Zhí Fú) 天辅 (Tiān Fǔ) 杜门 (Dù Mén) Xun 4　Ren Ren	螣蛇 (Téng Shé) 天英 (Tiān Yīng) 景门 (Jǐng Mén) Li 9　Wu Wu	太阴 (Tài Yīn) 禽芮 (Qín Ruì) 死门 (Sǐ Mén) Kun 2　Geng/Gui Geng/Gui
九天 (Jiǔ Tiān) 天冲 (Tiān Chōng) 伤门 (Shāng Mén) Zhen 3　Xin Xin	Yang (阳) Dun# 9 Hour: **JiaChen** **Fu Yin** ©Calvin Yap	六合 (Liù Hé) 天柱 (Tiān Zhù) 惊门 (Jīng Mén) Dui 7　Bing Bing
九地 (Jiǔ Dì) 天任 (Tiān Rèn) 生门 (Shēng Mén) Gen 8　Yi Yi	玄武 (Xuán Wǔ) 天蓬 (Tiān Péng) 休门 (Xiū Mén) Kan 1　Ji Ji	白虎 (Bái Hǔ) 天心 (Tiān Xīn) 开门 (Kāi Mén) Qian 6　Ding Ding

Yang (阳) Dun# 9 Hour: YiSi

直符(ZhíFú): 天辅(TiānFǔ) ; 直使(ZhíShǐ): 杜门(DùMén) ; 旬首(XúnShǒu): JiaChenRen

太阴 (Tài Yīn) 禽芮 (Qín Ruì) 生门 (Shēng Mén) Xun 4　Geng/Gui Ren	六合 (Liù Hé) 天柱 (Tiān Zhù) 伤门 (Shāng Mén) Li 9　Bing Wu	白虎 (Bái Hǔ) 天心 (Tiān Xīn) 杜门 (Dù Mén) Kun 2　Ding Geng/Gui
螣蛇 (Téng Shé) 天英 (Tiān Yīng) 休门 (Xiū Mén) Zhen 3　Wu Xin	Yang (阳) Dun# 9 Hour: **YiSi** ©Calvin Yap	玄武 (Xuán Wǔ) 天蓬 (Tiān Péng) 景门 (Jǐng Mén) Dui 7　Ji Bing
值符 (Zhí Fú) 天辅 (Tiān Fǔ) 开门 (Kāi Mén) Gen 8　Ren Yi	九天 (Jiǔ Tiān) 天冲 (Tiān Chōng) 惊门 (Jīng Mén) Kan 1　Xin Ji	九地 (Jiǔ Dì) 天任 (Tiān Rèn) 死门 (Sǐ Mén) Qian 6　Yi Ding

Yang (阳) Dun# 9 Hour: BingWu；直符(ZhíFú): 天辅(TiānFǔ)
直使(ZhíShǐ): 杜门(DùMén)；旬首(XúnShǒu): JiaChenRen

玄武 (Xuán Wǔ) 天蓬 (Tiān Péng) 开门 (Kāi Mén) Xun 4　Ji Ren	九地 (Jiǔ Dì) 天任 (Tiān Rèn) 休门 (Xiū Mén) Li 9　Yi Wu	九天 (Jiǔ Tiān) 天冲 (Tiān Chōng) 生门 (Shēng Mén) Kun 2　Xin Geng/Gui
白虎 (Bái Hǔ) 天心 (Tiān Xīn) 惊门 (Jīng Mén) Zhen 3　Ding Xin	Yang (阳) Dun# 9 Hour: **BingWu** ©Calvin Yap	值符 (Zhí Fú) 天辅 (Tiān Fǔ) 伤门 (Shāng Mén) Dui 7　Ren Bing
六合 (Liù Hé) 天柱 (Tiān Zhù) 死门 (Sǐ Mén) Gen 8　Bing Yi	太阴 (Tài Yīn) 禽芮 (Qín Ruì) 景门 (Jǐng Mén) Kan 1　Geng/Gui Ji	螣蛇 (Téng Shé) 天英 (Tiān Yīng) 杜门 (Dù Mén) Qian 6　Wu Ding

Yang (阳) Dun# 9 Hour: DingWei；直符(ZhíFú): 天辅(TiānFǔ)
直使(ZhíShǐ): 杜门(DùMén)；旬首(XúnShǒu): JiaChenRen

白虎 (Bái Hǔ) 天心 (Tiān Xīn) 休门 (Xiū Mén) Xun 4　Ding Ren	玄武 (Xuán Wǔ) 天蓬 (Tiān Péng) 生门 (Shēng Mén) Li 9　Ji Wu	九地 (Jiǔ Dì) 天任 (Tiān Rèn) 伤门 (Shāng Mén) Kun 2　Yi Geng/Gui
六合 (Liù Hé) 天柱 (Tiān Zhù) 开门 (Kāi Mén) Zhen 3　Bing Xin	Yang (阳) Dun# 9 Hour: **DingWei** **Fan Yin** ©Calvin Yap	九天 (Jiǔ Tiān) 天冲 (Tiān Chōng) 杜门 (Dù Mén) Dui 7　Xin Bing
太阴 (Tài Yīn) 禽芮 (Qín Ruì) 惊门 (Jīng Mén) Gen 8　Geng/Gui Yi	螣蛇 (Téng Shé) 天英 (Tiān Yīng) 死门 (Sǐ Mén) Kan 1　Wu Ji	值符 (Zhí Fú) 天辅 (Tiān Fǔ) 景门 (Jǐng Mén) Qian 6　Ren Ding

Yang (阳) Dun# 9 Hour: WuShen；直符(ZhíFú): 天辅(TiānFǔ)
直使(ZhíShǐ): 杜门(DùMén)；旬首(XúnShǒu): JiaChenRen

九天 (Jiǔ Tiān) 天冲 (Tiān Chōng) 死门 (Sǐ Mén) Xun 4　Xin Ren	值符 (Zhí Fú) 天辅 (Tiān Fǔ) 惊门 (Jīng Mén) Li 9　Ren Wu	螣蛇 (Téng Shé) 天英 (Tiān Yīng) 开门 (Kāi Mén) Kun 2　Wu Geng/Gui
九地 (Jiǔ Dì) 天任 (Tiān Rèn) 景门 (Jǐng Mén) Zhen 3　Yi Xin	Yang (阳) Dun# 9 Hour: **WuShen** ©Calvin Yap	太阴 (Tài Yīn) 禽芮 (Qín Ruì) 休门 (Xiū Mén) Dui 7　Geng/Gui Bing
玄武 (Xuán Wǔ) 天蓬 (Tiān Péng) 杜门 (Dù Mén) Gen 8　Ji Yi	白虎 (Bái Hǔ) 天心 (Tiān Xīn) 伤门 (Shāng Mén) Kan 1　Ding Ji	六合 (Liù Hé) 天柱 (Tiān Zhù) 生门 (Shēng Mén) Qian 6　Bing Ding

Yang (阳) Dun# 9 Hour: JiYou；直符(ZhíFú): 天辅(TiānFǔ)
直使(ZhíShǐ): 杜门(DùMén)；旬首(XúnShǒu): JiaChenRen

六合 (Liù Hé) 天柱 (Tiān Zhù) 伤门 (Shāng Mén) Xun 4　Bing Ren	白虎 (Bái Hǔ) 天心 (Tiān Xīn) 杜门 (Dù Mén) Li 9　Ding Wu	玄武 (Xuán Wǔ) 天蓬 (Tiān Péng) 景门 (Jǐng Mén) Kun 2　Ji Geng/Gui
太阴 (Tài Yīn) 禽芮 (Qín Ruì) 生门 (Shēng Mén) Zhen 3　Geng/Gui Xin	Yang (阳) Dun# 9 Hour: **JiYou** ©Calvin Yap	九地 (Jiǔ Dì) 天任 (Tiān Rèn) 死门 (Sǐ Mén) Dui 7　Yi Bing
螣蛇 (Téng Shé) 天英 (Tiān Yīng) 休门 (Xiū Mén) Gen 8　Wu Yi	值符 (Zhí Fú) 天辅 (Tiān Fǔ) 开门 (Kāi Mén) Kan 1　Ren Ji	九天 (Jiǔ Tiān) 天冲 (Tiān Chōng) 惊门 (Jīng Mén) Qian 6　Xin Ding

Yang (阳) Dun# 9 Hour: GengXu；直符(ZhíFú): 天辅(TiānFǔ)
直使(ZhíShǐ): 杜门(DùMén)；旬首(XúnShǒu): JiaChenRen

九地 (Jiǔ Dì) 天任 (Tiān Rèn) 惊门 (Jīng Mén) Xun 4　Yi Ren	九天 (Jiǔ Tiān) 天冲 (Tiān Chōng) 开门 (Kāi Mén) Li 9　Xin Wu	值符 (Zhí Fú) 天辅 (Tiān Fǔ) 休门 (Xiū Mén) Kun 2　Ren Geng/Gui
玄武 (Xuán Wǔ) 天蓬 (Tiān Péng) 死门 (Sǐ Mén) Zhen 3　Ji Xin	Yang (阳) Dun# 9 Hour: **GengXu** ©Calvin Yap	螣蛇 (Téng Shé) 天英 (Tiān Yīng) 生门 (Shēng Mén) Dui 7　Wu Bing
白虎 (Bái Hǔ) 天心 (Tiān Xīn) 景门 (Jǐng Mén) Gen 8　Ding Yi	六合 (Liù Hé) 天柱 (Tiān Zhù) 杜门 (Dù Mén) Kan 1　Bing Ji	太阴 (Tài Yīn) 禽芮 (Qín Ruì) 伤门 (Shāng Mén) Qian 6　Geng/Gui Ding

Yang (阳) Dun# 9 Hour: XinHai；直符(ZhíFú): 天辅(TiānFǔ)
直使(ZhíShǐ): 杜门(DùMén)；旬首(XúnShǒu): JiaChenRen

螣蛇 (Téng Shé) 天英 (Tiān Yīng) 生门 (Shēng Mén) Xun 4　Wu Ren	太阴 (Tài Yīn) 禽芮 (Qín Ruì) 伤门 (Shāng Mén) Li 9　Geng/Gui Wu	六合 (Liù Hé) 天柱 (Tiān Zhù) 杜门 (Dù Mén) Kun 2　Bing Geng/Gui
值符 (Zhí Fú) 天辅 (Tiān Fǔ) 休门 (Xiū Mén) Zhen 3　Ren Xin	Yang (阳) Dun# 9 Hour: **XinHai** ©Calvin Yap	白虎 (Bái Hǔ) 天心 (Tiān Xīn) 景门 (Jǐng Mén) Dui 7　Ding Bing
九天 (Jiǔ Tiān) 天冲 (Tiān Chōng) 开门 (Kāi Mén) Gen 8　Xin Yi	九地 (Jiǔ Dì) 天任 (Tiān Rèn) 惊门 (Jīng Mén) Kan 1　Yi Ji	玄武 (Xuán Wǔ) 天蓬 (Tiān Péng) 死门 (Sǐ Mén) Qian 6　Ji Ding

Yang (阳) Dun# 9 Hour: **RenZi** ；直符(ZhíFú): 天辅(TiānFǔ)
直使(ZhíShǐ): 杜门(DùMén) ；旬首(XúnShǒu): JiaChenRen

值符 (Zhí Fú) 天辅 (Tiān Fǔ) 景门 (Jǐng Mén) Xun 4 — Ren Ren	螣蛇 (Téng Shé) 天英 (Tiān Yīng) 死门 (Sǐ Mén) Li 9 — Wu Wu	太阴 (Tài Yīn) 禽芮 (Qín Ruì) 惊门 (Jīng Mén) Kun 2 — Geng/Gui Geng/Gui
九天 (Jiǔ Tiān) 天冲 (Tiān Chōng) 杜门 (Dù Mén) Zhen 3 — Xin Xin	Yang (阳) Dun# 9 Hour: **RenZi** **Fu Yin** ©Calvin Yap	六合 (Liù Hé) 天柱 (Tiān Zhù) 开门 (Kāi Mén) Dui 7 — Bing Bing
九地 (Jiǔ Dì) 天任 (Tiān Rèn) 伤门 (Shāng Mén) Gen 8 — Yi Yi	玄武 (Xuán Wǔ) 天蓬 (Tiān Péng) 生门 (Shēng Mén) Kan 1 — Ji Ji	白虎 (Bái Hǔ) 天心 (Tiān Xīn) 休门 (Xiū Mén) Qian 6 — Ding Ding

Yang (阳) Dun# 9 Hour: **GuiChou** ；直符(ZhíFú): 天辅(TiānFǔ)
直使(ZhíShǐ): 杜门(DùMén) ；旬首(XúnShǒu): JiaChenRen

九地 (Jiǔ Dì) 天任 (Tiān Rèn) 杜门 (Dù Mén) Xun 4 — Yi Yi	九天 (Jiǔ Tiān) 天冲 (Tiān Chōng) 景门 (Jǐng Mén) Li 9 — Xin Wu	值符 (Zhí Fú) 天辅 (Tiān Fǔ) 死门 (Sǐ Mén) Kun 2 — Ren Geng/Gui
玄武 (Xuán Wǔ) 天蓬 (Tiān Péng) 伤门 (Shāng Mén) Zhen 3 — Ji Xin	Yang (阳) Dun# 9 Hour: **GuiChou** ©Calvin Yap	螣蛇 (Téng Shé) 天英 (Tiān Yīng) 惊门 (Jīng Mén) Dui 7 — Wu Bing
白虎 (Bái Hǔ) 天心 (Tiān Xīn) 生门 (Shēng Mén) Gen 8 — Ding Yi	六合 (Liù Hé) 天柱 (Tiān Zhù) 休门 (Xiū Mén) Kan 1 — Bing Ji	太阴 (Tài Yīn) 禽芮 (Qín Ruì) 开门 (Kāi Mén) Qian 6 — Geng/Gui Ding

Chart: **+9JiaYin** (Yang Dun #9 JiaYin Xun)
JiaYin, YiMao, BingChen, DingSi, WuWu, JiWei, GengShen, XinYou, RenXu, GuiHai

Yang (阳) Dun# 9 Hour: **JiaYin** ；直符(ZhíFú): 天禽(TiānQín)
直使(ZhíShǐ): 死门(SǐMén) ；旬首(XúnShǒu): JiaYinGui

九地 (Jiǔ Dì) 天辅 (Tiān Fǔ) 杜门 (Dù Mén) Xun 4 — Ren Ren	九天 (Jiǔ Tiān) 天英 (Tiān Yīng) 景门 (Jǐng Mén) Li 9 — Wu Wu	值符 (Zhí Fú) 禽芮 (Qín Ruì) 死门 (Sǐ Mén) Kun 2 — Geng/Gui Geng/Gui
玄武 (Xuán Wǔ) 天冲 (Tiān Chōng) 伤门 (Shāng Mén) Zhen 3 — Xin Xin	Yang (阳) Dun# 9 Hour: **JiaYin** **Fu Yin** ©Calvin Yap	螣蛇 (Téng Shé) 天柱 (Tiān Zhù) 惊门 (Jīng Mén) Dui 7 — Bing Bing
白虎 (Bái Hǔ) 天任 (Tiān Rèn) 生门 (Shēng Mén) Gen 8 — Yi Yi	六合 (Liù Hé) 天蓬 (Tiān Péng) 休门 (Xiū Mén) Kan 1 — Ji Ji	太阴 (Tài Yīn) 天心 (Tiān Xīn) 开门 (Kāi Mén) Qian 6 — Ding Ding

Yang (阳) Dun# 9 Hour: **YiMao** ；直符(ZhíFú): 天禽(TiānQín)
直使(ZhíShǐ): 死门(SǐMén) ；旬首(XúnShǒu): JiaYinGui

太阴 (Tài Yīn) 天心 (Tiān Xīn) 生门 (Shēng Mén) Xun 4 — Ding Ren	六合 (Liù Hé) 天蓬 (Tiān Péng) 伤门 (Shāng Mén) Li 9 — Ji Wu	白虎 (Bái Hǔ) 天任 (Tiān Rèn) 杜门 (Dù Mén) Kun 2 — Yi Geng/Gui
螣蛇 (Téng Shé) 天柱 (Tiān Zhù) 休门 (Xiū Mén) Zhen 3 — Bing Xin	Yang (阳) Dun# 9 Hour: **YiMao** **Fan Yin** ©Calvin Yap	玄武 (Xuán Wǔ) 天冲 (Tiān Chōng) 景门 (Jǐng Mén) Dui 7 — Xin Bing
值符 (Zhí Fú) 禽芮 (Qín Ruì) 开门 (Kāi Mén) Gen 8 — Geng/Gui Yi	九天 (Jiǔ Tiān) 天英 (Tiān Yīng) 惊门 (Jīng Mén) Kan 1 — Wu Ji	九地 (Jiǔ Dì) 天辅 (Tiān Fǔ) 死门 (Sǐ Mén) Qian 6 — Ren Ding

Yang (阳) Dun# 9 Hour: **BingChen** ；直符(ZhíFú): 天禽(TiānQín)
直使(ZhíShǐ): 死门(SǐMén) ；旬首(XúnShǒu): JiaYinGui

玄武 (Xuán Wǔ) 天冲 (Tiān Chōng) 伤门 (Shāng Mén) Xun 4 — Xin Ren	九地 (Jiǔ Dì) 天辅 (Tiān Fǔ) 杜门 (Dù Mén) Li 9 — Ren Wu	九天 (Jiǔ Tiān) 天英 (Tiān Yīng) 景门 (Jǐng Mén) Kun 2 — Wu Geng/Gui
白虎 (Bái Hǔ) 天任 (Tiān Rèn) 生门 (Shēng Mén) Zhen 3 — Yi Xin	Yang (阳) Dun# 9 Hour: **BingChen** ©Calvin Yap	值符 (Zhí Fú) 禽芮 (Qín Ruì) 死门 (Sǐ Mén) Dui 7 — Geng/Gui Bing
六合 (Liù Hé) 天蓬 (Tiān Péng) 休门 (Xiū Mén) Gen 8 — Ji Yi	太阴 (Tài Yīn) 天心 (Tiān Xīn) 开门 (Kāi Mén) Kan 1 — Ding Ji	螣蛇 (Téng Shé) 天柱 (Tiān Zhù) 惊门 (Jīng Mén) Qian 6 — Bing Ding

Yang (阳) Dun# 9 Hour: **DingSi** ；直符(ZhíFú): 天禽(TiānQín)
直使(ZhíShǐ): 死门(SǐMén) ；旬首(XúnShǒu): JiaYinGui

白虎 (Bái Hǔ) 天任 (Tiān Rèn) 开门 (Kāi Mén) Xun 4 — Yi Ren	玄武 (Xuán Wǔ) 天冲 (Tiān Chōng) 休门 (Xiū Mén) Li 9 — Xin Wu	九地 (Jiǔ Dì) 天辅 (Tiān Fǔ) 生门 (Shēng Mén) Kun 2 — Ren Geng/Gui
六合 (Liù Hé) 天蓬 (Tiān Péng) 惊门 (Jīng Mén) Zhen 3 — Ji Xin	Yang (阳) Dun# 9 Hour: **DingSi** ©Calvin Yap	九天 (Jiǔ Tiān) 天英 (Tiān Yīng) 伤门 (Shāng Mén) Dui 7 — Wu Bing
太阴 (Tài Yīn) 天心 (Tiān Xīn) 死门 (Sǐ Mén) Gen 8 — Ding Yi	螣蛇 (Téng Shé) 天柱 (Tiān Zhù) 景门 (Jǐng Mén) Kan 1 — Bing Ji	值符 (Zhí Fú) 禽芮 (Qín Ruì) 杜门 (Dù Mén) Qian 6 — Geng/Gui Ding

Chart 1 — WuWu
```
Yang (阳) Dun# 9 Hour: WuWu；直符(ZhíFú): 天禽(TiānQín)
直使(ZhíShǐ): 死门(SǐMén)；旬首(XúnShǒu): JiaYinGui
```

九天 (Jiǔ Tiān)	值符 (Zhí Fú)	螣蛇 (Téng Shé)
天英 (Tiān Yīng)	禽芮 (Qín Ruì)	天柱 (Tiān Zhù)
景门 (Jǐng Mén)	死门 (Sǐ Mén)	惊门 (Jīng Mén)
Xun 4 Wu	Li 9 Geng/Gui	Kun 2 Bing
Ren	Wu	Geng/Gui
九地 (Jiǔ Dì)	Yang (阳) Dun# 9 Hour: **WuWu**	太阴 (Tài Yīn)
天辅 (Tiān Fǔ)		天心 (Tiān Xīn)
杜门 (Dù Mén)		开门 (Kāi Mén)
Zhen 3 Ren	©Calvin Yap	Dui 7 Ding
Xin		Bing
玄武 (Xuán Wǔ)	白虎 (Bái Hǔ)	六合 (Liù Hé)
天冲 (Tiān Chōng)	天任 (Tiān Rèn)	天蓬 (Tiān Péng)
伤门 (Shāng Mén)	生门 (Shēng Mén)	休门 (Xiū Mén)
Gen 8 Xin	Kan 1 Yi	Qian 6 Ji
Yi	Ji	Ding

Chart 2 — JiWei
```
Yang (阳) Dun# 9 Hour: JiWei；直符(ZhíFú): 天禽(TiānQín)
直使(ZhíShǐ): 死门(SǐMén)；旬首(XúnShǒu): JiaYinGui
```

六合 (Liù Hé)	白虎 (Bái Hǔ)	玄武 (Xuán Wǔ)
天蓬 (Tiān Péng)	天任 (Tiān Rèn)	天冲 (Tiān Chōng)
休门 (Xiū Mén)	生门 (Shēng Mén)	伤门 (Shāng Mén)
Xun 4 Ji	Li 9 Yi	Kun 2 Xin
Ren	Wu	Geng/Gui
太阴 (Tài Yīn)	Yang (阳) Dun# 9 Hour: **JiWei**	九地 (Jiǔ Dì)
天心 (Tiān Xīn)		天辅 (Tiān Fǔ)
开门 (Kāi Mén)		杜门 (Dù Mén)
Zhen 3 Ding	©Calvin Yap	Dui 7 Ren
Xin		Bing
螣蛇 (Téng Shé)	值符 (Zhí Fú)	九天 (Jiǔ Tiān)
天柱 (Tiān Zhù)	禽芮 (Qín Ruì)	天英 (Tiān Yīng)
惊门 (Jīng Mén)	死门 (Sǐ Mén)	景门 (Jǐng Mén)
Gen 8 Bing	Kan 1 Geng/Gui	Qian 6 Wu
Yi	Ji	Ding

Chart 3 — GengShen
```
Yang (阳) Dun# 9 Hour: GengShen；直符(ZhíFú): 天禽(TiānQín)
直使(ZhíShǐ): 死门(SǐMén)；旬首(XúnShǒu): JiaYinGui
```

九地 (Jiǔ Dì)	九天 (Jiǔ Tiān)	值符 (Zhí Fú)
天辅 (Tiān Fǔ)	天英 (Tiān Yīng)	禽芮 (Qín Ruì)
杜门 (Dù Mén)	景门 (Jǐng Mén)	死门 (Sǐ Mén)
Xun 4 Ren	Li 9 Wu	Kun 2 Geng/Gui
Ren	Wu	Geng/Gui
玄武 (Xuán Wǔ)	Yang (阳) Dun# 9	螣蛇 (Téng Shé)
天冲 (Tiān Chōng)	Hour: **GengShen**	天柱 (Tiān Zhù)
伤门 (Shāng Mén)	**Fu Yin**	惊门 (Jīng Mén)
Zhen 3 Xin	©Calvin Yap	Dui 7 Bing
Xin		Bing
白虎 (Bái Hǔ)	六合 (Liù Hé)	太阴 (Tài Yīn)
天任 (Tiān Rèn)	天蓬 (Tiān Péng)	天心 (Tiān Xīn)
生门 (Shēng Mén)	休门 (Xiū Mén)	开门 (Kāi Mén)
Gen 8 Yi	Kan 1 Ji	Qian 6 Ding
Yi	Ji	Ding

Chart 4 — XinYou
```
Yang (阳) Dun# 9 Hour: XinYou；直符(ZhíFú): 天禽(TiānQín)
直使(ZhíShǐ): 死门(SǐMén)；旬首(XúnShǒu): JiaYinGui
```

螣蛇 (Téng Shé)	太阴 (Tài Yīn)	六合 (Liù Hé)
天柱 (Tiān Zhù)	天心 (Tiān Xīn)	天蓬 (Tiān Péng)
惊门 (Jīng Mén)	开门 (Kāi Mén)	休门 (Xiū Mén)
Xun 4 Bing	Li 9 Ding	Kun 2 Ji
Ren	Wu	Geng/Gui
值符 (Zhí Fú)	Yang (阳) Dun# 9	白虎 (Bái Hǔ)
禽芮 (Qín Ruì)	Hour: **XinYou**	天任 (Tiān Rèn)
死门 (Sǐ Mén)		生门 (Shēng Mén)
Zhen 3 Geng/Gui	©Calvin Yap	Dui 7 Yi
Xin		Bing
九天 (Jiǔ Tiān)	九地 (Jiǔ Dì)	玄武 (Xuán Wǔ)
天英 (Tiān Yīng)	天辅 (Tiān Fǔ)	天冲 (Tiān Chōng)
景门 (Jǐng Mén)	杜门 (Dù Mén)	伤门 (Shāng Mén)
Gen 8 Wu	Kan 1 Ren	Qian 6 Xin
Yi	Ji	Ding

Chart 5 — RenXu
```
Yang (阳) Dun# 9 Hour: RenXu；直符(ZhíFú): 天禽(TiānQín)
直使(ZhíShǐ): 死门(SǐMén)；旬首(XúnShǒu): JiaYinGui
```

值符 (Zhí Fú)	螣蛇 (Téng Shé)	太阴 (Tài Yīn)
禽芮 (Qín Ruì)	天柱 (Tiān Zhù)	天心 (Tiān Xīn)
死门 (Sǐ Mén)	惊门 (Jīng Mén)	开门 (Kāi Mén)
Xun 4 Geng/Gui	Li 9 Bing	Kun 2 Ding
Ren	Wu	Geng/Gui
九天 (Jiǔ Tiān)	Yang (阳) Dun# 9	六合 (Liù Hé)
天英 (Tiān Yīng)	Hour: **RenXu**	天蓬 (Tiān Péng)
景门 (Jǐng Mén)		休门 (Xiū Mén)
Zhen 3 Wu	©Calvin Yap	Dui 7 Ji
Xin		Bing
九地 (Jiǔ Dì)	玄武 (Xuán Wǔ)	白虎 (Bái Hǔ)
天辅 (Tiān Fǔ)	天冲 (Tiān Chōng)	天任 (Tiān Rèn)
杜门 (Dù Mén)	伤门 (Shāng Mén)	生门 (Shēng Mén)
Gen 8 Ren	Kan 1 Xin	Qian 6 Yi
Yi	Ji	Ding

Chart 6 — GuiHai
```
Yang (阳) Dun# 9 Hour: GuiHai；直符(ZhíFú): 天禽(TiānQín)
直使(ZhíShǐ): 死门(SǐMén)；旬首(XúnShǒu): JiaYinGui
```

九地 (Jiǔ Dì)	九天 (Jiǔ Tiān)	值符 (Zhí Fú)
天辅 (Tiān Fǔ)	天英 (Tiān Yīng)	禽芮 (Qín Ruì)
杜门 (Dù Mén)	景门 (Jǐng Mén)	死门 (Sǐ Mén)
Xun 4 Ren	Li 9 Wu	Kun 2 Geng/Gui
Ren	Wu	Geng/Gui
玄武 (Xuán Wǔ)	Yang (阳) Dun# 9	螣蛇 (Téng Shé)
天冲 (Tiān Chōng)	Hour: **GuiHai**	天柱 (Tiān Zhù)
伤门 (Shāng Mén)	**Fu Yin**	惊门 (Jīng Mén)
Zhen 3 Xin	©Calvin Yap	Dui 7 Bing
Xin		Bing
白虎 (Bái Hǔ)	六合 (Liù Hé)	太阴 (Tài Yīn)
天任 (Tiān Rèn)	天蓬 (Tiān Péng)	天心 (Tiān Xīn)
生门 (Shēng Mén)	休门 (Xiū Mén)	开门 (Kāi Mén)
Gen 8 Yi	Kan 1 Ji	Qian 6 Ding
Yi	Ji	Ding

Yin Dun#1

Chart: -1JiaZi (Yin Dun #1 JiaZi Xun)
JiaZi, YiChou, BingYin, DingMao, WuChen, JiSi, GengWu, XinWei, RenShen, GuiYou

Yin (阴) Dun# 1 Hour: **JiaZi**；直符(ZhíFú): 天蓬(TiānPéng)
直使(ZhíShǐ): 休门(XiūMén)；旬首(XúnShǒu): JiaZiWu

玄武 (Xuán Wǔ) 天辅 (Tiān Fǔ) 杜门 (Dù Mén) Xun 4 — Ding Ding	白虎 (Bái Hǔ) 天英 (Tiān Yīng) 景门 (Jǐng Mén) Li 9 — Ji Ji	六合 (Liù Hé) 禽芮 (Qín Ruì) 死门 (Sǐ Mén) Kun 2 — Yi/Gui Yi/Gui
九地 (Jiǔ Dì) 天冲 (Tiān Chōng) 伤门 (Shāng Mén) Zhen 3 — Bing Bing	Yin (阴) Dun# 1 Hour: **JiaZi** **Fu Yin** ©Calvin Yap	太阴 (Tài Yīn) 天柱 (Tiān Zhù) 惊门 (Jīng Mén) Dui 7 — Xin Xin
九天 (Jiǔ Tiān) 天任 (Tiān Rèn) 生门 (Shēng Mén) Gen 8 — Geng Geng	值符 (Zhí Fú) 天蓬 (Tiān Péng) 休门 (Xiū Mén) Kan 1 — Wu Wu	螣蛇 (Téng Shé) 天心 (Tiān Xīn) 开门 (Kāi Mén) Qian 6 — Ren Ren

Yin (阴) Dun# 1 Hour: **YiChou**；直符(ZhíFú): 天蓬(TiānPéng)
直使(ZhíShǐ): 休门(XiūMén)；旬首(XúnShǒu): JiaZiWu

太阴 (Tài Yīn) 天柱 (Tiān Zhù) 开门 (Kāi Mén) Xun 4 — Ding Ding	螣蛇 (Téng Shé) 天心 (Tiān Xīn) 休门 (Xiū Mén) Li 9 — Ren Ji	值符 (Zhí Fú) 天蓬 (Tiān Péng) 生门 (Shēng Mén) Kun 2 — Wu Yi/Gui
六合 (Liù Hé) 禽芮 (Qín Ruì) 惊门 (Jīng Mén) Zhen 3 — Yi/Gui Bing	Yin (阴) Dun# 1 Hour: **YiChou** ©Calvin Yap	九天 (Jiǔ Tiān) 天任 (Tiān Rèn) 伤门 (Shāng Mén) Dui 7 — Geng Xin
白虎 (Bái Hǔ) 天英 (Tiān Yīng) 死门 (Sǐ Mén) Gen 8 — Ji Geng	玄武 (Xuán Wǔ) 天辅 (Tiān Fǔ) 景门 (Jǐng Mén) Kan 1 — Ding Wu	九地 (Jiǔ Dì) 天冲 (Tiān Chōng) 杜门 (Dù Mén) Qian 6 — Bing Ren

Yin (阴) Dun# 1 Hour: **BingYin**；直符(ZhíFú): 天蓬(TiānPéng)
直使(ZhíShǐ): 休门(XiūMén)；旬首(XúnShǒu): JiaZiWu

九天 (Jiǔ Tiān) 天任 (Tiān Rèn) 伤门 (Shāng Mén) Xun 4 — Geng Ding	九地 (Jiǔ Dì) 天冲 (Tiān Chōng) 杜门 (Dù Mén) Li 9 — Bing Ji	玄武 (Xuán Wǔ) 天辅 (Tiān Fǔ) 景门 (Jǐng Mén) Kun 2 — Ding Yi/Gui
值符 (Zhí Fú) 天蓬 (Tiān Péng) 生门 (Shēng Mén) Zhen 3 — Wu Bing	Yin (阴) Dun# 1 Hour: **BingYin** ©Calvin Yap	白虎 (Bái Hǔ) 天英 (Tiān Yīng) 死门 (Sǐ Mén) Dui 7 — Ji Xin
螣蛇 (Téng Shé) 天心 (Tiān Xīn) 休门 (Xiū Mén) Gen 8 — Ren Geng	太阴 (Tài Yīn) 天柱 (Tiān Zhù) 开门 (Kāi Mén) Kan 1 — Xin Wu	六合 (Liù Hé) 禽芮 (Qín Ruì) 惊门 (Jīng Mén) Qian 6 — Yi/Gui Ren

Yin (阴) Dun# 1 Hour: **DingMao**；直符(ZhíFú): 天蓬(TiānPéng)
直使(ZhíShǐ): 休门(XiūMén)；旬首(XúnShǒu): JiaZiWu

值符 (Zhí Fú) 天蓬 (Tiān Péng) 死门 (Sǐ Mén) Xun 4 — Wu Ding	九天 (Jiǔ Tiān) 天任 (Tiān Rèn) 惊门 (Jīng Mén) Li 9 — Geng Ji	九地 (Jiǔ Dì) 天冲 (Tiān Chōng) 开门 (Kāi Mén) Kun 2 — Bing Yi/Gui
螣蛇 (Téng Shé) 天心 (Tiān Xīn) 景门 (Jǐng Mén) Zhen 3 — Ren Bing	Yin (阴) Dun# 1 Hour: **DingMao** ©Calvin Yap	玄武 (Xuán Wǔ) 天辅 (Tiān Fǔ) 休门 (Xiū Mén) Dui 7 — Ding Xin
太阴 (Tài Yīn) 天柱 (Tiān Zhù) 杜门 (Dù Mén) Gen 8 — Xin Geng	六合 (Liù Hé) 禽芮 (Qín Ruì) 伤门 (Shāng Mén) Kan 1 — Yi/Gui Wu	白虎 (Bái Hǔ) 天英 (Tiān Yīng) 生门 (Shēng Mén) Qian 6 — Ji Ren

Yin (阴) Dun# 1 Hour: **WuChen**；直符(ZhíFú): 天蓬(TiānPéng)
直使(ZhíShǐ): 休门(XiūMén)；旬首(XúnShǒu): JiaZiWu

玄武 (Xuán Wǔ) 天辅 (Tiān Fǔ) 景门 (Jǐng Mén) Xun 4 — Ding Ding	白虎 (Bái Hǔ) 天英 (Tiān Yīng) 死门 (Sǐ Mén) Li 9 — Ji Ji	六合 (Liù Hé) 禽芮 (Qín Ruì) 惊门 (Jīng Mén) Kun 2 — Yi/Gui Yi/Gui
九地 (Jiǔ Dì) 天冲 (Tiān Chōng) 杜门 (Dù Mén) Zhen 3 — Bing Bing	Yin (阴) Dun# 1 Hour: **WuChen** **Fu Yin** ©Calvin Yap	太阴 (Tài Yīn) 天柱 (Tiān Zhù) 开门 (Kāi Mén) Dui 7 — Xin Xin
九天 (Jiǔ Tiān) 天任 (Tiān Rèn) 伤门 (Shāng Mén) Gen 8 — Geng Geng	值符 (Zhí Fú) 天蓬 (Tiān Péng) 生门 (Shēng Mén) Kan 1 — Wu Wu	螣蛇 (Téng Shé) 天心 (Tiān Xīn) 休门 (Xiū Mén) Qian 6 — Ren Ren

Yin (阴) Dun# 1 Hour: **JiSi**；直符(ZhíFú): 天蓬(TiānPéng)
直使(ZhíShǐ): 休门(XiūMén)；旬首(XúnShǒu): JiaZiWu

螣蛇 (Téng Shé) 天心 (Tiān Xīn) 惊门 (Jīng Mén) Xun 4 — Ren Ding	值符 (Zhí Fú) 天蓬 (Tiān Péng) 开门 (Kāi Mén) Li 9 — Wu Ji	九天 (Jiǔ Tiān) 天任 (Tiān Rèn) 休门 (Xiū Mén) Kun 2 — Geng Yi/Gui
太阴 (Tài Yīn) 天柱 (Tiān Zhù) 死门 (Sǐ Mén) Zhen 3 — Xin Bing	Yin (阴) Dun# 1 Hour: **JiSi** **Fan Yin** ©Calvin Yap	九地 (Jiǔ Dì) 天冲 (Tiān Chōng) 生门 (Shēng Mén) Dui 7 — Bing Xin
六合 (Liù Hé) 禽芮 (Qín Ruì) 景门 (Jǐng Mén) Gen 8 — Yi/Gui Geng	白虎 (Bái Hǔ) 天英 (Tiān Yīng) 杜门 (Dù Mén) Kan 1 — Ji Wu	玄武 (Xuán Wǔ) 天辅 (Tiān Fǔ) 伤门 (Shāng Mén) Qian 6 — Ding Ren

Yin (阴) Dun# 1 Hour: **GengWu** ; 直符(ZhíFú): 天蓬(TiānPéng)
直使(ZhíShǐ): 休门(XiūMén) ; 旬首(XúnShǒu): JiaZiWu

九地 (Jiǔ Dì) 天冲 (Tiān Chōng) 休门 (Xiū Mén) Xun 4 Bing Ding	玄武 (Xuán Wǔ) 天辅 (Tiān Fǔ) 生门 (Shēng Mén) Li 9 Ding Ji	白虎 (Bái Hǔ) 天英 (Tiān Yīng) 伤门 (Shāng Mén) Kun 2 Ji Yi/Gui
九天 (Jiǔ Tiān) 天任 (Tiān Rèn) 开门 (Kāi Mén) Zhen 3 Geng Bing	Yin (阴) Dun# 1 Hour: **GengWu** ©Calvin Yap	六合 (Liù Hé) 禽芮 (Qín Ruì) 杜门 (Dù Mén) Dui 7 Yi/Gui Xin
值符 (Zhí Fú) 天蓬 (Tiān Péng) 惊门 (Jīng Mén) Gen 8 Wu Geng	螣蛇 (Téng Shé) 天心 (Tiān Xīn) 死门 (Sǐ Mén) Kan 1 Ren Wu	太阴 (Tài Yīn) 天柱 (Tiān Zhù) 景门 (Jǐng Mén) Qian 6 Xin Ren

Yin (阴) Dun# 1 Hour: **XinWei** ; 直符(ZhíFú): 天蓬(TiānPéng)
直使(ZhíShǐ): 休门(XiūMén) ; 旬首(XúnShǒu): JiaZiWu

六合 (Liù Hé) 禽芮 (Qín Ruì) 生门 (Shēng Mén) Xun 4 Yi/Gui Ding	太阴 (Tài Yīn) 天柱 (Tiān Zhù) 伤门 (Shāng Mén) Li 9 Xin Ji	螣蛇 (Téng Shé) 天心 (Tiān Xīn) 杜门 (Dù Mén) Kun 2 Ren Yi/Gui
白虎 (Bái Hǔ) 天英 (Tiān Yīng) 休门 (Xiū Mén) Zhen 3 Ji Bing	Yin (阴) Dun# 1 Hour: **XinWei** ©Calvin Yap	值符 (Zhí Fú) 天蓬 (Tiān Péng) 景门 (Jǐng Mén) Dui 7 Wu Xin
玄武 (Xuán Wǔ) 天辅 (Tiān Fǔ) 开门 (Kāi Mén) Gen 8 Ding Geng	九地 (Jiǔ Dì) 天冲 (Tiān Chōng) 惊门 (Jīng Mén) Kan 1 Bing Wu	九天 (Jiǔ Tiān) 天任 (Tiān Rèn) 死门 (Sǐ Mén) Qian 6 Geng Ren

Yin (阴) Dun# 1 Hour: **RenShen** ; 直符(ZhíFú): 天蓬(TiānPéng)
直使(ZhíShǐ): 休门(XiūMén) ; 旬首(XúnShǒu): JiaZiWu

白虎 (Bái Hǔ) 天英 (Tiān Yīng) 惊门 (Jīng Mén) Xun 4 Ji Ding	六合 (Liù Hé) 禽芮 (Qín Ruì) 开门 (Kāi Mén) Li 9 Yi/Gui Ji	太阴 (Tài Yīn) 天柱 (Tiān Zhù) 休门 (Xiū Mén) Kun 2 Xin Yi/Gui
玄武 (Xuán Wǔ) 天辅 (Tiān Fǔ) 死门 (Sǐ Mén) Zhen 3 Ding Bing	Yin (阴) Dun# 1 Hour: **RenShen** ©Calvin Yap	螣蛇 (Téng Shé) 天心 (Tiān Xīn) 生门 (Shēng Mén) Dui 7 Ren Xin
九地 (Jiǔ Dì) 天冲 (Tiān Chōng) 景门 (Jǐng Mén) Gen 8 Bing Geng	九天 (Jiǔ Tiān) 天任 (Tiān Rèn) 杜门 (Dù Mén) Kan 1 Geng Wu	值符 (Zhí Fú) 天蓬 (Tiān Péng) 伤门 (Shāng Mén) Qian 6 Wu Ren

Yin (阴) Dun# 1 Hour: **GuiYou** ; 直符(ZhíFú): 天蓬(TiānPéng)
直使(ZhíShǐ): 休门(XiūMén) ; 旬首(XúnShǒu): JiaZiWu

太阴 (Tài Yīn) 天柱 (Tiān Zhù) 杜门 (Dù Mén) Xun 4 Xin Ding	螣蛇 (Téng Shé) 天心 (Tiān Xīn) 景门 (Jǐng Mén) Li 9 Ren Ji	值符 (Zhí Fú) 天蓬 (Tiān Péng) 死门 (Sǐ Mén) Kun 2 Wu Yi/Gui
六合 (Liù Hé) 禽芮 (Qín Ruì) 伤门 (Shāng Mén) Zhen 3 Yi/Gui Bing	Yin (阴) Dun# 1 Hour: **GuiYou** ©Calvin Yap	九天 (Jiǔ Tiān) 天任 (Tiān Rèn) 惊门 (Jīng Mén) Dui 7 Geng Xin
白虎 (Bái Hǔ) 天英 (Tiān Yīng) 生门 (Shēng Mén) Gen 8 Ji Geng	玄武 (Xuán Wǔ) 天辅 (Tiān Fǔ) 休门 (Xiū Mén) Kan 1 Ding Wu	九地 (Jiǔ Dì) 天冲 (Tiān Chōng) 开门 (Kāi Mén) Qian 6 Bing Ren

Chart: **-1JiaXu** (Yin Dun #1 JiaXu Xun)
JiaXu, YiHai, BingZi, DingChou, WuYin, JiMao, GengChen, XinSi, RenWu, GuiWei

Yin (阴) Dun# 1 Hour: **JiaXu** ; 直符(ZhíFú): 天英(TiānYīng)
直使(ZhíShǐ): 景门(JǐngMén) ; 旬首(XúnShǒu): JiaXuJi

螣蛇 (Téng Shé) 天辅 (Tiān Fǔ) 杜门 (Dù Mén) Xun 4 Ding Ding	值符 (Zhí Fú) 天英 (Tiān Yīng) 景门 (Jǐng Mén) Li 9 Ji Ji	九天 (Jiǔ Tiān) 禽芮 (Qín Ruì) 死门 (Sǐ Mén) Kun 2 Yi/Gui Yi/Gui
太阴 (Tài Yīn) 天冲 (Tiān Chōng) 伤门 (Shāng Mén) Zhen 3 Bing Bing	Yin (阴) Dun# 1 Hour: **JiaXu** **Fu Yin** ©Calvin Yap	九地 (Jiǔ Dì) 天柱 (Tiān Zhù) 惊门 (Jīng Mén) Dui 7 Xin Xin
六合 (Liù Hé) 天任 (Tiān Rèn) 生门 (Shēng Mén) Gen 8 Geng Geng	白虎 (Bái Hǔ) 天蓬 (Tiān Péng) 休门 (Xiū Mén) Kan 1 Wu Wu	玄武 (Xuán Wǔ) 天心 (Tiān Xīn) 开门 (Kāi Mén) Qian 6 Ren Ren

Yin (阴) Dun# 1 Hour: **YiHai** ; 直符(ZhíFú): 天英(TiānYīng)
直使(ZhíShǐ): 景门(JǐngMén) ; 旬首(XúnShǒu): JiaXuJi

太阴 (Tài Yīn) 天冲 (Tiān Chōng) 惊门 (Jīng Mén) Xun 4 Bing Ding	螣蛇 (Téng Shé) 天辅 (Tiān Fǔ) 开门 (Kāi Mén) Li 9 Ding Ji	值符 (Zhí Fú) 天英 (Tiān Yīng) 休门 (Xiū Mén) Kun 2 Ji Yi/Gui
六合 (Liù Hé) 天任 (Tiān Rèn) 死门 (Sǐ Mén) Zhen 3 Geng Bing	Yin (阴) Dun# 1 Hour: **YiHai** ©Calvin Yap	九天 (Jiǔ Tiān) 禽芮 (Qín Ruì) 生门 (Shēng Mén) Dui 7 Yi/Gui Xin
白虎 (Bái Hǔ) 天蓬 (Tiān Péng) 景门 (Jǐng Mén) Gen 8 Wu Geng	玄武 (Xuán Wǔ) 天心 (Tiān Xīn) 杜门 (Dù Mén) Kan 1 Ren Wu	九地 (Jiǔ Dì) 天柱 (Tiān Zhù) 伤门 (Shāng Mén) Qian 6 Xin Ren

Yin (阴) Dun# 1 Hour: BingZi；直符(ZhíFú): 天英(TiānYīng)
直使(ZhíShǐ): 景门(JǐngMén)；旬首(XúnShǒu): JiaXuJi

九天 (Jiǔ Tiān) 禽芮 (Qín Ruì) 生门 (Shēng Mén) Xun 4　Yi/Gui Ding	九地 (Jiǔ Dì) 天柱 (Tiān Zhù) 伤门 (Shāng Mén) Li 9　Xin Ji	玄武 (Xuán Wǔ) 天心 (Tiān Xīn) 杜门 (Dù Mén) Kun 2　Ren Yi/Gui
值符 (Zhí Fú) 天英 (Tiān Yīng) 休门 (Xiū Mén) Zhen 3　Ji Bing	Yin (阴) Dun# 1 Hour: **BingZi** ©Calvin Yap	白虎 (Bái Hǔ) 天蓬 (Tiān Péng) 景门 (Jǐng Mén) Dui 7　Wu Xin
螣蛇 (Téng Shé) 天辅 (Tiān Fǔ) 开门 (Kāi Mén) Gen 8　Ding Geng	太阴 (Tài Yīn) 天冲 (Tiān Chōng) 惊门 (Jīng Mén) Kan 1　Bing Wu	六合 (Liù Hé) 天任 (Tiān Rèn) 死门 (Sǐ Mén) Qian 6　Geng Ren

Yin (阴) Dun# 1 Hour: DingChou；直符(ZhíFú): 天英(TiānYīng)
直使(ZhíShǐ): 景门(JǐngMén)；旬首(XúnShǒu): JiaXuJi

值符 (Zhí Fú) 天英 (Tiān Yīng) 休门 (Xiū Mén) Xun 4　Ji	九天 (Jiǔ Tiān) 禽芮 (Qín Ruì) 生门 (Shēng Mén) Li 9　Yi/Gui Ji	九地 (Jiǔ Dì) 天柱 (Tiān Zhù) 伤门 (Shāng Mén) Kun 2　Xin Yi/Gui
螣蛇 (Téng Shé) 天辅 (Tiān Fǔ) 开门 (Kāi Mén) Zhen 3　Ding Bing	Yin (阴) Dun# 1 Hour: **DingChou** ©Calvin Yap	玄武 (Xuán Wǔ) 天心 (Tiān Xīn) 杜门 (Dù Mén) Dui 7　Ren Xin
太阴 (Tài Yīn) 天冲 (Tiān Chōng) 惊门 (Jīng Mén) Gen 8　Bing Geng	六合 (Liù Hé) 天任 (Tiān Rèn) 死门 (Sǐ Mén) Kan 1　Geng Wu	白虎 (Bái Hǔ) 天蓬 (Tiān Péng) 景门 (Jǐng Mén) Qian 6　Wu Ren

Yin (阴) Dun# 1 Hour: WuYin；直符(ZhíFú): 天英(TiānYīng)
直使(ZhíShǐ): 景门(JǐngMén)；旬首(XúnShǒu): JiaXuJi

玄武 (Xuán Wǔ) 天心 (Tiān Xīn) 伤门 (Shāng Mén) Xun 4　Ren Ding	白虎 (Bái Hǔ) 天蓬 (Tiān Péng) 杜门 (Dù Mén) Li 9　Wu Ji	六合 (Liù Hé) 天任 (Tiān Rèn) 景门 (Jǐng Mén) Kun 2　Geng Yi/Gui
九地 (Jiǔ Dì) 天柱 (Tiān Zhù) 生门 (Shēng Mén) Zhen 3　Xin Bing	Yin (阴) Dun# 1 Hour: **WuYin** **Fan Yin** ©Calvin Yap	太阴 (Tài Yīn) 天冲 (Tiān Chōng) 死门 (Sǐ Mén) Dui 7　Bing Xin
九天 (Jiǔ Tiān) 禽芮 (Qín Ruì) 休门 (Xiū Mén) Gen 8　Yi/Gui Geng	值符 (Zhí Fú) 天英 (Tiān Yīng) 开门 (Kāi Mén) Kan 1　Ji Wu	螣蛇 (Téng Shé) 天辅 (Tiān Fǔ) 惊门 (Jīng Mén) Qian 6　Ding Ren

Yin (阴) Dun# 1 Hour: JiMao；直符(ZhíFú): 天英(TiānYīng)
直使(ZhíShǐ): 景门(JǐngMén)；旬首(XúnShǒu): JiaXuJi

螣蛇 (Téng Shé) 天辅 (Tiān Fǔ) 景门 (Jǐng Mén) Xun 4　Ding Ding	值符 (Zhí Fú) 天英 (Tiān Yīng) 死门 (Sǐ Mén) Li 9　Ji Ji	九天 (Jiǔ Tiān) 禽芮 (Qín Ruì) 惊门 (Jīng Mén) Kun 2　Yi/Gui Yi/Gui
太阴 (Tài Yīn) 天冲 (Tiān Chōng) 杜门 (Dù Mén) Zhen 3　Bing Bing	Yin (阴) Dun# 1 Hour: **JiMao** **Fu Yin** ©Calvin Yap	九地 (Jiǔ Dì) 天柱 (Tiān Zhù) 开门 (Kāi Mén) Dui 7　Xin Xin
六合 (Liù Hé) 天任 (Tiān Rèn) 伤门 (Shāng Mén) Gen 8　Geng Geng	白虎 (Bái Hǔ) 天蓬 (Tiān Péng) 生门 (Shēng Mén) Kan 1　Wu Wu	玄武 (Xuán Wǔ) 天心 (Tiān Xīn) 休门 (Xiū Mén) Qian 6　Ren Ren

Yin (阴) Dun# 1 Hour: GengChen；直符(ZhíFú): 天英(TiānYīng)
直使(ZhíShǐ): 景门(JǐngMén)；旬首(XúnShǒu): JiaXuJi

九地 (Jiǔ Dì) 天柱 (Tiān Zhù) 死门 (Sǐ Mén) Xun 4　Xin Ding	玄武 (Xuán Wǔ) 天心 (Tiān Xīn) 惊门 (Jīng Mén) Li 9　Ren Ji	白虎 (Bái Hǔ) 天蓬 (Tiān Péng) 开门 (Kāi Mén) Kun 2　Wu Yi/Gui
九天 (Jiǔ Tiān) 禽芮 (Qín Ruì) 景门 (Jǐng Mén) Zhen 3　Yi/Gui Bing	Yin (阴) Dun# 1 Hour: **GengChen** ©Calvin Yap	六合 (Liù Hé) 天任 (Tiān Rèn) 休门 (Xiū Mén) Dui 7　Geng Xin
值符 (Zhí Fú) 天英 (Tiān Yīng) 杜门 (Dù Mén) Gen 8　Ji Geng	螣蛇 (Téng Shé) 天辅 (Tiān Fǔ) 伤门 (Shāng Mén) Kan 1　Ding Wu	太阴 (Tài Yīn) 天冲 (Tiān Chōng) 生门 (Shēng Mén) Qian 6　Bing Ren

Yin (阴) Dun# 1 Hour: XinSi；直符(ZhíFú): 天英(TiānYīng)
直使(ZhíShǐ): 景门(JǐngMén)；旬首(XúnShǒu): JiaXuJi

六合 (Liù Hé) 天任 (Tiān Rèn) 伤门 (Shāng Mén) Xun 4　Geng Ding	太阴 (Tài Yīn) 天冲 (Tiān Chōng) 杜门 (Dù Mén) Li 9　Bing Ji	螣蛇 (Téng Shé) 天辅 (Tiān Fǔ) 景门 (Jǐng Mén) Kun 2　Ding Yi/Gui
白虎 (Bái Hǔ) 天蓬 (Tiān Péng) 生门 (Shēng Mén) Zhen 3　Wu Bing	Yin (阴) Dun# 1 Hour: **XinSi** ©Calvin Yap	值符 (Zhí Fú) 天英 (Tiān Yīng) 死门 (Sǐ Mén) Dui 7　Ji Xin
玄武 (Xuán Wǔ) 天心 (Tiān Xīn) 休门 (Xiū Mén) Gen 8　Ren Geng	九地 (Jiǔ Dì) 天柱 (Tiān Zhù) 开门 (Kāi Mén) Kan 1　Xin Wu	九天 (Jiǔ Tiān) 禽芮 (Qín Ruì) 惊门 (Jīng Mén) Qian 6　Yi/Gui Ren

Yin (阴) Dun# 1 Hour: RenWu；直符(ZhíFú): 天英(TiānYīng)
直使(ZhíShǐ): 景门(JǐngMén)；旬首(XúnShǒu): JiaXuJi

白虎 (Bái Hǔ) 天蓬 (Tiān Péng) 开门 (Kāi Mén) Xun 4　Wu Ding	六合 (Liù Hé) 天任 (Tiān Rèn) 休门 (Xiū Mén) Li 9　Geng Ji	太阴 (Tài Yīn) 天冲 (Tiān Chōng) 生门 (Shēng Mén) Kun 2　Bing Yi/Gui
玄武 (Xuán Wǔ) 天心 (Tiān Xīn) 惊门 (Jǐng Mén) Zhen 3　Ren Bing	Yin (阴) Dun# 1 Hour: **RenWu** ©Calvin Yap	螣蛇 (Téng Shé) 天辅 (Tiān Fǔ) 伤门 (Shāng Mén) Dui 7　Ding Xin
九地 (Jiǔ Dì) 天柱 (Tiān Zhù) 死门 (Sǐ Mén) Gen 8　Xin Geng	九天 (Jiǔ Tiān) 禽芮 (Qín Ruì) 景门 (Jǐng Mén) Kan 1　Yi/Gui Wu	值符 (Zhí Fú) 天英 (Tiān Yīng) 杜门 (Dù Mén) Qian 6　Ji Ren

Yin (阴) Dun# 1 Hour: GuiWei；直符(ZhíFú): 天英(TiānYīng)
直使(ZhíShǐ): 景门(JǐngMén)；旬首(XúnShǒu): JiaXuJi

太阴 (Tài Yīn) 天冲 (Tiān Chōng) 杜门 (Dù Mén) Xun 4　Bing Ding	螣蛇 (Téng Shé) 天辅 (Tiān Fǔ) 景门 (Jǐng Mén) Li 9　Ding Ji	值符 (Zhí Fú) 天英 (Tiān Yīng) 死门 (Sǐ Mén) Kun 2　Ji Yi/Gui
六合 (Liù Hé) 天任 (Tiān Rèn) 伤门 (Shāng Mén) Zhen 3　Geng Bing	Yin (阴) Dun# 1 Hour: **GuiWei** ©Calvin Yap	九天 (Jiǔ Tiān) 禽芮 (Qín Ruì) 惊门 (Jǐng Mén) Dui 7　Yi/Gui Xin
白虎 (Bái Hǔ) 天蓬 (Tiān Péng) 生门 (Shēng Mén) Gen 8　Wu Geng	玄武 (Xuán Wǔ) 天心 (Tiān Xīn) 休门 (Xiū Mén) Kan 1　Ren Wu	九地 (Jiǔ Dì) 天柱 (Tiān Zhù) 开门 (Kāi Mén) Qian 6　Xin Ren

Chart: -1JiaShen (Yin Dun #1 JiaShen Xun)
JiaShen, YiYou, BingXu, DingHai, WuZi, JiChou, GengYin, XinMao, RenChen, GuiSi

Yin (阴) Dun# 1 Hour: JiaShen；直符(ZhíFú): 天任(TiānRèn)
直使(ZhíShǐ): 生门(ShēngMén)；旬首(XúnShǒu): JiaShenGeng

九地 (Jiǔ Dì) 天辅 (Tiān Fǔ) 杜门 (Dù Mén) Xun 4　Ding Ding	玄武 (Xuán Wǔ) 天英 (Tiān Yīng) 景门 (Jǐng Mén) Li 9　Ji Ji	白虎 (Bái Hǔ) 禽芮 (Qín Ruì) 死门 (Sǐ Mén) Kun 2　Yi/Gui Yi/Gui
九天 (Jiǔ Tiān) 天冲 (Tiān Chōng) 伤门 (Shāng Mén) Zhen 3　Bing Bing	Yin (阴) Dun# 1 Hour: **JiaShen** **Fu Yin** ©Calvin Yap	六合 (Liù Hé) 天柱 (Tiān Zhù) 惊门 (Jǐng Mén) Dui 7　Xin Xin
值符 (Zhí Fú) 天任 (Tiān Rèn) 生门 (Shēng Mén) Gen 8　Geng Geng	螣蛇 (Téng Shé) 天蓬 (Tiān Péng) 休门 (Xiū Mén) Kan 1　Wu Wu	太阴 (Tài Yīn) 天心 (Tiān Xīn) 开门 (Kāi Mén) Qian 6　Ren Ren

Yin (阴) Dun# 1 Hour: YiYou；直符(ZhíFú): 天任(TiānRèn)
直使(ZhíShǐ): 生门(ShēngMén)；旬首(XúnShǒu): JiaShenGeng

太阴 (Tài Yīn) 天心 (Tiān Xīn) 惊门 (Jǐng Mén) Xun 4　Ren Ding	螣蛇 (Téng Shé) 天蓬 (Tiān Péng) 开门 (Kāi Mén) Li 9　Wu Ji	值符 (Zhí Fú) 天任 (Tiān Rèn) 休门 (Xiū Mén) Kun 2　Geng Yi/Gui
六合 (Liù Hé) 天柱 (Tiān Zhù) 死门 (Sǐ Mén) Zhen 3　Xin Bing	Yin (阴) Dun# 1 Hour: **YiYou** **Fan Yin** ©Calvin Yap	九天 (Jiǔ Tiān) 天冲 (Tiān Chōng) 生门 (Shēng Mén) Dui 7　Bing Xin
白虎 (Bái Hǔ) 禽芮 (Qín Ruì) 景门 (Jǐng Mén) Gen 8　Yi/Gui Geng	玄武 (Xuán Wǔ) 天英 (Tiān Yīng) 杜门 (Dù Mén) Kan 1　Ji Wu	九地 (Jiǔ Dì) 天辅 (Tiān Fǔ) 伤门 (Shāng Mén) Qian 6　Ding Ren

Yin (阴) Dun# 1 Hour: BingXu；直符(ZhíFú): 天任(TiānRèn)
直使(ZhíShǐ): 生门(ShēngMén)；旬首(XúnShǒu): JiaShenGeng

九天 (Jiǔ Tiān) 天冲 (Tiān Chōng) 死门 (Sǐ Mén) Xun 4　Bing Ding	九地 (Jiǔ Dì) 天辅 (Tiān Fǔ) 惊门 (Jǐng Mén) Li 9　Ding Ji	玄武 (Xuán Wǔ) 天英 (Tiān Yīng) 开门 (Kāi Mén) Kun 2　Ji Yi/Gui
值符 (Zhí Fú) 天任 (Tiān Rèn) 景门 (Jǐng Mén) Zhen 3　Geng Bing	Yin (阴) Dun# 1 Hour: **BingXu** ©Calvin Yap	白虎 (Bái Hǔ) 禽芮 (Qín Ruì) 休门 (Xiū Mén) Dui 7　Yi/Gui Xin
螣蛇 (Téng Shé) 天蓬 (Tiān Péng) 杜门 (Dù Mén) Gen 8　Wu Geng	太阴 (Tài Yīn) 天心 (Tiān Xīn) 伤门 (Shāng Mén) Kan 1　Ren Wu	六合 (Liù Hé) 天柱 (Tiān Zhù) 生门 (Shēng Mén) Qian 6　Xin Ren

Yin (阴) Dun# 1 Hour: DingHai；直符(ZhíFú): 天任(TiānRèn)
直使(ZhíShǐ): 生门(ShēngMén)；旬首(XúnShǒu): JiaShenGeng

值符 (Zhí Fú) 天任 (Tiān Rèn) 开门 (Kāi Mén) Xun 4　Geng Ding	九天 (Jiǔ Tiān) 天冲 (Tiān Chōng) 休门 (Xiū Mén) Li 9　Bing Ji	九地 (Jiǔ Dì) 天辅 (Tiān Fǔ) 生门 (Shēng Mén) Kun 2　Ding Yi/Gui
螣蛇 (Téng Shé) 天蓬 (Tiān Péng) 惊门 (Jǐng Mén) Zhen 3　Wu Bing	Yin (阴) Dun# 1 Hour: **DingHai** ©Calvin Yap	玄武 (Xuán Wǔ) 天英 (Tiān Yīng) 伤门 (Shāng Mén) Dui 7　Ji Xin
太阴 (Tài Yīn) 天心 (Tiān Xīn) 死门 (Sǐ Mén) Gen 8　Ren Geng	六合 (Liù Hé) 天柱 (Tiān Zhù) 景门 (Jǐng Mén) Kan 1　Xin Wu	白虎 (Bái Hǔ) 禽芮 (Qín Ruì) 杜门 (Dù Mén) Qian 6　Yi/Gui Ren

Yin (阴) Dun# 1 Hour: **WuZi** ; 直符(ZhíFú): 天任(TiānRèn)
直使(ZhíShǐ): 生门(ShēngMén) ; 旬首(XúnShǒu): JiaShenGeng

玄武 (Xuán Wǔ) 天英 (Tiān Yīng) 生门 (Shēng Mén) Xun 4 Ji Ding	白虎 (Bái Hǔ) 禽芮 (Qín Ruì) 伤门 (Shāng Mén) Li 9 Yi/Gui Ji	六合 (Liù Hé) 天柱 (Tiān Zhù) 杜门 (Dù Mén) Kun 2 Xin
九地 (Jiǔ Dì) 天辅 (Tiān Fǔ) 休门 (Xiū Mén) Zhen 3 Ding Bing	Yin (阴) Dun# 1 Hour: **WuZi** ©Calvin Yap	太阴 (Tài Yīn) 天心 (Tiān Xīn) 景门 (Jǐng Mén) Dui 7 Ren Xin
九天 (Jiǔ Tiān) 天冲 (Tiān Chōng) 开门 (Kāi Mén) Gen 8 Bing Geng	值符 (Zhí Fú) 天任 (Tiān Rèn) 惊门 (Jīng Mén) Kan 1 Geng Wu	腾蛇 (Téng Shé) 天蓬 (Tiān Péng) 死门 (Sǐ Mén) Qian 6 Wu Ren

Yin (阴) Dun# 1 Hour: **JiChou** ; 直符(ZhíFú): 天任(TiānRèn)
直使(ZhíShǐ): 生门(ShēngMén) ; 旬首(XúnShǒu): JiaShenGeng

腾蛇 (Téng Shé) 天蓬 (Tiān Péng) 伤门 (Shāng Mén) Xun 4 Wu Ding	值符 (Zhi Fú) 天任 (Tiān Rèn) 杜门 (Dù Mén) Li 9 Geng Ji	九天 (Jiǔ Tiān) 天冲 (Tiān Chōng) 景门 (Jǐng Mén) Kun 2 Bing Yi/Gui
太阴 (Tài Yīn) 天心 (Tiān Xīn) 生门 (Shēng Mén) Zhen 3 Ren Bing	Yin (阴) Dun# 1 Hour: **JiChou** ©Calvin Yap	九地 (Jiǔ Dì) 天辅 (Tiān Fǔ) 死门 (Sǐ Mén) Dui 7 Ding Xin
六合 (Liù Hé) 天柱 (Tiān Zhù) 休门 (Xiū Mén) Gen 8 Xin Geng	白虎 (Bái Hǔ) 禽芮 (Qín Ruì) 开门 (Kāi Mén) Kan 1 Yi/Gui Wu	玄武 (Xuán Wǔ) 天英 (Tiān Yīng) 惊门 (Jīng Mén) Qian 6 Ji Ren

Yin (阴) Dun# 1 Hour: **GengYin** ; 直符(ZhíFú): 天任(TiānRèn)
直使(ZhíShǐ): 生门(ShēngMén) ; 旬首(XúnShǒu): JiaShenGeng

九地 (Jiǔ Dì) 天辅 (Tiān Fǔ) 开门 (Kāi Mén) Xun 4 Ding Ding	玄武 (Xuán Wǔ) 天英 (Tiān Yīng) 休门 (Xiū Mén) Li 9 Ji Ji	白虎 (Bái Hǔ) 禽芮 (Qín Ruì) 生门 (Shēng Mén) Kun 2 Yi/Gui Yi/Gui
九天 (Jiǔ Tiān) 天冲 (Tiān Chōng) 惊门 (Jīng Mén) Zhen 3 Bing Bing	Yin (阴) Dun# 1 Hour: **GengYin** **Fu Yin** ©Calvin Yap	六合 (Liù Hé) 天柱 (Tiān Zhù) 伤门 (Shāng Mén) Dui 7 Xin Xin
值符 (Zhi Fú) 天任 (Tiān Rèn) 死门 (Sǐ Mén) Gen 8 Geng Geng	腾蛇 (Téng Shé) 天蓬 (Tiān Péng) 景门 (Jǐng Mén) Kan 1 Wu Wu	太阴 (Tài Yīn) 天心 (Tiān Xīn) 杜门 (Dù Mén) Qian 6 Ren Ren

Yin (阴) Dun# 1 Hour: **XinMao** ; 直符(ZhíFú): 天任(TiānRèn)
直使(ZhíShǐ): 生门(ShēngMén) ; 旬首(XúnShǒu): JiaShenGeng

六合 (Liù Hé) 天柱 (Tiān Zhù) 景门 (Jǐng Mén) Xun 4 Xin Ding	太阴 (Tài Yīn) 天心 (Tiān Xīn) 死门 (Sǐ Mén) Li 9 Ren Ji	腾蛇 (Téng Shé) 天蓬 (Tiān Péng) 惊门 (Jīng Mén) Kun 2 Wu Yi/Gui
白虎 (Bái Hǔ) 禽芮 (Qín Ruì) 杜门 (Dù Mén) Zhen 3 Yi/Gui Bing	Yin (阴) Dun# 1 Hour: **XinMao** ©Calvin Yap	值符 (Zhi Fú) 天任 (Tiān Rèn) 开门 (Kāi Mén) Dui 7 Geng Xin
玄武 (Xuán Wǔ) 天英 (Tiān Yīng) 伤门 (Shāng Mén) Gen 8 Ji Geng	九地 (Jiǔ Dì) 天辅 (Tiān Fǔ) 生门 (Shēng Mén) Kan 1 Ding Wu	九天 (Jiǔ Tiān) 天冲 (Tiān Chōng) 休门 (Xiū Mén) Qian 6 Bing Ren

Yin (阴) Dun# 1 Hour: **RenChen** ; 直符(ZhíFú): 天任(TiānRèn)
直使(ZhíShǐ): 生门(ShēngMén) ; 旬首(XúnShǒu): JiaShenGeng

白虎 (Bái Hǔ) 禽芮 (Qín Ruì) 休门 (Xiū Mén) Xun 4 Yi/Gui Ding	六合 (Liù Hé) 天柱 (Tiān Zhù) 生门 (Shēng Mén) Li 9 Xin Ji	太阴 (Tài Yīn) 天心 (Tiān Xīn) 伤门 (Shāng Mén) Kun 2 Ren Yi/Gui
玄武 (Xuán Wǔ) 天英 (Tiān Yīng) 开门 (Kāi Mén) Zhen 3 Ji Bing	Yin (阴) Dun# 1 Hour: **RenChen** ©Calvin Yap	腾蛇 (Téng Shé) 天蓬 (Tiān Péng) 杜门 (Dù Mén) Dui 7 Wu Xin
九地 (Jiǔ Dì) 天辅 (Tiān Fǔ) 惊门 (Jīng Mén) Gen 8 Ding Geng	九天 (Jiǔ Tiān) 天冲 (Tiān Chōng) 死门 (Sǐ Mén) Kan 1 Bing Wu	值符 (Zhi Fú) 天任 (Tiān Rèn) 景门 (Jǐng Mén) Qian 6 Geng Ren

Yin (阴) Dun# 1 Hour: **GuiSi** ; 直符(ZhíFú): 天任(TiānRèn)
直使(ZhíShǐ): 生门(ShēngMén) ; 旬首(XúnShǒu): JiaShenGeng

太阴 (Tài Yīn) 天心 (Tiān Xīn) 杜门 (Dù Mén) Xun 4 Ren Ding	腾蛇 (Téng Shé) 天蓬 (Tiān Péng) 景门 (Jǐng Mén) Li 9 Wu Ji	值符 (Zhi Fú) 天任 (Tiān Rèn) 死门 (Sǐ Mén) Kun 2 Geng Yi/Gui
六合 (Liù Hé) 天柱 (Tiān Zhù) 伤门 (Shāng Mén) Zhen 3 Xin Bing	Yin (阴) Dun# 1 Hour: **GuiSi** **Fan Yin** ©Calvin Yap	九天 (Jiǔ Tiān) 天冲 (Tiān Chōng) 惊门 (Jīng Mén) Dui 7 Bing Xin
白虎 (Bái Hǔ) 禽芮 (Qín Ruì) 生门 (Shēng Mén) Gen 8 Yi/Gui Wu	玄武 (Xuán Wǔ) 天英 (Tiān Yīng) 休门 (Xiū Mén) Kan 1 Ji Wu	九地 (Jiǔ Dì) 天辅 (Tiān Fǔ) 开门 (Kāi Mén) Qian 6 Ding Ren

Chart: -1JiaWu (Yin Dun #1 JiaWu Xun)
JiaWu, YiWei, BingShen, DingYou, WuXu, JiHai, GengZi, XinChou, RenYin, GuiMao

---

Yin (阴) Dun# 1 Hour: **JiaWu** ; 直符(ZhíFú): 天柱(TiānZhù)
直使(ZhíShǐ): 惊门(JīngMén) ; 旬首(XúnShǒu): JiaWu/Xin

六合 (Liù Hé) 天辅 (Tiān Fǔ) 杜门 (Dù Mén) Xun 4　Ding Ding	太阴 (Tài Yīn) 天英 (Tiān Yīng) 景门 (Jǐng Mén) Li 9　Ji Ji	螣蛇 (Téng Shé) 禽芮 (Qín Ruì) 死门 (Sǐ Mén) Kun 2　Yi/Gui Yi/Gui
白虎 (Bái Hǔ) 天冲 (Tiān Chōng) 伤门 (Shāng Mén) Zhen 3　Bing Bing	Yin (阴) Dun# 1 Hour: **JiaWu** **Fu Yin** ©Calvin Yap	值符 (Zhí Fú) 天柱 (Tiān Zhù) 惊门 (Jīng Mén) Dui 7　Xin Xin
玄武 (Xuán Wǔ) 天任 (Tiān Rèn) 生门 (Shēng Mén) Gen 8　Geng Geng	九地 (Jiǔ Dì) 天蓬 (Tiān Péng) 休门 (Xiū Mén) Kan 1　Wu Wu	九天 (Jiǔ Tiān) 天心 (Tiān Xīn) 开门 (Kāi Mén) Qian 6　Ren Ren

Yin (阴) Dun# 1 Hour: **YiWei** ; 直符(ZhíFú): 天柱(TiānZhù)
直使(ZhíShǐ): 惊门(JīngMén) ; 旬首(XúnShǒu): JiaWu/Xin

太阴 (Tài Yīn) 天英 (Tiān Yīng) 伤门 (Shāng Mén) Xun 4　Ji Ding	螣蛇 (Téng Shé) 禽芮 (Qín Ruì) 杜门 (Dù Mén) Li 9　Yi/Gui Ji	值符 (Zhí Fú) 天柱 (Tiān Zhù) 景门 (Jǐng Mén) Kun 2　Xin Yi/Gui
六合 (Liù Hé) 天辅 (Tiān Fǔ) 生门 (Shēng Mén) Zhen 3　Ding Bing	Yin (阴) Dun# 1 Hour: **YiWei** ©Calvin Yap	九天 (Jiǔ Tiān) 天心 (Tiān Xīn) 死门 (Sǐ Mén) Dui 7　Ren Xin
白虎 (Bái Hǔ) 天冲 (Tiān Chōng) 开门 (Kāi Mén) Gen 8　Bing Geng	玄武 (Xuán Wǔ) 天任 (Tiān Rèn) 休门 (Xiū Mén) Kan 1　Geng Wu	九地 (Jiǔ Dì) 天蓬 (Tiān Péng) 惊门 (Jīng Mén) Qian 6　Wu Ren

Yin (阴) Dun# 1 Hour: **BingShen** ; 直符(ZhíFú): 天柱(TiānZhù)
直使(ZhíShǐ): 惊门(JīngMén) ; 旬首(XúnShǒu): JiaWu/Xin

九天 (Jiǔ Tiān) 天心 (Tiān Xīn) 景门 (Jǐng Mén) Xun 4　Ren Ding	九地 (Jiǔ Dì) 天蓬 (Tiān Péng) 死门 (Sǐ Mén) Li 9　Wu Ji	玄武 (Xuán Wǔ) 天任 (Tiān Rèn) 惊门 (Jīng Mén) Kun 2　Geng Yi/Gui
值符 (Zhí Fú) 天柱 (Tiān Zhù) 杜门 (Dù Mén) Zhen 3　Xin Bing	Yin (阴) Dun# 1 Hour: **BingShen** **Fan Yin** ©Calvin Yap	白虎 (Bái Hǔ) 天冲 (Tiān Chōng) 开门 (Kāi Mén) Dui 7　Bing Xin
螣蛇 (Téng Shé) 禽芮 (Qín Ruì) 伤门 (Shāng Mén) Gen 8　Yi/Gui Geng	太阴 (Tài Yīn) 天英 (Tiān Yīng) 生门 (Shēng Mén) Kan 1　Ji Wu	六合 (Liù Hé) 天辅 (Tiān Fǔ) 休门 (Xiū Mén) Qian 6　Ding Ren

Yin (阴) Dun# 1 Hour: **DingYou** ; 直符(ZhíFú): 天柱(TiānZhù)
直使(ZhíShǐ): 惊门(JīngMén) ; 旬首(XúnShǒu): JiaWu/Xin

值符 (Zhí Fú) 天柱 (Tiān Zhù) 惊门 (Jīng Mén) Xun 4　Xin Ding	九天 (Jiǔ Tiān) 天心 (Tiān Xīn) 开门 (Kāi Mén) Li 9　Ren Ji	九地 (Jiǔ Dì) 天蓬 (Tiān Péng) 休门 (Xiū Mén) Kun 2　Wu Yi/Gui
螣蛇 (Téng Shé) 禽芮 (Qín Ruì) 死门 (Sǐ Mén) Zhen 3　Yi/Gui Bing	Yin (阴) Dun# 1 Hour: **DingYou** ©Calvin Yap	玄武 (Xuán Wǔ) 天任 (Tiān Rèn) 生门 (Shēng Mén) Dui 7　Geng Xin
太阴 (Tài Yīn) 天英 (Tiān Yīng) 景门 (Jǐng Mén) Gen 8　Ji Geng	六合 (Liù Hé) 天辅 (Tiān Fǔ) 杜门 (Dù Mén) Kan 1　Ding Wu	白虎 (Bái Hǔ) 天冲 (Tiān Chōng) 伤门 (Shāng Mén) Qian 6　Bing Ren

Yin (阴) Dun# 1 Hour: **WuXu** ; 直符(ZhíFú): 天柱(TiānZhù)
直使(ZhíShǐ): 惊门(JīngMén) ; 旬首(XúnShǒu): JiaWu/Xin

玄武 (Xuán Wǔ) 天任 (Tiān Rèn) 开门 (Kāi Mén) Xun 4　Geng Ding	白虎 (Bái Hǔ) 天冲 (Tiān Chōng) 休门 (Xiū Mén) Li 9　Bing Ji	六合 (Liù Hé) 天辅 (Tiān Fǔ) 生门 (Shēng Mén) Kun 2　Ding Yi/Gui
九地 (Jiǔ Dì) 天蓬 (Tiān Péng) 惊门 (Jīng Mén) Zhen 3　Wu Bing	Yin (阴) Dun# 1 Hour: **WuXu** ©Calvin Yap	太阴 (Tài Yīn) 天英 (Tiān Yīng) 伤门 (Shāng Mén) Dui 7　Ji Xin
九天 (Jiǔ Tiān) 天心 (Tiān Xīn) 死门 (Sǐ Mén) Gen 8　Ren Geng	值符 (Zhí Fú) 天柱 (Tiān Zhù) 景门 (Jǐng Mén) Kan 1　Xin Wu	螣蛇 (Téng Shé) 禽芮 (Qín Ruì) 杜门 (Dù Mén) Qian 6　Yi/Gui Ren

Yin (阴) Dun# 1 Hour: **JiHai** ; 直符(ZhíFú): 天柱(TiānZhù)
直使(ZhíShǐ): 惊门(JīngMén) ; 旬首(XúnShǒu): JiaWu/Xin

螣蛇 (Téng Shé) 禽芮 (Qín Ruì) 景门 (Jǐng Mén) Xun 4　Yi/Gui Ding	值符 (Zhí Fú) 天柱 (Tiān Zhù) 死门 (Sǐ Mén) Li 9　Xin Ji	九天 (Jiǔ Tiān) 天心 (Tiān Xīn) 惊门 (Jīng Mén) Kun 2　Ren Yi/Gui
太阴 (Tài Yīn) 天英 (Tiān Yīng) 杜门 (Dù Mén) Zhen 3　Ji Bing	Yin (阴) Dun# 1 Hour: **JiHai** ©Calvin Yap	九地 (Jiǔ Dì) 天蓬 (Tiān Péng) 开门 (Kāi Mén) Dui 7　Wu Xin
六合 (Liù Hé) 天辅 (Tiān Fǔ) 伤门 (Shāng Mén) Gen 8　Ding Geng	白虎 (Bái Hǔ) 天冲 (Tiān Chōng) 生门 (Shēng Mén) Kan 1　Bing Wu	玄武 (Xuán Wǔ) 天任 (Tiān Rèn) 休门 (Xiū Mén) Qian 6　Geng Ren

Yin (阴) Dun# 1 Hour: **GengZi**；直符(ZhíFú): 天柱(TiānZhù)
直使(ZhíShǐ): 惊门(JīngMén)；旬首(XúnShǒu): JiaWu/Xin

九地 (Jiǔ Dì) 天蓬 (Tiān Péng) 生门 (Shēng Mén) Xun 4　　Wu 　　Ding	玄武 (Xuán Wǔ) 天任 (Tiān Rèn) 伤门 (Shāng Mén) Li 9　　Geng 　　Ji	白虎 (Bái Hǔ) 天冲 (Tiān Chōng) 杜门 (Dù Mén) Kun 2　　Bing 　　Yi/Gui
九天 (Jiǔ Tiān) 天心 (Tiān Xīn) 休门 (Xiū Mén) Zhen 3　　Ren 　　Bing	Yin (阴) Dun# 1 Hour: **GengZi** ©Calvin Yap	六合 (Liù Hé) 天辅 (Tiān Fǔ) 景门 (Jǐng Mén) Dui 7　　Ding 　　Xin
值符 (Zhí Fú) 天柱 (Tiān Zhù) 开门 (Kāi Mén) Gen 8　　Xin 　　Geng	腾蛇 (Téng Shé) 禽芮 (Qín Ruì) 惊门 (Jīng Mén) Kan 1　　Yi/Gui 　　Wu	太阴 (Tài Yīn) 天英 (Tiān Yīng) 死门 (Sǐ Mén) Qian 6　　Ji 　　Ren

Yin (阴) Dun# 1 Hour: **XinChou**；直符(ZhíFú): 天柱(TiānZhù)
直使(ZhíShǐ): 惊门(JīngMén)；旬首(XúnShǒu): JiaWu/Xin

六合 (Liù Hé) 天辅 (Tiān Fǔ) 死门 (Sǐ Mén) Xun 4　　Ding 　　Ding	太阴 (Tài Yīn) 天英 (Tiān Yīng) 惊门 (Jīng Mén) Li 9　　Ji	腾蛇 (Téng Shé) 禽芮 (Qín Ruì) 开门 (Kāi Mén) Kun 2　　Yi/Gui
白虎 (Bái Hǔ) 天冲 (Tiān Chōng) 景门 (Jǐng Mén) Zhen 3　　Bing 　　Bing	Yin (阴) Dun# 1 Hour: **XinChou** **Fu Yin** ©Calvin Yap	值符 (Zhí Fú) 天柱 (Tiān Zhù) 休门 (Xiū Mén) Dui 7　　Xin 　　Xin
玄武 (Xuán Wǔ) 天任 (Tiān Rèn) 杜门 (Dù Mén) Gen 8　　Geng 　　Geng	九地 (Jiǔ Dì) 天蓬 (Tiān Péng) 伤门 (Shāng Mén) Kan 1　　Wu 　　Wu	九天 (Jiǔ Tiān) 天心 (Tiān Xīn) 生门 (Shēng Mén) Qian 6　　Ren 　　Ren

Yin (阴) Dun# 1 Hour: **RenYin**；直符(ZhíFú): 天柱(TiānZhù)
直使(ZhíShǐ): 惊门(JīngMén)；旬首(XúnShǒu): JiaWu/Xin

白虎 (Bái Hǔ) 天冲 (Tiān Chōng) 休门 (Xiū Mén) Xun 4　　Bing 　　Ding	六合 (Liù Hé) 天辅 (Tiān Fǔ) 生门 (Shēng Mén) Li 9　　Ding 　　Ji	太阴 (Tài Yīn) 天英 (Tiān Yīng) 伤门 (Shāng Mén) Kun 2　　Ji 　　Yi/Gui
玄武 (Xuán Wǔ) 天任 (Tiān Rèn) 开门 (Kāi Mén) Zhen 3　　Geng 　　Bing	Yin (阴) Dun# 1 Hour: **RenYin** ©Calvin Yap	腾蛇 (Téng Shé) 禽芮 (Qin Ruì) 杜门 (Dù Mén) Dui 7　　Yi/Gui 　　Xin
九地 (Jiǔ Dì) 天蓬 (Tiān Péng) 惊门 (Jīng Mén) Gen 8　　Wu 　　Geng	九天 (Jiǔ Tiān) 天心 (Tiān Xīn) 死门 (Sǐ Mén) Kan 1　　Ren 　　Wu	值符 (Zhí Fú) 天柱 (Tiān Zhù) 景门 (Jǐng Mén) Qian 6　　Xin 　　Ren

Yin (阴) Dun# 1 Hour: **GuiMao**；直符(ZhíFú): 天柱(TiānZhù)
直使(ZhíShǐ): 惊门(JīngMén)；旬首(XúnShǒu): JiaWu/Xin

太阴 (Tài Yīn) 天英 (Tiān Yīng) 杜门 (Dù Mén) Xun 4　　Ji 　　Ding	腾蛇 (Téng Shé) 禽芮 (Qín Ruì) 景门 (Jǐng Mén) Li 9　　Yi/Gui 　　Ji	值符 (Zhí Fú) 天柱 (Tiān Zhù) 死门 (Sǐ Mén) Kun 2　　Xin 　　Yi/Gui
六合 (Liù Hé) 天辅 (Tiān Fǔ) 伤门 (Shāng Mén) Zhen 3　　Ding 　　Bing	Yin (阴) Dun# 1 Hour: **GuiMao** ©Calvin Yap	九天 (Jiǔ Tiān) 天心 (Tiān Xīn) 惊门 (Jīng Mén) Dui 7　　Ren 　　Xin
白虎 (Bái Hǔ) 天冲 (Tiān Chōng) 生门 (Shēng Mén) Gen 8　　Bing 　　Geng	玄武 (Xuán Wǔ) 天任 (Tiān Rèn) 休门 (Xiū Mén) Kan 1　　Geng 　　Wu	九地 (Jiǔ Dì) 天蓬 (Tiān Péng) 开门 (Kāi Mén) Qian 6　　Wu 　　Ren

Chart: **-1JiaChen** (Yin Dun #1 JiaChen Xun)
JiaChen, YiSi, BingWu, DingWei, WuShen, JiYou, GengXu, XinHai, RenZi, GuiChou

Yin (阴) Dun# 1 Hour: **JiaChen**；直符(ZhíFú): 天心(TiānXīn)
直使(ZhíShǐ): 开门(KāiMén)；旬首(XúnShǒu): JiaChenRen

白虎 (Bái Hǔ) 天辅 (Tiān Fǔ) 杜门 (Dù Mén) Xun 4　　Ding 　　Ding	六合 (Liù Hé) 天英 (Tiān Yīng) 景门 (Jǐng Mén) Li 9　　Ji 　　Ji	太阴 (Tài Yīn) 禽芮 (Qín Ruì) 死门 (Sǐ Mén) Kun 2　　Yi/Gui 　　Yi/Gui
玄武 (Xuán Wǔ) 天冲 (Tiān Chōng) 伤门 (Shāng Mén) Zhen 3　　Bing 　　Bing	Yin (阴) Dun# 1 Hour: **JiaChen** **Fu Yin** ©Calvin Yap	腾蛇 (Téng Shé) 天柱 (Tiān Zhù) 惊门 (Jīng Mén) Dui 7　　Xin 　　Xin
九地 (Jiǔ Dì) 天任 (Tiān Rèn) 生门 (Shēng Mén) Gen 8　　Geng 　　Geng	九天 (Jiǔ Tiān) 天蓬 (Tiān Péng) 休门 (Xiū Mén) Kan 1　　Wu 　　Wu	值符 (Zhí Fú) 天心 (Tiān Xīn) 开门 (Kāi Mén) Qian 6　　Ren 　　Ren

Yin (阴) Dun# 1 Hour: **YiSi**；直符(ZhíFú): 天心(TiānXīn)
直使(ZhíShǐ): 开门(KāiMén)；旬首(XúnShǒu): JiaChenRen

太阴 (Tài Yīn) 禽芮 (Qín Ruì) 死门 (Sǐ Mén) Xun 4　　Yi/Gui 　　Ding	腾蛇 (Téng Shé) 天柱 (Tiān Zhù) 惊门 (Jīng Mén) Li 9　　Xin 　　Ji	值符 (Zhí Fú) 天心 (Tiān Xīn) 开门 (Kāi Mén) Kun 2　　Ren 　　Yi/Gui
六合 (Liù Hé) 天英 (Tiān Yīng) 景门 (Jǐng Mén) Zhen 3　　Ji 　　Bing	Yin (阴) Dun# 1 Hour: **YiSi** ©Calvin Yap	九天 (Jiǔ Tiān) 天蓬 (Tiān Péng) 休门 (Xiū Mén) Dui 7　　Wu 　　Xin
白虎 (Bái Hǔ) 天辅 (Tiān Fǔ) 杜门 (Dù Mén) Gen 8　　Ding 　　Geng	玄武 (Xuán Wǔ) 天冲 (Tiān Chōng) 伤门 (Shāng Mén) Kan 1　　Bing 　　Wu	九地 (Jiǔ Dì) 天任 (Tiān Rèn) 生门 (Shēng Mén) Qian 6　　Geng 　　Ren

Yin (阴) Dun# 1 Hour: **BingWu**；直符(ZhíFú): 天心(TiānXīn)
直使(ZhíShǐ): 开门(KāiMén)；旬首(XúnShǒu): JiaChenRen

九天 (Jiǔ Tiān) 天蓬 (Tiān Péng) 开门 (Kāi Mén) Xun 4　Wu　Ding	九地 (Jiǔ Dì) 天任 (Tiān Rèn) 休门 (Xiū Mén) Li 9　Geng　Ji	玄武 (Xuán Wǔ) 天冲 (Tiān Chōng) 生门 (Shēng Mén) Kun 2　Bing　Yi/Gui
值符 (Zhí Fú) 天心 (Tiān Xīn) 惊门 (Jīng Mén) Zhen 3　Ren　Bing	Yin (阴) Dun# 1 Hour: **BingWu** ©Calvin Yap	白虎 (Bái Hǔ) 天辅 (Tiān Fǔ) 伤门 (Shāng Mén) Dui 7　Ding　Xin
螣蛇 (Téng Shé) 天柱 (Tiān Zhù) 死门 (Sǐ Mén) Gen 8　Xin　Geng	太阴 (Tài Yīn) 禽芮 (Qín Ruì) 景门 (Jǐng Mén) Kan 1　Yi/Gui　Wu	六合 (Liù Hé) 天英 (Tiān Yīng) 杜门 (Dù Mén) Qian 6　Ji　Ren

Yin (阴) Dun# 1 Hour: **DingWei**；直符(ZhíFú): 天心(TiānXīn)
直使(ZhíShǐ): 开门(KāiMén)；旬首(XúnShǒu): JiaChenRen

值符 (Zhí Fú) 天心 (Tiān Xīn) 休门 (Xiū Mén) Xun 4　Ren　Ding	九天 (Jiǔ Tiān) 天蓬 (Tiān Péng) 生门 (Shēng Mén) Li 9　Wu　Ji	九地 (Jiǔ Dì) 天任 (Tiān Rèn) 伤门 (Shāng Mén) Kun 2　Geng　Yi/Gui
螣蛇 (Téng Shé) 天柱 (Tiān Zhù) 开门 (Kāi Mén) Zhen 3　Xin　Bing	Yin (阴) Dun# 1 Hour: **DingWei** **Fan Yin** ©Calvin Yap	玄武 (Xuán Wǔ) 天冲 (Tiān Chōng) 杜门 (Dù Mén) Dui 7　Bing　Xin
太阴 (Tài Yīn) 禽芮 (Qín Ruì) 惊门 (Jīng Mén) Gen 8　Yi/Gui　Geng	六合 (Liù Hé) 天英 (Tiān Yīng) 死门 (Sǐ Mén) Kan 1　Ji　Wu	白虎 (Bái Hǔ) 天辅 (Tiān Fǔ) 景门 (Jǐng Mén) Qian 6　Ding　Ren

Yin (阴) Dun# 1 Hour: **WuShen**；直符(ZhíFú): 天心(TiānXīn)
直使(ZhíShǐ): 开门(KāiMén)；旬首(XúnShǒu): JiaChenRen

玄武 (Xuán Wǔ) 天冲 (Tiān Chōng) 死门 (Sǐ Mén) Xun 4　Bing　Ding	白虎 (Bái Hǔ) 天辅 (Tiān Fǔ) 惊门 (Jīng Mén) Li 9　Ding　Ji	六合 (Liù Hé) 天英 (Tiān Yīng) 开门 (Kāi Mén) Kun 2　Ji　Yi/Gui
九地 (Jiǔ Dì) 天任 (Tiān Rèn) 景门 (Jǐng Mén) Zhen 3　Geng　Bing	Yin (阴) Dun# 1 Hour: **WuShen** ©Calvin Yap	太阴 (Tài Yīn) 禽芮 (Qín Ruì) 休门 (Xiū Mén) Dui 7　Yi/Gui　Xin
九天 (Jiǔ Tiān) 天蓬 (Tiān Péng) 杜门 (Dù Mén) Gen 8　Wu　Geng	值符 (Zhí Fú) 天心 (Tiān Xīn) 伤门 (Shāng Mén) Kan 1　Ren　Wu	螣蛇 (Téng Shé) 天柱 (Tiān Zhù) 生门 (Shēng Mén) Qian 6　Xin　Ren

Yin (阴) Dun# 1 Hour: **JiYou**；直符(ZhíFú): 天心(TiānXīn)
直使(ZhíShǐ): 开门(KāiMén)；旬首(XúnShǒu): JiaChenRen

螣蛇 (Téng Shé) 天柱 (Tiān Zhù) 伤门 (Shāng Mén) Xun 4　Xin　Ding	值符 (Zhí Fú) 天心 (Tiān Xīn) 杜门 (Dù Mén) Li 9　Ren　Ji	九天 (Jiǔ Tiān) 天蓬 (Tiān Péng) 景门 (Jǐng Mén) Kun 2　Wu　Yi/Gui
太阴 (Tài Yīn) 禽芮 (Qín Ruì) 生门 (Shēng Mén) Zhen 3　Yi/Gui　Bing	Yin (阴) Dun# 1 Hour: **JiYou** ©Calvin Yap	九地 (Jiǔ Dì) 天任 (Tiān Rèn) 死门 (Sǐ Mén) Dui 7　Geng　Xin
六合 (Liù Hé) 天英 (Tiān Yīng) 休门 (Xiū Mén) Gen 8　Ji　Geng	白虎 (Bái Hǔ) 天辅 (Tiān Fǔ) 开门 (Kāi Mén) Kan 1　Ding　Wu	玄武 (Xuán Wǔ) 天冲 (Tiān Chōng) 惊门 (Jīng Mén) Qian 6　Bing　Ren

Yin (阴) Dun# 1 Hour: **GengXu**；直符(ZhíFú): 天心(TiānXīn)
直使(ZhíShǐ): 开门(KāiMén)；旬首(XúnShǒu): JiaChenRen

九地 (Jiǔ Dì) 天任 (Tiān Rèn) 惊门 (Jīng Mén) Xun 4　Geng　Ding	玄武 (Xuán Wǔ) 天冲 (Tiān Chōng) 开门 (Kāi Mén) Li 9　Bing　Ji	白虎 (Bái Hǔ) 天辅 (Tiān Fǔ) 休门 (Xiū Mén) Kun 2　Ding　Yi/Gui
九天 (Jiǔ Tiān) 天蓬 (Tiān Péng) 死门 (Sǐ Mén) Zhen 3　Wu　Bing	Yin (阴) Dun# 1 Hour: **GengXu** ©Calvin Yap	六合 (Liù Hé) 天英 (Tiān Yīng) 生门 (Shēng Mén) Dui 7　Ji　Xin
值符 (Zhí Fú) 天心 (Tiān Xīn) 景门 (Jǐng Mén) Gen 8　Ren　Geng	螣蛇 (Téng Shé) 天柱 (Tiān Zhù) 杜门 (Dù Mén) Kan 1　Xin　Wu	太阴 (Tài Yīn) 禽芮 (Qín Ruì) 伤门 (Shāng Mén) Qian 6　Yi/Gui　Ren

Yin (阴) Dun# 1 Hour: **XinHai**；直符(ZhíFú): 天心(TiānXīn)
直使(ZhíShǐ): 开门(KāiMén)；旬首(XúnShǒu): JiaChenRen

六合 (Liù Hé) 天英 (Tiān Yīng) 生门 (Shēng Mén) Xun 4　Ji　Ding	太阴 (Tài Yīn) 禽芮 (Qín Ruì) 伤门 (Shāng Mén) Li 9　Yi/Gui　Ji	螣蛇 (Téng Shé) 天柱 (Tiān Zhù) 杜门 (Dù Mén) Kun 2　Xin　Yi/Gui
白虎 (Bái Hǔ) 天辅 (Tiān Fǔ) 休门 (Xiū Mén) Zhen 3　Ding　Bing	Yin (阴) Dun# 1 Hour: **XinHai** ©Calvin Yap	值符 (Zhí Fú) 天心 (Tiān Xīn) 景门 (Jǐng Mén) Dui 7　Ren　Xin
玄武 (Xuán Wǔ) 天冲 (Tiān Chōng) 开门 (Kāi Mén) Gen 8　Bing　Geng	九地 (Jiǔ Dì) 天任 (Tiān Rèn) 惊门 (Jīng Mén) Kan 1　Geng　Wu	九天 (Jiǔ Tiān) 天蓬 (Tiān Péng) 死门 (Sǐ Mén) Qian 6　Wu　Ren

Yin (阴) Dun# 1 Hour: **RenZi**；直符(ZhíFú): 天心(TiānXīn)
直使(ZhíShǐ): 开门(KāiMén)；旬首(XúnShǒu): JiaChenRen

白虎 (Bái Hǔ) 天辅 (Tiān Fǔ) 景门 (Jǐng Mén) Xun 4　Ding Ding	六合 (Liù Hé) 天英 (Tiān Yīng) 死门 (Sǐ Mén) Li 9　Ji Ji	太阴 (Tài Yīn) 禽芮 (Qín Ruì) 惊门 (Jīng Mén) Kun 2　Yi/Gui Yi/Gui
玄武 (Xuán Wǔ) 天冲 (Tiān Chōng) 杜门 (Dù Mén) Zhen 3　Bing Bing	Yin (阴) Dun# 1 Hour: **RenZi** **Fu Yin** ©Calvin Yap	螣蛇 (Téng Shé) 天柱 (Tiān Zhù) 开门 (Kāi Mén) Dui 7　Xin Xin
九地 (Jiǔ Dì) 天任 (Tiān Rèn) 伤门 (Shāng Mén) Gen 8　Geng Geng	九天 (Jiǔ Tiān) 天蓬 (Tiān Péng) 生门 (Shēng Mén) Kan 1　Wu Wu	值符 (Zhí Fú) 天心 (Tiān Xīn) 休门 (Xiū Mén) Qian 6　Ren Ren

Yin (阴) Dun# 1 Hour: **GuiChou**；直符(ZhíFú): 天心(TiānXīn)
直使(ZhíShǐ): 开门(KāiMén)；旬首(XúnShǒu): JiaChenRen

太阴 (Tài Yīn) 禽芮 (Qín Ruì) 杜门 (Dù Mén) Xun 4　Yi/Gui Ding	螣蛇 (Téng Shé) 天柱 (Tiān Zhù) 景门 (Jǐng Mén) Li 9　Xin Ji	值符 (Zhí Fú) 天心 (Tiān Xīn) 死门 (Sǐ Mén) Kun 2　Ren Yi/Gui
六合 (Liù Hé) 天英 (Tiān Yīng) 伤门 (Shāng Mén) Zhen 3　Ji Bing	Yin (阴) Dun# 1 Hour: **GuiChou** ©Calvin Yap	九天 (Jiǔ Tiān) 天蓬 (Tiān Péng) 惊门 (Jīng Mén) Dui 7　Wu Xin
白虎 (Bái Hǔ) 天辅 (Tiān Fǔ) 生门 (Shēng Mén) Gen 8　Ding Geng	玄武 (Xuán Wǔ) 天冲 (Tiān Chōng) 休门 (Xiū Mén) Kan 1　Bing Wu	九地 (Jiǔ Dì) 天任 (Tiān Rèn) 开门 (Kāi Mén) Qian 6　Geng Ren

Chart: -1JiaYin (Yin Dun #1 JiaYin Xun)
JiaYin, YiMao, BingChen, DingSi, WuWu, JiWei, GengShen, XinYou, RenXu, GuiHai

Yin (阴) Dun# 1 Hour: **JiaYin**；直符(ZhíFú): 天禽(TiānQín)
直使(ZhíShǐ): 死门(SǐMén)；旬首(XúnShǒu): JiaYinGui

太阴 (Tài Yīn) 天辅 (Tiān Fǔ) 杜门 (Dù Mén) Xun 4　Ding Ding	螣蛇 (Téng Shé) 天英 (Tiān Yīng) 景门 (Jǐng Mén) Li 9　Ji Ji	值符 (Zhí Fú) 禽芮 (Qín Ruì) 死门 (Sǐ Mén) Kun 2　Yi/Gui Yi/Gui
六合 (Liù Hé) 天冲 (Tiān Chōng) 伤门 (Shāng Mén) Zhen 3　Bing Bing	Yin (阴) Dun# 1 Hour: **JiaYin** **Fu Yin** ©Calvin Yap	九天 (Jiǔ Tiān) 天柱 (Tiān Zhù) 惊门 (Jīng Mén) Dui 7　Xin Xin
白虎 (Bái Hǔ) 天任 (Tiān Rèn) 生门 (Shēng Mén) Gen 8　Geng Geng	玄武 (Xuán Wǔ) 天蓬 (Tiān Péng) 休门 (Xiū Mén) Kan 1　Wu Wu	九地 (Jiǔ Dì) 天心 (Tiān Xīn) 开门 (Kāi Mén) Qian 6　Ren Ren

Yin (阴) Dun# 1 Hour: **YiMao**；直符(ZhíFú): 天禽(TiānQín)
直使(ZhíShǐ): 死门(SǐMén)；旬首(XúnShǒu): JiaYinGui

太阴 (Tài Yīn) 天辅 (Tiān Fǔ) 死门 (Sǐ Mén) Xun 4　Ding Ding	螣蛇 (Téng Shé) 天英 (Tiān Yīng) 惊门 (Jīng Mén) Li 9　Ji Ji	值符 (Zhí Fú) 禽芮 (Qín Ruì) 开门 (Kāi Mén) Kun 2　Yi/Gui Yi/Gui
六合 (Liù Hé) 天冲 (Tiān Chōng) 景门 (Jǐng Mén) Zhen 3　Bing Bing	Yin (阴) Dun# 1 Hour: **YiMao** **Fu Yin** ©Calvin Yap	九天 (Jiǔ Tiān) 天柱 (Tiān Zhù) 休门 (Xiū Mén) Dui 7　Xin Xin
白虎 (Bái Hǔ) 天任 (Tiān Rèn) 杜门 (Dù Mén) Gen 8　Geng Geng	玄武 (Xuán Wǔ) 天蓬 (Tiān Péng) 伤门 (Shāng Mén) Kan 1　Wu Wu	九地 (Jiǔ Dì) 天心 (Tiān Xīn) 生门 (Shēng Mén) Qian 6　Ren Ren

Yin (阴) Dun# 1 Hour: **BingChen**；直符(ZhíFú): 天禽(TiānQín)
直使(ZhíShǐ): 死门(SǐMén)；旬首(XúnShǒu): JiaYinGui

九天 (Jiǔ Tiān) 天柱 (Tiān Zhù) 惊门 (Jīng Mén) Xun 4　Xin Ding	九地 (Jiǔ Dì) 天心 (Tiān Xīn) 开门 (Kāi Mén) Li 9　Ren Ji	玄武 (Xuán Wǔ) 天蓬 (Tiān Péng) 休门 (Xiū Mén) Kun 2　Wu Yi/Gui
值符 (Zhí Fú) 禽芮 (Qín Ruì) 死门 (Sǐ Mén) Zhen 3　Yi/Gui Bing	Yin (阴) Dun# 1 Hour: **BingChen** ©Calvin Yap	白虎 (Bái Hǔ) 天任 (Tiān Rèn) 生门 (Shēng Mén) Dui 7　Geng Xin
螣蛇 (Téng Shé) 天英 (Tiān Yīng) 景门 (Jǐng Mén) Gen 8　Ji Geng	太阴 (Tài Yīn) 天辅 (Tiān Fǔ) 杜门 (Dù Mén) Kan 1　Ding Wu	六合 (Liù Hé) 天冲 (Tiān Chōng) 伤门 (Shāng Mén) Qian 6　Bing Ren

Yin (阴) Dun# 1 Hour: **DingSi**；直符(ZhíFú): 天禽(TiānQín)
直使(ZhíShǐ): 死门(SǐMén)；旬首(XúnShǒu): JiaYinGui

值符 (Zhí Fú) 禽芮 (Qín Ruì) 杜门 (Dù Mén) Xun 4　Yi/Gui Ding	九天 (Jiǔ Tiān) 天柱 (Tiān Zhù) 景门 (Jǐng Mén) Li 9　Xin Ji	九地 (Jiǔ Dì) 天心 (Tiān Xīn) 死门 (Sǐ Mén) Kun 2　Ren Yi/Gui
螣蛇 (Téng Shé) 天英 (Tiān Yīng) 伤门 (Shāng Mén) Zhen 3　Ji Bing	Yin (阴) Dun# 1 Hour: **DingSi** ©Calvin Yap	玄武 (Xuán Wǔ) 天蓬 (Tiān Péng) 惊门 (Jīng Mén) Dui 7　Wu Xin
太阴 (Tài Yīn) 天辅 (Tiān Fǔ) 生门 (Shēng Mén) Gen 8　Ding Geng	六合 (Liù Hé) 天冲 (Tiān Chōng) 休门 (Xiū Mén) Kan 1　Bing Wu	白虎 (Bái Hǔ) 天任 (Tiān Rèn) 开门 (Kāi Mén) Qian 6　Geng Ren

Yin (阴) Dun# 1 Hour: **WuWu** ; 直符(ZhíFú): 天禽(TiānQín)
直使(ZhíShǐ): 死门(SǐMén) ; 旬首(XúnShǒu): JiaYinGui

玄武 (Xuán Wǔ) 天蓬 (Tiān Péng) 休门 (Xiū Mén) Xun 4　Wu Ding	白虎 (Bái Hǔ) 天任 (Tiān Rèn) 生门 (Shēng Mén) Li 9　Geng Ji	六合 (Liù Hé) 天冲 (Tiān Chōng) 伤门 (Shāng Mén) Kun 2　Bing Yi/Gui
九地 (Jiǔ Dì) 天心 (Tiān Xīn) 开门 (Kāi Mén) Zhen 3　Ren Bing	Yin (阴) Dun# 1 Hour: **WuWu** ©Calvin Yap	太阴 (Tài Yīn) 天辅 (Tiān Fǔ) 杜门 (Dù Mén) Dui 7　Ding Xin
九天 (Jiǔ Tiān) 天柱 (Tiān Zhù) 惊门 (Jīng Mén) Gen 8　Xin Geng	值符 (Zhí Fú) 禽芮 (Qín Ruì) 死门 (Sǐ Mén) Kan 1　Yi/Gui Wu	螣蛇 (Téng Shé) 天英 (Tiān Yīng) 景门 (Jǐng Mén) Qian 6　Ji Ren

Yin (阴) Dun# 1 Hour: **JiWei** ; 直符(ZhíFú): 天禽(TiānQín)
直使(ZhíShǐ): 死门(SǐMén) ; 旬首(XúnShǒu): JiaYinGui

螣蛇 (Téng Shé) 天英 (Tiān Yīng) 景门 (Jǐng Mén) Xun 4　Ji Ding	值符 (Zhí Fú) 禽芮 (Qín Ruì) 死门 (Sǐ Mén) Li 9　Yi/Gui Ji	九天 (Jiǔ Tiān) 天柱 (Tiān Zhù) 惊门 (Jīng Mén) Kun 2　Xin Yi/Gui
太阴 (Tài Yīn) 天辅 (Tiān Fǔ) 杜门 (Dù Mén) Zhen 3　Ding Bing	Yin (阴) Dun# 1 Hour: **JiWei** ©Calvin Yap	九地 (Jiǔ Dì) 天心 (Tiān Xīn) 开门 (Kāi Mén) Dui 7　Ren Xin
六合 (Liù Hé) 天冲 (Tiān Chōng) 伤门 (Shāng Mén) Gen 8　Bing Geng	白虎 (Bái Hǔ) 天任 (Tiān Rèn) 生门 (Shēng Mén) Kan 1　Geng Wu	玄武 (Xuán Wǔ) 天蓬 (Tiān Péng) 休门 (Xiū Mén) Qian 6　Wu Ren

Yin (阴) Dun# 1 Hour: **GengShen** ; 直符(ZhíFú): 天禽(TiānQín)
直使(ZhíShǐ): 死门(SǐMén) ; 旬首(XúnShǒu): JiaYinGui

九地 (Jiǔ Dì) 天心 (Tiān Xīn) 开门 (Kāi Mén) Xun 4　Ren Ding	玄武 (Xuán Wǔ) 天蓬 (Tiān Péng) 休门 (Xiū Mén) Li 9　Wu Ji	白虎 (Bái Hǔ) 天任 (Tiān Rèn) 生门 (Shēng Mén) Kun 2　Geng Yi/Gui
九天 (Jiǔ Tiān) 天柱 (Tiān Zhù) 惊门 (Jīng Mén) Zhen 3　Xin Bing	Yin (阴) Dun# 1 Hour: **GengShen** **Fan Yin** ©Calvin Yap	六合 (Liù Hé) 天冲 (Tiān Chōng) 伤门 (Shāng Mén) Dui 7　Bing Xin
值符 (Zhí Fú) 禽芮 (Qín Ruì) 死门 (Sǐ Mén) Gen 8　Yi/Gui Geng	螣蛇 (Téng Shé) 天英 (Tiān Yīng) 景门 (Jǐng Mén) Kan 1　Ji Wu	太阴 (Tài Yīn) 天辅 (Tiān Fǔ) 杜门 (Dù Mén) Qian 6　Ding Ren

Yin (阴) Dun# 1 Hour: **XinYou** ; 直符(ZhíFú): 天禽(TiānQín)
直使(ZhíShǐ): 死门(SǐMén) ; 旬首(XúnShǒu): JiaYinGui

六合 (Liù Hé) 天冲 (Tiān Chōng) 伤门 (Shāng Mén) Xun 4　Bing Ding	太阴 (Tài Yīn) 天辅 (Tiān Fǔ) 杜门 (Dù Mén) Li 9　Ding Ji	螣蛇 (Téng Shé) 天英 (Tiān Yīng) 景门 (Jǐng Mén) Kun 2　Ji Yi/Gui
白虎 (Bái Hǔ) 天任 (Tiān Rèn) 生门 (Shēng Mén) Zhen 3　Geng Bing	Yin (阴) Dun# 1 Hour: **XinYou** ©Calvin Yap	值符 (Zhí Fú) 禽芮 (Qín Ruì) 死门 (Sǐ Mén) Dui 7　Yi/Gui Xin
玄武 (Xuán Wǔ) 天蓬 (Tiān Péng) 休门 (Xiū Mén) Gen 8　Wu Geng	九地 (Jiǔ Dì) 天心 (Tiān Xīn) 开门 (Kāi Mén) Kan 1　Ren Wu	九天 (Jiǔ Tiān) 天柱 (Tiān Zhù) 惊门 (Jīng Mén) Qian 6　Xin Ren

Yin (阴) Dun# 1 Hour: **RenXu** ; 直符(ZhíFú): 天禽(TiānQín)
直使(ZhíShǐ): 死门(SǐMén) ; 旬首(XúnShǒu): JiaYinGui

白虎 (Bái Hǔ) 天任 (Tiān Rèn) 生门 (Shēng Mén) Xun 4　Geng Ding	六合 (Liù Hé) 天冲 (Tiān Chōng) 伤门 (Shāng Mén) Li 9　Bing Ji	太阴 (Tài Yīn) 天辅 (Tiān Fǔ) 杜门 (Dù Mén) Kun 2　Ding Yi/Gui
玄武 (Xuán Wǔ) 天蓬 (Tiān Péng) 休门 (Xiū Mén) Zhen 3　Wu Bing	Yin (阴) Dun# 1 Hour: **RenXu** ©Calvin Yap	螣蛇 (Téng Shé) 天英 (Tiān Yīng) 景门 (Jǐng Mén) Dui 7　Ji Xin
九地 (Jiǔ Dì) 天心 (Tiān Xīn) 开门 (Kāi Mén) Gen 8　Ren Geng	九天 (Jiǔ Tiān) 天柱 (Tiān Zhù) 惊门 (Jīng Mén) Kan 1　Xin Wu	值符 (Zhí Fú) 禽芮 (Qín Ruì) 死门 (Sǐ Mén) Qian 6　Yi/Gui Ren

Yin (阴) Dun# 1 Hour: **GuiHai** ; 直符(ZhíFú): 天禽(TiānQín)
直使(ZhíShǐ): 死门(SǐMén) ; 旬首(XúnShǒu): JiaYinGui

太阴 (Tài Yīn) 天辅 (Tiān Fǔ) 杜门 (Dù Mén) Xun 4　Ding Ding	螣蛇 (Téng Shé) 天英 (Tiān Yīng) 景门 (Jǐng Mén) Li 9　Ji Ji	值符 (Zhí Fú) 禽芮 (Qín Ruì) 死门 (Sǐ Mén) Kun 2　Yi/Gui Yi/Gui
六合 (Liù Hé) 天冲 (Tiān Chōng) 伤门 (Shāng Mén) Zhen 3　Bing Bing	Yin (阴) Dun# 1 Hour: **GuiHai** **Fu Yin** ©Calvin Yap	九天 (Jiǔ Tiān) 天柱 (Tiān Zhù) 惊门 (Jīng Mén) Dui 7　Xin Xin
白虎 (Bái Hǔ) 天任 (Tiān Rèn) 生门 (Shēng Mén) Gen 8　Geng Geng	玄武 (Xuán Wǔ) 天蓬 (Tiān Péng) 休门 (Xiū Mén) Kan 1　Wu Wu	九地 (Jiǔ Dì) 天心 (Tiān Xīn) 开门 (Kāi Mén) Qian 6　Ren Ren

Yin Dun#2

Chart: -2JiaZi (Yin Dun #2 JiaZi Xun)
JiaZi, YiChou, BingYin, DingMao, WuChen, JiSi, GengWu, XinWei, RenShen, GuiYou

---

Yin (阴) Dun# 2 Hour: **JiaZi**；直符(ZhíFú): 天芮(TiānRuì)
直使(ZhíShǐ): 死门(SǏMén)；旬首(XúnShǒu): JiaZiWu

太阴 (Tài Yīn) 天辅 (Tiān Fǔ) 杜门 (Dù Mén) Xun 4 Bing Bing	螣蛇 (Téng Shé) 天英 (Tiān Yīng) 景门 (Jǐng Mén) Li 9 Geng Geng	值符 (Zhí Fú) 禽芮 (Qín Ruì) 死门 (SǏ Mén) Kun 2 Wu/Ding Wu/Ding
六合 (Liù Hé) 天冲 (Tiān Chōng) 伤门 (Shāng Mén) Zhen 3 Yi Yi	Yin (阴) Dun# 2 Hour: **JiaZi** **Fu Yin** ©Calvin Yap	九天 (Jiǔ Tiān) 天柱 (Tiān Zhù) 惊门 (Jīng Mén) Dui 7 Ren Ren
白虎 (Bái Hǔ) 天任 (Tiān Rèn) 生门 (Shēng Mén) Gen 8 Xin Xin	玄武 (Xuán Wǔ) 天蓬 (Tiān Péng) 休门 (Xiū Mén) Kan 1 Ji Ji	九地 (Jiǔ Dì) 天心 (Tiān Xīn) 开门 (Kāi Mén) Qian 6 Gui Gui

Yin (阴) Dun# 2 Hour: **YiChou**；直符(ZhíFú): 天芮(TiānRuì)
直使(ZhíShǐ): 死门(SǏMén)；旬首(XúnShǒu): JiaZiWu

九天 (Jiǔ Tiān) 天柱 (Tiān Zhù) 休门 (Xiū Mén) Xun 4 Ren Bing	九地 (Jiǔ Dì) 天心 (Tiān Xīn) 生门 (Shēng Mén) Li 9 Gui Geng	玄武 (Xuán Wǔ) 天蓬 (Tiān Péng) 伤门 (Shāng Mén) Kun 2 Ji Wu/Ding
值符 (Zhí Fú) 禽芮 (Qín Ruì) 开门 (Kāi Mén) Zhen 3 Wu/Ding Yi	Yin (阴) Dun# 2 Hour: **YiChou** ©Calvin Yap	白虎 (Bái Hǔ) 天任 (Tiān Rèn) 杜门 (Dù Mén) Dui 7 Xin Ren
螣蛇 (Téng Shé) 天英 (Tiān Yīng) 惊门 (Jīng Mén) Gen 8 Geng Xin	太阴 (Tài Yīn) 天辅 (Tiān Fǔ) 死门 (SǏ Mén) Kan 1 Bing Ji	六合 (Liù Hé) 天冲 (Tiān Chōng) 景门 (Jǐng Mén) Qian 6 Yi Gui

Yin (阴) Dun# 2 Hour: **BingYin**；直符(ZhíFú): 天芮(TiānRuì)
直使(ZhíShǐ): 死门(SǏMén)；旬首(XúnShǒu): JiaZiWu

值符 (Zhí Fú) 禽芮 (Qín Ruì) 景门 (Jǐng Mén) Xun 4 Wu/Ding Bing	九天 (Jiǔ Tiān) 天柱 (Tiān Zhù) 死门 (SǏ Mén) Li 9 Ren Geng	九地 (Jiǔ Dì) 天心 (Tiān Xīn) 惊门 (Jīng Mén) Kun 2 Gui Wu/Ding
螣蛇 (Téng Shé) 天英 (Tiān Yīng) 杜门 (Dù Mén) Zhen 3 Geng Yi	Yin (阴) Dun# 2 Hour: **BingYin** ©Calvin Yap	玄武 (Xuán Wǔ) 天蓬 (Tiān Péng) 开门 (Kāi Mén) Dui 7 Ji Ren
太阴 (Tài Yīn) 天辅 (Tiān Fǔ) 伤门 (Shāng Mén) Gen 8 Bing Xin	六合 (Liù Hé) 天冲 (Tiān Chōng) 生门 (Shēng Mén) Kan 1 Yi Ji	白虎 (Bái Hǔ) 天任 (Tiān Rèn) 休门 (Xiū Mén) Qian 6 Xin Gui

Yin (阴) Dun# 2 Hour: **DingMao**；直符(ZhíFú): 天芮(TiānRuì)
直使(ZhíShǐ): 死门(SǏMén)；旬首(XúnShǒu): JiaZiWu

太阴 (Tài Yīn) 天辅 (Tiān Fǔ) 开门 (Kāi Mén) Xun 4 Bing Bing	螣蛇 (Téng Shé) 天英 (Tiān Yīng) 休门 (Xiū Mén) Li 9 Geng Geng	值符 (Zhí Fú) 禽芮 (Qín Ruì) 生门 (Shēng Mén) Kun 2 Wu/Ding Wu/Ding
六合 (Liù Hé) 天冲 (Tiān Chōng) 惊门 (Jīng Mén) Zhen 3 Yi Yi	Yin (阴) Dun# 2 Hour: **DingMao** **Fu Yin** ©Calvin Yap	九天 (Jiǔ Tiān) 天柱 (Tiān Zhù) 伤门 (Shāng Mén) Dui 7 Ren Ren
白虎 (Bái Hǔ) 天任 (Tiān Rèn) 死门 (SǏ Mén) Gen 8 Xin Xin	玄武 (Xuán Wǔ) 天蓬 (Tiān Péng) 景门 (Jǐng Mén) Kan 1 Ji Ji	九地 (Jiǔ Dì) 天心 (Tiān Xīn) 杜门 (Dù Mén) Qian 6 Gui Gui

Yin (阴) Dun# 2 Hour: **WuChen**；直符(ZhíFú): 天芮(TiānRuì)
直使(ZhíShǐ): 死门(SǏMén)；旬首(XúnShǒu): JiaZiWu

太阴 (Tài Yīn) 天辅 (Tiān Fǔ) 伤门 (Shāng Mén) Xun 4 Bing Bing	螣蛇 (Téng Shé) 天英 (Tiān Yīng) 杜门 (Dù Mén) Li 9 Geng Geng	值符 (Zhí Fú) 禽芮 (Qín Ruì) 景门 (Jǐng Mén) Kun 2 Wu/Ding Wu/Ding
六合 (Liù Hé) 天冲 (Tiān Chōng) 生门 (Shēng Mén) Zhen 3 Yi Yi	Yin (阴) Dun# 2 Hour: **WuChen** **Fu Yin** ©Calvin Yap	九天 (Jiǔ Tiān) 天柱 (Tiān Zhù) 死门 (SǏ Mén) Dui 7 Ren Ren
白虎 (Bái Hǔ) 天任 (Tiān Rèn) 休门 (Xiū Mén) Gen 8 Xin Xin	玄武 (Xuán Wǔ) 天蓬 (Tiān Péng) 开门 (Kāi Mén) Kan 1 Ji Ji	九地 (Jiǔ Dì) 天心 (Tiān Xīn) 惊门 (Jīng Mén) Qian 6 Gui Gui

Yin (阴) Dun# 2 Hour: **JiSi**；直符(ZhíFú): 天芮(TiānRuì)
直使(ZhíShǐ): 死门(SǏMén)；旬首(XúnShǒu): JiaZiWu

玄武 (Xuán Wǔ) 天蓬 (Tiān Péng) 生门 (Shēng Mén) Xun 4 Ji Bing	白虎 (Bái Hǔ) 天任 (Tiān Rèn) 伤门 (Shāng Mén) Li 9 Xin Geng	六合 (Liù Hé) 天冲 (Tiān Chōng) 杜门 (Dù Mén) Kun 2 Yi Wu/Ding
九地 (Jiǔ Dì) 天心 (Tiān Xīn) 休门 (Xiū Mén) Zhen 3 Gui Yi	Yin (阴) Dun# 2 Hour: **JiSi** ©Calvin Yap	太阴 (Tài Yīn) 天辅 (Tiān Fǔ) 景门 (Jǐng Mén) Dui 7 Bing Ren
九天 (Jiǔ Tiān) 天柱 (Tiān Zhù) 开门 (Kāi Mén) Gen 8 Ren Xin	值符 (Zhi Fú) 禽芮 (Qín Ruì) 惊门 (Jīng Mén) Kan 1 Wu/Ding Ji	螣蛇 (Téng Shé) 天英 (Tiān Yīng) 死门 (SǏ Mén) Qian 6 Geng Gui

Yin (阴) Dun# 2 Hour: **GengWu** ; 直符(ZhíFú): 天芮(TiānRuì)
直使(ZhíShǐ): 死门(SǐMén) ; 旬首(XúnShǒu): JiaZiWu

螣蛇 (Téng Shé) 天英 (Tiān Yīng) 杜门 (Dù Mén) Xun 4　Geng Bing	值符 (Zhí Fú) 禽芮 (Qín Ruì) 景门 (Jǐng Mén) Li 9　Wu/Ding Geng	九天 (Jiǔ Tiān) 天柱 (Tiān Zhù) 死门 (Sǐ Mén) Kun 2　Ren Wu/Ding
太阴 (Tài Yīn) 天辅 (Tiān Fǔ) 伤门 (Shāng Mén) Zhen 3　Bing Yi	Yin (阴) Dun# 2 Hour: **GengWu** ©Calvin Yap	九地 (Jiǔ Dì) 天心 (Tiān Xīn) 惊门 (Jīng Mén) Dui 7　Gui Ren
六合 (Liù Hé) 天冲 (Tiān Chōng) 生门 (Shēng Mén) Gen 8　Yi Xin	白虎 (Bái Hǔ) 天任 (Tiān Rèn) 休门 (Xiū Mén) Kan 1　Xin Ji	玄武 (Xuán Wǔ) 天蓬 (Tiān Péng) 开门 (Kāi Mén) Qian 6　Ji Gui

Yin (阴) Dun# 2 Hour: **XinWei** ; 直符(ZhíFú): 天芮(TiānRuì)
直使(ZhíShǐ): 死门(SǐMén) ; 旬首(XúnShǒu): JiaZiWu

九地 (Jiǔ Dì) 天心 (Tiān Xīn) 死门 (Sǐ Mén) Xun 4　Gui Bing	玄武 (Xuán Wǔ) 天蓬 (Tiān Péng) 惊门 (Jīng Mén) Li 9　Ji Geng	白虎 (Bái Hǔ) 天任 (Tiān Rèn) 开门 (Kāi Mén) Kun 2　Xin Wu/Ding
九天 (Jiǔ Tiān) 天柱 (Tiān Zhù) 景门 (Jǐng Mén) Zhen 3　Ren Yi	Yin (阴) Dun# 2 Hour: **XinWei** **Fan Yin** ©Calvin Yap	六合 (Liù Hé) 天冲 (Tiān Chōng) 休门 (Xiū Mén) Dui 7　Yi Ren
值符 (Zhí Fú) 禽芮 (Qín Ruì) 杜门 (Dù Mén) Gen 8　Wu/Ding Xin	螣蛇 (Téng Shé) 天英 (Tiān Yīng) 伤门 (Shāng Mén) Kan 1　Geng Ji	太阴 (Tài Yīn) 天辅 (Tiān Fǔ) 生门 (Shēng Mén) Qian 6　Bing Gui

Yin (阴) Dun# 2 Hour: **RenShen** ; 直符(ZhíFú): 天芮(TiānRuì)
直使(ZhíShǐ): 死门(SǐMén) ; 旬首(XúnShǒu): JiaZiWu

六合 (Liù Hé) 天冲 (Tiān Chōng) 惊门 (Jīng Mén) Xun 4　Yi Bing	太阴 (Tài Yīn) 天辅 (Tiān Fǔ) 开门 (Kāi Mén) Li 9　Bing Geng	螣蛇 (Téng Shé) 天英 (Tiān Yīng) 休门 (Xiū Mén) Kun 2　Geng Wu/Ding
白虎 (Bái Hǔ) 天任 (Tiān Rèn) 死门 (Sǐ Mén) Zhen 3　Xin Yi	Yin (阴) Dun# 2 Hour: **RenShen** ©Calvin Yap	值符 (Zhí Fú) 禽芮 (Qín Ruì) 生门 (Shēng Mén) Dui 7　Wu/Ding Ren
玄武 (Xuán Wǔ) 天蓬 (Tiān Péng) 景门 (Jǐng Mén) Gen 8　Ji Xin	九地 (Jiǔ Dì) 天心 (Tiān Xīn) 杜门 (Dù Mén) Kan 1　Gui Ji	九天 (Jiǔ Tiān) 天柱 (Tiān Zhù) 伤门 (Shāng Mén) Qian 6　Ren Gui

Yin (阴) Dun# 2 Hour: **GuiYou** ; 直符(ZhíFú): 天芮(TiānRuì)
直使(ZhíShǐ): 死门(SǐMén) ; 旬首(XúnShǒu): JiaZiWu

白虎 (Bái Hǔ) 天任 (Tiān Rèn) 杜门 (Dù Mén) Xun 4　Xin Bing	六合 (Liù Hé) 天冲 (Tiān Chōng) 景门 (Jǐng Mén) Li 9　Yi Geng	太阴 (Tài Yīn) 天辅 (Tiān Fǔ) 死门 (Sǐ Mén) Kun 2　Bing Wu/Ding
玄武 (Xuán Wǔ) 天蓬 (Tiān Péng) 伤门 (Shāng Mén) Zhen 3　Ji Yi	Yin (阴) Dun# 2 Hour: **GuiYou** ©Calvin Yap	螣蛇 (Téng Shé) 天英 (Tiān Yīng) 惊门 (Jīng Mén) Dui 7　Geng Ren
九地 (Jiǔ Dì) 天心 (Tiān Xīn) 生门 (Shēng Mén) Gen 8　Gui Xin	九天 (Jiǔ Tiān) 天柱 (Tiān Zhù) 休门 (Xiū Mén) Kan 1　Ren Ji	值符 (Zhí Fú) 禽芮 (Qín Ruì) 开门 (Kāi Mén) Qian 6　Wu/Ding Gui

---

Chart: **-2JiaXu** (Yin Dun #2 JiaXu Xun)
JiaXu, YiHai, BingZi, DingChou, WuYin, JiMao, GengChen, XinSi, RenWu, GuiWei

Yin (阴) Dun# 2 Hour: **JiaXu** ; 直符(ZhíFú): 天蓬(TiānPéng)
直使(ZhíShǐ): 休门(XiūMén) ; 旬首(XúnShǒu): JiaXuJi

玄武 (Xuán Wǔ) 天辅 (Tiān Fǔ) 杜门 (Dù Mén) Xun 4　Bing Bing	白虎 (Bái Hǔ) 天英 (Tiān Yīng) 景门 (Jǐng Mén) Li 9　Geng Geng	六合 (Liù Hé) 禽芮 (Qín Ruì) 死门 (Sǐ Mén) Kun 2　Wu/Ding Wu/Ding
九地 (Jiǔ Dì) 天冲 (Tiān Chōng) 伤门 (Shāng Mén) Zhen 3　Yi Yi	Yin (阴) Dun# 2 Hour: **JiaXu** **Fu Yin** ©Calvin Yap	太阴 (Tài Yīn) 天柱 (Tiān Zhù) 惊门 (Jīng Mén) Dui 7　Ren Ren
九天 (Jiǔ Tiān) 天任 (Tiān Rèn) 生门 (Shēng Mén) Gen 8　Xin Xin	值符 (Zhí Fú) 天蓬 (Tiān Péng) 休门 (Xiū Mén) Kan 1　Ji Ji	螣蛇 (Téng Shé) 天心 (Tiān Xīn) 开门 (Kāi Mén) Qian 6　Gui Gui

Yin (阴) Dun# 2 Hour: **YiHai** ; 直符(ZhíFú): 天蓬(TiānPéng)
直使(ZhíShǐ): 休门(XiūMén) ; 旬首(XúnShǒu): JiaXuJi

九天 (Jiǔ Tiān) 天任 (Tiān Rèn) 开门 (Kāi Mén) Xun 4　Xin Bing	九地 (Jiǔ Dì) 天冲 (Tiān Chōng) 休门 (Xiū Mén) Li 9　Yi Geng	玄武 (Xuán Wǔ) 天辅 (Tiān Fǔ) 生门 (Shēng Mén) Kun 2　Bing Wu/Ding
值符 (Zhí Fú) 天蓬 (Tiān Péng) 惊门 (Jīng Mén) Zhen 3　Ji Yi	Yin (阴) Dun# 2 Hour: **YiHai** ©Calvin Yap	白虎 (Bái Hǔ) 天英 (Tiān Yīng) 伤门 (Shāng Mén) Dui 7　Geng Ren
螣蛇 (Téng Shé) 天心 (Tiān Xīn) 死门 (Sǐ Mén) Gen 8　Gui Xin	太阴 (Tài Yīn) 天柱 (Tiān Zhù) 景门 (Jǐng Mén) Kan 1　Ren Ji	六合 (Liù Hé) 禽芮 (Qín Ruì) 杜门 (Dù Mén) Qian 6　Wu/Ding Gui

Yin (阴) Dun# 2 Hour: BingZi ; 直符(ZhíFú): 天蓬(TiānPéng)
直使(ZhíShǐ): 休门(XiūMén) ; 旬首(XúnShǒu): JiaXuJi

值符 (Zhí Fú) 天蓬 (Tiān Péng) 伤门 (Shāng Mén) Xun 4　Ji Bing	九天 (Jiǔ Tiān) 天任 (Tiān Rèn) 杜门 (Dù Mén) Li 9　Xin Geng	九地 (Jiǔ Dì) 天冲 (Tiān Chōng) 景门 (Jǐng Mén) Kun 2　Yi Wu/Ding
螣蛇 (Téng Shé) 天心 (Tiān Xīn) 生门 (Shēng Mén) Zhen 3　Gui Yi	Yin (阴) Dun# 2 Hour: **BingZi** ©Calvin Yap	玄武 (Xuán Wǔ) 天辅 (Tiān Fǔ) 死门 (Sǐ Mén) Dui 7　Bing Ren
太阴 (Tài Yīn) 天柱 (Tiān Zhù) 休门 (Xiū Mén) Gen 8　Ren Xin	六合 (Liù Hé) 禽芮 (Qín Ruì) 开门 (Kāi Mén) Kan 1　Wu/Ding Ji	白虎 (Bái Hǔ) 天英 (Tiān Yīng) 惊门 (Jīng Mén) Qian 6　Geng Gui

Yin (阴) Dun# 2 Hour: DingChou ; 直符(ZhíFú): 天蓬(TiānPéng)
直使(ZhíShǐ): 休门(XiūMén) ; 旬首(XúnShǒu): JiaXuJi

太阴 (Tài Yīn) 天柱 (Tiān Zhù) 死门 (Sǐ Mén) Xun 4　Ren Bing	螣蛇 (Téng Shé) 天心 (Tiān Xīn) 惊门 (Jīng Mén) Li 9　Gui Geng	值符 (Zhí Fú) 天蓬 (Tiān Péng) 开门 (Kāi Mén) Kun 2　Ji Wu/Ding
六合 (Liù Hé) 禽芮 (Qín Ruì) 景门 (Jǐng Mén) Zhen 3　Wu/Ding Yi	Yin (阴) Dun# 2 Hour: **DingChou** ©Calvin Yap	九天 (Jiǔ Tiān) 天任 (Tiān Rèn) 休门 (Xiū Mén) Dui 7　Xin Ren
白虎 (Bái Hǔ) 天英 (Tiān Yīng) 杜门 (Dù Mén) Gen 8　Geng Xin	玄武 (Xuán Wǔ) 天辅 (Tiān Fǔ) 伤门 (Shāng Mén) Kan 1　Bing Ji	九地 (Jiǔ Dì) 天冲 (Tiān Chōng) 生门 (Shēng Mén) Qian 6　Yi Gui

Yin (阴) Dun# 2 Hour: WuYin ; 直符(ZhíFú): 天蓬(TiānPéng)
直使(ZhíShǐ): 休门(XiūMén) ; 旬首(XúnShǒu): JiaXuJi

太阴 (Tài Yīn) 天柱 (Tiān Zhù) 景门 (Jǐng Mén) Xun 4　Ren Bing	螣蛇 (Téng Shé) 天心 (Tiān Xīn) 死门 (Sǐ Mén) Li 9　Gui Geng	值符 (Zhí Fú) 天蓬 (Tiān Péng) 惊门 (Jīng Mén) Kun 2　Ji Wu/Ding
六合 (Liù Hé) 禽芮 (Qín Ruì) 杜门 (Dù Mén) Zhen 3　Wu/Ding Yi	Yin (阴) Dun# 2 Hour: **WuYin** ©Calvin Yap	九天 (Jiǔ Tiān) 天任 (Tiān Rèn) 开门 (Kāi Mén) Dui 7　Xin Ren
白虎 (Bái Hǔ) 天英 (Tiān Yīng) 伤门 (Shāng Mén) Gen 8　Geng Xin	玄武 (Xuán Wǔ) 天辅 (Tiān Fǔ) 生门 (Shēng Mén) Kan 1　Bing Ji	九地 (Jiǔ Dì) 天冲 (Tiān Chōng) 休门 (Xiū Mén) Qian 6　Yi Gui

Yin (阴) Dun# 2 Hour: JiMao ; 直符(ZhíFú): 天蓬(TiānPéng)
直使(ZhíShǐ): 休门(XiūMén) ; 旬首(XúnShǒu): JiaXuJi

玄武 (Xuán Wǔ) 天辅 (Tiān Fǔ) 惊门 (Jīng Mén) Xun 4　Bing Bing	白虎 (Bái Hǔ) 天英 (Tiān Yīng) 开门 (Kāi Mén) Li 9　Geng Geng	六合 (Liù Hé) 禽芮 (Qín Ruì) 休门 (Xiū Mén) Kun 2　Wu/Ding Wu/Ding
九地 (Jiǔ Dì) 天冲 (Tiān Chōng) 死门 (Sǐ Mén) Zhen 3　Yi Yi	Yin (阴) Dun# 2 Hour: **JiMao** **Fu Yin** ©Calvin Yap	太阴 (Tài Yīn) 天柱 (Tiān Zhù) 生门 (Shēng Mén) Dui 7　Ren Ren
九天 (Jiǔ Tiān) 天任 (Tiān Rèn) 景门 (Jǐng Mén) Gen 8　Xin Xin	值符 (Zhí Fú) 天蓬 (Tiān Péng) 杜门 (Dù Mén) Kan 1　Ji Ji	螣蛇 (Téng Shé) 天心 (Tiān Xīn) 伤门 (Shāng Mén) Qian 6　Gui Gui

Yin (阴) Dun# 2 Hour: GengChen ; 直符(ZhíFú): 天蓬(TiānPéng)
直使(ZhíShǐ): 休门(XiūMén) ; 旬首(XúnShǒu): JiaXuJi

螣蛇 (Téng Shé) 天心 (Tiān Xīn) 休门 (Xiū Mén) Xun 4　Gui Bing	值符 (Zhí Fú) 天蓬 (Tiān Péng) 生门 (Shēng Mén) Li 9　Ji Geng	九天 (Jiǔ Tiān) 天任 (Tiān Rèn) 伤门 (Shāng Mén) Kun 2　Xin Wu/Ding
太阴 (Tài Yīn) 天柱 (Tiān Zhù) 开门 (Kāi Mén) Zhen 3　Ren Yi	Yin (阴) Dun# 2 Hour: **GengChen** **Fan Yin** ©Calvin Yap	九地 (Jiǔ Dì) 天冲 (Tiān Chōng) 杜门 (Dù Mén) Dui 7　Yi Ren
六合 (Liù Hé) 禽芮 (Qín Ruì) 惊门 (Jīng Mén) Gen 8　Wu/Ding Xin	白虎 (Bái Hǔ) 天英 (Tiān Yīng) 死门 (Sǐ Mén) Kan 1　Geng Ji	玄武 (Xuán Wǔ) 天辅 (Tiān Fǔ) 景门 (Jǐng Mén) Qian 6　Bing Gui

Yin (阴) Dun# 2 Hour: XinSi ; 直符(ZhíFú): 天蓬(TiānPéng)
直使(ZhíShǐ): 休门(XiūMén) ; 旬首(XúnShǒu): JiaXuJi

九地 (Jiǔ Dì) 天冲 (Tiān Chōng) 生门 (Shēng Mén) Xun 4　Yi Bing	玄武 (Xuán Wǔ) 天辅 (Tiān Fǔ) 伤门 (Shāng Mén) Li 9　Bing Geng	白虎 (Bái Hǔ) 天英 (Tiān Yīng) 杜门 (Dù Mén) Kun 2　Geng Wu/Ding
九天 (Jiǔ Tiān) 天任 (Tiān Rèn) 休门 (Xiū Mén) Zhen 3　Xin Yi	Yin (阴) Dun# 2 Hour: **XinSi** ©Calvin Yap	六合 (Liù Hé) 禽芮 (Qín Ruì) 景门 (Jǐng Mén) Dui 7　Wu/Ding Ren
值符 (Zhí Fú) 天蓬 (Tiān Péng) 开门 (Kāi Mén) Gen 8　Ji Xin	螣蛇 (Téng Shé) 天心 (Tiān Xīn) 惊门 (Jīng Mén) Kan 1　Gui Ji	太阴 (Tài Yīn) 天柱 (Tiān Zhù) 死门 (Sǐ Mén) Qian 6　Ren Gui

Yin (阴) Dun# 2 Hour: **RenWu** ; 直符(ZhíFú): 天蓬(TiānPéng)
直使(ZhíShǐ): 休门(XiūMén) ; 旬首(XúnShǒu): JiaXuJi

六合 (Liù Hé) 禽芮 (Qín Ruì) 惊门 (Jīng Mén) Xun 4 Wu/Ding Bing	太阴 (Tài Yīn) 天柱 (Tiān Zhù) 开门 (Kāi Mén) Li 9 Ren Geng	螣蛇(Téng Shé) 天心 (Tiān Xīn) 休门 (Xiū Mén) Kun 2 Gui Wu/Ding
白虎 (Bái Hǔ) 天英 (Tiān Yīng) 死门 (Sǐ Mén) Zhen 3 Geng Yi	Yin (阴) Dun# 2 Hour: **RenWu** ©Calvin Yap	值符 (Zhí Fú) 天蓬 (Tiān Péng) 生门 (Shēng Mén) Dui 7 Ji Ren
玄武 (Xuán Wǔ) 天辅 (Tiān Fǔ) 景门 (Jǐng Mén) Gen 8 Bing Xin	九地 (Jiǔ Dì) 天冲 (Tiān Chōng) 杜门 (Dù Mén) Kan 1 Yi Ji	九天 (Jiǔ Tiān) 天任 (Tiān Rèn) 伤门 (Shāng Mén) Qian 6 Xin Gui

Yin (阴) Dun# 2 Hour: **GuiWei** ; 直符(ZhíFú): 天蓬(TiānPéng)
直使(ZhíShǐ): 休门(XiūMén) ; 旬首(XúnShǒu): JiaXuJi

白虎 (Bái Hǔ) 天英 (Tiān Yīng) 杜门 (Dù Mén) Xun 4 Geng Bing	六合 (Liù Hé) 禽芮 (Qín Ruì) 景门 (Jǐng Mén) Li 9 Wu/Ding Geng	太阴 (Tài Yīn) 天柱 (Tiān Zhù) 死门 (Sǐ Mén) Kun 2 Ren Wu/Ding
玄武 (Xuán Wǔ) 天辅 (Tiān Fǔ) 伤门 (Shāng Mén) Zhen 3 Bing Yi	Yin (阴) Dun# 2 Hour: **GuiWei** ©Calvin Yap	螣蛇 (Téng Shé) 天心 (Tiān Xīn) 惊门 (Jīng Mén) Dui 7 Gui Ren
九地 (Jiǔ Dì) 天冲 (Tiān Chōng) 生门 (Shēng Mén) Gen 8 Yi Xin	九天 (Jiǔ Tiān) 天任 (Tiān Rèn) 休门 (Xiū Mén) Kan 1 Xin Ji	值符 (Zhí Fú) 天蓬 (Tiān Péng) 开门 (Kāi Mén) Qian 6 Ji Gui

Chart: **-2JiaShen** (Yin Dun #2 JiaShen Xun)
JiaShen, YiYou, BingXu, DingHai, WuZi, JiChou, GengYin, XinMao, RenChen, GuiSi

Yin (阴) Dun# 2 Hour: **JiaShen** ; 直符(ZhíFú): 天英(TiānYīng)
直使(ZhíShǐ): 景门(JǐngMén) ; 旬首(XúnShǒu): JiaShenGeng

螣蛇 (Téng Shé) 天辅 (Tiān Fǔ) 杜门 (Dù Mén) Xun 4 Bing Bing	值符 (Zhí Fú) 天英 (Tiān Yīng) 景门 (Jǐng Mén) Li 9 Geng Geng	九天 (Jiǔ Tiān) 禽芮 (Qín Ruì) 死门 (Sǐ Mén) Kun 2 Wu/Ding Wu/Ding
太阴 (Tài Yīn) 天冲 (Tiān Chōng) 伤门 (Shāng Mén) Zhen 3 Yi Yi	Yin (阴) Dun# 2 Hour: **JiaShen** **Fu Yin** ©Calvin Yap	九地 (Jiǔ Dì) 天柱 (Tiān Zhù) 惊门 (Jīng Mén) Dui 7 Ren Ren
六合 (Liù Hé) 天任 (Tiān Rèn) 生门 (Shēng Mén) Gen 8 Xin Xin	白虎 (Bái Hǔ) 天蓬 (Tiān Péng) 休门 (Xiū Mén) Kan 1 Ji Ji	玄武 (Xuán Wǔ) 天心 (Tiān Xīn) 开门 (Kāi Mén) Qian 6 Gui Gui

Yin (阴) Dun# 2 Hour: **YiYou** ; 直符(ZhíFú): 天英(TiānYīng)
直使(ZhíShǐ): 景门(JǐngMén) ; 旬首(XúnShǒu): JiaShenGeng

九天 (Jiǔ Tiān) 禽芮 (Qín Ruì) 惊门 (Jīng Mén) Xun 4 Wu/Ding Bing	九地 (Jiǔ Dì) 天柱 (Tiān Zhù) 开门 (Kāi Mén) Li 9 Ren Geng	玄武 (Xuán Wǔ) 天心 (Tiān Xīn) 休门 (Xiū Mén) Kun 2 Gui Wu/Ding
值符 (Zhí Fú) 天英 (Tiān Yīng) 死门 (Sǐ Mén) Zhen 3 Geng Yi	Yin (阴) Dun# 2 Hour: **YiYou** ©Calvin Yap	白虎 (Bái Hǔ) 天蓬 (Tiān Péng) 生门 (Shēng Mén) Dui 7 Ji Ren
螣蛇 (Téng Shé) 天辅 (Tiān Fǔ) 景门 (Jǐng Mén) Gen 8 Bing Xin	太阴 (Tài Yīn) 天冲 (Tiān Chōng) 杜门 (Dù Mén) Kan 1 Yi Ji	六合 (Liù Hé) 天任 (Tiān Rèn) 伤门 (Shāng Mén) Qian 6 Xin Gui

Yin (阴) Dun# 2 Hour: **BingXu** ; 直符(ZhíFú): 天英(TiānYīng)
直使(ZhíShǐ): 景门(JǐngMén) ; 旬首(XúnShǒu): JiaShenGeng

值符 (Zhí Fú) 天英 (Tiān Yīng) 生门 (Shēng Mén) Xun 4 Geng Bing	九天 (Jiǔ Tiān) 禽芮 (Qín Ruì) 伤门 (Shāng Mén) Li 9 Wu/Ding Geng	九地 (Jiǔ Dì) 天柱 (Tiān Zhù) 杜门 (Dù Mén) Kun 2 Ren Wu/Ding
螣蛇 (Téng Shé) 天辅 (Tiān Fǔ) 休门 (Xiū Mén) Zhen 3 Bing Yi	Yin (阴) Dun# 2 Hour: **BingXu** ©Calvin Yap	玄武 (Xuán Wǔ) 天心 (Tiān Xīn) 景门 (Jǐng Mén) Dui 7 Gui Ren
太阴 (Tài Yīn) 天冲 (Tiān Chōng) 开门 (Kāi Mén) Gen 8 Yi Xin	六合 (Liù Hé) 天任 (Tiān Rèn) 惊门 (Jīng Mén) Kan 1 Xin Ji	白虎 (Bái Hǔ) 天蓬 (Tiān Péng) 死门 (Sǐ Mén) Qian 6 Ji Gui

Yin (阴) Dun# 2 Hour: **DingHai** ; 直符(ZhíFú): 天英(TiānYīng)
直使(ZhíShǐ): 景门(JǐngMén) ; 旬首(XúnShǒu): JiaShenGeng

太阴 (Tài Yīn) 天冲 (Tiān Chōng) 休门 (Xiū Mén) Xun 4 Yi Bing	螣蛇 (Téng Shé) 天辅 (Tiān Fǔ) 生门 (Shēng Mén) Li 9 Bing Geng	值符 (Zhí Fú) 天英 (Tiān Yīng) 伤门 (Shāng Mén) Kun 2 Geng Wu/Ding
六合 (Liù Hé) 天任 (Tiān Rèn) 开门 (Kāi Mén) Zhen 3 Xin Yi	Yin (阴) Dun# 2 Hour: **DingHai** ©Calvin Yap	九天 (Jiǔ Tiān) 禽芮 (Qín Ruì) 杜门 (Dù Mén) Dui 7 Wu/Ding Ren
白虎 (Bái Hǔ) 天蓬 (Tiān Péng) 惊门 (Jīng Mén) Gen 8 Ji Xin	玄武 (Xuán Wǔ) 天心 (Tiān Xīn) 死门 (Sǐ Mén) Kan 1 Gui Ji	九地 (Jiǔ Dì) 天柱 (Tiān Zhù) 景门 (Jǐng Mén) Qian 6 Ren Gui

Yin (阴) Dun# 2 Hour: **WuZi**；直符(ZhíFú): 天英(TiānYīng)
直使(ZhíShǐ): 景门(JǐngMén)；句首(XúnShǒu): JiaShenGeng

太阴 (Tài Yīn) 天冲 (Tiān Chōng) 伤门 (Shāng Mén) Xun 4 — Yi / Bing	螣蛇 (Téng Shé) 天辅 (Tiān Fǔ) 杜门 (Dù Mén) Li 9 — Bing / Geng	值符 (Zhí Fú) 天英 (Tiān Yīng) 景门 (Jǐng Mén) Kun 2 — Geng / Wu/Ding
六合 (Liù Hé) 天任 (Tiān Rèn) 生门 (Shēng Mén) Zhen 3 — Xin / Yi	Yin (阴) Dun# 2 Hour: **WuZi** ©Calvin Yap	九天 (Jiǔ Tiān) 禽芮 (Qín Ruì) 死门 (Sǐ Mén) Dui 7 — Wu/Ding / Ren
白虎 (Bái Hǔ) 天蓬 (Tiān Péng) 休门 (Xiū Mén) Gen 8 — Ji / Xin	玄武 (Xuán Wǔ) 天心 (Tiān Xīn) 开门 (Kāi Mén) Kan 1 — Gui / Ji	九地 (Jiǔ Dì) 天柱 (Tiān Zhù) 惊门 (Jīng Mén) Qian 6 — Ren / Gui

Yin (阴) Dun# 2 Hour: **JiChou**；直符(ZhíFú): 天英(TiānYīng)
直使(ZhíShǐ): 景门(JǐngMén)；句首(XúnShǒu): JiaShenGeng

玄武 (Xuán Wǔ) 天心 (Tiān Xīn) 景门 (Jǐng Mén) Xun 4 — Gui / Bing	白虎 (Bái Hǔ) 天蓬 (Tiān Péng) 死门 (Sǐ Mén) Li 9 — Ji / Geng	六合 (Liù Hé) 天任 (Tiān Rèn) 惊门 (Jīng Mén) Kun 2 — Xin / Wu/Ding
天柱 (Tiān Zhù) 杜门 (Dù Mén) Zhen 3 — Ren / Yi	Yin (阴) Dun# 2 Hour: **JiChou** **Fan Yin** ©Calvin Yap	太阴 (Tài Yīn) 天冲 (Tiān Chōng) 开门 (Kāi Mén) Dui 7 — Yi / Ren
九天 (Jiǔ Tiān) 禽芮 (Qín Ruì) 伤门 (Shāng Mén) Gen 8 — Wu/Ding / Xin	值符 (Zhi Fú) 天英 (Tiān Yīng) 生门 (Shēng Mén) Kan 1 — Geng / Ji	螣蛇 (Téng Shé) 天辅 (Tiān Fǔ) 休门 (Xiū Mén) Qian 6 — Bing / Gui

Yin (阴) Dun# 2 Hour: **GengYin**；直符(ZhíFú): 天英(TiānYīng)
直使(ZhíShǐ): 景门(JǐngMén)；句首(XúnShǒu): JiaShenGeng

螣蛇 (Téng Shé) 天辅 (Tiān Fǔ) 死门 (Sǐ Mén) Xun 4 — Bing / Bing	值符 (Zhí Fú) 天英 (Tiān Yīng) 惊门 (Jīng Mén) Li 9 — Geng / Geng	九天 (Jiǔ Tiān) 禽芮 (Qín Ruì) 开门 (Kāi Mén) Kun 2 — Wu/Ding / Wu/Ding
太阴 (Tài Yīn) 天冲 (Tiān Chōng) 景门 (Jǐng Mén) Zhen 3 — Yi / Yi	Yin (阴) Dun# 2 Hour: **GengYin** **Fu Yin** ©Calvin Yap	九地 (Jiǔ Dì) 天柱 (Tiān Zhù) 休门 (Xiū Mén) Dui 7 — Ren / Ren
六合 (Liù Hé) 天任 (Tiān Rèn) 杜门 (Dù Mén) Gen 8 — Xin / Xin	白虎 (Bái Hǔ) 天蓬 (Tiān Péng) 伤门 (Shāng Mén) Kan 1 — Ji / Ji	玄武 (Xuán Wǔ) 天心 (Tiān Xīn) 生门 (Shēng Mén) Qian 6 — Gui / Gui

Yin (阴) Dun# 2 Hour: **XinMao**；直符(ZhíFú): 天英(TiānYīng)
直使(ZhíShǐ): 景门(JǐngMén)；句首(XúnShǒu): JiaShenGeng

九地 (Jiǔ Dì) 天柱 (Tiān Zhù) 伤门 (Shāng Mén) Xun 4 — Ren / Bing	玄武 (Xuán Wǔ) 天心 (Tiān Xīn) 杜门 (Dù Mén) Li 9 — Gui / Geng	白虎 (Bái Hǔ) 天蓬 (Tiān Péng) 景门 (Jǐng Mén) Kun 2 — Ji / Wu/Ding
九天 (Jiǔ Tiān) 禽芮 (Qín Ruì) 生门 (Shēng Mén) Zhen 3 — Wu/Ding / Yi	Yin (阴) Dun# 2 Hour: **XinMao** ©Calvin Yap	六合 (Liù Hé) 天任 (Tiān Rèn) 死门 (Sǐ Mén) Dui 7 — Xin / Ren
值符 (Zhí Fú) 天英 (Tiān Yīng) 休门 (Xiū Mén) Gen 8 — Geng / Xin	螣蛇 (Téng Shé) 天辅 (Tiān Fǔ) 开门 (Kāi Mén) Kan 1 — Bing / Ji	太阴 (Tài Yīn) 天冲 (Tiān Chōng) 惊门 (Jīng Mén) Qian 6 — Yi / Gui

Yin (阴) Dun# 2 Hour: **RenChen**；直符(ZhíFú): 天英(TiānYīng)
直使(ZhíShǐ): 景门(JǐngMén)；句首(XúnShǒu): JiaShenGeng

六合 (Liù Hé) 天任 (Tiān Rèn) 开门 (Kāi Mén) Xun 4 — Xin / Bing	太阴 (Tài Yīn) 天冲 (Tiān Chōng) 休门 (Xiū Mén) Li 9 — Yi / Geng	螣蛇 (Téng Shé) 天辅 (Tiān Fǔ) 生门 (Shēng Mén) Kun 2 — Bing / Wu/Ding
白虎 (Bái Hǔ) 天蓬 (Tiān Péng) 惊门 (Jīng Mén) Zhen 3 — Ji / Yi	Yin (阴) Dun# 2 Hour: **RenChen** ©Calvin Yap	值符 (Zhí Fú) 天英 (Tiān Yīng) 伤门 (Shāng Mén) Dui 7 — Geng / Ren
玄武 (Xuán Wǔ) 天心 (Tiān Xīn) 死门 (Sǐ Mén) Gen 8 — Gui / Xin	九地 (Jiǔ Dì) 天柱 (Tiān Zhù) 景门 (Jǐng Mén) Kan 1 — Ren / Ji	九天 (Jiǔ Tiān) 禽芮 (Qín Ruì) 杜门 (Dù Mén) Qian 6 — Wu/Ding / Gui

Yin (阴) Dun# 2 Hour: **GuiSi**；直符(ZhíFú): 天英(TiānYīng)
直使(ZhíShǐ): 景门(JǐngMén)；句首(XúnShǒu): JiaShenGeng

白虎 (Bái Hǔ) 天蓬 (Tiān Péng) 杜门 (Dù Mén) Xun 4 — Ji / Bing	六合 (Liù Hé) 天任 (Tiān Rèn) 景门 (Jǐng Mén) Li 9 — Xin / Geng	太阴 (Tài Yīn) 天冲 (Tiān Chōng) 死门 (Sǐ Mén) Kun 2 — Yi / Wu/Ding
玄武 (Xuán Wǔ) 天心 (Tiān Xīn) 伤门 (Shāng Mén) Zhen 3 — Gui / Yi	Yin (阴) Dun# 2 Hour: **GuiSi** ©Calvin Yap	螣蛇 (Téng Shé) 天辅 (Tiān Fǔ) 惊门 (Jīng Mén) Dui 7 — Bing / Ren
九地 (Jiǔ Dì) 天柱 (Tiān Zhù) 生门 (Shēng Mén) Gen 8 — Ren / Xin	九天 (Jiǔ Tiān) 禽芮 (Qín Ruì) 休门 (Xiū Mén) Kan 1 — Wu/Ding / Ji	值符 (Zhí Fú) 天英 (Tiān Yīng) 开门 (Kāi Mén) Qian 6 — Geng / Gui

Chart: -2JiaWu (Yin Dun #2 JiaWu Xun)
JiaWu, YiWei, BingShen, DingYou, WuXu, JiHai, GengZi, XinChou, RenYin, GuiMao

Yin (阴) Dun #2 Hour: **JiaWu** ; 直符(ZhíFú): 天任(TiānRèn)
直使(ZhíShǐ): 生门(ShēngMén) ; 旬首(XúnShǒu): JiaWu/Xin

九地 (Jiǔ Dì) 天辅 (Tiān Fǔ) 杜门 (Dù Mén) Xun 4　Bing Bing	玄武 (Xuán Wǔ) 天英 (Tiān Yīng) 景门 (Jǐng Mén) Li 9　Geng Geng	白虎 (Bái Hǔ) 禽芮 (Qín Ruì) 死门 (Sǐ Mén) Kun 2　Wu/Ding Wu/Ding
九天 (Jiǔ Tiān) 天冲 (Tiān Chōng) 伤门 (Shāng Mén) Zhen 3　Yi Yi	Yin (阴) Dun# 2 Hour: **JiaWu** **Fu Yin** ©Calvin Yap	六合 (Liù Hé) 天柱 (Tiān Zhù) 惊门 (Jīng Mén) Dui 7　Ren Ren
值符 (Zhí Fú) 天任 (Tiān Rèn) 生门 (Shēng Mén) Gen 8　Xin Xin	螣蛇 (Téng Shé) 天蓬 (Tiān Péng) 休门 (Xiū Mén) Kan 1　Ji Ji	太阴 (Tài Yīn) 天心 (Tiān Xīn) 开门 (Kāi Mén) Qian 6　Gui Gui

Yin (阴) Dun #2 Hour: **YiWei** ; 直符(ZhíFú): 天任(TiānRèn)
直使(ZhíShǐ): 生门(ShēngMén) ; 旬首(XúnShǒu): JiaWu/Xin

九天 (Jiǔ Tiān) 天冲 (Tiān Chōng) 惊门 (Jīng Mén) Xun 4　Yi Bing	九地 (Jiǔ Dì) 天辅 (Tiān Fǔ) 开门 (Kāi Mén) Li 9　Bing Geng	玄武 (Xuán Wǔ) 天英 (Tiān Yīng) 休门 (Xiū Mén) Kun 2　Geng Wu/Ding
值符 (Zhí Fú) 天任 (Tiān Rèn) 死门 (Sǐ Mén) Zhen 3　Xin Yi	Yin (阴) Dun# 2 Hour: **YiWei** ©Calvin Yap	白虎 (Bái Hǔ) 禽芮 (Qín Ruì) 生门 (Shēng Mén) Dui 7　Wu/Ding Ren
螣蛇 (Téng Shé) 天蓬 (Tiān Péng) 景门 (Jǐng Mén) Gen 8　Ji Xin	太阴 (Tài Yīn) 天心 (Tiān Xīn) 杜门 (Dù Mén) Kan 1　Gui Ji	六合 (Liù Hé) 天柱 (Tiān Zhù) 伤门 (Shāng Mén) Qian 6　Ren Gui

Yin (阴) Dun #2 Hour: **BingShen** ; 直符(ZhíFú): 天任(TiānRèn)
直使(ZhíShǐ): 生门(ShēngMén) ; 旬首(XúnShǒu): JiaWu/Xin

值符 (Zhí Fú) 天任 (Tiān Rèn) 死门 (Sǐ Mén) Xun 4　Xin Bing	九天 (Jiǔ Tiān) 天冲 (Tiān Chōng) 惊门 (Jīng Mén) Li 9　Yi Geng	九地 (Jiǔ Dì) 天辅 (Tiān Fǔ) 开门 (Kāi Mén) Kun 2　Bing Wu/Ding
螣蛇 (Téng Shé) 天蓬 (Tiān Péng) 景门 (Jǐng Mén) Zhen 3　Ji Yi	Yin (阴) Dun# 2 Hour: **BingShen** ©Calvin Yap	玄武 (Xuán Wǔ) 天英 (Tiān Yīng) 休门 (Xiū Mén) Dui 7　Geng Ren
太阴 (Tài Yīn) 天心 (Tiān Xīn) 杜门 (Dù Mén) Gen 8　Gui Xin	六合 (Liù Hé) 天柱 (Tiān Zhù) 伤门 (Shāng Mén) Kan 1　Ren Ji	白虎 (Bái Hǔ) 禽芮 (Qín Ruì) 生门 (Shēng Mén) Qian 6　Wu/Ding Gui

Yin (阴) Dun #2 Hour: **DingYou** ; 直符(ZhíFú): 天任(TiānRèn)
直使(ZhíShǐ): 生门(ShēngMén) ; 旬首(XúnShǒu): JiaWu/Xin

太阴 (Tài Yīn) 天心 (Tiān Xīn) 开门 (Kāi Mén) Xun 4　Gui Bing	螣蛇 (Téng Shé) 天蓬 (Tiān Péng) 休门 (Xiū Mén) Li 9　Ji Geng	值符 (Zhí Fú) 天任 (Tiān Rèn) 生门 (Shēng Mén) Kun 2　Xin Wu/Ding
六合 (Liù Hé) 天柱 (Tiān Zhù) 惊门 (Jīng Mén) Zhen 3　Ren Yi	Yin (阴) Dun# 2 Hour: **DingYou** **Fan Yin** ©Calvin Yap	九天 (Jiǔ Tiān) 天冲 (Tiān Chōng) 伤门 (Shāng Mén) Dui 7　Yi Ren
白虎 (Bái Hǔ) 禽芮 (Qín Ruì) 死门 (Sǐ Mén) Gen 8　Wu/Ding Xin	玄武 (Xuán Wǔ) 天英 (Tiān Yīng) 景门 (Jǐng Mén) Kan 1　Geng Ji	九地 (Jiǔ Dì) 天辅 (Tiān Fǔ) 杜门 (Dù Mén) Qian 6　Bing Gui

Yin (阴) Dun #2 Hour: **WuXu** ; 直符(ZhíFú): 天任(TiānRèn)
直使(ZhíShǐ): 生门(ShēngMén) ; 旬首(XúnShǒu): JiaWu/Xin

太阴 (Tài Yīn) 天心 (Tiān Xīn) 生门 (Shēng Mén) Xun 4　Gui Bing	螣蛇 (Téng Shé) 天蓬 (Tiān Péng) 伤门 (Shāng Mén) Li 9　Ji Geng	值符 (Zhí Fú) 天任 (Tiān Rèn) 杜门 (Dù Mén) Kun 2　Xin Wu/Ding
六合 (Liù Hé) 天柱 (Tiān Zhù) 休门 (Xiū Mén) Zhen 3　Ren Yi	Yin (阴) Dun# 2 Hour: **WuXu** **Fan Yin** ©Calvin Yap	九天 (Jiǔ Tiān) 天冲 (Tiān Chōng) 景门 (Jǐng Mén) Dui 7　Yi Ren
白虎 (Bái Hǔ) 禽芮 (Qín Ruì) 开门 (Kāi Mén) Gen 8　Wu/Ding Xin	玄武 (Xuán Wǔ) 天英 (Tiān Yīng) 惊门 (Jīng Mén) Kan 1　Geng Ji	九地 (Jiǔ Dì) 天辅 (Tiān Fǔ) 死门 (Sǐ Mén) Qian 6　Bing Gui

Yin (阴) Dun #2 Hour: **JiHai** ; 直符(ZhíFú): 天任(TiānRèn)
直使(ZhíShǐ): 生门(ShēngMén) ; 旬首(XúnShǒu): JiaWu/Xin

玄武 (Xuán Wǔ) 天英 (Tiān Yīng) 伤门 (Shāng Mén) Xun 4　Geng Bing	白虎 (Bái Hǔ) 禽芮 (Qín Ruì) 杜门 (Dù Mén) Li 9　Wu/Ding Geng	六合 (Liù Hé) 天柱 (Tiān Zhù) 景门 (Jǐng Mén) Kun 2　Ren Wu/Ding
九地 (Jiǔ Dì) 天辅 (Tiān Fǔ) 生门 (Shēng Mén) Zhen 3　Bing Yi	Yin (阴) Dun# 2 Hour: **JiHai** ©Calvin Yap	太阴 (Tài Yīn) 天心 (Tiān Xīn) 死门 (Sǐ Mén) Dui 7　Gui Ren
九天 (Jiǔ Tiān) 天冲 (Tiān Chōng) 休门 (Xiū Mén) Gen 8　Yi Xin	值符 (Zhí Fú) 天任 (Tiān Rèn) 开门 (Kāi Mén) Kan 1　Xin Ji	螣蛇 (Téng Shé) 天蓬 (Tiān Péng) 惊门 (Jīng Mén) Qian 6　Ji Gui

Yin (阴) Dun# 2 Hour: GengZi ; 直符(ZhíFú): 天任(TiānRèn)
直使(ZhíShǐ): 生门(ShēngMén) ; 旬首(XúnShǒu): JiaWu/Xin

螣蛇 (Téng Shé) 天蓬 (Tiān Péng) 开门(Kāi Mén) Xun 4　Ji	值符 (Zhí Fú) 天任 (Tiān Rèn) 休门(Xiū Mén) Li 9　Xin Geng	九天 (Jiǔ Tiān) 天冲 (Tiān Chōng) 生门(Shēng Mén) Kun 2　Wu/Ding
太阴 (Tài Yīn) 天心 (Tiān Xīn) 惊门(Jīng Mén) Zhen 3　Gui Yi	Yin (阴) Dun# 2 Hour: **GengZi** ©Calvin Yap	九地 (Jiǔ Dì) 天辅 (Tiān Fǔ) 伤门(Shāng Mén) Dui 7　Bing Ren
六合 (Liù Hé) 天柱 (Tiān Zhù) 死门(Sǐ Mén) Gen 8　Ren Xin	白虎 (Bái Hǔ) 禽芮 (Qín Ruì) 景门(Jǐng Mén) Kan 1　Wu/Ding Ji	玄武 (Xuán Wǔ) 天英 (Tiān Yīng) 杜门(Dù Mén) Qian 6　Geng Gui

Yin (阴) Dun# 2 Hour: XinChou ; 直符(ZhíFú): 天任(TiānRèn)
直使(ZhíShǐ): 生门(ShēngMén) ; 旬首(XúnShǒu): JiaWu/Xin

九地 (Jiǔ Dì) 天辅 (Tiān Fǔ) 景门(Jǐng Mén) Xun 4　Bing Bing	玄武 (Xuán Wǔ) 天英 (Tiān Yīng) 死门(Sǐ Mén) Li 9　Geng Geng	白虎 (Bái Hǔ) 禽芮 (Qín Ruì) 惊门(Jīng Mén) Kun 2　Wu/Ding
九天 (Jiǔ Tiān) 天冲 (Tiān Chōng) 杜门(Dù Mén) Zhen 3　Yi Yi	Yin (阴) Dun# 2 Hour: **XinChou** **Fu Yin** ©Calvin Yap	六合 (Liù Hé) 天柱 (Tiān Zhù) 开门(Kāi Mén) Dui 7　Ren Ren
值符 (Zhí Fú) 天任 (Tiān Rèn) 伤门(Shāng Mén) Gen 8　Xin Xin	螣蛇 (Téng Shé) 天蓬 (Tiān Péng) 生门(Shēng Mén) Kan 1　Ji Ji	太阴 (Tài Yīn) 天心 (Tiān Xīn) 休门(Xiū Mén) Qian 6　Gui Gui

Yin (阴) Dun# 2 Hour: RenYin ; 直符(ZhíFú): 天任(TiānRèn)
直使(ZhíShǐ): 生门(ShēngMén) ; 旬首(XúnShǒu): JiaWu/Xin

六合 (Liù Hé) 天柱 (Tiān Zhù) 休门(Xiū Mén) Xun 4　Ren Bing	太阴 (Tài Yīn) 天心 (Tiān Xīn) 生门(Shēng Mén) Li 9　Gui Geng	螣蛇 (Téng Shé) 天蓬 (Tiān Péng) 伤门(Shāng Mén) Kun 2　Ji Wu/Ding
白虎 (Bái Hǔ) 禽芮 (Qín Ruì) 开门(Kāi Mén) Zhen 3　Wu/Ding Yi	Yin (阴) Dun# 2 Hour: **RenYin** ©Calvin Yap	值符 (Zhí Fú) 天任 (Tiān Rèn) 杜门(Dù Mén) Dui 7　Xin Ren
玄武 (Xuán Wǔ) 天英 (Tiān Yīng) 惊门(Jīng Mén) Gen 8　Geng Xin	九地 (Jiǔ Dì) 天辅 (Tiān Fǔ) 死门(Sǐ Mén) Kan 1　Bing Ji	九天 (Jiǔ Tiān) 天冲 (Tiān Chōng) 景门(Jǐng Mén) Qian 6　Yi Gui

Yin (阴) Dun# 2 Hour: GuiMao ; 直符(ZhíFú): 天任(TiānRèn)
直使(ZhíShǐ): 生门(ShēngMén) ; 旬首(XúnShǒu): JiaWu/Xin

白虎 (Bái Hǔ) 禽芮 (Qín Ruì) 杜门(Dù Mén) Xun 4　Wu/Ding Bing	六合 (Liù Hé) 天柱 (Tiān Zhù) 景门(Jǐng Mén) Li 9　Ren Geng	太阴 (Tài Yīn) 天心 (Tiān Xīn) 死门(Sǐ Mén) Kun 2　Gui Wu/Ding
玄武 (Xuán Wǔ) 天英 (Tiān Yīng) 伤门(Shāng Mén) Zhen 3　Geng Yi	Yin (阴) Dun# 2 Hour: **GuiMao** ©Calvin Yap	螣蛇 (Téng Shé) 天蓬 (Tiān Péng) 惊门(Jīng Mén) Dui 7　Ji Ren
九地 (Jiǔ Dì) 天辅 (Tiān Fǔ) 生门(Shēng Mén) Gen 8　Bing Xin	九天 (Jiǔ Tiān) 天冲 (Tiān Chōng) 休门(Xiū Mén) Kan 1　Yi Ji	值符 (Zhí Fú) 天任 (Tiān Rèn) 开门(Kāi Mén) Qian 6　Xin Gui

Chart: -2JiaChen (Yin Dun #2 JiaChen Xun)
JiaChen, YiSi, BingWu, DingWei, WuShen, JiYou, GengXu, XinHai, RenZi, GuiChou

Yin (阴) Dun# 2 Hour: JiaChen ; 直符(ZhíFú): 天柱(TiānZhù)
直使(ZhíShǐ): 惊门(JīngMén) ; 旬首(XúnShǒu): JiaChenRen

六合 (Liù Hé) 天辅 (Tiān Fǔ) 杜门(Dù Mén) Xun 4　Bing Bing	太阴 (Tài Yīn) 天英 (Tiān Yīng) 景门(Jǐng Mén) Li 9　Geng Geng	螣蛇 (Téng Shé) 禽芮 (Qín Ruì) 死门(Sǐ Mén) Kun 2　Wu/Ding Wu/Ding
白虎 (Bái Hǔ) 天冲 (Tiān Chōng) 伤门(Shāng Mén) Zhen 3　Yi Yi	Yin (阴) Dun# 2 Hour: **JiaChen** **Fu Yin** ©Calvin Yap	值符 (Zhí Fú) 天柱 (Tiān Zhù) 惊门(Jīng Mén) Dui 7　Ren Ren
玄武 (Xuán Wǔ) 天任 (Tiān Rèn) 生门(Shēng Mén) Gen 8　Xin Xin	九地 (Jiǔ Dì) 天蓬 (Tiān Péng) 休门(Xiū Mén) Kan 1　Ji Ji	九天 (Jiǔ Tiān) 天心 (Tiān Xīn) 开门(Kāi Mén) Qian 6　Gui Gui

Yin (阴) Dun# 2 Hour: YiSi ; 直符(ZhíFú): 天柱(TiānZhù)
直使(ZhíShǐ): 惊门(JīngMén) ; 旬首(XúnShǒu): JiaChenRen

九天 (Jiǔ Tiān) 天心 (Tiān Xīn) 伤门(Shāng Mén) Xun 4　Gui Bing	九地 (Jiǔ Dì) 天蓬 (Tiān Péng) 杜门(Dù Mén) Li 9　Ji Geng	玄武 (Xuán Wǔ) 天任 (Tiān Rèn) 景门(Jǐng Mén) Kun 2　Xin Wu/Ding
值符 (Zhí Fú) 天柱 (Tiān Zhù) 生门(Shēng Mén) Zhen 3　Ren Yi	Yin (阴) Dun# 2 Hour: **YiSi** **Fan Yin** ©Calvin Yap	白虎 (Bái Hǔ) 天冲 (Tiān Chōng) 死门(Sǐ Mén) Dui 7　Yi Ren
螣蛇 (Téng Shé) 禽芮 (Qín Ruì) 休门(Xiū Mén) Gen 8　Wu/Ding Xin	太阴 (Tài Yīn) 天英 (Tiān Yīng) 开门(Kāi Mén) Kan 1　Geng Ji	六合 (Liù Hé) 天辅 (Tiān Fǔ) 惊门(Jīng Mén) Qian 6　Bing Gui

Yin (阴) Dun# 2 Hour: **BingWu**；直符(ZhíFú): 天柱(TiānZhù)
直使(ZhíShǐ): 惊门(JǐngMén)；旬首(XúnShǒu): JiaChenRen

值符 (Zhí Fú) 天柱 (Tiān Zhù) 景门 (Jǐng Mén) Xun 4　Ren Bing	九天 (Jiǔ Tiān) 天心 (Tiān Xīn) 死门 (Sǐ Mén) Li 9　Gui Geng	九地 (Jiǔ Dì) 天蓬 (Tiān Péng) 惊门 (Jǐng Mén) Kun 2　Ji Wu/Ding
螣蛇 (Téng Shé) 禽芮 (Qín Ruì) 杜门 (Dù Mén) Zhen 3　Wu/Ding Yi	Yin (阴) Dun# 2 Hour: **BingWu** ©Calvin Yap	玄武 (Xuán Wǔ) 天任 (Tiān Rèn) 开门 (Kāi Mén) Dui 7　Xin Ren
太阴 (Tài Yīn) 天英 (Tiān Yīng) 伤门 (Shāng Mén) Gen 8　Geng Xin	六合 (Liù Hé) 天辅 (Tiān Fǔ) 生门 (Shēng Mén) Kan 1　Bing Ji	白虎 (Bái Hǔ) 天冲 (Tiān Chōng) 休门 (Xiū Mén) Qian 6　Yi Gui

Yin (阴) Dun# 2 Hour: **DingWei**；直符(ZhíFú): 天柱(TiānZhù)
直使(ZhíShǐ): 惊门(JǐngMén)；旬首(XúnShǒu): JiaChenRen

太阴 (Tài Yīn) 天英 (Tiān Yīng) 惊门 (Jǐng Mén) Xun 4　Geng Bing	螣蛇 (Téng Shé) 禽芮 (Qín Ruì) 开门 (Kāi Mén) Li 9　Wu/Ding Geng	值符 (Zhí Fú) 天柱 (Tiān Zhù) 休门 (Xiū Mén) Kun 2　Ren Wu/Ding
六合 (Liù Hé) 天辅 (Tiān Fǔ) 死门 (Sǐ Mén) Zhen 3　Bing Yi	Yin (阴) Dun# 2 Hour: **DingWei** ©Calvin Yap	九天 (Jiǔ Tiān) 天心 (Tiān Xīn) 生门 (Shēng Mén) Dui 7　Gui Ren
白虎 (Bái Hǔ) 天冲 (Tiān Chōng) 景门 (Jǐng Mén) Gen 8　Yi Xin	玄武 (Xuán Wǔ) 天任 (Tiān Rèn) 杜门 (Dù Mén) Kan 1　Xin Ji	九地 (Jiǔ Dì) 天蓬 (Tiān Péng) 伤门 (Shāng Mén) Qian 6　Ji Gui

Yin (阴) Dun# 2 Hour: **WuShen**；直符(ZhíFú): 天柱(TiānZhù)
直使(ZhíShǐ): 惊门(JǐngMén)；旬首(XúnShǒu): JiaChenRen

太阴 (Tài Yīn) 天英 (Tiān Yīng) 开门 (Kāi Mén) Xun 4　Geng Bing	螣蛇 (Téng Shé) 禽芮 (Qín Ruì) 休门 (Xiū Mén) Li 9　Wu/Ding Geng	值符 (Zhí Fú) 天柱 (Tiān Zhù) 生门 (Shēng Mén) Kun 2　Ren Wu/Ding
六合 (Liù Hé) 天辅 (Tiān Fǔ) 惊门 (Jǐng Mén) Zhen 3　Bing Yi	Yin (阴) Dun# 2 Hour: **WuShen** ©Calvin Yap	九天 (Jiǔ Tiān) 天心 (Tiān Xīn) 伤门 (Shāng Mén) Dui 7　Gui Ren
白虎 (Bái Hǔ) 天冲 (Tiān Chōng) 死门 (Sǐ Mén) Gen 8　Yi Xin	玄武 (Xuán Wǔ) 天任 (Tiān Rèn) 景门 (Jǐng Mén) Kan 1　Xin Ji	九地 (Jiǔ Dì) 天蓬 (Tiān Péng) 杜门 (Dù Mén) Qian 6　Ji Gui

Yin (阴) Dun# 2 Hour: **JiYou**；直符(ZhíFú): 天柱(TiānZhù)
直使(ZhíShǐ): 惊门(JǐngMén)；旬首(XúnShǒu): JiaChenRen

玄武 (Xuán Wǔ) 天任 (Tiān Rèn) 景门 (Jǐng Mén) Xun 4　Xin Bing	白虎 (Bái Hǔ) 天冲 (Tiān Chōng) 死门 (Sǐ Mén) Li 9　Yi Geng	六合 (Liù Hé) 天辅 (Tiān Fǔ) 惊门 (Jǐng Mén) Kun 2　Bing Wu/Ding
九地 (Jiǔ Dì) 天蓬 (Tiān Péng) 杜门 (Dù Mén) Zhen 3　Ji Yi	Yin (阴) Dun# 2 Hour: **JiYou** ©Calvin Yap	太阴 (Tài Yīn) 天英 (Tiān Yīng) 开门 (Kāi Mén) Dui 7　Geng Ren
九天 (Jiǔ Tiān) 天心 (Tiān Xīn) 伤门 (Shāng Mén) Gen 8　Gui Xin	值符 (Zhí Fú) 天柱 (Tiān Zhù) 生门 (Shēng Mén) Kan 1　Ren Ji	螣蛇 (Téng Shé) 禽芮 (Qín Ruì) 休门 (Xiū Mén) Qian 6　Wu/Ding Gui

Yin (阴) Dun# 2 Hour: **GengXu**；直符(ZhíFú): 天柱(TiānZhù)
直使(ZhíShǐ): 惊门(JǐngMén)；旬首(XúnShǒu): JiaChenRen

螣蛇 (Téng Shé) 禽芮 (Qín Ruì) 生门 (Shēng Mén) Xun 4　Wu/Ding Bing	值符 (Zhí Fú) 天柱 (Tiān Zhù) 伤门 (Shāng Mén) Li 9　Ren Geng	九天 (Jiǔ Tiān) 天心 (Tiān Xīn) 杜门 (Dù Mén) Kun 2　Gui Wu/Ding
太阴 (Tài Yīn) 天英 (Tiān Yīng) 休门 (Xiū Mén) Zhen 3　Geng Yi	Yin (阴) Dun# 2 Hour: **GengXu** ©Calvin Yap	九地 (Jiǔ Dì) 天蓬 (Tiān Péng) 景门 (Jǐng Mén) Dui 7　Ji Ren
六合 (Liù Hé) 天辅 (Tiān Fǔ) 开门 (Kāi Mén) Gen 8　Bing Xin	白虎 (Bái Hǔ) 天冲 (Tiān Chōng) 惊门 (Jǐng Mén) Kan 1　Yi Ji	玄武 (Xuán Wǔ) 天任 (Tiān Rèn) 死门 (Sǐ Mén) Qian 6　Xin Gui

Yin (阴) Dun# 2 Hour: **XinHai**；直符(ZhíFú): 天柱(TiānZhù)
直使(ZhíShǐ): 惊门(JǐngMén)；旬首(XúnShǒu): JiaChenRen

九地 (Jiǔ Dì) 天蓬 (Tiān Péng) 死门 (Sǐ Mén) Xun 4　Ji Bing	玄武 (Xuán Wǔ) 天任 (Tiān Rèn) 惊门 (Jǐng Mén) Li 9　Xin Geng	白虎 (Bái Hǔ) 天冲 (Tiān Chōng) 开门 (Kāi Mén) Kun 2　Yi Wu/Ding
九天 (Jiǔ Tiān) 天心 (Tiān Xīn) 景门 (Jǐng Mén) Zhen 3　Gui Yi	Yin (阴) Dun# 2 Hour: **XinHai** ©Calvin Yap	六合 (Liù Hé) 天辅 (Tiān Fǔ) 休门 (Xiū Mén) Dui 7　Bing Ren
值符 (Zhí Fú) 天柱 (Tiān Zhù) 杜门 (Dù Mén) Gen 8　Ren Xin	螣蛇 (Téng Shé) 禽芮 (Qín Ruì) 伤门 (Shāng Mén) Kan 1　Wu/Ding Ji	太阴 (Tài Yīn) 天英 (Tiān Yīng) 生门 (Shēng Mén) Qian 6　Geng Gui

Yin (阴) Dun# 2 Hour: **RenZi**；直符(ZhíFú): 天柱(TiānZhù)
直使(ZhíShǐ): 惊门(JīngMén)；句首(XúnShǒu): JiaChenRen

六合 (Liù Hé) 天辅 (Tiān Fǔ) 休门 (Xiū Mén) Xun 4　Bing Bing	太阴 (Tài Yīn) 天英 (Tiān Yīng) 生门 (Shēng Mén) Li 9　Geng Geng	螣蛇 (Téng Shé) 禽芮 (Qín Ruì) 伤门 (Shāng Mén) Kun 2　Wu/Ding Wu/Ding
白虎 (Bái Hǔ) 天冲 (Tiān Chōng) 开门 (Kāi Mén) Zhen 3　Yi Yi	Yin (阴) Dun# 2 Hour: **RenZi** **Fu Yin** ©Calvin Yap	值符 (Zhi Fú) 天柱 (Tiān Zhù) 杜门 (Dù Mén) Dui 7　Ren Ren
玄武(Xuán Wǔ) 天任 (Tiān Rèn) 惊门 (Jīng Mén) Gen 8　Xin Xin	九地 (Jiǔ Dì) 天蓬 (Tiān Péng) 死门 (Sǐ Mén) Kan 1　Ji Ji	九天 (Jiǔ Tiān) 天心 (Tiān Xīn) 景门 (Jǐng Mén) Qian 6　Gui Gui

Yin (阴) Dun# 2 Hour: **GuiChou**；直符(ZhíFú): 天柱(TiānZhù)
直使(ZhíShǐ): 惊门(JīngMén)；句首(XúnShǒu): JiaChenRen

白虎 (Bái Hǔ) 天冲 (Tiān Chōng) 杜门 (Dù Mén) Xun 4　Yi	六合 (Liù Hé) 天辅 (Tiān Fǔ) 景门 (Jǐng Mén) Li 9　Bing Bing	太阴 (Tài Yīn) 天英 (Tiān Yīng) 死门 (Sǐ Mén) Kun 2　Geng Wu/Ding
玄武 (Xuán Wǔ) 天任 (Tiān Rèn) 伤门 (Shāng Mén) Zhen 3　Xin	Yin (阴) Dun# 2 Hour: **GuiChou** ©Calvin Yap	螣蛇 (Téng Shé) 禽芮 (Qín Ruì) 惊门 (Jīng Mén) Dui 7　Wu/Ding Ren
九地 (Jiǔ Dì) 天蓬 (Tiān Péng) 生门 (Shēng Mén) Gen 8　Ji Xin	九天 (Jiǔ Tiān) 天心 (Tiān Xīn) 休门 (Xiū Mén) Kan 1　Gui Ji	值符 (Zhi Fú) 天柱 (Tiān Zhù) 开门 (Kāi Mén) Qian 6　Ren Gui

Chart: **-2JiaYin** (Yin Dun #2 JiaYin Xun)
JiaYin, YiMao, BingChen, DingSi, WuWu, JiWei, GengShen, XinYou, RenXu, GuiHai

Yin (阴) Dun# 2 Hour: **JiaYin**；直符(ZhíFú): 天心(TiānXīn)
直使(ZhíShǐ): 开门(KāiMén)；句首(XúnShǒu): JiaYinGui

白虎 (Bái Hǔ) 天辅 (Tiān Fǔ) 杜门 (Dù Mén) Xun 4　Bing Bing	六合 (Liù Hé) 天英 (Tiān Yīng) 景门 (Jǐng Mén) Li 9　Geng Geng	太阴 (Tài Yīn) 禽芮 (Qín Ruì) 死门 (Sǐ Mén) Kun 2　Wu/Ding Wu/Ding
玄武 (Xuán Wǔ) 天冲 (Tiān Chōng) 伤门 (Shāng Mén) Zhen 3　Yi Yi	Yin (阴) Dun# 2 Hour: **JiaYin** **Fu Yin** ©Calvin Yap	螣蛇 (Téng Shé) 天柱 (Tiān Zhù) 惊门 (Jīng Mén) Dui 7　Ren Ren
九地 (Jiǔ Dì) 天任 (Tiān Rèn) 生门 (Shēng Mén) Gen 8　Xin Xin	九天 (Jiǔ Tiān) 天蓬 (Tiān Péng) 休门 (Xiū Mén) Kan 1　Ji Ji	值符 (Zhi Fú) 天心 (Tiān Xīn) 开门 (Kāi Mén) Qian 6　Gui Gui

Yin (阴) Dun# 2 Hour: **YiMao**；直符(ZhíFú): 天心(TiānXīn)
直使(ZhíShǐ): 开门(KāiMén)；句首(XúnShǒu): JiaYinGui

九天 (Jiǔ Tiān) 天蓬 (Tiān Péng) 死门 (Sǐ Mén) Xun 4　Ji Bing	九地 (Jiǔ Dì) 天任 (Tiān Rèn) 惊门 (Jīng Mén) Li 9　Xin Geng	玄武 (Xuán Wǔ) 天冲 (Tiān Chōng) 开门 (Kāi Mén) Kun 2　Yi Wu/Ding
值符 (Zhi Fú) 天心 (Tiān Xīn) 景门 (Jǐng Mén) Zhen 3　Gui Yi	Yin (阴) Dun# 2 Hour: **YiMao** ©Calvin Yap	白虎 (Bái Hǔ) 天辅 (Tiān Fǔ) 休门 (Xiū Mén) Dui 7　Bing Ren
螣蛇 (Téng Shé) 天柱 (Tiān Zhù) 杜门 (Dù Mén) Gen 8　Ren Xin	太阴 (Tài Yīn) 禽芮 (Qín Ruì) 伤门 (Shāng Mén) Kan 1　Wu/Ding Ji	六合 (Liù Hé) 天英 (Tiān Yīng) 生门 (Shēng Mén) Qian 6　Geng Gui

Yin (阴) Dun# 2 Hour: **BingChen**；直符(ZhíFú): 天心(TiānXīn)
直使(ZhíShǐ): 开门(KāiMén)；句首(XúnShǒu): JiaYinGui

值符 (Zhi Fú) 天心 (Tiān Xīn) 开门 (Kāi Mén) Xun 4　Gui Bing	九天 (Jiǔ Tiān) 天蓬 (Tiān Péng) 休门 (Xiū Mén) Li 9　Ji Geng	九地 (Jiǔ Dì) 天任 (Tiān Rèn) 生门 (Shēng Mén) Kun 2　Xin Wu/Ding
螣蛇 (Téng Shé) 天柱 (Tiān Zhù) 惊门 (Jīng Mén) Zhen 3　Ren Yi	Yin (阴) Dun# 2 Hour: **BingChen** **Fan Yin** ©Calvin Yap	玄武 (Xuán Wǔ) 天冲 (Tiān Chōng) 伤门 (Shāng Mén) Dui 7　Yi Ren
太阴 (Tài Yīn) 禽芮 (Qín Ruì) 死门 (Sǐ Mén) Gen 8　Wu/Ding Xin	六合 (Liù Hé) 天英 (Tiān Yīng) 景门 (Jǐng Mén) Kan 1　Geng Ji	白虎 (Bái Hǔ) 天辅 (Tiān Fǔ) 杜门 (Dù Mén) Qian 6　Bing Gui

Yin (阴) Dun# 2 Hour: **DingSi**；直符(ZhíFú): 天心(TiānXīn)
直使(ZhíShǐ): 开门(KāiMén)；句首(XúnShǒu): JiaYinGui

太阴 (Tài Yīn) 禽芮 (Qín Ruì) 休门 (Xiū Mén) Xun 4　Wu/Ding Bing	螣蛇 (Téng Shé) 天柱 (Tiān Zhù) 生门 (Shēng Mén) Li 9　Ren Geng	值符 (Zhi Fú) 天心 (Tiān Xīn) 伤门 (Shāng Mén) Kun 2　Gui Wu/Ding
六合 (Liù Hé) 天英 (Tiān Yīng) 开门 (Kāi Mén) Zhen 3　Geng Yi	Yin (阴) Dun# 2 Hour: **DingSi** ©Calvin Yap	九天 (Jiǔ Tiān) 天蓬 (Tiān Péng) 杜门 (Dù Mén) Dui 7　Ji Ren
白虎 (Bái Hǔ) 天辅 (Tiān Fǔ) 惊门 (Jīng Mén) Gen 8　Bing Xin	玄武 (Xuán Wǔ) 天冲 (Tiān Chōng) 死门 (Sǐ Mén) Kan 1　Yi Ji	九地 (Jiǔ Dì) 天任 (Tiān Rèn) 景门 (Jǐng Mén) Qian 6　Xin Gui

Yin (阴) Dun# 2 Hour: **WuWu** ; 直符(ZhíFú): 天心(TiānXīn)
直使(ZhíShǐ): 开门(KāiMén) ; 旬首(XúnShǒu): JiaYinGui

太阴 (Tài Yīn) 禽芮 (Qín Ruì) 死门 (Sǐ Mén) Xun 4 Wu/Ding Bing	螣蛇 (Téng Shé) 天柱 (Tiān Zhù) 惊门 (Jīng Mén) Li 9 Ren Geng	值符 (Zhí Fú) 天心 (Tiān Xīn) 开门 (Kāi Mén) Kun 2 Gui Wu/Ding
六合 (Liù Hé) 天英 (Tiān Yīng) 景门 (Jǐng Mén) Zhen 3 Geng Yi	Yin (阴) Dun# 2 Hour: **WuWu** ©Calvin Yap	九天 (Jiǔ Tiān) 天蓬 (Tiān Péng) 休门 (Xiū Mén) Dui 7 Ji Ren
白虎 (Bái Hǔ) 天辅 (Tiān Fǔ) 杜门 (Dù Mén) Gen 8 Bing Xin	玄武 (Xuán Wǔ) 天冲 (Tiān Chōng) 伤门 (Shāng Mén) Kan 1 Yi Ji	九地 (Jiǔ Dì) 天任 (Tiān Rèn) 生门 (Shēng Mén) Qian 6 Xin Gui

Yin (阴) Dun# 2 Hour: **JiWei** ; 直符(ZhíFú): 天心(TiānXīn)
直使(ZhíShǐ): 开门(KāiMén) ; 旬首(XúnShǒu): JiaYinGui

玄武 (Xuán Wǔ) 天冲 (Tiān Chōng) 伤门 (Shāng Mén) Xun 4 Yi Bing	白虎 (Bái Hǔ) 天辅 (Tiān Fǔ) 杜门 (Dù Mén) Li 9 Bing Geng	六合 (Liù Hé) 天英 (Tiān Yīng) 景门 (Jǐng Mén) Kun 2 Geng Wu/Ding
九地 (Jiǔ Dì) 天任 (Tiān Rèn) 生门 (Shēng Mén) Zhen 3 Xin Yi	Yin (阴) Dun# 2 Hour: **JiWei** ©Calvin Yap	太阴 (Tài Yīn) 禽芮 (Qín Ruì) 死门 (Sǐ Mén) Dui 7 Wu/Ding Ren
九天 (Jiǔ Tiān) 天蓬 (Tiān Péng) 休门 (Xiū Mén) Gen 8 Ji Xin	值符 (Zhí Fú) 天心 (Tiān Xīn) 开门 (Kāi Mén) Kan 1 Gui Ji	螣蛇 (Téng Shé) 天柱 (Tiān Zhù) 惊门 (Jīng Mén) Qian 6 Ren Gui

Yin (阴) Dun# 2 Hour: **GengShen** ; 直符(ZhíFú): 天心(TiānXīn)
直使(ZhíShǐ): 开门(KāiMén) ; 旬首(XúnShǒu): JiaYinGui

螣蛇 (Téng Shé) 天柱 (Tiān Zhù) 惊门 (Jīng Mén) Xun 4 Ren Bing	值符 (Zhí Fú) 天心 (Tiān Xīn) 开门 (Kāi Mén) Li 9 Gui Geng	九天 (Jiǔ Tiān) 天蓬 (Tiān Péng) 休门 (Xiū Mén) Kun 2 Ji Wu/Ding
太阴 (Tài Yīn) 禽芮 (Qín Ruì) 死门 (Sǐ Mén) Zhen 3 Wu/Ding Yi	Yin (阴) Dun# 2 Hour: **GengShen** ©Calvin Yap	九地 (Jiǔ Dì) 天任 (Tiān Rèn) 生门 (Shēng Mén) Dui 7 Xin Ren
六合 (Liù Hé) 天英 (Tiān Yīng) 景门 (Jǐng Mén) Gen 8 Geng Xin	白虎 (Bái Hǔ) 天辅 (Tiān Fǔ) 杜门 (Dù Mén) Kan 1 Bing Ji	玄武 (Xuán Wǔ) 天冲 (Tiān Chōng) 伤门 (Shāng Mén) Qian 6 Yi Gui

Yin (阴) Dun# 2 Hour: **XinYou** ; 直符(ZhíFú): 天心(TiānXīn)
直使(ZhíShǐ): 开门(KāiMén) ; 旬首(XúnShǒu): JiaYinGui

九地 (Jiǔ Dì) 天任 (Tiān Rèn) 生门 (Shēng Mén) Xun 4 Xin Bing	玄武 (Xuán Wǔ) 天冲 (Tiān Chōng) 伤门 (Shāng Mén) Li 9 Yi Geng	白虎 (Bái Hǔ) 天辅 (Tiān Fǔ) 杜门 (Dù Mén) Kun 2 Bing Wu/Ding
九天 (Jiǔ Tiān) 天蓬 (Tiān Péng) 休门 (Xiū Mén) Zhen 3 Ji Yi	Yin (阴) Dun# 2 Hour: **XinYou** ©Calvin Yap	六合 (Liù Hé) 天英 (Tiān Yīng) 景门 (Jǐng Mén) Dui 7 Geng Ren
值符 (Zhí Fú) 天心 (Tiān Xīn) 开门 (Kāi Mén) Gen 8 Gui Xin	螣蛇 (Téng Shé) 天柱 (Tiān Zhù) 惊门 (Jīng Mén) Kan 1 Ren Ji	太阴 (Tài Yīn) 禽芮 (Qín Ruì) 死门 (Sǐ Mén) Qian 6 Wu/Ding Gui

Yin (阴) Dun# 2 Hour: **RenXu** ; 直符(ZhíFú): 天心(TiānXīn)
直使(ZhíShǐ): 开门(KāiMén) ; 旬首(XúnShǒu): JiaYinGui

六合 (Liù Hé) 天英 (Tiān Yīng) 景门 (Jǐng Mén) Xun 4 Geng Bing	太阴 (Tài Yīn) 禽芮 (Qín Ruì) 死门 (Sǐ Mén) Li 9 Wu/Ding Geng	螣蛇 (Téng Shé) 天柱 (Tiān Zhù) 惊门 (Jīng Mén) Kun 2 Ren Wu/Ding
白虎 (Bái Hǔ) 天辅 (Tiān Fǔ) 杜门 (Dù Mén) Zhen 3 Bing Yi	Yin (阴) Dun# 2 Hour: **RenXu** ©Calvin Yap	值符 (Zhí Fú) 天心 (Tiān Xīn) 开门 (Kāi Mén) Dui 7 Gui Ren
玄武 (Xuán Wǔ) 天冲 (Tiān Chōng) 伤门 (Shāng Mén) Gen 8 Yi Xin	九地 (Jiǔ Dì) 天任 (Tiān Rèn) 生门 (Shēng Mén) Kan 1 Xin Ji	九天 (Jiǔ Tiān) 天蓬 (Tiān Péng) 休门 (Xiū Mén) Qian 6 Ji Gui

Yin (阴) Dun# 2 Hour: **GuiHai** ; 直符(ZhíFú): 天心(TiānXīn)
直使(ZhíShǐ): 开门(KāiMén) ; 旬首(XúnShǒu): JiaYinGui

白虎 (Bái Hǔ) 天辅 (Tiān Fǔ) 杜门 (Dù Mén) Xun 4 Bing Bing	六合 (Liù Hé) 天英 (Tiān Yīng) 景门 (Jǐng Mén) Li 9 Geng Geng	太阴 (Tài Yīn) 禽芮 (Qín Ruì) 死门 (Sǐ Mén) Kun 2 Wu/Ding Wu/Ding
玄武 (Xuán Wǔ) 天冲 (Tiān Chōng) 伤门 (Shāng Mén) Zhen 3 Yi Yi	Yin (阴) Dun# 2 Hour: **GuiHai** **Fu Yin** ©Calvin Yap	螣蛇 (Téng Shé) 天柱 (Tiān Zhù) 惊门 (Jīng Mén) Dui 7 Ren Ren
九地 (Jiǔ Dì) 天任 (Tiān Rèn) 生门 (Shēng Mén) Gen 8 Xin Xin	九天 (Jiǔ Tiān) 天蓬 (Tiān Péng) 休门 (Xiū Mén) Kan 1 Ji Ji	值符 (Zhí Fú) 天心 (Tiān Xīn) 开门 (Kāi Mén) Qian 6 Gui Gui

Yin Dun#3

<table>
<tr><td colspan="3" align="center">Chart: -3JiaZi (Yin Dun #3 JiaZi Xun)
JiaZi, YiChou, BingYin, DingMao, WuChen, JiSi, GengWu, XinWei, RenShen, GuiYou</td></tr>
</table>

Yin (阴) Dun# 3 Hour: JiaZi ; 直符(ZhíFú): 天冲(TiānChōng)
直使(ZhíShǐ): 伤门(ShāngMén) ; 旬首(XúnShǒu): JiaZiWu

九天 (Jiǔ Tiān) 天辅 (Tiān Fǔ) 杜门 (Dù Mén) Xun 4 Yi Yi	九地 (Jiǔ Dì) 天英 (Tiān Yīng) 景门 (Jǐng Mén) Li 9 Xin	玄武 (Xuán Wǔ) 禽芮 (Qín Ruì) 死门 (Sǐ Mén) Kun 2 Ji/Bing
值符 (Zhí Fú) 天冲 (Tiān Chōng) 伤门 (Shāng Mén) Zhen 3 Wu Wu	**Yin (阴) Dun# 3 Hour: JiaZi** **Fu Yin** ©Calvin Yap	白虎 (Bái Hǔ) 天柱 (Tiān Zhù) 惊门 (Jīng Mén) Dui 7 Gui Gui
腾蛇 (Téng Shé) 天任 (Tiān Rèn) 生门 (Shēng Mén) Gen 8 Ren Ren	太阴 (Tài Yīn) 天蓬 (Tiān Péng) 休门 (Xiū Mén) Kan 1 Geng Geng	六合 (Liù Hé) 天心 (Tiān Xīn) 开门 (Kāi Mén) Qian 6 Ding Ding

Yin (阴) Dun# 3 Hour: YiChou ; 直符(ZhíFú): 天冲(TiānChōng)
直使(ZhíShǐ): 伤门(ShāngMén) ; 旬首(XúnShǒu): JiaZiWu

值符 (Zhí Fú) 天冲 (Tiān Chōng) 休门 (Xiū Mén) Xun 4 Wu Yi	九天 (Jiǔ Tiān) 天辅 (Tiān Fǔ) 生门 (Shēng Mén) Li 9 Yi Xin	九地 (Jiǔ Dì) 天英 (Tiān Yīng) 伤门 (Shāng Mén) Kun 2 Xin Ji/Bing
腾蛇 (Téng Shé) 天任 (Tiān Rèn) 开门 (Kāi Mén) Zhen 3 Ren Wu	**Yin (阴) Dun# 3 Hour: YiChou** ©Calvin Yap	玄武 (Xuán Wǔ) 禽芮 (Qín Ruì) 杜门 (Dù Mén) Dui 7 Ji/Bing Gui
太阴 (Tài Yīn) 天蓬 (Tiān Péng) 惊门 (Jīng Mén) Gen 8 Geng Ren	六合 (Liù Hé) 天心 (Tiān Xīn) 死门 (Sǐ Mén) Kan 1 Ding Geng	白虎 (Bái Hǔ) 天柱 (Tiān Zhù) 景门 (Jǐng Mén) Qian 6 Gui Ding

Yin (阴) Dun# 3 Hour: BingYin ; 直符(ZhíFú): 天冲(TiānChōng)
直使(ZhíShǐ): 伤门(ShāngMén) ; 旬首(XúnShǒu): JiaZiWu

太阴 (Tài Yīn) 天蓬 (Tiān Péng) 死门 (Sǐ Mén) Xun 4 Geng Yi	腾蛇 (Téng Shé) 天任 (Tiān Rèn) 惊门 (Jīng Mén) Li 9 Ren Xin	值符 (Zhí Fú) 天冲 (Tiān Chōng) 开门 (Kāi Mén) Kun 2 Wu Ji/Bing
六合 (Liù Hé) 天心 (Tiān Xīn) 景门 (Jǐng Mén) Zhen 3 Ding Wu	**Yin (阴) Dun# 3 Hour: BingYin** ©Calvin Yap	九天 (Jiǔ Tiān) 天辅 (Tiān Fǔ) 休门 (Xiū Mén) Dui 7 Yi Gui
白虎 (Bái Hǔ) 天柱 (Tiān Zhù) 杜门 (Dù Mén) Gen 8 Gui Ren	玄武 (Xuán Wǔ) 禽芮 (Qín Ruì) 伤门 (Shāng Mén) Kan 1 Ji/Bing Geng	九地 (Jiǔ Dì) 天英 (Tiān Yīng) 生门 (Shēng Mén) Qian 6 Xin Ding

Yin (阴) Dun# 3 Hour: DingMao ; 直符(ZhíFú): 天冲(TiānChōng)
直使(ZhíShǐ): 伤门(ShāngMén) ; 旬首(XúnShǒu): JiaZiWu

白虎 (Bái Hǔ) 天柱 (Tiān Zhù) 生门 (Shēng Mén) Xun 4 Gui Yi	六合 (Liù Hé) 天心 (Tiān Xīn) 伤门 (Shāng Mén) Li 9 Ding Xin	太阴 (Tài Yīn) 天蓬 (Tiān Péng) 杜门 (Dù Mén) Kun 2 Geng Ji/Bing
玄武 (Xuán Wǔ) 禽芮 (Qín Ruì) 休门 (Xiū Mén) Zhen 3 Ji/Bing Wu	**Yin (阴) Dun# 3 Hour: DingMao** ©Calvin Yap	腾蛇 (Téng Shé) 天任 (Tiān Rèn) 景门 (Jǐng Mén) Dui 7 Ren Gui
九地 (Jiǔ Dì) 天英 (Tiān Yīng) 开门 (Kāi Mén) Gen 8 Xin Ren	九天 (Jiǔ Tiān) 天辅 (Tiān Fǔ) 惊门 (Jīng Mén) Kan 1 Yi Geng	值符 (Zhí Fú) 天冲 (Tiān Chōng) 死门 (Sǐ Mén) Qian 6 Wu Ding

Yin (阴) Dun# 3 Hour: WuChen ; 直符(ZhíFú): 天冲(TiānChōng)
直使(ZhíShǐ): 伤门(ShāngMén) ; 旬首(XúnShǒu): JiaZiWu

九天 (Jiǔ Tiān) 天辅 (Tiān Fǔ) 景门 (Jǐng Mén) Xun 4 Yi Yi	九地 (Jiǔ Dì) 天英 (Tiān Yīng) 死门 (Sǐ Mén) Li 9 Xin Xin	玄武 (Xuán Wǔ) 禽芮 (Qín Ruì) 惊门 (Jīng Mén) Kun 2 Ji/Bing Ji/Bing
值符 (Zhí Fú) 天冲 (Tiān Chōng) 杜门 (Dù Mén) Zhen 3 Wu Wu	**Yin (阴) Dun# 3 Hour: WuChen** **Fu Yin** ©Calvin Yap	白虎 (Bái Hǔ) 天柱 (Tiān Zhù) 开门 (Kāi Mén) Dui 7 Gui Gui
腾蛇 (Téng Shé) 天任 (Tiān Rèn) 伤门 (Shāng Mén) Gen 8 Ren Ren	太阴 (Tài Yīn) 天蓬 (Tiān Péng) 生门 (Shēng Mén) Kan 1 Geng Geng	六合 (Liù Hé) 天心 (Tiān Xīn) 休门 (Xiū Mén) Qian 6 Ding Ding

Yin (阴) Dun# 3 Hour: JiSi ; 直符(ZhíFú): 天冲(TiānChōng)
直使(ZhíShǐ): 伤门(ShāngMén) ; 旬首(XúnShǒu): JiaZiWu

太阴 (Tài Yīn) 天蓬 (Tiān Péng) 开门 (Kāi Mén) Xun 4 Geng Yi	腾蛇 (Téng Shé) 天任 (Tiān Rèn) 休门 (Xiū Mén) Li 9 Ren Xin	值符 (Zhí Fú) 天冲 (Tiān Chōng) 生门 (Shēng Mén) Kun 2 Wu Ji/Bing
六合 (Liù Hé) 天心 (Tiān Xīn) 惊门 (Jīng Mén) Zhen 3 Ding Wu	**Yin (阴) Dun# 3 Hour: JiSi** ©Calvin Yap	九天 (Jiǔ Tiān) 天辅 (Tiān Fǔ) 伤门 (Shāng Mén) Dui 7 Yi Gui
白虎 (Bái Hǔ) 天柱 (Tiān Zhù) 死门 (Sǐ Mén) Gen 8 Gui Ren	玄武 (Xuán Wǔ) 禽芮 (Qín Ruì) 景门 (Jǐng Mén) Kan 1 Ji/Bing Geng	九地 (Jiǔ Dì) 天英 (Tiān Yīng) 杜门 (Dù Mén) Qian 6 Xin Ding

Yin (阴) Dun# 3 Hour: **GengWu**；直符(ZhíFú): 天冲(TiānChōng)
直使(ZhíShǐ): 伤门(ShāngMén)；旬首(XúnShǒu): JiaZiWu

玄武 (Xuán Wǔ) 禽芮 (Qín Ruì) 惊门 (Jīng Mén) Xun 4 Ji/Bing Yi	白虎 (Bái Hǔ) 天柱 (Tiān Zhù) 开门 (Kāi Mén) Li 9 Gui Xin	六合 (Liù Hé) 天心 (Tiān Xīn) 休门 (Xiū Mén) Kun 2 Ding Ji/Bing
九地 (Jiǔ Dì) 天英 (Tiān Yīng) 死门 (Sǐ Mén) Zhen 3 Xin Wu	Yin (阴) Dun# 3 Hour: **GengWu** ©Calvin Yap	太阴 (Tài Yīn) 天蓬 (Tiān Péng) 生门 (Shēng Mén) Dui 7 Geng Gui
九天 (Jiǔ Tiān) 天辅 (Tiān Fǔ) 景门 (Jīng Mén) Gen 8 Yi Ren	值符 (Zhí Fú) 天冲 (Tiān Chōng) 杜门 (Dù Mén) Kan 1 Wu Geng	腾蛇 (Téng Shé) 天任 (Tiān Rèn) 伤门 (Shāng Mén) Qian 6 Ren Ding

Yin (阴) Dun# 3 Hour: **XinWei**；直符(ZhíFú): 天冲(TiānChōng)
直使(ZhíShǐ): 伤门(ShāngMén)；旬首(XúnShǒu): JiaZiWu

腾蛇 (Téng Shé) 天任 (Tiān Rèn) 休门 (Xiū Mén) Xun 4 Ren Yi	值符 (Zhí Fú) 天冲 (Tiān Chōng) 生门 (Shēng Mén) Li 9 Wu Xin	九天 (Jiǔ Tiān) 天辅 (Tiān Fǔ) 伤门 (Shāng Mén) Kun 2 Yi Ji/Bing
太阴 (Tài Yīn) 天蓬 (Tiān Péng) 开门 (Kāi Mén) Zhen 3 Geng Wu	Yin (阴) Dun# 3 Hour: **XinWei** ©Calvin Yap	九地 (Jiǔ Dì) 天英 (Tiān Yīng) 杜门 (Dù Mén) Dui 7 Xin Gui
六合 (Liù Hé) 天心 (Tiān Xīn) 惊门 (Jīng Mén) Gen 8 Ding Ren	白虎 (Bái Hǔ) 天柱 (Tiān Zhù) 死门 (Sǐ Mén) Kan 1 Gui Geng	玄武 (Xuán Wǔ) 禽芮 (Qín Ruì) 景门 (Jīng Mén) Qian 6 Ji/Bing Ding

Yin (阴) Dun# 3 Hour: **RenShen**；直符(ZhíFú): 天冲(TiānChōng)
直使(ZhíShǐ): 伤门(ShāngMén)；旬首(XúnShǒu): JiaZiWu

九地 (Jiǔ Dì) 天英 (Tiān Yīng) 伤门 (Shāng Mén) Xun 4 Xin Yi	玄武 (Xuán Wǔ) 禽芮 (Qín Ruì) 杜门 (Dù Mén) Li 9 Ji/Bing Xin	白虎 (Bái Hǔ) 天柱 (Tiān Zhù) 景门 (Jīng Mén) Kun 2 Gui Ji/Bing
九天 (Jiǔ Tiān) 天辅 (Tiān Fǔ) 生门 (Shēng Mén) Zhen 3 Yi Wu	Yin (阴) Dun# 3 Hour: **RenShen** ©Calvin Yap	六合 (Liù Hé) 天心 (Tiān Xīn) 死门 (Sǐ Mén) Dui 7 Ding Gui
值符 (Zhí Fú) 天冲 (Tiān Chōng) 休门 (Xiū Mén) Gen 8 Wu Ren	腾蛇 (Téng Shé) 天任 (Tiān Rèn) 开门 (Kāi Mén) Kan 1 Ren Geng	太阴 (Tài Yīn) 天蓬 (Tiān Péng) 惊门 (Jīng Mén) Qian 6 Geng Ding

Yin (阴) Dun# 3 Hour: **GuiYou**；直符(ZhíFú): 天冲(TiānChōng)
直使(ZhíShǐ): 伤门(ShāngMén)；旬首(XúnShǒu): JiaZiWu

六合 (Liù Hé) 天心 (Tiān Xīn) 杜门 (Dù Mén) Xun 4 Ding Yi	太阴 (Tài Yīn) 天蓬 (Tiān Péng) 景门 (Jīng Mén) Li 9 Geng Xin	腾蛇 (Téng Shé) 天任 (Tiān Rèn) 死门 (Sǐ Mén) Kun 2 Ren Ji/Bing
白虎 (Bái Hǔ) 天柱 (Tiān Zhù) 伤门 (Shāng Mén) Zhen 3 Gui Wu	Yin (阴) Dun# 3 Hour: **GuiYou** **Fan Yin** ©Calvin Yap	值符 (Zhí Fú) 天冲 (Tiān Chōng) 惊门 (Jīng Mén) Dui 7 Wu Gui
玄武 (Xuán Wǔ) 禽芮 (Qín Ruì) 生门 (Shēng Mén) Gen 8 Ji/Bing Ren	九地 (Jiǔ Dì) 天英 (Tiān Yīng) 休门 (Xiū Mén) Kan 1 Xin Geng	九天 (Jiǔ Tiān) 天辅 (Tiān Fǔ) 开门 (Kāi Mén) Qian 6 Yi Ding

Chart: -3JiaXu (Yin Dun #3 JiaXu Xun)
JiaXu, YiHai, BingZi, DingChou, WuYin, JiMao, GengChen, XinSi, RenWu, GuiWei

Yin (阴) Dun# 3 Hour: **JiaXu**；直符(ZhíFú): 天芮(TiānRuì)
直使(ZhíShǐ): 死门(SǐMén)；旬首(XúnShǒu): JiaXuJi

太阴 (Tài Yīn) 天辅 (Tiān Fǔ) 杜门 (Dù Mén) Xun 4 Yi Yi	腾蛇 (Téng Shé) 天英 (Tiān Yīng) 景门 (Jīng Mén) Li 9 Xin Xin	值符 (Zhí Fú) 禽芮 (Qín Ruì) 死门 (Sǐ Mén) Kun 2 Ji/Bing Ji/Bing
六合 (Liù Hé) 天冲 (Tiān Chōng) 伤门 (Shāng Mén) Zhen 3 Wu Wu	Yin (阴) Dun# 3 Hour: **JiaXu** **Fu Yin** ©Calvin Yap	九天 (Jiǔ Tiān) 天柱 (Tiān Zhù) 惊门 (Jīng Mén) Dui 7 Gui Gui
白虎 (Bái Hǔ) 天任 (Tiān Rèn) 生门 (Shēng Mén) Gen 8 Ren Ren	玄武 (Xuán Wǔ) 天蓬 (Tiān Péng) 休门 (Xiū Mén) Kan 1 Geng Geng	九地 (Jiǔ Dì) 天心 (Tiān Xīn) 开门 (Kāi Mén) Qian 6 Ding Ding

Yin (阴) Dun# 3 Hour: **YiHai**；直符(ZhíFú): 天芮(TiānRuì)
直使(ZhíShǐ): 死门(SǐMén)；旬首(XúnShǒu): JiaXuJi

值符 (Zhí Fú) 禽芮 (Qín Ruì) 休门 (Xiū Mén) Xun 4 Ji/Bing Yi	九天 (Jiǔ Tiān) 天柱 (Tiān Zhù) 生门 (Shēng Mén) Li 9 Gui Xin	九地 (Jiǔ Dì) 天心 (Tiān Xīn) 伤门 (Shāng Mén) Kun 2 Ding Ji/Bing
腾蛇 (Téng Shé) 天英 (Tiān Yīng) 开门 (Kāi Mén) Zhen 3 Xin Wu	Yin (阴) Dun# 3 Hour: **YiHai** ©Calvin Yap	玄武 (Xuán Wǔ) 天蓬 (Tiān Péng) 杜门 (Dù Mén) Dui 7 Geng Gui
太阴 (Tài Yīn) 天辅 (Tiān Fǔ) 惊门 (Jīng Mén) Gen 8 Yi Ren	六合 (Liù Hé) 天冲 (Tiān Chōng) 死门 (Sǐ Mén) Kan 1 Wu Geng	白虎 (Bái Hǔ) 天任 (Tiān Rèn) 景门 (Jīng Mén) Qian 6 Ren Ding

Yin (阴) Dun# 3 Hour: **BingZi** ; 直符(ZhíFú): 天芮(TiānRuì)
直使(ZhíShǐ): 死门(SǐMén) ; 旬首(XúnShǒu): JiaXuJi

太阴 (Tài Yīn) 天辅 (Tiān Fǔ) 景门 (Jǐng Mén) Xun 4　Yi 　Yi	螣蛇 (Téng Shé) 天英 (Tiān Yīng) 死门 (Sǐ Mén) Li 9　Xin 　Xin	值符 (Zhí Fú) 禽芮 (Qín Ruì) 惊门 (Jǐng Mén) Kun 2　Ji/Bing 　Ji/Bing
六合 (Liù Hé) 天冲 (Tiān Chōng) 杜门 (Dù Mén) Zhen 3　Wu 　Wu	Yin (阴) Dun# 3 Hour: **BingZi** **Fu Yin** ©Calvin Yap	九天 (Jiǔ Tiān) 天柱 (Tiān Zhù) 开门 (Kāi Mén) Dui 7　Gui 　Gui
白虎 (Bái Hǔ) 天任 (Tiān Rèn) 伤门 (Shāng Mén) Gen 8　Ren 　Ren	玄武 (Xuán Wǔ) 天蓬 (Tiān Péng) 生门 (Shēng Mén) Kan 1　Geng 　Geng	九地 (Jiǔ Dì) 天心 (Tiān Xīn) 休门 (Xiū Mén) Qian 6　Ding 　Ding

Yin (阴) Dun# 3 Hour: **DingChou** ; 直符(ZhíFú): 天芮(TiānRuì)
直使(ZhíShǐ): 死门(SǐMén) ; 旬首(XúnShǒu): JiaXuJi

白虎 (Bái Hǔ) 天任 (Tiān Rèn) 开门 (Kāi Mén) Xun 4　Ren 　Yi	六合 (Liù Hé) 天冲 (Tiān Chōng) 休门 (Xiū Mén) Li 9　Wu 　Xin	太阴 (Tài Yīn) 天辅 (Tiān Fǔ) 生门 (Shēng Mén) Kun 2　Yi 　Ji/Bing
玄武 (Xuán Wǔ) 天蓬 (Tiān Péng) 惊门 (Jǐng Mén) Zhen 3　Geng 　Wu	Yin (阴) Dun# 3 Hour: **DingChou** ©Calvin Yap	螣蛇 (Téng Shé) 天英 (Tiān Yīng) 伤门 (Shāng Mén) Dui 7　Xin 　Gui
九地 (Jiǔ Dì) 天心 (Tiān Xīn) 死门 (Sǐ Mén) Gen 8　Ding 　Ren	九天 (Jiǔ Tiān) 天柱 (Tiān Zhù) 景门 (Jǐng Mén) Kan 1　Gui 　Geng	值符 (Zhí Fú) 禽芮 (Qín Ruì) 杜门 (Dù Mén) Qian 6　Ji/Bing 　Ding

Yin (阴) Dun# 3 Hour: **WuYin** ; 直符(ZhíFú): 天芮(TiānRuì)
直使(ZhíShǐ): 死门(SǐMén) ; 旬首(XúnShǒu): JiaXuJi

九天 (Jiǔ Tiān) 天柱 (Tiān Zhù) 伤门 (Shāng Mén) Xun 4　Gui 　Yi	九地 (Jiǔ Dì) 天心 (Tiān Xīn) 杜门 (Dù Mén) Li 9　Ding 　Xin	玄武 (Xuán Wǔ) 天蓬 (Tiān Péng) 景门 (Jǐng Mén) Kun 2　Geng 　Ji/Bing
值符 (Zhí Fú) 禽芮 (Qín Ruì) 生门 (Shēng Mén) Zhen 3　Ji/Bing 　Wu	Yin (阴) Dun# 3 Hour: **WuYin** ©Calvin Yap	白虎 (Bái Hǔ) 天任 (Tiān Rèn) 死门 (Sǐ Mén) Dui 7　Ren 　Gui
螣蛇 (Téng Shé) 天英 (Tiān Yīng) 休门 (Xiū Mén) Gen 8　Xin 　Ren	太阴 (Tài Yīn) 天辅 (Tiān Fǔ) 开门 (Kāi Mén) Kan 1　Yi 　Geng	六合 (Liù Hé) 天冲 (Tiān Chōng) 惊门 (Jǐng Mén) Qian 6　Wu 　Ding

Yin (阴) Dun# 3 Hour: **JiMao** ; 直符(ZhíFú): 天芮(TiānRuì)
直使(ZhíShǐ): 死门(SǐMén) ; 旬首(XúnShǒu): JiaXuJi

太阴 (Tài Yīn) 天辅 (Tiān Fǔ) 生门 (Shēng Mén) Xun 4　Yi 　Yi	螣蛇 (Téng Shé) 天英 (Tiān Yīng) 伤门 (Shāng Mén) Li 9　Xin 　Xin	值符 (Zhí Fú) 禽芮 (Qín Ruì) 杜门 (Dù Mén) Kun 2　Ji/Bing 　Ji/Bing
六合 (Liù Hé) 天冲 (Tiān Chōng) 休门 (Xiū Mén) Zhen 3　Wu 　Wu	Yin (阴) Dun# 3 Hour: **JiMao** **Fu Yin** ©Calvin Yap	九天 (Jiǔ Tiān) 天柱 (Tiān Zhù) 景门 (Jǐng Mén) Dui 7　Gui 　Gui
白虎 (Bái Hǔ) 天任 (Tiān Rèn) 开门 (Kāi Mén) Gen 8　Ren 　Ren	玄武 (Xuán Wǔ) 天蓬 (Tiān Péng) 惊门 (Jǐng Mén) Kan 1　Geng 　Geng	九地 (Jiǔ Dì) 天心 (Tiān Xīn) 死门 (Sǐ Mén) Qian 6　Ding 　Ding

Yin (阴) Dun# 3 Hour: **GengChen** ; 直符(ZhíFú): 天芮(TiānRuì)
直使(ZhíShǐ): 死门(SǐMén) ; 旬首(XúnShǒu): JiaXuJi

玄武 (Xuán Wǔ) 天蓬 (Tiān Péng) 杜门 (Dù Mén) Xun 4　Geng 　Yi	白虎 (Bái Hǔ) 天任 (Tiān Rèn) 景门 (Jǐng Mén) Li 9　Ren 　Xin	六合 (Liù Hé) 天冲 (Tiān Chōng) 死门 (Sǐ Mén) Kun 2　Wu 　Ji/Bing
九地 (Jiǔ Dì) 天心 (Tiān Xīn) 伤门 (Shāng Mén) Zhen 3　Ding 　Wu	Yin (阴) Dun# 3 Hour: **GengChen** ©Calvin Yap	太阴 (Tài Yīn) 天辅 (Tiān Fǔ) 惊门 (Jǐng Mén) Dui 7　Yi 　Gui
九天 (Jiǔ Tiān) 天柱 (Tiān Zhù) 生门 (Shēng Mén) Gen 8　Gui 　Ren	值符 (Zhí Fú) 禽芮 (Qín Ruì) 休门 (Xiū Mén) Kan 1　Ji/Bing 　Geng	螣蛇 (Téng Shé) 天英 (Tiān Yīng) 开门 (Kāi Mén) Qian 6　Xin 　Ding

Yin (阴) Dun# 3 Hour: **XinSi** ; 直符(ZhíFú): 天芮(TiānRuì)
直使(ZhíShǐ): 死门(SǐMén) ; 旬首(XúnShǒu): JiaXuJi

螣蛇 (Téng Shé) 天英 (Tiān Yīng) 死门 (Sǐ Mén) Xun 4　Xin 　Yi	值符 (Zhí Fú) 禽芮 (Qín Ruì) 惊门 (Jǐng Mén) Li 9　Ji/Bing 　Xin	九天 (Jiǔ Tiān) 天柱 (Tiān Zhù) 开门 (Kāi Mén) Kun 2　Gui 　Ji/Bing
太阴 (Tài Yīn) 天辅 (Tiān Fǔ) 景门 (Jǐng Mén) Zhen 3　Yi 　Wu	Yin (阴) Dun# 3 Hour: **XinSi** ©Calvin Yap	九地 (Jiǔ Dì) 天心 (Tiān Xīn) 休门 (Xiū Mén) Dui 7　Ding 　Gui
六合 (Liù Hé) 天冲 (Tiān Chōng) 杜门 (Dù Mén) Gen 8　Wu 　Ren	白虎 (Bái Hǔ) 天任 (Tiān Rèn) 伤门 (Shāng Mén) Kan 1　Ren 　Geng	玄武 (Xuán Wǔ) 天蓬 (Tiān Péng) 生门 (Shēng Mén) Qian 6　Geng 　Ding

Yin (阴) Dun# 3 Hour: **RenWu**；直符(ZhíFú): 天芮(TiānRuì)
直使(ZhǐShǐ): 死门(SǐMén)；旬首(XúnShǒu): JiaXuJi

九地 (Jiǔ Dì) 天心 (Tiān Xīn) 惊门 (Jīng Mén) Xun 4　Ding Yi	玄武 (Xuán Wǔ) 天蓬 (Tiān Péng) 开门 (Kāi Mén) Li 9　Geng Xin	白虎 (Bái Hǔ) 天任 (Tiān Rèn) 休门 (Xiū Mén) Kun 2　Ren Ji/Bing
九天 (Jiǔ Tiān) 天柱 (Tiān Zhù) 死门 (Sǐ Mén) Zhen 3　Gui Wu	Yin (阴) Dun# 3 Hour: **RenWu** **Fan Yin** ©Calvin Yap	六合 (Liù Hé) 天冲 (Tiān Chōng) 生门 (Shēng Mén) Dui 7　Wu Gui
值符 (Zhí Fú) 禽芮 (Qín Ruì) 景门 (Jǐng Mén) Gen 8　Ji/Bing Ren	腾蛇 (Téng Shé) 天英 (Tiān Yīng) 杜门 (Dù Mén) Kan 1　Xin Geng	太阴 (Tài Yīn) 天辅 (Tiān Fǔ) 伤门 (Shāng Mén) Qian 6　Yi Ding

Yin (阴) Dun# 3 Hour: **GuiWei**；直符(ZhíFú): 天芮(TiānRuì)
直使(ZhǐShǐ): 死门(SǐMén)；旬首(XúnShǒu): JiaXuJi

六合 (Liù Hé) 天冲 (Tiān Chōng) 杜门 (Dù Mén) Xun 4　Wu Yi	太阴 (Tài Yīn) 天辅 (Tiān Fǔ) 景门 (Jǐng Mén) Li 9　Yi Xin	腾蛇 (Téng Shé) 天英 (Tiān Yīng) 死门 (Sǐ Mén) Kun 2　Xin Ji/Bing
白虎 (Bái Hǔ) 天任 (Tiān Rèn) 伤门 (Shāng Mén) Zhen 3　Ren Wu	Yin (阴) Dun# 3 Hour: **GuiWei** ©Calvin Yap	值符 (Zhí Fú) 禽芮 (Qín Ruì) 惊门 (Jīng Mén) Dui 7　Ji/Bing Gui
玄武 (Xuán Wǔ) 天蓬 (Tiān Péng) 生门 (Shēng Mén) Gen 8　Geng Ren	九地 (Jiǔ Dì) 天心 (Tiān Xīn) 休门 (Xiū Mén) Kan 1　Ding Geng	九天 (Jiǔ Tiān) 天柱 (Tiān Zhù) 开门 (Kāi Mén) Qian 6　Gui Ding

---

Chart: **-3JiaShen** (Yin Dun #3 JiaShen Xun)
JiaShen, YiYou, BingXu, DingHai, WuZi, JiChou, GengYin, XinMao, RenChen, GuiSi

Yin (阴) Dun# 3 Hour: **JiaShen**；直符(ZhíFú): 天蓬(TiānPéng)
直使(ZhǐShǐ): 休门(XiūMén)；旬首(XúnShǒu): JiaShenGeng

玄武 (Xuán Wǔ) 天辅 (Tiān Fǔ) 杜门 (Dù Mén) Xun 4　Yi Yi	白虎 (Bái Hǔ) 天英 (Tiān Yīng) 景门 (Jǐng Mén) Li 9　Xin Xin	六合 (Liù Hé) 禽芮 (Qín Ruì) 死门 (Sǐ Mén) Kun 2　Ji/Bing Ji/Bing
九地 (Jiǔ Dì) 天冲 (Tiān Chōng) 伤门 (Shāng Mén) Zhen 3　Wu Wu	Yin (阴) Dun# 3 Hour: **JiaShen** **Fu Yin** ©Calvin Yap	太阴 (Tài Yīn) 天柱 (Tiān Zhù) 惊门 (Jīng Mén) Dui 7　Gui Gui
九天 (Jiǔ Tiān) 天任 (Tiān Rèn) 生门 (Shēng Mén) Gen 8　Ren Ren	值符 (Zhí Fú) 天蓬 (Tiān Péng) 休门 (Xiū Mén) Kan 1　Geng Geng	腾蛇 (Téng Shé) 天心 (Tiān Xīn) 开门 (Kāi Mén) Qian 6　Ding Ding

Yin (阴) Dun# 3 Hour: **YiYou**；直符(ZhíFú): 天蓬(TiānPéng)
直使(ZhǐShǐ): 休门(XiūMén)；旬首(XúnShǒu): JiaShenGeng

值符 (Zhí Fú) 天蓬 (Tiān Péng) 开门 (Kāi Mén) Xun 4　Geng Yi	九天 (Jiǔ Tiān) 天任 (Tiān Rèn) 休门 (Xiū Mén) Li 9　Ren Xin	九地 (Jiǔ Dì) 天冲 (Tiān Chōng) 生门 (Shēng Mén) Kun 2　Wu Ji/Bing
腾蛇 (Téng Shé) 天心 (Tiān Xīn) 惊门 (Jīng Mén) Zhen 3　Ding Wu	Yin (阴) Dun# 3 Hour: **YiYou** ©Calvin Yap	玄武 (Xuán Wǔ) 天辅 (Tiān Fǔ) 伤门 (Shāng Mén) Dui 7　Yi Gui
太阴 (Tài Yīn) 天柱 (Tiān Zhù) 死门 (Sǐ Mén) Gen 8　Gui Ren	六合 (Liù Hé) 禽芮 (Qín Ruì) 景门 (Jǐng Mén) Kan 1　Ji/Bing Geng	白虎 (Bái Hǔ) 天英 (Tiān Yīng) 杜门 (Dù Mén) Qian 6　Xin Ding

Yin (阴) Dun# 3 Hour: **BingXu**；直符(ZhíFú): 天蓬(TiānPéng)
直使(ZhǐShǐ): 休门(XiūMén)；旬首(XúnShǒu): JiaShenGeng

太阴 (Tài Yīn) 天柱 (Tiān Zhù) 伤门 (Shāng Mén) Xun 4　Gui Yi	腾蛇 (Téng Shé) 天心 (Tiān Xīn) 杜门 (Dù Mén) Li 9　Ding Xin	值符 (Zhí Fú) 天蓬 (Tiān Péng) 景门 (Jǐng Mén) Kun 2　Geng Ji/Bing
六合 (Liù Hé) 禽芮 (Qín Ruì) 生门 (Shēng Mén) Zhen 3　Ji/Bing Wu	Yin (阴) Dun# 3 Hour: **BingXu** ©Calvin Yap	九天 (Jiǔ Tiān) 天任 (Tiān Rèn) 死门 (Sǐ Mén) Dui 7　Ren Gui
白虎 (Bái Hǔ) 天英 (Tiān Yīng) 休门 (Xiū Mén) Gen 8　Xin Ren	玄武 (Xuán Wǔ) 天辅 (Tiān Fǔ) 开门 (Kāi Mén) Kan 1　Yi Geng	九地 (Jiǔ Dì) 天冲 (Tiān Chōng) 惊门 (Jīng Mén) Qian 6　Wu Ding

Yin (阴) Dun# 3 Hour: **DingHai**；直符(ZhíFú): 天蓬(TiānPéng)
直使(ZhǐShǐ): 休门(XiūMén)；旬首(XúnShǒu): JiaShenGeng

白虎 (Bái Hǔ) 天英 (Tiān Yīng) 死门 (Sǐ Mén) Xun 4　Xin Yi	六合 (Liù Hé) 禽芮 (Qín Ruì) 惊门 (Jīng Mén) Li 9　Ji/Bing Xin	太阴 (Tài Yīn) 天柱 (Tiān Zhù) 开门 (Kāi Mén) Kun 2　Gui Ji/Bing
玄武 (Xuán Wǔ) 天辅 (Tiān Fǔ) 景门 (Jǐng Mén) Zhen 3　Yi Wu	Yin (阴) Dun# 3 Hour: **DingHai** ©Calvin Yap	腾蛇 (Téng Shé) 天心 (Tiān Xīn) 休门 (Xiū Mén) Dui 7　Ding Gui
九地 (Jiǔ Dì) 天冲 (Tiān Chōng) 杜门 (Dù Mén) Gen 8　Wu Ren	九天 (Jiǔ Tiān) 天任 (Tiān Rèn) 伤门 (Shāng Mén) Kan 1　Ren Geng	值符 (Zhí Fú) 天蓬 (Tiān Péng) 生门 (Shēng Mén) Qian 6　Geng Ding

Yin (阴) Dun# 3 Hour: WuZi；直符(ZhíFú): 天蓬(TiānPéng)
直使(ZhíShǐ): 休门(XiūMén)；旬首(XúnShǒu): JiaShenGeng

九天 (Jiǔ Tiān) 天任 (Tiān Rèn) 景门 (Jǐng Mén) Xun 4　Ren Yi	九地 (Jiǔ Dì) 天冲 (Tiān Chōng) 死门 (Sǐ Mén) Li 9　Wu Xin	玄武 (Xuán Wǔ) 天辅 (Tiān Fǔ) 惊门 (Jīng Mén) Kun 2　Yi Ji/Bing
值符 (Zhí Fú) 天蓬 (Tiān Péng) 杜门 (Dù Mén) Zhen 3　Geng Wu	Yin (阴) Dun# 3 Hour: **WuZi** ©Calvin Yap	白虎 (Bái Hǔ) 天英 (Tiān Yīng) 开门 (Kāi Mén) Dui 7　Xin Gui
螣蛇 (Téng Shé) 天心 (Tiān Xīn) 伤门 (Shāng Mén) Gen 8　Ding Ren	太阴 (Tài Yīn) 天柱 (Tiān Zhù) 生门 (Shēng Mén) Kan 1　Gui Geng	六合 (Liù Hé) 禽芮 (Qín Ruì) 休门 (Xiū Mén) Qian 6　Ji/Bing Ding

Yin (阴) Dun# 3 Hour: JiChou；直符(ZhíFú): 天蓬(TiānPéng)
直使(ZhíShǐ): 休门(XiūMén)；旬首(XúnShǒu): JiaShenGeng

太阴 (Tài Yīn) 天柱 (Tiān Zhù) 惊门 (Jīng Mén) Xun 4　Gui Yi	螣蛇 (Téng Shé) 天心 (Tiān Xīn) 开门 (Kāi Mén) Li 9　Ding Xin	值符 (Zhí Fú) 天蓬 (Tiān Péng) 休门 (Xiū Mén) Kun 2　Geng Ji/Bing
六合 (Liù Hé) 禽芮 (Qín Ruì) 死门 (Sǐ Mén) Zhen 3　Ji/Bing Wu	Yin (阴) Dun# 3 Hour: **JiChou** ©Calvin Yap	九天 (Jiǔ Tiān) 天任 (Tiān Rèn) 生门 (Shēng Mén) Dui 7　Ren Gui
白虎 (Bái Hǔ) 天英 (Tiān Yīng) 景门 (Jǐng Mén) Gen 8　Xin Ren	玄武 (Xuán Wǔ) 天辅 (Tiān Fǔ) 杜门 (Dù Mén) Kan 1　Yi Geng	九地 (Jiǔ Dì) 天冲 (Tiān Chōng) 伤门 (Shāng Mén) Qian 6　Wu Ding

Yin (阴) Dun# 3 Hour: GengYin；直符(ZhíFú): 天蓬(TiānPéng)
直使(ZhíShǐ): 休门(XiūMén)；旬首(XúnShǒu): JiaShenGeng

玄武 (Xuán Wǔ) 天辅 (Tiān Fǔ) 休门 (Xiū Mén) Xun 4　Yi Yi	白虎 (Bái Hǔ) 天英 (Tiān Yīng) 生门 (Shēng Mén) Li 9　Xin Xin	六合 (Liù Hé) 禽芮 (Qín Ruì) 伤门 (Shāng Mén) Kun 2　Ji/Bing Ji/Bing
九地 (Jiǔ Dì) 天冲 (Tiān Chōng) 开门 (Kāi Mén) Zhen 3　Wu Wu	Yin (阴) Dun# 3 Hour: **GengYin** **Fu Yin** ©Calvin Yap	太阴 (Tài Yīn) 天柱 (Tiān Zhù) 杜门 (Dù Mén) Dui 7　Gui Gui
九天 (Jiǔ Tiān) 天任 (Tiān Rèn) 惊门 (Jīng Mén) Gen 8　Ren Ren	值符 (Zhí Fú) 天蓬 (Tiān Péng) 死门 (Sǐ Mén) Kan 1　Geng Geng	螣蛇 (Téng Shé) 天心 (Tiān Xīn) 景门 (Jǐng Mén) Qian 6　Ding Ding

Yin (阴) Dun# 3 Hour: XinMao；直符(ZhíFú): 天蓬(TiānPéng)
直使(ZhíShǐ): 休门(XiūMén)；旬首(XúnShǒu): JiaShenGeng

螣蛇 (Téng Shé) 天心 (Tiān Xīn) 生门 (Shēng Mén) Xun 4　Ding Yi	值符 (Zhí Fú) 天蓬 (Tiān Péng) 伤门 (Shāng Mén) Li 9　Geng Xin	九天 (Jiǔ Tiān) 天任 (Tiān Rèn) 杜门 (Dù Mén) Kun 2　Ren Ji/Bing
太阴 (Tài Yīn) 天柱 (Tiān Zhù) 休门 (Xiū Mén) Zhen 3　Gui Wu	Yin (阴) Dun# 3 Hour: **XinMao** **Fan Yin** ©Calvin Yap	九地 (Jiǔ Dì) 天冲 (Tiān Chōng) 景门 (Jǐng Mén) Dui 7　Wu Gui
六合 (Liù Hé) 禽芮 (Qín Ruì) 开门 (Kāi Mén) Gen 8　Ji/Bing Ren	白虎 (Bái Hǔ) 天英 (Tiān Yīng) 惊门 (Jīng Mén) Kan 1　Xin Geng	玄武 (Xuán Wǔ) 天辅 (Tiān Fǔ) 死门 (Sǐ Mén) Qian 6　Yi Ding

Yin (阴) Dun# 3 Hour: RenChen；直符(ZhíFú): 天蓬(TiānPéng)
直使(ZhíShǐ): 休门(XiūMén)；旬首(XúnShǒu): JiaShenGeng

九地 (Jiǔ Dì) 天冲 (Tiān Chōng) 惊门 (Jīng Mén) Xun 4　Wu Yi	玄武 (Xuán Wǔ) 天辅 (Tiān Fǔ) 开门 (Kāi Mén) Li 9　Yi Xin	白虎 (Bái Hǔ) 天英 (Tiān Yīng) 休门 (Xiū Mén) Kun 2　Xin Ji/Bing
九天 (Jiǔ Tiān) 天任 (Tiān Rèn) 死门 (Sǐ Mén) Zhen 3　Ren Wu	Yin (阴) Dun# 3 Hour: **RenChen** ©Calvin Yap	六合 (Liù Hé) 禽芮 (Qín Ruì) 生门 (Shēng Mén) Dui 7　Ji/Bing Gui
值符 (Zhí Fú) 天蓬 (Tiān Péng) 景门 (Jǐng Mén) Gen 8　Geng Ren	螣蛇 (Téng Shé) 天心 (Tiān Xīn) 杜门 (Dù Mén) Kan 1　Ding Geng	太阴 (Tài Yīn) 天柱 (Tiān Zhù) 伤门 (Shāng Mén) Qian 6　Gui Ding

Yin (阴) Dun# 3 Hour: GuiSi；直符(ZhíFú): 天蓬(TiānPéng)
直使(ZhíShǐ): 休门(XiūMén)；旬首(XúnShǒu): JiaShenGeng

六合 (Liù Hé) 禽芮 (Qín Ruì) 杜门 (Dù Mén) Xun 4　Ji/Bing Yi	太阴 (Tài Yīn) 天柱 (Tiān Zhù) 景门 (Jǐng Mén) Li 9　Gui Xin	螣蛇 (Téng Shé) 天心 (Tiān Xīn) 死门 (Sǐ Mén) Kun 2　Ding Ji/Bing
白虎 (Bái Hǔ) 天英 (Tiān Yīng) 伤门 (Shāng Mén) Zhen 3　Xin Wu	Yin (阴) Dun# 3 Hour: **GuiSi** ©Calvin Yap	值符 (Zhí Fú) 天蓬 (Tiān Péng) 惊门 (Jīng Mén) Dui 7　Geng Gui
玄武 (Xuán Wǔ) 天辅 (Tiān Fǔ) 生门 (Shēng Mén) Gen 8　Yi Ren	九地 (Jiǔ Dì) 天冲 (Tiān Chōng) 休门 (Xiū Mén) Kan 1　Wu Geng	九天 (Jiǔ Tiān) 天任 (Tiān Rèn) 开门 (Kāi Mén) Qian 6　Ren Ding

Chart: -3JiaWu (Yin Dun #3 JiaWu Xun)
JiaWu, YiWei, BingShen, DingYou, WuXu, JiHai, GengZi, XinChou, RenYin, GuiMao

---

Yin (阴) Dun# 3 Hour: JiaWu ；直符(ZhíFú): 天英(TiānYīng)
直使(ZhíShǐ): 景门(JǐngMén) ；旬首(XúnShǒu): JiaWu/Xin

螣蛇 (Téng Shé) 天辅 (Tiān Fǔ) 杜门 (Dù Mén) Xun 4　Yi / Yi	值符 (Zhí Fú) 天英 (Tiān Yīng) 景门 (Jǐng Mén) Li 9　Xin / Xin	九天 (Jiǔ Tiān) 禽芮 (Qín Ruì) 死门 (Sǐ Mén) Kun 2　Ji/Bing / Ji/Bing
太阴 (Tài Yīn) 天冲 (Tiān Chōng) 伤门 (Shāng Mén) Zhen 3　Wu / Wu	Yin (阴) Dun# 3 Hour: **JiaWu** **Fu Yin** ©Calvin Yap	九地 (Jiǔ Dì) 天柱 (Tiān Zhù) 惊门 (Jīng Mén) Dui 7　Gui / Gui
六合 (Liù Hé) 天任 (Tiān Rèn) 生门 (Shēng Mén) Gen 8　Ren / Ren	白虎 (Bái Hǔ) 天蓬 (Tiān Péng) 休门 (Xiū Mén) Kan 1　Geng / Geng	玄武 (Xuán Wǔ) 天心 (Tiān Xīn) 开门 (Kāi Mén) Qian 6　Ding / Ding

Yin (阴) Dun# 3 Hour: YiWei ；直符(ZhíFú): 天英(TiānYīng)
直使(ZhíShǐ): 景门(JǐngMén) ；旬首(XúnShǒu): JiaWu/Xin

值符 (Zhí Fú) 天英 (Tiān Yīng) 惊门 (Jīng Mén) Xun 4　Xin / Yi	九天 (Jiǔ Tiān) 禽芮 (Qín Ruì) 开门 (Kāi Mén) Li 9　Ji/Bing / Xin	九地 (Jiǔ Dì) 天柱 (Tiān Zhù) 休门 (Xiū Mén) Kun 2　Gui / Ji/Bing
螣蛇 (Téng Shé) 天辅 (Tiān Fǔ) 死门 (Sǐ Mén) Zhen 3　Yi / Wu	Yin (阴) Dun# 3 Hour: **YiWei** ©Calvin Yap	玄武 (Xuán Wǔ) 天心 (Tiān Xīn) 生门 (Shēng Mén) Dui 7　Ding / Gui
太阴 (Tài Yīn) 天冲 (Tiān Chōng) 景门 (Jǐng Mén) Gen 8　Wu / Ren	六合 (Liù Hé) 天任 (Tiān Rèn) 杜门 (Dù Mén) Kan 1　Ren / Geng	白虎 (Bái Hǔ) 天蓬 (Tiān Péng) 伤门 (Shāng Mén) Qian 6　Geng / Ding

Yin (阴) Dun# 3 Hour: BingShen ；直符(ZhíFú): 天英(TiānYīng)
直使(ZhíShǐ): 景门(JǐngMén) ；旬首(XúnShǒu): JiaWu/Xin

太阴 (Tài Yīn) 天冲 (Tiān Chōng) 生门 (Shēng Mén) Xun 4　Wu / Yi	螣蛇 (Téng Shé) 天辅 (Tiān Fǔ) 伤门 (Shāng Mén) Li 9　Yi / Xin	值符 (Zhí Fú) 天英 (Tiān Yīng) 杜门 (Dù Mén) Kun 2　Xin / Ji/Bing
六合 (Liù Hé) 天任 (Tiān Rèn) 休门 (Xiū Mén) Zhen 3　Ren / Wu	Yin (阴) Dun# 3 Hour: **BingShen** ©Calvin Yap	九天 (Jiǔ Tiān) 禽芮 (Qín Ruì) 景门 (Jǐng Mén) Dui 7　Ji/Bing / Gui
白虎 (Bái Hǔ) 天蓬 (Tiān Péng) 开门 (Kāi Mén) Gen 8　Geng / Ren	玄武 (Xuán Wǔ) 天心 (Tiān Xīn) 惊门 (Jīng Mén) Kan 1　Ding / Geng	九地 (Jiǔ Dì) 天柱 (Tiān Zhù) 死门 (Sǐ Mén) Qian 6　Gui / Ding

Yin (阴) Dun# 3 Hour: DingYou ；直符(ZhíFú): 天英(TiānYīng)
直使(ZhíShǐ): 景门(JǐngMén) ；旬首(XúnShǒu): JiaWu/Xin

白虎 (Bái Hǔ) 天蓬 (Tiān Péng) 休门 (Xiū Mén) Xun 4　Geng / Yi	六合 (Liù Hé) 天任 (Tiān Rèn) 生门 (Shēng Mén) Li 9　Ren / Xin	太阴 (Tài Yīn) 天冲 (Tiān Chōng) 伤门 (Shāng Mén) Kun 2　Wu / Ji/Bing
玄武 (Xuán Wǔ) 天心 (Tiān Xīn) 开门 (Kāi Mén) Zhen 3　Ding / Wu	Yin (阴) Dun# 3 Hour: **DingYou** ©Calvin Yap	螣蛇 (Téng Shé) 天辅 (Tiān Fǔ) 杜门 (Dù Mén) Dui 7　Yi / Gui
九地 (Jiǔ Dì) 天柱 (Tiān Zhù) 惊门 (Jīng Mén) Gen 8　Gui / Ren	九天 (Jiǔ Tiān) 禽芮 (Qín Ruì) 死门 (Sǐ Mén) Kan 1　Ji/Bing / Geng	值符 (Zhí Fú) 天英 (Tiān Yīng) 景门 (Jǐng Mén) Qian 6　Xin / Ding

Yin (阴) Dun# 3 Hour: WuXu ；直符(ZhíFú): 天英(TiānYīng)
直使(ZhíShǐ): 景门(JǐngMén) ；旬首(XúnShǒu): JiaWu/Xin

九天 (Jiǔ Tiān) 禽芮 (Qín Ruì) 伤门 (Shāng Mén) Xun 4　Ji/Bing / Yi	九地 (Jiǔ Dì) 天柱 (Tiān Zhù) 杜门 (Dù Mén) Li 9　Gui / Xin	玄武 (Xuán Wǔ) 天心 (Tiān Xīn) 景门 (Jǐng Mén) Kun 2　Ding / Ji/Bing
值符 (Zhí Fú) 天英 (Tiān Yīng) 生门 (Shēng Mén) Zhen 3　Xin / Wu	Yin (阴) Dun# 3 Hour: **WuXu** ©Calvin Yap	白虎 (Bái Hǔ) 天蓬 (Tiān Péng) 死门 (Sǐ Mén) Dui 7　Geng / Gui
螣蛇 (Téng Shé) 天辅 (Tiān Fǔ) 休门 (Xiū Mén) Gen 8　Yi / Ren	太阴 (Tài Yīn) 天冲 (Tiān Chōng) 开门 (Kāi Mén) Kan 1　Wu / Geng	六合 (Liù Hé) 天任 (Tiān Rèn) 惊门 (Jīng Mén) Qian 6　Ren / Ding

Yin (阴) Dun# 3 Hour: JiHai ；直符(ZhíFú): 天英(TiānYīng)
直使(ZhíShǐ): 景门(JǐngMén) ；旬首(XúnShǒu): JiaWu/Xin

太阴 (Tài Yīn) 天冲 (Tiān Chōng) 景门 (Jǐng Mén) Xun 4　Wu / Yi	螣蛇 (Téng Shé) 天辅 (Tiān Fǔ) 死门 (Sǐ Mén) Li 9　Yi / Xin	值符 (Zhí Fú) 天英 (Tiān Yīng) 惊门 (Jīng Mén) Kun 2　Xin / Ji/Bing
六合 (Liù Hé) 天任 (Tiān Rèn) 杜门 (Dù Mén) Zhen 3　Ren / Wu	Yin (阴) Dun# 3 Hour: **JiHai** ©Calvin Yap	九天 (Jiǔ Tiān) 禽芮 (Qín Ruì) 开门 (Kāi Mén) Dui 7　Ji/Bing / Gui
白虎 (Bái Hǔ) 天蓬 (Tiān Péng) 伤门 (Shāng Mén) Gen 8　Geng / Ren	玄武 (Xuán Wǔ) 天心 (Tiān Xīn) 生门 (Shēng Mén) Kan 1　Ding / Geng	九地 (Jiǔ Dì) 天柱 (Tiān Zhù) 休门 (Xiū Mén) Qian 6　Gui / Ding

---

Yin (阴) Dun# 3 Hour: GengZi ; 直符(ZhíFú): 天英(TiānYīng)
直使(ZhíShǐ): 景门(JǐngMén) ; 旬首(XúnShǒu): JiaWu/Xin

玄武 (Xuán Wǔ) 天心 (Tiān Xīn) 死门 (Sǐ Mén) Xun 4 — Ding — Yi	白虎 (Bái Hǔ) 天蓬 (Tiān Péng) 惊门 (Jīng Mén) Li 9 — Geng — Xin	六合 (Liù Hé) 天任 (Tiān Rèn) 开门 (Kāi Mén) Kun 2 — Ren — Ji/Bing
九地 (Jiǔ Dì) 天柱 (Tiān Zhù) 景门 (Jǐng Mén) Zhen 3 — Gui — Wu	Yin (阴) Dun# 3 Hour: GengZi **Fan Yin** ©Calvin Yap	太阴 (Tài Yīn) 天冲 (Tiān Chōng) 休门 (Xiū Mén) Dui 7 — Wu — Gui
九天 (Jiǔ Tiān) 禽芮 (Qín Ruì) 杜门 (Dù Mén) Gen 8 — Ji/Bing — Ren	值符 (Zhí Fú) 天英 (Tiān Yīng) 伤门 (Shāng Mén) Kan 1 — Xin — Geng	螣蛇 (Téng Shé) 天辅 (Tiān Fǔ) 生门 (Shēng Mén) Qian 6 — Yi — Ding

Yin (阴) Dun# 3 Hour: XinChou ; 直符(ZhíFú): 天英(TiānYīng)
直使(ZhíShǐ): 景门(JǐngMén) ; 旬首(XúnShǒu): JiaWu/Xin

螣蛇 (Téng Shé) 天辅 (Tiān Fǔ) 伤门 (Shāng Mén) Xun 4 — Yi — Yi	值符 (Zhí Fú) 天英 (Tiān Yīng) 杜门 (Dù Mén) Li 9 — Xin — Xin	九天 (Jiǔ Tiān) 禽芮 (Qín Ruì) 景门 (Jǐng Mén) Kun 2 — Ji/Bing
太阴 (Tài Yīn) 天冲 (Tiān Chōng) 生门 (Shēng Mén) Zhen 3 — Wu — Wu	Yin (阴) Dun# 3 Hour: XinChou **Fu Yin** ©Calvin Yap	九地 (Jiǔ Dì) 天柱 (Tiān Zhù) 死门 (Sǐ Mén) Dui 7 — Gui — Gui
六合 (Liù Hé) 天任 (Tiān Rèn) 休门 (Xiū Mén) Gen 8 — Ren — Ren	白虎 (Bái Hǔ) 天蓬 (Tiān Péng) 开门 (Kāi Mén) Kan 1 — Geng — Geng	玄武 (Xuán Wǔ) 天心 (Tiān Xīn) 惊门 (Jīng Mén) Qian 6 — Ding — Ding

Yin (阴) Dun# 3 Hour: RenYin ; 直符(ZhíFú): 天英(TiānYīng)
直使(ZhíShǐ): 景门(JǐngMén) ; 旬首(XúnShǒu): JiaWu/Xin

九地 (Jiǔ Dì) 天柱 (Tiān Zhù) 开门 (Kāi Mén) Xun 4 — Gui — Yi	玄武 (Xuán Wǔ) 天心 (Tiān Xīn) 休门 (Xiū Mén) Li 9 — Ding — Xin	白虎 (Bái Hǔ) 天蓬 (Tiān Péng) 生门 (Shēng Mén) Kun 2 — Geng — Ji/Bing
九天 (Jiǔ Tiān) 禽芮 (Qín Ruì) 惊门 (Jīng Mén) Zhen 3 — Ji/Bing — Wu	Yin (阴) Dun# 3 Hour: RenYin ©Calvin Yap	六合 (Liù Hé) 天任 (Tiān Rèn) 伤门 (Shāng Mén) Dui 7 — Ren — Gui
值符 (Zhí Fú) 天英 (Tiān Yīng) 死门 (Sǐ Mén) Gen 8 — Xin — Ren	螣蛇 (Téng Shé) 天辅 (Tiān Fǔ) 景门 (Jǐng Mén) Kan 1 — Yi — Geng	太阴 (Tài Yīn) 天冲 (Tiān Chōng) 杜门 (Dù Mén) Qian 6 — Wu — Ding

Yin (阴) Dun# 3 Hour: GuiMao ; 直符(ZhíFú): 天英(TiānYīng)
直使(ZhíShǐ): 景门(JǐngMén) ; 旬首(XúnShǒu): JiaWu/Xin

六合 (Liù Hé) 天任 (Tiān Rèn) 杜门 (Dù Mén) Xun 4 — Ren — Yi	太阴 (Tài Yīn) 天冲 (Tiān Chōng) 景门 (Jǐng Mén) Li 9 — Wu — Xin	螣蛇 (Téng Shé) 天辅 (Tiān Fǔ) 死门 (Sǐ Mén) Kun 2 — Yi — Ji/Bing
白虎 (Bái Hǔ) 天蓬 (Tiān Péng) 伤门 (Shāng Mén) Zhen 3 — Geng — Wu	Yin (阴) Dun# 3 Hour: GuiMao ©Calvin Yap	值符 (Zhí Fú) 天英 (Tiān Yīng) 惊门 (Jīng Mén) Dui 7 — Xin — Gui
玄武 (Xuán Wǔ) 天心 (Tiān Xīn) 生门 (Shēng Mén) Gen 8 — Ding — Ren	九地 (Jiǔ Dì) 天柱 (Tiān Zhù) 休门 (Xiū Mén) Kan 1 — Gui — Geng	九天 (Jiǔ Tiān) 禽芮 (Qín Ruì) 开门 (Kāi Mén) Qian 6 — Ji/Bing — Ding

Chart: -3JiaChen (Yin Dun #3 JiaChen Xun)
JiaChen, YiSi, BingWu, DingWei, WuShen, JiYou, GengXu, XinHai, RenZi, GuiChou

Yin (阴) Dun# 3 Hour: JiaChen ; 直符(ZhíFú): 天任(TiānRèn)
直使(ZhíShǐ): 生门(ShēngMén) ; 旬首(XúnShǒu): JiaChenRen

九地 (Jiǔ Dì) 天辅 (Tiān Fǔ) 杜门 (Dù Mén) Xun 4 — Yi — Yi	玄武 (Xuán Wǔ) 天英 (Tiān Yīng) 景门 (Jǐng Mén) Li 9 — Xin — Xin	白虎 (Bái Hǔ) 禽芮 (Qín Ruì) 死门 (Sǐ Mén) Kun 2 — Ji/Bing — Ji/Bing
九天 (Jiǔ Tiān) 天冲 (Tiān Chōng) 伤门 (Shāng Mén) Zhen 3 — Wu — Wu	Yin (阴) Dun# 3 Hour: JiaChen **Fu Yin** ©Calvin Yap	六合 (Liù Hé) 天柱 (Tiān Zhù) 惊门 (Jīng Mén) Dui 7 — Gui — Gui
值符 (Zhí Fú) 天任 (Tiān Rèn) 生门 (Shēng Mén) Gen 8 — Ren — Ren	螣蛇 (Téng Shé) 天蓬 (Tiān Péng) 休门 (Xiū Mén) Kan 1 — Geng — Geng	太阴 (Tài Yīn) 天心 (Tiān Xīn) 开门 (Kāi Mén) Qian 6 — Ding — Ding

Yin (阴) Dun# 3 Hour: YiSi ; 直符(ZhíFú): 天任(TiānRèn)
直使(ZhíShǐ): 生门(ShēngMén) ; 旬首(XúnShǒu): JiaChenRen

值符 (Zhí Fú) 天任 (Tiān Rèn) 惊门 (Jīng Mén) Xun 4 — Ren — Yi	九天 (Jiǔ Tiān) 天冲 (Tiān Chōng) 开门 (Kāi Mén) Li 9 — Wu — Xin	九地 (Jiǔ Dì) 天辅 (Tiān Fǔ) 休门 (Xiū Mén) Kun 2 — Yi — Ji/Bing
螣蛇 (Téng Shé) 天蓬 (Tiān Péng) 死门 (Sǐ Mén) Zhen 3 — Geng — Wu	Yin (阴) Dun# 3 Hour: YiSi ©Calvin Yap	玄武 (Xuán Wǔ) 天英 (Tiān Yīng) 生门 (Shēng Mén) Dui 7 — Xin — Gui
太阴 (Tài Yīn) 天心 (Tiān Xīn) 景门 (Jǐng Mén) Gen 8 — Ding — Ren	六合 (Liù Hé) 天柱 (Tiān Zhù) 杜门 (Dù Mén) Kan 1 — Gui — Geng	白虎 (Bái Hǔ) 禽芮 (Qín Ruì) 伤门 (Shāng Mén) Qian 6 — Ji/Bing — Ding

Yin (阴) Dun# 3 Hour: BingWu ; 直符(ZhíFú): 天任(TiānRèn)
直使(ZhíShǐ): 生门(ShēngMén) ; 旬首(XúnShǒu): JiaChenRen

太阴 (Tài Yīn) 天心 (Tiān Xīn) 死门 (Sǐ Mén) Xun 4　Ding Yi	螣蛇 (Téng Shé) 天蓬 (Tiān Péng) 惊门 (Jīng Mén) Li 9　Geng Xin	值符 (Zhí Fú) 天任 (Tiān Rèn) 开门 (Kāi Mén) Kun 2　Ren Ji/Bing
六合 (Liù Hé) 天柱 (Tiān Zhù) 景门 (Jǐng Mén) Zhen 3　Gui Wu	Yin (阴) Dun# 3 Hour: **BingWu** **Fan Yin** ©Calvin Yap	九天 (Jiǔ Tiān) 天冲 (Tiān Chōng) 休门 (Xiū Mén) Dui 7　Wu Gui
白虎 (Bái Hǔ) 禽芮 (Qín Ruì) 杜门 (Dù Mén) Gen 8　Ji/Bing Ren	玄武 (Xuán Wǔ) 天英 (Tiān Yīng) 伤门 (Shāng Mén) Kan 1　Xin Geng	九地 (Jiǔ Dì) 天辅 (Tiān Fǔ) 生门 (Shēng Mén) Qian 6　Yi Ding

Yin (阴) Dun# 3 Hour: DingWei ; 直符(ZhíFú): 天任(TiānRèn)
直使(ZhíShǐ): 生门(ShēngMén) ; 旬首(XúnShǒu): JiaChenRen

白虎 (Bái Hǔ) 禽芮 (Qín Ruì) 开门 (Kāi Mén) Xun 4　Ji/Bing Yi	六合 (Liù Hé) 天柱 (Tiān Zhù) 休门 (Xiū Mén) Li 9　Gui Xin	太阴 (Tài Yīn) 天心 (Tiān Xīn) 生门 (Shēng Mén) Kun 2　Ding Ji/Bing
玄武 (Xuán Wǔ) 天英 (Tiān Yīng) 惊门 (Jīng Mén) Zhen 3　Xin Wu	Yin (阴) Dun# 3 Hour: **DingWei** ©Calvin Yap	螣蛇 (Téng Shé) 天蓬 (Tiān Péng) 伤门 (Shāng Mén) Dui 7　Geng Gui
九地 (Jiǔ Dì) 天辅 (Tiān Fǔ) 死门 (Sǐ Mén) Gen 8　Yi Ren	九天 (Jiǔ Tiān) 天冲 (Tiān Chōng) 景门 (Jǐng Mén) Kan 1　Wu Geng	值符 (Zhí Fú) 天任 (Tiān Rèn) 杜门 (Dù Mén) Qian 6　Ren Ding

Yin (阴) Dun# 3 Hour: WuShen ; 直符(ZhíFú): 天任(TiānRèn)
直使(ZhíShǐ): 生门(ShēngMén) ; 旬首(XúnShǒu): JiaChenRen

九天 (Jiǔ Tiān) 天冲 (Tiān Chōng) 生门 (Shēng Mén) Xun 4　Wu Yi	九地 (Jiǔ Dì) 天辅 (Tiān Fǔ) 伤门 (Shāng Mén) Li 9　Yi Xin	玄武 (Xuán Wǔ) 天英 (Tiān Yīng) 杜门 (Dù Mén) Kun 2　Xin Ji/Bing
值符 (Zhí Fú) 天任 (Tiān Rèn) 休门 (Xiū Mén) Zhen 3　Ren Wu	Yin (阴) Dun# 3 Hour: **WuShen** ©Calvin Yap	白虎 (Bái Hǔ) 禽芮 (Qín Ruì) 景门 (Jǐng Mén) Dui 7　Ji/Bing Gui
螣蛇 (Téng Shé) 天蓬 (Tiān Péng) 开门 (Kāi Mén) Gen 8　Geng Ren	太阴 (Tài Yīn) 天心 (Tiān Xīn) 惊门 (Jīng Mén) Kan 1　Ding Geng	六合 (Liù Hé) 天柱 (Tiān Zhù) 死门 (Sǐ Mén) Qian 6　Gui Ding

Yin (阴) Dun# 3 Hour: JiYou ; 直符(ZhíFú): 天任(TiānRèn)
直使(ZhíShǐ): 生门(ShēngMén) ; 旬首(XúnShǒu): JiaChenRen

太阴 (Tài Yīn) 天心 (Tiān Xīn) 伤门 (Shāng Mén) Xun 4　Ding Yi	螣蛇 (Téng Shé) 天蓬 (Tiān Péng) 杜门 (Dù Mén) Li 9　Geng Xin	值符 (Zhí Fú) 天任 (Tiān Rèn) 景门 (Jǐng Mén) Kun 2　Ren Ji/Bing
六合 (Liù Hé) 天柱 (Tiān Zhù) 生门 (Shēng Mén) Zhen 3　Gui Wu	Yin (阴) Dun# 3 Hour: **JiYou** **Fan Yin** ©Calvin Yap	九天 (Jiǔ Tiān) 天冲 (Tiān Chōng) 死门 (Sǐ Mén) Dui 7　Wu Gui
白虎 (Bái Hǔ) 禽芮 (Qín Ruì) 休门 (Xiū Mén) Gen 8　Ji/Bing Ren	玄武 (Xuán Wǔ) 天英 (Tiān Yīng) 开门 (Kāi Mén) Kan 1　Xin Geng	九地 (Jiǔ Dì) 天辅 (Tiān Fǔ) 惊门 (Jīng Mén) Qian 6　Yi Ding

Yin (阴) Dun# 3 Hour: GengXu ; 直符(ZhíFú): 天任(TiānRèn)
直使(ZhíShǐ): 生门(ShēngMén) ; 旬首(XúnShǒu): JiaChenRen

玄武 (Xuán Wǔ) 天英 (Tiān Yīng) 开门 (Kāi Mén) Xun 4　Xin Yi	白虎 (Bái Hǔ) 禽芮 (Qín Ruì) 休门 (Xiū Mén) Li 9　Ji/Bing Xin	六合 (Liù Hé) 天柱 (Tiān Zhù) 生门 (Shēng Mén) Kun 2　Gui Ji/Bing
九地 (Jiǔ Dì) 天辅 (Tiān Fǔ) 惊门 (Jīng Mén) Zhen 3　Yi Wu	Yin (阴) Dun# 3 Hour: **GengXu** ©Calvin Yap	太阴 (Tài Yīn) 天心 (Tiān Xīn) 伤门 (Shāng Mén) Dui 7　Ding Gui
九天 (Jiǔ Tiān) 天冲 (Tiān Chōng) 死门 (Sǐ Mén) Gen 8　Wu Ren	值符 (Zhí Fú) 天任 (Tiān Rèn) 景门 (Jǐng Mén) Kan 1　Ren Geng	螣蛇 (Téng Shé) 天蓬 (Tiān Péng) 杜门 (Dù Mén) Qian 6　Geng Ding

Yin (阴) Dun# 3 Hour: XinHai ; 直符(ZhíFú): 天任(TiānRèn)
直使(ZhíShǐ): 生门(ShēngMén) ; 旬首(XúnShǒu): JiaChenRen

螣蛇 (Téng Shé) 天蓬 (Tiān Péng) 景门 (Jǐng Mén) Xun 4　Geng Yi	值符 (Zhí Fú) 天任 (Tiān Rèn) 死门 (Sǐ Mén) Li 9　Ren Xin	九天 (Jiǔ Tiān) 天冲 (Tiān Chōng) 惊门 (Jīng Mén) Kun 2　Wu Ji/Bing
太阴 (Tài Yīn) 天心 (Tiān Xīn) 杜门 (Dù Mén) Zhen 3　Ding Wu	Yin (阴) Dun# 3 Hour: **XinHai** ©Calvin Yap	九地 (Jiǔ Dì) 天辅 (Tiān Fǔ) 开门 (Kāi Mén) Dui 7　Yi Gui
六合 (Liù Hé) 天柱 (Tiān Zhù) 伤门 (Shāng Mén) Gen 8　Gui Ren	白虎 (Bái Hǔ) 禽芮 (Qín Ruì) 生门 (Shēng Mén) Kan 1　Ji/Bing Geng	玄武 (Xuán Wǔ) 天英 (Tiān Yīng) 休门 (Xiū Mén) Qian 6　Xin Ding

Yin (阴) Dun# 3 Hour: RenZi ; 直符(ZhíFú): 天任(TiānRèn)
直使(ZhíShǐ): 生门(ShēngMén) ; 旬首(XúnShǒu): JiaChenRen

九地 (Jiǔ Dì) 天辅 (Tiān Fǔ) 休门 (Xiū Mén) Xun 4 Yi / Yi	玄武 (Xuán Wǔ) 天英 (Tiān Yīng) 生门 (Shēng Mén) Li 9 Xin	白虎 (Bái Hǔ) 禽芮 (Qín Ruì) 伤门 (Shāng Mén) Kun 2 Ji/Bing / Ji/Bing
九天 (Jiǔ Tiān) 天冲 (Tiān Chōng) 开门 (Kāi Mén) Zhen 3 Wu / Wu	Yin (阴) Dun# 3 Hour: **RenZi** **Fu Yin** ©Calvin Yap	六合 (Liù Hé) 天柱 (Tiān Zhù) 杜门 (Dù Mén) Dui 7 Gui / Gui
值符 (Zhí Fú) 天任 (Tiān Rèn) 惊门 (Jīng Mén) Gen 8 Ren / Ren	螣蛇 (Téng Shé) 天蓬 (Tiān Péng) 死门 (Sǐ Mén) Kan 1 Geng / Geng	太阴 (Tài Yīn) 天心 (Tiān Xīn) 景门 (Jīng Mén) Qian 6 Ding / Ding

Yin (阴) Dun# 3 Hour: GuiChou ; 直符(ZhíFú): 天任(TiānRèn)
直使(ZhíShǐ): 生门(ShēngMén) ; 旬首(XúnShǒu): JiaChenRen

六合 (Liù Hé) 天柱 (Tiān Zhù) 杜门 (Dù Mén) Xun 4 Gui / Yi	太阴 (Tài Yīn) 天心 (Tiān Xīn) 景门 (Jīng Mén) Li 9 Ding / Xin	螣蛇 (Téng Shé) 天蓬 (Tiān Péng) 死门 (Sǐ Mén) Kun 2 Geng / Ji/Bing
白虎 (Bái Hǔ) 禽芮 (Qín Ruì) 伤门 (Shāng Mén) Zhen 3 Ji/Bing / Wu	Yin (阴) Dun# 3 Hour: **GuiChou** ©Calvin Yap	值符 (Zhí Fú) 天任 (Tiān Rèn) 惊门 (Jīng Mén) Dui 7 Ren / Gui
玄武 (Xuán Wǔ) 天英 (Tiān Yīng) 生门 (Shēng Mén) Gen 8 Xin / Ren	九地 (Jiǔ Dì) 天辅 (Tiān Fǔ) 休门 (Xiū Mén) Kan 1 Yi / Geng	九天 (Jiǔ Tiān) 天冲 (Tiān Chōng) 开门 (Kāi Mén) Qian 6 Wu / Ding

---

Chart: -3JiaYin (Yin Dun #3 JiaYin Xun)
JiaYin, YiMao, BingChen, DingSi, WuWu, JiWei, GengShen, XinYou, RenXu, GuiHai

---

Yin (阴) Dun# 3 Hour: JiaYin ; 直符(ZhíFú): 天柱(TiānZhù)
直使(ZhíShǐ): 惊门(JīngMén) ; 旬首(XúnShǒu): JiaYinGui

六合 (Liù Hé) 天辅 (Tiān Fǔ) 杜门 (Dù Mén) Xun 4 Yi / Yi	太阴 (Tài Yīn) 天英 (Tiān Yīng) 景门 (Jīng Mén) Li 9 Xin / Xin	螣蛇 (Téng Shé) 禽芮 (Qín Ruì) 死门 (Sǐ Mén) Kun 2 Ji/Bing / Ji/Bing
白虎 (Bái Hǔ) 天冲 (Tiān Chōng) 伤门 (Shāng Mén) Zhen 3 Wu / Wu	Yin (阴) Dun# 3 Hour: **JiaYin** **Fu Yin** ©Calvin Yap	值符 (Zhí Fú) 天柱 (Tiān Zhù) 惊门 (Jīng Mén) Dui 7 Gui / Gui
玄武 (Xuán Wǔ) 天任 (Tiān Rèn) 生门 (Shēng Mén) Gen 8 Ren / Ren	九地 (Jiǔ Dì) 天蓬 (Tiān Péng) 休门 (Xiū Mén) Kan 1 Geng / Geng	九天 (Jiǔ Tiān) 天心 (Tiān Xīn) 开门 (Kāi Mén) Qian 6 Ding / Ding

Yin (阴) Dun# 3 Hour: YiMao ; 直符(ZhíFú): 天柱(TiānZhù)
直使(ZhíShǐ): 惊门(JīngMén) ; 旬首(XúnShǒu): JiaYinGui

值符 (Zhí Fú) 天柱 (Tiān Zhù) 伤门 (Shāng Mén) Xun 4 Gui / Yi	九天 (Jiǔ Tiān) 大心 (Tiān Xīn) 杜门 (Dù Mén) Li 9 Ding / Xin	九地 (Jiǔ Dì) 天蓬 (Tiān Péng) 景门 (Jīng Mén) Kun 2 Geng / Ji/Bing
螣蛇 (Téng Shé) 禽芮 (Qín Ruì) 生门 (Shēng Mén) Zhen 3 Ji/Bing / Wu	Yin (阴) Dun# 3 Hour: **YiMao** ©Calvin Yap	玄武 (Xuán Wǔ) 天任 (Tiān Rèn) 死门 (Sǐ Mén) Dui 7 Ren / Gui
太阴 (Tài Yīn) 天英 (Tiān Yīng) 休门 (Xiū Mén) Gen 8 Xin / Ren	六合 (Liù Hé) 天辅 (Tiān Fǔ) 开门 (Kāi Mén) Kan 1 Yi / Geng	白虎 (Bái Hǔ) 天冲 (Tiān Chōng) 惊门 (Jīng Mén) Qian 6 Wu / Ding

Yin (阴) Dun# 3 Hour: BingChen ; 直符(ZhíFú): 天柱(TiānZhù)
直使(ZhíShǐ): 惊门(JīngMén) ; 旬首(XúnShǒu): JiaYinGui

太阴 (Tài Yīn) 天英 (Tiān Yīng) 景门 (Jīng Mén) Xun 4 Xin / Yi	螣蛇 (Téng Shé) 禽芮 (Qín Ruì) 死门 (Sǐ Mén) Li 9 Ji/Bing / Xin	值符 (Zhí Fú) 天柱 (Tiān Zhù) 惊门 (Jīng Mén) Kun 2 Gui / Ji/Bing
六合 (Liù Hé) 天辅 (Tiān Fǔ) 杜门 (Dù Mén) Zhen 3 Yi / Wu	Yin (阴) Dun# 3 Hour: **BingChen** ©Calvin Yap	九天 (Jiǔ Tiān) 天心 (Tiān Xīn) 开门 (Kāi Mén) Dui 7 Ding / Gui
白虎 (Bái Hǔ) 天冲 (Tiān Chōng) 伤门 (Shāng Mén) Gen 8 Wu / Ren	玄武 (Xuán Wǔ) 天任 (Tiān Rèn) 生门 (Shēng Mén) Kan 1 Ren / Geng	九地 (Jiǔ Dì) 天蓬 (Tiān Péng) 休门 (Xiū Mén) Qian 6 Geng / Ding

Yin (阴) Dun# 3 Hour: DingSi ; 直符(ZhíFú): 天柱(TiānZhù)
直使(ZhíShǐ): 惊门(JīngMén) ; 旬首(XúnShǒu): JiaYinGui

白虎 (Bái Hǔ) 天冲 (Tiān Chōng) 惊门 (Jīng Mén) Xun 4 Wu / Yi	六合 (Liù Hé) 大辅 (Tiān Fǔ) 开门 (Kāi Mén) Li 9 Yi / Xin	太阴 (Tài Yīn) 天英 (Tiān Yīng) 休门 (Xiū Mén) Kun 2 Xin / Ji/Bing
玄武 (Xuán Wǔ) 天任 (Tiān Rèn) 死门 (Sǐ Mén) Zhen 3 Ren / Wu	Yin (阴) Dun# 3 Hour: **DingSi** ©Calvin Yap	螣蛇 (Téng Shé) 禽芮 (Qín Ruì) 生门 (Shēng Mén) Dui 7 Ji/Bing / Gui
九地 (Jiǔ Dì) 天蓬 (Tiān Péng) 景门 (Jīng Mén) Gen 8 Geng / Ren	九天 (Jiǔ Tiān) 天心 (Tiān Xīn) 杜门 (Dù Mén) Kan 1 Ding / Geng	值符 (Zhí Fú) 天柱 (Tiān Zhù) 伤门 (Shāng Mén) Qian 6 Gui / Ding

Yin (阴) Dun# 3 Hour: **WuWu** ; 直符(ZhíFú): 天柱(TiānZhù)
直使(ZhíShǐ): 惊门(JīngMén) ; 旬首(XúnShǒu): JiaYinGui

九天 (Jiǔ Tiān) 天心 (Tiān Xīn) 开门 (Kāi Mén) Xun 4 Ding Yi	九地 (Jiǔ Dì) 天蓬 (Tiān Péng) 休门 (Xiū Mén) Li 9 Geng Xin	玄武 (Xuán Wǔ) 天任 (Tiān Rèn) 生门 (Shēng Mén) Kun 2 Ren Ji/Bing
值符 (Zhí Fú) 天柱 (Tiān Zhù) 惊门 (Jīng Mén) Zhen 3 Gui Wu	Yin (阴) Dun# 3 Hour: **WuWu** **Fan Yin** ©Calvin Yap	白虎 (Bái Hǔ) 天冲 (Tiān Chōng) 伤门 (Shāng Mén) Dui 7 Wu Gui
螣蛇 (Téng Shé) 禽芮 (Qín Ruì) 死门 (Sǐ Mén) Gen 8 Ji/Bing Ren	太阴 (Tài Yīn) 天英 (Tiān Yīng) 景门 (Jǐng Mén) Kan 1 Xin Geng	六合 (Liù Hé) 天辅 (Tiān Fǔ) 杜门 (Dù Mén) Qian 6 Yi Ding

Yin (阴) Dun# 3 Hour: **JiWei** ; 直符(ZhíFú): 天柱(TiānZhù)
直使(ZhíShǐ): 惊门(JīngMén) ; 旬首(XúnShǒu): JiaYinGui

太阴 (Tài Yīn) 天英 (Tiān Yīng) 景门 (Jǐng Mén) Xun 4 Xin Yi	螣蛇 (Téng Shé) 禽芮 (Qín Ruì) 死门 (Sǐ Mén) Li 9 Ji/Bing Xin	值符 (Zhí Fú) 天柱 (Tiān Zhù) 惊门 (Jīng Mén) Kun 2 Gui Ji/Bing
六合 (Liù Hé) 天辅 (Tiān Fǔ) 杜门 (Dù Mén) Zhen 3 Yi Wu	Yin (阴) Dun# 3 Hour: **JiWei** ©Calvin Yap	九天 (Jiǔ Tiān) 天心 (Tiān Xīn) 开门 (Kāi Mén) Dui 7 Ding Gui
白虎 (Bái Hǔ) 天冲 (Tiān Chōng) 伤门 (Shāng Mén) Gen 8 Wu Ren	玄武 (Xuán Wǔ) 天任 (Tiān Rèn) 生门 (Shēng Mén) Kan 1 Ren Geng	九地 (Jiǔ Dì) 天蓬 (Tiān Péng) 休门 (Xiū Mén) Qian 6 Geng Ding

Yin (阴) Dun# 3 Hour: **GengShen** ; 直符(ZhíFú): 天柱(TiānZhù)
直使(ZhíShǐ): 惊门(JīngMén) ; 旬首(XúnShǒu): JiaYinGui

玄武 (Xuán Wǔ) 天任 (Tiān Rèn) 生门 (Shēng Mén) Xun 4 Ren Yi	白虎 (Bái Hǔ) 天冲 (Tiān Chōng) 伤门 (Shāng Mén) Li 9 Wu Xin	六合 (Liù Hé) 天辅 (Tiān Fǔ) 杜门 (Dù Mén) Kun 2 Yi Ji/Bing
九地 (Jiǔ Dì) 天蓬 (Tiān Péng) 休门 (Xiū Mén) Zhen 3 Geng Wu	Yin (阴) Dun# 3 Hour: **GengShen** ©Calvin Yap	太阴 (Tài Yīn) 天英 (Tiān Yīng) 景门 (Jǐng Mén) Dui 7 Xin Gui
九天 (Jiǔ Tiān) 天心 (Tiān Xīn) 开门 (Kāi Mén) Gen 8 Ding Ren	值符 (Zhí Fú) 天柱 (Tiān Zhù) 惊门 (Jīng Mén) Kan 1 Gui Geng	螣蛇 (Téng Shé) 禽芮 (Qín Ruì) 死门 (Sǐ Mén) Qian 6 Ji/Bing Ding

Yin (阴) Dun# 3 Hour: **XinYou** ; 直符(ZhíFú): 天柱(TiānZhù)
直使(ZhíShǐ): 惊门(JīngMén) ; 旬首(XúnShǒu): JiaYinGui

螣蛇 (Téng Shé) 禽芮 (Qín Ruì) 死门 (Sǐ Mén) Xun 4 Ji/Bing Yi	值符 (Zhí Fú) 天柱 (Tiān Zhù) 惊门 (Jīng Mén) Li 9 Gui Xin	九天 (Jiǔ Tiān) 天心 (Tiān Xīn) 开门 (Kāi Mén) Kun 2 Ding Ji/Bing
太阴 (Tài Yīn) 天英 (Tiān Yīng) 景门 (Jǐng Mén) Zhen 3 Xin Wu	Yin (阴) Dun# 3 Hour: **XinYou** ©Calvin Yap	九地 (Jiǔ Dì) 天蓬 (Tiān Péng) 休门 (Xiū Mén) Dui 7 Geng Gui
六合 (Liù Hé) 天辅 (Tiān Fǔ) 杜门 (Dù Mén) Gen 8 Yi Ren	白虎 (Bái Hǔ) 天冲 (Tiān Chōng) 伤门 (Shāng Mén) Kan 1 Wu Geng	玄武 (Xuán Wǔ) 天任 (Tiān Rèn) 生门 (Shēng Mén) Qian 6 Ren Ding

Yin (阴) Dun# 3 Hour: **RenXu** ; 直符(ZhíFú): 天柱(TiānZhù)
直使(ZhíShǐ): 惊门(JīngMén) ; 旬首(XúnShǒu): JiaYinGui

九地 (Jiǔ Dì) 天蓬 (Tiān Péng) 休门 (Xiū Mén) Xun 4 Geng Yi	玄武 (Xuán Wǔ) 天任 (Tiān Rèn) 生门 (Shēng Mén) Li 9 Ren Xin	白虎 (Bái Hǔ) 天冲 (Tiān Chōng) 伤门 (Shāng Mén) Kun 2 Wu Ji/Bing
九天 (Jiǔ Tiān) 天心 (Tiān Xīn) 开门 (Kāi Mén) Zhen 3 Ding Wu	Yin (阴) Dun# 3 Hour: **RenXu** ©Calvin Yap	六合 (Liù Hé) 天辅 (Tiān Fǔ) 杜门 (Dù Mén) Dui 7 Yi Gui
值符 (Zhí Fú) 天柱 (Tiān Zhù) 惊门 (Jīng Mén) Gen 8 Gui Ren	螣蛇 (Téng Shé) 禽芮 (Qín Ruì) 死门 (Sǐ Mén) Kan 1 Ji/Bing Geng	太阴 (Tài Yīn) 天英 (Tiān Yīng) 景门 (Jǐng Mén) Qian 6 Xin Ding

Yin (阴) Dun# 3 Hour: **GuiHai** ; 直符(ZhíFú): 天柱(TiānZhù)
直使(ZhíShǐ): 惊门(JīngMén) ; 旬首(XúnShǒu): JiaYinGui

六合 (Liù Hé) 天辅 (Tiān Fǔ) 杜门 (Dù Mén) Xun 4 Yi Yi	太阴 (Tài Yīn) 天英 (Tiān Yīng) 景门 (Jǐng Mén) Li 9 Xin Xin	螣蛇 (Téng Shé) 禽芮 (Qín Ruì) 死门 (Sǐ Mén) Kun 2 Ji/Bing Ji/Bing
白虎 (Bái Hǔ) 天冲 (Tiān Chōng) 伤门 (Shāng Mén) Zhen 3 Wu Wu	Yin (阴) Dun# 3 Hour: **GuiHai** **Fu Yin** ©Calvin Yap	值符 (Zhí Fú) 天柱 (Tiān Zhù) 惊门 (Jīng Mén) Dui 7 Gui Gui
玄武 (Xuán Wǔ) 天任 (Tiān Rèn) 生门 (Shēng Mén) Gen 8 Ren Ren	九地 (Jiǔ Dì) 天蓬 (Tiān Péng) 休门 (Xiū Mén) Kan 1 Geng Geng	九天 (Jiǔ Tiān) 天心 (Tiān Xīn) 开门 (Kāi Mén) Qian 6 Ding Ding

Yin Dun#4

Chart: -4JiaZi (Yin Dun #4 JiaZi Xun)
JiaZi, YiChou, BingYin, DingMao, WuChen, JiSi, GengWu, XinWei, RenShen, GuiYou

Yin (阴) Dun# 4 Hour: **JiaZi** ; 直符(ZhíFú): 天辅(TiānFǔ)
直使(ZhíShǐ): 杜门(DùMén) ; 旬首(XúnShǒu): JiaZiWu

值符 (Zhí Fú) 天辅 (Tiān Fǔ) 杜门 (Dù Mén) Xun 4　Wu Wu	九天 (Jiǔ Tiān) 天英 (Tiān Yīng) 景门 (Jǐng Mén) Li 9　Ren Ren	九地 (Jiǔ Dì) 禽芮 (Qín Ruì) 死门 (Sǐ Mén) Kun 2　Geng/Yi Geng/Yi
螣蛇 (Téng Shé) 天冲 (Tiān Chōng) 伤门 (Shāng Mén) Zhen 3　Ji Ji	Yin (阴) Dun# 4 Hour: **JiaZi** **Fu Yin** ©Calvin Yap	玄武 (Xuán Wǔ) 天柱 (Tiān Zhù) 惊门 (Jīng Mén) Dui 7　Ding Ding
太阴 (Tài Yīn) 天任 (Tiān Rèn) 生门 (Shēng Mén) Gen 8　Gui Gui	六合 (Liù Hé) 天蓬 (Tiān Péng) 休门 (Xiū Mén) Kan 1　Xin Xin	白虎 (Bái Hǔ) 天心 (Tiān Xīn) 开门 (Kāi Mén) Qian 6　Bing Bing

Yin (阴) Dun# 4 Hour: **YiChou** ; 直符(ZhíFú): 天辅(TiānFǔ)
直使(ZhíShǐ): 杜门(DùMén) ; 旬首(XúnShǒu): JiaZiWu

太阴 (Tài Yīn) 天任 (Tiān Rèn) 景门 (Jǐng Mén) Xun 4　Gui Wu	螣蛇 (Téng Shé) 天冲 (Tiān Chōng) 死门 (Sǐ Mén) Li 9　Ji Ren	值符 (Zhí Fú) 天辅 (Tiān Fǔ) 惊门 (Jīng Mén) Kun 2　Geng/Yi
六合 (Liù Hé) 天蓬 (Tiān Péng) 杜门 (Dù Mén) Zhen 3　Xin	Yin (阴) Dun# 4 Hour: **YiChou** ©Calvin Yap	九天 (Jiǔ Tiān) 天英 (Tiān Yīng) 开门 (Kāi Mén) Dui 7　Ren Ding
白虎 (Bái Hǔ) 天心 (Tiān Xīn) 伤门 (Shāng Mén) Gen 8　Bing Gui	玄武 (Xuán Wǔ) 天柱 (Tiān Zhù) 生门 (Shēng Mén) Kan 1　Ding Xin	九地 (Jiǔ Dì) 禽芮 (Qín Ruì) 休门 (Xiū Mén) Qian 6　Geng/Yi Bing

Yin (阴) Dun# 4 Hour: **BingYin** ; 直符(ZhíFú): 天辅(TiānFǔ)
直使(ZhíShǐ): 杜门(DùMén) ; 旬首(XúnShǒu): JiaZiWu

白虎 (Bái Hǔ) 天心 (Tiān Xīn) 生门 (Shēng Mén) Xun 4　Bing Wu	六合 (Liù Hé) 天蓬 (Tiān Péng) 伤门 (Shāng Mén) Li 9　Xin Ren	太阴 (Tài Yīn) 天任 (Tiān Rèn) 杜门 (Dù Mén) Kun 2　Gui Geng/Yi
玄武 (Xuán Wǔ) 天柱 (Tiān Zhù) 休门 (Xiū Mén) Zhen 3　Ding Ji	Yin (阴) Dun# 4 Hour: **BingYin** **Fan Yin** ©Calvin Yap	螣蛇 (Téng Shé) 天冲 (Tiān Chōng) 景门 (Jǐng Mén) Dui 7　Ji Ding
九地 (Jiǔ Dì) 禽芮 (Qín Ruì) 开门 (Kāi Mén) Gen 8　Geng/Yi Gui	九天 (Jiǔ Tiān) 天英 (Tiān Yīng) 惊门 (Jīng Mén) Kan 1　Ren Xin	值符 (Zhí Fú) 天辅 (Tiān Fǔ) 死门 (Sǐ Mén) Qian 6　Wu Bing

Yin (阴) Dun# 4 Hour: **DingMao** ; 直符(ZhíFú): 天辅(TiānFǔ)
直使(ZhíShǐ): 杜门(DùMén) ; 旬首(XúnShǒu): JiaZiWu

六合 (Liù Hé) 天蓬 (Tiān Péng) 惊门 (Jīng Mén) Xun 4　Xin Wu	太阴 (Tài Yīn) 天任 (Tiān Rèn) 开门 (Kāi Mén) Li 9　Gui Ren	螣蛇 (Téng Shé) 天冲 (Tiān Chōng) 休门 (Xiū Mén) Kun 2　Ji Geng/Yi
白虎 (Bái Hǔ) 天心 (Tiān Xīn) 死门 (Sǐ Mén) Zhen 3　Bing Ji	Yin (阴) Dun# 4 Hour: **DingMao** ©Calvin Yap	值符 (Zhí Fú) 天辅 (Tiān Fǔ) 生门 (Shēng Mén) Dui 7　Wu Ding
玄武 (Xuán Wǔ) 天柱 (Tiān Zhù) 景门 (Jǐng Mén) Gen 8　Ding Gui	九地 (Jiǔ Dì) 禽芮 (Qín Ruì) 杜门 (Dù Mén) Kan 1　Geng/Yi Xin	九天 (Jiǔ Tiān) 天英 (Tiān Yīng) 伤门 (Shāng Mén) Qian 6　Ren Bing

Yin (阴) Dun# 4 Hour: **WuChen** ; 直符(ZhíFú): 天辅(TiānFǔ)
直使(ZhíShǐ): 杜门(DùMén) ; 旬首(XúnShǒu): JiaZiWu

值符 (Zhí Fú) 天辅 (Tiān Fǔ) 伤门 (Shāng Mén) Xun 4　Wu Wu	九天 (Jiǔ Tiān) 天英 (Tiān Yīng) 杜门 (Dù Mén) Li 9　Ren Ren	九地 (Jiǔ Dì) 禽芮 (Qín Ruì) 景门 (Jǐng Mén) Kun 2　Geng/Yi Geng/Yi
螣蛇 (Téng Shé) 天冲 (Tiān Chōng) 生门 (Shēng Mén) Zhen 3　Ji Ji	Yin (阴) Dun# 4 Hour: **WuChen** **Fu Yin** ©Calvin Yap	玄武 (Xuán Wǔ) 天柱 (Tiān Zhù) 死门 (Sǐ Mén) Dui 7　Ding Ding
太阴 (Tài Yīn) 天任 (Tiān Rèn) 休门 (Xiū Mén) Gen 8　Gui Gui	六合 (Liù Hé) 天蓬 (Tiān Péng) 开门 (Kāi Mén) Kan 1　Xin Xin	白虎 (Bái Hǔ) 天心 (Tiān Xīn) 惊门 (Jīng Mén) Qian 6　Bing Bing

Yin (阴) Dun# 4 Hour: **JiSi** ; 直符(ZhíFú): 天辅(TiānFǔ)
直使(ZhíShǐ): 杜门(DùMén) ; 旬首(XúnShǒu): JiaZiWu

九天 (Jiǔ Tiān) 天英 (Tiān Yīng) 死门 (Sǐ Mén) Xun 4　Ren Wu	九地 (Jiǔ Dì) 禽芮 (Qín Ruì) 惊门 (Jīng Mén) Li 9　Geng/Yi Ren	玄武 (Xuán Wǔ) 天柱 (Tiān Zhù) 开门 (Kāi Mén) Kun 2　Ding Geng/Yi
值符 (Zhí Fú) 天辅 (Tiān Fǔ) 景门 (Jǐng Mén) Zhen 3　Wu Ji	Yin (阴) Dun# 4 Hour: **JiSi** ©Calvin Yap	白虎 (Bái Hǔ) 天心 (Tiān Xīn) 休门 (Xiū Mén) Dui 7　Bing Ding
螣蛇 (Téng Shé) 天冲 (Tiān Chōng) 杜门 (Dù Mén) Gen 8　Ji Gui	太阴 (Tài Yīn) 天任 (Tiān Rèn) 伤门 (Shāng Mén) Kan 1　Gui Xin	六合 (Liù Hé) 天蓬 (Tiān Péng) 生门 (Shēng Mén) Qian 6　Xin Bing

Yin (阴) Dun# 4 Hour: **GengWu**；直符(ZhíFú): 天辅(TiānFǔ)
直使(ZhíShǐ): 杜门(DùMén)；旬首(XúnShǒu): JiaZiWu

太阴 (Tài Yīn) 天任 (Tiān Rèn) 休门 (Xiū Mén) Xun 4 Gui Wu	螣蛇 (Téng Shé) 天冲 (Tiān Chōng) 生门 (Shēng Mén) Li 9 Ji Ren	值符 (Zhí Fú) 天辅 (Tiān Fǔ) 伤门 (Shāng Mén) Kun 2 Wu Geng/Yi
六合 (Liù Hé) 天蓬 (Tiān Péng) 开门 (Kāi Mén) Zhen 3 Xin Ji	Yin (阴) Dun# 4 Hour: **GengWu** ©Calvin Yap	九天 (Jiǔ Tiān) 天英 (Tiān Yīng) 杜门 (Dù Mén) Dui 7 Ren Ding
白虎 (Bái Hǔ) 天心 (Tiān Xīn) 惊门 (Jīng Mén) Gen 8 Bing Gui	玄武 (Xuán Wǔ) 天柱 (Tiān Zhù) 死门 (Sǐ Mén) Kan 1 Ding Xin	九地 (Jiǔ Dì) 禽芮 (Qín Ruì) 景门 (Jǐng Mén) Qian 6 Geng/Yi Bing

Yin (阴) Dun# 4 Hour: **XinWei**；直符(ZhíFú): 天辅(TiānFǔ)
直使(ZhíShǐ): 杜门(DùMén)；旬首(XúnShǒu): JiaZiWu

玄武 (Xuán Wǔ) 天柱 (Tiān Zhù) 开门 (Kāi Mén) Xun 4 Ding Wu	白虎 (Bái Hǔ) 天心 (Tiān Xīn) 休门 (Xiū Mén) Li 9 Bing Ren	六合 (Liù Hé) 天蓬 (Tiān Péng) 生门 (Shēng Mén) Kun 2 Xin Geng/Yi
九地 (Jiǔ Dì) 禽芮 (Qín Ruì) 惊门 (Jīng Mén) Zhen 3 Geng/Yi Ji	Yin (阴) Dun# 4 Hour: **XinWei** ©Calvin Yap	太阴 (Tài Yīn) 天任 (Tiān Rèn) 伤门 (Shāng Mén) Dui 7 Gui Ding
九天 (Jiǔ Tiān) 天英 (Tiān Yīng) 死门 (Sǐ Mén) Gen 8 Ren Gui	值符 (Zhí Fú) 天辅 (Tiān Fǔ) 景门 (Jǐng Mén) Kan 1 Wu Xin	螣蛇 (Téng Shé) 天冲 (Tiān Chōng) 杜门 (Dù Mén) Qian 6 Ji Bing

Yin (阴) Dun# 4 Hour: **RenShen**；直符(ZhíFú): 天辅(TiānFǔ)
直使(ZhíShǐ): 杜门(DùMén)；旬首(XúnShǒu): JiaZiWu

螣蛇 (Téng Shé) 天冲 (Tiān Chōng) 生门 (Shēng Mén) Xun 4 Ji Wu	值符 (Zhí Fú) 天辅 (Tiān Fǔ) 伤门 (Shāng Mén) Li 9 Wu Ren	九天 (Jiǔ Tiān) 天英 (Tiān Yīng) 杜门 (Dù Mén) Kun 2 Ren Geng/Yi
太阴 (Tài Yīn) 天任 (Tiān Rèn) 休门 (Xiū Mén) Zhen 3 Gui Ji	Yin (阴) Dun# 4 Hour: **RenShen** ©Calvin Yap	九地 (Jiǔ Dì) 禽芮 (Qín Ruì) 景门 (Jǐng Mén) Dui 7 Geng/Yi Ding
六合 (Liù Hé) 天蓬 (Tiān Péng) 开门 (Kāi Mén) Gen 8 Xin Gui	白虎 (Bái Hǔ) 天心 (Tiān Xīn) 惊门 (Jīng Mén) Kan 1 Bing Xin	玄武 (Xuán Wǔ) 天柱 (Tiān Zhù) 死门 (Sǐ Mén) Qian 6 Ding Bing

Yin (阴) Dun# 4 Hour: **GuiYou**；直符(ZhíFú): 天辅(TiānFǔ)
直使(ZhíShǐ): 杜门(DùMén)；旬首(XúnShǒu): JiaZiWu

九地 (Jiǔ Dì) 禽芮 (Qín Ruì) 杜门 (Dù Mén) Xun 4 Geng/Yi Wu	玄武 (Xuán Wǔ) 天柱 (Tiān Zhù) 景门 (Jǐng Mén) Li 9 Ding Ren	白虎 (Bái Hǔ) 天心 (Tiān Xīn) 死门 (Sǐ Mén) Kun 2 Bing Geng/Yi
九天 (Jiǔ Tiān) 天英 (Tiān Yīng) 伤门 (Shāng Mén) Zhen 3 Ren Ji	Yin (阴) Dun# 4 Hour: **GuiYou** ©Calvin Yap	六合 (Liù Hé) 天蓬 (Tiān Péng) 惊门 (Jīng Mén) Dui 7 Xin Ding
值符 (Zhí Fú) 天辅 (Tiān Fǔ) 生门 (Shēng Mén) Gen 8 Wu Gui	螣蛇 (Téng Shé) 天冲 (Tiān Chōng) 休门 (Xiū Mén) Kan 1 Ji Xin	太阴 (Tài Yīn) 天任 (Tiān Rèn) 开门 (Kāi Mén) Qian 6 Gui Bing

---

Chart: **-4JiaXu** (Yin Dun #4 JiaXu Xun)
JiaXu, YiHai, BingZi, DingChou, WuYin, JiMao, GengChen, XinSi, RenWu, GuiWei

Yin (阴) Dun# 4 Hour: **JiaXu**；直符(ZhíFú): 天冲(TiānChōng)
直使(ZhíShǐ): 伤门(ShāngMén)；旬首(XúnShǒu): JiaXuJi

九天 (Jiǔ Tiān) 天辅 (Tiān Fǔ) 杜门 (Dù Mén) Xun 4 Wu Wu	九地 (Jiǔ Dì) 天英 (Tiān Yīng) 景门 (Jǐng Mén) Li 9 Ren Ren	玄武 (Xuán Wǔ) 禽芮 (Qín Ruì) 死门 (Sǐ Mén) Kun 2 Geng/Yi Geng/Yi
值符 (Zhí Fú) 天冲 (Tiān Chōng) 伤门 (Shāng Mén) Zhen 3 Ji Ji	Yin (阴) Dun# 4 Hour: **JiaXu** **Fu Yin** ©Calvin Yap	白虎 (Bái Hǔ) 天柱 (Tiān Zhù) 惊门 (Jīng Mén) Dui 7 Ding Ding
螣蛇 (Téng Shé) 天任 (Tiān Rèn) 生门 (Shēng Mén) Gen 8 Gui Gui	太阴 (Tài Yīn) 天蓬 (Tiān Péng) 休门 (Xiū Mén) Kan 1 Xin Xin	六合 (Liù Hé) 天心 (Tiān Xīn) 开门 (Kāi Mén) Qian 6 Bing Bing

Yin (阴) Dun# 4 Hour: **YiHai**；直符(ZhíFú): 天冲(TiānChōng)
直使(ZhíShǐ): 伤门(ShāngMén)；旬首(XúnShǒu): JiaXuJi

太阴 (Tài Yīn) 天蓬 (Tiān Péng) 休门 (Xiū Mén) Xun 4 Xin Wu	螣蛇 (Téng Shé) 天任 (Tiān Rèn) 生门 (Shēng Mén) Li 9 Gui Ren	值符 (Zhí Fú) 天冲 (Tiān Chōng) 伤门 (Shāng Mén) Kun 2 Ji Geng/Yi
六合 (Liù Hé) 天心 (Tiān Xīn) 开门 (Kāi Mén) Zhen 3 Bing Ji	Yin (阴) Dun# 4 Hour: **YiHai** ©Calvin Yap	九天 (Jiǔ Tiān) 天辅 (Tiān Fǔ) 杜门 (Dù Mén) Dui 7 Wu Ding
白虎 (Bái Hǔ) 天柱 (Tiān Zhù) 惊门 (Jīng Mén) Gen 8 Ding Gui	玄武 (Xuán Wǔ) 禽芮 (Qín Ruì) 死门 (Sǐ Mén) Kan 1 Geng/Yi Xin	九地 (Jiǔ Dì) 天英 (Tiān Yīng) 景门 (Jǐng Mén) Qian 6 Ren Bing

Yin (阴) Dun# 4 Hour: **BingZi** ; 直符(ZhíFú): 天冲(TiānChōng) / 直使(ZhíShǐ): 伤门(ShāngMén) ; 旬首(XúnShǒu): JiaXuJi

白虎 (Bái Hǔ) 天柱 (Tiān Zhù) 死门 (Sǐ Mén) Xun 4　Ding Wu	六合 (Liù Hé) 天心 (Tiān Xīn) 惊门 (Jīng Mén) Li 9　Bing Ren	太阴 (Tài Yīn) 天蓬 (Tiān Péng) 开门 (Kāi Mén) Kun 2　Xin Geng/Yi
玄武 (Xuán Wǔ) 禽芮 (Qín Ruì) 景门 (Jǐng Mén) Zhen 3　Geng/Yi Ji	Yin (阴) Dun# 4 Hour: **BingZi** ©Calvin Yap	螣蛇 (Téng Shé) 天任 (Tiān Rèn) 休门 (Xiū Mén) Dui 7　Gui Ding
九地 (Jiǔ Dì) 天英 (Tiān Yīng) 杜门 (Dù Mén) Gen 8　Ren Gui	九天 (Jiǔ Tiān) 天辅 (Tiān Fǔ) 伤门 (Shāng Mén) Kan 1　Wu Xin	值符 (Zhí Fú) 天冲 (Tiān Chōng) 生门 (Shēng Mén) Qian 6　Ji Bing

Yin (阴) Dun# 4 Hour: **DingChou**; 直符(ZhíFú):天冲(TiānChōng) / 直使(ZhíShǐ): 伤门(ShāngMén) ; 旬首(XúnShǒu): JiaXuJi

六合 (Liù Hé) 天心 (Tiān Xīn) 生门 (Shēng Mén) Xun 4　Bing Wu	太阴 (Tài Yīn) 天蓬 (Tiān Péng) 伤门 (Shāng Mén) Li 9　Xin Ren	螣蛇 (Téng Shé) 天任 (Tiān Rèn) 杜门 (Dù Mén) Kun 2　Gui Geng/Yi
白虎 (Bái Hǔ) 天柱 (Tiān Zhù) 休门 (Xiū Mén) Zhen 3　Ding Ji	Yin (阴) Dun# 4 Hour: **DingChou** **Fan Yin** ©Calvin Yap	值符 (Zhí Fú) 天冲 (Tiān Chōng) 景门 (Jǐng Mén) Dui 7　Ji Ding
玄武 (Xuán Wǔ) 禽芮 (Qín Ruì) 开门 (Kāi Mén) Gen 8　Geng/Yi Gui	九地 (Jiǔ Dì) 天英 (Tiān Yīng) 惊门 (Jīng Mén) Kan 1　Ren Xin	九天 (Jiǔ Tiān) 天辅 (Tiān Fǔ) 死门 (Sǐ Mén) Qian 6　Wu Bing

Yin (阴) Dun# 4 Hour: **WuYin** ; 直符(ZhíFú): 天冲(TiānChōng) / 直使(ZhíShǐ): 伤门(ShāngMén) ; 旬首(XúnShǒu): JiaXuJi

值符 (Zhí Fú) 天冲 (Tiān Chōng) 景门 (Jǐng Mén) Xun 4　Ji Wu	九天 (Jiǔ Tiān) 天辅 (Tiān Fǔ) 死门 (Sǐ Mén) Li 9　Wu Ren	九地 (Jiǔ Dì) 天英 (Tiān Yīng) 惊门 (Jīng Mén) Kun 2　Ren Geng/Yi
螣蛇 (Téng Shé) 天任 (Tiān Rèn) 杜门 (Dù Mén) Zhen 3　Gui Ji	Yin (阴) Dun# 4 Hour: **WuYin** ©Calvin Yap	玄武 (Xuán Wǔ) 禽芮 (Qín Ruì) 开门 (Kāi Mén) Dui 7　Geng/Yi Ding
太阴 (Tài Yīn) 天蓬 (Tiān Péng) 伤门 (Shāng Mén) Gen 8　Xin Gui	六合 (Liù Hé) 天心 (Tiān Xīn) 生门 (Shēng Mén) Kan 1　Bing Xin	白虎 (Bái Hǔ) 天柱 (Tiān Zhù) 休门 (Xiū Mén) Qian 6　Ding Bing

Yin (阴) Dun# 4 Hour: **JiMao** ; 直符(ZhíFú): 天冲(TiānChōng) / 直使(ZhíShǐ): 伤门(ShāngMén) ; 旬首(XúnShǒu): JiaXuJi

九天 (Jiǔ Tiān) 天辅 (Tiān Fǔ) 开门 (Kāi Mén) Xun 4　Wu Wu	九地 (Jiǔ Dì) 天英 (Tiān Yīng) 休门 (Xiū Mén) Li 9　Ren Ren	玄武 (Xuán Wǔ) 禽芮 (Qín Ruì) 生门 (Shēng Mén) Kun 2　Geng/Yi Geng/Yi
值符 (Zhí Fú) 天冲 (Tiān Chōng) 惊门 (Jīng Mén) Zhen 3　Ji Ji	Yin (阴) Dun# 4 Hour: **JiMao** **Fu Yin** ©Calvin Yap	白虎 (Bái Hǔ) 天柱 (Tiān Zhù) 伤门 (Shāng Mén) Dui 7　Ding Ding
螣蛇 (Téng Shé) 天任 (Tiān Rèn) 死门 (Sǐ Mén) Gen 8　Gui Gui	太阴 (Tài Yīn) 天蓬 (Tiān Péng) 景门 (Jǐng Mén) Kan 1　Xin Xin	六合 (Liù Hé) 天心 (Tiān Xīn) 杜门 (Dù Mén) Qian 6　Bing Bing

Yin (阴) Dun# 4 Hour: **GengChen** ; 直符(ZhíFú): 天冲(TiānChōng) / 直使(ZhíShǐ): 伤门(ShāngMén) ; 旬首(XúnShǒu): JiaXuJi

太阴 (Tài Yīn) 天蓬 (Tiān Péng) 惊门 (Jīng Mén) Xun 4　Xin Wu	螣蛇 (Téng Shé) 天任 (Tiān Rèn) 开门 (Kāi Mén) Li 9　Gui Ren	值符 (Zhí Fú) 天冲 (Tiān Chōng) 休门 (Xiū Mén) Kun 2　Ji Geng/Yi
六合 (Liù Hé) 天心 (Tiān Xīn) 死门 (Sǐ Mén) Zhen 3　Bing Ji	Yin (阴) Dun# 4 Hour: **GengChen** ©Calvin Yap	九天 (Jiǔ Tiān) 天辅 (Tiān Fǔ) 生门 (Shēng Mén) Dui 7　Wu Ding
白虎 (Bái Hǔ) 天柱 (Tiān Zhù) 景门 (Jǐng Mén) Gen 8　Ding Gui	玄武 (Xuán Wǔ) 禽芮 (Qín Ruì) 杜门 (Dù Mén) Kan 1　Geng/Yi Xin	九地 (Jiǔ Dì) 天英 (Tiān Yīng) 伤门 (Shāng Mén) Qian 6　Ren Bing

Yin (阴) Dun# 4 Hour: **XinSi** ; 直符(ZhíFú): 天冲(TiānChōng) / 直使(ZhíShǐ): 伤门(ShāngMén) ; 旬首(XúnShǒu): JiaXuJi

玄武 (Xuán Wǔ) 禽芮 (Qín Ruì) 休门 (Xiū Mén) Xun 4　Geng/Yi Wu	白虎 (Bái Hǔ) 天柱 (Tiān Zhù) 生门 (Shēng Mén) Li 9　Ding Ren	六合 (Liù Hé) 天心 (Tiān Xīn) 伤门 (Shāng Mén) Kun 2　Bing Geng/Yi
九地 (Jiǔ Dì) 天英 (Tiān Yīng) 开门 (Kāi Mén) Zhen 3　Ren Ji	Yin (阴) Dun# 4 Hour: **XinSi** ©Calvin Yap	太阴 (Tài Yīn) 天蓬 (Tiān Péng) 杜门 (Dù Mén) Dui 7　Xin Xin
九天 (Jiǔ Tiān) 天辅 (Tiān Fǔ) 惊门 (Jīng Mén) Gen 8　Wu Gui	值符 (Zhí Fú) 天冲 (Tiān Chōng) 死门 (Sǐ Mén) Kan 1　Ji Xin	螣蛇 (Téng Shé) 天任 (Tiān Rèn) 景门 (Jǐng Mén) Qian 6　Gui Bing

<table>
<tr><td colspan="3">Yin (阴) Dun# 4 Hour: RenWu；直符(ZhíFú): 天冲(TiānChōng)
直使(ZhíShǐ): 伤门(ShāngMén)；旬首(XúnShǒu): JiaXuJi</td></tr>
<tr>
<td>螣蛇 (Téng Shé)
天任 (Tiān Rèn)
伤门 (Shāng Mén)
Xun 4　Gui
　　Wu</td>
<td>值符 (Zhí Fú)
天冲 (Tiān Chōng)
杜门 (Dù Mén)
Li 9　Ji
　　Ren</td>
<td>九天 (Jiǔ Tiān)
天辅 (Tiān Fǔ)
景门 (Jǐng Mén)
Kun 2　Wu
　　Geng/Yi</td>
</tr>
<tr>
<td>太阴 (Tài Yīn)
天蓬 (Tiān Péng)
生门 (Shēng Mén)
Zhen 3　Xin
　　Ji</td>
<td>Yin (阴) Dun# 4
Hour: RenWu

©Calvin Yap</td>
<td>九地 (Jiǔ Dì)
天英 (Tiān Yīng)
死门 (Sǐ Mén)
Dui 7　Ren
　　Ding</td>
</tr>
<tr>
<td>六合 (Liù Hé)
天心 (Tiān Xīn)
休门 (Xiū Mén)
Gen 8　Bing
　　Gui</td>
<td>白虎 (Bái Hǔ)
天柱 (Tiān Zhù)
开门 (Kāi Mén)
Kan 1　Ding
　　Xin</td>
<td>玄武 (Xuán Wǔ)
禽芮 (Qín Ruì)
惊门 (Jīng Mén)
Qian 6　Geng/Yi
　　Bing</td>
</tr>
</table>

<table>
<tr><td colspan="3">Yin (阴) Dun# 4 Hour: GuiWei；直符(ZhíFú): 天冲(TiānChōng)
直使(ZhíShǐ): 伤门(ShāngMén)；旬首(XúnShǒu): JiaXuJi</td></tr>
<tr>
<td>九地 (Jiǔ Dì)
天英 (Tiān Yīng)
杜门 (Dù Mén)
Xun 4　Ren
　　Wu</td>
<td>玄武 (Xuán Wǔ)
禽芮 (Qín Ruì)
景门 (Jǐng Mén)
Li 9　Geng/Yi
　　Ren</td>
<td>白虎 (Bái Hǔ)
天柱 (Tiān Zhù)
死门 (Sǐ Mén)
Kun 2　Ding
　　Geng/Yi</td>
</tr>
<tr>
<td>九天 (Jiǔ Tiān)
天辅 (Tiān Fǔ)
伤门 (Shāng Mén)
Zhen 3　Wu
　　Ji</td>
<td>Yin (阴) Dun# 4
Hour: GuiWei

©Calvin Yap</td>
<td>六合 (Liù Hé)
天心 (Tiān Xīn)
惊门 (Jīng Mén)
Dui 7　Bing
　　Ding</td>
</tr>
<tr>
<td>值符 (Zhí Fú)
天冲 (Tiān Chōng)
生门 (Shēng Mén)
Gen 8　Ji
　　Gui</td>
<td>螣蛇 (Téng Shé)
天任 (Tiān Rèn)
休门 (Xiū Mén)
Kan 1　Gui
　　Xin</td>
<td>太阴 (Tài Yīn)
天蓬 (Tiān Péng)
开门 (Kāi Mén)
Qian 6　Xin
　　Bing</td>
</tr>
</table>

<table>
<tr><td colspan="3">Chart: -4JiaShen (Yin Dun #4 JiaShen Xun)
JiaShen, YiYou, BingXu, DingHai, WuZi, JiChou, GengYin, XinMao, RenChen, GuiSi</td></tr>
</table>

<table>
<tr><td colspan="3">Yin (阴) Dun# 4 Hour: JiaShen；直符(ZhíFú): 天芮(TiānRuì)
直使(ZhíShǐ): 死门(SǐMén)；旬首(XúnShǒu): JiaShenGeng</td></tr>
<tr>
<td>太阴 (Tài Yīn)
天辅 (Tiān Fǔ)
杜门 (Dù Mén)
Xun 4　Wu
　　Wu</td>
<td>螣蛇 (Téng Shé)
天英 (Tiān Yīng)
景门 (Jǐng Mén)
Li 9　Ren
　　Ren</td>
<td>值符 (Zhí Fú)
禽芮 (Qín Ruì)
死门 (Sǐ Mén)
Kun 2　Geng/Yi
　　Geng/Yi</td>
</tr>
<tr>
<td>六合 (Liù Hé)
天冲 (Tiān Chōng)
伤门 (Shāng Mén)
Zhen 3　Ji
　　Ji</td>
<td>Yin (阴) Dun# 4
Hour: JiaShen
Fu Yin
©Calvin Yap</td>
<td>九天 (Jiǔ Tiān)
天柱 (Tiān Zhù)
惊门 (Jīng Mén)
Dui 7　Ding
　　Ding</td>
</tr>
<tr>
<td>白虎 (Bái Hǔ)
天任 (Tiān Rèn)
生门 (Shēng Mén)
Gen 8　Gui
　　Gui</td>
<td>玄武 (Xuán Wǔ)
天蓬 (Tiān Péng)
休门 (Xiū Mén)
Kan 1　Xin
　　Xin</td>
<td>九地 (Jiǔ Dì)
天心 (Tiān Xīn)
开门 (Kāi Mén)
Qian 6　Bing
　　Bing</td>
</tr>
</table>

<table>
<tr><td colspan="3">Yin (阴) Dun# 4 Hour: YiYou；直符(ZhíFú): 天芮(TiānRuì)
直使(ZhíShǐ): 死门(SǐMén)；旬首(XúnShǒu): JiaShenGeng</td></tr>
<tr>
<td>太阴 (Tài Yīn)
天辅 (Tiān Fǔ)
休门 (Xiū Mén)
Xun 4　Wu
　　Wu</td>
<td>螣蛇 (Téng Shé)
天英 (Tiān Yīng)
生门 (Shēng Mén)
Li 9　Ren
　　Ren</td>
<td>值符 (Zhí Fú)
禽芮 (Qín Ruì)
伤门 (Shāng Mén)
Kun 2　Geng/Yi
　　Geng/Yi</td>
</tr>
<tr>
<td>六合 (Liù Hé)
天冲 (Tiān Chōng)
开门 (Kāi Mén)
Zhen 3　Ji
　　Ji</td>
<td>Yin (阴) Dun# 4
Hour: YiYou
Fu Yin
©Calvin Yap</td>
<td>九天 (Jiǔ Tiān)
天柱 (Tiān Zhù)
杜门 (Dù Mén)
Dui 7　Ding
　　Ding</td>
</tr>
<tr>
<td>白虎 (Bái Hǔ)
天任 (Tiān Rèn)
惊门 (Jīng Mén)
Gen 8　Gui
　　Gui</td>
<td>玄武 (Xuán Wǔ)
天蓬 (Tiān Péng)
死门 (Sǐ Mén)
Kan 1　Xin
　　Xin</td>
<td>九地 (Jiǔ Dì)
天心 (Tiān Xīn)
景门 (Jǐng Mén)
Qian 6　Bing
　　Bing</td>
</tr>
</table>

<table>
<tr><td colspan="3">Yin (阴) Dun# 4 Hour: BingXu；直符(ZhíFú): 天芮(TiānRuì)
直使(ZhíShǐ): 死门(SǐMén)；旬首(XúnShǒu): JiaShenGeng</td></tr>
<tr>
<td>白虎 (Bái Hǔ)
天任 (Tiān Rèn)
景门 (Jǐng Mén)
Xun 4　Gui
　　Wu</td>
<td>六合 (Liù Hé)
天冲 (Tiān Chōng)
死门 (Sǐ Mén)
Li 9　Ji
　　Ren</td>
<td>太阴 (Tài Yīn)
天辅 (Tiān Fǔ)
惊门 (Jīng Mén)
Kun 2　Wu
　　Geng/Yi</td>
</tr>
<tr>
<td>玄武 (Xuán Wǔ)
天蓬 (Tiān Péng)
杜门 (Dù Mén)
Zhen 3　Xin
　　Ji</td>
<td>Yin (阴) Dun# 4
Hour: BingXu

©Calvin Yap</td>
<td>螣蛇 (Téng Shé)
天英 (Tiān Yīng)
开门 (Kāi Mén)
Dui 7　Ren
　　Ding</td>
</tr>
<tr>
<td>九地 (Jiǔ Dì)
天心 (Tiān Xīn)
伤门 (Shāng Mén)
Gen 8　Bing
　　Gui</td>
<td>九天 (Jiǔ Tiān)
天柱 (Tiān Zhù)
生门 (Shēng Mén)
Kan 1　Ding
　　Xin</td>
<td>值符 (Zhí Fú)
禽芮 (Qín Ruì)
休门 (Xiū Mén)
Qian 6　Geng/Yi
　　Bing</td>
</tr>
</table>

<table>
<tr><td colspan="3">Yin (阴) Dun# 4 Hour: DingHai；直符(ZhíFú): 天芮(TiānRuì)
直使(ZhíShǐ): 死门(SǐMén)；旬首(XúnShǒu): JiaShenGeng</td></tr>
<tr>
<td>六合 (Liù Hé)
天冲 (Tiān Chōng)
开门 (Kāi Mén)
Xun 4　Ji
　　Wu</td>
<td>太阴 (Tài Yīn)
天辅 (Tiān Fǔ)
休门 (Xiū Mén)
Li 9　Wu
　　Ren</td>
<td>螣蛇 (Téng Shé)
天英 (Tiān Yīng)
生门 (Shēng Mén)
Kun 2　Ren
　　Geng/Yi</td>
</tr>
<tr>
<td>白虎 (Bái Hǔ)
天任 (Tiān Rèn)
惊门 (Jīng Mén)
Zhen 3　Gui
　　Ji</td>
<td>Yin (阴) Dun# 4
Hour: DingHai

©Calvin Yap</td>
<td>值符 (Zhí Fú)
禽芮 (Qín Ruì)
伤门 (Shāng Mén)
Dui 7　Geng/Yi
　　Ding</td>
</tr>
<tr>
<td>玄武 (Xuán Wǔ)
天蓬 (Tiān Péng)
死门 (Sǐ Mén)
Gen 8　Xin
　　Gui</td>
<td>九地 (Jiǔ Dì)
天心 (Tiān Xīn)
景门 (Jǐng Mén)
Kan 1　Bing
　　Xin</td>
<td>九天 (Jiǔ Tiān)
天柱 (Tiān Zhù)
杜门 (Dù Mén)
Qian 6　Ding
　　Bing</td>
</tr>
</table>

Yin (阴) Dun# 4 Hour: WuZi ；直符(ZhíFú): 天芮(TiānRuì)
直使(ZhíShǐ): 死门(SǐMén) ；旬首(XúnShǒu): JiaShenGeng

值符 (Zhí Fú) 禽芮 (Qín Ruì) 伤门 (Shāng Mén) Xun 4　Geng/Yi Wu	九天 (Jiǔ Tiān) 天柱 (Tiān Zhù) 杜门 (Dù Mén) Li 9　Ding Ren	九地 (Jiǔ Dì) 天心 (Tiān Xīn) 景门 (Jǐng Mén) Kun 2　Bing Geng/Yi
螣蛇 (Téng Shé) 天英 (Tiān Yīng) 生门 (Shēng Mén) Zhen 3　Ren Ji	Yin (阴) Dun# 4 Hour: **WuZi** ©Calvin Yap	玄武 (Xuán Wǔ) 天蓬 (Tiān Péng) 死门 (Sǐ Mén) Dui 7　Xin Ding
太阴 (Tài Yīn) 天辅 (Tiān Fǔ) 休门 (Xiū Mén) Gen 8　Wu Gui	六合 (Liù Hé) 天冲 (Tiān Chōng) 开门 (Kāi Mén) Kan 1　Ji Xin	白虎 (Bái Hǔ) 天任 (Tiān Rèn) 惊门 (Jīng Mén) Qian 6　Gui Bing

Yin (阴) Dun# 4 Hour: JiChou ；直符(ZhíFú): 天芮(TiānRuì)
直使(ZhíShǐ): 死门(SǐMén) ；旬首(XúnShǒu): JiaShenGeng

九天 (Jiǔ Tiān) 天柱 (Tiān Zhù) 生门 (Shēng Mén) Xun 4　Ding Wu	九地 (Jiǔ Dì) 天心 (Tiān Xīn) 伤门 (Shāng Mén) Li 9　Bing Ren	玄武 (Xuán Wǔ) 天蓬 (Tiān Péng) 杜门 (Dù Mén) Kun 2　Xin Geng/Yi
值符 (Zhí Fú) 禽芮 (Qín Ruì) 休门 (Xiū Mén) Zhen 3　Geng/Yi Ji	Yin (阴) Dun# 4 Hour: **JiChou** ©Calvin Yap	白虎 (Bái Hǔ) 天任 (Tiān Rèn) 景门 (Jǐng Mén) Dui 7　Gui Ding
螣蛇 (Téng Shé) 天英 (Tiān Yīng) 惊门 (Jīng Mén) Gen 8　Ren Gui	太阴 (Tài Yīn) 天辅 (Tiān Fǔ) 开门 (Kāi Mén) Kan 1　Wu Xin	六合 (Liù Hé) 天冲 (Tiān Chōng) 死门 (Sǐ Mén) Qian 6　Ji Bing

Yin (阴) Dun# 4 Hour: GengYin ；直符(ZhíFú): 天芮(TiānRuì)
直使(ZhíShǐ): 死门(SǐMén) ；旬首(XúnShǒu): JiaShenGeng

太阴 (Tài Yīn) 天辅 (Tiān Fǔ) 杜门 (Dù Mén) Xun 4　Wu Wu	螣蛇 (Téng Shé) 天英 (Tiān Yīng) 景门 (Jǐng Mén) Li 9　Ren Ren	值符 (Zhí Fú) 禽芮 (Qín Ruì) 死门 (Sǐ Mén) Kun 2　Geng/Yi Geng/Yi
六合 (Liù Hé) 天冲 (Tiān Chōng) 伤门 (Shāng Mén) Zhen 3　Ji Ji	Yin (阴) Dun# 4 Hour: **GengYin** **Fu Yin** ©Calvin Yap	九天 (Jiǔ Tiān) 天柱 (Tiān Zhù) 惊门 (Jīng Mén) Dui 7　Ding Ding
白虎 (Bái Hǔ) 天任 (Tiān Rèn) 生门 (Shēng Mén) Gen 8　Gui Gui	玄武 (Xuán Wǔ) 天蓬 (Tiān Péng) 休门 (Xiū Mén) Kan 1　Xin Xin	九地 (Jiǔ Dì) 天心 (Tiān Xīn) 开门 (Kāi Mén) Qian 6　Bing Bing

Yin (阴) Dun# 4 Hour: XinMao ；直符(ZhíFú): 天芮(TiānRuì)
直使(ZhíShǐ): 死门(SǐMén) ；旬首(XúnShǒu): JiaShenGeng

玄武 (Xuán Wǔ) 天蓬 (Tiān Péng) 死门 (Sǐ Mén) Xun 4　Xin Wu	白虎 (Bái Hǔ) 天任 (Tiān Rèn) 惊门 (Jīng Mén) Li 9　Gui Ren	六合 (Liù Hé) 天冲 (Tiān Chōng) 开门 (Kāi Mén) Kun 2　Ji Geng/Yi
九地 (Jiǔ Dì) 天心 (Tiān Xīn) 景门 (Jǐng Mén) Zhen 3　Bing Ji	Yin (阴) Dun# 4 Hour: **XinMao** ©Calvin Yap	太阴 (Tài Yīn) 天辅 (Tiān Fǔ) 休门 (Xiū Mén) Dui 7　Wu Ding
九天 (Jiǔ Tiān) 天柱 (Tiān Zhù) 杜门 (Dù Mén) Gen 8　Ding Gui	值符 (Zhí Fú) 禽芮 (Qín Ruì) 伤门 (Shāng Mén) Kan 1　Geng/Yi Xin	螣蛇 (Téng Shé) 天英 (Tiān Yīng) 生门 (Shēng Mén) Qian 6　Ren Bing

Yin (阴) Dun# 4 Hour: RenChen ；直符(ZhíFú): 天芮(TiānRuì)
直使(ZhíShǐ): 死门(SǐMén) ；旬首(XúnShǒu): JiaShenGeng

螣蛇 (Téng Shé) 天英 (Tiān Yīng) 惊门 (Jīng Mén) Xun 4　Ren Wu	值符 (Zhí Fú) 禽芮 (Qín Ruì) 开门 (Kāi Mén) Li 9　Geng/Yi Ren	九天 (Jiǔ Tiān) 天柱 (Tiān Zhù) 休门 (Xiū Mén) Kun 2　Ding Geng/Yi
太阴 (Tài Yīn) 天辅 (Tiān Fǔ) 死门 (Sǐ Mén) Zhen 3　Wu Ji	Yin (阴) Dun# 4 Hour: **RenChen** ©Calvin Yap	九地 (Jiǔ Dì) 天心 (Tiān Xīn) 生门 (Shēng Mén) Dui 7　Bing Ding
六合 (Liù Hé) 天冲 (Tiān Chōng) 景门 (Jǐng Mén) Gen 8　Ji Gui	白虎 (Bái Hǔ) 天任 (Tiān Rèn) 杜门 (Dù Mén) Kan 1　Gui Xin	玄武 (Xuán Wǔ) 天蓬 (Tiān Péng) 伤门 (Shāng Mén) Qian 6　Xin Bing

Yin (阴) Dun# 4 Hour: GuiSi ；直符(ZhíFú): 天芮(TiānRuì)
直使(ZhíShǐ): 死门(SǐMén) ；旬首(XúnShǒu): JiaShenGeng

九地 (Jiǔ Dì) 天心 (Tiān Xīn) 杜门 (Dù Mén) Xun 4　Bing Wu	玄武 (Xuán Wǔ) 天蓬 (Tiān Péng) 景门 (Jǐng Mén) Li 9　Xin Ren	白虎 (Bái Hǔ) 天任 (Tiān Rèn) 死门 (Sǐ Mén) Kun 2　Gui Geng/Yi
九天 (Jiǔ Tiān) 天柱 (Tiān Zhù) 伤门 (Shāng Mén) Zhen 3　Ding Ji	Yin (阴) Dun# 4 Hour: **GuiSi** **Fan Yin** ©Calvin Yap	六合 (Liù Hé) 天冲 (Tiān Chōng) 惊门 (Jīng Mén) Dui 7　Ji Ding
值符 (Zhí Fú) 禽芮 (Qín Ruì) 生门 (Shēng Mén) Gen 8　Geng/Yi Gui	螣蛇 (Téng Shé) 天英 (Tiān Yīng) 休门 (Xiū Mén) Kan 1　Ren Xin	太阴 (Tài Yīn) 天辅 (Tiān Fǔ) 开门 (Kāi Mén) Qian 6　Wu Bing

Chart: **-4JiaWu** (Yin Dun #4 JiaWu Xun)
JiaWu, YiWei, BingShen, DingYou, WuXu, JiHai, GengZi, XinChou, RenYin, GuiMao

---

Yin (阴) Dun# 4 Hour: **JiaWu**；直符(ZhíFú): 天蓬(TiānPéng)
直使(ZhíShǐ): 休门(XiūMén)；旬首(XúnShǒu): JiaWu/Xin

玄武 (Xuán Wǔ)	白虎 (Bái Hǔ)	六合 (Liù Hé)
天辅 (Tiān Fǔ)	天英 (Tiān Yīng)	禽芮 (Qín Ruì)
杜门 (Dù Mén)	景门 (Jǐng Mén)	死门 (Sǐ Mén)
Xun 4　Wu　Wu	Li 9　Ren　Ren	Kun 2　Geng/Yi　Geng/Yi
九地 (Jiǔ Dì)	Yin (阴) Dun# 4	太阴 (Tài Yīn)
天冲 (Tiān Chōng)	Hour: **JiaWu**	天柱 (Tiān Zhù)
伤门 (Shāng Mén)	**Fu Yin**	惊门 (Jīng Mén)
Zhen 3　Ji　Ji	©Calvin Yap	Dui 7　Ding　Ding
九天 (Jiǔ Tiān)	值符 (Zhí Fú)	腾蛇 (Téng Shé)
天任 (Tiān Rèn)	天蓬 (Tiān Péng)	天心 (Tiān Xīn)
生门 (Shēng Mén)	休门 (Xiū Mén)	开门 (Kāi Mén)
Gen 8　Gui　Gui	Kan 1　Xin　Xin	Qian 6　Bing　Bing

Yin (阴) Dun# 4 Hour: **YiWei**；直符(ZhíFú): 天蓬(TiānPéng)
直使(ZhíShǐ): 休门(XiūMén)；旬首(XúnShǒu): JiaWu/Xin

太阴 (Tài Yīn)	腾蛇 (Téng Shé)	值符 (Zhí Fú)
天柱 (Tiān Zhù)	天心 (Tiān Xīn)	天蓬 (Tiān Péng)
开门 (Kāi Mén)	休门 (Xiū Mén)	生门 (Shēng Mén)
Xun 4　Ding　Wu	Li 9　Bing　Ren	Kun 2　Xin　Geng/Yi
六合 (Liù Hé)	Yin (阴) Dun# 4	九天 (Jiǔ Tiān)
禽芮 (Qín Ruì)	Hour: **YiWei**	天任 (Tiān Rèn)
惊门 (Jīng Mén)	©Calvin Yap	伤门 (Shāng Mén)
Zhen 3　Geng/Yi　Ji		Dui 7　Gui　Ding
白虎 (Bái Hǔ)	玄武 (Xuán Wǔ)	九地 (Jiǔ Dì)
天英 (Tiān Yīng)	天辅 (Tiān Fǔ)	天冲 (Tiān Chōng)
死门 (Sǐ Mén)	景门 (Jǐng Mén)	杜门 (Dù Mén)
Gen 8　Ren　Gui	Kan 1　Wu　Xin	Qian 6　Ji　Bing

Yin (阴) Dun# 4 Hour: **BingShen**；直符(ZhíFú): 天蓬(TiānPéng)
直使(ZhíShǐ): 休门(XiūMén)；旬首(XúnShǒu): JiaWu/Xin

白虎 (Bái Hǔ)	六合 (Liù Hé)	太阴 (Tài Yīn)
天英 (Tiān Yīng)	禽芮 (Qín Ruì)	天柱 (Tiān Zhù)
伤门 (Shāng Mén)	杜门 (Dù Mén)	景门 (Jǐng Mén)
Xun 4　Ren　Wu	Li 9　Geng/Yi　Ren	Kun 2　Ding　Geng/Yi
玄武 (Xuán Wǔ)	Yin (阴) Dun# 4	腾蛇 (Téng Shé)
天辅 (Tiān Fǔ)	Hour: **BingShen**	天心 (Tiān Xīn)
生门 (Shēng Mén)	©Calvin Yap	死门 (Sǐ Mén)
Zhen 3　Wu　Ji		Dui 7　Bing　Ding
九地 (Jiǔ Dì)	九天 (Jiǔ Tiān)	值符 (Zhí Fú)
天冲 (Tiān Chōng)	天任 (Tiān Rèn)	天蓬 (Tiān Péng)
休门 (Xiū Mén)	开门 (Kāi Mén)	惊门 (Jīng Mén)
Gen 8　Ji　Gui	Kan 1　Gui　Xin	Qian 6　Xin　Bing

Yin (阴) Dun# 4 Hour: **DingYou**；直符(ZhíFú): 天蓬(TiānPéng)
直使(ZhíShǐ): 休门(XiūMén)；旬首(XúnShǒu): JiaWu/Xin

六合 (Liù Hé)	太阴 (Tài Yīn)	腾蛇 (Téng Shé)
禽芮 (Qín Ruì)	天柱 (Tiān Zhù)	天心 (Tiān Xīn)
死门 (Sǐ Mén)	惊门 (Jīng Mén)	开门 (Kāi Mén)
Xun 4　Geng/Yi　Wu	Li 9　Ding　Ren	Kun 2　Bing　Geng/Yi
白虎 (Bái Hǔ)	Yin (阴) Dun# 4	值符 (Zhí Fú)
天英 (Tiān Yīng)	Hour: **DingYou**	天蓬 (Tiān Péng)
景门 (Jǐng Mén)	©Calvin Yap	休门 (Xiū Mén)
Zhen 3　Ren　Ji		Dui 7　Xin　Ding
玄武 (Xuán Wǔ)	九地 (Jiǔ Dì)	九天 (Jiǔ Tiān)
天辅 (Tiān Fǔ)	天冲 (Tiān Chōng)	天任 (Tiān Rèn)
杜门 (Dù Mén)	伤门 (Shāng Mén)	生门 (Shēng Mén)
Gen 8　Wu　Gui	Kan 1　Ji　Xin	Qian 6　Gui　Bing

Yin (阴) Dun# 4 Hour: **WuXu**；直符(ZhíFú): 天蓬(TiānPéng)
直使(ZhíShǐ): 休门(XiūMén)；旬首(XúnShǒu): JiaWu/Xin

值符 (Zhí Fú)	九天 (Jiǔ Tiān)	九地 (Jiǔ Dì)
天蓬 (Tiān Péng)	天任 (Tiān Rèn)	天冲 (Tiān Chōng)
景门 (Jǐng Mén)	死门 (Sǐ Mén)	惊门 (Jīng Mén)
Xun 4　Xin　Wu	Li 9　Gui　Ren	Kun 2　Ji　Geng/Yi
腾蛇 (Téng Shé)	Yin (阴) Dun# 4	玄武 (Xuán Wǔ)
天心 (Tiān Xīn)	Hour: **WuXu**	天辅 (Tiān Fǔ)
杜门 (Dù Mén)	©Calvin Yap	开门 (Kāi Mén)
Zhen 3　Bing　Ji		Dui 7　Wu　Ding
太阴 (Tài Yīn)	六合 (Liù Hé)	白虎 (Bái Hǔ)
天柱 (Tiān Zhù)	禽芮 (Qín Ruì)	天英 (Tiān Yīng)
伤门 (Shāng Mén)	生门 (Shēng Mén)	休门 (Xiū Mén)
Gen 8　Ding　Gui	Kan 1　Geng/Yi　Xin	Qian 6　Ren　Bing

Yin (阴) Dun# 4 Hour: **JiHai**；直符(ZhíFú): 天蓬(TiānPéng)
直使(ZhíShǐ): 休门(XiūMén)；旬首(XúnShǒu): JiaWu/Xin

九天 (Jiǔ Tiān)	九地 (Jiǔ Dì)	玄武 (Xuán Wǔ)
天任 (Tiān Rèn)	天冲 (Tiān Chōng)	天辅 (Tiān Fǔ)
惊门 (Jīng Mén)	开门 (Kāi Mén)	休门 (Xiū Mén)
Xun 4　Gui　Wu	Li 9　Ji　Ren	Kun 2　Wu　Geng/Yi
值符 (Zhí Fú)	Yin (阴) Dun# 4	白虎 (Bái Hǔ)
天蓬 (Tiān Péng)	Hour: **JiHai**	天英 (Tiān Yīng)
死门 (Sǐ Mén)	©Calvin Yap	生门 (Shēng Mén)
Zhen 3　Xin　Ji		Dui 7　Ren　Ding
腾蛇 (Téng Shé)	太阴 (Tài Yīn)	六合 (Liù Hé)
天心 (Tiān Xīn)	天柱 (Tiān Zhù)	禽芮 (Qín Ruì)
景门 (Jǐng Mén)	杜门 (Dù Mén)	伤门 (Shāng Mén)
Gen 8　Bing　Gui	Kan 1　Ding　Xin	Qian 6　Geng/Yi　Bing

Yin (阴) Dun# 4 Hour: **GengZi** ；直符(ZhíFú): 天蓬(TiānPéng)
直使(ZhíShǐ): 休门(XiūMén) ；旬首(XúnShǒu): JiaWu/Xin

太阴 (Tài Yīn) 天柱 (Tiān Zhù) 休门 (Xiū Mén) Xun 4　Ding Wu	螣蛇 (Téng Shé) 天心 (Tiān Xīn) 生门 (Shēng Mén) Li 9　Bing Ren	值符 (Zhí Fú) 天蓬 (Tiān Péng) 伤门 (Shāng Mén) Kun 2　Xin Geng/Yi
六合 (Liù Hé) 禽芮 (Qín Ruì) 开门 (Kāi Mén) Zhen 3　Geng/Yi Ji	Yin (阴) Dun# 4 Hour: GengZi ©Calvin Yap	九天 (Jiǔ Tiān) 天任 (Tiān Rèn) 杜门 (Dù Mén) Dui 7　Gui Ding
白虎 (Bái Hǔ) 天英 (Tiān Yīng) 惊门 (Jīng Mén) Gen 8　Ren Gui	玄武 (Xuán Wǔ) 天辅 (Tiān Fǔ) 死门 (Sǐ Mén) Kan 1　Wu Xin	九地 (Jiǔ Dì) 天冲 (Tiān Chōng) 景门 (Jǐng Mén) Qian 6　Ji Bing

Yin (阴) Dun# 4 Hour: **XinChou** ；直符(ZhíFú): 天蓬(TiānPéng)
直使(ZhíShǐ): 休门(XiūMén) ；旬首(XúnShǒu): JiaWu/Xin

玄武 (Xuán Wǔ) 天辅 (Tiān Fǔ) 生门 (Shēng Mén) Xun 4　Wu	白虎 (Bái Hǔ) 天英 (Tiān Yīng) 伤门 (Shāng Mén) Li 9　Ren Ren	六合 (Liù Hé) 禽芮 (Qín Ruì) 杜门 (Dù Mén) Kun 2　Geng/Yi Geng/Yi
九地 (Jiǔ Dì) 天冲 (Tiān Chōng) 休门 (Xiū Mén) Zhen 3　Ji Ji	Yin (阴) Dun# 4 Hour: XinChou Fu Yin ©Calvin Yap	太阴 (Tài Yīn) 天柱 (Tiān Zhù) 景门 (Jǐng Mén) Dui 7　Ding Ding
九天 (Jiǔ Tiān) 天任 (Tiān Rèn) 开门 (Kāi Mén) Gen 8　Gui Gui	值符 (Zhí Fú) 天蓬 (Tiān Péng) 惊门 (Jīng Mén) Kan 1　Xin Xin	螣蛇 (Téng Shé) 天心 (Tiān Xīn) 死门 (Sǐ Mén) Qian 6　Bing Bing

Yin (阴) Dun# 4 Hour: **RenYin** ；直符(ZhíFú): 天蓬(TiānPéng)
直使(ZhíShǐ): 休门(XiūMén) ；旬首(XúnShǒu): JiaWu/Xin

螣蛇 (Téng Shé) 天心 (Tiān Xīn) 惊门 (Jīng Mén) Xun 4　Bing Wu	值符 (Zhí Fú) 天蓬 (Tiān Péng) 开门 (Kāi Mén) Li 9　Xin Ren	九天 (Jiǔ Tiān) 天任 (Tiān Rèn) 休门 (Xiū Mén) Kun 2　Gui Geng/Yi
太阴 (Tài Yīn) 天柱 (Tiān Zhù) 死门 (Sǐ Mén) Zhen 3　Ding Ji	Yin (阴) Dun# 4 Hour: RenYin Fan Yin ©Calvin Yap	九地 (Jiǔ Dì) 天冲 (Tiān Chōng) 生门 (Shēng Mén) Dui 7　Ji Ding
六合 (Liù Hé) 禽芮 (Qín Ruì) 景门 (Jǐng Mén) Gen 8　Geng/Yi Gui	白虎 (Bái Hǔ) 天英 (Tiān Yīng) 杜门 (Dù Mén) Kan 1　Ren Xin	玄武 (Xuán Wǔ) 天辅 (Tiān Fǔ) 伤门 (Shāng Mén) Qian 6　Wu Bing

Yin (阴) Dun# 4 Hour: **GuiMao** ；直符(ZhíFú): 天蓬(TiānPéng)
直使(ZhíShǐ): 休门(XiūMén) ；旬首(XúnShǒu): JiaWu/Xin

九地 (Jiǔ Dì) 天冲 (Tiān Chōng) 杜门 (Dù Mén) Xun 4　Ji Wu	玄武 (Xuán Wǔ) 天辅 (Tiān Fǔ) 景门 (Jǐng Mén) Li 9　Wu Ren	白虎 (Bái Hǔ) 天英 (Tiān Yīng) 死门 (Sǐ Mén) Kun 2　Ren Geng/Yi
九天 (Jiǔ Tiān) 天任 (Tiān Rèn) 伤门 (Shāng Mén) Zhen 3　Gui Ji	Yin (阴) Dun# 4 Hour: GuiMao ©Calvin Yap	六合 (Liù Hé) 禽芮 (Qín Ruì) 惊门 (Jīng Mén) Dui 7　Geng/Yi Ding
值符 (Zhí Fú) 天蓬 (Tiān Péng) 生门 (Shēng Mén) Gen 8　Xin Gui	螣蛇 (Téng Shé) 天心 (Tiān Xīn) 休门 (Xiū Mén) Kan 1　Bing Xin	太阴 (Tài Yīn) 天柱 (Tiān Zhù) 开门 (Kāi Mén) Qian 6　Ding Bing

---

Chart: -4JiaChen (Yin Dun #4 JiaChen Xun)
JiaChen, YiSi, BingWu, DingWei, WuShen, JiYou, GengXu, XinHai, RenZi, GuiChou

Yin (阴) Dun# 4 Hour: **JiaChen** ；直符(ZhíFú): 天英(TiānYīng)
直使(ZhíShǐ): 景门(JǐngMén) ；旬首(XúnShǒu): JiaChenRen

螣蛇 (Téng Shé) 天辅 (Tiān Fǔ) 杜门 (Dù Mén) Xun 4　Wu Wu	值符 (Zhí Fú) 天英 (Tiān Yīng) 景门 (Jǐng Mén) Li 9　Ren Ren	九天 (Jiǔ Tiān) 禽芮 (Qín Ruì) 死门 (Sǐ Mén) Kun 2　Geng/Yi Geng/Yi
太阴 (Tài Yīn) 天冲 (Tiān Chōng) 伤门 (Shāng Mén) Zhen 3　Ji Ji	Yin (阴) Dun# 4 Hour: JiaChen Fu Yin ©Calvin Yap	九地 (Jiǔ Dì) 天柱 (Tiān Zhù) 惊门 (Jīng Mén) Dui 7　Ding Ding
六合 (Liù Hé) 天任 (Tiān Rèn) 生门 (Shēng Mén) Gen 8　Gui Gui	白虎 (Bái Hǔ) 天蓬 (Tiān Péng) 休门 (Xiū Mén) Kan 1　Xin Xin	玄武 (Xuán Wǔ) 天心 (Tiān Xīn) 开门 (Kāi Mén) Qian 6　Bing Bing

Yin (阴) Dun# 4 Hour: **YiSi** ；直符(ZhíFú): 天英(TiānYīng)
直使(ZhíShǐ): 景门(JǐngMén) ；旬首(XúnShǒu): JiaChenRen

太阴 (Tài Yīn) 天冲 (Tiān Chōng) 惊门 (Jīng Mén) Xun 4　Ji Wu	螣蛇 (Téng Shé) 天辅 (Tiān Fǔ) 开门 (Kāi Mén) Li 9　Wu Ren	值符 (Zhí Fú) 天英 (Tiān Yīng) 休门 (Xiū Mén) Kun 2　Ren Geng/Yi
六合 (Liù Hé) 天任 (Tiān Rèn) 死门 (Sǐ Mén) Zhen 3　Gui Ji	Yin (阴) Dun# 4 Hour: YiSi ©Calvin Yap	九天 (Jiǔ Tiān) 禽芮 (Qín Ruì) 生门 (Shēng Mén) Dui 7　Geng/Yi Ding
白虎 (Bái Hǔ) 天蓬 (Tiān Péng) 景门 (Jǐng Mén) Gen 8　Xin Gui	玄武 (Xuán Wǔ) 天心 (Tiān Xīn) 杜门 (Dù Mén) Kan 1　Bing Xin	九地 (Jiǔ Dì) 天柱 (Tiān Zhù) 伤门 (Shāng Mén) Qian 6　Ding Bing

Yin (阴) Dun# 4 Hour: **BingWu** ; 直符(ZhíFú): 天英(TiānYīng)
直使(ZhíShǐ): 景门(JǐngMén) ; 旬首(XúnShǒu): JiaChenRen

白虎 (Bái Hǔ) 天蓬 (Tiān Péng) 生门 (Shēng Mén) Xun 4 Xin Wu	六合 (Liù Hé) 天任 (Tiān Rèn) 伤门 (Shāng Mén) Li 9 Gui Ren	太阴 (Tài Yīn) 天冲 (Tiān Chōng) 杜门 (Dù Mén) Kun 2 Ji Geng/Yi
玄武 (Xuán Wǔ) 天心 (Tiān Xīn) 休门 (Xiū Mén) Zhen 3 Bing Ji	Yin (阴) Dun# 4 Hour: **BingWu** ©Calvin Yap	螣蛇 (Téng Shé) 天辅 (Tiān Fǔ) 景门 (Jǐng Mén) Dui 7 Wu Ding
九地 (Jiǔ Dì) 天柱 (Tiān Zhù) 开门 (Kāi Mén) Gen 8 Ding Gui	九天 (Jiǔ Tiān) 禽芮 (Qín Ruì) 惊门 (Jīng Mén) Kan 1 Geng/Yi Xin	值符 (Zhí Fú) 天英 (Tiān Yīng) 死门 (Sǐ Mén) Qian 6 Ren Bing

Yin (阴) Dun# 4 Hour: **DingWei** ; 直符(ZhíFú): 天英(TiānYīng)
直使(ZhíShǐ): 景门(JǐngMén) ; 旬首(XúnShǒu): JiaChenRen

六合 (Liù Hé) 天任 (Tiān Rèn) 休门 (Xiū Mén) Xun 4 Gui Wu	太阴 (Tài Yīn) 天冲 (Tiān Chōng) 生门 (Shēng Mén) Li 9 Ji Ren	螣蛇 (Téng Shé) 天辅 (Tiān Fǔ) 伤门 (Shāng Mén) Kun 2 Wu Geng/Yi
白虎 (Bái Hǔ) 天蓬 (Tiān Péng) 开门 (Kāi Mén) Zhen 3 Xin Ji	Yin (阴) Dun# 4 Hour: **DingWei** ©Calvin Yap	值符 (Zhí Fú) 天英 (Tiān Yīng) 杜门 (Dù Mén) Dui 7 Ren Ding
玄武 (Xuán Wǔ) 天心 (Tiān Xīn) 惊门 (Jīng Mén) Gen 8 Bing Gui	九地 (Jiǔ Dì) 天柱 (Tiān Zhù) 死门 (Sǐ Mén) Kan 1 Ding Xin	九天 (Jiǔ Tiān) 禽芮 (Qín Ruì) 景门 (Jǐng Mén) Qian 6 Geng/Yi Bing

Yin (阴) Dun# 4 Hour: **WuShen** ; 直符(ZhíFú): 天英(TiānYīng)
直使(ZhíShǐ): 景门(JǐngMén) ; 旬首(XúnShǒu): JiaChenRen

值符 (Zhí Fú) 天英 (Tiān Yīng) 伤门 (Shāng Mén) Xun 4 Ren Wu	九天 (Jiǔ Tiān) 禽芮 (Qín Ruì) 杜门 (Dù Mén) Li 9 Geng/Yi Ren	九地 (Jiǔ Dì) 天柱 (Tiān Zhù) 景门 (Jǐng Mén) Kun 2 Ding Geng/Yi
螣蛇 (Téng Shé) 天辅 (Tiān Fǔ) 生门 (Shēng Mén) Zhen 3 Wu Ji	Yin (阴) Dun# 4 Hour: **WuShen** ©Calvin Yap	玄武 (Xuán Wǔ) 天心 (Tiān Xīn) 死门 (Sǐ Mén) Dui 7 Bing Ding
太阴 (Tài Yīn) 天冲 (Tiān Chōng) 休门 (Xiū Mén) Gen 8 Ji Gui	六合 (Liù Hé) 天任 (Tiān Rèn) 开门 (Kāi Mén) Kan 1 Gui Xin	白虎 (Bái Hǔ) 天蓬 (Tiān Péng) 惊门 (Jīng Mén) Qian 6 Xin Bing

Yin (阴) Dun# 4 Hour: **JiYou** ; 直符(ZhíFú): 天英(TiānYīng)
直使(ZhíShǐ): 景门(JǐngMén) ; 旬首(XúnShǒu): JiaChenRen

九天 (Jiǔ Tiān) 禽芮 (Qín Ruì) 景门 (Jǐng Mén) Xun 4 Geng/Yi Wu	九地 (Jiǔ Dì) 天柱 (Tiān Zhù) 死门 (Sǐ Mén) Li 9 Ding Ren	玄武 (Xuán Wǔ) 天心 (Tiān Xīn) 惊门 (Jīng Mén) Kun 2 Bing Geng/Yi
值符 (Zhí Fú) 天英 (Tiān Yīng) 杜门 (Dù Mén) Zhen 3 Ren Ji	Yin (阴) Dun# 4 Hour: **JiYou** ©Calvin Yap	白虎 (Bái Hǔ) 天蓬 (Tiān Péng) 开门 (Kāi Mén) Dui 7 Xin Ding
螣蛇 (Téng Shé) 天辅 (Tiān Fǔ) 伤门 (Shāng Mén) Gen 8 Wu Gui	太阴 (Tài Yīn) 天冲 (Tiān Chōng) 生门 (Shēng Mén) Kan 1 Ji Xin	六合 (Liù Hé) 天任 (Tiān Rèn) 休门 (Xiū Mén) Qian 6 Gui Bing

Yin (阴) Dun# 4 Hour: **GengXu** ; 直符(ZhíFú): 天英(TiānYīng)
直使(ZhíShǐ): 景门(JǐngMén) ; 旬首(XúnShǒu): JiaChenRen

太阴 (Tài Yīn) 天冲 (Tiān Chōng) 死门 (Sǐ Mén) Xun 4 Ji Wu	螣蛇 (Téng Shé) 天辅 (Tiān Fǔ) 惊门 (Jīng Mén) Li 9 Wu Ren	值符 (Zhí Fú) 天英 (Tiān Yīng) 开门 (Kāi Mén) Kun 2 Ren Geng/Yi
六合 (Liù Hé) 天任 (Tiān Rèn) 景门 (Jǐng Mén) Zhen 3 Gui Ji	Yin (阴) Dun# 4 Hour: **GengXu** ©Calvin Yap	九天 (Jiǔ Tiān) 禽芮 (Qín Ruì) 休门 (Xiū Mén) Dui 7 Geng/Yi Ding
白虎 (Bái Hǔ) 天蓬 (Tiān Péng) 杜门 (Dù Mén) Gen 8 Xin Gui	玄武 (Xuán Wǔ) 天心 (Tiān Xīn) 伤门 (Shāng Mén) Kan 1 Bing Xin	九地 (Jiǔ Dì) 天柱 (Tiān Zhù) 生门 (Shēng Mén) Qian 6 Ding Bing

Yin (阴) Dun# 4 Hour: **XinHai** ; 直符(ZhíFú): 天英(TiānYīng)
直使(ZhíShǐ): 景门(JǐngMén) ; 旬首(XúnShǒu): JiaChenRen

玄武 (Xuán Wǔ) 天心 (Tiān Xīn) 伤门 (Shāng Mén) Xun 4 Bing Wu	白虎 (Bái Hǔ) 天蓬 (Tiān Péng) 杜门 (Dù Mén) Li 9 Xin Ren	六合 (Liù Hé) 天任 (Tiān Rèn) 景门 (Jǐng Mén) Kun 2 Gui Geng/Yi
九地 (Jiǔ Dì) 天柱 (Tiān Zhù) 生门 (Shēng Mén) Zhen 3 Ding Ji	Yin (阴) Dun# 4 Hour: **XinHai** **Fan Yin** ©Calvin Yap	太阴 (Tài Yīn) 天冲 (Tiān Chōng) 死门 (Sǐ Mén) Dui 7 Ji Ding
九天 (Jiǔ Tiān) 禽芮 (Qín Ruì) 休门 (Xiū Mén) Gen 8 Geng/Yi Gui	值符 (Zhí Fú) 天英 (Tiān Yīng) 开门 (Kāi Mén) Kan 1 Ren Xin	螣蛇 (Téng Shé) 天辅 (Tiān Fǔ) 惊门 (Jīng Mén) Qian 6 Wu Bing

Yin (阴) Dun# 4 Hour: RenZi ; 直符(ZhíFú): 天英(TiānYīng)
直使(ZhíShǐ): 景门(JǐngMén) ; 句首(XúnShǒu): JiaChenRen

螣蛇 (Téng Shé) 天辅 (Tiān Fǔ) 开门 (Kāi Mén) Xun 4 Wu Wu	值符 (Zhí Fú) 天英 (Tiān Yīng) 休门 (Xiū Mén) Li 9 Ren Ren	九天 (Jiǔ Tiān) 禽芮 (Qín Ruì) 生门 (Shēng Mén) Kun 2 Geng/Yi Geng/Yi
太阴 (Tài Yīn) 天冲 (Tiān Chōng) 惊门 (Jīng Mén) Zhen 3 Ji Ji	Yin (阴) Dun# 4 Hour: **RenZi** **Fu Yin** ©Calvin Yap	九地 (Jiǔ Dì) 天柱 (Tiān Zhù) 伤门 (Shāng Mén) Dui 7 Ding Ding
六合 (Liù Hé) 天任 (Tiān Rèn) 死门 (Sǐ Mén) Gen 8 Gui Gui	白虎 (Bái Hǔ) 天蓬 (Tiān Péng) 景门 (Jǐng Mén) Kan 1 Xin Xin	玄武 (Xuán Wǔ) 大心 (Tiān Xīn) 杜门 (Dù Mén) Qian 6 Bing Bing

Yin (阴) Dun# 4 Hour: GuiChou ; 直符(ZhíFú): 天英(TiānYīng)
直使(ZhíShǐ): 景门(JǐngMén) ; 句首(XúnShǒu): JiaChenRen

九地 (Jiǔ Dì) 天柱 (Tiān Zhù) 杜门 (Dù Mén) Xun 4 Ding Wu	玄武 (Xuán Wǔ) 大心 (Tiān Xīn) 景门 (Jǐng Mén) Li 9 Bing Ren	白虎 (Bái Hǔ) 天蓬 (Tiān Péng) 死门 (Sǐ Mén) Kun 2 Xin Geng/Yi
九天 (Jiǔ Tiān) 禽芮 (Qín Ruì) 伤门 (Shāng Mén) Zhen 3 Geng/Yi Ji	Yin (阴) Dun# 4 Hour: **GuiChou** ©Calvin Yap	六合 (Liù Hé) 天任 (Tiān Rèn) 惊门 (Jīng Mén) Dui 7 Gui Ding
值符 (Zhí Fú) 天英 (Tiān Yīng) 生门 (Shēng Mén) Gen 8 Ren Gui	螣蛇 (Téng Shé) 天辅 (Tiān Fǔ) 休门 (Xiū Mén) Kan 1 Wu Xin	太阴 (Tài Yīn) 天冲 (Tiān Chōng) 开门 (Kāi Mén) Qian 6 Ji Bing

Chart: -4JiaYin (Yin Dun #4 JiaYin Xun)
JiaYin, YiMao, BingChen, DingSi, WuWu, JiWei, GengShen, XinYou, RenXu, GuiHai

Yin (阴) Dun# 4 Hour: JiaYin ; 直符(ZhíFú): 天任(TiānRèn)
直使(ZhíShǐ): 生门(ShēngMén) ; 句首(XúnShǒu): JiaYinGui

九地 (Jiǔ Dì) 天辅 (Tiān Fǔ) 杜门 (Dù Mén) Xun 4 Wu Wu	玄武 (Xuán Wǔ) 天英 (Tiān Yīng) 景门 (Jǐng Mén) Li 9 Ren Ren	白虎 (Bái Hǔ) 禽芮 (Qín Ruì) 死门 (Sǐ Mén) Kun 2 Geng/Yi Geng/Yi
九天 (Jiǔ Tiān) 天冲 (Tiān Chōng) 伤门 (Shāng Mén) Zhen 3 Ji Ji	Yin (阴) Dun# 4 Hour: **JiaYin** **Fu Yin** ©Calvin Yap	六合 (Liù Hé) 天柱 (Tiān Zhù) 惊门 (Jīng Mén) Dui 7 Ding Ding
值符 (Zhí Fú) 天任 (Tiān Rèn) 生门 (Shēng Mén) Gen 8 Gui Gui	螣蛇 (Téng Shé) 天蓬 (Tiān Péng) 休门 (Xiū Mén) Kan 1 Xin Xin	太阴 (Tài Yīn) 大心 (Tiān Xīn) 开门 (Kāi Mén) Qian 6 Bing Bing

Yin (阴) Dun# 4 Hour: YiMao ; 直符(ZhíFú): 天任(TiānRèn)
直使(ZhíShǐ): 生门(ShēngMén) ; 句首(XúnShǒu): JiaYinGui

太阴 (Tài Yīn) 大心 (Tiān Xīn) 惊门 (Jīng Mén) Xun 4 Bing Wu	螣蛇 (Téng Shé) 天蓬 (Tiān Péng) 开门 (Kāi Mén) Li 9 Xin Ren	值符 (Zhí Fú) 天任 (Tiān Rèn) 休门 (Xiū Mén) Kun 2 Gui Geng/Yi
六合 (Liù Hé) 天柱 (Tiān Zhù) 死门 (Sǐ Mén) Zhen 3 Ding Ji	Yin (阴) Dun# 4 Hour: **YiMao** **Fan Yin** ©Calvin Yap	九天 (Jiǔ Tiān) 天冲 (Tiān Chōng) 生门 (Shēng Mén) Dui 7 Ji Ding
白虎 (Bái Hǔ) 禽芮 (Qín Ruì) 景门 (Jǐng Mén) Gen 8 Geng/Yi Gui	玄武 (Xuán Wǔ) 天英 (Tiān Yīng) 杜门 (Dù Mén) Kan 1 Ren Xin	九地 (Jiǔ Dì) 天辅 (Tiān Fǔ) 伤门 (Shāng Mén) Qian 6 Wu Bing

Yin (阴) Dun# 4 Hour: BingChen ; 直符(ZhíFú): 天任(TiānRèn)
直使(ZhíShǐ): 生门(ShēngMén) ; 句首(XúnShǒu): JiaYinGui

白虎 (Bái Hǔ) 禽芮 (Qín Ruì) 死门 (Sǐ Mén) Xun 4 Geng/Yi Wu	六合 (Liù Hé) 天柱 (Tiān Zhù) 惊门 (Jīng Mén) Li 9 Ding Ren	太阴 (Tài Yīn) 大心 (Tiān Xīn) 开门 (Kāi Mén) Kun 2 Bing Geng/Yi
玄武 (Xuán Wǔ) 天英 (Tiān Yīng) 景门 (Jǐng Mén) Zhen 3 Ren Ji	Yin (阴) Dun# 4 Hour: **BingChen** ©Calvin Yap	螣蛇 (Téng Shé) 天蓬 (Tiān Péng) 休门 (Xiū Mén) Dui 7 Xin Ding
九地 (Jiǔ Dì) 天辅 (Tiān Fǔ) 杜门 (Dù Mén) Gen 8 Wu Gui	九天 (Jiǔ Tiān) 天冲 (Tiān Chōng) 伤门 (Shāng Mén) Kan 1 Ji Xin	值符 (Zhí Fú) 天任 (Tiān Rèn) 生门 (Shēng Mén) Qian 6 Gui Bing

Yin (阴) Dun# 4 Hour: DingSi ; 直符(ZhíFú): 天任(TiānRèn)
直使(ZhíShǐ): 生门(ShēngMén) ; 句首(XúnShǒu): JiaYinGui

六合 (Liù Hé) 天柱 (Tiān Zhù) 开门 (Kāi Mén) Xun 4 Ding Wu	太阴 (Tài Yīn) 大心 (Tiān Xīn) 休门 (Xiū Mén) Li 9 Bing Ren	螣蛇 (Téng Shé) 天蓬 (Tiān Péng) 生门 (Shēng Mén) Kun 2 Xin Geng/Yi
白虎 (Bái Hǔ) 禽芮 (Qín Ruì) 惊门 (Jīng Mén) Zhen 3 Geng/Yi Ji	Yin (阴) Dun# 4 Hour: **DingSi** ©Calvin Yap	值符 (Zhí Fú) 天任 (Tiān Rèn) 伤门 (Shāng Mén) Dui 7 Gui Ding
玄武 (Xuán Wǔ) 天英 (Tiān Yīng) 死门 (Sǐ Mén) Gen 8 Ren Gui	九地 (Jiǔ Dì) 天辅 (Tiān Fǔ) 景门 (Jǐng Mén) Kan 1 Wu Xin	九天 (Jiǔ Tiān) 天冲 (Tiān Chōng) 杜门 (Dù Mén) Qian 6 Ji Bing

Yin (阴) Dun# 4 Hour: **WuWu** ; 直符(ZhíFú): 天任(TiānRèn)
直使(ZhíShǐ): 生门(ShēngMén) ; 旬首(XúnShǒu): JiaYinGui

值符 (Zhí Fú) 天任 (Tiān Rèn) 生门 (Shēng Mén) Xun 4　Gui Wu	九天 (Jiǔ Tiān) 天冲 (Tiān Chōng) 伤门 (Shāng Mén) Li 9　Ji Ren	九地 (Jiǔ Dì) 天辅 (Tiān Fǔ) 杜门 (Dù Mén) Kun 2　Wu Geng/Yi
腾蛇 (Téng Shé) 天蓬 (Tiān Péng) 休门 (Xiū Mén) Zhen 3　Xin Ji	Yin (阴) Dun# 4 Hour: **WuWu** ©Calvin Yap	玄武 (Xuán Wǔ) 天英 (Tiān Yīng) 景门 (Jǐng Mén) Dui 7　Ren Ding
太阴 (Tài Yīn) 天心 (Tiān Xīn) 开门 (Kāi Mén) Gen 8　Bing Gui	六合 (Liù Hé) 天柱 (Tiān Zhù) 惊门 (Jīng Mén) Kan 1　Ding Xin	白虎 (Bái Hǔ) 禽芮 (Qín Ruì) 死门 (Sǐ Mén) Qian 6　Geng/Yi Bing

Yin (阴) Dun# 4 Hour: **JiWei** ; 直符(ZhíFú): 天任(TiānRèn)
直使(ZhíShǐ): 生门(ShēngMén) ; 旬首(XúnShǒu): JiaYinGui

九天 (Jiǔ Tiān) 天冲 (Tiān Chōng) 伤门 (Shāng Mén) Xun 4　Ji Wu	九地 (Jiǔ Dì) 天辅 (Tiān Fǔ) 杜门 (Dù Mén) Li 9　Wu Ren	玄武 (Xuán Wǔ) 天英 (Tiān Yīng) 景门 (Jǐng Mén) Kun 2　Ren Geng/Yi
值符 (Zhí Fú) 天任 (Tiān Rèn) 生门 (Shēng Mén) Zhen 3　Gui Ji	Yin (阴) Dun# 4 Hour: **JiWei** ©Calvin Yap	白虎 (Bái Hǔ) 禽芮 (Qín Ruì) 死门 (Sǐ Mén) Dui 7　Geng/Yi Ding
腾蛇 (Téng Shé) 天蓬 (Tiān Péng) 休门 (Xiū Mén) Gen 8　Xin Gui	太阴 (Tài Yīn) 天心 (Tiān Xīn) 开门 (Kāi Mén) Kan 1　Bing Xin	六合 (Liù Hé) 天柱 (Tiān Zhù) 惊门 (Jīng Mén) Qian 6　Ding Bing

Yin (阴) Dun# 4 Hour: **GengShen** ; 直符(ZhíFú): 天任(TiānRèn)
直使(ZhíShǐ): 生门(ShēngMén) ; 旬首(XúnShǒu): JiaYinGui

太阴 (Tài Yīn) 天心 (Tiān Xīn) 开门 (Kāi Mén) Xun 4　Bing Wu	腾蛇 (Téng Shé) 天蓬 (Tiān Péng) 休门 (Xiū Mén) Li 9　Xin Ren	值符 (Zhí Fú) 天任 (Tiān Rèn) 生门 (Shēng Mén) Kun 2　Gui Geng/Yi
六合 (Liù Hé) 天柱 (Tiān Zhù) 惊门 (Jīng Mén) Zhen 3　Ding Ji	Yin (阴) Dun# 4 Hour: **GengShen** **Fan Yin** ©Calvin Yap	九天 (Jiǔ Tiān) 天冲 (Tiān Chōng) 伤门 (Shāng Mén) Dui 7　Ji Ding
白虎 (Bái Hǔ) 禽芮 (Qín Ruì) 死门 (Sǐ Mén) Gen 8　Geng/Yi Gui	玄武 (Xuán Wǔ) 天英 (Tiān Yīng) 景门 (Jǐng Mén) Kan 1　Ren Xin	九地 (Jiǔ Dì) 天辅 (Tiān Fǔ) 杜门 (Dù Mén) Qian 6　Wu Bing

Yin (阴) Dun# 4 Hour: **XinYou** ; 直符(ZhíFú): 天任(TiānRèn)
直使(ZhíShǐ): 生门(ShēngMén) ; 旬首(XúnShǒu): JiaYinGui

玄武 (Xuán Wǔ) 天英 (Tiān Yīng) 景门 (Jǐng Mén) Xun 4　Ren Wu	白虎 (Bái Hǔ) 禽芮 (Qín Ruì) 死门 (Sǐ Mén) Li 9　Geng/Yi Ren	六合 (Liù Hé) 天柱 (Tiān Zhù) 惊门 (Jīng Mén) Kun 2　Ding Geng/Yi
九地 (Jiǔ Dì) 天辅 (Tiān Fǔ) 杜门 (Dù Mén) Zhen 3　Wu Ji	Yin (阴) Dun# 4 Hour: **XinYou** ©Calvin Yap	太阴 (Tài Yīn) 天心 (Tiān Xīn) 开门 (Kāi Mén) Dui 7　Bing Ding
九天 (Jiǔ Tiān) 天冲 (Tiān Chōng) 伤门 (Shāng Mén) Gen 8　Ji Gui	值符 (Zhí Fú) 天任 (Tiān Rèn) 生门 (Shēng Mén) Kan 1　Gui Xin	腾蛇 (Téng Shé) 天蓬 (Tiān Péng) 休门 (Xiū Mén) Qian 6　Xin Bing

Yin (阴) Dun# 4 Hour: **RenXu** ; 直符(ZhíFú): 天任(TiānRèn)
直使(ZhíShǐ): 生门(ShēngMén) ; 旬首(XúnShǒu): JiaYinGui

腾蛇 (Téng Shé) 天蓬 (Tiān Péng) 休门 (Xiū Mén) Xun 4　Xin Wu	值符 (Zhí Fú) 天任 (Tiān Rèn) 生门 (Shēng Mén) Li 9　Gui Ren	九天 (Jiǔ Tiān) 天冲 (Tiān Chōng) 伤门 (Shāng Mén) Kun 2　Ji Geng/Yi
太阴 (Tài Yīn) 天心 (Tiān Xīn) 开门 (Kāi Mén) Zhen 3　Bing Ji	Yin (阴) Dun# 4 Hour: **RenXu** ©Calvin Yap	九地 (Jiǔ Dì) 天辅 (Tiān Fǔ) 杜门 (Dù Mén) Dui 7　Wu Ding
六合 (Liù Hé) 天柱 (Tiān Zhù) 惊门 (Jīng Mén) Gen 8　Ding Gui	白虎 (Bái Hǔ) 禽芮 (Qín Ruì) 死门 (Sǐ Mén) Kan 1　Geng/Yi Xin	玄武 (Xuán Wǔ) 天英 (Tiān Yīng) 景门 (Jǐng Mén) Qian 6　Ren Bing

Yin (阴) Dun# 4 Hour: **GuiHai** ; 直符(ZhíFú): 天任(TiānRèn)
直使(ZhíShǐ): 生门(ShēngMén) ; 旬首(XúnShǒu): JiaYinGui

九地 (Jiǔ Dì) 天辅 (Tiān Fǔ) 杜门 (Dù Mén) Xun 4　Wu Wu	玄武 (Xuán Wǔ) 天英 (Tiān Yīng) 景门 (Jǐng Mén) Li 9　Ren Ren	白虎 (Bái Hǔ) 禽芮 (Qín Ruì) 死门 (Sǐ Mén) Kun 2　Geng/Yi Geng/Yi
九天 (Jiǔ Tiān) 天冲 (Tiān Chōng) 伤门 (Shāng Mén) Zhen 3　Ji Ji	Yin (阴) Dun# 4 Hour: **GuiHai** **Fu Yin** ©Calvin Yap	六合 (Liù Hé) 天柱 (Tiān Zhù) 惊门 (Jīng Mén) Dui 7　Ding Ding
值符 (Zhí Fú) 天任 (Tiān Rèn) 生门 (Shēng Mén) Gen 8　Gui Gui	腾蛇 (Téng Shé) 天蓬 (Tiān Péng) 休门 (Xiū Mén) Kan 1　Xin Xin	太阴 (Tài Yīn) 天心 (Tiān Xīn) 开门 (Kāi Mén) Qian 6　Bing Bing

Yin Dun#5

Chart: -5JiaZi (Yin Dun #5 JiaZi Xun)
JiaZi, YiChou, BingYin, DingMao, WuChen, JiSi, GengWu, XinWei, RenShen, GuiYou

---

Yin (阴) Dun# 5 Hour: JiaZi；直符(ZhíFú): 天禽(TiānQín)
直使(ZhíShǐ): 死门(SǐMén)；旬首(XúnShǒu): JiaZiWu

太阴 (Tài Yīn) 天辅 (Tiān Fǔ) 杜门 (Dù Mén) Xun 4　　Ji Ji	螣蛇 (Téng Shé) 天英 (Tiān Yīng) 景门 (Jǐng Mén) Li 9　　Gui Gui	值符 (Zhí Fú) 禽芮 (Qín Ruì) 死门 (Sǐ Mén) Kun 2　　Xin/Wu Xin/Wu
六合 (Liù Hé) 天冲 (Tiān Chōng) 伤门 (Shāng Mén) Zhen 3　　Geng Geng	Yin (阴) Dun# 5 Hour: **JiaZi** **Fu Yin** ©Calvin Yap	九天 (Jiǔ Tiān) 天柱 (Tiān Zhù) 惊门 (Jǐng Mén) Dui 7　　Bing Bing
白虎 (Bái Hǔ) 天任 (Tiān Rèn) 生门 (Shēng Mén) Gen 8　　Ding Ding	玄武 (Xuán Wǔ) 天蓬 (Tiān Péng) 休门 (Xiū Mén) Kan 1　　Ren Ren	九地 (Jiǔ Dì) 天心 (Tiān Xīn) 开门 (Kāi Mén) Qian 6　　Yi Yi

Yin (阴) Dun# 5 Hour: YiChou；直符(ZhíFú): 天禽(TiānQín)
直使(ZhíShǐ): 死门(SǐMén)；旬首(XúnShǒu): JiaZiWu

白虎 (Bái Hǔ) 天任 (Tiān Rèn) 死门 (Sǐ Mén) Xun 4　　Ding Ji	六合 (Liù Hé) 天冲 (Tiān Chōng) 惊门 (Jǐng Mén) Li 9　　Geng Gui	太阴 (Tài Yīn) 天辅 (Tiān Fǔ) 开门 (Kāi Mén) Kun 2　　Ji Xin/Wu
玄武 (Xuán Wǔ) 天蓬 (Tiān Péng) 景门 (Jǐng Mén) Zhen 3　　Ren Geng	Yin (阴) Dun# 5 Hour: **YiChou** ©Calvin Yap	螣蛇 (Téng Shé) 天英 (Tiān Yīng) 休门 (Xiū Mén) Dui 7　　Gui Bing
九地 (Jiǔ Dì) 天心 (Tiān Xīn) 杜门 (Dù Mén) Gen 8　　Yi Ding	九天 (Jiǔ Tiān) 天柱 (Tiān Zhù) 伤门 (Shāng Mén) Kan 1　　Bing Ren	值符 (Zhí Fú) 禽芮 (Qín Ruì) 生门 (Shēng Mén) Qian 6　　Xin/Wu Yi

Yin (阴) Dun# 5 Hour: BingYin；直符(ZhíFú): 天禽(TiānQín)
直使(ZhíShǐ): 死门(SǐMén)；旬首(XúnShǒu): JiaZiWu

六合 (Liù Hé) 天冲 (Tiān Chōng) 惊门 (Jǐng Mén) Xun 4　　Geng Ji	太阴 (Tài Yīn) 天辅 (Tiān Fǔ) 开门 (Kāi Mén) Li 9　　Ji Gui	螣蛇 (Téng Shé) 天英 (Tiān Yīng) 休门 (Xiū Mén) Kun 2　　Gui Xin/Wu
白虎 (Bái Hǔ) 天任 (Tiān Rèn) 死门 (Sǐ Mén) Zhen 3　　Ding Geng	Yin (阴) Dun# 5 Hour: **BingYin** ©Calvin Yap	值符 (Zhí Fú) 禽芮 (Qín Ruì) 生门 (Shēng Mén) Dui 7　　Xin/Wu Bing
玄武 (Xuán Wǔ) 天蓬 (Tiān Péng) 景门 (Jǐng Mén) Gen 8　　Ren Ding	九地 (Jiǔ Dì) 天心 (Tiān Xīn) 杜门 (Dù Mén) Kan 1　　Yi Ren	九天 (Jiǔ Tiān) 天柱 (Tiān Zhù) 伤门 (Shāng Mén) Qian 6　　Bing Yi

Yin (阴) Dun# 5 Hour: DingMao；直符(ZhíFú): 天禽(TiānQín)
直使(ZhíShǐ): 死门(SǐMén)；旬首(XúnShǒu): JiaZiWu

九地 (Jiǔ Dì) 天心 (Tiān Xīn) 杜门 (Dù Mén) Xun 4　　Yi Ji	玄武 (Xuán Wǔ) 天蓬 (Tiān Péng) 景门 (Jǐng Mén) Li 9　　Ren Gui	白虎 (Bái Hǔ) 天任 (Tiān Rèn) 死门 (Sǐ Mén) Kun 2　　Ding Xin/Wu
九天 (Jiǔ Tiān) 天柱 (Tiān Zhù) 伤门 (Shāng Mén) Zhen 3　　Bing Geng	Yin (阴) Dun# 5 Hour: **DingMao** **Fan Yin** ©Calvin Yap	六合 (Liù Hé) 天冲 (Tiān Chōng) 惊门 (Jǐng Mén) Dui 7　　Geng Bing
值符 (Zhí Fú) 禽芮 (Qín Ruì) 生门 (Shēng Mén) Gen 8　　Xin/Wu Ding	螣蛇 (Téng Shé) 天英 (Tiān Yīng) 休门 (Xiū Mén) Kan 1　　Gui Ren	太阴 (Tài Yīn) 天辅 (Tiān Fǔ) 开门 (Kāi Mén) Qian 6　　Ji Yi

Yin (阴) Dun# 5 Hour: WuChen；直符(ZhíFú): 天禽(TiānQín)
直使(ZhíShǐ): 死门(SǐMén)；旬首(XúnShǒu): JiaZiWu

太阴 (Tài Yīn) 天辅 (Tiān Fǔ) 休门 (Xiū Mén) Xun 4　　Ji Ji	螣蛇 (Téng Shé) 天英 (Tiān Yīng) 生门 (Shēng Mén) Li 9　　Gui Gui	值符 (Zhí Fú) 禽芮 (Qín Ruì) 伤门 (Shāng Mén) Kun 2　　Xin/Wu Xin/Wu
六合 (Liù Hé) 天冲 (Tiān Chōng) 开门 (Kāi Mén) Zhen 3　　Geng Geng	Yin (阴) Dun# 5 Hour: **WuChen** **Fu Yin** ©Calvin Yap	九天 (Jiǔ Tiān) 天柱 (Tiān Zhù) 杜门 (Dù Mén) Dui 7　　Bing Bing
白虎 (Bái Hǔ) 天任 (Tiān Rèn) 惊门 (Jǐng Mén) Gen 8　　Ding Ding	玄武 (Xuán Wǔ) 天蓬 (Tiān Péng) 死门 (Sǐ Mén) Kan 1　　Ren Ren	九地 (Jiǔ Dì) 天心 (Tiān Xīn) 景门 (Jǐng Mén) Qian 6　　Yi Yi

Yin (阴) Dun# 5 Hour: JiSi；直符(ZhíFú): 天禽(TiānQín)
直使(ZhíShǐ): 死门(SǐMén)；旬首(XúnShǒu): JiaZiWu

值符 (Zhí Fú) 禽芮 (Qín Ruì) 景门 (Jǐng Mén) Xun 4　　Xin/Wu Ji	九天 (Jiǔ Tiān) 天柱 (Tiān Zhù) 死门 (Sǐ Mén) Li 9　　Bing Gui	九地 (Jiǔ Dì) 天心 (Tiān Xīn) 惊门 (Jǐng Mén) Kun 2　　Yi Xin/Wu
螣蛇 (Téng Shé) 天英 (Tiān Yīng) 杜门 (Dù Mén) Zhen 3　　Gui Geng	Yin (阴) Dun# 5 Hour: **JiSi** ©Calvin Yap	玄武 (Xuán Wǔ) 天蓬 (Tiān Péng) 开门 (Kāi Mén) Dui 7　　Ren Bing
太阴 (Tài Yīn) 天辅 (Tiān Fǔ) 伤门 (Shāng Mén) Gen 8　　Ji Ding	六合 (Liù Hé) 天冲 (Tiān Chōng) 生门 (Shēng Mén) Kan 1　　Geng Ren	白虎 (Bái Hǔ) 天任 (Tiān Rèn) 休门 (Xiū Mén) Qian 6　　Ding Yi

Yin (阴) Dun# 5 Hour: GengWu ; 直符(ZhíFú): 天禽(TiānQín)
直使(ZhíShǐ): 死门(SǐMén) ; 旬首(XúnShǒu): JiaZiWu

九天 (Jiǔ Tiān) 天柱 (Tiān Zhù) 开门 (Kāi Mén) Xun 4　Bing Ji	九地 (Jiǔ Dì) 天心 (Tiān Xīn) 休门 (Xiū Mén) Li 9　Yi Gui	玄武 (Xuán Wǔ) 天蓬 (Tiān Péng) 生门 (Shēng Mén) Kun 2　Ren Xin/Wu
值符 (Zhí Fú) 禽芮 (Qín Ruì) 惊门 (Jīng Mén) Zhen 3　Xin/Wu Geng	Yin (阴) Dun# 5 Hour: **GengWu** ©Calvin Yap	白虎 (Bái Hǔ) 天任 (Tiān Rèn) 伤门 (Shāng Mén) Dui 7　Ding Bing
螣蛇 (Téng Shé) 天英 (Tiān Yīng) 死门 (Sǐ Mén) Gen 8　Gui Ding	太阴 (Tài Yīn) 天辅 (Tiān Fǔ) 景门 (Jǐng Mén) Kan 1　Ji Ren	六合 (Liù Hé) 天冲 (Tiān Chōng) 杜门 (Dù Mén) Qian 6　Geng Yi

Yin (阴) Dun# 5 Hour: XinWei ; 直符(ZhíFú): 天禽(TiānQín)
直使(ZhíShǐ): 死门(SǐMén) ; 旬首(XúnShǒu): JiaZiWu

太阴 (Tài Yīn) 天辅 (Tiān Fǔ) 伤门 (Shāng Mén) Xun 4　Ji Ji	螣蛇 (Téng Shé) 天英 (Tiān Yīng) 杜门 (Dù Mén) Li 9　Gui Gui	值符 (Zhí Fú) 禽芮 (Qín Ruì) 景门 (Jǐng Mén) Kun 2　Xin/Wu Xin/Wu
六合 (Liù Hé) 天冲 (Tiān Chōng) 生门 (Shēng Mén) Zhen 3　Geng Geng	Yin (阴) Dun# 5 Hour: **XinWei** **Fu Yin** ©Calvin Yap	九天 (Jiǔ Tiān) 天柱 (Tiān Zhù) 死门 (Sǐ Mén) Dui 7　Bing Bing
白虎 (Bái Hǔ) 天任 (Tiān Rèn) 休门 (Xiū Mén) Gen 8　Ding Ding	玄武 (Xuán Wǔ) 天蓬 (Tiān Péng) 开门 (Kāi Mén) Kan 1　Ren Ren	九地 (Jiǔ Dì) 天心 (Tiān Xīn) 惊门 (Jīng Mén) Qian 6　Yi Yi

Yin (阴) Dun# 5 Hour: RenShen ; 直符(ZhíFú): 天禽(TiānQín)
直使(ZhíShǐ): 死门(SǐMén) ; 旬首(XúnShǒu): JiaZiWu

玄武 (Xuán Wǔ) 天蓬 (Tiān Péng) 生门 (Shēng Mén) Xun 4　Ren Ji	白虎 (Bái Hǔ) 天任 (Tiān Rèn) 伤门 (Shāng Mén) Li 9　Ding Gui	六合 (Liù Hé) 天冲 (Tiān Chōng) 杜门 (Dù Mén) Kun 2　Geng Xin/Wu
九地 (Jiǔ Dì) 天心 (Tiān Xīn) 休门 (Xiū Mén) Zhen 3　Yi Geng	Yin (阴) Dun# 5 Hour: **RenShen** ©Calvin Yap	太阴 (Tài Yīn) 天辅 (Tiān Fǔ) 景门 (Jǐng Mén) Dui 7　Ji Bing
九天 (Jiǔ Tiān) 天柱 (Tiān Zhù) 开门 (Kāi Mén) Gen 8　Bing Ding	值符 (Zhí Fú) 禽芮 (Qín Ruì) 惊门 (Jīng Mén) Kan 1　Xin/Wu Ren	螣蛇 (Téng Shé) 天英 (Tiān Yīng) 死门 (Sǐ Mén) Qian 6　Gui Yi

Yin (阴) Dun# 5 Hour: GuiYou ; 直符(ZhíFú): 天禽(TiānQín)
直使(ZhíShǐ): 死门(SǐMén) ; 旬首(XúnShǒu): JiaZiWu

螣蛇 (Téng Shé) 天英 (Tiān Yīng) 杜门 (Dù Mén) Xun 4　Gui Ji	值符 (Zhí Fú) 禽芮 (Qín Ruì) 景门 (Jǐng Mén) Li 9　Xin/Wu Gui	九天 (Jiǔ Tiān) 天柱 (Tiān Zhù) 死门 (Sǐ Mén) Kun 2　Bing Xin/Wu
太阴 (Tài Yīn) 天辅 (Tiān Fǔ) 伤门 (Shāng Mén) Zhen 3　Ji Geng	Yin (阴) Dun# 5 Hour: **GuiYou** ©Calvin Yap	九地 (Jiǔ Dì) 天心 (Tiān Xīn) 惊门 (Jīng Mén) Dui 7　Yi Bing
六合 (Liù Hé) 天冲 (Tiān Chōng) 生门 (Shēng Mén) Gen 8　Geng Ding	白虎 (Bái Hǔ) 天任 (Tiān Rèn) 休门 (Xiū Mén) Kan 1　Ding Ren	玄武 (Xuán Wǔ) 天蓬 (Tiān Péng) 开门 (Kāi Mén) Qian 6　Ren Yi

Chart: -5JiaXu (Yin Dun #5 JiaXu Xun)
JiaXu, YiHai, BingZi, DingChou, WuYin, JiMao, GengChen, XinSi, RenWu, GuiWei

Yin (阴) Dun# 5 Hour: JiaXu ; 直符(ZhíFú): 天辅(TiānFǔ)
直使(ZhíShǐ): 杜门(DùMén) ; 旬首(XúnShǒu): JiaXuJi

值符 (Zhí Fú) 天辅 (Tiān Fǔ) 杜门 (Dù Mén) Xun 4　Ji Ji	九天 (Jiǔ Tiān) 天英 (Tiān Yīng) 景门 (Jǐng Mén) Li 9　Gui Gui	九地 (Jiǔ Dì) 禽芮 (Qín Ruì) 死门 (Sǐ Mén) Kun 2　Xin/Wu Xin/Wu
螣蛇 (Téng Shé) 天冲 (Tiān Chōng) 伤门 (Shāng Mén) Zhen 3　Geng Geng	Yin (阴) Dun# 5 Hour: **JiaXu** **Fu Yin** ©Calvin Yap	玄武 (Xuán Wǔ) 天柱 (Tiān Zhù) 惊门 (Jīng Mén) Dui 7　Bing Bing
太阴 (Tài Yīn) 天任 (Tiān Rèn) 生门 (Shēng Mén) Gen 8　Ding Ding	六合 (Liù Hé) 天蓬 (Tiān Péng) 休门 (Xiū Mén) Kan 1　Ren Ren	白虎 (Bái Hǔ) 天心 (Tiān Xīn) 开门 (Kāi Mén) Qian 6　Yi Yi

Yin (阴) Dun# 5 Hour: YiHai ; 直符(ZhíFú): 天辅(TiānFǔ)
直使(ZhíShǐ): 杜门(DùMén) ; 旬首(XúnShǒu): JiaXuJi

白虎 (Bái Hǔ) 天心 (Tiān Xīn) 景门 (Jǐng Mén) Xun 4　Yi Ji	六合 (Liù Hé) 天蓬 (Tiān Péng) 死门 (Sǐ Mén) Li 9　Ren Gui	太阴 (Tài Yīn) 天任 (Tiān Rèn) 惊门 (Jīng Mén) Kun 2　Ding Xin/Wu
玄武 (Xuán Wǔ) 天柱 (Tiān Zhù) 杜门 (Dù Mén) Zhen 3　Bing Geng	Yin (阴) Dun# 5 Hour: **YiHai** **Fan Yin** ©Calvin Yap	螣蛇 (Téng Shé) 天冲 (Tiān Chōng) 开门 (Kāi Mén) Dui 7　Geng Bing
九地 (Jiǔ Dì) 禽芮 (Qín Ruì) 伤门 (Shāng Mén) Gen 8　Xin/Wu Ding	九天 (Jiǔ Tiān) 天英 (Tiān Yīng) 生门 (Shēng Mén) Kan 1　Gui Ren	值符 (Zhí Fú) 天辅 (Tiān Fǔ) 休门 (Xiū Mén) Qian 6　Ji Yi

Chart 1

Yin (阴) Dun# 5 Hour: **BingZi**；直符(ZhíFú): 天辅(TiānFǔ)
直使(ZhíShǐ): 杜门(DùMén)；旬首(XúnShǒu): JiaXuJi

六合 (Liù Hé) 天蓬 (Tiān Péng) 生门 (Shēng Mén) Xun 4　Ren　Ji	太阴 (Tài Yīn) 天任 (Tiān Rèn) 伤门 (Shāng Mén) Li 9　Ding　Gui	腾蛇 (Téng Shé) 天冲 (Tiān Chōng) 杜门 (Dù Mén) Kun 2　Geng　Xin/Wu
白虎 (Bái Hǔ) 天心 (Tiān Xīn) 休门 (Xiū Mén) Zhen 3　Yi　Geng	Yin (阴) Dun# 5 Hour: **BingZi** ©Calvin Yap	值符 (Zhí Fú) 天辅 (Tiān Fǔ) 景门 (Jǐng Mén) Dui 7　Ji　Bing
玄武 (Xuán Wǔ) 天柱 (Tiān Zhù) 开门 (Kāi Mén) Gen 8　Bing　Ding	九地 (Jiǔ Dì) 禽芮 (Qín Ruì) 惊门 (Jīng Mén) Kan 1　Xin/Wu　Ren	九天 (Jiǔ Tiān) 天英 (Tiān Yīng) 死门 (Sǐ Mén) Qian 6　Gui　Yi

Chart 2

Yin (阴) Dun# 5 Hour: **DingChou**；直符(ZhíFú): 天辅(TiānFǔ)
直使(ZhíShǐ): 杜门(DùMén)；旬首(XúnShǒu): JiaXuJi

九地 (Jiǔ Dì) 禽芮 (Qín Ruì) 惊门 (Jīng Mén) Xun 4　Xin/Wu　Ji	玄武 (Xuán Wǔ) 天柱 (Tiān Zhù) 开门 (Kāi Mén) Li 9　Bing　Gui	白虎 (Bái Hǔ) 天心 (Tiān Xīn) 休门 (Xiū Mén) Kun 2　Yi　Xin/Wu
九天 (Jiǔ Tiān) 天英 (Tiān Yīng) 死门 (Sǐ Mén) Zhen 3　Gui　Geng	Yin (阴) Dun# 5 Hour: **DingChou** ©Calvin Yap	六合 (Liù Hé) 天蓬 (Tiān Péng) 生门 (Shēng Mén) Dui 7　Ren　Bing
值符 (Zhí Fú) 天辅 (Tiān Fǔ) 景门 (Jǐng Mén) Gen 8　Ji　Ding	腾蛇 (Téng Shé) 天冲 (Tiān Chōng) 杜门 (Dù Mén) Kan 1　Geng　Ren	太阴 (Tài Yīn) 天任 (Tiān Rèn) 伤门 (Shāng Mén) Qian 6　Ding　Yi

Chart 3

Yin (阴) Dun# 5 Hour: **WuYin**；直符(ZhíFú): 天辅(TiānFǔ)
直使(ZhíShǐ): 杜门(DùMén)；旬首(XúnShǒu): JiaXuJi

太阴 (Tài Yīn) 天任 (Tiān Rèn) 伤门 (Shāng Mén) Xun 4　Ding　Ji	腾蛇 (Téng Shé) 天冲 (Tiān Chōng) 杜门 (Dù Mén) Li 9　Geng　Gui	值符 (Zhí Fú) 天辅 (Tiān Fǔ) 景门 (Jǐng Mén) Kun 2　Ji　Xin/Wu
六合 (Liù Hé) 天蓬 (Tiān Péng) 生门 (Shēng Mén) Zhen 3　Ren　Geng	Yin (阴) Dun# 5 Hour: **WuYin** ©Calvin Yap	九天 (Jiǔ Tiān) 天英 (Tiān Yīng) 死门 (Sǐ Mén) Dui 7　Gui　Bing
白虎 (Bái Hǔ) 天心 (Tiān Xīn) 休门 (Xiū Mén) Gen 8　Yi　Ding	玄武 (Xuán Wǔ) 天柱 (Tiān Zhù) 开门 (Kāi Mén) Kan 1　Bing　Ren	九地 (Jiǔ Dì) 禽芮 (Qín Ruì) 惊门 (Jīng Mén) Qian 6　Xin/Wu　Yi

Chart 4

Yin (阴) Dun# 5 Hour: **JiMao**；直符(ZhíFú): 天辅(TiānFǔ)
直使(ZhíShǐ): 杜门(DùMén)；旬首(XúnShǒu): JiaXuJi

值符 (Zhí Fú) 天辅 (Tiān Fǔ) 死门 (Sǐ Mén) Xun 4　Ji　Ji	九天 (Jiǔ Tiān) 天英 (Tiān Yīng) 惊门 (Jīng Mén) Li 9　Gui　Gui	九地 (Jiǔ Dì) 禽芮 (Qín Ruì) 开门 (Kāi Mén) Kun 2　Xin/Wu　Xin/Wu
腾蛇 (Téng Shé) 天冲 (Tiān Chōng) 景门 (Jǐng Mén) Zhen 3　Geng　Geng	Yin (阴) Dun# 5 Hour: **JiMao** **Fu Yin** ©Calvin Yap	玄武 (Xuán Wǔ) 天柱 (Tiān Zhù) 休门 (Xiū Mén) Dui 7　Bing　Bing
太阴 (Tài Yīn) 天任 (Tiān Rèn) 杜门 (Dù Mén) Gen 8　Ding　Ding	六合 (Liù Hé) 天蓬 (Tiān Péng) 伤门 (Shāng Mén) Kan 1　Ren　Ren	白虎 (Bái Hǔ) 天心 (Tiān Xīn) 生门 (Shēng Mén) Qian 6　Yi　Yi

Chart 5

Yin (阴) Dun# 5 Hour: **GengChen**；直符(ZhíFú): 天辅(TiānFǔ)
直使(ZhíShǐ): 杜门(DùMén)；旬首(XúnShǒu): JiaXuJi

九天 (Jiǔ Tiān) 天英 (Tiān Yīng) 休门 (Xiū Mén) Xun 4　Gui　Ji	九地 (Jiǔ Dì) 禽芮 (Qín Ruì) 生门 (Shēng Mén) Li 9　Xin/Wu　Gui	玄武 (Xuán Wǔ) 天柱 (Tiān Zhù) 伤门 (Shāng Mén) Kun 2　Bing　Xin/Wu
值符 (Zhí Fú) 天辅 (Tiān Fǔ) 开门 (Kāi Mén) Zhen 3　Ji　Geng	Yin (阴) Dun# 5 Hour: **GengChen** ©Calvin Yap	白虎 (Bái Hǔ) 天心 (Tiān Xīn) 杜门 (Dù Mén) Dui 7　Yi　Bing
腾蛇 (Téng Shé) 天冲 (Tiān Chōng) 惊门 (Jīng Mén) Gen 8　Geng　Ding	太阴 (Tài Yīn) 天任 (Tiān Rèn) 死门 (Sǐ Mén) Kan 1　Ding　Ren	六合 (Liù Hé) 天蓬 (Tiān Péng) 景门 (Jǐng Mén) Qian 6　Ren　Yi

Chart 6

Yin (阴) Dun# 5 Hour: **XinSi**；直符(ZhíFú): 天辅(TiānFǔ)
直使(ZhíShǐ): 杜门(DùMén)；旬首(XúnShǒu): JiaXuJi

太阴 (Tài Yīn) 天任 (Tiān Rèn) 开门 (Kāi Mén) Xun 4　Ding　Ji	腾蛇 (Téng Shé) 天冲 (Tiān Chōng) 休门 (Xiū Mén) Li 9　Geng　Gui	值符 (Zhí Fú) 天辅 (Tiān Fǔ) 生门 (Shēng Mén) Kun 2　Ji　Xin/Wu
六合 (Liù Hé) 天蓬 (Tiān Péng) 惊门 (Jīng Mén) Zhen 3　Ren　Geng	Yin (阴) Dun# 5 Hour: **XinSi** ©Calvin Yap	九天 (Jiǔ Tiān) 天英 (Tiān Yīng) 伤门 (Shāng Mén) Dui 7　Gui　Bing
白虎 (Bái Hǔ) 天心 (Tiān Xīn) 死门 (Sǐ Mén) Gen 8　Yi　Ding	玄武 (Xuán Wǔ) 天柱 (Tiān Zhù) 景门 (Jǐng Mén) Kan 1　Bing　Ren	九地 (Jiǔ Dì) 禽芮 (Qín Ruì) 杜门 (Dù Mén) Qian 6　Xin/Wu　Yi

Yin (阴) Dun# 5 Hour: **RenWu** ; 直符(ZhíFú): 天辅(TiānFǔ)
直使(ZhíShǐ): 杜门(DùMén) ; 旬首(XúnShǒu): JiaXuJi

玄武 (Xuán Wǔ) 天柱 (Tiān Zhù) 生门 (Shēng Mén) Xun 4 — Bing Ji	白虎 (Bái Hǔ) 天心 (Tiān Xīn) 伤门 (Shāng Mén) Li 9 — Yi Gui	六合 (Liù Hé) 天蓬 (Tiān Péng) 杜门 (Dù Mén) Kun 2 — Ren Xin/Wu
九地 (Jiǔ Dì) 禽芮 (Qín Ruì) 休门 (Xiū Mén) Zhen 3 — Xin/Wu Geng	Yin (阴) Dun# 5 Hour: **RenWu** ©Calvin Yap	太阴 (Tài Yīn) 天任 (Tiān Rèn) 景门 (Jǐng Mén) Dui 7 — Ding Bing
九天 (Jiǔ Tiān) 天英 (Tiān Yīng) 开门 (Kāi Mén) Gen 8 — Gui Ding	值符 (Zhí Fú) 天辅 (Tiān Fǔ) 惊门 (Jīng Mén) Kan 1 — Ji Ren	螣蛇 (Téng Shé) 天冲 (Tiān Chōng) 死门 (Sǐ Mén) Qian 6 — Geng Yi

Yin (阴) Dun# 5 Hour: **GuiWei** ; 直符(ZhíFú): 天辅(TiānFǔ)
直使(ZhíShǐ): 杜门(DùMén) ; 旬首(XúnShǒu): JiaXuJi

螣蛇 (Téng Shé) 天冲 (Tiān Chōng) 杜门 (Dù Mén) Xun 4 — Geng Ji	值符 (Zhí Fú) 天辅 (Tiān Fǔ) 景门 (Jǐng Mén) Li 9 — Ji Gui	九天 (Jiǔ Tiān) 天英 (Tiān Yīng) 死门 (Sǐ Mén) Kun 2 — Gui Xin/Wu
太阴 (Tài Yīn) 天任 (Tiān Rèn) 伤门 (Shāng Mén) Zhen 3 — Ding Geng	Yin (阴) Dun# 5 Hour: **GuiWei** ©Calvin Yap	九地 (Jiǔ Dì) 禽芮 (Qín Ruì) 惊门 (Jīng Mén) Dui 7 — Xin/Wu Bing
六合 (Liù Hé) 天蓬 (Tiān Péng) 生门 (Shēng Mén) Gen 8 — Ren Ding	白虎 (Bái Hǔ) 天心 (Tiān Xīn) 休门 (Xiū Mén) Kan 1 — Yi Ren	玄武 (Xuán Wǔ) 天柱 (Tiān Zhù) 开门 (Kāi Mén) Qian 6 — Bing Yi

---

Chart: -5JiaShen (Yin Dun #5 JiaShen Xun)
JiaShen, YiYou, BingXu, DingHai, WuZi, JiChou, GengYin, XinMao, RenChen, GuiSi

Yin (阴) Dun# 5 Hour: **JiaShen** ; 直符(ZhíFú): 天冲(TiānChōng)
直使(ZhíShǐ): 伤门(ShāngMén) ; 旬首(XúnShǒu): JiaShenGeng

九天 (Jiǔ Tiān) 天辅 (Tiān Fǔ) 杜门 (Dù Mén) Xun 4 — Ji Ji	九地 (Jiǔ Dì) 天英 (Tiān Yīng) 景门 (Jǐng Mén) Li 9 — Gui Gui	玄武 (Xuán Wǔ) 禽芮 (Qín Ruì) 死门 (Sǐ Mén) Kun 2 — Xin/Wu Xin/Wu
值符 (Zhí Fú) 天冲 (Tiān Chōng) 伤门 (Shāng Mén) Zhen 3 — Geng Geng	Yin (阴) Dun# 5 Hour: **JiaShen** **Fu Yin** ©Calvin Yap	白虎 (Bái Hǔ) 天柱 (Tiān Zhù) 惊门 (Jīng Mén) Dui 7 — Bing Bing
螣蛇 (Téng Shé) 天任 (Tiān Rèn) 生门 (Shēng Mén) Gen 8 — Ding Ding	太阴 (Tài Yīn) 天蓬 (Tiān Péng) 休门 (Xiū Mén) Kan 1 — Ren Ren	六合 (Liù Hé) 天心 (Tiān Xīn) 开门 (Kāi Mén) Qian 6 — Yi Yi

Yin (阴) Dun# 5 Hour: **YiYou** ; 直符(ZhíFú): 天冲(TiānChōng)
直使(ZhíShǐ): 伤门(ShāngMén) ; 旬首(XúnShǒu): JiaShenGeng

白虎 (Bái Hǔ) 天柱 (Tiān Zhù) 休门 (Xiū Mén) Xun 4 — Bing Ji	六合 (Liù Hé) 天心 (Tiān Xīn) 生门 (Shēng Mén) Li 9 — Yi Gui	太阴 (Tài Yīn) 天蓬 (Tiān Péng) 伤门 (Shāng Mén) Kun 2 — Ren Xin/Wu
玄武 (Xuán Wǔ) 禽芮 (Qín Ruì) 开门 (Kāi Mén) Zhen 3 — Xin/Wu Geng	Yin (阴) Dun# 5 Hour: **YiYou** ©Calvin Yap	螣蛇 (Téng Shé) 天任 (Tiān Rèn) 杜门 (Dù Mén) Dui 7 — Ding Bing
九地 (Jiǔ Dì) 天英 (Tiān Yīng) 惊门 (Jīng Mén) Gen 8 — Gui Ding	九天 (Jiǔ Tiān) 天辅 (Tiān Fǔ) 死门 (Sǐ Mén) Kan 1 — Ji Ren	值符 (Zhí Fú) 天冲 (Tiān Chōng) 景门 (Jǐng Mén) Qian 6 — Geng Yi

Yin (阴) Dun# 5 Hour: **BingXu** ; 直符(ZhíFú): 天冲(TiānChōng)
直使(ZhíShǐ): 伤门(ShāngMén) ; 旬首(XúnShǒu): JiaShenGeng

六合 (Liù Hé) 天心 (Tiān Xīn) 死门 (Sǐ Mén) Xun 4 — Yi Ji	太阴 (Tài Yīn) 天蓬 (Tiān Péng) 惊门 (Jīng Mén) Li 9 — Ren Gui	螣蛇 (Téng Shé) 天任 (Tiān Rèn) 开门 (Kāi Mén) Kun 2 — Ding Xin/Wu
白虎 (Bái Hǔ) 天柱 (Tiān Zhù) 景门 (Jǐng Mén) Zhen 3 — Bing Geng	Yin (阴) Dun# 5 Hour: **BingXu** **Fan Yin** ©Calvin Yap	值符 (Zhí Fú) 天冲 (Tiān Chōng) 休门 (Xiū Mén) Dui 7 — Geng Bing
玄武 (Xuán Wǔ) 禽芮 (Qín Ruì) 杜门 (Dù Mén) Gen 8 — Xin/Wu Ding	九地 (Jiǔ Dì) 天英 (Tiān Yīng) 伤门 (Shāng Mén) Kan 1 — Gui Ren	九天 (Jiǔ Tiān) 天辅 (Tiān Fǔ) 生门 (Shēng Mén) Qian 6 — Ji Yi

Yin (阴) Dun# 5 Hour: **DingHai** ; 直符(ZhíFú): 天冲(TiānChōng)
直使(ZhíShǐ): 伤门(ShāngMén) ; 旬首(XúnShǒu): JiaShenGeng

九地 (Jiǔ Dì) 天英 (Tiān Yīng) 生门 (Shēng Mén) Xun 4 — Gui Ji	玄武 (Xuán Wǔ) 禽芮 (Qín Ruì) 伤门 (Shāng Mén) Li 9 — Xin/Wu Gui	白虎 (Bái Hǔ) 天柱 (Tiān Zhù) 杜门 (Dù Mén) Kun 2 — Bing Xin/Wu
九天 (Jiǔ Tiān) 天辅 (Tiān Fǔ) 休门 (Xiū Mén) Zhen 3 — Ji Geng	Yin (阴) Dun# 5 Hour: **DingHai** ©Calvin Yap	六合 (Liù Hé) 天心 (Tiān Xīn) 景门 (Jǐng Mén) Dui 7 — Yi Bing
值符 (Zhí Fú) 天冲 (Tiān Chōng) 开门 (Kāi Mén) Gen 8 — Geng Ding	螣蛇 (Téng Shé) 天任 (Tiān Rèn) 惊门 (Jīng Mén) Kan 1 — Ding Ren	太阴 (Tài Yīn) 天蓬 (Tiān Péng) 死门 (Sǐ Mén) Qian 6 — Ren Yi

Yin (阴) Dun# 5 Hour: **WuZi**；直符(ZhíFú): 天冲(TiānChōng)
直使(ZhíShǐ): 伤门(ShāngMén)；旬首(XúnShǒu): JiaShenGeng

太阴 (Tài Yīn) 天蓬 (Tiān Péng) 景门 (Jīng Mén) Xun 4　Ren Ji	螣蛇 (Téng Shé) 天任 (Tiān Rèn) 死门 (Sǐ Mén) Li 9　Ding Gui	值符 (Zhí Fú) 天冲 (Tiān Chōng) 惊门 (Jīng Mén) Kun 2　Geng Xin/Wu
六合 (Liù Hé) 天心 (Tiān Xīn) 杜门 (Dù Mén) Zhen 3　Yi Geng	Yin (阴) Dun# 5 Hour: **WuZi** ©Calvin Yap	九天 (Jiǔ Tiān) 天辅 (Tiān Fǔ) 开门 (Kāi Mén) Dui 7　Ji Bing
白虎 (Bái Hǔ) 天柱 (Tiān Zhù) 伤门 (Shāng Mén) Gen 8　Bing Ding	玄武 (Xuán Wǔ) 禽芮 (Qín Ruì) 生门 (Shēng Mén) Kan 1　Xin/Wu Ren	九地 (Jiǔ Dì) 天英 (Tiān Yīng) 休门 (Xiū Mén) Qian 6　Gui Yi

Yin (阴) Dun# 5 Hour: **JiChou**；直符(ZhíFú): 天冲(TiānChōng)
直使(ZhíShǐ): 伤门(ShāngMén)；旬首(XúnShǒu): JiaShenGeng

值符 (Zhí Fú) 天冲 (Tiān Chōng) 开门 (Kāi Mén) Xun 4　Geng Ji	九天 (Jiǔ Tiān) 天辅 (Tiān Fǔ) 休门 (Xiū Mén) Li 9　Ji Gui	九地 (Jiǔ Dì) 天英 (Tiān Yīng) 生门 (Shēng Mén) Kun 2　Gui Xin/Wu
螣蛇 (Téng Shé) 天任 (Tiān Rèn) 惊门 (Jīng Mén) Zhen 3　Ding Geng	Yin (阴) Dun# 5 Hour: **JiChou** ©Calvin Yap	玄武 (Xuán Wǔ) 禽芮 (Qín Ruì) 伤门 (Shāng Mén) Dui 7　Xin/Wu Bing
太阴 (Tài Yīn) 天蓬 (Tiān Péng) 死门 (Sǐ Mén) Gen 8　Ren Ding	六合 (Liù Hé) 天心 (Tiān Xīn) 景门 (Jīng Mén) Kan 1　Yi Ren	白虎 (Bái Hǔ) 天柱 (Tiān Zhù) 杜门 (Dù Mén) Qian 6　Bing Yi

Yin (阴) Dun# 5 Hour: **GengYin**；直符(ZhíFú): 天冲(TiānChōng)
直使(ZhíShǐ): 伤门(ShāngMén)；旬首(XúnShǒu): JiaShenGeng

九天 (Jiǔ Tiān) 天辅 (Tiān Fǔ) 惊门 (Jīng Mén) Xun 4　Ji Ji	九地 (Jiǔ Dì) 天英 (Tiān Yīng) 开门 (Kāi Mén) Li 9　Gui Gui	玄武 (Xuán Wǔ) 禽芮 (Qín Ruì) 休门 (Xiū Mén) Kun 2　Xin/Wu Xin/Wu
值符 (Zhí Fú) 天冲 (Tiān Chōng) 死门 (Sǐ Mén) Zhen 3　Geng Geng	Yin (阴) Dun# 5 Hour: **GengYin** **Fu Yin** ©Calvin Yap	白虎 (Bái Hǔ) 天柱 (Tiān Zhù) 生门 (Shēng Mén) Dui 7　Bing Bing
螣蛇 (Téng Shé) 天任 (Tiān Rèn) 景门 (Jīng Mén) Gen 8　Ding Ding	太阴 (Tài Yīn) 天蓬 (Tiān Péng) 杜门 (Dù Mén) Kan 1　Ren Ren	六合 (Liù Hé) 天心 (Tiān Xīn) 伤门 (Shāng Mén) Qian 6　Yi Yi

Yin (阴) Dun# 5 Hour: **XinMao**；直符(ZhíFú): 天冲(TiānChōng)
直使(ZhíShǐ): 伤门(ShāngMén)；旬首(XúnShǒu): JiaShenGeng

太阴 (Tài Yīn) 天蓬 (Tiān Péng) 休门 (Xiū Mén) Xun 4　Ren Ji	螣蛇 (Téng Shé) 天任 (Tiān Rèn) 生门 (Shēng Mén) Li 9　Ding Gui	值符 (Zhí Fú) 天冲 (Tiān Chōng) 伤门 (Shāng Mén) Kun 2　Geng Xin/Wu
六合 (Liù Hé) 天心 (Tiān Xīn) 开门 (Kāi Mén) Zhen 3　Yi Geng	Yin (阴) Dun# 5 Hour: **XinMao** ©Calvin Yap	九天 (Jiǔ Tiān) 天辅 (Tiān Fǔ) 杜门 (Dù Mén) Dui 7　Ji Bing
白虎 (Bái Hǔ) 天柱 (Tiān Zhù) 惊门 (Jīng Mén) Gen 8　Bing Ding	玄武 (Xuán Wǔ) 禽芮 (Qín Ruì) 死门 (Sǐ Mén) Kan 1　Xin/Wu Ren	九地 (Jiǔ Dì) 天英 (Tiān Yīng) 景门 (Jīng Mén) Qian 6　Gui Yi

Yin (阴) Dun# 5 Hour: **RenChen**；直符(ZhíFú): 天冲(TiānChōng)
直使(ZhíShǐ): 伤门(ShāngMén)；旬首(XúnShǒu): JiaShenGeng

玄武 (Xuán Wǔ) 禽芮 (Qín Ruì) 伤门 (Shāng Mén) Xun 4　Xin/Wu Ji	白虎 (Bái Hǔ) 天柱 (Tiān Zhù) 杜门 (Dù Mén) Li 9　Bing Gui	六合 (Liù Hé) 天心 (Tiān Xīn) 景门 (Jīng Mén) Kun 2　Yi Xin/Wu
九地 (Jiǔ Dì) 天英 (Tiān Yīng) 生门 (Shēng Mén) Zhen 3　Gui Geng	Yin (阴) Dun# 5 Hour: **RenChen** ©Calvin Yap	太阴 (Tài Yīn) 天蓬 (Tiān Péng) 死门 (Sǐ Mén) Dui 7　Ren Bing
九天 (Jiǔ Tiān) 天辅 (Tiān Fǔ) 休门 (Xiū Mén) Gen 8　Ji Ding	值符 (Zhí Fú) 天冲 (Tiān Chōng) 开门 (Kāi Mén) Kan 1　Geng Ren	螣蛇 (Téng Shé) 天任 (Tiān Rèn) 惊门 (Jīng Mén) Qian 6　Ding Yi

Yin (阴) Dun# 5 Hour: **GuiSi**；直符(ZhíFú): 天冲(TiānChōng)
直使(ZhíShǐ): 伤门(ShāngMén)；旬首(XúnShǒu): JiaShenGeng

螣蛇 (Téng Shé) 天任 (Tiān Rèn) 杜门 (Dù Mén) Xun 4　Ding Ji	值符 (Zhí Fú) 天冲 (Tiān Chōng) 景门 (Jīng Mén) Li 9　Geng Gui	九天 (Jiǔ Tiān) 天辅 (Tiān Fǔ) 死门 (Sǐ Mén) Kun 2　Ji Xin/Wu
太阴 (Tài Yīn) 天蓬 (Tiān Péng) 伤门 (Shāng Mén) Zhen 3　Ren Geng	Yin (阴) Dun# 5 Hour: **GuiSi** ©Calvin Yap	九地 (Jiǔ Dì) 天英 (Tiān Yīng) 惊门 (Jīng Mén) Dui 7　Gui Bing
六合 (Liù Hé) 天心 (Tiān Xīn) 生门 (Shēng Mén) Gen 8　Yi Ding	白虎 (Bái Hǔ) 天柱 (Tiān Zhù) 休门 (Xiū Mén) Kan 1　Bing Ren	玄武 (Xuán Wǔ) 禽芮 (Qín Ruì) 开门 (Kāi Mén) Qian 6　Xin/Wu Yi

---

<table>
<tr><td colspan="3" align="center">Chart: -5JiaWu (Yin Dun #5 JiaWu Xun)
JiaWu, YiWei, BingShen, DingYou, WuXu, JiHai, GengZi, XinChou, RenYin, GuiMao</td></tr>
</table>

Yin (阴) Dun# 5 Hour: JiaWu；直符(ZhíFú): 天芮(TiānRuì)
直使(ZhíShǐ): 死门(SǐMén)；旬首(XúnShǒu): JiaWu/Xin

太阴 (Tài Yīn) 天辅 (Tiān Fǔ) 杜门 (Dù Mén) Xun 4 Ji Ji	螣蛇 (Téng Shé) 天英 (Tiān Yīng) 景门 (Jǐng Mén) Li 9 Gui Gui	值符 (Zhí Fú) 禽芮 (Qín Ruì) 死门 (Sǐ Mén) Kun 2 Xin/Wu Xin/Wu
六合 (Liù Hé) 天冲 (Tiān Chōng) 伤门 (Shāng Mén) Zhen 3 Geng Geng	Yin (阴) Dun# 5 Hour: **JiaWu** **Fu Yin** ©Calvin Yap	九天 (Jiǔ Tiān) 天柱 (Tiān Zhù) 惊门 (Jīng Mén) Dui 7 Bing Bing
白虎 (Bái Hǔ) 天任 (Tiān Rèn) 生门 (Shēng Mén) Gen 8 Ding Ding	玄武 (Xuán Wǔ) 天蓬 (Tiān Péng) 休门 (Xiū Mén) Kan 1 Ren Ren	九地 (Jiǔ Dì) 天心 (Tiān Xīn) 开门 (Kāi Mén) Qian 6 Yi Yi

Yin (阴) Dun# 5 Hour: YiWei；直符(ZhíFú): 天芮(TiānRuì)
直使(ZhíShǐ): 死门(SǐMén)；旬首(XúnShǒu): JiaWu/Xin

白虎 (Bái Hǔ) 天任 (Tiān Rèn) 休门 (Xiū Mén) Xun 4 Ding	六合 (Liù Hé) 天冲 (Tiān Chōng) 生门 (Shēng Mén) Li 9 Geng Gui	太阴 (Tài Yīn) 天辅 (Tiān Fǔ) 伤门 (Shāng Mén) Kun 2 Ji Xin/Wu
玄武 (Xuán Wǔ) 天蓬 (Tiān Péng) 开门 (Kāi Mén) Zhen 3 Ren Geng	Yin (阴) Dun# 5 Hour: **YiWei** ©Calvin Yap	螣蛇 (Téng Shé) 天英 (Tiān Yīng) 杜门 (Dù Mén) Dui 7 Gui Bing
九地 (Jiǔ Dì) 天心 (Tiān Xīn) 惊门 (Jīng Mén) Gen 8 Yi Ding	九天 (Jiǔ Tiān) 天柱 (Tiān Zhù) 死门 (Sǐ Mén) Kan 1 Bing Ren	值符 (Zhí Fú) 禽芮 (Qín Ruì) 景门 (Jǐng Mén) Qian 6 Xin/Wu Yi

Yin (阴) Dun# 5 Hour: BingShen；直符(ZhíFú): 天芮(TiānRuì)
直使(ZhíShǐ): 死门(SǐMén)；旬首(XúnShǒu): JiaWu/Xin

六合 (Liù Hé) 天冲 (Tiān Chōng) 景门 (Jǐng Mén) Xun 4 Geng Ji	太阴 (Tài Yīn) 天辅 (Tiān Fǔ) 死门 (Sǐ Mén) Li 9 Ji Gui	螣蛇 (Téng Shé) 天英 (Tiān Yīng) 惊门 (Jīng Mén) Kun 2 Gui Xin/Wu
白虎 (Bái Hǔ) 天任 (Tiān Rèn) 杜门 (Dù Mén) Zhen 3 Ding Geng	Yin (阴) Dun# 5 Hour: **BingShen** ©Calvin Yap	值符 (Zhí Fú) 禽芮 (Qín Ruì) 开门 (Kāi Mén) Dui 7 Xin/Wu Bing
玄武 (Xuán Wǔ) 天蓬 (Tiān Péng) 伤门 (Shāng Mén) Gen 8 Ren Ding	九地 (Jiǔ Dì) 天心 (Tiān Xīn) 生门 (Shēng Mén) Kan 1 Yi Ren	九天 (Jiǔ Tiān) 天柱 (Tiān Zhù) 休门 (Xiū Mén) Qian 6 Bing Yi

Yin (阴) Dun# 5 Hour: DingYou；直符(ZhíFú): 天芮(TiānRuì)
直使(ZhíShǐ): 死门(SǐMén)；旬首(XúnShǒu): JiaWu/Xin

九地 (Jiǔ Dì) 天心 (Tiān Xīn) 开门 (Kāi Mén) Xun 4 Yi Ji	玄武 (Xuán Wǔ) 天蓬 (Tiān Péng) 休门 (Xiū Mén) Li 9 Ren Gui	白虎 (Bái Hǔ) 天任 (Tiān Rèn) 生门 (Shēng Mén) Kun 2 Ding Xin/Wu
九天 (Jiǔ Tiān) 天柱 (Tiān Zhù) 惊门 (Jīng Mén) Zhen 3 Bing Geng	Yin (阴) Dun# 5 Hour: **DingYou** **Fan Yin** ©Calvin Yap	六合 (Liù Hé) 天冲 (Tiān Chōng) 伤门 (Shāng Mén) Dui 7 Geng Bing
值符 (Zhí Fú) 禽芮 (Qín Ruì) 死门 (Sǐ Mén) Gen 8 Xin/Wu Ding	螣蛇 (Téng Shé) 天英 (Tiān Yīng) 景门 (Jǐng Mén) Kan 1 Gui Ren	太阴 (Tài Yīn) 天辅 (Tiān Fǔ) 杜门 (Dù Mén) Qian 6 Ji Yi

Yin (阴) Dun# 5 Hour: WuXu；直符(ZhíFú): 天芮(TiānRuì)
直使(ZhíShǐ): 死门(SǐMén)；旬首(XúnShǒu): JiaWu/Xin

太阴 (Tài Yīn) 天辅 (Tiān Fǔ) 伤门 (Shāng Mén) Xun 4 Ji Ji	螣蛇 (Téng Shé) 天英 (Tiān Yīng) 杜门 (Dù Mén) Li 9 Gui Gui	值符 (Zhí Fú) 禽芮 (Qín Ruì) 景门 (Jǐng Mén) Kun 2 Xin/Wu Xin/Wu
六合 (Liù Hé) 天冲 (Tiān Chōng) 生门 (Shēng Mén) Zhen 3 Geng Geng	Yin (阴) Dun# 5 Hour: **WuXu** **Fu Yin** ©Calvin Yap	九天 (Jiǔ Tiān) 天柱 (Tiān Zhù) 死门 (Sǐ Mén) Dui 7 Bing Bing
白虎 (Bái Hǔ) 天任 (Tiān Rèn) 休门 (Xiū Mén) Gen 8 Ding Ding	玄武 (Xuán Wǔ) 天蓬 (Tiān Péng) 开门 (Kāi Mén) Kan 1 Ren Ren	九地 (Jiǔ Dì) 天心 (Tiān Xīn) 惊门 (Jīng Mén) Qian 6 Yi Yi

Yin (阴) Dun# 5 Hour: JiHai；直符(ZhíFú): 天芮(TiānRuì)
直使(ZhíShǐ): 死门(SǐMén)；旬首(XúnShǒu): JiaWu/Xin

值符 (Zhí Fú) 禽芮 (Qín Ruì) 生门 (Shēng Mén) Xun 4 Xin/Wu Ji	九天 (Jiǔ Tiān) 天柱 (Tiān Zhù) 伤门 (Shāng Mén) Li 9 Bing Gui	九地 (Jiǔ Dì) 天心 (Tiān Xīn) 杜门 (Dù Mén) Kun 2 Yi Xin/Wu
螣蛇 (Téng Shé) 天英 (Tiān Yīng) 休门 (Xiū Mén) Zhen 3 Gui Geng	Yin (阴) Dun# 5 Hour: **JiHai** ©Calvin Yap	玄武 (Xuán Wǔ) 天蓬 (Tiān Péng) 景门 (Jǐng Mén) Dui 7 Ren Bing
太阴 (Tài Yīn) 天辅 (Tiān Fǔ) 开门 (Kāi Mén) Gen 8 Ji Ding	六合 (Liù Hé) 天冲 (Tiān Chōng) 惊门 (Jīng Mén) Kan 1 Geng Ren	白虎 (Bái Hǔ) 天任 (Tiān Rèn) 死门 (Sǐ Mén) Qian 6 Ding Yi

---

Yin (阴) Dun# 5 Hour: **GengZi** ；直符(ZhíFú): 天芮(TiānRuì)
直使(ZhíShǐ): 死门(SǐMén) ；旬首(XúnShǒu): JiaWu/Xin

Xun 4	Li 9	Kun 2
九天 (Jiǔ Tiān) 天柱 (Tiān Zhù) 杜门 (Dù Mén) Xun 4　Bing Ji	九地 (Jiǔ Dì) 天心 (Tiān Xīn) 景门 (Jǐng Mén) Li 9　Yi Gui	玄武 (Xuán Wǔ) 天蓬 (Tiān Péng) 死门 (Sǐ Mén) Kun 2　Ren Xin/Wu
值符 (Zhí Fú) 禽芮 (Qín Ruì) 伤门 (Shāng Mén) Zhen 3　Xin/Wu Geng	Yin (阴) Dun# 5 Hour: **GengZi** ©Calvin Yap	白虎 (Bái Hǔ) 天任 (Tiān Rèn) 惊门 (Jīng Mén) Dui 7　Ding Bing
腾蛇 (Téng Shé) 天英 (Tiān Yīng) 生门 (Shēng Mén) Gen 8　Gui Ding	太阴 (Tài Yīn) 天辅 (Tiān Fǔ) 休门 (Xiū Mén) Kan 1　Ji Ren	六合 (Liù Hé) 天冲 (Tiān Chōng) 开门 (Kāi Mén) Qian 6　Geng Yi

Yin (阴) Dun# 5 Hour: **XinChou** ；直符(ZhíFú): 天芮(TiānRuì)
直使(ZhíShǐ): 死门(SǐMén) ；旬首(XúnShǒu): JiaWu/Xin

Xun 4	Li 9	Kun 2
太阴 (Tài Yīn) 天辅 (Tiān Fǔ) 死门 (Sǐ Mén) Xun 4　Ji	腾蛇 (Téng Shé) 天英 (Tiān Yīng) 惊门 (Jīng Mén) Li 9　Gui	值符 (Zhí Fú) 禽芮 (Qín Ruì) 开门 (Kāi Mén) Kun 2　Xin/Wu Xin/Wu
六合 (Liù Hé) 天冲 (Tiān Chōng) 景门 (Jǐng Mén) Zhen 3　Geng Geng	Yin (阴) Dun# 5 Hour: **XinChou** **Fu Yin** ©Calvin Yap	九天 (Jiǔ Tiān) 天柱 (Tiān Zhù) 休门 (Xiū Mén) Dui 7　Bing Bing
白虎 (Bái Hǔ) 天任 (Tiān Rèn) 杜门 (Dù Mén) Gen 8　Ding Ding	玄武 (Xuán Wǔ) 天蓬 (Tiān Péng) 伤门 (Shāng Mén) Kan 1　Ren Ren	九地 (Jiǔ Dì) 天心 (Tiān Xīn) 生门 (Shēng Mén) Qian 6　Yi Yi

Yin (阴) Dun# 5 Hour: **RenYin** ；直符(ZhíFú): 天芮(TiānRuì)
直使(ZhíShǐ): 死门(SǐMén) ；旬首(XúnShǒu): JiaWu/Xin

Xun 4	Li 9	Kun 2
玄武 (Xuán Wǔ) 天蓬 (Tiān Péng) 惊门 (Jīng Mén) Xun 4　Ren Ji	白虎 (Bái Hǔ) 天任 (Tiān Rèn) 开门 (Kāi Mén) Li 9　Ding Gui	六合 (Liù Hé) 天冲 (Tiān Chōng) 休门 (Xiū Mén) Kun 2　Geng Xin/Wu
九地 (Jiǔ Dì) 天心 (Tiān Xīn) 死门 (Sǐ Mén) Zhen 3　Yi Geng	Yin (阴) Dun# 5 Hour: **RenYin** ©Calvin Yap	太阴 (Tài Yīn) 天辅 (Tiān Fǔ) 生门 (Shēng Mén) Dui 7　Ji Bing
九天 (Jiǔ Tiān) 天柱 (Tiān Zhù) 景门 (Jǐng Mén) Gen 8　Bing Ding	值符 (Zhí Fú) 禽芮 (Qín Ruì) 杜门 (Dù Mén) Kan 1　Xin/Wu Ren	腾蛇 (Téng Shé) 天英 (Tiān Yīng) 伤门 (Shāng Mén) Qian 6　Gui Yi

Yin (阴) Dun# 5 Hour: **GuiMao** ；直符(ZhíFú): 天芮(TiānRuì)
直使(ZhíShǐ): 死门(SǐMén) ；旬首(XúnShǒu): JiaWu/Xin

Xun 4	Li 9	Kun 2
腾蛇 (Téng Shé) 天英 (Tiān Yīng) 杜门 (Dù Mén) Xun 4　Gui Ji	值符 (Zhí Fú) 禽芮 (Qín Ruì) 景门 (Jǐng Mén) Li 9　Xin/Wu Gui	九天 (Jiǔ Tiān) 天柱 (Tiān Zhù) 死门 (Sǐ Mén) Kun 2　Bing Xin/Wu
太阴 (Tài Yīn) 天辅 (Tiān Fǔ) 伤门 (Shāng Mén) Zhen 3　Ji Geng	Yin (阴) Dun# 5 Hour: **GuiMao** ©Calvin Yap	九地 (Jiǔ Dì) 天心 (Tiān Xīn) 惊门 (Jīng Mén) Dui 7　Yi Bing
六合 (Liù Hé) 天冲 (Tiān Chōng) 生门 (Shēng Mén) Gen 8　Geng Geng	白虎 (Bái Hǔ) 天任 (Tiān Rèn) 休门 (Xiū Mén) Kan 1　Ding Ren	玄武 (Xuán Wǔ) 天蓬 (Tiān Péng) 开门 (Kāi Mén) Qian 6　Ren Yi

---

Chart: **-5JiaChen** (Yin Dun #5 JiaChen Xun)
JiaChen, YiSi, BingWu, DingWei, WuShen, JiYou, GengXu, XinHai, RenZi, GuiChou

Yin (阴) Dun# 5 Hour: **JiaChen** ；直符(ZhíFú): 天蓬(TiānPéng)
直使(ZhíShǐ): 休门(XiūMén) ；旬首(XúnShǒu): JiaChenRen

Xun 4	Li 9	Kun 2
玄武 (Xuán Wǔ) 天辅 (Tiān Fǔ) 杜门 (Dù Mén) Xun 4　Ji Ji	白虎 (Bái Hǔ) 天英 (Tiān Yīng) 景门 (Jǐng Mén) Li 9　Gui Gui	六合 (Liù Hé) 禽芮 (Qín Ruì) 死门 (Sǐ Mén) Kun 2　Xin/Wu Xin/Wu
九地 (Jiǔ Dì) 天冲 (Tiān Chōng) 伤门 (Shāng Mén) Zhen 3　Geng Geng	Yin (阴) Dun# 5 Hour: **JiaChen** **Fu Yin** ©Calvin Yap	太阴 (Tài Yīn) 天柱 (Tiān Zhù) 惊门 (Jīng Mén) Dui 7　Bing Bing
九天 (Jiǔ Tiān) 天任 (Tiān Rèn) 生门 (Shēng Mén) Gen 8　Ding Ding	值符 (Zhí Fú) 天蓬 (Tiān Péng) 休门 (Xiū Mén) Kan 1　Ren Ren	腾蛇 (Téng Shé) 天心 (Tiān Xīn) 开门 (Kāi Mén) Qian 6　Yi Yi

Yin (阴) Dun# 5 Hour: **YiSi** ；直符(ZhíFú): 天蓬(TiānPéng)
直使(ZhíShǐ): 休门(XiūMén) ；旬首(XúnShǒu): JiaChenRen

Xun 4	Li 9	Kun 2
白虎 (Bái Hǔ) 天英 (Tiān Yīng) 开门 (Kāi Mén) Xun 4　Gui Ji	六合 (Liù Hé) 禽芮 (Qín Ruì) 休门 (Xiū Mén) Li 9　Xin/Wu Gui	太阴 (Tài Yīn) 天柱 (Tiān Zhù) 生门 (Shēng Mén) Kun 2　Bing Xin/Wu
玄武 (Xuán Wǔ) 天辅 (Tiān Fǔ) 惊门 (Jīng Mén) Zhen 3　Ji Geng	Yin (阴) Dun# 5 Hour: **YiSi** ©Calvin Yap	腾蛇 (Téng Shé) 天心 (Tiān Xīn) 伤门 (Shāng Mén) Dui 7　Yi Bing
九地 (Jiǔ Dì) 天冲 (Tiān Chōng) 死门 (Sǐ Mén) Gen 8　Geng Geng	九天 (Jiǔ Tiān) 天任 (Tiān Rèn) 景门 (Jǐng Mén) Kan 1　Ding Ren	值符 (Zhí Fú) 天蓬 (Tiān Péng) 杜门 (Dù Mén) Qian 6　Ren Yi

Chart 1

Yin (阴) Dun# 5 Hour: **BingWu**；直符(ZhíFú): 天蓬(TiānPéng)
直使(ZhíShǐ): 休门(XiūMén)；旬首(XúnShǒu): JiaChenRen

六合 (Liù Hé) 禽芮 (Qín Ruì) 伤门 (Shāng Mén) Xun 4　Xin/Wu　Ji	太阴 (Tài Yīn) 天柱 (Tiān Zhù) 杜门 (Dù Mén) Li 9　Bing　Gui	螣蛇 (Téng Shé) 天心 (Tiān Xīn) 景门 (Jǐng Mén) Kun 2　Yi　Xin/Wu
白虎 (Bái Hǔ) 天英 (Tiān Yīng) 生门 (Shēng Mén) Zhen 3　Gui　Geng	Yin (阴) Dun# 5 Hour: **BingWu** ©Calvin Yap	值符 (Zhí Fú) 天蓬 (Tiān Péng) 死门 (Sǐ Mén) Dui 7　Ren　Bing
玄武 (Xuán Wǔ) 天辅 (Tiān Fǔ) 休门 (Xiū Mén) Gen 8　Ji　Ding	九地 (Jiǔ Dì) 天冲 (Tiān Chōng) 开门 (Kāi Mén) Kan 1　Geng　Ren	九天 (Jiǔ Tiān) 天任 (Tiān Rèn) 惊门 (Jīng Mén) Qian 6　Ding　Yi

Chart 2

Yin (阴) Dun# 5 Hour: **DingWei**；直符(ZhíFú): 天蓬(TiānPéng)
直使(ZhíShǐ): 休门(XiūMén)；旬首(XúnShǒu): JiaChenRen

九地 (Jiǔ Dì) 天冲 (Tiān Chōng) 死门 (Sǐ Mén) Xun 4　Geng　Ji	玄武 (Xuán Wǔ) 天辅 (Tiān Fǔ) 惊门 (Jīng Mén) Li 9　Ji　Gui	白虎 (Bái Hǔ) 天英 (Tiān Yīng) 开门 (Kāi Mén) Kun 2　Gui　Xin/Wu
九天 (Jiǔ Tiān) 天任 (Tiān Rèn) 景门 (Jǐng Mén) Zhen 3　Ding　Geng	Yin (阴) Dun# 5 Hour: **DingWei** ©Calvin Yap	六合 (Liù Hé) 禽芮 (Qín Ruì) 休门 (Xiū Mén) Dui 7　Xin/Wu　Bing
值符 (Zhí Fú) 天蓬 (Tiān Péng) 杜门 (Dù Mén) Gen 8　Ren　Ding	螣蛇 (Téng Shé) 天心 (Tiān Xīn) 伤门 (Shāng Mén) Kan 1　Yi　Ren	太阴 (Tài Yīn) 天柱 (Tiān Zhù) 生门 (Shēng Mén) Qian 6　Bing　Yi

Chart 3

Yin (阴) Dun# 5 Hour: **WuShen**；直符(ZhíFú): 天蓬(TiānPéng)
直使(ZhíShǐ): 休门(XiūMén)；旬首(XúnShǒu): JiaChenRen

太阴 (Tài Yīn) 天柱 (Tiān Zhù) 景门 (Jǐng Mén) Xun 4　Bing　Ji	螣蛇 (Téng Shé) 天心 (Tiān Xīn) 死门 (Sǐ Mén) Li 9　Yi　Gui	值符 (Zhí Fú) 天蓬 (Tiān Péng) 惊门 (Jīng Mén) Kun 2　Ren　Xin/Wu
六合 (Liù Hé) 禽芮 (Qín Ruì) 杜门 (Dù Mén) Zhen 3　Xin/Wu　Geng	Yin (阴) Dun# 5 Hour: **WuShen** ©Calvin Yap	九天 (Jiǔ Tiān) 天任 (Tiān Rèn) 开门 (Kāi Mén) Dui 7　Ding　Bing
白虎 (Bái Hǔ) 天英 (Tiān Yīng) 伤门 (Shāng Mén) Gen 8　Gui　Ding	玄武 (Xuán Wǔ) 天辅 (Tiān Fǔ) 生门 (Shēng Mén) Kan 1　Ji　Ren	九地 (Jiǔ Dì) 天冲 (Tiān Chōng) 休门 (Xiū Mén) Qian 6　Geng　Yi

Chart 4

Yin (阴) Dun# 5 Hour: **JiYou**；直符(ZhíFú): 天蓬(TiānPéng)
直使(ZhíShǐ): 休门(XiūMén)；旬首(XúnShǒu): JiaChenRen

值符 (Zhí Fú) 天蓬 (Tiān Péng) 惊门 (Jīng Mén) Xun 4　Ren　Ji	九天 (Jiǔ Tiān) 天任 (Tiān Rèn) 开门 (Kāi Mén) Li 9　Ding　Gui	九地 (Jiǔ Dì) 天冲 (Tiān Chōng) 休门 (Xiū Mén) Kun 2　Geng　Xin/Wu
螣蛇 (Téng Shé) 天心 (Tiān Xīn) 死门 (Sǐ Mén) Zhen 3　Yi　Geng	Yin (阴) Dun# 5 Hour: **JiYou** ©Calvin Yap	玄武 (Xuán Wǔ) 天辅 (Tiān Fǔ) 生门 (Shēng Mén) Dui 7　Ji　Bing
太阴 (Tài Yīn) 天柱 (Tiān Zhù) 景门 (Jǐng Mén) Gen 8　Bing　Ding	六合 (Liù Hé) 禽芮 (Qín Ruì) 杜门 (Dù Mén) Kan 1　Xin/Wu　Ren	白虎 (Bái Hǔ) 天英 (Tiān Yīng) 伤门 (Shāng Mén) Qian 6　Gui　Yi

Chart 5

Yin (阴) Dun# 5 Hour: **GengXu**；直符(ZhíFú): 天蓬(TiānPéng)
直使(ZhíShǐ): 休门(XiūMén)；旬首(XúnShǒu): JiaChenRen

九天 (Jiǔ Tiān) 天任 (Tiān Rèn) 休门 (Xiū Mén) Xun 4　Ding　Ji	九地 (Jiǔ Dì) 天冲 (Tiān Chōng) 生门 (Shēng Mén) Li 9　Geng　Gui	玄武 (Xuán Wǔ) 天辅 (Tiān Fǔ) 伤门 (Shāng Mén) Kun 2　Ji　Xin/Wu
值符 (Zhí Fú) 天蓬 (Tiān Péng) 开门 (Kāi Mén) Zhen 3　Ren　Geng	Yin (阴) Dun# 5 Hour: **GengXu** ©Calvin Yap	白虎 (Bái Hǔ) 天英 (Tiān Yīng) 杜门 (Dù Mén) Dui 7　Gui　Bing
螣蛇 (Téng Shé) 天心 (Tiān Xīn) 惊门 (Jīng Mén) Gen 8　Yi　Ding	太阴 (Tài Yīn) 天柱 (Tiān Zhù) 死门 (Sǐ Mén) Kan 1　Bing　Ren	六合 (Liù Hé) 禽芮 (Qín Ruì) 景门 (Jǐng Mén) Qian 6　Xin/Wu　Yi

Chart 6

Yin (阴) Dun# 5 Hour: **XinHai**；直符(ZhíFú): 天蓬(TiānPéng)
直使(ZhíShǐ): 休门(XiūMén)；旬首(XúnShǒu): JiaChenRen

太阴 (Tài Yīn) 天柱 (Tiān Zhù) 生门 (Shēng Mén) Xun 4　Bing　Ji	螣蛇 (Téng Shé) 天心 (Tiān Xīn) 伤门 (Shāng Mén) Li 9　Yi　Gui	值符 (Zhí Fú) 天蓬 (Tiān Péng) 杜门 (Dù Mén) Kun 2　Ren　Xin/Wu
六合 (Liù Hé) 禽芮 (Qín Ruì) 休门 (Xiū Mén) Zhen 3　Xin/Wu　Geng	Yin (阴) Dun# 5 Hour: **XinHai** ©Calvin Yap	九天 (Jiǔ Tiān) 天任 (Tiān Rèn) 景门 (Jǐng Mén) Dui 7　Ding　Bing
白虎 (Bái Hǔ) 天英 (Tiān Yīng) 开门 (Kāi Mén) Gen 8　Gui　Ding	玄武 (Xuán Wǔ) 天辅 (Tiān Fǔ) 惊门 (Jīng Mén) Kan 1　Ji　Ren	九地 (Jiǔ Dì) 天冲 (Tiān Chōng) 死门 (Sǐ Mén) Qian 6　Geng

Yin (阴) Dun# 5 Hour: RenZi ; 直符(ZhíFú): 天蓬(TiānPéng)
直使(ZhíShǐ): 休门(XiūMén) ; 旬首(XúnShǒu): JiaChenRen

玄武 (Xuán Wǔ) 天辅 (Tiān Fǔ) 惊门 (Jīng Mén) Xun 4 Ji Ji	白虎 (Bái Hǔ) 天英 (Tiān Yīng) 开门 (Kāi Mén) Li 9 Gui Gui	六合 (Liù Hé) 禽芮 (Qín Ruì) 休门 (Xiū Mén) Kun 2 Xin/Wu Xin/Wu
九地 (Jiǔ Dì) 天冲 (Tiān Chōng) 死门 (Sǐ Mén) Zhen 3 Geng Geng	Yin (阴) Dun# 5 Hour: **RenZi** **Fu Yin** ©Calvin Yap	太阴 (Tài Yīn) 天柱 (Tiān Zhù) 生门 (Shēng Mén) Dui 7 Bing Bing
九天 (Jiǔ Tiān) 天任 (Tiān Rèn) 景门 (Jǐng Mén) Gen 8 Ding Ding	值符 (Zhí Fú) 天蓬 (Tiān Péng) 杜门 (Dù Mén) Kan 1 Ren Ren	腾蛇 (Téng Shé) 天心 (Tiān Xīn) 伤门 (Shāng Mén) Qian 6 Yi Yi

Yin (阴) Dun# 5 Hour: GuiChou ; 直符(ZhíFú): 天蓬(TiānPéng)
直使(ZhíShǐ): 休门(XiūMén) ; 旬首(XúnShǒu): JiaChenRen

腾蛇 (Téng Shé) 天心 (Tiān Xīn) 杜门 (Dù Mén) Xun 4 Yi Ji	值符 (Zhí Fú) 天蓬 (Tiān Péng) 景门 (Jǐng Mén) Li 9 Ren Gui	九天 (Jiǔ Tiān) 天任 (Tiān Rèn) 死门 (Sǐ Mén) Kun 2 Ding Xin/Wu
太阴 (Tài Yīn) 天柱 (Tiān Zhù) 伤门 (Shāng Mén) Zhen 3 Bing Geng	Yin (阴) Dun# 5 Hour: **GuiChou** **Fan Yin** ©Calvin Yap	九地 (Jiǔ Dì) 天冲 (Tiān Chōng) 惊门 (Jīng Mén) Dui 7 Geng Bing
六合 (Liù Hé) 禽芮 (Qín Ruì) 生门 (Shēng Mén) Gen 8 Xin/Wu Ding	白虎 (Bái Hǔ) 天英 (Tiān Yīng) 休门 (Xiū Mén) Kan 1 Gui Ren	玄武 (Xuán Wǔ) 天辅 (Tiān Fǔ) 开门 (Kāi Mén) Qian 6 Ji Yi

---

Chart: -5JiaYin (Yin Dun #5 JiaYin Xun)
JiaYin, YiMao, BingChen, DingSi, WuWu, JiWei, GengShen, XinYou, RenXu, GuiHai

---

Yin (阴) Dun# 5 Hour: JiaYin ; 直符(ZhíFú): 天英(TiānYīng)
直使(ZhíShǐ): 景门(JǐngMén) ; 旬首(XúnShǒu): JiaYinGui

腾蛇 (Téng Shé) 天辅 (Tiān Fǔ) 杜门 (Dù Mén) Xun 4 Ji Ji	值符 (Zhí Fú) 天英 (Tiān Yīng) 景门 (Jǐng Mén) Li 9 Gui Gui	九天 (Jiǔ Tiān) 禽芮 (Qín Ruì) 死门 (Sǐ Mén) Kun 2 Xin/Wu Xin/Wu
太阴 (Tài Yīn) 天冲 (Tiān Chōng) 伤门 (Shāng Mén) Zhen 3 Geng Geng	Yin (阴) Dun# 5 Hour: **JiaYin** **Fu Yin** ©Calvin Yap	九地 (Jiǔ Dì) 天柱 (Tiān Zhù) 惊门 (Jīng Mén) Dui 7 Bing Bing
六合 (Liù Hé) 天任 (Tiān Rèn) 生门 (Shēng Mén) Gen 8 Ding Ding	白虎 (Bái Hǔ) 天蓬 (Tiān Péng) 休门 (Xiū Mén) Kan 1 Ren Ren	玄武 (Xuán Wǔ) 天心 (Tiān Xīn) 开门 (Kāi Mén) Qian 6 Yi Yi

Yin (阴) Dun# 5 Hour: YiMao ; 直符(ZhíFú): 天英(TiānYīng)
直使(ZhíShǐ): 景门(JǐngMén) ; 旬首(XúnShǒu): JiaYinGui

白虎 (Bái Hǔ) 天蓬 (Tiān Péng) 惊门 (Jīng Mén) Xun 4 Ren Ji	六合 (Liù Hé) 天任 (Tiān Rèn) 开门 (Kāi Mén) Li 9 Ding Gui	太阴 (Tài Yīn) 天冲 (Tiān Chōng) 休门 (Xiū Mén) Kun 2 Geng Xin/Wu
玄武 (Xuán Wǔ) 天心 (Tiān Xīn) 死门 (Sǐ Mén) Zhen 3 Yi Geng	Yin (阴) Dun# 5 Hour: **YiMao** ©Calvin Yap	腾蛇 (Téng Shé) 天辅 (Tiān Fǔ) 生门 (Shēng Mén) Dui 7 Ji Bing
九地 (Jiǔ Dì) 天柱 (Tiān Zhù) 景门 (Jǐng Mén) Gen 8 Bing Ding	九天 (Jiǔ Tiān) 禽芮 (Qín Ruì) 杜门 (Dù Mén) Kan 1 Xin/Wu Ren	值符 (Zhí Fú) 天英 (Tiān Yīng) 伤门 (Shāng Mén) Qian 6 Gui Yi

Yin (阴) Dun# 5 Hour: BingChen ; 直符(ZhíFú): 天英(TiānYīng)
直使(ZhíShǐ): 景门(JǐngMén) ; 旬首(XúnShǒu): JiaYinGui

六合 (Liù Hé) 天任 (Tiān Rèn) 生门 (Shēng Mén) Xun 4 Ding Ji	太阴 (Tài Yīn) 天冲 (Tiān Chōng) 伤门 (Shāng Mén) Li 9 Geng Gui	腾蛇 (Téng Shé) 天辅 (Tiān Fǔ) 杜门 (Dù Mén) Kun 2 Ji Xin/Wu
白虎 (Bái Hǔ) 天蓬 (Tiān Péng) 休门 (Xiū Mén) Zhen 3 Ren Geng	Yin (阴) Dun# 5 Hour: **BingChen** ©Calvin Yap	值符 (Zhí Fú) 天英 (Tiān Yīng) 景门 (Jǐng Mén) Dui 7 Gui Bing
玄武 (Xuán Wǔ) 天心 (Tiān Xīn) 开门 (Kāi Mén) Gen 8 Yi Ding	九地 (Jiǔ Dì) 天柱 (Tiān Zhù) 惊门 (Jīng Mén) Kan 1 Bing Ren	九天 (Jiǔ Tiān) 禽芮 (Qín Ruì) 死门 (Sǐ Mén) Qian 6 Xin/Wu Yi

Yin (阴) Dun# 5 Hour: DingSi ; 直符(ZhíFú): 天英(TiānYīng)
直使(ZhíShǐ): 景门(JǐngMén) ; 旬首(XúnShǒu): JiaYinGui

九地 (Jiǔ Dì) 天柱 (Tiān Zhù) 休门 (Xiū Mén) Xun 4 Bing Ji	玄武 (Xuán Wǔ) 天心 (Tiān Xīn) 生门 (Shēng Mén) Li 9 Yi Gui	白虎 (Bái Hǔ) 天蓬 (Tiān Péng) 伤门 (Shāng Mén) Kun 2 Ren Xin/Wu
九天 (Jiǔ Tiān) 禽芮 (Qín Ruì) 开门 (Kāi Mén) Zhen 3 Xin/Wu Geng	Yin (阴) Dun# 5 Hour: **DingSi** ©Calvin Yap	六合 (Liù Hé) 天任 (Tiān Rèn) 杜门 (Dù Mén) Dui 7 Ding Bing
值符 (Zhí Fú) 天英 (Tiān Yīng) 惊门 (Jīng Mén) Gen 8 Gui Ding	腾蛇 (Téng Shé) 天辅 (Tiān Fǔ) 死门 (Sǐ Mén) Kan 1 Ji Ren	太阴 (Tài Yīn) 天冲 (Tiān Chōng) 景门 (Jǐng Mén) Qian 6 Geng Yi

Yin (阴) Dun# 5 Hour: **WuWu** ; 直符(ZhíFú): 天英(TiānYīng)
直使(ZhíShǐ): 景门(JǐngMén) ; 旬首(XúnShǒu): JiaYinGui

太阴 (Tài Yīn) 天冲 (Tiān Chōng) 伤门 (Shāng Mén) Xun 4　Geng 　　Ji	螣蛇 (Téng Shé) 天辅 (Tiān Fǔ) 杜门 (Dù Mén) Li 9　Ji 　　Gui	值符 (Zhí Fú) 天英 (Tiān Yīng) 景门 (Jǐng Mén) Kun 2　Gui 　　Xin/Wu
六合 (Liù Hé) 天任 (Tiān Rèn) 生门 (Shēng Mén) Zhen 3　Ding 　　Geng	Yin (阴) Dun# 5 Hour: **WuWu** ©Calvin Yap	九天 (Jiǔ Tiān) 禽芮 (Qín Ruì) 死门 (Sǐ Mén) Dui 7　Xin/Wu 　　Bing
白虎 (Bái Hǔ) 天蓬 (Tiān Péng) 休门 (Xiū Mén) Gen 8　Ren 　　Ding	玄武 (Xuán Wǔ) 天心 (Tiān Xīn) 开门 (Kāi Mén) Kan 1　Yi 　　Ren	九地 (Jiǔ Dì) 天柱 (Tiān Zhù) 惊门 (Jǐng Mén) Qian 6　Bing 　　Yi

Yin (阴) Dun# 5 Hour: **JiWei** ; 直符(ZhíFú): 天英(TiānYīng)
直使(ZhíShǐ): 景门(JǐngMén) ; 旬首(XúnShǒu): JiaYinGui

值符 (Zhí Fú) 天英 (Tiān Yīng) 景门 (Jǐng Mén) Xun 4　Gui 　　Ji	九天 (Jiǔ Tiān) 禽芮 (Qín Ruì) 死门 (Sǐ Mén) Li 9　Xin/Wu 　　Gui	九地 (Jiǔ Dì) 天柱 (Tiān Zhù) 惊门 (Jīng Mén) Kun 2　Bing 　　Xin/Wu
螣蛇 (Téng Shé) 天辅 (Tiān Fǔ) 杜门 (Dù Mén) Zhen 3　Ji 　　Geng	Yin (阴) Dun# 5 Hour: **JiWei** ©Calvin Yap	玄武 (Xuán Wǔ) 天心 (Tiān Xīn) 开门 (Kāi Mén) Dui 7　Yi 　　Bing
太阴 (Tài Yīn) 天冲 (Tiān Chōng) 伤门 (Shāng Mén) Gen 8　Geng 　　Ding	六合 (Liù Hé) 天任 (Tiān Rèn) 生门 (Shēng Mén) Kan 1　Ding 　　Ren	白虎 (Bái Hǔ) 天蓬 (Tiān Péng) 休门 (Xiū Mén) Qian 6　Ren 　　Yi

Yin (阴) Dun# 5 Hour: **GengShen** ; 直符(ZhíFú): 天英(TiānYīng)
直使(ZhíShǐ): 景门(JǐngMén) ; 旬首(XúnShǒu): JiaYinGui

九天 (Jiǔ Tiān) 禽芮 (Qín Ruì) 死门 (Sǐ Mén) Xun 4　Xin/Wu 　　Ji	九地 (Jiǔ Dì) 天柱 (Tiān Zhù) 惊门 (Jǐng Mén) Li 9　Bing 　　Gui	玄武 (Xuán Wǔ) 天心 (Tiān Xīn) 开门 (Kāi Mén) Kun 2　Yi 　　Xin/Wu
值符 (Zhí Fú) 天英 (Tiān Yīng) 景门 (Jǐng Mén) Zhen 3　Gui 　　Geng	Yin (阴) Dun# 5 Hour: **GengShen** ©Calvin Yap	白虎 (Bái Hǔ) 天蓬 (Tiān Péng) 休门 (Xiū Mén) Dui 7　Ren 　　Bing
螣蛇 (Téng Shé) 天辅 (Tiān Fǔ) 杜门 (Dù Mén) Gen 8　Ji 　　Ding	太阴 (Tài Yīn) 天冲 (Tiān Chōng) 伤门 (Shāng Mén) Kan 1　Geng 　　Ren	六合 (Liù Hé) 天任 (Tiān Rèn) 生门 (Shēng Mén) Qian 6　Ding 　　Yi

Yin (阴) Dun# 5 Hour: **XinYou** ; 直符(ZhíFú): 天英(TiānYīng)
直使(ZhíShǐ): 景门(JǐngMén) ; 旬首(XúnShǒu): JiaYinGui

太阴 (Tài Yīn) 天冲 (Tiān Chōng) 伤门 (Shāng Mén) Xun 4　Geng 　　Ji	螣蛇 (Téng Shé) 天辅 (Tiān Fǔ) 杜门 (Dù Mén) Li 9　Ji 　　Gui	值符 (Zhí Fú) 天英 (Tiān Yīng) 景门 (Jǐng Mén) Kun 2　Gui 　　Xin/Wu
六合 (Liù Hé) 天任 (Tiān Rèn) 生门 (Shēng Mén) Zhen 3　Ding 　　Geng	Yin (阴) Dun# 5 Hour: **XinYou** ©Calvin Yap	九天 (Jiǔ Tiān) 禽芮 (Qín Ruì) 死门 (Sǐ Mén) Dui 7　Xin/Wu 　　Bing
白虎 (Bái Hǔ) 天蓬 (Tiān Péng) 休门 (Xiū Mén) Gen 8　Ren 　　Ding	玄武 (Xuán Wǔ) 天心 (Tiān Xīn) 开门 (Kāi Mén) Kan 1　Yi 　　Ren	九地 (Jiǔ Dì) 天柱 (Tiān Zhù) 惊门 (Jǐng Mén) Qian 6　Bing 　　Yi

Yin (阴) Dun# 5 Hour: **RenXu** ; 直符(ZhíFú): 天英(TiānYīng)
直使(ZhíShǐ): 景门(JǐngMén) ; 旬首(XúnShǒu): JiaYinGui

玄武 (Xuán Wǔ) 天心 (Tiān Xīn) 开门 (Kāi Mén) Xun 4　Yi 　　Ji	白虎 (Bái Hǔ) 天蓬 (Tiān Péng) 休门 (Xiū Mén) Li 9　Ren 　　Gui	六合 (Liù Hé) 天任 (Tiān Rèn) 生门 (Shēng Mén) Kun 2　Ding 　　Xin/Wu
九地 (Jiǔ Dì) 天柱 (Tiān Zhù) 惊门 (Jǐng Mén) Zhen 3　Bing 　　Geng	Yin (阴) Dun# 5 Hour: **RenXu** Fan Yin ©Calvin Yap	太阴 (Tài Yīn) 天冲 (Tiān Chōng) 伤门 (Shāng Mén) Dui 7　Geng 　　Bing
九天 (Jiǔ Tiān) 禽芮 (Qín Ruì) 死门 (Sǐ Mén) Gen 8　Xin/Wu 　　Ding	值符 (Zhí Fú) 天英 (Tiān Yīng) 景门 (Jǐng Mén) Kan 1　Gui 　　Ren	螣蛇 (Téng Shé) 天辅 (Tiān Fǔ) 杜门 (Dù Mén) Qian 6　Ji 　　Yi

Yin (阴) Dun# 5 Hour: **GuiHai** ; 直符(ZhíFú): 天英(TiānYīng)
直使(ZhíShǐ): 景门(JǐngMén) ; 旬首(XúnShǒu): JiaYinGui

螣蛇 (Téng Shé) 天辅 (Tiān Fǔ) 杜门 (Dù Mén) Xun 4　Ji 　　Ji	值符 (Zhí Fú) 天英 (Tiān Yīng) 景门 (Jǐng Mén) Li 9　Gui 　　Gui	九天 (Jiǔ Tiān) 禽芮 (Qín Ruì) 死门 (Sǐ Mén) Kun 2　Xin/Wu 　　Xin/Wu
太阴 (Tài Yīn) 天冲 (Tiān Chōng) 伤门 (Shāng Mén) Zhen 3　Geng 　　Geng	Yin (阴) Dun# 5 Hour: **GuiHai** Fu Yin ©Calvin Yap	九地 (Jiǔ Dì) 天柱 (Tiān Zhù) 惊门 (Jǐng Mén) Dui 7　Bing 　　Bing
六合 (Liù Hé) 天任 (Tiān Rèn) 生门 (Shēng Mén) Gen 8　Ding 　　Ding	白虎 (Bái Hǔ) 天蓬 (Tiān Péng) 休门 (Xiū Mén) Kan 1　Ren 　　Ren	玄武 (Xuán Wǔ) 天心 (Tiān Xīn) 开门 (Kāi Mén) Qian 6　Yi 　　Yi

Yin Dun#6

Chart: **-6JiaZi** (Yin Dun #6 JiaZi Xun)
JiaZi, YiChou, BingYin, DingMao, WuChen, JiSi, GengWu, XinWei, RenShen, GuiYou

Yin (阴) Dun# 6 Hour: **JiaZi**；直符(ZhíFú): 天心(TiānXīn)
直使(ZhíShǐ): 开门(KāiMén)；旬首(XúnShǒu): JiaZiWu

白虎 (Bái Hǔ) 天辅 (Tiān Fǔ) 杜门 (Dù Mén) Xun 4　Geng Geng	六合 (Liù Hé) 天英 (Tiān Yīng) 景门 (Jǐng Mén) Li 9　Ding Ding	太阴 (Tài Yīn) 禽芮 (Qín Ruì) 死门 (Sǐ Mén) Kun 2　Ren/Ji Ren/Ji
玄武 (Xuán Wǔ) 天冲 (Tiān Chōng) 伤门 (Shāng Mén) Zhen 3　Xin Xin	Yin (阴) Dun# 6 Hour: **JiaZi** **Fu Yin** ©Calvin Yap	螣蛇 (Téng Shé) 天柱 (Tiān Zhù) 惊门 (Jīng Mén) Dui 7　Yi Yi
九地 (Jiǔ Dì) 天任 (Tiān Rèn) 生门 (Shēng Mén) Gen 8　Bing Bing	九天 (Jiǔ Tiān) 天蓬 (Tiān Péng) 休门 (Xiū Mén) Kan 1　Gui Gui	值符 (Zhí Fú) 天心 (Tiān Xīn) 开门 (Kāi Mén) Qian 6　Wu Wu

Yin (阴) Dun# 6 Hour: **YiChou**；直符(ZhíFú): 天心(TiānXīn)
直使(ZhíShǐ): 开门(KāiMén)；旬首(XúnShǒu): JiaZiWu

六合 (Liù Hé) 天英 (Tiān Yīng) 死门 (Sǐ Mén) Xun 4　Ding Geng	太阴 (Tài Yīn) 禽芮 (Qín Ruì) 惊门 (Jīng Mén) Li 9　Ren/Ji Ding	螣蛇 (Téng Shé) 天柱 (Tiān Zhù) 开门 (Kāi Mén) Kun 2　Yi Ren/Ji
白虎 (Bái Hǔ) 天辅 (Tiān Fǔ) 景门 (Jǐng Mén) Zhen 3　Geng Xin	Yin (阴) Dun# 6 Hour: **YiChou** ©Calvin Yap	值符 (Zhí Fú) 天心 (Tiān Xīn) 休门 (Xiū Mén) Dui 7　Wu Yi
玄武 (Xuán Wǔ) 天冲 (Tiān Chōng) 杜门 (Dù Mén) Gen 8　Xin Bing	九地 (Jiǔ Dì) 天任 (Tiān Rèn) 伤门 (Shāng Mén) Kan 1　Bing Gui	九天 (Jiǔ Tiān) 天蓬 (Tiān Péng) 生门 (Shēng Mén) Qian 6　Gui Wu

Yin (阴) Dun# 6 Hour: **BingYin**；直符(ZhíFú): 天心(TiānXīn)
直使(ZhíShǐ): 开门(KāiMén)；旬首(XúnShǒu): JiaZiWu

九地 (Jiǔ Dì) 天任 (Tiān Rèn) 开门 (Kāi Mén) Xun 4　Bing Geng	玄武 (Xuán Wǔ) 天冲 (Tiān Chōng) 休门 (Xiū Mén) Li 9　Xin Ding	白虎 (Bái Hǔ) 天辅 (Tiān Fǔ) 生门 (Shēng Mén) Kun 2　Geng Ren/Ji
九天 (Jiǔ Tiān) 天蓬 (Tiān Péng) 惊门 (Jīng Mén) Zhen 3　Gui Xin	Yin (阴) Dun# 6 Hour: **BingYin** ©Calvin Yap	六合 (Liù Hé) 天英 (Tiān Yīng) 伤门 (Shāng Mén) Dui 7　Ding Yi
值符 (Zhí Fú) 天心 (Tiān Xīn) 死门 (Sǐ Mén) Gen 8　Wu Bing	螣蛇 (Téng Shé) 天柱 (Tiān Zhù) 景门 (Jǐng Mén) Kan 1　Yi Gui	太阴 (Tài Yīn) 禽芮 (Qín Ruì) 杜门 (Dù Mén) Qian 6　Ren/Ji Wu

Yin (阴) Dun# 6 Hour: **DingMao**；直符(ZhíFú): 天心(TiānXīn)
直使(ZhíShǐ): 开门(KāiMén)；旬首(XúnShǒu): JiaZiWu

螣蛇 (Téng Shé) 天柱 (Tiān Zhù) 休门 (Xiū Mén) Xun 4　Yi Geng	值符 (Zhí Fú) 天心 (Tiān Xīn) 生门 (Shēng Mén) Li 9　Wu Ding	九天 (Jiǔ Tiān) 天蓬 (Tiān Péng) 伤门 (Shāng Mén) Kun 2　Gui Ren/Ji
太阴 (Tài Yīn) 禽芮 (Qín Ruì) 开门 (Kāi Mén) Zhen 3　Ren/Ji Xin	Yin (阴) Dun# 6 Hour: **DingMao** ©Calvin Yap	九地 (Jiǔ Dì) 天任 (Tiān Rèn) 杜门 (Dù Mén) Dui 7　Bing Yi
六合 (Liù Hé) 天英 (Tiān Yīng) 惊门 (Jīng Mén) Gen 8　Ding Bing	白虎 (Bái Hǔ) 天辅 (Tiān Fǔ) 死门 (Sǐ Mén) Kan 1　Geng Gui	玄武 (Xuán Wǔ) 天冲 (Tiān Chōng) 景门 (Jǐng Mén) Qian 6　Xin Wu

Yin (阴) Dun# 6 Hour: **WuChen**；直符(ZhíFú): 天心(TiānXīn)
直使(ZhíShǐ): 开门(KāiMén)；旬首(XúnShǒu): JiaZiWu

白虎 (Bái Hǔ) 天辅 (Tiān Fǔ) 死门 (Sǐ Mén) Xun 4　Geng Geng	六合 (Liù Hé) 天英 (Tiān Yīng) 惊门 (Jīng Mén) Li 9　Ding Ding	太阴 (Tài Yīn) 禽芮 (Qín Ruì) 开门 (Kāi Mén) Kun 2　Ren/Ji Ren/Ji
玄武 (Xuán Wǔ) 天冲 (Tiān Chōng) 景门 (Jǐng Mén) Zhen 3　Xin Xin	Yin (阴) Dun# 6 Hour: **WuChen** **Fu Yin** ©Calvin Yap	螣蛇 (Téng Shé) 天柱 (Tiān Zhù) 休门 (Xiū Mén) Dui 7　Yi Yi
九地 (Jiǔ Dì) 天任 (Tiān Rèn) 杜门 (Dù Mén) Gen 8　Bing Bing	九天 (Jiǔ Tiān) 天蓬 (Tiān Péng) 伤门 (Shāng Mén) Kan 1　Gui Gui	值符 (Zhí Fú) 天心 (Tiān Xīn) 生门 (Shēng Mén) Qian 6　Wu Wu

Yin (阴) Dun# 6 Hour: **JiSi**；直符(ZhíFú): 天心(TiānXīn)
直使(ZhíShǐ): 开门(KāiMén)；旬首(XúnShǒu): JiaZiWu

太阴 (Tài Yīn) 禽芮 (Qín Ruì) 伤门 (Shāng Mén) Xun 4　Ren/Ji Geng	螣蛇 (Téng Shé) 天柱 (Tiān Zhù) 杜门 (Dù Mén) Li 9　Yi Ding	值符 (Zhí Fú) 天心 (Tiān Xīn) 景门 (Jǐng Mén) Kun 2　Wu Ren/Ji
六合 (Liù Hé) 天英 (Tiān Yīng) 生门 (Shēng Mén) Zhen 3　Ding Xin	Yin (阴) Dun# 6 Hour: **JiSi** ©Calvin Yap	九天 (Jiǔ Tiān) 天蓬 (Tiān Péng) 死门 (Sǐ Mén) Dui 7　Gui Yi
白虎 (Bái Hǔ) 天辅 (Tiān Fǔ) 休门 (Xiū Mén) Gen 8　Geng Bing	玄武 (Xuán Wǔ) 天冲 (Tiān Chōng) 开门 (Kāi Mén) Kan 1　Xin Gui	九地 (Jiǔ Dì) 天任 (Tiān Rèn) 惊门 (Jīng Mén) Qian 6　Bing Wu

Yin (阴) Dun# 6 Hour: **GengWu**；直符(ZhíFú): 天心(TiānXīn)
直使(ZhíShǐ): 开门(KāiMén)；旬首(XúnShǒu): JiaZiWu

值符 (Zhí Fú) 天心 (Tiān Xīn) 惊门 (Jǐng Mén) Xun 4　Wu Geng	九天 (Jiǔ Tiān) 天蓬 (Tiān Péng) 开门 (Kāi Mén) Li 9　Gui Ding	九地 (Jiǔ Dì) 天任 (Tiān Rèn) 休门 (Xiū Mén) Kun 2　Bing Ren/Ji
螣蛇 (Téng Shé) 天柱 (Tiān Zhù) 死门 (Sǐ Mén) Zhen 3　Yi Xin	Yin (阴) Dun# 6 Hour: **GengWu** **Fan Yin** ©Calvin Yap	玄武 (Xuán Wǔ) 天冲 (Tiān Chōng) 生门 (Shēng Mén) Dui 7　Xin Yi
太阴 (Tài Yīn) 禽芮 (Qín Ruì) 景门 (Jǐng Mén) Gen 8　Ren/Ji Bing	六合 (Liù Hé) 天英 (Tiān Yīng) 杜门 (Dù Mén) Kan 1　Ding Gui	白虎 (Bái Hǔ) 天辅 (Tiān Fǔ) 伤门 (Shāng Mén) Qian 6　Geng Wu

Yin (阴) Dun# 6 Hour: **XinWei**；直符(ZhíFú): 天心(TiānXīn)
直使(ZhíShǐ): 开门(KāiMén)；旬首(XúnShǒu): JiaZiWu

九天 (Jiǔ Tiān) 天蓬 (Tiān Péng) 生门 (Shēng Mén) Xun 4　Gui Geng	九地 (Jiǔ Dì) 天任 (Tiān Rèn) 伤门 (Shāng Mén) Li 9　Bing Ding	玄武 (Xuán Wǔ) 天冲 (Tiān Chōng) 杜门 (Dù Mén) Kun 2　Xin Ren/Ji
值符 (Zhí Fú) 天心 (Tiān Xīn) 休门 (Xiū Mén) Zhen 3　Wu Xin	Yin (阴) Dun# 6 Hour: **XinWei** ©Calvin Yap	白虎 (Bái Hǔ) 天辅 (Tiān Fǔ) 景门 (Jǐng Mén) Dui 7　Geng Yi
螣蛇 (Téng Shé) 天柱 (Tiān Zhù) 开门 (Kāi Mén) Gen 8　Yi Bing	太阴 (Tài Yīn) 禽芮 (Qín Ruì) 惊门 (Jǐng Mén) Kan 1　Ren/Ji Gui	六合 (Liù Hé) 天英 (Tiān Yīng) 死门 (Sǐ Mén) Qian 6　Ding Wu

Yin (阴) Dun# 6 Hour: **RenShen**；直符(ZhíFú): 天心(TiānXīn)
直使(ZhíShǐ): 开门(KāiMén)；旬首(XúnShǒu): JiaZiWu

太阴 (Tài Yīn) 禽芮 (Qín Ruì) 景门 (Jǐng Mén) Xun 4　Ren/Ji Geng	螣蛇 (Téng Shé) 天柱 (Tiān Zhù) 死门 (Sǐ Mén) Li 9　Yi Ding	值符 (Zhí Fú) 天心 (Tiān Xīn) 惊门 (Jǐng Mén) Kun 2　Wu Ren/Ji
六合 (Liù Hé) 天英 (Tiān Yīng) 杜门 (Dù Mén) Zhen 3　Ding Xin	Yin (阴) Dun# 6 Hour: **RenShen** ©Calvin Yap	九天 (Jiǔ Tiān) 天蓬 (Tiān Péng) 开门 (Kāi Mén) Dui 7　Gui Yi
白虎 (Bái Hǔ) 天辅 (Tiān Fǔ) 伤门 (Shāng Mén) Gen 8　Geng Bing	玄武 (Xuán Wǔ) 天冲 (Tiān Chōng) 生门 (Shēng Mén) Kan 1　Xin Gui	九地 (Jiǔ Dì) 天任 (Tiān Rèn) 休门 (Xiū Mén) Qian 6　Bing Wu

Yin (阴) Dun# 6 Hour: **GuiYou**；直符(ZhíFú): 天心(TiānXīn)
直使(ZhíShǐ): 开门(KāiMén)；旬首(XúnShǒu): JiaZiWu

玄武 (Xuán Wǔ) 天冲 (Tiān Chōng) 杜门 (Dù Mén) Xun 4　Xin Geng	白虎 (Bái Hǔ) 天辅 (Tiān Fǔ) 景门 (Jǐng Mén) Li 9　Geng Ding	六合 (Liù Hé) 天英 (Tiān Yīng) 死门 (Sǐ Mén) Kun 2　Ding Ren/Ji
九地 (Jiǔ Dì) 天任 (Tiān Rèn) 伤门 (Shāng Mén) Zhen 3　Bing Xin	Yin (阴) Dun# 6 Hour: **GuiYou** ©Calvin Yap	太阴 (Tài Yīn) 禽芮 (Qín Ruì) 惊门 (Jǐng Mén) Dui 7　Ren/Ji Yi
九天 (Jiǔ Tiān) 天蓬 (Tiān Péng) 生门 (Shēng Mén) Gen 8　Gui Bing	值符 (Zhí Fú) 天心 (Tiān Xīn) 休门 (Xiū Mén) Kan 1　Wu Gui	螣蛇 (Téng Shé) 天柱 (Tiān Zhù) 开门 (Kāi Mén) Qian 6　Yi Wu

Chart: **-6JiaXu** (Yin Dun #6 JiaXu Xun)
JiaXu, YiHai, BingZi, DingChou, WuYin, JiMao, GengChen, XinSi, RenWu, GuiWei

Yin (阴) Dun# 6 Hour: **JiaXu**；直符(ZhíFú): 天禽(TiānQín)
直使(ZhíShǐ): 死门(SǐMén)；旬首(XúnShǒu): JiaXuJi

太阴 (Tài Yīn) 天辅 (Tiān Fǔ) 杜门 (Dù Mén) Xun 4　Geng Geng	螣蛇 (Téng Shé) 天英 (Tiān Yīng) 景门 (Jǐng Mén) Li 9　Ding Ding	值符 (Zhí Fú) 禽芮 (Qín Ruì) 死门 (Sǐ Mén) Kun 2　Ren/Ji Ren/Ji
六合 (Liù Hé) 天冲 (Tiān Chōng) 伤门 (Shāng Mén) Zhen 3　Xin Xin	Yin (阴) Dun# 6 Hour: **JiaXu** **Fu Yin** ©Calvin Yap	九天 (Jiǔ Tiān) 天柱 (Tiān Zhù) 惊门 (Jǐng Mén) Dui 7　Yi Yi
白虎 (Bái Hǔ) 天任 (Tiān Rèn) 生门 (Shēng Mén) Gen 8　Bing Bing	玄武 (Xuán Wǔ) 天蓬 (Tiān Péng) 休门 (Xiū Mén) Kan 1　Gui Gui	九地 (Jiǔ Dì) 天心 (Tiān Xīn) 开门 (Kāi Mén) Qian 6　Wu Wu

Yin (阴) Dun# 6 Hour: **YiHai**；直符(ZhíFú): 天禽(TiānQín)
直使(ZhíShǐ): 死门(SǐMén)；旬首(XúnShǒu): JiaXuJi

六合 (Liù Hé) 天冲 (Tiān Chōng) 死门 (Sǐ Mén) Xun 4　Xin Geng	太阴 (Tài Yīn) 天辅 (Tiān Fǔ) 惊门 (Jǐng Mén) Li 9　Geng Ding	螣蛇 (Téng Shé) 天英 (Tiān Yīng) 开门 (Kāi Mén) Kun 2　Ding Ren/Ji
白虎 (Bái Hǔ) 天任 (Tiān Rèn) 景门 (Jǐng Mén) Zhen 3　Bing Xin	Yin (阴) Dun# 6 Hour: **YiHai** ©Calvin Yap	值符 (Zhí Fú) 禽芮 (Qín Ruì) 休门 (Xiū Mén) Dui 7　Ren/Ji Yi
玄武 (Xuán Wǔ) 天蓬 (Tiān Péng) 杜门 (Dù Mén) Gen 8　Gui Bing	九地 (Jiǔ Dì) 天心 (Tiān Xīn) 伤门 (Shāng Mén) Kan 1　Wu Gui	九天 (Jiǔ Tiān) 天柱 (Tiān Zhù) 生门 (Shēng Mén) Qian 6　Yi Wu

Yin (阴) Dun# 6 Hour: BingZi；直符(ZhíFú): 天禽(TiānQín)
直使(ZhíShǐ): 死门(SǐMén)；旬首(XúnShǒu): JiaXuJi

九地 (Jiǔ Dì) 天心 (Tiān Xīn) 惊门 (Jīng Mén) Xun 4　Wu Geng	玄武 (Xuán Wǔ) 天蓬 (Tiān Péng) 开门 (Kāi Mén) Li 9　Gui Ding	白虎 (Bái Hǔ) 天任 (Tiān Rèn) 休门 (Xiū Mén) Kun 2　Bing Ren/Ji
九天 (Jiǔ Tiān) 天柱 (Tiān Zhù) 死门 (Sǐ Mén) Zhen 3　Yi Xin	Yin (阴) Dun# 6 Hour: **BingZi** **Fan Yin** ©Calvin Yap	六合 (Liù Hé) 天冲 (Tiān Chōng) 生门 (Shēng Mén) Dui 7　Xin Yi
值符 (Zhí Fú) 禽芮 (Qín Ruì) 景门 (Jǐng Mén) Gen 8　Ren/Ji Bing	腾蛇 (Téng Shé) 天英 (Tiān Yīng) 杜门 (Dù Mén) Kan 1　Ding Gui	太阴 (Tài Yīn) 天辅 (Tiān Fǔ) 伤门 (Shāng Mén) Qian 6　Geng Wu

Yin (阴) Dun# 6 Hour: DingChou；直符(ZhíFú): 天禽(TiānQín)
直使(ZhíShǐ): 死门(SǐMén)；旬首(XúnShǒu): JiaXuJi

腾蛇 (Téng Shé) 天英 (Tiān Yīng) 杜门 (Dù Mén) Xun 4　Ding Geng	值符 (Zhí Fú) 禽芮 (Qín Ruì) 景门 (Jǐng Mén) Li 9　Ren/Ji Ding	九天 (Jiǔ Tiān) 天柱 (Tiān Zhù) 死门 (Sǐ Mén) Kun 2　Yi Ren/Ji
太阴 (Tài Yīn) 天辅 (Tiān Fǔ) 伤门 (Shāng Mén) Zhen 3　Geng Xin	Yin (阴) Dun# 6 Hour: **DingChou** ©Calvin Yap	九地 (Jiǔ Dì) 天心 (Tiān Xīn) 惊门 (Jīng Mén) Dui 7　Wu Yi
六合 (Liù Hé) 天冲 (Tiān Chōng) 生门 (Shēng Mén) Gen 8　Xin Bing	白虎 (Bái Hǔ) 天任 (Tiān Rèn) 休门 (Xiū Mén) Kan 1　Bing Gui	玄武 (Xuán Wǔ) 天蓬 (Tiān Péng) 开门 (Kāi Mén) Qian 6　Gui Wu

Yin (阴) Dun# 6 Hour: WuYin；直符(ZhíFú): 天禽(TiānQín)
直使(ZhíShǐ): 死门(SǐMén)；旬首(XúnShǒu): JiaXuJi

白虎 (Bái Hǔ) 天任 (Tiān Rèn) 休门 (Xiū Mén) Xun 4　Bing Geng	六合 (Liù Hé) 天冲 (Tiān Chōng) 生门 (Shēng Mén) Li 9　Xin Ding	太阴 (Tài Yīn) 天辅 (Tiān Fǔ) 伤门 (Shāng Mén) Kun 2　Geng Ren/Ji
玄武 (Xuán Wǔ) 天蓬 (Tiān Péng) 开门 (Kāi Mén) Zhen 3　Gui Xin	Yin (阴) Dun# 6 Hour: **WuYin** ©Calvin Yap	腾蛇 (Téng Shé) 天英 (Tiān Yīng) 杜门 (Dù Mén) Dui 7　Ding Yi
九地 (Jiǔ Dì) 天心 (Tiān Xīn) 惊门 (Jīng Mén) Gen 8　Wu Bing	九天 (Jiǔ Tiān) 天柱 (Tiān Zhù) 死门 (Sǐ Mén) Kan 1　Yi Gui	值符 (Zhí Fú) 禽芮 (Qín Ruì) 景门 (Jǐng Mén) Qian 6　Ren/Ji Wu

Yin (阴) Dun# 6 Hour: JiMao；直符(ZhíFú): 天禽(TiānQín)
直使(ZhíShǐ): 死门(SǐMén)；旬首(XúnShǒu): JiaXuJi

太阴 (Tài Yīn) 天辅 (Tiān Fǔ) 景门 (Jǐng Mén) Xun 4　Geng Geng	腾蛇 (Téng Shé) 天英 (Tiān Yīng) 死门 (Sǐ Mén) Li 9　Ding Ding	值符 (Zhí Fú) 禽芮 (Qín Ruì) 惊门 (Jīng Mén) Kun 2　Ren/Ji Ren/Ji
六合 (Liù Hé) 天冲 (Tiān Chōng) 杜门 (Dù Mén) Zhen 3　Xin Xin	Yin (阴) Dun# 6 Hour: **JiMao** **Fu Yin** ©Calvin Yap	九天 (Jiǔ Tiān) 天柱 (Tiān Zhù) 开门 (Kāi Mén) Dui 7　Yi Yi
白虎 (Bái Hǔ) 天任 (Tiān Rèn) 伤门 (Shāng Mén) Gen 8　Bing Bing	玄武 (Xuán Wǔ) 天蓬 (Tiān Péng) 生门 (Shēng Mén) Kan 1　Gui Gui	九地 (Jiǔ Dì) 天心 (Tiān Xīn) 休门 (Xiū Mén) Qian 6　Wu Wu

Yin (阴) Dun# 6 Hour: GengChen；直符(ZhíFú): 天禽(TiānQín)
直使(ZhíShǐ): 死门(SǐMén)；旬首(XúnShǒu): JiaXuJi

值符 (Zhí Fú) 禽芮 (Qín Ruì) 开门 (Kāi Mén) Xun 4　Ren/Ji Geng	九天 (Jiǔ Tiān) 天柱 (Tiān Zhù) 休门 (Xiū Mén) Li 9　Yi Ding	九地 (Jiǔ Dì) 天心 (Tiān Xīn) 生门 (Shēng Mén) Kun 2　Wu Ren/Ji
腾蛇 (Téng Shé) 天英 (Tiān Yīng) 惊门 (Jīng Mén) Zhen 3　Ding Xin	Yin (阴) Dun# 6 Hour: **GengChen** ©Calvin Yap	玄武 (Xuán Wǔ) 天蓬 (Tiān Péng) 伤门 (Shāng Mén) Dui 7　Gui Yi
太阴 (Tài Yīn) 天辅 (Tiān Fǔ) 死门 (Sǐ Mén) Gen 8　Geng Bing	六合 (Liù Hé) 天冲 (Tiān Chōng) 景门 (Jǐng Mén) Kan 1　Xin Gui	白虎 (Bái Hǔ) 天任 (Tiān Rèn) 杜门 (Dù Mén) Qian 6　Bing Wu

Yin (阴) Dun# 6 Hour: XinSi；直符(ZhíFú): 天禽(TiānQín)
直使(ZhíShǐ): 死门(SǐMén)；旬首(XúnShǒu): JiaXuJi

九天 (Jiǔ Tiān) 天柱 (Tiān Zhù) 伤门 (Shāng Mén) Xun 4　Yi Geng	九地 (Jiǔ Dì) 天心 (Tiān Xīn) 杜门 (Dù Mén) Li 9　Wu Ding	玄武 (Xuán Wǔ) 天蓬 (Tiān Péng) 景门 (Jǐng Mén) Kun 2　Gui Ren/Ji
值符 (Zhí Fú) 禽芮 (Qín Ruì) 生门 (Shēng Mén) Zhen 3　Ren/Ji Xin	Yin (阴) Dun# 6 Hour: **XinSi** ©Calvin Yap	白虎 (Bái Hǔ) 天任 (Tiān Rèn) 死门 (Sǐ Mén) Dui 7　Bing Yi
腾蛇 (Téng Shé) 天英 (Tiān Yīng) 休门 (Xiū Mén) Gen 8　Ding Bing	太阴 (Tài Yīn) 天辅 (Tiān Fǔ) 开门 (Kāi Mén) Kan 1　Geng Gui	六合 (Liù Hé) 天冲 (Tiān Chōng) 惊门 (Jīng Mén) Qian 6　Xin Wu

Yin (阴) Dun# 6 Hour: **RenWu** ；直符(ZhíFú): 天禽(TiānQín)
直使(ZhíShǐ): 死门(SǐMén) ；旬首(XúnShǒu): JiaXuJi

太阴 (Tài Yīn) 天辅 (Tiān Fǔ) 生门 (Shēng Mén) Xun 4　Geng Geng	螣蛇 (Téng Shé) 天英 (Tiān Yīng) 伤门 (Shāng Mén) Li 9　Ding Ding	值符 (Zhí Fú) 禽芮 (Qín Ruì) 杜门 (Dù Mén) Kun 2　Ren/Ji Ren/Ji
六合 (Liù Hé) 天冲 (Tiān Chōng) 休门 (Xiū Mén) Zhen 3　Xin Xin	Yin (阴) Dun# 6 Hour: **RenWu** **Fu Yin** ©Calvin Yap	九天 (Jiǔ Tiān) 天柱 (Tiān Zhù) 景门 (Jǐng Mén) Dui 7　Yi Yi
白虎 (Bái Hǔ) 天任 (Tiān Rèn) 开门 (Kāi Mén) Gen 8　Bing Bing	玄武 (Xuán Wǔ) 天蓬 (Tiān Péng) 惊门 (Jīng Mén) Kan 1　Gui Gui	九地 (Jiǔ Dì) 天心 (Tiān Xīn) 死门 (Sǐ Mén) Qian 6　Wu Wu

Yin (阴) Dun# 6 Hour: **GuiWei** ；直符(ZhíFú): 天禽(TiānQín)
直使(ZhíShǐ): 死门(SǐMén) ；旬首(XúnShǒu): JiaXuJi

玄武 (Xuán Wǔ) 天蓬 (Tiān Péng) 杜门 (Dù Mén) Xun 4　Gui Geng	白虎 (Bái Hǔ) 天任 (Tiān Rèn) 景门 (Jǐng Mén) Li 9　Bing Ding	六合 (Liù Hé) 天冲 (Tiān Chōng) 死门 (Sǐ Mén) Kun 2　Xin Ren/Ji
九地 (Jiǔ Dì) 天心 (Tiān Xīn) 伤门 (Shāng Mén) Zhen 3　Wu Xin	Yin (阴) Dun# 6 Hour: **GuiWei** ©Calvin Yap	太阴 (Tài Yīn) 天辅 (Tiān Fǔ) 惊门 (Jǐng Mén) Dui 7　Geng Yi
九天 (Jiǔ Tiān) 天柱 (Tiān Zhù) 生门 (Shēng Mén) Gen 8　Yi Bing	值符 (Zhí Fú) 禽芮 (Qín Ruì) 休门 (Xiū Mén) Kan 1　Ren/Ji Gui	螣蛇 (Téng Shé) 天英 (Tiān Yīng) 开门 (Kāi Mén) Qian 6　Ding Wu

Chart: -6JiaShen (Yin Dun #6 JiaShen Xun)
JiaShen, YiYou, BingXu, DingHai, WuZi, JiChou, GengYin, XinMao, RenChen, GuiSi

Yin (阴) Dun# 6 Hour: **JiaShen** ；直符(ZhíFú): 天辅(TiānFǔ)
直使(ZhíShǐ): 杜门(DùMén) ；旬首(XúnShǒu): JiaShenGeng

值符 (Zhí Fú) 天辅 (Tiān Fǔ) 杜门 (Dù Mén) Xun 4　Geng Geng	九天 (Jiǔ Tiān) 天英 (Tiān Yīng) 景门 (Jǐng Mén) Li 9　Ding Ding	九地 (Jiǔ Dì) 禽芮 (Qín Ruì) 死门 (Sǐ Mén) Kun 2　Ren/Ji Ren/Ji
螣蛇 (Téng Shé) 天冲 (Tiān Chōng) 伤门 (Shāng Mén) Zhen 3　Xin Xin	Yin (阴) Dun# 6 Hour: **JiaShen** **Fu Yin** ©Calvin Yap	玄武 (Xuán Wǔ) 天柱 (Tiān Zhù) 惊门 (Jǐng Mén) Dui 7　Yi Yi
太阴 (Tài Yīn) 天任 (Tiān Rèn) 生门 (Shēng Mén) Gen 8　Bing Bing	六合 (Liù Hé) 天蓬 (Tiān Péng) 休门 (Xiū Mén) Kan 1　Gui Gui	白虎 (Bái Hǔ) 天心 (Tiān Xīn) 开门 (Kāi Mén) Qian 6　Wu Wu

Yin (阴) Dun# 6 Hour: **YiYou** ；直符(ZhíFú): 天辅(TiānFǔ)
直使(ZhíShǐ): 杜门(DùMén) ；旬首(XúnShǒu): JiaShenGeng

六合 (Liù Hé) 天蓬 (Tiān Péng) 景门 (Jǐng Mén) Xun 4　Gui Geng	太阴 (Tài Yīn) 天任 (Tiān Rèn) 死门 (Sǐ Mén) Li 9　Bing Ding	螣蛇 (Téng Shé) 天冲 (Tiān Chōng) 惊门 (Jīng Mén) Kun 2　Xin Ren/Ji
白虎 (Bái Hǔ) 天心 (Tiān Xīn) 杜门 (Dù Mén) Zhen 3　Wu Xin	Yin (阴) Dun# 6 Hour: **YiYou** ©Calvin Yap	值符 (Zhí Fú) 天辅 (Tiān Fǔ) 开门 (Kāi Mén) Dui 7　Geng Yi
玄武 (Xuán Wǔ) 天柱 (Tiān Zhù) 伤门 (Shāng Mén) Gen 8　Yi Bing	九地 (Jiǔ Dì) 禽芮 (Qín Ruì) 生门 (Shēng Mén) Kan 1　Ren/Ji Gui	九天 (Jiǔ Tiān) 天英 (Tiān Yīng) 休门 (Xiū Mén) Qian 6　Ding Wu

Yin (阴) Dun# 6 Hour: **BingXu** ；直符(ZhíFú): 天辅(TiānFǔ)
直使(ZhíShǐ): 杜门(DùMén) ；旬首(XúnShǒu): JiaShenGeng

九地 (Jiǔ Dì) 禽芮 (Qín Ruì) 生门 (Shēng Mén) Xun 4　Ren/Ji Geng	玄武 (Xuán Wǔ) 天柱 (Tiān Zhù) 伤门 (Shāng Mén) Li 9　Yi Ding	白虎 (Bái Hǔ) 天心 (Tiān Xīn) 杜门 (Dù Mén) Kun 2　Wu Ren/Ji
九天 (Jiǔ Tiān) 天英 (Tiān Yīng) 休门 (Xiū Mén) Zhen 3　Ding Xin	Yin (阴) Dun# 6 Hour: **BingXu** ©Calvin Yap	六合 (Liù Hé) 天蓬 (Tiān Péng) 景门 (Jǐng Mén) Dui 7　Gui Yi
值符 (Zhí Fú) 天辅 (Tiān Fǔ) 开门 (Kāi Mén) Gen 8　Geng Bing	螣蛇 (Téng Shé) 天冲 (Tiān Chōng) 惊门 (Jīng Mén) Kan 1　Xin Gui	太阴 (Tài Yīn) 天任 (Tiān Rèn) 死门 (Sǐ Mén) Qian 6　Bing Wu

Yin (阴) Dun# 6 Hour: **DingHai** ；直符(ZhíFú): 天辅(TiānFǔ)
直使(ZhíShǐ): 杜门(DùMén) ；旬首(XúnShǒu): JiaShenGeng

螣蛇 (Téng Shé) 天冲 (Tiān Chōng) 惊门 (Jīng Mén) Xun 4　Xin Geng	值符 (Zhí Fú) 天辅 (Tiān Fǔ) 开门 (Kāi Mén) Li 9　Geng Ding	九天 (Jiǔ Tiān) 天英 (Tiān Yīng) 休门 (Xiū Mén) Kun 2　Ding Ren/Ji
太阴 (Tài Yīn) 天任 (Tiān Rèn) 死门 (Sǐ Mén) Zhen 3　Bing Xin	Yin (阴) Dun# 6 Hour: **DingHai** ©Calvin Yap	九地 (Jiǔ Dì) 禽芮 (Qín Ruì) 生门 (Shēng Mén) Dui 7　Ren/Ji Yi
六合 (Liù Hé) 天蓬 (Tiān Péng) 景门 (Jǐng Mén) Gen 8　Gui Bing	白虎 (Bái Hǔ) 天心 (Tiān Xīn) 杜门 (Dù Mén) Kan 1　Wu Gui	玄武 (Xuán Wǔ) 天柱 (Tiān Zhù) 伤门 (Shāng Mén) Qian 6　Yi Wu

Yin (阴) Dun# 6 Hour: WuZi；直符(ZhíFú): 天辅(TiānFǔ)
直使(ZhíShǐ): 杜门(DùMén)；旬首(XúnShǒu): JiaShenGeng

白虎 (Bái Hǔ) 天心 (Tiān Xīn) 伤门 (Shāng Mén) Xun 4　Wu　Geng	六合 (Liù Hé) 天蓬 (Tiān Péng) 杜门 (Dù Mén) Li 9　Gui　Ding	太阴 (Tài Yīn) 天任 (Tiān Rèn) 景门 (Jǐng Mén) Kun 2　Bing　Ren/Ji
玄武 (Xuán Wǔ) 天柱 (Tiān Zhù) 生门 (Shēng Mén) Zhen 3　Yi　Xin	Yin (阴) Dun# 6 Hour: **WuZi** **Fan Yin** ©Calvin Yap	螣蛇 (Téng Shé) 天冲 (Tiān Chōng) 死门 (Sǐ Mén) Dui 7　Xin　Yi
九地 (Jiǔ Dì) 禽芮 (Qín Ruì) 休门 (Xiū Mén) Gen 8　Ren/Ji　Bing	九天 (Jiǔ Tiān) 天英 (Tiān Yīng) 开门 (Kāi Mén) Kan 1　Ding　Gui	值符 (Zhí Fú) 天辅 (Tiān Fǔ) 惊门 (Jǐng Mén) Qian 6　Geng　Wu

Yin (阴) Dun# 6 Hour: JiChou；直符(ZhíFú): 天辅(TiānFǔ)
直使(ZhíShǐ): 杜门(DùMén)；旬首(XúnShǒu): JiaShenGeng

太阴 (Tài Yīn) 天任 (Tiān Rèn) 死门 (Sǐ Mén) Xun 4　Bing　Geng	螣蛇 (Téng Shé) 天冲 (Tiān Chōng) 惊门 (Jǐng Mén) Li 9　Xin　Ding	值符 (Zhí Fú) 天辅 (Tiān Fǔ) 开门 (Kāi Mén) Kun 2　Geng　Ren/Ji
六合 (Liù Hé) 天蓬 (Tiān Péng) 景门 (Jǐng Mén) Zhen 3　Gui　Xin	Yin (阴) Dun# 6 Hour: **JiChou** ©Calvin Yap	九天 (Jiǔ Tiān) 天英 (Tiān Yīng) 休门 (Xiū Mén) Dui 7　Ding　Yi
白虎 (Bái Hǔ) 天心 (Tiān Xīn) 杜门 (Dù Mén) Gen 8　Wu　Bing	玄武 (Xuán Wǔ) 天柱 (Tiān Zhù) 伤门 (Shāng Mén) Kan 1　Yi　Gui	九地 (Jiǔ Dì) 禽芮 (Qín Ruì) 生门 (Shēng Mén) Qian 6　Ren/Ji　Wu

Yin (阴) Dun# 6 Hour: GengYin；直符(ZhíFú): 天辅(TiānFǔ)
直使(ZhíShǐ): 杜门(DùMén)；旬首(XúnShǒu): JiaShenGeng

值符 (Zhí Fú) 天辅 (Tiān Fǔ) 休门 (Xiū Mén) Xun 4　Geng　Geng	九天 (Jiǔ Tiān) 天英 (Tiān Yīng) 生门 (Shēng Mén) Li 9　Ding　Ding	九地 (Jiǔ Dì) 禽芮 (Qín Ruì) 伤门 (Shāng Mén) Kun 2　Ren/Ji　Ren/Ji
螣蛇 (Téng Shé) 天冲 (Tiān Chōng) 开门 (Kāi Mén) Zhen 3　Xin　Xin	Yin (阴) Dun# 6 Hour: **GengYin** **Fu Yin** ©Calvin Yap	玄武 (Xuán Wǔ) 天柱 (Tiān Zhù) 杜门 (Dù Mén) Dui 7　Yi　Yi
太阴 (Tài Yīn) 天任 (Tiān Rèn) 惊门 (Jǐng Mén) Gen 8　Bing　Bing	六合 (Liù Hé) 天蓬 (Tiān Péng) 死门 (Sǐ Mén) Kan 1　Gui　Gui	白虎 (Bái Hǔ) 天心 (Tiān Xīn) 景门 (Jǐng Mén) Qian 6　Wu　Wu

Yin (阴) Dun# 6 Hour: XinMao；直符(ZhíFú): 天辅(TiānFǔ)
直使(ZhíShǐ): 杜门(DùMén)；旬首(XúnShǒu): JiaShenGeng

九天 (Jiǔ Tiān) 天英 (Tiān Yīng) 开门 (Kāi Mén) Xun 4　Ding　Geng	九地 (Jiǔ Dì) 禽芮 (Qín Ruì) 休门 (Xiū Mén) Li 9　Ren/Ji　Ding	玄武 (Xuán Wǔ) 天柱 (Tiān Zhù) 生门 (Shēng Mén) Kun 2　Yi　Ren/Ji
值符 (Zhí Fú) 天辅 (Tiān Fǔ) 惊门 (Jǐng Mén) Zhen 3　Geng　Xin	Yin (阴) Dun# 6 Hour: **XinMao** ©Calvin Yap	白虎 (Bái Hǔ) 天心 (Tiān Xīn) 伤门 (Shāng Mén) Dui 7　Wu　Yi
螣蛇 (Téng Shé) 天冲 (Tiān Chōng) 死门 (Sǐ Mén) Gen 8　Xin　Bing	太阴 (Tài Yīn) 天任 (Tiān Rèn) 景门 (Jǐng Mén) Kan 1　Bing　Gui	六合 (Liù Hé) 天蓬 (Tiān Péng) 杜门 (Dù Mén) Qian 6　Gui　Wu

Yin (阴) Dun# 6 Hour: RenChen；直符(ZhíFú): 天辅(TiānFǔ)
直使(ZhíShǐ): 杜门(DùMén)；旬首(XúnShǒu): JiaShenGeng

太阴 (Tài Yīn) 天任 (Tiān Rèn) 生门 (Shēng Mén) Xun 4　Bing　Geng	螣蛇 (Téng Shé) 天冲 (Tiān Chōng) 伤门 (Shāng Mén) Li 9　Xin　Ding	值符 (Zhí Fú) 天辅 (Tiān Fǔ) 杜门 (Dù Mén) Kun 2　Geng　Ren/Ji
六合 (Liù Hé) 天蓬 (Tiān Péng) 休门 (Xiū Mén) Zhen 3　Gui　Xin	Yin (阴) Dun# 6 Hour: **RenChen** ©Calvin Yap	九天 (Jiǔ Tiān) 天英 (Tiān Yīng) 景门 (Jǐng Mén) Dui 7　Ding　Yi
白虎 (Bái Hǔ) 天心 (Tiān Xīn) 开门 (Kāi Mén) Gen 8　Wu　Bing	玄武 (Xuán Wǔ) 天柱 (Tiān Zhù) 惊门 (Jǐng Mén) Kan 1　Yi　Gui	九地 (Jiǔ Dì) 禽芮 (Qín Ruì) 死门 (Sǐ Mén) Qian 6　Ren/Ji　Wu

Yin (阴) Dun# 6 Hour: GuiSi；直符(ZhíFú): 天辅(TiānFǔ)
直使(ZhíShǐ): 杜门(DùMén)；旬首(XúnShǒu): JiaShenGeng

玄武 (Xuán Wǔ) 天柱 (Tiān Zhù) 杜门 (Dù Mén) Xun 4　Yi　Geng	白虎 (Bái Hǔ) 天心 (Tiān Xīn) 景门 (Jǐng Mén) Li 9　Wu　Ding	六合 (Liù Hé) 天蓬 (Tiān Péng) 死门 (Sǐ Mén) Kun 2　Gui　Ren/Ji
九地 (Jiǔ Dì) 禽芮 (Qín Ruì) 伤门 (Shāng Mén) Zhen 3　Ren/Ji　Xin	Yin (阴) Dun# 6 Hour: **GuiSi** ©Calvin Yap	太阴 (Tài Yīn) 天任 (Tiān Rèn) 惊门 (Jǐng Mén) Dui 7　Bing　Yi
九天 (Jiǔ Tiān) 天英 (Tiān Yīng) 生门 (Shēng Mén) Gen 8　Ding　Bing	值符 (Zhí Fú) 天辅 (Tiān Fǔ) 休门 (Xiū Mén) Kan 1　Geng　Gui	螣蛇 (Téng Shé) 天冲 (Tiān Chōng) 开门 (Kāi Mén) Qian 6　Xin　Wu

Chart: -6JiaWu (Yin Dun #6 JiaWu Xun)
JiaWu, YiWei, BingShen, DingYou, WuXu, JiHai, GengZi, XinChou, RenYin, GuiMao

Yin (阴) Dun# 6 Hour: **JiaWu**；直符(ZhíFú): 天冲(TiānChōng)
直使(ZhíShǐ): 伤门(ShāngMén)；旬首(XúnShǒu): JiaWu/Xin

九天 (Jiǔ Tiān) 天辅 (Tiān Fǔ) 杜门 (Dù Mén) Xun 4　Geng Geng	九地 (Jiǔ Dì) 天英 (Tiān Yīng) 景门 (Jǐng Mén) Li 9　Ding Ding	玄武 (Xuán Wǔ) 禽芮 (Qín Ruì) 死门 (Sǐ Mén) Kun 2　Ren/Ji Ren/Ji
值符 (Zhí Fú) 天冲 (Tiān Chōng) 伤门 (Shāng Mén) Zhen 3　Xin Xin	Yin (阴) Dun# 6 Hour: **JiaWu** **Fu Yin** ©Calvin Yap	白虎 (Bái Hǔ) 天柱 (Tiān Zhù) 惊门 (Jīng Mén) Dui 7　Yi Yi
腾蛇 (Téng Shé) 天任 (Tiān Rèn) 生门 (Shēng Mén) Gen 8　Bing Bing	太阴 (Tài Yīn) 天蓬 (Tiān Péng) 休门 (Xiū Mén) Kan 1　Gui Gui	六合 (Liù Hé) 天心 (Tiān Xīn) 开门 (Kāi Mén) Qian 6　Wu Wu

Yin (阴) Dun# 6 Hour: **YiWei**；直符(ZhíFú): 天冲(TiānChōng)
直使(ZhíShǐ): 伤门(ShāngMén)；旬首(XúnShǒu): JiaWu/Xin

六合 (Liù Hé) 天心 (Tiān Xīn) 休门 (Xiū Mén) Xun 4　Wu Geng	太阴 (Tài Yīn) 天蓬 (Tiān Péng) 生门 (Shēng Mén) Li 9　Gui Ding	腾蛇 (Téng Shé) 天任 (Tiān Rèn) 伤门 (Shāng Mén) Kun 2　Bing Ren/Ji
白虎 (Bái Hǔ) 天柱 (Tiān Zhù) 开门 (Kāi Mén) Zhen 3　Yi Xin	Yin (阴) Dun# 6 Hour: **YiWei** **Fan Yin** ©Calvin Yap	值符 (Zhí Fú) 天冲 (Tiān Chōng) 杜门 (Dù Mén) Dui 7　Xin Yi
玄武 (Xuán Wǔ) 禽芮 (Qín Ruì) 惊门 (Jīng Mén) Gen 8　Ren/Ji Bing	九地 (Jiǔ Dì) 天英 (Tiān Yīng) 死门 (Sǐ Mén) Kan 1　Ding Gui	九天 (Jiǔ Tiān) 天辅 (Tiān Fǔ) 景门 (Jǐng Mén) Qian 6　Geng Wu

Yin (阴) Dun# 6 Hour: **BingShen**；直符(ZhíFú): 天冲(TiānChōng)
直使(ZhíShǐ): 伤门(ShāngMén)；旬首(XúnShǒu): JiaWu/Xin

九地 (Jiǔ Dì) 天英 (Tiān Yīng) 死门 (Sǐ Mén) Xun 4　Ding Geng	玄武 (Xuán Wǔ) 禽芮 (Qín Ruì) 惊门 (Jīng Mén) Li 9　Ren/Ji Ding	白虎 (Bái Hǔ) 天柱 (Tiān Zhù) 开门 (Kāi Mén) Kun 2　Yi Ren/Ji
九天 (Jiǔ Tiān) 天辅 (Tiān Fǔ) 景门 (Jǐng Mén) Zhen 3　Geng Xin	Yin (阴) Dun# 6 Hour: **BingShen** ©Calvin Yap	六合 (Liù Hé) 天心 (Tiān Xīn) 休门 (Xiū Mén) Dui 7　Wu Yi
值符 (Zhí Fú) 天冲 (Tiān Chōng) 杜门 (Dù Mén) Gen 8　Xin Bing	腾蛇 (Téng Shé) 天任 (Tiān Rèn) 伤门 (Shāng Mén) Kan 1　Bing Gui	太阴 (Tài Yīn) 天蓬 (Tiān Péng) 生门 (Shēng Mén) Qian 6　Gui Wu

Yin (阴) Dun# 6 Hour: **DingYou**；直符(ZhíFú): 天冲(TiānChōng)
直使(ZhíShǐ): 伤门(ShāngMén)；旬首(XúnShǒu): JiaWu/Xin

腾蛇 (Téng Shé) 天任 (Tiān Rèn) 生门 (Shēng Mén) Xun 4　Bing Geng	值符 (Zhí Fú) 天冲 (Tiān Chōng) 伤门 (Shāng Mén) Li 9　Xin Ding	九天 (Jiǔ Tiān) 天辅 (Tiān Fǔ) 杜门 (Dù Mén) Kun 2　Geng Ren/Ji
太阴 (Tài Yīn) 天蓬 (Tiān Péng) 休门 (Xiū Mén) Zhen 3　Gui Xin	Yin (阴) Dun# 6 Hour: **DingYou** ©Calvin Yap	九地 (Jiǔ Dì) 天英 (Tiān Yīng) 景门 (Jǐng Mén) Dui 7　Ding Yi
六合 (Liù Hé) 天心 (Tiān Xīn) 开门 (Kāi Mén) Gen 8　Wu Bing	白虎 (Bái Hǔ) 天柱 (Tiān Zhù) 惊门 (Jīng Mén) Kan 1　Yi Gui	玄武 (Xuán Wǔ) 禽芮 (Qín Ruì) 死门 (Sǐ Mén) Qian 6　Ren/Ji Wu

Yin (阴) Dun# 6 Hour: **WuXu**；直符(ZhíFú): 天冲(TiānChōng)
直使(ZhíShǐ): 伤门(ShāngMén)；旬首(XúnShǒu): JiaWu/Xin

白虎 (Bái Hǔ) 天柱 (Tiān Zhù) 景门 (Jǐng Mén) Xun 4　Yi Geng	六合 (Liù Hé) 天心 (Tiān Xīn) 死门 (Sǐ Mén) Li 9　Wu Ding	太阴 (Tài Yīn) 天蓬 (Tiān Péng) 惊门 (Jīng Mén) Kun 2　Gui Ren/Ji
玄武 (Xuán Wǔ) 禽芮 (Qín Ruì) 杜门 (Dù Mén) Zhen 3　Ren/Ji Xin	Yin (阴) Dun# 6 Hour: **WuXu** ©Calvin Yap	腾蛇 (Téng Shé) 天任 (Tiān Rèn) 开门 (Kāi Mén) Dui 7　Bing Yi
九地 (Jiǔ Dì) 天英 (Tiān Yīng) 伤门 (Shāng Mén) Gen 8　Ding Bing	九天 (Jiǔ Tiān) 天辅 (Tiān Fǔ) 生门 (Shēng Mén) Kan 1　Geng Gui	值符 (Zhí Fú) 天冲 (Tiān Chōng) 休门 (Xiū Mén) Qian 6　Xin Wu

Yin (阴) Dun# 6 Hour: **JiHai**；直符(ZhíFú): 天冲(TiānChōng)
直使(ZhíShǐ): 伤门(ShāngMén)；旬首(XúnShǒu): JiaWu/Xin

太阴 (Tài Yīn) 天蓬 (Tiān Péng) 开门 (Kāi Mén) Xun 4　Gui Geng	腾蛇 (Téng Shé) 天任 (Tiān Rèn) 休门 (Xiū Mén) Li 9　Bing Ding	值符 (Zhí Fú) 天冲 (Tiān Chōng) 生门 (Shēng Mén) Kun 2　Xin Ren/Ji
六合 (Liù Hé) 天心 (Tiān Xīn) 惊门 (Jīng Mén) Zhen 3　Wu Xin	Yin (阴) Dun# 6 Hour: **JiHai** ©Calvin Yap	九天 (Jiǔ Tiān) 天辅 (Tiān Fǔ) 伤门 (Shāng Mén) Dui 7　Geng Yi
白虎 (Bái Hǔ) 天柱 (Tiān Zhù) 死门 (Sǐ Mén) Gen 8　Yi Bing	玄武 (Xuán Wǔ) 禽芮 (Qín Ruì) 景门 (Jǐng Mén) Kan 1　Ren/Ji Gui	九地 (Jiǔ Dì) 天英 (Tiān Yīng) 杜门 (Dù Mén) Qian 6　Ding Wu

Chart 1 — Yin (阴) Dun# 6 Hour: **GengZi**；直符(ZhíFú): 天冲(TiānChōng)

直使(ZhíShǐ): 伤门(ShāngMén)；旬首(XúnShǒu): JiaWu/Xin

值符 (Zhí Fú) 天冲 (Tiān Chōng) 惊门 (Jīng Mén) Xun 4　Xin Geng	九天 (Jiǔ Tiān) 天辅 (Tiān Fǔ) 开门 (Kāi Mén) Li 9　Geng Ding	九地 (Jiǔ Dì) 天英 (Tiān Yīng) 休门 (Xiū Mén) Kun 2　Ding Ren/Ji
螣蛇 (Téng Shé) 天任 (Tiān Rèn) 死门 (Sǐ Mén) Zhen 3　Bing Xin	Yin (阴) Dun# 6 Hour: **GengZi** ©Calvin Yap	玄武 (Xuán Wǔ) 禽芮 (Qín Ruì) 生门 (Shēng Mén) Dui 7　Ren/Ji Yi
太阴 (Tài Yīn) 天蓬 (Tiān Péng) 景门 (Jǐng Mén) Gen 8　Gui Bing	六合 (Liù Hé) 天心 (Tiān Xīn) 杜门 (Dù Mén) Kan 1　Wu Gui	白虎 (Bái Hǔ) 天柱 (Tiān Zhù) 伤门 (Shāng Mén) Qian 6　Yi Wu

Chart 2 — Yin (阴) Dun# 6 Hour: **XinChou**；直符(ZhíFú): 冲(TiānChōng)

直使(ZhíShǐ): 伤门(ShāngMén)；旬首(XúnShǒu): JiaWu/Xin

九天 (Jiǔ Tiān) 天辅 (Tiān Fǔ) 休门 (Xiū Mén) Xun 4　Geng Geng	九地 (Jiǔ Dì) 天英 (Tiān Yīng) 生门 (Shēng Mén) Li 9　Ding Ding	玄武 (Xuán Wǔ) 禽芮 (Qín Ruì) 伤门 (Shāng Mén) Kun 2　Ren/Ji Ren/Ji
值符 (Zhí Fú) 天冲 (Tiān Chōng) 开门 (Kāi Mén) Zhen 3　Xin Xin	Yin (阴) Dun# 6 Hour: **XinChou** **Fu Yin** ©Calvin Yap	白虎 (Bái Hǔ) 天柱 (Tiān Zhù) 杜门 (Dù Mén) Dui 7　Yi Yi
螣蛇 (Téng Shé) 天任 (Tiān Rèn) 惊门 (Jīng Mén) Gen 8　Bing Bing	太阴 (Tài Yīn) 天蓬 (Tiān Péng) 死门 (Sǐ Mén) Kan 1　Gui Gui	六合 (Liù Hé) 天心 (Tiān Xīn) 景门 (Jǐng Mén) Qian 6　Wu Wu

Chart 3 — Yin (阴) Dun# 6 Hour: **RenYin**；直符(ZhíFú): 天冲(TiānChōng)

直使(ZhíShǐ): 伤门(ShāngMén)；旬首(XúnShǒu): JiaWu/Xin

太阴 (Tài Yīn) 天蓬 (Tiān Péng) 伤门 (Shāng Mén) Xun 4　Gui Geng	螣蛇 (Téng Shé) 天任 (Tiān Rèn) 杜门 (Dù Mén) Li 9　Bing Ding	值符 (Zhí Fú) 天冲 (Tiān Chōng) 景门 (Jǐng Mén) Kun 2　Xin Ren/Ji
六合 (Liù Hé) 天心 (Tiān Xīn) 生门 (Shēng Mén) Zhen 3　Wu Xin	Yin (阴) Dun# 6 Hour: **RenYin** ©Calvin Yap	九天 (Jiǔ Tiān) 天辅 (Tiān Fǔ) 死门 (Sǐ Mén) Dui 7　Geng Yi
白虎 (Bái Hǔ) 天柱 (Tiān Zhù) 休门 (Xiū Mén) Gen 8　Yi Bing	玄武 (Xuán Wǔ) 禽芮 (Qín Ruì) 开门 (Kāi Mén) Kan 1　Ren/Ji Gui	九地 (Jiǔ Dì) 天英 (Tiān Yīng) 惊门 (Jīng Mén) Qian 6　Ding Wu

Chart 4 — Yin (阴) Dun# 6 Hour: **GuiMao**；直符(ZhíFú): 天冲(TiānChōng)

直使(ZhíShǐ): 伤门(ShāngMén)；旬首(XúnShǒu): JiaWu/Xin

玄武 (Xuán Wǔ) 禽芮 (Qín Ruì) 杜门 (Dù Mén) Xun 4　Ren/Ji Geng	白虎 (Bái Hǔ) 天柱 (Tiān Zhù) 景门 (Jǐng Mén) Li 9　Yi Ding	六合 (Liù Hé) 天心 (Tiān Xīn) 死门 (Sǐ Mén) Kun 2　Wu Ren/Ji
九地 (Jiǔ Dì) 天英 (Tiān Yīng) 伤门 (Shāng Mén) Zhen 3　Ding Xin	Yin (阴) Dun# 6 Hour: **GuiMao** ©Calvin Yap	太阴 (Tài Yīn) 天蓬 (Tiān Péng) 惊门 (Jīng Mén) Dui 7　Gui Yi
九天 (Jiǔ Tiān) 天辅 (Tiān Fǔ) 生门 (Shēng Mén) Gen 8　Geng Bing	值符 (Zhí Fú) 天冲 (Tiān Chōng) 休门 (Xiū Mén) Kan 1　Xin Gui	螣蛇 (Téng Shé) 天任 (Tiān Rèn) 开门 (Kāi Mén) Qian 6　Bing Wu

Chart: -6JiaChen (Yin Dun #6 JiaChen Xun)

JiaChen, YiSi, BingWu, DingWei, WuShen, JiYou, GengXu, XinHai, RenZi, GuiChou

Chart 5 — Yin (阴) Dun# 6 Hour: **JiaChen**；直符(ZhíFú): 天芮(TiānRuì)

直使(ZhíShǐ): 死门(SǐMén)；旬首(XúnShǒu): JiaChenRen

太阴 (Tài Yīn) 天辅 (Tiān Fǔ) 杜门 (Dù Mén) Xun 4　Geng Geng	螣蛇 (Téng Shé) 天英 (Tiān Yīng) 景门 (Jǐng Mén) Li 9　Ding Ding	值符 (Zhí Fú) 禽芮 (Qín Ruì) 死门 (Sǐ Mén) Kun 2　Ren/Ji Ren/Ji
六合 (Liù Hé) 天冲 (Tiān Chōng) 伤门 (Shāng Mén) Zhen 3　Xin Xin	Yin (阴) Dun# 6 Hour: **JiaChen** **Fu Yin** ©Calvin Yap	九天 (Jiǔ Tiān) 天柱 (Tiān Zhù) 惊门 (Jīng Mén) Dui 7　Yi Yi
白虎 (Bái Hǔ) 天任 (Tiān Rèn) 生门 (Shēng Mén) Gen 8　Bing Bing	玄武 (Xuán Wǔ) 天蓬 (Tiān Péng) 休门 (Xiū Mén) Kan 1　Gui Gui	九地 (Jiǔ Dì) 天心 (Tiān Xīn) 开门 (Kāi Mén) Qian 6　Wu Wu

Chart 6 — Yin (阴) Dun# 6 Hour: **YiSi**；直符(ZhíFú): 天芮(TiānRuì)

直使(ZhíShǐ): 死门(SǐMén)；旬首(XúnShǒu): JiaChenRen

六合 (Liù Hé) 天冲 (Tiān Chōng) 休门 (Xiū Mén) Xun 4　Xin Geng	太阴 (Tài Yīn) 天辅 (Tiān Fǔ) 生门 (Shēng Mén) Li 9　Geng Ding	螣蛇 (Téng Shé) 天英 (Tiān Yīng) 伤门 (Shāng Mén) Kun 2　Ding Ren/Ji
白虎 (Bái Hǔ) 天任 (Tiān Rèn) 开门 (Kāi Mén) Zhen 3　Bing Xin	Yin (阴) Dun# 6 Hour: **YiSi** ©Calvin Yap	值符 (Zhí Fú) 禽芮 (Qín Ruì) 杜门 (Dù Mén) Dui 7　Ren/Ji Yi
玄武 (Xuán Wǔ) 天蓬 (Tiān Péng) 惊门 (Jīng Mén) Gen 8　Gui Bing	九地 (Jiǔ Dì) 天心 (Tiān Xīn) 死门 (Sǐ Mén) Kan 1　Wu Gui	九天 (Jiǔ Tiān) 天柱 (Tiān Zhù) 景门 (Jǐng Mén) Qian 6　Yi Wu

Yin (阴) Dun# 6 Hour: BingWu；直符(ZhíFú): 天芮(TiānRuì)
直使(ZhíShǐ): 死门(SǐMén)；旬首(XúnShǒu): JiaChenRen

九地 (Jiǔ Dì) 天心 (Tiān Xīn) 景门 (Jǐng Mén) Xun 4　Wu Geng	玄武 (Xuán Wǔ) 天蓬 (Tiān Péng) 死门 (Sǐ Mén) Li 9　Gui Ding	白虎 (Bái Hǔ) 天任 (Tiān Rèn) 惊门 (Jīng Mén) Kun 2　Bing Ren/Ji
九天 (Jiǔ Tiān) 天柱 (Tiān Zhù) 杜门 (Dù Mén) Zhen 3　Yi Xin	Yin (阴) Dun# 6 Hour: BingWu **Fan Yin** ©Calvin Yap	六合 (Liù Hé) 天冲 (Tiān Chōng) 开门 (Kāi Mén) Dui 7　Xin Yi
值符 (Zhí Fú) 禽芮 (Qín Ruì) 伤门 (Shāng Mén) Gen 8　Ren/Ji Bing	腾蛇 (Téng Shé) 天英 (Tiān Yīng) 生门 (Shēng Mén) Kan 1　Ding Gui	太阴 (Tài Yīn) 天辅 (Tiān Fǔ) 休门 (Xiū Mén) Qian 6　Geng Wu

Yin (阴) Dun# 6 Hour: DingWei；直符(ZhíFú): 天芮(TiānRuì)
直使(ZhíShǐ): 死门(SǐMén)；旬首(XúnShǒu): JiaChenRen

腾蛇 (Téng Shé) 天英 (Tiān Yīng) 开门 (Kāi Mén) Xun 4　Ding Geng	值符 (Zhí Fú) 禽芮 (Qín Ruì) 休门 (Xiū Mén) Li 9　Ren/Ji Ding	九天 (Jiǔ Tiān) 天柱 (Tiān Zhù) 生门 (Shēng Mén) Kun 2　Yi Ren/Ji
太阴 (Tài Yīn) 天辅 (Tiān Fǔ) 惊门 (Jīng Mén) Zhen 3　Geng Xin	Yin (阴) Dun# 6 Hour: DingWei ©Calvin Yap	九地 (Jiǔ Di) 天心 (Tiān Xīn) 伤门 (Shāng Mén) Dui 7　Wu Yi
六合 (Liù Hé) 天冲 (Tiān Chōng) 死门 (Sǐ Mén) Gen 8　Xin Bing	白虎 (Bái Hǔ) 天任 (Tiān Rèn) 景门 (Jǐng Mén) Kan 1　Bing Gui	玄武 (Xuán Wǔ) 天蓬 (Tiān Péng) 杜门 (Dù Mén) Qian 6　Gui Wu

Yin (阴) Dun# 6 Hour: WuShen；直符(ZhíFú): 天芮(TiānRuì)
直使(ZhíShǐ): 死门(SǐMén)；旬首(XúnShǒu): JiaChenRen

白虎 (Bái Hǔ) 天任 (Tiān Rèn) 伤门 (Shāng Mén) Xun 4　Bing Geng	六合 (Liù Hé) 天冲 (Tiān Chōng) 杜门 (Dù Mén) Li 9　Xin Ding	太阴 (Tài Yīn) 天辅 (Tiān Fǔ) 景门 (Jǐng Mén) Kun 2　Geng Ren/Ji
玄武 (Xuán Wǔ) 天蓬 (Tiān Péng) 生门 (Shēng Mén) Zhen 3　Gui Xin	Yin (阴) Dun# 6 Hour: WuShen ©Calvin Yap	腾蛇 (Téng Shé) 天英 (Tiān Yīng) 死门 (Sǐ Mén) Dui 7　Ding Yi
九地 (Jiǔ Dì) 天心 (Tiān Xīn) 休门 (Xiū Mén) Gen 8　Wu Bing	九天 (Jiǔ Tiān) 天柱 (Tiān Zhù) 开门 (Kāi Mén) Kan 1　Yi Gui	值符 (Zhí Fú) 禽芮 (Qín Ruì) 惊门 (Jīng Mén) Qian 6　Ren/Ji Wu

Yin (阴) Dun# 6 Hour: JiYou；直符(ZhíFú): 天芮(TiānRuì)
直使(ZhíShǐ): 死门(SǐMén)；旬首(XúnShǒu): JiaChenRen

太阴 (Tài Yīn) 天辅 (Tiān Fǔ) 生门 (Shēng Mén) Xun 4　Geng Geng	腾蛇 (Téng Shé) 天英 (Tiān Yīng) 伤门 (Shāng Mén) Li 9　Ding Ding	值符 (Zhí Fú) 禽芮 (Qín Ruì) 杜门 (Dù Mén) Kun 2　Ren/Ji Ren/Ji
六合 (Liù Hé) 天冲 (Tiān Chōng) 休门 (Xiū Mén) Zhen 3　Xin Xin	Yin (阴) Dun# 6 Hour: JiYou **Fu Yin** ©Calvin Yap	九天 (Jiǔ Tiān) 天柱 (Tiān Zhù) 景门 (Jǐng Mén) Dui 7　Yi Yi
白虎 (Bái Hǔ) 天任 (Tiān Rèn) 开门 (Kāi Mén) Gen 8　Bing Bing	玄武 (Xuán Wǔ) 天蓬 (Tiān Péng) 惊门 (Jīng Mén) Kan 1　Gui Gui	九地 (Jiǔ Dì) 天心 (Tiān Xīn) 死门 (Sǐ Mén) Qian 6　Wu Wu

Yin (阴) Dun# 6 Hour: GengXu；直符(ZhíFú): 天芮(TiānRuì)
直使(ZhíShǐ): 死门(SǐMén)；旬首(XúnShǒu): JiaChenRen

值符 (Zhí Fú) 禽芮 (Qín Ruì) 杜门 (Dù Mén) Xun 4　Ren/Ji Geng	九天 (Jiǔ Tiān) 天柱 (Tiān Zhù) 景门 (Jǐng Mén) Li 9　Yi Ding	九地 (Jiǔ Dì) 天心 (Tiān Xīn) 死门 (Sǐ Mén) Kun 2　Wu Ren/Ji
腾蛇 (Téng Shé) 天英 (Tiān Yīng) 伤门 (Shāng Mén) Zhen 3　Ding Xin	Yin (阴) Dun# 6 Hour: GengXu ©Calvin Yap	玄武 (Xuán Wǔ) 天蓬 (Tiān Péng) 惊门 (Jīng Mén) Dui 7　Gui Yi
太阴 (Tài Yīn) 天辅 (Tiān Fǔ) 生门 (Shēng Mén) Gen 8　Geng Bing	六合 (Liù Hé) 天冲 (Tiān Chōng) 休门 (Xiū Mén) Kan 1　Xin Gui	白虎 (Bái Hǔ) 天任 (Tiān Rèn) 开门 (Kāi Mén) Qian 6　Bing Wu

Yin (阴) Dun# 6 Hour: XinHai；直符(ZhíFú): 天芮(TiānRuì)
直使(ZhíShǐ): 死门(SǐMén)；旬首(XúnShǒu): JiaChenRen

九天 (Jiǔ Tiān) 天柱 (Tiān Zhù) 死门 (Sǐ Mén) Xun 4　Yi Geng	九地 (Jiǔ Dì) 天心 (Tiān Xīn) 惊门 (Jīng Mén) Li 9　Wu Ding	玄武 (Xuán Wǔ) 天蓬 (Tiān Péng) 开门 (Kāi Mén) Kun 2　Gui Ren/Ji
值符 (Zhí Fú) 禽芮 (Qín Ruì) 景门 (Jǐng Mén) Zhen 3　Ren/Ji Xin	Yin (阴) Dun# 6 Hour: XinHai ©Calvin Yap	白虎 (Bái Hǔ) 天任 (Tiān Rèn) 休门 (Xiū Mén) Dui 7　Bing Yi
腾蛇 (Téng Shé) 天英 (Tiān Yīng) 杜门 (Dù Mén) Gen 8　Ding Bing	太阴 (Tài Yīn) 天辅 (Tiān Fǔ) 伤门 (Shāng Mén) Kan 1　Geng Gui	六合 (Liù Hé) 天冲 (Tiān Chōng) 生门 (Shēng Mén) Qian 6　Xin Wu

Yin (阴) Dun# 6 Hour: RenZi ; 直符(ZhíFú): 天芮(TiānRuì)
直使(ZhíShǐ): 死门(SǐMén) ; 旬首(XúnShǒu): JiaChenRen

太阴 (Tài Yīn) 天辅 (Tiān Fǔ) 惊门 (Jīng Mén) Xun 4　Geng Geng	螣蛇 (Téng Shé) 天英 (Tiān Yīng) 开门 (Kāi Mén) Li 9　Ding Ding	值符 (Zhí Fú) 禽芮 (Qín Ruì) 休门 (Xiū Mén) Kun 2　Ren/Ji Ren/Ji
六合 (Liù Hé) 天冲 (Tiān Chōng) 死门 (Sǐ Mén) Zhen 3　Xin Xin	Yin (阴) Dun# 6 Hour: **RenZi** **Fu Yin** ©Calvin Yap	九天 (Jiǔ Tiān) 天柱 (Tiān Zhù) 生门 (Shēng Mén) Dui 7　Yi Yi
白虎 (Bái Hǔ) 天任 (Tiān Rèn) 景门 (Jǐng Mén) Gen 8　Bing Bing	玄武 (Xuán Wǔ) 天蓬 (Tiān Péng) 杜门 (Dù Mén) Kan 1　Gui Gui	九地 (Jiǔ Dì) 天心 (Tiān Xīn) 伤门 (Shāng Mén) Qian 6　Wu Wu

Yin (阴) Dun# 6 Hour: GuiChou ; 直符(ZhíFú): 天芮(TiānRuì)
直使(ZhíShǐ): 死门(SǐMén) ; 旬首(XúnShǒu): JiaChenRen

玄武 (Xuán Wǔ) 天蓬 (Tiān Péng) 杜门 (Dù Mén) Xun 4　Gui Geng	白虎 (Bái Hǔ) 天任 (Tiān Rèn) 景门 (Jǐng Mén) Li 9　Bing Ding	六合 (Liù Hé) 天冲 (Tiān Chōng) 死门 (Sǐ Mén) Kun 2　Xin Ren/Ji
九地 (Jiǔ Dì) 天心 (Tiān Xīn) 伤门 (Shāng Mén) Zhen 3　Wu Xin	Yin (阴) Dun# 6 Hour: **GuiChou** ©Calvin Yap	太阴 (Tài Yīn) 天辅 (Tiān Fǔ) 惊门 (Jīng Mén) Dui 7　Geng Yi
九天 (Jiǔ Tiān) 天柱 (Tiān Zhù) 生门 (Shēng Mén) Gen 8　Yi Bing	值符 (Zhí Fú) 禽芮 (Qín Ruì) 休门 (Xiū Mén) Kan 1　Ren/Ji Gui	螣蛇 (Téng Shé) 天英 (Tiān Yīng) 开门 (Kāi Mén) Qian 6　Ding Wu

Chart: -6JiaYin (Yin Dun #6 JiaYin Xun)
JiaYin, YiMao, BingChen, DingSi, WuWu, JiWei, GengShen, XinYou, RenXu, GuiHai

Yin (阴) Dun# 6 Hour: JiaYin ; 直符(ZhíFú): 天蓬(TiānPéng)
直使(ZhíShǐ): 休门(XiūMén) ; 旬首(XúnShǒu): JiaYinGui

玄武 (Xuán Wǔ) 天辅 (Tiān Fǔ) 杜门 (Dù Mén) Xun 4　Geng Geng	白虎 (Bái Hǔ) 天英 (Tiān Yīng) 景门 (Jǐng Mén) Li 9　Ding Ding	六合 (Liù Hé) 禽芮 (Qín Ruì) 死门 (Sǐ Mén) Kun 2　Ren/Ji Ren/Ji
九地 (Jiǔ Dì) 天冲 (Tiān Chōng) 伤门 (Shāng Mén) Zhen 3　Xin Xin	Yin (阴) Dun# 6 Hour: **JiaYin** **Fu Yin** ©Calvin Yap	太阴 (Tài Yīn) 天柱 (Tiān Zhù) 惊门 (Jīng Mén) Dui 7　Yi Yi
九天 (Jiǔ Tiān) 天任 (Tiān Rèn) 生门 (Shēng Mén) Gen 8　Bing Bing	值符 (Zhí Fú) 天蓬 (Tiān Péng) 休门 (Xiū Mén) Kan 1　Gui Gui	螣蛇 (Téng Shé) 天心 (Tiān Xīn) 开门 (Kāi Mén) Qian 6　Wu Wu

Yin (阴) Dun# 6 Hour: YiMao ; 直符(ZhíFú): 天蓬(TiānPéng)
直使(ZhíShǐ): 休门(XiūMén) ; 旬首(XúnShǒu): JiaYinGui

六合 (Liù Hé) 禽芮 (Qín Ruì) 开门 (Kāi Mén) Xun 4　Ren/Ji Geng	太阴 (Tài Yīn) 天柱 (Tiān Zhù) 休门 (Xiū Mén) Li 9　Yi	螣蛇 (Téng Shé) 天心 (Tiān Xīn) 生门 (Shēng Mén) Kun 2　Wu Ren/Ji
白虎 (Bái Hǔ) 天英 (Tiān Yīng) 惊门 (Jīng Mén) Zhen 3　Ding Xin	Yin (阴) Dun# 6 Hour: **YiMao** ©Calvin Yap	值符 (Zhí Fú) 天蓬 (Tiān Péng) 伤门 (Shāng Mén) Dui 7　Gui Yi
玄武 (Xuán Wǔ) 天辅 (Tiān Fǔ) 死门 (Sǐ Mén) Gen 8　Geng Bing	九地 (Jiǔ Dì) 天冲 (Tiān Chōng) 景门 (Jǐng Mén) Kan 1　Xin Gui	九天 (Jiǔ Tiān) 天任 (Tiān Rèn) 杜门 (Dù Mén) Qian 6　Bing Wu

Yin (阴) Dun# 6 Hour: BingChen ; 直符(ZhíFú): 天蓬(TiānPéng)
直使(ZhíShǐ): 休门(XiūMén) ; 旬首(XúnShǒu): JiaYinGui

九地 (Jiǔ Dì) 天冲 (Tiān Chōng) 伤门 (Shāng Mén) Xun 4　Xin Geng	玄武 (Xuán Wǔ) 天辅 (Tiān Fǔ) 杜门 (Dù Mén) Li 9　Geng Ding	白虎 (Bái Hǔ) 天英 (Tiān Yīng) 景门 (Jǐng Mén) Kun 2　Ding Ren/Ji
九天 (Jiǔ Tiān) 天任 (Tiān Rèn) 生门 (Shēng Mén) Zhen 3　Bing Xin	Yin (阴) Dun# 6 Hour: **BingChen** ©Calvin Yap	六合 (Liù Hé) 禽芮 (Qín Ruì) 死门 (Sǐ Mén) Dui 7　Ren/Ji Yi
值符 (Zhí Fú) 天蓬 (Tiān Péng) 休门 (Xiū Mén) Gen 8　Gui Bing	螣蛇 (Téng Shé) 天心 (Tiān Xīn) 开门 (Kāi Mén) Kan 1　Wu Gui	太阴 (Tài Yīn) 天柱 (Tiān Zhù) 惊门 (Jīng Mén) Qian 6　Yi Wu

Yin (阴) Dun# 6 Hour: DingSi ; 直符(ZhíFú): 天蓬(TiānPéng)
直使(ZhíShǐ): 休门(XiūMén) ; 旬首(XúnShǒu): JiaYinGui

螣蛇 (Téng Shé) 天心 (Tiān Xīn) 死门 (Sǐ Mén) Xun 4　Wu Geng	值符 (Zhí Fú) 天蓬 (Tiān Péng) 惊门 (Jīng Mén) Li 9　Gui Ding	九天 (Jiǔ Tiān) 天任 (Tiān Rèn) 开门 (Kāi Mén) Kun 2　Bing Ren/Ji
太阴 (Tài Yīn) 天柱 (Tiān Zhù) 景门 (Jǐng Mén) Zhen 3　Yi Xin	Yin (阴) Dun# 6 Hour: **DingSi** **Fan Yin** ©Calvin Yap	九地 (Jiǔ Dì) 天冲 (Tiān Chōng) 休门 (Xiū Mén) Dui 7　Xin Yi
六合 (Liù Hé) 禽芮 (Qín Ruì) 杜门 (Dù Mén) Gen 8　Ren/Ji Bing	白虎 (Bái Hǔ) 天英 (Tiān Yīng) 伤门 (Shāng Mén) Kan 1　Ding Gui	玄武 (Xuán Wǔ) 天辅 (Tiān Fǔ) 生门 (Shēng Mén) Qian 6　Geng Wu

Yin (阴) Dun# 6 Hour: **WuWu**；直符(ZhíFú): 天蓬(TiānPéng)
直使(ZhíShǐ): 休门(XiūMén)；旬首(XúnShǒu): JiaYinGui

白虎 (Bái Hǔ) 天英 (Tiān Yīng) 景门 (Jǐng Mén) Xun 4　Ding Geng	六合 (Liù Hé) 禽芮 (Qín Ruì) 死门 (Sǐ Mén) Li 9　Ding	太阴 (Tài Yīn) 天柱 (Tiān Zhù) 惊门 (Jīng Mén) Kun 2　Yi Ren/Ji
玄武 (Xuán Wǔ) 天辅 (Tiān Fǔ) 杜门 (Dù Mén) Zhen 3　Geng Xin	Yin (阴) Dun# 6 Hour: **WuWu** ©Calvin Yap	螣蛇 (Téng Shé) 天心 (Tiān Xīn) 开门 (Kāi Mén) Dui 7　Wu Yi
九地 (Jiǔ Dì) 天冲 (Tiān Chōng) 伤门 (Shāng Mén) Gen 8　Xin Bing	九天 (Jiǔ Tiān) 天任 (Tiān Rèn) 生门 (Shēng Mén) Kan 1　Bing Gui	值符 (Zhí Fú) 天蓬 (Tiān Péng) 休门 (Xiū Mén) Qian 6　Gui Wu

Yin (阴) Dun# 6 Hour: **JiWei**；直符(ZhíFú): 天蓬(TiānPéng)
直使(ZhíShǐ): 休门(XiūMén)；旬首(XúnShǒu): JiaYinGui

太阴 (Tài Yīn) 天柱 (Tiān Zhù) 惊门 (Jīng Mén) Xun 4　Yi Geng	螣蛇 (Téng Shé) 天心 (Tiān Xīn) 开门 (Kāi Mén) Li 9　Wu	值符 (Zhí Fú) 天蓬 (Tiān Péng) 休门 (Xiū Mén) Kun 2　Gui Ren/Ji
六合 (Liù Hé) 禽芮 (Qín Ruì) 死门 (Sǐ Mén) Zhen 3　Ren/Ji Xin	Yin (阴) Dun# 6 Hour: **JiWei** ©Calvin Yap	九天 (Jiǔ Tiān) 天任 (Tiān Rèn) 生门 (Shēng Mén) Dui 7　Bing Yi
白虎 (Bái Hǔ) 天英 (Tiān Yīng) 景门 (Jǐng Mén) Gen 8　Ding Bing	玄武 (Xuán Wǔ) 天辅 (Tiān Fǔ) 杜门 (Dù Mén) Kan 1　Geng Gui	九地 (Jiǔ Dì) 天冲 (Tiān Chōng) 伤门 (Shāng Mén) Qian 6　Xin Wu

Yin (阴) Dun# 6 Hour: **GengShen**；直符(ZhíFú): 天蓬(TiānPéng)
直使(ZhíShǐ): 休门(XiūMén)；旬首(XúnShǒu): JiaYinGui

值符 (Zhí Fú) 天蓬 (Tiān Péng) 休门 (Xiū Mén) Xun 4　Gui Geng	九天 (Jiǔ Tiān) 天任 (Tiān Rèn) 生门 (Shēng Mén) Li 9　Bing Ding	九地 (Jiǔ Dì) 天冲 (Tiān Chōng) 伤门 (Shāng Mén) Kun 2　Xin Ren/Ji
螣蛇 (Téng Shé) 天心 (Tiān Xīn) 开门 (Kāi Mén) Zhen 3　Wu Xin	Yin (阴) Dun# 6 Hour: **GengShen** ©Calvin Yap	玄武 (Xuán Wǔ) 天辅 (Tiān Fǔ) 杜门 (Dù Mén) Dui 7　Geng Yi
太阴 (Tài Yīn) 天柱 (Tiān Zhù) 惊门 (Jīng Mén) Gen 8　Yi Bing	六合 (Liù Hé) 禽芮 (Qín Ruì) 死门 (Sǐ Mén) Kan 1　Ren/Ji Gui	白虎 (Bái Hǔ) 天英 (Tiān Yīng) 景门 (Jǐng Mén) Qian 6　Ding Wu

Yin (阴) Dun# 6 Hour: **XinYou**；直符(ZhíFú): 天蓬(TiānPéng)
直使(ZhíShǐ): 休门(XiūMén)；旬首(XúnShǒu): JiaYinGui

九天 (Jiǔ Tiān) 天任 (Tiān Rèn) 生门 (Shēng Mén) Xun 4　Bing Geng	九地 (Jiǔ Dì) 天冲 (Tiān Chōng) 伤门 (Shāng Mén) Li 9　Xin Ding	玄武 (Xuán Wǔ) 天辅 (Tiān Fǔ) 杜门 (Dù Mén) Kun 2　Geng Ren/Ji
值符 (Zhí Fú) 天蓬 (Tiān Péng) 休门 (Xiū Mén) Zhen 3　Gui Xin	Yin (阴) Dun# 6 Hour: **XinYou** ©Calvin Yap	白虎 (Bái Hǔ) 天英 (Tiān Yīng) 景门 (Jǐng Mén) Dui 7　Ding Yi
螣蛇 (Téng Shé) 天心 (Tiān Xīn) 开门 (Kāi Mén) Gen 8　Wu Bing	太阴 (Tài Yīn) 天柱 (Tiān Zhù) 惊门 (Jīng Mén) Kan 1　Yi Gui	六合 (Liù Hé) 禽芮 (Qín Ruì) 死门 (Sǐ Mén) Qian 6　Ren/Ji Wu

Yin (阴) Dun# 6 Hour: **RenXu**；直符(ZhíFú): 天蓬(TiānPéng)
直使(ZhíShǐ): 休门(XiūMén)；旬首(XúnShǒu): JiaYinGui

太阴 (Tài Yīn) 天柱 (Tiān Zhù) 惊门 (Jīng Mén) Xun 4　Yi Geng	螣蛇 (Téng Shé) 天心 (Tiān Xīn) 开门 (Kāi Mén) Li 9　Wu	值符 (Zhí Fú) 天蓬 (Tiān Péng) 休门 (Xiū Mén) Kun 2　Gui Ren/Ji
六合 (Liù Hé) 禽芮 (Qín Ruì) 死门 (Sǐ Mén) Zhen 3　Ren/Ji Xin	Yin (阴) Dun# 6 Hour: **RenXu** ©Calvin Yap	九天 (Jiǔ Tiān) 天任 (Tiān Rèn) 生门 (Shēng Mén) Dui 7　Bing Yi
白虎 (Bái Hǔ) 天英 (Tiān Yīng) 景门 (Jǐng Mén) Gen 8　Ding Bing	玄武 (Xuán Wǔ) 天辅 (Tiān Fǔ) 杜门 (Dù Mén) Kan 1　Geng Gui	九地 (Jiǔ Dì) 天冲 (Tiān Chōng) 伤门 (Shāng Mén) Qian 6　Xin Wu

Yin (阴) Dun# 6 Hour: **GuiHai**；直符(ZhíFú): 天蓬(TiānPéng)
直使(ZhíShǐ): 休门(XiūMén)；旬首(XúnShǒu): JiaYinGui

玄武 (Xuán Wǔ) 天辅 (Tiān Fǔ) 杜门 (Dù Mén) Xun 4　Geng Geng	白虎 (Bái Hǔ) 天英 (Tiān Yīng) 景门 (Jǐng Mén) Li 9　Ding	六合 (Liù Hé) 禽芮 (Qín Ruì) 死门 (Sǐ Mén) Kun 2　Ren/Ji Ren/Ji
九地 (Jiǔ Dì) 天冲 (Tiān Chōng) 伤门 (Shāng Mén) Zhen 3　Xin Xin	Yin (阴) Dun# 6 Hour: **GuiHai** **Fu Yin** ©Calvin Yap	太阴 (Tài Yīn) 天柱 (Tiān Zhù) 惊门 (Jīng Mén) Dui 7　Yi Yi
九天 (Jiǔ Tiān) 天任 (Tiān Rèn) 生门 (Shēng Mén) Gen 8　Bing Bing	值符 (Zhí Fú) 天蓬 (Tiān Péng) 休门 (Xiū Mén) Kan 1　Gui Gui	螣蛇 (Téng Shé) 天心 (Tiān Xīn) 开门 (Kāi Mén) Qian 6　Wu Wu

Yin Dun#7

Chart: **-7JiaZi** (Yin Dun #7 JiaZi Xun)
JiaZi, YiChou, BingYin, DingMao, WuChen, JiSi, GengWu, XinWei, RenShen, GuiYou

Yin (阴) Dun# 7 Hour: JiaZi ; 直符(ZhíFú): 天柱(TiānZhù)
直使(ZhíShǐ): 惊门(JīngMén) ; 句首(XúnShǒu): JiaZiWu

六合 (Liù Hé) 天辅 (Tiān Fǔ) 杜门 (Dù Mén) Xun 4　Xin Xin	太阴 (Tài Yīn) 天英 (Tiān Yīng) 景门 (Jǐng Mén) Li 9　Bing Bing	螣蛇 (Téng Shé) 禽芮 (Qín Ruì) 死门 (Sǐ Mén) Kun 2　Gui/Geng Gui/Geng
白虎 (Bái Hǔ) 天冲 (Tiān Chōng) 伤门 (Shāng Mén) Zhen 3　Ren Ren	Yin (阴) Dun# 7 Hour: **JiaZi** **Fu Yin** ©Calvin Yap	值符 (Zhí Fú) 天柱 (Tiān Zhù) 惊门 (Jīng Mén) Dui 7　Wu Wu
玄武 (Xuán Wǔ) 天任 (Tiān Rèn) 生门 (Shēng Mén) Gen 8　Yi Yi	九地 (Jiǔ Dì) 天蓬 (Tiān Péng) 休门 (Xiū Mén) Kan 1　Ding Ding	九天 (Jiǔ Tiān) 天心 (Tiān Xīn) 开门 (Kāi Mén) Qian 6　Ji Ji

Yin (阴) Dun# 7 Hour: YiChou ; 直符(ZhíFú): 天柱(TiānZhù)
直使(ZhíShǐ): 惊门(JīngMén) ; 句首(XúnShǒu): JiaZiWu

九地 (Jiǔ Dì) 天蓬 (Tiān Péng) 伤门 (Shāng Mén) Xun 4　Ding Xin	玄武 (Xuán Wǔ) 天任 (Tiān Rèn) 杜门 (Dù Mén) Li 9　Yi Bing	白虎 (Bái Hǔ) 天冲 (Tiān Chōng) 景门 (Jǐng Mén) Kun 2　Ren Gui/Geng
九天 (Jiǔ Tiān) 天心 (Tiān Xīn) 生门 (Shēng Mén) Zhen 3　Ji Ren	Yin (阴) Dun# 7 Hour: **YiChou** ©Calvin Yap	六合 (Liù Hé) 天辅 (Tiān Fǔ) 死门 (Sǐ Mén) Dui 7　Xin Wu
值符 (Zhí Fú) 天柱 (Tiān Zhù) 休门 (Xiū Mén) Gen 8　Wu Yi	螣蛇 (Téng Shé) 禽芮 (Qín Ruì) 开门 (Kāi Mén) Kan 1　Gui/Geng Ding	太阴 (Tài Yīn) 天英 (Tiān Yīng) 惊门 (Jīng Mén) Qian 6　Bing Ji

Yin (阴) Dun# 7 Hour: BingYin ; 直符(ZhíFú): 天柱(TiānZhù)
直使(ZhíShǐ): 惊门(JīngMén) ; 句首(XúnShǒu): JiaZiWu

螣蛇 (Téng Shé) 禽芮 (Qín Ruì) 景门 (Jǐng Mén) Xun 4　Gui/Geng Xin	值符 (Zhí Fú) 天柱 (Tiān Zhù) 死门 (Sǐ Mén) Li 9　Wu Bing	九天 (Jiǔ Tiān) 天心 (Tiān Xīn) 惊门 (Jīng Mén) Kun 2　Ji Gui/Geng
太阴 (Tài Yīn) 天英 (Tiān Yīng) 杜门 (Dù Mén) Zhen 3　Bing Ren	Yin (阴) Dun# 7 Hour: **BingYin** ©Calvin Yap	九地 (Jiǔ Dì) 天蓬 (Tiān Péng) 开门 (Kāi Mén) Dui 7　Ding Wu
六合 (Liù Hé) 天辅 (Tiān Fǔ) 伤门 (Shāng Mén) Gen 8　Xin Yi	白虎 (Bái Hǔ) 天冲 (Tiān Chōng) 生门 (Shēng Mén) Kan 1　Ren Ding	玄武 (Xuán Wǔ) 天任 (Tiān Rèn) 休门 (Xiū Mén) Qian 6　Yi Ji

Yin (阴) Dun# 7 Hour: DingMao ; 直符(ZhíFú): 天柱(TiānZhù)
直使(ZhíShǐ): 惊门(JīngMén) ; 句首(XúnShǒu): JiaZiWu

玄武 (Xuán Wǔ) 天任 (Tiān Rèn) 惊门 (Jīng Mén) Xun 4　Yi Xin	白虎 (Bái Hǔ) 天冲 (Tiān Chōng) 开门 (Kāi Mén) Li 9　Ren Bing	六合 (Liù Hé) 天辅 (Tiān Fǔ) 休门 (Xiū Mén) Kun 2　Xin Gui/Geng
九地 (Jiǔ Dì) 天蓬 (Tiān Péng) 死门 (Sǐ Mén) Zhen 3　Ding Ren	Yin (阴) Dun# 7 Hour: **DingMao** ©Calvin Yap	太阴 (Tài Yīn) 天英 (Tiān Yīng) 生门 (Shēng Mén) Dui 7　Bing Wu
九天 (Jiǔ Tiān) 天心 (Tiān Xīn) 景门 (Jǐng Mén) Gen 8　Ji Yi	值符 (Zhí Fú) 天柱 (Tiān Zhù) 杜门 (Dù Mén) Kan 1　Wu Ding	螣蛇 (Téng Shé) 禽芮 (Qín Ruì) 伤门 (Shāng Mén) Qian 6　Gui/Geng Ji

Yin (阴) Dun# 7 Hour: WuChen ; 直符(ZhíFú): 天柱(TiānZhù)
直使(ZhíShǐ): 惊门(JīngMén) ; 句首(XúnShǒu): JiaZiWu

六合 (Liù Hé) 天辅 (Tiān Fǔ) 开门 (Kāi Mén) Xun 4　Xin Xin	太阴 (Tài Yīn) 天英 (Tiān Yīng) 休门 (Xiū Mén) Li 9　Bing Bing	螣蛇 (Téng Shé) 禽芮 (Qín Ruì) 生门 (Shēng Mén) Kun 2　Gui/Geng Gui/Geng
白虎 (Bái Hǔ) 天冲 (Tiān Chōng) 惊门 (Jīng Mén) Zhen 3　Ren Ren	Yin (阴) Dun# 7 Hour: **WuChen** **Fu Yin** ©Calvin Yap	值符 (Zhí Fú) 天柱 (Tiān Zhù) 伤门 (Shāng Mén) Dui 7　Wu Wu
玄武 (Xuán Wǔ) 天任 (Tiān Rèn) 死门 (Sǐ Mén) Gen 8　Yi Yi	九地 (Jiǔ Dì) 天蓬 (Tiān Péng) 景门 (Jǐng Mén) Kan 1　Ding Ding	九天 (Jiǔ Tiān) 天心 (Tiān Xīn) 杜门 (Dù Mén) Qian 6　Ji Ji

Yin (阴) Dun# 7 Hour: JiSi ; 直符(ZhíFú): 天柱(TiānZhù)
直使(ZhíShǐ): 惊门(JīngMén) ; 句首(XúnShǒu): JiaZiWu

白虎 (Bái Hǔ) 天冲 (Tiān Chōng) 景门 (Jǐng Mén) Xun 4　Ren Xin	六合 (Liù Hé) 天辅 (Tiān Fǔ) 死门 (Sǐ Mén) Li 9　Xin Bing	太阴 (Tài Yīn) 天英 (Tiān Yīng) 惊门 (Jīng Mén) Kun 2　Bing Gui/Geng
玄武 (Xuán Wǔ) 天任 (Tiān Rèn) 杜门 (Dù Mén) Zhen 3　Yi Ren	Yin (阴) Dun# 7 Hour: **JiSi** ©Calvin Yap	螣蛇 (Téng Shé) 禽芮 (Qín Ruì) 开门 (Kāi Mén) Dui 7　Gui/Geng Wu
九地 (Jiǔ Dì) 天蓬 (Tiān Péng) 伤门 (Shāng Mén) Gen 8　Ding Yi	九天 (Jiǔ Tiān) 天心 (Tiān Xīn) 生门 (Shēng Mén) Kan 1　Ji Ding	值符 (Zhí Fú) 天柱 (Tiān Zhù) 休门 (Xiū Mén) Qian 6　Wu Ji

Yin (阴) Dun# 7 Hour: GengWu；直符(ZhíFú): 天柱(TiānZhù)
直使(ZhíShǐ): 惊门(JǐngMén)；旬首(XúnShǒu): JiaZiWu

太阴 (Tài Yīn) 天英 (Tiān Yīng) 生门 (Shēng Mén) Xun 4　Bing Xin	螣蛇 (Téng Shé) 禽芮 (Qín Ruì) 伤门 (Shāng Mén) Li 9　Gui/Geng Bing	值符 (Zhí Fú) 天柱 (Tiān Zhù) 杜门 (Dù Mén) Kun 2　Wu Gui/Geng
六合 (Liù Hé) 天辅 (Tiān Fǔ) 休门 (Xiū Mén) Zhen 3　Xin Ren	Yin (阴) Dun# 7 Hour: **GengWu** ©Calvin Yap	九天 (Jiǔ Tiān) 天心 (Tiān Xīn) 景门 (Jǐng Mén) Dui 7　Ji Wu
白虎 (Bái Hǔ) 天冲 (Tiān Chōng) 开门 (Kāi Mén) Gen 8　Ren Yi	玄武 (Xuán Wǔ) 天任 (Tiān Rèn) 惊门 (Jǐng Mén) Kan 1　Yi Ding	九地 (Jiǔ Dì) 天蓬 (Tiān Péng) 死门 (Sǐ Mén) Qian 6　Ding Ji

Yin (阴) Dun# 7 Hour: XinWei；直符(ZhíFú): 天柱(TiānZhù)
直使(ZhíShǐ): 惊门(JǐngMén)；旬首(XúnShǒu): JiaZiWu

值符 (Zhí Fú) 天柱 (Tiān Zhù) 死门 (Sǐ Mén) Xun 4　Wu Xin	九天 (Jiǔ Tiān) 天心 (Tiān Xīn) 惊门 (Jǐng Mén) Li 9　Ji Bing	九地 (Jiǔ Dì) 天蓬 (Tiān Péng) 开门 (Kāi Mén) Kun 2　Ding Gui/Geng
螣蛇 (Téng Shé) 禽芮 (Qín Ruì) 景门 (Jǐng Mén) Zhen 3　Gui/Geng Ren	Yin (阴) Dun# 7 Hour: **XinWei** ©Calvin Yap	玄武 (Xuán Wǔ) 天任 (Tiān Rèn) 休门 (Xiū Mén) Dui 7　Yi Wu
太阴 (Tài Yīn) 天英 (Tiān Yīng) 杜门 (Dù Mén) Gen 8　Bing Yi	六合 (Liù Hé) 天辅 (Tiān Fǔ) 伤门 (Shāng Mén) Kan 1　Xin Ding	白虎 (Bái Hǔ) 天冲 (Tiān Chōng) 生门 (Shēng Mén) Qian 6　Ren Ji

Yin (阴) Dun# 7 Hour: RenShen；直符(ZhíFú): 天柱(TiānZhù)
直使(ZhíShǐ): 惊门(JǐngMén)；旬首(XúnShǒu): JiaZiWu

九天 (Jiǔ Tiān) 天心 (Tiān Xīn) 休门 (Xiū Mén) Xun 4　Ji Xin	九地 (Jiǔ Dì) 天蓬 (Tiān Péng) 生门 (Shēng Mén) Li 9　Ding Bing	玄武 (Xuán Wǔ) 天任 (Tiān Rèn) 伤门 (Shāng Mén) Kun 2　Yi Gui/Geng
值符 (Zhí Fú) 天柱 (Tiān Zhù) 开门 (Kāi Mén) Zhen 3　Wu Ren	Yin (阴) Dun# 7 Hour: **RenShen** **Fan Yin** ©Calvin Yap	白虎 (Bái Hǔ) 天冲 (Tiān Chōng) 杜门 (Dù Mén) Dui 7　Ren Wu
螣蛇 (Téng Shé) 禽芮 (Qín Ruì) 惊门 (Jǐng Mén) Gen 8　Gui/Geng Yi	太阴 (Tài Yīn) 天英 (Tiān Yīng) 死门 (Sǐ Mén) Kan 1　Bing Ding	六合 (Liù Hé) 天辅 (Tiān Fǔ) 景门 (Jǐng Mén) Qian 6　Xin Ji

Yin (阴) Dun# 7 Hour: GuiYou；直符(ZhíFú): 天柱(TiānZhù)
直使(ZhíShǐ): 惊门(JǐngMén)；旬首(XúnShǒu): JiaZiWu

太阴 (Tài Yīn) 天英 (Tiān Yīng) 杜门 (Dù Mén) Xun 4　Bing Xin	螣蛇 (Téng Shé) 禽芮 (Qín Ruì) 景门 (Jǐng Mén) Li 9　Gui/Geng Bing	值符 (Zhí Fú) 天柱 (Tiān Zhù) 死门 (Sǐ Mén) Kun 2　Wu Gui/Geng
六合 (Liù Hé) 天辅 (Tiān Fǔ) 伤门 (Shāng Mén) Zhen 3　Xin Ren	Yin (阴) Dun# 7 Hour: **GuiYou** ©Calvin Yap	九天 (Jiǔ Tiān) 天心 (Tiān Xīn) 惊门 (Jǐng Mén) Dui 7　Ji Wu
白虎 (Bái Hǔ) 天冲 (Tiān Chōng) 生门 (Shēng Mén) Gen 8　Ren Yi	玄武 (Xuán Wǔ) 天任 (Tiān Rèn) 休门 (Xiū Mén) Kan 1　Yi Ding	九地 (Jiǔ Dì) 天蓬 (Tiān Péng) 开门 (Kāi Mén) Qian 6　Ding Ji

Chart: -7JiaXu (Yin Dun #7 JiaXu Xun)
JiaXu, YiHai, BingZi, DingChou, WuYin, JiMao, GengChen, XinSi, RenWu, GuiWei

Yin (阴) Dun# 7 Hour: JiaXu；直符(ZhíFú): 天心(TiānXīn)
直使(ZhíShǐ): 开门(KāiMén)；旬首(XúnShǒu): JiaXuJi

白虎 (Bái Hǔ) 天辅 (Tiān Fǔ) 杜门 (Dù Mén) Xun 4　Xin Xin	六合 (Liù Hé) 天英 (Tiān Yīng) 景门 (Jǐng Mén) Li 9　Bing Bing	太阴 (Tài Yīn) 禽芮 (Qín Ruì) 死门 (Sǐ Mén) Kun 2　Gui/Geng Gui/Geng
玄武 (Xuán Wǔ) 天冲 (Tiān Chōng) 伤门 (Shāng Mén) Zhen 3　Ren Ren	Yin (阴) Dun# 7 Hour: **JiaXu** **Fu Yin** ©Calvin Yap	螣蛇 (Téng Shé) 天柱 (Tiān Zhù) 惊门 (Jǐng Mén) Dui 7　Wu Wu
九地 (Jiǔ Dì) 天任 (Tiān Rèn) 生门 (Shēng Mén) Gen 8　Yi Yi	九天 (Jiǔ Tiān) 天蓬 (Tiān Péng) 休门 (Xiū Mén) Kan 1　Ding Ding	值符 (Zhí Fú) 天心 (Tiān Xīn) 开门 (Kāi Mén) Qian 6　Ji Ji

Yin (阴) Dun# 7 Hour: YiHai；直符(ZhíFú): 天心(TiānXīn)
直使(ZhíShǐ): 开门(KāiMén)；旬首(XúnShǒu): JiaXuJi

九地 (Jiǔ Dì) 天任 (Tiān Rèn) 死门 (Sǐ Mén) Xun 4　Yi Xin	玄武 (Xuán Wǔ) 天冲 (Tiān Chōng) 惊门 (Jǐng Mén) Li 9　Ren Bing	白虎 (Bái Hǔ) 天辅 (Tiān Fǔ) 开门 (Kāi Mén) Kun 2　Xin Gui/Geng
九天 (Jiǔ Tiān) 天蓬 (Tiān Péng) 景门 (Jǐng Mén) Zhen 3　Ding Ren	Yin (阴) Dun# 7 Hour: **YiHai** ©Calvin Yap	六合 (Liù Hé) 天英 (Tiān Yīng) 休门 (Xiū Mén) Dui 7　Bing Wu
值符 (Zhí Fú) 天心 (Tiān Xīn) 杜门 (Dù Mén) Gen 8　Ji Yi	螣蛇 (Téng Shé) 天柱 (Tiān Zhù) 伤门 (Shāng Mén) Kan 1　Wu Ding	太阴 (Tài Yīn) 禽芮 (Qín Ruì) 生门 (Shēng Mén) Qian 6　Gui/Geng Ji

Yin (阴) Dun# 7 Hour: **BingZi**；直符(ZhíFú): 天心(TiānXīn)
直使(ZhíShǐ): 开门(KāiMén)；旬首(XúnShǒu): JiaXuJi

腾蛇 (Téng Shé) 天柱 (Tiān Zhù) 开门 (Kāi Mén) Xun 4　Wu Xin	值符 (Zhí Fú) 天心 (Tiān Xīn) 休门 (Xiū Mén) Li 9　Ji Bing	九天 (Jiǔ Tiān) 天蓬 (Tiān Péng) 生门 (Shēng Mén) Kun 2　Ding Gui/Geng
太阴 (Tài Yīn) 禽芮 (Qín Ruì) 惊门 (Jīng Mén) Zhen 3　Gui/Geng Ren	Yin (阴) Dun# 7 Hour: **BingZi** ©Calvin Yap	九地 (Jiǔ Dì) 天任 (Tiān Rèn) 伤门 (Shāng Mén) Dui 7　Yi Wu
六合 (Liù Hé) 天英 (Tiān Yīng) 死门 (Sǐ Mén) Gen 8　Bing Yi	白虎 (Bái Hǔ) 天辅 (Tiān Fǔ) 景门 (Jǐng Mén) Kan 1　Xin Ding	玄武 (Xuán Wǔ) 天冲 (Tiān Chōng) 杜门 (Dù Mén) Qian 6　Ren Ji

Yin (阴) Dun# 7 Hour: **DingChou**；直符(ZhíFú): 天心(TiānXīn)
直使(ZhíShǐ): 开门(KāiMén)；旬首(XúnShǒu): JiaXuJi

玄武 (Xuán Wǔ) 天冲 (Tiān Chōng) 休门 (Xiū Mén) Xun 4　Ren Xin	白虎 (Bái Hǔ) 天辅 (Tiān Fǔ) 生门 (Shēng Mén) Li 9　Xin Bing	六合 (Liù Hé) 天英 (Tiān Yīng) 伤门 (Shāng Mén) Kun 2　Bing Gui/Geng
九地 (Jiǔ Dì) 天任 (Tiān Rèn) 开门 (Kāi Mén) Zhen 3　Yi Ren	Yin (阴) Dun# 7 Hour: **DingChou** ©Calvin Yap	太阴 (Tài Yīn) 禽芮 (Qín Ruì) 杜门 (Dù Mén) Dui 7　Gui/Geng Wu
九天 (Jiǔ Tiān) 天蓬 (Tiān Péng) 惊门 (Jīng Mén) Gen 8　Ding Yi	值符 (Zhí Fú) 天心 (Tiān Xīn) 死门 (Sǐ Mén) Kan 1　Ji Ding	腾蛇 (Téng Shé) 天柱 (Tiān Zhù) 景门 (Jǐng Mén) Qian 6　Wu Ji

Yin (阴) Dun# 7 Hour: **WuYin**；直符(ZhíFú): 天心(TiānXīn)
直使(ZhíShǐ): 开门(KāiMén)；旬首(XúnShǒu): JiaXuJi

六合 (Liù Hé) 天英 (Tiān Yīng) 死门 (Sǐ Mén) Xun 4　Bing Xin	太阴 (Tài Yīn) 禽芮 (Qín Ruì) 惊门 (Jīng Mén) Li 9　Gui/Geng Bing	腾蛇 (Téng Shé) 天柱 (Tiān Zhù) 开门 (Kāi Mén) Kun 2　Wu Gui/Geng
白虎 (Bái Hǔ) 天辅 (Tiān Fǔ) 景门 (Jǐng Mén) Zhen 3　Xin Ren	Yin (阴) Dun# 7 Hour: **WuYin** ©Calvin Yap	值符 (Zhí Fú) 天心 (Tiān Xīn) 休门 (Xiū Mén) Dui 7　Ji Wu
玄武 (Xuán Wǔ) 天冲 (Tiān Chōng) 杜门 (Dù Mén) Gen 8　Ren Yi	九地 (Jiǔ Dì) 天任 (Tiān Rèn) 伤门 (Shāng Mén) Kan 1　Yi Ding	九天 (Jiǔ Tiān) 天蓬 (Tiān Péng) 生门 (Shēng Mén) Qian 6　Ding Ji

Yin (阴) Dun# 7 Hour: **JiMao**；直符(ZhíFú): 天心(TiānXīn)
直使(ZhíShǐ): 开门(KāiMén)；旬首(XúnShǒu): JiaXuJi

白虎 (Bái Hǔ) 天辅 (Tiān Fǔ) 伤门 (Shāng Mén) Xun 4　Xin Xin	六合 (Liù Hé) 天英 (Tiān Yīng) 杜门 (Dù Mén) Li 9　Bing Bing	太阴 (Tài Yīn) 禽芮 (Qín Ruì) 景门 (Jǐng Mén) Kun 2　Gui/Geng Gui/Geng
玄武 (Xuán Wǔ) 天冲 (Tiān Chōng) 生门 (Shēng Mén) Zhen 3　Ren Ren	Yin (阴) Dun# 7 Hour: **JiMao** **Fu Yin** ©Calvin Yap	腾蛇 (Téng Shé) 天柱 (Tiān Zhù) 死门 (Sǐ Mén) Dui 7　Wu Wu
九地 (Jiǔ Dì) 天任 (Tiān Rèn) 休门 (Xiū Mén) Gen 8　Yi Yi	九天 (Jiǔ Tiān) 天蓬 (Tiān Péng) 开门 (Kāi Mén) Kan 1　Ding Ding	值符 (Zhí Fú) 天心 (Tiān Xīn) 惊门 (Jīng Mén) Qian 6　Ji Ji

Yin (阴) Dun# 7 Hour: **GengChen**；直符(ZhíFú): 天心(TiānXīn)
直使(ZhíShǐ): 开门(KāiMén)；旬首(XúnShǒu): JiaXuJi

太阴 (Tài Yīn) 禽芮 (Qín Ruì) 惊门 (Jīng Mén) Xun 4　Gui/Geng Xin	腾蛇 (Téng Shé) 天柱 (Tiān Zhù) 开门 (Kāi Mén) Li 9　Wu Bing	值符 (Zhí Fú) 天心 (Tiān Xīn) 休门 (Xiū Mén) Kun 2　Ji Gui/Geng
六合 (Liù Hé) 天英 (Tiān Yīng) 死门 (Sǐ Mén) Zhen 3　Bing Ren	Yin (阴) Dun# 7 Hour: **GengChen** ©Calvin Yap	九天 (Jiǔ Tiān) 天蓬 (Tiān Péng) 生门 (Shēng Mén) Dui 7　Ding Wu
白虎 (Bái Hǔ) 天辅 (Tiān Fǔ) 景门 (Jǐng Mén) Gen 8　Xin Yi	玄武 (Xuán Wǔ) 天冲 (Tiān Chōng) 杜门 (Dù Mén) Kan 1　Ren Ding	九地 (Jiǔ Dì) 天任 (Tiān Rèn) 伤门 (Shāng Mén) Qian 6　Yi Ji

Yin (阴) Dun# 7 Hour: **XinSi**；直符(ZhíFú): 天心(TiānXīn)
直使(ZhíShǐ): 开门(KāiMén)；旬首(XúnShǒu): JiaXuJi

值符 (Zhí Fú) 天心 (Tiān Xīn) 生门 (Shēng Mén) Xun 4　Ji Xin	九天 (Jiǔ Tiān) 天蓬 (Tiān Péng) 伤门 (Shāng Mén) Li 9　Ding Bing	九地 (Jiǔ Dì) 天任 (Tiān Rèn) 杜门 (Dù Mén) Kun 2　Yi Gui/Geng
腾蛇 (Téng Shé) 天柱 (Tiān Zhù) 休门 (Xiū Mén) Zhen 3　Wu Ren	Yin (阴) Dun# 7 Hour: **XinSi** **Fan Yin** ©Calvin Yap	玄武 (Xuán Wǔ) 天冲 (Tiān Chōng) 景门 (Jǐng Mén) Dui 7　Ren Wu
太阴 (Tài Yīn) 禽芮 (Qín Ruì) 开门 (Kāi Mén) Gen 8　Gui/Geng Yi	六合 (Liù Hé) 天英 (Tiān Yīng) 惊门 (Jīng Mén) Kan 1　Bing Ding	白虎 (Bái Hǔ) 天辅 (Tiān Fǔ) 死门 (Sǐ Mén) Qian 6　Xin Ji

Yin (阴) Dun# 7 Hour: **RenWu** ; 直符(ZhíFú): 天心(TiānXīn)
直使(ZhíShǐ): 开门(KāiMén) ; 旬首(XúnShǒu): JiaXuJi

九天 (Jiǔ Tiān) 天蓬 (Tiān Péng) 景门 (Jǐng Mén) Xun 4 — Ding / Xin	九地 (Jiǔ Dì) 天任 (Tiān Rèn) 死门 (Sǐ Mén) Li 9 — Yi / Bing	玄武(Xuán Wǔ) 天冲 (Tiān Chōng) 惊门 (Jīng Mén) Kun 2 — Ren / Gui/Geng
值符 (Zhí Fú) 天心 (Tiān Xīn) 杜门 (Dù Mén) Zhen 3 — Ji / Ren	Yin (阴) Dun# 7 Hour: **RenWu** ©Calvin Yap	白虎 (Bái Hǔ) 天辅 (Tiān Fǔ) 开门 (Kāi Mén) Dui 7 — Xin / Wu
螣蛇 (Téng Shé) 天柱 (Tiān Zhù) 伤门 (Shāng Mén) Gen 8 — Wu / Yi	太阴 (Tài Yīn) 禽芮 (Qín Ruì) 生门 (Shēng Mén) Kan 1 — Gui/Geng / Ding	六合 (Liù Hé) 天英 (Tiān Yīng) 休门 (Xiū Mén) Qian 6 — Bing / Ji

Yin (阴) Dun# 7 Hour: **GuiWei** ; 直符(ZhíFú): 天心(TiānXīn)
直使(ZhíShǐ): 开门(KāiMén) ; 旬首(XúnShǒu): JiaXuJi

太阴 (Tài Yīn) 禽芮 (Qín Ruì) 杜门 (Dù Mén) Xun 4 — Gui/Geng / Xin	螣蛇 (Téng Shé) 天柱 (Tiān Zhù) 景门 (Jǐng Mén) Li 9 — Wu / Bing	值符 (Zhí Fú) 天心 (Tiān Xīn) 死门 (Sǐ Mén) Kun 2 — Ji / Gui/Geng
六合 (Liù Hé) 天英 (Tiān Yīng) 伤门 (Shāng Mén) Zhen 3 — Bing / Ren	Yin (阴) Dun# 7 Hour: **GuiWei** ©Calvin Yap	九天 (Jiǔ Tiān) 天蓬 (Tiān Péng) 惊门 (Jīng Mén) Dui 7 — Ding / Wu
白虎 (Bái Hǔ) 天辅 (Tiān Fǔ) 生门 (Shēng Mén) Gen 8 — Xin / Yi	玄武 (Xuán Wǔ) 天冲 (Tiān Chōng) 休门 (Xiū Mén) Kan 1 — Ren / Ding	九地 (Jiǔ Dì) 天任 (Tiān Rèn) 开门 (Kāi Mén) Qian 6 — Yi / Ji

---

Chart: -7JiaShen (Yin Dun #7 JiaShen Xun)
JiaShen, YiYou, BingXu, DingHai, WuZi, JiChou, GengYin, XinMao, RenChen, GuiSi

Yin (阴) Dun# 7 Hour: **JiaShen** ; 直符(ZhíFú): 天禽(TiānQín)
直使(ZhíShǐ): 死门(SǐMén) ; 旬首(XúnShǒu): JiaShenGeng

太阴 (Tài Yīn) 天辅 (Tiān Fǔ) 杜门 (Dù Mén) Xun 4 — Xin / Xin	螣蛇 (Téng Shé) 天英 (Tiān Yīng) 景门 (Jǐng Mén) Li 9 — Bing / Bing	值符 (Zhí Fú) 禽芮 (Qín Ruì) 死门 (Sǐ Mén) Kun 2 — Gui/Geng / Gui/Geng
六合 (Liù Hé) 天冲 (Tiān Chōng) 伤门 (Shāng Mén) Zhen 3 — Ren / Ren	Yin (阴) Dun# 7 Hour: **JiaShen** **Fu Yin** ©Calvin Yap	九天 (Jiǔ Tiān) 天柱 (Tiān Zhù) 惊门 (Jīng Mén) Dui 7 — Wu / Wu
白虎 (Bái Hǔ) 天任 (Tiān Rèn) 生门 (Shēng Mén) Gen 8 — Yi / Yi	玄武 (Xuán Wǔ) 天蓬 (Tiān Péng) 休门 (Xiū Mén) Kan 1 — Ding / Ding	九地 (Jiǔ Dì) 天心 (Tiān Xīn) 开门 (Kāi Mén) Qian 6 — Ji / Ji

Yin (阴) Dun# 7 Hour: **YiYou** ; 直符(ZhíFú): 天禽(TiānQín)
直使(ZhíShǐ): 死门(SǐMén) ; 旬首(XúnShǒu): JiaShenGeng

九地 (Jiǔ Dì) 天心 (Tiān Xīn) 死门 (Sǐ Mén) Xun 4 — Ji / Xin	玄武 (Xuán Wǔ) 天蓬 (Tiān Péng) 惊门 (Jīng Mén) Li 9 — Ding / Bing	白虎 (Bái Hǔ) 天任 (Tiān Rèn) 开门 (Kāi Mén) Kun 2 — Yi / Gui/Geng
九天 (Jiǔ Tiān) 天柱 (Tiān Zhù) 景门 (Jǐng Mén) Zhen 3 — Wu / Ren	Yin (阴) Dun# 7 Hour: **YiYou** **Fan Yin** ©Calvin Yap	六合 (Liù Hé) 天冲 (Tiān Chōng) 休门 (Xiū Mén) Dui 7 — Ren / Wu
值符 (Zhí Fú) 禽芮 (Qín Ruì) 杜门 (Dù Mén) Gen 8 — Gui/Geng / Yi	螣蛇 (Téng Shé) 天英 (Tiān Yīng) 伤门 (Shāng Mén) Kan 1 — Bing / Ding	太阴 (Tài Yīn) 天辅 (Tiān Fǔ) 生门 (Shēng Mén) Qian 6 — Xin / Ji

Yin (阴) Dun# 7 Hour: **BingXu** ; 直符(ZhíFú): 天禽(TiānQín)
直使(ZhíShǐ): 死门(SǐMén) ; 旬首(XúnShǒu): JiaShenGeng

螣蛇 (Téng Shé) 天英 (Tiān Yīng) 惊门 (Jīng Mén) Xun 4 — Bing / Xin	值符 (Zhí Fú) 禽芮 (Qín Ruì) 开门 (Kāi Mén) Li 9 — Gui/Geng / Bing	九天 (Jiǔ Tiān) 天柱 (Tiān Zhù) 休门 (Xiū Mén) Kun 2 — Wu / Gui/Geng
太阴 (Tài Yīn) 天辅 (Tiān Fǔ) 死门 (Sǐ Mén) Zhen 3 — Xin / Ren	Yin (阴) Dun# 7 Hour: **BingXu** ©Calvin Yap	九地 (Jiǔ Dì) 天心 (Tiān Xīn) 生门 (Shēng Mén) Dui 7 — Ji / Wu
六合 (Liù Hé) 天冲 (Tiān Chōng) 景门 (Jǐng Mén) Gen 8 — Ren / Yi	白虎 (Bái Hǔ) 天任 (Tiān Rèn) 杜门 (Dù Mén) Kan 1 — Yi / Ding	玄武 (Xuán Wǔ) 天蓬 (Tiān Péng) 伤门 (Shāng Mén) Qian 6 — Ding / Ji

Yin (阴) Dun# 7 Hour: **DingHai** ; 直符(ZhíFú): 天禽(TiānQín)
直使(ZhíShǐ): 死门(SǐMén) ; 旬首(XúnShǒu): JiaShenGeng

玄武 (Xuán Wǔ) 天蓬 (Tiān Péng) 杜门 (Dù Mén) Xun 4 — Ding / Xin	白虎 (Bái Hǔ) 天任 (Tiān Rèn) 景门 (Jǐng Mén) Li 9 — Yi / Bing	六合 (Liù Hé) 天冲 (Tiān Chōng) 死门 (Sǐ Mén) Kun 2 — Ren / Gui/Geng
九地 (Jiǔ Dì) 天心 (Tiān Xīn) 伤门 (Shāng Mén) Zhen 3 — Ji / Ren	Yin (阴) Dun# 7 Hour: **DingHai** ©Calvin Yap	太阴 (Tài Yīn) 天辅 (Tiān Fǔ) 惊门 (Jīng Mén) Dui 7 — Xin / Wu
九天 (Jiǔ Tiān) 天柱 (Tiān Zhù) 生门 (Shēng Mén) Gen 8 — Wu / Yi	值符 (Zhí Fú) 禽芮 (Qín Ruì) 休门 (Xiū Mén) Kan 1 — Gui/Geng / Ding	螣蛇 (Téng Shé) 天英 (Tiān Yīng) 开门 (Kāi Mén) Qian 6 — Bing / Ji

Yin (阴) Dun# 7 Hour: **WuZi**；直符(ZhíFú): 天禽(TiānQín)
直使(ZhíShǐ): 死门(SǐMén)；旬首(XúnShǒu): JiaShenGeng

六合 (Liù Hé) 天冲 (Tiān Chōng) 休门 (Xiū Mén) Xun 4　Ren　Xin	太阴 (Tài Yīn) 天辅 (Tiān Fǔ) 生门 (Shēng Mén) Li 9　Xin　Bing	螣蛇 (Téng Shé) 天英 (Tiān Yīng) 伤门 (Shāng Mén) Kun 2　Bing　Gui/Geng
白虎 (Bái Hǔ) 天任 (Tiān Rèn) 开门 (Kāi Mén) Zhen 3　Yi　Ren	Yin (阴) Dun# 7 Hour: **WuZi** ©Calvin Yap	值符 (Zhí Fú) 禽芮 (Qín Ruì) 杜门 (Dù Mén) Dui 7　Gui/Geng　Wu
玄武 (Xuán Wǔ) 天蓬 (Tiān Péng) 惊门 (Jīng Mén) Gen 8　Ding　Yi	九地 (Jiǔ Dì) 天心 (Tiān Xīn) 死门 (Sǐ Mén) Kan 1　Ji　Ding	九天 (Jiǔ Tiān) 天柱 (Tiān Zhù) 景门 (Jǐng Mén) Qian 6　Wu　Ji

Yin (阴) Dun# 7 Hour: **JiChou**；直符(ZhíFú): 天禽(TiānQín)
直使(ZhíShǐ): 死门(SǐMén)；旬首(XúnShǒu): JiaShenGeng

白虎 (Bái Hǔ) 天任 (Tiān Rèn) 景门 (Jǐng Mén) Xun 4　Yi　Xin	六合 (Liù Hé) 天冲 (Tiān Chōng) 死门 (Sǐ Mén) Li 9　Ren　Bing	太阴 (Tài Yīn) 天辅 (Tiān Fǔ) 惊门 (Jīng Mén) Kun 2　Xin　Gui/Geng
玄武 (Xuán Wǔ) 天蓬 (Tiān Péng) 杜门 (Dù Mén) Zhen 3　Ding　Ren	Yin (阴) Dun# 7 Hour: **JiChou** ©Calvin Yap	螣蛇 (Téng Shé) 天英 (Tiān Yīng) 开门 (Kāi Mén) Dui 7　Bing　Wu
九地 (Jiǔ Dì) 天柱 (Tiān Zhù) 伤门 (Shāng Mén) Gen 8　Ji　Yi	九天 (Jiǔ Tiān) 天心 (Tiān Xīn) 生门 (Shēng Mén) Kan 1　Wu　Ding	值符 (Zhí Fú) 禽芮 (Qín Ruì) 休门 (Xiū Mén) Qian 6　Gui/Geng　Ji

Yin (阴) Dun# 7 Hour: **GengYin**；直符(ZhíFú): 天禽(TiānQín)
直使(ZhíShǐ): 死门(SǐMén)；旬首(XúnShǒu): JiaShenGeng

太阴 (Tài Yīn) 天辅 (Tiān Fǔ) 开门 (Kāi Mén) Xun 4　Xin　Xin	螣蛇 (Téng Shé) 天英 (Tiān Yīng) 休门 (Xiū Mén) Li 9　Bing　Bing	值符 (Zhí Fú) 禽芮 (Qín Ruì) 生门 (Shēng Mén) Kun 2　Gui/Geng　Gui/Geng
六合 (Liù Hé) 天冲 (Tiān Chōng) 惊门 (Jīng Mén) Zhen 3　Ren　Ren	Yin (阴) Dun# 7 Hour: **GengYin** **Fu Yin** ©Calvin Yap	九天 (Jiǔ Tiān) 天柱 (Tiān Zhù) 伤门 (Shāng Mén) Dui 7　Wu　Wu
白虎 (Bái Hǔ) 天任 (Tiān Rèn) 死门 (Sǐ Mén) Gen 8　Yi　Yi	玄武 (Xuán Wǔ) 天蓬 (Tiān Péng) 景门 (Jǐng Mén) Kan 1　Ding　Ding	九地 (Jiǔ Dì) 天心 (Tiān Xīn) 杜门 (Dù Mén) Qian 6　Ji　Ji

Yin (阴) Dun# 7 Hour: **XinMao**；直符(ZhíFú): 天禽(TiānQín)
直使(ZhíShǐ): 死门(SǐMén)；旬首(XúnShǒu): JiaShenGeng

值符 (Zhí Fú) 禽芮 (Qín Ruì) 伤门 (Shāng Mén) Xun 4　Gui/Geng　Xin	九天 (Jiǔ Tiān) 天柱 (Tiān Zhù) 杜门 (Dù Mén) Li 9　Wu　Bing	九地 (Jiǔ Dì) 天心 (Tiān Xīn) 景门 (Jǐng Mén) Kun 2　Ji　Gui/Geng
螣蛇 (Téng Shé) 天英 (Tiān Yīng) 生门 (Shēng Mén) Zhen 3　Bing　Ren	Yin (阴) Dun# 7 Hour: **XinMao** ©Calvin Yap	玄武 (Xuán Wǔ) 天蓬 (Tiān Péng) 死门 (Sǐ Mén) Dui 7　Ding　Wu
太阴 (Tài Yīn) 天辅 (Tiān Fǔ) 休门 (Xiū Mén) Gen 8　Xin　Yi	六合 (Liù Hé) 天冲 (Tiān Chōng) 开门 (Kāi Mén) Kan 1　Ren　Ding	白虎 (Bái Hǔ) 天任 (Tiān Rèn) 惊门 (Jīng Mén) Qian 6　Yi　Ji

Yin (阴) Dun# 7 Hour: **RenChen**；直符(ZhíFú): 天禽(TiānQín)
直使(ZhíShǐ): 死门(SǐMén)；旬首(XúnShǒu): JiaShenGeng

九天 (Jiǔ Tiān) 天柱 (Tiān Zhù) 生门 (Shēng Mén) Xun 4　Wu　Xin	九地 (Jiǔ Dì) 天心 (Tiān Xīn) 伤门 (Shāng Mén) Li 9　Ji　Bing	玄武 (Xuán Wǔ) 天蓬 (Tiān Péng) 杜门 (Dù Mén) Kun 2　Ding　Gui/Geng
值符 (Zhí Fú) 禽芮 (Qín Ruì) 休门 (Xiū Mén) Zhen 3　Gui/Geng　Ren	Yin (阴) Dun# 7 Hour: **RenChen** ©Calvin Yap	白虎 (Bái Hǔ) 天任 (Tiān Rèn) 景门 (Jǐng Mén) Dui 7　Yi　Wu
螣蛇 (Téng Shé) 天英 (Tiān Yīng) 开门 (Kāi Mén) Gen 8　Bing　Yi	太阴 (Tài Yīn) 天辅 (Tiān Fǔ) 惊门 (Jīng Mén) Kan 1　Xin　Ding	六合 (Liù Hé) 天冲 (Tiān Chōng) 死门 (Sǐ Mén) Qian 6　Ren　Ji

Yin (阴) Dun# 7 Hour: **GuiSi**；直符(ZhíFú): 天禽(TiānQín)
直使(ZhíShǐ): 死门(SǐMén)；旬首(XúnShǒu): JiaShenGeng

太阴 (Tài Yīn) 天辅 (Tiān Fǔ) 杜门 (Dù Mén) Xun 4　Xin　Xin	螣蛇 (Téng Shé) 天英 (Tiān Yīng) 景门 (Jǐng Mén) Li 9　Bing　Bing	值符 (Zhí Fú) 禽芮 (Qín Ruì) 死门 (Sǐ Mén) Kun 2　Gui/Geng　Gui/Geng
六合 (Liù Hé) 天冲 (Tiān Chōng) 伤门 (Shāng Mén) Zhen 3　Ren　Ren	Yin (阴) Dun# 7 Hour: **GuiSi** **Fu Yin** ©Calvin Yap	九天 (Jiǔ Tiān) 天柱 (Tiān Zhù) 惊门 (Jīng Mén) Dui 7　Wu　Wu
白虎 (Bái Hǔ) 天任 (Tiān Rèn) 生门 (Shēng Mén) Gen 8　Yi　Yi	玄武 (Xuán Wǔ) 天蓬 (Tiān Péng) 休门 (Xiū Mén) Kan 1　Ding　Ding	九地 (Jiǔ Dì) 天心 (Tiān Xīn) 开门 (Kāi Mén) Qian 6　Ji　Ji

Chart: **-7JiaWu** (Yin Dun #7 JiaWu Xun)
JiaWu, YiWei, BingShen, DingYou, WuXu, JiHai, GengZi, XinChou, RenYin, GuiMao

Yin (阴) Dun# 7 Hour: **JiaWu**；直符(ZhíFú): 天辅(TiānFǔ)
直使(ZhíShǐ): 杜门(DùMén)；旬首(XúnShǒu): JiaWu/Xin

值符 (Zhí Fú) 天辅 (Tiān Fǔ) 杜门 (Dù Mén) Xun 4　Xin Xin	九天 (Jiǔ Tiān) 天英 (Tiān Yīng) 景门 (Jǐng Mén) Li 9　Bing Bing	九地 (Jiǔ Dì) 禽芮 (Qín Ruì) 死门 (Sǐ Mén) Kun 2　Gui/Geng Gui/Geng
腾蛇 (Téng Shé) 天冲 (Tiān Chōng) 伤门 (Shāng Mén) Zhen 3　Ren Ren	Yin (阴) Dun# 7 Hour: **JiaWu** **Fu Yin** ©Calvin Yap	玄武 (Xuán Wǔ) 天柱 (Tiān Zhù) 惊门 (Jīng Mén) Dui 7　Wu Wu
太阴 (Tài Yīn) 天任 (Tiān Rèn) 生门 (Shēng Mén) Gen 8　Yi Yi	六合 (Liù Hé) 天蓬 (Tiān Péng) 休门 (Xiū Mén) Kan 1　Ding Ding	白虎 (Bái Hǔ) 天心 (Tiān Xīn) 开门 (Kāi Mén) Qian 6　Ji Ji

Yin (阴) Dun# 7 Hour: **YiWei**；直符(ZhíFú): 天辅(TiānFǔ)
直使(ZhíShǐ): 杜门(DùMén)；旬首(XúnShǒu): JiaWu/Xin

九地 (Jiǔ Dì) 禽芮 (Qín Ruì) 景门 (Jǐng Mén) Xun 4　Gui/Geng Xin	玄武 (Xuán Wǔ) 天柱 (Tiān Zhù) 死门 (Sǐ Mén) Li 9　Wu	白虎 (Bái Hǔ) 天心 (Tiān Xīn) 惊门 (Jīng Mén) Kun 2　Ji Gui/Geng
九天 (Jiǔ Tiān) 天英 (Tiān Yīng) 杜门 (Dù Mén) Zhen 3　Bing Ren	Yin (阴) Dun# 7 Hour: **YiWei** ©Calvin Yap	六合 (Liù Hé) 天蓬 (Tiān Péng) 开门 (Kāi Mén) Dui 7　Ding Wu
值符 (Zhí Fú) 天辅 (Tiān Fǔ) 伤门 (Shāng Mén) Gen 8　Xin	腾蛇 (Téng Shé) 天冲 (Tiān Chōng) 生门 (Shēng Mén) Kan 1　Ren Ding	太阴 (Tài Yīn) 天任 (Tiān Rèn) 休门 (Xiū Mén) Qian 6　Yi Ji

Yin (阴) Dun# 7 Hour: **BingShen**；直符(ZhíFú): 天辅(TiānFǔ)
直使(ZhíShǐ): 杜门(DùMén)；旬首(XúnShǒu): JiaWu/Xin

腾蛇 (Téng Shé) 天冲 (Tiān Chōng) 生门 (Shēng Mén) Xun 4　Ren Xin	值符 (Zhí Fú) 天辅 (Tiān Fǔ) 伤门 (Shāng Mén) Li 9　Xin Bing	九天 (Jiǔ Tiān) 天英 (Tiān Yīng) 杜门 (Dù Mén) Kun 2　Bing Gui/Geng
太阴 (Tài Yīn) 天任 (Tiān Rèn) 休门 (Xiū Mén) Zhen 3　Yi Ren	Yin (阴) Dun# 7 Hour: **BingShen** ©Calvin Yap	九地 (Jiǔ Dì) 禽芮 (Qín Ruì) 景门 (Jǐng Mén) Dui 7　Gui/Geng Wu
六合 (Liù Hé) 天蓬 (Tiān Péng) 开门 (Kāi Mén) Gen 8　Ding Yi	白虎 (Bái Hǔ) 天心 (Tiān Xīn) 惊门 (Jīng Mén) Kan 1　Ji Ding	玄武 (Xuán Wǔ) 天柱 (Tiān Zhù) 死门 (Sǐ Mén) Qian 6　Wu Ji

Yin (阴) Dun# 7 Hour: **DingYou**；直符(ZhíFú): 天辅(TiānFǔ)
直使(ZhíShǐ): 杜门(DùMén)；旬首(XúnShǒu): JiaWu/Xin

玄武 (Xuán Wǔ) 天柱 (Tiān Zhù) 惊门 (Jīng Mén) Xun 4　Wu Xin	白虎 (Bái Hǔ) 天心 (Tiān Xīn) 开门 (Kāi Mén) Li 9　Ji Bing	六合 (Liù Hé) 天蓬 (Tiān Péng) 休门 (Xiū Mén) Kun 2　Ding Gui/Geng
九地 (Jiǔ Dì) 禽芮 (Qín Ruì) 死门 (Sǐ Mén) Zhen 3　Gui/Geng Ren	Yin (阴) Dun# 7 Hour: **DingYou** ©Calvin Yap	太阴 (Tài Yīn) 天任 (Tiān Rèn) 生门 (Shēng Mén) Dui 7　Yi Wu
九天 (Jiǔ Tiān) 天英 (Tiān Yīng) 景门 (Jǐng Mén) Gen 8　Bing Yi	值符 (Zhí Fú) 天辅 (Tiān Fǔ) 杜门 (Dù Mén) Kan 1　Xin Ding	腾蛇 (Téng Shé) 天冲 (Tiān Chōng) 伤门 (Shāng Mén) Qian 6　Ren Ji

Yin (阴) Dun# 7 Hour: **WuXu**；直符(ZhíFú): 天辅(TiānFǔ)
直使(ZhíShǐ): 杜门(DùMén)；旬首(XúnShǒu): JiaWu/Xin

六合 (Liù Hé) 天蓬 (Tiān Péng) 伤门 (Shāng Mén) Xun 4　Ding Xin	太阴 (Tài Yīn) 天任 (Tiān Rèn) 杜门 (Dù Mén) Li 9　Yi Bing	腾蛇 (Téng Shé) 天冲 (Tiān Chōng) 景门 (Jǐng Mén) Kun 2　Ren Gui/Geng
白虎 (Bái Hǔ) 天心 (Tiān Xīn) 生门 (Shēng Mén) Zhen 3　Ji Ren	Yin (阴) Dun# 7 Hour: **WuXu** ©Calvin Yap	值符 (Zhí Fú) 天辅 (Tiān Fǔ) 死门 (Sǐ Mén) Dui 7　Xin Wu
玄武 (Xuán Wǔ) 天柱 (Tiān Zhù) 休门 (Xiū Mén) Gen 8　Wu Yi	九地 (Jiǔ Dì) 禽芮 (Qín Ruì) 开门 (Kāi Mén) Kan 1　Gui/Geng Ding	九天 (Jiǔ Tiān) 天英 (Tiān Yīng) 惊门 (Jīng Mén) Qian 6　Bing Ji

Yin (阴) Dun# 7 Hour: **JiHai**；直符(ZhíFú): 天辅(TiānFǔ)
直使(ZhíShǐ): 杜门(DùMén)；旬首(XúnShǒu): JiaWu/Xin

白虎 (Bái Hǔ) 天心 (Tiān Xīn) 死门 (Sǐ Mén) Xun 4　Ji Xin	六合 (Liù Hé) 天蓬 (Tiān Péng) 惊门 (Jīng Mén) Li 9　Ding Bing	太阴 (Tài Yīn) 天任 (Tiān Rèn) 开门 (Kāi Mén) Kun 2　Yi Gui/Geng
玄武 (Xuán Wǔ) 天柱 (Tiān Zhù) 景门 (Jǐng Mén) Zhen 3　Wu Ren	Yin (阴) Dun# 7 Hour: **JiHai** **Fan Yin** ©Calvin Yap	腾蛇 (Téng Shé) 天冲 (Tiān Chōng) 休门 (Xiū Mén) Dui 7　Ren Wu
九地 (Jiǔ Dì) 禽芮 (Qín Ruì) 杜门 (Dù Mén) Gen 8　Gui/Geng Yi	九天 (Jiǔ Tiān) 天英 (Tiān Yīng) 伤门 (Shāng Mén) Kan 1　Bing Ding	值符 (Zhí Fú) 天辅 (Tiān Fǔ) 生门 (Shēng Mén) Qian 6　Xin Ji

Yin (阴) Dun# 7 Hour: GengZi ；直符(ZhíFú): 天辅(TiānFǔ)
直使(ZhíShǐ): 杜门(DùMén) ；旬首(XúnShǒu): JiaWu/Xin

太阴 (Tài Yīn) 天任 (Tiān Rèn) 休门 (Xiū Mén) Xun 4　Yi Xin	螣蛇 (Téng Shé) 天冲 (Tiān Chōng) 生门 (Shēng Mén) Li 9　Ren	值符 (Zhi Fú) 天辅 (Tiān Fǔ) 伤门 (Shāng Mén) Kun 2　Xin Bing　Gui/Geng
六合 (Liù Hé) 天蓬 (Tiān Péng) 开门 (Kāi Mén) Zhen 3　Ding Ren	Yin (阴) Dun# 7 Hour: **GengZi** ©Calvin Yap	九天 (Jiǔ Tiān) 天英 (Tiān Yīng) 杜门 (Dù Mén) Dui 7　Bing Wu
白虎 (Bái Hǔ) 天心 (Tiān Xīn) 惊门 (Jīng Mén) Gen 8　Ji Yi	玄武 (Xuán Wǔ) 天柱 (Tiān Zhù) 死门 (Sǐ Mén) Kan 1　Wu Ding	九地 (Jiǔ Dì) 禽芮 (Qín Ruì) 景门 (Jǐng Mén) Qian 6 Gui/Geng Ji

Yin (阴) Dun# 7 Hour: XinChou ；直符(ZhíFú): 天辅(TiānFǔ)
直使(ZhíShǐ): 杜门(DùMén) ；旬首(XúnShǒu): JiaWu/Xin

值符 (Zhi Fú) 天辅 (Tiān Fǔ) 开门 (Kāi Mén) Xun 4　Xin Xin	九天 (Jiǔ Tiān) 天英 (Tiān Yīng) 休门 (Xiū Mén) Li 9　Bing	九地 (Jiǔ Dì) 禽芮 (Qín Ruì) 生门 (Shēng Mén) Kun 2　Gui/Geng Gui/Geng
螣蛇 (Téng Shé) 天冲 (Tiān Chōng) 惊门 (Jīng Mén) Zhen 3　Ren Ren	Yin (阴) Dun# 7 Hour: **XinChou** **Fu Yin** ©Calvin Yap	玄武 (Xuán Wǔ) 天柱 (Tiān Zhù) 伤门 (Shāng Mén) Dui 7　Wu Wu
太阴 (Tài Yīn) 天任 (Tiān Rèn) 死门 (Sǐ Mén) Gen 8　Yi Yi	六合 (Liù Hé) 天蓬 (Tiān Péng) 景门 (Jǐng Mén) Kan 1　Ding Ding	白虎 (Bái Hǔ) 天心 (Tiān Xīn) 杜门 (Dù Mén) Qian 6　Ji Ji

Yin (阴) Dun# 7 Hour: RenYin ；直符(ZhíFú): 天辅(TiānFǔ)
直使(ZhíShǐ): 杜门(DùMén) ；旬首(XúnShǒu): JiaWu/Xin

九天 (Jiǔ Tiān) 天英 (Tiān Yīng) 生门 (Shēng Mén) Xun 4　Bing Xin	九地 (Jiǔ Dì) 禽芮 (Qín Ruì) 伤门 (Shāng Mén) Li 9　Gui/Geng Bing	玄武 (Xuán Wǔ) 天柱 (Tiān Zhù) 杜门 (Dù Mén) Kun 2　Wu Gui/Geng
值符 (Zhi Fú) 天辅 (Tiān Fǔ) 休门 (Xiū Mén) Zhen 3　Xin Ren	Yin (阴) Dun# 7 Hour: **RenYin** ©Calvin Yap	白虎 (Bái Hǔ) 天心 (Tiān Xīn) 景门 (Jǐng Mén) Dui 7　Ji Wu
螣蛇 (Téng Shé) 天冲 (Tiān Chōng) 开门 (Kāi Mén) Gen 8　Ren Yi	太阴 (Tài Yīn) 天任 (Tiān Rèn) 惊门 (Jīng Mén) Kan 1　Yi Ding	六合 (Liù Hé) 天蓬 (Tiān Péng) 死门 (Sǐ Mén) Qian 6　Ding Ji

Yin (阴) Dun# 7 Hour: GuiMao ；直符(ZhíFú): 天辅(TiānFǔ)
直使(ZhíShǐ): 杜门(DùMén) ；旬首(XúnShǒu): JiaWu/Xin

太阴 (Tài Yīn) 天任 (Tiān Rèn) 杜门 (Dù Mén) Xun 4　Yi Xin	螣蛇 (Téng Shé) 天冲 (Tiān Chōng) 景门 (Jǐng Mén) Li 9　Ren	值符 (Zhi Fú) 天辅 (Tiān Fǔ) 死门 (Sǐ Mén) Kun 2　Xin Gui/Geng
六合 (Liù Hé) 天蓬 (Tiān Péng) 伤门 (Shāng Mén) Zhen 3　Ding Ren	Yin (阴) Dun# 7 Hour: **GuiMao** ©Calvin Yap	九天 (Jiǔ Tiān) 天英 (Tiān Yīng) 惊门 (Jīng Mén) Dui 7　Bing Wu
白虎 (Bái Hǔ) 天心 (Tiān Xīn) 生门 (Shēng Mén) Gen 8　Ji Yi	玄武 (Xuán Wǔ) 天柱 (Tiān Zhù) 休门 (Xiū Mén) Kan 1　Wu Ding	九地 (Jiǔ Dì) 禽芮 (Qín Ruì) 开门 (Kāi Mén) Qian 6 Gui/Geng Ji

Chart: -7JiaChen (Yin Dun #7 JiaChen Xun)
JiaChen, YiSi, BingWu, DingWei, WuShen, JiYou, GengXu, XinHai, RenZi, GuiChou

Yin (阴) Dun# 7 Hour: JiaChen ；直符(ZhíFú): 天冲(TiānChōng)
直使(ZhíShǐ): 伤门(ShāngMén) ；旬首(XúnShǒu): JiaChenRen

九天 (Jiǔ Tiān) 天辅 (Tiān Fǔ) 杜门 (Dù Mén) Xun 4　Xin Xin	九地 (Jiǔ Dì) 天英 (Tiān Yīng) 景门 (Jǐng Mén) Li 9　Bing Bing	玄武 (Xuán Wǔ) 禽芮 (Qín Ruì) 死门 (Sǐ Mén) Kun 2　Gui/Geng Gui/Geng
值符 (Zhi Fú) 天冲 (Tiān Chōng) 伤门 (Shāng Mén) Zhen 3　Ren Ren	Yin (阴) Dun# 7 Hour: **JiaChen** **Fu Yin** ©Calvin Yap	白虎 (Bái Hǔ) 天柱 (Tiān Zhù) 惊门 (Jīng Mén) Dui 7　Wu Wu
螣蛇 (Téng Shé) 天任 (Tiān Rèn) 生门 (Shēng Mén) Gen 8　Yi Yi	太阴 (Tài Yīn) 天蓬 (Tiān Péng) 休门 (Xiū Mén) Kan 1　Ding Ding	六合 (Liù Hé) 天心 (Tiān Xīn) 开门 (Kāi Mén) Qian 6　Ji Ji

Yin (阴) Dun# 7 Hour: YiSi ；直符(ZhíFú): 天冲(TiānChōng)
直使(ZhíShǐ): 伤门(ShāngMén) ；旬首(XúnShǒu): JiaChenRen

九地 (Jiǔ Dì) 天英 (Tiān Yīng) 休门 (Xiū Mén) Xun 4　Bing Xin	玄武 (Xuán Wǔ) 禽芮 (Qín Ruì) 生门 (Shēng Mén) Li 9　Gui/Geng Bing	白虎 (Bái Hǔ) 天柱 (Tiān Zhù) 伤门 (Shāng Mén) Kun 2　Wu Gui/Geng
九天 (Jiǔ Tiān) 天辅 (Tiān Fǔ) 开门 (Kāi Mén) Zhen 3　Xin Ren	Yin (阴) Dun# 7 Hour: **YiSi** ©Calvin Yap	六合 (Liù Hé) 天心 (Tiān Xīn) 杜门 (Dù Mén) Dui 7　Ji Wu
值符 (Zhi Fú) 天冲 (Tiān Chōng) 惊门 (Jīng Mén) Gen 8　Ren Yi	螣蛇 (Téng Shé) 天任 (Tiān Rèn) 死门 (Sǐ Mén) Kan 1　Yi Ding	太阴 (Tài Yīn) 天蓬 (Tiān Péng) 景门 (Jǐng Mén) Qian 6　Ding Ji

Yin (阴) Dun# 7 Hour: BingWu ; 直符(ZhíFú): 天冲(TiānChōng)
直使(ZhíShǐ): 伤门(ShāngMén) ; 旬首(XúnShǒu): JiaChenRen

螣蛇 (Téng Shé) 天任 (Tiān Rèn) 死门 (Sǐ Mén) Xun 4　　Yi　Xin	值符 (Zhí Fú) 天冲 (Tiān Chōng) 惊门 (Jīng Mén) Li 9　　Ren	九天 (Jiǔ Tiān) 天辅 (Tiān Fǔ) 开门 (Kāi Mén) Kun 2　Xin　Gui/Geng
太阴 (Tài Yīn) 天蓬 (Tiān Péng) 景门 (Jǐng Mén) Zhen 3　Ding　Ren	Yin (阴) Dun# 7 Hour: **BingWu** ©Calvin Yap	九地 (Jiǔ Dì) 天英 (Tiān Yīng) 休门 (Xiū Mén) Dui 7　Bing　Wu
六合 (Liù Hé) 天心 (Tiān Xīn) 杜门 (Dù Mén) Gen 8　Ji　Yi	白虎 (Bái Hǔ) 天柱 (Tiān Zhù) 伤门 (Shāng Mén) Kan 1　Wu　Ding	玄武 (Xuán Wǔ) 禽芮 (Qín Ruì) 生门 (Shēng Mén) Qian 6　Gui/Geng　Ji

Yin (阴) Dun# 7 Hour: DingWei ; 直符(ZhíFú): 天冲(TiānChōng)
直使(ZhíShǐ): 伤门(ShāngMén) ; 旬首(XúnShǒu): JiaChenRen

玄武 (Xuán Wǔ) 禽芮 (Qín Ruì) 生门 (Shēng Mén) Xun 4　Gui/Geng　Xin	白虎 (Bái Hǔ) 天柱 (Tiān Zhù) 伤门 (Shāng Mén) Li 9　Wu　Bing	六合 (Liù Hé) 天心 (Tiān Xīn) 杜门 (Dù Mén) Kun 2　Ji　Gui/Geng
九地 (Jiǔ Dì) 天英 (Tiān Yīng) 休门 (Xiū Mén) Zhen 3　Bing　Ren	Yin (阴) Dun# 7 Hour: **DingWei** ©Calvin Yap	太阴 (Tài Yīn) 天蓬 (Tiān Péng) 景门 (Jǐng Mén) Dui 7　Ding　Wu
九天 (Jiǔ Tiān) 天辅 (Tiān Fǔ) 开门 (Kāi Mén) Gen 8　Xin　Yi	值符 (Zhí Fú) 天冲 (Tiān Chōng) 惊门 (Jīng Mén) Kan 1　Ren　Ding	螣蛇 (Téng Shé) 天任 (Tiān Rèn) 死门 (Sǐ Mén) Qian 6　Yi　Ji

Yin (阴) Dun# 7 Hour: WuShen ; 直符(ZhíFú): 天冲(TiānChōng)
直使(ZhíShǐ): 伤门(ShāngMén) ; 旬首(XúnShǒu): JiaChenRen

六合 (Liù Hé) 天心 (Tiān Xīn) 景门 (Jǐng Mén) Xun 4　Ji　Xin	太阴 (Tài Yīn) 天蓬 (Tiān Péng) 死门 (Sǐ Mén) Li 9　Ding　Bing	螣蛇 (Téng Shé) 天任 (Tiān Rèn) 惊门 (Jīng Mén) Kùn 2　Yi　Gui/Geng
白虎 (Bái Hǔ) 天柱 (Tiān Zhù) 杜门 (Dù Mén) Zhen 3　Wu　Ren	Yin (阴) Dun# 7 Hour: **WuShen** **Fan Yin** ©Calvin Yap	值符 (Zhí Fú) 天冲 (Tiān Chōng) 开门 (Kāi Mén) Dui 7　Ren　Wu
玄武(Xuán Wǔ) 禽芮 (Qín Ruì) 伤门 (Shāng Mén) Gen 8　Gui/Geng　Yi	九地 (Jiǔ Dì) 天英 (Tiān Yīng) 生门 (Shēng Mén) Kan 1　Bing　Ding	九天 (Jiǔ Tiān) 天辅 (Tiān Fǔ) 休门 (Xiū Mén) Qian 6　Xin　Ji

Yin (阴) Dun# 7 Hour: JiYou ; 直符(ZhíFú): 天冲(TiānChōng)
直使(ZhíShǐ): 伤门(ShāngMén) ; 旬首(XúnShǒu): JiaChenRen

白虎 (Bái Hǔ) 天柱 (Tiān Zhù) 开门 (Kāi Mén) Xun 4　Wu　Xin	六合 (Liù Hé) 天心 (Tiān Xīn) 休门 (Xiū Mén) Li 9　Ji　Bing	太阴 (Tài Yīn) 天蓬 (Tiān Péng) 生门 (Shēng Mén) Kun 2　Ding　Gui/Geng
玄武 (Xuán Wǔ) 禽芮 (Qín Ruì) 惊门 (Jīng Mén) Zhen 3　Gui/Geng　Ren	Yin (阴) Dun# 7 Hour: **JiYou** ©Calvin Yap	螣蛇 (Téng Shé) 天任 (Tiān Rèn) 伤门 (Shāng Mén) Dui 7　Yi　Wu
九地 (Jiǔ Dì) 天英 (Tiān Yīng) 死门 (Sǐ Mén) Gen 8　Bing　Yi	九天 (Jiǔ Tiān) 天辅 (Tiān Fǔ) 景门 (Jǐng Mén) Kan 1　Xin　Ding	值符 (Zhí Fú) 天冲 (Tiān Chōng) 杜门 (Dù Mén) Qian 6　Ren　Ji

Yin (阴) Dun# 7 Hour: GengXu ; 直符(ZhíFú): 天冲(TiānChōng)
直使(ZhíShǐ): 伤门(ShāngMén) ; 旬首(XúnShǒu): JiaChenRen

太阴 (Tài Yīn) 天蓬 (Tiān Péng) 惊门 (Jīng Mén) Xun 4　Ding　Xin	螣蛇 (Téng Shé) 天任 (Tiān Rèn) 开门 (Kāi Mén) Li 9　Yi　Bing	值符 (Zhí Fú) 天冲 (Tiān Chōng) 休门 (Xiū Mén) Kun 2　Ren　Gui/Geng
六合 (Liù Hé) 天心 (Tiān Xīn) 死门 (Sǐ Mén) Zhen 3　Ji　Ren	Yin (阴) Dun# 7 Hour: **GengXu** ©Calvin Yap	九天 (Jiǔ Tiān) 天辅 (Tiān Fǔ) 生门 (Shēng Mén) Dui 7　Xin　Wu
白虎 (Bái Hǔ) 天柱 (Tiān Zhù) 景门 (Jǐng Mén) Gen 8　Wu　Yi	玄武 (Xuán Wǔ) 禽芮 (Qín Ruì) 杜门 (Dù Mén) Kan 1　Gui/Geng　Ding	九地 (Jiǔ Dì) 天英 (Tiān Yīng) 伤门 (Shāng Mén) Qian 6　Bing　Ji

Yin (阴) Dun# 7 Hour: XinHai ; 直符(ZhíFú): 天冲(TiānChōng)
直使(ZhíShǐ): 伤门(ShāngMén) ; 旬首(XúnShǒu): JiaChenRen

值符 (Zhí Fú) 天冲 (Tiān Chōng) 休门 (Xiū Mén) Xun 4　Ren　Xin	九天 (Jiǔ Tiān) 天辅 (Tiān Fǔ) 生门 (Shēng Mén) Li 9　Xin　Bing	九地 (Jiǔ Dì) 天英 (Tiān Yīng) 伤门 (Shāng Mén) Kun 2　Bing　Gui/Geng
螣蛇 (Téng Shé) 天任 (Tiān Rèn) 开门 (Kāi Mén) Zhen 3　Yi　Ren	Yin (阴) Dun# 7 Hour: **XinHai** ©Calvin Yap	玄武 (Xuán Wǔ) 禽芮 (Qín Ruì) 杜门 (Dù Mén) Dui 7　Gui/Geng　Wu
太阴 (Tài Yīn) 天蓬 (Tiān Péng) 惊门 (Jīng Mén) Gen 8　Ding　Yi	六合 (Liù Hé) 天心 (Tiān Xīn) 死门 (Sǐ Mén) Kan 1　Ji　Ding	白虎 (Bái Hǔ) 天柱 (Tiān Zhù) 景门 (Jǐng Mén) Qian 6　Wu　Ji

Yin (阴) Dun# 7 Hour: RenZi；直符(ZhíFú): 天冲(TiānChōng)
直使(ZhíShǐ): 伤门(ShāngMén)；旬首(XúnShǒu): JiaChenRen

九天 (Jiǔ Tiān) 天辅 (Tiān Fǔ) 伤门 (Shāng Mén) Xun 4　　Xin 　　　Xin	九地 (Jiǔ Dì) 天英 (Tiān Yīng) 杜门 (Dù Mén) Li 9　　Bing 　　　Bing	玄武 (Xuán Wǔ) 禽芮 (Qín Ruì) 景门 (Jǐng Mén) Kun 2　Gui/Geng 　　　Gui/Geng
值符 (Zhí Fú) 天冲 (Tiān Chōng) 生门 (Shēng Mén) Zhen 3　Ren 　　　Ren	Yin (阴) Dun# 7 Hour: **RenZi** **Fu Yin** ©Calvin Yap	白虎 (Bái Hǔ) 天柱 (Tiān Zhù) 死门 (Sǐ Mén) Dui 7　　Wu 　　　Wu
腾蛇 (Téng Shé) 天任 (Tiān Rèn) 休门 (Xiū Mén) Gen 8　　Yi 　　　Yi	太阴 (Tài Yīn) 天蓬 (Tiān Péng) 开门 (Kāi Mén) Kan 1　　Ding 　　　Ding	六合 (Liù Hé) 天心 (Tiān Xīn) 惊门 (Jīng Mén) Qian 6　　Ji 　　　Ji

Yin (阴) Dun# 7 Hour: GuiChou；直符(ZhíFú): 冲(TiānChōng)
直使(ZhíShǐ): 伤门(ShāngMén)；旬首(XúnShǒu): JiaChenRen

太阴 (Tài Yīn) 天蓬 (Tiān Péng) 杜门 (Dù Mén) Xun 4　　Ding 　　　Xin	腾蛇 (Téng Shé) 天任 (Tiān Rèn) 景门 (Jǐng Mén) Li 9　　Yi 　　　Bing	值符 (Zhí Fú) 天冲 (Tiān Chōng) 死门 (Sǐ Mén) Kun 2　　Ren 　　　Gui/Geng
六合 (Liù Hé) 天心 (Tiān Xīn) 伤门 (Shāng Mén) Zhen 3　Ji 　　　Ren	Yin (阴) Dun# 7 Hour: **GuiChou** ©Calvin Yap	九天 (Jiǔ Tiān) 天辅 (Tiān Fǔ) 惊门 (Jīng Mén) Dui 7　　Xin 　　　Wu
白虎 (Bái Hǔ) 天柱 (Tiān Zhù) 生门 (Shēng Mén) Gen 8　　Wu 　　　Yi	玄武 (Xuán Wǔ) 禽芮 (Qín Ruì) 休门 (Xiū Mén) Kan 1　Gui/Geng 　　　Ding	九地 (Jiǔ Dì) 天英 (Tiān Yīng) 开门 (Kāi Mén) Qian 6　　Bing 　　　Ji

---

Chart: -7JiaYin (Yin Dun #7 JiaYin Xun)
JiaYin, YiMao, BingChen, DingSi, WuWu, JiWei, GengShen, XinYou, RenXu, GuiHai

Yin (阴) Dun# 7 Hour: JiaYin；直符(ZhíFú): 天芮(TiānRuì)
直使(ZhíShǐ): 死门(SǐMén)；旬首(XúnShǒu): JiaYinGui

太阴 (Tài Yīn) 天辅 (Tiān Fǔ) 杜门 (Dù Mén) Xun 4　　Xin 　　　Xin	腾蛇 (Téng Shé) 天英 (Tiān Yīng) 景门 (Jǐng Mén) Li 9　　Bing 　　　Bing	值符 (Zhí Fú) 禽芮 (Qín Ruì) 死门 (Sǐ Mén) Kun 2　Gui/Geng 　　　Gui/Geng
六合 (Liù Hé) 天冲 (Tiān Chōng) 伤门 (Shāng Mén) Zhen 3　Ren 　　　Ren	Yin (阴) Dun# 7 Hour: **JiaYin** **Fu Yin** ©Calvin Yap	九天 (Jiǔ Tiān) 天柱 (Tiān Zhù) 惊门 (Jīng Mén) Dui 7　　Wu 　　　Wu
白虎 (Bái Hǔ) 天任 (Tiān Rèn) 生门 (Shēng Mén) Gen 8　　Yi 　　　Yi	玄武 (Xuán Wǔ) 天蓬 (Tiān Péng) 休门 (Xiū Mén) Kan 1　　Ding 　　　Ding	九地 (Jiǔ Dì) 天心 (Tiān Xīn) 开门 (Kāi Mén) Qian 6　　Ji 　　　Ji

Yin (阴) Dun# 7 Hour: YiMao；直符(ZhíFú): 天芮(TiānRuì)
直使(ZhíShǐ): 死门(SǐMén)；旬首(XúnShǒu): JiaYinGui

九地 (Jiǔ Dì) 天心 (Tiān Xīn) 休门 (Xiū Mén) Xun 4　　Ji 　　　Xin	玄武 (Xuán Wǔ) 天蓬 (Tiān Péng) 生门 (Shēng Mén) Li 9　　Ding 　　　Bing	白虎 (Bái Hǔ) 天任 (Tiān Rèn) 伤门 (Shāng Mén) Kun 2　　Yi 　　　Gui/Geng
九天 (Jiǔ Tiān) 天柱 (Tiān Zhù) 开门 (Kāi Mén) Zhen 3　Wu 　　　Ren	Yin (阴) Dun# 7 Hour: **YiMao** **Fan Yin** ©Calvin Yap	六合 (Liù Hé) 天冲 (Tiān Chōng) 杜门 (Dù Mén) Dui 7　　Ren 　　　Wu
值符 (Zhí Fú) 禽芮 (Qín Ruì) 惊门 (Jīng Mén) Gen 8　Gui/Geng 　　　Yi	腾蛇 (Téng Shé) 天英 (Tiān Yīng) 死门 (Sǐ Mén) Kan 1　　Bing 　　　Ding	太阴 (Tài Yīn) 天辅 (Tiān Fǔ) 景门 (Jǐng Mén) Qian 6　　Xin 　　　Ji

Yin (阴) Dun# 7 Hour: BingChen；直符(ZhíFú): 天芮(TiānRuì)
直使(ZhíShǐ): 死门(SǐMén)；旬首(XúnShǒu): JiaYinGui

腾蛇 (Téng Shé) 天英 (Tiān Yīng) 景门 (Jǐng Mén) Xun 4　　Bing 　　　Xin	值符 (Zhí Fú) 禽芮 (Qín Ruì) 死门 (Sǐ Mén) Li 9　Gui/Geng 　　　Bing	九天 (Jiǔ Tiān) 天柱 (Tiān Zhù) 惊门 (Jīng Mén) Kun 2　　Wu 　　　Gui/Geng
太阴 (Tài Yīn) 天辅 (Tiān Fǔ) 杜门 (Dù Mén) Zhen 3　Xin 　　　Ren	Yin (阴) Dun# 7 Hour: **BingChen** ©Calvin Yap	九地 (Jiǔ Dì) 天心 (Tiān Xīn) 开门 (Kāi Mén) Dui 7　　Ji 　　　Wu
六合 (Liù Hé) 天冲 (Tiān Chōng) 伤门 (Shāng Mén) Gen 8　　Ren 　　　Yi	白虎 (Bái Hǔ) 天任 (Tiān Rèn) 生门 (Shēng Mén) Kan 1　　Yi 　　　Ding	玄武 (Xuán Wǔ) 天蓬 (Tiān Péng) 休门 (Xiū Mén) Qian 6　　Ding 　　　Ji

Yin (阴) Dun# 7 Hour: DingSi；直符(ZhíFú): 天芮(TiānRuì)
直使(ZhíShǐ): 死门(SǐMén)；旬首(XúnShǒu): JiaYinGui

玄武 (Xuán Wǔ) 天蓬 (Tiān Péng) 开门 (Kāi Mén) Xun 4　　Ding 　　　Xin	白虎 (Bái Hǔ) 天任 (Tiān Rèn) 休门 (Xiū Mén) Li 9　　Yi 　　　Bing	六合 (Liù Hé) 天冲 (Tiān Chōng) 生门 (Shēng Mén) Kun 2　　Ren 　　　Gui/Geng
九地 (Jiǔ Dì) 天心 (Tiān Xīn) 惊门 (Jīng Mén) Zhen 3　Ji 　　　Ren	Yin (阴) Dun# 7 Hour: **DingSi** ©Calvin Yap	太阴 (Tài Yīn) 天辅 (Tiān Fǔ) 伤门 (Shāng Mén) Dui 7　　Xin 　　　Wu
九天 (Jiǔ Tiān) 天柱 (Tiān Zhù) 死门 (Sǐ Mén) Gen 8　　Wu 　　　Yi	值符 (Zhí Fú) 禽芮 (Qín Ruì) 景门 (Jǐng Mén) Kan 1　Gui/Geng 　　　Ding	腾蛇 (Téng Shé) 天英 (Tiān Yīng) 杜门 (Dù Mén) Qian 6　　Bing 　　　Ji

Yin (阴) Dun# 7 Hour: WuWu ; 直符(ZhíFú): 天芮(TiānRuì)
直使(ZhíShǐ): 死门(SǐMén) ; 旬首(XúnShǒu): JiaYinGui

六合 (Liù Hé) 天冲 (Tiān Chōng) 伤门 (Shāng Mén) Xun 4 Ren Xin	太阴 (Tài Yīn) 天辅 (Tiān Fǔ) 杜门 (Dù Mén) Li 9 Xin Bing	螣蛇 (Téng Shé) 天英 (Tiān Yīng) 景门 (Jǐng Mén) Kun 2 Bing Gui/Geng
白虎 (Bái Hǔ) 天任 (Tiān Rèn) 生门 (Shēng Mén) Zhen 3 Yi Ren	Yin (阴) Dun# 7 Hour: WuWu ©Calvin Yap	值符 (Zhí Fú) 禽芮 (Qín Ruì) 死门 (Sǐ Mén) Dui 7 Gui/Geng Wu
玄武 (Xuán Wǔ) 天蓬 (Tiān Péng) 休门 (Xiū Mén) Gen 8 Ding Yi	九地 (Jiǔ Dì) 天心 (Tiān Xīn) 开门 (Kāi Mén) Kan 1 Ji Ding	九天 (Jiǔ Tiān) 天柱 (Tiān Zhù) 惊门 (Jīng Mén) Qian 6 Wu Ji

Yin (阴) Dun# 7 Hour: JiWei ; 直符(ZhíFú): 天芮(TiānRuì)
直使(ZhíShǐ): 死门(SǐMén) ; 旬首(XúnShǒu): JiaYinGui

白虎 (Bái Hǔ) 天任 (Tiān Rèn) 生门 (Shēng Mén) Xun 4 Yi Xin	六合 (Liù Hé) 天冲 (Tiān Chōng) 伤门 (Shāng Mén) Li 9 Ren Bing	太阴 (Tài Yīn) 天辅 (Tiān Fǔ) 杜门 (Dù Mén) Kun 2 Xin Gui/Geng
玄武 (Xuán Wǔ) 天蓬 (Tiān Péng) 休门 (Xiū Mén) Zhen 3 Ding Ren	Yin (阴) Dun# 7 Hour: JiWei ©Calvin Yap	螣蛇 (Téng Shé) 天英 (Tiān Yīng) 景门 (Jǐng Mén) Dui 7 Bing Wu
九地 (Jiǔ Dì) 天心 (Tiān Xīn) 开门 (Kāi Mén) Gen 8 Ji Yi	九天 (Jiǔ Tiān) 天柱 (Tiān Zhù) 惊门 (Jīng Mén) Kan 1 Wu Ding	值符 (Zhí Fú) 禽芮 (Qín Ruì) 死门 (Sǐ Mén) Qian 6 Gui/Geng Ji

Yin (阴) Dun# 7 Hour: GengShen ; 直符(ZhíFú): 天芮(TiānRuì)
直使(ZhíShǐ): 死门(SǐMén) ; 旬首(XúnShǒu): JiaYinGui

太阴 (Tài Yīn) 天辅 (Tiān Fǔ) 杜门 (Dù Mén) Xun 4 Xin Xin	螣蛇 (Téng Shé) 天英 (Tiān Yīng) 景门 (Jǐng Mén) Li 9 Bing Bing	值符 (Zhí Fú) 禽芮 (Qín Ruì) 死门 (Sǐ Mén) Kun 2 Gui/Geng Gui/Geng
六合 (Liù Hé) 天冲 (Tiān Chōng) 伤门 (Shāng Mén) Zhen 3 Ren Ren	Yin (阴) Dun# 7 Hour: GengShen Fu Yin ©Calvin Yap	九天 (Jiǔ Tiān) 天柱 (Tiān Zhù) 惊门 (Jīng Mén) Dui 7 Wu Wu
白虎 (Bái Hǔ) 天任 (Tiān Rèn) 生门 (Shēng Mén) Gen 8 Yi Yi	玄武 (Xuán Wǔ) 天蓬 (Tiān Péng) 休门 (Xiū Mén) Kan 1 Ding Ding	九地 (Jiǔ Dì) 天心 (Tiān Xīn) 开门 (Kāi Mén) Qian 6 Ji Ji

Yin (阴) Dun# 7 Hour: XinYou ; 直符(ZhíFú): 天芮(TiānRuì)
直使(ZhíShǐ): 死门(SǐMén) ; 旬首(XúnShǒu): JiaYinGui

值符 (Zhí Fú) 禽芮 (Qín Ruì) 死门 (Sǐ Mén) Xun 4 Gui/Geng Xin	九天 (Jiǔ Tiān) 天柱 (Tiān Zhù) 惊门 (Jīng Mén) Li 9 Wu Bing	九地 (Jiǔ Dì) 天心 (Tiān Xīn) 开门 (Kāi Mén) Kun 2 Ji Gui/Geng
螣蛇 (Téng Shé) 天英 (Tiān Yīng) 景门 (Jǐng Mén) Zhen 3 Bing Ren	Yin (阴) Dun# 7 Hour: XinYou ©Calvin Yap	玄武 (Xuán Wǔ) 天蓬 (Tiān Péng) 休门 (Xiū Mén) Dui 7 Ding Wu
太阴 (Tài Yīn) 天辅 (Tiān Fǔ) 杜门 (Dù Mén) Gen 8 Xin Yi	六合 (Liù Hé) 天冲 (Tiān Chōng) 伤门 (Shāng Mén) Kan 1 Ren Ding	白虎 (Bái Hǔ) 天任 (Tiān Rèn) 生门 (Shēng Mén) Qian 6 Yi Ji

Yin (阴) Dun# 7 Hour: RenXu ; 直符(ZhíFú): 天芮(TiānRuì)
直使(ZhíShǐ): 死门(SǐMén) ; 旬首(XúnShǒu): JiaYinGui

九天 (Jiǔ Tiān) 天柱 (Tiān Zhù) 惊门 (Jīng Mén) Xun 4 Wu Xin	九地 (Jiǔ Dì) 天心 (Tiān Xīn) 开门 (Kāi Mén) Li 9 Ji Bing	玄武 (Xuán Wǔ) 天蓬 (Tiān Péng) 休门 (Xiū Mén) Kun 2 Ding Gui/Geng
值符 (Zhí Fú) 禽芮 (Qín Ruì) 死门 (Sǐ Mén) Zhen 3 Gui/Geng Ren	Yin (阴) Dun# 7 Hour: RenXu ©Calvin Yap	白虎 (Bái Hǔ) 天任 (Tiān Rèn) 生门 (Shēng Mén) Dui 7 Yi Wu
螣蛇 (Téng Shé) 天英 (Tiān Yīng) 景门 (Jǐng Mén) Gen 8 Bing Yi	太阴 (Tài Yīn) 天辅 (Tiān Fǔ) 杜门 (Dù Mén) Kan 1 Xin Ding	六合 (Liù Hé) 天冲 (Tiān Chōng) 伤门 (Shāng Mén) Qian 6 Ren Ji

Yin (阴) Dun# 7 Hour: GuiHai ; 直符(ZhíFú): 天芮(TiānRuì)
直使(ZhíShǐ): 死门(SǐMén) ; 旬首(XúnShǒu): JiaYinGui

太阴 (Tài Yīn) 天辅 (Tiān Fǔ) 杜门 (Dù Mén) Xun 4 Xin Xin	螣蛇 (Téng Shé) 天英 (Tiān Yīng) 景门 (Jǐng Mén) Li 9 Bing Bing	值符 (Zhí Fú) 禽芮 (Qín Ruì) 死门 (Sǐ Mén) Kun 2 Gui/Geng Gui/Geng
六合 (Liù Hé) 天冲 (Tiān Chōng) 伤门 (Shāng Mén) Zhen 3 Ren Ren	Yin (阴) Dun# 7 Hour: GuiHai Fu Yin ©Calvin Yap	九天 (Jiǔ Tiān) 天柱 (Tiān Zhù) 惊门 (Jīng Mén) Dui 7 Wu Wu
白虎 (Bái Hǔ) 天任 (Tiān Rèn) 生门 (Shēng Mén) Gen 8 Yi Yi	玄武 (Xuán Wǔ) 天蓬 (Tiān Péng) 休门 (Xiū Mén) Kan 1 Ding Ding	九地 (Jiǔ Dì) 天心 (Tiān Xīn) 开门 (Kāi Mén) Qian 6 Ji Ji

Yin Dun#8

Chart: -8JiaZi (Yin Dun #8 JiaZi Xun)
JiaZi, YiChou, BingYin, DingMao, WuChen, JiSi, GengWu, XinWei, RenShen, GuiYou

Yin (阴) Dun# 8 Hour: **JiaZi**; 直符(ZhíFú): 天任(TiānRèn)
直使(ZhíShǐ): 生门(ShēngMén); 旬首(XúnShǒu): JiaZiWu

九地 (Jiŭ Dì) 天辅 (Tiān Fǔ) 杜门 (Dù Mén) Xun 4　Ren Ren	玄武 (Xuán Wǔ) 天英 (Tiān Yīng) 景门 (Jǐng Mén) Li 9　Yi Yi	白虎 (Bái Hǔ) 禽芮 (Qín Ruì) 死门 (Sǐ Mén) Kun 2　Ding/Xin Ding/Xin
九天 (Jiŭ Tiān) 天冲 (Tiān Chōng) 伤门 (Shāng Mén) Zhen 3　Gui Gui	Yin (阴) Dun# 8 Hour: **JiaZi** **Fu Yin** ©Calvin Yap	六合 (Liù Hé) 天柱 (Tiān Zhù) 惊门 (Jīng Mén) Dui 7　Ji Ji
值符 (Zhí Fú) 天任 (Tiān Rèn) 生门 (Shēng Mén) Gen 8　Wu Wu	螣蛇 (Téng Shé) 天蓬 (Tiān Péng) 休门 (Xiū Mén) Kan 1　Bing Bing	太阴 (Tài Yīn) 天心 (Tiān Xīn) 开门 (Kāi Mén) Qian 6　Geng Geng

Yin (阴) Dun# 8 Hour: **YiChou**; 直符(ZhíFú): 天任(TiānRèn)
直使(ZhíShǐ): 生门(ShēngMén); 旬首(XúnShǒu): JiaZiWu

螣蛇 (Téng Shé) 天蓬 (Tiān Péng) 惊门 (Jīng Mén) Xun 4　Bing Ren	值符 (Zhí Fú) 天任 (Tiān Rèn) 开门 (Kāi Mén) Li 9　Wu Yi	九天 (Jiŭ Tiān) 天冲 (Tiān Chōng) 休门 (Xiū Mén) Kun 2　Gui Ding/Xin
太阴 (Tài Yīn) 天心 (Tiān Xīn) 死门 (Sǐ Mén) Zhen 3　Geng Gui	Yin (阴) Dun# 8 Hour: **YiChou** ©Calvin Yap	九地 (Jiŭ Dì) 天辅 (Tiān Fǔ) 生门 (Shēng Mén) Dui 7　Ren Ji
六合 (Liù Hé) 天柱 (Tiān Zhù) 景门 (Jǐng Mén) Gen 8　Ji Wu	白虎 (Bái Hǔ) 禽芮 (Qín Ruì) 杜门 (Dù Mén) Kan 1　Ding/Xin Bing	玄武 (Xuán Wǔ) 天英 (Tiān Yīng) 伤门 (Shāng Mén) Qian 6　Yi Geng

Yin (阴) Dun# 8 Hour: **BingYin**; 直符(ZhíFú): 天任(TiānRèn)
直使(ZhíShǐ): 生门(ShēngMén); 旬首(XúnShǒu): JiaZiWu

玄武 (Xuán Wǔ) 天英 (Tiān Yīng) 死门 (Sǐ Mén) Xun 4　Yi Ren	白虎 (Bái Hǔ) 禽芮 (Qín Ruì) 惊门 (Jīng Mén) Li 9　Ding/Xin Yi	六合 (Liù Hé) 天柱 (Tiān Zhù) 开门 (Kāi Mén) Kun 2　Ji Ding/Xin
九地 (Jiŭ Dì) 天辅 (Tiān Fǔ) 景门 (Jǐng Mén) Zhen 3　Ren Gui	Yin (阴) Dun# 8 Hour: **BingYin** ©Calvin Yap	太阴 (Tài Yīn) 天心 (Tiān Xīn) 休门 (Xiū Mén) Dui 7　Geng Ji
九天 (Jiŭ Tiān) 天冲 (Tiān Chōng) 杜门 (Dù Mén) Gen 8　Gui Wu	值符 (Zhí Fú) 天任 (Tiān Rèn) 伤门 (Shāng Mén) Kan 1　Wu Bing	螣蛇 (Téng Shé) 天蓬 (Tiān Péng) 生门 (Shēng Mén) Qian 6　Bing Geng

Yin (阴) Dun# 8 Hour: **DingMao**; 直符(ZhíFú): 天任(TiānRèn)
直使(ZhíShǐ): 生门(ShēngMén); 旬首(XúnShǒu): JiaZiWu

太阴 (Tài Yīn) 天心 (Tiān Xīn) 开门 (Kāi Mén) Xun 4　Geng Ren	螣蛇 (Téng Shé) 天蓬 (Tiān Péng) 休门 (Xiū Mén) Li 9　Bing Yi	值符 (Zhí Fú) 天任 (Tiān Rèn) 生门 (Shēng Mén) Kun 2　Wu Ding/Xin
六合 (Liù Hé) 天柱 (Tiān Zhù) 惊门 (Jīng Mén) Zhen 3　Ji Gui	Yin (阴) Dun# 8 Hour: **DingMao** **Fan Yin** ©Calvin Yap	九天 (Jiŭ Tiān) 天冲 (Tiān Chōng) 伤门 (Shāng Mén) Dui 7　Gui Ji
白虎 (Bái Hǔ) 禽芮 (Qín Ruì) 死门 (Sǐ Mén) Gen 8　Ding/Xin Wu	玄武 (Xuán Wǔ) 天英 (Tiān Yīng) 景门 (Jǐng Mén) Kan 1　Yi Bing	九地 (Jiŭ Dì) 天辅 (Tiān Fǔ) 杜门 (Dù Mén) Qian 6　Ren Geng

Yin (阴) Dun# 8 Hour: **WuChen**; 直符(ZhíFú): 天任(TiānRèn)
直使(ZhíShǐ): 生门(ShēngMén); 旬首(XúnShǒu): JiaZiWu

九地 (Jiŭ Dì) 天辅 (Tiān Fǔ) 生门 (Shēng Mén) Xun 4　Ren Ren	玄武 (Xuán Wǔ) 天英 (Tiān Yīng) 伤门 (Shāng Mén) Li 9　Yi Yi	白虎 (Bái Hǔ) 禽芮 (Qín Ruì) 杜门 (Dù Mén) Kun 2　Ding/Xin Ding/Xin
九天 (Jiŭ Tiān) 天冲 (Tiān Chōng) 休门 (Xiū Mén) Zhen 3　Gui Gui	Yin (阴) Dun# 8 Hour: **WuChen** **Fu Yin** ©Calvin Yap	六合 (Liù Hé) 天柱 (Tiān Zhù) 景门 (Jǐng Mén) Dui 7　Ji Ji
值符 (Zhí Fú) 天任 (Tiān Rèn) 开门 (Kāi Mén) Gen 8　Wu Wu	螣蛇 (Téng Shé) 天蓬 (Tiān Péng) 惊门 (Jīng Mén) Kan 1　Bing Bing	太阴 (Tài Yīn) 天心 (Tiān Xīn) 死门 (Sǐ Mén) Qian 6　Geng Geng

Yin (阴) Dun# 8 Hour: **JiSi**; 直符(ZhíFú): 天任(TiānRèn)
直使(ZhíShǐ): 生门(ShēngMén); 旬首(XúnShǒu): JiaZiWu

六合 (Liù Hé) 天柱 (Tiān Zhù) 伤门 (Shāng Mén) Xun 4　Ji Ren	太阴 (Tài Yīn) 天心 (Tiān Xīn) 杜门 (Dù Mén) Li 9　Geng Yi	螣蛇 (Téng Shé) 天蓬 (Tiān Péng) 景门 (Jǐng Mén) Kun 2　Bing Ding/Xin
白虎 (Bái Hǔ) 禽芮 (Qín Ruì) 生门 (Shēng Mén) Zhen 3　Ding/Xin Gui	Yin (阴) Dun# 8 Hour: **JiSi** ©Calvin Yap	值符 (Zhí Fú) 天任 (Tiān Rèn) 死门 (Sǐ Mén) Dui 7　Wu Ji
玄武 (Xuán Wǔ) 天英 (Tiān Yīng) 休门 (Xiū Mén) Gen 8　Yi Wu	九地 (Jiŭ Dì) 天辅 (Tiān Fǔ) 开门 (Kāi Mén) Kan 1　Ren Bing	九天 (Jiŭ Tiān) 天冲 (Tiān Chōng) 惊门 (Jīng Mén) Qian 6　Gui Geng

Yin (阴) Dun# 8 Hour: **GengWu** ; 直符(ZhíFú): 天任(TiānRèn)
直使(ZhíShǐ): 生门(ShēngMén) ; 旬首(XúnShǒu): JiaZiWu

白虎 (Bái Hǔ) 禽芮 (Qín Ruì) 开门 (Kāi Mén) Xun 4　Ding/Xin Ren	六合 (Liù Hé) 天柱 (Tiān Zhù) 休门 (Xiū Mén) Li 9　Ji Yi	太阴 (Tài Yīn) 天心 (Tiān Xīn) 生门 (Shēng Mén) Kun 2　Geng Ding/Xin
玄武 (Xuán Wǔ) 天英 (Tiān Yīng) 惊门 (Jīng Mén) Zhen 3　Yi Gui	Yin (阴) Dun# 8 Hour: **GengWu** ©Calvin Yap	螣蛇 (Téng Shé) 天蓬 (Tiān Péng) 伤门 (Shāng Mén) Dui 7　Bing Ji
九地 (Jiǔ Dì) 天辅 (Tiān Fǔ) 死门 (Sǐ Mén) Gen 8　Ren Wu	九天 (Jiǔ Tiān) 天冲 (Tiān Chōng) 景门 (Jǐng Mén) Kan 1　Gui Bing	值符 (Zhí Fú) 天任 (Tiān Rèn) 杜门 (Dù Mén) Qian 6　Wu Geng

Yin (阴) Dun# 8 Hour: **XinWei** ; 直符(ZhíFú): 天任(TiānRèn)
直使(ZhíShǐ): 生门(ShēngMén) ; 旬首(XúnShǒu): JiaZiWu

太阴 (Tài Yīn) 天心 (Tiān Xīn) 景门 (Jǐng Mén) Xun 4　Geng Ren	螣蛇 (Téng Shé) 天蓬 (Tiān Péng) 死门 (Sǐ Mén) Li 9　Bing Yi	值符 (Zhí Fú) 天任 (Tiān Rèn) 惊门 (Jīng Mén) Kun 2　Wu Ding/Xin
六合 (Liù Hé) 天柱 (Tiān Zhù) 杜门 (Dù Mén) Zhen 3　Ji Gui	Yin (阴) Dun# 8 Hour: **XinWei** **Fan Yin** ©Calvin Yap	九天 (Jiǔ Tiān) 天冲 (Tiān Chōng) 开门 (Kāi Mén) Dui 7　Gui Ji
白虎 (Bái Hǔ) 禽芮 (Qín Ruì) 伤门 (Shāng Mén) Gen 8　Ding/Xin Wu	玄武 (Xuán Wǔ) 天英 (Tiān Yīng) 生门 (Shēng Mén) Kan 1　Yi Bing	九地 (Jiǔ Dì) 天辅 (Tiān Fǔ) 休门 (Xiū Mén) Qian 6　Ren Geng

Yin (阴) Dun# 8 Hour: **RenShen** ; 直符(ZhíFú): 天任(TiānRèn)
直使(ZhíShǐ): 生门(ShēngMén) ; 旬首(XúnShǒu): JiaZiWu

值符 (Zhí Fú) 天任 (Tiān Rèn) 休门 (Xiū Mén) Xun 4　Wu Ren	九天 (Jiǔ Tiān) 天冲 (Tiān Chōng) 生门 (Shēng Mén) Li 9　Gui Yi	九地 (Jiǔ Dì) 天辅 (Tiān Fǔ) 伤门 (Shāng Mén) Kun 2　Ren Ding/Xin
螣蛇 (Téng Shé) 天蓬 (Tiān Péng) 开门 (Kāi Mén) Zhen 3　Bing Gui	Yin (阴) Dun# 8 Hour: **RenShen** ©Calvin Yap	玄武 (Xuán Wǔ) 天英 (Tiān Yīng) 杜门 (Dù Mén) Dui 7　Yi Ji
太阴 (Tài Yīn) 天心 (Tiān Xīn) 惊门 (Jīng Mén) Gen 8　Geng Wu	六合 (Liù Hé) 天柱 (Tiān Zhù) 死门 (Sǐ Mén) Kan 1　Ji Bing	白虎 (Bái Hǔ) 禽芮 (Qín Ruì) 景门 (Jǐng Mén) Qian 6　Ding/Xin Geng

Yin (阴) Dun# 8 Hour: **GuiYou** ; 直符(ZhíFú): 天任(TiānRèn)
直使(ZhíShǐ): 生门(ShēngMén) ; 旬首(XúnShǒu): JiaZiWu

九天 (Jiǔ Tiān) 天冲 (Tiān Chōng) 杜门 (Dù Mén) Xun 4　Gui Ren	九地 (Jiǔ Dì) 天辅 (Tiān Fǔ) 景门 (Jǐng Mén) Li 9　Ren Yi	玄武 (Xuán Wǔ) 天英 (Tiān Yīng) 死门 (Sǐ Mén) Kun 2　Yi Ding/Xin
值符 (Zhí Fú) 天任 (Tiān Rèn) 伤门 (Shāng Mén) Zhen 3　Wu Gui	Yin (阴) Dun# 8 Hour: **GuiYou** ©Calvin Yap	白虎 (Bái Hǔ) 禽芮 (Qín Ruì) 惊门 (Jīng Mén) Dui 7　Ding/Xin Ji
螣蛇 (Téng Shé) 天蓬 (Tiān Péng) 生门 (Shēng Mén) Gen 8　Bing Wu	太阴 (Tài Yīn) 天心 (Tiān Xīn) 休门 (Xiū Mén) Kan 1　Geng Bing	六合 (Liù Hé) 天柱 (Tiān Zhù) 开门 (Kāi Mén) Qian 6　Ji Geng

---

Chart: -8JiaXu (Yin Dun #8 JiaXu Xun)
JiaXu, YiHai, BingZi, DingChou, WuYin, JiMao, GengChen, XinSi, RenWu, GuiWei

Yin (阴) Dun# 8 Hour: **JiaXu** ; 直符(ZhíFú): 天柱(TiānZhù)
直使(ZhíShǐ): 惊门(JīngMén) ; 旬首(XúnShǒu): JiaXuJi

六合 (Liù Hé) 天辅 (Tiān Fǔ) 杜门 (Dù Mén) Xun 4　Ren Ren	太阴 (Tài Yīn) 天英 (Tiān Yīng) 景门 (Jǐng Mén) Li 9　Yi Yi	螣蛇 (Téng Shé) 禽芮 (Qín Ruì) 死门 (Sǐ Mén) Kun 2　Ding/Xin Ding/Xin
白虎 (Bái Hǔ) 天冲 (Tiān Chōng) 伤门 (Shāng Mén) Zhen 3　Gui Gui	Yin (阴) Dun# 8 Hour: **JiaXu** **Fu Yin** ©Calvin Yap	值符 (Zhí Fú) 天柱 (Tiān Zhù) 惊门 (Jīng Mén) Dui 7　Ji Ji
玄武 (Xuán Wǔ) 天任 (Tiān Rèn) 生门 (Shēng Mén) Gen 8　Wu Wu	九地 (Jiǔ Dì) 天蓬 (Tiān Péng) 休门 (Xiū Mén) Kan 1　Bing Bing	九天 (Jiǔ Tiān) 天心 (Tiān Xīn) 开门 (Kāi Mén) Qian 6　Geng Geng

Yin (阴) Dun# 8 Hour: **YiHai** ; 直符(ZhíFú): 天柱(TiānZhù)
直使(ZhíShǐ): 惊门(JīngMén) ; 旬首(XúnShǒu): JiaXuJi

螣蛇 (Téng Shé) 禽芮 (Qín Ruì) 伤门 (Shāng Mén) Xun 4　Ding/Xin Ren	值符 (Zhí Fú) 天柱 (Tiān Zhù) 杜门 (Dù Mén) Li 9　Ji Yi	九天 (Jiǔ Tiān) 天心 (Tiān Xīn) 景门 (Jǐng Mén) Kun 2　Geng Ding/Xin
太阴 (Tài Yīn) 天英 (Tiān Yīng) 生门 (Shēng Mén) Zhen 3　Yi Gui	Yin (阴) Dun# 8 Hour: **YiHai** ©Calvin Yap	九地 (Jiǔ Dì) 天蓬 (Tiān Péng) 死门 (Sǐ Mén) Dui 7　Bing Ji
六合 (Liù Hé) 天辅 (Tiān Fǔ) 休门 (Xiū Mén) Gen 8　Ren Wu	白虎 (Bái Hǔ) 天冲 (Tiān Chōng) 开门 (Kāi Mén) Kan 1　Gui Bing	玄武 (Xuán Wǔ) 天任 (Tiān Rèn) 惊门 (Jīng Mén) Qian 6　Wu Geng

---

Yin (阴) Dun# 8 Hour: BingZi；直符(ZhíFú): 天柱(TiānZhù)
直使(ZhíShǐ): 惊门(JǐngMén)；旬首(XúnShǒu): JiaXuJi

玄武 (Xuán Wǔ) 天任 (Tiān Rèn) 景门 (Jǐng Mén) Xun 4　Wu Ren	白虎 (Bái Hǔ) 天冲 (Tiān Chōng) 死门 (Sǐ Mén) Li 9　Gui Yi	六合 (Liù Hé) 天辅 (Tiān Fǔ) 惊门 (Jǐng Mén) Kun 2　Ren Ding/Xin
九地 (Jiǔ Dì) 天蓬 (Tiān Péng) 杜门 (Dù Mén) Zhen 3　Bing Gui	Yin (阴) Dun# 8 Hour: **BingZi** ©Calvin Yap	太阴 (Tài Yīn) 天英 (Tiān Yīng) 开门 (Kāi Mén) Dui 7　Yi Ji
九天 (Jiǔ Tiān) 天心 (Tiān Xīn) 伤门 (Shāng Mén) Gen 8　Geng Wu	值符 (Zhí Fú) 天柱 (Tiān Zhù) 生门 (Shēng Mén) Kan 1　Ji Bing	螣蛇 (Téng Shé) 禽芮 (Qín Ruì) 休门 (Xiū Mén) Qian 6　Ding/Xin Geng

Yin (阴) Dun# 8 Hour: DingChou；直符(ZhíFú): 天柱(TiānZhù)
直使(ZhíShǐ): 惊门(JǐngMén)；旬首(XúnShǒu): JiaXuJi

太阴 (Tài Yīn) 天英 (Tiān Yīng) 惊门 (Jǐng Mén) Xun 4　Yi Ren	螣蛇 (Téng Shé) 禽芮 (Qín Ruì) 开门 (Kāi Mén) Li 9　Ding/Xin Yi	值符 (Zhí Fú) 天柱 (Tiān Zhù) 休门 (Xiū Mén) Kun 2　Ji Ding/Xin
六合 (Liù Hé) 天辅 (Tiān Fǔ) 死门 (Sǐ Mén) Zhen 3　Ren Gui	Yin (阴) Dun# 8 Hour: **DingChou** ©Calvin Yap	九天 (Jiǔ Tiān) 天心 (Tiān Xīn) 生门 (Shēng Mén) Dui 7　Geng Ji
白虎 (Bái Hǔ) 天冲 (Tiān Chōng) 景门 (Jǐng Mén) Gen 8　Gui Wu	玄武 (Xuán Wǔ) 天任 (Tiān Rèn) 杜门 (Dù Mén) Kan 1　Wu Bing	九地 (Jiǔ Dì) 天蓬 (Tiān Péng) 伤门 (Shāng Mén) Qian 6　Bing Geng

Yin (阴) Dun# 8 Hour: WuYin；直符(ZhíFú): 天柱(TiānZhù)
直使(ZhíShǐ): 惊门(JǐngMén)；旬首(XúnShǒu): JiaXuJi

九地 (Jiǔ Dì) 天蓬 (Tiān Péng) 开门 (Kāi Mén) Xun 4　Bing Ren	玄武 (Xuán Wǔ) 天任 (Tiān Rèn) 休门 (Xiū Mén) Li 9　Wu Yi	白虎 (Bái Hǔ) 天冲 (Tiān Chōng) 生门 (Shēng Mén) Kun 2　Gui Ding/Xin
九天 (Jiǔ Tiān) 天心 (Tiān Xīn) 惊门 (Jǐng Mén) Zhen 3　Geng Gui	Yin (阴) Dun# 8 Hour: **WuYin** ©Calvin Yap	六合 (Liù Hé) 天辅 (Tiān Fǔ) 伤门 (Shāng Mén) Dui 7　Ren Ji
值符 (Zhí Fú) 天柱 (Tiān Zhù) 死门 (Sǐ Mén) Gen 8　Ji Wu	螣蛇 (Téng Shé) 禽芮 (Qín Ruì) 景门 (Jǐng Mén) Kan 1　Ding/Xin Bing	太阴 (Tài Yīn) 天英 (Tiān Yīng) 杜门 (Dù Mén) Qian 6　Yi Geng

Yin (阴) Dun# 8 Hour: JiMao；直符(ZhíFú): 天柱(TiānZhù)
直使(ZhíShǐ): 惊门(JǐngMén)；旬首(XúnShǒu): JiaXuJi

六合 (Liù Hé) 天辅 (Tiān Fǔ) 景门 (Jǐng Mén) Xun 4　Ren Ren	太阴 (Tài Yīn) 天英 (Tiān Yīng) 死门 (Sǐ Mén) Li 9　Yi Yi	螣蛇 (Téng Shé) 禽芮 (Qín Ruì) 惊门 (Jǐng Mén) Kun 2　Ding/Xin Ding/Xin
白虎 (Bái Hǔ) 天冲 (Tiān Chōng) 杜门 (Dù Mén) Zhen 3　Gui Gui	Yin (阴) Dun# 8 Hour: **JiMao** **Fu Yin** ©Calvin Yap	值符 (Zhí Fú) 天柱 (Tiān Zhù) 开门 (Kāi Mén) Dui 7　Ji Ji
玄武 (Xuán Wǔ) 天任 (Tiān Rèn) 伤门 (Shāng Mén) Gen 8　Wu Wu	九地 (Jiǔ Dì) 天蓬 (Tiān Péng) 生门 (Shēng Mén) Kan 1　Bing Bing	九天 (Jiǔ Tiān) 天心 (Tiān Xīn) 休门 (Xiū Mén) Qian 6　Geng Geng

Yin (阴) Dun# 8 Hour: GengChen；直符(ZhíFú): 天柱(TiānZhù)
直使(ZhíShǐ): 惊门(JǐngMén)；旬首(XúnShǒu): JiaXuJi

白虎 (Bái Hǔ) 天冲 (Tiān Chōng) 生门 (Shēng Mén) Xun 4　Gui Ren	六合 (Liù Hé) 天辅 (Tiān Fǔ) 伤门 (Shāng Mén) Li 9　Ren Yi	太阴 (Tài Yīn) 天英 (Tiān Yīng) 杜门 (Dù Mén) Kun 2　Yi Ding/Xin
玄武 (Xuán Wǔ) 天任 (Tiān Rèn) 休门 (Xiū Mén) Zhen 3　Wu Gui	Yin (阴) Dun# 8 Hour: **GengChen** ©Calvin Yap	螣蛇 (Téng Shé) 禽芮 (Qín Ruì) 景门 (Jǐng Mén) Dui 7　Ding/Xin Ji
九地 (Jiǔ Dì) 天蓬 (Tiān Péng) 开门 (Kāi Mén) Gen 8　Bing Wu	九天 (Jiǔ Tiān) 天心 (Tiān Xīn) 惊门 (Jǐng Mén) Kan 1　Geng Bing	值符 (Zhí Fú) 天柱 (Tiān Zhù) 死门 (Sǐ Mén) Qian 6　Ji Geng

Yin (阴) Dun# 8 Hour: XinSi；直符(ZhíFú): 天柱(TiānZhù)
直使(ZhíShǐ): 惊门(JǐngMén)；旬首(XúnShǒu): JiaXuJi

太阴 (Tài Yīn) 天英 (Tiān Yīng) 死门 (Sǐ Mén) Xun 4　Yi Ren	螣蛇 (Téng Shé) 禽芮 (Qín Ruì) 惊门 (Jǐng Mén) Li 9　Ding/Xin Yi	值符 (Zhí Fú) 天柱 (Tiān Zhù) 开门 (Kāi Mén) Kun 2　Ji Ding/Xin
六合 (Liù Hé) 天辅 (Tiān Fǔ) 景门 (Jǐng Mén) Zhen 3　Ren Gui	Yin (阴) Dun# 8 Hour: **XinSi** ©Calvin Yap	九天 (Jiǔ Tiān) 天心 (Tiān Xīn) 休门 (Xiū Mén) Dui 7　Geng Ji
白虎 (Bái Hǔ) 天冲 (Tiān Chōng) 杜门 (Dù Mén) Gen 8　Gui Wu	玄武 (Xuán Wǔ) 天任 (Tiān Rèn) 伤门 (Shāng Mén) Kan 1　Wu Bing	九地 (Jiǔ Dì) 天蓬 (Tiān Péng) 生门 (Shēng Mén) Qian 6　Bing Geng

Yin (阴) Dun# 8 Hour: **RenWu** ; 直符(ZhíFú): 天柱(TiānZhù)
直使(ZhíShǐ): 惊门(JīngMén) ; 旬首(XúnShǒu): JiaXuJi

值符 (Zhí Fú) 天柱 (Tiān Zhù) 休门 (Xiū Mén) Xun 4 Ji Ren	九天 (Jiǔ Tiān) 天心 (Tiān Xīn) 生门 (Shēng Mén) Li 9 Geng Yi	九地 (Jiǔ Dì) 天蓬 (Tiān Péng) 伤门 (Shāng Mén) Kun 2 Bing Ding/Xin
螣蛇 (Téng Shé) 禽芮 (Qín Ruì) 开门 (Kāi Mén) Zhen 3 Ding/Xin Gui	Yin (阴) Dun# 8 Hour: **RenWu** ©Calvin Yap	玄武 (Xuán Wǔ) 天任 (Tiān Rèn) 杜门 (Dù Mén) Dui 7 Wu Ji
太阴 (Tài Yīn) 天英 (Tiān Yīng) 惊门 (Jīng Mén) Gen 8 Yi Wu	六合 (Liù Hé) 天辅 (Tiān Fǔ) 死门 (Sǐ Mén) Kan 1 Ren Bing	白虎 (Bái Hǔ) 天冲 (Tiān Chōng) 景门 (Jǐng Mén) Qian 6 Gui Geng

Yin (阴) Dun# 8 Hour: **GuiWei** ; 直符(ZhíFú): 天柱(TiānZhù)
直使(ZhíShǐ): 惊门(JīngMén) ; 旬首(XúnShǒu): JiaXuJi

九天 (Jiǔ Tiān) 天心 (Tiān Xīn) 杜门 (Dù Mén) Xun 4 Geng Ren	九地 (Jiǔ Dì) 天蓬 (Tiān Péng) 景门 (Jǐng Mén) Li 9 Bing Yi	玄武 (Xuán Wǔ) 天任 (Tiān Rèn) 死门 (Sǐ Mén) Kun 2 Wu Ding/Xin
值符 (Zhí Fú) 天柱 (Tiān Zhù) 伤门 (Shāng Mén) Zhen 3 Ji Gui	Yin (阴) Dun# 8 Hour: **GuiWei** **Fan Yin** ©Calvin Yap	白虎 (Bái Hǔ) 天冲 (Tiān Chōng) 惊门 (Jīng Mén) Dui 7 Gui Ji
螣蛇 (Téng Shé) 禽芮 (Qín Ruì) 生门 (Shēng Mén) Gen 8 Ding/Xin Wu	太阴 (Tài Yīn) 天英 (Tiān Yīng) 休门 (Xiū Mén) Kan 1 Yi Bing	六合 (Liù Hé) 天辅 (Tiān Fǔ) 开门 (Kāi Mén) Qian 6 Ren Geng

Chart: **-8JiaShen** (Yin Dun #8 JiaShen Xun)
JiaShen, YiYou, BingXu, DingHai, WuZi, JiChou, GengYin, XinMao, RenChen, GuiSi

Yin (阴) Dun# 8 Hour: **JiaShen** ; 直符(ZhíFú): 天心(TiānXīn)
直使(ZhíShǐ): 开门(KāiMén) ; 旬首(XúnShǒu): JiaShenGeng

白虎 (Bái Hǔ) 天辅 (Tiān Fǔ) 杜门 (Dù Mén) Xun 4 Ren Ren	六合 (Liù Hé) 天英 (Tiān Yīng) 景门 (Jǐng Mén) Li 9 Yi Yi	太阴 (Tài Yīn) 禽芮 (Qín Ruì) 死门 (Sǐ Mén) Kun 2 Ding/Xin Ding/Xin
玄武 (Xuán Wǔ) 天冲 (Tiān Chōng) 伤门 (Shāng Mén) Zhen 3 Gui Gui	Yin (阴) Dun# 8 Hour: **JiaShen** **Fu Yin** ©Calvin Yap	螣蛇 (Téng Shé) 天柱 (Tiān Zhù) 惊门 (Jīng Mén) Dui 7 Ji Ji
九地 (Jiǔ Dì) 天任 (Tiān Rèn) 生门 (Shēng Mén) Gen 8 Wu Wu	九天 (Jiǔ Tiān) 天蓬 (Tiān Péng) 休门 (Xiū Mén) Kan 1 Bing Bing	值符 (Zhí Fú) 天心 (Tiān Xīn) 开门 (Kāi Mén) Qian 6 Geng Geng

Yin (阴) Dun# 8 Hour: **YiYou** ; 直符(ZhíFú): 天心(TiānXīn)
直使(ZhíShǐ): 开门(KāiMén) ; 旬首(XúnShǒu): JiaShenGeng

螣蛇 (Téng Shé) 天柱 (Tiān Zhù) 死门 (Sǐ Mén) Xun 4 Ji Ren	值符 (Zhí Fú) 天心 (Tiān Xīn) 惊门 (Jīng Mén) Li 9 Geng Yi	九天 (Jiǔ Tiān) 天蓬 (Tiān Péng) 开门 (Kāi Mén) Kun 2 Bing Ding/Xin
太阴 (Tài Yīn) 禽芮 (Qín Ruì) 景门 (Jǐng Mén) Zhen 3 Ding/Xin Gui	Yin (阴) Dun# 8 Hour: **YiYou** ©Calvin Yap	九地 (Jiǔ Dì) 天任 (Tiān Rèn) 休门 (Xiū Mén) Dui 7 Wu Ji
六合 (Liù Hé) 天英 (Tiān Yīng) 杜门 (Dù Mén) Gen 8 Yi Wu	白虎 (Bái Hǔ) 天辅 (Tiān Fǔ) 伤门 (Shāng Mén) Kan 1 Ren Bing	玄武 (Xuán Wǔ) 天冲 (Tiān Chōng) 生门 (Shēng Mén) Qian 6 Gui Geng

Yin (阴) Dun# 8 Hour: **BingXu** ; 直符(ZhíFú): 天心(TiānXīn)
直使(ZhíShǐ): 开门(KāiMén) ; 旬首(XúnShǒu): JiaShenGeng

玄武 (Xuán Wǔ) 天冲 (Tiān Chōng) 开门 (Kāi Mén) Xun 4 Gui Ren	白虎 (Bái Hǔ) 天辅 (Tiān Fǔ) 休门 (Xiū Mén) Li 9 Ren Yi	六合 (Liù Hé) 天英 (Tiān Yīng) 生门 (Shēng Mén) Kun 2 Yi Ding/Xin
九地 (Jiǔ Dì) 天任 (Tiān Rèn) 惊门 (Jīng Mén) Zhen 3 Wu Gui	Yin (阴) Dun# 8 Hour: **BingXu** ©Calvin Yap	太阴 (Tài Yīn) 禽芮 (Qín Ruì) 伤门 (Shāng Mén) Dui 7 Ding/Xin Ji
九天 (Jiǔ Tiān) 天蓬 (Tiān Péng) 死门 (Sǐ Mén) Gen 8 Bing Wu	值符 (Zhí Fú) 天心 (Tiān Xīn) 景门 (Jǐng Mén) Kan 1 Geng Bing	螣蛇 (Téng Shé) 天柱 (Tiān Zhù) 杜门 (Dù Mén) Qian 6 Ji Geng

Yin (阴) Dun# 8 Hour: **DingHai** ; 直符(ZhíFú): 天心(TiānXīn)
直使(ZhíShǐ): 开门(KāiMén) ; 旬首(XúnShǒu): JiaShenGeng

太阴 (Tài Yīn) 禽芮 (Qín Ruì) 休门 (Xiū Mén) Xun 4 Ding/Xin Ren	螣蛇 (Téng Shé) 天柱 (Tiān Zhù) 生门 (Shēng Mén) Li 9 Ji Yi	值符 (Zhí Fú) 天心 (Tiān Xīn) 伤门 (Shāng Mén) Kun 2 Geng Ding/Xin
六合 (Liù Hé) 天英 (Tiān Yīng) 开门 (Kāi Mén) Zhen 3 Yi Gui	Yin (阴) Dun# 8 Hour: **DingHai** ©Calvin Yap	九天 (Jiǔ Tiān) 天蓬 (Tiān Péng) 杜门 (Dù Mén) Dui 7 Bing Ji
白虎 (Bái Hǔ) 天辅 (Tiān Fǔ) 惊门 (Jīng Mén) Gen 8 Ren Wu	玄武 (Xuán Wǔ) 天冲 (Tiān Chōng) 死门 (Sǐ Mén) Kan 1 Gui Bing	九地 (Jiǔ Dì) 天任 (Tiān Rèn) 景门 (Jǐng Mén) Qian 6 Wu Geng

---

Yin (阴) Dun# 8 Hour: WuZi ; 直符(ZhíFú): 天心(TiānXīn)
直使(ZhíShǐ): 开门(KāiMén) ; 旬首(XúnShǒu): JiaShenGeng

九地 (Jiǔ Dì) 天任 (Tiān Rèn) 死门 (Sǐ Mén) Xun 4　Wu Ren	玄武 (Xuán Wǔ) 天冲 (Tiān Chōng) 惊门 (Jīng Mén) Li 9　Gui 　Yi	白虎 (Bái Hǔ) 天辅 (Tiān Fǔ) 开门 (Kāi Mén) Kun 2　Ren Ding/Xin
九天 (Jiǔ Tiān) 天蓬 (Tiān Péng) 景门 (Jīng Mén) Zhen 3　Bing Gui	Yin (阴) Dun# 8 Hour: **WuZi** ©Calvin Yap	六合 (Liù Hé) 天英 (Tiān Yīng) 休门 (Xiū Mén) Dui 7　Yi Ji
值符 (Zhí Fú) 天心 (Tiān Xīn) 杜门 (Dù Mén) Gen 8　Geng Wu	腾蛇 (Téng Shé) 天柱 (Tiān Zhù) 伤门 (Shāng Mén) Kan 1　Ji Bing	太阴 (Tài Yīn) 禽芮 (Qín Ruì) 生门 (Shēng Mén) Qian 6　Ding/Xin Geng

Yin (阴) Dun# 8 Hour: JiChou ; 直符(ZhíFú): 天心(TiānXīn)
直使(ZhíShǐ): 开门(KāiMén) ; 旬首(XúnShǒu): JiaShenGeng

六合 (Liù Hé) 天英 (Tiān Yīng) 伤门 (Shāng Mén) Xun 4　Yi Ren	太阴 (Tài Yīn) 禽芮 (Qín Ruì) 杜门 (Dù Mén) Li 9　Ding/Xin Yi	腾蛇 (Téng Shé) 天柱 (Tiān Zhù) 景门 (Jīng Mén) Kun 2　Ji Ding/Xin
白虎 (Bái Hǔ) 天辅 (Tiān Fǔ) 生门 (Shēng Mén) Zhen 3　Ren Gui	Yin (阴) Dun# 8 Hour: **JiChou** ©Calvin Yap	值符 (Zhí Fú) 天心 (Tiān Xīn) 死门 (Sǐ Mén) Dui 7　Geng Ji
玄武 (Xuán Wǔ) 天冲 (Tiān Chōng) 休门 (Xiū Mén) Gen 8　Gui Wu	九地 (Jiǔ Dì) 天任 (Tiān Rèn) 开门 (Kāi Mén) Kan 1　Wu Bing	九天 (Jiǔ Tiān) 天蓬 (Tiān Péng) 惊门 (Jīng Mén) Qian 6　Bing Geng

Yin (阴) Dun# 8 Hour: GengYin ; 直符(ZhíFú): 天心(TiānXīn)
直使(ZhíShǐ): 开门(KāiMén) ; 旬首(XúnShǒu): JiaShenGeng

白虎 (Bái Hǔ) 天辅 (Tiān Fǔ) 惊门 (Jīng Mén) Xun 4　Ren Ren	六合 (Liù Hé) 天英 (Tiān Yīng) 开门 (Kāi Mén) Li 9　Yi Yi	太阴 (Tài Yīn) 禽芮 (Qín Ruì) 休门 (Xiū Mén) Kun 2　Ding/Xin Ding/Xin
玄武 (Xuán Wǔ) 天冲 (Tiān Chōng) 死门 (Sǐ Mén) Zhen 3　Gui Gui	Yin (阴) Dun# 8 Hour: **GengYin** **Fu Yin** ©Calvin Yap	腾蛇 (Téng Shé) 天柱 (Tiān Zhù) 生门 (Shēng Mén) Dui 7　Ji Ji
九地 (Jiǔ Dì) 天任 (Tiān Rèn) 景门 (Jīng Mén) Gen 8　Wu Wu	九天 (Jiǔ Tiān) 天蓬 (Tiān Péng) 杜门 (Dù Mén) Kan 1　Bing Bing	值符 (Zhí Fú) 天心 (Tiān Xīn) 伤门 (Shāng Mén) Qian 6　Geng Geng

Yin (阴) Dun# 8 Hour: XinMao ; 直符(ZhíFú): 天心(TiānXīn)
直使(ZhíShǐ): 开门(KāiMén) ; 旬首(XúnShǒu): JiaShenGeng

太阴 (Tài Yīn) 禽芮 (Qín Ruì) 生门 (Shēng Mén) Xun 4　Ding/Xin Ren	腾蛇 (Téng Shé) 天柱 (Tiān Zhù) 伤门 (Shāng Mén) Li 9　Ji Yi	值符 (Zhí Fú) 天心 (Tiān Xīn) 杜门 (Dù Mén) Kun 2　Geng Ding/Xin
六合 (Liù Hé) 天英 (Tiān Yīng) 休门 (Xiū Mén) Zhen 3　Yi Gui	Yin (阴) Dun# 8 Hour: **XinMao** ©Calvin Yap	九天 (Jiǔ Tiān) 天蓬 (Tiān Péng) 景门 (Jīng Mén) Dui 7　Bing Ji
白虎 (Bái Hǔ) 天辅 (Tiān Fǔ) 开门 (Kāi Mén) Gen 8　Ren Wu	玄武 (Xuán Wǔ) 天冲 (Tiān Chōng) 惊门 (Jīng Mén) Kan 1　Gui Bing	九地 (Jiǔ Dì) 天任 (Tiān Rèn) 死门 (Sǐ Mén) Qian 6　Wu Geng

Yin (阴) Dun# 8 Hour: RenChen ; 直符(ZhíFú): 天心(TiānXīn)
直使(ZhíShǐ): 开门(KāiMén) ; 旬首(XúnShǒu): JiaShenGeng

值符 (Zhí Fú) 天心 (Tiān Xīn) 景门 (Jīng Mén) Xun 4　Geng Ren	九天 (Jiǔ Tiān) 天蓬 (Tiān Péng) 死门 (Sǐ Mén) Li 9　Bing Yi	九地 (Jiǔ Dì) 天任 (Tiān Rèn) 惊门 (Jīng Mén) Kun 2　Wu Ding/Xin
腾蛇 (Téng Shé) 天柱 (Tiān Zhù) 杜门 (Dù Mén) Zhen 3　Ji Gui	Yin (阴) Dun# 8 Hour: **RenChen** **Fan Yin** ©Calvin Yap	玄武 (Xuán Wǔ) 天冲 (Tiān Chōng) 开门 (Kāi Mén) Dui 7　Gui Ji
太阴 (Tài Yīn) 禽芮 (Qín Ruì) 伤门 (Shāng Mén) Gen 8　Ding/Xin Wu	六合 (Liù Hé) 天英 (Tiān Yīng) 生门 (Shēng Mén) Kan 1　Yi Bing	白虎 (Bái Hǔ) 天辅 (Tiān Fǔ) 休门 (Xiū Mén) Qian 6　Ren Geng

Yin (阴) Dun# 8 Hour: GuiSi ; 直符(ZhíFú): 天心(TiānXīn)
直使(ZhíShǐ): 开门(KāiMén) ; 旬首(XúnShǒu): JiaShenGeng

九天 (Jiǔ Tiān) 天蓬 (Tiān Péng) 杜门 (Dù Mén) Xun 4　Bing Ren	九地 (Jiǔ Dì) 天任 (Tiān Rèn) 景门 (Jīng Mén) Li 9　Wu Yi	玄武 (Xuán Wǔ) 天冲 (Tiān Chōng) 死门 (Sǐ Mén) Kun 2　Gui Ding/Xin
值符 (Zhí Fú) 天心 (Tiān Xīn) 伤门 (Shāng Mén) Zhen 3　Geng Gui	Yin (阴) Dun# 8 Hour: **GuiSi** ©Calvin Yap	白虎 (Bái Hǔ) 天辅 (Tiān Fǔ) 惊门 (Jīng Mén) Dui 7　Ren Ji
腾蛇 (Téng Shé) 天柱 (Tiān Zhù) 生门 (Shēng Mén) Gen 8　Ji Wu	太阴 (Tài Yīn) 禽芮 (Qín Ruì) 休门 (Xiū Mén) Kan 1　Ding/Xin Bing	六合 (Liù Hé) 天英 (Tiān Yīng) 开门 (Kāi Mén) Qian 6　Yi Geng

---

Chart: -8JiaWu (Yin Dun #8 JiaWu Xun)
JiaWu, YiWei, BingShen, DingYou, WuXu, JiHai, GengZi, XinChou, RenYin, GuiMao

---

Yin (阴) Dun# 8 Hour: **JiaWu**；直符(ZhíFú): 天禽(TiānQín)
直使(ZhíShǐ): 死门(SǐMén)；旬首(XúnShǒu): JiaWu/Xin

太阴 (Tài Yīn)	螣蛇 (Téng Shé)	值符 (Zhí Fú)
天辅 (Tiān Fǔ)	天英 (Tiān Yīng)	禽芮 (Qín Ruì)
杜门 (Dù Mén)	景门 (Jǐng Mén)	死门 (Sǐ Mén)
Xun 4　　Ren	Li 9　　Yi	Kun 2　Ding/Xin
Ren	Yi	Ding/Xin
六合 (Liù Hé)	Yin (阴) Dun# 8	九天 (Jiǔ Tiān)
天冲 (Tiān Chōng)	Hour: **JiaWu**	天柱 (Tiān Zhù)
伤门 (Shāng Mén)	**Fu Yin**	惊门 (Jǐng Mén)
Zhen 3　　Gui	©Calvin Yap	Dui 7　　Ji
Gui		Ji
白虎 (Bái Hǔ)	玄武 (Xuán Wǔ)	九地 (Jiǔ Dì)
天任 (Tiān Rèn)	天蓬 (Tiān Péng)	天心 (Tiān Xīn)
生门 (Shēng Mén)	休门 (Xiū Mén)	开门 (Kāi Mén)
Gen 8　　Wu	Kan 1　　Bing	Qian 6　Geng
Wu	Bing	Geng

Yin (阴) Dun# 8 Hour: **YiWei**；直符(ZhíFú): 天禽(TiānQín)
直使(ZhíShǐ): 死门(SǐMén)；旬首(XúnShǒu): JiaWu/Xin

螣蛇 (Téng Shé)	值符 (Zhí Fú)	九天 (Jiǔ Tiān)
天英 (Tiān Yīng)	禽芮 (Qín Ruì)	天柱 (Tiān Zhù)
死门 (Sǐ Mén)	惊门 (Jǐng Mén)	开门 (Kāi Mén)
Xun 4　　Yi	Li 9　Ding/Xin	Kun 2　　Ji
Ren	Yi	Ding/Xin
太阴 (Tài Yīn)	Yin (阴) Dun# 8	九地 (Jiǔ Dì)
天辅 (Tiān Fǔ)	Hour: **YiWei**	天心 (Tiān Xīn)
景门 (Jǐng Mén)		休门 (Xiū Mén)
Zhen 3　　Ren	©Calvin Yap	Dui 7　Geng
Gui		Ji
六合 (Liù Hé)	白虎 (Bái Hǔ)	玄武 (Xuán Wǔ)
天冲 (Tiān Chōng)	天任 (Tiān Rèn)	天蓬 (Tiān Péng)
杜门 (Dù Mén)	伤门 (Shāng Mén)	生门 (Shēng Mén)
Gen 8　　Gui	Kan 1　　Wu	Qian 6　Bing
Wu	Bing	Geng

Yin (阴) Dun# 8 Hour: **BingShen**；直符(ZhíFú): 天禽(TiānQín)
直使(ZhíShǐ): 死门(SǐMén)；旬首(XúnShǒu): JiaWu/Xin

玄武 (Xuán Wǔ)	白虎 (Bái Hǔ)	六合 (Liù Hé)
天蓬 (Tiān Péng)	天任 (Tiān Rèn)	天冲 (Tiān Chōng)
惊门 (Jǐng Mén)	开门 (Kāi Mén)	休门 (Xiū Mén)
Xun 4　　Bing	Li 9　　Wu	Kun 2　　Gui
Ren	Yi	Ding/Xin
九地 (Jiǔ Dì)	Yin (阴) Dun# 8	太阴 (Tài Yīn)
天心 (Tiān Xīn)	Hour: **BingShen**	天辅 (Tiān Fǔ)
死门 (Sǐ Mén)		生门 (Shēng Mén)
Zhen 3　　Geng	©Calvin Yap	Dui 7　　Ren
Gui		Ji
九天 (Jiǔ Tiān)	值符 (Zhí Fú)	螣蛇 (Téng Shé)
天柱 (Tiān Zhù)	禽芮 (Qín Ruì)	天英 (Tiān Yīng)
景门 (Jǐng Mén)	杜门 (Dù Mén)	伤门 (Shāng Mén)
Gen 8　　Ji	Kan 1　Ding/Xin	Qian 6　　Yi
Wu	Bing	Geng

Yin (阴) Dun# 8 Hour: **DingYou**；直符(ZhíFú): 天禽(TiānQín)
直使(ZhíShǐ): 死门(SǐMén)；旬首(XúnShǒu): JiaWu/Xin

太阴 (Tài Yīn)	螣蛇 (Téng Shé)	值符 (Zhí Fú)
天辅 (Tiān Fǔ)	天英 (Tiān Yīng)	禽芮 (Qín Ruì)
杜门 (Dù Mén)	景门 (Jǐng Mén)	死门 (Sǐ Mén)
Xun 4　　Ren	Li 9　　Yi	Kun 2　Ding/Xin
Ren	Yi	Ding/Xin
六合 (Liù Hé)	Yin (阴) Dun# 8	九天 (Jiǔ Tiān)
天冲 (Tiān Chōng)	Hour: **DingYou**	天柱 (Tiān Zhù)
伤门 (Shāng Mén)	**Fu Yin**	惊门 (Jǐng Mén)
Zhen 3　　Gui	©Calvin Yap	Dui 7　　Ji
Gui		Ji
白虎 (Bái Hǔ)	玄武 (Xuán Wǔ)	九地 (Jiǔ Dì)
天任 (Tiān Rèn)	天蓬 (Tiān Péng)	天心 (Tiān Xīn)
生门 (Shēng Mén)	休门 (Xiū Mén)	开门 (Kāi Mén)
Gen 8　　Wu	Kan 1　　Bing	Qian 6　Geng
Wu	Bing	Geng

Yin (阴) Dun# 8 Hour: **WuXu**；直符(ZhíFú): 天禽(TiānQín)
直使(ZhíShǐ): 死门(SǐMén)；旬首(XúnShǒu): JiaWu/Xin

九地 (Jiǔ Dì)	玄武 (Xuán Wǔ)	白虎 (Bái Hǔ)
天心 (Tiān Xīn)	天蓬 (Tiān Péng)	天任 (Tiān Rèn)
休门 (Xiū Mén)	生门 (Shēng Mén)	伤门 (Shāng Mén)
Xun 4　　Geng	Li 9　　Bing	Kun 2　　Wu
Ren	Yi	Ding/Xin
九天 (Jiǔ Tiān)	Yin (阴) Dun# 8	六合 (Liù Hé)
天柱 (Tiān Zhù)	Hour: **WuXu**	天冲 (Tiān Chōng)
开门 (Kāi Mén)	**Fan Yin**	杜门 (Dù Mén)
Zhen 3　　Ji	©Calvin Yap	Dui 7　　Gui
Gui		Ji
值符 (Zhí Fú)	螣蛇 (Téng Shé)	太阴 (Tài Yīn)
禽芮 (Qín Ruì)	天英 (Tiān Yīng)	天辅 (Tiān Fǔ)
惊门 (Jǐng Mén)	死门 (Sǐ Mén)	景门 (Jǐng Mén)
Gen 8　Ding/Xin	Kan 1　　Yi	Qian 6　Ren
Wu	Bing	Geng

Yin (阴) Dun# 8 Hour: **JiHai**；直符(ZhíFú): 天禽(TiānQín)
直使(ZhíShǐ): 死门(SǐMén)；旬首(XúnShǒu): JiaWu/Xin

六合 (Liù Hé)	太阴 (Tài Yīn)	螣蛇 (Téng Shé)
天冲 (Tiān Chōng)	天辅 (Tiān Fǔ)	天英 (Tiān Yīng)
景门 (Jǐng Mén)	死门 (Sǐ Mén)	惊门 (Jǐng Mén)
Xun 4　　Gui	Li 9　　Ren	Kun 2　　Yi
Ren	Yi	Ding/Xin
白虎 (Bái Hǔ)	Yin (阴) Dun# 8	值符 (Zhí Fú)
天任 (Tiān Rèn)	Hour: **JiHai**	禽芮 (Qín Ruì)
杜门 (Dù Mén)		开门 (Kāi Mén)
Zhen 3　　Wu	©Calvin Yap	Dui 7　Ding/Xin
Gui		Ji
玄武 (Xuán Wǔ)	九地 (Jiǔ Dì)	九天 (Jiǔ Tiān)
天蓬 (Tiān Péng)	天心 (Tiān Xīn)	天柱 (Tiān Zhù)
伤门 (Shāng Mén)	生门 (Shēng Mén)	休门 (Xiū Mén)
Gen 8　　Bing	Kan 1　　Geng	Qian 6　　Ji
Wu	Bing	Geng

Yin (阴) Dun# 8 Hour: **GengZi**；直符(ZhíFú): 天禽(TiānQín)
直使(ZhíShǐ): 死门(SǐMén)；旬首(XúnShǒu): JiaWu/Xin

白虎 (Bái Hǔ) 天任 (Tiān Rèn) 开门 (Kāi Mén) Xun 4　　Wu 　　　Ren	六合 (Liù Hé) 天冲 (Tiān Chōng) 休门 (Xiū Mén) Li 9　　Gui 　　　Yi	太阴 (Tài Yīn) 天辅 (Tiān Fǔ) 生门 (Shēng Mén) Kun 2　　Ren 　　　Ding/Xin
玄武 (Xuán Wǔ) 天蓬 (Tiān Péng) 惊门 (Jīng Mén) Zhen 3　　Bing 　　　Gui	Yin (阴) Dun# 8 Hour: **GengZi** ©Calvin Yap	腾蛇 (Téng Shé) 天英 (Tiān Yīng) 伤门 (Shāng Mén) Dui 7　　Yi 　　　Ji
九地 (Jiǔ Dì) 天心 (Tiān Xīn) 死门 (Sǐ Mén) Gen 8　　Geng 　　　Wu	九天 (Jiǔ Tiān) 天柱 (Tiān Zhù) 景门 (Jīng Mén) Kan 1　　Ji 　　　Bing	值符 (Zhí Fú) 禽芮 (Qín Ruì) 杜门 (Dù Mén) Qian 6　　Ding/Xin 　　　Geng

Yin (阴) Dun# 8 Hour: **XinChou**；直符(ZhíFú): 天禽(TiānQín)
直使(ZhíShǐ): 死门(SǐMén)；旬首(XúnShǒu): JiaWu/Xin

太阴 (Tài Yīn) 天辅 (Tiān Fǔ) 伤门 (Shāng Mén) Xun 4　　Ren 　　　Ren	腾蛇 (Téng Shé) 天英 (Tiān Yīng) 杜门 (Dù Mén) Li 9　　Yi 　　　Yi	值符 (Zhí Fú) 禽芮 (Qín Ruì) 景门 (Jīng Mén) Kun 2　　Ding/Xin 　　　Ding/Xin
六合 (Liù Hé) 天冲 (Tiān Chōng) 生门 (Shēng Mén) Zhen 3　　Gui 　　　Gui	Yin (阴) Dun# 8 Hour: **XinChou** **Fu Yin** ©Calvin Yap	九天 (Jiǔ Tiān) 天柱 (Tiān Zhù) 死门 (Sǐ Mén) Dui 7　　Ji 　　　Ji
白虎 (Bái Hǔ) 天任 (Tiān Rèn) 休门 (Xiū Mén) Gen 8　　Wu 　　　Wu	玄武 (Xuán Wǔ) 天蓬 (Tiān Péng) 开门 (Kāi Mén) Kan 1　　Bing 　　　Bing	九地 (Jiǔ Dì) 天心 (Tiān Xīn) 惊门 (Jīng Mén) Qian 6　　Geng 　　　Geng

Yin (阴) Dun# 8 Hour: **RenYin**；直符(ZhíFú): 天禽(TiānQín)
直使(ZhíShǐ): 死门(SǐMén)；旬首(XúnShǒu): JiaWu/Xin

值符 (Zhí Fú) 禽芮 (Qín Ruì) 生门 (Shēng Mén) Xun 4　　Ding/Xin 　　　Ren	九天 (Jiǔ Tiān) 天柱 (Tiān Zhù) 伤门 (Shāng Mén) Li 9　　Ji 　　　Yi	九地 (Jiǔ Dì) 天心 (Tiān Xīn) 杜门 (Dù Mén) Kun 2　　Geng 　　　Ding/Xin
腾蛇 (Téng Shé) 天英 (Tiān Yīng) 休门 (Xiū Mén) Zhen 3　　Yi 　　　Gui	Yin (阴) Dun# 8 Hour: **RenYin** ©Calvin Yap	玄武 (Xuán Wǔ) 天蓬 (Tiān Péng) 景门 (Jīng Mén) Dui 7　　Bing 　　　Ji
太阴 (Tài Yīn) 天辅 (Tiān Fǔ) 开门 (Kāi Mén) Gen 8　　Ren 　　　Wu	六合 (Liù Hé) 天冲 (Tiān Chōng) 惊门 (Jīng Mén) Kan 1　　Gui 　　　Bing	白虎 (Bái Hǔ) 天任 (Tiān Rèn) 死门 (Sǐ Mén) Qian 6　　Wu 　　　Geng

Yin (阴) Dun# 8 Hour: **GuiMao**；直符(ZhíFú): 天禽(TiānQín)
直使(ZhíShǐ): 死门(SǐMén)；旬首(XúnShǒu): JiaWu/Xin

九天 (Jiǔ Tiān) 天柱 (Tiān Zhù) 杜门 (Dù Mén) Xun 4　　Ji 　　　Ren	九地 (Jiǔ Dì) 天心 (Tiān Xīn) 景门 (Jīng Mén) Li 9　　Geng 　　　Yi	玄武 (Xuán Wǔ) 天蓬 (Tiān Péng) 死门 (Sǐ Mén) Kun 2　　Bing 　　　Ding/Xin
值符 (Zhí Fú) 禽芮 (Qín Ruì) 伤门 (Shāng Mén) Zhen 3　　Ding/Xin 　　　Gui	Yin (阴) Dun# 8 Hour: **GuiMao** ©Calvin Yap	白虎 (Bái Hǔ) 天任 (Tiān Rèn) 惊门 (Jīng Mén) Dui 7　　Wu 　　　Ji
腾蛇 (Téng Shé) 天英 (Tiān Yīng) 生门 (Shēng Mén) Gen 8　　Yi 　　　Wu	太阴 (Tài Yīn) 天辅 (Tiān Fǔ) 休门 (Xiū Mén) Kan 1　　Ren 　　　Bing	六合 (Liù Hé) 天冲 (Tiān Chōng) 开门 (Kāi Mén) Qian 6　　Gui 　　　Geng

---

Chart: -8JiaChen (Yin Dun #8 JiaChen Xun)
JiaChen, YiSi, BingWu, DingWei, WuShen, JiYou, GengXu, XinHai, RenZi, GuiChou

Yin (阴) Dun# 8 Hour: **JiaChen**；直符(ZhíFú): 天辅(TiānFǔ)
直使(ZhíShǐ): 杜门(DùMén)；旬首(XúnShǒu): JiaChenRen

值符 (Zhí Fú) 天辅 (Tiān Fǔ) 杜门 (Dù Mén) Xun 4　　Ren 　　　Ren	九天 (Jiǔ Tiān) 天英 (Tiān Yīng) 景门 (Jīng Mén) Li 9　　Yi 　　　Yi	九地 (Jiǔ Dì) 禽芮 (Qín Ruì) 死门 (Sǐ Mén) Kun 2　　Ding/Xin 　　　Ding/Xin
腾蛇 (Téng Shé) 天冲 (Tiān Chōng) 伤门 (Shāng Mén) Zhen 3　　Gui 　　　Gui	Yin (阴) Dun# 8 Hour: **JiaChen** **Fu Yin** ©Calvin Yap	玄武 (Xuán Wǔ) 天柱 (Tiān Zhù) 惊门 (Jīng Mén) Dui 7　　Ji 　　　Ji
太阴 (Tài Yīn) 天任 (Tiān Rèn) 生门 (Shēng Mén) Gen 8　　Wu 　　　Wu	六合 (Liù Hé) 天蓬 (Tiān Péng) 休门 (Xiū Mén) Kan 1　　Bing 　　　Bing	白虎 (Bái Hǔ) 天心 (Tiān Xīn) 开门 (Kāi Mén) Qian 6　　Geng 　　　Geng

Yin (阴) Dun# 8 Hour: **YiSi**；直符(ZhíFú): 天辅(TiānFǔ)
直使(ZhíShǐ): 杜门(DùMén)；旬首(XúnShǒu): JiaChenRen

腾蛇 (Téng Shé) 天冲 (Tiān Chōng) 景门 (Jīng Mén) Xun 4　　Gui 　　　Ren	值符 (Zhí Fú) 天辅 (Tiān Fǔ) 死门 (Sǐ Mén) Li 9　　Ren 　　　Yi	九天 (Jiǔ Tiān) 天英 (Tiān Yīng) 惊门 (Jīng Mén) Kun 2　　Yi 　　　Ding/Xin
太阴 (Tài Yīn) 天任 (Tiān Rèn) 杜门 (Dù Mén) Zhen 3　　Wu 　　　Gui	Yin (阴) Dun# 8 Hour: **YiSi** ©Calvin Yap	九地 (Jiǔ Dì) 禽芮 (Qín Ruì) 开门 (Kāi Mén) Dui 7　　Ding/Xin 　　　Ji
六合 (Liù Hé) 天蓬 (Tiān Péng) 伤门 (Shāng Mén) Gen 8　　Bing 　　　Wu	白虎 (Bái Hǔ) 天心 (Tiān Xīn) 生门 (Shēng Mén) Kan 1　　Geng 　　　Bing	玄武 (Xuán Wǔ) 天柱 (Tiān Zhù) 休门 (Xiū Mén) Qian 6　　Ji 　　　Geng

Yin (阴) Dun# 8 Hour: BingWu；直符(ZhíFú): 天辅(TiānFǔ)
直使(ZhíShǐ): 杜门(DùMén)；旬首(XúnShǒu): JiaChenRen

玄武 (Xuán Wǔ) 天柱 (Tiān Zhù) 生门 (Shēng Mén) Xun 4 Ji Ren	白虎 (Bái Hǔ) 天心 (Tiān Xīn) 伤门 (Shāng Mén) Li 9 Geng Yi	六合 (Liù Hé) 天蓬 (Tiān Péng) 杜门 (Dù Mén) Kun 2 Bing Ding/Xin
九地 (Jiǔ Dì) 禽芮 (Qín Ruì) 休门 (Xiū Mén) Zhen 3 Ding/Xin Gui	Yin (阴) Dun# 8 Hour: **BingWu** ©Calvin Yap	太阴 (Tài Yīn) 天任 (Tiān Rèn) 景门 (Jǐng Mén) Dui 7 Wu Ji
九天 (Jiǔ Tiān) 天英 (Tiān Yīng) 开门 (Kāi Mén) Gen 8 Yi Wu	值符 (Zhí Fú) 天辅 (Tiān Fù) 惊门 (Jīng Mén) Kan 1 Ren Bing	螣蛇 (Téng Shé) 天冲 (Tiān Chōng) 死门 (Sǐ Mén) Qian 6 Gui Geng

Yin (阴) Dun# 8 Hour: DingWei；直符(ZhíFú): 天辅(TiānFǔ)
直使(ZhíShǐ): 杜门(DùMén)；旬首(XúnShǒu): JiaChenRen

太阴 (Tài Yīn) 天任 (Tiān Rèn) 惊门 (Jīng Mén) Xun 4 Wu Ren	螣蛇 (Téng Shé) 天冲 (Tiān Chōng) 开门 (Kāi Mén) Li 9 Gui Yi	值符 (Zhí Fú) 天辅 (Tiān Fù) 休门 (Xiū Mén) Kun 2 Ren Ding/Xin
六合 (Liù Hé) 天蓬 (Tiān Péng) 死门 (Sǐ Mén) Zhen 3 Bing Gui	Yin (阴) Dun# 8 Hour: **DingWei** ©Calvin Yap	九天 (Jiǔ Tiān) 天英 (Tiān Yīng) 生门 (Shēng Mén) Dui 7 Yi Ji
白虎 (Bái Hǔ) 天心 (Tiān Xīn) 景门 (Jǐng Mén) Gen 8 Geng Wu	玄武 (Xuán Wǔ) 天柱 (Tiān Zhù) 杜门 (Dù Mén) Kan 1 Ji Bing	九地 (Jiǔ Dì) 禽芮 (Qín Ruì) 伤门 (Shāng Mén) Qian 6 Ding/Xin Geng

Yin (阴) Dun# 8 Hour: WuShen；直符(ZhíFú): 天辅(TiānFǔ)
直使(ZhíShǐ): 杜门(DùMén)；旬首(XúnShǒu): JiaChenRen

九地 (Jiǔ Dì) 禽芮 (Qín Ruì) 伤门 (Shāng Mén) Xun 4 Ding/Xin Ren	玄武 (Xuán Wǔ) 天柱 (Tiān Zhù) 杜门 (Dù Mén) Li 9 Ji Yi	白虎 (Bái Hǔ) 天心 (Tiān Xīn) 景门 (Jǐng Mén) Kun 2 Geng Ding/Xin
九天 (Jiǔ Tiān) 天英 (Tiān Yīng) 生门 (Shēng Mén) Zhen 3 Yi Gui	Yin (阴) Dun# 8 Hour: **WuShen** ©Calvin Yap	六合 (Liù Hé) 天蓬 (Tiān Péng) 死门 (Sǐ Mén) Dui 7 Bing Ji
值符 (Zhí Fú) 天辅 (Tiān Fù) 休门 (Xiū Mén) Gen 8 Ren Wu	螣蛇 (Téng Shé) 天冲 (Tiān Chōng) 开门 (Kāi Mén) Kan 1 Gui Bing	太阴 (Tài Yīn) 天任 (Tiān Rèn) 惊门 (Jīng Mén) Qian 6 Wu Geng

Yin (阴) Dun# 8 Hour: JiYou；直符(ZhíFú): 天辅(TiānFǔ)
直使(ZhíShǐ): 杜门(DùMén)；旬首(XúnShǒu): JiaChenRen

六合 (Liù Hé) 天蓬 (Tiān Péng) 死门 (Sǐ Mén) Xun 4 Bing Ren	太阴 (Tài Yīn) 天任 (Tiān Rèn) 惊门 (Jīng Mén) Li 9 Wu Yi	螣蛇 (Téng Shé) 天冲 (Tiān Chōng) 开门 (Kāi Mén) Kun 2 Gui Ding/Xin
白虎 (Bái Hǔ) 天心 (Tiān Xīn) 景门 (Jǐng Mén) Zhen 3 Geng Gui	Yin (阴) Dun# 8 Hour: **JiYou** ©Calvin Yap	值符 (Zhí Fú) 天辅 (Tiān Fù) 休门 (Xiū Mén) Dui 7 Ren Ji
玄武 (Xuán Wǔ) 天柱 (Tiān Zhù) 杜门 (Dù Mén) Gen 8 Ji Wu	九地 (Jiǔ Dì) 禽芮 (Qín Ruì) 伤门 (Shāng Mén) Kan 1 Ding/Xin Bing	九天 (Jiǔ Tiān) 天英 (Tiān Yīng) 生门 (Shēng Mén) Qian 6 Yi Geng

Yin (阴) Dun# 8 Hour: GengXu；直符(ZhíFú): 天辅(TiānFǔ)
直使(ZhíShǐ): 杜门(DùMén)；旬首(XúnShǒu): JiaChenRen

白虎 (Bái Hǔ) 天心 (Tiān Xīn) 休门 (Xiū Mén) Xun 4 Geng Ren	六合 (Liù Hé) 天蓬 (Tiān Péng) 生门 (Shēng Mén) Li 9 Bing Yi	太阴 (Tài Yīn) 天任 (Tiān Rèn) 伤门 (Shāng Mén) Kun 2 Wu Ding/Xin
玄武 (Xuán Wǔ) 天柱 (Tiān Zhù) 开门 (Kāi Mén) Zhen 3 Ji Gui	Yin (阴) Dun# 8 Hour: **GengXu** **Fan Yin** ©Calvin Yap	螣蛇 (Téng Shé) 天冲 (Tiān Chōng) 杜门 (Dù Mén) Dui 7 Gui Ji
九地 (Jiǔ Dì) 禽芮 (Qín Ruì) 惊门 (Jīng Mén) Gen 8 Ding/Xin Wu	九天 (Jiǔ Tiān) 天英 (Tiān Yīng) 死门 (Sǐ Mén) Kan 1 Yi Bing	值符 (Zhí Fú) 天辅 (Tiān Fù) 景门 (Jǐng Mén) Qian 6 Ren Geng

Yin (阴) Dun# 8 Hour: XinHai；直符(ZhíFú): 天辅(TiānFǔ)
直使(ZhíShǐ): 杜门(DùMén)；旬首(XúnShǒu): JiaChenRen

太阴 (Tài Yīn) 天任 (Tiān Rèn) 开门 (Kāi Mén) Xun 4 Wu Ren	螣蛇 (Téng Shé) 天冲 (Tiān Chōng) 休门 (Xiū Mén) Li 9 Gui Yi	值符 (Zhí Fú) 天辅 (Tiān Fù) 生门 (Shēng Mén) Kun 2 Ren Ding/Xin
六合 (Liù Hé) 天蓬 (Tiān Péng) 惊门 (Jīng Mén) Zhen 3 Bing Gui	Yin (阴) Dun# 8 Hour: **XinHai** ©Calvin Yap	九天 (Jiǔ Tiān) 天英 (Tiān Yīng) 伤门 (Shāng Mén) Dui 7 Yi Ji
白虎 (Bái Hǔ) 天心 (Tiān Xīn) 死门 (Sǐ Mén) Gen 8 Geng Wu	玄武 (Xuán Wǔ) 天柱 (Tiān Zhù) 景门 (Jǐng Mén) Kan 1 Ji Bing	九地 (Jiǔ Dì) 禽芮 (Qín Ruì) 杜门 (Dù Mén) Qian 6 Ding/Xin Geng

Yin (阴) Dun# 8 Hour: RenZi；直符(ZhíFú): 天辅(TiānFǔ)
直使(ZhíShǐ): 杜门(DùMén)；旬首(XúnShǒu): JiaChenRen

值符 (Zhí Fú) 天辅 (Tiān Fǔ) 生门 (Shēng Mén) Xun 4　Ren Ren	九天 (Jiǔ Tiān) 天英 (Tiān Yīng) 伤门 (Shāng Mén) Li 9　Yi Yi	九地 (Jiǔ Dì) 禽芮 (Qín Ruì) 杜门 (Dù Mén) Kun 2　Ding/Xin Ding/Xin
螣蛇 (Téng Shé) 天冲 (Tiān Chōng) 休门 (Xiū Mén) Zhen 3　Gui Gui	Yin (阴) Dun# 8 Hour: **RenZi** **Fu Yin** ©Calvin Yap	玄武 (Xuán Wǔ) 天柱 (Tiān Zhù) 景门 (Jǐng Mén) Dui 7　Ji Ji
太阴 (Tài Yīn) 天任 (Tiān Rèn) 开门 (Kāi Mén) Gen 8　Wu Wu	六合 (Liù Hé) 天蓬 (Tiān Péng) 惊门 (Jīng Mén) Kan 1　Bing Bing	白虎 (Bái Hǔ) 天心 (Tiān Xīn) 死门 (Sǐ Mén) Qian 6　Geng Geng

Yin (阴) Dun# 8 Hour: GuiChou；直符(ZhíFú): 天辅(TiānFǔ)
直使(ZhíShǐ): 杜门(DùMén)；旬首(XúnShǒu): JiaChenRen

九天 (Jiǔ Tiān) 天英 (Tiān Yīng) 杜门 (Dù Mén) Xun 4　Yi Ren	九地 (Jiǔ Dì) 禽芮 (Qín Ruì) 景门 (Jǐng Mén) Li 9　Ding/Xin Yi	玄武 (Xuán Wǔ) 天柱 (Tiān Zhù) 死门 (Sǐ Mén) Kun 2　Ji Ding/Xin
值符 (Zhí Fú) 天辅 (Tiān Fǔ) 伤门 (Shāng Mén) Zhen 3　Ren Gui	Yin (阴) Dun# 8 Hour: **GuiChou** ©Calvin Yap	白虎 (Bái Hǔ) 天心 (Tiān Xīn) 惊门 (Jīng Mén) Dui 7　Geng Ji
螣蛇 (Téng Shé) 天冲 (Tiān Chōng) 生门 (Shēng Mén) Gen 8　Gui Wu	太阴 (Tài Yīn) 天任 (Tiān Rèn) 休门 (Xiū Mén) Kan 1　Wu Bing	六合 (Liù Hé) 天蓬 (Tiān Péng) 开门 (Kāi Mén) Qian 6　Bing Geng

---

Chart: -8JiaYin (Yin Dun #8 JiaYin Xun)
JiaYin, YiMao, BingChen, DingSi, WuWu, JiWei, GengShen, XinYou, RenXu, GuiHai

Yin (阴) Dun# 8 Hour: JiaYin；直符(ZhíFú): 天冲(TiānChōng)
直使(ZhíShǐ): 伤门(ShāngMén)；旬首(XúnShǒu): JiaYinGui

九天 (Jiǔ Tiān) 天辅 (Tiān Fǔ) 杜门 (Dù Mén) Xun 4　Ren Ren	九地 (Jiǔ Dì) 天英 (Tiān Yīng) 景门 (Jǐng Mén) Li 9　Yi Yi	玄武 (Xuán Wǔ) 禽芮 (Qín Ruì) 死门 (Sǐ Mén) Kun 2　Ding/Xin Ding/Xin
值符 (Zhí Fú) 天冲 (Tiān Chōng) 伤门 (Shāng Mén) Zhen 3　Gui Gui	Yin (阴) Dun# 8 Hour: **JiaYin** **Fu Yin** ©Calvin Yap	白虎 (Bái Hǔ) 天柱 (Tiān Zhù) 惊门 (Jīng Mén) Dui 7　Ji Ji
螣蛇 (Téng Shé) 天任 (Tiān Rèn) 生门 (Shēng Mén) Gen 8　Wu Wu	太阴 (Tài Yīn) 天蓬 (Tiān Péng) 休门 (Xiū Mén) Kan 1　Bing Bing	六合 (Liù Hé) 天心 (Tiān Xīn) 开门 (Kāi Mén) Qian 6　Geng Geng

Yin (阴) Dun# 8 Hour: YiMao；直符(ZhíFú): 天冲(TiānChōng)
直使(ZhíShǐ): 伤门(ShāngMén)；旬首(XúnShǒu): JiaYinGui

螣蛇 (Téng Shé) 天任 (Tiān Rèn) 休门 (Xiū Mén) Xun 4　Wu Ren	值符 (Zhí Fú) 天冲 (Tiān Chōng) 生门 (Shēng Mén) Li 9　Gui Yi	九天 (Jiǔ Tiān) 天辅 (Tiān Fǔ) 伤门 (Shāng Mén) Kun 2　Ren Ding/Xin
太阴 (Tài Yīn) 天蓬 (Tiān Péng) 开门 (Kāi Mén) Zhen 3　Bing Gui	Yin (阴) Dun# 8 Hour: **YiMao** ©Calvin Yap	九地 (Jiǔ Dì) 天英 (Tiān Yīng) 杜门 (Dù Mén) Dui 7　Yi Ji
六合 (Liù Hé) 天心 (Tiān Xīn) 惊门 (Jīng Mén) Gen 8　Geng Wu	白虎 (Bái Hǔ) 天柱 (Tiān Zhù) 死门 (Sǐ Mén) Kan 1　Ji Bing	玄武 (Xuán Wǔ) 禽芮 (Qín Ruì) 景门 (Jǐng Mén) Qian 6　Ding/Xin Geng

Yin (阴) Dun# 8 Hour: BingChen；直符(ZhíFú): 天冲(TiānChōng)
直使(ZhíShǐ): 伤门(ShāngMén)；旬首(XúnShǒu): JiaYinGui

玄武 (Xuán Wǔ) 禽芮 (Qín Ruì) 死门 (Sǐ Mén) Xun 4　Ding/Xin Ren	白虎 (Bái Hǔ) 天柱 (Tiān Zhù) 惊门 (Jīng Mén) Li 9　Ji Yi	六合 (Liù Hé) 天心 (Tiān Xīn) 开门 (Kāi Mén) Kun 2　Geng Ding/Xin
九地 (Jiǔ Dì) 天英 (Tiān Yīng) 景门 (Jǐng Mén) Zhen 3　Yi Gui	Yin (阴) Dun# 8 Hour: **BingChen** ©Calvin Yap	太阴 (Tài Yīn) 天蓬 (Tiān Péng) 休门 (Xiū Mén) Dui 7　Bing Ji
九天 (Jiǔ Tiān) 天辅 (Tiān Fǔ) 杜门 (Dù Mén) Gen 8　Ren Wu	值符 (Zhí Fú) 天冲 (Tiān Chōng) 伤门 (Shāng Mén) Kan 1　Gui Bing	螣蛇 (Téng Shé) 天任 (Tiān Rèn) 生门 (Shēng Mén) Qian 6　Wu Geng

Yin (阴) Dun# 8 Hour: DingSi；直符(ZhíFú): 天冲(TiānChōng)
直使(ZhíShǐ): 伤门(ShāngMén)；旬首(XúnShǒu): JiaYinGui

太阴 (Tài Yīn) 天蓬 (Tiān Péng) 生门 (Shēng Mén) Xun 4　Bing Ren	螣蛇 (Téng Shé) 天任 (Tiān Rèn) 伤门 (Shāng Mén) Li 9　Wu Yi	值符 (Zhí Fú) 天冲 (Tiān Chōng) 杜门 (Dù Mén) Kun 2　Gui Ding/Xin
六合 (Liù Hé) 天心 (Tiān Xīn) 休门 (Xiū Mén) Zhen 3　Geng Gui	Yin (阴) Dun# 8 Hour: **DingSi** ©Calvin Yap	九天 (Jiǔ Tiān) 天辅 (Tiān Fǔ) 景门 (Jǐng Mén) Dui 7　Ren Ji
白虎 (Bái Hǔ) 天柱 (Tiān Zhù) 开门 (Kāi Mén) Gen 8　Ji Wu	玄武 (Xuán Wǔ) 禽芮 (Qín Ruì) 惊门 (Jīng Mén) Kan 1　Ding/Xin Bing	九地 (Jiǔ Dì) 天英 (Tiān Yīng) 死门 (Sǐ Mén) Qian 6　Yi Geng

Yin (阴) Dun# 8 Hour: WuWu ; 直符(ZhíFú): 天冲(TiānChōng) ; 直使(ZhíShǐ): 伤门(ShāngMén) ; 旬首(XúnShǒu): JiaYinGui

九地 (Jiǔ Dì) 天英 (Tiān Yīng) 景门 (Jǐng Mén) Xun 4　Yi Ren	玄武 (Xuán Wǔ) 禽芮 (Qín Ruì) 死门 (Sǐ Mén) Li 9　Ding/Xin Yi	白虎 (Bái Hǔ) 天柱 (Tiān Zhù) 惊门 (Jīng Mén) Kun 2　Ji Ding/Xin
九天 (Jiǔ Tiān) 天辅 (Tiān Fǔ) 杜门 (Dù Mén) Zhen 3　Ren Gui	Yin (阴) Dun# 8 Hour: **WuWu** ©Calvin Yap	六合 (Liù Hé) 天心 (Tiān Xīn) 开门 (Kāi Mén) Dui 7　Geng Ji
值符 (Zhí Fú) 天冲 (Tiān Chōng) 伤门 (Shāng Mén) Gen 8　Gui Wu	螣蛇 (Téng Shé) 天任 (Tiān Rèn) 生门 (Shēng Mén) Kan 1　Wu Bing	太阴 (Tài Yīn) 天蓬 (Tiān Péng) 休门 (Xiū Mén) Qian 6　Bing Geng

Yin (阴) Dun# 8 Hour: JiWei ; 直符(ZhíFú): 天冲(TiānChōng) ; 直使(ZhíShǐ): 伤门(ShāngMén) ; 旬首(XúnShǒu): JiaYinGui

六合 (Liù Hé) 天心 (Tiān Xīn) 开门 (Kāi Mén) Xun 4　Geng Ren	太阴 (Tài Yīn) 天蓬 (Tiān Péng) 休门 (Xiū Mén) Li 9　Bing Yi	螣蛇 (Téng Shé) 天任 (Tiān Rèn) 生门 (Shēng Mén) Kun 2　Wu Ding/Xin
白虎 (Bái Hǔ) 天柱 (Tiān Zhù) 惊门 (Jīng Mén) Zhen 3　Ji Gui	Yin (阴) Dun# 8 Hour: **JiWei** **Fan Yin** ©Calvin Yap	值符 (Zhí Fú) 天冲 (Tiān Chōng) 伤门 (Shāng Mén) Dui 7　Gui Ji
玄武 (Xuán Wǔ) 禽芮 (Qín Ruì) 死门 (Sǐ Mén) Gen 8　Ding/Xin Wu	九地 (Jiǔ Dì) 天英 (Tiān Yīng) 景门 (Jǐng Mén) Kan 1　Yi Bing	九天 (Jiǔ Tiān) 天辅 (Tiān Fǔ) 杜门 (Dù Mén) Qian 6　Ren Geng

Yin (阴) Dun# 8 Hour: GengShen ; 直符(ZhíFú): 天冲(TiānChōng) ; 直使(ZhíShǐ): 伤门(ShāngMén) ; 旬首(XúnShǒu): JiaYinGui

白虎 (Bái Hǔ) 天柱 (Tiān Zhù) 惊门 (Jīng Mén) Xun 4　Ji Ren	六合 (Liù Hé) 天心 (Tiān Xīn) 开门 (Kāi Mén) Li 9　Geng Yi	太阴 (Tài Yīn) 天蓬 (Tiān Péng) 休门 (Xiū Mén) Kun 2　Bing Ding/Xin
玄武 (Xuán Wǔ) 禽芮 (Qín Ruì) 死门 (Sǐ Mén) Zhen 3　Ding/Xin Gui	Yin (阴) Dun# 8 Hour: **GengShen** ©Calvin Yap	螣蛇 (Téng Shé) 天任 (Tiān Rèn) 生门 (Shēng Mén) Dui 7　Wu Ji
九地 (Jiǔ Dì) 天英 (Tiān Yīng) 景门 (Jǐng Mén) Gen 8　Yi Wu	九天 (Jiǔ Tiān) 天辅 (Tiān Fǔ) 杜门 (Dù Mén) Kan 1　Ren Bing	值符 (Zhí Fú) 天冲 (Tiān Chōng) 伤门 (Shāng Mén) Qian 6　Gui Geng

Yin (阴) Dun# 8 Hour: XinYou ; 直符(ZhíFú): 天冲(TiānChōng) ; 直使(ZhíShǐ): 伤门(ShāngMén) ; 旬首(XúnShǒu): JiaYinGui

太阴 (Tài Yīn) 天蓬 (Tiān Péng) 休门 (Xiū Mén) Xun 4　Bing Ren	螣蛇 (Téng Shé) 天任 (Tiān Rèn) 生门 (Shēng Mén) Li 9　Wu Yi	值符 (Zhí Fú) 天冲 (Tiān Chōng) 伤门 (Shāng Mén) Kun 2　Gui Ding/Xin
六合 (Liù Hé) 天心 (Tiān Xīn) 开门 (Kāi Mén) Zhen 3　Geng Gui	Yin (阴) Dun# 8 Hour: **XinYou** ©Calvin Yap	九天 (Jiǔ Tiān) 天辅 (Tiān Fǔ) 杜门 (Dù Mén) Dui 7　Ren Ji
白虎 (Bái Hǔ) 天柱 (Tiān Zhù) 惊门 (Jīng Mén) Gen 8　Ji Wu	玄武 (Xuán Wǔ) 禽芮 (Qín Ruì) 死门 (Sǐ Mén) Kan 1　Ding/Xin Bing	九地 (Jiǔ Dì) 天英 (Tiān Yīng) 景门 (Jǐng Mén) Qian 6　Yi Geng

Yin (阴) Dun# 8 Hour: RenXu ; 直符(ZhíFú): 天冲(TiānChōng) ; 直使(ZhíShǐ): 伤门(ShāngMén) ; 旬首(XúnShǒu): JiaYinGui

值符 (Zhí Fú) 天冲 (Tiān Chōng) 伤门 (Shāng Mén) Xun 4　Gui Ren	九天 (Jiǔ Tiān) 天辅 (Tiān Fǔ) 杜门 (Dù Mén) Li 9　Ren Yi	九地 (Jiǔ Dì) 天英 (Tiān Yīng) 景门 (Jǐng Mén) Kun 2　Yi Ding/Xin
螣蛇 (Téng Shé) 天任 (Tiān Rèn) 生门 (Shēng Mén) Zhen 3　Wu Gui	Yin (阴) Dun# 8 Hour: **RenXu** ©Calvin Yap	玄武 (Xuán Wǔ) 禽芮 (Qín Ruì) 死门 (Sǐ Mén) Dui 7　Ding/Xin Ji
太阴 (Tài Yīn) 天蓬 (Tiān Péng) 休门 (Xiū Mén) Gen 8　Bing Wu	六合 (Liù Hé) 天心 (Tiān Xīn) 开门 (Kāi Mén) Kan 1　Geng Bing	白虎 (Bái Hǔ) 天柱 (Tiān Zhù) 惊门 (Jīng Mén) Qian 6　Ji Geng

Yin (阴) Dun# 8 Hour: GuiHai ; 直符(ZhíFú): 天冲(TiānChōng) ; 直使(ZhíShǐ): 伤门(ShāngMén) ; 旬首(XúnShǒu): JiaYinGui

九天 (Jiǔ Tiān) 天辅 (Tiān Fǔ) 杜门 (Dù Mén) Xun 4　Ren Ren	九地 (Jiǔ Dì) 天英 (Tiān Yīng) 景门 (Jǐng Mén) Li 9　Yi Yi	玄武 (Xuán Wǔ) 禽芮 (Qín Ruì) 死门 (Sǐ Mén) Kun 2　Ding/Xin Ding/Xin
值符 (Zhí Fú) 天冲 (Tiān Chōng) 伤门 (Shāng Mén) Zhen 3　Gui Gui	Yin (阴) Dun# 8 Hour: **GuiHai** **Fu Yin** ©Calvin Yap	白虎 (Bái Hǔ) 天柱 (Tiān Zhù) 惊门 (Jīng Mén) Dui 7　Ji Ji
螣蛇 (Téng Shé) 天任 (Tiān Rèn) 生门 (Shēng Mén) Gen 8　Wu Wu	太阴 (Tài Yīn) 天蓬 (Tiān Péng) 休门 (Xiū Mén) Kan 1　Bing Bing	六合 (Liù Hé) 天心 (Tiān Xīn) 开门 (Kāi Mén) Qian 6　Geng Geng

Yin Dun#9

Chart: **-9JiaZi** (Yin Dun #9 JiaZi Xun)
JiaZi, YiChou, BingYin, DingMao, WuChen, JiSi, GengWu, XinWei, RenShen, GuiYou

Yin (阴) Dun# 9 Hour: **JiaZi**；直符(ZhíFú): 天英(TiānYīng)
直使(ZhíShǐ): 景门(JǐngMén)；旬首(XúnShǒu): JiaZiWu

螣蛇 (Téng Shé) 天辅 (Tiān Fǔ) 杜门 (Dù Mén) Xun 4　Gui Gui	值符 (Zhí Fú) 天英 (Tiān Yīng) 景门 (Jǐng Mén) Li 9　Wu Wu	九天 (Jiǔ Tiān) 禽芮 (Qín Ruì) 死门 (Sǐ Mén) Kun 2　Bing/Ren Bing/Ren
太阴 (Tài Yīn) 天冲 (Tiān Chōng) 伤门 (Shāng Mén) Zhen 3　Ding Ding	Yin (阴) Dun# 9 Hour: **JiaZi** **Fu Yin** ©Calvin Yap	九地 (Jiǔ Dì) 天柱 (Tiān Zhù) 惊门 (Jīng Mén) Dui 7　Geng Geng
六合 (Liù Hé) 天任 (Tiān Rèn) 生门 (Shēng Mén) Gen 8　Ji Ji	白虎 (Bái Hǔ) 天蓬 (Tiān Péng) 休门 (Xiū Mén) Kan 1　Yi Yi	玄武 (Xuán Wǔ) 天心 (Tiān Xīn) 开门 (Kāi Mén) Qian 6　Xin Xin

Yin (阴) Dun# 9 Hour: **YiChou**；直符(ZhíFú): 天英(TiānYīng)
直使(ZhíShǐ): 景门(JǐngMén)；旬首(XúnShǒu): JiaZiWu

玄武 (Xuán Wǔ) 天心 (Tiān Xīn) 惊门 (Jīng Mén) Xun 4　Xin Gui	白虎 (Bái Hǔ) 天蓬 (Tiān Péng) 开门 (Kāi Mén) Li 9　Yi Wu	六合 (Liù Hé) 天任 (Tiān Rèn) 休门 (Xiū Mén) Kun 2　Ji Bing/Ren
九地 (Jiǔ Dì) 天柱 (Tiān Zhù) 死门 (Sǐ Mén) Zhen 3　Geng Ding	Yin (阴) Dun# 9 Hour: **YiChou** **Fan Yin** ©Calvin Yap	太阴 (Tài Yīn) 天冲 (Tiān Chōng) 生门 (Shēng Mén) Dui 7　Ding Geng
九天 (Jiǔ Tiān) 禽芮 (Qín Ruì) 景门 (Jǐng Mén) Gen 8　Bing/Ren Ji	值符 (Zhí Fú) 天英 (Tiān Yīng) 杜门 (Dù Mén) Kan 1　Wu Yi	螣蛇 (Téng Shé) 天辅 (Tiān Fǔ) 伤门 (Shāng Mén) Qian 6　Gui Xin

Yin (阴) Dun# 9 Hour: **BingYin**；直符(ZhíFú): 天英(TiānYīng)
直使(ZhíShǐ): 景门(JǐngMén)；旬首(XúnShǒu): JiaZiWu

太阴 (Tài Yīn) 天冲 (Tiān Chōng) 生门 (Shēng Mén) Xun 4　Ding Gui	螣蛇 (Téng Shé) 天辅 (Tiān Fǔ) 伤门 (Shāng Mén) Li 9　Gui Wu	值符 (Zhí Fú) 天英 (Tiān Yīng) 杜门 (Dù Mén) Kun 2　Wu Bing/Ren
六合 (Liù Hé) 天任 (Tiān Rèn) 休门 (Xiū Mén) Zhen 3　Ji Ding	Yin (阴) Dun# 9 Hour: **BingYin** ©Calvin Yap	九天 (Jiǔ Tiān) 禽芮 (Qín Ruì) 景门 (Jǐng Mén) Dui 7　Bing/Ren Geng
白虎 (Bái Hǔ) 天蓬 (Tiān Péng) 开门 (Kāi Mén) Gen 8　Yi Ji	玄武 (Xuán Wǔ) 天心 (Tiān Xīn) 惊门 (Jīng Mén) Kan 1　Xin Yi	九地 (Jiǔ Dì) 天柱 (Tiān Zhù) 死门 (Sǐ Mén) Qian 6　Geng Xin

Yin (阴) Dun# 9 Hour: **DingMao**；直符(ZhíFú): 天英(TiānYīng)
直使(ZhíShǐ): 景门(JǐngMén)；旬首(XúnShǒu): JiaZiWu

九天 (Jiǔ Tiān) 禽芮 (Qín Ruì) 休门 (Xiū Mén) Xun 4　Bing/Ren Gui	九地 (Jiǔ Dì) 天柱 (Tiān Zhù) 生门 (Shēng Mén) Li 9　Geng Wu	玄武 (Xuán Wǔ) 天心 (Tiān Xīn) 伤门 (Shāng Mén) Kun 2　Xin Bing/Ren
值符 (Zhí Fú) 天英 (Tiān Yīng) 开门 (Kāi Mén) Zhen 3　Wu Ding	Yin (阴) Dun# 9 Hour: **DingMao** ©Calvin Yap	白虎 (Bái Hǔ) 天蓬 (Tiān Péng) 杜门 (Dù Mén) Dui 7　Yi Geng
螣蛇 (Téng Shé) 天辅 (Tiān Fǔ) 惊门 (Jīng Mén) Gen 8　Gui Ji	太阴 (Tài Yīn) 天冲 (Tiān Chōng) 死门 (Sǐ Mén) Kan 1　Ding Yi	六合 (Liù Hé) 天任 (Tiān Rèn) 景门 (Jǐng Mén) Qian 6　Ji Xin

Yin (阴) Dun# 9 Hour: **WuChen**；直符(ZhíFú): 天英(TiānYīng)
直使(ZhíShǐ): 景门(JǐngMén)；旬首(XúnShǒu): JiaZiWu

螣蛇 (Téng Shé) 天辅 (Tiān Fǔ) 伤门 (Shāng Mén) Xun 4　Gui Gui	值符 (Zhí Fú) 天英 (Tiān Yīng) 杜门 (Dù Mén) Li 9　Wu Wu	九天 (Jiǔ Tiān) 禽芮 (Qín Ruì) 景门 (Jǐng Mén) Kun 2　Bing/Ren Bing/Ren
太阴 (Tài Yīn) 天冲 (Tiān Chōng) 生门 (Shēng Mén) Zhen 3　Ding Ding	Yin (阴) Dun# 9 Hour: **WuChen** **Fu Yin** ©Calvin Yap	九地 (Jiǔ Dì) 天柱 (Tiān Zhù) 死门 (Sǐ Mén) Dui 7　Geng Geng
六合 (Liù Hé) 天任 (Tiān Rèn) 休门 (Xiū Mén) Gen 8　Ji Ji	白虎 (Bái Hǔ) 天蓬 (Tiān Péng) 开门 (Kāi Mén) Kan 1　Yi Yi	玄武 (Xuán Wǔ) 天心 (Tiān Xīn) 惊门 (Jīng Mén) Qian 6　Xin Xin

Yin (阴) Dun# 9 Hour: **JiSi**；直符(ZhíFú): 天英(TiānYīng)
直使(ZhíShǐ): 景门(JǐngMén)；旬首(XúnShǒu): JiaZiWu

九地 (Jiǔ Dì) 天柱 (Tiān Zhù) 景门 (Jǐng Mén) Xun 4　Geng Gui	玄武 (Xuán Wǔ) 天心 (Tiān Xīn) 死门 (Sǐ Mén) Li 9　Xin Wu	白虎 (Bái Hǔ) 天蓬 (Tiān Péng) 惊门 (Jīng Mén) Kun 2　Yi Bing/Ren
九天 (Jiǔ Tiān) 禽芮 (Qín Ruì) 杜门 (Dù Mén) Zhen 3　Bing/Ren Ding	Yin (阴) Dun# 9 Hour: **JiSi** ©Calvin Yap	六合 (Liù Hé) 天任 (Tiān Rèn) 开门 (Kāi Mén) Dui 7　Ji Geng
值符 (Zhí Fú) 天英 (Tiān Yīng) 伤门 (Shāng Mén) Gen 8　Wu Ji	螣蛇 (Téng Shé) 天辅 (Tiān Fǔ) 生门 (Shēng Mén) Kan 1　Gui Yi	太阴 (Tài Yīn) 天冲 (Tiān Chōng) 休门 (Xiū Mén) Qian 6　Ding Xin

Yin (阴) Dun# 9 Hour: GengWu；直符(ZhíFú): 天英(TiānYīng)
直使(ZhíShǐ): 景门(JǐngMén)；旬首(XúnShǒu): JiaZiWu

六合 (Liù Hé) 天任 (Tiān Rèn) 死门 (Sǐ Mén) Xun 4　Ji Gui	太阴 (Tài Yīn) 天冲 (Tiān Chōng) 惊门 (Jīng Mén) Li 9　Ding Wu	螣蛇 (Téng Shé) 天辅 (Tiān Fǔ) 开门 (Kāi Mén) Kun 2　Gui Bing/Ren
白虎 (Bái Hǔ) 天蓬 (Tiān Péng) 景门 (Jǐng Mén) Zhen 3　Yi Ding	Yin (阴) Dun# 9 Hour: **GengWu** ©Calvin Yap	值符 (Zhí Fú) 天英 (Tiān Yīng) 休门 (Xiū Mén) Dui 7　Wu Geng
玄武 (Xuán Wǔ) 天心 (Tiān Xīn) 杜门 (Dù Mén) Gen 8　Xin Ji	九地 (Jiǔ Dì) 天柱 (Tiān Zhù) 伤门 (Shāng Mén) Kan 1　Geng Yi	九天 (Jiǔ Tiān) 禽芮 (Qín Ruì) 生门 (Shēng Mén) Qian 6　Bing/Ren Xin

Yin (阴) Dun# 9 Hour: XinWei；直符(ZhíFú): 天英(TiānYīng)
直使(ZhíShǐ): 景门(JǐngMén)；旬首(XúnShǒu): JiaZiWu

白虎 (Bái Hǔ) 天蓬 (Tiān Péng) 伤门 (Shāng Mén) Xun 4　Yi Gui	六合 (Liù Hé) 天任 (Tiān Rèn) 杜门 (Dù Mén) Li 9　Ji Wu	太阴 (Tài Yīn) 天冲 (Tiān Chōng) 景门 (Jǐng Mén) Kun 2　Ding Bing/Ren
玄武 (Xuán Wǔ) 天心 (Tiān Xīn) 生门 (Shēng Mén) Zhen 3　Xin Ding	Yin (阴) Dun# 9 Hour: **XinWei** ©Calvin Yap	螣蛇 (Téng Shé) 天辅 (Tiān Fǔ) 死门 (Sǐ Mén) Dui 7　Gui Geng
九地 (Jiǔ Dì) 天柱 (Tiān Zhù) 休门 (Xiū Mén) Gen 8　Geng Ji	九天 (Jiǔ Tiān) 禽芮 (Qín Ruì) 开门 (Kāi Mén) Kan 1　Bing/Ren Yi	值符 (Zhí Fú) 天英 (Tiān Yīng) 惊门 (Jīng Mén) Qian 6　Wu Xin

Yin (阴) Dun# 9 Hour: RenShen；直符(ZhíFú): 天英(TiānYīng)
直使(ZhíShǐ): 景门(JǐngMén)；旬首(XúnShǒu): JiaZiWu

太阴 (Tài Yīn) 天冲 (Tiān Chōng) 开门 (Kāi Mén) Xun 4　Ding Gui	螣蛇 (Téng Shé) 天辅 (Tiān Fǔ) 休门 (Xiū Mén) Li 9　Gui Wu	值符 (Zhí Fú) 天英 (Tiān Yīng) 生门 (Shēng Mén) Kun 2　Wu Bing/Ren
六合 (Liù Hé) 天任 (Tiān Rèn) 惊门 (Jīng Mén) Zhen 3　Ji Ding	Yin (阴) Dun# 9 Hour: **RenShen** ©Calvin Yap	九天 (Jiǔ Tiān) 禽芮 (Qín Ruì) 伤门 (Shāng Mén) Dui 7　Bing/Ren Geng
白虎 (Bái Hǔ) 天蓬 (Tiān Péng) 死门 (Sǐ Mén) Gen 8　Yi Ji	玄武 (Xuán Wǔ) 天心 (Tiān Xīn) 景门 (Jǐng Mén) Kan 1　Xin Yi	九地 (Jiǔ Dì) 天柱 (Tiān Zhù) 杜门 (Dù Mén) Qian 6　Geng Xin

Yin (阴) Dun# 9 Hour: GuiYou；直符(ZhíFú): 天英(TiānYīng)
直使(ZhíShǐ): 景门(JǐngMén)；旬首(XúnShǒu): JiaZiWu

值符 (Zhí Fú) 天英 (Tiān Yīng) 杜门 (Dù Mén) Xun 4　Wu Gui	九天 (Jiǔ Tiān) 禽芮 (Qín Ruì) 景门 (Jǐng Mén) Li 9　Bing/Ren Wu	九地 (Jiǔ Dì) 天柱 (Tiān Zhù) 死门 (Sǐ Mén) Kun 2　Geng Bing/Ren
螣蛇 (Téng Shé) 天辅 (Tiān Fǔ) 伤门 (Shāng Mén) Zhen 3　Gui Ding	Yin (阴) Dun# 9 Hour: **GuiYou** ©Calvin Yap	玄武 (Xuán Wǔ) 天心 (Tiān Xīn) 惊门 (Jīng Mén) Dui 7　Xin Geng
太阴 (Tài Yīn) 天冲 (Tiān Chōng) 生门 (Shēng Mén) Gen 8　Ding Ji	六合 (Liù Hé) 天任 (Tiān Rèn) 休门 (Xiū Mén) Kan 1　Ji Yi	白虎 (Bái Hǔ) 天蓬 (Tiān Péng) 开门 (Kāi Mén) Qian 6　Yi Xin

Chart: **-9JiaXu** (Yin Dun #9 JiaXu Xun)
JiaXu, YiHai, BingZi, DingChou, WuYin, JiMao, GengChen, XinSi, RenWu, GuiWei

Yin (阴) Dun# 9 Hour: JiaXu；直符(ZhíFú): 天任(TiānRèn)
直使(ZhíShǐ): 生门(ShēngMén)；旬首(XúnShǒu): JiaXuJi

九地 (Jiǔ Dì) 天辅 (Tiān Fǔ) 杜门 (Dù Mén) Xun 4　Gui Gui	玄武 (Xuán Wǔ) 天英 (Tiān Yīng) 景门 (Jǐng Mén) Li 9　Wu Wu	白虎 (Bái Hǔ) 禽芮 (Qín Ruì) 死门 (Sǐ Mén) Kun 2　Bing/Ren Bing/Ren
九天 (Jiǔ Tiān) 天冲 (Tiān Chōng) 伤门 (Shāng Mén) Zhen 3　Ding Ding	Yin (阴) Dun# 9 Hour: **JiaXu** **Fu Yin** ©Calvin Yap	六合 (Liù Hé) 天柱 (Tiān Zhù) 惊门 (Jīng Mén) Dui 7　Geng Geng
值符 (Zhí Fú) 天任 (Tiān Rèn) 生门 (Shēng Mén) Gen 8　Ji Ji	螣蛇 (Téng Shé) 天蓬 (Tiān Péng) 休门 (Xiū Mén) Kan 1　Yi Yi	太阴 (Tài Yīn) 天心 (Tiān Xīn) 开门 (Kāi Mén) Qian 6　Xin Xin

Yin (阴) Dun# 9 Hour: YiHai；直符(ZhíFú): 天任(TiānRèn)
直使(ZhíShǐ): 生门(ShēngMén)；旬首(XúnShǒu): JiaXuJi

玄武 (Xuán Wǔ) 天英 (Tiān Yīng) 惊门 (Jīng Mén) Xun 4　Wu Gui	白虎 (Bái Hǔ) 禽芮 (Qín Ruì) 开门 (Kāi Mén) Li 9　Bing/Ren Wu	六合 (Liù Hé) 天柱 (Tiān Zhù) 休门 (Xiū Mén) Kun 2　Geng Bing/Ren
九地 (Jiǔ Dì) 天辅 (Tiān Fǔ) 死门 (Sǐ Mén) Zhen 3　Gui Ding	Yin (阴) Dun# 9 Hour: **YiHai** ©Calvin Yap	太阴 (Tài Yīn) 天心 (Tiān Xīn) 生门 (Shēng Mén) Dui 7　Xin Geng
九天 (Jiǔ Tiān) 天冲 (Tiān Chōng) 景门 (Jǐng Mén) Gen 8　Ding Ji	值符 (Zhí Fú) 天任 (Tiān Rèn) 杜门 (Dù Mén) Kan 1　Ji Yi	螣蛇 (Téng Shé) 天蓬 (Tiān Péng) 伤门 (Shāng Mén) Qian 6　Yi Xin

Yin (阴) Dun# 9 Hour: **BingZi**；直符(ZhíFú): 天任(TiānRèn)
直使(ZhíShǐ): 生门(ShēngMén)；旬首(XúnShǒu): JiaXuJi

太阴 (Tài Yīn) 天心 (Tiān Xīn) 死门 (Sǐ Mén) Xun 4　Xin Gui	螣蛇 (Téng Shé) 天蓬 (Tiān Péng) 惊门 (Jīng Mén) Li 9　Yi Wu	值符 (Zhí Fú) 天任 (Tiān Rèn) 开门 (Kāi Mén) Kun 2　Ji Bing/Ren
六合 (Liù Hé) 天柱 (Tiān Zhù) 景门 (Jǐng Mén) Zhen 3　Geng Ding	Yin (阴) Dun# 9 Hour: **BingZi** **Fan Yin** ©Calvin Yap	九天 (Jiǔ Tiān) 天冲 (Tiān Chōng) 休门 (Xiū Mén) Dui 7　Ding Geng
白虎 (Bái Hǔ) 禽芮 (Qín Ruì) 杜门 (Dù Mén) Gen 8　Bing/Ren Ji	玄武 (Xuán Wǔ) 天英 (Tiān Yīng) 伤门 (Shāng Mén) Kan 1　Wu Yi	九地 (Jiǔ Dì) 天辅 (Tiān Fǔ) 生门 (Shēng Mén) Qian 6　Gui Xin

Yin (阴) Dun# 9 Hour: **DingChou**；直符(ZhíFú): 天任(TiānRèn)
直使(ZhíShǐ): 生门(ShēngMén)；旬首(XúnShǒu): JiaXuJi

九天 (Jiǔ Tiān) 天冲 (Tiān Chōng) 开门 (Kāi Mén) Xun 4　Ding Gui	九地 (Jiǔ Dì) 天辅 (Tiān Fǔ) 休门 (Xiū Mén) Li 9　Gui Wu	玄武 (Xuán Wǔ) 天英 (Tiān Yīng) 生门 (Shēng Mén) Kun 2　Wu Bing/Ren
值符 (Zhí Fú) 天任 (Tiān Rèn) 惊门 (Jīng Mén) Zhen 3　Ji Ding	Yin (阴) Dun# 9 Hour: **DingChou** ©Calvin Yap	白虎 (Bái Hǔ) 禽芮 (Qín Ruì) 伤门 (Shāng Mén) Dui 7　Bing/Ren Geng
螣蛇 (Téng Shé) 天蓬 (Tiān Péng) 死门 (Sǐ Mén) Gen 8　Yi Ji	太阴 (Tài Yīn) 天心 (Tiān Xīn) 景门 (Jǐng Mén) Kan 1　Xin Yi	六合 (Liù Hé) 天柱 (Tiān Zhù) 杜门 (Dù Mén) Qian 6　Geng Xin

Yin (阴) Dun# 9 Hour: **WuYin**；直符(ZhíFú): 天任(TiānRèn)
直使(ZhíShǐ): 生门(ShēngMén)；旬首(XúnShǒu): JiaXuJi

螣蛇 (Téng Shé) 天蓬 (Tiān Péng) 生门 (Shēng Mén) Xun 4　Yi Gui	值符 (Zhí Fú) 天任 (Tiān Rèn) 伤门 (Shāng Mén) Li 9　Ji Wu	九天 (Jiǔ Tiān) 天冲 (Tiān Chōng) 杜门 (Dù Mén) Kun 2　Ding Bing/Ren
太阴 (Tài Yīn) 天心 (Tiān Xīn) 休门 (Xiū Mén) Zhen 3　Xin Ding	Yin (阴) Dun# 9 Hour: **WuYin** ©Calvin Yap	九地 (Jiǔ Dì) 天辅 (Tiān Fǔ) 景门 (Jǐng Mén) Dui 7　Gui Geng
六合 (Liù Hé) 天柱 (Tiān Zhù) 开门 (Kāi Mén) Gen 8　Geng Ji	白虎 (Bái Hǔ) 禽芮 (Qín Ruì) 惊门 (Jīng Mén) Kan 1　Bing/Ren Yi	玄武 (Xuán Wǔ) 天英 (Tiān Yīng) 死门 (Sǐ Mén) Qian 6　Wu Xin

Yin (阴) Dun# 9 Hour: **JiMao**；直符(ZhíFú): 天任(TiānRèn)
直使(ZhíShǐ): 生门(ShēngMén)；旬首(XúnShǒu): JiaXuJi

九地 (Jiǔ Dì) 天辅 (Tiān Fǔ) 伤门 (Shāng Mén) Xun 4　Gui Gui	玄武 (Xuán Wǔ) 天英 (Tiān Yīng) 杜门 (Dù Mén) Li 9　Wu Wu	白虎 (Bái Hǔ) 禽芮 (Qín Ruì) 景门 (Jǐng Mén) Kun 2　Bing/Ren Bing/Ren
九天 (Jiǔ Tiān) 天冲 (Tiān Chōng) 生门 (Shēng Mén) Zhen 3　Ding Ding	Yin (阴) Dun# 9 Hour: **JiMao** **Fu Yin** ©Calvin Yap	六合 (Liù Hé) 天柱 (Tiān Zhù) 死门 (Sǐ Mén) Dui 7　Geng Geng
值符 (Zhí Fú) 天任 (Tiān Rèn) 休门 (Xiū Mén) Gen 8　Ji Ji	螣蛇 (Téng Shé) 天蓬 (Tiān Péng) 开门 (Kāi Mén) Kan 1　Yi Yi	太阴 (Tài Yīn) 天心 (Tiān Xīn) 惊门 (Jīng Mén) Qian 6　Xin Xin

Yin (阴) Dun# 9 Hour: **GengChen**；直符(ZhíFú): 天任(TiānRèn)
直使(ZhíShǐ): 生门(ShēngMén)；旬首(XúnShǒu): JiaXuJi

六合 (Liù Hé) 天柱 (Tiān Zhù) 开门 (Kāi Mén) Xun 4　Geng Gui	太阴 (Tài Yīn) 天心 (Tiān Xīn) 休门 (Xiū Mén) Li 9　Xin Wu	螣蛇 (Téng Shé) 天蓬 (Tiān Péng) 生门 (Shēng Mén) Kun 2　Yi Bing/Ren
白虎 (Bái Hǔ) 禽芮 (Qín Ruì) 惊门 (Jīng Mén) Zhen 3　Bing/Ren Ding	Yin (阴) Dun# 9 Hour: **GengChen** ©Calvin Yap	值符 (Zhí Fú) 天任 (Tiān Rèn) 伤门 (Shāng Mén) Dui 7　Ji Geng
玄武 (Xuán Wǔ) 天英 (Tiān Yīng) 死门 (Sǐ Mén) Gen 8　Wu Ji	九地 (Jiǔ Dì) 天辅 (Tiān Fǔ) 景门 (Jǐng Mén) Kan 1　Gui Yi	九天 (Jiǔ Tiān) 天冲 (Tiān Chōng) 杜门 (Dù Mén) Qian 6　Ding Xin

Yin (阴) Dun# 9 Hour: **XinSi**；直符(ZhíFú): 天任(TiānRèn)
直使(ZhíShǐ): 生门(ShēngMén)；旬首(XúnShǒu): JiaXuJi

白虎 (Bái Hǔ) 禽芮 (Qín Ruì) 景门 (Jǐng Mén) Xun 4　Bing/Ren Gui	六合 (Liù Hé) 天柱 (Tiān Zhù) 死门 (Sǐ Mén) Li 9　Geng Wu	太阴 (Tài Yīn) 天心 (Tiān Xīn) 惊门 (Jīng Mén) Kun 2　Xin Bing/Ren
玄武 (Xuán Wǔ) 天英 (Tiān Yīng) 杜门 (Dù Mén) Zhen 3　Wu Ding	Yin (阴) Dun# 9 Hour: **XinSi** ©Calvin Yap	螣蛇 (Téng Shé) 天蓬 (Tiān Péng) 开门 (Kāi Mén) Dui 7　Yi Geng
九地 (Jiǔ Dì) 天辅 (Tiān Fǔ) 伤门 (Shāng Mén) Gen 8　Gui Ji	九天 (Jiǔ Tiān) 天冲 (Tiān Chōng) 生门 (Shēng Mén) Kan 1　Ding Yi	值符 (Zhí Fú) 天任 (Tiān Rèn) 休门 (Xiū Mén) Qian 6　Ji Xin

Yin (阴) Dun# 9 Hour: **RenWu** ；直符(ZhíFú): 天任(TiānRèn)
直使(ZhíShǐ): 生门(ShēngMén) ；旬首(XúnShǒu): JiaXuJi

太阴 (Tài Yīn) 天心 (Tiān Xīn) 休门 (Xiū Mén) Xun 4 Xin Gui	螣蛇 (Téng Shé) 天蓬 (Tiān Péng) 生门 (Shēng Mén) Li 9 Yi Wu	值符 (Zhí Fú) 天任 (Tiān Rèn) 伤门 (Shāng Mén) Kun 2 Ji Bing/Ren
六合 (Liù Hé) 天柱 (Tiān Zhù) 开门 (Kāi Mén) Zhen 3 Geng Ding	Yin (阴) Dun# 9 Hour: **RenWu** **Fan Yin** ©Calvin Yap	九天 (Jiǔ Tiān) 天冲 (Tiān Chōng) 杜门 (Dù Mén) Dui 7 Ding Geng
白虎 (Bái Hǔ) 禽芮 (Qín Ruì) 惊门 (Jīng Mén) Gen 8 Bing/Ren Ji	玄武 (Xuán Wǔ) 天英 (Tiān Yīng) 死门 (Sǐ Mén) Kan 1 Wu Yi	九地 (Jiǔ Dì) 天辅 (Tiān Fǔ) 景门 (Jǐng Mén) Qian 6 Gui Xin

Yin (阴) Dun# 9 Hour: **GuiWei** ；直符(ZhíFú): 天任(TiānRèn)
直使(ZhíShǐ): 生门(ShēngMén) ；旬首(XúnShǒu): JiaXuJi

值符 (Zhí Fú) 天任 (Tiān Rèn) 杜门 (Dù Mén) Xun 4 Ji Gui	九天 (Jiǔ Tiān) 天冲 (Tiān Chōng) 景门 (Jǐng Mén) Li 9 Ding Wu	九地 (Jiǔ Dì) 天辅 (Tiān Fǔ) 死门 (Sǐ Mén) Kun 2 Gui Bing/Ren
螣蛇 (Téng Shé) 天蓬 (Tiān Péng) 伤门 (Shāng Mén) Zhen 3 Yi Ding	Yin (阴) Dun# 9 Hour: **GuiWei** ©Calvin Yap	玄武 (Xuán Wǔ) 天英 (Tiān Yīng) 惊门 (Jīng Mén) Dui 7 Wu Geng
太阴 (Tài Yīn) 天心 (Tiān Xīn) 生门 (Shēng Mén) Gen 8 Xin Ji	六合 (Liù Hé) 天柱 (Tiān Zhù) 休门 (Xiū Mén) Kan 1 Geng Yi	白虎 (Bái Hǔ) 禽芮 (Qín Ruì) 开门 (Kāi Mén) Qian 6 Bing/Ren Xin

---

Chart: **-9JiaShen** (Yin Dun #9 JiaShen Xun)
JiaShen, YiYou, BingXu, DingHai, WuZi, JiChou, GengYin, XinMao, RenChen, GuiSi

Yin (阴) Dun# 9 Hour: **JiaShen** ；直符(ZhíFú): 天柱(TiānZhù)
直使(ZhíShǐ): 惊门(JīngMén) ；旬首(XúnShǒu): JiaShenGeng

六合 (Liù Hé) 天辅 (Tiān Fǔ) 杜门 (Dù Mén) Xun 4 Gui Gui	太阴 (Tài Yīn) 天英 (Tiān Yīng) 景门 (Jǐng Mén) Li 9 Wu Wu	螣蛇 (Téng Shé) 禽芮 (Qín Ruì) 死门 (Sǐ Mén) Kun 2 Bing/Ren Bing/Ren
白虎 (Bái Hǔ) 天冲 (Tiān Chōng) 伤门 (Shāng Mén) Zhen 3 Ding Ding	Yin (阴) Dun# 9 Hour: **JiaShen** **Fu Yin** ©Calvin Yap	值符 (Zhí Fú) 天柱 (Tiān Zhù) 惊门 (Jīng Mén) Dui 7 Geng Geng
玄武 (Xuán Wǔ) 天任 (Tiān Rèn) 生门 (Shēng Mén) Gen 8 Ji Ji	九地 (Jiǔ Dì) 天蓬 (Tiān Péng) 休门 (Xiū Mén) Kan 1 Yi Yi	九天 (Jiǔ Tiān) 天心 (Tiān Xīn) 开门 (Kāi Mén) Qian 6 Xin Xin

Yin (阴) Dun# 9 Hour: **YiYou** ；直符(ZhíFú): 天柱(TiānZhù)
直使(ZhíShǐ): 惊门(JīngMén) ；旬首(XúnShǒu): JiaShenGeng

玄武 (Xuán Wǔ) 天任 (Tiān Rèn) 伤门 (Shāng Mén) Xun 4 Ji Gui	白虎 (Bái Hǔ) 天冲 (Tiān Chōng) 杜门 (Dù Mén) Li 9 Ding Wu	六合 (Liù Hé) 天辅 (Tiān Fǔ) 景门 (Jǐng Mén) Kun 2 Gui Bing/Ren
九地 (Jiǔ Dì) 天蓬 (Tiān Péng) 生门 (Shēng Mén) Zhen 3 Yi Ding	Yin (阴) Dun# 9 Hour: **YiYou** ©Calvin Yap	太阴 (Tài Yīn) 天英 (Tiān Yīng) 死门 (Sǐ Mén) Dui 7 Wu Geng
九天 (Jiǔ Tiān) 天心 (Tiān Xīn) 休门 (Xiū Mén) Gen 8 Xin Ji	值符 (Zhí Fú) 天柱 (Tiān Zhù) 开门 (Kāi Mén) Kan 1 Geng Yi	螣蛇 (Téng Shé) 禽芮 (Qín Ruì) 惊门 (Jīng Mén) Qian 6 Bing/Ren Xin

Yin (阴) Dun# 9 Hour: **BingXu** ；直符(ZhíFú): 天柱(TiānZhù)
直使(ZhíShǐ): 惊门(JīngMén) ；旬首(XúnShǒu): JiaShenGeng

太阴 (Tài Yīn) 天英 (Tiān Yīng) 景门 (Jǐng Mén) Xun 4 Wu Gui	螣蛇 (Téng Shé) 禽芮 (Qín Ruì) 死门 (Sǐ Mén) Li 9 Bing/Ren Wu	值符 (Zhí Fú) 天柱 (Tiān Zhù) 惊门 (Jīng Mén) Kun 2 Geng Bing/Ren
六合 (Liù Hé) 天辅 (Tiān Fǔ) 杜门 (Dù Mén) Zhen 3 Gui Ding	Yin (阴) Dun# 9 Hour: **BingXu** ©Calvin Yap	九天 (Jiǔ Tiān) 天心 (Tiān Xīn) 开门 (Kāi Mén) Dui 7 Xin Geng
白虎 (Bái Hǔ) 天冲 (Tiān Chōng) 伤门 (Shāng Mén) Gen 8 Ding Ji	玄武 (Xuán Wǔ) 天任 (Tiān Rèn) 生门 (Shēng Mén) Kan 1 Ji Yi	九地 (Jiǔ Dì) 天蓬 (Tiān Péng) 休门 (Xiū Mén) Qian 6 Yi Xin

Yin (阴) Dun# 9 Hour: **DingHai** ；直符(ZhíFú): 天柱(TiānZhù)
直使(ZhíShǐ): 惊门(JīngMén) ；旬首(XúnShǒu): JiaShenGeng

九天 (Jiǔ Tiān) 天心 (Tiān Xīn) 惊门 (Jīng Mén) Xun 4 Xin Gui	九地 (Jiǔ Dì) 天蓬 (Tiān Péng) 开门 (Kāi Mén) Li 9 Yi Wu	玄武 (Xuán Wǔ) 天任 (Tiān Rèn) 休门 (Xiū Mén) Kun 2 Ji Bing/Ren
值符 (Zhí Fú) 天柱 (Tiān Zhù) 死门 (Sǐ Mén) Zhen 3 Geng Ding	Yin (阴) Dun# 9 Hour: **DingHai** **Fan Yin** ©Calvin Yap	白虎 (Bái Hǔ) 天冲 (Tiān Chōng) 生门 (Shēng Mén) Dui 7 Ding Geng
螣蛇 (Téng Shé) 禽芮 (Qín Ruì) 景门 (Jǐng Mén) Gen 8 Bing/Ren Ji	太阴 (Tài Yīn) 天英 (Tiān Yīng) 杜门 (Dù Mén) Kan 1 Wu Yi	六合 (Liù Hé) 天辅 (Tiān Fǔ) 伤门 (Shāng Mén) Qian 6 Gui Xin

Chart 1

Yin (阴) Dun# 9 Hour: **WuZi**；直符(ZhíFú): 天柱(TiānZhù)
直使(ZhíShǐ): 惊门(JǐngMén)；旬首(XúnShǒu): JiaShenGeng

螣蛇 (Téng Shé) 禽芮 (Qín Ruì) 开门 (Kāi Mén) Xun 4　Bing/Ren Gui	值符 (Zhí Fú) 天柱 (Tiān Zhù) 休门 (Xiū Mén) Li 9　Geng Wu	九天 (Jiǔ Tiān) 天心 (Tiān Xīn) 生门 (Shēng Mén) Kun 2　Xin Bing/Ren
太阴 (Tài Yīn) 天英 (Tiān Yīng) 惊门 (Jǐng Mén) Zhen 3　Wu Ding	Yin (阴) Dun# 9 Hour: **WuZi** ©Calvin Yap	九地 (Jiǔ Dì) 天蓬 (Tiān Péng) 伤门 (Shāng Mén) Dui 7　Yi Geng
六合 (Liù Hé) 天辅 (Tiān Fú) 死门 (Sǐ Mén) Gen 8　Gui Ji	白虎 (Bái Hǔ) 天冲 (Tiān Chōng) 景门 (Jǐng Mén) Kan 1　Ding Yi	玄武 (Xuán Wǔ) 天任 (Tiān Rèn) 杜门 (Dù Mén) Qian 6　Ji Xin

Chart 2

Yin (阴) Dun# 9 Hour: **JiChou**；直符(ZhíFú): 天柱(TiānZhù)
直使(ZhíShǐ): 惊门(JǐngMén)；旬首(XúnShǒu): JiaShenGeng

九地 (Jiǔ Dì) 天蓬 (Tiān Péng) 景门 (Jǐng Mén) Xun 4　Yi Gui	玄武 (Xuán Wǔ) 天任 (Tiān Rèn) 死门 (Sǐ Mén) Li 9　Ji Wu	白虎 (Bái Hǔ) 天冲 (Tiān Chōng) 惊门 (Jǐng Mén) Kun 2　Ding Bing/Ren
九天 (Jiǔ Tiān) 天心 (Tiān Xīn) 杜门 (Dù Mén) Zhen 3　Xin Ding	Yin (阴) Dun# 9 Hour: **JiChou** ©Calvin Yap	六合 (Liù Hé) 天辅 (Tiān Fú) 开门 (Kāi Mén) Dui 7　Gui Geng
值符 (Zhí Fú) 天柱 (Tiān Zhù) 伤门 (Shāng Mén) Gen 8　Geng Ji	螣蛇 (Téng Shé) 禽芮 (Qín Ruì) 生门 (Shēng Mén) Kan 1　Bing/Ren Yi	太阴 (Tài Yīn) 天英 (Tiān Yīng) 休门 (Xiū Mén) Qian 6　Wu Xin

Chart 3

Yin (阴) Dun# 9 Hour: **GengYin**；直符(ZhíFú): 天柱(TiānZhù)
直使(ZhíShǐ): 惊门(JǐngMén)；旬首(XúnShǒu): JiaShenGeng

六合 (Liù Hé) 天辅 (Tiān Fú) 生门 (Shēng Mén) Xun 4　Gui Gui	太阴 (Tài Yīn) 天英 (Tiān Yīng) 伤门 (Shāng Mén) Li 9　Wu Wu	螣蛇 (Téng Shé) 禽芮 (Qín Ruì) 杜门 (Dù Mén) Kun 2　Bing/Ren Bing/Ren
白虎 (Bái Hǔ) 天冲 (Tiān Chōng) 休门 (Xiū Mén) Zhen 3　Ding Ding	Yin (阴) Dun# 9 Hour: **GengYin** **Fu Yin** ©Calvin Yap	值符 (Zhí Fú) 天柱 (Tiān Zhù) 景门 (Jǐng Mén) Dui 7　Geng Geng
玄武 (Xuán Wǔ) 天任 (Tiān Rèn) 开门 (Kāi Mén) Gen 8　Ji Ji	九地 (Jiǔ Dì) 天蓬 (Tiān Péng) 惊门 (Jǐng Mén) Kan 1　Yi Yi	九天 (Jiǔ Tiān) 天心 (Tiān Xīn) 死门 (Sǐ Mén) Qian 6　Xin Xin

Chart 4

Yin (阴) Dun# 9 Hour: **XinMao**；直符(ZhíFú): 天柱(TiānZhù)
直使(ZhíShǐ): 惊门(JǐngMén)；旬首(XúnShǒu): JiaShenGeng

白虎 (Bái Hǔ) 天冲 (Tiān Chōng) 死门 (Sǐ Mén) Xun 4　Ding Gui	六合 (Liù Hé) 天辅 (Tiān Fú) 惊门 (Jǐng Mén) Li 9　Gui Wu	太阴 (Tài Yīn) 天英 (Tiān Yīng) 开门 (Kāi Mén) Kun 2　Wu Bing/Ren
玄武 (Xuán Wǔ) 天任 (Tiān Rèn) 景门 (Jǐng Mén) Zhen 3　Ji Ding	Yin (阴) Dun# 9 Hour: **XinMao** ©Calvin Yap	螣蛇 (Téng Shé) 禽芮 (Qín Ruì) 休门 (Xiū Mén) Dui 7　Bing/Ren Geng
九地 (Jiǔ Dì) 天蓬 (Tiān Péng) 杜门 (Dù Mén) Gen 8　Yi Ji	九天 (Jiǔ Tiān) 天心 (Tiān Xīn) 伤门 (Shāng Mén) Kan 1　Xin Yi	值符 (Zhí Fú) 天柱 (Tiān Zhù) 生门 (Shēng Mén) Qian 6　Geng Xin

Chart 5

Yin (阴) Dun# 9 Hour: **RenChen**；直符(ZhíFú): 天柱(TiānZhù)
直使(ZhíShǐ): 惊门(JǐngMén)；旬首(XúnShǒu): JiaShenGeng

太阴 (Tài Yīn) 天英 (Tiān Yīng) 休门 (Xiū Mén) Xun 4　Wu Gui	螣蛇 (Téng Shé) 禽芮 (Qín Ruì) 生门 (Shēng Mén) Li 9　Bing/Ren Wu	值符 (Zhí Fú) 天柱 (Tiān Zhù) 伤门 (Shāng Mén) Kun 2　Geng Bing/Ren
六合 (Liù Hé) 天辅 (Tiān Fú) 开门 (Kāi Mén) Zhen 3　Gui Ding	Yin (阴) Dun# 9 Hour: **RenChen** ©Calvin Yap	九天 (Jiǔ Tiān) 天心 (Tiān Xīn) 杜门 (Dù Mén) Dui 7　Xin Geng
白虎 (Bái Hǔ) 天冲 (Tiān Chōng) 惊门 (Jǐng Mén) Gen 8　Ding Ji	玄武 (Xuán Wǔ) 天任 (Tiān Rèn) 死门 (Sǐ Mén) Kan 1　Ji Yi	九地 (Jiǔ Dì) 天蓬 (Tiān Péng) 景门 (Jǐng Mén) Qian 6　Yi Xin

Chart 6

Yin (阴) Dun# 9 Hour: **GuiSi**；直符(ZhíFú): 天柱(TiānZhù)
直使(ZhíShǐ): 惊门(JǐngMén)；旬首(XúnShǒu): JiaShenGeng

值符 (Zhí Fú) 天柱 (Tiān Zhù) 杜门 (Dù Mén) Xun 4　Geng Gui	九天 (Jiǔ Tiān) 天心 (Tiān Xīn) 景门 (Jǐng Mén) Li 9　Xin Wu	九地 (Jiǔ Dì) 天蓬 (Tiān Péng) 死门 (Sǐ Mén) Kun 2　Yi Bing/Ren
螣蛇 (Téng Shé) 禽芮 (Qín Ruì) 伤门 (Shāng Mén) Zhen 3　Bing/Ren Ding	Yin (阴) Dun# 9 Hour: **GuiSi** ©Calvin Yap	玄武 (Xuán Wǔ) 天任 (Tiān Rèn) 惊门 (Jǐng Mén) Dui 7　Ji Geng
太阴 (Tài Yīn) 天英 (Tiān Yīng) 生门 (Shēng Mén) Gen 8　Wu Ji	六合 (Liù Hé) 天辅 (Tiān Fú) 休门 (Xiū Mén) Kan 1　Gui Yi	白虎 (Bái Hǔ) 天冲 (Tiān Chōng) 开门 (Kāi Mén) Qian 6　Ding Xin

Chart: -9JiaWu (Yin Dun #9 JiaWu Xun)
JiaWu, YiWei, BingShen, DingYou, WuXu, JiHai, GengZi, XinChou, RenYin, GuiMao

---

Yin (阴) Dun# 9 Hour: JiaWu ；直符(ZhíFú): 天心(TiānXīn)
直使(ZhíShǐ): 开门(KāiMén) ；旬首(XúnShǒu): JiaWu/Xin

白虎 (Bái Hǔ) 天辅 (Tiān Fǔ) 杜门 (Dù Mén) Xun 4 Gui Gui	六合 (Liù Hé) 天英 (Tiān Yīng) 景门 (Jǐng Mén) Li 9 Wu Wu	太阴 (Tài Yīn) 禽芮 (Qín Ruì) 死门 (Sǐ Mén) Kun 2 Bing/Ren Bing/Ren
玄武 (Xuán Wǔ) 天冲 (Tiān Chōng) 伤门 (Shāng Mén) Zhen 3 Ding Ding	Yin (阴) Dun# 9 Hour: **JiaWu** **Fu Yin** ©Calvin Yap	螣蛇 (Téng Shé) 天柱 (Tiān Zhù) 惊门 (Jīng Mén) Dui 7 Geng Geng
九地 (Jiǔ Dì) 天任 (Tiān Rèn) 生门 (Shēng Mén) Gen 8 Ji Ji	九天 (Jiǔ Tiān) 天蓬 (Tiān Péng) 休门 (Xiū Mén) Kan 1 Yi Yi	值符 (Zhi Fú) 天心 (Tiān Xīn) 开门 (Kāi Mén) Qian 6 Xin Xin

Yin (阴) Dun# 9 Hour: YiWei ；直符(ZhíFú): 天心(TiānXīn)
直使(ZhíShǐ): 开门(KāiMén) ；旬首(XúnShǒu): JiaWu/Xin

玄武 (Xuán Wǔ) 天冲 (Tiān Chōng) 死门 (Sǐ Mén) Xun 4 Ding Gui	白虎 (Bái Hǔ) 天辅 (Tiān Fǔ) 惊门 (Jīng Mén) Li 9 Gui Wu	六合 (Liù Hé) 天英 (Tiān Yīng) 开门 (Kāi Mén) Kun 2 Wu Bing/Ren
九地 (Jiǔ Dì) 天任 (Tiān Rèn) 景门 (Jǐng Mén) Zhen 3 Ji Ding	Yin (阴) Dun# 9 Hour: **YiWei** ©Calvin Yap	太阴 (Tài Yīn) 禽芮 (Qín Ruì) 休门 (Xiū Mén) Dui 7 Bing/Ren Geng
九天 (Jiǔ Tiān) 天蓬 (Tiān Péng) 杜门 (Dù Mén) Gen 8 Yi Yi	值符 (Zhi Fú) 天心 (Tiān Xīn) 伤门 (Shāng Mén) Kan 1 Xin Yi	螣蛇 (Téng Shé) 天柱 (Tiān Zhù) 生门 (Shēng Mén) Qian 6 Geng Xin

---

Yin (阴) Dun# 9 Hour: BingShen ；直符(ZhíFú): 天心(TiānXīn)
直使(ZhíShǐ): 开门(KāiMén) ；旬首(XúnShǒu): JiaWu/Xin

太阴 (Tài Yīn) 禽芮 (Qín Ruì) 开门 (Kāi Mén) Xun 4 Bing/Ren Gui	螣蛇 (Téng Shé) 天柱 (Tiān Zhù) 休门 (Xiū Mén) Li 9 Geng Wu	值符 (Zhí Fú) 天心 (Tiān Xīn) 生门 (Shēng Mén) Kun 2 Xin Bing/Ren
六合 (Liù Hé) 天英 (Tiān Yīng) 惊门 (Jīng Mén) Zhen 3 Wu Ding	Yin (阴) Dun# 9 Hour: **BingShen** ©Calvin Yap	九天 (Jiǔ Tiān) 天蓬 (Tiān Péng) 伤门 (Shāng Mén) Dui 7 Yi Geng
白虎 (Bái Hǔ) 天辅 (Tiān Fǔ) 死门 (Sǐ Mén) Gen 8 Gui Ji	玄武 (Xuán Wǔ) 天冲 (Tiān Chōng) 景门 (Jǐng Mén) Kan 1 Ding Yi	九地 (Jiǔ Dì) 天任 (Tiān Rèn) 杜门 (Dù Mén) Qian 6 Ji Xin

Yin (阴) Dun# 9 Hour: DingYou ；直符(ZhíFú): 天心(TiānXīn)
直使(ZhíShǐ): 开门(KāiMén) ；旬首(XúnShǒu): JiaWu/Xin

九天 (Jiǔ Tiān) 天蓬 (Tiān Péng) 休门 (Xiū Mén) Xun 4 Yi Gui	九地 (Jiǔ Dì) 天任 (Tiān Rèn) 生门 (Shēng Mén) Li 9 Ji Wu	玄武 (Xuán Wǔ) 天冲 (Tiān Chōng) 伤门 (Shāng Mén) Kun 2 Ding Bing/Ren
值符 (Zhí Fú) 天心 (Tiān Xīn) 开门 (Kāi Mén) Zhen 3 Xin Ding	Yin (阴) Dun# 9 Hour: **DingYou** ©Calvin Yap	白虎 (Bái Hǔ) 天辅 (Tiān Fǔ) 杜门 (Dù Mén) Dui 7 Gui Geng
螣蛇 (Téng Shé) 天柱 (Tiān Zhù) 惊门 (Jīng Mén) Gen 8 Geng Ji	太阴 (Tài Yīn) 禽芮 (Qín Ruì) 死门 (Sǐ Mén) Kan 1 Bing/Ren Yi	六合 (Liù Hé) 天英 (Tiān Yīng) 景门 (Jǐng Mén) Qian 6 Wu Xin

---

Yin (阴) Dun# 9 Hour: WuXu ；直符(ZhíFú): 天心(TiānXīn)
直使(ZhíShǐ): 开门(KāiMén) ；旬首(XúnShǒu): JiaWu/Xin

螣蛇 (Téng Shé) 天柱 (Tiān Zhù) 死门 (Sǐ Mén) Xun 4 Geng Gui	值符 (Zhí Fú) 天心 (Tiān Xīn) 惊门 (Jīng Mén) Li 9 Xin Wu	九天 (Jiǔ Tiān) 天蓬 (Tiān Péng) 开门 (Kāi Mén) Kun 2 Yi Bing/Ren
太阴 (Tài Yīn) 禽芮 (Qín Ruì) 景门 (Jǐng Mén) Zhen 3 Bing/Ren Ding	Yin (阴) Dun# 9 Hour: **WuXu** ©Calvin Yap	九地 (Jiǔ Dì) 天任 (Tiān Rèn) 休门 (Xiū Mén) Dui 7 Ji Geng
六合 (Liù Hé) 天英 (Tiān Yīng) 杜门 (Dù Mén) Gen 8 Wu Ji	白虎 (Bái Hǔ) 天辅 (Tiān Fǔ) 伤门 (Shāng Mén) Kan 1 Gui Yi	玄武 (Xuán Wǔ) 天冲 (Tiān Chōng) 生门 (Shēng Mén) Qian 6 Ding Xin

Yin (阴) Dun# 9 Hour: JiHai ；直符(ZhíFú): 天心(TiānXīn)
直使(ZhíShǐ): 开门(KāiMén) ；旬首(XúnShǒu): JiaWu/Xin

九地 (Jiǔ Dì) 天任 (Tiān Rèn) 伤门 (Shāng Mén) Xun 4 Ji Gui	玄武 (Xuán Wǔ) 天冲 (Tiān Chōng) 杜门 (Dù Mén) Li 9 Ding Wu	白虎 (Bái Hǔ) 天辅 (Tiān Fǔ) 景门 (Jǐng Mén) Kun 2 Gui Bing/Ren
九天 (Jiǔ Tiān) 天蓬 (Tiān Péng) 生门 (Shēng Mén) Zhen 3 Yi Ding	Yin (阴) Dun# 9 Hour: **JiHai** ©Calvin Yap	六合 (Liù Hé) 天英 (Tiān Yīng) 死门 (Sǐ Mén) Dui 7 Wu Geng
值符 (Zhí Fú) 天心 (Tiān Xīn) 休门 (Xiū Mén) Gen 8 Xin Ji	螣蛇 (Téng Shé) 天柱 (Tiān Zhù) 开门 (Kāi Mén) Kan 1 Geng Yi	太阴 (Tài Yīn) 禽芮 (Qín Ruì) 惊门 (Jīng Mén) Qian 6 Bing/Ren Xin

---

Yin (阴) Dun# 9 Hour: **GengZi**；直符(ZhíFú): 天心(TiānXīn)
直使(ZhíShǐ): 开门(KāiMén)；旬首(XúnShǒu): JiaWu/Xin

六合 (Liù Hé) 天英 (Tiān Yīng) 惊门 (Jīng Mén) Xun 4 Gui	太阴 (Tài Yīn) 禽芮 (Qín Ruì) 开门 (Kāi Mén) Li 9 Bing/Ren Wu	螣蛇 (Téng Shé) 天柱 (Tiān Zhù) 休门 (Xiū Mén) Kun 2 Geng Bing/Ren
白虎 (Bái Hǔ) 天辅 (Tiān Fǔ) 死门 (Sǐ Mén) Zhen 3 Gui Ding	Yin (阴) Dun# 9 Hour: **GengZi** ©Calvin Yap	值符 (Zhí Fú) 天心 (Tiān Xīn) 生门 (Shēng Mén) Dui 7 Xin Geng
玄武 (Xuán Wǔ) 天冲 (Tiān Chōng) 景门 (Jǐng Mén) Gen 8 Ding Ji	九地 (Jiǔ Dì) 天任 (Tiān Rèn) 杜门 (Dù Mén) Kan 1 Ji Yi	九天 (Jiǔ Tiān) 天蓬 (Tiān Péng) 伤门 (Shāng Mén) Qian 6 Yi Xin

Yin (阴) Dun# 9 Hour: **XinChou**；直符(ZhíFú): 天心(TiānXīn)
直使(ZhíShǐ): 开门(KāiMén)；旬首(XúnShǒu): JiaWu/Xin

白虎 (Bái Hǔ) 天辅 (Tiān Fǔ) 生门 (Shēng Mén) Xun 4 Gui	六合 (Liù Hé) 天英 (Tiān Yīng) 伤门 (Shāng Mén) Li 9 Wu	太阴 (Tài Yīn) 禽芮 (Qín Ruì) 杜门 (Dù Mén) Kun 2 Bing/Ren Bing/Ren
玄武 (Xuán Wǔ) 天冲 (Tiān Chōng) 休门 (Xiū Mén) Zhen 3 Ding Ding	Yin (阴) Dun# 9 Hour: **XinChou** **Fu Yin** ©Calvin Yap	螣蛇 (Téng Shé) 天柱 (Tiān Zhù) 景门 (Jǐng Mén) Dui 7 Geng Geng
九地 (Jiǔ Dì) 天任 (Tiān Rèn) 开门 (Kāi Mén) Gen 8 Ji Ji	九天 (Jiǔ Tiān) 天蓬 (Tiān Péng) 惊门 (Jīng Mén) Kan 1 Yi Yi	值符 (Zhí Fú) 天心 (Tiān Xīn) 死门 (Sǐ Mén) Qian 6 Xin Xin

Yin (阴) Dun# 9 Hour: **RenYin**；直符(ZhíFú): 天心(TiānXīn)
直使(ZhíShǐ): 开门(KāiMén)；旬首(XúnShǒu): JiaWu/Xin

太阴 (Tài Yīn) 禽芮 (Qín Ruì) 景门 (Jǐng Mén) Xun 4 Bing/Ren Gui	螣蛇 (Téng Shé) 天柱 (Tiān Zhù) 死门 (Sǐ Mén) Li 9 Geng Wu	值符 (Zhí Fú) 天心 (Tiān Xīn) 惊门 (Jīng Mén) Kun 2 Xin Bing/Ren
六合 (Liù Hé) 天英 (Tiān Yīng) 杜门 (Dù Mén) Zhen 3 Wu Ding	Yin (阴) Dun# 9 Hour: **RenYin** ©Calvin Yap	九天 (Jiǔ Tiān) 天蓬 (Tiān Péng) 开门 (Kāi Mén) Dui 7 Yi Geng
白虎 (Bái Hǔ) 天辅 (Tiān Fǔ) 伤门 (Shāng Mén) Gen 8 Gui Ji	玄武 (Xuán Wǔ) 天冲 (Tiān Chōng) 生门 (Shēng Mén) Kan 1 Ding Yi	九地 (Jiǔ Dì) 天任 (Tiān Rèn) 休门 (Xiū Mén) Qian 6 Ji Xin

Yin (阴) Dun# 9 Hour: **GuiMao**；直符(ZhíFú): 天心(TiānXīn)
直使(ZhíShǐ): 开门(KāiMén)；旬首(XúnShǒu): JiaWu/Xin

值符 (Zhi Fú) 天心 (Tiān Xīn) 杜门 (Dù Mén) Xun 4 Xin Gui	九天 (Jiǔ Tiān) 天蓬 (Tiān Péng) 景门 (Jǐng Mén) Li 9 Yi Wu	九地 (Jiǔ Dì) 天任 (Tiān Rèn) 死门 (Sǐ Mén) Kun 2 Ji Bing/Ren
螣蛇 (Téng Shé) 天柱 (Tiān Zhù) 伤门 (Shāng Mén) Zhen 3 Geng Ding	Yin (阴) Dun# 9 Hour: **GuiMao** **Fan Yin** ©Calvin Yap	玄武 (Xuán Wǔ) 天冲 (Tiān Chōng) 惊门 (Jīng Mén) Dui 7 Ding Geng
太阴 (Tài Yīn) 禽芮 (Qín Ruì) 生门 (Shēng Mén) Gen 8 Bing/Ren Ji	六合 (Liù Hé) 天英 (Tiān Yīng) 休门 (Xiū Mén) Kan 1 Wu Yi	白虎 (Bái Hǔ) 天辅 (Tiān Fǔ) 开门 (Kāi Mén) Qian 6 Gui Xin

---

Chart: **-9JiaChen** (Yin Dun #9 JiaChen Xun)
JiaChen, YiSi, BingWu, DingWei, WuShen, JiYou, GengXu, XinHai, RenZi, GuiChou

Yin (阴) Dun# 9 Hour: **JiaChen**；直符(ZhíFú): 天禽(TiānQín)
直使(ZhíShǐ): 死门(SǐMén)；旬首(XúnShǒu): JiaChenRen

太阴 (Tài Yīn) 天辅 (Tiān Fǔ) 杜门 (Dù Mén) Xun 4 Gui Gui	螣蛇 (Téng Shé) 天英 (Tiān Yīng) 景门 (Jǐng Mén) Li 9 Wu Wu	值符 (Zhi Fú) 禽芮 (Qín Ruì) 死门 (Sǐ Mén) Kun 2 Bing/Ren Bing/Ren
六合 (Liù Hé) 天冲 (Tiān Chōng) 伤门 (Shāng Mén) Zhen 3 Ding Ding	Yin (阴) Dun# 9 Hour: **JiaChen** **Fu Yin** ©Calvin Yap	九天 (Jiǔ Tiān) 天柱 (Tiān Zhù) 惊门 (Jīng Mén) Dui 7 Geng Geng
白虎 (Bái Hǔ) 天任 (Tiān Rèn) 生门 (Shēng Mén) Gen 8 Ji Ji	玄武 (Xuán Wǔ) 天蓬 (Tiān Péng) 休门 (Xiū Mén) Kan 1 Yi Yi	九地 (Jiǔ Dì) 天心 (Tiān Xīn) 开门 (Kāi Mén) Qian 6 Xin Xin

Yin (阴) Dun# 9 Hour: **YiSi**；直符(ZhíFú): 天禽(TiānQín)
直使(ZhíShǐ): 死门(SǐMén)；旬首(XúnShǒu): JiaChenRen

玄武 (Xuán Wǔ) 天蓬 (Tiān Péng) 死门 (Sǐ Mén) Xun 4 Yi Gui	白虎 (Bái Hǔ) 天任 (Tiān Rèn) 惊门 (Jīng Mén) Li 9 Ji Wu	六合 (Liù Hé) 天冲 (Tiān Chōng) 开门 (Kāi Mén) Kun 2 Ding Bing/Ren
九地 (Jiǔ Dì) 天心 (Tiān Xīn) 景门 (Jǐng Mén) Zhen 3 Xin Ding	Yin (阴) Dun# 9 Hour: **YiSi** ©Calvin Yap	太阴 (Tài Yīn) 天辅 (Tiān Fǔ) 休门 (Xiū Mén) Dui 7 Gui Geng
九天 (Jiǔ Tiān) 天柱 (Tiān Zhù) 杜门 (Dù Mén) Gen 8 Geng Ji	值符 (Zhi Fú) 禽芮 (Qín Ruì) 伤门 (Shāng Mén) Kan 1 Bing/Ren Yi	螣蛇 (Téng Shé) 天英 (Tiān Yīng) 生门 (Shēng Mén) Qian 6 Wu Xin

Chart 1

Yin (阴) Dun# 9 Hour: **BingWu**；直符(ZhíFú): 天禽(TiānQín)
直使(ZhíShǐ): 死门(SǐMén)；旬首(XúnShǒu): JiaChenRen

太阴 (Tài Yīn) 天辅 (Tiān Fǔ) 惊门 (Jīng Mén) Xun 4　Gui Gui	螣蛇 (Téng Shé) 天英 (Tiān Yīng) 开门 (Kāi Mén) Li 9　Wu Wu	值符 (Zhí Fú) 禽芮 (Qín Ruì) 休门 (Xiū Mén) Kun 2　Bing/Ren Bing/Ren
六合 (Liù Hé) 天冲 (Tiān Chōng) 死门 (Sǐ Mén) Zhen 3　Ding Ding	Yin (阴) Dun# 9 Hour: **BingWu** **Fu Yin** ©Calvin Yap	九天 (Jiǔ Tiān) 天柱 (Tiān Zhù) 生门 (Shēng Mén) Dui 7　Geng Geng
白虎 (Bái Hǔ) 天任 (Tiān Rèn) 景门 (Jǐng Mén) Gen 8　Ji Ji	玄武 (Xuán Wǔ) 天蓬 (Tiān Péng) 杜门 (Dù Mén) Kan 1　Yi Yi	九地 (Jiǔ Dì) 天心 (Tiān Xīn) 伤门 (Shāng Mén) Qian 6　Xin Xin

Chart 2

Yin (阴) Dun# 9 Hour: **DingWei**；直符(ZhíFú): 天禽(TiānQín)
直使(ZhíShǐ): 死门(SǐMén)；旬首(XúnShǒu): JiaChenRen

九天 (Jiǔ Tiān) 天柱 (Tiān Zhù) 杜门 (Dù Mén) Xun 4　Geng Gui	九地 (Jiǔ Dì) 天心 (Tiān Xīn) 景门 (Jǐng Mén) Li 9　Xin Wu	玄武 (Xuán Wǔ) 天蓬 (Tiān Péng) 死门 (Sǐ Mén) Kun 2　Yi Bing/Ren
值符 (Zhí Fú) 禽芮 (Qín Ruì) 伤门 (Shāng Mén) Zhen 3　Bing/Ren Ding	Yin (阴) Dun# 9 Hour: **DingWei** ©Calvin Yap	白虎 (Bái Hǔ) 天任 (Tiān Rèn) 惊门 (Jīng Mén) Dui 7　Ji Geng
螣蛇 (Téng Shé) 天英 (Tiān Yīng) 生门 (Shēng Mén) Gen 8　Wu Ji	太阴 (Tài Yīn) 天辅 (Tiān Fǔ) 休门 (Xiū Mén) Kan 1　Gui Yi	六合 (Liù Hé) 天冲 (Tiān Chōng) 开门 (Kāi Mén) Qian 6　Ding Xin

Chart 3

Yin (阴) Dun# 9 Hour: **WuShen**；直符(ZhíFú): 天禽(TiānQín)
直使(ZhíShǐ): 死门(SǐMén)；旬首(XúnShǒu): JiaChenRen

螣蛇 (Téng Shé) 天英 (Tiān Yīng) 休门 (Xiū Mén) Xun 4　Wu Gui	值符 (Zhí Fú) 禽芮 (Qín Ruì) 生门 (Shēng Mén) Li 9　Bing/Ren Wu	九天 (Jiǔ Tiān) 天柱 (Tiān Zhù) 伤门 (Shāng Mén) Kun 2　Geng Bing/Ren
太阴 (Tài Yīn) 天辅 (Tiān Fǔ) 开门 (Kāi Mén) Zhen 3　Gui Ding	Yin (阴) Dun# 9 Hour: **WuShen** ©Calvin Yap	九地 (Jiǔ Dì) 天心 (Tiān Xīn) 杜门 (Dù Mén) Dui 7　Xin Geng
六合 (Liù Hé) 天冲 (Tiān Chōng) 惊门 (Jīng Mén) Gen 8　Ding Ji	白虎 (Bái Hǔ) 天任 (Tiān Rèn) 死门 (Sǐ Mén) Kan 1　Ji Yi	玄武 (Xuán Wǔ) 天蓬 (Tiān Péng) 景门 (Jǐng Mén) Qian 6　Yi Xin

Chart 4

Yin (阴) Dun# 9 Hour: **JiYou**；直符(ZhíFú): 天禽(TiānQín)
直使(ZhíShǐ): 死门(SǐMén)；旬首(XúnShǒu): JiaChenRen

九地 (Jiǔ Dì) 天心 (Tiān Xīn) 景门 (Jǐng Mén) Xun 4　Xin Gui	玄武 (Xuán Wǔ) 天蓬 (Tiān Péng) 死门 (Sǐ Mén) Li 9　Yi Wu	白虎 (Bái Hǔ) 天任 (Tiān Rèn) 惊门 (Jīng Mén) Kun 2　Ji Bing/Ren
九天 (Jiǔ Tiān) 天柱 (Tiān Zhù) 杜门 (Dù Mén) Zhen 3　Geng Ding	Yin (阴) Dun# 9 Hour: **JiYou** **Fan Yin** ©Calvin Yap	六合 (Liù Hé) 天冲 (Tiān Chōng) 开门 (Kāi Mén) Dui 7　Ding Geng
值符 (Zhí Fú) 禽芮 (Qín Ruì) 伤门 (Shāng Mén) Gen 8　Bing/Ren Ji	螣蛇 (Téng Shé) 天英 (Tiān Yīng) 生门 (Shēng Mén) Kan 1　Wu Yi	太阴 (Tài Yīn) 天辅 (Tiān Fǔ) 休门 (Xiū Mén) Qian 6　Gui Xin

Chart 5

Yin (阴) Dun# 9 Hour: **GengXu**；直符(ZhíFú): 天禽(TiānQín)
直使(ZhíShǐ): 死门(SǐMén)；旬首(XúnShǒu): JiaChenRen

六合 (Liù Hé) 天冲 (Tiān Chōng) 开门 (Kāi Mén) Xun 4　Ding Gui	太阴 (Tài Yīn) 天辅 (Tiān Fǔ) 休门 (Xiū Mén) Li 9　Gui Wu	螣蛇 (Téng Shé) 天英 (Tiān Yīng) 生门 (Shēng Mén) Kun 2　Wu Bing/Ren
白虎 (Bái Hǔ) 天任 (Tiān Rèn) 惊门 (Jīng Mén) Zhen 3　Ji Ding	Yin (阴) Dun# 9 Hour: **GengXu** ©Calvin Yap	值符 (Zhí Fú) 禽芮 (Qín Ruì) 伤门 (Shāng Mén) Dui 7　Bing/Ren Geng
玄武 (Xuán Wǔ) 天蓬 (Tiān Péng) 死门 (Sǐ Mén) Gen 8　Yi Ji	九地 (Jiǔ Dì) 天心 (Tiān Xīn) 景门 (Jǐng Mén) Kan 1　Xin Yi	九天 (Jiǔ Tiān) 天柱 (Tiān Zhù) 杜门 (Dù Mén) Qian 6　Geng Xin

Chart 6

Yin (阴) Dun# 9 Hour: **XinHai**；直符(ZhíFú): 天禽(TiānQín)
直使(ZhíShǐ): 死门(SǐMén)；旬首(XúnShǒu): JiaChenRen

白虎 (Bái Hǔ) 天任 (Tiān Rèn) 伤门 (Shāng Mén) Xun 4　Ji Gui	六合 (Liù Hé) 天冲 (Tiān Chōng) 杜门 (Dù Mén) Li 9　Ding Wu	太阴 (Tài Yīn) 天辅 (Tiān Fǔ) 景门 (Jǐng Mén) Kun 2　Gui Bing/Ren
玄武 (Xuán Wǔ) 天蓬 (Tiān Péng) 生门 (Shēng Mén) Zhen 3　Yi Ding	Yin (阴) Dun# 9 Hour: **XinHai** ©Calvin Yap	螣蛇 (Téng Shé) 天英 (Tiān Yīng) 死门 (Sǐ Mén) Dui 7　Wu Geng
九地 (Jiǔ Dì) 天心 (Tiān Xīn) 休门 (Xiū Mén) Gen 8　Xin Ji	九天 (Jiǔ Tiān) 天柱 (Tiān Zhù) 开门 (Kāi Mén) Kan 1　Geng Yi	值符 (Zhí Fú) 禽芮 (Qín Ruì) 惊门 (Jīng Mén) Qian 6　Bing/Ren Xin

Yin (阴) Dun# 9 Hour: RenZi；直符(ZhíFú): 天禽(TiānQín)
直使(ZhíShǐ): 死门(SǐMén)；旬首(XúnShǒu): JiaChenRen

太阴 (Tài Yīn) 天辅 (Tiān Fǔ) 生门 (Shēng Mén) Xun 4　Gui Gui	螣蛇 (Téng Shé) 天英 (Tiān Yīng) 伤门 (Shāng Mén) Li 9　Wu Wu	值符 (Zhí Fú) 禽芮 (Qín Ruì) 杜门 (Dù Mén) Kun 2　Bing/Ren Bing/Ren
六合 (Liù Hé) 天冲 (Tiān Chōng) 休门 (Xiū Mén) Zhen 3　Ding Ding	Yin (阴) Dun# 9 Hour: **RenZi** **Fu Yin** ©Calvin Yap	九天 (Jiǔ Tiān) 天柱 (Tiān Zhù) 景门 (Jǐng Mén) Dui 7　Geng Geng
白虎 (Bái Hǔ) 天任 (Tiān Rèn) 开门 (Kāi Mén) Gen 8　Ji Ji	玄武 (Xuán Wǔ) 天蓬 (Tiān Péng) 惊门 (Jīng Mén) Kan 1　Yi Yi	九地 (Jiǔ Dì) 天心 (Tiān Xīn) 死门 (Sǐ Mén) Qian 6　Xin Xin

Yin (阴) Dun# 9 Hour: GuiChou；直符(ZhíFú): 天禽(TiānQín)
直使(ZhíShǐ): 死门(SǐMén)；旬首(XúnShǒu): JiaChenRen

值符 (Zhi Fú) 禽芮 (Qín Ruì) 杜门 (Dù Mén) Xun 4　Bing/Ren Gui	九天 (Jiǔ Tiān) 天柱 (Tiān Zhù) 景门 (Jǐng Mén) Li 9　Geng Wu	九地 (Jiǔ Dì) 天心 (Tiān Xīn) 死门 (Sǐ Mén) Kun 2　Xin Bing/Ren
螣蛇 (Téng Shé) 天英 (Tiān Yīng) 伤门 (Shāng Mén) Zhen 3　Wu Ding	Yin (阴) Dun# 9 Hour: **GuiChou** ©Calvin Yap	玄武 (Xuán Wǔ) 天蓬 (Tiān Péng) 惊门 (Jīng Mén) Dui 7　Yi Geng
太阴 (Tài Yīn) 天辅 (Tiān Fǔ) 生门 (Shēng Mén) Gen 8　Gui Ji	六合 (Liù Hé) 天冲 (Tiān Chōng) 休门 (Xiū Mén) Kan 1　Ding Yi	白虎 (Bái Hǔ) 天任 (Tiān Rèn) 开门 (Kāi Mén) Qian 6　Ji Xin

---

Chart: -9JiaYin (Yin Dun #9 JiaYin Xun)
JiaYin, YiMao, BingChen, DingSi, WuWu, JiWei, GengShen, XinYou, RenXu, GuiHai

---

Yin (阴) Dun# 9 Hour: JiaYin；直符(ZhíFú): 天辅(TiānFǔ)
直使(ZhíShǐ): 杜门(DùMén)；旬首(XúnShǒu): JiaYinGui

值符 (Zhí Fú) 天辅 (Tiān Fǔ) 杜门 (Dù Mén) Xun 4　Gui Gui	九天 (Jiǔ Tiān) 天英 (Tiān Yīng) 景门 (Jǐng Mén) Li 9　Wu Wu	九地 (Jiǔ Dì) 禽芮 (Qín Ruì) 死门 (Sǐ Mén) Kun 2　Bing/Ren Bing/Ren
螣蛇 (Téng Shé) 天冲 (Tiān Chōng) 伤门 (Shāng Mén) Zhen 3　Ding Ding	Yin (阴) Dun# 9 Hour: **JiaYin** **Fu Yin** ©Calvin Yap	玄武 (Xuán Wǔ) 天柱 (Tiān Zhù) 惊门 (Jīng Mén) Dui 7　Geng Geng
太阴 (Tài Yīn) 天任 (Tiān Rèn) 生门 (Shēng Mén) Gen 8　Ji Ji	六合 (Liù Hé) 天蓬 (Tiān Péng) 休门 (Xiū Mén) Kan 1　Yi Yi	白虎 (Bái Hǔ) 天心 (Tiān Xīn) 开门 (Kāi Mén) Qian 6　Xin Xin

Yin (阴) Dun# 9 Hour: YiMao；直符(ZhíFú): 天辅(TiānFǔ)
直使(ZhíShǐ): 杜门(DùMén)；旬首(XúnShǒu): JiaYinGui

玄武 (Xuán Wǔ) 天柱 (Tiān Zhù) 景门 (Jǐng Mén) Xun 4　Geng Gui	白虎 (Bái Hǔ) 天心 (Tiān Xīn) 死门 (Sǐ Mén) Li 9　Xin Wu	六合 (Liù Hé) 天蓬 (Tiān Péng) 惊门 (Jīng Mén) Kun 2　Yi Bing/Ren
九地 (Jiǔ Dì) 禽芮 (Qín Ruì) 杜门 (Dù Mén) Zhen 3　Bing/Ren Ding	Yin (阴) Dun# 9 Hour: **YiMao** ©Calvin Yap	太阴 (Tài Yīn) 天任 (Tiān Rèn) 开门 (Kāi Mén) Dui 7　Ji Geng
九天 (Jiǔ Tiān) 天英 (Tiān Yīng) 伤门 (Shāng Mén) Gen 8　Wu Ji	值符 (Zhí Fú) 天辅 (Tiān Fǔ) 生门 (Shēng Mén) Kan 1　Gui Yi	螣蛇 (Téng Shé) 天冲 (Tiān Chōng) 休门 (Xiū Mén) Qian 6　Ding Xin

Yin (阴) Dun# 9 Hour: BingChen；直符(ZhíFú): 天辅(TiānFǔ)
直使(ZhíShǐ): 杜门(DùMén)；旬首(XúnShǒu): JiaYinGui

太阴 (Tài Yīn) 天任 (Tiān Rèn) 生门 (Shēng Mén) Xun 4　Ji Gui	螣蛇 (Téng Shé) 天冲 (Tiān Chōng) 伤门 (Shāng Mén) Li 9　Ding Wu	值符 (Zhí Fú) 天辅 (Tiān Fǔ) 杜门 (Dù Mén) Kun 2　Gui Bing/Ren
六合 (Liù Hé) 天蓬 (Tiān Péng) 休门 (Xiū Mén) Zhen 3　Yi Ding	Yin (阴) Dun# 9 Hour: **BingChen** ©Calvin Yap	九天 (Jiǔ Tiān) 天英 (Tiān Yīng) 景门 (Jǐng Mén) Dui 7　Wu Geng
白虎 (Bái Hǔ) 天心 (Tiān Xīn) 开门 (Kāi Mén) Gen 8　Xin Ji	玄武 (Xuán Wǔ) 天柱 (Tiān Zhù) 惊门 (Jīng Mén) Kan 1　Geng Yi	九地 (Jiǔ Dì) 禽芮 (Qín Ruì) 死门 (Sǐ Mén) Qian 6　Bing/Ren Xin

Yin (阴) Dun# 9 Hour: DingSi；直符(ZhíFú): 天辅(TiānFǔ)
直使(ZhíShǐ): 杜门(DùMén)；旬首(XúnShǒu): JiaYinGui

九天 (Jiǔ Tiān) 天英 (Tiān Yīng) 惊门 (Jīng Mén) Xun 4　Wu Gui	九地 (Jiǔ Dì) 禽芮 (Qín Ruì) 开门 (Kāi Mén) Li 9　Bing/Ren Wu	玄武 (Xuán Wǔ) 天柱 (Tiān Zhù) 休门 (Xiū Mén) Kun 2　Geng Bing/Ren
值符 (Zhí Fú) 天辅 (Tiān Fǔ) 死门 (Sǐ Mén) Zhen 3　Gui Ding	Yin (阴) Dun# 9 Hour: **DingSi** ©Calvin Yap	白虎 (Bái Hǔ) 天心 (Tiān Xīn) 生门 (Shēng Mén) Dui 7　Xin Geng
螣蛇 (Téng Shé) 天冲 (Tiān Chōng) 景门 (Jǐng Mén) Gen 8　Ding Ji	太阴 (Tài Yīn) 天任 (Tiān Rèn) 杜门 (Dù Mén) Kan 1　Ji Yi	六合 (Liù Hé) 天蓬 (Tiān Péng) 伤门 (Shāng Mén) Qian 6　Yi Xin

Yin (阴) Dun# 9 Hour: **WuWu**；直符(ZhíFú): 天辅(TiānFǔ)
直使(ZhíShǐ): 杜门(DùMén)；旬首(XúnShǒu): JiaYinGui

螣蛇 (Téng Shé) 天冲 (Tiān Chōng) 伤门 (Shāng Mén) Xun 4　Ding Gui	值符 (Zhí Fú) 天辅 (Tiān Fǔ) 杜门 (Dù Mén) Li 9　Gui Wu	九天 (Jiǔ Tiān) 天英 (Tiān Yīng) 景门 (Jǐng Mén) Kun 2　Wu Bing/Ren
太阴 (Tài Yīn) 天任 (Tiān Rèn) 生门 (Shēng Mén) Zhen 3　Ji Ding	Yin (阴) Dun# 9 Hour: **WuWu** ©Calvin Yap	九地 (Jiǔ Dì) 禽芮 (Qín Ruì) 死门 (Sǐ Mén) Dui 7　Bing/Ren Geng
六合 (Liù Hé) 天蓬 (Tiān Péng) 休门 (Xiū Mén) Gen 8　Yi Ji	白虎 (Bái Hǔ) 天心 (Tiān Xīn) 开门 (Kāi Mén) Kan 1　Xin Yi	玄武 (Xuán Wǔ) 天柱 (Tiān Zhù) 惊门 (Jīng Mén) Qian 6　Geng Xin

Yin (阴) Dun# 9 Hour: **JiWei**；直符(ZhíFú): 天辅(TiānFǔ)
直使(ZhíShǐ): 杜门(DùMén)；旬首(XúnShǒu): JiaYinGui

九地 (Jiǔ Dì) 禽芮 (Qín Ruì) 死门 (Sǐ Mén) Xun 4　Bing/Ren Gui	玄武 (Xuán Wǔ) 天柱 (Tiān Zhù) 惊门 (Jīng Mén) Li 9　Geng Wu	白虎 (Bái Hǔ) 天心 (Tiān Xīn) 开门 (Kāi Mén) Kun 2　Xin Bing/Ren
九天 (Jiǔ Tiān) 天英 (Tiān Yīng) 景门 (Jǐng Mén) Zhen 3　Wu Ding	Yin (阴) Dun# 9 Hour: **JiWei** ©Calvin Yap	六合 (Liù Hé) 天蓬 (Tiān Péng) 休门 (Xiū Mén) Dui 7　Yi Geng
值符 (Zhí Fú) 天辅 (Tiān Fǔ) 杜门 (Dù Mén) Gen 8　Gui Ji	螣蛇 (Téng Shé) 天冲 (Tiān Chōng) 伤门 (Shāng Mén) Kan 1　Ding Yi	太阴 (Tài Yīn) 天任 (Tiān Rèn) 生门 (Shēng Mén) Qian 6　Ji Xin

Yin (阴) Dun# 9 Hour: **GengShen**；直符(ZhíFú): 天辅(TiānFǔ)
直使(ZhíShǐ): 杜门(DùMén)；旬首(XúnShǒu): JiaYinGui

六合 (Liù Hé) 天蓬 (Tiān Péng) 休门 (Xiū Mén) Xun 4　Yi Gui	太阴 (Tài Yīn) 天任 (Tiān Rèn) 生门 (Shēng Mén) Li 9　Ji Wu	螣蛇 (Téng Shé) 天冲 (Tiān Chōng) 伤门 (Shāng Mén) Kun 2　Ding Bing/Ren
白虎 (Bái Hǔ) 天心 (Tiān Xīn) 开门 (Kāi Mén) Zhen 3　Xin Ding	Yin (阴) Dun# 9 Hour: **GengShen** ©Calvin Yap	值符 (Zhí Fú) 天辅 (Tiān Fǔ) 杜门 (Dù Mén) Dui 7　Gui Geng
玄武 (Xuán Wǔ) 天柱 (Tiān Zhù) 惊门 (Jīng Mén) Gen 8　Geng Ji	九地 (Jiǔ Dì) 禽芮 (Qín Ruì) 死门 (Sǐ Mén) Kan 1　Bing/Ren Yi	九天 (Jiǔ Tiān) 天英 (Tiān Yīng) 景门 (Jǐng Mén) Qian 6　Wu Xin

Yin (阴) Dun# 9 Hour: **XinYou**；直符(ZhíFú): 天辅(TiānFǔ)
直使(ZhíShǐ): 杜门(DùMén)；旬首(XúnShǒu): JiaYinGui

白虎 (Bái Hǔ) 天心 (Tiān Xīn) 开门 (Kāi Mén) Xun 4　Xin Gui	六合 (Liù Hé) 天蓬 (Tiān Péng) 休门 (Xiū Mén) Li 9　Yi Wu	太阴 (Tài Yīn) 天任 (Tiān Rèn) 生门 (Shēng Mén) Kun 2　Ji Bing/Ren
玄武 (Xuán Wǔ) 天柱 (Tiān Zhù) 惊门 (Jīng Mén) Zhen 3　Geng Ding	Yin (阴) Dun# 9 Hour: **XinYou** **Fan Yin** ©Calvin Yap	螣蛇 (Téng Shé) 天冲 (Tiān Chōng) 伤门 (Shāng Mén) Dui 7　Ding Geng
九地 (Jiǔ Dì) 禽芮 (Qín Ruì) 死门 (Sǐ Mén) Gen 8　Bing/Ren Ji	九天 (Jiǔ Tiān) 天英 (Tiān Yīng) 景门 (Jǐng Mén) Kan 1　Wu Yi	值符 (Zhí Fú) 天辅 (Tiān Fǔ) 杜门 (Dù Mén) Qian 6　Gui Xin

Yin (阴) Dun# 9 Hour: **RenXu**；直符(ZhíFú): 天辅(TiānFǔ)
直使(ZhíShǐ): 杜门(DùMén)；旬首(XúnShǒu): JiaYinGui

太阴 (Tài Yīn) 天任 (Tiān Rèn) 生门 (Shēng Mén) Xun 4　Ji Gui	螣蛇 (Téng Shé) 天冲 (Tiān Chōng) 伤门 (Shāng Mén) Li 9　Ding Wu	值符 (Zhí Fú) 天辅 (Tiān Fǔ) 杜门 (Dù Mén) Kun 2　Gui Bing/Ren
六合 (Liù Hé) 天蓬 (Tiān Péng) 休门 (Xiū Mén) Zhen 3　Yi Ding	Yin (阴) Dun# 9 Hour: **RenXu** ©Calvin Yap	九天 (Jiǔ Tiān) 天英 (Tiān Yīng) 景门 (Jǐng Mén) Dui 7　Wu Geng
白虎 (Bái Hǔ) 天心 (Tiān Xīn) 开门 (Kāi Mén) Gen 8　Xin Ji	玄武 (Xuán Wǔ) 天柱 (Tiān Zhù) 惊门 (Jīng Mén) Kan 1　Geng Yi	九地 (Jiǔ Dì) 禽芮 (Qín Ruì) 死门 (Sǐ Mén) Qian 6　Bing/Ren Xin

Yin (阴) Dun# 9 Hour: **GuiHai**；直符(ZhíFú): 天辅(TiānFǔ)
直使(ZhíShǐ): 杜门(DùMén)；旬首(XúnShǒu): JiaYinGui

值符 (Zhí Fú) 天辅 (Tiān Fǔ) 杜门 (Dù Mén) Xun 4　Gui Gui	九天 (Jiǔ Tiān) 天英 (Tiān Yīng) 景门 (Jǐng Mén) Li 9　Wu Wu	九地 (Jiǔ Dì) 禽芮 (Qín Ruì) 死门 (Sǐ Mén) Kun 2　Bing/Ren Bing/Ren
螣蛇 (Téng Shé) 天冲 (Tiān Chōng) 伤门 (Shāng Mén) Zhen 3　Ding Ding	Yin (阴) Dun# 9 Hour: **GuiHai** **Fu Yin** ©Calvin Yap	玄武 (Xuán Wǔ) 天柱 (Tiān Zhù) 惊门 (Jīng Mén) Dui 7　Geng Geng
太阴 (Tài Yīn) 天任 (Tiān Rèn) 生门 (Shēng Mén) Gen 8　Ji Ji	六合 (Liù Hé) 天蓬 (Tiān Péng) 休门 (Xiū Mén) Kan 1　Yi Yi	白虎 (Bái Hǔ) 天心 (Tiān Xīn) 开门 (Kāi Mén) Qian 6　Xin Xin

Courses

Note: the courses are subject to change. Please check http://www.fengshui-hacks.com/ for up to date information.

Road to Practitioner Program

Specialised Chinese Meta-Physics Courses

Supplementary Classes

- Qi Men Dun Jia for Working Professional

- Basic Fengshui for house selection

- Ultimate Date Selection Course (10 Officers, 28 constellation, Dong Gong, Xuan Kong Da Gua, Qi Men Dun Jia.)

- Mei Hua Yi Shu and Yijing Divination

- Face Reading

- Palm Reading

INDEX

194, 197, 200, 203, 206, 209, 212, 215

Wood, 43, 44, 47, 48, 49, 50, 54

Xiū Mén, 61, 62, 63, 64

Zhí Fú, 70, 71, 72

Zhí Rùn, 31

Zhōu Yú, 22

Zhūgě Liàng, 22, 23

* 9 7 8 9 8 1 1 4 1 1 0 7 6 *